BUTTERWORTHS EMPLOYMENT LAW HANDBOOK

BUTTERWORTHS EMPLOYMENT LAW HANDBOOK

Sixth Edition

Edited by
PETER WALLINGTON, MA, LLM
Barrister at Law,
Sometime Professor of Law at the University of Lancaster
and Brunel University

BUTTERWORTHS
LONDON, DUBLIN, EDINBURGH
1993

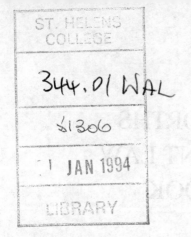
United Kingdom	Butterworth & Co (Publishers) Ltd, 88 Kingsway, LONDON WC2B 6AB and 4 Hill Street, EDINBURGH EH2 3JZ
Australia	Butterworths Pty Ltd, SYDNEY, MELBOURNE, BRISBANE, ADELAIDE, PERTH, CANBERRA and HOBART
Belgium	Butterworth & Co (Publishers) Ltd, BRUSSELS
Canada	Butterworth Canada Ltd, TORONTO and VANCOUVER
Ireland	Butterworth (Ireland) Ltd, DUBLIN
Malaysia	Malayan Law Journal Sdn Bhd, KUALA LUMPUR
New Zealand	Butterworths of New Zealand Ltd, WELLINGTON and AUCKLAND
Puerto Rico	Equity de Puerto Rico, Inc, HATO REY
Singapore	Malayan Law Journal Pte Ltd, SINGAPORE
USA	Butterworth Legal Publishers, AUSTIN, Texas; BOSTON, Massachusetts; CLEARWATER, Florida (D & S Publishers); ORFORD, New Hampshire (Equity Publishing); ST PAUL, Minnesota; and SEATTLE, Washington

A CIP catalogue record for this book is available from the British Library.

ISBN 0 406 02234 8

Typeset by Kerrypress Ltd, Luton, Beds
Printed in Great Britain by Mackays of Chatham PLC, Chatham, Kent

EDITOR'S INTRODUCTION TO THE SIXTH EDITION

Since the first edition of this Handbook was published in 1980, no edition has had to incorporate such a volume of change in legislation, both in form and in substance, as this sixth edition.

The changes in form derive from the two major consolidating Acts of 1992, namely the Trade Union and Labour Relations (Consolidation) Act and the Social Security Contributions and Benefits Act. Effectively TULR(C)A brings together the whole body of primary legislation on trade unions, collective rights and industrial action, whilst SSCBA consolidates, inter alia, the legislation on statutory sick pay and statutory maternity pay.

The substantive changes are primarily contained in the Trade Union Reform and Employment Rights Act 1993, which is the most far-reaching piece of employment legislation since the Employment Protection Act 1975. The 1993 Act consists mainly of amendments to the principal individual and collective consolidation Acts, the Employment Protection (Consolidation) Act 1978 and the Trade Union and Labour Relations (Consolidation) Act 1992, and, therefore, its provisions are largely incorporated into those Acts in this Handbook.

Substantial new European material, including relevant parts of the Maastricht Treaty and the most important Health and Safety Regulations (which came into force on 1 January 1993 in implementation of the EC's programme of Health and Safety Directives) have been included in this edition.

This major revision of the content of the Handbook has provided the opportunity to reorganise the layout so that it is more convenient to use. The book is now arranged as follows.

Part 1 contains Statutes. These are in chronological order and, where there are two or more from the same year, they appear in order of Chapter number.

Part 2 contains Statutory Instruments. This section has been expanded to include a larger selection of Statutory Instruments made under the Health and Safety at Work etc Act 1974, and greater coverage of Statutory Instruments relevant to the jurisdiction of Industrial Tribunals. These appear in chronological order.

Part 3 contains European materials: the Treaty of Rome, as amended by the Maastricht Treaty, and its Protocols; the EC Social Charter of 1989; and relevant Regulations, Directives and Recommendations. These appear in chronological order.

Part 4 contains Statutory Codes of Practice, including the revised Codes on Picketing, Time off for Trade Union Duties and Activities, and Trade Union Ballots on Industrial Action. The materials in this Part are Crown copyright.

Part 5 contains miscellaneous materials, namely EAT Practice Directions, the TUC's Bridlington Agreement, the relevant parts of the European Convention on Human Rights, the 1961 European Social Charter and the most relevant ILO Conventions. In addition, a list of useful addresses and telephone numbers is included.

The Handbook is indexed and cross-referenced by paragraph numbers, and is annotated to indicate the sources of changes incorporated into the text. Annotations also refer to subordinate legislation and Codes of Practice made under the enabling powers concerned, although these references are not intended to be comprehensive.

Amendments and insertions to the text are indicated by square brackets and repeals are indicated by ellipses. Where material is omitted (eg as outside the scope of the work or because it merely amends other legislation) the reason for the omission is indicated in brackets in italics.

The law is stated as at 1 July 1993 (the date of Royal Assent of the Trade Union Reform and Employment Rights Act). All material available at the time of going to press which affects the law prospectively has been incorporated. It is indicated either by incorporation in the text with appropriate annotations or in the notes following the relevant text. Prospectively repealed text is printed in italics and prospective insertions are in square brackets.

The Trade Union Reform and Employment Rights Act 1993 is subject to the usual staged implementation of major legislation by commencement order. The first order, the Trade Union Reform and Employment Rights Act 1993 (Commencement No 1 and Transitional Provisions) Order 1993, SI 1993/1908, was made on 27 July 1993. It is reproduced in full at paras [1435]-[1442]. The order specifies commencement dates for almost all the provisions of the Act apart from those affecting maternity rights (which under EC Directive 92/85 must be in force by 18 October 1994), the new code on written particulars of terms of employment (likely to commence at the end of November 1993, according to a Department of Employment Press Release of 1 July 1993) and those provisions with commencement dates stipulated in the Act itself.

The major part of the Act commenced on 30 August 1993 as follows: Part I (except ss 7, 8, 9 and 14), the provisions enabling the making of new Regulations for Tribunals and the EAT (but no draft Regulations had been published by that date), and changes in unfair dismissal protection other than those linked to maternity rights.

Commencement dates have, so far as possible, been incorporated at proof stage into the notes to the relevant provisions, but it has not been possible to cross-reference fully the transitional provisions of the order at this late stage, and readers should take care to check the order itself for any transitional provisions and the events to which a commencement date relates. Commencement dates and information about commencement orders are only given for provisions coming into effect after 1 July 1988.

For reasons of space, Part II of the Wages Act 1986 (Wages Councils), which was repealed with effect from 30 August 1993, has been omitted.

In editing the Handbook, I have received much assistance from the comments of users too numerous to thank individually: those comments are much appreciated. I am grateful to the editorial staff at Butterworths and I am indebted to all involved for their enthusiastic, tolerant and professional approach. Responsibility for the vagaries of selection is mine alone.

PETER WALLINGTON
TEMPLE, EC4

September 1993

CONTENTS

PART 2 STATUTORY INSTRUMENTS

PART 3 EUROPEAN COMMUNITY MATERIALS

SECTION A: CONSTITUTIONAL MATERIALS

SECTION B: REGULATIONS, DIRECTIVES AND RECOMMENDATIONS

PART 4 STATUTORY CODES OF PRACTICE

PART 5 MISCELLANEOUS MATERIALS

(a) INTERNATIONAL LAW MATERIALS

(b) EMPLOYMENT APPEAL TRIBUNAL PRACTICE DIRECTIONS

(c) MISCELLANEOUS MATERIALS

PART 1
STATUTES

STATUTES

APPORTIONMENT ACT 1870

(1870 c 35)

An Act for the better Apportionment of Rents and other periodical Payments
[1 August 1870]

1 Short title

This Act may be cited for all purposes as "The Apportionment Act 1870."   **[1]**

2 Rents, etc to be apportionable in respect of time

. . . All rents, annuities, dividends, and other periodical payments in the nature of income (whether reserved or made payable under an instrument in writing or otherwise) shall, like interest on money lent, be considered as accruing from day to day, and shall be apportionable in respect of time accordingly.   **[2]**

NOTE

Words omitted repealed by the Statute Law Revision (No 2) Act 1893.

3, 4 *(Outside the scope of this work.)*

5 Interpretation

In the construction of this Act—

The word "rents" includes rent service, rentcharge, and rent seck, and also tithes and all periodical payments or renderings in lieu of or in the nature of rent or tithe.

The word "annuities" includes salaries and pensions.

The word "dividends" includes (besides dividends strictly so called) all payments made by the name of dividend, bonus or otherwise out of the revenue of trading or other public companies, divisable between all or any of the members of such respective companies, whether such payments shall be usually made or declared, at any fixed times or otherwise; and all such divisable revenue shall, for the purposes of this Act, be deemed to have accrued by equal daily increment during or within the period for or in respect of which the payment of the same revenue shall be declared or expressed to be made, but the said word "dividend" does not include payments in the nature of a return or reimbursement of capital.   **[3]**

6 *(Outside the scope of this work.)*

7 Nor where stipulation made to the contrary

The provisions of this Act shall not extend to any case in which it is or shall be expressly stipulated that no apportionment shall take place.   **[4]**

DISABLED PERSONS (EMPLOYMENT) ACT 1944
(1944 c 10)

ARRANGEMENT OF SECTIONS

Disabled persons

An Act to make further and better provision for enabling persons handicapped by disablement to secure employment, or work on their own account, and for purposes connected therewith

[1 March 1944]

Disabled persons

1 Definition of "disabled person"

(1) In this Act the expression "disabled person" means a person who, on account of injury, disease, or congenital deformity, is substantially handicapped in obtaining or keeping employment, or in undertaking work on his own account, of a kind which apart from that injury, disease or deformity would be suited to his age, experience and qualifications; and the expression "disablement", in relation to any person, shall be construed accordingly.

(2) For the purposes of the definitions contained in the preceding subsection, the expression "disease" shall be construed as including a physical or mental condition arising from imperfect development of any organ. **[5]**

2–5 (*Repealed by the Employment and Training Act 1973, s 14, Sch 3, para 2, Sch 4.*)

Provisions for enabling registered disabled persons to obtain employment or to undertake work on their own account

6 Register of disabled persons

(1) The Minister shall establish and maintain a register of disabled persons (in this Act referred to as "the register").

(2) The register shall be kept in such form, and entries therein, and alterations and removals of entries therein and therefrom, shall be made in such manner, as the Minister may determine.

(3) A person whose name is for the time being in the register is in this Act referred to as a "person registered as handicapped by disablement".

(4) The Minister may make regulations prescribing the manner in which the fact that a person's name is for the time being in the register may be proved, including, without prejudice to the generality of this power, regulations as to the issue of certificates for that purpose and as to the custody, use and delivery up thereof.   **[6]**

NOTE

Regulations under sub-s (4): The Disabled Persons (Registration) Regulations 1945, SR & O 1945/938, regs 8–10 (not reproduced).

7, 8 ((*Relating to the register of disabled persons) omitted for reasons of space.*)

9 Obligations as to employment of quota of registered persons in substantial staffs

(1) It shall be the duty of a person who has a substantial number of employees to give employment to persons registered as handicapped by disablement to the number that is his quota as ascertained in accordance with the next succeeding section, and, where he is not already doing so at times when vacancies occur, to allocate vacancies for that purpose; and the said duty shall be enforceable to the extent and in manner hereinafter in this section provided in the case of a person to whom this section applies, that is to say, a person who for the time being has, or in accordance with his normal practice and apart from transitory circumstances would have, in his employment persons to the number of not less than twenty (or such lower number as may be specified by an order made by the Minister for the time being in force).

(2) Subject to the provisions of the two next succeeding subsections, a person to whom this section applies shall not at any time take, or offer to take, into his employment any person other than a person registered as handicapped by disablement, if immediately after the taking in of that person the number of persons so registered in the employment of the person to whom this section applies (excluding persons employed by him in an employment of a class then designated under section twelve of this Act) would be less than his quota.

(3) Subsection (2) of this section shall not apply to a person's taking, or offering to take, into his employment at any time a person whom apart from that subsection it would have been his duty to take into his employment at that time either—

(a) by virtue of any Act, whether passed before or after the passing of this Act; or

(b) by virtue of an agreement to reinstate him in his employment entered into before the date appointed for the coming into operation of subsection (2) of this section.

(4) Subsection (2) of this section shall not apply to a person's taking, or offering to take, into his employment any person in accordance with a permit issued by the Minister under the subsequent provisions of this Act in that behalf.

(5) A person to whom this section applies who for the time being has in his employment a person registered as handicapped by disablement shall not, unless he has reasonable cause for doing so, discontinue the employment of that person, if immediately after the discontinuance the number of persons so registered in the employment of the person to whom this section applies (excluding persons employed by him in an employment of a class then designated under section twelve of this Act) would be less than his quota:

Provided that this subsection shall not have effect if immediately after the discontinuance the employer would no longer be a person to whom this section applies.

(6) Any person who contravenes subsection (2) or subsection (5) of this section shall be guilty of an offence and shall be liable on summary conviction to a fine not exceeding [level 3 on the standard scale] or to imprisonment for a term not exceeding three months, or to both such fine and such imprisonment.

(7) A prosecution for a contravention of subsection (5) of this section shall not be instituted against any person unless—

(a) the matter has been referred to a district advisory committee;
(b) the committee, before considering the matter, has notified that person so as to give him an opportunity of making within a period not shorter than seven days from the sending or giving of the notification to him such representations to the committee as he may desire, either orally or in writing as he may desire; and
(c) the committee has made a report to the Minister.

On any such prosecution it shall not be necessary to prove compliance with the preceding provisions of this subsection unless the defendant so requires, and, if he so requires, a certificate purporting to be signed by or on behalf of the chairman of a district advisory committee that the matter in question has been referred to the committee under this subsection and that a notification and report has been made by them as therein provided shall be sufficient evidence of the facts stated therein until the contrary is shown.   [7]

NOTES

Sub-s (6): maximum fine increased and converted to a level on the standard scale by the Criminal Justice Act 1982, ss 37, 38, 46.

No order has been made under sub-s (1) as at 1 July 1993.

10 Determination of employers' quotas

(1) The quota at any time of a person to whom section nine of this Act applies shall be a number ascertained in accordance with the provisions of this section.

(2) There shall be—

(a) a standard percentage; and
(b) a special percentage, either greater or smaller than the standard percentage, for employment in any trade or industry, or in any branch or part of any trade or industry, or for employment with any class of employer, being

employment to which it appears to the Minister that a percentage other than the standard percentage ought to be assigned on the ground of its having distinctive characteristics as respects its suitability for disabled persons.

(3) The standard percentage and any special percentage shall be such as may be specified by order made by the Minister, after consultation with such organisations representing employers and workers respectively, or both employers and workers, as he thinks fit, and an order assigning a special percentage shall contain such provisions as may appear to the Minister to be requisite for more particularly defining for the purposes of this section the trade or industry, branch or part of a trade or industry, or class of employer, to employment in which or with whom the percentage is assigned.

(4) The quota at any time of a person to whom section nine of this Act applies shall be the number ascertained by applying to the number of all the persons then in his employment (excluding persons employed by him in an employment of a class then designated under section twelve of this Act)—

    (a) so far as they consist of persons employed by him in an employment other than one to which a special percentage is then assigned, the standard percentage; and

    (b) so far as they consist of persons employed by him in an employment to which a special percentage is then assigned, that percentage:

Provided that if the number so ascertained includes or consists of a fraction less than one half the fraction shall be disregarded, and if the number so ascertained includes or consists of a fraction being one half or more the quota shall be the nearest higher whole number.

(5) On an application in that behalf being made in the prescribed manner by any person to whom section nine of this Act applies representing that his quota, if ascertained in accordance with the last preceding subsection, or with that subsection together with any direction for the time being in force under this subsection, would be too great having regard to the particular circumstances in which all or any of the persons employed by him are employed, the Minister, if he is satisfied, after referring the application to a district advisory committee for their recommendations and considering their recommendations, that the representation is well founded, may direct that, during any such period ending not later than twelve months from the date of the direction as may be therein specified, the standard percentage, or any special percentage, or both, shall be reduced as specified in the direction for the purposes of the operation of the last preceding subsection in relation to the applicant.

(6) The Minister shall, on an application in that behalf being made in the prescribed manner by any person to whom section nine of this Act applies and on his giving to the Minister all such information relevant to the application as he may require, determine what percentage of the number of all the persons in the employment of the applicant (excluding persons employed by him in an employment of a class for the time being designated under section twelve of this Act) his quota, as ascertained in accordance with the preceding provisions of this section, is likely to represent over any period ending not later than twelve months from the date of the determination, and shall furnish the applicant with a certificate stating that percentage and the period as respects which the determination was made, and the applicant shall be deemed to have in his employment at any time during the period stated in the certificate persons registered as handicapped by disablement to the number of his quota if the number of such persons then in his employment (excluding as aforesaid) reaches the percentage stated in the certificate of the number of all the persons then in his employment (excluding as aforesaid). **[8]**

NOTE
The "standard percentage" currently prescribed under sub-s (3) is 3%: Disabled Persons (Standard Percentage) Order 1946, SR & O 1946/1258. See also the Disabled Persons (Special Percentage) (No 1) Order 1946, SR & O 1946/236, specifying 0.1% for certain employments.

11 Permits for employment of persons not registered where quota condition not satisfied

(1) On an application in that behalf being made in the prescribed manner by any person to whom section nine of this Act applies, the Minister may grant a permit for the purposes of subsection (4) of that section if it appears to him to be expedient so to do having regard to the nature of the work for which the applicant desires to take a person or persons into his employment and the qualifications and the suitability for the work of any person or persons registered as handicapped by disablement who may be available therefor, or if he is satisfied that there is no such person or an insufficient number of such persons available therefor.

(2) A permit may be granted either unconditionally or subject to any conditions relating to the employment of the person or persons to whom the permit relates, and may be granted as respects the employment either of one or more persons specified or described therein or of a specified number of persons.

(3) If on an application being made as aforesaid the Minister is not satisfied that the case is one in which any permit, or such a permit as is applied for, ought to be granted, or is of opinion that conditions to which the applicant objects ought to be attached to a grant, then, if the applicant so requests, the Minister shall refer the application to a district advisory committee for their recommendations and shall determine what permit (if any) ought to be granted, and subject to what conditions (if any), only after considering the recommendations of the committee. **[9]**

NOTE
Prescribed forms of application: see the Disabled Persons (General) Regulations 1945, SR & O 1945/1558, reg 4.

12 Appropriation of vacancies in certain employments to registered persons only

(1) The Minister may, after consultation with such organisations representing [employers and workers respectively, or both employers and workers, as he thinks fit, by order designate classes of employment as classes to which this section is to apply, being such classes of employment as appear to him to afford specially suitable opportunities for the employment of disabled persons.

(2) Subject as mentioned in the next succeeding subsection no person shall take, or offer to take, into his employment in an employment of a class to which this section applies any person other than a person registered as handicapped by disablement, or cause or permit a person in his employment other than a person registered as handicapped by disablement to take up with him employment of a class to which this section applies.

(3) The provisions as to taking a person into employment in pursuance of a statutory or contractual obligation, and as to permits, of subsections (3) and (4) of section nine, and of section eleven, of this Act shall have effect in relation to the last preceding subsection as they have effect in relation to subsection (2) of section nine of this Act.

(4) Any person who contravenes subsection (2) of this section shall be guilty of an offence and shall be liable on summary conviction to a fine not exceeding [level 3 on the standard scale] or to imprisonment for a term not exceeding three months, or to both such fine and such imprisonment.   **[10]**

NOTE

Sub-s (4): maximum fine increased and converted to a level on the standard scale by the Criminal Justice Act 1982, ss 37, 38, 46.

13 Provisions for interpretation, etc, of preceding sections

(1) In this Act references to employment shall be construed as references to any relationship, whether entered into for business or other purposes, the legal character of which is that of master and servant, or is that of master and apprentice or a relationship similar to that of master and apprentice.

(2) In this Act references to taking into employment shall be construed—

(a) as including references to the engagement by an employer of a person previously in his employment, but not if the new period of employment begins immediately on the ending of an earlier period or after an interval attributable to the employed person's illness or being on holiday or to other temporary causes;

(b) as not including any reference to the taking into his employment, by a person taking over a business or establishment at any time in succession to, or jointly with, another person who was carrying it on immediately before that time, of a person employed in that business or establishment immediately before that time.

(3) With respect to part-time employment, or to employment part-time with one employer and part-time with another or with the same employer part-time in one class of employment and part-time in another, the Minister may make regulations prescribing the extent and manner to and in which such employment is to be regarded for the purposes of this Act.

(4) Where a person who is a trustee or is acting in any other fiduciary capacity has employees the expenses (if any) of whose employment are or would be chargeable in his accounts in that capacity, he shall be treated for the purposes of the provisions of this Act relating to the duty of employers to give employment to persons registered as handicapped by disablement as one person in relation to that capacity and a different person in relation to any other capacity.

(5) The fact that the making, termination or variation of a contract involves a contravention of any of the provisions of this Act relating to the duty of employers to give employment to persons registered as handicapped by disablement, or of the last preceding section, shall not affect the operation in law of the contract, or of its termination or variation, as the case may be.

(6) Where a person registered as handicapped by disablement ceases to be so registered at a time when he is in employment with any employer, and for any period thereafter continues, either without any interval or with such interval only as is mentioned in paragraph (a) of subsection (2) of this section, in employment with that employer, or with a person taking over in succession (whether directly or indirectly) to, or jointly with, that employer a business or establishment in which the person who was so registered was employed at that time, he shall, for the purposes of the application of this Act during that period to that employer or to any person taking over as aforesaid, be treated as if he had continued to be a person so registered.

          [11]

14 Records to be kept by employers

(1) Every person to whom section nine of this Act applies shall record particulars showing the number of persons employed by him, the number of persons registered as handicapped by disablement employed by him, and the names of such persons respectively, and particulars of all other matters which may be relevant for showing compliance on his part with the provisions of subsections (2) and (5) of that section, being particulars giving all such information, and recorded in such form, as may be requisite for that purpose.

(2) Every person who employs any person or persons in employment of a class designated under section twelve of this Act shall record particulars showing his or their name or names, and particulars of all other matters which may be relevant for showing compliance on his part with the provisions of subsection (2) of that section, being particulars giving all such information, and recorded in such form, as may be requisite for that purpose.

(3) The Minister may make regulations as to the matters of which particulars ought to be recorded under this section, the nature of the particulars proper to be recorded, and the form appropriate for the recording thereof, and records conforming in any respect with regulations so made shall be treated as sufficient in that respect for the purposes of this section.

(4) A person as respects whose employees records of such particulars as are mentioned in subsection (1) or (2) of this section are made shall preserve them for such period as may be prescribed, and shall on being required so to do by a person authorised by the Minister in that behalf produce them for his inspection.

(5) On a prosecution for an offence under subsection (2) or (5) of section nine of this Act, or for an offence under subsection (2) of section twelve of this Act, a record of such particulars as are mentioned in subsection (1) or (2), as the case may be, of this section made by or on behalf of a person by whom the offence is alleged to have been committed shall be sufficient evidence, until the contrary is shown, of the facts stated therein.

(6) If any person contravenes or fails to comply with any of the provisions applicable to him of subsection (1), (2) or (4) of this section, he shall be guilty of an offence and shall be liable on summary conviction to a fine not exceeding [level 2 on the standard scale], and if a failure to produce records in respect of which a person has been convicted under this subsection is continued after conviction, he shall, unless he proves that the failure is due to his not having made or not having preserved the required records, be guilty of a further offence and liable on summary conviction to a fine not exceeding five pounds for each day on which the failure is so continued.

(7) If any person includes, or causes or knowingly allows to be included, in a record of such particulars as are mentioned in subsection (1) or (2) of this section, any particulars which he knows to be false in a material respect, or for purposes connected with this Act produces or furnishes, or causes or knowingly allows to be produced or furnished, any record or information which he knows to be false in a material respect, he shall be guilty of an offence and shall be liable on summary conviction to a fine not exceeding [level 3 on the standard scale] or to imprisonment for a term not exceeding three months, or to both such fine and such imprisonment.   [12]

NOTES

  Sub-s (6): first-mentioned maximum fine previously increased by the Criminal Law Act 1977, s 31(6), and converted to a level on the standard scale by the Criminal Justice Act 1982, ss 37, 46.
  Sub-s (7): maximum fine increased and converted to a level on the standard scale by the Criminal Justice Act 1982, ss 37, 38, 46.

15 Provision for registered persons who are seriously disabled of employment, or work on their own account, under special conditions

(1) Facilities may be provided as specified in this section for enabling persons registered as handicapped by disablement who by reason of the nature or severity of their disablement are unlikely either at any time or until after the lapse of a prolonged period to be able otherwise to obtain employment, or to undertake work on their own account (whether because employment or such work would not be available to them or because they would be unlikely to be able to compete therein on terms comparable as respects earnings and security with those enjoyed by persons engaged therein who are not subject to disablement), to obtain employment or to undertake such work under special conditions, and for the training of such persons for the employment or work in question.

(2) The nature of the facilities to be provided under this section shall be such as the Minister may determine, and the Minister may with the approval of the Treasury make arrangements for the provision thereof by any of one or more companies which may be formed for that purpose and incorporated under the Companies Act 1929, [or the Companies Act 1948] at his instance, being a company required by its constitution to apply its profits, if any, or other income in promoting its objects and prohibited thereby from paying any dividend to its members, or by any association or body, being an association or body so required and prohibited, which appears to the Minister to be able and willing to provide the requisite facilities in an efficient and proper manner.

(3) The objects of any company to be formed for the purposes of this section may include all such objects as appear to the Minister to be requisite for enabling it to act effectively for those purposes, and any such company shall be constituted so as to enable all or any of its operations to be controlled by the Minister or persons acting on his behalf as may appear to the Minister to be requisite.

(4) The Minister, or with his authorisation any such company association or body as aforesaid providing facilities under this section, may defray or contribute towards expenses incurred by persons for whom facilities are provided under this section in travelling to and from the place where they are employed or work or where training is provided, and may make payments to or in respect of such persons, up to such amounts as the Minister may with the approval of the Treasury determine and in such manner as he may determine.

(5) Payments may be made by the Minister—

    (a) in respect of the expenses of the formation and incorporation of any such company as aforesaid,

    (b) to any such company association or body as aforesaid in respect of expenses incurred by them in providing facilities under this section, or of expenses incurred by them under the last preceding subsection, and

    (c) to any local authority in respect of expenses incurred by them under any enactment conferring powers on them in that behalf in providing under arrangements made between the Minister and the authority facilities approved by him for any of the purposes mentioned in subsection (1) of this section, in defraying or contributing towards expenses incurred by persons for whom such facilities are so provided in travelling as mentioned in the last preceding subsection, or in making payments to or in respect of such persons,

up to such amounts as the Minister may with the approval of the Treasury determine.

(6) Expenses incurred by the Minister under this section shall be defrayed out of moneys provided by Parliament. **[13]**

NOTE

Sub-s (2): amended by the Companies Act 1948, s 457(b). No equivalent amendment has been made to accommodate the enactment of the Companies Act 1985: see the Companies Consolidation (Consequential Provisions) Act 1985, Sch 2.

Administration

16 Preference for ex-service men and women

The Minister shall so exercise his discretion in selecting persons for . . . facilities under section fifteen of this Act at any time while it appears to him that they cannot for the time being be provided for all persons in need of them, . . . as to secure that, so far as consistent with the efficient exercise of his powers, preference shall be given to persons . . . who have served whole time in the armed forces of the Crown or in the merchant navy or the mercantile marine . . . **[14]**

NOTE

First and second words omitted repealed by the Employment and Training Act 1973, s 14(2), Sch 3 para 2, Sch 4; third and fourth words omitted repealed by the Armed Forces Act 1981, s 28, Sch 5, Pt I.

17 (*Provides, together with Sch 2, for the setting up of a national advisory council and district advisory committees.*)

18 Officers, etc

(1) The Minister, with the approval of the Treasury as to numbers and remuneration, may appoint officers and servants to act for the purposes of this Act, and may, in lieu of or in addition to appointing persons under this section, arrange with any government department that officers or servants of that department shall act for the purposes of this Act.

(2) There shall be paid to officers and servants appointed under this section such salaries or remuneration as the Treasury may determine, and the expenses of the payment thereof, and any other administrative expenses incurred for the purposes of this Act by any government department, shall be defrayed out of moneys provided by Parliament. **[15]**

19 Provisions as to offences

(1) Proceedings for an offence under this Act shall not be instituted in England except by or with the consent of the Minister or by an officer authorised in that behalf by special or general directions of the Minister.

(2) Notwithstanding any provision in any Act prescribing the period within which summary proceedings may be commenced, proceedings for an offence under this Act may be commenced at any time within the period of three months from the date on which evidence, sufficient in the opinion of the Minister to justify a prosecution for the offence, comes to his knowledge, or within the period of twelve months from the date on which the offence was committed, whichever period last expires, and for the purposes of this subsection a certificate purporting to be signed

by or on behalf of the Minister as to the date on which such evidence as aforesaid came to his knowledge shall be conclusive evidence thereof.

(3) Where the person convicted of an offence under this Act in respect of which a fine up to a maximum amount of [level 3 on the standard scale] may be imposed under any of the preceding provisions thereof is a body corporate, the maximum amount of the fine which may be imposed on that body shall be [level 5 on the standard scale] in lieu of [level 3 on the standard scale].

(4) Where an offence under this Act has been committed by a body corporate, every person who at the time of the commission of the offence was a director or officer of the body corporate, or was purporting to act in any such capacity, shall be deemed to be guilty of that offence, unless he proves that the contravention was committed without his consent or connivance and that he exercised all such diligence to prevent the commission of the offence as he ought to have exercised having regard to the nature of his functions in that capacity and to all the circumstances.

(5) Proceedings against a person for an offence under this Act alleged to have been committed outside Great Britain may be taken before the appropriate court in Great Britain having jurisdiction in the place where that person is for the time being.

(6) Subsection (2) of this section shall in its application to Scotland have effect as if for the reference to evidence sufficient to justify a prosecution there were substituted a reference to evidence sufficient to justify a report to the Lord Advocate with a view to consideration of the question of prosecution.   **[16]**

NOTE

Sub-s (3): maximum fines increased and converted to levels on the standard scale by the Criminal Justice Act 1982, ss 37, 38, 46.

20 Regulations and orders

(1) The Minister may make regulations for prescribing anything which under this Act is to be prescribed.

(2) Any regulations or order made by the Minister under this Act shall, as soon as may be after the making thereof, be laid before Parliament, and if either House of Parliament within the period of twenty-eight days beginning with the day on which any such regulations or order are or is laid before it resolves that the regulations or order be annulled, the regulations or order shall thereupon become void, without prejudice, however, to the validity of anything previously done thereunder or to the making of new regulations or a new order.

In reckoning any such period of twenty-eight days as aforesaid, no account shall be taken of any time during which Parliament is dissolved or prorogued, or during which both Houses are adjourned for more than four days.

(3) . . .

(4) An order made under this Act may be varied or revoked by a subsequent order.   **[17]**

NOTE

Sub-s (3): repealed by the Statute Law Revision Act 1963.

Application, commencement, etc

21 Application as respects a place of employment, and nationality

(1) In the provisions of this Act relating to the duty of employers to give employment to persons registered as handicapped by disablement or to employments of classes designated under section twelve of this Act, references to employment shall be construed, subject to the provisions of the next succeeding subsection, as references to employment in Great Britain.

(2) In the said provisions of this Act references to employment shall include references to employment in the capacity of master or of a member of the crew of a British ship (other than a ship employed exclusively outside Great Britain) if the owner or managing owner or person having the management of the ship is resident or has his principal place of business in Great Britain:

Provided that subsection (2) of section nine of this Act and subsection (2) of section twelve thereof shall, in relation to the taking into employment of a person in any such capacity as aforesaid or the taking up by a person employed in any such capacity as aforesaid of an employment of a class designated under section twelve of this Act, have effect only if the engagement under which he is taken into employment is entered into, or if his employment in the employment of that class begins, in Great Britain.

(3) This Act shall, subject as may be prescribed, apply to persons who are not British subjects in the same manner as it applies to persons who are British subjects. **[18]**

22 (*Provides for the application of certain parts of the Act to Northern Ireland.*)

23 Short title, interpretation and commencement

(1) This Act may be cited as the Disabled Persons (Employment) Act 1944.

(2) References in this Act to any enactment shall be construed as references to that enactment as amended by or under any other enactment.

(3) . . . **[19]**

NOTE

Sub-s (3): repealed by the Statute Law Revision Act 1950.

(*Sch 1 repealed with savings by the Armed Forces Act 1981, s 28(2), Sch 5, Pt I; Sch 2 omitted (see note to s 17).*)

EQUAL PAY ACT 1970

(1970 c 41)

ARRANGEMENT OF SECTIONS

An Act to prevent discrimination, as regards terms and conditions of employment between men and women

[29 May 1970]

1 Requirement of equal treatment for men and women in same employment

[(1) If the terms of a contract under which a woman is employed at an establishment in Great Britain do not include (directly or by reference to a collective agreement or otherwise) an equality clause they shall be deemed to include one.

(2) An equality clause is a provision which relates to terms (whether concerned with pay or not) of a contract under which a woman is employed (the "woman's contract"), and has the effect that—

(a) where the woman is employed on like work with a man in the same employment—

(i) if (apart from the equality clause) any term of the woman's contract is or becomes less favourable to the woman than a term of a similar kind in the contract under which that man is employed, that term of the woman's contract shall be treated as so modified as not to be less favourable, and

(ii) if (apart from the equality clause) at any time the woman's contract does not include a term corresponding to a term benefiting that man included in the contract under which he is employed, the woman's contract shall be treated as including such a term;

(b) where the woman is employed on work rated as equivalent with that of a man in the same employment—

(i) if (apart from the equality clause) any term of the woman's contract determined by the rating of the work is or becomes less favourable to the woman than a term of a similar kind in the contract under which that man is employed, that term of the woman's contract shall be treated as so modified as not to be less favourable, and

(ii) if (apart from the equality clause) at any time the woman's contract does not include a term corresponding to a term benefiting that man included in the contract under which he is employed and determined by the rating of the work, the woman's contract shall be treated as including such a term;

[(c) where a woman is employed on work which, not being work in relation to which paragraph (a) or (b) above applies, is, in terms of the demands made on her (for instance under such headings as effort, skill and decision), of equal value to that of a man in the same employment—

(i) if (apart from the equality clause) any term of the woman's contract is or becomes less favourable to the woman than a term of a similar kind in the contract under which that man is employed, that term of the woman's contract shall be treated as so modified as not to be less favourable, and

(ii) if (apart from the equality clause) at any time the woman's contract does not include a term corresponding to a term benefiting that man included in the contract under which he is employed, the woman's contract shall be treated as including such a term].

[(3) An equality clause shall not operate in relation to a variation between the woman's contract and the man's contract if the employer proves that the variation is genuinely due to a material factor which is not the difference of sex and that factor—

    (a) in the case of an equality clause falling within subsection (2)(a) or (b) above, must be a material difference between the woman's case and the man's; and

    (b) in the case of an equality clause falling within subsection (2)(c) above, may be such a material difference.]]

(4) A woman is to be regarded as employed on like work with men if, but only if, her work and theirs is of the same or a broadly similar nature, and the differences (if any) between the things she does and the things they do are not of practical importance in relation to terms and conditions of employment; and accordingly in comparing her work with theirs regard shall be had to the frequency or otherwise with which any such differences occur in practice as well as to the nature and extent of the differences.

(5) A woman is to be regarded as employed on work rated as equivalent with that of any men if, but only if, her job and their job have been given an equal value, in terms of the demand made on a worker under various headings (for instance effort, skill, decision), on a study undertaken with a view to evaluating in those terms the jobs to be done by all or any of the employees in an undertaking or group of undertakings, or would have been given an equal value but for the evaluation being made on a system setting different values for men and women on the same demand under any heading.

(6) Subject to the following subsections, for purposes of this section—

    (a) "employed" means employed under a contract of service or of apprenticeship or a contract personally to execute any work or labour, and related expressions shall be construed accordingly;

    (b) ...

    (c) two employers are to be treated as associated if one is a company of which the other (directly or indirectly) has control or if both are companies of which a third person (directly or indirectly) has control,

[and men shall be treated as in the same employment with a woman if they are men employed by her employer or any associated employer at the same establishment or at establishments in Great Britain which include that one and at which common terms and conditions of employment are observed either generally or for employees of the relevant classes].

(7) ...

[(8) This section shall apply to—

    (a) service for purposes of a Minister of the Crown or government department, other than service of a person holding a statutory office, or

    (b) service on behalf of the Crown for purposes of a person holding a statutory office or purposes of a statutory body,

as it applies to employment by a private person, and shall so apply as if references to a contract of employment included references to the terms of service.

(9) Subsection (8) does not apply in relation to service in—

    (a) the naval, military or air forces of the Crown, ...

    (b) ...

(10) In this section "statutory body" means a body set up by or in pursuance of an enactment, and "statutory office" means an office so set up; and service "for purposes of" a Minister of the Crown or government department does not include service in any office in Schedule 2 (Ministerial offices) to the House of Commons Disqualification Act 1975 as for the time being in force.]

[(10A) This section applies in relation to service as a relevant member of the House of Commons staff as in relation to service for the purposes of a Minister of the Crown or government department, and accordingly applies as if references to a contract of employment included references to the terms of service of such a member.

In this subsection "relevant member of the House of Commons staff" has the same meaning as in section 139 of the Employment Protection (Consolidation) Act 1978; and subsections (4) to (9) of that section (person to be treated as employer of House of Commons staff) apply, with any necessary modifications, for the purposes of this section.]

[(10B)This section applies in relation to employment as a relevant member of the House of Lords staff as in relation to other employment.

In this subsection "relevant member of the House of Lords staff" has the same meaning as in section 139A of the Employment Protection (Consolidation) Act 1978; and subsection (6) of that section applies for the purposes of this section.]

[(11) For the purposes of this Act it is immaterial whether the law which (apart from this subsection) is the [law applicable to] a contract is the law of any part of the United Kingdom or not.

(12) In this Act "Great Britain" includes such of the territorial waters of the United Kingdom as are adjacent to Great Britain.

(13) Provisions of this section and [sections 2 and 2A] below framed with reference to women and their treatment relative to men are to be read as applying equally in a converse case to men and their treatment relative to women.] **[20]**

NOTES

Sub-ss (1), (8): substituted by the Sex Discrimination Act 1975, s 8(1), (6), Sch 1, Pt I.

Sub-s (2): substituted by the Sex Discrimination Act 1975, s 8(1); para (c) added by the Equal Pay (Amendment) Regulations 1983, SI 1983/1794, reg 2(1).

Sub-s (3): further substituted by SI 1983/1794, reg 2(2).

Sub-s (6): para (b) repealed and words at the end of sub-s (6) added by the Sex Discrimination Act 1975, s 8(6), Sch 1, Pt I.

Sub-s (7): repealed by the Sex Discrimination Act 1975, s 8(6), Sch 1, Pt I.

Sub-s (9): added by the Sex Discrimination Act 1975, s 8(6), Sch 1, Pt I; para (b) and the word "or" preceding it repealed by the Armed Forces Act 1981, s 28, Sch 5, Pt I.

Sub-s (10): added by the Sex Discrimination Act 1975, s 8(6), Sch 1, Pt I.

Sub-s (10A): added by the Trade Union and Labour Relations (Consolidation) Act 1992, s 300(2), Sch 2, para 3(1), (2).

Sub-s (10B): inserted by the Trade Union Reform and Employment Rights Act 1993, s 49(1), Sch 7, para 8, as from a day to be appointed.

Sub-s (11): added by the Sex Discrimination Act 1975, s 8(6), Sch 1, Pt I; words in square brackets substituted by the Contracts (Applicable Law) Act 1990, s 5, Sch 4.

Sub-s (12): added by the Sex Discrimination Act 1975, s 8(6), Sch 1, Pt I.

Sub-s (13): added by the Sex Discrimination Act 1975, s 8(6), Sch 1, Pt I; words in square brackets substituted by SI 1983/1794, reg 3(2).

2 Disputes as to, and enforcement of, requirement of equal treatment

[(1) Any claim in respect of the contravention of a term modified or included by virtue of an equality clause, including a claim for arrears of remuneration or damages in respect of the contravention, may be presented by way of a complaint to an industrial tribunal.

(1A)   Where a dispute arises in relation to the effect of an equality clause the employer may apply to an industrial tribunal for an order declaring the rights of the employer and the employee in relation to the matter in question.]

(2) Where it appears to the Secretary of State that there may be a question whether the employer of any women is or has been [contravening a term modified or included by virtue of their equality clauses], but that it is not reasonable to expect them to take steps to have the question determined, the question may be referred by him [as respects all or any of them] to an industrial tribunal and shall be dealt with as if the reference were of a claim by the women [or woman] against the employer.

(3) Where it appears to the court in which any proceedings are pending that a claim or counter-claim in respect of the operation of an [equality clause] could more conveniently be disposed of separately by an industrial tribunal, the court may direct that the claim or counter-claim shall be struck out; and (without prejudice to the foregoing) where in proceedings before any court a question arises as to the operation of an [equality clause], the court may on the application of any party to the proceedings or otherwise refer that question, or direct it to be referred by a party to the proceedings, to an industrial tribunal for determination by the tribunal, and may stay or sist the proceedings in the meantime.

(4) No claim in respect of the operation of an [equality clause] relating to a woman's employment shall be referred to an industrial tribunal otherwise than by virtue of subsection (3) above, if she has not been employed in the employment within the six months preceding the date of the reference.

(5) A woman shall not be entitled, in proceedings brought in respect of a failure to comply with an [equality clause] (including proceedings before an industrial tribunal), to be awarded any payment by way of arrears of remuneration or damages in respect of a time earlier than two years before the date on which the proceedings were instituted.

(6), (7) . . .   [21]

NOTES
Sub-s (1): substituted by the Sex Discrimination Act 1975, s 8(6), Sch 1, Pt I.
Sub-s (1A): inserted by the Sex Discrimination Act 1975, s 8(6), Sch 1, Pt I.
Sub-ss (2)-(5): amended by the Sex Discrimination Act 1975, s 8(6), Sch, Pt I.
Sub-s (6): repealed by the Sex Discrimination Act 1975, s 8(6), Sch 1, Pt I.
Sub-s (7): repealed by the Employment Protection (Consolidation) Act 1978, s 159(3), Sch 17.

[2A Procedure before tribunal in certain cases

(1) Where on a complaint or reference made to an industrial tribunal under section 2 above, a dispute arises as to whether any work is of equal value as mentioned in section 1(2)(c) above the tribunal shall not determine that question unless—

    (a) it is satisfied that there are no reasonable grounds for determining that the work is of equal value as so mentioned; or

    (b) it has required a member of the panel of independent experts to prepare a report with respect to that question and has received that report.

(2) Without prejudice to the generality of paragraph (a) of subsection (1) above, there shall be taken, for the purposes of that paragraph, to be no reasonable grounds for determining that the work of a woman is of equal value as mentioned in section 1(2)(c) above if—

    (a) that work and the work of the man in question have been given different values on a study such as is mentioned in section 1(5) above; and

(b) there are no reasonable grounds for determining that the evaluation contained in the study was (within the meaning of subsection (3) below) made on a system which discriminates on grounds of sex.

(3) An evaluation contained in a study such as is mentioned in section 1(5) above is made on a system which discriminates on grounds of sex where a difference, or coincidence, between values set by that system on different demands under the same or different headings is not justifiable irrespective of the sex of the person on whom those demands are made.

(4) In paragraph (b) of subsection (1) above the reference to a member of the panel of independent experts is a reference to a person who is for the time being designated by the Advisory, Conciliation and Arbitration Service for the purposes of that paragraph as such a member, being neither a member of the Council of that Service nor one of its officers or servants.]   **[22–23]**

NOTE

Added by the Equal Pay (Amendment) Regulations 1983, SI 1983/1794, reg 3(1).

3–5 (*S 3 repealed by the Sex Discrimination Act 1986, s 9, Schedule, Pt II (for savings, see s 9(3)); s 4 repealed by the Wages Act 1986, s 32(2), Sch 5, Pt II; s 5 (reference of agricultural wages orders to Central Arbitration Committee) omitted.*)

6 Exclusion from ss 1 to 5 of pensions etc

[(1) [An equality clause shall not] operate in relation to terms—

    (a) affected by compliance with the laws regulating the employment of women, or

    (b) affording special treatment to women in connection with pregnancy or childbirth.

    (1A) An equality clause . . . —

    (a) shall operate in relation to terms relating to membership of an occupational pension scheme (within the meaning of the Social Security Pensions Act 1975) *so far as those terms relate to any matter in respect of which the scheme has to conform with the equal access requirements of Part IV of that Act; but*

    (b) subject to this, shall not operate in relation to terms related to death or retirement, or to any provision made in connection with death or retirement [other than a term or provision which, in relation to retirement, affords access to opportunities for promotion transfer or training or provides for a woman's dismissal or demotion].]

(2) Any reference in this section to retirement includes retirement, whether voluntary or not, on grounds of age, length of service or incapacity [and the reference in subsection (1A) above to a woman's dismissal shall be construed in accordance with section 82(1A) of the Sex Discrimination Act 1975 as a reference to her dismissal from employment].   **[24]**

NOTES

Sub-s (1): substituted together with sub-s (1A) for original sub-s (1) by the Sex Discrimination Act 1975, s 8(6), Sch 1, Pt I; words in square brackets substituted by the Sex Discrimination Act 1986, s 9(1), (3), Schedule, Pt II.

Sub-s (1A): substituted together with sub-s (1) by the Sex Discrimination Act 1975, s 8(6), Sch 1, Pt I; words omitted repealed by the Sex Discrimination Act 1986, s 9, Schedule, Pt II; words in square brackets

added by ss 2, 9(1) of the 1986 Act; italicised words repealed by the Social Security Act 1989, s 23, Sch 5, Pt II, para 13, as from a day to be appointed. The following words will then replace those repealed:
  "which is also an employment-related benefit scheme, within the meaning of Schedule 5 to the Social Security Act 1989, so far as those terms relate to any matter in respect of which the scheme has to comply with the principle of equal treatment in accordance with that Schedule; but"
Sub-s (2): words in square brackets added by the Sex Discrimination Act 1986, s 2.

7 Service pay

(1) The Secretary of State or Defence Council shall not make, or recommend to Her Majesty the making of, any instrument relating to the terms and conditions of service of members of the naval, military or air forces of the Crown . . ., if the instrument has the effect of making a distinction, as regards pay, allowances or leave, between men and women who are members of those forces . . ., not being a distinction fairly attributable to differences between the obligations undertaken by men and those undertaken by women as such members as aforesaid.

(2) The Secretary of State or Defence Council may refer to the [Central Arbitration Committee] for their advice any question whether a provision made or proposed to be made by any such instrument as is referred to in subsection (1) above ought to be regarded for purposes of this section as making a distinction not permitted by that subsection. **[25]**

NOTES
Sub-s (1): words omitted repealed by the Armed Forces Act 1981, s 28, Sch 5, Part I.
Sub-s (2): words in square brackets originally substituted by the Employment Protection Act 1975, s 125(1), Sch 16, Part IV and continue to have effect by virtue of the Trade Union and Labour Relations (Consolidation) Act 1992, s 300(2), Sch 2, para 3.

8 (*Repealed by the Sex Discrimination Act 1975, s 8(6), Sch 1, Pt I, para 4.*)

9 Commencement

(1) . . . the foregoing provisions of this Act shall come into force on the 29th December 1975 and references in this Act to its commencement shall be construed as referring to the coming into force of those provisions on that date.

(2)–(5) . . . **[26]**

NOTES
Sub-s (1): words omitted repealed by the Sex Discrimination Act 1975, s 8(6), Sch 1, Part I.
Sub-ss (2)–(5): repealed by the Sex Discrimination Act 1975, s 8(6), Sch 1, Part I.

10 (*Repealed by the Sex Discrimination Act 1986, s 9, Schedule, Pt II.*)

11 Short title, interpretation and extent

(1) This Act may be cited as the Equal Pay Act 1970.

(2) In this Act the expression "man" and "woman" shall be read as applying to persons of whatever age.

(3) This Act shall not extend to Northern Ireland. **[27]**

EUROPEAN COMMUNITIES ACT 1972
(1972 c 68)

ARRANGEMENT OF SECTIONS

PART I
GENERAL PROVISIONS

An Act to make provision in connection with the enlargement of the European Communities to include the United Kingdom, together with (for certain purposes) the Channel Islands, the Isle of Man and Gibraltar
                                                       [17 October 1972]

NOTE

    The Parts of this Act which have been reproduced here are those which govern the status in UK law of the European Community Treaties and legislation, and empower the incorporation of Community legislation into UK law.

PART I
GENERAL PROVISIONS

1 Short title and interpretation

(1) This Act may be cited as the European Communities Act 1972.

    (2) In this Act . . . —

    "the Communities" means the European Economic Community, the European Coal and Steel Community and the European Atomic Energy Community;

    "the Treaties" or "the Community Treaties" means, subject to subsection (3) below, the pre-accession treaties, that is to say, those described in Part I of Schedule I to this Act, taken with—

      (a) the treaty relating to the accession of the United Kingdom to the European Economic Community and to the European Atomic Energy Community, signed at Brussels on the 22nd January 1972; and

      (b) the decision, of the same date, of the Council of the European Communities relating to the accession of the United Kingdom to the European Coal and Steel Community; [and

      (c) the treaty relating to the accession of the Hellenic Republic to the European Economic Community and to the European Atomic Energy Community, signed at Athens on 28th May 1979; and

(d) the decision, of 24th May 1979, of the Council relating to the accession of the Hellenic Republic to the European Coal and Steel Community;] [and

(e) the decisions, of 7th May 1985 and of 24th June 1988, of the Council on the Communities' system of own resources; and

(f) the undertaking by the Representatives of the Governments of the member States, as confirmed at their meeting within the Council on 24th June 1988 in Luxembourg, to make payments to finance the Communities' general budget for the financial year 1988; and] [and

(g) the treaty relating to the accession of the Kingdom of Spain and the Portuguese Republic to the European Economic Community and to the European Atomic Energy Community, signed at Lisbon and Madrid on 12th June 1985; and

(h) the decision, of 11th June 1985, of the Council relating to the accession of the Kingdom of Spain and the Portuguese Republic to the European Coal and Steel Community;] [and

(j) the following provisions of the Single European Act signed at Luxembourg and The Hague on 17th and 28th February 1986, namely Title II (amendment of the treaties establishing the Communities) and, so far as they relate to any of the Communities or any Community institution, the preamble and Titles I (common provisions) and IV (general and final provisions);] [and

(k) Titles II, III and IV of the Treaty on European Union signed at Maastricht on 7th February 1992, together with the other provisions of the Treaty so far as they relate to those Titles, and the Protocols adopted at Maastricht on that date and annexed to the Treaty establishing the European Community with the exception of the Protocol on Social Policy on page 117 of Cm 1934]

and any other treaty entered into by any of the Communities, with or without any of the member States, or entered into, as a treaty ancillary to any of the Treaties, by the United Kingdom;

and any expression defined in Schedule I to this Act has the meaning there given to it.

(3) If Her Majesty by Order in Council declares that a treaty specified in the Order is to be regarded as one of the Community Treaties as herein defined, the Order shall be conclusive that it is to be so regarded; but a treaty entered into by the United Kingdom after the 22nd January 1972, other than a pre-accession treaty to which the United Kingdom accedes on terms settled on or before that date, shall not be so regarded unless it is so specified, nor be so specified unless a draft of the Order in Council has been approved by resolution of each House of Parliament.

(4) For purposes of subsections (2) and (3) above, "treaty" includes any international agreement, and any protocol or annex to a treaty or international agreement.　　　　　　　　　　　　　　　　　　　　　　　　　　　　　　**[28]**

NOTES

Sub-s (2): words omitted repealed by the Interpretation Act 1978, s 25(1), Sch 3; paras (c), (d) added by the European Communities (Greek Accession) Act 1979, s 1; paras (e), (f) added by the European Communities (Finance) Act 1985, s 1, substituted by the European Communities (Finance) Act 1988, s 1; paras (g), (h) added by the European Communities (Spanish and Portuguese Accession) Act 1985, s 1; para (j) added by the European Communities (Amendment) Act 1986, s 1; para (k) added by the European Communities (Amendment) Act 1993, s 1(1), as from 23 July 1993.

By virtue of s 7 of the European Communities (Amendment) Act 1993, that Act (and therefore the insertion of para (k) in sub-s (2) above) "shall come into force only when each House of Parliament has come to a Resolution on a motion tabled by a Minister of the Crown considering the question of adopting the Protocol on Social Policy". Such Resolutions were passed by the House of Lords on 22 July 1993 and by the House of Commons on 23 July 1993. The Treaty was ratified by the United Kingdom on 2 August 1993.

---

2 General implementation of Treaties

(1) All such rights, powers, liabilities, obligations and restrictions from time to time created or arising by or under the Treaties, and all such remedies and procedures from time to time provided for by or under the Treaties, as in accordance with the Treaties are without further enactment to be given legal effect or used in the United Kingdom shall be recognised and available in law, and be enforced, allowed and followed accordingly; and the expression "enforceable Community right" and similar expressions shall be read as referring to one to which this subsection applies.

(2) Subject to Schedule 2 to this Act, at any time after its passing Her Majesty may by Order in Council, and any designated Minister or department may by regulations, make provision—

(a) for the purpose of implementing any Community obligation of the United Kingdom, or enabling any such obligation to be implemented, or of enabling any rights enjoyed or to be enjoyed by the United Kingdom under or by virtue of the Treaties to be exercised; or

(b) for the purpose of dealing with matters arising out of or related to any such obligation or rights or the coming into force, or the operation from time to time, of subsection (1) above;

and in the exercise of any statutory power or duty, including any power to give directions or to legislate by means of orders, rules, regulations or other subordinate instrument, the person entrusted with the power or duty may have regard to the objects of the Communities and to any such obligation or rights as aforesaid.

In this subsection "designated Minister or department" means such Minister of the Crown or government department as may from time to time be designated by Order in Council in relation to any matter or for any purpose, but subject to such restrictions or conditions (if any) as may be specified by the Order in Council.

(3) There shall be charged on and issued out of the Consolidated Fund or, if so determined by the Treasury, the National Loans Fund the amounts required to meet any Community obligation to make payments to any of the Communities or member States, or any Community obligation in respect of contributions to the capital or reserves of the European Investment Bank or in respect of loans to the Bank, or to redeem any notes or obligations issued or created in respect of any such Community obligation; and, except as otherwise provided by or under any enactment,—

(a) any other expenses incurred under or by virtue of the Treaties or this Act by any Minister of the Crown or government department may be paid out of moneys provided by Parliament; and

(b) any sums received under or by virtue of the Treaties or this Act by any Minister of the Crown or government department, save for such sums as may be required for disbursements permitted by any other enactment, shall be paid into the Consolidated Fund or, if so determined by the Treasury, the National Loans Fund.

(4) The provision that may be made under subsection (2) above includes, subject to Schedule 2 to this Act, any such provision (of any such extent) as might be made by Act of Parliament, and any enactment passed or to be passed, other than one contained in this Part of this Act, shall be construed and have effect subject to the foregoing provisions of this section; but, except as may be provided by any Act passed after this Act, Schedule 2 shall have effect in connection with the powers conferred

by this and the following sections of this Act to make Orders in Council and regulations.

(5), (6) ...   [29]

3 Decisions on, and proof of, Treaties and Community instruments, etc

(1) For the purposes of all legal proceedings any question as to the meaning or effect of any of the Treaties, or as to the validity, meaning or effect of any Community instrument, shall be treated as a question of law (and, if not referred to the European Court, be for determination as such in accordance with the principles laid down by and any relevant [decision of the European Court or any court attached thereto)].

(2) Judicial notice shall be taken of the Treaties, of the Official Journal of the Communities and of any decision of, or expression of opinion by, the European Court [or any court attached thereto] on any such question as aforesaid; and the Official Journal shall be admissible as evidence of any instrument or other act thereby communicated of any of the Communities or of any Community institution.

(3) Evidence of any instrument issued by a Community institution, including any judgment or order of the European Court [or any court attached thereto], or of any document in the custody of a Community institution, or any entry in or extract from such a document, may be given in any legal proceedings by production of a copy certified as a true copy by an official of that institution; and any document purporting to be such a copy shall be received in evidence without proof of the official position or handwriting of the person signing the certificate.

(4) Evidence of any Community instrument may also be given in any legal proceedings—
   (a) by production of a copy purporting to be printed by the Queen's Printer;
   (b) where the instrument is in the custody of a government department (including a department of the Government of Northern Ireland), by production of a copy certified on behalf of the department to be a true copy by an officer of the department generally or specially authorised so to do;

and any document purporting to be such a copy as is mentioned in paragraph (b) above of an instrument in the custody of a department shall be received in evidence without proof of the official position or handwriting of the person signing the certificate, or of his authority to do so, or of the document being in the custody of the department.

(5) In any legal proceedings in Scotland evidence of any matter given in a manner authorised by this section shall be sufficient evidence of it.   [30]

4–12 (*Ss 4–6, 11, 12 outside the scope of this work; s 7(1), (2) repealed by the Agriculture (Miscellaneous Provisions) Act 1976, s 26(3), Sch 4, Pt I; s 7(3), (4) repealed by the Food Act 1984, s 134, Sch 11; s 8 repealed by the Films Act 1985, s 7(1), Sch 2; s 9 repealed by the Companies Consolidation (Consequential Provisions) Act 1985, s 29, Sch 1; s 10 repealed by the Restrictive Trade Practices Act 1976, s 44(6), Sch 6.*)

SCHEDULES

SCHEDULE 1

Section 1

DEFINITIONS RELATING TO COMMUNITIES

PART I
THE PRE-ACCESSION TREATIES

1. The "E.C.S.C. Treaty", that is to say, the Treaty establishing the European Coal and Steel Community, signed at Paris on the 18th April 1951.

2. The "E.E.C. Treaty", that is to say, the Treaty establishing the European Economic Community, signed at Rome on the 25th March 1957.

3. The "Euratom Treaty", that is to say, the Treaty establishing the European Atomic Energy Community, signed at Rome on the 25th March 1957.

4. The Convention on certain Institutions common to the European Communities, signed at Rome on the 25th March 1957.

5. The Treaty establishing a single Council and a single Commission of the European Communities, signed at Brussels on the 8th April 1965.

6. The Treaty amending certain Budgetary Provisions of the Treaties establishing the European Communities and of the Treaty establishing a single Council and a single Commission of the European Communities, signed at Luxembourg on the 22nd April 1970.

7. Any treaty entered into before the 22nd January 1972 by any of the Communities (with or without any of the member States) or, as a treaty ancillary to any treaty included in this Part of this Schedule, by the member States (with or without any other country).   **[31]**

PART II
OTHER DEFINITIONS

"Economic Community", "Coal and Steel Community" and "Euratom" mean respectively the European Economic Community, the European Coal and Steel Community and the European Atomic Energy Community.

"Community customs duty" means, in relation to any goods, such duty of customs as may from time to time be fixed for those goods by directly applicable Community provision as the duty chargeable on importation into member States.

"Community institution" means any institution of any of the Communities or common to the Communities; and any reference to an institution of a particular Community shall include one common to the Communities when it acts for that Community, and similarly with references to a committee, officer or servant of a particular Community.

"Community instrument" means any instrument issued by a Community institution.

"Community obligation" means any obligation created or arising by or under the Treaties, whether an enforceable Community obligation or not.

"Enforceable Community right" and similar expressions shall be construed in accordance with section 2(1) of this Act.

"Entry date" means the date on which the United Kingdom becomes a member of the Communities.

"European Court" means the Court of Justice of the European Communities.

"Member", in the expression "member State", refers to membership of the Communities.
    [32]

SCHEDULE 2

Section 2

PROVISIONS AS TO SUBORDINATE LEGISLATION

1.—(1) The powers conferred by section 2(2) of this Act to make provision for the purposes mentioned in section 2(2)(a) and (b) shall not include power—

(a) to make any provision imposing or increasing taxation; or

(b) to make any provision taking effect from a date earlier than that of the making of the instrument containing the provision; or

(c) to confer any power to legislate by means of orders, rules, regulations or other subordinate instrument, other than rules of procedure for any court or tribunal; or

(d) to create any new criminal offence punishable with imprisonment for more than two years or punishable on summary conviction with imprisonment for more than three months or with a fine of more than [level 5 on the standard scale] (if not calculated on a daily basis) or with a fine of more than [£100 a day].

(2) Sub-paragraph (1)(c) above shall not be taken to preclude the modification of a power to legislate conferred otherwise than under section 2(2), or the extension of any such power to purposes of the like nature as those for which it was conferred; and a power to give directions as to matters of administration is not to be regarded as a power to legislate within the meaning of sub-paragraph (1)(c).

2.—(1) Subject to paragraph 3 below, where a provision contained in any section of this Act confers power to make regulations (otherwise than by modification or extension of an existing power), the power shall be exercisable by statutory instrument.

(2) Any statutory instrument containing an Order in Council or regulations made in the exercise of a power so conferred, if made without a draft having been approved by resolution of each House of Parliament, shall be subject to annulment in pursuance of a resolution of either House.

3. Nothing in paragraph 2 above shall apply to any Order in Council made by the Governor of Northern Ireland or to any regulations made by a Minister or department of the Government of Northern Ireland; but where a provision contained in any section of this Act confers power to make such an Order in Council or regulations, then any Order in Council or regulations made in the exercise of that power, if made without a draft having been approved by resolution of each House of the Parliament of Northern Ireland, shall be subject to negative resolution within the meaning of section 41(6) of the Interpretation Act (Northern Ireland) 1954 as if the Order or regulations were a statutory instrument within the meaning of that Act. **[33]**

4, 5 (*Outside the scope of this work.*)

NOTE

Para 1: first-mentioned maximum fine increased and converted to a level on the standard scale by the Criminal Justice Act 1982, ss 37, 40, 46; second amendment made by the Criminal Law Act 1977, s 32(3).

HEALTH AND SAFETY AT WORK ETC ACT 1974

(1974 c 37)

ARRANGEMENT OF SECTIONS

PART I

HEALTH, SAFETY AND WELFARE IN CONNECTION WITH WORK, AND CONTROL OF DANGEROUS SUBSTANCES AND CERTAIN EMISSIONS INTO THE ATMOSPHERE

Preliminary

PART IV
MISCELLANEOUS AND GENERAL

*An Act to make further provision for securing the health, safety and welfare of persons
at work, for protecting others against risks to health or safety in connection with
the activities of persons at work, for controlling the keeping and use and
preventing the unlawful acquisition, possession and use of dangerous substances,
and for controlling certain emissions into the atmosphere; to make further
provision with respect to the employment medical advisory service; to amend the
law relating to building regulations, and the Building (Scotland) Act 1959; and
for connected purposes*

[31 July 1974]

NOTES

Ss 29–32 and Sch 4 were repealed by the Employment Protection Act 1975, ss 116, 125(3), Sch 15, Pt I, Sch 18. Ss 61–74, 76 and Schs 5, 6 were repealed by the Building Act 1984, s 133(2), Sch 7. S 79 was repealed by the Companies Consolidation (Consequential Provisions) Act 1985, s 29, Sch 1.

The following provisions, which are outside the scope of this work, amend or repeal other legislation or enact transitional provisions, are omitted: ss 5, 55–60, 75, 77, 78, 83, Schs 6–10. The rest of the Act is printed in full.

The Act confers extensive powers to make subordinate legislation. Considerations of space preclude reference to all orders made under the Act, for details of which specialist works on Health and Safety should be consulted.

PART I

HEALTH, SAFETY AND WELFARE IN CONNECTION WITH WORK, AND CONTROL OF
DANGEROUS SUBSTANCES AND CERTAIN EMISSIONS INTO THE ATMOSPHERE

Preliminary

1 Preliminary

(1) The provisions of this Part shall have effect with a view to—

    (a) securing the health, safety and welfare of persons at work;

    (b) protecting persons other than persons at work against risks to health or safety arising out of or in connection with the activities of persons at work;

    (c) controlling the keeping and use of explosive or highly flammable or otherwise dangerous substances, and generally preventing the unlawful acquisition, possession and use of such substances; *and*

    (d) *controlling the emission into the atmosphere of noxious or offensive substances from premises of any class prescribed for the purposes of this paragraph.*

(2) The provisions of this Part relating to the making of health and safety regulations ... and the preparation and approval of codes of practice shall in particular have effect with a view to enabling the enactments specified in the third column of Schedule 1 and the regulations, orders and other instruments in force under those enactments to be progressively replaced by a system of regulations and approved codes of practice operating in combination with the other provisions of this Part and designed to maintain or improve the standards of health, safety and welfare established by or under those enactments.

(3) For the purposes of this Part risks arising out of or in connection with the activities of persons at work shall be treated as including risks attributable to the manner of conducting an undertaking, the plant or substances used for the purposes of an undertaking and the condition of premises so used or any part of them.

(4) References in this Part to the general purposes of this Part are references to the purposes mentioned in subsection (1) above.   **[34]**

NOTES
    Sub-s (1): words in italics repealed by the Environmental Protection Act 1990, s 162, Sch 16, Part I, as from a day to be appointed.
    Sub-s (2): words omitted repealed by the Employment Protection Act 1975, ss 116, 125(3), Sch 15, para 1, Sch 18.
    See also the Consumer Protection Act 1987, s 39 (which enacts Sch 3 to that Act (amendments to the Health and Safety at Work, etc Act 1974), and provides "and accordingly, the general purposes of that Part [ie Part I of the 1974 Act] shall include the purpose of protecting persons from the risks protection from which would not be afforded by virtue of that Part but for those amendments").
    See further, in relation to the extension of the general purposes of Part I, the Offshore Safety Act 1992, ss 1(1), 2(1).

General duties

2 General duties of employers to their employees

(1) It shall be the duty of every employer to ensure, so far as is reasonably practicable, the health, safety and welfare at work of all his employees.

(2) Without prejudice to the generality of an employer's duty under the preceding subsection, the matters to which that duty extends include in particular—

    (a) the provision and maintenance of plant and systems of work that are, so far as is reasonably practicable, safe and without risks to health;

    (b) arrangements for ensuring, so far as is reasonably practicable, safety and absence of risks to health in connection with the use, handling, storage and transport of articles and substances;

(c) the provision of such information, instruction, training and supervision as is necessary to ensure, so far as is reasonably practicable, the health and safety at work of his employees;

(d) so far as is reasonably practicable as regards any place of work under the employer's control, the maintenance of it in a condition that is safe and without risks to health and the provision and maintenance of means of access to and egress from it that are safe and without such risks;

(e) the provision and maintenance of a working environment for his employees that is, so far as is reasonably practicable, safe, without risks to health, and adequate as regards facilities and arrangements for their welfare at work.

(3) Except in such cases as may be prescribed, it shall be the duty of every employer to prepare and as often as may be appropriate revise a written statement of his general policy with respect to the health and safety at work of his employees and the organisation and arrangements for the time being in force for carrying out that policy, and to bring the statement and any revision of it to the notice of all his employees.

(4) Regulations made by the Secretary of State may provide for the appointment in prescribed cases by recognised trade unions (within the meaning of the regulations) of safety representatives from amongst the employees, and those representatives shall represent the employees in consultations with the employers under subsection (6) below and shall have such other functions as may be prescribed.

(5) ...

(6) It shall be the duty of every employer to consult any such representatives with a view to the making and maintenance of arrangements which will enable him and his employees to co-operate effectively in promoting and developing measures to ensure the health and safety at work of the employees, and in checking the effectiveness of such measures.

(7) In such cases as may be prescribed it shall be the duty of every employer, if requested to do so by the safety representatives mentioned in [subsection (4)] above, to establish, in accordance with regulations made by the Secretary of State, a safety committee having the function of keeping under review the measures taken to ensure the health and safety at work of his employees and such other functions as may be prescribed.   **[35]**

NOTES

Sub-s (3): see the Employers' Health and Safety Policy Statements (Exceptions) Regulations 1975, SI 1975/1584, which exempt employers with fewer than 5 employees from the requirements of sub-s (3).

Sub-ss (4), (7): see the Safety Representatives and Safety Committees Regulations 1977, SI 1977/500 (paras **[1057]**–**[1069]**).

Sub-s (5): repealed by the Employment Protection Act 1975, ss 116, 125(3), Sch 15, para 2, Sch 18.

Sub-s (7): words in square brackets substituted by the Employment Protection Act 1975, ss 116, 125(3), Sch 15, para 2, Sch 18.

3 General duties of employers and self-employed to persons other than their employees

(1) It shall be the duty of every employer to conduct his undertaking in such a way as to ensure, so far as is reasonably practicable, that persons not in his employment who may be affected thereby are not thereby exposed to risks to their health or safety.

(2) It shall be the duty of every self-employed person to conduct his undertaking in such a way as to ensure, so far as is reasonably practicable, that he and other persons (not being his employees) who may be affected thereby are not thereby exposed to risks to their health or safety.

(3) In such cases as may be prescribed, it shall be the duty of every employer and every self-employed person, in the prescribed circumstances and in the prescribed manner, to give to persons (not being his employees) who may be affected by the way in which he conducts his undertaking the prescribed information about such aspects of the way in which he conducts his undertaking as might affect their health or safety.   **[36]**

NOTES

The definition of "self-employed person" is extended by the Health and Safety (Genetic Manipulation) Regulations 1989, SI 1989/1810, to cover persons engaged in genetic manipulation, as defined in the regulations, who are not employees.

Modified, in relation to Enforcement in Great Britain in relation to relevant machinery for use at work, by the Supply of Machinery (Safety) Regulations 1992, SI 1992/3073, reg 28, Sch 6, para 1.

4 General duties of persons concerned with premises to persons other than their employees

(1) This section has effect for imposing on persons duties in relation to those who—

(a) are not their employees; but

(b) use non-domestic premises made available to them as a place of work or as a place where they may use plant or substances provided for their use there,

and applies to premises so made available and other non-domestic premises used in connection with them.

(2) It shall be the duty of each person who has, to any extent, control of premises to which this section applies or of the means of access thereto or egress therefrom or of any plant or substance in such premises to take such measures as it is reasonable for a person in his position to take to ensure, so far as is reasonably practicable, that the premises, all means of access thereto or egress therefrom available for use by persons using the premises, and any plant or substance in the premises or, as the case may be, provided for use there, is or are safe and without risks to health.

(3) Where a person has, by virtue of any contract or tenancy, an obligation of any extent in relation to—

(a) the maintenance or repair of any premises to which this section applies or any means of access thereto or egress therefrom; or

(b) the safety of or the absence of risks to health arising from plant or substances in any such premises;

that person shall be treated, for the purposes of subsection (2) above, as being a person who has control of the matters to which his obligation extends.

(4) Any reference in this section to a person having control of any premises or matter is a reference to a person having control of the premises or matter in connection with the carrying on by him of a trade, business or other undertaking (whether for profit or not).   **[37–38]**

5 (*Prevention of harmful emissions into atmosphere: omitted (also prospectively repealed by the Environmental Protection Act 1990, s 162(2), Sch 16, Pt I).*)

6 General duties of manufacturers etc as regards articles and substances for use at work

[(1) It shall be the duty of any person who designs, manufactures, imports or supplies any article for use at work or any article of fairground equipment—

(a) to ensure, so far as is reasonably practicable, that the article is so designed and constructed that it will be safe and without risks to health at all times when it is being set, used, cleaned or maintained by a person at work;

(b) to carry out or arrange for the carrying out of such testing and examination as may be necessary for the performance of the duty imposed on him by the preceding paragraph;

(c) to take such steps as are necessary to secure that persons supplied by that person with the article are provided with adequate information about the use for which the article is designed or has been tested and about any conditions necessary to ensure that it will be safe and without risks to health at all such times as are mentioned in paragraph (a) above and when it is being dismantled or disposed of; and

(d) to take such steps as are necessary to secure, so far as is reasonably practicable, that persons so supplied are provided with all such revisions of information provided to them by virtue of the preceding paragraph as are necessary by reason of its becoming known that anything gives rise to a serious risk to health or safety.

(1A) It shall be the duty of any person who designs, manufactures, imports or supplies any article of fairground equipment—

(a) to ensure, so far as is reasonably practicable, that the article is so designed and constructed that it will be safe and without risks to health at all times when it is being used for or in connection with the entertainment of members of the public;

(b) to carry out or arrange for the carrying out of such testing and examination as may be necessary for the performance of the duty imposed on him by the preceding paragraph;

(c) to take such steps as are necessary to secure that persons supplied by that person with the article are provided with adequate information about the use for which the article is designed or has been tested and about any conditions necessary to ensure that it will be safe and without risks to health at all times when it is being used for or in connection with the entertainment of members of the public; and

(d) to take such steps as are necessary to secure, so far as is reasonably practicable, that persons so supplied are provided with all such revisions of information provided to them by virtue of the preceding paragraph as are necessary by reason of its becoming known that anything gives rise to a serious risk to health or safety.]

(2) It shall be the duty of any person who undertakes the design or manufacture of any article for use at work [or of any article of fairground equipment] to carry out or arrange for the carrying out of any necessary research with a view to the discovery and, so far as is reasonably practicable, the elimination or minimisation of any risks to health or safety to which the design or article may give rise.

(3) It shall be the duty of any person who erects or installs any article for use at work in any premises where that article is to be used by persons at work [or who erects or installs any article of fairground equipment] to ensure, so far as is reasonably practicable, that nothing about the way in which [the article is erected or installed makes it unsafe or a risk to health at any such time as is mentioned in paragraph (a)

of subsection (1) or, as the case may be, in paragraph (a) of subsection (1) or (1A) above.]

[(4) It shall be the duty of any person who manufactures, imports or supplies any substance—

    (a) to ensure, so far as is reasonably practicable, that the substance will be safe and without risks to health at all times when it is being used, handled, processed, stored or transported by a person at work or in premises to which section 4 above applies;

    (b) to carry out or arrange for the carrying out of such testing and examination as may be necessary for the performance of the duty imposed on him by the preceding paragraph;

    (c) to take such steps as are necessary to secure that persons supplied by that person with the substance are provided with adequate information about any risks to health or safety to which the inherent properties of the substance may give rise, about the results of any relevant tests which have been carried out on or in connection with the substance and about any conditions necessary to ensure that the substance will be safe and without risks to health at all such times as are mentioned in paragraph (a) above and when the substance is being disposed of; and

    (d) to take such steps as are necessary to secure, so far as is reasonably practicable, that persons so supplied are provided with all such revisions of information provided to them by virtue of the preceding paragraph as are necessary by reason of its becoming known that anything gives rise to a serious risk to health or safety.]

(5) It shall be the duty of any person who undertakes the manufacture of any [substance] to carry out or arrange for the carrying out of any necessary research with a view to the discovery and, so far as is reasonably practicable, the elimination or minimisation of any risks to health or safety to which the substance may give rise [at all such times as are mentioned in paragraph (a) of subsection (4) above].

(6) Nothing in the preceding provisions of this section shall be taken to require a person to repeat any testing, examination or research which has been carried out otherwise than by him or at his instance, in so far as it is reasonable for him to rely on the results thereof for the purposes of those provisions.

(7) Any duty imposed on any person by any of the preceding provisions of this section shall extend only to things done in the course of a trade, business or other undertaking carried on by him (whether for profit or not) and to matters within his control.

(8) Where a person designs, manufactures, imports or supplies an article [for use at work or an article of fairground equipment and does so for or to another] on the basis of a written undertaking by that other to take specified steps sufficient to ensure, so far as is reasonably practicable, that the article will be safe and without risks to health [at all such times as are mentioned in paragraph (a) of subsection (1) or, as the case may be, in paragraph (a) of subsection (1) or (1A) above], the undertaking shall have the effect of relieving the first-mentioned person from the duty imposed [by virtue of that paragraph] above to such extent as is reasonable having regard to the terms of the undertaking.

[(8A) Nothing in subsection (7) or (8) above shall relieve any person who imports any article or substance from any duty in respect of anything which—

    (a) in the case of an article designed outside the United Kingdom, was done by and in the course of any trade, profession or other undertaking carried on by, or was within the control of, the person who designed the article; or

(b) in the case of an article or substance manufactured outside the United Kingdom, was done by and in the course of any trade, profession or other undertaking carried on by, or was within the control of, the person who manufactured the article or substance.]

(9) Where a person ("the ostensible supplier") supplies any [article or substance] to another ("the customer") under a hire-purchase agreement, conditional sale agreement or credit-sale agreement, and the ostensible supplier—

(a) carries on the business of financing the acquisition of goods by others by means of such agreements; and

(b) in the course of that business acquired his interest in the article or substance supplied to the customer as a means of financing its acquisition by the customer from a third person ("the effective supplier"),

the effective supplier and not the ostensible supplier shall be treated for the purposes of this section as supplying the article or substance to the customer, and any duty imposed by the preceding provisions of this section on suppliers shall accordingly fall on the effective supplier and not on the ostensible supplier.

[(10) For the purposes of this section an absence of safety or a risk to health shall be disregarded in so far as the case in or in relation to which it would arise is shown to be one the occurrence of which could not reasonably be foreseen; and in determining whether any duty imposed by virtue of paragraph (a) of subsection (1), (1A) or (4) above has been performed regard shall be had to any relevant information or advice which has been provided to any person by the person by whom the article has been designed, manufactured, imported or supplied or, as the case may be, by the person by whom the substance has been manufactured, imported or supplied.] **[39]**

NOTES

Sub-ss (1), (1A): substituted for sub-s (1), as originally enacted, by the Consumer Protection Act 1987, s 36, Sch 3, para 1(1), (2).

Sub-ss (2), (3), (5), (8), (9): amended by the Consumer Protection Act 1987, s 36, Sch 3, para 1(1), (3), (4), (6), (7), (9).

Sub-ss (4), (10): substituted by the Consumer Protection Act 1987, s 36, Sch 3, para 1(1), (5), (10).

Sub-s (8A): inserted by the Consumer Protection Act 1987, s 36, Sch 3, para 1(1), (8).

Modified, in relation to exposure to noise, by the Noise at Work Regulations 1989, SI 1989/1790, reg 12.

Modified, in relation to first (and then further) leases of any article for use at work or any article of fairground equipment, by the Health and Safety (Leasing Arrangements) Regulations 1992, SI 1992/1524, regs 3, 4 (replacing SI 1980/907).

See also the Supply of Machinery (Safety) Regulations 1992, SI 1992/3073, which prescribe safety standards for specified machinery manufactured in the UK or imported from outside the EC, and modify certain provisions of this Act in relation to such machinery.

See further: the Health and Safety (Enforcing Authority) Regulations 1989, SI 1989/1903, reg 4(5).

7 General duties of employees at work

It shall be the duty of every employee while at work—

(a) to take reasonable care for the health and safety of himself and of other persons who may be affected by his acts or omissions at work; and

(b) as regards any duty or requirement imposed on his employer or any other person by or under any of the relevant statutory provisions, to co-operate with him so far as is necessary to enable that duty or requirement to be performed or complied with. **[40]**

NOTE

See also the Management of Health and Safety at Work Regulations 1992, SI 1992/2051, reg 12, and paras 76–78 of the Approved Code of Practice issued in supplementation of the regulations.

8 Duty not to interfere with or misuse things provided pursuant to certain provisions

No person shall intentionally or recklessly interfere with or misuse anything provided in the interests of health, safety or welfare in pursuance of any of the relevant statutory provisions.   **[41]**

9 Duty not to charge employees for things done or provided pursuant to certain specific requirements

No employer shall levy or permit to be levied on any employee of his any charge in respect of anything done or provided in pursuance of any specific requirement of the relevant statutory provisions.   **[42]**

The Health and Safety Commission and the Health and Safety Executive

10 Establishment of the Commission and the Executive

(1) There shall be two bodies corporate to be called the Health and Safety Commission and the Health and Safety Executive which shall be constituted in accordance with the following provisions of this section.

(2) The Health and Safety Commission (hereafter in this Act referred to as "the Commission") shall consist of a chairman appointed by the Secretary of State and not less than six nor more than nine other members appointed by the Secretary of State in accordance with subsection (3) below.

(3) Before appointing the members of the Commission (other than the chairman) the Secretary of State shall—

(a) as to three of them, consult such organisations representing employers as he considers appropriate;

(b) as to three others, consult such organisations representing employees as he considers appropriate; and

(c) as to any other members he may appoint, consult such organisations representing local authorities and such other organisations, including professional bodies, the activities of whose members are concerned with matters relating to any of the general purposes of this Part, as he considers appropriate.

(4) The Secretary of State may appoint one of the members to be deputy chairman of the Commission.

(5) The Health and Safety Executive (hereafter in this Act referred to as "the Executive") shall consist of three persons of whom one shall be appointed by the Commission with the approval of the Secretary of State to be the director of the Executive and the others shall be appointed by the Commission with the like approval after consultation with the said director.

(6) The provisions of Schedule 2 shall have effect with respect to the Commission and the Executive.

(7) The functions of the Commission and of the Executive, and of their officers and servants, shall be performed on behalf of the Crown.

[(8) For the purposes of any civil proceedings arising out of those functions, the Crown Proceedings Act 1947 and the Crown Suits (Scotland) Act 1857 shall apply to the Commission and the Executive as if they were government departments within

the meaning of the said Act of 1947 or, as the case may be, public departments within
the meaning of the said Act of 1857.]   [43]

NOTE
   Sub-s (8): added by the Employment Protection Act 1975, s 116, Sch 15, para 3.

11 General functions of the Commission and the Executive

(1) In addition to the other functions conferred on the Commission by virtue of this
Act, but subject to subsection (3) below, it shall be the general duty of the Commission
to do such things and make such arrangements as it considers appropriate for the
general purposes of this Part . . .

   (2) It shall be the duty of the Commission . . .—

   (a) to assist and encourage persons concerned with matters relevant to any of
       the general purposes of this Part to further those purposes;
   (b) to make such arrangements as it considers appropriate for the carrying out
       of research, the publication of the results of research and the provision of
       training and information in connection with those purposes, and to
       encourage research and the provision of training and information in that
       connection by others;
   (c) to make such arrangements as it considers appropriate for securing that
       government   departments,   employers,   employees,   organisations
       representing employers and employees respectively, and other persons
       concerned with matters relevant to any of those purposes are provided with
       an information and advisory service and are kept informed of, and
       adequately advised on, such matters;
   (d) to submit from time to time to the authority having power to make
       regulations under any of the relevant statutory provisions such proposals
       as the Commission considers appropriate for the making of regulations
       under that power.

   (3) It shall be the duty of the Commission—

   (a) to submit to the Secretary of State from time to time particulars of what it
       proposes to do for the purpose of performing its functions; and
   (b) subject to the following paragraph, to ensure that its activities are in
       accordance with proposals approved by the Secretary of State; and
   (c) to give effect to any directions given to it by the Secretary of State.

   (4) In addition to any other functions conferred on the Executive by virtue of this
Part, it shall be the duty of the Executive—

   (a) to exercise on behalf of the Commission such of the Commission's
       functions as the Commission directs it to exercise; and
   (b) to give effect to any directions given to it by the Commission otherwise
       than in pursuance of paragraph (a) above;

but, except for the purpose of giving effect to directions given to the Commission by
the Secretary of State, the Commission shall not give to the Executive any directions
as to the enforcement of any of the relevant statutory provisions in a particular case.

   (5) Without prejudice to subsection (2) above, it shall be the duty of the
Executive, if so requested by a Minister of the Crown—

   (a) to provide him with information about the activities of the Executive in
       connection with any matter with which he is concerned; and
   (b) to provide him with advice on any matter with which he is concerned on
       which relevant expert advice is obtainable from any of the officers or
       servants of the Executive but which is not relevant to any of the general
       purposes of this Part.

(6) The Commission and the Executive shall, subject to any directions given to it in pursuance of this Part, have power to do anything (except borrow money) which is calculated to facilitate, or is conducive or incidental to, the performance of any function of the Commission or, as the case may be, the Executive (including a function conferred on it by virtue of this subsection). **[44]**

NOTE

Sub-ss (1), (2): words omitted repealed by the Employment Protection Act 1975, ss 116, 125(3), Sch 15, para 4, Sch 18.

12 Control of the Commission by the Secretary of State

The Secretary of State may—

(a) approve, with or without modifications, any proposals submitted to him in pursuance of section 11(3)(a);

(b) give to the Commission at any time such directions as he thinks fit with respect to its functions (including directions modifying its functions, but not directions conferring on it functions other than any of which it was deprived by previous directions given by virtue of this paragraph), and any directions which it appears to him requisite or expedient to give in the interests of the safety of the State. **[45]**

13 Other powers of the Commission

(1) The Commission shall have power—

(a) to make agreements with any government department or other person for that department or person to perform on behalf of the Commission or the Executive (with or without payment) any of the functions of the Commission or, as the case may be, of the Executive;

(b) subject to subsection (2) below, to make agreements with any Minister of the Crown, government department or other public authority for the Commission to perform on behalf of that Minister, department or authority (with or without payment) functions exercisable by the Minister, department or authority (including, in the case of a Minister, functions not conferred by an enactment), being functions which in the opinion of the Secretary of State can appropriately be performed by the Commission in connection with any of the Commission's functions;

(c) to provide (with or without payment) services or facilities required otherwise than for the general purposes of this Part in so far as they are required by any government department or other public authority in connection with the exercise by that department or authority of any of its functions;

(d) to appoint persons or committees of persons to provide the Commission with advice in connection with any of its functions and (without prejudice to the generality of the following paragraph) to pay to persons so appointed such remuneration as the Secretary of State may with the approval of the Minister for the Civil Service determine;

(e) in connection with any of the functions of the Commission, to pay to any person such travelling and subsistence allowances and such compensation for loss of remunerative time as the Secretary of State may with the approval of the Minister for the Civil Service determine;

(f) to carry out or arrange for or make payments in respect of research into any matter connected with any of the Commission's functions, and to disseminate or arrange for or make payments in respect of the dissemination of information derived from such research;

(g) to include, in any arrangements made by the Commission for the provision of facilities or services by it or on its behalf, provision for the making of payments to the Commission or any person acting on its behalf by other parties to the arrangements and by persons who use those facilities or services.

(2) Nothing in subsection (1)(b) shall authorise the Commission to perform any function of a Minister, department or authority which consists of a power to make regulations or other instruments of a legislative character.   [46]

14 Power of the Commission to direct investigations and inquiries

(1) This section applies to the following matters, that is to say any accident, occurrence, situation or other matter whatsoever which the Commission thinks it necessary or expedient to investigate for any of the general purposes of this Part or with a view to the making of regulations for those purposes; and for the purposes of this subsection it is immaterial whether the Executive is or is not responsible for securing the enforcement of such (if any) of the relevant statutory provisions as relate to the matter in question.

(2) The Commission may at any time—

(a) direct the Executive or authorise any other person to investigate and make a special report on any matter to which this section applies; or

(b) with the consent of the Secretary of State direct an inquiry to be held into any such matter;

. . .

(3) Any inquiry held by virtue of subsection (2)(b) above shall be held in accordance with regulations made for the purposes of this subsection by the Secretary of State, and shall be held in public except where or to the extent that the regulations provide otherwise.

(4) Regulations made for the purposes of subsection (3) above may in particular include provision—

(a) conferring on the person holding any such inquiry, and any person assisting him in the inquiry, powers of entry and inspection;

(b) conferring on any such person powers of summoning witnesses to give evidence or produce documents and power to take evidence on oath and administer oaths or require the making of declarations;

(c) requiring any such inquiry to be held otherwise than in public where or to the extent that a Minister of the Crown so directs.

(5) In the case of a special report made by virtue of subsection (2)(a) above or a report made by the person holding an inquiry held by virtue of subsection (2)(b) above, the Commission may cause the report, or so much of it as the Commission thinks fit, to be made public at such time and in such manner as the Commission thinks fit.

(6) The Commission—

(a) in the case of an investigation and special report made by virtue of subsection (2)(a) above (otherwise than by an officer or servant of the Executive), may pay to the person making it such remuneration and expenses as the Secretary of State may, with the approval of the Minister for the Civil Service, determine;

(b) in the case of an inquiry held by virtue of subsection (2)(b) above, may pay to the person holding it and to any assessor appointed to assist him such remuneration and expenses, and to persons attending the inquiry as witnesses such expenses, as the Secretary of State may, with the like approval, determine; and

(c) may, to such extent as the Secretary of State may determine, defray the other costs, if any, of any such investigation and special report or inquiry.

(7) Where an inquiry is directed to be held by virtue of subsection (2)(b) above into any matter to which this section applies arising in Scotland, being a matter which causes the death of any person, no inquiry with regard to that death shall, unless the Lord Advocate otherwise directs, be held in pursuance of the Fatal Accidents [and Sudden Deaths Inquiry (Scotland) Act 1976].   **[47]**

NOTES
Sub-s (2): words omitted repealed by the Employment Protection Act 1975, ss 116, 125(3), Sch 15, para 5, Sch 18.
Sub-s (7): words in square brackets substituted by the Fatal Accidents and Sudden Deaths Inquiry (Scotland) Act 1976, s 8(1), Sch 1, para 4.
The regulations made under sub-s (3) are the Health and Safety Inquiries (Procedure) Regulations 1975, SI 1975/335, as amended by the Inquiries Procedure (Amendment) Regulations 1976, SI 1976/1246.

Health and Safety regulations and approved codes of practice

15 Health and safety regulations

[(1) Subject to the provisions of section 50, the Secretary of State, the Minister of Agriculture, Fisheries and Food or the Secretary of State and that Minister acting jointly shall have power to make regulations under this section for any of the general purposes of this Part (and regulations so made are in this Part referred to as "health and safety regulations").]

(2) Without prejudice to the generality of the preceding subsection, health and safety regulations may for any of the general purposes of this Part make provision for any of the purposes mentioned in Schedule 3.

(3) Health and safety regulations—
(a) may repeal or modify any of the existing statutory provisions;
(b) may exclude or modify in relation to any specified class of case any of the provisions of sections 2 to 9 or any of the existing statutory provisions;
(c) may make a specified authority or class of authorities responsible, to such extent as may be specified, for the enforcement of any of the relevant statutory provisions.

(4) Health and safety regulations—
(a) may impose requirements by reference to the approval of the Commission or any other specified body or person;
(b) may provide for references in the regulations to any specified document to operate as references to that document as revised or re-issued from time to time.

(5) Health and safety regulations—
(a) may provide (either unconditionally or subject to conditions, and with or without limit of time) for exemptions from any requirement or prohibition imposed by or under any of the relevant statutory provisions;
(b) may enable exemptions from any requirement or prohibition imposed by or under any of the relevant statutory provisions to be granted (either unconditionally or subject to conditions, and with or without limit of time) by any specified person or by any person authorised in that behalf by a specified authority.

(6) Health and safety regulations—

    (a) may specify the persons or classes of persons who, in the event of a contravention of a requirement or prohibition imposed by or under the regulations, are to be guilty of an offence, whether in addition to or to the exclusion of other persons or classes of persons;

    (b) may provide for any specified defence to be available in proceedings for any offence under the relevant statutory provisions either generally or in specified circumstances;

    (c) may exclude proceedings on indictment in relation to offences consisting of a contravention of a requirement or prohibition imposed by or under any of the existing statutory provisions, sections 2 to 9 or health and safety regulations;

    (d) may restrict the punishments [(other than the maximum fine on conviction on indictment)] which can be imposed in respect of any such offence as is mentioned in paragraph (c) above.

    [(e) in the case of regulations made for any purpose mentioned in section 1(1) of the Offshore Safety Act 1992, may provide that any offence consisting of a contravention of the regulations, or of any requirement or prohibition imposed by or under them, shall be punishable on conviction on indictment by imprisonment for a term not exceeding two years, or a fine, or both.]

(7) Without prejudice to section 35, health and safety regulations may make provision for enabling offences under any of the relevant statutory provisions to be treated as having been committed at any specified place for the purpose of bringing any such offence within the field of responsibility of any enforcing authority or conferring jurisdiction on any court to entertain proceedings for any such offence.

(8) Health and safety regulations may take the form of regulations applying to particular circumstances only or to a particular case only (for example, regulations applying to particular premises only).

(9) If an Order in Council is made under section 84(3) providing that this section shall apply to or in relation to persons, premises or work outside Great Britain then, notwithstanding the Order, health and safety regulations shall not apply to or in relation to aircraft in flight, vessels, hovercraft or offshore installations outside Great Britain or persons at work outside Great Britain in connection with submarine cables or submarine pipelines except in so far as the regulations expressly so provide.

(10) In this section "specified" means specified in health and safety regulations.

                                                      [48]

NOTES

Sub-s (1): substituted by the Employment Protection Act 1975, s 116, Sch 15, para 6.

Sub-s (6): in para (d), words in square brackets added by the Criminal Law Act 1977, s 65, Sch 12; para (e) added by the Offshore Safety Act 1992, s 4(1), (6).

See further, for additional provision as to the power to make regulations under this section: the Offshore Safety Act 1992, ss 1(2), 2(2).

A very large number of regulations has been made under this section. Specialist Health and Safety publications should be consulted for a full list. Those regulations reproduced in Part 2 of this volume are: the Safety Representatives and Safety Committees Regulations 1977, SI 1977/500 (as amended by SI 1992/2051); the Reporting of Injuries, Diseases and Dangerous Occurrences Regulations 1985, SI 1985/2023 (as amended by SI 1989/1457); the Control of Substances Hazardous to Health Regulations 1988, SI 1988/1657 (as amended by SI 1990/2026, SI 1991/2431, SI 1992/2382, SI 1993/745); the Health and Safety Information for Employees Regulations 1989, SI 1989/682; the Management of Health and Safety at Work Regulations 1992, SI 1992/2051; the Health and Safety (Display Screen Equipment) Regulations 1992, SI 1992/2792; and the Manual Handling Operations Regulations 1992, SI 1992/2793.

16 Approval of codes of practice by the Commission

(1) For the purpose of providing practical guidance with respect to the requirements of any provision of sections 2 to 7 or of health and safety regulations or of any of the existing statutory provisions, the Commission may, subject to the following subsection . . .—

    (a) approve and issue such codes of practice (whether prepared by it or not) as in its opinion are suitable for that purpose;

    (b) approve such codes of practice issued or proposed to be issued otherwise than by the Commission as in its opinion are suitable for that purpose.

(2) The Commission shall not approve a code of practice under subsection (1) above without the consent of the Secretary of State, and shall, before seeking his consent, consult—

    (a) any government department or other body that appears to the Commission to be appropriate (and, in particular, in the case of a code relating to electromagnetic radiations, the National Radiological Protection Board); and

    (b) such government departments and other bodies, if any, as in relation to any matter dealt with in the code, the Commission is required to consult under this section by virtue of directions given to it by the Secretary of State.

(3) Where a code of practice is approved by the Commission under subsection (1) above, the Commission shall issue a notice in writing—

    (a) identifying the code in question and stating the date on which its approval by the Commission is to take effect; and

    (b) specifying for which of the provisions mentioned in subsection (1) above the code is approved.

(4) The Commission may—

    (a) from time to time revise the whole or any part of any code of practice prepared by it in pursuance of this section;

    (b) approve any revision or proposed revision of the whole or any part of any code of practice for the time being approved under this section;

and the provisions of subsections (2) and (3) above shall, with the necessary modifications, apply in relation to the approval of any revision under this subsection as they apply in relation to the approval of a code of practice under subsection (1) above.

(5) The Commission may at any time with the consent of the Secretary of State withdraw its approval from any code of practice approved under this section, but before seeking his consent shall consult the same government departments and other bodies as it would be required to consult under subsection (2) above it it were proposing to approve the code.

(6) Where under the preceding subsection the Commission withdraws its approval from a code of practice approved under this section, the Commission shall issue a notice in writing identifying the code in question and stating the date on which its approval of it is to cease to have effect.

(7) References in this part to an approved code of practice are references to that code as it has effect for the time being by virtue of any revision of the whole or any part of it approved under this section.

(8) The power of the Commission under subsection (1)(b) above to approve a code of practice issued or proposed to be issued otherwise than by the Commission shall include power to approve a part of such a code of practice; and accordingly in this Part "code of practice" may be read as including a part of such a code of practice.

17 Use of approved codes of practice in criminal proceedings

(1) A failure on the part of any person to observe any provision of an approved code of practice shall not of itself render him liable to any civil or criminal proceedings; but where in any criminal proceedings a party is alleged to have committed an offence by reason of a contravention of any requirement or prohibition imposed by or under any such provision as is mentioned in section 16(1) being a provision for which there was an approved code of practice at the time of the alleged contravention, the following subsection shall have effect with respect to that code in relation to those proceedings.

(2) Any provision of the code of practice which appears to the court to be relevant to the requirement or prohibition alleged to have been contravened shall be admissible in evidence in the proceedings; and if it is proved that there was at any material time a failure to observe any provision of the code which appears to the court to be relevant to any matter which it is necessary for the prosecution to prove in order to establish a contravention of that requirement or prohibition, that matter shall be taken as proved unless the court is satisfied that the requirement or prohibition was in respect of that matter complied with otherwise than by way of observance of that provision of the code.

(3) In any criminal proceedings—

(a) a document purporting to be a notice issued by the Commission under section 16 shall be taken to be such a notice unless the contrary is proved; and

(b) a code of practice which appears to the court to be the subject of such a notice shall be taken to be the subject of that notice unless the contrary is proved.   **[50]**

Enforcement

18 Authorities responsible for enforcement of the relevant statutory provisions

(1) It shall be the duty of the Executive to make adequate arrangements for the enforcement of the relevant statutory provisions except to the extent that some other authority or class of authorities is by any of those provisions or by regulations under subsection (2) below made responsible for their enforcement.

(2) The Secretary of State may by regulations—

(a) make local authorities responsible for the enforcement of the relevant statutory provisions to such extent as may be prescribed;

(b) make provision for enabling responsibility for enforcing any of the relevant statutory provisions to be, to such extent as may be determined under the regulations—

(i) transferred from the Executive to local authorities or from local authorities to the Executive; or

(ii) assigned to the Executive or to local authorities for the purpose of removing any uncertainty as to what are by virtue of this subsection their respective responsibilities for the enforcement of those provisions;

and any regulations made in pursuance of paragraph (b) above shall include provision for securing that any transfer or assignment effected under the regulations is brought to the notice of persons affected by it.

(3) Any provision made by regulations under the preceding subsection shall have effect subject to any provision made by health and safety regulations . . . in pursuance of section 15(3)(c).

(4) It shall be the duty of every local authority—

    (a) to make adequate arrangements for the enforcement within their area of the relevant statutory provisions to the extent that they are by any of those provisions or by regulations under subsection (2) above made responsible for their enforcement; and

    (b) to perform the duty imposed on them by the preceding paragraph and any other functions conferred on them by any of the relevant statutory provisions in accordance with such guidance as the Commission may give them.

(5) Where any authority other than . . . the Executive or a local authority is by any of the relevant statutory provisions or by regulations under subsection (2) above made responsible for the enforcement of any of those provisions to any extent, it shall be the duty of that authority—

    (a) to make adequate arrangements for the enforcement of those provisions to that extent; and

    (b) to perform the duty imposed on the authority by the preceding paragraph and any other functions conferred on the authority by any of the relevant statutory provisions in accordance with such guidance as the Commission may give to the authority.

(6) Nothing in the provisions of this Act or of any regulations made thereunder charging any person in Scotland with the enforcement of any of the relevant statutory provisions shall be construed as authorising that person to institute proceedings for any offence.

(7) In this Part—

    (a) "enforcing authority" means the Executive or any other authority which is by any of the relevant statutory provisions or by regulations under subsection (2) above made responsible for the enforcement of any of those provisions to any extent; and

    (b) any reference to an enforcing authority's field of responsibility is a reference to the field over which that authority's responsibility for the enforcement of those provisions extends for the time being;

but where by virtue of paragraph (a) of section 13(1) the performance of any function of the Commission or the Executive is delegated to a government department or person, references to the Commission or the Executive (or to an enforcing authority where that authority is the Executive) in any provision of this Part which relates to that function shall, so far as may be necessary to give effect to any agreement under that paragraph, be construed as references to that department or person; and accordingly any reference to the field of responsibility of an enforcing authority shall be construed as a reference to the field over which that department or person for the time being performs such a function.   **[51]**

NOTES

  Sub-ss (3), (5): words omitted repealed by the Employment Protection Act 1975, ss 116, 125(3), Sch 15, para 8, Sch 18.

  Regulations under this section: see the Health and Safety (Enforcing Authority) Regulations 1989, SI 1989/1903 (replacing SI 1977/746).

19 Appointment of inspectors

(1) Every enforcing authority may appoint as inspectors (under whatever title it may from time to time determine) such persons having suitable qualifications as it thinks necessary for carrying into effect the relevant statutory provisions within its field of responsibility, and may terminate any appointment made under this section.

(2) Every appointment of a person as an inspector under this section shall be made by an instrument in writing specifying which of the powers conferred on inspectors by the relevant statutory provisions are to be exercisable by the person appointed; and an inspector shall in right of his appointment under this section—

  (a) be entitled to exercise only such of those powers as are so specified; and
  (b) be entitled to exercise the powers so specified only within the field of responsibility of the authority which appointed him.

(3) So much of an inspector's instrument of appointment as specifies the powers which he is entitled to exercise may be varied by the enforcing authority which appointed him.

(4) An inspector shall, if so required when exercising or seeking to exercise any power conferred on him by any of the relevant statutory provisions, produce his instrument of appointment or a duly authenticated copy thereof.   **[52]**

NOTES
  Modified, in relation to vessels for use at work, by the Simple Pressure Vessels (Safety) Regulations 1991, SI 1991/2749, Sch 5.
  Modified, in relation to enforcement in Great Britain in relation to relevant machinery for use at work, by the Supply of Machinery (Safety) Regulations 1992, SI 1992/3073, reg 28, Sch 6, para 1.

20 Powers of inspectors

(1) Subject to the provisions of section 19 and this section, an inspector may, for the purpose of carrying into effect any of the relevant statutory provisions within the field of responsibility of the enforcing authority which appointed him, exercise the powers set out in subsection (2) below.

(2) The powers of an inspector referred to in the preceding subsection are the following, namely—

  (a) at any reasonable time (or, in a situation which in his opinion is or may be dangerous, at any time) to enter any premises which he has reason to believe it is necessary for him to enter for the purpose mentioned in subsection (1) above;
  (b) to take with him a constable if he has reasonable cause to apprehend any serious obstruction in the execution of his duty;
  (c) without prejudice to the preceding paragraph, on entering any premises by virtue of paragraph (a) above to take with him—
    (i) any other person duly authorised by his (the inspector's) enforcing authority; and
    (ii) any equipment or materials required for any purpose for which the power of entry is being exercised;
  (d) to make such examination and investigation as may in any circumstances be necessary for the purpose mentioned in subsection (1) above;
  (e) as regards any premises which he has power to enter, to direct that those premises or any part of them, or anything therein, shall be left undisturbed (whether generally or in particular respects) for so long as is reasonably necessary for the purpose of any examination or investigation under paragraph (d) above;

(f)   to take such measurements and photographs and make such recordings as he considers necessary for the purpose of any examination or investigation under paragraph (d) above;

(g)   to take samples of any articles or substances found in any premises which he has power to enter, and of the atmosphere in or in the vicinity of any such premises;

(h)   in the case of any article or substance found in any premises which he has power to enter, being an article or substance which appears to him to have caused or to be likely to cause danger to health or safety, to cause it to be dismantled or subjected to any process or test (but not so as to damage or destroy it unless this is in the circumstances necessary for the purpose mentioned in subsection (1) above);

(i)   in the case of any such article or substance as is mentioned in the preceding paragraph, to take possession of it and detain it for so long as is necessary for all or any of the following purposes, namely—

    (i)   to examine it and do to it anything which he has power to do under that paragraph;

    (ii)   to ensure that it is not tampered with before his examination of it is completed;

    (iii)   to ensure that it is available for use as evidence in any proceedings for an offence under any of the relevant statutory provisions or any proceedings relating to a notice under section 21 or 22;

(j)   to require any person whom he has reasonable cause to believe to be able to give any information relevant to any examination or investigation under paragraph (d) above to answer (in the absence of persons other than a person nominated by him to be present and any persons whom the inspector may allow to be present) such questions as the inspector thinks fit to ask and to sign a declaration of the truth of his answers;

(k)   to require the production of, inspect, and take copies of or of any entry in—

    (i)   any books or documents which by virtue of any of the relevant statutory provisions are required to be kept; and

    (ii)   any other books or documents which it is necessary for him to see for the purposes of any examination or investigation under paragraph (d) above;

(l)   to require any person to afford him such facilities and assistance with respect to any matters or things within that person's control or in relation to which that person has responsibilities as are necessary to enable the inspector to exercise any of the powers conferred on him by this section;

(m)   any other power which is necessary for the purpose mentioned in subsection (1) above.

(3) The Secretary of State may by regulations make provision as to the procedure to be followed in connection with the taking of samples under subsection (2)(g) above (including provision as to the way in which samples that have been so taken are to be dealt with).

(4) Where an inspector proposes to exercise the power conferred by subsection (2)(h) above in the case of an article or substance found in any premises, he shall, if so requested by a person who at the time is present in and has responsibilities in relation to those premises, cause anything which is to be done by virtue of that power to be done in the presence of that person unless the inspector considers that its being done in that person's presence would be prejudicial to the safety of the State.

(5) Before exercising the power conferred by subsection (2)(h) above in the case of any article or substance, an inspector shall consult such persons as appear to him appropriate for the purpose of ascertaining what dangers, if any, there may be in doing anything which he proposes to do under that power.

(6) Where under the power conferred by subsection (2)(i) above an inspector takes possession of any article or substance found in any premises, he shall leave there, either with a responsible person or, if that is impracticable, fixed in a conspicuous position, a notice giving particulars of that article or substance sufficient to identify it and stating that he has taken possession of it under that power; and before taking possession of any such substance under that power an inspector shall, if it is practicable for him to do so, take a sample thereof and give to a responsible person at the premises a portion of the sample marked in a manner sufficient to identify it.

(7) No answer given by a person in pursuance of a requirement imposed under subsection (2)(j) above shall be admissible in evidence against that person or the husband or wife of that person in any proceedings.

(8) Nothing in this section shall be taken to compel the production by any person of a document of which he would on grounds of legal professional privilege be entitled to withhold production on an order for discovery in an action in the High Court or, as the case may be, on an order for the production of documents in an action in the Court of Session.   **[53]**

NOTES
Modified, in relation to vessels for use at work, by the Simple Pressure Vessels (Safety) Regulations 1991, SI 1991/2749, Sch 5.
Modified, in relation to enforcement in Great Britain in relation to relevant machinery for use at work, by the Supply of Machinery (Safety) Regulations 1992, SI 1992/3073, reg 28, Sch 6, para 1.

21 Improvement notices

If an inspector is of the opinion that a person—

    (a) is contravening one or more of the relevant statutory provisions; or
    (b) has contravened one or more of those provisions in circumstances that make it likely that the contravention will continue or be repeated,

he may serve on him a notice (in this Part referred to as "an improvement notice") stating that he is of that opinion, specifying the provision or provisions as to which he is of that opinion, giving particulars of the reasons why he is of that opinion, and requiring that person to remedy the contravention or, as the case may be, the matters occasioning it within such period (ending not earlier than the period within which an appeal against the notice can be brought under section 24) as may be specified in the notice.   **[54]**

NOTES
Modified, in relation to vessels for use at work, by the Simple Pressure Vessels (Safety) Regulations 1991, SI 1991/2749, Sch 5.
Modified, in relation to enforcement in Great Britain in relation to relevant machinery for use at work, by the Supply of Machinery (Safety) Regulations 1992, SI 1992/3073, reg 28, Sch 6, para 1.

22 Prohibition notices

(1) This section applies to any activities which are being or are [likely] to be carried on by or under the control of any person, being activities to or in relation to which any of the relevant statutory provisions apply or will, if the activities are so carried on, apply.

(2) If as regards any activities to which this section applies an inspector is of the opinion that, as carried on or [likely] to be carried on by or under the control of the person in question, the activities involve or, as the case may be, will involve a risk of serious personal injury, the inspector may serve on that person a notice (in this Part referred to as "a prohibition notice").

(3) A prohibition notice shall—

(a) state that the inspector is of the said opinion;

(b) specify the matters which in his opinion give or, as the case may be, will give rise to the said risk;

(c) where in his opinion any of those matters involves or, as the case may be, will involve a contravention of any of the relevant statutory provisions, state that he is of that opinion, specify the provision or provisions as to which he is of that opinion, and give particulars of the reasons why he is of that opinion; and

(d) direct that the activities to which the notice relates shall not be carried on by or under the control of the person on whom the notice is served unless the matters specified in the notice in pursuance of paragraph (b) above and any associated contraventions of provisions so specified in pursuance of paragraph (c) above have been remedied.

[(4) A direction contained in a prohibition notice in pursuance of subsection (3)(d) above shall take effect—

(a) at the end of the period specified in the notice; or

(b) if the notice so declares, immediately.] **[55]**

NOTES

Sub-ss (1), (2): words substituted by the Consumer Protection Act 1987, s 3, Sch 3, para 2(a).

Sub-s (4): substituted by the Consumer Protection Act 1987, s 3, Sch 3, para 2(b).

See further, in relation to the definition of work: the Genetic Manipulation Regulations 1989, SI 1989/1810, reg 3.

Modified, in relation to enforcement in Great Britain in relation to relevant machinery for use at work, by the Supply of Machinery (Safety) Regulations 1992, SI 1992/3073, reg 28, Sch 6, para 1.

23 Provisions supplementary to ss 21 and 22

(1) in this section "a notice" means an improvement notice or a prohibition notice.

(2) A notice may (but need not) include directions as to the measures to be taken to remedy any contravention or matter to which the notice relates; and any such directions—

(a) may be framed to any extent by reference to any approved code of practice; and

(b) may be framed so as to afford the person on whom the notice is served a choice between different ways of remedying the contravention or matter.

(3) Where any of the relevant statutory provisions applies to a building or any matter connected with a building and an inspector proposes to serve an improvement notice relating to a contravention of that provision in connection with that building or matter, the notice shall not direct any measures to be taken to remedy the contravention of that provision which are more onerous than those necessary to secure conformity with the requirements of any building regulations for the time being in force to which that building or matter would be required to conform if the relevant building were being newly erected unless the provision in question imposes specific requirements more onerous than the requirements of any such building regulations to which the building or matter would be required to conform as aforesaid.

In this subsection "the relevant building", in the case of a building, means that building, and, in the case of a matter connected with a building, means the building with which the matter is connected.

(4) Before an inspector serves in connection with any premises used or about to be used as a place of work a notice requiring or likely to lead to the taking of measures affecting the means of escape in case of fire with which the premises are or ought to be provided, he shall consult the fire authority.

In this subsection "fire authority" has the meaning assigned by section 43(1) of the Fire Precautions Act 1971.

(5) Where an improvement notice or a prohibition notice which is not to take immediate effect has been served—

    (a) the notice may be withdrawn by an inspector at any time before the end of the period specified therein in pursuance of section 21 or section 22(4) as the case may be; and

    (b) the period so specified may be extended or further extended by an inspector at any time when an appeal against the notice is not pending.

    (6) . . .   **[56]**

NOTES

Sub-s (6): makes special provision in relation to the Buildings (Scotland) Act 1959, and is omitted.

Modified, in relation to vessels for use at work, by the Simple Pressure Vessels (Safety) Regulations 1991, SI 1991/2749, Sch 5.

Modified, in relation to enforcement in Great Britain in relation to relevant machinery for use at work, by the Supply of Machinery (Safety) Regulations 1992, SI 1992/3073, reg 28, Sch 6, para 1.

24 Appeal against improvement or prohibition notice

(1) In this section "a notice" means an improvement notice or a prohibition notice.

(2) A person on whom a notice is served may within such period from the date of its service as may be prescribed appeal to an industrial tribunal; and on such an appeal the tribunal may either cancel or affirm the notice and, if it affirms it, may do so either in its original form or with such modifications as the tribunal may in the circumstances think fit.

(3) Where an appeal under this section is brought against a notice within the period allowed under the preceding subsection, then—

    (a) in the case of an improvement notice, the bringing of the appeal shall have the effect of suspending the operation of the notice until the appeal is finally disposed of or, if the appeal is withdrawn, until the withdrawal of the appeal;

    (b) in the case of a prohibition notice, the bringing of the appeal shall have the like effect if, but only if, on the application of the appellant the tribunal so directs (and then only from the giving of the direction).

(4) One or more assessors may be appointed for the purposes of any proceedings brought before an industrial tribunal under this section.   **[57]**

NOTES

For the procedure on appeal, including the time limit prescribed for the purpose of sub-s (2), see the Industrial Tribunals (Improvement and Prohibition Notices Appeals) Regulations 1974, SI 1974/1925, below, paras **[1022]–[1026]**.

See further, in relation to circumstances in which the notices may be cancelled: the Low Voltage Electrical Equipment (Safety) Regulations 1989, SI 1989/728, reg 2; the Construction Products Regulations 1991, SI 1991/1620, reg 33.

Modified, in relation to vessels for use at work, by the Simple Pressure Vessels (Safety) Regulations 1991, SI 1991/2749, Sch 5.

Modified, in relation to enforcement in Great Britain in relation to relevant machinery for use at work, by the Supply of Machinery (Safety) Regulations 1992, SI 1992/3073, reg 28, Sch 6, para 1.

25 Power to deal with cause of imminent danger

(1) Where, in the case of any article or substance found by him in any premises which he has power to enter, an inspector has reasonable cause to believe that, in the circumstances in which he finds it, the article or substance is a cause of imminent danger of serious personal injury, he may seize it and cause it to be rendered harmless (whether by destruction or otherwise).

(2) Before there is rendered harmless under this section—

(a) any article that forms part of a batch of similar articles; or
(b) any substance,

the inspector shall, if it is practicable for him to do so, take a sample thereof and give to a responsible person at the premises where the article or substance was found by him a portion of the sample marked in a manner sufficient to identify it.

(3) As soon as may be after any article or substance has been seized and rendered harmless under this section, the inspector shall prepare and sign a written report giving particulars of the circumstances in which the article or substance was seized and so dealt with by him, and shall—

(a) give a signed copy of the report to a responsible person at the premises where the article or substance was found by him; and
(b) unless that person is the owner of the article or substance, also serve a signed copy of the report on the owner;

and if, where paragraph (b) above applies, the inspector cannot after reasonable enquiry ascertain the name or address of the owner, the copy may be served on him by giving it to the person to whom a copy was given under the preceding paragraph.
[58]

NOTE
Modified, in relation to enforcement in Great Britain in relation to relevant machinery for use at work, by the Supply of Machinery (Safety) Regulations 1992, SI 1992/3073, reg 28, Sch 6, para 1.

[25A Power of customs officer to detain articles and substances

(1) A customs officer may, for the purpose of facilitating the exercise or performance by any enforcing authority or inspector of any of the powers or duties of the authority or inspector under any of the relevant statutory provisions, seize any imported article or imported substance and detain it for not more than two working days.

(2) Anything seized and detained under this section shall be dealt with during the period of its detention in such manner as the Commissioners of Customs and Excise may direct.

(3) In subsection (1) above the reference to two working days is a reference to a period of forty-eight hours calculated from the time when the goods in question are seized but disregarding so much of any period as falls on a Saturday or Sunday or on Christmas Day, Good Friday or a day which is a bank holiday under the Banking and Financial Dealings Act 1971 in the part of Great Britain where the goods are seized.]
[59]

NOTES
Inserted, by the Consumer Protection Act 1987, s 36, Sch 3, para 3.
Modified, in relation to vessels for use at work, by the Simple Pressure Vessels (Safety) Regulations 1991, SI 1991/2749, Sch 5.

Modified, in relation to enforcement in Great Britain in relation to relevant machinery for use at work, by the Supply of Machinery (Safety) Regulations 1992, SI 1992/3073, reg 28, Sch 6, para 1.

26 Power of enforcing authorities to indemnify their inspectors

Where an action has been brought against an inspector in respect of an act done in the execution or purported execution of any of the relevant statutory provisions and the circumstances are such that he is not legally entitled to require the enforcing authority which appointed him to indemnify him, that authority may, nevertheless, indemnify him against the whole or part of any damages and costs or expenses which he may have been ordered to pay or may have incurred, if the authority is satisfied that he honestly believed that the act complained of was within his powers and that his duty as an inspector required or entitled him to do it.   [60]

NOTES
    Modified, in relation to vessels for use at work, by the Simple Pressure Vessels (Safety) Regulations 1991, SI 1991/2749, Sch 5.
    Modified, in relation to enforcement in Great Britain in relation to relevant machinery for use at work, by the Supply of Machinery (Safety) Regulations 1992, SI 1992/3073, reg 28, Sch 6, para 1.

Obtaining and disclosure of information

27 Obtaining of information by the Commission, the Executive, enforcing authorities etc

(1) For the purpose of obtaining—

   (a) any information which the Commission needs for the discharge of its functions; or

   (b) any information which an enforcing authority needs for the discharge of the authority's functions,

the Commission may, with the consent of the Secretary of State, serve on any person a notice requiring that person to furnish to the Commission or, as the case may be, to the enforcing authority in question such information about such matters as may be specified in the notice, and to do so in such form and manner and within such time as may be so specified.

   In this subsection "consent" includes a general consent extending to cases of any stated description.

   (2) Nothing in section 9 of the Statistics of Trade Act 1947 (which restricts the disclosure of information obtained under that Act) shall prevent or penalise—

   (a) the disclosure by a Minister of the Crown to the Commission or the Executive of information obtained under that Act about any undertaking within the meaning of that Act, being information consisting of the names and addresses of the persons carrying on the undertaking, the nature of the undertaking's activities, the numbers of persons of different descriptions who work in the undertaking, the addresses or places where activities of the undertaking are or were carried on, the nature of the activities carried on there, or the numbers of persons of different descriptions who work or worked in the undertaking there; . . .

   (b) . . .

   (3) In the preceding subsection any reference to a Minister of the Crown, the Commission, [or the Executive] includes respectively a reference to an officer of his or of that body and also, in the case of a reference to the Commission, includes a reference to—

   (a) a person performing any functions of the Commission or the Executive on its behalf by virtue of section 13(1)(a);

   (b) an officer of a body which is so performing any such functions; and

   (c) an adviser appointed in pursuance of section 13(1)(d).

   (4) A person to whom information is disclosed in pursuance of subsection (2) above shall not use the information for a purpose other than a purpose of the Commission or, as the case may be, of the Executive.   **[61]**

NOTES

  Sub-s (2): words omitted repealed by the Employment Act 1989, ss 29(3), (4), Sch 6, para 10, Sch 7, Part I.

  Sub-s (3): words substituted by the Employment Act 1989, s 29(3), Sch 6, para 10.

  Modified, in relation to vessels for use at work, by the Simple Pressure Vessels (Safety) Regulations 1991, SI 1991/2749, Sch 5.

  Modified, in relation to enforcement in Great Britain in relation to relevant machinery for use at work, by the Supply of Machinery (Safety) Regulations 1992, SI 1992/3073, reg 28, Sch 6, para 1.

[27A Information communicated by the Commissioners of Customs and Excise

(1) If they think it appropriate to do so for the purpose of facilitating the exercise or performance by any person to whom subsection (2) below applies of any of that person's powers or duties under any of the relevant statutory provisions, the Commissioners of Customs and Excise may authorise the disclosure to that person of any information obtained for the purposes of the exercise by the Commissioners of their functions in relation to imports.

(2) This subsection applies to an enforcing authority and to an inspector.

(3) A disclosure of information made to any person under subsection (1) above shall be made in such manner as may be directed by the Commissioners of Customs and Excise and may be made through such persons acting on behalf of that person as may be so directed.

(4) Information may be disclosed to a person under subsection (1) above whether or not the disclosure of the information has been requested by or on behalf of that person.]   **[62]**

NOTES

  Inserted by the Consumer Protection Act 1987, s 36, Sch 3, para 4.

  Modified, in relation to vessels for use at work, by the Simple Pressure Vessels (Safety) Regulations 1991, SI 1991/2749, Sch 5.

  Modified, in relation to enforcement in Great Britain in relation to relevant machinery for use at work, by the Supply of Machinery (Safety) Regulations 1992, SI 1992/3073, reg 28, Sch 6, para 1.

28 Restrictions on disclosure of information

(1) In this and the two following subsections—

   (a) "relevant information" means information obtained by a person under section 27(1) or furnished to any person [under section 27A above or] in pursuance of a requirement imposed by any of the relevant statutory provisions; and

   (b) "the recipient", in relation to any relevant information, means the person by whom that information was so obtained or to whom that information was so furnished, as the case may be.

(2) Subject to the following subsection, no relevant information shall be disclosed without the consent of the person by whom it was furnished.

(3) The preceding subsection shall not apply to—

   (a) disclosure of information to the Commission, the Executive, a government department or any enforcing authority;

(b) without prejudice to paragraph (a) above, disclosure by the recipient of information to any person for the purpose of any function conferred on the recipient by or under any of the relevant statutory provisions;

(c) without prejudice to paragraph (a) above, disclosure by the recipient of information to—

(i) an officer of a local authority who is authorised by that authority to receive it,

[(ii) an officer of the National Rivers Authority or of a water undertaker, sewerage undertaker, water authority or water development board who is authorised by that Authority, undertaker, authority or board to receive it,]

(iii) an officer of a river purification board who is authorised by that board to receive it, or

(iv) a constable authorised by a chief officer of police to receive it;

(d) disclosure by the recipient of information in a form calculated to prevent it from being identified as relating to a particular person or case;

(e) disclosure of information for the purposes of any legal proceedings or any investigation or inquiry held by virtue of section 14(2), or for the purposes of a report of any such proceedings or inquiry or of a special report made by virtue of section 14(2).

(4) In the preceding subsection any reference to the Commission, the Executive, a government department or an enforcing authority includes respectively a reference to an officer of that body or authority (including, in the case of an enforcing authority, any inspector appointed by it), and also, in the case of a reference to the Commission, includes a reference to—

(a) a person performing any functions of the Commission or the Executive on its behalf by virtue of section 13(1)(a);

(b) an officer of a body which is so performing any such functions; and

(c) an adviser appointed in pursuance of section 13(1)(d).

(5) A person to whom information is disclosed in pursuance of subsection (3) above shall not use the information for a purpose other than—

(a) in a case falling within paragraph (a) of that subsection, a purpose of the Commission or of the Executive or of the government department in question, or the purposes of the enforcing authority in question in connection with the relevant statutory provisions, as the case may be;

(b) in the case of information given to an officer of a [body which is a local authority, the National Rivers Authority, a water undertaker, a sewerage undertaker, a water authority, a river purification board or a water development board, the purposes of the body] in connection with the relevant statutory provisions or any enactment whatsoever relating to public health, public safety or the protection of the environment;

(c) in the case of information given to a constable, the purposes of the police in connection with the relevant statutory provisions or any enactment whatsoever relating to public health, public safety or the safety of the State.

[(6) References in subsections (3) and (5) above to a local authority include . . . a joint authority established by Part IV of the Local Government Act 1985.]

(7) A person shall not disclose any information obtained by him as a result of the exercise of any power conferred by section 14(4)(a) or 20 (including, in particular, any information with respect to any trade secret obtained by him in any premises entered by him by virtue of any such power) except—

(a) for the purposes of his functions; or

(b) for the purposes of any legal proceedings or any investigation or inquiry held by virtue of section 14(2) or for the purposes of a report of any such proceedings or inquiry or of a special report made by virtue of section 14(2); or

(c) with the relevant consent.

In this subsection "the relevant consent" means, in the case of information furnished in pursuance of a requirement imposed under section 20, the consent of the person who furnished it, and, in any other case, the consent of a person having responsibilities in relation to the premises where the information was obtained.

(8) Notwithstanding anything in the preceding subsection an inspector shall, in circumstances in which it is necessary to do so for the purpose of assisting in keeping persons (or the representatives of persons) employed at any premises adequately informed about matters affecting their health, safety and welfare, give to such persons or their representatives the following descriptions of information, that is to say—

(a) factual information obtained by him as mentioned in that subsection which relates to those premises or anything which was or is therein or was or is being done therein; and

(b) information with respect to any action which he has taken or proposes to take in or in connection with those premises in the performance of his functions;

and, where an inspector does as aforesaid, he shall give the like information to the employer of the first-mentioned persons.

[(9) Notwithstanding anything in subsection (7) above, a person who has obtained such information as is referred to in that subsection may furnish to a person who appears to him to be likely to be a party to any civil proceedings arising out of any accident, occurrence, situation or other matter, a written statement of relevant facts observed by him in the course of exercising any of the powers referred to in that subsection.]

[(10) For the purposes of this section the Broads Authority shall be treated as a local authority.]   **[63]**

NOTES
Sub-s (1): words in square brackets inserted by the Consumer Protection Act 1987, s 36, Sch 3, para 5.
Sub-ss (3), (5): words in square brackets substituted by the Water Act 1989, s 190, Sch 25, para 46.
Sub-s (6): substituted by the Local Government Act 1985, s 84, Sch 14, para 52; words omitted repealed by the Education Reform Act 1988, s 237, Sch 13, Part I.
Sub-s (9): added by the Employment Protection Act 1975, s 116, Sch 15, para 9.
Sub-s (10): added by the Norfolk and Suffolk Broads Act 1988, s 21, Sch 6, para 13.
Modified by the Waste Regulation and Disposal (Authorities) Order 1985, SI 1985/1884, art 10, Sch 3.
Modified, in relation to vessels for use at work, by the Simple Pressure Vessels (Safety) Regulations 1991, SI 1991/2749, Sch 5.
Modified, in relation to enforcement in Great Britain in relation to relevant machinery for use at work, by the Supply of Machinery (Safety) Regulations 1992, SI 1992/3073, reg 28, Sch 6, para 1.

29–32 (*Repealed by the Employment Protection Act 1975, ss 116, 125(3), Sch 15, para 10, Sch 18.*)

Provisions as to offences

33 Offences

(1) It is an offence for a person—

(a) to fail to discharge a duty to which he is subject by virtue of sections 2 to 7;

(b) to contravene section 8 or 9;

(c) to contravene any health and safety regulations . . . or any requirement or prohibition imposed under any such regulations (including any requirement or prohibition to which he is subject by virtue of the terms of or any condition or restriction attached to any licence, approval, exemption or other authority issued, given or granted under the regulations);

(d) to contravene any requirement imposed by or under regulations under section 14 or intentionally to obstruct any person in the exercise of his powers under that section;

(e) to contravene any requirement imposed by an inspector under section 20 or 25;

(f) to prevent or attempt to prevent any other person from appearing before an inspector or from answering any question to which an inspector may by virtue of section 20(2) require an answer;

(g) to contravene any requirement or prohibition imposed by an improvement notice or a prohibition notice (including any such notice as modified on appeal);

(h) intentionally to obstruct an inspector in the exercise or performance of his powers or duties [or to obstruct a customs officer in the exercise of his powers under section 25A];

(i) to contravene any requirement imposed by a notice under section 27(1);

(j) to use or disclose any information in contravention of section 27(4) or 28;

(k) to make a statement which he knows to be false or recklessly to make a statement which is false where the statement is made—

    (i) in purported compliance with a requirement to furnish any information imposed by or under any of the relevant statutory provisions; or

    (ii) for the purpose of obtaining the issue of a document under any of the relevant statutory provisions to himself or another person;

(l) intentionally to make a false entry in any register, book, notice or other document required by or under any of the relevant statutory provisions to be kept, served or given or, with intent to deceive, to made use of any such entry which he knows to be false;

(m) with intent to deceive, to . . . use a document issued or authorised to be issued under any of the relevant statutory provisions or required for any purpose thereunder or to make or have in his possession a document so closely resembling any such document as to be calculated to deceive;

(n) falsely to pretend to be an inspector;

(o) to fail to comply with an order made by a court under section 42.

[(1A) Subject to any provision made by virtue of section 15(6)(d), a person guilty of an offence under subsection (1)(a) above consisting of failing to discharge a duty to which he is subject by virtue of sections 2 to 6 shall be liable—

(a) on summary conviction, to a fine not exceeding £20,000;

(b) on conviction on indictment, to a fine.]

(2) A person guilty of an offence under paragraph (d), (f), (h) or (n) of subsection (1) above, or of an offence under paragraph (e) of that subsection consisting of contravening a requirement imposed by an inspector under section 20, shall be liable on summary conviction to a fine not exceeding [level 5 on the standard scale];

[(2A) A person guilty of an offence under subsection (1)(g) or (o) above shall be liable—

(a) on summary conviction, to imprisonment for a term not exceeding six months, or a fine not exceeding £20,000, or both;

(b) on conviction on indictment, to imprisonment for a term not exceeding two years, or a fine, or both.]

(3) Subject to any provision made by virtue of section 15(6)(d) [or (e)] or by virtue of paragraph 2(2) of Schedule 3, a person guilty of [an offence under subsection (1) above not falling within subsection (1A), (2) or (2A) above], or of an offence under any of the existing statutory provisions, being an offence for which no other penalty is specified, shall be liable—

    (a) on summary conviction, to a fine not exceeding [the prescribed sum];

    (b) on conviction on indictment—

        (i) if the offence is one to which this sub-paragraph applies, to imprisonment for a term not exceeding two years, or a fine, or both;

        (ii) if the offence is not one to which the preceding sub-paragraph applies, to a fine.

(4) Subsection (3)(b)(i) above applies to the following offences—

    (a) an offence consisting of contravening any of the relevant statutory provisions by doing otherwise than under the authority of a licence issued by the Executive . . . something for the doing of which such a licence is necessary under the relevant statutory provisions;

    (b) an offence consisting of contravening a term of or a condition or restriction attached to any such licence as is mentioned in the preceding paragraph;

    (c) an offence consisting of acquiring or attempting to acquire, possessing or using an explosive article or substance (within the meaning of any of the relevant statutory provisions) in contravention of any of the relevant statutory provisions;

    (d) . . .

    (e) an offence under subsection (1)(j) above.

(5), (6) . . .　　　　　　　　　　　　　　　　　　　　　　　　　　　**[64]**

NOTES

    Sub-s (1): words omitted in para (c) repealed by the Employment Protection Act 1975, ss 116, 125(3), Sch 15, para 11, Sch 18; in sub-para (h) words in square brackets added by the Consumer Protection Act 1987, s 36, Sch 3, para 6; words omitted in para (m) repealed by the Forgery and Counterfeiting Act 1981, s 30, Schedule, Part I.

    Sub-s (1A): inserted by the Offshore Safety Act 1992, s 4(2), (6).

    Sub-s (2): maximum fine increased by the Criminal Law Act 1977, s 31, Sch 6, and converted to a level on the standard scale by the Criminal Justice Act 1982, ss 37, 46.

    Sub-s (2A): inserted by the Offshore Safety Act 1992, s 4(3), (6).

    Sub-s (3): first words in square brackets added and second words in square brackets substituted by the Offshore Safety Act 1992, s 4(4), (6); final words in square brackets substituted by the Magistrates' Courts Act 1980, s 32(2).

    Sub-s (4): words omitted in para (a) repealed by the Employment Protection Act 1975, ss 116, 125(3), Sch 15, para 11, Sch 18; para (d) repealed by the Offshore Safety Act 1992, ss 4(5), (6), 7(2), Sch 2.

    Sub-s (5): repealed by the Offshore Safety Act 1992, ss 4(5), (6), 7(2), Sch 2.

    Sub-s (6): repealed by the Forgery and Counterfeiting Act 1981, s 30, Schedule, Part I.

34 Extension of time for bringing summary proceedings

(1) Where—

    (a) a special report on any matter to which section 14 of this Act applies is made by virtue of subsection (2)(a) of that section; or

    (b) a report is made by the person holding an inquiry into any such matter by virtue of subsection (2)(b) of that section; or

    (c) a coroner's inquest is held touching the death of any person whose death may have been caused by an accident which happened while he was at work or by a disease which he contracted or probably contracted at work or by any accident, act or omission which occurred in connection with the work of any person whatsoever; or

    (d) a public inquiry into any death that may have been so caused is held under the Fatal Accidents Inquiry (Scotland) Act 1895 or the Fatal Accidents and Sudden Deaths Inquiry (Scotland) Act 1906,

and it appears from the report or, in a case falling within paragraph (c) or (d) above, from the proceedings at the inquest or inquiry, that any of the relevant statutory provisions was contravened at a time which is material in relation to the subject-matter of the report, inquest or inquiry, summary proceedings against any person liable to be proceeded against in respect of the contravention may be commenced at any time within three months of the making of the report or, in a case falling within paragraph (c) or (d) above, within three months of the conclusion of the inquest or inquiry.

(2) Where an offence under any of the relevant statutory provisions is committed by reason of a failure to do something at or within a time fixed by or under any of those provisions, the offence shall be deemed to continue until that thing is done.

(3) Summary proceedings for an offence to which this subsection applies may be commenced at any time within six months from the date on which there comes to the knowledge of a responsible enforcing authority evidence sufficient in the opinion of that authority to justify a prosecution for that offence; and for the purposes of this subsection—

(a) a certificate of an enforcing authority stating that such evidence came to its knowledge on a specified date shall be conclusive evidence of that fact; and

(b) a document purporting to be such a certificate and to be signed by or on behalf of the enforcing authority in question shall be presumed to be such a certificate unless the contrary is proved.

(4) The preceding subsection applies to any offence under any of the relevant statutory provisions which a person commits by virtue of any provision or requirement to which he is subject as the designer, manufacturer, importer or supplier of any thing; and in that subsection "responsible enforcing authority" means an enforcing authority within whose field of responsibility the offence in question lies, whether by virtue of section 35 or otherwise.

(5) In the application of subsection (3) above to Scotland—

(a) for the words from "there comes" to "that offence" there shall be substituted the words "evidence, sufficient in the opinion of the enforcing authority to justify a report to the Lord Advocate with a view to consideration of the question of prosecution, comes to the knowledge of the authority";

(b) at the end of paragraph (b) there shall be added the words "and

(c) section 23(2) of the Summary Jurisdiction (Scotland) Act 1954 (date of commencement of proceedings) shall have effect as it has effect for the purposes of that section.".

[(6) In the application of subsection (4) above to Scotland, after the words "applies to" there shall be inserted the words "any offence under section 33(1)(c) above where the health and safety regulations concerned were made for the general purpose mentioned in section 18(1) of the Gas Act 1986 and".] **[65]**

NOTES

Sub-s (6): added by the Gas Act 1986, s 67(1), Sch 7, para 18.

Modified, in relation to vessels for use at work, by the Simple Pressure Vessels (Safety) Regulations 1991, SI 1991/2749, Sch 5.

Modified, in relation to enforcement in Great Britain in relation to relevant machinery for use at work, by the Supply of Machinery (Safety) Regulations 1992, SI 1992/3073, reg 28, Sch 6, para 1.

35 Venue

An offence under any of the relevant statutory provisions committed in connection with any plant or substance may, if necessary for the purpose of bringing the offence within the field of responsibility of any enforcing authority or conferring jurisdiction on any court to entertain proceedings for the offence, be treated as having been committed at the place where that plant or substance is for the time being.   **[66]**

NOTES

  Modified, in relation to vessels for use at work, by the Simple Pressure Vessels (Safety) Regulations 1991, SI 1991/2749, Sch 5.

  Modified, in relation to enforcement in Great Britain in relation to relevant machinery for use at work, by the Supply of Machinery (Safety) Regulations 1992, SI 1992/3073, reg 28, Sch 6, para 1.

36 Offences due to fault of other person

(1) Where the commission by any person of an offence under any of the relevant statutory provisions is due to the act or default of some other person, that other person shall be guilty of the offence, and a person may be charged with and convicted of the offence by virtue of this subsection whether or not proceedings are taken against the first-mentioned person.

  (2) Where there would be or have been the commission of an offence under section 33 by the Crown but for the circumstance that that section does not bind the Crown, and that fact is due to the act or default of a person other than the Crown, that person shall be guilty of the offence which, but for that circumstance, the Crown would be committing or would have committed, and may be charged with and convicted of that offence accordingly.

  (3) The preceding provisions of this section are subject to any provision made by virtue of section 15(6).   **[67]**

NOTE

  Modified, in relation to enforcement in Great Britain in relation to relevant machinery for use at work, by the Supply of Machinery (Safety) Regulations 1992, SI 1992/3073, reg 28, Sch 6, para 1.

37 Offences by bodies corporate

(1) Where an offence under any of the relevant statutory provisions committed by a body corporate is proved to have been committed with the consent or connivance of, or to have been attributable to any neglect on the part of, any director, manager, secretary or other similar officer of the body corporate or a person who was purporting to act in any such capacity, he as well as the body corporate shall be guilty of that offence and shall be liable to be proceeded against and punished accordingly.

  (2) Where the affairs of a body corporate are managed by its members, the preceding subsection shall apply in relation to the acts and defaults of a member in connection with his functions of management as if he were a director of the body corporate.   **[68]**

NOTE

  Modified, in relation to enforcement in Great Britain in relation to relevant machinery for use at work, by the Supply of Machinery (Safety) Regulations 1992, SI 1992/3073, reg 28, Sch 6, para 1.

38 Restriction on institution of proceedings in England and Wales

Proceedings for an offence under any of the relevant statutory provisions shall not, in England and Wales, be instituted except by an inspector or by or with the consent of the Director of Public Prosecutions.   **[69]**

39 Prosecutions by inspectors

(1) An inspector, if authorised in that behalf by the enforcing authority which appointed him, may, although not of counsel or a solicitor, prosecute before a magistrates' court proceedings for an offence under any of the relevant statutory provisions.

(2) This section shall not apply to Scotland.   **[70]**

40 Onus of proving limits of what is practicable etc

In any proceedings for an offence under any of the relevant statutory provisions consisting of a failure to comply with a duty or requirement to do something so far as is practicable or so far as is reasonably practicable, or to use the best practicable means to do something, it shall be for the accused to prove (as the case may be) that it was not practicable or not reasonably practicable to do more than was in fact done to satisfy the duty or requirement, or that there was no better practicable means than was in fact used to satisfy the duty or requirement.   **[71]**

41 Evidence

(1) Where an entry is required by any of the relevant statutory provisions to be made in any register or other record, the entry, if made, shall, as against the person by or on whose behalf it was made, be admissible as evidence or in Scotland sufficient evidence of the facts stated therein.

(2) Where an entry which is so required to be so made with respect to the observance of any of the relevant statutory provisions has not been made, that fact shall be admissible as evidence or in Scotland sufficient evidence that that provision has not been observed.   **[72]**

42 Power of court to order cause of offence to be remedied or, in certain cases, forfeiture

(1) Where a person is convicted of an offence under any of the relevant statutory provisions in respect of any matters which appear to the court to be matters which it is in his power to remedy, the court may, in addition to or instead of imposing any punishment, order him, within such time as may be fixed by the order, to take such steps as may be specified in the order for remedying the said matters.

(2) The time fixed by an order under subsection (1) above may be extended or further extended by order of the court on an application made before the end of that time as originally fixed or as extended under this subsection, as the case may be.

(3) Where a person is ordered under subsection (1) above to remedy any matters, that person shall not be liable under any of the relevant statutory provisions in respect of those matters in so far as they continue during the time fixed by the order or any further time allowed under subsection (2) above.

(4) Subject to the following subsection, the court by or before which a person is convicted of an offence such as is mentioned in section 33(4)(c) in respect of any such explosive article or substance as is there mentioned may order the article or substance in question to be forfeited and either destroyed or dealt with in such other manner as the court may order.

(5) The court shall not order anything to be forfeited under the preceding subsection where a person claiming to be the owner of or otherwise interested in it applies to be heard by the court, unless an opportunity has been given to him to show cause why the order should not be made. **[73]**

NOTE
　Modified, in relation to enforcement in Great Britain in relation to relevant machinery for use at work, by the Supply of Machinery (Safety) Regulations 1992, SI 1992/3073, reg 28, Sch 6, para 1.

Financial provisions

43 Financial provisions

(1) It shall be the duty of the Secretary of State to pay to the Commission such sums as are approved by the Treasury and as he considers appropriate for the purpose of enabling the Commission to perform its functions; and it shall be the duty of the Commission to pay to the Executive such sums as the Commission considers appropriate for the purpose of enabling the Executive to perform its functions.

(2) Regulations may provide for such fees as may be fixed by or determined under the regulations to be payable for or in connection with the performance by or on behalf of any authority to which this subsection applies of any function conferred on that authority by or under any of the relevant statutory provisions.

(3) Subsection (2) above applies to the following authorities, namely the Commission, the Executive, the Secretary of State, . . . every enforcing authority, and any other person on whom any function is conferred by or under any of the relevant statutory provisions.

(4) Regulations under this section may specify the person by whom any fee payable under the regulations is to be paid; but no such fee shall be made payable by a person in any of the following capacities, namely an employee, a person seeking employment, a person training for employment, and a person seeking training for employment.

(5) Without prejudice to section 82(3), regulations under this section may fix or provide for the determination of different fees in relation to different functions, or in relation to the same function in different circumstances.

[(6) The power to make regulations under this section shall be exercisable by the Secretary of State, the Minister of Agriculture, Fisheries and Food or the Secretary of State and that Minister acting jointly.]

(7) ...

(8) In subsection (4) above the references to a person training for employment and a person seeking training for employment shall include respectively a person attending an industrial rehabilitation course provided by virtue of the Employment and Training Act 1973 and a person seeking to attend such a course.

(9) For the purposes of this section the performance by an inspector of his functions shall be treated as the performance by the enforcing authority which appointed him of functions conferred on that authority by or under any of the relevant statutory provisions.   **[74]**

NOTES
   Sub-s (3): words omitted repealed by the Employment Protection Act 1975, ss 116, 125(3), Sch 15, para 12, Sch 18.
   Sub-s (6): substituted, and sub-s (7) repealed, by the Employment Protection Act 1975, s 116, Sch 15, para 12.
   The current regulations prescribing fees are the Health and Safety (Fees) Regulations 1990, 1991, 1992 and 1993, SI 1990/1380, SI 1991/1921, SI 1992/1752, SI 1993/1321.

Miscellaneous and supplementary

44 Appeals in connection with licensing provisions in the relevant statutory provisions

(1) Any person who is aggrieved by a decision of an authority having power to issue licences (other than . . . nuclear site licences) under any of the relevant statutory provisions—

   (a) refusing to issue him a licence, to renew a licence held by him, or to transfer to him a licence held by another;
   (b) issuing him a licence on or subject to any term, condition or restriction whereby he is aggrieved;
   (c) varying or refusing to vary any term, condition or restriction on or subject to which a licence is held by him; or
   (d) revoking a licence held by him,

may appeal to the Secretary of State.

(2) The Secretary of State may, in such cases as he considers it appropriate to do so, having regard to the nature of the questions which appear to him to arise, direct that an appeal under this section shall be determined on his behalf by a person appointed by him for that purpose.

(3) Before the determination of an appeal the Secretary of State shall ask the appellant and the authority against whose decision the appeal is brought whether they wish to appear and be heard on the appeal and—

   (a) the appeal may be determined without a hearing of the parties if both of them express a wish not to appear and be heard as aforesaid;
   (b) the Secretary of State shall, if either of the parties expresses a wish to appear and be heard, afford to both of them an opportunity of so doing.

(4) The Tribunals and Inquiries Act [1992] shall apply to a hearing held by a person appointed in pursuance of subsection (2) above to determine an appeal as it applies to a statutory inquiry held by the Secretary of State, but as if in [section 10(1)] of that Act (statement of reasons for decisions) the reference to any decision taken by the Secretary of State included a reference to a decision taken on his behalf by that person.

(5) A person who determines an appeal under this section on behalf of the Secretary of State and the Secretary of State, if he determines such an appeal, may give such directions as he considers appropriate to give effect to his determination.

(6) The Secretary of State may pay to any person appointed to hear or determine an appeal under this section on his behalf such remuneration and allowances as the Secretary of State may with the approval of the Minister for the Civil Service determine.

(7) In this section—

    (a) "licence" means a licence under any of the relevant statutory provisions other than [a nuclear site licence];

    (b) "nuclear site licence" means a licence to use a site for the purpose of installing or operating a nuclear installation within the meaning of the following subsection.

(8) For the purposes of the preceding subsection "nuclear installation" means—

    (a) a nuclear reactor (other than such a reactor comprised in a means of transport, whether by land, water or air); or

    (b) any other installation of such class or description as may be prescribed for the purposes of this paragraph or section 1(1)(b) of the Nuclear Installations Act 1965, being an installation designed or adapted for—

        (i) the production or use of atomic energy; or

        (ii) the carrying out of any process which is preparatory or ancillary to the production or use of atomic energy and which involves or is capable of causing the emission of ionising radiations; or

        (iii) the storage, processing or disposal of nuclear fuel or of bulk quantities of other radioactive matter, being matter which has been produced or irradiated in the course of the production or use of nuclear fuel;

and in this subsection—

"atomic energy" has the meaning assigned by the Atomic Energy Act 1946;

"nuclear reactor" means any plant (including any machinery, equipment or appliance, whether affixed to land or not) designed or adapted for the production of atomic energy by a fission process in which a controlled chain reaction can be maintained without an additional source of neutrons.

[75]

NOTES

    Sub-s (1): words omitted repealed by the Employment Protection Act 1975, ss 116, 125 (3), Sch 15, para 13, Sch 18.

    Sub-s (4): words in square brackets substituted by the Tribunals and Inquiries Act 1992, s 18(1), Sch 3, para 9.

    Sub-s (7): words in square brackets substituted by the Employment Protection Act 1975, s 116, Sch 15, para 13.

---

45 Default powers

(1) Where, in the case of a local authority who are an enforcing authority, the Commission is of the opinion that an investigation should be made as to whether that

local authority have failed to perform any of their enforcement functions the Commission may make a report to the Secretary of State.

(2) The Secretary of State may, after considering a report submitted to him under the preceding subsection, cause a local inquiry to be held; and the provisions of subsections (2) to (5) of section 250 of the Local Government Act 1972 as to local inquiries shall, without prejudice to the generality of subsection (1) of that section, apply to a local inquiry so held as they apply to a local inquiry held in pursuance of that section.

(3) If the Secretary of State is satisfied, after having caused a local inquiry to be held into the matter, that a local authority have failed to perform any of their enforcement functions, he may make an order declaring the authority to be in default.

(4) An order made by virtue of the preceding subsection which declares an authority to be in default may, for the purpose of remedying the default, direct the authority (hereafter in this section referred to as "the defaulting authority") to perform such of their enforcement functions as are specified in the order in such manner as may be so specified and may specify the time or times within which those functions are to be performed by the authority.

(5) If the defaulting authority fail to comply with any direction contained in such an order the Secretary of State may, instead of enforcing the order by mandamus, make an order transferring to the Executive such of the enforcement functions of the defaulting authority as he thinks fit.

(6) Where any enforcement functions of the defaulting authority are transferred in pursuance of the preceding subsection, the amount of any expenses which the Executive certifies were incurred by it in performing those functions shall on demand be paid to it by the defaulting authority.

(7) Any expenses which in pursuance of the preceding subsection are required to be paid by the defaulting authority in respect of any enforcement functions transferred in pursuance of this section shall be defrayed by the authority in the like manner, and shall be debited to the like account, as if the enforcement functions had not been transferred and the expenses had been incurred by the authority in performing them.

(8) Where the defaulting authority are required to defray any such expenses the authority shall have the like powers for the purpose of raising the money for defraying those expenses as they would have had for the purpose of raising money required for defraying expenses incurred for the purpose of the enforcement functions in question.

(9) An order transferring any enforcement functions of the defaulting authority in pursuance of subsection (5) above may provide for the transfer to the Executive of such of the rights, liabilities and obligations of the authority as the Secretary of State considers appropriate; and where such an order is revoked the Secretary of State may, by the revoking order or a subsequent order, make such provision as he considers appropriate with respect to any rights, liabilities and obligations held by the Executive for the purposes of the transferred enforcement functions.

(10) The Secretary of State may by order vary or revoke any order previously made by him in pursuance of this section.

(11) In this section "enforcement functions", in relation to a local authority, means the functions of the authority as an enforcing authority.

(12) In the application of this section to Scotland—

(a) in subsection (2) for the words "subsections (2) to (5) of section 250 of the

Local Government Act 1972" there shall be substituted the words "subsections (2) to (8) of section 210 of the Local Government (Scotland) Act 1973", except that before 16th May 1975 for the said words there shall be substituted the words "subsections (2) to (9) of section 355 of the Local Government (Scotland) Act 1947";

(b) in subsection (5) the words "instead of enforcing the order by mandamus" shall be omitted.   [76]

46 Service of notices

(1) Any notice required or authorised by any of the relevant statutory provisions to be served on or given to an inspector may be served or given by delivering it to him or by leaving it at, or sending it by post to, his office.

(2) Any such notice required or authorised to be served on or given to a person other than an inspector may be served or given by delivering it to him, or by leaving it at his proper address, or by sending it by post to him at that address.

(3) Any such notice may—

(a) in the case of a body corporate, be served on or given to the secretary or clerk of that body;

(b) in the case of a partnership, be served on or given to a partner or a person having the control or management of the partnership business or, in Scotland, the firm.

(4) For the purposes of this section and of section 26 of the Interpretation Act 1889 (service of documents by post) in its application to this section, the proper address of any person on or to whom any such notice is to be served or given shall be his last known address, except that—

(a) in the case of a body corporate or their secretary or clerk, it shall be the address of the registered or principal office of that body;

(b) in the case of a partnership or a person having the control or the management of the partnership business, it shall be the principal office of the partnership;

and for the purposes of this subsection the principal office of a company registered outside the United Kingdom or of a partnership carrying on business outside the United Kingdom shall be their principal office within the United Kingdom.

(5) If the person to be served with or given any such notice has specified an address within the United Kingdom other than his proper address within the meaning of subsection (4) above as the one at which he or someone on his behalf will accept notices of the same description as that notice, that address shall also be treated for the purposes of this section and section 26 of the Interpretation Act 1889 as his proper address.

(6) Without prejudice to any other provision of this section, any such notice required or authorised to be served on or given to the owner or occupier of any premises (whether a body corporate or not) may be served or given by sending it by post to him at those premises, or by addressing it by name to the person on or to whom it is to be served or given and delivering it to some responsible person who is or appears to be resident or employed in the premises.

(7) If the name or the address of any owner or occupier of premises on or to whom any such notice as aforesaid is to be served or given cannot after reasonable inquiry be ascertained, the notice may be served or given by addressing it to the person on or to whom it is to be served or given by the description of "owner" or "occupier" of

the premises (describing them) to which the notice relates, and by delivering it to some responsible person who is or appears to be resident or employed in the premises, or, if there is no such person to whom it can be delivered, by affixing it or a copy of it to some conspicuous part of the premises.

(8) The preceding provisions of this section shall apply to the sending or giving of a document as they apply to the giving of a notice.   [77]

NOTE
Interpretation Act 1889: see now the Interpretation Act 1978, s 25(2).

47 Civil Liability

(1) Nothing in this Part shall be construed—

   (a) as conferring a right of action in any civil proceedings in respect of any failure to comply with any duty imposed by sections 2 to 7 or any contravention of section 8; or

   (b) as affecting the extent (if any) to which breach of a duty imposed by any of the existing statutory provisions is actionable; or

   (c) as affecting the operation of section 12 of the Nuclear Installations Act 1965 (right to compensation by virtue of certain provisions of that Act).

(2) Breach of a duty imposed by health and safety regulations . . . shall, so far as it causes damage, be actionable except in so far as the regulations provide otherwise.

(3) No provision made by virtue of section 15(6)(b) shall afford a defence in any civil proceedings, whether brought by virtue of subsection (2) above or not; but as regards any duty imposed as mentioned in subsection (2) above health and safety regulations . . . may provide for any defence specified in the regulations to be available in any action for breach of that duty.

(4) Subsections (1)(a) and (2) above are without prejudice to any right of action which exists apart from the provisions of this Act, and subsection (3) above is without prejudice to any defence which may be available apart from the provisions of the regulations there mentioned.

(5) Any term of an agreement which purports to exclude or restrict the operation of subsection (2) above, or any liability arising by virtue of that subsection shall be void, except in so far as health and safety regulations . . . provide otherwise.

(6) In this section "damage" includes the death of, or injury to, any person (including any disease and any impairment of a person's physical or mental condition).   [78]

NOTES
Sub-ss (2), (3): words omitted repealed by the Employment Protection Act 1975, ss 116, 125(3), Sch 15, para 14, Sch 18.
Sub-s (5): words omitted repealed by the Employment Protection Act 1975, s 116, Sch 15, para 14.

48 Application to Crown

(1) Subject to the provisions of this section, the provisions of this Part, except sections 21 to 25 and 33 to 42, and of regulations made under this Part shall bind the Crown.

(2) Although they do not bind the Crown, sections 33 to 42 shall apply to persons in the public service of the Crown as they apply to other persons.

(3) For the purposes of this Part and regulations made thereunder persons in the service of the Crown shall be treated as employees of the Crown whether or not they would be so treated apart from this subsection.

(4) Without prejudice to section 15(5), the Secretary of State may, to the extent that it appears to him requisite or expedient to do so in the interests of the safety of the State or the safe custody of persons lawfully detained, by order exempt the Crown either generally or in particular respects from all or any of the provisions of this Part which would, by virtue of subsection (1) above, bind the Crown.

(5) The power to make orders under this section shall be exercisable by statutory instrument, and any such order may be varied or revoked by a subsequent order.

(6) Nothing in this section shall authorise proceedings to be brought against Her Majesty in her private capacity, and this subsection shall be construed as if section 38(3) of the Crown Proceedings Act 1947 (interpretation of references in that Act to Her Majesty in her private capacity) were contained in this Act.   **[79]**

NOTE

See further, in relation to the powers of the Secretary of State under sub-s (4): the Atomic Weapons Establishment Act 1991, Schedule, para 7(1).

49 Adaptation of enactments to metric units or appropriate metric units

(1) [Regulations made under this subsection may amend]—

- (a) any of the relevant statutory provisions; or
- (b) any provision of an enactment which relates to any matter relevant to any of the general purposes of this Part but is not among the relevant statutory provisions; or
- (c) any provision of an instrument made or having effect under any such enactment as is mentioned in the preceding paragraph,

by substituting an amount or quantity expressed in metric units for an amount or quantity not so expressed or by substituting an amount or quantity expressed in metric units of a description specified in the regulations for an amount or quantity expressed in metric units of a different description.

(2) The amendments shall be such as to preserve the effect of the provisions mentioned except to such extent as in the opinion of the [authority making the regulations] is necessary to obtain amounts expressed in convenient and suitable terms.

(3) Regulations made . . . under this subsection may, in the case of a provision which falls within any of paragraphs (a) to (c) of subsection (1) above and contains words which refer to units other than metric units, repeal those words [if the authority making the regulations] is of the opinion that those words could be omitted without altering the effect of that provision.

[(4) The power to make regulations under this section shall be exercisable by the Secretary of State, the Minister of Agriculture, Fisheries and Food or the Secretary of State and that Minister acting jointly.]   **[80]**

NOTES

Sub-ss (1)–(3): words in square brackets substituted and words omitted from sub-s (3) repealed by the Employment Protection Act 1975, ss 116, 125(3), Sch 15, para 15(1), Sch 18.

Sub-s (4): substituted by the Employment Protection Act 1975, s 116, Sch 15, para 15(2).

50 Regulations under the relevant statutory provisions

[(1) Where any power to make regulations under any of the relevant statutory provisions is exercisable by the Secretary of State, the Minister of Agriculture, Fisheries and Food or both of them acting jointly that power may be exercised either so as to give effect (with or without modifications) to proposals submitted by the Commission under section 11(2)(d) or independently of any such proposals; but the authority who is to exercise the power shall not exercise it independently of proposals from the Commission unless he has consulted the Commission and such other bodies as appear to him to be appropriate.]

(2) Where the [authority who is to exercise any such power as is mentioned in subsection (1) above proposes to exercise that power] so as to give effect to any such proposals as are there mentioned with modifications, he shall, before making the regulations, consult the Commission.

(3) Where the Commission proposes to submit [under section 11(2)(d)] any such proposals as are mentioned in subsection (1) above except proposals for the making of regulations under section 43(2), it shall, before so submitting them, consult—

    (a) any government department or other body that appears to the Commission to be appropriate (and, in particular, in the case of proposals for the making of regulations under section 18(2), any body representing local authorities that so appears, and, in the case of proposals for the making of regulations relating to electro-magnetic radiations, the National Radiological Protection Board);

    (b) such government departments and other bodies, if any, as, in relation to any matter dealt with in the proposals, the Commission is required to consult under this subsection by virtue of directions given to it by the Secretary of State.

    (4),(5) ...   [81]

NOTES

    Sub-s (1): substituted by the Employment Protection Act 1975, s 116, Sch 15, para 16(1).

    Sub-ss (2), (3): words in square brackets substituted by the Employment Protection Act 1975, s 116, Sch 15, para 16(2), (3).

    Sub-ss (4), (5): repealed by the Employment Protection Act 1975, ss 116, 125(3), Sch 15, para 16(4), Sch 18.

51 Exclusion of application to domestic employment

Nothing in this Part shall apply in relation to a person by reason only that he employs another, or is himself employed, as a domestic servant in a private household.

[82]

52 Meaning of work and at work

(1) For the purposes of this Part—

    (a) "work" means work as an employee or as a self-employed person;

    (b) an employee is at work throughout the time when he is in the course of his employment, but not otherwise; and

    (c) a self-employed person is at work throughout such time as he devotes to work as a self-employed person;

and, subject to the following subsection, the expressions "work" and "at work", in whatever context, shall be construed accordingly.

(2) Regulations made under this subsection may—

(a) extend the meaning of "work" and "at work" for the purposes of this Part; and

(b) in that connection provide for any of the relevant statutory provisions to have effect subject to such adaptations as may be specified in the regulations.

[(3) The power to make regulations under subsection (2) above shall be exercisable by the Secretary of State, the Minister of Agriculture, Fisheries and Food or the Secretary of State and that Minister acting jointly.] **[83]**

NOTES
Sub-s (3): substituted for the original sub-ss (3), (4), by the Employment Protection Act 1975, s 116, Sch 15, para 17.
See the Health and Safety (Genetic Manipulation) Regulations 1989, SI 1989/1810, and the Health and Safety (Dangerous Pathogens) Regulations 1981, SI 1981/1011, which extend the definition of "work" to cover activities involving genetic manipulation and the handling or keeping of a listed dangerous pathogen respectively. See also the Health and Safety (Training for Employment) Regulations 1990, SI 1990/1380, which extend the definitions of "work" and "at work" respectively to cover persons engaged in specified training.
See further: the Offshore Installations and Pipelines Works (First-Aid) Regulations 1989, SI 1989/1671, reg 4.

53 General interpretation of Part I

(1) In this Part, unless the context otherwise requires—

. . . . .

"article for use at work" means—

(a) any plant designed for use or operation (whether exclusively or not) by persons at work, and

(b) any article designed for use as a component in any such plant;

["article of fairground equipment" means any fairground equipment or any article designed for use as a component in any such equipment;]

"code of practice" (without prejudice to section 16(8)) includes a standard, a specification and any other documentary form of practical guidance;

"the Commission" has the meaning assigned by section 10(2);

"conditional sale agreement" means an agreement for the sale of goods under which the purchase price or part of it is payable by instalments, and the property in the goods is to remain in the seller (notwithstanding that the buyer is to be in possession of the goods) until such conditions as to the payment of instalments or otherwise as may be specified in the agreement are fulfilled;

"contract of employment" means a contract of employment or apprenticeship (whether express or implied and, if express, whether oral or in writing);

"credit-sale agreement" means an agreement for the sale of goods, under which the purchase price or part of it is payable by instalments, but which is not a conditional sale agreement;

["customs officer" means an officer within the meaning of the Customs and Excise Management Act 1979;]

"domestic premises" means premises occupied as a private dwelling (including any garden, yard, garage, outhouse or other appurtenance of such premises which is not used in common by the occupants of more than one such dwelling), and "non-domestic premises" shall be construed accordingly;

"employee" means an individual who works under a contract of employment, and related expressions shall be construed accordingly;

"enforcing authority" has the meaning assigned by section 18(7);

"the Executive" has the meaning assigned by section 10(5);
"the existing statutory provisions" means the following provisions while and
to the extent that they remain in force, namely the provisions of the Acts
mentioned in Schedule 1 which are specified in the third column of that
Schedule and of the regulations, orders or other instruments of a legislative
character made or having effect under any provision so specified;

. . . . .

["fairground equipment" means any fairground ride, any similar plant which
is designed to be in motion for entertainment purposes with members of
the public on or inside it or any plant which is designed to be used by
members of the public for entertainment purposes either as a slide or for
bouncing upon, and in this definition the reference to plant which is
designed to be in motion with members of the public on or inside it includes
a reference to swings, dodgems and other plant which is designed to be in
motion wholly or partly under the control of, or to be put in motion by, a
member of the public;]
"the general purposes of this Part" has the meaning assigned by section 1;
"health and safety regulations" has the meaning assigned by section 15(1);
"hire-purchase agreement" means an agreement other than a conditional sale
agreement, under which—

(a) goods are bailed or (in Scotland) hired in return for periodical
payments by the person to whom they are bailed or hired; and
(b) the property in the goods will pass to that person if the terms of the
agreement are complied with and one or more of the following occurs:

(i) the exercise of an option to purchase by that person;
(ii) the doing of any other specified act by any party to the agreement;
(iii) the happening of any other event;

and "hire-purchase" shall be construed accordingly;
"improvement notice" means a notice under section 21;
"inspector" means an inspector appointed under section 19;

. . . . .

"local authority" means—

(a) in relation to England and Wales, a county council, . . ., a district
council, a London borough council, the Common Council of the City
of London, the Sub-Treasurer of the Inner Temple or the Under-
Treasurer of the Middle Temple,
(b) in relation to Scotland, a regional, islands or district council except
that before 16th May 1975 it means a town council or county council;

["micro-organism" includes any microscopic biological entity which is capable
of replication;]
"offshore installation" means any installation which is intended for underwater
exploitation of mineral resources or exploration with a view to such
exploitation;
"personal injury" includes any disease and any impairment of a person's
physical or mental condition;
"plant" includes any machinery, equipment or appliance;
"premises" includes any place and, in particular, includes—

(a) any vehicle, vessel, aircraft or hovercraft,
(b) any installation on land (including the foreshore and other land
intermittently covered by water), any offshore installation, and any
other installation (whether floating, or resting on the seabed or the

subsoil thereof, or resting on other land covered with water or the subsoil thereof), and

(c) any tent or movable structure;

"prescribed" means prescribed by regulations made by the Secretary of State;

"prohibition notice" means a notice under section 22;

. . . . .

"the relevant statutory provisions" means—

(a) the provisions of this Part and of any health and safety regulations . . .; and

(b) the existing statutory provisions;

"self-employed person" means an individual who works for gain or reward otherwise than under a contract of employment, whether or not he himself employs others;

"substance" means any natural or artificial substance [(including micro-organisms)], whether in solid or liquid form or in the form of a gas or vapour;

. . . . .

"supply", where the reference is to supplying articles or substances, means supplying them by way of sale, lease, hire or hire-purchase, whether as principal or agent for another.

(2)–(6) . . .   **[84]**

NOTES

Sub-s (1): definitions "article of fairground equipment", "customs officer", "fairground equipment", "micro-organism" added by the Consumer Protection Act 1987, s 36, Sch 3, para 7; in definition "substance" words in square brackets added by the Consumer Protection Act 1987, s 36, Sch 3, para 7; definition "substance for use at work" repealed by the Consumer Protection Act 1987, s 48, Sch 5; in definition "local authority" words omitted repealed by the Local Government Act 1985, s 102, Sch 17; other words omitted repealed by the Employment Protection Act, ss 116, 125(3), Sch 15, para 18, Sch 18.

Sub-ss (2)–(6): repealed by the Employment Protection Act 1975, ss 116, 125(3), Sch 15, para 18, Sch 18.

54 Application of Part I to Isles of Scilly

This Part, in its application to the Isles of Scilly, shall apply as if those Isles were a local government area and the Council of those Isles were a local authority.   **[85]**

55–76 (*Ss 55–60 (Employment Medical Advisory Service), 75 (which amend the Buildings (Scotland) Act 1959), are omitted; ss 61–64, 76 repealed by the Building Act 1984, s 133(2), Sch 7.*)

PART IV

MISCELLANEOUS AND GENERAL

77–79 (*Ss 77, 78 (which amend other Acts) are omitted; s 79 repealed by the Companies Consolidation (Consequential Provisions) Act 1985, s 29, Sch 1.*)

80 General power to repeal or modify Acts and instruments

(1) Regulations made under this subsection may repeal or modify any provision to which this subsection applies if it appears to the authority making the regulations that

the repeal or, as the case may be, the modification of that provision is expedient in consequence of or in connection with any provision made by or under Part I.

(2) Subsection (1) above applies to any provision, not being among the relevant statutory provisions, which—

    (a) is contained in this Act or in any other Act passed before or in the same Session as this Act; or

    (b) is contained in any regulations, order or other instrument of a legislative character which was made under an Act before the passing of this Act; or

    (c) applies, excludes or for any other purpose refers to any of the relevant statutory provisions and is contained in any Act not falling within paragraph (a) above or in any regulations, order or other instrument of a legislative character which is made under an Act but does not fall within paragraph (b) above.

[(2A) Subsection (1) above shall apply to provisions in the Employment Protection (Consolidation) Act 1978 which re-enact provisions previously contained in the Redundancy Payments Act 1965, the Contracts of Employment Act 1972 and the Trade Union and Labour Relations Act 1974 as it applies to provisions contained in Acts passed before or in the same session as this Act.]

(3) Without prejudice to the generality of subsection (1) above, the modifications which may be made by regulations thereunder include modifications relating to the enforcement of provisions to which this section applies (including the appointment of persons for the purpose of such enforcement, and the powers of persons so appointed).

[(4) The power to make regulations under subsection (1) above shall be exercisable by the Secretary of State, the Minister of Agriculture, Fisheries and Food or the Secretary of State and that Minister acting jointly; but the authority who is to exercise the power shall, before exercising it, consult such bodies as appear to him to be appropriate.

(5) In this section "the relevant statutory provisions" has the same meaning as in Part I.]

(6) ...   **[86]**

NOTES

    Sub-s (2A): inserted by the Employment Protection (Consolidation) Act 1978, s 159(2), Sch 16, para 17.

    Sub-ss (4), (5): substituted for the original sub-ss (4)–(6) by the Employment Protection Act 1975, s 116, Sch 15, para 19.

    By virtue of the Clean Air Act 1993, s 67(1), Sch 4, para 1 (commencement 27 August 1993: ibid s 68(2)), sub-s (1) above shall apply to provisions in that Act which re-enact provisions previously contained in an Act passed before or in the same session as that Act as it applies to provisions so contained.

81 Expenses and receipts

There shall be paid out of money provided by Parliament—

    (a) any expenses incurred by a Minister of the Crown or government department for the purposes of this Act; and

    (b) any increase attributable to the provisions of this Act in the sums payable under any other Act out of money so provided;

and any sums received by a Minister of the Crown or government department by virtue of this Act shall be paid into the Consolidated Fund.   **[87]**

82 General provisions as to interpretation and regulations

(1) In this Act—

    (a) "Act" includes a provisional order confirmed by an Act;

    (b) "contravention" includes failure to comply, and "contravene" has a corresponding meaning;

    (c) "modifications" includes additions, omissions and amendments, and related expressions shall be construed accordingly;

    (d) any reference to a Part, section or Schedule not otherwise identified is a reference to that Part or section of, or Schedule to, this Act.

(2) Except in so far as the context otherwise requires, any reference in this Act to an enactment is a reference to it as amended, and includes a reference to it as applied, by or under any other enactment, including this Act.

(3) Any power conferred by Part I or II or this Part to make regulations—

    (a) includes power to make different provision by the regulations for different circumstances or cases and to include in the regulations such incidental, supplemental and transitional provisions as the authority making the regulations considers appropriate in connection with the regulations; and

    (b) shall be exercisable by statutory instrument, which shall be subject to annulment in pursuance of a resolution of either House of Parliament.

[88]

83 ((*Amendments and repeals) omitted.*)

84 Extent, and application of Act

(1) This Act, except—

    (a) Part I and this Part so far as may be necessary to enable regulations under section 15 . . . to be made and operate for the purpose mentioned in paragraph 2 of Schedule 3; and

    (b) paragraph . . . 3 of Schedule 9,

does not extend to Northern Ireland.

(2) Part III, except section 75 and Schedule 7, does not extend to Scotland.

(3) Her Majesty may by order in Council provide that the provisions of Parts I and II and this Part shall, to such extent and for such purposes as may be specified in the Order, apply (with or without modification) to or in relation to persons, premises, work, articles, substances and other matters (of whatever kind) outside Great Britain as those provisions apply within Great Britain or within a part of Great Britain so specified.

For the purposes of this subsection "premises", "work" and "substance" have the same meanings as they have for the purposes of Part I.

(4) An Order in Council under subsection (3) above—

    (a) may make different provision for different circumstances or cases;

    (b) may (notwithstanding that this may affect individuals or bodies corporate outside the United Kingdom) provide for any of the provisions mentioned in that subsection, as applied by such an Order, to apply to individuals whether or not they are British subjects and to bodies corporate whether or not they are incorporated under the law of any part of the United Kingdom;

(c) may make provision for conferring jurisdiction on any court or class of courts specified in the Order with respect to offences under Part I committed outside Great Britain or with respect to causes of action arising by virtue of section 47(2) in respect of acts or omissions taking place outside Great Britain, and for the determination, in accordance with the law in force in such part of Great Britain as may be specified in the Order, of questions arising out of such acts or omissions;

(d) may exclude from the operation of section 3 of the Territorial Waters Jurisdiction Act 1878 (consents required for prosecutions) proceedings for offences under any provision of Part I committed outside Great Britain;

(e) may be varied or revoked by a subsequent Order in Council under this section;

and any such Order shall be subject to annulment in pursuance of a resolution of either House of Parliament.

(5) . . .

(6) Any jurisdiction conferred on any court under this section shall be without prejudice to any jurisdiction exercisable apart from this section by that or any other court.   [89]

NOTES

Sub-s (1): second words omitted repealed by the House of Commons Disqualification Act 1975, s 10(2), Sch 3; other words omitted repealed by the Employment Protection Act 1975, ss 116, 125(3), Sch 15, para 20.

Sub-s (5): repealed by the Offshore Safety Act 1992, ss 3(1), 7(2), Sch 2.

The powers under this section have been exercised by the Health and Safety at Work etc Act 1974 (Application outside Great Britain) Order 1989, SI 1989/840, revoking and replacing SI 1977/1232, which applies ss 1–59, 80–82 of the Act, with appropriate modifications, to various offshore activities.

85 Short title and commencement

(1) This Act may be cited as the Health and Safety at Work etc. Act 1974.

(2) This Act shall come into operation on such day as the Secretary of State may by order made by statutory instrument appoint, and different days may be appointed under this subsection for different purposes.

(3) An order under this section may contain such transitional provisions and savings as appear to the Secretary of State to be necessary or expedient in connection with the provisions thereby brought into force, including such adaptations of those provisions or any provision of this Act then in force as appear to him to be necessary or expedient in consequence of the partial operation of this Act (whether before or after the day appointed by the order).   [90]

SCHEDULES

SCHEDULE 1

Sections 1, 53

EXISTING ENACTMENTS WHICH ARE RELEVANT STATUTORY PROVISIONS

Chapter	Short title	Provisions which are relevant statutory provisions
1875 c. 17	The Explosives Act 1875	The whole Act except sections 30 to 32, 80 and 116 to 121.
1882 c. 22	The Boiler Explosions Act 1882	The whole Act.
1890 c. 35	The Boiler Explosions Act 1890	The whole Act.
1906 c. 14	The Alkali, &c Works Regulation Act 1906	The whole Act.
1909 c. 43	The Revenue Act 1909	Section 11.
1919 c. 23	The Anthrax Prevention Act 1919	The whole Act.
1920 c. 65	The Employment of Women, Young Persons and Children Act 1920	The whole Act.
1922 c. 35	The Celluloid and Cinematograph Film Act 1922	The whole Act.
1923 c. 17	The Explosives Act 1923	The whole Act.
1926 c. 43	The Public Health (Smoke Abatement) Act 1926	The whole Act.
1928 c. 32	The Petroleum (Consolidation) Act 1928	The whole Act.
1936 c. 22	The Hours of Employment (Conventions) Act 1936	The whole Act except section 5.
1936 c. 27	The Petroleum (Transfer of Licences) Act 1936	The whole Act.
1937 c. 45	The Hydrogen Cyanide (Fumigation) Act 1937	The whole Act.
1945 c. 19	The Ministry of Fuel and Power Act 1945	Section 1(1) so far as it relates to maintaining and improving the safety, health and welfare of persons employed in or about mines and quarries in Great Britain.
1946 c. 59	The Coal Industry Nationalisation Act 1946	Section 42(1) and (2).
1948 c. 37	The Radioactive Substances Act 1948	Section 5(1)(a).
1951 c 21	The Alkali, &c Works Regulations (Scotland) Act 1951	The whole Act.
1951 c. 58	The Fireworks Act 1951	Sections 4 and 7.
1952 c. 60	The Agriculture (Poisonous Substances) Act 1952	The whole Act.
1953 c. 47	The Emergency Laws (Miscellaneous Provisions) Act 1953	Section 3.

Chapter	Short title	Provisions which are relevant statutory provisions
1954 c. 70	The Mines and Quarries Act 1954	The whole Act except section 151.
1956 c. 49	The Agriculture (Safety, Health and Welfare Provisions) Act 1956	The whole Act.
1961 c. 34	The Factories Act 1961	The whole Act except section 135.
1961 c. 64	The Public Health Act 1961	Section 73.
1962 c. 58	The Pipe-lines Act 1962	Sections 20 to 26, 33, 34 and 42, Schedule 5.
1963 c. 41	The Offices, Shops and Railway Premises Act 1963	The whole Act.
1965 c. 57	The Nuclear Installations Act 1965	Sections 1, 3 to 6, 22 and [24A], Schedule 2.
1969 c. 10	The Mines and Quarries (Tips) Act 1969	Sections 1 to 10.
1971 c. 20	The Mines Management Act 1971	The whole Act.
1972 c. 28	The Employment Medical Advisory Service Act 1972	The whole Act except sections 1 and 6 and Schedule 1.

[91]

NOTES

Words omitted repealed by the Sex Discrimination Act 1986, s 9, Schedule, Part III; in the entry relating to the Nuclear Installations Act 1965, figure in square brackets substituted by the Atomic Energy Act 1989, s 6(3).

Modified by the Offshore Safety Act 1992, ss 1(1), 2(1).

SCHEDULE 2

Section 10

ADDITIONAL PROVISIONS RELATING TO CONSTITUTION ETC, OF THE
COMMISSION AND EXECUTIVE

Tenure of office

1. Subject to paragraphs 2 to 4 below, a person shall hold and vacate office as a member or as chairman or deputy chairman in accordance with the terms of the instrument appointing him to that office.

2. A person may at any time resign his office as a member or as chairman or deputy chairman by giving the Secretary of State a notice in writing signed by that person and stating that he resigns that office.

3.—(1) If a member becomes or ceases to be the chairman or deputy chairman, the Secretary of State may vary the terms of the instrument appointing him to be a member so as to alter the date on which he is to vacate office as a member.

(2) If the chairman or deputy chairman ceases to be a member he shall cease to be chairman or deputy chairman, as the case may be.

4.—(1) If the Secretary of State is satisfied that a member—

(a) has been absent from meetings of the Commission for a period longer than six consecutive months without the permission of the Commission; or

(b) has become bankrupt or made an arrangement with his creditors; or

(c) is incapacitated by physical or mental illness; or

(d) is otherwise unable or unfit to discharge the functions of a member, the Secretary of State may declare his office as a member to be vacant and shall notify the declaration in such manner as the Secretary of State thinks fit; and thereupon the office shall become vacant.

(2) In the application of the preceding sub-paragraph to Scotland for the references in paragraph (b) to a member's having become bankrupt and to a member's having made an arrangement with his creditors there shall be substituted respectively references to sequestration of a member's estate having been awarded and to a member's having made a trust deed for behoof of his creditors or a composition contract.

Remuneration etc. of members

5. The Commission may pay to each member such remuneration and allowances as the Secretary of State may determine.

6. The Commission may pay or make provision for paying, to or in respect of any member, such sums by way of pension, superannuation allowances and gratuities as the Secretary of State may determine.

7. Where a person ceases to be a member otherwise than on the expiry of his term of office and it appears to the Secretary of State that there are special circumstances which make it right for him to receive compensation, the Commission may make to him a payment of such amount as the Secretary of State may determine.

Proceedings

8. The quorum of the Commission and the arrangements relating to meetings of the Commission shall be such as the Commission may determine.

9. The validity of any proceedings of the Commission shall not be affected by any vacancy among the members or by any defect in the appointment of a member.

Staff

10. It shall be the duty of the Executive to provide for the Commission such officers and servants as are requisite for the proper discharge of the Commission's functions; and any reference in this Act to an officer or servant of the Commission is a reference to an officer or servant provided for the Commission in pursuance of this paragraph.

11. The Executive may appoint such officers and servants as it may determine with the consent of the Secretary of State as to numbers and terms and conditions of service.

12. The Commission shall pay to the Minister for the Civil Service, at such times in each accounting year as may be determined by that Minister subject to any directions of the Treasury, sums of such amounts as he may so determine for the purposes of this paragraph as being equivalent to the increase during that year of such liabilities of his as are attributable to the provision of pensions, allowances or gratuities to or in respect of persons who are or have been in the service of the Executive in so far as that increase results from the service of those persons during that accounting year and to the expense to be incurred in administering those pensions, allowances or gratuities.

Performance of functions

13. The Commission may authorise any member of the Commission or any officer or servant of the Commission or of the Executive to perform on behalf of the Commission such of the Commission's functions (including the function conferred on the Commission by this paragraph) as are specified in the authorisation.

Accounts and reports

14.—(1) It shall be the duty of the Commission—
  (a) to keep proper accounts and proper records in relation to the accounts;
  (b) to prepare in respect of each accounting year a statement of accounts in such form as the Secretary of State may direct with the approval of the Treasury; and
  (c) to send copies of the statement to the Secretary of State and the Comptroller and Auditor General before the end of the month of November next following the accounting year to which the statement relates.

(2) The Comptroller and Auditor General shall examine, certify and report on each statement received by him in pursuance of this Schedule and shall lay copies of each statement and of his report before each House of Parliament.

15. It shall be the duty of the Commission to make to the Secretary of State, as soon as possible after the end of each accounting year, a report on the performance of its functions during that year; and the Secretary of State shall lay before each House of Parliament a copy of each report made to him in pursuance of this paragraph.

Supplemental

16. The Secretary of State shall not make a determination or give his consent in pursuance of paragraph 5, 6, 7 or 11 of this Schedule except with the approval of the Minister for the Civil Service.

17. The fixing of the common seal of the Commission shall be authenticated by the signature of the secretary of the Commission or some other person authorised by the Commission to act for that purpose.

18. A document purporting to be duly executed under the seal of the Commission shall be received in evidence and shall, unless the contrary is proved, be deemed to be so executed.

19. In the preceding provisions of this Schedule—

   (a) "accounting year" means the period of twelve months ending with 31st March in any year except that the first accounting year of the Commission shall, if the Secretary of State so directs, be such period shorter or longer than twelve months (but not longer than two years) as is specified in the direction; and

   (b) "the chairman", "a deputy chairman" and "a member" mean respectively the chairman, a deputy chairman and a member of the Commission.

20. (1) The preceding provisions of this Schedule (except paragraphs 10 to 12 and 15) shall have effect in relation to the Executive as if—

   (a) for any reference to the Commission there were substituted a reference to the Executive;

   (b) for any reference to the Secretary of State in paragraphs 2 to 4 and 19 and the first such reference in paragraph 7 there were substituted a reference to the Commission;

   (c) for any reference to the Secretary of State in paragraphs 5 to 7 (except the first such reference in paragraph 7) there were substituted a reference to the Commission acting with the consent of the Secretary of State;

   (d) for any reference to the chairman there were substituted a reference to the director, and any reference to the deputy chairman were omitted;

   (e) in paragraph 14(1)(c) for the words from "Secretary" to "following" there were substituted the words "Commission by such date as the Commission may direct after the end of".

(2) It shall be the duty of the Commission to include in or send with the copies of the statement sent by it as required by paragraph 14(1)(c) of this Schedule copies of the statement sent to it by the Executive in pursuance of the said paragraph 14(1)(c) as adapted by the preceding sub-paragraph.

(3) The terms of an instrument appointing a person to be a member of the Executive shall be such as the Commission may determine with the approval of the Secretary of State and the Minister for the Civil Service. **[92]**

SCHEDULE 3

Section 15

SUBJECT-MATTER OF HEALTH AND SAFETY REGULATIONS

1.—(1) Regulating or prohibiting—

   (a) the manufacture, supply or use of any plant;

   (b) the manufacture, supply, keeping or use of any substance;

   (c) the carrying on of any process or the carrying out of any operation.

(2) Imposing requirements with respect to the design, construction, guarding, siting, installation, commissioning, examination, repair, maintenance, alteration, adjustment, dismantling, testing or inspection of any plant.

(3) Imposing requirements with respect to the marking of any plant or of any articles used or designed for use as components in any plant, and in that connection regulating or restricting the use of specified markings.

(4) Imposing requirements with respect to the testing, labelling or examination of any substance.

(5) Imposing requirements with respect to the carrying out of research in connection with any activity mentioned in sub-paragraphs (1) to (4) above.

2.—(1) Prohibiting the importation into the United Kingdom or the landing or unloading there of articles or substances of any specified description, whether absolutely or unless conditions imposed by or under the regulations are complied with.

(2) Specifying, in a case where an act or omission in relation to such an importation, landing or unloading as is mentioned in the preceding sub-paragraph constitutes an offence under a provision of this Act and of [the Customs and Excise Acts 1979], the Act under which the offence is to be punished.

3.—(1) Prohibiting or regulating the transport of articles or substances of any specified description.

(2) Imposing requirements with respect to the manner and means of transporting articles or substances of any specified description, including requirements with respect to the construction, testing and marking of containers and means of transport and the packaging and labelling of articles or substances in connection with their transport.

4.—(1) Prohibiting the carrying on of any specified activity or the doing of any specified thing except under the authority and in accordance with the terms and conditions of a licence, or except with the consent or approval of specified authority.

(2) Providing for the grant, renewal, variation, transfer and revocation of licences (including the variation and revocation of conditions attached to licences).

5. Requiring any person, premises or thing to be registered in any specified circumstances or as a condition of the carrying on of any specified activity or the doing of any specified thing.

6.—(1) Requiring, in specified circumstances, the appointment (whether in a specified capacity or not) of persons (or persons with specified qualifications or experience, or both) to perform specified functions, and imposing duties or conferring powers on persons appointed (whether in pursuance of the regulations or not) to perform specified functions.

(2) Restricting the performance of specified functions to persons possessing specified qualifications or experience.

7. Regulating or prohibiting the employment in specified circumstances of all persons or any class of persons.

8.—(1) Requiring the making of arrangements for securing the health of persons at work or other persons, including arrangements for medical examinations and health surveys.

(2) Requiring the making of arrangements for monitoring the atmospheric or other conditions in which persons work.

9. Imposing requirements with respect to any matter affecting the conditions in which persons work, including in particular such matters as the structural condition and stability of premises, the means of access to and egress from premises, cleanliness, temperature, lighting, ventilation, overcrowding, noise, vibrations, ionising and other radiations, dust and fumes.

10. Securing the provision of specified welfare facilities for persons at work, including in particular such things as an adequate water supply, sanitary conveniences, washing and bathing facilities, ambulance and first-aid arrangements, cloakroom accommodation, sitting facilities and refreshment facilities.

11. Imposing requirements with respect to the provision and use in specified circumstances of protective clothing or equipment, including affording protection against the weather.

12. Requiring in specified circumstances the taking of specified precautions in connection with the risk of fire.

13.—(1) Prohibiting or imposing requirements in connection with the emission into the atmosphere of any specified gas, smoke or dust or any other specified substance whatsoever.

(2) Prohibiting or imposing requirements in connection with the emission of noise, vibrations or any ionising or other radiations.

(3) Imposing requirements with respect to the monitoring of any such emission as is mentioned in the preceding sub-paragraphs.

14. Imposing requirements with respect to the instruction, training and supervision of persons at work.

15.—(1) Requiring, in specified circumstances, specified matters to be notified in a specified manner to specified persons.

(2) Empowering inspectors in specified circumstances to require persons to submit written particulars of measures proposed to be taken to achieve compliance with any of the relevant statutory provisions.

16. Imposing requirements with respect to the keeping and preservation of records and other documents, including plans and maps.

17. Imposing requirements with respect to the management of animals.

18. The following purposes as regards premises of any specified description where persons work, namely—

 (a) requiring precautions to be taken against dangers to which the premises or persons therein are or may be exposed by reason of conditions (including natural conditions) existing in the vicinity;

 (b) securing that persons in the premises leave them in specified circumstances.

19. Conferring, in specified circumstances involving a risk of fire or explosion, power to search a person or any article which a person has with him for the purpose of ascertaining whether he has in his possession any article of a specified kind likely in those circumstances to cause a fire or explosion, and power to seize and dispose of any article of that kind found on such a search.

20. Restricting, prohibiting or requiring the doing of any specified thing where any accident or other occurrence of a specified kind has occurred.

21. As regards cases of any specified class, being a class such that the variety in the circumstances of particular cases within it calls for the making of special provision for particular cases, any of the following purposes, namely—

 (a) conferring on employers or other persons power to make rules or give directions with respect to matters affecting health or safety;

 (b) requiring employers or other persons to make rules with respect to any such matters;

 (c) empowering specified persons to require employers or other persons either to make rules with respect to any such matters or to modify any such rules previously made by virtue of this paragraph; and

 (d) making admissible in evidence without further proof, in such circumstances and subject to such conditions as may be specified, documents which purport to be copies of rules or rules of any specified class made under this paragraph.

22. Conferring on any local or public authority power to make byelaws with respect to any specified matter, specifying the authority or person by whom any byelaws made in the exercise of that power need to be confirmed, and generally providing for the procedure to be followed in connection with the making of any such byelaws.

Interpretation

23.—(1) In this Schedule "specified" means specified in health and safety regulations.

(2) It is hereby declared that the mention in this Schedule of a purpose that falls within any more general purpose mentioned therein is without prejudice to the generality of the more general purpose. **[93]**

NOTE
Para 2: sub-para (2) amended by the Customs and Excise Management Act 1979, s 177(1), Sch 4, para 12, Table, Part I.

(Sch 4 repealed by the Employment Protection Act 1975, ss 116, 125(3), Sch 15, para 21, Sch 18; Schs 5, 6 repealed by the Building Act 1984, s 133(2), Sch 7; Schs 7 (which amends the Buildings (Scotland) Act 1959), 8 (transitional provisions with respect to fire certificates), 9 (minor and consequential amendments), 10 (repeals) omitted.)

REHABILITATION OF OFFENDERS ACT 1974

(1974 c 53)

ARRANGEMENT OF SECTIONS

PART I

GENERAL PROVISIONS

An Act to rehabilitate offenders who have not been reconvicted of any serious offence for periods of years, to penalise the unauthorised disclosure of their previous convictions, to amend the law of defamation, and for purposes connected therewith

[31 July 1974]

1 Rehabilitated persons and spent convictions

(1) Subject to subsection (2) below, where an individual has been convicted, whether before or after the commencement of this Act, of any offence or offences, and the following conditions are satisfied, that is to say—

(a) he did not have imposed on him in respect of that conviction a sentence which is excluded from rehabilitation under this Act; and
(b) he has not had imposed on him in respect of a subsequent conviction during

the rehabilitation period applicable to the first-mentioned conviction in accordance with section 6 below a sentence which is excluded from rehabilitation under this Act;

then, after the end of the rehabilitation period so applicable (including, where appropriate, any extension under section 6(4) below of the period originally applicable to the first-mentioned conviction) or, where that rehabilitation period ended before the commencement of this Act, after the commencement of this Act, that individual shall for the purposes of this Act be treated as a rehabilitated person in respect of the first-mentioned conviction and that conviction shall for those purposes be treated as spent.

(2) A person shall not become a rehabilitated person for the purposes of this Act in respect of a conviction unless he has served or otherwise undergone or complied with any sentence imposed on him in respect of that conviction; but the following shall not, by virtue of this subsection, prevent a person from becoming a rehabilitated person for those purposes—

(a) failure to pay a fine or other sum adjudged to be paid by or imposed on a conviction, or breach of a condition of a recognizance or of a bond of caution to keep the peace or be of good behaviour;

(b) breach of any condition or requirement applicable in relation to a sentence which renders the person to whom it applies liable to be dealt with for the offence for which the sentence was imposed, or, where the sentence was a suspended sentence of imprisonment, liable to be dealt with in respect of that sentence (whether or not, in any case, he is in fact so dealt with);

(c) failure to comply with any requirement of a suspended sentence supervision order.

[(2A) Where in respect of a conviction a person has been sentenced to imprisonment with an order under section 47(1) of the Criminal Law Act 1977, he is to be treated for the purposes of subsection (2) above as having served the sentence as soon as he completes service of so much of the sentence as was by that order required to be served in prison.]

(3) In this Act "sentence" includes any order made by a court in dealing with a person in respect of his conviction of any offence or offences, other than—

(a) an order for committal or any other order made in default of payment of any fine or other sum adjudged to be paid by or imposed on a conviction, or for want of sufficient distress to satisfy any such fine or other sum;

(b) an order dealing with a person in respect of a suspended sentence of imprisonment.

(4) In this Act, references to a conviction, however expressed, include references—

(a) to a conviction by or before a court outside Great Britain; and

(b) to any finding (other than a finding linked with a finding of insanity) in any criminal proceedings . . . that a person has committed an offence or done the act or made the omission charged;

and notwithstanding anything in section 9 of the Criminal Justice (Scotland) Act 1949 or [section 1C] of the Powers of Criminal Courts Act 1973 (conviction of a person . . . discharged to be deemed not to be a conviction) a conviction in respect of which an order is made [discharging the person concerned] absolutely or conditionally shall be treated as a conviction for the purposes of this Act and the person in question may become a rehabilitated person in respect of that conviction and the conviction a spent conviction for those purposes accordingly.   **[94]**

NOTES

Sub-s (2A): inserted by the Criminal Law Act 1977, s 47, Sch 9, para 11.

Sub-s (4): first words omitted repealed by the Children Act 1989, s 108(7), Sch 15; first and final words in square brackets substituted and second words omitted repealed by the Criminal Justice Act 1991, ss 100, 101(2), Sch 11, para 20, Sch 13.

The reference in sub-s (2)(a) to a fine or other sum adjudged to be paid by or imposed on a conviction does not include a reference to an amount payable under a confiscation order made under the Drug Trafficking Offences Act 1986, the Criminal Justice (Scotland) Act 1987, or under the Criminal Justice Act 1988. See, respectively, the Drug Trafficking Offences Act 1986, s 39(3), the Criminal Justice (Scotland) Act 1987, s 45(2) and the Criminal Justice Act 1988, s 170(1), Sch 15, para 47.

2, 3 (*Deal respectively with findings of service disciplinary proceedings and proceedings of children's hearings under the Social Work (Scotland) Act 1968.*)

4 Effect of rehabilitation

(1) Subject to sections 7 and 8 below, a person who has become a rehabilitated person for the purposes of this Act in respect of a conviction shall be treated for all purposes in law as a person who has not committed or been charged with or prosecuted for or convicted of or sentenced for the offence or offences which were the subject of that conviction; and, notwithstanding the provisions of any other enactment or rule of law to the contrary, but subject as aforesaid—

    (a) no evidence shall be admissible in any proceedings before a judicial authority exercising its jurisdiction or functions in Great Britain to prove that any such person has committed or been charged with or prosecuted for or convicted of or sentenced for any offence which was the subject of a spent conviction; and

    (b) a person shall not, in any such proceedings, be asked, and, if asked, shall not be required to answer, any question relating to his past which cannot be answered without acknowledging or referring to a spent conviction or spent convictions or any circumstances ancillary thereto.

(2) Subject to the provisions of any order made under subsection (4) below, where a question seeking information with respect to a person's previous convictions, offences, conduct or circumstances is put to him or to any other person otherwise than in proceedings before a judicial authority—

    (a) the question shall be treated as not relating to spent convictions or to any circumstances ancillary to spent convictions, and the answer thereto may be framed accordingly; and

    (b) the person questioned shall not be subjected to any liability or otherwise prejudiced in law by reason of any failure to acknowledge or disclose a spent conviction or any circumstances ancillary to a spent conviction in his answer to the question.

(3) Subject to the provisions of any order made under subsection (4) below,—

    (a) any obligation imposed on any person by any rule of law or by the provisions of any agreement or arrangement to disclose any matters to any other person shall not extend to requiring him to disclose a spent conviction or any circumstances ancillary to a spent conviction (whether the conviction is his own or another's); and

    (b) a conviction which has become spent or any circumstances ancillary thereto, or any failure to disclose a spent conviction or any such circumstances, shall not be a proper ground for dismissing or excluding a person from any office, profession, occupation or employment, or for prejudicing him in any way in any occupation or employment.

(4) The Secretary of State may by order—

(a) make such provision as seems to him appropriate for excluding or modifying the application of either or both of paragraphs (a) and (b) of subsection (2) above in relation to questions put in such circumstances as may be specified in the order;

(b) provide for such exceptions from the provisions of subsection (3) above as seem to him appropriate, in such cases or classes of case, and in relation to convictions of such a description, as may be specified in the order.

(5) For the purposes of this section and section 7 below any of the following are circumstances ancillary to a conviction, that is to say—

(a) the offence or offences which were the subject of that conviction;

(b) the conduct constituting that offence or those offences; and

(c) any process or proceedings preliminary to that conviction, any sentence imposed in respect of that conviction, any proceedings (whether by way of appeal or otherwise) for reviewing that conviction or any such sentence, and anything done in pursuance of or undergone in compliance with any such sentence.

(6) For the purposes of this section and section 7 below "proceedings before a judicial authority" includes, in addition to proceedings before any of the ordinary courts of law, proceedings before any tribunal, body or person having power—

(a) by virtue of any enactment, law, custom or practice;

(b) under the rules governing any association, institution, profession, occupation or employment; or

(c) under any provision of an agreement providing for arbitration with respect to questions arising thereunder;

to determine any question affecting the rights, privileges, obligations or liabilities of any person, or to receive evidence affecting the determination of any such question.

[95]

NOTES

See further the Financial Services Act 1986, s 189, Sch 14, and the Banking Act 1987, s 95, which restrict the application of this section in the circumstances there specified.

Orders under this section: Rehabilitation of Offenders Act 1974 (Exceptions) Order 1975, SI 1975/1023, as amended by SI 1986/1249, SI 1986/2268, below, paras [1027]–[1035].

5 Rehabilitation periods for particular sentences

(1) The sentences excluded from rehabilitation under this Act are—

(a) a sentence of imprisonment for life;

(b) a sentence of imprisonment [, youth custody] [detention in a young offender institution] or corrective training for a term exceeding thirty months;

(c) a sentence of preventive detention; . . .

(d) a sentence of detention during Her Majesty's pleasure or for life, [or under section 205(2) or (3) of the Criminal Procedure (Scotland) Act 1975,] or for a term exceeding thirty months, passed under section 53 of the Children and Young Persons Act 1933 [(young offenders convicted of grave crimes) or under section 206 of the said Act of 1975 (detention of children convicted on indictment)] [or a corresponding court-martial punishment];

[(e) a sentence of custody for life]

and any other sentence is a sentence subject to rehabilitation under this Act.

[(1A) In subsection (1)(d) above "corresponding court-martial punishment" means a punishment awarded under section 71A(3) or (4) of the Army Act 1955, section 71A(3) or (4) of the Air Force Act 1955 or section 43A(3) or (4) of the Naval Discipline Act 1957.]

(2) For the purposes of this Act—

  (a) the rehabilitation period applicable to a sentence specified in the first column of Table A below is the period specified in the second column of that Table in relation to that sentence, or, where the sentence was imposed on a person who was under [eighteen years of age] at the date of his conviction, half that period; and

  (b) the rehabilitation period applicable to a sentence specified in the first column of Table B below is the period specified in the second column of that Table in relation to that sentence;

reckoned in either case from the date of the conviction in respect of which the sentence was imposed.

TABLE A

Rehabilitation periods subject to reduction by half for persons [under 18]

Sentence	Rehabilitation period
A sentence of imprisonment [detention in a young offender institution] [or youth custody] or corrective training for a term exceeding six months but not exceeding thirty months.	Ten years
A sentence of cashiering, discharge with ignominy or dismissal with disgrace from Her Majesty's service.	Ten years
A sentence of imprisonment [detention in a young offender institution] [or youth custody] for a term not exceeding six months.	Seven years
A sentence of dismissal from Her Majesty's service.	Seven years
Any sentence of detention in respect of a conviction in service disciplinary proceedings.	Five years
A fine or any other sentence subject to rehabilitation under this Act, not being a sentence to which Table B below or any of subsections (3) to (8) below applies.	Five years

TABLE B

Rehabilitation periods for certain sentences confined to young offenders

Sentence	Rehabilitation period
A sentence of Borstal training.	Seven years
[A custodial order under Schedule 5A to the Army Act 1955 or the Air Force Act 1955, or under Schedule 4A to the Naval Discipline Act 1957, where the maximum period of detention specified in the order is more than six months.	Seven years]
[A custodial order under section 71AA of the Army Act 1955 or the Air Force Act 1955, or under section 43AA of the Naval Discipline Act 1957, where the maximum period of detention specified in the order is more than six months.	Seven years]
A sentence of detention for a term exceeding six months	Five years

but not exceeding thirty months passed under section 53 of the said Act of 1933 or under section [206 of the Criminal Procedure (Scotland) Act 1975.]	
A sentence of detention for a term not exceeding six months passed under either of those provisions.	Three years
An order for detention in a detention centre made under [section 4 of the Criminal Justice Act 1982,]section 4 of the Criminal Justice Act 1961 . . .	Three years
[A custodial order under any of the Schedules to the said Acts of 1955 and 1957 mentioned above, where the maximum period of detention specified in the order is six months or less.	Three years]
[A custodial order under section 71AA of the said Acts of 1955, or section 43AA of the said Act of 1957, where the maximum period of detention specified in the order is six months or less.	Three years]

(3) The rehabilitation period applicable—

    (a) to an order discharging a person absolutely for an offence; and

    (b) to the discharge by a children's hearing under section 43(2) of the Social Work (Scotland) Act 1968 of the referral of a child's case;

shall be six months from the date of conviction.

(4) Where in respect of a conviction a person was conditionally discharged, bound over to keep the peace or be of good behaviour, or placed on probation, the rehabilitation period applicable to the sentence shall be one year from the date of conviction or a period beginning with that date and ending when the order for conditional discharge or probation order or (as the case may be) the recognisance or bond of caution to keep the peace or be of good behaviour ceases or ceased to have effect, whichever is the longer.

(5) Where in respect of a conviction any of the following sentences was imposed, that is to say—

    (a) an order under section 57 of the Children and Young Persons Act 1933 or section 61 of the Children and Young Persons (Scotland) Act 1937 committing the person convicted to the care of a fit person;

    (b) a supervision order under any provision of either of those Acts or of the Children and Young Persons Act 1963;

    [(c) an order under section 413 of the Criminal Procedure (Scotland) Act 1975 committing a child for the purpose of his undergoing residential training;]

    (d) an approved school order under section 61 of the said Act of 1937;

    (e) . . . a supervision order under any provision of the Children and Young Persons Act 1969; or

    (f) a supervision requirement under any provision of the Social Work (Scotland) Act 1968;

    [(g) a community supervision order under Schedule 5A to the Army Act 1955 or the Air Force Act 1955, or under Schedule 4A to the Naval Discipline Act 1957;

    (h) . . .]

the rehabilitation period applicable to the sentence shall be one year from the date of conviction or a period beginning with that date and ending when the order or requirement ceases or ceased to have effect, whichever is the longer.

(6) Where in respect of a conviction any of the following orders was made, that is to say—

(a) an order under section 54 of the said Act of 1933 committing the person convicted to custody in a remand home;

(b) an approved school order under section 57 of the said Act of 1933; or

(c) an attendance centre order under section 19 of the Criminal Justice Act 1948;

the rehabilitation period applicable to the sentence shall be a period beginning with the date of conviction and ending one year after the date on which the order ceases or ceased to have effect.

(7) Where in respect of a conviction a hospital order under [Part III of the Mental Health Act 1983] or under Part V of the Mental Health (Scotland) Act 1960 (with or without [a restriction order] was made, the rehabilitation period applicable to the sentence shall be the period of five years from the date of conviction or a period beginning with that date and ending two years after the date on which the hospital order ceases or ceased to have effect, whichever is the longer.

(8) Where in respect of a conviction an order was made imposing on the person convicted any disqualification, disability, prohibition or other penalty, the rehabilitation period applicable to the sentence shall be a period beginning with the date of conviction and ending on the date on which the disqualification, disability, prohibition or penalty (as the case may be) ceases or ceased to have effect.

(9) For the purposes of this section—

(a) "sentence of imprisonment" includes a sentence of detention [under section 207 or 415 of the Criminal Procedure (Scotland) Act 1975] and a sentence of penal servitude, and "term of imprisonment" shall be construed accordingly;

(b) consecutive terms of imprisonment or of detention under section 53 of the said Act of 1933 or [section 206 of the said Act of 1975] and terms which are wholly or partly concurrent (being terms of imprisonment or detention imposed in respect of offences of which a person was convicted in the same proceedings) shall be treated as a single term;

(c) no account shall be taken of any subsequent variation, made by a court in dealing with a person in respect of a suspended sentence of imprisonment, of the term originally imposed; and

(d) a sentence imposed by a court outside Great Britain shall be treated as a sentence of that one of the descriptions mentioned in this section which most nearly corresponds to the sentence imposed.

(10) References in this section to the period during which a probation order, or a . . . supervision order under the Children and Young Persons Act 1969, or a supervision requirement under the Social Work (Scotland) Act 1968, is or was in force include references to any period during which any order or requirement to which this subsection applies, being an order or requirement made or imposed directly or indirectly in substitution for the first-mentioned order or requirement, is or was in force.

This subsection applies—

(a) to any such order or requirement as is mentioned above in this subsection;

(b) to any order having effect under section 25(2) of the said Act of 1969 as if it were a training school order in Northern Ireland; and

(c) to any supervision order made under section 72(2) of the said Act of 1968 and having effect as a supervision order under the Children and Young Persons Act (Northern Ireland) 1950.

[(10A) The reference in subsection (5) above to the period during which a reception order has effect includes a reference to any subsequent period during which by virtue of the order having been made the Social Work (Scotland) Act 1968 or the Children and Young Persons Act (Northern Ireland) 1968 has effect in relation to the person in respect of whom the order was made and subsection (10) above shall accordingly have effect in relation to any such subsequent period.]

(11) The Secretary of State may by order—

(a) substitute different periods or terms for any of the periods or terms mentioned in subsections (1) to (8) above; and

(b) substitute a different age for the age mentioned in subsection (2)(a) above.

[96]

NOTES

Sub-s (1): in para (b) first amendment in square brackets made by the Criminal Justice Act 1982, ss 77, 78, Sch 14, para 36, second amendment in square brackets made by the Criminal Justice Act 1988, s 123(6), Sch 8, para 9(a); in paras (c), (e) amendments made by the Criminal Justice Act 1982, ss 77, 78, Sch 14, para 36, Sch 16; in para (d), first and second amendments in square brackets made by the Criminal Justice (Scotland) Act 1980, s 83(2), Sch 7, para 24; final amendment in para (d) made by the Armed Forces Act 1976, s 22, Sch 9, para 20(4).

Sub-ss (1A), (10A): added by the Armed Forces Act 1976, s 22, Sch 9, paras 20(5), 21(3).

Sub-s (2): in para (a) and heading to Table A, words in square brackets substituted (with additional effect in relation to any sentence imposed on any person who was convicted before 1 October 1992 and was aged 17 at the date of his conviction) by the Criminal Justice Act 1991, ss 68, 101(1), Sch 8, para 5, Sch 12, para 22; in Table A first and third amendments in square brackets made by the Criminal Justice Act 1988, s 123(6), Sch 8, para 9(b), second and fourth amendments in square brackets made by the Criminal Justice Act 1982, s 77, Sch 14, para 37; in Table B, words omitted repealed and third amendment in square brackets made by the Criminal Justice (Scotland) Act 1980, s 83(2), Sch 7, para 24, first and fifth amendments in square brackets made by the Armed Forces Act 1976, s 22, Sch 9, para 21(1), second and sixth amendments in square brackets made by the Armed Forces Act 1981, s 28, Sch 4, para 2, fourth amendment in square brackets made by the Criminal Justice Act 1982, s 77, Sch 14, para 37.

Sub-s (5): para (c) substituted by the Criminal Justice (Scotland) Act 1980, s 83(2), Sch 7, para 24; words omitted in para (e) repealed by the Children Act 1989, s 108(7), Sch 15; paras (g), (h) added by the Armed Forces Act 1976, s 22, Sch 9, para 21(2); para (h) repealed with savings by the Armed Forces Act 1991, s 26, Sch 3, for savings see SI 1991/2719, art 3.

Sub-s (7): first amendment made by the Mental Health Act 1983, s 148, Sch 4, para 39; second amendment made by the Mental Health (Amendment) Act 1982, s 65(1), Sch 3, para 49.

Sub-s (9): amended by the Criminal Justice (Scotland) Act 1980, s 83(2), Sch 7, para 24.

Sub-s (10): words omitted repealed by the Children Act 1989, s 108(7), Sch 15.

6 The rehabilitation period applicable to a conviction

(1) Where only one sentence is imposed in respect of a conviction (not being a sentence excluded from rehabilitation under this Act) the rehabilitation period applicable to the conviction is, subject to the following provisions of this section, the period applicable to the sentence in accordance with section 5 above.

(2) Where more than one sentence is imposed in respect of a conviction (whether or not in the same proceedings) and none of the sentences imposed is excluded from rehabilitation under this Act, then, subject to the following provisions of this section, if the periods applicable to those sentences in accordance with section 5 above differ, the rehabilitation period applicable to the conviction shall be the longer or the longest (as the case may be) of those periods.

(3) Without prejudice to subsection (2) above, where in respect of a conviction a person was conditionally discharged or placed on probation and after the end of the rehabilitation period applicable to the conviction in accordance with subsection (1) or (2) above he is dealt with, in consequence of a breach of conditional discharge or probation, for the offence for which the order for conditional discharge or probation order was made, then, if the rehabilitation period applicable to the conviction in accordance with subsection (2) above (taking into account any sentence imposed when he is so dealt with) ends later than the rehabilitation period previously applicable to the conviction, he shall be treated for the purposes of this Act as not

having become a rehabilitated person in respect of that conviction, and the conviction shall for those purposes be treated as not having become spent, in relation to any period falling before the end of the new rehabilitation period.

(4) Subject to subsection (5) below, where during the rehabilitation period applicable to a conviction—

(a) the person convicted is convicted of a further offence; and

(b) no sentence excluded from rehabilitation under this Act is imposed on him in respect of the later conviction;

if the rehabilitation period applicable in accordance with this section to either of the convictions would end earlier than the period so applicable in relation to the other, the rehabilitation period which would (apart from this subsection) end the earlier shall be extended so as to end at the same time as the other rehabilitation period.

(5) Where the rehabilitation period applicable to a conviction is the rehabilitation period applicable in accordance with section 5(8) above to an order imposing on a person any disqualification, disability, prohibition or other penalty, the rehabilitation period applicable to another conviction shall not by virtue of subsection (4) above be extended by reference to that period; but if any other sentence is imposed in respect of the first-mentioned conviction for which a rehabilitation period is prescribed by any other provision of section 5 above, the rehabilitation period applicable to another conviction shall, where appropriate, be extended under subsection (4) above by reference to the rehabilitation period applicable in accordance with that section to that sentence or, where more than one such sentence is imposed, by reference to the longer or longest of the periods so applicable to those sentences, as if the period in question were the rehabilitation period applicable to the first-mentioned conviction.

(6) Subject to subsection (7) below, for the purposes of subsection (4)(*a*) above there shall be disregarded—

(a) any conviction in England and Wales of [a summary offence or of a scheduled offence (within the meaning of [section 22 of the Magistrates' Courts Act 1980] tried summarily in pursuance of subsection (2) of that section (summary trial where value involved is small);]

(b) any conviction in Scotland of an offence which is not excluded from the jurisdiction of inferior courts of summary jurisdiction by virtue of section 4 of the Summary Jurisdiction (Scotland) Act 1954 (certain crimes not to be tried in inferior courts of summary jurisdiction); and

(c) any conviction by or before a court outside Great Britain of an offence in respect of conduct which, if it had taken place in any part of Great Britain, would not have constituted an offence under the law in force in that part of Great Britain.

(7) Notwithstanding subsection (6) above, a conviction in service disciplinary proceedings shall not be disregarded for the purposes of subsection (4)(a) above.

[97]

NOTE

Sub-s (6): amended by the Criminal Law Act 1977, Sch 12; further amended by the Magistrates' Courts Act 1980, s 154, Sch 7, para 134.

7 Limitations on rehabilitation under this Act, etc

(1) Nothing in section 4(1) above shall affect—

(a) any right of Her Majesty, by virtue of Her Royal prerogative or otherwise, to grant a free pardon, to quash any conviction or sentence, or to commute any sentence;

(b) the enforcement by any process or proceedings of any fine or other sum adjudged to be paid by or imposed on a spent conviction;

(c) the issue of any process for the purpose of proceedings in respect of any breach of a condition or requirement applicable to a sentence imposed in respect of a spent conviction; or

(d) the operation of any enactment by virtue of which, in consequence of any conviction, a person is subject, otherwise than by way of sentence, to any disqualification, disability, prohibition or other penalty the period of which extends beyond the rehabilitation period applicable in accordance with section 6 above to the conviction.

(2) Nothing in section 4(1) above shall affect the determination of any issue, or prevent the admission or requirement of any evidence, relating to a person's previous convictions or to circumstances ancillary thereto—

(a) in any criminal proceedings before a court in Great Britain (including any appeal or reference in a criminal matter);

(b) in any service disciplinary proceedings or in any proceedings on appeal from any service disciplinary proceedings;

[(c) in any proceedings relating to adoption, the marriage of any minor, the exercise of the inherent jurisdiction of the High Court with respect to minors or the provision by any person of accommodation, care or schooling for minors;

(cc) in any proceedings brought under the Children Act 1989;]

[(d) in any proceedings relating to the variation or discharge of a supervision order under the Children and Young Persons Act 1969, or on appeal from any such proceedings;]

(e) in any proceedings before a children's hearing under the Social Work (Scotland) Act 1968 or on appeal from any such hearing; or

(f) in any proceedings in which he is a party or a witness, provided that, on the occasion when the issue or the admission or requirement of the evidence falls to be determined, he consents to the determination of the issue or, as the case may be, the admission or requirement of the evidence notwithstanding the provisions of section 4(1); [or,

(g) . . .]

In the application of this subsection to Scotland, "minor" means a child under the age of eighteen, . . .

(3) If at any stage in any proceedings before a judicial authority in Great Britain (not being proceedings to which, by virtue of any of paragraphs (a) to (e) of subsection (2) above or of any order for the time being in force under subsection (4) below, section 4(1) above has no application, or proceedings to which section 8 below applies) the authority is satisfied, in the light of any considerations which appear to it to be relevant (including any evidence which has been or may thereafter be put before it), that justice cannot be done in the case except by admitting or requiring evidence relating to a person's spent convictions or to circumstances ancillary thereto, that authority may admit or, as the case may be, require the evidence in question notwithstanding the provisions of subsection (1) of section 4 above, and may determine any issue to which the evidence relates in disregard, so far as necessary, of those provisions.

(4) The Secretary of State may by order exclude the application of section 4(1) above in relation to any proceedings specified in the order (other than proceedings to which section 8 below applies) to such extent and for such purposes as may be so specified.

(5) No order made by a court with respect to any person otherwise than on a conviction shall be included in any list or statement of that person's previous convictions given or made to any court which is considering how to deal with him in respect of any offence.   **[97A]**

NOTE
Sub-s 2: paras (c), (cc), (d) substituted for paras (c), (d) as originally enacted by the Children Act 1989, s 108(5), Sch 13, para 35; para (g) repealed by the Banking Act 1987, s 108(2), Sch 7, Part I; words omitted repealed by the Age of Legal Capacity (Scotland) Act 1991, s 10, Sch 2.

8 (*Defamation actions: omitted.*)

9 Unauthorised disclosure of spent convictions

(1) In this section—

"official record" means a record kept for the purposes of its functions by any court, police force, Government department, local or other public authority in Great Britain, or a record kept, in Great Britain or elsewhere, for the purposes of any of Her Majesty's forces, being in either case a record containing information about persons convicted of offences; and

"specified information" means information imputing that a named or otherwise identifiable rehabilitated living person has committed or been charged with or prosecuted for or convicted of or sentenced for any offence which is the subject of a spent conviction.

(2) Subject to the provisions of any order made under subsection (5) below, any person who, in the course of his official duties, has or at any time has had custody of or access to any official record or the information contained therein, shall be guilty of an offence if, knowing or having reasonable cause to suspect that any specified information he has obtained in the course of those duties is specified information, he discloses it, otherwise than in the course of those duties, to another person.

(3) In any proceedings for an offence under subsection (2) above it shall be a defence for the defendant (or, in Scotland, the accused person) to show that the disclosure was made—

(a) to the rehabilitated person or to another person at the express request of the rehabilitated person; or

(b) to a person whom he reasonably believed to be the rehabilitated person or to another person at the express request of a person whom he reasonably believed to be the rehabilitated person.

(4) Any person who obtains any specified information from any official record by means of any fraud, dishonesty or bribe shall be guilty of an offence.

(5) The Secretary of State may by order make such provision as appears to him to be appropriate for excepting the disclosure of specified information derived from an official record from the provisions of subsection (2) above in such cases or classes of case as may be specified in the order.

(6) Any person guilty of an offence under subsection (2) above shall be liable on summary conviction to a fine not exceeding [level 4 on the standard scale].

(7) Any person guilty of an offence under subsection (4) above shall be liable on summary conviction to a fine not exceeding [level 5 on the standard scale] or to imprisonment for a term not exceeding six months, or to both.

(8) Proceedings for an offence under subsection (2) above shall not, in England and Wales, be instituted except by or on behalf of the Director of Public Prosecutions.
[97B]

NOTE
Sub-ss (6), (7): maximum fines increased and converted to levels on the standard scale by the Criminal Justice Act 1982, ss 37, 38, 46.

10 Orders

(1) Any power of the Secretary of State to make an order under any provision of this Act shall be exercisable by statutory instrument, and an order made under any provision of this Act except section 11 below may be varied or revoked by a subsequent order made under that provision.

(2) No order shall be made by the Secretary of State under any provision of this Act other than section 11 below unless a draft of it has been laid before, and approved by resolution of, each House of Parliament.   **[98]**

11 Citation, commencement and extent

(1) This Act may be cited as the Rehabilitation of Offenders Act 1974.

(2) This Act shall come into force on 1st July 1975 or such earlier day as the Secretary of State may by order appoint.

(3) This Act shall not apply to Northern Ireland.   **[99]**

SEX DISCRIMINATION ACT 1975

(1975 c 65)

ARRANGEMENT OF SECTIONS

PART I
DISCRIMINATION TO WHICH ACT APPLIES

PART II
DISCRIMINATION IN THE EMPLOYMENT FIELD

Discrimination by employers

PART III

DISCRIMINATION IN OTHER FIELDS

Barristers

Advocates

PART IV

OTHER UNLAWFUL ACTS

PART V

GENERAL EXCEPTIONS FROM PARTS II TO IV

PART VI

EQUAL OPPORTUNITIES COMMISSION

Codes of practice

PART VII
ENFORCEMENT

PART VIII
SUPPLEMENTAL

SCHEDULES

An Act to render unlawful certain kinds of sex discrimination and discrimination on the ground of marriage, and establish a Commission with the function of working towards the elimination of such discrimination and promoting equality of opportunity between men and women generally; and for related purposes

[12 November 1975]

NOTE

Parts of this Act are outside the scope of this work: ss 22–35, 36 (discrimination in fields other than employment), Sch 2 (related provisions) and ss 78, 79 (provisions relating to education). These, together with Sch 1, which amends the Equal Pay Act 1970, and Schs 5, 6 (minor amendments and repeals) are omitted.

PART I
DISCRIMINATION TO WHICH ACT APPLIES

1 Sex discrimination against women

(1) A person discriminates against a woman in any circumstances relevant for the purposes of any provision of this Act if—

    (a) on the ground of her sex he treats her less favourably than he treats or would treat a man, or

    (b) he applies to her a requirement or condition which he applies or would apply equally to a man but—

        (i) which is such that the proportion of women who can comply with it is considerably smaller than the proportion of men who can comply with it, and

        (ii) which he cannot show to be justifiable irrespective of the sex of the person to whom it is applied, and

        (iii) which is to her detriment because she cannot comply with it.

(2) If a person treats or would treat a man differently according to the man's marital status, his treatment of a woman is for the purposes of subsection (1)(a) to be compared to his treatment of a man having the like marital status. **[100]**

2 Sex discrimination against men

(1) Section 1, and the provisions of Parts II and III relating to sex discrimination against women, are to be read as applying equally to the treatment of men, and for that purpose shall have effect with such modifications as are requisite.

(2) In the application of subsection (1) no account shall be taken of special treatment afforded to women in connection with pregnancy or childbirth. **[101]**

3 Discrimination against married persons in employment field

(1) A person discriminates against a married person of either sex in any circumstances relevant for the purposes of any provision of Part II if—

    (a) on the ground of his or her marital status he treats that person less favourably than he treats or would treat an unmarried person of the same sex, or

    (b) he applies to that person a requirement or condition which he applies or would apply equally to an unmarried person but—

        (i) which is such that the proportion of married persons who can comply with it is considerably smaller than the proportion of unmarried persons of the same sex who can comply with it, and

        (ii) which he cannot show to be justifiable irrespective of the marital status of the person to whom it is applied, and

(iii) which is to that person's detriment because he cannot comply with it.

(2) For the purposes of subsection (1), a provision of Part II framed with reference to discrimination against women shall be treated as applying equally to the treatment of men, and for that purpose shall have effect with such modifications as are requisite. **[102]**

4 Discrimination by way of victimisation

(1) A person ("the discriminator") discriminates against another person ("the person victimised") in any circumstances relevant for the purposes of any provision of this Act if he treats the person victimised less favourably than in those circumstances he treats or would treat other persons, and does so by reason that the person victimised has—

    (a) brought proceedings against the discriminator or any other person under this Act or the Equal Pay Act 1970, or

    (b) given evidence or information in connection with proceedings brought by any person against the discriminator or any other person under this Act or the Equal Pay Act 1970, or

    (c) otherwise done anything under or by reference to this Act or the Equal Pay Act 1970 in relation to the discriminator or any other person, or

    (d) alleged that the discriminator or any other person has committed an act which (whether or not the allegation so states) would amount to a contravention of this Act or give rise to a claim under the Equal Pay Act 1970,

or by reason that the discriminator knows the person victimised intends to do any of those things, or suspects the person victimised has done, or intends to do, any of them.

(2) Subsection (1) does not apply to treatment of a person by reason of any allegation made by him if the allegation was false and not made in good faith.

(3) For the purposes of subsection (1), a provision of Part II or III framed with reference to discrimination against women shall be treated as applying equally to the treatment of men and for that purpose shall have effect with such modifications as are requisite. **[103]**

NOTES

    Sub-s (1): in paras (a)–(c), after the words "Equal Pay Act 1970" there are added the words "or Part I of Schedule 5 to the Social Security Act 1989" by the Social Security Act 1989, s 23, Sch 5, Pt II, para 14(1)(a), as from a day to be appointed; at the end of para (d) there are added the words "or proceedings under Part I of Schedule 5 to the Social Security Act 1989" by para 14(1)(b) of Sch 5, Pt II to the 1989 Act, as from a day to be appointed.

    See the general note to the Social Security Act 1989, below.

5 Interpretation

(1) In this Act—

    (a) references to discrimination refer to any discrimination falling within sections 1 to 4; and

    (b) references to sex discrimination refer to any discrimination falling within section 1 or 2,

and related expressions shall be construed accordingly.

(2) In this Act—

"woman" includes a female of any age, and
"man" includes a male of any age.

(3) A comparison of the cases of persons of different sex or marital status under section 1(1) or 3(1) must be such that the relevant circumstances in the one case are the same, or not materially different, in the other.   **[104]**

PART II

DISCRIMINATION IN THE EMPLOYMENT FIELD

Discrimination by employers

6 Discrimination against applicants and employees

(1) It is unlawful for a person, in relation to employment by him at an establishment in Great Britain, to discriminate against a woman—

    (a) in the arrangements he makes for the purpose of determining who should be offered that employment, or

    (b) in the terms on which he offers her that employment, or

    (c) by refusing or deliberately omitting to offer her that employment.

(2) It is unlawful for a person, in the case of a woman employed by him at an establishment in Great Britain, to discriminate against her—

    (a) in the way he affords her access to opportunities for promotion, transfer or training, or to any other benefits, facilities or services, or by refusing or deliberately omitting to afford her access to them, or

    (b) by dismissing her, or subjecting her to any other detriment.

(3) . . .

(4) Subsections (1)(b) and (2) do not apply to provision in relation to death or retirement [*except in so far as, in their application to provision in relation to retirement, they* render it unlawful for a person to discriminate against a woman—

    (a) in such of the terms on which he offers her employment as make provision in relation to the way in which he will afford her access to opportunities for promotion, transfer or training or as provide for her dismissal or demotion; or

    (b) in the way he affords her access to opportunities for promotion, transfer or training or by refusing or deliberately omitting to afford her access to any such opportunities; or

    (c) by dismissing her or subjecting her to any detriment which results in her dismissal or consists in or involves her demotion].

(5) Subject to section 8(3), subsection (1)(b) does not apply to any provision for the payment of money which, if the woman in question were given the employment, would be included (directly . . . or otherwise) in the contract under which she was employed.

(6) Subsection (2) does not apply to benefits consisting of the payment of money when the provision of those benefits is regulated by the woman's contract of employment.

(7) Subsection (2) does not apply to benefits, facilities or services of any description if the employer is concerned with the provision (for payment or not) of benefits, facilities or services of that description to the public, or to a section of the public comprising the woman in question, unless—

    (a) that provision differs in a material respect from the provision of the benefits, facilities or services by the employer to his employees, or

(b) the provision of the benefits, facilities or services to the woman in question is regulated by her contract of employment, or

(c) the benefits, facilities or services relate to training. **[105]**

NOTES

Sub-s (3): repealed by the Sex Discrimination Act 1986, ss 1(1), 9(2), Schedule, Pt II.

Sub-s (4): words in square brackets added by the Sex Discrimination Act 1986, s 2(1); words italicised therein substituted by the Social Security Act 1989, s 23, Sch 5, Pt II, para 14(2), as follows, as from a day to be appointed—

"except as provided in subsections (4A) and (4B) below.

(4A) Subsection (4) does not prevent the application of subsections (1)(b) and (2) to provision in relation to retirement in so far as those subsections".

The remainder of sub-s (4) following the insertion will then become part of sub-s (4A), and sub-ss (4), (4A) will appear as follows:

(4) Subsections (1)(b) and (2) do not apply to provision in relation to death or retirement except as provided in subsections (4A) and (4B) below.

(4A) Subsection (4) does not prevent the application of subsections (1)(b) and (2) to provision in relation to retirement in so far as those subsections render it unlawful for a person to discriminate against a woman—

   (a) in such of the terms on which he offers her employment as make provision in relation to the way in which he will afford her access to opportunities for promotion, transfer or training or as provide for her dismissal or demotion; or

   (b) in the way he affords her access to opportunities for promotion, transfer or training or by refusing or deliberately omitting to afford her access to any such opportunities; or

   (c) by dismissing her or subjecting her to any detriment which results in her dismissal or consists in or involves her demotion.

Sub-ss (4B), (4C): inserted by the Social Security Act 1989, s 23, Sch 5, Pt II, para 14(3), as from a day to be appointed, as follows—

"(4B) Subsection (4) does not prevent the application of subsections (1)(b) and (2) to provision in relation to death or retirement in so far as those subsections render it unlawful for a person to discriminate against a woman—

   (a) in such of the terms on which he offers her employment as make provision in relation to the way in which he will afford her access to any benefits, facilities or services under an occupational pension scheme; or

   (b) in the way he affords her access to any such benefits, facilities or services; or

   (c) by refusing or deliberately omitting to afford her access to any such benefits, facilities or services; or

   (d) by subjecting her to any detriment in connection with any such scheme;

   but an act of discrimination is rendered unlawful by virtue of this subsection only to the extent that the act relates to a matter in respect of which an occupational pension scheme has to comply with the principle of equal treatment in accordance with Part I of Schedule 5 to the Social Security Act 1989.

(4C) In the application of subsection (4B) to discrimination against married persons of either sex, Part I of Schedule 5 to the Social Security Act 1989 shall be taken to apply to less favourable treatment of married persons on the basis of their marital status as it applies in relation to less favourable treatment of persons on the basis of sex, and references to persons of either sex shall be construed accordingly.".

Sub-s (5): words omitted repealed by the Sex Discrimination Act 1986, s 9, Schedule, Pt II.

Sub-s (8): added by the Social Security Act 1989, s 23, Sch 5, Pt II, para 14, as from a day to be appointed, as follows—

"(8) In this section "occupational pension scheme" means an occupational pension scheme, within the meaning of the Social Security Pensions Act 1975, which is also an employment-related benefit scheme, within the meaning of Schedule 5 to the Social Security Act 1989.".

Modified, in relation to governing bodies with delegated budgets, by the Education (Modification of Enactments Relating to Employment) Order 1989, SI 1989/901, art 3, Schedule.

7 Exception where sex is a genuine occupational qualification

(1) In relation to sex discrimination—

   (a) section 6(1)(a) or (c) does not apply to any employment where being a man is a genuine occupational qualification for the job, and

   (b) section 6(2)(a) does not apply to opportunities for promotion or transfer to, or training for, such employment.

(2) Being a man is a genuine occupational qualification for a job only where—

(a) the essential nature of the job calls for a man for reasons of physiology (excluding physical strength or stamina) or, in dramatic performances or other entertainment, for reasons of authenticity, so that the essential nature of the job would be materially different if carried out by a woman; or

(b) the job needs to be held by a man to preserve decency or privacy because—

    (i) it is likely to involve physical contact with men in circumstances where they might reasonably object to its being carried out by a woman, or

    (ii) the holder of the job is likely to do his work in circumstances where men might reasonably object to the presence of a woman because they are in a state of undress or are using sanitary facilities; or

[(ba) the job is likely to involve the holder of the job doing his work, or living, in a private home and needs to be held by a man because objection might reasonably be taken to allowing to a woman—

    (i) the degree of physical or social contact with a person living in the home, or

    (ii) the knowledge of intimate details of such a person's life,

which is likely, because of the nature or circumstances of the job or of the home, to be allowed to, or available to, the holder of the job; or]

(c) the nature or location of the establishment makes it impracticable for the holder of the job to live elsewhere than in premises provided by the employer, and—

    (i) the only such premises which are available for persons holding that kind of job are lived in, or normally lived in, by men and are not equipped with separate sleeping accommodation for women and sanitary facilities which could be used by women in privacy from men, and

    (ii) it is not reasonable to expect the employer either to equip those premises with such accommodation and facilities or to provide other premises for women; or

(d) the nature of the establishment, or of the part of it within which the work is done, requires the job to be held by a man because—

    (i) it is, or is part of, a hospital, prison or other establishment for persons requiring special care, supervision or attention, and

    (ii) those persons are all men (disregarding any woman whose presence is exceptional), and

    (iii) it is reasonable, having regard to the essential character of the establishment or that part, that the job should not be held by a woman; or

(e) the holder of the job provides individuals with personal services promoting their welfare or education, or similar personal services, and those services can most effectively be provided by a man, or

(f) . . .

(g) the job needs to be held by a man because it is likely to involve the performance of duties outside the United Kingdom in a country whose laws or customs are such that the duties could not, or could not effectively, be performed by a woman, or

(h) the job is one of two to be held by a married couple.

(3) Subsection (2) applies where some only of the duties of the job fall within paragraphs (a) to (g) as well as where all of them do.

(4) Paragraph (a), (b), (c), (d), (e) . . . or (g) of subsection (2) does not apply in relation to the filling of a vacancy at a time when the employer already has male employees—

    (a) who are capable of carrying out the duties falling within that paragraph, and

    (b) whom it would be reasonable to employ on those duties, and

    (c) whose numbers are sufficient to meet the employer's likely requirements in respect of those duties without undue inconvenience.   **[106]**

NOTES

Sub-s (2): para (ba) inserted by the Sex Discrimination Act 1986, s 1(2); para (f) repealed with savings by the Employment Act 1989, ss 3(1), (2), 29(4), (6), 53(2), Sch 7, Pt II, Sch 9, para 1.

Sub-s (4): omitted letter repealed by the Employment Act 1989, s 29(4), Sch 7, Pt II, Sch 9.

Modified, in relation to governing bodies with delegated budgets, by the Education (Modification of Enactments Relating to Employment) Order 1989, SI 1989/901, art 3, Schedule.

8 Equal Pay Act 1970

(1) . . .

(2) Section 1(1) of the Equal Pay Act 1970 (as set out in subsection (1) above) does not apply in determining for the purposes of section 6(1)(b) of this Act the terms on which employment is offered.

(3) Where a person offers a woman employment on certain terms, and if she accepted the offer then, by virtue of an equality clause, any of those terms would fall to be modified, or any additional term would fall to be included, the offer shall be taken to contravene section 6(1)(b).

(4) Where a person offers a woman employment on certain terms, and subsection (3) would apply but for the fact that, on her acceptance of the offer, section 1(3) of the Equal Pay Act 1970 (as set out in subsection (1) above) would prevent the equality clause from operating, the offer shall be taken not to contravene section 6(1)(b).

(5) An act does not contravene section 6(2) if—

    (a) it contravenes a term modified or included by virtue of an equality clause, or

    (b) it would contravene such a term but for the fact that the equality clause is prevented from operating by section 1(3) of the Equal Pay Act 1970.

(6) . . .   **[107]**

NOTE

Sub-ss (1), (6): amend the Equal Pay Act 1970, ss 1–3.

9 Discrimination against contract workers

(1) This section applies to any work for a person ("the principal") which is available for doing by individuals ("contract workers") who are employed not by the principal himself but by another person, who supplies them under a contract made with the principal.

(2) It is unlawful for the principal, in relation to work to which this section applies, to discriminate against a woman who is a contract worker—

    (a) in the terms on which he allows her to do that work, or

    (b) by not allowing her to do it or continue to do it, or

    (c) in the way he affords her access to any benefits, facilities or services or by refusing or deliberately omitting to afford her access to them, or

(d) by subjecting her to any other detriment.

(3) The principal does not contravene subsection (2)(b) by doing any act in relation to a woman at a time when if the work were to be done by a person taken into his employment being a man would be a genuine occupational qualification for the job.

(4) Subsection (2)(c) does not apply to' benefits, facilities or services of any description if the principal is concerned with the provision (for payment or not) of benefits, facilities or services of that description to the public, or to a section of the public to which the woman belongs, unless that provision differs in a material respect from the provision of the benefits, facilities or services by the principal to his contract workers.   **[108]**

NOTE
Modified, in relation to governing bodies with delegated budgets, by the Education (Modification of Enactments Relating to Employment) Order 1989, SI 1989/901, art 3, Schedule.

10 Meaning of employment at establishment in Great Britain

(1) For the purposes of this Part and section 1 of the Equal Pay Act 1970 ("the relevant purposes"), employment is to be regarded as being at an establishment in Great Britain unless the employee does his work wholly or mainly outside Great Britain.

(2) Subsection (1) does not apply to—

(a) employment on board a ship registered at a port of registry in Great Britain, or

(b) employment on aircraft or hovercraft registered in the United Kingdom and operated by a person who has his principal place of business, or is ordinarily resident, in Great Britain;

but for the relevant purposes such employment is to be regarded as being at an establishment in Great Britain unless the employee does his work wholly outside Great Britain.

(3) In the case of employment on board a ship registered at a port of registry in Great Britain (except where the employee does his work wholly outside Great Britain, and outside any area added under subsection (5)) the ship shall for the relevant purposes be deemed to be the establishment.

(4) Where work is not done at an establishment it shall be treated for the relevant purposes as done at the establishment from which it is done or (where it is not done from any establishment) at the establishment with which it has the closest connection.

(5) In relation to employment concerned with *exploration of the sea bed or subsoil or the exploitation of their natural resources*, Her Majesty may by Order in Council provide that subsections (1) and (2) shall each have effect as if the last reference to Great Britain included any area for the time being designated under section 1(7) of the Continental Shelf Act 1964 , except an area or part of an area in which the law of Northern Ireland applies.

(6) An Order in Council under subsection (5) may provide that, in relation to employment to which the Order applies, this Part and section 1 of the Equal Pay Act 1970 are to have effect with such modifications as are specified in the Order.

(7) An Order in Council under subsection (5) shall be of no effect unless a draft of the Order was laid before and approved by each House of Parliament.   **[109]**

Discrimination by other bodies

11 Partnerships

(1) It is unlawful for a firm . . ., in relation to a position as partner in the firm, to discriminate against a woman—

 (a) in the arrangements they make for the purpose of determining who should be offered that position, or

 (b) in the terms on which they offer her that position, or

 (c) by refusing or deliberately omitting to offer her that position, or

 (d) in a case where the woman already holds that position—

  (i) in the way they afford her access to any benefits, facilities or services, or by refusing or deliberately omitting to afford her access to them, or

  (ii) by expelling her from that position, or subjecting her to any other detriment.

(2) Subsection (1) shall apply in relation to persons proposing to form themselves into a partnership as it applies in relation to a firm.

(3) Subsection (1)(a) and (c) do not apply to a position as partner where, if it were employment, being a man would be a genuine occupational qualification for the job.

(4) Subsection (1)(b) and (d) do not apply to provision made in relation to death or retirement [except in so far as, in their application to provision made in relation to retirement, they render it unlawful for a firm to discriminate against a woman—

 (a) in such of the terms on which they offer her a position as partner as provide for her expulsion from that position; or

 (b) by expelling her from a position as partner or subjecting her to any detriment which results in her expulsion from such a position.]

(5) In the case of a limited partnership references in subsection (1) to a partner shall be construed as references to a general partner as defined in section 3 of the Limited Partnerships Act 1907. **[110]**

12 Trade unions etc

(1) This section applies to an organisation of workers, an organisation of employers, or any other organisation whose members carry on a particular profession or trade for the purposes of which the organisation exists.

(2) It is unlawful for an organisation to which this section applies, in the case of a woman who is not a member of the organisation, to discriminate against her—

 (a) in the terms on which it is prepared to admit her to membership, or

 (b) by refusing, or deliberately omitting to accept, her application for membership.

(3) It is unlawful for an organisation to which this section applies, in the case of a woman who is a member of the organisation, to discriminate against her—

(a) in the way it affords her access to any benefits, facilities or services, or by refusing or deliberately omitting to afford her access to them, or

(b) by depriving her of membership, or varying the terms on which she is a member, or

(c) by subjecting her to any other detriment.

(4) This section does not apply to provision made in relation to the death or retirement from work of a member.   **[111]**

13 Qualifying bodies

(1) It is unlawful for an authority or body which can confer an authorisation or qualification which is needed for, or facilitates, engagement in a particular profession or trade to discriminate against a woman—

(a) in the terms on which it is prepared to confer on her that authorisation or qualification, or

(b) by refusing or deliberately omitting to grant her application for it, or

(c) by withdrawing it from her or varying the terms on which she holds it.

(2) Where an authority or body is required by law to satisfy itself as to his good character before conferring on a person an authorisation or qualification which is needed for, or facilitates, his engagement in any profession or trade then, without prejudice to any other duty to which it is subject, that requirement shall be taken to impose on the authority or body a duty to have regard to any evidence tending to show that he, or any of his employees, or agents (whether past or present), has practised unlawful discrimination in, or in connection with, the carrying on of any profession or trade.

(3) In this section—

(a) "authorisation or qualification" includes recognition, registration, enrolment, approval and certification,

(b) "confer" includes renew or extend.

(4) Subsection (1) does not apply to discrimination which is rendered unlawful by section 22 or 23.   **[112]**

[14 Persons concerned with provision of vocational training

(1) It is unlawful, in the case of a woman seeking or undergoing training which would help fit her for any employment, for any person who provides, or makes arrangements for the provision of, facilities for such training to discriminate against her—

(a) in the terms on which that person affords her access to any training course or other facilities concerned with such training, or

(b) by refusing or deliberately omitting to afford her such access, or

(c) by terminating her training, or

(d) by subjecting her to any detriment during the course of her training.

(2) Subsection (1) does not apply to—

(a) discrimination which is rendered unlawful by section 6(1) or (2) or section 22 or 23, or

(b) discrimination which would be rendered unlawful by any of those provisions but for the operation of any other provision of this Act.]

                                        [113]

NOTE
Substituted by the Employment Act 1989, s 7(1).

15 Employment agencies

(1) It is unlawful for an employment agency to discriminate against a woman—

    (a) in the terms on which the agency offers to provide any of its services, or

    (b) by refusing or deliberately omitting to provide any of its services, or

    (c) in the way it provides any of its services.

(2) It is unlawful for a local education authority or an education authority to do any act in the performance of its functions under section 8 of the Employment and Training Act 1973 which constitutes discrimination.

(3) References in subsection (1) to the services of an employment agency include guidance on careers and any other services related to employment.

(4) This section does not apply if the discrimination only concerns employment which the employer could lawfully refuse to offer the woman.

(5) An employment agency or local education authority *or an education authority* shall not be subject to any liability under this section if it proves—

    (a) that it acted in reliance on a statement made to it by the employer to the effect that, by reason of the operation of subsection (4), its action would not be unlawful, and

    (b) that it was reasonable for it to rely on the statement.

(6) A person who knowingly or recklessly makes a statement such as is referred to in subsection (5)(a) which in a material respect is false or misleading commits an offence, and shall be liable on summary conviction to a fine not exceeding [level 5 on the standard scale]. **[114]**

NOTES
Sub-s (2): substituted by the Trade Union Reform and Employment Rights Act 1993, s 49(2), Sch 8, para 8(a), as from a day to be appointed, as follows—
(2) It is unlawful for a local education authority or education authority or any other person to do any act in providing services in pursuance of arrangements made, or a direction given, under section 10 of the Employment and Training Act 1973, which constitutes discrimination.
Sub-s (5): for the words in italics there are substituted the words ", education authority or other person" by the Trade Union Reform and Employment Rights Act 1993, s 49(2), Sch 8, para 8(b), as from a day to be appointed.
Sub-s (6): maximum fine increased and converted to a level on the standard scale by the Criminal Justice Act 1982, ss 37, 38, 46.

16 Manpower Services Commission etc

[(1) It is unlawful for the [Secretary of State . . .] to discriminate in the provision of facilities or services under section 2 of the Employment and Training Act 1973.]

[(1A) It is unlawful for Scottish Enterprise or Highlands and Islands Enterprise to discriminate in the provision of facilities or services under such arrangements as are mentioned in section 2(3) of the Enterprise and New Towns (Scotland) Act 1990 (arrangements analogous to arrangements in pursuance of section 2 of the said Act of 1973).]

(2) This section does not apply in a case where—

    (a) section 14 applies, or

    (b) the [Secretary of State] is acting as an employment agency. **[115]**

Special cases

17 Police

(1) For the purposes of this Part, the holding of the office of constable shall be treated as employment—

   (a) by the chief officer of police as respects any act done by him in relation to a constable or that office;

   (b) by the police authority as respects any act done by them in relation to a constable or that office.

(2) Regulations made under section 33, 34 or 35 of the Police Act 1964 shall not treat men and women differently except—

   (a) as to requirements relating to height, uniform or equipment, or allowances in lieu of uniform or equipment, or

   (b) so far as special treatment is accorded to women in connection with pregnancy or childbirth, or

   (c) in relation to pensions to or in respect of special constables or police cadets.

(3) Nothing in this Part renders unlawful any discrimination between male and female constables as to matters such as are mentioned in subsection (2)(a).

(4) There shall be paid out of the police fund—

   (a) any compensation, costs or expenses awarded against a chief officer of police in any proceedings brought against him under this Act, and any costs or expenses incurred by him in any such proceedings so far as not recovered by him in the proceedings; and

   (b) any sum required by a chief officer of police for the settlement of any claim made against him under this Act if the settlement is approved by the police authority.

(5) Any proceedings under this Act which, by virtue of subsection (1), would lie against a chief officer of police shall be brought against the chief officer of police for the time being or, in the case of a vacancy in that office, against the person for the time being performing the functions of that office; and references in subsection (4) to the chief officer of police shall be construed accordingly.

(6) Subsections (1) and (3) apply to a police cadet and appointment as a police cadet as they apply to a constable and the office of constable.

(7) In this section—

   "chief officer of police"—

      (a) in relation to a person appointed, or an appointment falling to be made, under a specified Act, has the same meaning as in the Police Act 1964,

      (b) in relation to any other person or appointment means the officer who has the direction and control of the body of constables or cadets in question;

   "police authority"—

      (a) in relation to a person appointed, or an appointment falling to be made, under a specified Act, has the same meaning as in the Police Act 1964,

(b) in relation to any other person or appointment, means the authority by whom the person in question is or on appointment would be paid;

"police cadet" means any person appointed to undergo training with a view to becoming a constable;

"police fund" in relation to a chief officer of police within paragraph (a) of the above definition of that term has the same meaning as in the Police Act 1964, and in any other case means money provided by the police authority;

"specified Act" means the Metropolitan Police Act 1829, the City of London Police Act 1839 or the Police Act 1964.

(8) In the application of this section to Scotland, in subsection (7) for any reference to the Police Act 1964 there shall be substituted a reference to the Police (Scotland) Act 1967, and for the reference to sections 33, 34 and 35 of the former Act in subsection (2) there shall be substituted a reference to sections 26 and 27 of the latter Act.

[116]

18 Prison officers

(1) Nothing in this Part renders unlawful any discrimination between male and female prison officers as to requirements relating to height.

(2) . . .   [117]

NOTE

Sub-s (2): amends the Prison Act 1952, s 7(2).

19 Ministers of religion etc

(1) Nothing in this Part applies to employment for purposes of an organised religion where the employment is limited to one sex so as to comply with the doctrines of the religion or avoid offending the religious susceptibilities of a significant number of its followers.

(2) Nothing in section 13 applies to an authorisation or qualification (as defined in that section) for purposes of an organised religion where the authorisation or qualification is limited to one sex so as to comply with the doctrines of the religion or avoid offending the religious susceptibilities of a significant number of its followers.

[118]

20 Midwives

(1) [Until 1st September 1983] section 6(1) does not apply to employment as a midwife.

(2) [Until 1st September 1983] section 6(2)(a) does not apply to promotion, transfer or training as a midwife.

(3) [Until 1st September 1983] section 14 does not apply to training as a midwife.

(4), (5) . . .   [119]

NOTES

Sub-ss (1), (2), (3): words in square brackets inserted by the Sex Discrimination Act 1975 (Amendment of section 20) Order 1983, SI 1983/1202, art 2.

Sub-ss (4), (5): repealed by the Nurses, Midwives and Health Visitors Act 1979, s 23(5), Sch 8.

21 Mineworkers

(1) ...

(2) *Throughout the Coal Mines Regulations Act 1908, for "workman" or "man" there is substituted "worker", and for "workmen" or "men" there is substituted "workers".*   **[120]**

NOTE
Sub-s (1): repealed by the Employment Act 1989, s 29(4), Sch 7, Pt III.
Sub-s (2): amends the Coal Mines Regulation Act 1908. Repealed by the Coal Industry Act 1992, s 2, Schedule, Pt II, as from a day to be appointed.

PART III
DISCRIMINATION IN OTHER FIELDS

22–35 (*Outside the scope of this work.*)

Barristers

[35A Discrimination by, or in relation to, barristers

(1) It is unlawful for a barrister or barrister's clerk, in relation to any offer of a pupillage or tenancy, to discriminate against a woman—

    (a) in the arrangements which are made for the purpose of determining to whom it should be offered;

    (b) in respect of any terms on which it is offered; or

    (c) by refusing, or deliberately omitting, to offer it to her.

(2) It is unlawful for a barrister or barrister's clerk, in relation to a woman who is a pupil or tenant in the chambers in question, to discriminate against her—

    (a) in respect of any terms applicable to her as a pupil or tenant;

    (b) in the opportunities for training, or gaining experience, which are afforded or denied to her;

    (c) in the benefits, facilities or services which are afforded or denied to her; or

    (d) by terminating her pupillage or by subjecting her to any pressure to leave the chambers or other detriment.

(3) It is unlawful for any person, in relation to the giving, withholding or acceptance of instructions to a barrister, to discriminate against any person.

(4) In this section—

    "barrister's clerk" includes any person carrying out any of the functions of a barrister's clerk; and

    "pupil", "pupillage", "tenancy" and "tenant" have the meaning commonly associated with their use in the context of a set of barristers' chambers.

(5) This section does not apply to Scotland.]   **[120A]**

NOTE
Commencement: 1 January 1991.
Inserted with savings by the Courts and Legal Services Act 1990, s 64(1); for savings see Sch 19, para 1 thereof.

Advocates

[35B Discrimination by, or in relation to, advocates

(1) It is unlawful for an advocate, in relation to taking any person as his pupil, to discriminate against a woman—

    (a) in the arrangements which are made for the purpose of determining whom he will take as his pupil;

    (b) in respect of any terms on which he offers to take her as his pupil; or

    (c) by refusing, or deliberately omitting, to take her as his pupil.

(2) It is unlawful for an advocate, in relation to a woman who is a pupil, to discriminate against her—

    (a) in respect of any terms applicable to her as a pupil;

    (b) in the opportunities for training, or gaining experience, which are afforded or denied to her;

    (c) in the benefits, facilities or services which are afforded or denied to her; or

    (d) by terminating her the relationship or by subjecting her to any pressure to terminate the relationship or other detriment.

(3) It is unlawful for any person, in relation to the giving, withholding or acceptance of instructions to an advocate, to discriminate against a woman.

(4) In this section—

"advocate" means a member of the Faculty of Advocates practising as such; and

"pupil"has the meaning commonly associated its use in the context of a person training to be an advocate.

(5) Section 3 applies for the purposes of this section as it applies for the purposes of any provision of Part II.

(6) This section does not apply to England and Wales.]   **[120B]**

NOTE
Commencement: 1 January 1991.
Inserted with savings by the Courts and Legal Services Act 1990, s 65(1).

36 (*Outside the scope of this work.*)

PART IV

OTHER UNLAWFUL ACTS

37 Discriminatory practices

(1) In this section "discriminatory practice" means the application of a requirement or condition which results in an act of discrimination which is unlawful by virtue of any provision of Part II or III taken with section 1(1)(b) or 3(1)(b) or which would be likely to result in such an act of discrimination if the persons to whom it is applied were not all of one sex.

(2) A person acts in contravention of this section if and so long as—

    (a) he applies a discriminatory practice, or

    (b) he operates practices or other arrangements which in any circumstances would call for the application by him of a discriminatory practice.

(3) Proceedings in respect of a contravention of this section shall be brought only by the Commission in accordance with sections 67 to 71 of this Act.   **[121]**

38 Discriminatory advertisements

(1) It is unlawful to publish or cause to be published an advertisement which indicates, or might reasonably be understood as indicating, an intention by a person to do any act which is or might be unlawful by virtue of Part II or III.

(2) Subsection (1) does not apply to an advertisement if the intended act would not in fact be unlawful.

(3) For the purposes of subsection (1), use of a job description with a sexual connotation (such as "waiter", "salesgirl", "postman" or "stewardess") shall be taken to indicate an intention to discriminate, unless the advertisement contains an indication to the contrary.

(4) The publisher of an advertisement made unlawful by subsection (1) shall not be subject to any liability under that subsection in respect of the publication of the advertisement if he proves—

    (a) that the advertisement was published in reliance on a statement made to him by the person who caused it to be published to the effect that, by reason of the operation of subsection (2), the publication would not be unlawful, and

    (b) that it was reasonable for him to rely on the statement.

(5) A person who knowingly or recklessly makes a statement such as is referred to in subsection (4) which in a material respect is false or misleading commits an offence, and shall be liable on summary conviction to a fine not exceeding [level 5 on the standard scale].   **[122]**

NOTE

Sub-s (5): maximum fine increased and converted to a level on the standard scale by the Criminal Justice Act 1982, ss 37, 38, 46.

39 Instructions to discriminate

It is unlawful for a person—

    (a) who has authority over another person, or

    (b) in accordance with whose wishes that other person is accustomed to act,

to instruct him to do any act which is unlawful by virtue of Part II or III, or procure or attempt to procure the doing by him of any such act.   **[123]**

40 Pressure to discriminate

(1) It is unlawful to induce, or attempt to induce, a person to do any act which contravenes Part II or III by—

    (a) providing or offering to provide him with any benefit, or

    (b) subjecting or threatening to subject him to any detriment.

(2) An offer or threat is not prevented from falling within subsection (1) because it is not made directly to the person in question, if it is made in such a way that he is likely to hear of it.   **[124]**

41 Liability of employers and principals

(1) Anything done by a person in the course of his employment shall be treated for the purposes of this Act as done by his employer as well as by him, whether or not it was done with the employer's knowledge or approval.

(2) Anything done by a person as agent for another person with the authority (whether express or implied, and whether precedent or subsequent) of that other person shall be treated for the purposes of this Act as done by that other person as well as by him.

(3) In proceedings brought under this Act against any person in respect of an act alleged to have been done by an employee of his it shall be a defence for that person to prove that he took such steps as were reasonably practicable to prevent the employee from doing that act, or from doing in the course of his employment acts of that description.   **[125]**

NOTE
    Modified, in relation to governing bodies with delegated budgets, by the Education (Modification of Enactments Relating to Employment) Order 1989, SI 1989/901, art 3, Schedule.

42 Aiding unlawful acts

(1) A person who knowingly aids another person to do an act made unlawful by this Act shall be treated for the purposes of this Act as himself doing an unlawful act of the like description.

(2) For the purposes of subsection (1) an employee or agent for whose act the employer or principal is liable under section 41 (or would be so liable but for section 41(3)) shall be deemed to aid the doing of the act by the employer or principal.

(3) A person does not under this section knowingly aid another to do an unlawful act if—

(a) he acts in reliance on a statement made to him by that other person that, by reason of any provision of this Act, the act which he aids would not be unlawful, and

(b) it is reasonable for him to rely on the statement.

(4) A person who knowingly or recklessly makes a statement such as is referred to in subsection (3)(a) which in a material respect is false or misleading commits an offence, and shall be liable on summary conviction to a fine not exceeding [level 5 on the standard scale].

                                                                              [126]

NOTE
    Sub-s (4): maximum fine increased and converted to a level on the standard scale by the Criminal Justice Act 1982, ss 37, 38, 46.

PART V
GENERAL EXCEPTIONS FROM PARTS II TO IV

43 Charities

(1) Nothing in Parts II to IV shall—

(a) be construed as affecting a provision to which this subsection applies, or

(b) render unlawful an act which is done in order to give effect to such a provision.

(2) Subsection (1) applies to a provision for conferring benefits on persons of one sex only (disregarding any benefits to persons of the opposite sex which are exceptional or are relatively insignificant), being a provision which is contained in a charitable instrument.

[(3) In this section "charitable instrument" means an enactment or other instrument passed or made for charitable purposes, or an enactment or other instrument so far as it relates to charitable purposes, and in Scotland includes the governing instrument of an endowment or of an educational endowment as those expressions are defined in section 135(1) of the Education (Scotland) Act 1962.

In the application of this section to England and Wales, "charitable purposes" means purposes which are exclusively charitable according to the law of England and Wales.] **[127]**

NOTE
Sub-s (3): substituted for original sub-ss (3), (4) by the Sex Discrimination Act 1975 (Amendment of section 43) Order 1977, SI 1977/528.

44 Sport etc

Nothing in Parts II to IV shall, in relation to any sport, game or other activity of a competitive nature where the physical strength, stamina or physique of the average woman puts her at a disadvantage to the average man, render unlawful any act related to the participation of a person as a competitor in events involving that activity which are confined to competitors of one sex. **[127A]**

45 Insurance

Nothing in Parts II to IV shall render unlawful the treatment of a person in relation to an annuity, life assurance policy, accident insurance policy, or similar matter involving the assessment of risk, where the treatment—

    (a)   was effected by reference to actuarial or other data from a source on which it was reasonable to rely, and

    (b)   was reasonable having regard to the data and any other relevant factors. **[127B]**

46 Communal accommodation

(1) In this section "communal accommodation" means residential accommodation which includes dormitories or other shared sleeping accommodation which for reasons of privacy or decency should be used by men only, or by women only (but which may include some shared sleeping accommodation for men, and some for women, or some ordinary sleeping accommodation).

(2) In this section "communal accommodation" also includes residential accommodation all or part of which should be used by men only, or by women only, because of the nature of the sanitary facilities serving the accommodation.

(3) Nothing in Part II or III shall render unlawful sex discrimination in the admission of persons to communal accommodation if the accommodation is managed in a way which, given the exigencies of the situation, comes as near as may be to fair and equitable treatment of men and women.

(4) In applying subsection (3) account shall be taken of—

    (a) whether and how far it is reasonable to expect that the accommodation should be altered or extended, or that further alternative accommodation should be provided; and

    (b) the frequency of the demand or need for use of the accommodation by men as compared with women.

(5) Nothing in Part II or III shall render unlawful sex discrimination against a woman, or against a man, as respects the provision of any benefit, facility or service if—

    (a) the benefit, facility or service cannot properly and effectively be provided except for those using communal accommodation, and

    (b) in the relevant circumstances the woman or, as the case may be, the man could lawfully be refused the use of the accommodation by virtue of subsection (3).

(6) Neither subsection (3) nor subsection (5) is a defence to an act of sex discrimination under Part II unless such arrangements as are reasonably practicable are made to compensate for the detriment caused by the discrimination; but in considering under subsection (5)(b) whether the use of communal accommodation could lawfully be refused (in a case based on Part II), it shall be assumed that the requirements of this subsection have been complied with as respects subsection (3).

(7) Section 25 shall not apply to sex discrimination within subsection (3) or (5).

(8) This section is without prejudice to the generality of section 35(1)(c).

[128]

47 Discriminatory training by certain bodies

(1) Nothing in Parts II to IV shall render unlawful any act done in relation to particular work by [any person] in, or in connection with—

    (a) affording women only, or men only, access to facilities for training which would help to fit them for that work, or

    (b) encouraging women only, or men only, to take advantage of opportunities for doing that work,

where [it reasonably appears to that person] that at any time within the 12 months immediately preceding the doing of the act there were no persons of the sex in question doing that work in Great Britain, or the number of persons of that sex doing the work in Great Britain was comparatively small.

(2) Where in relation to particular work [it reasonably appears to any person] that although the condition for the operation of subsection (1) is not met for the whole of Great Britain it is met for an area within Great Britain, nothing in Parts II to IV shall render unlawful any act done by [that person] in, or in connection with—

    (a) affording persons who are of the sex in question, and who appear likely to take up that work in that area, access to facilities for training which would help to fit them for that work, or

    (b) encouraging persons of that sex to take advantage of opportunities in the area for doing that work.

(3) Nothing in Parts II to IV shall render unlawful any act done by [any person] in, or in connection with, affording persons access to facilities for training which would help to fit them for employment, where [it reasonably appears to that person] that those persons are in special need of training by reason of the period for which

they have been discharging domestic or family responsibilities to the exclusion of regular full time employment.

The discrimination in relation to which this subsection applies may result from confining the training to persons who have been discharging domestic or family responsibilities, or from the way persons are selected for training, or both.

[(4) The preceding provisions of this section shall not apply in relation to any discrimination which is rendered unlawful by section 6.] **[129]**

NOTES
Sub-ss (1)-(3): words in square brackets substituted by the Sex Discrimination Act 1986, s 4(1)-(3).
Sub-s (4): substituted by the Sex Discrimination Act 1986, s 4(1), (4).

48 Other discriminatory training etc

(1) Nothing in Parts II to IV shall render unlawful any act done by an employer in relation to particular work in his employment, being an act done in, or in connection with,—

   (a) affording his female employees only, or his male employees only, access to facilities for training which would help to fit them for that work, or

   (b) encouraging women only, or men only, to take advantage of opportunities for doing that work,

where at any time within the twelve months immediately preceding the doing of the act there were no persons of the sex in question among those doing that work or the number of persons of that sex doing the work was comparatively small.

(2) Nothing in section 12 shall render unlawful any act done by an organisation to which that section applies in, or in connection with,—

   (a) affording female members of the organisation only, or male members of the organisation only, access to facilities for training which would help to fit them for holding a post of any kind in the organisation, or

   (b) encouraging female members only, or male members only, to take advantage of opportunities for holding such posts in the organisation,

where at any time within the twelve months immediately preceding the doing of the act there were no persons of the sex in question among persons holding such posts in the organisation or the number of persons of that sex holding such posts was comparatively small.

(3) Nothing in Parts II to IV shall render unlawful any act done by an organisation to which section 12 applies in, or in connection with, encouraging women only, or men only, to become members of the organisation where at any time within the twelve months immediately preceding the doing of the act there were no persons of the sex in question among those members or the number of persons of that sex among the members was comparatively small. **[130]**

49 Trade unions etc: elective bodies

(1) If an organisation to which section 12 applies comprises a body the membership of which is wholly or mainly elected, nothing in section 12 shall render unlawful provision which ensures that a minimum number of persons of one sex are members of the body—

   (a) by reserving seats on the body for persons of that sex, or

   (b) by making extra seats on the body available (by election or co-option or

otherwise) for persons of that sex on occasions when the number of persons
of that sex in the other seats is below the minimum,

where in the opinion of the organisation the provision is in the circumstances needed
to secure a reasonable lower limit to the number of members of that sex serving on
the body; and nothing in Parts II to IV shall render unlawful any act done in order to
give effect to such a provision.

(2) This section shall not be taken as making lawful—

   (a) discrimination in the arrangements for determining the persons entitled to
      vote in an election of members of the body, or otherwise to choose the
      persons to serve on the body, or

   (b) discrimination in any arrangements concerning membership of the
      organisation itself.   **[131]**

50 Indirect access to benefits etc

(1) References in this Act to the affording by any person of access to benefits,
facilities or services are not limited to benefits, facilities or services provided by that
person himself, but include any means by which it is in that person's power to
facilitate access to benefits, facilities or services provided by any other person (the
"actual provider").

(2) Where by any provision of this Act the affording by any person of access to
benefits, facilities or services in a discriminatory way is in certain circumstances
prevented from being unlawful, the effect of the provision shall extend also to the
liability under this Act of any actual provider.   **[132]**

[51 Acts done for purposes of protection of women

(1) Nothing in the following provisions, namely—

   (a) Part II,

   (b) Part III so far as it applies to vocational training, or

   (c) Part IV so far as it has effect in relation to the provisions mentioned in
      paragraphs (a) and (b),

shall render unlawful any act done by a person in relation to a woman if—

   (i) it was necessary for that person to do it in order to comply with a
      requirement of an existing statutory provision concerning the protection
      of women, or

   (ii) it was necessary for that person to do it in order to comply with a
      requirement of a relevant statutory provision (within the meaning of Part
      I of the Health and Safety at Work etc Act 1974) and it was done by that
      person for the purpose of the protection of the woman in question (or of
      any class of women that included that woman).

(2) In subsection (1)—

   (a) the reference in paragraph (i) of that subsection to an existing statutory
      provision concerning the protection of women is a reference to any such
      provision having effect for the purpose of protecting women as regards—

      (i) pregnancy or maternity, or

      (ii) other circumstances giving rise to risks specifically affecting women,

      whether the provision relates only to such protection or to the protection
      of any other class of persons as well; and

(b) the reference in paragraph (ii) of that subsection to the protection of a particular woman or class of women is a reference to the protection of that woman or those women as regards any circumstances falling within paragraph (a)(i) or (ii) above.

(3) In this section "existing statutory provision" means (subject to subsection (4)) any provision of—

(a) an Act passed before this Act, or

(b) an instrument approved or made by or under such an Act (including one approved or made after the passing of this Act).

(4) Where an Act passed after this Act re-enacts (with or without modification) a provision of an Act passed before this Act, that provision as re-enacted shall be treated for the purposes of subsection (3) as if it continued to be contained in an Act passed before this Act.] **[133]**

NOTE

Commencement: 16 January 1990.
Substituted with savings, together with s 51A, by the Employment Act 1989, ss 3(1), (3), 29(6), Sch 9, para 1.

[51A Acts done under statutory authority to be exempt from certain provisions of Part III

(1) Nothing in—

(a) the relevant provisions of Part III, or

(b) Part IV so far as it has effect in relation to those provisions,

shall render unlawful any act done by a person if it was necessary for that person to do it in order to comply with a requirement of an existing statutory provision within the meaning of section 51.

(2) In subsection (1) "the relevant provisions of Part III" means the provisions of that Part except so far as they apply to vocational training.] **[134]**

NOTE

Commencement: 16 January 1990.
Substituted with savings, together with new s 51, for s 51 as originally enacted and amended by the Sex Discrimination Act 1986, Sch 4, by the Employment Act 1989, ss 3(3), 29(6), Sch 9.

52 Acts safeguarding national security

(1) Nothing in Parts II to IV shall render unlawful an act done for the purpose of safeguarding national security.

(2) A certificate purporting to be signed by or on behalf of a Minister of the Crown and certifying that an act specified in the certificate was done for the purpose of safeguarding national security shall be conclusive evidence that it was done for that purpose.

(3) A document purporting to be a certificate such as is mentioned in subsection (2) shall be received in evidence and, unless the contrary is proved, shall be deemed to be such a certificate. **[135]**

NOTE

The Sex Discrimination (Amendment) Order 1988, SI 1988/249, provides that sub-ss (2), (3) shall "cease to have effect in relation to the determination of the question whether any act is rendered unlawful by virtue of Part II of that Act, or by Part III of that Act as it applies to vocational training, or by Part IV of that Act taken with Part II or with Part III as it so applies".

[52A Construction of references to vocational training

In the following provisions, namely—

    (a) sections 51 and 51A, and

    (b) the provisions of any Order in Council modifying the effect of section 52,

"vocational training" includes advanced vocational training and retraining; and any reference to vocational training in those provisions shall be construed as including a reference to vocational guidance.] **[136]**

NOTE
    Commencement: 1 January 1990.
    Inserted with savings by the Employment Act 1989, ss 3(1), (4), 29(6), Sch 9, para 1.

PART VI
EQUAL OPPORTUNITIES COMMISSION

53 Establishment and duties of Commission

(1) There shall be a body of Commissioners named the Equal Opportunities Commission, consisting of at least eight but not more than fifteen individuals each appointed by the Secretary of State on a full-time or part-time basis, which shall have the following duties—

    (a) to work towards the elimination of discrimination,

    (b) to promote equality of opportunity between men and women generally, and

    (c) to keep under review the working of this Act and the Equal Pay Act 1970 and, when they are so required by the Secretary of State or otherwise think it necessary, draw up and submit to the Secretary of State proposals for amending them.

(2) The Secretary of State shall appoint—

    (a) one of the Commissioners to be chairman of the Commission, and

    (b) either one or two of the Commissioners (as the Secretary of State thinks fit) to be deputy chairman or deputy chairmen of the Commission.

(3) The Secretary of State may by order amend subsection (1) so far as it regulates the number of Commissioners.

(4) Schedule 3 shall have effect with respect to the Commission. **[137]**

54 Research and education

(1) The Commission may undertake or assist (financially or otherwise) the undertaking by other persons of any research, and any educational activities, which appear to the Commission necessary or expedient for the purposes of section 53(1).

(2) The Commission may make charges for educational or other facilities or services made available by them. **[138]**

55 Review of discriminatory provisions in health and safety legislation

(1) Without prejudice to the generality of section 53(1), the Commission, in pursuance of the duties imposed by paragraphs (a) and (b) of that subsection—

    (a) shall keep under review the relevant statutory provisions in so far as they require men and women to be treated differently, and

    (b) if so required by the Secretary of State, make to him a report on any matter specified by him which is connected with those duties and concerns the relevant statutory provisions.

Any such report shall be made within the time specified by the Secretary of State, and the Secretary of State shall cause the report to be published.

(2) Whenever the Commission think it necessary, they shall draw up and submit to the Secretary of State proposals for amending the relevant statutory provisions.

(3) The Commission shall carry out their duties in relation to the relevant statutory provisions in consultation with the Health and Safety Commission.

(4) In this section "the relevant statutory provisions" has the meaning given by section 53 of the Health and Safety at Work etc Act 1974.   **[139]**

56 Annual reports

(1) As soon as practicable after the end of each calendar year the Commission shall make to the Secretary of State a report on their activities during the year (an "annual report").

(2) Each annual report shall include a general survey of developments, during the period to which it relates, in respect of matters falling within the scope of the Commission's duties.

(3) The Secretary of State shall lay a copy of every annual report before each House of Parliament, and shall cause the report to be published.   **[140]**

[Codes of practice

56A Codes of practice

(1) The Commission may issue codes of practice containing such practical guidance as the Commission think fit for either or both of the following purposes, namely—

    (a) the elimination of discrimination in the field of employment;

    (b) the promotion of equality of opportunity in that field between men and women.

(2) When the Commission propose to issue a code of practice, they shall prepare and publish a draft of that code, shall consider any representations made to them about the draft and may modify the draft accordingly.

(3) In the course of preparing any draft code of practice for eventual publication under subsection (2) the Commission shall consult with—

    (a) such organisations or associations of organisations representative of employers or of workers; and

    (b) such other organisations, or bodies,

as appear to the Commission to be appropriate.

(4) If the Commission determine to proceed with the draft, they shall transmit the draft to the Secretary of State who shall—

    (a) if he approves of it, lay it before both Houses of Parliament; and

    (b) if he does not approve of it, publish details of his reasons for withholding approval.

(5) If, within the period of forty days beginning with the day on which a copy of a draft code of practice is laid before each House of Parliament, or, if such copies are laid on different days, with the later of the two days, either House so resolves, no further proceedings shall be taken thereon, but without prejudice to the laying before Parliament of a new draft.

(6) In reckoning the period of forty days referred to in subsection (5), no account shall be taken of any period during which Parliament is dissolved or prorogued or during which both Houses are adjourned for more than four days.

(7) If no such resolution is passed as is referred to in subsection (5), the Commission shall issue the code in the form of the draft and the code shall come into effect on such day as the Secretary of State may by order appoint.

(8) Without prejudice to section 81(4), an order under subsection (7) may contain such transitional provisions or savings as appear to the Secretary of State to be necessary or expedient in connection with the code of practice thereby brought into operation.

(9) The Commission may from time to time revise the whole or any part of a code of practice issued under this section and issue that revised code, and subsections (2) to (8) shall apply (with appropriate modifications) to such a revised code as they apply to the first issue of a code.

(10) A failure on the part of any person to observe any provision of a code of practice shall not of itself render him liable to any proceedings; but in any proceedings under this Act [or the Equal Pay Act 1970] before an industrial tribunal any code of practice issued under this section shall be admissible in evidence, and if any provision of such a code appears to the tribunal to be relevant to any question arising in the proceedings it shall be taken into account in determining that question.

(11) Without prejudice to subsection (1), a code of practice issued under this section may include such practical guidance as the Commission think fit as to what steps it is reasonably practicable for employers to take for the purpose of preventing their employees from doing in the course of their employment acts made unlawful by this Act.] **[141]**

NOTES

Inserted, with preceding cross-heading, by the Race Relations Act 1976, s 79(4), Sch 4, para 1.
Sub-s (10): words in square brackets inserted by the Trade Union Reform and Employment Rights Act 1993, s 49(1), Sch 7, para 15, as from 30 August 1993 (SI 1993/1908).
The only Code of Practice relating to employment made under this section is the Code of Practice for the Elimination of Discrimination on the Grounds of Sex and Marriage and the Promotion of Equality of Opportunity in Employment (1985). This is reprinted below (para **[3065]**).

Investigations

57 Power to conduct formal investigations

(1) Without prejudice to their general power to do anything requisite for the performance of their duties under section 53(1), the Commission may if they think fit, and shall if required by the Secretary of State, conduct a formal investigation for any purpose connected with the carrying out of those duties.

(2) The Commission may, with the approval of the Secretary of State, appoint, on a full-time or part-time basis, one or more individuals as additional Commissioners for the purposes of a formal investigation.

(3) The Commission may nominate one or more Commissioners, with or without one or more additional Commissioners, to conduct a formal investigation on their behalf, and may delegate any of their functions in relation to the investigation to the persons so nominated. **[142]**

58 Terms of reference

(1) The Commission shall not embark on a formal investigation unless the requirements of this section have been complied with.

(2) Terms of reference for the investigation shall be drawn up by the Commission or, if the Commission were required by the Secretary of State to conduct the investigation, by the Secretary of State after consulting the Commission.

(3) It shall be the duty of the Commission to give general notice of the holding of the investigation unless the terms of reference confine it to activities of persons named in them, but in such a case the Commission shall in the prescribed manner give those persons notice of the holding of the investigation.

[(3A) Where the terms of reference of the investigation confine it to activities of persons named in them and the Commission in the course of it propose to investigate any act made unlawful by this Act which they believe that a person so named may have done, the Commission shall—

(a) inform that person of their belief and of their proposal to investigate the act in question; and

(b) offer him an opportunity of making oral or written representations with regard to it (or both oral and written representations if he thinks fit);

and a person so named who avails himself of an opportunity under this subsection of making oral representations may be represented—

(i) by counsel or a solicitor; or

(ii) by some other person of his choice, not being a person to whom the Commission object on the ground that he is unsuitable.]

(4) The Commission or, if the Commission were required by the Secretary of State to conduct the investigation, the Secretary of State after consulting the Commission may from time to time revise the terms of reference; and subsections (1), [(3) and (3A)] shall apply to the revised investigation and terms of reference as they applied to the original. **[143]**

NOTES
Sub-s (3A): inserted by the Race Relations Act 1976, s 79(4), Sch 4, para 2.
Sub-s (4): words in square brackets substituted by the Race Relations Act 1976, s 79(4), Sch 4, para 2.

59 Power to obtain information

(1) For the purposes of a formal investigation the Commission, by a notice in the prescribed form served on him in the prescribed manner,—

(a) may require any person to furnish such written information as may be described in the notice, and may specify the time at which, and the manner and form in which, the information is to be furnished;

(b) may require any person to attend at such time and place as is specified in the notice and give oral information about, and produce all documents in his possession or control relating to, any matter specified in the notice.

(2) Except as provided by section 69, a notice shall be served under subsection (1) only where—

(a) service of the notice was authorised by an order made by or on behalf of the Secretary of State, or

(b) the terms of reference of the investigation state that the Commission believe that a person named in them may have done or may be doing acts of all or any of the following descriptions—

(i) unlawful discriminatory acts,

(ii) contraventions of section 37,

(iii) contraventions of sections 38, 39 or 40, and

(iv) acts in breach of a term modified or included by virtue of an equality clause,

and confine the investigation to those acts.

(3) A notice under subsection (1) shall not require a person—

(a) to give information, or produce any documents, which he could not be compelled to give in evidence, or produce, in civil proceedings before the High Court or the Court of Session, or

(b) to attend at any place unless the necessary expenses of his journey to and from that place are paid or tendered to him.

(4) If a person fails to comply with a notice served on him under subsection (1) or the Commission has reasonable cause to believe that he intends not to comply with it, the Commission may apply to a county court for an order requiring him to comply with it or with such directions for the like purpose as may be contained in the order; and [section 55 (penalty for neglecting or refusing to give evidence) of the County Courts Act 1984] shall apply to failure without reasonable excuse to comply with any such order as it applies in the cases there provided.

(5) In the application of subsection (4) to Scotland—

(a) for the reference to a county court there shall be substituted a reference to a sheriff court, and

(b) for the words after "order; and" to the end of the subsection there shall be substituted the words "paragraph 73 of the First Schedule to the Sheriff Courts (Scotland) Act 1907 (power of sheriff to grant second diligence for compelling the attendances of witnesses or havers) shall apply to any such order as it applies in proceedings in the sheriff court".

(6) A person commits an offence if he—

(a) wilfully alters, suppresses, conceals or destroys a document which he has been required by a notice or order under this section to produce, or

(b) in complying with such a notice or order, knowingly or recklessly makes any statement which is false in a material particular,

and shall be liable on summary conviction to a fine not exceeding [level 5 on the standard scale].

(7) Proceedings for an offence under subsection (6) may (without prejudice to any jurisdiction exercisable apart from this subsection) be instituted—

(a) against any person at any place at which he has an office or other place of business;

(b) against an individual at any place where he resides, or at which he is for the time being. **[144]**

NOTES

Sub-s (4): words in square brackets substituted by the County Courts Act 1984, s 148(1), Sch 2, Pt V, para 54.

Sub-s (6): maximum fine increased and converted to a level on the standard scale by the Criminal Justice Act 1982, ss 37, 38, 46.

Regulations under this section: the Sex Discrimination (Formal Investigations) Regulations 1975, SI 1975/1993, as amended by SI 1977/843 (below, para **[1036]**).

60 Recommendations and reports on formal investigations

(1) If in the light of any of their findings in a formal investigation it appears to the Commission necessary or expedient, whether during the course of the investigation or after its conclusion,—

    (a) to make to any persons, with a view to promoting equality of opportunity between men and women who are affected by any of their activities, recommendations for changes in their policies or procedures, or as to any other matters, or

    (b) to make to the Secretary of State any recommendations, whether for changes in the law or otherwise,

the Commission shall make those recommendations accordingly.

(2) The Commission shall prepare a report of their findings in any formal investigation conducted by them.

(3) If the formal investigation is one required by the Secretary of State—

    (a) the Commission shall deliver the report to the Secretary of State, and

    (b) the Secretary of State shall cause the report to be published,

and unless required by the Secretary of State the Commission shall not publish the report.

(4) If the formal investigation is not one required by the Secretary of State, the Commission shall either publish the report, or make it available for inspection in accordance with subsection (5).

(5) Where under subsection (4) a report is to be made available for inspection, any person shall be entitled, on payment of such fee (if any) as may be determined by the Commission—

    (a) to inspect the report during ordinary office hours and take copies of all or any part of the report, or

    (b) to obtain from the Commission a copy, certified by the Commission to be correct, of the report.

(6) The Commission may if they think fit determine that the right conferred by subsection (5)(a) shall be exercisable in relation to a copy of the report instead of, or in addition to, the original.

(7) The Commission shall give general notice of the place or places where, and the times when, reports may be inspected under subsection (5).   **[145]**

61 Restriction on disclosure of information

(1) No information given to the Commission by any person ("the informant") in connection with a formal investigation shall be disclosed by the Commission, or by any person who is or has been a Commissioner, additional Commissioner or employee of the Commission, except—

    (a) on the order of any court, or

    (b) with the informant's consent, or

    (c) in the form of a summary or other general statement published by the Commission which does not identify the informant or any other person to whom the information relates, or

(d) in a report of the investigation published by the Commission or made available for inspection under section 60(5), or

(e) to the Commissioners, additional Commissioners or employees of the Commission, or, so far as may be necessary for the proper performance of the functions of the Commission, to other persons, or

(f) for the purpose of any civil proceedings under this Act to which the Commission are a party, or any criminal proceedings.

(2) Any person who discloses information in contravention of subsection (1) commits an offence and shall be liable on summary conviction to a fine not exceeding [level 5 on the standard scale].

(3) In preparing any report for publication or for inspection the Commission shall exclude, so far as is consistent with their duties and the object of the report, any matter which relates to the private affairs of any individual or business interests of any person where the publication of that matter might, in the opinion of the Commission, prejudicially affect that individual or person.   **[146]**

NOTE

Sub-s (2): maximum fine increased and converted to a level on the standard scale by the Criminal Justice Act 1982, ss 37, 38, 46.

PART VII

ENFORCEMENT

General

[62 Restriction of proceedings for breach of Act

(1) Except as provided by this Act no proceedings, whether civil or criminal, shall lie against any person in respect of an act by reason that the act is unlawful by virtue of a provision of this Act.

(2) Subsection (1) does not preclude the making of an order of certiorari, mandamus or prohibition.

(3) In Scotland, subsection (1) does not preclude the exercise of the jurisdiction of the Court of Session to entertain an application for reduction or suspension of any order or determination, or otherwise to consider the validity of any order or determination, or to require reasons for any order or determination to be stated.]

[147]

NOTE

Substituted by the Race Relations Act 1976, s 79(4), Sch 4, para 3.

Enforcement in employment field

63 Jurisdiction of industrial tribunals

(1) A complaint by any person ("the complainant") that another person ("the respondent")—

(a) has committed an act of discrimination against the complainant which is unlawful by virtue of Part II, or

(b) is by virtue of section 41 or 42 to be treated as having committed such an act of discrimination against the complainant,

may be presented to an industrial tribunal.

(2) Subsection (1) does not apply to a complaint under section 13(1) of an act in respect of which an appeal, or proceedings in the nature of an appeal, may be brought under any enactment.   **[148]**

64 Conciliation in employment cases

(1) Where a complaint has been presented to an industrial tribunal under section 63, or under section 2(1) of the Equal Pay Act 1970, and a copy of the complaint has been sent to a conciliation officer, it shall be the duty of the conciliation officer—

(a) if he is requested to do so both by the complainant and the respondent, or

(b) if, in the absence of requests by the complainant and the respondent, he considers that he could act under this subsection with a reasonable prospect of success,

to endeavour to promote a settlement of the complaint without its being determined by an industrial tribunal.

(2) Where, before a complaint such as is mentioned in subsection (1) has been presented to an industrial tribunal, a request is made to a conciliation officer to make his services available in the matter by a person who, if the complaint were so presented, would be the complainant or respondent, subsection (1) shall apply as if the complaint had been so presented and a copy of it had been sent to the conciliation officer.

(3) In proceeding under subsection (1) or (2), a conciliation officer shall where appropriate have regard to the desirability of encouraging the use of other procedures available for the settlement of grievances.

(4) Anything communicated to a conciliation officer in connection with the performance of his functions under this section shall not be admissible in evidence in any proceedings before an industrial tribunal except with the consent of the person who communicated it to that officer.   **[149]**

65 Remedies on complaint under section 63

(1) Where an industrial tribunal finds that a complaint presented to it under section 63 is well-founded the tribunal shall make such of the following as it considers just and equitable—

(a) an order declaring the rights of the complainant and the respondent in relation to the act to which the complaint relates;

(b) an order requiring the respondent to pay to the complainant compensation of an amount corresponding to any damages he could have been ordered by a county court or by a sheriff court to pay to the complainant if the complaint had fallen to be dealt with under section 66;

(c) a recommendation that the respondent take within a specified period action appearing to the tribunal to be practicable for the purpose of obviating or reducing the adverse effect on the complainant of any act of discrimination to which the complaint relates.

(2) The amount of compensation awarded to a person under subsection (1)(b) shall not exceed the [limit for the time being imposed by] [section 75 of the Employment Protection (Consolidation) Act 1978].

(3) If without reasonable justification the respondent to a complaint fails to comply with a recommendation made by an industrial tribunal under subsection (1)(c), then, if they think it just and equitable to do so—

   (a) the tribunal may [(subject to the limit in subsection (2))] increase the amount of compensation required to be paid to the complainant in respect of the complaint by an order made under subsection (1)(b), or

   (b) if an order under subsection (1)(b) could have been made but was not, the tribunal may make such an order.   **[150]**

NOTES

Sub-s (2): words in first pair of square brackets substituted by the Employment Protection Act 1975, s 125(1), Sch 16, Pt IV, para 18(1), (2); words in second pair of square brackets substituted by the Employment Protection (Consolidation Act) 1978, s 159(2), Sch 16, para 20(1). The current limit is £11,000 (from 1 June 1993; previously £10,000).

Sub-s (3): in para (a), words in square brackets inserted by the Race Relations Act 1976, s 79(4), Sch 4, para 4.

Enforcement of Part III

66 Claims under Part III

(1) A claim by any person ("the claimant") that another person ("the respondent")—

   (a) has committed an act of discrimination against the claimant which is unlawful by virtue of Part III, or

   (b) is by virtue of section 41 or 42 to be treated as having committed such an act of discrimination against the claimant,

may be made the subject of civil proceedings in like manner as any other claim in tort or (in Scotland) in reparation for breach of statutory duty.

(2) Proceedings under subsection (1)—

   (a) shall be brought in England and Wales only in a county court, and

   (b) shall be brought in Scotland only in a sheriff court.

(3) As respects an unlawful act of discrimination falling within section 1(1)(b) (or, where this section is applied by section 65(1)(b), section 3(1)(b)) no award of damages shall be made if the respondent proves that the requirement or condition in question was not applied with the intention of treating the claimant unfavourably on the ground of his sex or marital status as the case may be,

(4) For the avoidance of doubt it is hereby declared that damages in respect of an unlawful act of discrimination may include compensation for injury to feelings whether or not they include compensation under any other head.

(5) Civil proceedings in respect of a claim by any person that he has been discriminated against in contravention of section 22 or 23 by a body to which section 25(1) applies shall not be instituted unless the claimant has given notice of the claim to the Secretary of State and either the Secretary of State has by notice informed the claimant that the Secretary of State does not require further time to consider the matter, or the period of two months has elapsed since the claimant gave notice to the Secretary of State; but nothing in this subsection applies to a counterclaim.

[(5A) In Scotland, when any proceedings are brought under this section, in addition to the service on the defender of a copy of the summons or initial writ initiating the action a copy thereof shall be sent as soon as practicable to the Commission in a manner to be prescribed by Act of Sederunt.]

(6) For the purposes of proceedings under subsection (1)—

   (a) [section 63(1) (assessors) of the County Courts Act 1984] shall apply with the omission of the words "on the application of any party", and

   (b) the remuneration of assessors appointed under the said section [63(1)] shall be at such rate as may be determined by the Lord Chancellor with the approval of the Minister for the Civil Service.

(7) For the purposes of proceedings before the sheriff, provision may be made by Act of Sederunt for the appointment of assessors by him, and the remuneration of any assessors so appointed shall be at such rates as the Lord President of the Court of Session with the approval of the Minister for the Civil Service may determine.

(8) A county court or sheriff court shall have jurisdiction to entertain proceedings under subsection (1) with respect to an act done on a ship, aircraft or hovercraft outside its district, including such an act done outside Great Britain.　　　　**[151]**

NOTES
Sub-s (2): amendment in square brackets made by the Race Relations Act 1976, s 79(4), Sch 4, para 5.
Sub-s (5A): inserted by the Race Relations Act 1976, s 79(4), Sch 4, para 5.
Sub-s (6): amended by the County Courts Act 1984, s 148(1), Sch 2, para 55.

Non-discrimination notices

67 Issue of non-discrimination notice

(1) This section applies to—

    (a) an unlawful discriminatory act, and
    (b) a contravention of section 37, and
    (c) a contravention of section 38, 39 or 40, and
    (d) an act in breach of a term modified or included by virtue of an equality clause,

and so applies whether or not proceedings have been brought in respect of the act.

(2) If in the course of a formal investigation the Commission become satisfied that a person is committing, or has committed, any such acts, the Commission may in the prescribed manner serve on him a notice in the prescribed form ("a non-discrimination notice") requiring him—

    (a) not to commit any such acts, and
    (b) where compliance with paragraph (a) involves changes in any of his practices or other arrangements—

        (i) to inform the Commission that he has effected those changes and what those changes are, and
        (ii) to take such steps as may be reasonably required by the notice for the purpose of affording that information to other persons concerned.

(3) A non-discrimination notice may also require the person on whom it is served to furnish the Commission with such other information as may be reasonably required by the notice in order to verify that the notice has been complied with.

(4) The notice may specify the time at which, and the manner and form in which, any information is to be furnished to the Commission, but the time at which any information is to be furnished in compliance with the notice shall not be later than five years after the notice has become final.

(5) The Commission shall not serve a non-discrimination notice in respect of any person unless they have first—

    (a) given him notice that they are minded to issue a non-discrimination notice in his case, specifying the grounds on which they contemplate doing so, and
    (b) offered him an opportunity of making oral or written representations in the

matter (or both oral and written representations if he thinks fit) within a period of not less than 28 days specified in the notice, and

(c) taken account of any representations so made by him.

(6) Subsection (2) does not apply to any acts in respect of which the Secretary of State could exercise the powers conferred on him by section 25(2) and (3); but if the Commission become aware of any such acts they shall give notice of them to the Secretary of State.

(7) Section 59(4) shall apply to requirements under subsection (2)(b), (3) and (4) contained in a non-discrimination notice which has become final as it applies to requirements in a notice served under section 59(1). **[152]**

NOTE

For the prescribed form of non-discrimination notice, see the Sex Discrimination (Formal Investigations) Regulations 1975, SI 1975/1993, reg 6 and Sch 2 (as substituted by SI 1977/843), below, paras **[1041]** and **[1043]**.

68 Appeal against non-discrimination notice

(1) Not later than six weeks after a non-discrimination notice is served on any person he may appeal against any requirement of the notice—

(a) to an industrial tribunal, so far as the requirement relates to acts which are within the jurisdiction of the tribunal;

(b) to a county court or to a sheriff court so far as the requirement relates to acts which are within the jurisdiction of the court and are not within the jurisdiction of an industrial tribunal.

(2) Where the court or tribunal considers a requirement in respect of which an appeal is brought under subsection (1) to be unreasonable because it is based on an incorrect finding of fact or for any other reason, the court or tribunal shall quash the requirement.

(3) On quashing a requirement under subsection (2) the court or tribunal may direct that the non-discrimination notice shall be treated as if, in place of the requirement quashed, it had contained a requirement in terms specified in the direction.

(4) Subsection (1) does not apply to a requirement treated as included in a non-discrimination notice by virtue of a direction under subsection (3). **[153]**

NOTE

For the procedure on appeals see the Industrial Tribunals (Non-discrimination Notices Appeals) Regulations 1977, SI 1977/1094, below, para **[1098]**.

69 Investigation as to compliance with non-discrimination notice

(1) If—

(a) the terms of reference of a formal investigation state that its purpose is to determine whether any requirements of a non-discrimination notice are or have been carried out, but section 59(2)(b) does not apply, and

(b) section 58(3) is complied with in relation to the investigation on a date ("the commencement date") not later than the expiration of the period of five years beginning when the non-discrimination notice became final,

the Commission may within the period referred to in subsection (2) serve notices under section 59(1) for the purposes of the investigation without needing to obtain the consent of the Secretary of State.

(2) The said period begins on the commencement date and ends on the later of the following dates—

    (a) the date on which the period of five years mentioned in subsection (1)(b) expires;

    (b) the date two years after the commencement date.   **[154]**

70 Register of non-discrimination notices

(1) The Commission shall establish and maintain a register ("the register") of non-discrimination notices which have become final.

(2) Any person shall be entitled, on payment of such fee (if any) as may be determined by the Commission,—

    (a) to inspect the register during ordinary office hours and take copies of any entry, or

    (b) to obtain from the Commission a copy, certified by the Commission to be correct, of any entry in the register.

(3) The Commission may, if they think fit, determine that the right conferred by subsection (2)(a) shall be exercisable in relation to a copy of the register instead of, or in addition to, the original.

(4) The Commission shall give general notice of the place or places where, and the times when, the register or a copy of it may be inspected.   **[155]**

Other enforcement by Commission

71 Persistent discrimination

(1) If, during the period of five years beginning on the date on which either of the following became final in the case of any person, namely,—

    (a) a non-discrimination notice served on him,

    (b) a finding by a court or tribunal under section 63 or 66, or section 2 of the Equal Pay Act 1970, that he has done an unlawful discriminatory act or an act in breach of a term modified or included by virtue of an equality clause,

it appears to the Commission that unless restrained he is likely to do one or more acts falling within paragraph (b), or contravening section 37, the Commission may apply to a county court for an injunction, or to the sheriff court for an order, restraining him from doing so; and the court, if satisfied that the application is well-founded, may grant the injunction or order in the terms applied for or in more limited terms.

(2) In proceedings under this section the Commission shall not allege that the person to whom the proceedings relate has done an act which is within the jurisdiction of an industrial tribunal unless a finding by an industrial tribunal that he did that act has become final.   **[156]**

72 Enforcement of ss 38 to 40

(1) Proceedings in respect of a contravention of section 38, 39 or 40 shall be brought only by the Commission in accordance with the following provisions of this section.

(2) The proceedings shall be—

    (a) an application for a decision whether the alleged contravention occurred, or

(b) an application under subsection (4) below,

or both.

(3) An application under subsection (2)(a) shall be made—

(a) in a case based on any provision of Part II, to an industrial tribunal, and

(b) in any other case to a county court or sheriff court.

(4) If it appears to the Commission—

(a) that a person has done an act which by virtue of section 38, 39 or 40 was unlawful, and

(b) that unless restrained he is likely to do further acts which by virtue of that section are unlawful,

the Commission may apply to a county court for an injunction, or to a sheriff court for an order, restraining him from doing such acts; and the court, if satisfied that the application is well-founded, may grant the injunction or ... order in the terms applied for or more limited terms.

(5) In proceedings under subsection (4) the Commission shall not allege that the person to whom the proceedings relate has done an act which is unlawful under this Act and within the jurisdiction of an industrial tribunal unless a finding by an industrial tribunal that he did that act has become final. **[157]**

NOTE

Sub-s (4): word omitted repealed by the Race Relations Act 1976, s 79(4), (5), Sch 4, para 6, Sch 5.

73 Preliminary action in employment cases

(1) With a view to making an application under section 71(1) or 72(4) in relation to a person the Commission may present to an industrial tribunal a complaint that he has done an act within the jurisdiction of an industrial tribunal, and if the tribunal considers that the complaint is well-founded they shall make a finding to that effect and, if they think it just and equitable to do so in the case of an act contravening any provision of Part II may also (as if the complaint had been presented by the person discriminated against) make an order such as is referred to in section 65(1)(a), or a recommendation such as is referred to in section 65(1)(c), or both.

(2) Subsection (1) is without prejudice to the jurisdiction conferred by section 72(2).

(3) Any finding of an industrial tribunal under—

(a) this Act, or

(b) the Equal Pay Act 1970,

in respect of any act shall, if it has become final, be treated as conclusive—

(i) by the county court or sheriff court on an application under section 71(1) or 72(4) or in proceedings on an equality clause,

(ii) by an industrial tribunal on a complaint made by the person affected by the act under section 63 or in relation to an equality clause.

(4) In sections 71 and 72 and this section, the acts "within the jurisdiction of an industrial tribunal" are those in respect of which such jurisdiction is conferred by sections 63 and 72 and by section 2 of the Equal Pay Act 1970. **[158]**

Help for persons suffering discrimination

74 Help for aggrieved persons in obtaining information etc

(1) With a view to helping a person ("the person aggrieved") who considers he may have been discriminated against in contravention of this Act to decide whether to institute proceedings and, if he does so, to formulate and present his case in the most effective manner, the Secretary of State shall by order prescribe—

    (a) forms by which the person aggrieved may question the respondent on his reasons for doing any relevant act, or on any other matter which is or may be relevant;

    (b) forms by which the respondent may if he so wishes reply to any questions.

(2) Where the person aggrieved questions the respondent (whether in accordance with an order under subsection (1) or not)—

    (a) the question, and any reply by the respondent (whether in accordance with such an order or not) shall, subject to the following provisions of this section, be admissible as evidence in the proceedings;

    (b) if it appears to the court or tribunal that the respondent deliberately, and without reasonable excuse, omitted to reply within a reasonable period or that his reply is evasive or equivocal, the court or tribunal may draw any inference from that fact that it considers it just and equitable to draw, including an inference that he committed an unlawful act.

(3) The Secretary of State may by order—

    (a) prescribe the period within which questions must be duly served in order to be admissible under subsection (2)(a), and

    (b) prescribe the manner in which a question, and any reply by the respondent, may be duly served.

(4) Rules may enable the court entertaining a claim under section 66 to determine, before the date fixed for the hearing of the claim, whether a question or reply is admissible under this section or not.

(5) This section is without prejudice to any other enactment or rule of law regulating interlocutory and preliminary matters in proceedings before a county court, sheriff court or industrial tribunal, and has effect subject to any enactment or rule of law regulating the admissibility of evidence in such proceedings.

(6) In this section "respondent" includes a prospective respondent and "rules"—

    (a) in relation to county court proceedings, means county court rules;

    (b) in relation to sheriff court proceedings, means sheriff court rules.   **[159]**

NOTE
    Order under this section: the Sex Discrimination (Questions and Replies) Order 1975, SI 1975/2048, as amended by SI 1977/844, below, para **[1044]**.

75 Assistance by Commission

(1) Where, in relation to proceedings or prospective proceedings either under this Act or in respect of an equality clause, an individual who is an actual or prospective complainant or claimant applies to the Commission for assistance under this section, the Commission shall consider the application and may grant it if they think fit to do so on the ground that—

    (a) the case raises a question of principle, or

    (b) it is unreasonable, having regard to the complexity of the case or the applicant's position in relation to the respondent or another person involved or any other matter, to expect the applicant to deal with the case unaided,

or by reason of any other special consideration.

(2) Assistance by the Commission under this section may include—

(a) giving advice;

(b) procuring or attempting to procure the settlement of any matter in dispute;

(c) arranging for the giving of advice or assistance by a solicitor or counsel;

(d) arranging for representation by any person including all such assistance as is usually given by a solicitor or counsel in the steps preliminary or incidental to any proceedings, or in arriving at or giving effect to a compromise to avoid or bring to an end any proceedings,

[(e) any other form of assistance which the Commission may consider appropriate,]

but paragraph (d) shall not affect the law and practice regulating the descriptions of persons who may appear in, conduct, defend and address the court in, any proceedings.

(3) In so far as expenses are incurred by the Commission in providing the applicant with assistance under this section the recovery of those expenses (as taxed or assessed in such manner as may be prescribed by rules or regulations) shall constitute a first charge for the benefit of the Commission—

(a) on any costs or expenses which (whether by virtue of a judgment or order of a court or tribunal or an agreement or otherwise) are payable to the applicant by any other person in respect of the matter in connection with which the assistance is given, and

(b) so far as relates to any costs or expenses, on his rights under any compromise or settlement arrived at in connection with that matter to avoid or bring to an end any proceedings.

(4) The charge conferred by subsection (3) is subject to any charge under the [Legal Aid Act 1988], or any charge or obligation for payment in priority to other debts under the [Legal Aid (Scotland) Act 1986], and is subject to any provision in [either of those Acts for payment of any sum to the Legal Aid Board or into the Scottish Legal Aid Fund].

(5) In this section "respondent" includes a prospective respondent and "rules or regulations"—

(a) in relation to county court proceedings, means county court rules;

(b) in relation to sheriff court proceedings, means sheriff court rules;

(c) in relation to industrial tribunal proceedings, means regulations made under [paragraph 1 of Schedule 9 to the Employment Protection (Consolidation) Act 1978]. **[160]**

NOTES

Sub-s (2): para (e) added by the Race Relations Act 1976, s 79(4), Sch 4, para 7.

Sub-s (4): words in first and third square brackets substituted by the Legal Aid Act 1988, s 45, Sch 5, para 6; words in second square brackets substituted by the Legal Aid (Scotland) Act 1986, s 45(1), Sch 3, para 5.

Sub-s (5): para (c) amended by the Employment Protection (Consolidation) Act 1978, s 159(2), Sch 16, para 20(2).

Modifications: any reference to solicitors etc modified to include references to recognised bodies, by the Solicitors' Incorporated Practices Order 1991, SI 1991/2684, arts 4, 5, Sch 1.

Period within which proceedings to be brought

76 Period within which proceedings to be brought

(1) An industrial tribunal shall not consider a complaint under section 63 unless it is presented to the tribunal before the end of the period of three months beginning when the act complained of was done.

(2) A county court or a sheriff court shall not consider a claim under section 66 unless proceedings in respect of the claim are instituted before the end of—

    [(a) the period of six months beginning when the act complained of was done; or

    (b) in a case to which section 66(5) applies, the period of eight months so beginning.]

    [(3) An industrial tribunal, county court or sheriff court shall not consider an application under section 72(2)(a) unless it is made before the end of the period of six months beginning when the act to which it relates was done; and a county court or sheriff court shall not consider an application under section 72(4) unless it is made before the end of the period of five years so beginning.]

    (4) An industrial tribunal shall not consider a complaint under section 73(1) unless it is presented to the tribunal before the end of the period of six months beginning when the act complained of was done.

    (5) A court or tribunal may nevertheless consider any such complaint, claim or application which is out of time if, in all the circumstances of the case, it considers that it is just and equitable to do so.

    (6) For the purposes of this section—

    (a) where the inclusion of any term in a contract renders the making of the contract an unlawful act that act shall be treated as extending throughout the duration of the contract, and

    (b) any act extending over a period shall be treated as done at the end of that period, and

    (c) a deliberate omission shall be treated as done when the person in question decided upon it,

and in the absence of evidence establishing the contrary a person shall be taken for the purposes of this section to decide upon an omission when he does an act inconsistent with doing the omitted act or, if he has done no such inconsistent act, when the period expires within which he might reasonably have been expected to do the omitted act if it was to be done.   **[161]**

NOTES
    Sub-s (2): words in square brackets substituted by the Race Relations Act 1976, s 79(4), Sch 4, para 8(a).
    Sub-s (3): substituted by the Race Relations Act 1976, s 79(4), Sch 4, para 8(b).

PART VIII

SUPPLEMENTAL

77 Validity and revision of contracts

(1) A term of a contract is void where—

    (a) its inclusion renders the making of the contract unlawful by virtue of this Act, or

(b) it is included in furtherance of an act rendered unlawful by this Act, or

(c) it provides for the doing of an act which would be rendered unlawful by this Act.

(2) Subsection (1) does not apply to a term the inclusion of which constitutes, or is in furtherance of, or provides for, unlawful discrimination against a party to the contract, but the term shall be unenforceable against that party.

(3) A term in a contract which purports to exclude or limit any provision of this Act or the Equal Pay Act 1970 is unenforceable by any person in whose favour the term would operate apart from this subsection.

(4) Subsection (3) does not apply—

(a) to a contract settling a complaint to which section 63(1) of this Act or section 2 of the Equal Pay Act 1970 applies where the contract is made with the assistance of a conciliation officer;

(b) to a contract settling a claim to which section 66 applies.

(5) On the application of any person interested in a contract to which subsection (2) applies, a county court or sheriff court may make such order as it thinks just for removing or modifying any term made unenforceable by that subsection; but such an order shall not be made unless all persons affected have been given notice of the application (except where under rules of court notice may be dispensed with) and have been afforded an opportunity to make representations to the court.

(6) An order under subsection (5) may include provision as respects any period before the making of the order. **[162]**

NOTES

Sub-s (4): para (aa) inserted by the Trade Union Reform and Employment Rights Act 1993, s 39(2), Sch 6, para 1(a), as from 30 August 1993 (SI 1993/1908), as follows—

"(aa) to a contract settling a complaint to which section 63(1) of this Act or section 2 of the Equal Pay Act 1970 applies if the conditions regulating compromise contracts under this Act are satisfied in relation to the contract;".

Sub-ss (4A)–(4C): inserted by the Trade Union Reform and Employment Rights Act 1993, s 39(2), Sch 6, para 1(b), as from 30 August 1993 (SI 1993/1908), as follows—

"(4A) The conditions regulating compromise contracts under this Act are that—

(a) the contract must be in writing;

(b) the contract must relate to the particular complaint;

(c) the complainant must have received independent legal advice from a qualified lawyer as to the terms and effect of the proposed contract and in particular its effect on his ability to pursue his complaint before an industrial tribunal;

(d) there must be in force, when the adviser gives the advice, a policy of insurance covering the risk of a claim by the complainant in respect of loss arising in consequence of the advice;

(e) the contract must identify the adviser; and

(f) the contract must state that the conditions regulating compromise contracts under this Act are satisfied.

(4B) In subsection (4A)—

"independent", in relation to legal advice to the complainant, means that it is given by a lawyer who is not acting for the other party or for a person who is connected with that other party; and

"qualified lawyer" means—

(a) as respects proceedings in England and Wales—

(i) a barrister, whether in practice as such or employed to give legal advice, or

(ii) a solicitor of the Supreme Court who holds a practising certificate;

(b) as respects proceedings in Scotland—

(i) an advocate, whether in practice as such or employed to give legal advice, or

(ii) a solicitor who holds a practising certificate.

(4C) For the purposes of subsection (4B) any two persons are to be treated as "connected" if one is a company of which the other (directly or indirectly) has control, or if both are companies of which a third person (directly or indirectly) has control.".

78, 79 (*Relate to education; outside the scope of this work.*)

80 Power to amend certain provisions of Act

(1) The Secretary of State may by an order the draft of which has been approved by each House of Parliament—

    (a) amend any of the following provisions, namely, sections 6(3), 7, 19, 20(1), (2) and (3), 31(2), 32, 34, 35 and 43 to 48 (including any such provision as amended by a previous order under this subsection);

    (b) amend or repeal any of the following provisions, namely, sections 11(4), 12(4), 33 and 49 (including any such provision as amended by a previous order under this subsection);

    (c) amend Part II, III or IV so as to render lawful an act which, apart from the amendment, would be unlawful by reason of section 6(1) or (2), 29(1), 30 or 31;

    (d) ...

(2) The Secretary of State shall not lay before Parliament the draft of an order under subsection (1) unless he has consulted the Commission about the contents of the draft.

(3) An order under subsection (1)(c) may make such amendments to the list of provisions given in subsection (1)(a) as in the opinion of the Secretary of State are expedient having regard to the contents of the order. **[163]**

NOTES

Sub-s (1): para (d) repealed by the Sex Discrimination Act 1986, s 9(2), Schedule, Pt II.

The only relevant orders made to date under this section amend ss 20 (SI 1983/1202) and 43 (SI 1977/528). See those sections respectively for details.

81 Orders

(1) Any power of the Secretary of State to make orders under the provisions of this Act (except sections . . . 27, . . . and 59(2)) shall be exercisable by statutory instrument.

(2) An order made by the Secretary of State under the preceding provisions of this Act (except sections . . . 27, ..., 59(2) and 80(1)) shall be subject to annulment in pursuance of a resolution of either House of Parliament.

(3) Subsections (1) and (2) do not apply to an order under section 78 or 79, but—

    (a) an order under section 78 which modifies an enactment, and

    (b) any order under section 79 other than one which relates to an endowment to which section [115 of the Education (Scotland) Act 1980] (small endowments) applies,

shall be made by statutory instrument subject to annulment in pursuance of a resolution of either House of Parliament.

(4) An order under this Act may make different provision in relation to different cases or classes of case, may exclude certain cases or classes of case, and may contain transitional provisions and savings.

(5) Any power conferred by this Act to make orders includes power (exercisable in the like manner and subject to the like conditions) to vary or revoke any order so made. **[164]**

NOTE

Sub-ss (1), (2): first words in both subsections omitted repealed by the Employment Act 1989, s 29(4), Sch 7, Pt II; second words in both subsections omitted repealed by the Sex Discrimination Act 1986, s 9(2), Schedule, Pt I.

Sub-s (3): words in square brackets substituted by the Education (Scotland) Act 1980, s 136(2), Sch 4, para 10.

82 General interpretation provisions

(1) In this Act, unless the context otherwise requires—

"access" shall be construed in accordance with section 50;

"act" includes a deliberate omission;

"advertisement" includes every form of advertisement, whether to the public or not, and whether in a newspaper or other publication, by television or radio, by display of notices, signs, labels, showcards or goods, by distribution of samples, circulars, catalogues, price lists or other material by exhibition of pictures, models or films, or in any other way, and references to the publishing of advertisements shall be construed accordingly;

"associated employer" shall be construed in accordance with subsection (2);

["board of management", in relation to a self-governing school, has the same meaning as in the Education (Scotland) Act 1980;]

["Board of management" in relation to a college of further education within the meaning of Part I of the Further and Higher Education (Scotland) Act 1992, has the same meaning as in that Part;]

"the Commission" means the Equal Opportunities Commission;

"Commissioner" means a member of the Commission;

. . . . .

"designate" shall be construed in accordance with subsection (3);

"discrimination" and related terms shall be construed in accordance with section 5(1);

"dispose", in relation to premises, includes granting a right to occupy the premises, and any reference to acquiring premises shall be construed accordingly;

"education" includes any form of training or instruction;

"education authority" and "educational establishment" in relation to Scotland have the same meaning as they have respectively in section [135(1) of the Education (Scotland) Act 1980];

"employment" means employment under a contract of service or of apprenticeship or a contract personally to execute any work or labour, and related expressions shall be construed accordingly;

"employment agency" means a person who, for profit or not, provides services for the purpose of finding employment for workers or supplying employers with workers;

"equality clause" has the meaning given in section 1(2) of the Equal Pay Act 1970 (as set out in section 8(1) of this Act);

"estate agent" means a person who, by way of profession or trade, provides services for the purpose of finding premises for persons seeking to acquire them or assisting in the disposal of premises;

"final" shall be construed in accordance with subsection (4);

"firm" has the meaning given by section 4 of the Partnership Act 1890;

"formal investigation" means an investigation under section 57;

"further education" has the meaning given by [section 41(3) of the Education

Act 1944 as read with section 14 of the Further and Higher Education Act 1992] and in Scotland has the meaning given by section [135(1) of the Education (Scotland) Act 1980];

"general notice", in relation to any person, means a notice published by him at a time and a manner appearing to him suitable for securing that the notice is seen within a reasonable time by persons likely to be affected by it;

"genuine occupational qualification" shall be construed in accordance with section 7(2);

"Great Britain" includes such of the territorial waters of the United Kingdom as are adjacent to Great Britain;

"independent school" has the meaning given by section 114(1) of the Education Act 1944 and in Scotland has the meaning given by section [135(1) of the Education (Scotland) Act 1980];

. . . . .

"man" includes a male of any age;

"managers" has the same meaning for Scotland as in section [135(1) of the Education (Scotland) Act 1980];

"near relative" shall be construed in accordance with subsection (5);

"non-discrimination notice" means a notice under section 67;

"notice" means a notice in writing;

"prescribed" means prescribed by regulations made by the Secretary of State by statutory instrument;

"profession" includes any vocation or occupation;

"proprietor", in relation to any school, has the meaning given by section 114(1) of the Education Act 1944 and in Scotland has the meaning given by section [135(1) of the Education (Scotland) Act 1980];

"pupil", in Scotland, includes a student of any age;

"retirement" includes retirement (whether voluntary or not) on grounds of age, length of service or incapacity;

"school" has the meaning given by section 114(1) of the Education Act 1944, and in Scotland has the meaning given by section [135(1) of the Education (Scotland) Act 1980];

"school education" has the same meaning given by section [135(1) of the Education (Scotland) Act 1980];

["self-governing school" has the same meaning as in the Education (Scotland) Act 1980;]

"trade" includes any business;

"training" includes any form of education or instruction;

"university" includes a university college and the college, school or hall of a university;

"upper limit of compulsory school age" means, subject to section 9 of the Education Act 1962, the age that is that limit by virtue of section 35 of the Education Act 1944 and the Order in Council made under that section;

"woman" includes a female of any age.

[(1A) References in this Act to the dismissal of a person from employment or to the expulsion of a person from a position as partner include references—

(a) to the termination of that person's employment or partnership by the expiration of any period (including a period expiring by reference to an event or circumstance), not being a termination immediately after which the employment or partnership is renewed on the same terms; and

(b) to the termination of that person's employment or partnership by any act of his (including the giving of notice) in circumstances such that he is entitled to terminate it without notice by reason of the conduct of the employer or, as the case may be, the conduct of the other partners.]

(2) For the purposes of this Act two employers are to be treated as associated if one is a company of which the other (directly or indirectly) has control or if both are companies of which a third person (directly or indirectly) has control.

(3) Any power conferred by this Act to designate establishments or persons may be exercised either by naming them or by identifying them by reference to a class or other description.

(4) For the purposes of this Act a non-discrimination notice or a finding by a court or tribunal becomes final when an appeal against the notice or finding is dismissed, withdrawn or abandoned or when the time for appealing expires without an appeal having been brought; and for this purpose an appeal against a non-discrimination notice shall be taken to be dismissed if, notwithstanding that a requirement of the notice is quashed on appeal, a direction is given in respect of it under section 68(3).

(5) For the purposes of this Act a person is a near relative of another if that person is the wife or husband, or parent or child, a grandparent or grandchild, or a brother or sister of the other (whether of full blood or half-blood or by affinity), and "child" includes an illegitimate child and the wife or husband of an illegitimate child.

(6) Except so far as the context otherwise requires, any reference in this Act to an enactment shall be construed as a reference to that enactment as amended by or under any other enactment including this Act.

(7) In this Act, except where otherwise indicated—

(a) a reference to a numbered Part, section or Schedule is a reference to the Part or section of, or the Schedule to, this Act so numbered, and

(b) a reference in a section to a numbered subsection is a reference to the subsection of that section so numbered, and

(c) a reference in a section, subsection or Schedule to a numbered paragraph is a reference to the paragraph of that section, subsection or Schedule so numbered, and

(d) a reference to any provision of an Act (including this Act) includes a Schedule incorporated in the Act by that provision. [165]

NOTES

Sub-s (1): first definition "board of management" inserted by the Self-Governing Schools etc (Scotland) Act 1989, s 82(1), Sch 10, para 5(1), (4); second definition "Board of management" inserted by the Further and Higher Education (Scotland) Act 1992, s 62, Sch 9, para 4(5); definition "conciliation officer" repealed by the Employment Protection Act 1975, s 125(3), Sch 18; in definition "further education", first words in square brackets substituted by the Further and Higher Education Act 1992, s 93, Sch 8, Pt II, para 82; definition "industrial tribunal" repealed by the Industrial Training Act 1982, s 20, Sch 3, para 5(b), Sch 4; definition "self-governing school" inserted by the Self-Governing Schools etc (Scotland) Act 1989, s 82(1), Sch 10, para 5(4); definition "upper limit of compulsory school age" repealed as from a day to be appointed by the Education Act 1993, s 307(1), Sch 19, para 60, Sch 21, Pt II. All other amendments made by the Education (Scotland) Act 1980, s 136(2), Sch 4, para 11.

Sub-s (1A): added by the Sex Discrimination Act 1986, s 2.

Modified, in relation to governing bodies with delegated budgets, by the Education (Modification of Enactments Relating to Employment) Order 1989, SI 1989/901, art 3, Schedule.

83 Transitional and commencement provisions, amendments and repeals

(1) The provisions of Schedule 4 shall have effect for making transitional provision for the purposes of this Act.

(2) Parts II to VII shall come into operation on such day as the Secretary of State may by order appoint, and different days may be so appointed for different provisions and for different purposes.

(3) Subject to subsection (4)—

   (a) the enactments specified in Schedule 5 shall have effect subject to the amendments specified in that Schedule (being minor amendments or amendments consequential on the preceding provisions of this Act), and

   (b) the enactments specified in Schedule 6 are hereby repealed to the extent shown in column 3 of that Schedule.

(4) The Secretary of State shall by order provide for the coming into operation of the amendments contained in Schedule 5 and the repeals contained in Schedule 6, and those amendments and repeals shall have effect only as provided by an order so made.

(5) An order under this section may make such transitional provision as appears to the Secretary of State to be necessary or expedient in connection with the provisions thereby brought into operation, including such adaptations of those provisions, or of any provisions of this Act then in operation, as appear to the Secretary of State necessary or expedient in consequence of the partial operation of this Act.   **[166]**

84 Financial provisions

There shall be defrayed out of money provided by Parliament—

   (a) sums required by the Secretary of State for making payments under paragraph 5 or 14 of Schedule 3, and for defraying any other expenditure falling to be made by him under or by virtue of this Act;

   (b) payments falling to be made under section 66(6)(b) or (7) in respect of the remuneration of assessors; and

   (c) any increase attributable to the provisions of this Act in the sums payable out of money provided by Parliament under any other Act.   **[167]**

85 Application to Crown

(1) This Act applies—

   (a) to an act done by or for purposes of a Minister of the Crown or government department, or

   (b) to an act done on behalf of the Crown by a statutory body, or a person holding a statutory office,

as it applies to an act done by a private person.

(2) Parts II and IV apply to—

   (a) service for purposes of a Minister of the Crown or government department, other than service of a person holding a statutory office, or

   (b) service on behalf of the Crown for purposes of a person holding a statutory office or purposes of a statutory body,

as they apply to employment by a private person, and shall so apply as if references to a contract of employment included references to the terms of service.

(3) Subsections (1) and (2) have effect subject to section 17.

(4) Subsections (1) and (2) do not apply in relation to service in—

   (a) the naval, military or air forces of the Crown, . . .

   (b) . . .

(5) Nothing in this Act shall render unlawful discrimination in admission to the Army Cadet Force, Air Training Corps, Sea Cadet Corps or Combined Cadet Force,

or any other cadet training corps for the time being administered by the Ministry of Defence.

(6) This Act (except section 8(1) and (6)) does not apply to employment in the case of which the employee may be required to serve in support of a force . . . mentioned in subsection (4) . . .

(7) Subsection (2) of section 10 shall have effect in relation to any ship, aircraft or hovercraft belonging to or possessed by Her Majesty in right of the Government of the United Kingdom as it has effect in relation to a ship, aircraft or hovercraft mentioned in paragraph (a) or (b) of that subsection, and section 10(5) shall apply accordingly.

(8) The provisions of Parts II to IV of the Crown Proceedings Act 1947 shall apply to proceedings against the Crown under this Act as they apply to proceedings in England and Wales which by virtue of section 23 of that Act are treated for the purposes of Part II of that Act as civil proceedings by or against the Crown, except that in their application to proceedings under this Act section 20 of that Act (removal of proceedings from county court to High Court) shall not apply.

(9) The provisions of Part V of the Crown Proceedings Act 1947 shall apply to proceedings against the Crown under this Act as they apply to proceedings in Scotland which by virtue of the said Part are treated as civil proceedings by or against the Crown, except that in their application to proceedings under this Act the proviso to section 44 of that Act (removal of proceedings from the sheriff court to the Court of Session) shall not apply.

(10) In this section "statutory body" means a body set up by or in pursuance of an enactment, and "statutory office" means an office so set up; and service "for purposes of" a Minister of the Crown or government department does not include service in any office in Schedule 2 (Ministerial offices) to the House of Commons Disqualification Act 1975 as for the time being in force. **[168]**

NOTE

Sub-ss (4), (6): words omitted repealed by the Armed Forces Act 1981, s 28(2), Sch 5, Pt I.

[85A Application to House of Commons staff

(1) Parts II and IV apply to an act done by an employer of a relevant member of the House of Commons staff, and to service as such a member, as they apply to an act done by and to service for the purposes of a Minister of the Crown or government department, and accordingly apply as if references to a contract of employment included references to the terms of service of such a member.

(2) In this section "relevant member of the House of Commons staff" has the same meaning as in section 139 of the Employment Protection (Consolidation) Act 1978; and subsections (4) to (9) of that section (person to be treated as employer of House of Commons staff) apply, with any necessary modifications, for the purposes of Parts II and IV as they apply by virtue of this section.] **[169]**

NOTE

Inserted by the Trade Union and Labour Relations (Consolidation) Act 1992, s 300(2), Sch 2, para 6.

[85B Application to House of Lords staff

(1) Parts II and IV apply in relation to employment as a relevant member of the House of Lords staff as they apply in relation to other employment.

(2) In this section "relevant member of the House of Lords staff" has the same meaning as in section 139A of the Employment Protection (Consolidation) Act 1978; and subsection (6) of that section applies for the purposes of this section.] **[169A]**

NOTE
Inserted by the Trade Union Reform and Employment Rights Act 1993, s 49(1), Sch 7, para 9, as from a day to be appointed.

86 Government appointments outside section 6

(1) This section applies to any appointment by a Minister of the Crown or government department to an office or post where section 6 does not apply in relation to the appointment.

(2) In making the appointment, and in making the arrangements for determining who should be offered the office or post, the Minister of the Crown or government department shall not do an act which would be unlawful under section 6 if the Crown were the employer for the purposes of this Act. **[170]**

87 Short title and extent

(1) This Act may be cited as the Sex Discrimination Act 1975.

(2) This Act (except paragraph 16 of Schedule 3) does not extend to Northern Ireland. **[171]**

SCHEDULES

(Schs 1 (amendments to the Equal Pay Act 1970), 2 (transitional exemption orders in education) omitted.)

SCHEDULE 3
Section 53

EQUAL OPPORTUNITIES COMMISSION

Incorporation and status

1. On the appointment by the Secretary of State of the first Commissioners, the Commission shall come into existence as a body corporate with perpetual succession and a common seal.

2.—(1) The Commission is not an emanation of the Crown, and shall not act or be treated as the servant or agent of the Crown.

(2) Accordingly—

  (a) neither the Commission nor a Commissioner or member of its staff as such is entitled to any status, immunity, privilege or exemption enjoyed by the Crown;
  (b) the Commissioners and members of the staff of the Commission as such are not civil servants; and
  (c) the Commission's property is not property of, or held on behalf of, the Crown.

Tenure of office of Commissioners

3.—(1) A Commissioner shall hold and vacate his office in accordance with the terms of his appointment.

(2) A person shall not be appointed a Commissioner for more than five years.

(3) With the consent of the Commissioner concerned, the Secretary of State may alter the terms of an appointment so as to make a full-time Commissioner into a part-time Commissioner or vice versa, or for any other purpose.

(4) A Commissioner may resign by notice to the Secretary of State.

(5) The Secretary of State may terminate the appointment of a Commissioner if satisfied that—

    (a) without the consent of the Commission, he failed to attend the meetings of the Commission during a continuous period of six months beginning not earlier than nine months before the termination; or

    (b) he is an undischarged bankrupt, or has made an arrangement with his creditors, or is insolvent within the meaning of paragraph 9(2) of Schedule 3 to the Conveyancing and Feudal Reform (Scotland) Act 1970; or

    (c) he is by reason of physical or mental illness, or for any other reason, incapable of carrying out his duties.

(6) Past service as a Commissioner is no bar to re-appointment.

Tenure of office of chairman and deputy chairmen

4.—(1) The chairman and each deputy chairman shall hold and vacate his office in accordance with the terms of his appointment, and may resign by notice to the Secretary of State.

(2) The office of the chairman or a deputy chairman is vacated if he ceases to be a Commissioner.

(3) Past service as chairman or a deputy chairman is no bar to re-appointment.

Remuneration of Commissioners

5. The Secretary of State may pay, or make such payments towards the provision of, such remuneration, pensions, allowances or gratuities to or in respect of the Commissioners or any of them as, with the consent of the Minister for the Civil Service, he may determine.

6. Where a person ceases to be a Commissioner otherwise than on the expiry of his term of office, and it appears to the Secretary of State that there are special circumstances which make it right for that person to receive compensation, the Secretary of State may with the consent of the Minister for the Civil Service direct the Commission to make to that person a payment of such amount as, with the consent of that Minister, the Secretary of State may determine.

Additional Commissioners

7.—(1) Paragraphs 2(2), 3(1) and (6), and 6 shall apply to additional Commissioners appointed under section 57(2) as they apply to Commissioners.

(2) The Commission may pay, or make such payments towards the provision of, such remuneration, pensions, allowances or gratuities to or in respect of an additional Commissioner as the Secretary of State, with the consent of the Minister for the Civil Service, may determine.

(3) With the approval of the Secretary of State and the consent of the additional Commissioner concerned, the Commission may alter the terms of an appointment of an additional Commissioner so as to make a full-time additional Commissioner into a part-time additional Commissioner or vice versa, or for any other purpose.

(4) An additional Commissioner may resign by notice to the Commission.

(5) The Secretary of State, or the Commission acting with the approval of the Secretary of State, may terminate the appointment of an additional Commissioner if satisfied that—

    (a) without reasonable excuse he failed to carry out the duties for which he was appointed during a continuous period of three months beginning not earlier than six months before the termination; or

(b)   he is a person such as is mentioned in paragraph 3(5)(b); or
(c)   he is by reason of physical or mental illness, or for any other reason, incapable of carrying out his duties.

(6) The appointment of an additional Commissioner shall terminate at the conclusion of the investigation for which he was appointed, if not sooner.

Staff

8. The Commission may, after consultation with the Secretary of State, appoint such officers and servants as they think fit, subject to the approval of the Minister for the Civil Service as to numbers and as to remuneration and other terms and conditions of service.

9.—(1) Employment with the Commission shall be included among the kinds of employment to which a superannuation scheme under section 1 of the Superannuation Act 1972 can apply, and accordingly in Schedule 1 to that Act (in which those kinds of employment are listed) the words "Equal Opportunities Commission" shall be inserted at the appropriate place in alphabetical order.

(2) Where a person who is employed by the Commission and is by reference to that employment a participant in a scheme under section 1 of the Superannuation Act 1972 becomes a Commissioner or an additional Commissioner, the Minister for the Civil Service may determine that his service as a Commissioner or additional Commissioner shall be treated for the purposes of the scheme as service as an employee of the Commission; and his rights under the scheme shall not be affected by paragraph 5 or 7(2).

10. The Employers' Liability (Compulsory Insurance) Act 1969 shall not require insurance to be effected by the Commission.

Proceedings and business

11.—(1) Subject to the provisions of this Act, the Commission may make arrangements for the regulation of their proceedings and business, and may vary or revoke those arrangements.

(2) The arrangements may, with the approval of the Secretary of State, provide for the discharge under the general direction of the Commission of any of the Commission's functions by a committee of the Commission, or by two or more Commissioners.

(3) Anything done by or in relation to a committee, or Commissioners, in the discharge of the Commission's functions shall have the same effect as if done by or in relation to the Commission.

12. The validity of any proceedings of the Commission shall not be affected by any vacancy among the members of the Commission or by any defect in the appointment of any Commissioner or additional Commissioner.

13. The quorum for meetings of the Commission shall in the first instance be determined by a meeting of the Commission attended by not less than five Commissioners.

Finance

14. The Secretary of State shall pay to the Commission expenses incurred or to be incurred by it under paragraphs 6, 7 and 8, and, with the consent of the Minister for the Civil Service and the Treasury, shall pay to the Commission such sums as the Secretary of State thinks fit for enabling the Commission to meet other expenses.

[15.—(1) The accounting year of the Commission shall be the twelve months ending on 31st March.

(2) It shall be the duty of the Commission—
(a)   to keep proper accounts and proper records in relation to the accounts;
(b)   to prepare in respect of each accounting year a statement of accounts in such form as the Secretary of State may direct with the approval of the Treasury; and
(c)   to send copies of the statement to the Secretary of State and the Comptroller and

Auditor General before the end of the month of November next following the accounting year to which the statement relates.

(3) The Comptroller and Auditor General shall examine, certify and report on each statement received by him in pursuance of this Schedule and shall lay copies of each statement and of his report before each House of Parliament.]

[Disqualification Acts]

16. ... **[172]**

NOTE
Para 15: substituted by the Race Relations Act 1976, s 79(4), Sch 4, para 9.
Para 16: amends the House of Commons Disqualification Act 1975, Sch 1, Pts II, III, and the Northern Ireland Assembly Disqualification Act 1975, Sch 1, Pts II, III.

SCHEDULE 4

Section 83

TRANSITIONAL PROVISIONS

1, 2. ...

3.—(1) Until a date specified by order made by the Secretary of State the courses of training to be undergone by men as a condition of [registration as midwives under the the Nurses, Midwives and Health Visitors Act 1979] must be courses approved in writing by or on behalf of the Secretary of State for the purposes of this paragraph.

(2), (3) ...

(4) An order under this paragraph shall be laid in draft before each House of Parliament, and section 6(1) of the Statutory Instruments Act 1946 (Parliamentary control by negative resolution of draft instruments) shall apply accordingly.

4. ...

5.—(1) Section 6 of the Equal Pay Act 1970 (as amended by paragraph 3 of Schedule 1 to this Act) shall apply as if the references to death or retirement in subsection (1A)(b) of the said section 6 included references to sums payable on marriage in pursuance of a contract of employment made before the passing of this Act, or the commutation, at any time, of the right to such sums.

(2) In relation to service within section 1(8) of the said Act of 1970 (service of the Crown) for the reference in this paragraph to a contract of employment made before the passing of this Act there shall be substituted a reference to terms of service entered into before the passing of this Act. **[173]**

NOTES
Paras 1, 2: spent.
Para 3: words in square brackets in sub-para (1) substituted, and sub-paras (2), (3) repealed, by the Nurses, Midwives and Health Visitors Act 1979, s 23(4), (5), Sch 7, para 26, Sch 8.
Order under para 3: Sex Discrimination (Midwives) (Specified Date) Order 1983, SI 1983/1841 (specifying 1 January 1984 as the specified date).
Para 4: (education) omitted.

(Schs 5, 6 (minor amendments and repeals) omitted.)

RACE RELATIONS ACT 1976
(1976 c 74)

ARRANGEMENT OF SECTIONS

PART I
DISCRIMINATION TO WHICH ACT APPLIES

PART II
DISCRIMINATION IN THE EMPLOYMENT FIELD

Discrimination by employers

Discrimination by other bodies

Police

PART III
DISCRIMINATION IN OTHER FIELDS

Barristers

Advocates

PART IV
OTHER UNLAWFUL ACTS

PART V
CHARITIES

PART VI
GENERAL EXCEPTIONS FROM PARTS II TO IV

PART VII
THE COMMISSION FOR RACIAL EQUALITY

General

Codes of practice

Investigations

PART VIII
ENFORCEMENT

General

Enforcement in employment field

Enforcement of Part III

Non-discrimination notices

PART X
SUPPLEMENTAL

An Act to make fresh provision with respect to discrimination on racial grounds and relations between people of different racial groups; and to make in the Sex Discrimination Act 1975 amendments for bringing provisions in that Act relating to its administration and enforcement into conformity with the corresponding provisions in this Act

[22 November 1976]

NOTE
    Parts of this Act are outside the scope of this work: ss 17–27 (discrimination in fields other than employment) and 67 (designated county courts and sheriff courts). These are omitted, together with s 79 (transitional and commencement provisions, amendments and repeals) and Schs 2 (transitional provisions), 4, 5 (amendments of other Acts; repeals).

PART I
DISCRIMINATION TO WHICH ACT APPLIES

1 Racial discrimination

(1) A person discriminates against another in any circumstances relevant for the purposes of any provision of this Act if—

    (a)   on racial grounds he treats that other less favourably than he treats or would treat other persons; or

    (b)   he applies to that other a requirement or condition which he applies or would apply equally to persons not of the same racial group as that other but—

    (i) which is such that the proportion of persons of the same racial group as that other who can comply with it is considerably smaller than the proportion of persons not of that racial group who can comply with it; and

    (ii) which he cannot show to be justifiable irrespective of the colour, race, nationality or ethnic or national origins of the person to whom it is applied; and

    (iii) which is to the detriment of that other because he cannot comply with it.

(2) It is hereby declared that, for the purposes of this Act, segregating a person from other persons on racial grounds is treating him less favourably than they are treated.   **[174]**

2 Discrimination by way of victimisation

(1) A person ("the discriminator") discriminates against another person ("the person victimised") in any circumstances relevant for the purposes of any provision of this Act if he treats the person victimised less favourably than in those circumstances he treats or would treat other persons, and does so by reason that the person victimised has—

    (a) brought proceedings against the discriminator or any other person under this Act; or

    (b) given evidence or information in connection with proceedings brought by any person against the discriminator or any other person under this Act; or

    (c) otherwise done anything under or by reference to this Act in relation to the discriminator or any other person; or

    (d) alleged that the discriminator or any other person has committed an act which (whether or not the allegation so states) would amount to a contravention of this Act,

or by reason that the discriminator knows that the person victimised intends to do any of those things, or suspects that the person victimised has done, or intends to do, any of them.

(2) Subsection (1) does not apply to treatment of a person by reason of any allegation made by him if the allegation was false and not made in good faith.

                                               [175]

3 Meaning of "racial grounds", "racial group" etc

(1) In this Act, unless the context otherwise requires—

    "racial grounds" means any of the following grounds, namely colour, race nationality or ethnic or national origins;

    "racial group" means a group of persons defined by reference to colour, race, nationality or ethnic or national origins, and references to a person's racial group refer to any racial group into which he falls.

(2) The fact that a racial group comprises two or more distinct racial groups does not prevent it from constituting a particular racial group for the purposes of this Act.

    (3) In this Act—

(a) references to discrimination refer to any discrimination falling within section 1 or 2; and

(b) references to racial discrimination refer to any discrimination falling within section 1,

and related expressions shall be construed accordingly.

(4) A comparison of the case of a person of a particular racial group with that of a person not of that group under section 1(1) must be such that the relevant circumstances in the one case are the same, or not materially different, in the other.

[176]

PART II

DISCRIMINATION IN THE EMPLOYMENT FIELD

Discrimination by employers

4 Discrimination against applicants and employees

(1) It is unlawful for a person, in relation to employment by him at an establishment in Great Britain, to discriminate against another—

(a) in the arrangements he makes for the purpose of determining who should be offered that employment; or

(b) in the terms on which he offers him that employment; or

(c) by refusing or deliberately omitting to offer him that employment.

(2) It is unlawful for a person, in the case of a person employed by him at an establishment in Great Britain, to discriminate against that employee—

(a) in the terms of employment which he affords him; or

(b) in the way he affords him access to opportunities for promotion, transfer or training, or to any other benefits, facilities or services, or by refusing or deliberately omitting to afford him access to them; or

(c) by dismissing him, or subjecting him to any other detriment.

(3) Except in relation to discrimination falling within section 2, subsections (1) and (2) do not apply to employment for the purposes of a private household.

(4) Subsection (2) does not apply to benefits, facilities or services of any description if the employer is concerned with the provision (for payment or not) of benefits, facilities or services of that description to the public, or to a section of the public comprising the employee in question, unless—

(a) that provision differs in a material respect from the provision of the benefits, facilities or services by the employer to his employees; or

(b) the provision of the benefits, facilities or services to the employee in question is regulated by his contract of employment; or

(c) the benefits, facilities or services relate to training. **[177]**

NOTE

Modified, in relation to governing bodies with delegated budgets, by the Education (Modification of Enactments Relating to Employment) Order 1989, SI 1989/901, art 3, Schedule.

5 Exceptions for genuine occupational qualifications

(1) In relation to racial discrimination—

(a) section 4(1)(a) or (c) does not apply to any employment where being of a particular racial group is a genuine occupational qualification for the job; and

(b) section 4(2)(b) does not apply to opportunities for promotion or transfer to, or training for, such employment.

(2) Being of a particular racial group is a genuine occupational qualification for a job only where—

(a) the job involves participation in a dramatic performance or other entertainment in a capacity for which a person of that racial group is required for reasons of authenticity; or

(b) the job involves participation as an artist's or photographic model in the production of a work of art, visual image or sequence of visual images for which a person of that racial group is required for reasons of authenticity; or

(c) the job involves working in a place where food or drink is (for payment or not) provided to and consumed by members of the public or a section of the public in a particular setting for which, in that job, a person of that racial group is required for reasons of authenticity; or

(d) the holder of the job provides persons of that racial group with personal services promoting their welfare, and those services can most effectively be provided by a person of that racial group.

(3) Subsection (2) applies where some only of the duties of the job fall within paragraph (a), (b), (c) or (d) as well as where all of them do.

(4) Paragraph (a), (b), (c) or (d) of subsection (2) does not apply in relation to the filling of a vacancy at a time when the employer already has employees of the racial group in question—

(a) who are capable of carrying out the duties falling within that paragraph; and

(b) whom it would be reasonable to employ on those duties; and

(c) whose numbers are sufficient to meet the employer's likely requirements in respect of those duties without undue inconvenience. **[178]**

NOTE

Modified, in relation to governing bodies with delegated budgets, by the Education (Modification of Enactments Relating to Employment) Order 1989, SI 1989/901, art 3, Schedule.

6 Exception for employment intended to provide training in skills to be exercised outside Great Britain

Nothing in section 4 shall render unlawful any act done by an employer for the benefit of a person not ordinarily resident in Great Britain in or in connection with employing him at an establishment in Great Britain, where the purpose of that employment is to provide him with training in skills which he appears to the employer to intend to exercise wholly outside Great Britain. **[179]**

7 Discrimination against contract workers

(1) This section applies to any work for a person ("the principal") which is available for doing by individuals ("contract workers") who are employed not by the principal himself but by another person, who supplies them under a contract made with the principal.

(2) It is unlawful for the principal, in relation to work to which this section applies, to discriminate against a contract worker—

(a) in the terms on which he allows him to do that work; or

(b) by not allowing him to do it or continue to do it; or

(c) in the way he affords him access to any benefits, facilities or services or by refusing or deliberately omitting to afford him access to them; or

(d) by subjecting him to any other detriment.

(3) The principal does not contravene subsection (2)(b) by doing any act in relation to a person not of a particular racial group at a time when, if the work were to be done by a person taken into the principal's employment, being of that racial group would be a genuine occupational qualification for the job.

(4) Nothing in this section shall render unlawful any act done by the principal for the benefit of a contract worker not ordinarily resident in Great Britain in or in connection with allowing him to do work to which this section applies, where the purpose of his being allowed to do that work is to provide him with training in skills which he appears to the principal to intend to exercise wholly outside Great Britain.

(5) Subsection (2)(c) does not apply to benefits, facilities or services of any description if the principal is concerned with the provision (for payment or not) of benefits, facilities or services of that description to the public, or to a section of the public to which the contract worker in question belongs, unless that provision differs in a material respect from the provision of the benefits, facilities or services by the principal to his contract workers. **[180]**

NOTE
Modified, in relation to governing bodies with delegated budgets, by the Education (Modification of Enactments Relating to Employment) Order 1989, SI 1989/901, art 3, Schedule.

8 Meaning of employment at establishment in Great Britain

(1) For the purposes of this Part ("the relevant purposes"), employment is to be regarded as being at an establishment in Great Britain unless the employee does his work wholly or mainly outside Great Britain.

(2) In relation to—

(a) employment on board a ship registered at a port of registry in Great Britain; or

(b) employment on an aircraft or hovercraft registered in the United Kingdom and operated by a person who has his principal place of business, or is ordinarily resident in Great Britain, other than an aircraft or hovercraft while so operated in pursuance of a contract with a person who has his principal place of business, or is ordinarily resident, outside the United Kingdom,

subsection (1) shall have effect as if the words "or mainly" were omitted.

(3) In the case of employment on board a ship registered at a port of registry in Great Britain (except where the employee does his work wholly outside Great Britain) the ship shall for the relevant purposes be deemed to be the establishment.

(4) Where work is not done at an establishment it shall be treated for the relevant purposes as done at the establishment from which it is done or (where it is not done from any establishment) at the establishment with which it has the closest connection.

(5) In relation to employment concerned with *exploration of the sea bed or subsoil or the exploitation of their natural resources*, Her Majesty may by Order in Council provide that subsections (1) to (3) shall have effect as if in both subsection (1) and subsection (3) the last reference to Great Britain included any area for the time being designated under section 1(7) of the Continental Shelf Act 1964, except an area or part of an area in which the law of Northern Ireland applies.

(6) An Order in Council under subsection (5) may provide that, in relation to the employment to which the Order applies, this Part is to have effect with such modifications as are specified in the Order.

(7) An Order in Council under subsection (5) shall be of no effect unless a draft of the Order has been laid before and approved by resolution of each House of Parliament. **[181]**

NOTES

Sub-s (5): for the words in italics there are substituted the words "any activity falling within section 23(2) of the Oil and Gas (Enterprise) Act 1982", and after "1964" there are inserted the words "or specified under section 22(5) of the Oil and Gas (Enterprise) Act 1982", by the Oil and Gas (Enterprise) Act 1982, s 37, Sch 3, para 36, as from a day to be appointed.

Order under this section: the Race Relations (Offshore Employment) Order 1987, SI 1987/929.

See further the Employment (Continental Shelf) Act 1978, which modifies the territorial effect of this Act.

9 Exception for seamen recruited abroad

(1) Nothing in section 4 shall render unlawful any act done by an employer in or in connection with employment by him on any ship in the case of a person who applied or was engaged for that employment outside Great Britain.

(2) Nothing in section 7 shall, as regards work to which that section applies, render unlawful any act done by the principal in or in connection with such work on any ship in the case of a contract worker who was engaged outside Great Britain by the person by whom he is supplied.

(3) Subsections (1) and (2) do not apply to employment or work concerned with *exploration of the sea bed or subsoil or the exploitation of their natural resources* in any area for the time being designated under section 1(7) of the Continental Shelf Act 1964, not being an area or part of an area in which the law of Northern Ireland applies.

(4) For the purposes of subsection (1) a person brought to Great Britain with a view to his entering into an agreement in Great Britain to be employed on any ship shall be treated as having applied for the employment outside Great Britain. **[182]**

NOTE

Sub-s (3): for the words in italics there are substituted the words "any activity falling within section 23(2) of the Oil and Gas (Enterprise) Act 1982", and after "1964" there are inserted the words "or specified under section 22(5) of the Oil and Gas (Enterprise) Act 1982", by the Oil and Gas (Enterprise) Act 1982, s 37, Sch 3, para 36, as from a day to be appointed.

Discrimination by other bodies

10 Partnerships

(1) It is unlawful for a firm consisting of six or more partners, in relation to a position as partner in the firm, to discriminate against a person—

    (a) in the arrangements they make for the purpose of determining who should be offered that position; or

    (b) in the terms on which they offer him that position; or

    (c) by refusing or deliberately omitting to offer him that position; or

    (d) in a case where the person already holds that position—

        (i) in the way they afford him access to any benefits, facilities or services, or by refusing or deliberately omitting to afford him access to them; or

(ii) by expelling him from that position, or subjecting him to any other detriment.

(2) Subsection (1) shall apply in relation to persons proposing to form themselves into a partnership as it applies in relation to a firm.

(3) Subsection (1)(a) and (c) do not apply to a position as partner where, if it were employment, being of a particular racial group would be a genuine occupational qualification for the job.

(4) In the case of a limited partnership references in this section to a partner shall be construed as references to a general partner as defined in section 3 of the Limited Partnerships Act 1907.   **[183]**

11 Trade unions etc

(1) This section applies to an organisation of workers, an organisation of employers, or any other organisation whose members carry on a particular profession or trade for the purposes of which the organisation exists.

(2) It is unlawful for an organisation to which this section applies, in the case of a person who is not a member of the organisation, to discriminate against him—

(a) in the terms on which it is prepared to admit him to membership; or

(b) by refusing, or deliberately omitting to accept, his application for membership.

(3) It is unlawful for an organisation to which this section applies, in the case of a person who is a member of the organisation, to discriminate against him—

(a) in the way it affords him access to any benefits, facilities or services, or by refusing or deliberately omitting to afford him access to them; or

(b) by depriving him of membership, or varying the terms on which he is a member; or

(c) by subjecting him to any other detriment.   **[184]**

12 Qualifying bodies

(1) It is unlawful for an authority or body which can confer an authorisation or qualification which is needed for, or facilitates, engagement in a particular profession or trade to discriminate against a person—

(a) in the terms on which it is prepared to confer on him that authorisation or qualification; or

(b) by refusing, or deliberately omitting to grant, his application for it; or

(c) by withdrawing it from him or varying the terms on which he holds it.

(2) In this section—

(a) "authorisation or qualification" includes recognition, registration, enrolment, approval and certification;

(b) "confer" includes renew or extend.

(3) Subsection (1) does not apply to discrimination which is rendered unlawful by section 17 or 18.   **[185]**

[13 Persons concerned with provision of vocational training

(1) It is unlawful, in the case of an individual seeking or undergoing training which would help fit him for any employment, for any person who provides, or makes

arrangements for the provision of, facilities for such training to discriminate against him—

    (a) in the terms on which that person affords him access to any training course or other facilities concerned with such training; or

    (b) by refusing or deliberately omitting to afford him such access; or

    (c) by terminating his training; or

    (d) by subjecting him to any detriment during the course of his training.

  (2) Subsection (1) does not apply to—

    (a) discrimination which is rendered unlawful by section 4(1) or (2) or section 17 or 18; or

    (b) discrimination which would be rendered unlawful by any of those provisions but for the operation of any other provision of this Act.]

                                                                 [186]

NOTE

Substituted by the Employment Act 1989, s 7(2).

14 Employment agencies

(1) It is unlawful for an employment agency to discriminate against a person—

    (a) in the terms on which the agency offers to provide any of its services; or

    (b) by refusing or deliberately omitting to provide any of its services; or

    (c) in the way it provides any of its services.

  (2) It is unlawful for a local education authority or an education authority to do any act in the performance of its functions under section 8 of the Employment and Training Act 1973 which constitutes discrimination.

  (3) References in subsection (1) to the services of an employment agency include guidance on careers and any other services related to employment.

  (4) This section does not apply if the discrimination only concerns employment which the employer could lawfully refuse to offer the person in question.

  (5) An employment agency or local education authority *or an education authority* shall not be subject to any liability under this section if it proves—

    (a) that it acted in reliance on a statement made to it by the employer to the effect that, by reason of the operation of subsection (4), its action would not be unlawful; and

    (b) that it was reasonable for it to rely on the statement.

  (6) A person who knowingly or recklessly makes a statement such as is referred to in subsection (5)(a) which in a material respect is false or misleading commits an offence, and shall be liable on summary conviction to a fine not exceeding [level 5 on the standard scale].   **[187]**

NOTES

    Sub-s (2): substituted by the Trade Union Reform and Employment Rights Act 1993, s 49(2), Sch 8, para 9(a), as from a day to be appointed, as follows—

    "(2) It is unlawful for a local education authority or education authority or any other person to do any act in providing services in pursuance of arrangements made, or a direction given, under section 10 of the Employment and Training Act 1973 which constitutes discrimination.".

    Sub-s (5): for the words in italics there are substituted the words ", education authority or other person" by the Trade Union Reform and Employment Rights Act 1993, s 49(2), Sch 8, para 9(b), as from a day to be appointed.

    Sub-s (6): maximum fine increased and converted to a level on the standard scale by the Criminal Justice Act 1982, ss 37, 38, 46.

15 Manpower Services Commission etc

[(1) It is unlawful for the [Secretary of State . . .] to discriminate in the provision of facilities or services under section 2 of the Employment and Training Act 1973.]

[(1A) It is unlawful for Scottish Enterprise or Highlands and Islands Enterprise to discriminate in the provision of facilities or services under such arrangements as are mentioned in section 2(3) of the Enterprise and New Towns (Scotland) Act 1990 (arrangements analogous to arrangements in pursuance of section 2 of the said Act of 1973).]

(2) This section does not apply in a case where—

(a) section 13 applies; or

(b) the [Secretary of State] is acting as an employment agency. **[188]**

NOTES

Sub-s (1): substituted by the Employment and Training Act 1981, s 9, Sch 2, Pt II, para 20; amendment in square brackets made by the Employment Act 1988, s 33, Sch 3, Pt II, para 12(2); words omitted repealed by the Employment Act 1989, s 29(4), Sch 7, Pt I.

Sub-s (1A): added by the Enterprise and New Towns (Scotland) Act 1990, s 18.

Sub-s (2): words in square brackets substituted by the Employment Act 1989, s 29(3), Sch 6, para 15.

Police

16 Police

(1) For the purposes of this Part, the holding of the office of constable shall be treated as employment—

(a) by the chief officer of police as respects any act done by him in relation to a constable or that office;

(b) by the police authority as respects any act done by them in relation to a constable or that office.

(2) There shall be paid out of the police fund—

(a) any compensation, costs or expenses awarded against a chief officer of police in any proceedings brought against him under this Act, and any costs or expenses incurred by him in any such proceedings so far as not recovered by him in the proceedings; and

(b) any sum required by a chief officer of police for the settlement of any claim made against him under this Act if the settlement is approved by the police authority.

(3) Any proceedings under this Act which, by virtue of subsection (1), would lie against a chief officer of police shall be brought against the chief officer of police for the time being or, in the case of a vacancy in that office, against the person for the time being performing the functions of that office; and references in subsection (2) to the chief officer of police shall be construed accordingly.

(4) Subsection (1) applies to a police cadet and appointment as a police cadet as it applies to a constable and the office of constable.

(5) In this section—

"chief officer of police"—

(a) in relation to a person appointed, or an appointment falling to be made, under a specified Act, has the same meaning as in the Police Act,

(b) in relation to any other person or appointment, means the officer who has the direction and control of the body of constables or cadets in question;

"the Police Act" means, for England and Wales, the Police Act 1964 or, for Scotland, the Police (Scotland) Act 1967;

"police authority"—

(a) in relation to a person appointed, or an appointment falling to be made, under a specified Act, has the same meaning as in the Police Act,

(b) in relation to any other person or appointment, means the authority by whom the person in question is or on appointment would be paid;

"police cadet" means any person appointed to undergo training with a view to becoming a constable;

"police fund" in relation to a chief officer of police within paragraph (a) of the above definition of that term has the same meaning as in the Police Act, and in any other case means money provided by the police authority;

"specified Act" means the Metropolitan Police Act 1829, the City of London Police Act 1839 or the Police Act. **[189]**

PART III

DISCRIMINATION IN OTHER FIELDS

17–26 (*Outside the scope of this work.*)

[Barristers

26A Discrimination by, or in relation to, barristers

(1) It is unlawful for a barrister or barrister's clerk, in relation to any offer of a pupillage or tenancy, to discriminate against a person—

(a) in the arrangements which are made for the purpose of determining to whom it should be offered;

(b) in respect of any terms on which it is offered; or

(c) by refusing, or deliberately omitting, to offer it to him.

(2) It is unlawful for a barrister or barrister's clerk, in relation to a pupil or tenant in the chambers in question, to discriminate against him—

(a) in respect of any terms applicable to him as a pupil or tenant;

(b) in the opportunities for training, or gaining experience, which are afforded or denied to him;

(c) in the benefits, facilities or services which are afforded or denied to him; or

(d) by terminating his pupillage or by subjecting him to any pressure to leave the chambers or other detriment.

(3) It is unlawful for any person, in relation to the giving, withholding or acceptance of instructions to a barrister, to discriminate against any person.

(4) In this section—

"barrister's clerk" includes any person carrying out any of the functions of a barrister's clerk; and

"pupil", "pupillage", "tenancy" and "tenant" have the meaning commonly associated with their use in the context of a set of barristers' chambers.

(5) This section does not apply to Scotland.] **[189A]**

NOTE

Commencement: 1 January 1991.

Inserted with savings by the Courts and Legal Services Act 1990, s 64(2); for savings see Sch 19, para 1 thereof.

[Advocates

26B Discrimination by, or in relation to, advocates

(1) It is unlawful for an advocate, in relation to taking any person as his pupil, to discriminate against a person—

(a) in the arrangements which he makes for the purpose of determining whom he will take as his pupil;

(b) in respect of any terms on which he offers to take any person as his pupil; or

(c) by refusing, or deliberately omitting, to take a person as his pupil.

(2) It is unlawful for an advocate, in relation to a person who is a pupil, to discriminate against him—

(a) in respect of any terms applicable to him as a pupil;

(b) in the opportunities for training, or gaining experience, which are afforded or denied to him;

(c) in the benefits, facilities or services which are afforded or denied to him; or

(d) by terminating her the relationship or by subjecting him to any pressure to terminate the relationship or other detriment.

(3) It is unlawful for any person, in relation to the giving, withholding or acceptance of instructions to an advocate, to discriminate against any person.

(4) In this section—

"advocate" means a member of the Faculty of Advocates practising as such; and

"pupil"has the meaning commonly associated its use in the context of a person training to be an advocate.

(5) Section 3 applies for the purposes of this section as it applies for the purposes of any provision of Part II.

(6) This section does not apply to England and Wales.] **[189B]**

NOTE
Commencement: 1 January 1991.
Inserted with savings by the Courts and Legal Services Act 1990, s 65(2).

27 (*Outside the scope of this work.*)

PART IV
OTHER UNLAWFUL ACTS

28 Discriminatory practices

(1) In this section "discriminatory practice" means the application of a requirement or condition which results in an act of discrimination which is unlawful by virtue of any provision of Part II or III taken with section 1(1)(b), or which would be likely to result in such an act of discrimination if the persons to whom it is applied included persons of any particular racial group as regards which there has been no occasion for applying it.

(2) A person acts in contravention of this section if and so long as—

(a) he applies a discriminatory practice; or

(b) he operates practices or other arrangements which in any circumstances would call for the application by him of a discriminatory practice.

(3) Proceedings in respect of a contravention of this section shall be brought only by the Commission in accordance with sections 58 to 62. **[190]**

29 Discriminatory advertisements

(1) It is unlawful to publish or to cause to be published an advertisement which indicates, or might reasonably be understood as indicating, an intention by a person to do an act of discrimination, whether the doing of that act by him would be lawful or, by virtue of Part II or III, unlawful.

(2) Subsection (1) does not apply to an advertisement—

(a) if the intended act would be lawful by virtue of any of sections 5, 6, 7(3) and (4), 10(3), 26, 34(2)(b), 35 to 39 and 41; or

(b) if the advertisement relates to the services of an employment agency (within the meaning of section 14(1)) and the intended act only concerns employment which the employer could by virtue of section 5, 6 or 7(3) or (4) lawfully refuse to offer to persons against whom the advertisement indicates an intention to discriminate.

(3) Subsection (1) does not apply to an advertisement which indicates that persons of any class defined otherwise than by reference to colour, race or ethnic or national origins are required for employment outside Great Britain.

(4) The publisher of an advertisement made unlawful by subsection (1) shall not be subject to any liability under that subsection in respect of the publication of the advertisement if he proves—

(a) that the advertisement was published in reliance on a statement made to him by the person who caused it to be published to the effect that, by reason of the operation of subsection (2) or (3), the publication would not be unlawful; and

(b) that it was reasonable for him to rely on the statement.

(5) A person who knowingly or recklessly makes a statement such as is mentioned in subsection (4)(a) which in a material respect is false or misleading commits an offence, and shall be liable on summary conviction to a fine not exceeding [level 5 on the standard scale]. **[191]**

NOTE

Sub-s (5): maximum fine increased and converted to a level on the standard scale by the Criminal Justice Act 1982, ss 37, 38, 46.

30 Instructions to discriminate

It is unlawful for a person—

(a) who has authority over another person; or

(b) in accordance with whose wishes that other person is accustomed to act,

to instruct him to do any act which is unlawful by virtue of Part II or III, or procure or attempt to procure the doing by him of any such act. **[192]**

31 Pressure to discriminate

(1) It is unlawful to induce, or attempt to induce, a person to do any act which contravenes Part II or III.

(2) An attempted inducement is not prevented from falling within subsection (1) because it is not made directly to the person in question, if it is made in such a way that he is likely to hear of it.   **[193]**

32 Liability of employers and principals

(1) Anything done by a person in the course of his employment shall be treated for the purposes of this Act (except as regards offences thereunder) as done by his employer as well as by him, whether or not it was done with the employer's knowledge or approval.

(2) Anything done by a person as agent for another person with the authority (whether express or implied, and whether precedent or subsequent) of that other person shall be treated for the purposes of this Act (except as regards offences thereunder) as done by that other person as well as by him.

(3) In proceedings brought under this Act against any person in respect of an act alleged to have been done by an employee of his it shall be a defence for that person to prove that he took such steps as were reasonably practicable to prevent the employee from doing that act, or from doing in the course of his employment acts of that description.   **[194]**

NOTE

Modified, in relation to governing bodies with delegated budgets, by the Education (Modification of Enactments Relating to Employment) Order 1989, SI 1989/901, art 3, Schedule.

33 Aiding unlawful acts

(1) A person who knowingly aids another person to do an act made unlawful by this Act shall be treated for the purposes of this Act as himself doing an unlawful act of the like description.

(2) For the purposes of subsection (1) an employee or agent for whose act the employer or principal is liable under section 32 (or would be so liable but for section 32(3)) shall be deemed to aid the doing of the act by the employer or principal.

(3) A person does not under this section knowingly aid another to do an unlawful act if—

(a) he acts in reliance on a statement made to him by that other person that, by reason of any provision of this Act, the act which he aids would not be unlawful; and

(b) it is reasonable for him to rely on the statement.

(4) A person who knowingly or recklessly makes a statement such as is mentioned in subsection (3)(a) which in a material respect is false or misleading commits an offence, and shall be liable on summary conviction to a fine not exceeding [level 5 on the standard scale].   **[195]**

NOTE

Sub-s (4): maximum fine increased and converted to a level on the standard scale by the Criminal Justice Act 1982, ss 37, 38, 46.

PART V
CHARITIES

34 Charities

(1) A provision which is contained in a charitable instrument (whenever that instrument took or takes effect) and which provides for conferring benefits on persons of a class defined by reference to colour shall have effect for all purposes as if it provided for conferring the like benefits—

(a) on persons of the class which results if the restriction by reference to colour is disregarded; or

(b) where the original class is defined by reference to colour only, on persons generally;

but nothing in this subsection shall be taken to alter the effect of any provision as regards any time before the coming into operation of this subsection.

(2) Nothing in Parts II to IV shall—

(a) be construed as affecting a provision to which this subsection applies; or

(b) render unlawful an act which is done in order to give effect to such a provision.

(3) Subsection (2) applies to any provision which is contained in a charitable instrument (whenever that instrument took or takes effect) and which provides for conferring benefits on persons of a class defined otherwise than by reference to colour (including a class resulting from the operation of subsection (1)).

(4) In this section "charitable instrument" means an enactment or other instrument passed or made for charitable purposes, or an enactment or other instrument so far as it relates to charitable purposes, and in Scotland includes the governing instrument of an endowment or of an educational endowment as those expressions are defined in section 135(1) of the Education (Scotland) Act 1962.

In the application of this section to England and Wales, "charitable purposes" means purposes which are exclusively charitable according to the law of England and Wales.   **[196]**

NOTE

The definitions referred to in sub-s (4) as being in s 135 of the Education (Scotland) Act 1962 have been repealed and re-enacted in s 122(1) of the Education (Scotland) Act 1980, but no consequential amendment to sub-s (4) has been made.

PART VI
GENERAL EXCEPTIONS FROM PARTS II TO IV

35 Special needs of racial groups in regard to education, training or welfare

Nothing in Parts II to IV shall render unlawful any act done in affording persons of a particular racial group access to facilities or services to meet the special needs of persons of that group in regard to their education, training or welfare, or any ancillary benefits.   **[197]**

36 Provision of education or training for persons not ordinarily resident in Great Britain

Nothing in Parts II to IV shall render unlawful any act done by a person for the benefit of persons not ordinarily resident in Great Britain in affording them access to facilities for education or training or any ancillary benefits, where it appears to him that the persons in question do not intend to remain in Great Britain after their period of education or training there.   **[198]**

37 Discriminatory training by certain bodies

(1) Nothing in Parts II to IV shall render unlawful any act done in relation to particular work by [any person] in or in connection with—

   (a) affording only persons of a particular racial group access to facilities for training which would help to fit them for that work; or
   (b) encouraging only persons of a particular racial group to take advantage of opportunities for doing that work,

where [it reasonably appears to that person] that at any time within the twelve months immediately preceding the doing of the act—

   (i) there were no persons of that group among those doing that work in Great Britain; or
   (ii) the proportion of persons of that group among those doing that work in Great Britain was small in comparison with the proportion of persons of that group among the population of Great Britain.

(2) Where in relation to particular work [it reasonably appears to any person] that although the condition for the operation of subsection (1) is not met for the whole of Great Britain it is met for an area within Great Britain, nothing in Parts II to IV shall render unlawful any act done by [that person] in or in connection with—

   (a) affording persons who are of the racial group in question, and who appear likely to take up that work in that area, access to facilities for training which would help to fit them for that work; or
   (b) encouraging persons of that group to take advantage of opportunities in the area for doing that work.

[(3) The preceding provisions of this section shall not apply to any discrimination which is rendered unlawful by section 4(1) or (2).]   **[199]**

NOTES
Sub-ss (1), (2): words in square brackets substituted by the Employment Act 1989, s 7(3)(a), (b).
Sub-s (3): substituted by the Employment Act 1989, s 7(3)(c).

38 Other discriminatory training etc

(1) Nothing in Parts II to IV shall render unlawful any act done by an employer in relation to particular work in his employment at a particular establishment in Great Britain, being an act done in or in connection with—

   (a) affording only those of his employees working at that establishment who are of a particular racial group access to facilities for training which would help to fit them for that work; or
   (b) encouraging only persons of a particular racial group to take advantage of opportunities for doing that work at that establishment,

where any of the conditions in subsection (2) was satisfied at any time within the twelve months immediately preceding the doing of the act.

(2) Those conditions are—

   (a) that there are no persons of the racial group in question among those doing that work at that establishment; or
   (b) that the proportion of persons of that group among those doing that work

at that establishment is small in comparison with the proportion of persons of that group—

(i) among all those employed by that employer there; or

(ii) among the population of the area from which that employer normally recruits persons for work in his employment at that establishment.

(3) Nothing in section 11 shall render unlawful any act done by an organisation to which that section applies in or in connection with—

(a) affording only members of the organisation who are of a particular racial group access to facilities for training which would help to fit them for holding a post of any kind in the organisation; or

(b) encouraging only members of the organisation who are of a particular racial group to take advantage of opportunities for holding such posts in the organisation,

where either of the conditions in subsection (4) was satisfied at any time within the twelve months immediately preceding the doing of the act.

(4) Those conditions are—

(a) that there are no persons of the racial group in question among persons holding such posts in that organisation; or

(b) that the proportion of persons of that group among those holding such posts in that organisation is small in comparison with the proportion of persons of that group among the members of the organisation.

(5) Nothing in Parts II to IV shall render unlawful any act done by an organisation to which section 11 applies in or in connection with encouraging only persons of a particular racial group to become members of the organisation where at any time within the twelve months immediately preceding the doing of the act—

(a) no persons of that group were members of the organisation; or

(b) the proportion of persons of that group among members of the organisation was small in comparison with the proportion of persons of that group among those eligible for membership of the organisation.

(6) Section 8 (meaning of employment at establishment in Great Britain) shall apply for the purposes of this section as if this section were contained in Part II.

[200]

39 Sports and competitions

Nothing in Parts II to IV shall render unlawful any act whereby a person discriminates against another on the basis of that other's nationality or place of birth or the length of time for which he has been resident in a particular area or place, if the act is done—

(a) in selecting one or more persons to represent a country, place or area, or any related association, in any sport or game; or

(b) in pursuance of the rules of any competition so far as they relate to eligibility to compete in any sport or game. **[201]**

40 Indirect access to benefits etc

(1) References in this Act to the affording by any person of access to benefits, facilities or services are not limited to benefits, facilities or services provided by that person himself, but include any means by which it is in that person's power to

facilitate access to benefits, facilities or services provided by any other person (the "actual provider").

(2) Where by any provision of this Act the affording by any person of access to benefits, facilities or services in a discriminatory way is in certain circumstances prevented from being unlawful, the effect of the provision shall extend also to the liability under this Act of any actual provider.   **[202]**

41 Acts done under statutory authority etc

(1) Nothing in Parts II to IV shall render unlawful any act of discrimination done—

    (a)   in pursuance of any enactment or Order in Council; or

    (b)   in pursuance of any instrument made under any enactment by a Minister of the Crown; or

    (c)   in order to comply with any condition or requirement imposed by a Minister of the Crown (whether before or after the passing of this Act) by virtue of any enactment.

References in this subsection to an enactment, Order in Council or instrument include an enactment, Order in Council or instrument passed or made after the passing of this Act.

(2) Nothing in Parts II to IV shall render unlawful any act whereby a person discriminates against another on the basis of that other's nationality or place of ordinary residence or the length of time for which he has been present or resident in or outside the United Kingdom or an area within the United Kingdom, if that Act is done—

    (a)   in pursuance of any arrangements made (whether before or after the passing of this Act) by or with the approval of, or for the time being approved by, a Minister of the Crown; or

    (b)   in order to comply with any condition imposed (whether before or after the passing of this Act) by a Minister of the Crown.   **[203]**

42 Acts safeguarding national security

Nothing in Parts II to IV shall render unlawful an act done for the purpose of safeguarding national security.   **[204]**

PART VII

THE COMMISSION FOR RACIAL EQUALITY

General

43 Establishment and duties of Commission

(1) There shall be a body of Commissioners named the Commission for Racial Equality consisting of at least eight but not more than fifteen individuals each appointed by the Secretary of State on a full-time or part-time basis, which shall have the following duties—

    (a)   to work towards the elimination of discrimination;

    (b)   to promote equality of opportunity, and good relations, between persons of different racial groups generally; and

    (c)   to keep under review the working of this Act and, when they are so required by the Secretary of State or otherwise think it necessary, draw up and submit to the Secretary of State proposals for amending it.

(2) The Secretary of State shall appoint—

(a) one of the Commissioners to be chairman of the Commission; and

(b) either one or more of the Commissioners (as the Secretary of State thinks fit) to be deputy chairman or deputy chairmen of the Commission.

(3) The Secretary of State may by order amend subsection (1) so far as it regulates the number of Commissioners.

(4) Schedule 1 shall have effect with respect to the Commission.

(5) The Race Relations Board and the Community Relations Commission are hereby abolished.   [205]

44 Assistance to organisations

(1) The Commission may give financial or other assistance to any organisation appearing to the Commission to be concerned with the promotion of equality of opportunity, and good relations, between persons of different racial groups, but shall not give any such financial assistance out of money provided (through the Secretary of State) by Parliament except with the approval of the Secretary of State given with the consent of the Treasury.

(2) Except in so far as other arrangements for their discharge are made and approved under paragraph 13 of Schedule 1—

(a) the Commission's functions under subsection (1); and

(b) other functions of the Commission in relation to matters connected with the giving of such financial or other assistance as is mentioned in that subsection,

shall be discharged under the general direction of the Commission by a committee of the Commission consisting of at least three but not more than five Commissioners, of whom one shall be the deputy chairman or one of the deputy chairmen of the Commission.   [206]

45 Research and education

(1) The Commission may undertake or assist (financially or otherwise) the undertaking by other persons of any research, and any educational activities, which appear to the Commission necessary or expedient for the purposes of section 43(1).

(2) The Commission may make charges for educational or other facilities or services made available by them.   [207]

46 Annual reports

(1) As soon as practicable after the end of each calendar year the Commission shall make to the Secretary of State a report on their activities during the year (an "annual report").

(2) Each annual report shall include a general survey of developments, during the period to which it relates, in respect of matters falling within the scope of the Commission's functions.

(3) The Secretary of State shall lay a copy of every annual report before each House of Parliament, and shall cause the report to be published. **[208]**

Codes of practice

47 Codes of practice

(1) The Commission may issue codes of practice containing such practical guidance as the Commission think fit for [all or any] of the following purposes, namely—

   (a) the elimination of discrimination in the field of employment;

   (b) the promotion of equality of opportunity in that field between persons of different racial groups;

  [(c) the elimination of discrimination in the field of housing . . .;

   (d) the promotion of equality of opportunity in the field of . . . housing between persons of different racial groups].

(2) When the Commission propose to issue a code of practice, they shall prepare and publish a draft of that code, shall consider any representations made to them about the draft and may modify the draft accordingly.

(3) In the course of preparing any draft code of practice [relating to the field of employment] for eventual publication under subsection (2) the Commission shall consult with—

   (a) such organisations or associations of organisations representative of employers or of workers; and

   (b) such other organisations, or bodies,

as appear to the Commission to be appropriate.

[(3A) In the course of preparing any draft code of practice relating to the field of . . . housing for eventual publication under subsection (2) the Commission shall consult with such organisations or bodies as appear to the Commission to be appropriate having regard to the content of the draft code.]

(4) If the Commission determine to proceed with [a draft code of practice], they shall transmit the draft to the Secretary of State who shall—

   (a) if he approves of it, lay it before both Houses of Parliament; and

   (b) if he does not approve of it, publish details of his reasons for withholding approval.

(5) If, within the period of forty days beginning with the day on which a copy of a draft code of practice is laid before each House of Parliament, or, if such copies are laid on different days, with the later of the two days, either House so resolves, no further proceedings shall be taken thereon, but without prejudice to the laying before Parliament of a new draft.

(6) In reckoning the period of forty days referred to in subsection (5), no account shall be taken of any period during which Parliament is dissolved or prorogued or during which both Houses are adjourned for more than four days.

(7) If no such resolution is passed as is referred to in subsection (5), the Commission shall issue the code in the form of the draft and the code shall come into effect on such day as the Secretary of State may by order appoint.

(8) Without prejudice to section 74(3), an order under subsection (7) may contain such transitional provisions or savings as appear to the Secretary of State to be necessary or expedient in connection with the code of practice thereby brought into operation.

(9) The Commission may from time to time revise the whole or any part of a code of practice issued under this section and issue that revised code, and subsections (2) to (8) shall apply (with appropriate modifications) to such a revised code as they apply to the first issue of a code.

(10) A failure on the part of any person to observe any provision of a code of practice shall not of itself render him liable to any proceedings; but in any proceedings under this Act before an industrial tribunal [a county court or, in Scotland, a sheriff court] any code of practice issued under this section shall be admissible in evidence, and if any provision of such a code appears to the tribunal [or the court] to be relevant to any question arising in the proceedings it shall be taken into account in determining that question.

(11) Without prejudice to subsection (1), a code of practice issued under this section may include such practical guidance as the Commission think fit as to what steps it is reasonably practicable for employers to take for the purpose of preventing their employees from doing in the course of their employment acts made unlawful by this Act.   [209]

NOTES

Sub-s (1): first words in square brackets substituted, and sub-paras (c), (d) added, by the Housing Act 1988, s 137(2); words omitted repealed by the Local Government and Housing Act 1989, ss 180, 194(4), Sch 12, Pt II.

Sub-ss (3), (10): words in square brackets inserted by the Housing Act 1988, s 137(3), (5).

Sub-s (3A): inserted by the Housing Act 1988, s 137(3); word omitted repealed by the Local Government and Housing Act 1989, ss 180, 194(4), Sch 12, Pt II.

Sub-s (4): words in square brackets substituted by the Housing Act 1988, s 137(4).

The only relevant code made under this section is the Code of Practice for the Elimination of Racial Discrimination and the Promotion of Equality of Opportunity in Employment 1983, printed below, para [3056]. Other Codes of Practice relate to rented and non-rented housing.

Investigations

48 Power to conduct formal investigations

(1) Without prejudice to their general power to do anything requisite for the performance of their duties under section 43(1), the Commission may if they think fit, and shall if required by the Secretary of State, conduct a formal investigation for any purpose connected with the carrying out of those duties.

(2) The Commission may, with the approval of the Secretary of State, appoint, on a full-time or part-time basis, one or more individuals as additional Commissioners for the purposes of a formal investigation.

(3) The Commission may nominate one or more Commissioners, with or without one or more additional Commissioners, to conduct a formal investigation on their behalf, and may delegate any of their functions in relation to the investigation to the persons so nominated.   [210]

49 Terms of reference

(1) The Commission shall not embark on a formal investigation unless the requirements of this section have been complied with.

(2) Terms of reference for the investigation shall be drawn up by the Commission or, if the Commission were required by the Secretary of State to conduct the investigation, by the Secretary of State after consulting the Commission.

(3) It shall be the duty of the Commission to give general notice of the holding of the investigation unless the terms of reference confine it to activities of persons named in them, but in such a case the Commission shall in the prescribed manner give those persons notice of the holding of the investigation.

(4) Where the terms of reference of the investigation confine it to activities of persons named in them and the Commission in the course of it propose to investigate any act made unlawful by this Act which they believe that a person so named may have done, the Commission shall—

    (a) inform that person of their belief and of their proposal to investigate the act in question; and

    (b) offer him an opportunity of making oral or written representations with regard to it (or both oral and written representations if he thinks fit);

and a person so named who avails himself of an opportunity under this subsection of making oral representations may be represented—

    (i) by counsel or a solicitor; or

    (ii) by some other person of his choice, not being a person to whom the Commission object on the ground that he is unsuitable.

(5) The Commission or, if the Commission were required by the Secretary of State to conduct the investigation, the Secretary of State after consulting the Commission may from time to time revise the terms of reference; and subsections (1), (3) and (4) shall apply to the revised investigation and terms of reference as they applied to the original.   **[211]**

50 Power to obtain information

(1) For the purposes of a formal investigation the Commission, by a notice in the prescribed form served on him in the prescribed manner—

    (a) may require any person to furnish such written information as may be described in the notice, and may specify the time at which, and the manner and form in which, the information is to be furnished;

    (b) may require any person to attend at such time and place as is specified in the notice and give oral information about, and produce all documents in his possession or control relating to, any matter specified in the notice.

(2) Except as provided by section 60, a notice shall be served under subsection (1) only where—

    (a) service of the notice was authorised by an order made by the Secretary of State; or

    (b) the terms of reference of the investigation state that the Commission believe that a person named in them may have done or may be doing acts of all or any of the following descriptions—

        (i) unlawful discriminatory acts;

        (ii) contraventions of section 28; and

        (iii) contraventions of sections 29, 30 or 31,

    and confine the investigation to those acts.

(3) A notice under subsection (1) shall not require a person—

    (a) to give information, or produce any documents, which he could not be compelled to give in evidence, or produce, in civil proceedings before the High Court or the Court of Session; or

    (b) to attend at any place unless the necessary expenses of his journey to and from that place are paid or tendered to him.

(4) If a person fails to comply with a notice served on him under subsection (1) or the Commission have reasonable cause to believe that he intends not to comply with it, the Commission may apply to a county court or, in Scotland, a sheriff court for an order requiring him to comply with it or with such directions for the like purpose as may be contained in the order.

(5) [Section 55 of the County Courts Act 1984] (penalty for neglecting witness summons) shall apply to failure without reasonable excuse to comply with an order of a county court under subsection (4) as it applies in the cases provided in the [said section 55]; and paragraph 73 of Schedule 1 to the Sheriff Courts (Scotland) Act 1907 (power of sheriff to grant second diligence for compelling the attendance of witnesses or havers) shall apply to an order of a sheriff court under subsection (4) as it applies in proceedings in the sheriff court.

(6) A person commits an offence if he—

    (a) wilfully alters, suppresses, conceals or destroys a document which he has been required by a notice or order under this section to produce; or

    (b) in complying with such a notice or order, knowingly or recklessly makes any statement which is false in a material particular,

and shall be liable on summary conviction to a fine not exceeding [level 5 on the standard scale].

(7) Proceedings for an offence under subsection (6) may (without prejudice to any jurisdiction exercisable apart from this subsection) be instituted—

    (a) against any person at any place at which he has an office or other place of business;

    (b) against an individual at any place where he resides, or at which he is for the time being. **[212]**

NOTES

Sub-s (5): words in square brackets substituted by the County Courts Act 1984, s 148(1), Sch 2, Pt V, para 61.

Sub-s (6): maximum fine increased and converted to a level on the standard scale by the Criminal Justice Act 1982, ss 37, 38, 46.

Order under this section: the Race Relations (Formal Investigations) Regulations 1977, SI 1977/841, below, para **[1082]**.

51 Recommendations and reports on formal investigations

(1) If in the light of any of their findings in a formal investigation it appears to the Commission necessary or expedient, whether during the course of the investigation or after its conclusion—

    (a) to make to any person, with a view to promoting equality of opportunity between persons of different racial groups who are affected by any of his activities, recommendations for changes in his policies or procedures, or as to any other matters; or

    (b) to make to the Secretary of State any recommendations, whether for changes in the law or otherwise,

the Commission shall make those recommendations accordingly.

(2) The Commission shall prepare a report of their findings in any formal investigation conducted by them.

(3) If the formal investigation is one required by the Secretary of State—

    (a) the Commission shall deliver the report to the Secretary of State; and

    (b) the Secretary of State shall cause the report to be published, and, unless required by the Secretary of State, the Commission shall not publish the report.

(4) If the formal investigation is not one required by the Secretary of State, the Commission shall either publish the report, or make it available for inspection in accordance with subsection (5).

(5) Where under subsection (4) a report is to be made available for inspection, any person shall be entitled, on payment of such fee (if any) as may be determined by the Commission—

(a) to inspect the report during ordinary office hours and take copies of all or any part of the report; or

(b) to obtain from the Commission a copy, certified by the Commission to be correct, of the report.

(6) The Commission may, if they think fit, determine that the right conferred by subsection (5)(a) shall be exercisable in relation to a copy of the report instead of, or in addition to, the original.

(7) The Commission shall give general notice of the place or places where, and the times when, reports may be inspected under subsection (5). [213]

52 Restriction on disclosure of information

(1) No information given to the Commission by any person ("the informant") in connection with a formal investigation shall be disclosed by the Commission, or by any person who is or has been a Commissioner, additional Commissioner or employee of the Commission, except—

(a) on the order of any court; or

(b) with the informant's consent; or

(c) in the form of a summary or other general statement published by the Commission which does not identify the informant or any other person to whom the information relates; or

(d) in a report of the investigation published by the Commission or made available for inspection under section 51(5); or

(e) to the Commissioners, additional Commissioners or employees of the Commission, or, so far as may be necessary for the proper performance of the functions of the Commission, to other persons; or

(f) for the purpose of any civil proceedings under this Act to which the Commission are a party, or any criminal proceedings.

(2) Any person who discloses information in contravention of subsection (1) commits an offence and shall be liable on summary conviction to a fine not exceeding [level 5 on the standard scale].

(3) In preparing any report for publication or for inspection the Commission shall exclude, so far as is consistent with their duties and the object of the report, any matter which relates to the private affairs of any individual or the business interests of any person where the publication of that matter might, in the opinion of the Commission, prejudicially affect that individual or person. [214]

NOTE
   Sub-s (2): maximum fine increased and converted to a level on the standard scale by the Criminal Justice Act 1982, ss 37, 38, 46.

PART VIII
ENFORCEMENT

General

53 Restriction of proceedings for breach of Act

(1) Except as provided by this Act no proceedings, whether civil or criminal, shall lie against any person in respect of an act by reason that the act is unlawful by virtue of a provision of this Act.

(2) Subsection (1) does not preclude the making of an order of certiorari, mandamus or prohibition.

(3) In Scotland, subsection (1) does not preclude the exercise of the jurisdiction of the Court of Session to entertain an application for reduction or suspension of any order or determination or otherwise to consider the validity of any order or determination, or to require reasons for any order or determination to be stated.

[215]

Enforcement in employment field

54 Jurisdiction of industrial tribunals

(1) A complaint by any person ("the complainant") that another person ("the respondent")—

> (a) has committed an act of discrimination against the complainant which is unlawful by virtue of Part II; or
> (b) is by virtue of section 32 or 33 to be treated as having committed such an act of discrimination against the complainant,

may be presented to an industrial tribunal.

(2) Subsection (1) does not apply to a complaint under section 12(1) of an act in respect of which an appeal, or proceedings in the nature of an appeal, may be brought under any enactment, or to a complaint to which section 75(8) applies. [216]

55 Conciliation in employment cases

(1) Where a complaint has been presented to an industrial tribunal under section 54 and a copy of the complaint has been sent to a conciliation officer, it shall be the duty of the conciliation officer—

> (a) if he is requested to do so both by the complainant and by the respondent; or
> (b) if, in the absence of requests by the complainant and the respondent, he considers that he could act under this subsection with a reasonable prospect of success,

to endeavour to promote a settlement of the complaint without its being determined by an industrial tribunal.

(2) Where, before a complaint such as is mentioned in subsection (1) has been presented to an industrial tribunal, a request is made to a conciliation officer to make his services available in the matter by a person who, if the complaint were so

presented, would be the complainant or respondent, subsection (1) shall apply as if the complaint had been so presented and a copy of it had been sent to the conciliation officer.

(3) In proceeding under subsection (1) or (2), a conciliation officer shall where appropriate have regard to the desirability of encouraging the use of other procedures available for the settlement of grievances.

(4) Anything communicated to a conciliation officer in connection with the performance of his functions under this section shall not be admissible in evidence in any proceedings before an industrial tribunal except with the consent of the person who communicated it to that officer. **[217]**

56 Remedies on complaint under s 54

(1) Where an industrial tribunal finds that a complaint presented to it under section 54 is well-founded, the tribunal shall make such of the following as it considers just and equitable—

    (a) an order declaring the rights of the complainant and the respondent in relation to the act to which the complaint relates;

    (b) an order requiring the respondent to pay to the complainant compensation of an amount corresponding to any damages he could have been ordered by a county court or by a sheriff court to pay to the complainant if the complaint had fallen to be dealt with under section 57;

    (c) a recommendation that the respondent take within a specified period action appearing to the tribunal to be practicable for the purpose of obviating or reducing the adverse effect on the complainant of any act of discrimination to which the complaint relates.

(2) The amount of compensation awarded to a person under subsection (1)(b) shall not exceed the limit for the time being imposed by [section 75 of the Employment Protection (Consolidation) Act 1978].

(3) Where compensation falls to be awarded in respect of any act both under the Sex Discrimination Act 1975 and this Act, the aggregate of the following amounts of compensation awarded by an industrial tribunal, that is to say—

    (a) any compensation awarded under the said Act of 1975; and

    (b) any compensation awarded under subsection (1)(b),

shall not exceed the limit referred to in subsection (2).

(4) If without reasonable justification the respondent to a complaint fails to comply with a recommendation made by an industrial tribunal under subsection (1)(c), then, if it thinks it just and equitable to do so—

    (a) the tribunal may (subject to the limit in subsection (2)) increase the amount of compensation required to be paid to the complainant in respect of the complaint by an order made under subsection (1)(b); or

    (b) if an order under subsection (1)(b) could have been made but was not, the tribunal may make such an order. **[218]**

NOTE

Sub-s (2): words in square brackets substituted by the Employment Protection (Consolidation) Act 1978, s 159(2), Sch 16, para 25(2).

The current limit on compensation is £11,000, as from 1 June 1993. The previous limit was £10,000.

Enforcement of Part III

57 Claims under Part III

(1) A claim by any person ("the claimant") that another person ("the respondent")—

(a) has committed an act of discrimination against the claimant which is unlawful by virtue of Part III; or

(b) is by virtue of section 32 or 33 to be treated as having committed such an act of discrimination against the claimant, may be made the subject of civil proceedings in like manner as any other claim in tort or (in Scotland) in reparation for breach of statutory duty.

(2) Proceedings under subsection (1)—

(a) shall, in England and Wales, be brought only in a designated county court; and

(b) shall, in Scotland, be brought only in a sheriff court.

(3) As respects an unlawful act of discrimination falling within section 1(1)(b), no award of damages shall be made if the respondent proves that the requirement or condition in question was not applied with the intention of treating the claimant unfavourably on racial grounds.

(4) For the avoidance of doubt it is hereby declared that damages in respect of an unlawful act of discrimination may include compensation for injury to feelings whether or not they include compensation under any other head.

(5) Civil proceedings in respect of a claim by any person that he has been discriminated against in contravention of section 17 or 18 by a body to which section 19(1) applies shall not be instituted unless the claimant has given notice of the claim to the Secretary of State and either the Secretary of State has by notice informed the claimant that the Secretary of State does not require further time to consider the matter, or the period of two months has elapsed since the claimant gave notice to the Secretary of State; but nothing in this subsection applies to a counterclaim.

(6) In Scotland, when any proceedings are brought under this section, in addition to the service on the defender of a copy of the summons or initial writ initiating the action a copy thereof shall be sent as soon as practicable to the Commission in a manner to be prescribed by Act of Sederunt.   **[219]**

Non-discrimination notices

58 Issue of non-discrimination notice

(1) This section applies to—

(a) an unlawful discriminatory act; and

(b) an act contravening section 28; and

(c) an act contravening section 29, 30 or 31,

and so applies whether or not proceedings have been brought in respect of the act.

(2) If in the course of a formal investigation the Commission become satisfied that a person is committing, or has committed, any such acts, the Commission may in the prescribed manner serve on him a notice in the prescribed form ("a non-discrimination notice") requiring him—

(a) not to commit any such acts; and

(b) where compliance with paragraph (a) involves changes in any of his practices or other arrangements—

(i) to inform the Commission that he has effected those changes and what those changes are; and

(ii) to take such steps as may be reasonably required by the notice for the purpose of affording that information to other persons concerned.

(3) A non-discrimination notice may also require the person on whom it is served to furnish the Commission with such other information as may be reasonably required by the notice in order to verify that the notice has been complied with.

(4) The notice may specify the time at which, and the manner and form in which, any information is to be furnished to the Commission, but the time at which any information is to be furnished in compliance with the notice shall not be later than five years after the notice has become final.

(5) The Commission shall not serve a non-discrimination notice in respect of any person unless they have first—

(a) given him notice that they are minded to issue a non-discrimination notice in his case, specifying the grounds on which they contemplate doing so; and

(b) offered him an opportunity of making oral or written representations in the matter (or both oral and written representations if he thinks fit) within a period of not less than 28 days specified in the notice; and

(c) taken account of any representations so made by him.

(6) Subsection (2) does not apply to any acts in respect of which the Secretary of State could exercise the powers conferred on him by section 19(2) and (3); but if the Commission become aware of any such acts they shall give notice of them to the Secretary of State.

(7) Section 50(4) shall apply to requirements under subsection (2)(b), (3) and (4) contained in a non-discrimination notice which has become final as it applies to requirements in a notice served under section 50(1). [220]

NOTE

For the prescribed form of non-discrimination notice see the Race Relations (Formal Investigations) Regulations 1977, SI 1977/841, reg 6, Sch 2, below, paras [1087] and [1089].

59 Appeal against non-discrimination notice

(1) Not later than six weeks after a non-discrimination notice is served on any person he may appeal against any requirement of the notice—

(a) to an industrial tribunal, so far as the requirement relates to acts which are within the jurisdiction of the tribunal;

(b) to a designated county court or a sheriff court, so far as the requirement relates to acts which are within the jurisdiction of the court and are not within the jurisdiction of an industrial tribunal.

(2) Where the tribunal or court considers a requirement in respect of which an appeal is brought under subsection (1) to be unreasonable because it is based on an incorrect finding of fact or for any other reason, the tribunal or court shall quash the requirement.

(3) On quashing a requirement under subsection (2) the tribunal or court may direct that the non-discrimination notice shall be treated as if, in place of the requirement quashed, it had contained a requirement in terms specified in the direction.

(4) Subsection (1) does not apply to a requirement treated as included in a non-discrimination notice by virtue of a direction under subsection (3).   **[221]**

NOTE

For the procedure on appeals see the Industrial Tribunals (Non-discrimination Notices Appeals) Regulations 1977, SI 1977/1094, below, para **[1098]**.

60 Investigation as to compliance with non-discrimination notice

(1) If—

(a) the terms of reference of a formal investigation state that its purpose is to determine whether any requirements of a non-discrimination notice are being or have been carried out, but section 50(2)(b) does not apply; and

(b) section 49(3) is complied with in relation to the investigation on a date ("the commencement date") not later than the expiration of the period of five years beginning when the non-discrimination notice became final,

the Commission may within the period referred to in subsection (2) serve notices under section 50(1) for the purposes of the investigation without needing to obtain the consent of the Secretary of State.

(2) The said period begins on the commencement date and ends on 'the later of the following dates—

(a) the date on which the period of five years mentioned in subsection (1)(b) expires;

(b) the date two years after the commencement date.   **[222]**

61 Register of non-discrimination notices

(1) The Commission shall establish and maintain a register ("the register") of non-discrimination notices which have become final.

(2) Any person shall be entitled, on payment of such fee (if any) as may be determined by the Commission—

(a) to inspect the register during ordinary office hours and take copies of any entry; or

(b) to obtain from the Commission a copy, certified by the Commission to be correct, of any entry in the register.

(3) The Commission may, if they think fit, determine that the right conferred by subsection (2)(a) shall be exercisable in relation to a copy of the register instead of, or in addition to, the original.

(4) The Commission shall give general notice of the place or places where, and the times when, the register or a copy of it may be inspected.   **[223]**

Other enforcement by Commission

62 Persistent discrimination

(1) If, during the period of five years beginning on the date on which any of the following became final in the case of any person, namely—

(a) a non-discrimination notice served on him; or

(b) a finding by a tribunal or court under section 54 or 57 that he has done an unlawful discriminatory act; or (c)　a finding by a court in proceedings under section 19 or 20 of the Race Relations Act 1968 that he has done an act which was unlawful by virtue of any provision of Part I of that Act,

it appears to the Commission that unless restrained he is likely to do one or more acts falling within paragraph (b), or contravening section 28, the Commission may apply to a designated county court for an injunction, or to a sheriff court for an order, restraining him from doing so; and the court, if satisfied that the application is well-founded, may grant the injunction or order in the terms applied for or in more limited terms.

(2)　In proceedings under this section the Commission shall not allege that the person to whom the proceedings relate has done an act falling within subsection (1)(b) or contravening section 28 which is within the jurisdiction of an industrial tribunal unless a finding by an industrial tribunal that he did that act has become final.

[224]

63　Enforcement of ss 29 to 31

(1)　Proceedings in respect of a contravention of section 29, 30 or 31 shall be brought only by the Commission in accordance with the following provisions of this section.

(2)　The proceedings shall be—
(a)　an application for a decision whether the alleged contravention occurred; or
(b)　an application under subsection (4),

or both.

(3)　An application under subsection (2)(a) shall be made—
(a)　in a case based on any provision of Part II, to an industrial tribunal; and
(b)　in any other case, to a designated county court or a sheriff court.

(4)　If it appears to the Commission—
(a)　that a person has done an act which by virtue of section 29, 30 or 31 was unlawful; and
(b)　that unless restrained he is likely to do further acts which by virtue of that section are unlawful,

the Commission may apply to a designated county court for an injunction, or to a sheriff court for an order, restraining him from doing such acts; and the court, if satisfied that the application is well-founded, may grant the injunction or order in the terms applied for or more limited terms.

(5)　In proceedings under subsection (4) the Commission shall not allege that the person to whom the proceedings relate has done an act which is unlawful under this Act and within the jurisdiction of an industrial tribunal unless a finding by an industrial tribunal that he did that act has become final.　　　　**[225]**

64　Preliminary action in employment cases

(1)　With a view to making an application under section 62(1) or 63(4) in relation to a person the Commission may present to an industrial tribunal a complaint that he has done an act within the jurisdiction of an industrial tribunal, and if the tribunal considers that the complaint is well-founded it shall make a finding to that effect and, if it thinks it just and equitable to do so in the case of an act contravening any provision of Part II may also (as if the complaint had been presented by the person discriminated against) make an order such as is referred to in section 56(1)(a), or a recommendation such as is referred to in section 56(1)(c), or both.

(2) Subsection (1) is without prejudice to the jurisdiction conferred by section 63(2).

(3) In sections 62 and 63 and this section, the acts "within the jurisdiction of an industrial tribunal" are those in respect of which such jurisdiction is conferred by sections 54 and 63. **[226]**

Help for persons suffering discrimination

65 Help for aggrieved persons in obtaining information etc

(1) With a view to helping a person ("the person aggrieved") who considers he may have been discriminated against in contravention of this Act to decide whether to institute proceedings and, if he does so, to formulate and present his case in the most effective manner, the Secretary of State shall by order prescribe—

  (a) forms by which the person aggrieved may question the respondent on his reasons for doing any relevant act, or on any other matter which is or may be relevant; and

  (b) forms by which the respondent may if he so wishes reply to any questions.

(2) Where the person aggrieved questions the respondent (whether in accordance with an order under subsection (1) or not)—

  (a) the question, and any reply by the respondent (whether in accordance with such an order or not) shall, subject to the following provisions of this section, be admissible as evidence in the proceedings;

  (b) if it appears to the court or tribunal that the respondent deliberately, and without reasonable excuse, omitted to reply within a reasonable period or that his reply is evasive or equivocal, the court or tribunal may draw any inference from that fact that it considers it just and equitable to draw, including an inference that he committed an unlawful act.

(3) The Secretary of State may by order—

  (a) prescribe the period within which questions must be duly served in order to be admissible under subsection (2)(a); and

  (b) prescribe the manner in which a question, and any reply by the respondent, may be duly served.

(4) Rules may enable the court entertaining a claim under section 57 to determine, before the date fixed for the hearing of the claim, whether a question or reply is admissible under this section or not.

(5) This section is without prejudice to any other enactment or rule of law regulating interlocutory and preliminary matters in proceedings before a county court, sheriff court or industrial tribunal, and has effect subject to any enactment or rule of law regulating the admissibility of evidence in such proceedings.

(6) In this section "respondent" includes a prospective respondent and "rules"—

  (a) in relation to county court proceedings, means county court rules;

  (b) in relation to sheriff court proceedings, means sheriff court rules. **[227]**

NOTE

The order made under this section is the Race Relations (Questions and Replies) Order 1977, SI 1977/842, below, para **[1090]**.

66 Assistance by Commission

(1) Where, in relation to proceedings or prospective proceedings under this Act, an individual who is an actual or prospective complainant or claimant applies to the Commission for assistance under this section, the Commission shall consider the application and may grant it if they think fit to do so—

(a) on the ground that the case raises a question of principle; or

(b) on the ground that it is unreasonable, having regard to the complexity of the case, or to the applicant's position in relation to the respondent or another person involved, or to any other matter, to expect the applicant to deal with the case unaided; or

(c) by reason of any other special consideration.

(2) Assistance by the Commission under this section may include—

(a) giving advice;

(b) procuring or attempting to procure the settlement of any matter in dispute;

(c) arranging for the giving of advice or assistance by a solicitor or counsel;

(d) arranging for representation by any person, including all such assistance as is usually given by a solicitor or counsel in the steps preliminary or incidental to any proceedings, or in arriving at or giving effect to a compromise to avoid or bring to an end any proceedings;

(e) any other form of assistance which the Commission may consider appropriate,

but paragraph (d) shall not affect the law and practice regulating the descriptions of persons who may appear in, conduct, defend, and address the court in, any proceedings.

(3) Where under subsection (1) an application for assistance under this section is made in writing, the Commission shall, within the period of two months beginning when the application is received—

(a) consider the application after making such enquiries as they think fit; and

(b) decide whether or not to grant it; and

(c) inform the applicant of their decision, stating whether or not assistance under this section is to be provided by the Commission and, if so, what form it will take.

(4) If, in a case where subsection (3) applies, the Commission within the period of two months there mentioned give notice to the applicant that, in relation to his application—

(a) the period of two months allowed them by that subsection is by virtue of the notice extended to three months; and

(b) the reference to two months in section 68(3) is by virtue of the notice to be read as a reference to three months,

subsection (3) and section 68(3) shall have effect accordingly.

(5) In so far as expenses are incurred by the Commission in providing the applicant with assistance under this section, the recovery of those expenses (as taxed or assessed in such manner as may be prescribed by rules or regulations) shall constitute a first charge for the benefit of the Commission—

(a) on any costs or expenses which (whether by virtue of a judgment or order of a court or tribunal or an agreement or otherwise) are payable to the applicant by any other person in respect of the matter in connection with which the assistance is given; and

(b) so far as relates to any costs or expenses, on his rights under any compromise or settlement arrived at in connection with that matter to avoid or bring to an end any proceedings.

(6) The charge conferred by subsection (5) is subject to any charge under the [Legal Aid Act 1988], or any charge or obligation for payment in priority to other debts under [the Legal Aid (Scotland) Act 1986], and is subject to any provision in [either of those Acts for payment of any sum to the Legal Aid Board or into the Scottish Legal Aid Fund].

(7) In this section "respondent" includes a prospective respondent and "rules or regulations"—

(a) in relation to county court proceedings, means county court rules;
(b) in relation to sheriff court proceedings, means sheriff court rules;
(c) in relation to industrial tribunal proceedings, means regulations made under [paragraph 1 of Schedule 9 to the Employment Protection (Consolidation) Act 1978].

[228]

NOTES

Sub-s (6): words in first and third pairs of square brackets substituted by the Legal Aid Act 1988, s 45(1), (3), Sch 5, para 7; words in second pair of square brackets substituted by the Legal Aid (Scotland) Act 1986, s 45(1), Sch 3, para 6.

Sub-s (7): words in square brackets substituted by the Employment Protection (Consolidation) Act 1978, s 159(2), Sch 16, para 25.

67 (*Sheriff courts and designated county courts.*)

Period within which proceedings to be brought

68 Period within which proceedings to be brought

(1) An industrial tribunal shall not consider a complaint under section 54 unless it is presented to the tribunal before the end of the period of three months beginning when the act complained of was done.

(2) A county court or a sheriff court shall not consider a claim under section 57 unless proceedings in respect of the claim are instituted before the end of—

(a) the period of six months beginning when the act complained of was done; or

(b) in a case to which section 57(5) applies, the period of eight months so beginning.

(3) Where, in relation to proceedings or prospective proceedings by way of a claim under section 57, an application for assistance under section 66 is made to the Commission before the end of the period of six or, as the case may be, eight months mentioned in paragraph (a) or (b) of subsection (2), the period allowed by that paragraph for instituting proceedings in respect of the claim shall be extended by two months.

(4) An industrial tribunal, county court or sheriff court shall not consider an application under section 63(2)(a) unless it is made before the end of the period of six months beginning when the act to which it relates was done; and a county court or sheriff court shall not consider an application under section 63(4) unless it is made before the end of the period of five years so beginning.

(5) An industrial tribunal shall not consider a complaint under section 64(1) unless it is presented to the tribunal before the end of the period of six months beginning when the act complained of was done.

(6) A court or tribunal may nevertheless consider any such complaint, claim or application which is out of time if, in all the circumstances of the case, it considers that it is just and equitable to do so.

(7) For the purposes of this section—

(a) when the inclusion of any term in a contract renders the making of the contract an unlawful act, that act shall be treated as extending throughout the duration of the contract; and

(b) any act extending over a period shall be treated as done at the end of that period; and

(c) a deliberate omission shall be treated as done when the person in question decided upon it;

and in the absence of evidence establishing the contrary a person shall be taken for the purposes of this section to decide upon an omission when he does an act inconsistent with doing the omitted act or, if he has done no such inconsistent act, when the period expires within which he might reasonably have been expected to do the omitted act if it was to be done.   **[229]**

Evidence

69 Evidence

(1) Any finding by a court under section 19 or 20 of the Race Relations Act 1968, or by a court or industrial tribunal under this Act, in respect of any act shall, if it has become final, be treated as conclusive in any proceedings under this Act.

(2) In any proceedings under this Act a certificate signed by or on behalf of a Minister of the Crown and certifying—

(a) that any arrangements or conditions specified in the certificate were made, approved or imposed by a Minister of the Crown and were in operation at a time or throughout a period so specified; or

(b) that an act specified in the certificate was done for the purpose of safeguarding national security,

shall be conclusive evidence of the matters certified.

(3) A document purporting to be a certificate such as is mentioned in subsection (2) shall be received in evidence and, unless the contrary is proved, shall be deemed to be such a certificate.   **[230]**

70 *((Pt IX) Repealed by the Public Order Act 1986, s 40(3), Sch 3.)*

PART X
SUPPLEMENTAL

71 Local authorities: general statutory duty

Without prejudice to their obligation to comply with any other provision of this Act, it shall be the duty of every local authority to make appropriate arrangements with a view to securing that their various functions are carried out with due regard to the need—

(a) to eliminate unlawful racial discrimination; and

(b) to promote equality of opportunity and good relations, between persons of different racial groups [;

and in this section "local authority" includes . . . a joint authority established by Part IV of the Local Government Act 1985.]

[The Broads Authority shall be treated as a local authority for the purposes of this section.]   [231]

NOTE
First words in square brackets added by the Local Government Act 1985, s 84, Sch 14, Pt II, para 54; words omitted repealed by the Education Reform Act 1988, s 237(2), Sch 13, Pt I; final words in square brackets added by the Norfolk and Suffolk Broads Act 1988, s 21, Sch 6, para 16.

72 Validity and revision of contracts

(1) A term of a contract is void where—

   (a) its inclusion renders the making of the contract unlawful by virtue of this Act; or
   (b) it is included in furtherance of an act rendered unlawful by this Act; or
   (c) it provides for the doing of an act which would be rendered unlawful by this Act.

(2) Subsection (1) does not apply to a term the inclusion of which constitutes, or is in furtherance of, or provides for, unlawful discrimination against a party to the contract, but the term shall be unenforceable against that party.

(3) A term in a contract which purports to exclude or limit any provision of this Act is unenforceable by any person in whose favour the term would operate apart from this subsection.

(4) Subsection (3) does not apply—

   (a) to a contract settling a complaint to which section 54(1) applies where the contract is made with the assistance of a conciliation officer; or
   (b) to a contract settling a claim to which section 57 applies.

(5) On the application of any person interested in a contract to which subsection (2) applies, a designated county court or a sheriff court may make such order as it thinks just for removing or modifying any term made unenforceable by that subsection; but such an order shall not be made unless all persons affected have been given notice of the application (except where under rules of court notice may be dispensed with) and have been afforded an opportunity to make representations to the court.

(6) An order under subsection (5) may include provision as respects any period before the making of the order.   [232]

NOTES
Sub-s (4): para (aa) inserted by the Trade Union Reform and Employment Rights Act 1993, s 39(2), Sch 6, para 2(a), as from 30 August 1993 (SI 1993/1908), as follows—
   "(aa) to a contract settling a complaint to which section 54(1) applies if the conditions regulating compromise contracts under this Act are satisfied in relation to the contract;".
Sub-ss (4A)–(4C): inserted by the Trade Union Reform and Employment Rights Act 1993, s 39(2), Sch 6, para 2(b), as from 30 August 1993 (SI 1993/1908), as follows—
   "(4A)   The conditions regulating compromise contracts under this Act are that—
   (a)   the contract must be in writing;
   (b)   the contract must relate to the particular complaint;
   (c)   the complainant must have received independent legal advice from a qualified lawyer as to the terms and effect of the proposed contract and in particular its effect on his ability to pursue his complaint before an industrial tribunal;
   (d)   there must be in force, when the adviser gives the advice, a policy of insurance covering the risk of a claim by the complainant in respect of loss arising in consequence of the advice;

(e)   the contract must identify the adviser; and
(f)   the contract must state that the conditions regulating compromise contracts under this Act are satisfied.

(4B) In subsection (4A)—
"independent", in relation to legal advice to the complainant, means that it is given by a lawyer who is not acting for the other party or for a person who is connected with that other party; and
"qualified lawyer" means—
(a)   as respects proceedings in England and Wales—
     (i)   a barrister, whether in practice as such or employed to give legal advice, or
     (ii)   a solicitor of the Supreme Court who holds a practising certificate.
(b)   as respects proceedings in Scotland—
     (i)   an advocate, whether in practice as such or employed to give legal advice, or
     (ii)   a solicitor who holds a practising certificate.

(4C) For the purposes of subsection (4B) any two persons are to be treated as "connected" if one is a company of which the other (directly or indirectly) has control, or if both are companies of which a third person (directly or indirectly) has control.".

73 Power to amend certain provisions of Act

(1) The Secretary of State may by an order the draft of which has been approved by each House of Parliament—

(a)   amend or repeal section 9 (including that section as amended by a previous order under this subsection);

(b)   amend Part II, III or IV so as to render lawful an act which, apart from the amendment, would be unlawful by reason of section 4(1) or (2), 20(1), 21, 24 or 25;

(c)   amend section 10(1) or 25(1)(a) so as to alter the number of partners or members specified in that provision.

(2) The Secretary of State shall not lay before Parliament the draft of an order under subsection (1) unless he has consulted the Commission about the contents of the draft.   **[233]**

NOTE
Up to 1 September 1993 no orders have been made under this section.

74 Orders and regulations

(1) Any power of a Minister of the Crown to make orders or regulations under the provisions of this Act (except [section] 50(2)(a)) shall be exercisable by statutory instrument.

(2) An order made by a Minister of the Crown under the preceding provisions of this Act (except sections . . . 50(2)(a) and 73(1)), and any regulations made under section 75(5)(a), shall be subject to annulment in pursuance of a resolution of either House of Parliament.

(3) An order under this Act may make different provision in relation to different cases or classes of case, may exclude certain cases or classes of case, and may contain transitional provisions and savings.

(4) Any power conferred by this Act to make orders includes power (exercisable in the like manner and subject to the like conditions) to vary or revoke any order so made.

(5) Any document purporting to be an order made by the Secretary of State under section . . . 50(2)(a) and to be signed by him or on his behalf shall be received in evidence, and shall, unless the contrary is proved, be deemed to be made by him.

NOTES

Sub-s (1): word in square brackets substituted by the Employment Act 1989, s 29(3), Sch 6, para 16.
Sub-ss (2), (5): words omitted repealed by the Employment Act 1989, s 29(4), Sch 7, Pt II.

75 Application to Crown etc

(1) This Act applies—

    (a) to an act done by or for purposes of a Minister of the Crown or government department; or

    (b) to an act done on behalf of the Crown by a statutory body, or a person holding a statutory office,

as it applies to an act done by a private person.

(2) Parts II and IV apply to—

    (a) service for purposes of a Minister of the Crown or government department, other than service of a person holding a statutory office; or

    (b) service on behalf of the Crown for purposes of a person holding a statutory office or purposes of a statutory body; or

    (c) service in the armed forces,

as they apply to employment by a private person, and shall so apply as if references to a contract of employment included references to the terms of service.

(3) Subsections (1) and (2) have effect subject to section 16.

(4) Subsection (2) of section 8 and subsection (4) of section 27 shall have effect in relation to any ship, aircraft or hovercraft belonging to or possessed by Her Majesty in right of the Government of the United Kingdom as it has effect in relation to a ship, aircraft or hovercraft such as is mentioned in paragraph (a) or (b) of the subsection in question; and section 8(3) shall apply accordingly.

(5) Nothing in this Act shall—

    (a) invalidate any rules (whether made before or after the passing of this Act) restricting employment in the service of the Crown or by any public body prescribed for the purposes of this subsection by regulations made by the Minister for the Civil Service to persons of particular birth, nationality, descent or residence; or

    (b) render unlawful the publication, display or implementation of any such rules, or the publication of advertisements stating the gist of any such rules.

In this subsection "employment" includes service of any kind, and "public body" means a body of persons, whether corporate or unincorporate, carrying on a service or undertaking of a public nature.

(6) The provisions of Parts II to IV of the Crown Proceedings Act 1947 shall apply to proceedings against the Crown under this Act as they apply to proceedings in England and Wales which by virtue of section 23 of that Act are treated for the purposes of Part II of that Act as civil proceedings by or against the Crown, except that in their application to proceedings under this Act section 20 of that Act (removal of proceedings from county court to High Court) shall not apply.

(7) The provisions of Part V of the Crown Proceedings Act 1947 shall apply to proceedings against the Crown under this Act as they apply to proceedings in Scotland which by virtue of the said Part are treated as civil proceedings by or against the Crown, except that in their application to proceedings under this Act the proviso to section 44 of that Act (removal of proceedings from the sheriff court to the Court of Session) shall not apply.

(8) This subsection applies to any complaint by a person ("the complainant") that another person—

(a) has committed an act of discrimination against the complainant which is unlawful by virtue of section 4; or

(b) is by virtue of section 32 or 33 to be treated as having committed such an act of discrimination against the complainant,

if at the time when the act complained of was done the complainant was serving in the armed forces and the discrimination in question relates to his service in those forces.

(9) Section 54(1) shall not apply to a complaint to which subsection (8) applies, but any such complaint may be made, and if made shall be dealt with, in accordance with whichever of the following provisions for the redress of complaints is appropriate, namely section 130 of the Naval Discipline Act 1957, section 180 or 181 of the Army Act 1955 or section 180 or 181 of the Air Force Act 1955.

(10) In this section—

(a) "the armed forces" means any of the naval, military or air forces of the Crown . . .;

(b) "statutory body" means a body set up by or in pursuance of an enactment, and "statutory office" means an office so set up; and

(c) service "for purposes of" a Minister of the Crown or government department does not include service in any office in Schedule 2 (Ministerial offices) to the House of Commons Disqualification Act 1975 as for the time being in force.   **[235]**

NOTES

Sub-s (10): words omitted in para (a) repealed by the Armed Forces Act 1981, s 28(2), Sch 5, Pt I.

The Race Relations (Prescribed Public Bodies) Regulations 1984, SI 1984/218, as amended by the Race Relations (Prescribed Public Bodies) (Amendment) Regulations 1985, SI 1985/1309, and the Race Relations (Prescribed Public Bodies) (Amendment) (No 2) Regulations 1985, SI 1985/1757, list the following as prescribed bodies for the purposes of s 75:

Armouries
Bank of England
British Council
British Museum
British Museum (Natural History)
Civil Aviation Authority
Development Commission
House of Commons (as respects the employment of relevant members of the House of Commons staff)
Imperial War Museum
Metropolitan Police Office (as respects the employment of members of the metropolitan civil staffs)
National Audit Office
National Economic Development Office
National Environment Research Council
National Gallery
National Galleries of Scotland
National Library of Scotland
National Maritime Museum
National Museums of Scotland
National Portrait Gallery
Royal Air Force Museum
Royal Commission on Ancient and Historical Monuments in Wales
Royal Commission on the Ancient and Historical Monuments of Scotland
Royal Commission on Historical Manuscripts
Royal Commission on Historical Monuments (England)
Science Museum
Science and Engineering Research Council
Tate Gallery
United Kingdom Atomic Energy Authority
Victoria and Albert Museum

Wallace Collection
Regulation 1(2) of the 1984 Regs defines "members of the metropolitan civil staffs" as: "persons who are employed under the Commissioner of Police for the Metropolis or the Receiver for the Metropolitan Police District and are not constables and whose salaries are paid out of the Metropolitan Police Fund".

Reg 1(2) of the 1985 Regs defines "relevant members of the House of Commons staff" as "any person appointed by the House of Commons Commission" and "any member of Mr Speaker's personal staff".

[75A Application to House of Commons Staff

(1) Parts II and IV apply to an act done by an employer of a relevant member of the House of Commons staff, and to service as such a member, as they apply to an act done by and to service for the purposes of a Minister of the Crown or government department, and accordingly apply as if references to a contract of employment included references to the terms of service of such a member.

(2) In this section "relevant member of the House of Commons staff" has the same meaning as in section 139 of the Employment Protection (Consolidation) Act 1978; and subsections (4) to (9) of that section (person to be treated as employer of House of Commons staff) apply, with any necessary modifications, for the purposes of Parts II and IV as they apply by virtue of this section.]   [236]

NOTE
Commencement: 16 October 1992.
Inserted by the Trade Union and Labour Relations (Consolidation) Act 1992, s 300(2), Sch 2, para 7.

[75B Application to House of Lords Staff

(1) Parts II and IV apply in relation to employment as a relevant member of the House of Lords staff as they apply in relation to other employment.

(2) In this section "relevant member of the House of Lords staff" has the same meaning as in section 139A of the Employment Protection (Consolidation) Act 1978; and subsection (6) of that section applies for the purposes of this section.]   [236A]

NOTE
Inserted by the Trade Union Reform and Employment Rights Act 1993, s 49(1), Sch 7, para 10, as from a day to be appointed.

76 Government appointments outside s 4

(1) This section applies to any appointment by a Minister of the Crown or government department to an office or post where section 4 does not apply in relation to the appointment.

(2) In making the appointment, and in making the arrangements for determining who should be offered the office or post, the Minister of the Crown or government department shall not do an act which would be unlawful under section 4 if the Crown were the employer for the purposes of this Act.   [237]

77 Financial provisions

There shall be defrayed out of money provided by Parliament—

   (a) sums required by the Secretary of State for making payments under paragraph 5 or 16 of Schedule 1 or paragraph 12 of Schedule 2, and for defraying any other expenditure falling to be made by him under or by virtue of this Act;

   (b) any expenses incurred by the Secretary of State with the consent of the Treasury in undertaking, or financially assisting the undertaking by other persons of, research into any matter connected with relations between persons of different racial groups;

(c) payments falling to be made under section 67(5) in respect of the remuneration of assessors; and

(d) any increase attributable to the provisions of this Act in the sums payable out of money provided by Parliament under any other Act.   **[238]**

78 General interpretation provisions

(1) In this Act, unless the context otherwise requires—

"access" shall be construed in accordance with section 40;

"act" includes a deliberate omission;

"advertisement" includes every form of advertisement or notice, whether to the public or not, and whether in a newspaper or other publication, by television or radio, by display of notices, signs, labels, showcards or goods, by distribution of samples, circulars, catalogues, price lists or other material, by exhibition of pictures, models or films, or in any other way, and references to the publishing of advertisements shall be construed accordingly;

["board of management" in relation to a self-governing school, has the same meaning as in the Education (Scotland) Act 1980;]

["board of management" in relation to a college of further education within the meaning of Part I of the Further and Higher Education (Scotland) Act 1992, has the same meaning as in that Part;]

"the Commission" means the Commission for Racial Equality;

"Commissioner" means a member of the Commission;

"designated county court" has the meaning given by section 67(1);

"discrimination" and related terms shall be construed in accordance with section 3(3);

"dispose", in relation to premises, includes granting a right to occupy the premises, and any reference to acquiring premises shall be construed accordingly;

"education" includes any form of training or instruction;

"education authority" and "educational establishment" have for Scotland the same meaning as they have respectively in section [135(1) of the Education (Scotland) Act 1980];

"employment" means employment under a contract of service or of apprenticeship or a contract personally to execute any work or labour, and related expressions shall be construed accordingly;

"employment agency" means a person who, for profit or not, provides services for the purpose of finding employment for workers or supplying employers with workers;

"estate agent" means a person who, by way of profession or trade, provides services for the purpose of finding premises for persons seeking to acquire them or assisting in the disposal of premises;

"final" shall be construed in accordance with subsection (4);

"firm" has the meaning given by section 4 of the Partnership Act 1890;

"formal investigation" means an investigation under section 48;

"further education" has . . . for Scotland the meaning given by [section 135(1) of the Education (Scotland) Act 1980];

"general notice", in relation to any person, means a notice published by him at a time and in a manner appearing to him suitable for securing that the notice is seen within a reasonable time by persons likely to be affected by it;

"genuine occupational qualification" shall be construed in accordance with section 5;

"Great Britain" includes such of the territorial waters of the United Kingdom
as are adjacent to Great Britain;

"independent school" has for England and Wales the meaning given by section
114(1) of the Education Act 1944, and for Scotland the meaning given by
section [135(1) of the Education (Scotland) Act 1980];

. . . . .

"managers" has for Scotland the same meaning as in section [135(1) of the
Education (Scotland) Act 1980];

"Minister of the Crown" includes the Treasury and the Defence Council;

"nationality" includes citizenship;

"near relative" shall be construed in accordance with subsection (5);

"non-discrimination notice" means a notice under section 58;

"notice" means a notice in writing;

"prescribed" means prescribed by regulations made by the Secretary of State;

"profession" includes any vocation or occupation;

"proprietor", in relation to a school, has for England and Wales the meaning
given by section 114(1) of the Education Act 1944, and for Scotland the
meaning given by section [135(1) of the Education (Scotland) Act 1980];

"pupil" in Scotland includes a student of any age;

"racial grounds" and "racial group" have the meaning given by section 3(1);

"school" has for England and Wales the meaning given by section 114(1) of
the Education Act 1944, and for Scotland the meaning given by section
[135(1) of the Education (Scotland) Act 1980];

"school education" has for Scotland the meaning given by section [135(1) of
the Education (Scotland) Act 1980];

["self-governing school" has the same meaning as in the Education (Scotland
Act 1980;]

"trade" includes any business;

"training" includes any form of education or instruction;

"university" includes a university college and the college, school or hall of a
university;

*"upper limit of compulsory school age" for England and Wales means, subject
to section 9 of the Education Act 1962, the age that is that limit by virtue
of section 35 of the Education Act 1944 and the Order in Council made
under that section.*

(2) It is hereby declared that in this Act "premises", unless the context otherwise
requires, includes land of any description.

(3) Any power conferred by this Act to designate establishments or persons may
be exercised either by naming them or by identifying them by reference to a class or
other description.

(4) For the purposes of this Act a non-discrimination notice or a finding by a
court or tribunal becomes final when an appeal against the notice or finding is
dismissed, withdrawn or abandoned or when the time for appealing expires without
an appeal having been brought; and for this purpose an appeal against a non-
discrimination notice shall be taken to be dismissed if, notwithstanding that a
requirement of the notice is quashed on appeal, a direction is given in respect of it
under section 59(3).

(5) For the purposes of this Act a person is a near relative of another if that person
is the wife or husband, a parent or child, a grandparent or grandchild, or a brother or
sister of the other (whether of full blood or half-blood or by affinity), and "child"
includes an illegitimate child and the wife or husband of an illegitimate child.

(6) Except so far as the context otherwise requires, any reference in this Act to an enactment shall be construed as a reference to that enactment as amended by or under any other enactment, including this Act.

(7) In this Act, except where otherwise indicated—

(a) a reference to a numbered Part, section or Schedule is a reference to the Part or section of, or the Schedule to, this Act so numbered; and

(b) a reference in a section to a numbered subsection is a reference to the subsection of that section so numbered; and

(c) a reference in a section, subsection or Schedule to a numbered paragraph is a reference to the paragraph of that section, subsection or Schedule so numbered; and

(d) a reference to any provision of an Act (including this Act) includes a Schedule incorporated in the Act by that provision.   **[239]**

NOTES
   Sub-s (1): first definition "board of management" inserted by the Self-Governing Schools etc (Scotland) Act 1989, s 82(1), Sch 10, para 6(4); second definition "board of management" inserted by the Further and Higher Education (Scotland) Act 1992, s 93, Sch 9, para 5(5); words omitted in definition "further education" repealed by the Education Reform Act 1988, s 237, Sch 13, Pt II; definition "industrial tribunal" repealed by the Industrial Training Act 1982, s 20, Sch 3, para 7(b), Sch 4; definition "upper limit of compulsory school age" repealed as from a day to be appointed by the Education Act 1993, s 307(1), Sch 19, para 67, Sch 21, Pt II. All other amendments made by the Education (Scotland) Act 1980, s 136(2), Sch 4, para 15.

79 (*Transitional and commencement provisions, amendments and repeals.*)

80 Short title and extent

(1) This Act may be cited as the Race Relations Act 1976.

(2) ...   **[240]–[241]**

NOTE
   Sub-s (2): relates to Northern Ireland.

SCHEDULES

SCHEDULE 1

Section 43

THE COMMISSION FOR RACIAL EQUALITY

Incorporation and status

1. On the appointment by the Secretary of State of the first Commissioners, the Commission shall come into existence as a body corporate.

2.—(1) The Commission is not an emanation of the Crown, and shall not act or be treated as the servant or agent of the Crown.

(2) Accordingly—

(a) neither the Commission nor a Commissioner or member of its staff as such is entitled to any status, immunity, privilege or exemption enjoyed by the Crown;

(b) the Commissioners and members of the staff of the Commission as such are not civil servants; and

(c) the Commission's property is not property of, or held on behalf of, the Crown.

Tenure of office of Commissioners

3.—(1) A Commissioner shall hold and vacate his office in accordance with the terms of his appointment.

(2) A person shall not be appointed a Commissioner for more than five years.

(3) With the consent of the Commissioner concerned, the Secretary of State may alter the terms of an appointment so as to make a full-time Commissioner into a part-time Commissioner or vice versa, or for any other purpose.

(4) A Commissioner may resign by notice to the Secretary of State.

(5) The Secretary of State may terminate the appointment of a Commissioner if satisfied that—

   (a) without the consent of the Commission, he failed to attend the meetings of the Commission during a continuous period of six months beginning not earlier than nine months before the termination; or

   (b) he is an undischarged bankrupt, or has made an arrangement with his creditors, or is insolvent within the meaning of paragraph 9(2) of Schedule 3 to the Conveyancing and Feudal Reform (Scotland) Act 1970; or

   (c) he is by reason of physical or mental illness, or for any other reason, incapable of carrying out his duties.

(6) Past service as a Commissioner is no bar to re-appointment.

Tenure of office of chairman and deputy chairmen

4.—(1) The chairman and each deputy chairman shall hold and vacate his office in accordance with the terms of his appointment, and may resign by notice to the Secretary of State.

(2) The office of the chairman or a deputy chairman is vacated if he ceases to be a Commissioner.

(3) Past service as chairman or a deputy chairman is no bar to re-appointment.

Remuneration of Commissioners

5. The Secretary of State may pay, or make such payments towards the provision of, such remuneration, pensions, allowances or gratuities to or in respect of the Commissioners or any of them as, with the consent of the Minister for the Civil Service, he may determine.

6. Where a person ceases to be a Commissioner otherwise than on the expiry of his term of office, and it appears to the Secretary of State that there are special circumstances which make it right for that person to receive compensation, the Secretary of State may, with the consent of the Minister for the Civil Service, direct the Commission to make to that person a payment of such amount as, with the consent of that Minister, the Secretary of State may determine.

Additional Commissioners

7.—(1) Paragraphs 2(2), 3(1) and (6), and 6 shall apply to additional Commissioners appointed under section 48(2) as they apply to Commissioners.

(2) The Commission may pay, or make such payments towards the provision of, such remuneration, pensions, allowances or gratuities to or in respect of an additional Commissioner as the Secretary of State, with the consent of the Minister for the Civil Service, may determine.

(3) With the approval of the Secretary of State and the consent of the additional Commissioner concerned, the Commission may alter the terms of an appointment of an additional Commissioner so as to make a full-time additional Commissioner into a part-time additional Commissioner or vice versa, or for any other purpose.

(4) An additional Commissioner may resign by notice to the Commission.

(5) The Secretary of State, or the Commission acting with the approval of the Secretary of State, may terminate the appointment of an additional Commissioner if satisfied that—

    (a) without reasonable excuse he failed to carry out the duties for which he was appointed during a continuous period of three months beginning not earlier than six months before the termination; or

    (b) he is a person such as is mentioned in paragraph 3(5)(b); or

    (c) he is by reason of physical or mental illness, or for any other reason, incapable of carrying out his duties.

(6) The appointment of an additional Commissioner shall terminate at the conclusion of the investigation for which he was appointed, if not sooner.

Staff

8. The Commission may, after consultation with the Secretary of State, appoint such officers and servants as they think fit, subject to the approval of the Minister for the Civil Service as to numbers and as to remuneration and other terms and conditions of service.

9.—(1) Employment with the Commission shall be included among the kinds of employment to which a superannuation scheme under section 1 of the Superannuation Act 1972 can apply, and accordingly in Schedule 1 to that Act (in which those kinds of employment are listed) the words "Commission for Racial Equality" shall be inserted after the words "Commission on Industrial Relations."

(2) Where a person who is employed by the Commission and is by reference to that employment a participant in a scheme under section 1 of the Superannuation Act 1972 becomes a Commissioner or an additional Commissioner, the Minister for the Civil Service may determine that his service as a Commissioner or additional Commissioner shall be treated for the purposes of the scheme as service as an employee of the Commission.

10.—(1) In this paragraph—

    "the new Commission" means the Commission for Racial Equality;

    "present Commission employee" means a person who immediately before the repeal date is employed by the Community Relations Commission;

    "private pension scheme" means a scheme for the payment of pensions, allowances or gratuities other than one made under section 1 of the Superannuation Act 1972;

    "the repeal date" means the date on which the repeal of the Race Relations Act 1968 by this Act takes effect.

(2) If a present Commission employee enters the employment of the new Commission on the repeal date and on so doing elects to be covered for his service in that employment by a private pension scheme in which he was a participant in respect of his service in the employment of the Community Relations Commission the new Commission may make such payments towards the provision of benefits to or in respect of him under that scheme (or any other private pension scheme replacing it) as may be determined by the new Commission with the consent of the Secretary of State given with the approval of the Minister for the Civil Service; and it shall be the duty of the new Commission and those Ministers in the exercise of their functions under this sub-paragraph to ensure that his rights under the scheme do not become less advantageous than they were when he entered the employment of the new Commission.

(3) Where a person who is employed by the new Commission and is in respect of that employment a participant in a private pension scheme becomes a Commissioner or an additional Commissioner, his service as a Commissioner or additional Commissioner may be treated for the purposes of the scheme as service as an employee of the new Commission.

11. The Employers' Liability (Compulsory Insurance) Act 1969 shall not require insurance to be effected by the Commission.

Advisory committees

12. The Commission may, with the approval of the Secretary of State, appoint advisory committees for the purpose of such of their functions as they think fit.

Proceedings and business

13.—(1) Subject to the provisions of this Act—

(a) the Commission shall discharge their functions in accordance with arrangements made by the Commission and approved by the Secretary of State; and

(b) arrangements so made and approved may provide for the discharge under the general direction of the Commission of any of the Commission's functions by a committee of the Commission, or by two or more Commissioners.

(2) Anything done by or in relation to a committee of the Commission or Commissioners, in the discharge of the Commission's functions shall have the same effect as if done by or in relation to the Commission.

14. The validity of any proceedings of the Commission shall not be affected by any vacancy among the members of the Commission or by any defect in the appointment of any Commissioner or additional Commissioner.

15. The quorum for meetings of the Commission shall in the first instance be determined by a meeting of the Commission attended by not less than five Commissioners.

Finance

16. The Secretary of State shall pay to the Commission expenses incurred or to be incurred by them under paragraph 6, 7, 8 or 10 of this Schedule or paragraph 7 of Schedule 2, and, with the consent of the Minister for the Civil Service and the Treasury, shall pay to the Commission such sums as the Secretary of State thinks fit for enabling the Commission to meet other expenses.

17.—(1) The accounting year of the Commission shall be the twelve months ending on 31st March.

(2) It shall be the duty of the Commission—

(a) to keep proper accounts and proper records in relation to the accounts;

(b) to prepare in respect of each accounting year a statement of accounts in such form as the Secretary of State may direct with the approval of the Treasury; and

(c) to send copies of the statement to the Secretary of State and the Comptroller and Auditor General before the end of the month of November next following the accounting year to which the statement relates.

(3) The Comptroller and Auditor General shall examine, certify and report on each statement received by him in pursuance of this Schedule and shall lay copies of each statement and of his report before each House of Parliament.

Disqualification Acts

18. . . .   [242]

NOTE

Para 18: amends the House of Commons Disqualification Act 1975, Sch 1, Pts II, III, and the Northern Ireland Assembly Disqualification Act 1975, Sch 1, Pts II, III.

(Schs 2 (transitional provisions), 4 (amendments, repeals) omitted; Sch 3 repealed by the Trade Union and Labour Relations (Consolidation) Act 1992, s 300(1), Sch 1.)

PATENTS ACT 1977

(1977 c 37)

ARRANGEMENT OF SECTIONS

PART I
NEW DOMESTIC LAW

Employees' inventions

PART III
MISCELLANEOUS AND GENERAL

Supplemental

*An Act to establish a new law of patents applicable to future patents and applications
for patents; to amend the law of patents applicable to existing patents and
applications for patents; to give effect to certain international conventions on
patents; and for connected purposes*

[29 July 1977]

NOTE

Only those sections of this Act concerned with inventions made by employees are reproduced here, ie
ss 39–43 (and s 132 which makes provision as to the extent, etc of the Act). For definitions within the Act
see s 130 (not reproduced).

PART I
NEW DOMESTIC LAW

1–38 (*Outside the scope of this work.*)

Employees' inventions

39 Right to employees' inventions

(1) Notwithstanding anything in any rule of law, an invention made by an employee
shall, as between him and his employer, be taken to belong to his employer for the
purposes of this Act and all other purposes if—

> (a) it was made in the course of the normal duties of the employee or in the
> course of duties falling outside his normal duties, but specifically assigned
> to him, and the circumstances in either case were such that an invention
> might reasonably be expected to result from the carrying out of his duties;
> or

(b) the invention was made in the course of the duties of the employee and, at the time of making the invention, because of the nature of his duties and the particular responsibilities arising from the nature of his duties he had a special obligation to further the interests of the employer's undertaking.

(2) Any other invention made by an employee shall, as between him and his employer, be taken for those purposes to belong to the employee.

[(3) Where by virtue of this section an invention belongs, as between him and his employer, to an employee, nothing done—

(a) by or on behalf of the employee or any person claiming under him for the purposes of pursuing an application for a patent, or

(b) by any person for the purpose of performing or working the invention,

shall be taken to infringe any copyright or design right to which, as between him and his employer, his employer is entitled in any model or document relating to the invention.]   [243]

NOTE

Sub-s (3): added by the Copyright, Designs and Patents Act 1988, s 295, Sch 5, para 11(1).

40 Compensation of employees for certain inventions

(1) Where it appears to the court or the comptroller on an application made by an employee within the prescribed period that the employee has made an invention belonging to the employer for which a patent has been granted, that the patent is (having regard among other things to the size and nature of the employer's undertaking) of outstanding benefit to the employer and that by reason of those facts it is just that the employee should be awarded compensation to be paid by the employer, the court or the comptroller may award him such compensation of an amount determined under section 41 below.

(2) Where it appears to the court or the comptroller on an application made by an employee within the prescribed period that—

(a) a patent has been granted for an invention made by and belonging to the employee;

(b) his rights in the invention, or in any patent or application for a patent for the invention, have since the appointed day been assigned to the employer or an exclusive licence under the patent or application has since the appointed day been granted to the employer;

(c) the benefit derived by the employee from the contract of assignment, assignation or grant or any ancillary contract ("the relevant contract") is inadequate in relation to the benefit derived by the employer from the patent; and

(d) by reason of those facts it is just that the employee should be awarded compensation to be paid by the employer in addition to the benefit derived from the relevant contract;

the court or the comptroller may award him such compensation of an amount determined under section 41 below.

(3) Subsections (1) and (2) above shall not apply to the invention of an employee where a relevant collective agreement provides for the payment of compensation in respect of inventions of the same description as that invention to employees of the same description as that employee.

(4) Subsection (2) above shall have effect notwithstanding anything in the relevant contract or any agreement applicable to the invention (other than any such collective agreement).

(5) If it appears to the comptroller on an application under this section that the application involves matters which would more properly be determined by the court, he may decline to deal with it.

(6) In this section—

"the prescribed period", in relation to proceedings before the court, means the period prescribed by rules of court, and

"relevant collective agreement" means a collective agreement within the meaning of [the Trade Union and Labour Relations (Consolidation) Act 1992], made by or on behalf of a trade union to which the employee belongs, and by the employer or an employers' association to which the employer belongs which is in force at the time of the making of the invention.

(7) References in this section to an invention belonging to an employer or employee are references to it so belonging as between the employer and the employee.

[244]

NOTES
Sub-s (6): words in square brackets substituted by the Trade Union and Labour Relations (Consolidation) Act 1992, s 300(2), Sch 2, para 9.
The relevant regulation under this section is the Patent Rules 1990, SI 1990/2384, rule 59.

41 Amount of compensation

(1) An award of compensation to an employee under section 40(1) or (2) above in relation to a patent for an invention shall be such as will secure for the employee a fair share (having regard to all the circumstances) of the benefit which the employer has derived, or may reasonably be expected to derive, from the patent or from the assignment, assignation or grant to a person connected with the employer of the property or any right in the invention or the property in, or any right in or under, an application for that patent.

(2) For the purposes of subsection (1) above the amount of any benefit derived or expected to be derived by an employer from the assignment, assignation or grant of—

(a) the property in, or any right in or under, a patent for the invention or an application for such a patent; or

(b) the property or any right in the invention;

to a person connected with him shall be taken to be the amount which could reasonably be expected to be so derived by the employer if that person had not been connected with him.

(3) Where the Crown or a Research Council in its capacity as employer assigns or grants the property in, or any right in or under, an invention, patent or application for a patent to a body having among its functions that of developing or exploiting inventions resulting from public research and does so for no consideration or only a nominal consideration, any benefit derived from the invention, patent or application by that body shall be treated for the purposes of the foregoing provisions of this section as so derived by the Crown or, as the case may be, Research Council.

In this subsection "Research Council" means a body which is a Research Council for the purposes of the Science and Technology Act 1965.

(4) In determining the fair share of the benefit to be secured for an employee in respect of a patent for an invention which has always belonged to an employer, the court or the comptroller shall, among other things, take the following matters into account, that is to say—

(a) the nature of the employee's duties, his remuneration and the other advantages he derives or has derived from his employment or has derived in relation to the invention under this Act;

(b) the effort and skill which the employee has devoted to making the invention;

(c) the effort and skill which any other person has devoted to making the invention jointly with the employee concerned, and the advice and other assistance contributed by any other employee who is not a joint inventor of the invention; and

(d) the contribution made by the employer to the making, developing and working of the invention by the provision of advice, facilities and other assistance, by the provision of opportunities and by his managerial and commercial skill and activities.

(5) In determining the fair share of the benefit to be secured for an employee in respect of a patent for an invention which originally belonged to him, the court or the comptroller shall, among other things, take the following matters into account, that is to say—

(a) any conditions in a licence or licences granted under this Act or otherwise in respect of the invention or the patent;

(b) the extent to which the invention was made jointly by the employee with any other person; and

(c) the contribution made by the employer to the making, developing and working of the invention as mentioned in subsection (4)(d) above.

(6) Any order for the payment of compensation under section 40 above may be an order for the payment of a lump sum or for periodical payment, or both.

(7) Without prejudice to section 32 of the Interpretation Act 1889 (which provides that a statutory power may in general be exercised from time to time), the refusal of the court or the comptroller to make any such order on an application made by an employee under section 40 above shall not prevent a further application being made under that section by him or any successor in title of his.

(8) Where the court or the comptroller has made any such order, the court or he may on the application of either the employer or the employee vary or discharge it or suspend any provision of the order and revive any provision so suspended, and section 40(5) above shall apply to the application as it applies to an application under that section.

(9) In England and Wales any sums awarded by the comptroller under section 40 above shall, if a county court so orders, be recoverable by execution issued from the county court or otherwise as if they were payable under an order of that court.

(10) In Scotland an order made under section 40 above by the comptroller for the payment of any sums may be enforced in like manner as a recorded decree arbitral.

(11) In Northern Ireland an order made under section 40 above by the comptroller for the payment of any sums may be enforced as if it were a money judgment.

[245]

NOTES

Section modified in its application to the Isle of Man by the Patents Act (Isle of Man) Order 1978, SI 1978/621.

The relevant regulation in relation to sub-s (8) is the Patent Rules 1990, SI 1990/2384, rule 60.

42 Enforceability of contracts relating to employees' inventions

(1) This section applies to any contract (whenever made) relating to inventions made by an employee, being a contract entered into by him—

(a) with the employer (alone or with another); or

(b) with some other person at the request of the employer or in pursuance of the employee's contract of employment.

(2) Any term in a contract to which this section applies which diminishes the employee's rights in inventions of any description made by him after the appointed day and the date of the contract, or in or under patents for those inventions or applications for such patents, shall be unenforceable against him to the extent that it diminishes his rights in an invention of that description so made, or in or under a patent for such an invention or an application for any such patent.

(3) Subsection (2) above shall not be construed as derogating from any duty of confidentiality owed to his employer by an employee by virtue of any rule of law or otherwise.

(4) This section applies to any arrangement made with a Crown employee by or on behalf of the Crown as his employer as it applies to any contract made between an employee and an employer other than the Crown, and for the purposes of this section "Crown employee" means a person employed under or for the purposes of a government department or any officer or body exercising on behalf of the Crown functions conferred by any enactment [or a person serving in the naval, military or air forces of the Crown]. [246]

NOTE

Words in square brackets added by the Armed Forces Act 1981, s 22(1), (2).

43 Supplementary

(1) Sections 39 to 42 above shall not apply to an invention made before the appointed day.

(2) Sections 39 to 42 above shall not apply to an invention made by an employee unless at the time he made the invention one of the following conditions was satisfied in his case, that is to say—

(a) he was mainly employed in the United Kingdom; or

(b) he was not mainly employed anywhere or his place of employment could not be determined, but his employer had a place of business in the United Kingdom to which the employee was attached, whether or not he was also attached elsewhere.

(3) In section 39 to 42 above and this section, except so far as the context otherwise requires, references to the making of an invention by an employee are references to his making it alone or jointly with any other person, but do not include references to his merely contributing advice or other assistance in the making of an invention by another employee.

(4) Any references [in sections 39 to 42] above to a patent and to a patent being granted are respectively references to a patent or other protection and to its being granted whether under the law of the United Kingdom or the law in force in any other country or under any treaty or international convention.

(5) For the purposes of sections 40 and 41 above the benefit derived or expected to be derived by an employer from a patent shall, where he dies before any award is made under section 40 above in respect of the patent, include any benefit derived or

expected to be derived from the patent by his personal representatives or by any person in whom it was vested by their assent.

(6) Where an employee dies before an award is made under section 40 above in respect of a patented invention made by him, his personal representatives or their successors in title may exercise his right to make or proceed with an application for compensation under section (1) or (2) of that section.

(7) In sections 40 and 41 above and this section "benefit" means benefit in money or money's worth.

(8) Section 533 of the Income and Corporation Taxes Act 1970 (definition of connected persons) shall apply for determining for the purposes of section 41(2) above whether one person is connected with another as it applies for determining that question for the purposes of the Tax Acts. **[247]**

NOTE
Sub-s (4): words in square brackets substituted by the Copyright, Designs and Patents Act 1988, s 295, Sch 5, para 11(2).

44–95 (*Ss 44–83, 86, 87, 89–95 outside the scope of this work; ss 84, 85, 88 repealed by the Copyright, Designs and Patents Act 1988, ss 295, 303(2), Sch 5, para 23, Sch 8.*)

PART III
MISCELLANEOUS AND GENERAL

96–121 (*S 96 repealed by the Supreme Court Act 1981, s 152(4), Sch 7; ss 97–103, 105–113, 116–121 outside the scope of this work; ss 104, 114, 115 repealed by the Copyright, Designs and Patents Act 1988, s 303(2), Sch 8.*)

Supplemental

122–131 (*Outside the scope of this work.*)

132 Short title, extent, commencement, consequential amendments and repeals

(1) This Act may be cited as the Patents Act 1977.

(2) This Act shall extend to the Isle of Man, subject to any modifications contained in an Order made by Her Majesty in Council, and accordingly, subject to any such order, references in this Act to the United Kingdom shall be construed as including references to the Isle of Man.

(3) For the purposes of this Act the territorial waters of the United Kingdom shall be treated as part of the United Kingdom.

(4) This Act applies to acts done in an area designated by order under section 1(7) of the Continental Shelf Act 1964, [or specified by Order under section 22(5) of the Oil and Gas (Enterprise) Act 1982 in connection with any activity falling within section 23(2) of that Act], as it applies to acts done in the United Kingdom.

(5) This Act (except sections 77(6), (7) and (9), 78(7) and (8), this subsection and the repeal of section 41 of the 1949 Act) shall come into operation on such day as may be appointed by the Secretary of State by order, and different days may be appointed under this subsection for different purposes.

(6), (7) . . .   **[248]**

NOTES
   Sub-s (4): words in square brackets substituted by the Oil and Gas (Enterprise) Act 1982, s 37(1), Sch 3, para 39.
   Sub-ss (6), (7): amendments and repeals (omitted).

(Schs 1–6 outside the scope of this work.)

UNFAIR CONTRACT TERMS ACT 1977
(1977 c 50)

ARRANGEMENT OF SECTIONS

PART I
AMENDMENT OF LAW FOR ENGLAND AND WALES AND NORTHERN IRELAND

Introductory

PART II
AMENDMENT OF LAW FOR SCOTLAND

An Act to impose further limits on the extent to which under the law of England and Wales and Northern Ireland civil liability for breach of contract, or for negligence or other breach of duty, can be avoided by means of contract terms and otherwise, and under the law of Scotland civil liability can be avoided by means of contract terms

[26 October 1977]

PART I

AMENDMENT OF LAW FOR ENGLAND AND WALES AND NORTHERN IRELAND

Introductory

1 Scope of Part I

(1) For the purposes of this Part of this Act, "negligence" means the breach—

   (a) of any obligation, arising from the express or implied terms of a contract, to take reasonable care or exercise reasonable skill in the performance of the contract;

   (b) of any common law duty to take reasonable care or exercise reasonable skill (but not any stricter duty);

   (c) of the common duty of care imposed by the Occupiers' Liability Act 1957 or the Occupiers' Liability Act (Northern Ireland) 1957.

   (2) This Part of this Act is subject to Part III; and in relation to contracts, the operation of sections 2 to 4 and 7 is subject to the exceptions made by Schedule 1.

   (3) In the case of both contract and tort, sections 2 to 7 apply (except where the contrary is stated in section 6(4)) only to business liability, that is liability for breach of obligations or duties arising—

   (a) from things done or to be done by a person in the course of a business (whether his own business or another's); or

   (b) from the occupation of premises used for business purposes of the occupier;

and references to liability are to be read accordingly [but liability of an occupier of premises for breach of an obligation or duty towards a person obtaining access to the premises for recreational or educational purposes, being liability for loss or damage suffered by reason of the dangerous state of the premises, is not a business liability of the occupier unless granting that person such access for the purposes concerned falls within the business purposes of the occupier].

(4) In relation to any breach of duty or obligation, it is immaterial for any purpose of this Part of this Act whether the breach was inadvertent or intentional, or whether liability for it arises directly or vicariously.   **[249]**

NOTE

Sub-s (3): words in square brackets added by the Occupiers' Liability Act 1984, s 2.

Avoidance of liability for negligence, breach of contract, etc

2 Negligence liability

(1) A person cannot by reference to any contract term or to a notice given to persons generally or to particular persons exclude or restrict his liability for death or personal injury resulting from negligence.

(2) In the case of other loss or damage, a person cannot so exclude or restrict his liability for negligence except in so far as the term or notice satisfies the requirement of reasonableness.

(3) Where a contract term or notice purports to exclude or restrict liability for negligence a person's agreement to or awareness of it is not of itself to be taken as indicating his voluntary acceptance of any risk.   **[250]**

3 Liability arising in contract

(1) This section applies as between contracting parties where one of them deals as consumer or on the other's written standard terms of business.

(2) As against that party, the other cannot by reference to any contract term—

    (a) when himself in breach of contract, exclude or restrict any liability of his in respect of the breach; or

    (b) claim to be entitled—

        (i) to render a contractual performance substantially different from that which was reasonably expected of him, or

        (ii) in respect of the whole or any part of his contractual obligation, to render no performance at all,

except in so far as (in any of the cases mentioned above in this subsection) the contract term satisfies the requirement of reasonableness.   **[251]**

4 Unreasonable indemnity clauses

(1) A person dealing as consumer cannot by reference to any contract term be made to indemnify another person (whether a party to the contract or not) in respect of liability that may be incurred by the other for negligence or breach of contract, except in so far as the contract term satisfies the requirement of reasonableness.

(2) This section applies whether the liability in question—

    (a) is directly that of the person to be indemnified or is incurred by him vicariously;

    (b) is to the person dealing as consumer or to someone else.   **[252]**

5–7 (*Ss 5 (guarantees of consumer goods), 6 (sale and hire-purchase), 7 (miscellaneous contracts under which goods pass) outside the scope of this work.*)

Other provisions about contracts

8 (*Amends the Misrepresentation Act 1987.*)

9 Effect of breach

(1) Where for reliance upon it a contract term has to satisfy the requirement of reasonableness, it may be found to do so and be given effect accordingly notwithstanding that the contract has been terminated either by breach or by a party electing to treat it as repudiated.

(2) Where on a breach the contract is nevertheless affirmed by a party entitled to treat it as repudiated, this does not of itself exclude the requirement of reasonableness in relation to any contract term. **[252A]**

10 Evasion by means of secondary contract

A person is not bound by any contract term prejudicing or taking away rights of his which arise under, or in connection with the performance of, another contract, so far as those rights extend to the enforcement of another's liability which this Part of this Act prevents that other from excluding or restricting. **[253]**

Explanatory provisions

11 The "reasonableness" test

(1) In relation to a contract term, the requirement of reasonableness for the purposes of this Part of this Act, section 3 of the Misrepresentation Act 1967 and section 3 of the Misrepresentation Act (Northern Ireland) 1967 is that the term shall have been a fair and reasonable one to be included having regard to the circumstances which were, or ought reasonably to have been, known to or in the contemplation of the parties when the contract was made.

(2) In determining for the purposes of section 6 or 7 above whether a contract term satisfies the requirement of reasonableness, regard shall be had in particular to the matters specified in Schedule 2 to this Act; but this subsection does not prevent the court or arbitrator from holding, in accordance with any rule of law, that a term which purports to exclude or restrict any relevant liability is not a term of the contract.

(3) In relation to a notice (not being a notice having contractual effect), the requirement of reasonableness under this Act is that it should be fair and reasonable to allow reliance on it, having regard to all the circumstances obtaining when the liability arose or (but for the notice) would have arisen.

(4) Where by reference to a contract term or notice a person seeks to restrict liability to a specified sum of money, and the question arises (under this or any other Act) whether the term or notice satisfies the requirement of reasonableness, regard shall be had in particular (but without prejudice to subsection (2) above in the case of contract terms) to—

    (a) the resources which he could expect to be available to him for the purpose of meeting the liability should it arise; and

    (b) how far it was open to him to cover himself by insurance.

(5) It is for those claiming that a contract term or notice satisfies the requirement of reasonableness to show that it does.   [254]

12 "Dealing as consumer"

(1) A party to a contract "deals as consumer" in relation to another party if—

(a) he neither makes the contract in the course of a business nor holds himself out as doing so; and

(b) the other party does make the contract in the course of a business; and

(c) in the case of a contract governed by the law of sale of goods or hire-purchase, or by section 7 of this Act, the goods passing under or in pursuance of the contract are of a type ordinarily supplied for private use or consumption.

(2) But on a sale by auction or by competitive tender the buyer is not in any circumstances to be regarded as dealing as consumer.

(3) Subject to this, it is for those claiming that a party does not deal as consumer to show that he does not.   [255]

13 Varieties of exemption clause

(1) To the extent that this Part of this Act prevents the exclusion or restriction of any liability it also prevents—

(a) making the liability or its enforcement subject to restrictive or onerous conditions;

(b) excluding or restricting any right or remedy in respect of the liability, or subjecting a person to any prejudice in consequence of his pursuing any such right or remedy;

(c) excluding or restricting rules of evidence or procedure;

and (to that extent) sections 2 and 5 to 7 also prevent excluding or restricting liability by reference to terms and notices which exclude or restrict the relevant obligation or duty.

(2) But an agreement in writing to submit present or future differences to arbitration is not to be treated under this Part of this Act as excluding or restricting any liability.   [256]

14 Interpretation of Part I

In this Part of this Act—

"business" includes a profession and the activities of any government department or local or public authority;

"goods" has the same meaning as in [the Sale of Goods Act 1979];

"hire-purchase agreement" has the same meaning as in the Consumer Credit Act 1974;

"negligence" has the meaning given by section 1(1);

"notice" includes an announcement, whether or not in writing, and any other communication or pretended communication; and

"personal injury" includes any disease and any impairment of physical or mental condition.   [257]

NOTE
Words in square brackets in definition "goods" substituted by the Sale of Goods Act 1979, s 63(1), Sch 2, para 20.

PART II

AMENDMENT OF LAW FOR SCOTLAND

15 Scope of Part II

(1) This Part of this Act . . . is subject to Part III of this Act, and does not affect the validity of any discharge or indemnity given by a person in consideration of the receipt by him of compensation in settlement of any claim which he has.

(2) Subject to subsection (3) below, sections 16 to 18 of this Act apply to any contract only to the extent that the contract—

(a) relates to the transfer of the ownership or possession of goods from one person to another (with or without work having been done on them);

(b) constitutes a contract of service or apprenticeship;

(c) relates to services of whatever kind, including (without prejudice to the foregoing generality) carriage, deposit and pledge, care and custody, mandate, agency, loan and services relating to the use of land;

(d) relates to the liability of an occupier of land to persons entering upon or using that land;

(e) relates to a grant of any right or permission to enter upon or use land not amounting to an estate or interest in the land.

(3) Notwithstanding anything in subsection (2) above, sections 16 to 18—

(a) do not apply to any contract to the extent that the contract—

(i) is a contract of insurance (including a contract to pay an annuity on human life);

(ii) relates to the formation, constitution or dissolution of any body corporate or unincorporated association or partnership;

(b) apply to —

a contract of marine salvage or towage;

a charter party of a ship or hovercraft;

a contract for the carriage of goods by ship or hovercraft; or,

a contract to which subsection (4) below relates,

only to the extent that—

(i) both parties deal or hold themselves out as dealing in the course of a business (and then only in so far as the contract purports to exclude or restrict liability for breach of duty in respect of death or personal injury); or

(ii) the contract is a consumer contract (and then only in favour of the consumer).

(4) This subsection relates to a contract in pursuance of which goods are carried by ship or hovercraft and which either—

(a) specifies ship or hovercraft as the means of carriage over part of the journey to be covered; or

(b) makes no provision as to the means of carriage and does not exclude ship or hovercraft as that means,

in so far as the contract operates for and in relation to the carriage of the goods by that means. **[258]**

NOTE
Sub-s (1): words omitted repealed by the Law Reform (Miscellaneous Provisions) (Scotland) Act 1990, ss 68(1), (2), 74, Sch 9.

16 Liability for breach of duty

(1) [Subject to subsection (1A) below,] where a term of a contract [or a provision of a notice given to persons generally or to particular persons] purports to exclude or restrict liability for breach of duty arising in the course of any business or from the occupation of any premises used for business purposes of the occupier, that term—

    (a) shall be void in any case where such exclusion or restriction is in respect of death or personal injury;

    (b) shall, in any other case, have no effect if it was not fair and reasonable to incorporate the term [or provision] in the contract [or, as the case may be, if it is not fair and reasonable to allow reliance on the provision].

    [(1A) Nothing in paragraph (b) of subsection (1) above shall be taken as implying that a provision of a notice has effect in circumstances where, apart from that paragraph, it would not have effect.]

(2) Subsection (1)(a) above does not affect the validity of any discharge and indemnity given by a person, or in connection with an award to him of compensation for pneumoconiosis attributable to employment in the coal industry, in respect of any further claim arising from his contracting that disease.

(3) Where under subsection (1) above a term of a contract [or a provision of a notice] is void or has no effect, the fact that a person agreed to, or was aware of, the term [or provision] shall not of itself be sufficient evidence that he knowingly and voluntarily assumed any risk. **[259]**

NOTES
Sub-ss (1), (3): words in square brackets inserted by the Law Reform (Miscellaneous Provisions) (Scotland) Act 1990, s 68(1), (3)(a), (c).
Sub-s (1A): inserted by the Law Reform (Miscellaneous Provisions) (Scotland) Act 1990, s 68(1), (3)(b).

17 Control of unreasonable exemptions in consumer or standard form contracts

(1) Any term of a contract which is a consumer contract or a standard form contract shall have no effect for the purpose of enabling a party to the contract—

    (a) who is in breach of a contractual obligation, to exclude or restrict any liability of his to the consumer or customer in respect of the breach;

    (b) in respect of a contractual obligation, to render no performance, or to render a performance substantially different from that which the consumer or customer reasonably expected from the contract;

if it was not fair and reasonable to incorporate the term in the contract.

(2) In this section "customer" means a party to a standard form contract who deals on the basis of written standard terms of business of the other party to the contract who himself deals in the course of a business. **[260]**

18 Unreasonable indemnity clauses in consumer contracts

(1) Any term of a contract which is a consumer contract shall have no effect for the purpose of making the consumer indemnify another person (whether a party to the

contract or not) in respect of liability which that other person may incur as a result of breach of duty or breach of contract, if it was not fair and reasonable to incorporate the term in the contract.

(2) In this section "liability" means liability arising in the course of any business or from the occupation of any premises used for business purposes of the occupier.

[261]

19–21 *(Ss 19 (guarantees of consumer goods), 20 (sale and hire purchase contracts), 21 (other contracts for the supply of goods) omitted.)*

22 Consequence of breach

For the avoidance of doubt, where any provision of this Part of this Act requires that the incorporation of a term in a contract must be fair and reasonable for the term to have effect—

> (a) if that requirement is satisfied, the term may be given effect to notwithstanding that the contract has been terminated in consequence of breach of that contract;
>
> (b) for the term to be given effect to, that requirement must be satisfied even where a party who is entitled to rescind the contract elects not to rescind it. **[261A]**

23 Evasion by means of secondary contract

Any term of a contract shall be void which purports to exclude or restrict, or has the effect of excluding or restricting—

> (a) the exercise, by a party to any other contract, of any right or remedy which arises in respect of that other contract in consequence of breach of duty, or of obligation, liability for which could not by virtue of the provisions of this Part of this Act be excluded or restricted by a term of that other contract;
>
> (b) the application of the provisions of this Part of this Act in respect of that or any other contract. **[262]**

24 The "reasonableness" test

(1) In determining for the purposes of this Part of this Act whether it was fair and reasonable to incorporate a term in a contract, regard shall be had only to the circumstances which were, or ought reasonably to have been, known to or in the contemplation of the parties to the contract at the time the contract was made.

(2) In determining for the purposes of section 20 or 21 of this Act whether it was fair and reasonable to incorporate a term in a contract, regard shall be had in particular to the matters specified in Schedule 2 to this Act; but this subsection shall not prevent a court or arbiter from holding, in accordance with any rule of law, that a term which purports to exclude or restrict any relevant liability is not a term of the contract.

[(2A) In determining for the purposes of this Part of this Act whether it is fair and reasonable to allow reliance on a provision of a notice (not being a notice having contractual effect), regard shall be had to all the circumstances obtaining when the liability arose or (but for the provision) would have arisen.]

(3) Where a term in a contract [or a provision of a notice] purports to restrict liability to a specified sum of money, and the question arises for the purposes of this Part of this Act whether it was fair and reasonable to incorporate the term in the contract, [or whether it is fair and reasonable to allow reliance on the provision,] then, without prejudice to subsection (2) above, [in the case of a term in a contract] regard shall be had in particular to—

    (a) the resources which the party seeking to rely on that term [or provision] could expect to be available to him for the purpose of meeting the liability should it arise;

    (b) how far it was open to that party to cover himself by insurance.

(4) The onus of proving that it was fair and reasonable to incorporate a term in a contract [or that it is fair and reasonable to allow reliance on a provision of a notice] shall lie on the party so contending.   **[263]**

NOTES

Sub-s (2A): inserted by the Law Reform (Miscellaneous Provisions) (Scotland) Act 1990, s 68(1), (4)(a).

Sub-ss (3), (4): words in square brackets inserted by the Law Reform (Miscellaneous Provisions) (Scotland) Act 1990, s 68(1), (4)(b), (c).

25 Interpretation of Part II

(1) In this Part of this Act—

"breach of duty" means the breach—

    (a) of any obligation, arising from the express or implied terms of a contract, to take reasonable care or exercise reasonable skill in the performance of the contract;

    (b) of any common law duty to take reasonable care or exercise reasonable skill;

    (c) of the duty of reasonable care imposed by section 2(1) of the Occupiers' Liability (Scotland) Act 1960;

"business" includes a profession and the activities of any government department or local or public authority;

"consumer" has the meaning assigned to that expression in the definition in this section of "consumer contract";

"consumer contract" means a contract (not being a contract of sale by auction or competitive tender) in which—

    (a) one party to the contract deals, and the other party to the contract ("the consumer") does not deal or hold himself out as dealing, in the course of a business, and

    (b) in the case of a contract such as is mentioned in section 15(2)(a) of this Act, the goods are of a type ordinarily supplied for private use or consumption;

and for the purposes of this Part of this Act the onus of proving that a contract is not to be regarded as a consumer contract shall lie on the party so contending;

"goods" has the same meaning as in [the Sale of Goods Act 1979];

"hire-purchase agreement" has the same meaning as in section 189(1) of the Consumer Credit Act 1974;

["notice" includes an announcement, whether or not in writing, and any other communication or pretended communication;]

"personal injury" includes any disease and any impairment of physical or mental condition.

(2) In relation to any breach of duty or obligation, it is immaterial for any purpose of this Part of this Act whether the act or omission giving rise to that breach was inadvertent or intentional, or whether liability for it arises directly or vicariously.

(3) In this Part of this Act, any reference to excluding or restricting any liability includes—

    (a) making the liability or its enforcement subject to any restrictive or onerous conditions;

    (b) excluding or restricting any right or remedy in respect of the liability, or subjecting a person to any prejudice in consequence of his pursuing any such right or remedy;

    (c) excluding or restricting any rule of evidence or procedure;

    (d) . . .,

but does not include an agreement to submit any question to arbitration.

(4) . . .

(5) In sections 15 and 16 and 19 to 21 of this Act, any reference to excluding or restricting any liability for breach of an obligation or duty shall include a reference to excluding or restricting the obligation or duty itself.   [264]

NOTES

    Sub-s (1): words in square brackets in definition "goods" substituted by the Sale of Goods Act 1979, s 63, Sch 2, para 22; definition "notice" inserted by the Law Reform (Miscellaneous Provisions) (Scotland) Act 1990, s 68(1), (5)(a).

    Sub-ss (3)(d), (4): repealed by the Law Reform (Miscellaneous Provisions) (Scotland) Act 1990, ss 68(1), (5)(b), 74, Sch 9.

PART III

PROVISIONS APPLYING TO WHOLE OF UNITED KINGDOM

Miscellaneous

26 (*(International supply contracts) omitted.*)

27 Choice of law clauses

(1) Where the [law applicable to] a contract is the law of any part of the United Kingdom only by choice of the parties (and apart from that choice would be the law of some country outside the United Kingdom) sections 2 to 7 and 16 to 21 of this Act do not operate as part [of the law applicable to the contract].

(2) This Act has effect notwithstanding any contract term which applies or purports to apply the law of some country outside the United Kingdom, where (either or both)—

    (a) the term appears to the court, or arbitrator or arbiter to have been imposed wholly or mainly for the purpose of enabling the party imposing it to evade the operation of this Act; or

    (b) in the making of the contract one of the parties dealt as consumer, and he was then habitually resident in the United Kingdom, and the essential steps necessary for the making of the contract were taken there, whether by him or others on his behalf.

(3) In the application of subsection (2) above to Scotland, for paragraph (b) there shall be substituted—

"(b) the contract is a consumer contract as defined in Part II of this Act, and the consumer at the date when the contract was made was habitually resident in the United Kingdom, and the essential steps necessary for the making of the contract were taken there, whether by him or others on his behalf.".

[264A]

NOTE

Sub-s (1): words in square brackets substituted and inserted by the Contracts (Applicable Law) Act 1990, s 5, Sch 4, para 4.

28–30 (*Ss 28 (temporary provision for sea carriage of passengers), 29 (saving for other relevant legislation) omitted; s 30 repealed by the Consumer Safety Act 1978, s 10(1), Sch 3.*)

General

31 Commencement; amendments; repeals

(1) This Act comes into force on 1st February 1978.

(2) Nothing in this Act applies to contracts made before the date on which it comes into force; but subject to this, it applies to liability for any loss or damage which is suffered on or after that date.

(3) The enactments specified in Schedule 3 to this Act are amended as there shown.

(4) The enactments specified in Schedule 4 to this Act are repealed to the extent specified in column 3 of that Schedule. **[265]**

32 Citation and extent

(1) This Act may be cited as the Unfair Contract Terms Act 1977.

(2) Part I of this Act extends to England and Wales and to Northern Ireland; but it does not extend to Scotland.

(3) Part II of this Act extends to Scotland only.

(4) This Part of this Act extends to the whole of the United Kingdom. **[266]**

SCHEDULES

SCHEDULE 1

Section 1(2)

SCOPE OF SECTIONS 2 TO 4 AND 7

1. Sections 2 to 4 of this Act do not extend to—
   (a) any contract of insurance (including a contract to pay an annuity on human life);
   (b) any contract so far as it relates to the creation or transfer of an interest in land, or to the termination of such an interest, whether by extinction, merger, surrender, forfeiture or otherwise;

(c) any contract so far as it relates to the creation or transfer of a right or interest in any patent, trade mark, copyright [or design right], registered design, technical or commercial information or other intellectual property, or relates to the termination of any such right or interest;

(d) any contract so far as it relates—

    (i) to the formation or dissolution of a company (which means any body corporate or unincorporated association and includes a partnership), or

    (ii) to its constitution or the rights or obligations of its corporators or members;

(e) any contract so far as it relates to the creation or transfer of securities or of any right or interest in securities.

2. Section 2(1) extends to—

(a) any contract of marine salvage or towage;

(b) any charterparty of a ship or hovercraft; and

(c) any contract for the carriage of goods by ship or hovercraft;

but subject to this sections 2 to 4 and 7 do not extend to any such contract except in favour of a person dealing as a consumer.

3. Where goods are carried by ship or hovercraft in pursuance of a contract which either—

(a) specifies that as a means of carriage over part of the journey to be covered, or

(b) makes no provision as to the means of carriage and does not exclude that means,

then sections 2(2), 3 and 4 do not, except in favour of a person dealing as consumer, extend to the contract as it operates for and in relation to the carriage of the goods by that means.

4. Section 2(1) and (2) do not extend to a contract of employment, except in favour of the employee.

5. Section 2(1) does not affect the validity of any discharge and indemnity given by a person, on or in connection with an award to him of compensation for pneumoconiosis attributable to employment in the coal industry, in respect of any further claim arising from his contracting that disease. **[267]**

NOTES

Para 1: words in square brackets inserted by the Copyright, Designs and Patents Act 1988, s 303(1), Sch 7, para 24.

By virtue of the Patents, Designs and Marks Act 1986, s 2, Sch 2, para 1(2)(f), the reference in para 1(c) above to a trade mark includes a reference to a registered service mark.

SCHEDULE 2

Sections 11(2), 24(2)

"GUIDELINES" FOR APPLICATION OF REASONABLENESS TEST

The matters to which regard is to be had in particular for the purposes of sections 6(3), 7(3) and (4), 20 and 21 are any of the following which appear to be relevant—

(a) the strength of the bargaining positions of the parties relative to each other, taking into account (among other things) alternative means by which the customer's requirements could have been met;

(b) whether the customer received an inducement to agree to the term, or in accepting it had an opportunity of entering into a similar contract with other persons, but without having to accept a similar term;

(c) whether the customer knew or ought reasonably to have known of the existence and extent of the term (having regard, among other things, to any custom of the trade and any previous course of dealing between the parties);

(d) where the term excludes or restricts any relevant liability if some condition is not complied with, whether it was reasonable at the time of the contract to expect that compliance with that condition would be practicable;

(e) whether the goods were manufactured, processed or adapted to the special order of the customer. **[267A]**

(Schs 3, 4 are concerned with amendments and repeals and are omitted.)

STATE IMMUNITY ACT 1978

(1978 c 33)

An Act to make new provision with respect to proceedings in the United Kingdom by or against other States; to provide for the effect of judgments given against the United Kingdom in the courts of States parties to the European Convention on State Immunity; to make new provision with respect to the immunities and privileges of heads of State; and for connected purposes

[20 July 1978]

NOTE

Only sections of this Act relevant to employment law are reproduced here.

PART I

PROCEEDINGS IN UNITED KINGDOM BY OR AGAINST OTHER STATES

Immunity from jurisdiction

1 General immunity from jurisdiction

(1) A State is immune from the jurisdiction of the courts of the United Kingdom except as provided in the following provisions of this Part of this Act.

(2) A court shall give effect to the immunity conferred by this section even though the State does not appear in the proceedings in question.   **[268]**

Exceptions from immunity

2, 3 (*Outside the scope of this work.*)

4 Contracts of employment

(1) A State is not immune as respects proceedings relating to a contract of employment between the State and an individual where the contract was made in the United Kingdom or the work is to be wholly or partly performed there.

(2) Subject to subsections (3) and (4) below, this section does not apply if—

  (a) at the time when the proceedings are brought the individual is a national of the State concerned; or

  (b) at the time when the contract was made the individual was neither a national of the United Kingdom nor habitually resident there; or

  (c) the parties to the contract have otherwise agreed in writing.

(3) Where the work is for an office, agency or establishment maintained by the State in the United Kingdom for commercial purposes, subsection (2) (a) and (b) above do not exclude the application of this section unless the individual was, at the time when the contract was made, habitually resident in that State.

(4) Subsection (2)(c) above does not exclude the application of this section where the law of the United Kingdom requires the proceedings to be brought before a court of the United Kingdom.

(5) In subsection (2)(b) above "national of the United Kingdom" [means—

  (a) a British citizen, a British Dependent Territories citizen [, a British National (Overseas)] or a British Overseas citizen; or

(b) a person who under the British Nationality Act 1981 is a British subject; or

(c) a British protected person (within the meaning of that Act)].

(6) In this section "proceedings relating to a contract of employment" includes proceedings between the parties to such a contract in respect of any statutory rights or duties to which they are entitled or subject as employer or employee.   [269]

NOTE
  Sub-s (5): words in first (outer) pair of square brackets substituted by the British Nationality Act 1981, s 52(6), Sch 7; words in second (inner) pair of square brackets inserted by the Hong Kong (British Nationality) Order 1986, SI 1986/948, art 8, Schedule.

5–13 (*Outside the scope of this work.*)

Supplementary provisions

14, 15 (*Outside the scope of this work.*)

16 Excluded matters

(1) This Part of this Act does not affect any immunity or privilege conferred by the Diplomatic Privileges Act 1964 or the Consular Relations Act 1968; and—

(a) section 4 above does not apply to proceedings concerning the employment of the members of a mission within the meaning of the Convention scheduled to the said Act of 1964 or of the members of a consular post within the meaning of the Convention scheduled to the said Act of 1968;

(b) section 6(1) above does not apply to proceedings concerning a State's title to or its possession of property used for the purposes of a diplomatic mission.

(2) This Part of this Act does not apply to proceedings relating to anything done by or in relation to the armed forces of a State while present in the United Kingdom and, in particular, has effect subject to the Visiting Forces Act 1952.

(3) This Part of this Act does not apply to proceedings to which section 17(6) of the Nuclear Installations Act 1965 applies.

(4) This Part of this Act does not apply to criminal proceedings.

(5) . . .   [270]

NOTE
  Sub-s (5): (relates to s 11) omitted.

17–19 (*Outside the scope of this work.*)

PART III

MISCELLANEOUS AND SUPPLEMENTARY

20–22 (*Outside the scope of this work.*)

23 Short title, repeals commencement and extent

(1) This Act may be cited as the State Immunity Act 1978.

(2) . . .

(3) Subject to subsection (4) below, Parts I and II of this Act do not apply to proceedings in respect of matters that occurred before the date of the coming into force of this Act and, in particular—

(a) sections 2(2) and 13(3) do not apply to any prior agreement, and
(b) sections 3, 4 and 9 do not apply to any transaction, contract or arbitration agreement,

entered into before that date.

(4) Section 12 above applies to any proceedings instituted after the coming into force of this Act.

(5) This Act shall come into force on such date as may be specified by an order made by the Lord Chancellor by statutory instrument.

(6) This Act extends to Northern Ireland.

(7) Her Majesty may by Order in Council extend any of the provisions of this Act, with or without modification, to any dependent territory. [271]–[273]

NOTE
Sub-s (2): repeals the Administration of Justice (Miscellaneous Provisions) Act 1938, s 13, and the Law Reform (Miscellaneous Provisions) (Scotland) Act 1940, s 7.

EMPLOYMENT PROTECTION (CONSOLIDATION) ACT 1978
(1978 c 44)

ARRANGEMENT OF SECTIONS

PART I
PARTICULARS OF TERMS OF EMPLOYMENT

Written particulars of terms of employment

PART I
EMPLOYMENT PARTICULARS

Written particulars of employment

Itemised pay statements

Enforcement of rights under Part I

PART II
RIGHTS ARISING IN COURSE OF EMPLOYMENT

Guarantee payments

Suspension from work on medical grounds

PART V
UNFAIR DISMISSAL

PART VI
REDUNDANCY PAYMENTS

Part VII
Insolvency of Employer

Part VIII
Resolution of Disputes Relating to Employment

Industrial tribunals

Recoupment of certain benefits

Conciliation officers

An Act to consolidate certain enactments relating to the rights of employees arising out of their employment; and certain enactments relating to the insolvency of employers; to industrial tribunals; to recoupment of certain benefits; to conciliation officers; and to the Employment Appeal Tribunal.   [31 July 1978]

NOTE

This Act originally consolidated the major employment protection legislation within the jurisdiction of industrial tribunals. It has since been subjected to numerous amendments, and those parts relating to collective labour relations were repealed and re-consolidated by the Trade Union and Labour Relations Act 1992. Substantial further amendments and substitutions are prospectively made by the Trade Union Reform and Employment Rights Act 1993. That Act is to be brought into force in stages, as indicated in notes to individual sections. Provisions of this Act prospectively repealed are printed in italics. New sections not yet in force (including some new sections which occupy the vacancy created by sections repealed by the 1992 Act) are printed at the relevant point in the text, with annotations as to source. In order not to overburden the text, the new sections which will replace ss 1–6 and 33–48 of the 1978 Act, and which are enacted by the 1993 Act, are printed grouped together with appropriate cross-references. This is intended to provide a source of reference to both the versions of the legislation.

The Act is printed in full as currently in force, except for ss 157, 158 (application to Northern Ireland and Isle of Man) and Schs 16, 17 (amendments and repeals).

NOTE

Ss 1–6, which are printed in italics below, are substituted en bloc by new ss 1–6 by the Trade Union Reform and Employment Rights Act 1993, s 26, Sch 4, as from a day to be appointed. The new ss 1–6 are printed after the italicised original sections, beginning at para **[280A]** below. At the time of going to press it was understood that a commencement date of late November 1993 was planned, but no relevant Commencement Order had been made.

PART I

PARTICULARS OF TERMS OF EMPLOYMENT

Written particulars of terms of employment

1 *Written particulars of terms of employment*

(1) Not later than thirteen weeks after [the beginning of an employee's employment] with an employer, the employer shall give to the employee a written statement in accordance with the following provisions of this section.

(2) An employer shall in a statement under this section—

   (a) identify the parties;

   (b) specify the date when the employment began;

   [(c) specify the date on which the employee's period of continuous employment began (taking into account any employment with a previous employer which counts towards that period)].

(3) A statement under this section shall contain the following particulars of the terms of employment as at a specified date not more than one week before the statement is given, that is to say—

    (a) the scale or rate of remuneration, or the method of calculating remuneration,

    (b) the intervals at which remuneration is paid (that is, whether weekly or monthly or by some other period),

    (c) any terms and conditions relating to hours of work (including any terms and conditions relating to normal working hours),

    (d) any terms and conditions relating to—

        (i) entitlement to holidays, including public holidays, and holiday pay (the particulars given being sufficient to enable the employee's entitlement, including any entitlement to accrued holiday pay on the termination of employment, to be precisely calculated),

        (ii) incapacity for work due to sickness or injury, including any provision for sick pay,

        (iii) pensions and pension schemes,

    (e) the length of notice which the employee is obliged to give and entitled to receive to determine his contract of employment, and

    (f) the title of the job which the employee is employed to do:

Provided that paragraph (d)(iii) shall not apply to the employees of any body or authority if the employees' pension rights depend on the terms of a pension scheme established under any provision contained in or having effect under an Act of Parliament and the body or authority are required by any such provision to give to new employees information concerning their pension rights, or concerning the determination of questions affecting their pension rights.

(4) Subject to subsection (5) [and section 2A(1)], every statement given to an employee under this section shall include a note—

    (a) specifying any disciplinary rules applicable to the employee, or referring to a document which is reasonably accessible to the employee and which specifies such rules;

    (b) specifying, by description or otherwise—

        (i) a person to whom the employee can apply if he is dissatisfied with any disciplinary decision relating to him; and

        (ii) a person to whom the employee can apply for the purpose of seeking redress of any grievance relating to his employment,

    and the manner in which any such application should be made;

    (c) where there are further steps consequent upon any such application, explaining those steps or referring to a document which is reasonably accessible to the employee and which explains them; and

    (d) stating whether a contracting-out certificate is in force for the employment in respect of which the statement is given.

(5) The provisions of paragraph (a) to (c) of subsection (4) shall not apply to rules, disciplinary decisions, grievances or procedures relating to health or safety at work.

(6) The definition of week given by section 153(1) does not apply for the purposes of this section. **[274]**

NOTES

    Substituted, together with ss 2, 2A, 4–6, by new ss 1–6, by the Trade Union Reform and Employment Rights Act 1993, s 26, Sch 4, as from a day to be appointed. For new ss 1–6 see paras **[280A]** et seq below.

    Sub-s (1): words in square brackets substituted by the Employment Act 1982, s 20, Sch 2, para 8(1)(a).

Sub-s (2): para (c) substituted by the Employment Act 1982, s 20, Sch 2, para 8(1)(b).
Sub-s (4): words in square brackets added with savings by the Employment Act 1989, ss 29(3), Sch 6, para 18, Sch 9.

2 Supplementary provisions relating to statements under s 1

(1) If there are no particulars to be entered under any of the heads of paragraph (d) of subsection (3) of section 1, or under any of the other provisions of section 1(2) and (3), that fact shall be stated.

(2) If the contract is for a fixed term, the statement given under section 1 shall state the date when the contract expires.

(3) A statement given under section 1 may, for all or any of the particulars to be given by the statement, refer the employee to some document which the employee has reasonable opportunities of reading in the course of his employment or which is made reasonably accessible to him in some other way.

[(4) No statement need be given under section 1 where—

(a) the employee's employment began not more than six months after the end of earlier employment with the same employer,

(b) a statement under that section, and any information subsequently required under section 4, was duly given to the employee in respect of his earlier employment, and

(c) the terms of his present employment are the same as those of his earlier employment and any other matters falling within section 1(4) of which particulars were to be given by that statement are also unchanged,

but without prejudice to the operation of subsection (1) of section 4 if there is subsequently a change in his terms of employment or in any of those matters.]

[275]

NOTES
Substituted, together with ss 1, 2A, 4–6, by new ss 1–6, by the Trade Union Reform and Employment Rights Act 1993, s 26, Sch 4, as from a day to be appointed. For new ss 1–6 see paras **[280A]** et seq below.
Sub-s (4): substituted by the Employment Act 1982, s 20, Sch 2, para 8(2); further substituted with savings by the Employment Act 1989, ss 13(2), 29(6), Sch 9; for further savings see SI 1990/189, reg 3(1).

[2A Particulars of disciplinary procedures not required where less than 20 employees

(1) The note which, by virtue of subsection (4) of section 1, is required to be included in a statement given to an employee under that section need not comply with the following provisions of that subsection, namely—

(a) paragraph (a),

(b) in paragraph (b), sub-paragraph (i) and the words following sub-paragraph (ii) so far as relating to sub-paragraph (i), and

(c) paragraph (c),

if on the date when the employee's employment began the relevant number of employees was less than twenty.

(2) In subsection (1) "the relevant number of employees", in relation to an employee, means the number of employees employed by his employer added to the number of employees employed by any associated employer.]

[276]

NOTES
Inserted with savings by the Employment Act 1989, ss 13(3), 29(6), Sch 9; for further savings see SI 1990/189, reg 3(1).

Substituted, together with ss 1, 2, 4–6, by new ss 1–6, by the Trade Union Reform and Employment Rights Act 1993, s 26, Sch 4, as from a day to be appointed. For new ss 1–6 see paras **[280A]** et seq below.

3 *(Repealed by the Employment Act 1982, s 21(3), Sch 4. For new s 3, as substituted by the Trade Union Reform and Employment Rights Act 1993, s 26, Sch 4, as from a day to be appointed, see para [280C] below.)*

4 Changes in terms of employment

(1) If after the date to which a statement given under section 1 relates there is a change in the terms of employment to be included, or referred to, in that statement the employer shall, not more than one month after the change, inform the employee of the nature of the change by a written statement and, if he does not leave a copy of the statement with the employee, shall preserve the statement and ensure that the employee has reasonable opportunities of reading it in the course of his employment, or that it is made reasonably accessible to him in some other way.

(2) A statement given under subsection (1) may, for all or any of the particulars to be given by the statement, refer the employee to some document which the employee has reasonable opportunities of reading in the course of his employment, or which is made reasonably accessible to him in some other way.

(3) If, in referring in the statement given under section 1 or under subsection (1) of this section to any such document, the employer indicates to the employee that future changes in the terms of which the particulars are given in the document will be entered up in the document (or recorded by some other means for the information of persons referring to the document), the employer need not under subsection (1) inform the employee of any such change if it is duly entered up or recorded not later than one month after the change is made.

(4) Where, after an employer has given to an employee a written statement in accordance with section 1—

> *(a) the name of the employer (whether an individual or a body corporate or partnership) is changed, without any change in the identity of the employer, or*
> *(b) the identity of the employer is changed, in such circumstances that, . . ., the continuity of the employee's period of employment is not broken,*

and (in either case) the change does not involve any change in the terms (other than the names of the parties) included or referred to in the statement, then, the person who, immediately after the change, is the employer shall not be required to give to the employee a statement in accordance with section 1, but, subject to subsection (5), the change shall be treated as a change falling within subsection (1) of this section.

(5) A written statement under this section which informs an employee of such a change in his terms of employment as is referred to in subsection (4)(b) shall specify the date on which the employee's [period of continuous employment] began.

[(6) Any reference in subsection (1), (3) or (4) to the terms of employment which were to be, or were, included or referred to in a statement given under section 1 shall be construed as including a reference to any other matters falling within section 1(2)(c) and (4) of which particulars were to be given by that statement.] **[277]**

NOTES

Substituted, together with ss 1–2A, 5, 5A, 6, by new ss 1–6, by the Trade Union Reform and Employment Rights Act 1993, s 26, Sch 4, as from a day to be appointed. For new ss 1–6 see paras **[280A]** et seq below.

Sub-s (4): words omitted repealed by the Employment Act 1982, ss 20, 21(3), Sch 2, para 8(3)(a), Sch 4.

Sub-s (5): words in square brackets substituted by the Employment Act 1982, s 20, Sch 2, para 8(3)(b).

Sub-s (6): added with savings by the Employment Act 1989, ss 13(4), 29(6), Sch 9.

5 Exclusion of certain contracts in writing

[(1)] Sections 1 and 4 shall not apply to an employee if and so long as the following conditions are fulfilled in relation to him, that is to say—

(a) *the employee's contract of employment is a contract which has been reduced to writing in one or more documents and which contains express terms affording the particulars to be given under each of the paragraphs in subsection (3) of section 1, and under each head of paragraph (d) of that subsection;*

(b) *there has been given to the employee a copy of the contract (with any variations made from time to time), or he has reasonable opportunities of reading such a copy in the course of his employment, or such a copy is made reasonably accessible to him in some other way; and*

(c) *such a note as is mentioned in section 1(4) has been given to the employee or he has reasonable opportunities of reading such a note in the course of his employment or such a note is made reasonably accessible to him in some other way:*

. . .

[(2) If on the date when the employee's employment began the relevant number of employees was less than twenty, any reference in subsection (1)(c) to such a note as is there mentioned shall be construed as including a reference to such a note as is mentioned in section 1(4) as it has effect with the omission of the provisions specified in section 2A(1)(a) to (c).

(3) In subsection (2) "the relevant number of employees" has the meaning given by section 2A(2).]   **[278]**

NOTES

Substituted, together with ss 1–2A, 4, 5A, 6, by new ss 1–6, by the Trade Union Reform and Employment Rights Act 1993, s 26, Sch 4, as from a day to be appointed. For new ss 1–6 see paras **[280A]** et seq below.

Sub-s (1): numbered with savings by the Employment Act 1989, ss 13(5), 29(6), Sch 9, for further savings see SI 1990/189, reg 3(1); words omitted repealed by the Employment Act 1982, s 21(3), Sch 4.

Sub-ss (2), (3): added with savings by the Employment Act 1989, ss 13(5), 29(6), Sch 9; for further savings see SI 1990/189, reg 3(1).

[5A Employees becoming or ceasing to be excluded from ss 1 to 4

(1) Sections 1 to 4 shall apply to an employee who at any time comes or ceases to come within the exceptions from those sections provided for by section 5, 141, 144, 145 or 146(4) to (7), or under section 149, as if his employment with his employer terminated or began at that time.

(2) Subsection (1) of section 1 shall apply to an employee who ceases to come within the exception provided by section 5 with the substitution for the words "thirteen weeks" of the words "one month".

(3) The fact that section 1 is directed to apply to an employee as if his employment began on his ceasing to come within one of the exceptions referred to in subsection (1) shall not affect the obligation under subsection (2)(b) of that section to specify the date on which his employment actually began.]   **[279]**

NOTES

Inserted with savings by the Employment Act 1982, s 20, Sch 2, para 8(4).
Substituted, together with ss 1–2A, 5, 6, by new ss 1–6, by the Trade Union Reform and Employment Rights Act 1993, s 26, Sch 4, as from a day to be appointed. For new ss 1–6 see paras [**280A**] et seq below.

6 Power of Secretary of State to require further particulars

The Secretary of State may by order provide that section 1 shall have effect as if such further particulars as may be specified in the order were included in the particulars to be included in a statement, under that section, and, for that purpose, the order may include such provisions amending section 1(1), (2) and (3) as appear to the Secretary of State to be expedient.   **[280]**

NOTES

Substituted, along with ss 1–2A, 5, 5A, by new ss 1–6, by the Trade Union Reform and Employment Rights Act 1993, s 26, Sch 4, as from a day to be appointed. For new ss 1–6 see paras [**280A**] et seq below.
No orders have been made under this section at the time of going to press.

NOTE

The Trade Union Reform and Employment Rights Act 1993, s 26, Sch 4, substitutes the following ss 1–6 for those printed in italics above, as from a day to be appointed:

[Part I

Employment Particulars

Written particulars of employment

1 Employer's duty to give statement of employment particulars

(1) Not later than two months after the beginning of an employee's employment with an employer, the employer shall give to the employee a written statement which may, subject to subsection (3) of section 2, be given in instalments before the end of that period.

(2) The statement shall contain particulars of—

    (a) the names of the employer and employee,

    (b) the date when the employment began, and

    (c) the date on which the employee's period of continuous employment began (taking into account any employment with a previous employer which counts towards that period).

(3) The statement shall also contain particulars, as at a specified date not more than seven days before the statement or instalment of the statement containing them is given, of—

    (a) the scale or rate of remuneration or the method of calculating remuneration,

    (b) the intervals at which remuneration is paid (that is, weekly, monthly or other specified intervals),

    (c) any terms and conditions relating to hours of work (including any terms and conditions relating to normal working hours),

    (d) any terms and conditions relating to any of the following—

        (i) entitlement to holidays, including public holidays, and holiday pay (the particulars given being sufficient to enable the employee's entitlement, including any entitlement to accrued holiday pay on the termination of employment, to be precisely calculated),

        (ii) incapacity for work due to sickness or injury, including any provision for sick pay, and

(iii) pensions and pension schemes,
(e) the length of notice which the employee is obliged to give and entitled to receive to terminate his contract of employment,
(f) the title of the job which the employee is employed to do or a brief description of the work for which the employee is employed,
(g) where the employment is not intended to be permanent, the period for which it is expected to continue or, if it is for a fixed term, the date when it is to end,
(h) either the place of work or, where the employee is required or permitted to work at various places, an indication of that and of the address of the employer,
(j) any collective agreements which directly affect the terms and conditions of the employment including, where the employer is not a party, the persons by whom they were made, and
(k) where the employee is required to work outside the United Kingdom for a period of more than one month—

 (i) the period for which he is to work outside the United Kingdom,
 (ii) the currency in which remuneration is to be paid while he is working outside the United Kingdom,
 (iii) any additional remuneration payable to him, and any benefits to be provided to or in respect of him, by reason of his being required to work outside the United Kingdom, and
 (iv) any terms and conditions relating to his return to the United Kingdom.

(4) Subsection (3)(d)(iii) shall not apply to the employees of any body or authority if—

 (a) the employees' pension rights depend on the terms of a pension scheme established under any provision contained in or having effect under any Act of Parliament, and
 (b) the body or authority are required by any such provision to give to new employees information concerning their pension rights or the determination of questions affecting their pension rights.]   **[280A]**

NOTES
Substituted by the Trade Union Reform and Employment Rights Act 1993, s 26, Sch 4, as from a day to be appointed.
It is submitted that the reference in sub-s (1) to sub-s (3) of section 2 should be a reference to sub-s (4) of that section.

[2 Section 1: supplementary

(1) If, in the case of a statement under section 1, there are no particulars to be entered under any of the heads of paragraph (d) or (k) of subsection (3) of that section, or under any of the other paragraphs of subsection (2) or (3) of that section, that fact shall be stated.

(2) A statement under section 1—

 (a) may refer the employee to the provisions of some other document which—

  (i) the employee has reasonable opportunities of reading in the course of his employment, or
  (ii) is made reasonably accessible to him in some other way,

 for particulars of any of the matters specified in heads (ii) and (iii) of paragraph (d) of subsection (3) of section 1, and

 (b) may refer the employee to the law, or, subject to subsection (3), to the provisions of any collective agreement which directly affects the terms and conditions of the employment, for particulars of either of the matters specified in paragraph (e) of that subsection.

(3) A statement under section 1 may refer the employee to the provisions of a collective agreement under subsection (2)(b) if, and only if, it is an agreement which—

    (a) the employee has reasonable opportunities of reading in the course of his employment, or

    (b) is made reasonably accessible to him in some other way.

(4) The particulars required by section 1(2) and the following provisions of subsection (3)—

    (a) paragraphs (a) to (c),

    (b) head (i) of paragraph (d),

    (c) paragraph (f), and

    (d) paragraph (h),

shall be included in a single document (in this Part referred to as the "principal statement").

(5) Where before the end of the period of two months after the beginning of his employment an employee is to begin to work outside the United Kingdom for a period of more than one month, the statement under section 1 shall be given to him not later than the time when he leaves the United Kingdom in order to begin so to work.

(6) A statement shall be given to a person under section 1 notwithstanding that his employment ends before the end of the period within which the statement is required to be given.] **[280B]**

NOTES

Substituted by the Trade Union Reform and Employment Rights Act 1993, s 26, Sch 4, as from a day to be appointed.

[3 Statement to include note about disciplinary procedures

(1) A statement under section 1 shall include a note—

    (a) specifying any disciplinary rules applicable to the employee or referring the employee to the provisions of a document which—

        (i) the employee has reasonable opportunities of reading in the course of his employment, or

        (ii) is made reasonably accessible to him in some other way,

    and which specifies such rules,

    (b) specifying, by description or otherwise—

        (i) a person to whom the employee can apply if he is dissatisfied with any disciplinary decision relating to him, and

        (ii) a person to whom the employee can apply for the purpose of seeking redress of any grievance relating to his employment,

    and the manner in which any such application should be made,

    (c) where there are further steps consequent on any such application, explaining those steps or referring to the provisions of a document which—

        (i) the employee has reasonable opportunities of reading in the course of his employment, or

        (ii) is made reasonably accessible to him in some other way,

    and which explains them, and

    (d) stating whether a contracting-out certificate is in force for the employment.

(2) Subsection (1)(a) to (c) shall not apply to rules, disciplinary decisions, grievances or procedures relating to health or safety at work.

(3) The note need not comply with the following provisions of subsection (1)—

    (a) paragraph (a),

    (b) in paragraph (b), sub-paragraph (i) and the words following sub-paragraph (ii) so far as relating to sub-paragraph (i), and

    (c) paragraph (c),

if on the date when the employee's employment began the relevant number of employees was less than twenty.

(4) In subsection (3) "the relevant number of employees", in relation to an employee, means the number of employees employed by his employer added to the number of employees employed by any associated employer.]   **[280C]**

NOTES

    Substituted by the Trade Union Reform and Employment Rights Act 1993, s 26, Sch 4, as from a day to be appointed.

[4 Employer's duty to give statement of changes

(1) If, after the date to which a statement given under section 1 relates, or, where no such statement is given, after the end of the period within which a statement under section 1 is required to be given, there is a change in any of the matters particulars of which are required by sections 1 to 3 to be included or referred to in a statement under section 1, the employer shall at the earliest opportunity and, in any event, not later than—

    (a) one month after the change, or

    (b) where the change results from the employee being required to work outside the United Kingdom for a period of more than one month, the time when he leaves the United Kingdom in order to begin so to work, if that is earlier,

give to the employee a written statement containing particulars of the change.

(2) In a case where the statement under section 1 is given in instalments, subsection (1) applies—

    (a) in relation to—

        (i) matters particulars of which are required to be (whether they are or not) included in the instalment comprising the principal statement, and

        (ii) other matters particulars of which are included or referred to in that instalment;

    (b) in relation to matters particulars of which are included or referred to in any other instalment; and

    (c) in relation to any change occurring after the end of the two-month period within which a statement under section 1 is required to be given in matters particulars of which were required to be included in the statement given under section 1 but which were not included in any instalment;

as it applies in relation to matters particulars of which are required to be included or referred to in a statement under section 1 not given in instalments.

(3) A statement under subsection (1)—

    (a) may refer the employee to the provisions of some other document which—

        (i) the employee has reasonable opportunities of reading in the course of his employment, or

        (ii) is made reasonably accessible to him in some other way,

    for a change in any of the matters specified in sections 1(3)(d) (ii) and (iii and 3(1)(a) and (c), and

(b) may refer the employee to the law, or, subject to subsection (4), to the provisions of any collective agreement which directly affects the terms and conditions of the employment, for a change in either of the matters specified in section 1(3)(e).

(4) A statement under subsection (1) may refer the employee to the provisions of a collective agreement under subsection (3)(b) if, and only if, it is an agreement which—

(a) the employee has reasonable opportunities of reading in the course of his employment, or

(b) is made reasonably accessible to him in some other way.

(5) Where after an employer has given to an employee a statement under section 1—

(a) either—

(i) the name of the employer (whether an individual or a body corporate or partnership) is changed without any change in the identity of the employer, or

(ii) the identity of the employer is changed in circumstances in which the continuity of the employee's period of employment is not broken, and

(b) the change does not involve any change in any of the matters (other than the names of the parties) particulars of which are required by sections 1 to 3 to be included in the statement,

the person who immediately after the change is the employer shall not be required to give to the employee a statement under section 1 but the change shall be treated as a change falling within subsection (1) of this section.

(6) A statement under subsection (1) which informs an employee of a change such as is referred to in subsection (5)(a)(ii) shall specify the date on which the employee's period of continuous employment began.]   **[280D]**

NOTES

Substituted by the Trade Union Reform and Employment Rights Act 1993, s 26, Sch 4, as from a day to be appointed.

[5 Exclusion of sections 1 to 4 in case of certain employees

(1) Sections 1 to 4 shall not apply to an employee if—

(a) his employment continues for less than one month, or

(b) he is employed under a contract which normally involves employment for less than eight hours weekly.

(2) Sections 1 to 4 shall apply to an employee who at any time comes or ceases to come within the exceptions from those sections provided for by subsection (1)(b) and sections 141 and 144, and under section 149, as if his employment with his employer terminated or began at that time.

(3) The fact that section 1 is directed by subsection (2) to apply to an employee as if his employment began on his ceasing to come within the exceptions referred to in that subsection shall not affect the obligation under section 1(2)(b) to specify the date on which his employment actually began.]   **[280E]**

NOTES

Substituted by the Trade Union Reform and Employment Rights Act 1993, s 26, Sch 4, as from a day to be appointed.

[6 Power of Secretary of State to require particulars of further matters

The Secretary of State may by order provide that section 1 shall have effect as if particulars of such further matters as may be specified in the order were included in the particulars required by that section; and, for that purpose, the order may include such provisions amending that section as appear to the Secretary of State to be expedient.]   **[280F]**

NOTES

Substituted by the Trade Union Reform and Employment Rights Act 1993, s 26, Sch 4, as from a day to be appointed.

7 *(Repealed by the Employment Act 1982, s 21(3), Sch 4.)*

Itemised pay statements

8 Right to itemised pay statement

Every employee shall have the right to be given by his employer at or before the time at which any payment of wages or salary is made to him an itemised pay statement, in writing, containing the following particulars, that is to say—

    (a) the gross amount of the wages or salary;

    (b) the amounts of any variable and, subject to section 9, any fixed deductions from that gross amount and the purposes for which they are made;

    (c) the net amount of wages or salary payable; and

    (d) where different parts of the net amount are paid in different ways, the amount and method of payment of each part-payment.   **[281]**

9 Standing statement of fixed deductions

(1) A pay statement given in accordance with section 8 need not contain separate particulars of a fixed deduction if it contains instead an aggregate amount of fixed deductions, including that deduction, and the employer has given to the employee, at or before the time at which that pay statement is given, a standing statement of fixed deductions, in writing, which contains the following particulars of each deduction comprised in that aggregate amount, that is to say,—

    (a) the amount of the deduction;

    (b) the intervals at which the deduction is to be made; and

    (c) the purpose for which it is made,

and which, in accordance with subsection (4), is effective at the date on which the pay statement is given.

(2) A standing statement of fixed deductions may be amended, whether by addition of a new deduction or by a change in the particulars or cancellation of an existing deduction, by notice in writing, containing particulars of the amendment, given by the employer to the employee.

(3) An employer who has given to an employee a standing statement of fixed deductions shall, within the period of twelve months beginning with the date on which the first standing statement was given and at intervals of not more than twelve months thereafter, re-issue it in a consolidated form incorporating any amendments notified in accordance with subsection (2).

(4) A standing statement of fixed deductions shall become effective, for the purposes of subsection (1), on the date on which it is given to the employee and shall cease to have effect on the expiration of the period of twelve months beginning with that date, or, where it is re-issued in accordance with subsection (3), the expiration of the period of twelve months beginning with the date on which it was last re-issued.

[282]

10 Power to amend ss 8 and 9

The Secretary of State may by order—

    (a) vary the provisions of sections 8 and 9 as to the particulars which must be included in a pay statement or a standing statement of fixed deductions by adding items to or removing items from the particulars listed in those sections or by amending any such particulars; and

    (b) vary the provisions of section 9(3) and (4) so as to shorten or extend the periods of twelve months referred to in those subsections, or those periods as varied from time to time under this section.   **[283]**

Enforcement of rights under Part I

11 References to industrial tribunals

(1) Where an employer does not give an employee a statement as required by section 1 or 4(1) or 8 [(that is to say, either because he gives him no statement or because the statement he gives does not comply with those requirements)], the employee may require a reference to be made to an industrial tribunal to determine what particulars ought to have been included or referred to in a statement so as to comply with the requirements of the relevant section.

    (2) Where—

    (a) a statement purporting to be a statement under section 1 or 4(1), or

    (b) a pay statement or a standing statement of fixed deductions, purporting to comply with section 8 or 9(1),

has been given to an employee, and a question arises as to the particulars which ought to have been included or referred to in the statement so as to comply with the requirements of this Part, either the employer or the employee may require that question to be referred to and determined by an industrial tribunal.

(3) Where a statement under section 1 or 4(1) given by an employer to an employee contains such an indication as is mentioned in section 4(3), and

    (a) any particulars purporting to be particulars of a change to which that indication relates are entered up or recorded in accordance with that indication, and

    (b) a question arises as to the particulars which ought to have been so entered up or recorded,

either the employer or the employee may require that question to be referred to and determined by an industrial tribunal.

(4) In this section, a question as to the particulars which ought to have been included—

    (a) in a pay statement, or in a standing statement of fixed deductions, does not include a question solely as to the accuracy of an amount stated in any such particulars;

(b) in *a note under section 1(4)* [the note required by section 3 to be included in the statement under section 1], does not include any question whether the employment is, has been or will be contracted-out employment for the purposes of Part III of the Social Security Pensions Act 1975.

(5) Where, on a reference under subsection (1), an industrial tribunal determines particulars as being those which ought to have been included or referred to in a statement given under section 1 or 4(1) the employer shall be deemed to have given to the employee a statement in which those particulars were included, or referred to, as specified in the decision of the tribunal.

(6) On determining a reference under subsection (2)(a) an industrial tribunal may either confirm the particulars as included or referred to in the statement given by the employer, or may amend those particulars, or may substitute other particulars for them, as the tribunal may determine to be appropriate; and the statement shall be deemed to have been given by the employer to the employee in accordance with the decision of the tribunal.

(7) On determining a reference under subsection (3), an industrial tribunal may either confirm the particulars to which the reference relates, or may amend those particulars or may substitute other particulars for them, as the tribunal may determine to be appropriate; and particulars of the change to which the reference relates shall be deemed to have been entered up or recorded in accordance with the decision of the tribunal.

(8) Where on a reference under this section an industrial tribunal finds that an employer has failed to give an employee any pay statement in accordance with section 8 or that a pay statement or standing statement of fixed deductions does not, in relation to a deduction, contain the particulars required to be included in that statement by that section or section 9(1)—

(a) the tribunal shall make a declaration to that effect; and

(b) where the tribunal further finds that any unnotified deductions have been made from the pay of the employee during the period of thirteen weeks immediately preceding the date of the application for the reference (whether or not the deductions were made in breach of the contract of employment), the tribunal may order the employer to pay the employee a sum not exceeding the aggregate of the unnotified deductions so made.

In this subsection "unnotified deduction" means a deduction made without the employer giving the employee, in any pay statement or standing statement of fixed deductions, the particulars of that deduction required by section 8 or 9(1).

(9) An industrial tribunal shall not entertain a reference under this section in a case where the employment to which the reference relates has ceased unless an application requiring the reference to be made was made

[(a)] before the end of the period of three months beginning with the date on which the employment ceased [or—

(b) within such further period as the tribunal considers reasonable in a case where it is satisfied that it was not reasonably practicable for the application to be made before the end of that period of three months].

[284]

NOTES

Sub-ss (1), (9): words in square brackets inserted by the Trade Union Reform and Employment Rights Act 1993, s 49(2), Sch 8, para 10(a), (c), as from a day to be appointed.

Sub-ss (3), (7): repealed by the Trade Union Reform and Employment Rights Act 1993, s 51, Sch 10, as from a day to be appointed.

Sub-s (4): words in italics prospectively repealed, and words in square brackets prospectively substituted, by the Trade Union Reform and Employment Rights Act 1993, s 49(2), Sch 8, para 10(b), as from a day to be appointed.

PART II

RIGHTS ARISING IN COURSE OF EMPLOYMENT

Guarantee payments

12 Right to guarantee payment

(1) Where an employee throughout a day during any part of which he would normally be required to work in accordance with his contract of employment is not provided with work by his employer by reason of—

(a) a diminution in the requirements of the employer's business for work of the kind which the employee is employed to do, or

(b) any other occurrence affecting the normal working of the employer's business in relation to work of the kind which the employee is employed to do,

he shall, subject to the following provisions of this Act, be entitled to be paid by his employer a payment, referred to in this Act as a guarantee payment, in respect of that day, and in this section and sections 13 and 16—

(i) such a day is referred to as a "workless day", and

(ii) "workless period" has a corresponding meaning.

(2) In this section and sections 13 to 17, "day" means the period of twenty-four hours from midnight to midnight, and where a period of employment begun on any day extends over midnight into the following day, or would normally so extend, then—

(a) if the employment before midnight is, or would normally be, of longer duration than that after midnight, that period of employment shall be treated as falling wholly on the first day; and

(b) in any other case, that period of employment shall be treated as falling wholly on the second day. [285]

13 General exclusions from right under s 12

[(1) An employee shall not be entitled to a guarantee payment unless he has been continuously employed for a period of not less than one month ending with the day before that in respect of which the guarantee payment is claimed.

(2) An employee who is employed—

(a) under a contract for a fixed term of three months or less, or

(b) under a contract made in contemplation of the performance of a specific task which is not expected to last for more than three months,

shall not be entitled to a guarantee payment unless he has been continuously employed for a period of more than three months ending with the day before that in respect of which the guarantee payment is claimed.]

[(3)] An employee shall not be entitled to a guarantee payment in respect of a workless day if the failure to provide him with work occurs in consequence of a [strike, lock-out or other industrial action] involving any employee of his employer or of an associated employer.

[(4)] An employee shall not be entitled to a guarantee payment in respect of a workless day if—

(a) his employer has offered to provide alternative work for that day which is suitable in all the circumstances whether or not work which the employee is under his contract employed to perform, and the employee has unreasonably refused that offer; or

(b) he does not comply with reasonable requirements imposed by his employer with a view to ensuring that his services are available.   **[286]**

NOTES

Sub-ss (1), (2): inserted with savings, and previous sub-ss (1), (2) renumbered (3), (4), by the Employment Act 1982, s 20, Sch 2, para 1.

Sub-s (3): words substituted by the Employment Act 1982, s 21, Sch 3, Pt II, para 15.

14 Calculation of guarantee payment

(1) Subject to the limits set by section 15, the amount of a guarantee payment payable to an employee in respect of any day shall be the sum produced by multiplying the number of normal working hours on that day by the guaranteed hourly rate, and, accordingly, no guarantee payment shall be payable to an employee in whose case there are no normal working hours on the day in question.

(2) Subject to subsection (3), the guaranteed hourly rate in relation to an employee shall be the amount of one week's pay divided by—

(a) the number of normal working hours in a week for that employee when employed under the contract of employment in force on the day in respect of which the guarantee payment is payable; or

(b) where the number of such normal working hours differs from week to week or over a longer period, the average number of such hours calculated by dividing by twelve the total number of the employee's normal working hours during the period of twelve weeks ending with the last complete week before the day in respect of which the guarantee payment is payable; or

(c) in a case falling within paragraph (b) but where the employee has not been employed for a sufficient period to enable the calculation to be made under that paragraph, a number which fairly represents the number of normal working hours in a week having regard to such of the following considerations as are appropriate in the circumstances, that is to say—

(i) the average number of normal working hours in a week which the employee could expect in accordance with the terms of his contract;

(ii) the average number of such hours of other employees engaged in relevant comparable employment with the same employer.

(3) If in any case an employee's contract has been varied, or a new contract has been entered into, in connection with a period of short-time working, subsection (2) shall have effect as if for the reference to the day in respect of which the guarantee payment is payable there was substituted a reference to the last day on which the original contract was in force.   **[287]**

15 Limits on amount of and entitlement to guarantee payment

(1) The amount of a guarantee payment payable to an employee in respect of any day shall not exceed [£14.10].

(2) An employee shall not be entitled to guarantee payments in respect of more than the specified number of days in [any period of three months].

(3) The specified number of days for the purposes of subsection (2) shall be, subject to subsection (4),—

(a) the number of days, not exceeding five, on which the employee normally works in a week under the contract of employment in force on the day in respect of which the guarantee payment is claimed; or

(b) where that number of days varies from week to week or over a longer period, the average number of such days, not exceeding five, calculated by dividing by twelve the total number of such days during the period of twelve weeks ending with the last complete week before the day in respect of which the guarantee payment is claimed, and rounding up the resulting figure to the next whole number; or

(c) in a case falling within paragraph (b) but where the employee has not been employed for a sufficient period to enable the calculation to be made under that paragraph, a number which fairly represents the number of the employee's normal working days in a week, not exceeding five, having regard to such of the following considerations as are appropriate in the circumstances, that is to say,—

　(i) the average number of normal working days in a week which the employee could expect in accordance with the terms of his contract;

　(ii) the average number of such days of other employees engaged in relevant comparable employment with the same employer.

(4) If in any case an employee's contract has been varied or a new contract has been entered into, in connection with a period of short-time working, subsection (3) shall have effect as if for the references to the day in respect of which the guarantee payment is claimed there were substituted references to the last day on which the original contract was in force.

(5) The Secretary of State may vary any of the limits referred to in this section, and may in particular vary the [length of the period] referred to in subsection (2), after a review under section 148, by order made in accordance with that section.

[288]

NOTES

Sub-s (1): sum in square brackets substituted by the Employment Protection (Variation of Limits) Order 1992, SI 1992/312, art 2, as from 1 April 1992. The previous amount (as from 1 April 1991) was £13.65; from 1 April 1990 the amount was £12.65. There was no annual increase in 1993.

Sub-ss (2), (5): words in square brackets substituted by the Employment Act 1980, ss 14, 20, Sch 1, para 8.

16 Supplementary provisions relating to guarantee payments

(1) Subject to subsection (2), a right to a guarantee payment shall not affect any right of an employee in relation to remuneration under his contract of employment (in this section referred to as "contractual remuneration").

(2) Any contractual remuneration paid to an employee in respect of a workless day shall go towards discharging any liability of the employer to pay a guarantee payment in respect of that day, and conversely any guarantee payment paid in respect of a day shall go towards discharging any liability of the employer to pay contractual remuneration in respect of that day.

(3) For the purposes of subsection (2), contractual remuneration shall be treated as paid in respect of a workless day—

(a) where it is expressed to be calculated or payable by reference to that day or any part of that day, to the extent that it is so expressed; and

(b) in any other case, to the extent that it represents guaranteed remuneration, rather than remuneration for work actually done, and is referable to that day when apportioned rateably between that day and any other workless period falling within the period in respect of which the remuneration is paid.

(4) The Secretary of State may by order provide that in relation to any description of employees the provisions of sections 12(2), 14 and 15(3) (as originally enacted or as varied under section 15(5)) and of subsections (1) to (3), and, so far as they apply for the purposes of those provisions, the provisions of Schedule 14 shall have effect subject to such modifications and adaptations as may be prescribed by the order.

[289]

17 Complaint to industrial tribunal

(1) An employee may present a complaint to an industrial tribunal that his employer has failed to pay the whole or any part of a guarantee payment to which the employee is entitled.

(2) An industrial tribunal shall not entertain a complaint relating to a guarantee payment in respect of any day unless the complaint is presented to the tribunal before the end of the period of three months beginning with that day or within such further period as the tribunal considers reasonable in a case where it is satisfied that it was not reasonably practicable for the complaint to be presented within the period of three months.

(3) Where an industrial tribunal finds a complaint under subsection (1) well-founded, the tribunal shall order the employer to pay the complainant the amount of guarantee payment which it finds is due to him.   **[290]**

18 Exemption orders

(1) If at any time there is in force a collective agreement, or a wages order, whereby employees to whom the agreement or order relates have a right to guaranteed remuneration and on the application of all the parties to the agreement or, as the case may be, of the *council or* Board making the order, the appropriate Minister, having regard to the provisions of the agreement or order, is satisfied that section 12 should not apply to those employees, he may make an order under this section excluding those employees from the operation of that section.

(2) In subsection (1), a wages order means an order made under any of the following provisions, that is to say—

   [(a)   section 14 of the Wages Act 1986];
   (b)   section 3 of the Agricultural Wages Act 1948;
   (c)   section 3 of the Agricultural Wages (Scotland) Act 1949.

(3) In subsection (1), "the appropriate Minister" means—

   (a)   as respects a collective agreement or such an order as is referred to in subsection (2)*(a) or* (c), the Secretary of State;
   (b)   as respects such an order as is referred to in subsection (2)(b), the Minister of Agriculture, Fisheries and Food.

(4) The Secretary of State shall not make an order under this section in respect of an agreement unless—

   (a)   the agreement provides for procedures to be followed (whether by arbitration or otherwise) in cases where an employee claims that his employer has failed to pay the whole or any part of any guaranteed remuneration to which the employee is entitled under the agreement, and that those procedures include a right to arbitration or adjudication by an independent referee or body in cases where (by reason of an equality of votes or otherwise) a decision cannot otherwise be reached; or

(b) the agreement indicates that an employee to whom the agreement relates may present a complaint to an industrial tribunal that his employer has failed to pay the whole or any part of any guaranteed remuneration to which the employee is entitled under the agreement;

and where an order under this section is in force in respect of such an agreement as is described in paragraph (b) an industrial tribunal shall have jurisdiction over such a complaint as if it were a complaint falling within section 17.

(5) Without prejudice to section 154(4), an order under this section may be varied or revoked by a subsequent order thereunder, whether in pursuance of an application made by all or any of the parties to the agreement in question, or, as the case may be, by the *council or* Board which made the order in question, or without any such application.
[291]

NOTES

Sub-ss (1), (2), (3), (5): words in italics repealed by the Trade Union Reform and Employment Rights Act 1993, s 51, Sch 10, as from 30 August 1993 (SI 1993/1908) below para **[1435]**.

Sub-s (2)(a): substituted by the Wages Act 1986, s 32(1), (3), Sch 4, para 7, Sch 6, para 7.

At the time of going to press the following Guarantee Payments Exemption Orders had been made: No 1 (SI 1977/156) Federation of Civil Engineering Contracts; No 2 (SI 1977/157) National Federation of Demolition Contractors; No 3 (SI 1977/158) National Joint Council for the Building Industry; No 5 (SI 1977/902) British Footwear Manufacturers' Federation; No 6 (SI 1977/1096) Steeplejacks and Lightning Conductor Engineers; No 7 (SI 1977/1158) Paper and Board Industry; No 8 (SI 1977/1322) Smiths Food Group; No 9 (SI 1977/1349) British Leather Federation; No 10 (SI 1977/1522) Fibreboard Packing Case Industry; No 11 (SI 1977/1523) Henry Wiggin & Co Ltd; No 12 (SI 1977/1583) Refractory Users Federation; No 13 (SI 1977/1601) Multiwall Sack Manufacturers; No 14 (SI 1977/2032) Tudor Food Products; No 15 (SI 1978/153) British Carton Association; No 16 (SI 1978/429) Henry Wiggin & Co; No 17 (SI 1978/737) NJC for Workshops for the Blind; No 18 (SI 1978/826) Employers' Federation of Card Clothing Manufacturers; No 19 (SI 1979/1403) NJC for the Motor Vehicle Repair Industry; No 21 (SI 1981/6) Plant Hire Working Rule Agreement; No 23 (SI 1987/1757) National Agreement for Wire and Wire Rope Industries (revoking No 4); No 24 (SI 1989/1326) Rowntree Mackintosh Confectionary Ltd (revoking No 22 as amended); No 25 (SI 1989/1575) Building and Allied Trades Joint Industrial Council (revoking No 20); No 26 (SI 1989/2163) Airflow Streamlines; No 27 (SI 1990/927) G & G Kynock plc; and No 28 (SI 1990/2330).

Suspension from work on medical grounds

19 Right to remuneration on suspension on medical grounds

(1) An employee who is suspended from work by his employer on medical grounds in consequence of—

(a) any requirement imposed by or under any provision of any enactment or of any instrument made under any enactment, or

(b) any recommendation in any provision of a code of practice issued or approved under section 16 of the Health and Safety at Work etc Act 1974,

which is a provision for the time being specified in Schedule 1 shall, subject to the following provisions of this Act, be entitled to be paid by his employer remuneration while he is so suspended for a period not exceeding twenty-six weeks.

(2) For the purposes of this section and sections 20 to 22 and 61, an employee shall be regarded as suspended from work only if, and so long as, he continues to be employed by his employer, but is not provided with work or does not perform the work he normally performed before the suspension.

(3) The Secretary of State may by order add provisions to or remove provisions from the list of specified provisions in Schedule 1. **[292]**

20 General exclusions from right under s 19

[(1) An employee shall not be entitled to remuneration under section 19 unless he has been continuously employed for a period of not less than one month ending with the day before that on which the suspension begins.

(2) An employee who is employed—

(a) under a contract for a fixed term of three months or less, or
(b) under a contract made in contemplation of the performance of a specific task which is not expected to last for more than three months,

shall not be entitled to remuneration under section 19 unless he has been continuously employed for a period of more than three months ending with the day before that on which the suspension begins.]

[(3)] An employee shall not be entitled to remuneration under section 19 in respect of any period during which he is incapable of work by reason of disease or bodily or mental disablement.

[(4)] An employee shall not be entitled to remuneration under section 19 in respect of any period during which—

(a) his employer has offered to provide him with suitable alternative work, whether or not work which the employee is under his contract, or was under the contract in force before the suspension, employed to perform, and the employee has unreasonably refused to perform that work; or
(b) he does not comply with reasonable requirements imposed by his employer with a view to ensuring that his services are available.   **[293]**

NOTES
Sub-ss (1), (2): inserted with savings and previous sub-ss (1), (2) renumbered (3), (4) by the Employment Act 1982, s 20, Sch 2, para 2.

21 Calculation of remuneration

(1) The amount of remuneration payable by an employer to an employee under section 19 shall be a week's pay in respect of each week of the period of suspension referred to in subsection (1) of that section, and if in any week remuneration is payable in respect only of part of that week the amount of a week's pay shall be reduced proportionately.

(2) Subject to subsection (3), a right to remuneration under section 19 shall not affect any right of an employee in relation to remuneration under his contract of employment (in this section referred to as "contractual remuneration").

(3) Any contractual remuneration paid by an employer to an employee in respect of any period shall go towards discharging the employer's liability under section 19 in respect of that period, and conversely any payment of remuneration in discharge of an employer's liability under section 19 in respect of any period shall go towards discharging any obligation of the employer to pay contractual remuneration in respect of that period.   **[294]**

22 Complaint to industrial tribunal

(1) An employee may present a complaint to an industrial tribunal that his employer has failed to pay the whole or any part of remuneration to which the employee is entitled under section 19.

(2) An industrial tribunal shall not entertain a complaint relating to remuneration under section 19 in respect of any day unless the complaint is presented to the tribunal before the end of the period of three months beginning with that day, or within such further period as the tribunal considers reasonable in a case where it is satisfied that it was not reasonably practicable for the complaint to be presented within the period of three months.

(3) Where an industrial tribunal finds a complaint under subsection (1) well-founded the tribunal shall order the employer to pay the complainant the amount of remuneration which it finds is due to him.   **[295]**

[Right not to suffer detriment in health and safety cases

22A Right not to suffer detriment in health and safety cases

(1) An employee has the right not to be subjected to any detriment by any act, or any deliberate failure to act, by his employer done on the ground that—

    (a) having been designated by the employer to carry out activities in connection with preventing or reducing risks to health and safety at work, he carried out, or proposed to carry out, any such activities,

    (b) being a representative of workers on matters of health and safety at work, or a member of a safety committee—

        (i) in accordance with arrangements established under or by virtue of any enactment, or

        (ii) by reason of being acknowledged as such by the employer,

    he performed, or proposed to perform, any functions as such a representative or a member of such a committee,

    (c) being an employee at a place where—

        (i) there was no such representative or safety committee, or

        (ii) there was such a representative or safety committee but it was not reasonably practicable for the employee to raise the matter by those means,

    he brought to his employer's attention, by reasonable means, circumstances connected with his work which he reasonably believed were harmful or potentially harmful to health or safety,

    (d) in circumstances of danger which he reasonably believed to be serious and imminent and which he could not reasonably have been expected to avert, he left, or proposed to leave, or (while the danger persisted) refused to return to, his place of work or any dangerous part of his place of work, or

    (e) in circumstances of danger which he reasonably believed to be serious and imminent, he took, or proposed to take, appropriate steps to protect himself or other persons from the danger.

(2) For the purposes of subsection (1)(e) whether steps which an employee took, or proposed to take, were appropriate shall be judged by reference to all the circumstances including, in particular, his knowledge and the facilities and advice available to him at the time.

(3) An employee shall not be regarded as having been subjected to any detriment on the ground specified in subsection (1)(e) if the employer shows that it was, or would have been, so negligent for the employee to take the steps which he took, or proposed to take, that a reasonable employer might have treated him as the employer did.

(4) Except where an employee is dismissed in circumstances in which, by virtue of section 142, section 54 does not apply to the dismissal, this section shall not apply where the detriment in question amounts to dismissal.]   **[295A]**

NOTE
Inserted, with preceding cross-heading and ss 22B, 22C, by the Trade Union Reform and Employment Rights Act 1993, s 28, Sch 5, para 1, as from 30 August 1993 (SI 1993/1908), below, para **[1435]**).

[22B Proceedings for contravention of section 22A

(1) An employee may present a complaint to an industrial tribunal on the ground that he has been subjected to a detriment in contravention of section 22A.

(2) On such a complaint it shall be for the employer to show the ground on which any act, or deliberate failure to act, was done.

(3) An industrial tribunal shall not consider a complaint under this section unless it is presented—

   (a) before the end of the period of three months beginning with the date of the act or failure to act to which the complaint relates or, where that act or failure is part of a series of similar acts or failures, the last of them, or
   (b) where the tribunal is satisfied that it was not reasonably practicable for the complaint to be presented before the end of that period, within such further period as it considers reasonable.

(4) For the purposes of subsection (3)—

   (a) where an act extends over a period, the "date of the act" means the last day of that period, and
   (b) a deliberate failure to act shall be treated as done when it was decided on;

and, in the absence of evidence establishing the contrary, an employer shall be taken to decide on a failure to act when he does an act inconsistent with doing the failed act or, if he has done no such inconsistent act, when the period expires within which he might reasonably have been expected to do the failed act if it was to be done.]   **[295B]**

NOTE
Inserted by the Trade Union Reform and Employment Rights Act 1993, s 28, Sch 5, as from 30 August 1993 (SI 1993/1908), below, para **[1435]**).

[22C Remedies

(1) Where the industrial tribunal finds that a complaint under section 22B is well-founded, it shall make a declaration to that effect and may make an award of compensation to be paid to the complainant in respect of the act or failure to act complained of.

(2) The amount of the compensation awarded shall be such as the tribunal considers just and equitable in all the circumstances having regard to the infringement complained of and to any loss which is attributable to the act or failure which infringed his right.

(3) The loss shall be taken to include—

   (a) any expenses reasonably incurred by the complainant in consequence of the act or failure complained of, and
   (b) loss of any benefit which he might reasonably be expected to have had but for that act or failure.

(4) In ascertaining the loss, the tribunal shall apply the same rule concerning the duty of a person to mitigate his loss as applies to damages recoverable under the common law of England and Wales or Scotland.

(5) Where the tribunal finds that the act or failure complained of was to any extent caused or contributed to by action of the complainant, it shall reduce the amount of the compensation by such proportion as it considers just and equitable having regard to that finding.] **[295C]**

NOTE

Inserted by the Trade Union Reform and Employment Rights Act 1993, s 28, Sch 5, as from 30 August 1993 (SI 1993/1908), below, para **[1435]**).

Trade union membership and activities

23–26A *(Repealed by the Trade Union and Labour Relations (Consolidation) Act 1992, s 300(1), Sch 1. See now ibid ss 146–151.)*

Time off work

27, 28 *(Repealed by the Trade Union and Labour Relations (Consolidation) Act 1992, s 300(1), Sch 1. See now ibid ss 168–170.)*

29 Time off for public duties

(1) An employer shall permit an employee of his who is—
    (a) a justice of the peace;
    (b) a member of a local authority;
    [(bb) a member of the Broads Authority;]
    (c) a member of any statutory tribunal;
    [(cc) a member of, in England and Wales, a board of visitors appointed under section 6(2) of the Prison Act 1952 or, in Scotland, a visiting committee appointed under section 19(3) of the Prisons (Scotland) Act 1989 or constituted by virtue of rules made under section 39, as read with section 8(1), of that Act;]
    (d) a member of [a National Health Service trust or], in England and Wales, a Regional Health Authority [an Area Health Authority or a District] Health Authority [or a Family Practitioner Committee] or, in Scotland, a Health Board;
    (e) a member of, in England and Wales, the managing or governing body of an educational establishment maintained by a local education authority, or, in Scotland, a school . . . council or the governing body of a [designated institution or a central institution]; . . .
    [(ee) a member of the governing body of a grant-maintained school;]
    [(ef) a member of the governing body of a [further education corporation or] higher education corporation; or]
    [(ef) a member of a school board or of the board of management of a self-governing school;]
    [(eg) a member of the board of management of a college of further education; or]
    (f) a member of, in England and Wales, [the National Rivers Authority or, in Scotland, a] river purification board,

to take time off, subject to and in accordance with subsection (4), during the employee's working hours for the purposes of performing any of the duties of his office or, as the case may be, his duties as such a member.

(2) In subsection (1)—

(a) "local authority" in relation to England and Wales includes the Common Council of the City of London but otherwise has the same meaning as in the Local Government Act 1972, and in relation to Scotland has the same meaning as in the Local Government (Scotland) Act 1973;

(b) "Regional Health Authority" . . . "Area Health Authority" [and District Health Authority] [and "Family Practitioner Committee"] have the same meaning as in the National Health Service Act 1977, and "Health Board" has the same meaning as in the National Health Service (Scotland) Act 1972;

(c) "local education authority" means the authority designated by section 192(1) of the Local Government Act 1972, ["school council" means a body appointed under section 125(1) of the Local Government (Scotland) Act 1973, "board of management", where it appears in paragraph (ef) as inserted by the Self-Governing Schools etc (Scotland) Act 1989, "central institution" and "self-governing school" have the same meanings as in section 135(1) of the Education (Scotland) Act 1980, "school board" has the same meaning as in section 1(1) of the School Boards (Scotland) Act 1988, "board of management", where it appears and "college of further education" have the same meanings as in section 36(1) of the Further and Higher Education (Scotland) Act 1992 and "designated institution" has the same meaning as in Part II of that Act of 1992]; and

(d) "river purification board" means a board established under section 135 of the Local Government (Scotland) Act 1973.

(3) For the purposes of subsection (1) the duties of a member of a body referred to in paragraphs (b) to (f) of that subsection are:—

(a) attendance at a meeting of the body or any of its committees or sub-committees;

(b) the doing of any other thing approved by the body, or anything of a class so approved, for the purpose of the discharge of the functions of the body or of any of its committees or sub-committees.

(4) The amount of time off which an employee is to be permitted to take under this section and the occasions on which and any conditions subject to which time off may be so taken are those that are reasonable in all the circumstances having regard, in particular, to the following:—

(a) how much time off is required for the performance of the duties of the office or as a member of the body in question, and how much time off is required for the performance of the particular duty;

(b) how much time off the employee has already been permitted under this section or [sections 168 and 170 of the Trade Union and Labour Relations (Consolidation) Act 1992 (time off for trade union duties and activities)];

(c) the circumstances of the employer's business and the effect of the employee's absence on the running of that business.

(5) The Secretary of State may by order—

(a) modify the provisions of subsection (1) by adding any office or body to, or removing any office or body from, that subsection or by altering the description of any office or body in that subsection; and

(b) modify the provisions of subsection (3).

(6) An employee may present a complaint to an industrial tribunal that his employer has failed to permit him to take time off as required by this section.

_____ [296]

NOTES

Sub-s (1): para (bb) added by the Norfolk and Suffolk Broads Act 1988, s 21, Sch 6, para 19; para (cc) added by SI 1990/1870, art 2; in para (d) first words in square brackets added by the National Health Service and Community Care Act 1990, s 66(1), Sch 9, para 20, second words in square brackets added by the Health Services Act 1980, ss 1, 2, Sch 1, Pt I, final words in square brackets added by SI 1985/39, art 8; in para (e), first words omitted repealed, and words in square brackets substituted, by the Further and Higher Education (Scotland) Act 1992, s 62, Sch 9, para 6(a), Sch 10, second word omitted repealed by the Education Reform Act 1988, s 237, Sch 12, Pt I, para 23, Sch 13, Pt III; para (ee) added by the Education Reform Act 1988, s 237, Sch 12, Pt I, para 23; first para (ef) added by the Education Reform Act 1988, s 237, Sch 12, Pt III, para 80, words in square brackets therein added by the Further and Higher Education Act 1992, s 93, Sch 8, Pt II, para 89; second para (ef) added by the Self-Governing Schools etc (Scotland) Act 1989, s 82(1), Sch 10, para 7; para (eg) added by the Further and Higher Education (Scotland) Act 1992, s 62, Sch 9, para 6(b); in para (f) words in square brackets substituted by the Water Act 1989, s 190, Sch 25, para 56.

Sub-s (2): in para (b), words omitted repealed and first words in square brackets inserted by the Health Services Act 1980, ss 1, 2, Sch 1, Pt I; second words in square brackets inserted by SI 1985/39, art 8; words in square brackets in para (c) substituted by the Further and Higher Education (Scotland) Act 1992, s 62, Sch 9, para 6(c).

Sub-s (4): in para (b), words in square brackets substituted by the Trade Union and Labour Relations (Consolidation) Act 1992, s 300(2), Sch 2, para 11.

See further, in relation to remuneration for such time off: the Local Government and Housing Act 1989, s 10.

Family Practitioner Committee: to be construed as a reference to a Family Health Services Authority by virtue of the National Health Service and Community Care Act 1990, s 2(1), (2).

The orders under this section are those the effect of which is indicated in the foregoing notes.

30 Provisions as to industrial tribunals

(1) An industrial tribunal shall not consider [a complaint under section 29 that an employer has failed to permit an employee to take time off] unless it is presented within three months of the date when the failure occurred or within such further period as the tribunal considers reasonable in a case where it is satisfied that it was not reasonably practicable for the complaint to be presented within the period of three months.

(2) Where an industrial tribunal finds [such a complaint] well-founded, the tribunal shall make a declaration to that effect and may make an award of compensation to be paid by the employer to the employee which shall be of such amount as the tribunal considers just and equitable in all the circumstances having regard to the employer's default in failing to permit time off to be taken by the employee and to any loss sustained by the employee which is attributable to the matters complained of.

(3) . . . [297]

NOTES

Sub-s (1): words in square brackets substituted for paras (a) and (b) as originally enacted by the Trade Union and Labour Relations (Consolidation) Act 1992, s 300(2), Sch 2, para 12(a).

Sub-s (2): words in square brackets substituted by the Trade Union and Labour Relations (Consolidation) Act 1992, s 300(2), Sch 2, para 12(b).

Sub-s (3): repealed by the Trade Union and Labour Relations (Consolidation) Act 1992, s 300, Sch 1, Sch 2, para 12(c).

31 Time off to look for work or make arrangements for training

(1) An employee who is given notice of dismissal by reason of redundancy shall, subject to the following provisions of this section, be entitled before the expiration of his notice to be allowed by his employer reasonable time off during the employee's

working hours in order to look for new employment or make arrangements for training for future employment.

(2) An employee shall not be entitled to time off under this section unless, on whichever is the later of the following dates, that is to say—

(a) the date on which the notice is due to expire; or

(b) the date on which it would expire were it the notice required to be given by section 49(1),

he will have been or, as the case may be, would have been continuously employed for a period of two years or more.

(3) An employee who is allowed time off during his working hours under subsection (1) shall, subject to the following provisions of this section, be entitled to be paid remuneration by his employer for the period of absence at the appropriate hourly rate.

(4) The appropriate hourly rate in relation to an employee shall be the amount of one week's pay divided by—

(a) the number of normal working hours in a week for that employee when employed under the contract of employment in force on the day when notice was given; or

(b) where the number of such normal working hours differs from week to week or over a longer period, the average number of such hours calculated by dividing by twelve the total number of the employee's normal working hours during the period of twelve weeks ending with the last complete week before the day on which notice was given.

(5) If an employer unreasonably refuses to allow an employee time off from work under this section, the employee shall, subject to subsection (9), be entitled to be paid an amount equal to the remuneration to which he would have been entitled under subsection (3) if he had been allowed the time off.

(6) An employee may present a complaint to an industrial tribunal on the ground that his employer has unreasonably refused to allow him time off under this section or has failed to pay the whole or any part of any amount to which the employee is entitled under subsection (3) or (5).

(7) An industrial tribunal shall not entertain a complaint under subsection (6) unless it is presented to the tribunal within the period of three months beginning with the day on which it is alleged that the time off should have been allowed, or within such further period as the tribunal considers reasonable in a case where it is satisfied that it was not reasonably practicable for the complaint to be presented within the period of three months.

(8) If on a complaint under subsection (6) the tribunal finds the grounds of the complaint well-founded it shall make a declaration to that effect and shall order the employer to pay to the employee the amount which it finds due to him.

(9) The amount—

(a) of an employer's liability to pay remuneration under subsection (3); or

(b) which may be ordered by a tribunal to be paid by an employer under subsection (8),

or, where both paragraphs (a) and (b) are applicable, the aggregate amount of the liabilities referred to in those paragraphs, shall not exceed, in respect of the notice period of any employee, two-fifths of a week's pay of that employee.

(10) Subject to subsection (11), a right to any amount under subsection (3) or (5) shall not affect any right of an employee in relation to remuneration under the contract of employment (in this section referred to as "contractual remuneration").

(11) Any contractual remuneration paid to an employee in respect of a period when he takes time off for the purposes referred to in subsection (1) shall go towards discharging any liability of the employer to pay remuneration under subsection (3) in respect of that period, and conversely any payment of remuneration under subsection (3) in respect of a period shall go towards discharging any liability of the employer to pay contractual remuneration in respect of that period.   [298]

[31A Time off for ante-natal care

(1) An employee who is pregnant and who has, on the advice of a registered medical practitioner, registered midwife or registered health visitor, made an appointment to attend at any place for the purpose of receiving ante-natal care shall, subject to the following provisions of this section, have the right not to be unreasonably refused time off during her working hours to enable her to keep the appointment.

(2) Subject to subsection (3), an employer shall not be required by virtue of this section to permit an employee to take time off to keep an appointment unless, if he requests he to do so, she produces for his inspection—

    (a) a certificate from a registered medical practitioner, registered midwife or registered health visitor stating that the employee is pregnant, and

    (b) an appointment card or some other document showing that the appointment has been made.

(3) Subsection (2) shall not apply where the employee's appointment is the first appointment during her pregnancy for which she seeks permission to take time off in accordance with subsection (1).

(4) An employee who is permitted to take time off during her working hours in accordance with subsection (1) shall be entitled to be paid remuneration by her employer for the period of absence at the appropriate hourly rate.

(5) The appropriate hourly rate in relation to an employee shall be the amount of one week's pay divided by—

    (a) the number of normal working hours in a week for that employee when employed under the contract of employment in force on the day when the time off is taken; or

    (b) where the number of such normal working hours differs from week to week or over a longer period, the average number of such hours calculated by dividing by twelve the total number of the employee's normal working hours during the period of twelve weeks ending with the last complete week before the day on which the time off is taken; or

    (c) in a case falling within paragraph (b) but where the employee has not been employed for a sufficient period to enable the calculation to be made under that paragraph, a number which fairly represents the number of normal working hours in a week having regard to such of the following considerations as are appropriate in the circumstances, that is to say,—

        (i) the average number of normal working hours in a week which the employee could expect in accordance with the terms of her contract;

        (ii) the average number of such hours of other employees engaged in relevant comparable employment with the same employer.

(6) An employee may present a complaint to an industrial tribunal that her employer has unreasonably refused her time off as required by this section or that he has failed to pay her the whole or part of any amount to which she is entitled under subsection (4).

(7) An industrial tribunal shall not entertain a complaint under subsection (6) unless it is presented within the period of three months beginning with the day of the appointment concerned, or within such further period as the tribunal considers reasonable in a case where it is satisfied that it was not reasonably practicable for the complaint to be presented within the period of three months.

(8) Where on a complaint under subsection (6) the tribunal finds the complaint well-founded it shall make a declaration to that effect; and

    (a) if the complaint is that the employer has unreasonably refused the employee time off, the tribunal shall order the employer to pay to the employee an amount equal to the remuneration to which she would have been entitled under subsection (4) if the time off had not been refused; and

    (b) if the complaint is that the employer has failed to pay the employee the whole or part of any amount to which she is entitled under subsection (4), the tribunal shall order the employer to pay to the employee the amount which it finds due to her.

(9) Subject to subsection (10), a right to any amount under subsection (4) shall not affect any right of an employee in relation to remuneration under her contract of employment (in this section referred to as "contractual remuneration").

(10) Any contractual remuneration paid to an employee in respect of a period of time off under this section shall go towards discharging any liability of the employer to pay remuneration under subsection (4) in respect of that period, and conversely any payment of remuneration under subsection (4) in respect of a period shall go towards discharging any liability of the employer to pay contractual remuneration in respect of that period.

(11) Until the coming into operation of section 10 of the Nurses, Midwives and Health Visitors Act 1979, this section shall have effect as if for any reference to a registered midwife or registered health visitor there were substituted a reference to a certified midwife.] **[299]**

NOTE
Inserted by the Employment Act 1980, s 13.

[32 Meaning of "working hours"

For the purposes of sections 29 to 31A the working hours of an employee shall be taken to be any time when in accordance with his contract of employment he is required to be at work.] **[300]**

NOTES
Commencement: 16 October 1992 (Trade Union and Labour Relation (Consolidation) Act 1992, s 302.)
Substituted by the Trade Union and Labour Relations (Consolidation) Act 1992, s 300(2), Sch 2, para 13.

PART III

MATERNITY

NOTE
This Part (ss 33, 45–48, printed in italics below) is substituted by the Trade Union Reform and Employment Rights Act 1993, s 23. Sch 2, as from a day to be appointed. The substituted Pt III (ss 33–47) is printed after the italicised original part, beginning at para [**305A**] below. It is likely that the substitution will take effect in October 1994; see the note to the substituted Pt III below.

General provisions

33 Rights of employee in connection with pregnancy and confinement

(1) An employee who is absent from work wholly or partly because of pregnancy or confinement shall, subject to the following provisions of this Act,—

    (a) ...

    (b) be entitled to return to work.

(2) Schedule 2 shall have effect for the purpose of supplementing the following provisions of this Act in relation to an employee's right to return to work.

(3) An employee shall be entitled to the [right] referred to in subsection (1) whether or not a contract of employment subsists during the period of her absence but, subject to subsection (4), she shall not be so entitled unless—

    (a) she continues to be employed by her employer (whether or not she is at work) until immediately before the beginning of the eleventh week before the expected week of confinement;

    (b) she has at the beginning of that eleventh week been continuously employed for a period of not less than two years; ...

    (c) ...

    [(d) ... *she informs her employer in writing at least twenty-one days before her absence begins or, if that is not reasonably practicable, as soon as reasonably practicable,—*

        (i) that he will be (or is) absent from work wholly or partly because of pregnancy or confinement,

        (ii) that she intends to return to work with her employer, and

        (iii) of the expected week of confinement or, if the confinement has occurred, the date of confinement].

[(3A) Where not earlier than forty-nine days after the beginning of the expected week of confinement (or the date of confinement) notified under subsection (3)(d) an employee is requested in accordance with subsection (3B) by her employer or a successor of his to give him written confirmation that she intends to return to work, she shall not be entitled to the right to return unless she gives that confirmation within fourteen days of receiving the request or, if that is not reasonably practicable, as soon as reasonably practicable.

(3B) A request under subsection (3A) shall be made in writing and shall be accompanied by a written statement of the effect of that subsection.]

(4) An employee who has been dismissed by her employer for a reason falling within section 60(1)(a) or (b) and has not been re-engaged in accordance with that section, shall be entitled to the [right] referred to in subsection (1) of this section notwithstanding that she has thereby ceased to be employed before the beginning of the eleventh week before the expected week of confinement if, but for that dismissal, she would at the beginning of that eleventh week have been continuously employed for a period of not less than two years, but she shall not be entitled to the right ... *unless she informs her employer (in writing if he so requests), before or as soon as reasonably practicable after the dismissal takes effect, that she intends to return to work with him.*

In this subsection "dismiss" and "dismissal" have the same meaning as they have for the purposes of Part V.

(5) An employee shall not be entitled to [the right] referred to in subsection (1) unless, if requested to do so by her employer, she produces for his inspection a

certificate from a registered medical practitioner or a [registered midwife] stating the expected week of her confinement.

(6) *The Secretary of State may by order vary the periods of two years referred to in subsection (3) and (4), or those periods as varied from time to time under this subsection, but no such order shall be made unless a draft of the order has been laid before Parliament and approved by resolution of each House of Parliament.* **[301]**

NOTES
Substituted, along with ss 45–48, by new ss 33–47, by the Trade Union Reform and Employment Rights Act 1993, s 23, as from a day to be appointed. For new ss 33–47, see paras **[305A]** et seq below. It is likely that the substitution will take effect in October 1994; see the note to the substituted Pt III below.
Sub-s (1): para (a) repealed by the Social Security Act 1986, s 86, Sch 11.
Sub-s (3): first word in square brackets substituted by the Social Security Act 1986, s 86, Sch 10, Pt IV, para 75; in para (b) word omitted repealed by the Employment Act 1980, s 20, Sch 2; para (c) repealed by the Social Security Act 1986, s 86, Sch 11; para (d) added by the Employment Act 1980, s 11(1).
Sub-ss (3A), (3B): inserted by the Employment Act 1980, s 11(2).
Sub-s (4): word in square brackets substituted by the Social Security Act 1986, s 86, Sch 10, Pt IV, para 75; words omitted repealed by the Social Security Act 1986, s 86, Sch 11.
Sub-s (5): first words in square brackets substituted by the Social Security Act 1986, s 86, Sch 10, Pt IV, para 75; second words in square brackets substituted by the Nurses, Midwives and Health Visitors Act 1979, s 23(4), Sch 7, para 31.

34 – 44 *((Maternity pay) repealed by the Social Security Act 1986, s 86(2), Sch 11. The equivalent provisions have since been consolidated in the Social Security (Contributions and Benefits) Act 1992, ss 164–171, below, paras [626]–[633]. For new ss 34 – 44, as substituted for the original ss 33, 45 – 48 by the Trade Union Reform and Employment Rights Act 1993, s 23, as from a day to be appointed, see paras [305B] et seq below.)*

Right to return to work

45 Right to return to work

(1) The right to return to work of an employee who has been absent from work wholly or partly because of pregnancy or confinement is, subject to the following provisions of this Act, a right to return to work with her original employer, or, where appropriate, his successor, at any time before the end of the period of twenty-nine weeks beginning with the week in which the date of confinement falls, in the job in which she was employed under the original contract of employment and on terms and conditions not less favourable than those which would have been applicable to her if she had not been so absent.

(2) In subsection (1) "terms and conditions not less favourable than those which would have been applicable to her if she had not been so absent" means, as regards seniority, pension rights and other similar rights, that the period or periods of employment prior to the employee's absence shall be regarded as continuous with her employment following that absence [but subject to the requirements of paragraph 5 of Schedule 5 to the Social Security Act 1989 (credit for the period of absence in certain cases)].

(3) If an employee is entitled to return to work in accordance with subsection (1), but it is not practicable by reason of redundancy for the employer to permit her so to return to work she shall be entitled, where there is a suitable available vacancy, to be offered alternative employment with her employer (or his successor), or an associated employer, under a new contract of employment complying with subsection (4).

(4) The new contract of employment must be such that—

(a) *the work to be done under the contract is of a kind which is both suitable in relation to the employee and appropriate for her to do in the circumstances; and*

(b) *the provisions of the new contract as to the capacity and place in which she is to be employed and as to the other terms and conditions of her employment are not substantially less favourable to her than if she had returned to work in accordance with subsection (1).* **[302]**

NOTES

Substituted, along with ss 33, 46–48, by new ss 33–47, by the Trade Union Reform and Employment Rights Act 1993, s 23, as from a day to be appointed. For new ss 33–47, see paras **[305A]** et seq below. It is likely that the substitution will take effect in October 1994; see the note to the substituted Pt III below.

Sub-s (2): words in square brackets added by the Social Security Act 1989, s 23, Sch 5, Pt II, para 15, as from a day to be appointed.

Modified by the Social Security Act 1986, s 49, Sch 4, Pt III, para 15, and in relation to governing bodies with delegated budgets, by the Education (Modification of Enactments Relating to Employment) Order 1989, SI 1989/901, art 3.

46 Enforcement of rights under s 45

The remedies of an employee for infringement of either of the rights mentioned in section 45 are those conferred by or by virtue of the provisions of sections 47, 56 and 86 and Schedule 2. **[303]**

NOTE

Substituted, along with ss 33, 45, 47, 48, by new ss 33–47, by the Trade Union Reform and Employment Rights Act 1993, s 23, as from a day to be appointed. For new ss 33–47, see paras **[305A]** et seq below. It is likely that the substitution will take effect in October 1994; see the note to the substituted Pt III below.

Modified by the Social Security Act 1986, s 49, Sch 4, Pt III, para 15, and in relation to governing bodies with delegated budgets, by the Education (Modification of Enactments Relating to Employment) Order 1989, SI 1989/901, art 3.

47 Exercise of right to return to work

(1) An employee shall exercise her right to return to work by [giving written notice to] the employer (who may be her original employer or a successor of that employer) at least [twenty-one] days before the day on which she proposes to return of her proposal to return on that day (in this section referred to as the "notified day of return").

(2) An employer may postpone an employee's return to work until a date not more than four weeks after the notified day of return if he notifies her before that day that for specified reasons he is postponing her return until that date, and accordingly she will be entitled to return to work with him on that date.

(3) Subject to subsection (4), an employee may—

(a) *postpone her return to work until a date not exceeding four weeks from the notified day of return, notwithstanding that that date falls after the end of the period of twenty-nine weeks mentioned in section 45(1); and*

(b) *where no day of return has been notified to the employer, extend the time during which she may exercise her right to return in accordance with subsection (1), so that she returns to work not later than four weeks from the expiration of the said period of twenty-nine weeks;*

if before the notified day of return or, as the case may be, the expiration of the period of twenty-nine weeks she gives the employer a certificate from a registered medical practitioner stating that by reason of disease or bodily or mental disablement she will be incapable of work on the notified day of return or the expiration of that period, as the case may be.

(4) Where an employee has once exercised a right of postponement or extension under subsection (3)(a) or (b), she shall not again be entitled to exercise a right of postponement or extension under that subsection in connection with the same return to work.

(5) If an employee has notified a day of return but there is an interruption of work (whether due to industrial action or some other reason) which renders it unreasonable to expect the employee to return to work on the notified day of return, she may instead return to work when work resumes after the interruption or as soon as reasonably practicable thereafter.

(6) If no day of return has been notified and there is an interruption of work (whether due to industrial action or some other reason) which renders it unreasonable to expect the employee to return to work before the expiration of the period of twenty-nine weeks referred to in section 45(1), or which appears likely to have that effect, and in consequence the employee does not notify a day of return, the employee may exercise her right to return in accordance with sub-section (1) so that she returns to work at any time before the end of the period of [twenty-eight] days from the end of the interruption notwithstanding that she returns to work outside the said period of twenty-nine weeks.

(7) Where the employee has either—

> *(a) exercised the right under subsection (3)(b) to extend the period during which she may exercise her right to return; or*
> *(b) refrained from notifying the day of return in the circumstances described in subsection (6),*

the other of those subsections shall apply as if for the reference to the expiration of the period of twenty-nine weeks there were substituted a reference to the expiration of the further period of four weeks or, as the case may be, of the period of [twenty-eight] days from the end of the interruption of work.

(8) Where—

> *(a) an employee's return is postponed under subsection (2) or (3)(a), or*
> *(b) the employee returns to work on a day later than the notified day of return in the circumstances described in subsection (5),*

then, subject to subsection (4), references in those subsections and in sections 56 and 86 and Schedule 2 to the notified day of return shall be construed as references to the day to which the return is postponed or, as the case may be, that later day.

[304]

NOTES
    Substituted, along with ss 33, 45, 46, 48, by new ss 33–47, by the Trade Union Reform and Employment Rights Act 1993, s 23, as from a day to be appointed. For new ss 33–47, see paras **[305A]** et seq below. It is likely that the substitution will take effect in October 1994; see the note to the substituted Pt III below.
    Sub-ss (1), (6), (7): words in square brackets substituted by the Employment Act 1980, s 11(3).
    Modified by the Social Security Act 1986, s 49, Sch 4, Pt III, para 15, and in relation to governing bodies with delegated budgets, by the Education (Modification of Enactments Relating to Employment) Order 1989, SI 1989/901, art 3.

48 Contractual right to return to work

(1) An employee who has a right both under this Act and under a contract of employment, or otherwise, to return to work, may not exercise the two rights

separately but may in returning to work take advantage of whichever right is, in any particular respect, the more favourable.

(2) The provisions of sections 45, 46, 47, 56 and 86 and paragraphs 1 to 4 and 6 of Schedule 2 shall apply, subject to any modifications necessary to give effect to any more favourable contractual terms, to the exercise of the composite right described in subsection (1) as they apply to the exercise of the right to return conferred solely by this Part. **[305]**

NOTES

Substituted, along with ss 33, 45–47, by new ss 33–47, by the Trade Union Reform and Employment Rights Act 1993, s 23, as from a day to be appointed. For new ss 33–47, see paras **[305A]** et seq below. It is likely that the substitution will take effect in October 1994; see the note to the substituted Pt III below.

Modified by the Social Security Act 1986, s 49, Sch 4, Pt III, para 15, and in relation to governing bodies with delegated budgets, by the Education (Modification of Enactments Relating to Employment) Order 1989, SI 1989/901, art 3.

NOTE

A new Pt III of the Act is substituted for the Pt III printed in italics above by the Trade Union Reform and Employment Rights Act 1993, ss 23, 25, Schs 2, 3. The provisions are intended to implement parts of EC Council Directive 92/85 (below, paras **[2264]**–**[2281]**) which is required to be put into domestic law by 18 October 1994. It is likely that that date will be the date of commencement of the new Pt III.

[PART III

MATERNITY

General right to maternity leave

[33 General right to maternity leave

(1) An employee who is absent from work at any time during her maternity leave period shall, subject to sections 36 and 37, be entitled to the benefit of the terms and conditions of employment which would have been applicable to her if she had not been absent (and had not been pregnant or given birth to a child).

(2) Subsection (1) does not confer any entitlement to remuneration.]   **[305A]**

NOTE

Substituted by the Trade Union Reform and Employment Rights Act 1993, s 23(1)(a), (2), as from a day to be appointed.

[34 Commencement of maternity leave period

(1) Subject to subsection (2), an employee's maternity leave period commences with—

    (a) the date which, in accordance with section 36, she notifies to her employer as the date on which she intends her period of absence from work in exercise of her right to maternity leave to commence, or

    (b) if earlier, the first day on which she is absent from work wholly or partly because of pregnancy or childbirth after the beginning of the sixth week before the expected week of childbirth.

(2) Where childbirth occurs before the day with which the employee's maternity leave period would otherwise commence, her maternity leave period shall commence with the day on which childbirth occurs.

(3) The Secretary of State may by order vary either of the provisions of subsections (1) and (2).

(4) No order shall be made under subsection (3) unless a draft of the order has been laid before Parliament and approved by a resolution of each House of Parliament.]   **[305B]**

NOTE
Substituted by the Trade Union Reform and Employment Rights Act 1993, s 23(1)(a), (2), as from a day to be appointed.

[35 Duration of maternity leave period

(1) Subject to subsections (2) and (3), an employee's maternity leave period shall continue for the period of fourteen weeks from its commencement or until the birth of the child, if later.

(2) Subject to subsection (3), where any requirement imposed by or under any provision of any enactment or of any instrument made under any enactment, other than a provision for the time being specified in an order made under section 45(3), prohibits her working for any period after the end of the period mentioned in subsection (1) by reason of her having recently given birth, her maternity leave period shall continue until the expiry of that later period.

(3) Where an employee is dismissed after the commencement of her maternity leave period but before the time when (apart from this subsection) that period would end, the period ends at the time of the dismissal.

(4) The Secretary of State may by order vary any of the provisions of this section.

(5) No order shall be made under subsection (4) unless a draft of the order has been laid before Parliament and approved by a resolution of each House of Parliament.]   **[305C]**

NOTE
Substituted by the Trade Union Reform and Employment Rights Act 1993, s 23(1)(a), (2), as from a day to be appointed.

[36 Notice of commencement of leave

(1) An employee shall not have the right conferred by section 33 unless—

    (a) she notifies her employer of the date (within the restriction imposed by subsection (2)) ("the notified leave date") on which she intends her period of absence from work in exercise of her right to maternity leave to commence—

        (i) not less than twenty-one days before that date, or
        (ii) if that is not reasonably practicable, as soon as is reasonably practicable,

    (b) where she is first absent from work wholly or partly because of pregnancy or childbirth before the notified leave date or before she has notified such a date and after the beginning of the sixth week before the expected week of childbirth, she notifies her employer as soon as is reasonably practicable that she is absent for that reason, or

    (c) where childbirth occurs before the notified leave date or before she has notified such a date, she notifies her employer that she has given birth as soon as is reasonably practicable after the birth,

and any notice she is required to give under paragraphs (a) to (c) shall, if her employer so requests, be given in writing.

(2) No date may be notified under subsection (1)(a) which occurs before the beginning of the eleventh week before the expected week of childbirth.

(3) Where, in the case of an employee, either paragraph (b) or (c) of subsection (1) has fallen to be satisfied, and has been so satisfied, nothing in paragraph (a) of that subsection shall impose any requirement on the employee.] **[305D]**

NOTE
Substituted by the Trade Union Reform and Employment Rights Act 1993, s 23(1)(a), (2), as from a day to be appointed.

[37 Requirement to inform employer of pregnancy etc

(1) An employee shall not have the right conferred by section 33 unless she informs her employer in writing at least twenty-one days before her maternity leave period commences or, if that is not reasonably practicable, as soon as is reasonably practicable—

  (a) that she is pregnant, and
  (b) of the expected week of childbirth or, if the childbirth has occurred, the date on which it occurred.

(2) An employee shall not have the right conferred by section 33 unless, if requested to do so by her employer, she produces for his inspection a certificate from a registered medical practitioner or a registered midwife stating the expected week of childbirth.] **[305E]**

NOTE
Substituted by the Trade Union Reform and Employment Rights Act 1993, s 23(1)(a), (2), as from a day to be appointed.

[37A Requirement to inform employer of return during maternity leave period

(1) An employee who intends to return to work earlier than the end of her maternity leave period shall give to her employer not less than seven days notice of the date on which she intends to return.

(2) If an employee returns to work as mentioned in subsection (1) without notifying her employer of her intention to do so or without giving him the notice required by that subsection her employer shall be entitled to postpone her return to a date such as will secure, subject to subsection (3), that he has seven days notice of her return.

(3) An employer is not entitled under subsection (2) to postpone an employee's return to work to a date after the end of her maternity leave period.

(4) If an employee who has been notified under subsection (2) that she is not to return to work before the date specified by her employer does return to work before that date the employer shall be under no contractual obligation to pay her remuneration until the date specified by him as the date on which she may return.] **[305F]**

NOTE
Substituted by the Trade Union Reform and Employment Rights Act 1993, s 23(1)(a), (2), as from a day to be appointed.

[38 Special provision where redundancy during maternity leave period

(1) Where during an employee's maternity leave period it is not practicable by reason of redundancy for the employer to continue to employ her under her existing contract of employment, she shall be entitled, where there is a suitable available vacancy, to be offered (before the ending of her employment under that contract) alternative employment with her employer or his successor, or an associated employer, under a new contract of employment which complies with subsection (2) (and takes effect immediately on the ending of her employment under the previous contract).

(2) The new contract of employment must be such that—

    (a) the work to be done under the contract is of a kind which is both suitable in relation to the employee and appropriate for her to do in the circumstances; and

    (b) the provisions of the new contract as to the capacity and place in which she is to be employed and as to the other terms and conditions of her employment are not substantially less favourable to her than if she had continued to be employed under the previous contract.]   **[305G]**

NOTE
    Substituted by the Trade Union Reform and Employment Rights Act 1993, s 23(1)(a), (2), as from a day to be appointed.

[38A Contractual right to maternity leave

(1) An employee who has the right to maternity leave under section 33 and a right to maternity leave under a contract of employment or otherwise may not exercise the two rights separately but may, in taking maternity leave, take advantage of whichever right is, in any particular respect, the more favourable.

(2) The provisions of sections 34 to 38 shall apply, subject to any modifications necessary to give effect to any more favourable contractual terms, to the exercise of the composite right described in subsection (1) as they apply to the exercise of the right under section 33.]   **[305H]**

NOTE
    Substituted by the Trade Union Reform and Employment Rights Act 1993, s 23(1)(a), (2), as from a day to be appointed.

[Right to return to work

39 Right to return to work

(1) An employee who—

    (a) has the right conferred by section 33, and

    (b) has, at the beginning of the eleventh week before the expected week of childbirth, been continuously employed for a period of not less than two years,

shall also have the right to return to work at any time during the period beginning at the end of her maternity leave period and ending twenty-nine weeks after the beginning of the week in which childbirth occurs.

(2) An employee's right to return to work under this section is the right to return to work with the person who was her employer before the end of her maternity leave period, or (where appropriate) his successor, in the job in which she was then employed—

    (a) on terms and conditions as to remuneration not less favourable than those which would have been applicable to her had she not been absent from work at any time since the commencement of her maternity leave period,

    (b) with her seniority, pension rights and similar rights as they would have been if the period or periods of her employment prior to the end of her maternity leave period were continuous with her employment following her return to work (but subject to the requirements of paragraph 5 of Schedule 5 to the Social Security Act 1989 (credit for the period of absence in certain cases)), and

    (c) otherwise on terms and conditions no less favourable than those which would have been applicable to her had she not been absent from work after the end of her maternity leave period.

(3) The Secretary of State may by order vary the period of two years specified in subsection (1) or that period as so varied.

(4) No order shall be made under subsection (3) unless a draft of the order has been laid before Parliament and approved by a resolution of each House of Parliament.]   **[305I]**

NOTE

Substituted by the Trade Union Reform and Employment Rights Act 1993, s 23(1)(b), Sch 2, as from a day to be appointed.

[40 Requirement to give notice of return to employer

(1) An employee shall not have the right to return to work under section 39 unless she includes with the information required by section 37(1) the information that she intends to exercise the right.

(2) Where, not earlier than twenty-one days before the end of her maternity leave period, an employee is requested in accordance with subsection (3) by her employer, or a successor of his, to give him written confirmation that she intends to exercise the right to return to work under section 39, the employee shall not be entitled to that right unless she gives the requested confirmation within fourteen days of receiving the request or, if that is not reasonably practicable, as soon as is reasonably practicable.

(3) A request under subsection (2) shall be—

    (a) made in writing, and

    (b) accompanied by a written statement of the effect of that subsection.]

                                                               [305J]

NOTE

Substituted by the Trade Union Reform and Employment Rights Act 1993, s 23(1)(b), Sch 2, as from a day to be appointed.

[41 Special provision where redundancies occur before return to work

(1) Where an employee has the right to return to work under section 39, but it is not practicable by reason of redundancy for the employer to permit her to return in accordance with that right, she shall be entitled, where there is a suitable available vacancy, to be offered alternative employment with her employer (or his successor), or an associated employer, under a new contract of employment complying with subsection (2).

(2) The new contract of employment must be such that—

(a) the work to be done under the contract is of a kind which is both suitable in relation to the employee and appropriate for her to do in the circumstances; and

(b) the provisions of the new contract as to the capacity and place in which she is to be employed and as to the other terms and conditions of her employment are not substantially less favourable to her than if she had returned to work pursuant to her right to return.]   **[305K]**

NOTE
Substituted by the Trade Union Reform and Employment Rights Act 1993, s 23(1)(b), Sch 2, as from a day to be appointed.

[42 Exercise of right to return to work

(1) An employee shall exercise the right to return to work under section 39 by giving written notice to the employer (who may be her employer before the end of her maternity leave period or a successor of his) at least twenty-one days before the day on which she proposes to return of her proposal to return on that day (the "notified day of return").

(2) An employer may postpone an employee's return to work until a date not more than four weeks after the notified day of return if he notifies her before that day that for specified reasons he is postponing her return until that date, and accordingly she will be entitled to return to work with him on that date.

(3) Subject to subsection (4), an employee may—

(a) postpone her return to work until a date not exceeding four weeks from the notified day of return, notwithstanding that that date falls after the end of the period of twenty-nine weeks beginning with the week in which childbirth occurred; and

(b) where no day of return has been notified to the employer, extend the time during which she may exercise her right to return in accordance with subsection (1), so that she returns to work not later than four weeks from the end of that period of twenty-nine weeks;

if, before the notified day of return (or the end of the period of twenty-nine weeks), she gives the employer a certificate from a registered medical practitioner stating that by reason of disease or bodily or mental disablement she will be incapable of work on the notified day of return (or the end of that period).

(4) Where an employee has once exercised a right of postponement or extension under subsection (3)(a) or (b), she shall not again be entitled to exercise a right of postponement or extension under that subsection in connection with the same return to work.

(5) If an employee has notified a day of return but there is an interruption of work (whether due to industrial action or some other reason) which renders it unreasonable to expect the employee to return to work on the notified day of return, she may instead return to work when work resumes after the interruption or as soon as reasonably practicable afterwards.

(6) If—

(a) no day of return has been notified,

(b) there is an interruption of work (whether due to industrial action or some other reason) which renders it unreasonable to expect the employee to return to work before the end of the period of twenty-nine weeks beginning with the week in which childbirth occurred, or which appears likely to have that effect, and

(c) in consequence, the employee does not notify a day of return,

the employee may exercise her right to return in accordance with subsection (1) so that she returns to work at any time before the end of the period of twenty-eight days from the end of the interruption notwithstanding that she returns to work outside the period of twenty-nine weeks.

(7) Where the employee has either—

(a) exercised the right under subsection (3)(b) to extend the period during which she may exercise her right to return; or

(b) refrained from notifying the day of return in the circumstances described in subsection (6),

the other of those subsections shall apply as if for the reference to the end of the period of twenty-nine weeks there were substituted a reference to the end of the further period of four weeks or, as the case may be, of the period of twenty-eight days from the end of the interruption of work.]   [305L]

NOTE
Substituted by the Trade Union Reform and Employment Rights Act 1993, s 23(1)(b), Sch 2, as from a day to be appointed.

[43 Supplementary

(1) Schedule 2 shall have effect for the purpose of supplementing the preceding sections in relation to an employee's right to return to work under section 39.

(2) Sections 56 and 86 also have effect for that purpose.

(3) Subject to subsection (4), in sections 56 and 86 and Schedule 2 "notified day of return" has the same meaning as in section 42.

(4) Where—

(a) an employee's return is postponed under subsection (2) or (3)(a) of section 42, or

(b) the employee returns to work on a day later than the notified day of return in the circumstances described in subsection (5) of that section,

then, subject to subsection (4) of that section, references in those subsections and in sections 56 and 86 and Schedule 2 to the notified day of return shall be construed as references to the day to which the return is postponed or that later day.]   [305M]

NOTE
Substituted by the Trade Union Reform and Employment Rights Act 1993, s 23(1)(b), Sch 2, as from a day to be appointed.

[44 Contractual rights

(1) An employee who has the right to return to work under section 39 and a right to return to work after absence because of pregnancy or childbirth under a contract of employment or otherwise may not exercise the two rights separately but may, in returning to work, take advantage of whichever right is, in any particular respect, the more favourable.

(2) The provisions of sections 39, 41 to 43, 56 and 86 and paragraphs 1 to 4 and 6 of Schedule 2 shall apply, subject to any modifications necessary to give effect to any more favourable contractual terms, to the exercise of the composite right described in subsection (1) as they apply to the exercise of the right to return to work under section 39.]   [305N]

NOTE
Substituted by the Trade Union Reform and Employment Rights Act 1993, s 23(1)(b), Sch 2, as from a day to be appointed.

[Suspension from work on maternity grounds

45 Suspension from work on maternity grounds

(1) For the purposes of sections 46 and 47 an employee is suspended on maternity grounds where, in consequence of—

(a) any requirement imposed by or under any relevant provision of any enactment or of any instrument made under any enactment, or

(b) any recommendation in any relevant provision of a code of practice issued or approved under section 16 of the Health and Safety at Work etc. Act 1974,

she is suspended from work by her employer on the ground that she is pregnant, has recently given birth or is breastfeeding a child.

(2) For the purposes of this section, sections 46 and 47 and section 61 an employee shall be regarded as suspended from work only if, and so long as, she continues to be employed by her employer, but is not provided with work or (disregarding alternative work for the purposes of section 46) does not perform the work she normally performed before the suspension.

(3) For the purposes of subsection (1) a provision is a "relevant provision" if it is for the time being specified as a relevant provision in an order made by the Secretary of State under this subsection.]   **[305O]**

NOTE
Substituted by the Trade Union Reform and Employment Rights Act 1993, s 25, Sch 3, as from a day to be appointed.

[46 Right to offer of alternative work

(1) Where an employer has available suitable alternative work for an employee the employee has a right to be offered to be provided with it before being suspended on maternity grounds.

(2) For alternative work to be suitable for an employee for the purposes of this section—

(a) the work must be of a kind which is both suitable in relation to her and appropriate for her to do in the circumstances; and

(b) the terms and conditions applicable to her for performing the work, if they differ from the corresponding terms and conditions applicable to her for performing the work she normally performs under her contract of employment, must not be substantially less favourable to her than those corresponding terms and conditions.

(3) An employee may present a complaint to an industrial tribunal that her employer has failed to offer to provide her with work in contravention of subsection (1).

(4) An industrial tribunal shall not entertain a complaint under subsection (3) unless it is presented to the tribunal before the end of the period of three months beginning with the first day of the suspension, or within such further period as the

tribunal considers reasonable in a case where it is satisfied that it was not reasonably practicable for the complaint to be presented within the period of three months.

(5) Where the tribunal finds the complaint well-founded it may make an award of compensation to be paid by the employer to the employee.

(6) The amount of the compensation shall be such as the tribunal considers just and equitable in all the circumstances having regard to the infringement of the complainant's right under subsection (1) by the employer's failure complained of and to any loss sustained by the complainant which is attributable to that failure.]

[305P]

NOTE
Substituted by the Trade Union Reform and Employment Rights Act 1993, s 25, Sch 3, as from a day to be appointed.

[47 Right to remuneration on suspension

(1) An employee who is suspended on maternity grounds shall be entitled to be paid remuneration by her employer while she is so suspended.

(2) An employee shall not be entitled to remuneration under this section in respect of any period during which her employer has offered to provide her with work which is suitable alternative work for the purposes of section 46 and the employee has unreasonably refused to perform that work.

(3) The amount of remuneration payable by an employer to an employee under this section shall be a week's pay in respect of each week of the period of suspension; and if in any week remuneration is payable in respect only of part of that week the amount of a week's pay shall be reduced proportionately.

(4) Subject to subsection (5), a right to remuneration under this section shall not affect any right of an employee in relation to remuneration under her contract of employment (in subsection (5) referred to as "contractual remuneration").

(5) Any contractual remuneration paid by an employer to an employee in respect of any period shall go towards discharging the employer's liability under this section in respect of that period; and, conversely, any payment of remuneration in discharge of an employer's liability under this section in respect of any period shall go towards discharging any obligation of the employer to pay contractual remuneration in respect of that period.

(6) An employee may present a complaint to an industrial tribunal that her employer has failed to pay the whole or any part of remuneration to which she is entitled under this section.

(7) An industrial tribunal shall not entertain a complaint relating to remuneration under this section in respect of any day unless the complaint is presented to the tribunal before the end of the period of three months beginning with that day, or within such further period as the tribunal considers reasonable in a case where it is satisfied that it was not reasonably practicable for the complaint to be presented within the period of three months.

(8) Where an industrial tribunal finds a complaint under subsection (6) well-founded the tribunal shall order the employer to pay the complainant the amount of remuneration which it finds is due to her.]   [305Q]

NOTE
Substituted by the Trade Union Reform and Employment Rights Act 1993, s 25, Sch 3, as from a day to be appointed.

PART IV

TERMINATION OF EMPLOYMENT

49 Rights of employer and employee to a minimum period of notice

(1) The notice required to be given by an employer to terminate the contract of employment of a person who has been continuously employed for [one month] or more—

(a) shall be not less than one week's notice if his period of continuous employment is less than two years;

(b) shall be not less than one week's notice for each year of continuous employment if his period of continuous employment is two years or more but less than twelve years; and

(c) shall be not less than twelve weeks' notice if his period of continuous employment is twelve years or more.

(2) The notice required to be given by an employee who has been continuously employed for [one month] or more to terminate his contract of employment shall be not less than one week.

(3) Any provision for shorter notice in any contract of employment with a person who has been continuously employed for [one month] or more shall have effect subject to the foregoing subsections, but this section shall not be taken to prevent either party from waiving his right to notice on any occasion, or from accepting a payment in lieu of notice.

(4) Any contract of employment of a person who has been continuously employed for [three months] or more which is a contract for a term certain of [one month] or less shall have effect as if it were for an indefinite period and, accordingly, subsections (1) and (2) shall apply to the contract.

[(4A) Subsections (1) and (2) do not apply to a contract made in contemplation of the performance of a specific task which is not expected to last for more than three months unless the employee has been continuously employed for a period of more than three months.]

(5) It is hereby declared that this section does not affect any right of either party to treat the contract as terminable without notice by reason of such conduct by the other party as would have enabled him so to treat it before the passing of this Act.

(6) The definition of week given by section 153(1) does not apply for the purposes of this section.   **[306]**

NOTES

Sub-ss (1)–(4): words in square brackets substituted with savings by the Employment Act 1982, s 20, Sch 2, para 3(1), (2).

Sub-s (4A): inserted subject to savings savings by the Employment Act 1982, s 20, Sch 2, para 3(3).

50 Rights of employee in period of notice

(1) If an employer gives notice to terminate the contract of employment of a person who has been continuously employed for [one month] or more, the provisions of Schedule 3 shall have effect as respects the liability of the employer for the period of notice required by section 49(1).

(2) If an employee who has been continuously employed for [one month] or more gives notice to terminate his contract of employment, the provisions of Schedule 3

shall have effect as respects the liability of the employer for the period of notice required by section 49(2).

(3) This section shall not apply in relation to a notice given by the employer or the employee if the notice to be given by the employer to terminate the contract must be at least one week more than the notice required by section 49(1).　　　**[307]**

NOTE

Sub-ss (1), (2): words in square brackets substituted with savings by the Employment Act 1982, s 20, Sch 2, para 3(1).

51 Measure of damages in proceedings against employers

If an employer fails to give the notice required by section 49, the rights conferred by section 50 (with Schedule 3) shall be taken into account in assessing his liability for breach of the contract.　　　**[308]**

52 Statutory contracts

Sections 49 and 50 shall apply in relation to a contract all or any of the terms of which are terms which take effect by virtue of any provision contained in or having effect under an Act of Parliament, whether public or local, as they apply in relation to any other contract; and the reference in this section to an Act of Parliament includes, subject to any express provision to the contrary, an Act passed after this Act. **[309]**

53 Written statement of reasons for dismissal

(1) An employee shall be entitled—
  (a) if he is given by his employer notice of termination of his contract of employment;
  (b) if his contract of employment is terminated by his employer without notice; or
  (c) if, where he is employed under a contract for a fixed term, that term expires without being renewed under the same contract,

to be provided by his employer, on request, within fourteen days of that request, with a written statement giving particulars of the reasons for his dismissal.

(2) An employee shall not be entitled to a written statement under subsection (1) unless on the effective date of termination he has been, or will have been, continuously employed for a period of [[not less than two years] ending with that date].

[(2A) An employee shall be entitled (without making any request and irrespective of whether or not she has been continuously employed for any period) to be provided by her employer with a written statement giving particulars of the reasons for her dismissal if she is dismissed—
  (a) at any time while she is pregnant, or
  (b) after childbirth in circumstances in which her maternity leave period ends by reason of the dismissal.]

(3) A written statement provided under this section shall be admissible in evidence in any proceedings.

(4) A complaint may be presented to an industrial tribunal by an employee *against his employer* on the ground that the employer unreasonably *refused to provide*

a written statement under subsection (1) or that the particulars of reasons given in purported compliance with *that subsection* are inadequate or untrue, and if the tribunal finds the complaint well-founded—

(a) it may make a declaration as to what it finds the employer's reasons were for dismissing the employee; and

(b) it shall make an award that the employer pay to the employee a sum equal to the amount of two weeks' pay.

(5) An industrial tribunal shall not entertain a complaint under this section relating to the reasons for a dismissal unless it is presented to the tribunal at such a time that the tribunal would, in accordance with section 67(2) or (4), entertain a complaint of unfair dismissal in respect of that dismissal presented at the same time.

[310]

NOTES

Sub-s (2): words in first (outer) pair of square brackets substituted by the Employment Act 1982, s 20, Sch 2, para 4; words in second (inner) pair of square brackets substituted with savings by the Employment Act 1989, ss 15(1), 29(6), Sch 9; for further savings see, SI 1990/189, art 3(2), which provides that the previous period (six months) continued to apply if the period of continuous employment of the employee began before 26 February 1990.

Sub-s (2A): inserted by the Trade Union Reform and Employment Rights Act 1993, s 24(4), as from a day to be appointed (likely to be October 1994).

Sub-s (4): first set of words in italics are repealed, for the second set of words in italics there are substituted the words "failed to provide a written statement under this section", and for the third set of words in italics there are substituted the words "this section", by the Trade Union Reform and Employment Rights Act 1993, ss 49(2), 51, Sch 8, para 11, Sch 10, as from 30 August 1993 (SI 1993/1908, below, para [1435]).

Modified, in relation to governing bodies with delegated budgets, by the Education (Modification of Enactments Relating to Employment) Order 1989, SI 1989/901, arts 3, 4.

PART V

UNFAIR DISMISSAL

Right not to be unfairly dismissed

54 Right of employee not to be unfairly dismissed

(1) In every employment to which this section applies every employee shall have the right not to be unfairly dismissed by his employer.

(2) This section applies to every employment except in so far as its application is excluded by or under any provision of this Part or by sections 141 to 149.   [311]

NOTE

Modified, in relation to governing bodies with delegated budgets, by the Education (Modification of Enactments Relating to Employment) Order 1989, SI 1989/901, arts 3, 4.

Meaning of unfair dismissal

55 Meaning of "dismissal"

(1) In this Part, except as respects a case to which section 56 applies, "dismissal" and "dismiss" shall be construed in accordance with the following provisions of this section

(2) Subject to subsection (3), an employee shall be treated as dismissed by his employer if, but only if,—

(a) the contract under which he is employed by the employer is terminated by the employer, whether it is so terminated by notice or without notice, or

   (b) where under that contract he is employed for a fixed term, that term expires without being renewed under the same contract, or

   (c) the employee terminates that contract, with or without notice, in circumstances such that he is entitled to terminate it without notice by reason of the employer's conduct.

(3) Where an employer gives notice to an employee to terminate his contract of employment and, at a time within the period of that notice, the employee gives notice to the employer to terminate the contract of employment on a date earlier than the date on which the employer's notice is due to expire, the employee shall for the purposes of this Part be taken to be dismissed by his employer, and the reasons for the dismissal shall be taken to be the reasons for which the employer's notice is given.

(4) In this Part "the effective date of termination"—

   (a) in relation to an employee whose contract of employment is terminated by notice, whether given by his employer or by the employee, means the date on which that notice expires;

   (b) in relation to an employee whose contract of employment is terminated without notice, means the date on which the termination takes effect; and

   (c) in relation to an employee who is employed under a contract for a fixed term, where that term expires without being renewed under the same contract, means the date on which that term expires.

[(5) Where the contract of employment is terminated by the employer and the notice required by section 49 to be given by an employer would, if duly given on the material date, expire on a date later than the effective date of termination (as defined by subsection (4)) then, for the purposes of sections 53(2), 64(1)(a), *64A* and 73(3) and paragraph 8(3) of Schedule 14, the later date shall be treated as the effective date of termination in relation to the dismissal.

(6) Where the contract of employment is terminated by the employee and—

   (a) the material date does not fall during a period of notice given by the employer to terminate that contract; and

   (b) had the contract been terminated not by the employee but by notice given on the material date by the employer, that notice would have been required by section 49 to expire on a date later than the effective date of termination (as defined by subsection (4)),

then, for the purposes of sections 64(1)(a), *64A* and 73(3) and paragraph 8(3) of Schedule 14, the later date shall be treated as the effective date of termination in relation to the dismissal.

(7) "Material date" means—

   (a) in subsection (5), the date when notice of termination was given by the employer or (where no notice was given) the date when the contract of employment was terminated by the employer; and

   (b) in subsection (6), the date when notice of termination was given by the employee or (where no notice was given) the date when the contract of employment was terminated by the employee.]   [312]

NOTES

Sub-ss (5)–(7): substituted for original sub-s (5) by the Employment Act 1982, s 21, Sch 3, Pt I, para 1; words in italics in sub-ss (5), (6) repealed by the Trade Union Reform and Employment Rights Act 1993, s 51, Sch 10, as from 30 August 1993 (SI 1993/1908, below, para [**1435**]).

Modified, in relation to governing bodies with delegated budgets, by the Education (Modification of Enactments Relating to Employment) Order 1989, SI 1989/901, arts 3, 4.

56 Failure to permit women to return to work after confinement treated as dismissal

Where an employee *is entitled to return to work and has exercised her right to return in accordance with section 47* [has the right to return to work under section 39 and has exercised it in accordance with section 42] but is not permitted to return to work, then [subject to section 56A] she shall be treated for the purposes of this Part as if she had been employed until the notified day of return, and, if she would not otherwise be so treated, as having been continuously employed until that day, and as if she had been dismissed with effect from that day for the reason for which she was not permitted to return.   **[313]**

NOTE

Words in italics substituted by words immediately following in square brackets, by the Trade Union Reform and Employment Rights Act 1993, s 49(2), Sch 8, para 12, as from a day to be appointed. Words in square brackets inserted by the Employment Act 1980, s 20, Sch 2, para 11.

Modified, in relation to governing bodies with delegated budgets, by the Education (Modification of Enactments Relating to Employment) Order 1989, SI 1989/901, arts 3, 4.

[56A Exclusion of s 56 in certain cases

(1) Section 56 shall not apply in relation to an employee if—

    (a) immediately before *her absence began* [the end of her maternity leave period or, if it ends by reason of dismissal, immediately before the dismissal] the number of employees employed by her employer, added to the number employed by any associated employer of his, did not exceed five, and

    (b) it is not reasonably practicable for the employer (who may be the same employer or a successor of his) to permit her to return to work in accordance with *section 45(1)* [section 39], or for him or an associated employer to offer her employment under a contract of employment satisfying the conditions specified in subsection (3).

(2) Section 56 shall not apply in relation to an employee if—

    (a) it is not reasonably practicable for a reason other than redundancy for the employer (who may be the same employer or a successor of his) to permit her to return to work in accordance with *section 45(1)* [section 39], and

    (b) he or an associated employer offers her employment under a contract of employment satisfying the conditions specified in subsection (3), and

    (c) she accepts or unreasonably refuses that offer.

(3) The conditions referred to in subsections (1) and (2) are—

    (a) that the work to be done under the contract is of a kind which is both suitable in relation to the employee and appropriate for her to do in the circumstances; and

    (b) that the provisions of the contract as to the capacity and place in which she is to be employed and as to the other terms and conditions of her employment are not substantially less favourable to her than if she had returned to work in accordance with *section 45(1)* [section 39].

(4) Where on a complaint of unfair dismissal any question arises as to whether the operation of section 56 is excluded by subsection (1) or (2), it shall be for the employer to show that the provisions of that subsection were satisfied in relation to the complainant.]   **[314]**

NOTES

Inserted by the Employment Act 1980, s 12.

Sub-ss (1), (2), (3): words in italics substituted by the words in each case immediately following in square brackets, by the Trade Union Reform and Employment Rights Act 1993, s 49(2), Sch 8, para 13, as from a day to be appointed.

Modified, in relation to governing bodies with delegated budgets, by the Education (Modification of Enactments Relating to Employment) Order 1989, SI 1989/901, arts 3, 4.

See also the Employment Protection (Employment in Aided Schools) Order 1981, SI 1981/847, for the application of this section to employment in aided schools.

57 General provisions relating to fairness of dismissal

(1) In determining for the purposes of this Part whether the dismissal of an employee was fair or unfair, it shall be for the employer to show—

    (a) what was the reason (or, if there was more than one, the principal reason) for the dismissal, and

    (b) that it was a reason falling within subsection (2) or some other substantial reason of a kind such as to justify the dismissal of an employee holding the position which that employee held.

(2) In subsection (1)(b) the reference to a reason falling within this subsection is a reference to a reason which—

    (a) related to the capability or qualifications of the employee for performing work of the kind which he was employed by the employer to do, or

    (b) related to the conduct of the employee, or

    (c) was that the employee was redundant, or

    (d) was that the employee could not continue to work in the position which he held without contravention (either on his part or on that of his employer) of a duty or restriction imposed by or under an enactment.

(3) Where the employer has fulfilled the requirements of subsection (1), then, [subject to *sections 59 to 61*, [sections 57A to 61] and to sections 152, 153 and 238 of the Trade Union and Labour Relations (Consolidation) Act 1992 (provisions as to dismissal on ground of trade union membership or activities or in connection with industrial action),] the determination of the question whether the dismissal was fair or unfair, having regard to the reason shown by the employer, shall depend on whether [in the circumstances (including the size and administrative resources of the employer's undertaking) the employer acted reasonably or unreasonably in treating it as a sufficient reason for dismissing the employee; and that question shall be determined in accordance with equity and the substantial merits of the case.]

(4) In this section, in relation to an employee,—

    (a) "capability" means capability assessed by reference to skill, aptitude, health or any other physical or mental quality;

    (b) "qualifications" means any degree, diploma or other academic, technical or professional qualification relevant to the position which the employee held.   **[315]**

NOTES

Sub-s (3): first words in square brackets substituted by the Trade Union and Labour Relations (Consolidation) Act 1992, s 300(2), Sch 2, para 14, and words in italics therein, substituted by the words thereafter in square brackets, by the Trade Union Reform and Employment Rights Act 1993, s 28, Sch 5, para 2, as from 30 August 1993 (SI 1993/1908, below, para [**1435**]); final words in square brackets substituted by the Employment Act 1980, s 6.

[57A Dismissal in health and safety cases

(1) The dismissal of an employee by an employer shall be regarded for the purposes of this Part as having been unfair if the reason for it (or, if more than one, the principal reason) was that the employee—

(a) having been designated by the employer to carry out activities in connection with preventing or reducing risks to health and safety at work, carried out, or proposed to carry out, any such activities,

(b) being a representative of workers on matters of health and safety at work, or a member of a safety committee—

    (i) in accordance with arrangements established under or by virtue of any enactment, or

    (ii) by reason of being acknowledged as such by the employer,

performed, or proposed to perform, any functions as such a representative or a member of such a committee,

(c) being an employee at a place where—

    (i) there was no such representative or safety committee, or

    (ii) there was such a representative or safety committee but it was not reasonably practicable for the employee to raise the matter by those means,

brought to his employer's attention, by reasonable means, circumstances connected with his work which he reasonably believed were harmful or potentially harmful to health or safety,

(d) in circumstances of danger which he reasonably believed to be serious and imminent and which he could not reasonably have been expected to avert, left, or proposed to leave, or (while the danger persisted) refused to return to, his place of work or any dangerous part of his place of work, or

(e) in circumstances of danger which he reasonably believed to be serious and imminent, took, or proposed to take, appropriate steps to protect himself or other persons from the danger.

(2) For the purposes of subsection (1)(e) whether steps which an employee took, or proposed to take, were appropriate shall be judged by reference to all the circumstances including, in particular, his knowledge and the facilities and advice available to him at the time.

(3) Where the reason (or, if more than one, the principal reason) for the dismissal of an employee was that specified in subsection (1)(e), the dismissal shall not be regarded as having been unfair if the employer shows that it was, or would have been, so negligent for the employee to take the steps which he took, or proposed to take, that a reasonable employer might have dismissed him for taking, or proposing to take, them.]   **[315A]**

NOTE

Inserted by the Trade Union Reform and Employment Rights Act 1993, s 28, Sch 5, para 3, as from 30 August 1993 (SI 1993/1908, below, para [**1435**]).

58, 58A (*S 58 repealed by the Trade Union and Labour Relations (Consolidation) Act 1992, s 300(1), Sch 1; s 58A repealed by the Employment Act 1988, s 33, Sch 4.*)

59 Dismissal on ground of redundancy

[(1)] Where the reason or principal reason for the dismissal of an employee was that *he* was redundant, but it is shown that the circumstances constituting the redundancy applied equally to one or more other employees in the same undertaking who held positions similar to that held by *him* [the employee] and who have not been dismissed by the [employer, and either—

(a) that the reason (or, if more than one, the principal reason) for which the employee was selected for dismissal was an inadmissible reason; or]

(b) that *he* [the employee] was selected for dismissal in contravention of a customary arrangement or agreed procedure relating to redundancy and there were no special reasons justifying a departure from that arrangement or procedure *in his case* [in the case of the employee],

then, for the purposes of this Part, the dismissal shall be regarded as unfair.

[(2) For the purposes of this section "inadmissible", in relation to a reason, means that it is one of those specified in section [57A(1) (read with (2) and (3)),] 60(a) to (e) [or 60A(1) (read with (2) and (3))].]

[(3) For the purposes of this Part "a redundancy case" means a case where the reason or principal reason for the dismissal was that the employee was redundant but the equal application of the circumstances to non-dismissed employees is also shown.]   [316]

NOTES

Sub-s (1): numbered as such by the Trade Union Reform and Employment Rights Act 1993, s 24(2); words in italics, substituted, in each case, by the words in square brackets immediately following, by the Trade Union Reform and Employment Rights Act 1993, s 49(2), Sch 8, para 14(a), (b), as from 30 August 1993 (SI 1993/1908, below, para [**1435**]. Para (a) and the words in square brackets immediately preceding it substituted by *ibid*, s 24(2), as from 30 August 1993 (SI 1993/1908).

Sub-s (2): inserted by the Trade Union Reform and Employment Rights Act 1993, s 24(2) as from 30 August 1993 (SI 1993/1908); words in first pair of square brackets inserted by s 28, Sch 5, para 4 thereof, and words in second pair of square brackets added by s 29(2) thereof, as from 30 August 1993 (SI 1993/1908).

Sub-s (3): inserted by the Trade Union Reform and Employment Rights Act 1993, s 49(2), Sch 8, para 14(c), as from 30 August 1993 (SI 1993/1908).

60 Dismissal on ground of pregnancy

(1) An employee shall be treated for the purposes of this Part as unfairly dismissed if the reason or principal reason for her dismissal is that she is pregnant or is any other reason connected with her pregnancy, except one of the following reasons—

(a) *that at the effective date of termination she is or will have become, because of her pregnancy, incapable of adequately doing the work which she is employed to do;*

(b) *that, because of her pregnancy, she cannot or will not be able to continue after that date to do that work without contravention (either by her or her employer) of a duty or restriction imposed by or under any enactment.*

(2) An employee shall be treated for the purposes of this Part as unfairly dismissed if her employer dismisses her for a reason mentioned in subsection (1)(a) or (b), but neither he nor any successor of his, where there is a suitable available vacancy, makes her an offer before or on the effective date of termination to engage her under a new contract of employment complying with subsection (3).

(3) The new contract of employment must—

(a) *take effect immediately on the ending of employment under the previous contract, or, where that employment ends on a Friday, Saturday or Sunday, on or before the next Monday after that Friday, Saturday or Sunday;*

(b) *be such that the work to be done under the contract is of a kind which is both suitable in relation to the employee and appropriate for her to do in the circumstances; and*

(c) *be such that the provisions of the new contract as to the capacity and place in which she is to be employed and as to the other terms and conditions of her employment are not substantially less favourable to her than the corresponding provisions of the previous contract.*

(4) On a complaint of unfair dismissal on the ground of failure to offer to engage an employee as mentioned in subsection (2), it shall be for the employer to show that he or a successor made an offer to engage her in compliance with subsections (2) and (3) or, as the case may be, that there was no suitable available vacancy for her.

(5) Section 55(3) shall not apply in a case where an employer gives notice to an employee to terminate her contract of employment for a reason mentioned in subsection (1)(a) or (b).   **[317]**

NOTE

Substituted by the Trade Union Reform and Employment Rights Act 1993, s 24(1), as from a day to be appointed, as follows—

"60 Dismissal on ground of pregnancy or childbirth

An employee shall be treated for the purposes of this Part as unfairly dismissed if—

(a) the reason (or, if there is more than one, the principal reason) for her dismissal is that she is pregnant or any other reason connected with her pregnancy,

(b) her maternity leave period is ended by the dismissal and the reason (or, if there is more than one, the principal reason) for her dismissal is that she has given birth to a child or any other reason connected with her having given birth to a child,

(c) the reason (or, if there is more than one, the principal reason) for her dismissal, where her contract of employment was terminated after the end of her maternity leave period, is that she took, or availed herself of the benefits of, maternity leave,

(d) the reason (or, if there is more than one, the principal reason) for her dismissal, where—

(i) before the end of her maternity leave period, she gave to her employer a certificate from a registered medical practitioner stating that by reason of disease or bodily or mental disablement she would be incapable of work after the end of that period, and

(ii) her contract of employment was terminated within the four week period following the end of her maternity leave period in circumstances where she continued to be incapable of work and the certificate relating to her incapacity remained current,

is that she has given birth to a child or any other reason connected with her having given birth to a child,

(e) the reason (or, if there is more than one, the principal reason) for her dismissal is a requirement or recommendation such as is referred to in section 45(1), or

(f) her maternity leave period is ended by the dismissal, and the reason (or, if there is more than one, the principal reason) for her dismissal is that she is redundant and section 38 has not been complied with.

For the purposes of paragraph (c) above a woman "takes maternity leave" if she is absent from work during her maternity leave period and a woman "avails herself of the benefits of maternity leave" if, during her maternity leave period, she avails herself of the benefit of any of the terms and conditions of her employment preserved by section 33 during that period.".

[60A Dismissal on grounds of assertion of statutory right

(1) The dismissal of an employee by an employer shall be regarded for the purposes of this Part as having been unfair if the reason for it (or, if more than one, the principal reason) was that the employee—

(a) brought proceedings against the employer to enforce a right of his which is a relevant statutory right; or

(b) alleged that the employer had infringed a right of his which is a relevant statutory right.

(2) It is immaterial for the purposes of subsection (1) whether the employee has the right or not and whether it has been infringed or not, but, for that subsection to apply, the claim to the right and that it has been infringed must be made in good faith.

(3) It shall be sufficient for subsection (1) to apply that the employee, without specifying the right, made it reasonably clear to the employer what the right claimed to have been infringed was.

(4) The following statutory rights are relevant for the purposes of this section, namely—

(a) any right conferred by—

     (i)   this Act, or

     (ii)   the Wages Act 1986,

for which the remedy for its infringement is by way of a complaint or reference to an industrial tribunal;

  (b)   the right conferred by section 49 (minimum notice);

  (c)   the rights conferred by the following provisions of the Trade Union and Labour Relations (Consolidation) Act 1992, namely, sections 68, 86, 146, 168, 169 and 170 (deductions from pay, union activities and time off).]

                                                               [317A]

NOTE

Inserted by the Trade Union Reform and Employment Rights Act 1993, s 29(1), as from 30 August 1993 (SI 1993/1908, below, para [**1435**]).

61 Dismissal of replacement

(1) Where an employer—

  (a)   on engaging an employee informs the employee in writing that his employment will be terminated on the *return to work of* [resumption of work by] another employee who is, or will be, absent wholly or partly because of pregnancy or *confinement*; [childbirth] and

  (b)   dismisses the first-mentioned employee in order to make it possible to give work to the other employee;

then, for the purposes of section 57(1)(b), but without prejudice to the application of section 57(3), the dismissal shall be regarded as having been for a substantial reason of a kind such as to justify the dismissal of an employee holding the position which that employee held.

   (2)   Where an employer—

  (a)   on engaging an employee informs the employee in writing that his employment will be terminated on the end of a suspension such as is referred to in section 19 [or 45] of another employee; and

  (b)   dismisses the first-mentioned employee in order to make it possible to allow the *other employee to resume his original work* [resumption of work by the other employee];

then, for the purposes of section 57(1)(b), but without prejudice to the application of section 57 (3), the dismissal shall be regarded as having been for a substantial reason of a kind such as to justify the dismissal of an employee holding the position which that employee held.   **[318]**

NOTES

Words in italics, substituted in each case by the words in square brackets immediately following and words in square brackets in sub-s(2)(a) inserted, by the Trade Union Reform and Employment Rights Act 1993, s 49(2), Sch 8, para 15, as from a day to be appointed.

62, 62A *(Repealed by the Trade Union and Labour Relations (Consolidation) Act 1992, s 300(1), Sch 1. See now ibid, ss 237, 238.)*

63 Pressure on employer to dismiss unfairly

In determining, for the purposes of this Part any question as to the reason, or principal reason, for which an employee was dismissed or any question whether the reason or principal reason for which an employee was dismissed was a reason fulfilling the requirements of section 57(1)(b) or whether the employer acted reasonably in treating it as a sufficient reason for dismissing him,—

(a) no account shall be taken of any pressure which, by calling, organising, procuring or financing a strike or other industrial action, or threatening to do so, was exercised on the employer to dismiss the employee, and

(b) any such question shall be determined as if no such pressure had been exercised.	**[319]**

Exclusion of section 54

64 Qualifying period and upper age limit

(1) . . ., section 54 does not apply to the dismissal of an employee from any employment if the employee—

(a) was not continuously employed for a period of not less than [two years] ending with the effective date of termination, or

[(b) attained the following age on or before the effective date of termination, that is to say—

(i) if in the undertaking in which he was employed there was a normal retiring age for an employee holding the position which he held and the age was the same whether the employee holding that position was a man or a woman, that normal retiring age; and

(ii) in any other case, the age of sixty-five.]

(2) If an employee is dismissed by reason of any such requirement or recommendation as is referred to in section 19(1), subsection (1)(a) shall have effect in relation to that dismissal as if for the words ["two years"] there were substituted the words ["one month"].

[(3) Subsection (1) shall not apply to the dismissal of an employee if it is shown that the reason (or, if more than one, the principal reason) for the dismissal or, in a redundancy case, for selecting the employee for dismissal, was an inadmissible reason.

(4) For the purposes of subsection (3) "inadmissible", in relation to a reason, means that it is one of those specified in section [57A(1) (read with (2) and (3))] 60(a) to (e) [or 60A(1) (read with (2) and (3))].

(5) Subsection (1) shall not apply to a case falling within section 60(f).]	**[320]**

NOTES

Sub-s (1): words omitted repealed by the Trade Union and Labour Relations (Consolidation) Act 1992, s 300(1), Sch 1; in para (a), words in square brackets substituted by SI 1985/782, arts 3, 5; para (b) substituted by the Sex Discrimination Act 1986, s 3.

Sub-s (2): first words in square brackets substituted by SI 1985/782, arts 4, 5; final words in square brackets substituted by the Employment Act 1982, s 20, Sch 2, para 5(1)(b).

Sub-s (3): previous sub-section (not reproduced) repealed by the Trade Union and Labour Relations (Consolidation) Act 1992, s 300(1), Sch 1.

Sub-ss (3)–(5): added by the Trade Union Reform and Employment Rights Act 1993, s 24(3), as from 30 August 1993 (SI 1993/1908, below, para [**1435**]); words in square brackets in sub-s (4) inserted by *ibid*, ss 28, 29(3) Sch 5, para 5, as from 30 August (SI 1993/1908, below, para [**1435**]).

[64A Extended qualifying period where no more than twenty employees

(1) Subject to subsection (2), section 54 does not apply to the dismissal of an employee from any employment if—

(a) the period (ending with the effective date of termination) during which the

employee was continuously employed did not exceed two years; and
  (b) *at no time during that period did the number of employees employed by the employer for the time being of the dismissed employee, added to the number employed by any associated employer, exceed twenty.*

  (2) *Subsection (1) shall not apply to the dismissal of an employee by reason of any such requirement or recommendation as is referred to in section 19(1), . . .]*

[321]

NOTES

Inserted by the Employment Act 1980, s 8(1).

Repealed by the Trade Union Reform and Employment Rights Act 1993, ss 49(1), 51, Sch 7, para 2, Sch 10, as from 30 August 1993 (SI 1993/1908, below, para [**1435**]).

Sub-s (1): operation excluded except in any case where the period of continuous employment begins before 1 June 1985, by the Unfair Dismissal (Variation of Qualifying Period) Order 1985, SI 1985/782, arts 3, 5.

Sub-s (2): words omitted repealed by the Trade Union and Labour Relations (Consolidation) Act 1992, s 300(1), Sch 1.

65 Exclusion in respect of dismissal procedures agreement

(1) An application may be made jointly to the Secretary of State by all the parties to a dismissal procedures agreement to make an order designating that agreement for the purposes of this section.

(2) On any such application the Secretary of State may make such an order if he is satisfied—

  (a) that every trade union which is a party to the dismissal procedures agreement is an independent trade union;
  (b) that the agreement provides for procedures to be followed in cases where an employee claims that he has been, or is in the course of being, unfairly dismissed;
  (c) that those procedures are available without discrimination to all employees falling within any description to which the agreement applies;
  (d) that the remedies provided by the agreement in respect of unfair dismissal are on the whole as beneficial as (but not necessarily identical with) those provided in respect of unfair dismissal by this Part;
  (e) that the procedures provided by the agreement include a right to arbitration or adjudication by an independent referee, or by a tribunal or other independent body, in cases where (by reason of an equality of votes or for any other reason) a decision cannot otherwise be reached; and
  (f) that the provisions of the agreement are such that it can be determined with reasonable certainty whether a particular employee is one to whom the agreement applies or not.

(3) Where a dismissal procedures agreement is designated by an order under this section which is for the time being in force, the provisions of that agreement relating to dismissal shall have effect in substitution for any rights under section 54; and accordingly that section shall not apply to the dismissal of an employee from any employment if it is employment to which, and he is an employee to whom, those provisions of the agreement apply.

(4) Subsection (3) shall not apply to the *right not to be unfairly dismissed for any reason mentioned in subsection (1) or (2) of section 60* [right conferred by section 60 or 60A(1)].

[322]

NOTE

Sub-s (4): words in italics, substituted by words in square brackets immediately following, by the Trade Union Reform and Employment Rights Act 1993, s 49(2), Sch 8, para 16, as from 30 August 1993 (so far as relating to s 60A(1) of this Act) (SI 1993/1908, below, para [**1435**]).

66 Revocation of exclusion order under s 65

(1) ...

(2) If [at any time when an order under section 65 is in force in respect of a dismissal procedures agreement the Secretary of State is satisfied, whether on an application by any of the parties to the agreement or otherwise] either—

(a) that it is the desire of all the parties to the dismissal procedures agreement that the order should be revoked, or

(b) that the agreement has ceased to fulfil all the conditions specified in section 65(2),

the Secretary of State shall revoke the order by a further order made under this section.

(3) Any order made under this section may contain such transitional provisions as appear to the Secretary of State to be appropriate in the circumstances, and, in particular, may direct—

(a) that, notwithstanding section 65(3), an employee shall not be excluded from his rights under section 54 where the effective date of termination falls within a transitional period which is specified in the order and is a period ending with the date on which the order under this section takes effect and shall have an extended time for presenting a complaint under section 67 in respect of a dismissal where the effective date of termination falls within that period, and

(b) that in determining any complaint of unfair dismissal presented by an employee to whom the dismissal procedures agreement applies, where the effective date of termination falls within that transitional period, an industrial tribunal shall have regard to such considerations (in addition to those specified in this Part and paragraph 2 of Schedule 9) as may be specified in the order. [323]

NOTES

Sub-s (1): repealed by the Employment Act 1980, s 20, Sch 1, para 13, Sch 2.

Sub-s (2): words in square brackets substituted by the Employment Act 1980, s 20, Sch 1, para 13, Sch 2.

Remedies for unfair dismissal

67 Complaint to industrial tribunal

(1) A complaint may be presented to an industrial tribunal against an employer by any person (in this Part referred to as the complainant) that he was unfairly dismissed by the employer.

(2) Subject to subsection (4), an industrial tribunal shall not consider a complaint under this section unless it is presented to the tribunal before the end of the period of three months beginning with the effective date of termination or within such further period as the tribunal considers reasonable in a case where it is satisfied that it was not reasonably practicable for the complaint to be presented before the end of the period of three months.

(3) ...

(4) An industrial tribunal shall consider a complaint under this section if, where the dismissal is with notice, the complaint is presented after the notice is given notwithstanding that it is presented before the effective date of termination and in relation to such a complaint the provisions of this Act, so far as they relate to unfair dismissal, shall have effect—

(a) as if references to a complaint by a person that he was unfairly dismissed by his employer included references to a complaint by a person that his employer has given him notice in such circumstances that he will be unfairly dismissed when the notice expires;

(b) as if references to reinstatement included references to the withdrawal of the notice by the employer;

(c) as if references to the effective date of termination included references to the date which would be the effective date of termination on the expiry of the notice; and

(d) as if references to an employee ceasing to be employed included references to an employee having been given notice of dismissal.   **[324]**

NOTE
   Sub-s (3): repealed by the Trade Union and Labour Relations (Consolidation) Act 1992, s 300(1), Sch 1.

68 Remedies for unfair dismissal

(1) Where on a complaint under section 67 an industrial tribunal finds that the grounds of the complaint are well-founded, it shall explain to the complainant what orders for reinstatement or re-engagement may be made under section 69 and in what circumstances they may be made, and shall ask him whether he wishes the tribunal to make such an order, and if he does express such a wish the tribunal may make an order under section 69.

(2) If on a complaint under section 67 the tribunal finds that the grounds of the complaint are well-founded and no order is made under section 69, the tribunal shall make an award of compensation for unfair dismissal, calculated in accordance with [sections 72 to 76], to be paid by the employer to the employee.   **[325]**

NOTES
   Sub-s (2): amended by the Employment Act 1982, s 21, Sch 3, Pt II, para 21.

69 Order for reinstatement or re-engagement

(1) An order under this section may be an order for reinstatement (in accordance with subsections (2) and (3)) or an order for re-engagement (in accordance with subsection (4)), as the industrial tribunal may decide, and in the latter case may be on such terms as the tribunal may decide.

(2) An order for reinstatement is an order that the employer shall treat the complainant in all respects as if he had not been dismissed, and on making such an order the tribunal shall specify—

(a) any amount payable by the employer in respect of any benefit which the complainant might reasonably be expected to have had but for the dismissal, including arrears of pay, for the period between the date of termination of employment and the date of reinstatement;

(b) any rights and privileges, including seniority and pension rights, which must be restored to the employee; and

(c) the date by which the order must be complied with.

(3) Without prejudice to the generality of subsection (2), if the complainant would have benefited from an improvement in his terms and conditions of employment had he not been dismissed, an order for reinstatement shall require him to be treated as if he had benefited from that improvement from the date on which he would have done so but for being dismissed.

(4) An order for re-engagement is an order that the complainant be engaged by the employer, or by a successor of the employer or by an associated employer, in employment comparable to that from which he was dismissed or other suitable employment, and on making such an order the tribunal shall specify the terms on which re-engagement is to take place including—

(a) the identity of the employer;

(b) the nature of the employment;

(c) the remuneration for the employment;

(d) any amount payable by the employer in respect of any benefit which the complainant might reasonably be expected to have had but for the dismissal, including arrears of pay, for the period between the date of termination of employment and the date of re-engagement;

(e) any rights and privileges, including seniority and pension rights, which must be restored to the employee; and

(f) the date by which the order must be complied with.

(5) In exercising its discretion under this section the tribunal shall first consider whether to make an order for reinstatement and in so doing shall take into account the following considerations, that is to say—

(a) whether the complainant wishes to be reinstated;

(b) whether it is practicable for the employer to comply with an order for reinstatement;

(c) where the complainant caused or contributed to some extent to the dismissal, whether it would be just to order his reinstatement.

(6) If the tribunal decides not to make an order for reinstatement it shall then consider whether to make an order for re-engagement and if so on what terms; and in so doing the tribunal shall take into account the following considerations, that is to say—

(a) any wish expressed by the complainant as to the nature of the order to be made;

(b) whether it is practicable for the employer or, as the case may be, a successor or associated employer to comply with an order for re-engagement;

(c) where the complainant caused or contributed to some extent to the dismissal, whether it would be just to order his re-engagement and if so on what terms;

and except in a case where the tribunal takes into account contributory fault under paragraph (c) it shall, if it orders re-engagement, do so on terms which are, so far as is reasonably practicable, as favourable as an order for reinstatement.   [326]

70 Supplementary provisions relating to s 69

(1) Where in any case an employer has engaged a permanent replacement for a dismissed employee, the tribunal shall not take that fact into account in determining, for the purposes of subsection (5)(b) or (6)(b) of section 69, whether it is practicable to comply with an order for reinstatement or re-engagement unless the employer shows—

(a) that it was not practicable for him to arrange for the dismissed employee's work to be done without engaging a permanent replacement; or

(b) that he engaged the replacement after the lapse of a reasonable period, without having heard from the dismissed employee that he wished to be reinstated or re-engaged, and that when the employer engaged the replacement it was no longer reasonable for him to arrange for the dismissed employee's work to be done except by a permanent replacement.

(2) In calculating for the purpose of subsection (2)(a) or (4)(d) of section 69 any amount payable by the employer, the tribunal shall take into account, so as to reduce the employer's liability, any sums received by the complainant in respect of the period between the date of termination of employment and the date of reinstatement or re-engagement by way of—

    (a) wages in lieu of notice or ex gratia payments paid by the employer;

    (b) remuneration paid in respect of employment with another employer;

and such other benefits as the tribunal thinks appropriate in the circumstances.

                                                    [327]

71 Enforcement of s 69 order and compensation

(1) If an order under section 69 is made and the complainant is reinstated or, as the case may be, re-engaged but the terms of the order are not fully complied with, then, subject to *section 75*, an industrial tribunal shall make an award of compensation, to be paid by the employer to the employee, of such amount as the tribunal thinks fit having regard to the loss sustained by the complainant in consequence of the failure to comply fully with the terms of the order.

[(1A) Subsection (1) is subject to section 75 except that the limit imposed by that section may be exceeded to the extent necessary to enable the award fully to reflect the amount specified as payable under section 69(2)(a) or (4)(d), as the case may be.]

(2) Subject to subsection (1), if an order under section 69 is made but the complainant is not reinstated or, as the case may be, re-engaged in accordance with the order—

    (a) the tribunal shall make an award of compensation for unfair dismissal, calculated in accordance with [sections 72 to 76], to be paid by the employer to the employee; and

    (b) [unless] [the case is one where this paragraph is excluded or] the employer satisfies the tribunal that it was not practicable to comply with the order, the tribunal shall make an additional award of compensation to be paid by the employer to the employee of an amount—

        (i) where the dismissal is of a description referred to in subsection (3), not less than twenty-six nor more than fifty-two weeks' pay, or

        (ii) in any other case, not less than thirteen nor more than twenty-six weeks' pay.

[(2A) Subsection (2)(b) is excluded where the reason (or, if more than one, the principal reason) for the dismissal or, in a redundancy case, for selecting the employee for dismissal, was an inadmissible reason.

(2B) For the purposes of subsection (2A) a reason is "inadmissible" if it is one of those specified in section 57A(1)(a) and (b).]

(3) The descriptions of dismissal in respect of which an employer may incur a higher additional award in accordance with subsection (2)(b)(i) are the following, that is to say—

    (a) ...

    (b) a dismissal which is an act of discrimination within the meaning of the Sex Discrimination Act 1975 which is unlawful by virtue of that Act;

    (c) a dismissal which is an act of discrimination within the meaning of the Race Relations Act 1976 which is unlawful by virtue of that Act.

(4) Where in any case an employer has engaged a permanent replacement for a dismissed employee the tribunal shall not take that fact into account in determining,

for the purposes of subsection (2)(b) whether it was practicable to comply with the order for reinstatement or re-engagement unless the employer shows that it was not practicable for him to arrange for the dismissed employee's work to be done without engaging a permanent replacement.

(5) Where in any case an industrial tribunal makes an award of compensation for unfair dismissal, calculated in accordance with [sections 72 to 76], and the tribunal finds that the complainant has unreasonably prevented an order under section 69 from being complied with, it shall, without prejudice to the generality of section 74(4), take that conduct into account as a failure on the part of the complainant to mitigate his loss.   **[328]**

NOTES
Sub-s (1): for the words in italics, there are substituted the words "subsection (1A)", by the Trade Union Reform and Employment Rights Act 1993, s 30(1), (2)(a), as from 30 August 1993 (SI 1993/1908, below, para [**1435**]).
Sub-s (1A): inserted by the Trade Union Reform and Employment Rights Act 1993, s 30(1), (2)(b), as from 30 August 1993 (SI 1993/1908).
Sub-s (2): in para (a) words in square brackets substituted by the Employment Act 1982, s 21, Sch 3, Pt II, para 22, Sch 4; in para (b) first word in square brackets substituted by the Trade Union and Labour Relations (Consolidation) Act 1992, s 300(2), Sch 2, para 15; second words in square brackets inserted by the Trade Union Reform and Employment Rights Act 1993, s 28, Sch 5, para 6(a), as from 30 August 1993 (SI 1993/1908).
Sub-ss (2A), (2B): inserted by the Trade Union Reform and Employment Rights Act 1993, s 28, Sch 5, para 6(b), as from 30 August 1993 (SI 1993/1908).
Sub-s (3): para (a) repealed by the Employment Act 1982, s 21(3), Sch 4.
Sub-s (5): words in square brackets substituted by the Employment Act 1982, s 21, Sch 3, para 22.

Amount of compensation

[72 Compensation for unfair dismissal

[(1)] Where a tribunal makes an award of compensation for unfair dismissal under section 68(2) or 71(2)(a) the award shall consist of—

   (a) a basic award calculated in accordance with section 73, and
   (b) a compensatory award calculated in accordance with section 74.]

[(2) Where the reason (or, if more than one, the principal reason) for the dismissal or, in a redundancy case, for selecting the employee for dismissal, was an inadmissible reason, then, unless—

   (a) the complainant does not request the tribunal to make an order under section 69, or
   (b) the case falls within section 73(2),

the award shall include a special award calculated in accordance with section 75A.

(3) For the purposes of subsection (2) a reason is "inadmissible" if it is one of those specified in section 57A(1)(a) and (b).]   **[329]**

NOTES
Commencement: 16 October 1992 (Trade Union and Labour Relations (Consolidation) Act 1992, s 302.)
Substituted by the the Trade Union and Labour Relations (Consolidation) Act 1992, s 300(2), Sch 2, para 16.
Sub-s (1): numbered by the Trade Union Reform and Employment Rights Act 1993, s 28, Sch 5, para 7, as from 30 August 1993 (SI 1993/1908).
Sub-ss (2), (3): added by the Trade Union Reform and Employment Rights Act 1993, s 28, Sch 5, para 7, as from 30 August 1993 (SI 1993/1908).

72A *(Repealed by the Trade Union and Labour Relations (Consolidation) Act 1992, s 300(1), Sch 1; see now ibid s 155 (para [819] below.)*

73 Calculation of basic award

(1) The amount of the basic award shall be the amount calculated in accordance with subsections (3) to (6) [(6A)], subject to—

    (a) subsection (2) of this section (which provides for an award of two weeks' pay in certain redundancy cases);

    (b) . . .

    [(ba) subsection (7A) (which provides for the amount of the award to be reduced where the employee has unreasonably refused an offer of reinstatement);

    (bb) subsection (7B) (which provides for the amount of the award to be reduced because of the employee's conduct;]

    (c) . . .

    (d) subsection (9) (which provides for the amount of the award to be reduced where the employee received a payment in respect of redundancy); and

    (e) section 76 (which prohibits compensation being awarded under this Part and under the Sex Discrimination Act 1975 or the Race Relations Act 1976 in respect of the same matter).

(2) The amount of the basic award shall be two weeks' pay where the tribunal finds that the reason or principal reason for the dismissal of the employee was that he was redundant and the employee—

    (a) by virtue of section 82(5) or (6) is not, or if he were otherwise entitled would not be, entitled to a redundancy payment; or

    (b) by virtue of the operation of section 84(1) is not treated as dismissed for the purposes of Part VI.

(3) The amount of the basic award shall be calculated by reference to the period, ending with the effective date of termination, during which the employee has been continuously employed, by starting at the end of that period and reckoning backwards the numbers of years of employment falling within that period, and allowing—

    (a) one and a half weeks' pay for each such year of employment . . . in which the employee was not below the age of forty-one;

    [(b) one week's pay for each year of employment not falling within paragraph (a) . . . in which the employee was not below the age of twenty-two; and

    (c) half a week's pay for each such year of employment not falling within either of paragraphs (a) and (b)].

(4) Where, in reckoning the number of years of employment in accordance with subsection (3), twenty years of employment have been reckoned no account shall be taken of any year of employment earlier than those twenty years.

[(4A), (4B) . . .]

(5) Where in the case of an employee the effective date of termination is after the specified anniversary the amount of the basic award calculated in accordance with subsections (3) and (4) shall be reduced by the appropriate fraction.

(6) In subsection (5) ["the specified anniversary" in relation to an employee means the sixty-fourth anniversary of the day of his birth], and "the appropriate fraction" means the fraction of which—

    (a) the numerator is the number of whole months reckoned from the specified anniversary in the period beginning with that anniversary and ending with the effective date of termination; and

    (b) the denominator is twelve.

[(6A) Where the reason (or, if more than one, the principal reason) for the dismissal or, in a redundancy case, for selecting the employee for dismissal, was an inadmissible reason the amount of the basic award (before any reduction under the following provisions of this section) shall not be less than £2,700.

(6B)   For the purposes of this section a reason is "inadmissible" if it is one of those specified in section 57A(1)(a) and (b).

(6C)   The Secretary of State may by order increase the sum specified in subsection (6A).

(6D)   No order shall be made under subsection (6C) unless a draft of the order has been laid before Parliament and approved by a resolution of each House of Parliament.]

(7) . . .

[(7A)   Where the tribunal finds that the complainant has unreasonably refused an offer by the employer which if accepted would have the effect of reinstating the complainant in his employment in all respects as if he had not been dismissed, the tribunal shall reduce or further reduce the amount of the basic award to such extent as it considers just and equitable having regard to that finding.

(7B)   Where the tribunal considers that any conduct of the complainant before the dismissal (or, where the dismissal was with notice, before the notice was given) . . . was such that it would be just and equitable to reduce or further reduce the amount of the basic award to any extent, the tribunal shall reduce or further reduce that amount accordingly.]

[(7C)   Subsection (7B) does not apply *where the reason or principal reason for the dismissal was that the employee was redundant* [in a redundancy case, unless the reason for selecting the employee for dismissal was an inadmissible reason; and in that event subsection (7B) shall apply only to so much of the basic award as is payable because of subsection (6A)].]

(8) . . .

(9)   The amount of the basic award shall be reduced or, as the case may be, be further reduced, by the amount of any redundancy payment awarded by the tribunal under Part VI in respect of the same dismissal or of any payment made by the employer to the employee on the ground that the dismissal was by reason of redundancy, whether in pursuance of Part VI or otherwise.   **[330]**

NOTES
   Sub-s (1): figure in italics substituted by figure in square brackets thereafter by the Trade Union Reform and Employment Rights Act 1993, s 28, Sch 5, para 8(a), as from 30 August 1993 (SI 1993/1908, below, para [1435]); para (b) repealed by the Employment Act 1982, s 21(3), Sch 4; paras (ba), (bb) added and para (c) repealed by the Employment Act 1980, ss 9, 20, Sch 2.
   Sub-s (3): paras (b), (c) substituted by the Employment Act 1980, s 9; words omitted repealed with savings by the Employment Act 1982, ss 20, 21(3), Sch 2, para 5(2), Sch 4.
   Sub-ss (4A), (4B): inserted by the Employment Act 1982, s 4(1); repealed by the Trade Union and Labour Relations (Consolidation) Act 1992, s 300(1), Sch 1.
   Sub-s (6): words in square brackets substituted by the Sex Discrimination Act 1986, s 3(2), (3).
   Sub-ss (6A)–(6D): inserted by the Trade Union Reform and Employment Rights Act 1993, s 28, Sch 5, para 8(b), as from 30 August 1993 (SI 1993/1908).
   Sub-s (7): repealed by the Employment Act 1982, ss 4(2)(a), 21(3), Sch 4.
   Sub-s (7A): added by the Employment Act 1980, s 9.
   Sub-s (7B): added by the Employment Act 1980, s 9; words omitted repealed by the Employment Act 1982, ss 4(2)(b), 21(3), Sch 4.
   Sub-s (7C): added by the Employment Act 1982, s 4(2); substituted by the Trade Union and Labour Relations (Consolidation) Act 1992, s 300(2), Sch 2, para 17; words in italics substituted by words in square brackets immediately thereafter, by the Trade Union Reform and Employment Rights Act 1993, s 28, Sch 5, para 8(c), as from 30 August 1993 (SI 1993/1908).
   Sub-s (8): repealed by the Employment Act 1980, ss 9, 20, Sch 2.

74 Calculation of compensatory award

(1) Subject to *sections 75 and 76* [subsection (8) and section 76], the amount of the compensatory award shall be such amount as the tribunal considers just and equitable in all the circumstances having regard to the loss sustained by the complainant in consequence of the dismissal in so far as that loss is attributable to action taken by the employer.

(2) The said loss shall be taken to include—

    (a) any expenses reasonably incurred by the complainant in consequence of the dismissal, and

    (b) subject to subsection (3), loss of any benefit which he might reasonably be expected to have had but for the dismissal.

(3) The said loss, in respect of any loss of any entitlement or potential entitlement to, or expectation of, a payment on account of dismissal by reason of redundancy, whether in pursuance of Part VI or otherwise, shall include only the loss referable to the amount, if any, by which the amount of that payment would have exceeded the amount of a basic award (apart from any reduction under [section 73(7A) to (9)]) in respect of the same dismissal.

(4) In ascertaining the said loss the tribunal shall apply the same rule concerning the duty of a person to mitigate his loss as applies to damages recoverable under the common law of England and Wales or of Scotland, as the case may be.

(5) In determining, for the purposes of subsection (1), how far any loss sustained by the complainant was attributable to action taken by the employer no account shall be taken of any pressure which, by calling, organising, procuring or financing a strike or other industrial action, or threatening to do so, was exercised on the employer to dismiss the employee, and that question shall be determined as if no such pressure had been exercised.

(6) Where the tribunal finds that the dismissal was to any extent caused or contributed to by any action of the complainant it shall reduce the amount of the compensatory award by such proportion as it considers just and equitable having regard to that finding.

(7) If the amount of any payment made by the employer to the employee on the ground that the dismissal was by reason of redundancy, whether in pursuance of Part VI or otherwise, exceeds the amount of the basic award which would be payable but for section 73(9) that excess shall go to reduce the amount of the compensatory award.

[(8) Subsection (1) is subject also to section 75 except that, in the case of an award of compensation under section 71(2)(a) where an additional award falls to be made, the limit imposed by section 75 may be exceeded to the extent necessary to enable the award fully to reflect the amount specified as payable under section 69(2)(a) or (4)(d), as the case may be, if that limit would otherwise reduce the amount of the compensatory award when added to the additional award.] **[331]**

NOTES

    Sub-s (1): words in italics substituted by words in square brackets thereafter, by the Trade Union Reform and Employment Rights Act 1993, s 30(1), (3)(a), as from 30 August 1993 (SI 1993/1908, below, para [**1435**]).

    Sub-s (3): words in square brackets substituted by the Employment Act 1982, s 21, Sch 3, Pt II, para 23.

    Sub-s (8): added by the Trade Union Reform and Employment Rights Act 1993, s 30(1), (3)(b), as from 30 August 1993 (SI 1993/1908).

75 Limit on compensation

(1) The amount of compensation awarded to a person under section 71(1) or of a compensatory award to a person calculated in accordance with section 74 shall [(save where the exception in section 71(1A) or 74(8) applies)] not exceed [£11,000].

(2) The Secretary of State may by order increase the said limit of [£8,000] or that limit as from time to time increased under this subsection, but no such order shall be made unless a draft of the order has been laid before Parliament and approved by a resolution of each House of Parliament.

(3) It is hereby declared for the avoidance of doubt that the limit imposed by this section applies to the amount which the industrial tribunal would, apart from this section, otherwise award in respect of the subject matter of the complaint after taking into account any payment made by the respondent to the complainant in respect of that matter and any reduction in the amount of the award required by any enactment or rule of law.   **[332]**

NOTES
Sub-s (1): first words in square brackets inserted by the Trade Union Reform and Employment Rights Act 1993, s 30(1), (4), as from 30 August 1993 (SI 1993/1908, below, para **[1435]**). Sum of £11,000 substituted by the Unfair Dismissal (Increase of Compensation Limit) Order 1993, SI 1993/1348, art 2, where the "appropriate date" as defined in art 3 (below, para **[1434]**) falls on or after 1 June 1993. The most recent previous limits were £10,000 (from 1 April 1991: SI 1991/466) and £8,925 (from 1 April 1989: SI 1989/527).
Sub-s (2): sum in square brackets substituted by SI 1984/2020, arts 3, 4; not subsequently amended, despite the increase in the limit specified in sub-s (1).

75A (*Repealed by the Trade Union and Labour Relations (Consolidation) Act 1992, s 300(1), Sch 1. See now ibid s 158.*)

[75A Calculation of special award

(1) Subject to the following provisions of this section, the amount of the special award shall be—

  (a) one week's pay multiplied by 104, or
  (b) £13,400,

whichever is the greater, but shall not exceed £26,800.

(2) Where the award of compensation is made under section 71(2)(a) then, unless the employer satisfies the tribunal that it was not practicable to comply with the preceding order under section 69, the amount of the special award shall be increased to—

  (a) one week's pay multiplied by 156, or
  (b) £20,100,

whichever is the greater, but subject to the following provisions of this section.

(3) In a case where the amount of the basic award is reduced under section 73(5), the amount of the special award shall be reduced by the same fraction.

(4) Where the tribunal considers that any conduct of the complainant before the dismissal (or, where the dismissal was with notice, before the notice was given) was such that it would be just and equitable to reduce or further reduce the amount of the special award to any extent, the tribunal shall reduce or further reduce that amount accordingly.

(5) Where the tribunal finds that the complainant has unreasonably—

(a) prevented an order under section 69 from being complied with, or

(b) refused an offer by the employer (made otherwise than in compliance with such an order) which if accepted would have the effect of reinstating the complainant in his employment in all respects as if he had not been dismissed,

the tribunal shall reduce or further reduce the amount of the special award to such extent as it considers just and equitable having regard to that finding.

(6) Where the employer has engaged a permanent replacement for the complainant, the tribunal shall not take that fact into account in determining for the purposes of subsection (2) whether it was practicable to comply with an order under section 69 unless the employer shows that it was not practicable for him to arrange for the complainant's work to be done without engaging a permanent replacement.

(7) The Secretary of State may by order increase any of the sums specified in subsections (1) and (2).

(8) No order shall be made under subsection (7) unless a draft of the order has been laid before Parliament and approved by a resolution of each House of Parliament.]   [332A]

NOTE
Inserted by the Trade Union Reform and Employment Rights Act 1993, s 28, Sch 5, para 9, as from 30 August 1993 (SI 1993/1908, below, para [**1435**]).

76 Compensation for act which is both sex or racial discrimination (or both) and unfair dismissal

(1) Where compensation falls to be awarded in respect of any act both under the provisions of this Act relating to unfair dismissal and under one or both of the following Acts, namely the Sex Discrimination Act 1975 and the Race Relations Act 1976, an industrial tribunal shall not award compensation under any one of those two or, as the case may be, three Acts in respect of any loss or other matter which is or has been taken into account under the other or any other of them by the tribunal or another industrial tribunal in awarding compensation on the same or another complaint in respect of that act.

(2) Without prejudice to section 75 (whether as enacted or as applied by section 65 of the Sex Discrimination Act 1975 or section 56 of the Race Relations Act 1976) in a case to which subsection (1) applies, the aggregate of the following amounts of compensation awarded by an industrial tribunal, that is to say—

(a) any compensation awarded under the said Act of 1975; and

(b) any compensation awarded under the said Act of 1976; and

(c) any compensation awarded under section 71 (1) or, as the case may be, which is calculated in accordance with section 74,

shall not exceed the limit for the time being imposed by section 75.   [333]

76A–79 *(Ss 76A, 77–79 repealed by the Trade Union and Labour Relations (Consolidation) Act 1992, s 300(1), Sch 1. See now ibid ss 160–166. Ss 76B, 76C repealed by the Employment Act 1982, s 21(3), Sch 4. New ss 77, 77A, 78, 78A and 79 are inserted by the Trade Union Reform and Employment Rights Act 1993, s 28, Sch 5, para 10, as from 30 August 1993: these are set out below.)*

[Interim relief

77 Interim relief pending determination of complaint of unfair dismissal

(1) An employee who presents a complaint to an industrial tribunal that he has been unfairly dismissed by his employer and that the reason (or, if more than one, the principal reason) for the dismissal was one of those specified in section 57A(1)(a) and (b) may apply to the tribunal for interim relief.

(2) The tribunal shall not entertain an application for interim relief unless it is presented to the tribunal before the end of the period of seven days immediately following the effective date of termination (whether before, on or after that date).

(3) The tribunal shall determine the application for interim relief as soon as practicable after receiving the application.

(4) The tribunal shall give to the employer (not later than seven days before the date of the hearing) a copy of the application together with notice of the date, time and place of the hearing.

(5) The tribunal shall not exercise any power it has of postponing the hearing of an application for interim relief except where it is satisfied that special circumstances exist which justify it in doing so.]   [333A]

NOTE
    Inserted by the Trade Union Reform and Employment Rights Act 1993, s 28, Sch 5, para 10, as from 30 August 1993 (SI 1993/1908, below, para [1435]).

[77A Procedure on hearing of application and making of order

(1) If on hearing an employee's application for interim relief it appears to the tribunal that it is likely that on determining the complaint to which the application relates the tribunal will find that the reason (or, if more than one, the principal reason) for his dismissal was one of those specified in section 57A(1)(a) and (b) the following provisions shall apply.

(2) The tribunal shall announce its findings and explain to both parties (if present) what powers the tribunal may exercise on the application and in what circumstances it will exercise them, and shall ask the employer (if present) whether he is willing, pending the determination or settlement of the complaint—

  (a) to reinstate the employee, that is to say, to treat him in all respects as if he had not been dismissed, or

  (b) if not, to re-engage him in another job on terms and conditions not less favourable than those which would have been applicable to him if he had not been dismissed.

(3) For this purpose "terms and conditions not less favourable than those which would have been applicable to him if he had not been dismissed" means, as regards seniority, pension rights and other similar rights, that the period prior to the dismissal should be regarded as continuous with his employment following the dismissal.

(4) If the employer states that he is willing to reinstate the employee, the tribunal shall make an order to that effect.

(5) If the employer states that he is willing to re-engage the employee in another job and specifies the terms and conditions on which he is willing to do so, the tribunal shall ask the employee whether he is willing to accept the job on those terms and conditions; and—

(a) if the employee is willing to accept the job on those terms and conditions, the tribunal shall make an order to that effect, and

(b) if he is not, then, if the tribunal is of the opinion that the refusal is reasonable, the tribunal shall make an order for the continuation of his contract of employment, but otherwise the tribunal shall make no order.

(6) If on the hearing of an application for interim relief the employer fails to attend before the tribunal, or states that he is unwilling either to reinstate the employee or re-engage him as mentioned in subsection (2), the tribunal shall make an order for the continuation of the employee's contract of employment.] **[333B]**

NOTE

Inserted by the Trade Union Reform and Employment Rights Act 1993, s 28, Sch 5, para 10, as from 30 August 1993 (SI 1993/1908, below, para **[1435]**).

[78 Orders for continuation of contract of employment

(1) An order under section 77A for the continuation of a contract of employment is an order that the contract of employment continue in force—

(a) for the purposes of pay or of any other benefit derived from the employment, seniority, pension rights and other similar matters, and

(b) for the purposes of determining for any purpose the period for which the employee has been continuously employed,

from the date of its termination (whether before or after the making of the order) until the determination or settlement of the complaint.

(2) Where the tribunal makes such an order it shall specify in the order the amount which is to be paid by the employer to the employee by way of pay in respect of each normal pay period, or part of any such period, falling between the date of dismissal and the determination or settlement of the complaint.

(3) Subject as follows, the amount so specified shall be that which the employee could reasonably have been expected to earn during that period, or part, and shall be paid—

(a) in the case of payment for any such period falling wholly or partly after the making of the order, on the normal pay day for that period, and

(b) in the case of a payment for any past period, within such time as may be specified in the order.

(4) If an amount is payable in respect only of part of a normal pay period, the amount shall be calculated by reference to the whole period and reduced proportionately.

(5) Any payment made to an employee by an employer under his contract of employment, or by way of damages for breach of that contract, in respect of a normal pay period, or part of any such period, shall go towards discharging the employer's liability in respect of that period under subsection (2); and, conversely, any payment under that subsection in respect of a period shall go towards discharging any liability of the employer under, or in respect of breach of, the contract of employment in respect of that period.

(6) If an employee, on or after being dismissed by his employer, receives a lump sum which, or part of which, is in lieu of wages but is not referable to any normal pay period, the tribunal shall take the payment into account in determining the amount of pay to be payable in pursuance of any such order.

(7) For the purposes of this section, the amount which an employee could reasonably have been expected to earn, his normal pay period and the normal pay day for each such period shall be determined as if he had not been dismissed.]

[333C]

NOTE
Inserted by the Trade Union Reform and Employment Rights Act 1993, s 28, Sch 5, para 10, as from 30 August 1993 (SI 1993/1908, below, para [**1435**]).

[78A Application for variation or revocation of order

(1) At any time between the making of an order under section 77A and the determination or settlement of the complaint, the employer or the employee may apply to an industrial tribunal for the revocation or variation of the order on the ground of a relevant change of circumstances since the making of the order.

(2) Sections 77 and 77A apply in relation to such an application as in relation to an original application for interim relief except that, in the case of an application by the employer, section 77(4) has effect with the substitution of a reference to the employee for the reference to the employer.] [333D]

NOTE
Inserted by the Trade Union Reform and Employment Rights Act 1993, s 28, Sch 5, para 10, as from 30 August 1993 (SI 1993/1908, below, para [**1435**]).

[79 Consequence of failure to comply with order

(1) If on the application of an employee an industrial tribunal is satisfied that the employer has not complied with the terms of an order for the reinstatement or re-engagement of the employee under section 77A(4) or (5), the tribunal shall—

(a) make an order for the continuation of the employee's contract of employment, and
(b) order the employer to pay the employee such compensation as the tribunal considers just and equitable in all the circumstances having regard—
   (i) to the infringement of the employee's right to be reinstated or re-engaged in pursuance of the order, and
   (ii) to any loss suffered by the employee in consequence of the non-compliance.

(2) Section 78 applies to an order under subsection (1)(a) as in relation to an order under section 77A.

(3) If on the application of an employee an industrial tribunal is satisfied that the employer has not complied with the terms of an order for the continuation of a contract of employment, the following provisions apply.

(4) If the non-compliance consists of a failure to pay an amount by way of pay specified in the order, the tribunal shall determine the amount owed by the employer on the date of the determination.

(5) If on that date the tribunal also determines the employee's complaint that he has been unfairly dismissed, it shall specify that amount separately from any other sum awarded to the employee.

(6) In any other case, the tribunal shall order the employer to pay the employee such compensation as the tribunal considers just and equitable in all the circumstances having regard to any loss suffered by the employee in consequence of the non-compliance.] [333E]

NOTE
Inserted by the Trade Union Reform and Employment Rights Act 1993, s 28, Sch 5, para 10, as from 30 August 1993 (SI 1993/1908, below, para [1435]).

Teachers in aided schools

80 Teacher in aided school dismissed on requirement of local education authority

(1) Where a teacher in an aided school is dismissed by the governors . . . of the school in pursuance of a requirement of the local education authority under paragraph (a) of the proviso to section 24(2) of the Education Act 1944, this Part shall have effect in relation to the dismissal as if—

(a) the local education authority had at all material times been the teacher's employer, and

(b) the local education authority had dismissed him, and the reason or principal reason for which they did so had been the reason or principal reason for which they required his dismissal.

(2) For the purposes of a complaint under section 67 as applied by this section—

(a) section 71(2)(b) shall have effect as if for the words "not practicable to comply" there were substituted the words "not practicable for the local education authority to permit compliance"; and

(b) section 74(5) shall have effect as if any reference to the employer were a reference to the local education authority.   [334]

NOTES
Sub-s(1): words omitted repealed by the Education Act 1980, s 1(3), Sch 1, para 30.
Modified, in relation to governing bodies with delegated budgets, by the Education (Modification of Enactments Relating to Employment) Order 1989, SI 1989/901, arts 3, 4.

PART VI
REDUNDANCY PAYMENTS

Right to redundancy payment

81 General provisions as to right to redundancy payment

(1) Where an employee who has been continuously employed for the requisite period—

(a) is dismissed by his employer by reason of redundancy, or

(b) is laid off or kept on short-time to the extent specified in subsection (1) of section 88 and complies with the requirements of that section,

then, subject to the following provisions of this Act, the employer shall be liable to pay to him a sum (in this Act referred to as a "redundancy payment") calculated in accordance with Schedules 4, 13 and 14.

(2) For the purposes of this Act an employee who is dismissed shall be taken to be dismissed by reason of redundancy if the dismissal is attributable wholly or mainly to—

(a) the fact that his employer has ceased, or intends to cease, to carry on the business for the purposes of which the employee was employed by him, or has ceased, or intends to cease, to carry on that business in the place where the employee was so employed, or

, (b) the fact that the requirements of that business for employees to carry out
work of a particular kind, or for employees to carry out work of a particular
kind in the place where he was so employed, have ceased or diminished
or are expected to cease or diminish.

For the purposes of this subsection, the business of the employer together with
the business or businesses of his associated employers shall be treated as one unless
either of the conditions specified in this subsection would be satisfied without so
treating those businesses.

[(2A) For the purposes of subsection (2) the activities carried on by a local
education authority with respect to the schools maintained by it and the activities
carried on by the governors of those schools shall be treated as one business unless
either of the conditions specified in subsection (2) would be satisfied without so
treating them.]

(3) In subsection (2), "cease" means cease either permanently or temporarily and
from whatsoever cause, and "diminish" has a corresponding meaning.

(4) For the purposes of subsection (1), the requisite period is the period of two
years ending with the relevant date, . . .   **[335]**

NOTES
Sub-s (2A): added by the Employment Act 1982, s 21, Sch 3, Pt I, para 2(1).
Sub-s (4): words omitted repealed with savings by the Employment Act 1982, ss 20, 21(3), Sch 2, para
6(2), Sch 4.
This section and ss 82 and 84 and Sch 4 are modified in their application to certain public sector
employees by the Redundancy Payments (Local Government) (Modification) Order 1983, SI 1983/1160,
as amended by SI 1989/532, SI 1990/826, SI 1991/818.
See further: the Dock Work Act 1989, s 5.

82 General exclusions from right to redundancy payment

[(1) An employee shall not be entitled to a redundancy payment if he has before the
relevant date attained the following age, that is to say—

(a) in a case where—

(i) in the business for the purposes of which he was employed there was
a normal retiring age of less than sixty-five for an employee holding
the position which he held, and
(ii) the age was the same whether the employee holding that position was
a man or a woman,

that normal retiring age; and

(b) in any other case, the age of sixty-five.]

(2) Except as provided by section 92, an employee shall not be entitled to a
redundancy payment by reason of dismissal where his employer, being entitled to
terminate his contract of employment without notice by reason of the employee's
conduct, terminates it either—

(a) without notice, or
(b) by giving shorter notice than that which, in the absence of such conduct,
the employer would be required to give to terminate the contract, or
(c) by giving notice (not being such shorter notice as is mentioned in paragraph
(b)) which includes, or is accompanied by, a statement in writing that the
employer would, by reason of the employee's conduct, be entitled to
terminate the contract without notice.

(3) If an employer makes an employee an offer (whether in writing or not) before
the ending of his employment under the previous contract to renew his contract of

employment, or to re-engage him under a new contract of employment, so that the renewal or re-engagement would take effect either immediately on the ending of his employment under the previous contract or after an interval of not more than four weeks thereafter, the provisions of subsections (5) and (6) shall have effect.

(4) For the purposes of the application of subsection (3) to a contract under which the employment ends on a Friday, Saturday or Sunday—

(a) the renewal or re-engagement shall be treated as taking effect immediately on the ending of the employment under the previous contract if it takes effect on or before the next Monday after that Friday, Saturday or Sunday; and

(b) the interval of four weeks shall be calculated as if the employment had ended on that Monday.

(5) If an employer makes an employee such an offer as is referred to in subsection (3) and either—

(a) the provisions of the contract as renewed, or of the new contract, as to the capacity and place in which he would be employed, and as to the other terms and conditions of his employment, would not differ from the corresponding provisions of the previous contract; or

(b) the first-mentioned provisions would differ (wholly or in part) from those corresponding provisions, but the offer constitutes an offer of suitable employment in relation to the employee;

and in either case the employee unreasonably refuses that offer, he shall not be entitled to a redundancy payment by reason of his dismissal.

(6) If an employee's contract of employment is renewed, or he is re-engaged under a new contract of employment, in pursuance of such an offer as is referred to in subsection (3), and the provisions of the contract as renewed, or of the new contract, as to the capacity and place in which he is employed, and as to the other terms and conditions of his employment, differ (wholly or in part) from the corresponding provisions of the previous contract but the employment is suitable in relation to the employee, and during the trial period referred to in section 84 the employee unreasonably terminates the contract, or unreasonably gives notice to terminate it and the contract is thereafter, in consequence, terminated, he shall not be entitled to a redundancy payment by reason of his dismissal from employment under the previous contract.

(7) Any reference in this section to re-engagement by the employer shall be construed as including a reference to re-engagement by the employer or by any associated employer, and any reference in this section to an offer made by the employer shall be construed as including a reference to an offer made by an associated employer.   [336]

NOTES

Sub-s (1): substituted by the Employment Act 1989, ss 16(1), 29(6), Sch 9.

Modified by the Local Government Reorganisation (Compensation) Regulations 1986, SI 1986/151, regs 3, 4, Schedule, Pt II.

Modified by the Education (Reorganisation in Inner London) (Compensation) Regulations 1989, SI 1989/1139, regs 3(6), 4(4), (6), (8), Schedule, Pt III.

This section and ss 81 and 84 and Sch 4 are modified in their application to certain public sector employees by the Redundancy Payments (Local Government) (Modification) Order 1983, SI 1983/1160, as amended by SI 1989/532, SI 1990/826, SI 1991/818.

83 Dismissal by employer

(1) In this Part, except as respects a case to which section 86 applies, "dismiss" and "dismissal" shall, subject to sections 84, 85 and 93, be construed in accordance with subsection (2).

(2) An employee shall be treated as dismissed by his employer if, but only if,—

(a) the contract under which he is employed by the employer is terminated by the employer, whether it is so terminated by notice or without notice, or

(b) where under that contract he is employed for a fixed term, that term expires without being renewed under the same contract, or

(c) the employee terminates that contract with or without notice, in circumstances (not falling within section 92(4)) such that he is entitled to terminate it without notice by reason of the employer's conduct.   **[337]**

84 Renewal of contract or re-engagement

(1) If an employee's contract of employment is renewed, or he is re-engaged under a new contract of employment in pursuance of an offer (whether in writing or not) made by his employer before the ending of his employment under the previous contract, and the renewal or re-engagement takes effect either immediately on the ending of that employment or after an interval of not more than four weeks thereafter, then, subject to subsections (3) to (6), the employee shall not be regarded as having been dismissed by his employer by reason of the ending of his employment under the previous contract.

(2) For the purposes of the application of subsection (1) to a contract under which the employment ends on a Friday, Saturday or Sunday—

(a) the renewal or re-engagement shall be treated as taking effect immediately on the ending of the employment if it takes effect on or before the Monday after that Friday, Saturday or Sunday, and

(b) the interval of four weeks referred to in that subsection shall be calculated as if the employment had ended on that Monday.

(3) If, in a case to which subsection (1) applies, the provisions of the contract as renewed, or of the new contract, as to the capacity and place in which the employee is employed, and as to the other terms and conditions of his employment, differ (wholly or in part) from the corresponding provisions of the previous contract, there shall be a trial period in relation to the contract as renewed, or the new contract (whether or not there has been a previous trial period under this section).

(4) The trial period shall begin with the ending of the employee's employment under the previous contract and end with the expiration of the period of four weeks beginning with the date on which the employee starts work under the contract as renewed, or the new contract, or such longer period as may be agreed in accordance with the next following subsection for the purpose of retraining the employee for employment under that contract.

(5) Any such agreement shall—

(a) be made between the employer and the employee or his representative before the employee starts work under the contract as renewed or, as the case may be, the new contract;

(b) be in writing;

(c) specify the date of the end of the trial period; and

(d) specify the terms and conditions of employment which will apply in the employee's case after the end of that period.

(6) If during the trial period—

(a) the employee, for whatever reason, terminates the contract, or gives notice to terminate it and the contract is thereafter, in consequence, terminated; or

(b) the employer, for a reason connected with or arising out of the change to the renewed, or new, employment, terminates the contract, or gives notice to terminate it and the contract is thereafter, in consequence, terminated,

then, unless the employee's contract of employment is again renewed, or he is again re-engaged under a new contract of employment, in circumstances such that subsection (1) again applies, he shall be treated as having been dismissed on the date on which his employment under the previous contract or, if there has been more than one trial period, the original contract ended for the reason for which he was then dismissed or would have been dismissed had the offer (or original offer) of renewed, or new, employment not been made, or, as the case may be, for the reason which resulted in that offer being made.

(7) Any reference in this section to re-engagement by the employer shall be construed as including a reference to re-engagement by the employer or by any associated employer, and any reference in this section to an offer made by the employer shall be construed as including a reference to an offer made by an associated employer. **[338]**

NOTE

This section and ss 81, and 82 and Sch 4 are modified in their application to certain public sector employees by the Redundancy Payments (Local Government) (Modification) Order 1983, SI 1983/1160, as amended by SI 1989/532, SI 1990/826, SI 1991/818.

85 Employee anticipating expiry of employer's notice

(1) The provisions of this section shall have effect where—

(a) an employer gives notice to an employee to terminate the contract of employment, and

(b) at a time within the obligatory period of that notice, the employee gives notice in writing to the employer to terminate the contract of employment on a date earlier than the date on which the employer's notice is due to expire.

(2) Subject to the following provisions of this section, in the circumstances specified in subsection (1) the employee shall, for the purposes of this Part, be taken to be dismissed by his employer.

(3) If, before the employee's notice is due to expire, the employer gives him notice in writing—

(a) requiring him to withdraw his notice terminating the contract of employment as mentioned in subsection (1)(b) and to continue in the employment until the date on which the employer's notice expires, and

(b) stating that, unless he does so, the employer will contest any liability to pay to him a redundancy payment in respect of the termination of his contract of employment,

but the employee does not comply with the requirements of that notice, the employee shall not be entitled to a redundancy payment by virtue of subsection (2) except as provided by subsection (4).

(4) Where, in the circumstances specified in subsection (1), the employer has given notice to the employee under subsection (3), and on a reference to a tribunal it appears to the tribunal, having regard both to the reasons for which the employee

(3) For the purpose mentioned in subsection (2), no account shall be taken of any week for which an employee is laid off or kept on short-time where the lay-off or short-time is wholly or mainly attributable to a strike or a lock-out (within the meaning of paragraph 24 of Schedule 13) whether the strike or lock-out is in the trade or industry in which the employee is employed or not and whether it is in Great Britain or elsewhere.

(4) Where the employer gives a counter-notice within seven days after the service of a notice of intention to claim, and does not withdraw the counter-notice by a subsequent notice in writing, the employee shall not be entitled to a redundancy payment in pursuance of the notice of intention to claim except in accordance with a decision of an industrial tribunal.

(5) The period allowed for the purposes of subsection (2)(a) of section 88 is as follows, that is to say,—

(a) if the employer does not give a counter-notice within seven days after the service of the notice of intention to claim, that period is three weeks after the end of those seven days;

(b) if the employer gives a counter-notice within those seven days, but withdraws it by a subsequent notice in writing, that period is three weeks after the service of the notice of withdrawal;

(c) if the employer gives a counter-notice within those seven days and does not so withdraw it, and a question as to the right of the employee to a redundancy payment in pursuance of the notice of intention to claim is referred to a tribunal, that period is three weeks after the tribunal has notified to the employee its decision on that reference.

(6) For the purposes of paragraph (c) of subsection (5) no account shall be taken of any appeal against the decision of the tribunal, or of any requirement to the tribunal to state a case for the opinion of the High Court or the Court of Session, or of any proceedings or decision in consequence of such an appeal or requirement.   **[343]**

90 The relevant date

(1) Subject to the following provisions of this section, for the purposes of the provisions of this Act so far as they relate to redundancy payments, "the relevant date", in relation to the dismissal of an employee—

(a) where his contract of employment is terminated by notice, whether given by his employer or by the employee, means the date on which that notice expires;

(b) where his contract of employment is terminated without notice, means the date on which the termination takes effect;

(c) where he is employed under a contract for a fixed term and that term expires as mentioned in subsection (2)(b) of section 83, means the date on which that term expires;

(d) where he is treated, by virtue of subsection (6) of section 84, as having been dismissed on the termination of his employment under a previous contract, means—

(i) for the purposes of section 101, the date which is the relevant date as defined by paragraph (a), (b) or (c) in relation to the renewed, or new, contract, or, where there has been more than one trial period under section 84, the last such contract; and

(ii) for the purposes of any other provision, the date which is the relevant date as defined by paragraph (a), (b) or (c) in relation to the previous contract, or, where there has been more than one trial period under section 84, the original contract; and

(e) where he is taken to be dismissed by virtue of section 85(2), means the date on which the employee's notice to terminate his contract of employment expires.

(2) "The relevant date", in relation to a notice of intention to claim or a right to a redundancy payment in pursuance of such a notice,—

(a) in a case falling within paragraph (a) of subsection (1) of section 88, means the date on which the last of the four or more consecutive weeks before the service of the notice came to an end, and

(b) in a case falling within paragraph (b) of that subsection, means the date on which the last of the series of six or more weeks before the service of the notice came to an end.

(3) Where the notice required to be given by an employer to terminate a contract of employment by section 49(1) would, if duly given when notice of termination was given by the employer, or (where no notice was given) when the contract of employment was terminated by the employer, expire on a date later than the relevant date as defined by subsection (1), then for the purposes of section 81(4) and paragraph 1 of Schedule 4 and paragraph 8(4) of Schedule 14, that later date shall be treated as the relevant date in relation to the dismissal.   **[344]**

91 Reference of questions to tribunal

(1) Any question arising under this Part as to the right of an employee to a redundancy payment, or as to the amount of a redundancy payment, shall be referred to and determined by an industrial tribunal.

(2) For the purposes of any such reference, an employee who has been dismissed by his employer shall, unless the contrary is proved, be presumed to have been so dismissed by reason of redundancy.

(3) In relation to lay-off or short-time, the questions which may be referred to and determined by an industrial tribunal, as mentioned in subsection (1), shall include any question whether an employee will become entitled to a redundancy payment if he is not dismissed by his employer and he terminates his contract of employment as mentioned in subsection (2)(a) of section 88; and any such question shall for the purposes of this Part be taken to be a question as to the right of the employee to a redundancy payment.   **[345]**

92 Special provisions as to termination of contract in cases of misconduct or industrial dispute

(1) Where at any such time as is mentioned in subsection (2), an employee who—

(a) has been given notice by his employer to terminate his contract of employment, or

(b) has given notice to his employer under subsection (1) of section 88,

takes part in a strike, in such circumstances that the employer is entitled, by reason of his taking part in the strike, to treat the contract of employment as terminable without notice, and the employer for that reason terminates the contract as mentioned in subsection (2) of section 82, that subsection shall not apply to that termination of the contract.

(2) The times referred to in subsection (1) are—

(a) in a case falling within paragraph (a) of that subsection any time within the obligatory period of the employer's notice (as defined by section 85(5)), and

(b) in a case falling within paragraph (b) of subsection (1), any time after the service of the notice mentioned in that paragraph.

(3) Where at any such time as is mentioned in subsection (2) an employee's contract of employment, otherwise than by reason of his taking part in a strike, is terminated by his employer in the circumstances specified in subsection (2) of section 82, and is so terminated as mentioned therein, and on a reference to an industrial tribunal it appears to the tribunal, in the circumstances of the case, to be just and equitable that the employee should receive the whole or part of any redundancy payment to which he would have been entitled apart from section 82(2), the tribunal may determine that the employer shall be liable to pay to the employee—

(a) the whole of the redundancy payment to which the employee would have been so entitled, or

(b) such part of that redundancy payment as the tribunal thinks fit.

(4) Where an employee terminates his contract of employment without notice, being entitled to do so by reason of a lock-out by his employer, section 83(2)(c) shall not apply to that termination of the contract.

(5) In this section "strike" and "lock-out" each has the meaning given by paragraph 24 of Schedule 13.   **[346]**

93 Implied or constructive termination of contract

(1) Where in accordance with any enactment or rule of law—

(a) any act on the part of an employer, or

(b) any event affecting an employer (including, in the case of an individual, his death),

operates so as to terminate a contract under which an employee is employed by him, that act or event shall for the purposes of this Part be treated as a termination of the contract by the employer, if apart from this subsection it would not constitute a termination of the contract by him and, in particular, the provisions of sections 83, 84 and 90 shall apply accordingly.

(2) Where subsection (1) applies, and the employee's contract of employment is not renewed, and he is not re-engaged under a new contract of employment, so as to be treated, by virtue of section 84(1), as not having been dismissed, he shall, without prejudice to section 84(6), be taken for the purposes of this Part to be dismissed by reason of redundancy if the circumstances in which his contract is not so renewed and he is not so re-engaged are wholly or mainly attributable to one or other of the facts specified in paragraphs (a) and (b) of section 81(2).

(3) For the purposes of subsection (2), section 81(2)(a), in so far as it relates to the employer ceasing or intending to cease to carry on the business, shall be construed as if the reference to the employer included a reference to any person to whom, in consequence of the act or event in question, power to dispose of the business has passed.

(4) In this section, any reference to section 84(1) includes a reference to that subsection as applied by section 94(2) or as so applied and (where appropriate) modified by section 95(2), and where section 84(1) applies as so modified the references in subsection (2) of this section to renewal of or re-engagement under a contract of employment shall be construed as including references to renewal of or re-engagement in employment otherwise than under a contract of employment.   **[347]**

NOTE

Sub-s (4): repealed by the Trade Union Reform and Employment Rights Act 1993, s 51, Sch 10, as from 30 August 1993 (SI 1993/1908, below, para [**1435**]).

94 Change of ownership of business

(1) The provisions of this section shall have effect where—

(a) *a change occurs (whether by virtue of a sale or other disposition or by operation of law) in the ownership of a business for the purposes of which a person is employed, or of a part of such a business, and*

(b) *in connection with that change the person by whom the employee is employed immediately before the change occurs (in this section referred to as "the previous owner") terminates the employee's contract of employment, whether by notice or without notice.*

(2) If, by agreement with the employee, the person who immediately after the change occurs is the owner of the business, or of the part of the business in question, as the case may be (in this section referred to as "the new owner"), renews the employee's contract of employment (with the substitution of the new owner for the previous owner) or re-engages him under a new contract of employment, sections 84 and 90 shall have effect as if the renewal or re-engagement had been a renewal or re-engagement by the previous owner (without any substitution of the new owner for the previous owner).

(3) If the new owner offers to renew the employee's contract of employment (with the substitution of the new owner for the previous owner) or to re-engage him under a new contract of employment, subsections (3) to (6) of section 82 shall have effect, subject to subsection (4), in relation to that offer as they would have had effect in relation to the like offer made by the previous owner.

(4) For the purposes of the operation, in accordance with subsection (3), of subsections (3) to (6) of section 82 in relation to an offer made by the new owner—

(a) *the offer shall not be treated as one whereby the provisions of the contract as renewed, or of the new contract, as the case may be, would differ from the corresponding provisions of the contract as in force immediately before the dismissal by reason only that the new owner would be substituted for the previous owner as the employer, and*

(b) *no account shall be taken of that substitution in determining whether the refusal of the offer was unreasonable or, as the case may be, whether the employee acted reasonably in terminating the renewed, or new, employment during the trial period referred to in section 84.*

(5) The preceding provisions of this section shall have effect (subject to the necessary modifications) in relation to a case where—

(a) *the persons by whom a business, or part of a business, is owned immediately before a change is one of the persons by whom (whether as partners, trustees or otherwise) it is owned immediately after the change, or*

(b) *the person by whom a business, or part of a business, is owned immediately before a change (whether as partners, trustees or otherwise) include the person by whom, or include one or more of the persons by whom, it is owned immediately after the change,*

as those provisions have effect where the previous owner and the new owner are wholly different persons.

(6) Sections 82(7) and 84(7) shall not apply in any case to which this section applies.

(7) Nothing in this section shall be construed as requiring any variation of a contract of employment by agreement between the parties to be treated as constituting a termination of the contract. **[348]**

NOTE
Repealed by the Trade Union Reform and Employment Rights Act 1993, s 51, Sch 10, as from 30 August 1993 (SI 1993/1908, below, para **[1435]**).

95 Transfer to Crown employment

(1) Section 94 shall apply to a transfer of functions from a person not acting on behalf of the Crown (in this section referred to as the transferor) to a government department or any other officer or body exercising functions on behalf of the Crown (in this section referred to as the transferee) as that section applies to a transfer of a business, but with the substitution for references to the previous owner and new owner of references to the transferor and transferee respectively.

(2) In so far as the renewal or re-engagement of the employee by the transferee is in employment otherwise than under a contract of employment—

(a) references in section 94 (and in sections 82(4) to (6), 84 and 90 as they apply by virtue of that section) to a contract of employment or to the terms of such a contract shall be construed as references to employment otherwise than under such a contract and to the terms of such employment; and

(b) references in subsection (4) of section 94, as modified by subsection (1) of this section, to the substitution of the transferee for the transferor shall be construed as references to the substitution of employment by the transferee otherwise than under a contract of employment for employment by the transferor under such a contract. **[349]**

NOTE
Repealed by the Trade Union Reform and Employment Rights Act 1993, s 51, Sch 10, as from 30 August 1993 (SI 1993/1908, below, para **[1435]**).

96 Exemption orders

(1) If at any time there is in force an agreement between one or more employers or organisations of employers and one or more trade unions representing employees, whereby employees to whom the agreement applies have a right in certain circumstances to payments on the termination of their contracts of employment, and, on the application of all the parties to the agreement, the Secretary of State, having regard to the provisions of the agreement, is satisfied that section 81 should not apply to those employees, he may make an order under this section in respect of that agreement.

(2) The Secretary of State shall not make an order under this section in respect of an agreement unless the agreement indicates (in whatsoever terms) the willingness of the parties to it to submit to an industrial tribunal such questions as are mentioned in paragraph (b) of subsection (3).

(3) Where an order under this section is in force in respect of an agreement—

(a) section 81 shall not have effect in relation to any employee who immediately before the relevant date is an employee to whom the agreement applies, but

(b) section 91 shall have effect in relation to any question arising under the agreement as to the right of an employee to a payment on the termination of his employment, or as to the amount of such a payment, as if the payment were a redundancy payment and the question arose under this Part.

(4) Any order under this section may be revoked by a subsequent order thereunder, whether in pursuance of an application made by all or any of the parties to the agreement in question or without any such application.   **[350]**

NOTE
    Order under this section: Redundancy Payments (Exemption) Order 1980, SI 1980/1052 (certain employees of Lancashire County Council).

97 *(Repealed by the Employment Act 1980, s 20, Sch 2.)*

98 Exclusion or reduction of redundancy payment on account of pension rights

(1) The Secretary of State shall by regulations make provision for excluding the right to a redundancy payment, or reducing the amount of any redundancy payment, in such cases as may be prescribed by the regulations, being cases in which an employee has (whether by virtue of any statutory provision or otherwise) a right or claim (whether legally enforceable or not) to a periodical payment or lump sum by way of pension, gratuity or superannuation allowance which is to be paid by reference to his employment by a particular employer and is to be paid, or to begin to be paid, at the time when he leaves that employment or within such period thereafter as may be prescribed by the regulations.

(2) Provision shall be made by any such regulations for securing that the right to a redundancy payment shall not be excluded, and that the amount of a redundancy payment shall not be reduced, by reason of any right or claim to a periodical payment or lump sum, in so far as that payment or lump sum represents such compensation as is mentioned in section 118(1) and is payable under a statutory provision, whether made or passed before, on or after the passing of this Act.

(3) In relation to any case where, under section 85 or 92 or 110, an industrial tribunal determines that an employer is liable to pay part (but not the whole) of a redundancy payment, any reference in this section to a redundancy payment, or to the amount of a redundancy payment, shall be construed as a reference to that part of the redundancy payment, or to the amount of that part, as the case may be. **[351]**

99 Public offices, etc

(1) Without prejudice to any exemption or immunity of the Crown, section 81 shall not apply to any person in respect of any employment which—

(a) is employment in a public office for the purposes of section 38 of the Superannuation Act 1965, or

(b) whether by virtue of that Act or otherwise, is treated for the purposes of pensions and other superannuation benefits as service in the civil service of the State, . . .

(c) . . .

(2) Without prejudice to any exemption or immunity of the Crown, section 81 shall not apply to any person in respect of his employment in any capacity under the Government of an overseas territory (as defined by section 114).   **[352]**

NOTES
Sub-s (1): words omitted repealed by the National Health Service and Community Care Act 1990, s 66(2), Sch 10.

100 Domestic servants

(1) For the purposes of the application of the provisions of this Part to an employee who is employed as a domestic servant in a private household, those provisions *(except section 94)* shall apply as if the household were a business and the maintenance of the household were the carrying on of that business by the employer.

(2) . . . section 81 shall not apply to any person in respect of employment as a domestic servant in a private household, where the employer is the father, mother, grandfather, grandmother, stepfather, stepmother, son, daughter, grandson, granddaughter, stepson, stepdaughter, brother, sister, half-brother, or half-sister of the employee.   [353]

NOTES
Sub-s (1): words in italics repealed by the Trade Union Reform and Employment Rights Act 1993, s 51, Sch 10, as from 30 August 1993 (SI 1993/1908, below, para [1435]).
Sub-s (2): words omitted repealed by the Employment Act 1982, s 21, Sch 4.

101 Claims for redundancy payments

(1) Notwithstanding anything in the preceding provisions of this Part, an employee shall not be entitled to a redundancy payment unless, before the end of the period of six months beginning with the relevant date—

    (a) the payment has been agreed and paid, or

    (b) the employee has made a claim for the payment by notice in writing given to the employer, or

    (c) a question as to the right of the employee to the payment, or as to the amount of the payment, has been referred to an industrial tribunal, or

    (d) a complaint relating to his dismissal has been presented by the employee under section 67.

(2) An employee shall not by virtue of subsection (1) lose his right to a redundancy payment if, during the period of six months immediately following the period mentioned in that subsection, the employee—

    (a) makes such a claim as is referred to in paragraph (b) of that subsection,

    (b) refers to a tribunal such a question as is referred to in paragraph (c) of that subsection, or

    (c) makes such a complaint as is referred to in paragraph (d) of that subsection,

and it appears to the tribunal to be just and equitable that the employee should receive a redundancy payment having regard to the reason shown by the employee for his failure to take any such step as is referred to in paragraph (a), (b) or (c) of this subsection within the period mentioned in subsection (1), and to all the other relevant circumstances.   [354]

102 Written particulars of redundancy payment

(1) On making any redundancy payment, otherwise than in pursuance of a decision of a tribunal which specifies the amount of the payment to be made, the employer shall give to the employee a written statement indicating how the amount of the payment has been calculated.

(2) Any employer who without reasonable excuse fails to comply with subsection (1) shall be guilty of an offence and liable on summary conviction to a fine not exceeding [level 1 on the standard scale].

(3) If an employer fails to comply with the requirements of subsection (1), then (without prejudice to any proceedings for an offence under subsection (2)) the employee may by notice in writing to the employer require him to give to the employee a written statement complying with those requirements within such period (not being less than one week beginning with the day on which the notice is given) as may be specified in the notice; and if the employer without reasonable excuse fails to comply with the notice he shall be guilty of an offence under this subsection and liable on summary conviction—

    (a) if it is his first conviction of an offence under this subsection, to a fine not exceeding £20, or

    (b) in any other case, to a fine not exceeding £100.   [355]

NOTES

Sub-s (2): maximum fine increased and converted to a level on the standard scale by the Criminal Justice Act 1982, ss 37, 38, 46.

Sub-s (3): enhanced penalty on a subsequent conviction now abolished, maximum fine on any conviction increased and converted to level 3 on the standard scale by the Criminal Justice Act 1982, ss 35, 37, 38, 46.

Redundancy Fund

103–105 *(S 103 repealed with savings by the Employment Act 1990, s 16(2), Sch 3; ss 104, 104A repealed, with savings in the case of s 104, by the Employment Act 1989, ss 17(a), 29(4), (6), Sch 7, Pt II, Sch 9, para 4; s 105 repealed by the Employment Act 1990, ss 13(4), 16(2), Sch 3.)*

106 Payments out of fund to employees

(1) Where an employee claims that his employer is liable to pay to him an employer's payment, and either—

    (a) that the employee has taken all reasonable steps (other than legal proceedings) to recover the payment from the employer and that the employer has refused or failed to pay it, or has paid part of it and has refused or failed to pay the balance, or

    (b) that the employer is insolvent and that the whole or part of the payment remains unpaid,

the employee may apply to the Secretary of State for a payment under this section.

[(1A) In this Act "employer's payment", in relation to an employee, means—

    (a) a redundancy payment which his employer is liable to pay to him under the foregoing provisions of this Part, or

    (b) a payment which his employer is, under an agreement in respect of which an order is in force under section 96, liable to make to him on the termination of his contract of employment.

(1B) In relation to a case where, under section 85, 92 or 110, an industrial tribunal determines that an employer is liable to pay only part of a redundancy payment, the reference in subsection (1A)(a) above to a redundancy payment shall be construed as a reference to that part of the redundancy payment.]

(2) If on an application under this section the Secretary of State is satisfied—

(a) that the employee is entitled to the employer's payment;

(b) that either of the conditions specified in subsection (1) is fulfilled; and

(c) that, in a case where the employer's payment is such a payment as is mentioned in paragraph (b) . . . of [subsection (1A)], the employee's right to the payment arises by virtue of a [period of continuous employment] (computed in accordance with the provisions of the agreement in question) which is not less than [two years],

the Secretary of State shall pay to the employee out of [the National Insurance Fund] a sum calculated in accordance with Schedule 7, reduced by so much (if any) of the employer's payment as has been paid.

(3) Where the Secretary of State pays a sum to an employee in respect of an employer's payment—

(a) all rights and remedies of the employee with respect to the employer's payment, or (if the Secretary of State has paid only part of it) all his rights and remedies with respect to that part of the employer's payment, shall be transferred to and vest in the Secretary of State; and

(b) any decision of an industrial tribunal requiring the employer's payment to be paid to the employee shall have effect as if it required that payment, or, as the case may be, that part of it which the Secretary of State has paid, to be paid to the Secretary of State;

and any moneys recovered by the Secretary of State by virtue of this subsection shall be paid into [the National Insurance Fund].

(4) . . .

(5) For the purposes of this section an employer shall be taken to be insolvent if—

[(a) he has been adjudged bankrupt or has made a composition or arrangement with his creditors;

(b) he has died and his estate falls to be administered in accordance with an order under section [421 of the Insolvency Act 1986]; or]

(c) where the employer is a company, a winding-up order [or an administration order] has been made with respect to it or a resolution for voluntary winding-up has been passed with respect to it, or a receiver or manager of its undertaking has been duly appointed, or possession has been taken, by or on behalf of the holders of any debentures secured by a floating charge, of any property of the company comprised in or subject to the charge [or [a voluntary arrangement proposed for the purposes of Part I of the Insolvency Act 1986 is approved under that Part]].

(6) In the application of this section to Scotland, for paragraphs (a), (b) and (c) of subsection (5) there shall be substituted the following paragraphs:—

(a) an award of sequestration has been made on his estate, or he has executed a trust deed for his creditors or entered into a composition contract;

(b) he has died and a judicial factor appointed under section [11A of the Judicial Factors (Scotland) Act 1989] is required by the provisions of that section to divide his insolvent estate among his creditors; or

(c) where the employer is a company, a winding-up order [or an administration order] has been made or a resolution for voluntary winding-up is passed with respect to it or a receiver of its undertaking is duly appointed [or [a voluntary arrangement proposed for the purposes of Part I of the Insolvency Act 1986 is approved under that Part]].

(7) In this section "legal proceedings" does not include any proceedings before an industrial tribunal, but includes any proceedings to enforce a decision or award of an industrial tribunal.   **[356]**

NOTES
Sub-ss (1A), (1B): added with savings by the Employment Act 1989, s 29(3), (6), Sch 6, para 21(2), Sch 9.

Sub-s (2): words omitted repealed by the Wages Act 1986, s 32(2), Sch 5, Pt I; words in first pair of square brackets substituted with savings by the Employment Act 1989, s 29(3), (6), Sch 6, para 21(3), Sch 9; words in second and third pairs of square brackets substituted with savings by the Employment Act 1982, s 20, Sch 2, para 6(4); final words in square brackets substituted by the Employment Act 1990, s 16(1), Sch 2, para 1(3).

Sub-s (3): words in square brackets substituted by the Employment Act 1990, s 16(1), Sch 2, para 1(3).

Sub-s (4): repealed with savings by the Employment Act 1989, ss 29(3), (4), (6), Sch 6, para 21(4), Sch 7, Pt II, Sch 9.

Sub-s (5): paras (a), (b) substituted with savings and in para (c) first words in square brackets and words in second (outer) pair of square brackets added with savings by the Insolvency Act 1985, s 235, Sch 8, para 31, for savings see the Insolvency Act 1986, s 437, Sch 11; in para (b) words in square brackets and in para (c) words in third (inner) pair of square brackets substituted with savings by the Insolvency Act 1986, ss 437, 439(2), Schs 11, 14.

Sub-s (6): para (b) amended by the Bankruptcy (Scotland) Act 1985, s 75(1), Sch 7, para 14(1); para (c) amended by the Insolvency Act 1985, s 235, Sch 8, para 31 and the Insolvency Act 1986, s 439(2), Sch 14; for savings see s 437 of and Sch 11 to the 1986 Act.

107 Supplementary provisions relating to applications under s 106

(1) Where an employee makes an application to the Secretary of State under section 106, the Secretary of State may, by notice in writing given to the employer, require the employer to provide the Secretary of State with such information, and to produce for examination on behalf of the Secretary of State documents in his custody or under his control of such descriptions, as the Secretary of State may reasonably require for the purpose of determining whether the application is well-founded.

(2) If any person on whom a notice is served under this section fails without reasonable excuse to comply with a requirement imposed by the notice, he shall be guilty of an offence and liable on summary conviction to a fine not exceeding [level 3 on the standard scale].

(3) Any person who—

    (a) in providing any information required by a notice under this section, makes a statement which he knows to be false in a material particular, or recklessly makes a statement which is false in a material particular, or

    (b) produces for examination in accordance with any such notice a document which to his knowledge has been wilfully falsified,

shall be guilty of an offence under this subsection.

(4) A person guilty of an offence under subsection (3) shall be liable on summary conviction to a fine not exceeding the prescribed sum or to imprisonment for a term not exceeding three months or both, or on conviction on indictment to a fine or to imprisonment for a term not exceeding two years or both.

(5) In subsection (4) above "the prescribed sum" means—

    (a) in England and Wales, the prescribed sum within the meaning of [section 32 of the Magistrates' Courts Act 1980] (that is to say, £1,000 or another sum fixed by order under [section 143 of that Act] to take account of changes in the value of money);

    (b) in Scotland, the prescribed sum within the meaning of section 289B of the Criminal Procedure (Scotland) Act 1975 (that is to say, £1,000 or another sum fixed by an order made under section 289D of that Act for that purpose).   **[357]**

[108 References to tribunal relating to payments under s 106

(1) Where on an application made to the Secretary of State for a payment under section 106 it is claimed that an employer is liable to pay an employer's payment, there shall be referred to an industrial tribunal—

(a) any question as to the liability of the employer to pay the employer's payment; and

(b) any question as to the amount of the sum payable in accordance with Schedule 7.

(2) For the purposes of any reference under this section an employee who has been dismissed by his employer shall, unless the contrary is proved, be presumed to have been so dismissed by reason of redundancy.]   **[358]**

109 *(Repealed by the Employment Act 1990, s 16(2), Sch 3.)*

Miscellaneous and supplemental

110 Strike during currency of employer's notice to terminate contract

(1) The provisions of this section shall have effect where, after an employer has given notice to an employee to terminate his contract of employment (in this section referred to as a "notice of termination")—

(a) the employee begins to take part in a strike of employees of the employer, and

(b) the employer serves on him a notice in writing (in this section referred to as a "notice of extension") requesting him to agree to extend the contract of employment beyond the time of expiry by an additional period comprising as many available days as the number of working days lost by striking (in this section referred to as "the proposed period of extension").

(2) A notice of extension shall indicate the reasons for which the employer makes the request contained in the notice, and shall state that unless either—

(a) the employee complies with the request, or

(b) the employer is satisfied that, in consequence of sickness, injury or otherwise, he is unable to comply with it, or that (notwithstanding that he is able to comply with it) in the circumstances it is reasonable for him not to do so,

the employer will contest any liability to pay him a redundancy payment in respect of the dismissal effected by the notice of termination.

(3) For the purposes of this section an employee shall be taken to comply with the request contained in a notice of extension if, but only if, on each available day

within the proposed period of extension, he attends at his proper or usual place of work and is ready and willing to work, whether he has signified his agreement to the request in any other way or not.

(4) Where an employee on whom a notice of extension has been served—

(a) complies with the request contained in the notice, or

(b) does not comply with it, but attends at his proper or usual place of work and is ready and willing to work on one or more (but not all) of the available days within the proposed period of extension,

the notice of termination shall have effect, and shall be deemed at all material times to have had effect, as if the period specified in it had (in a case falling within paragraph (a)) been extended beyond the time of expiry by an additional period equal to the proposed period of extension or (in a case falling within paragraph (b)) had been extended beyond the time of expiry up to the end of the day (or, if more than one, the last of the days) on which he so attends and is ready and willing to work; and section 50 and Schedule 3 shall apply accordingly as if the period of notice required by section 49 were extended to a corresponding extent.

(5) Subject to subsection (6), if an employee on whom a notice of extension is served in pursuance of subsection (1) does not comply with the request contained in the notice, he shall not be entitled to a redundancy payment by reason of the dismissal effected by the notice of termination, unless the employer agrees to pay such a payment to him notwithstanding that the request has not been complied with.

(6) Where a notice of extension has been served, and on a reference to an industrial tribunal it appears to the tribunal that the employee has not complied with the request contained in the notice and the employer has not agreed to pay a redundancy payment in respect of the dismissal in question, but that the employee was unable to comply with the request, or it was reasonable for him not to comply with it, as mentioned in subsection (2)(b) the tribunal may determine that the employer shall be liable to pay to the employee—

(a) the whole of any redundancy payment to which the employee would have been entitled apart from subsection (5), or

(b) such part of any such redundancy payment as the tribunal thinks fit.

(7) The service of a notice of extension, and any extension, by virtue of subsection (4) of the period specified in a notice of termination,—

(a) shall not affect any right either of the employer or of the employee to terminate the contract of employment (whether before, at or after the time of expiry) by a further notice or without notice, and

(b) shall not affect the operation of sections 81 to 102 in relation to any such termination of the contract of employment.

(8) In this section any reference to the number of working days lost by striking is a reference to the number of working days in the period beginning with the date of service of the notice of termination and ending with the time of expiry which are days on which the employee in question takes part in a strike of employees of the employer.

(9) In this section, "strike" has the meaning given by paragraph 24 of Schedule 13, "time of expiry", in relation to a notice of termination, means the time at which the notice would expire apart from this section, "working day", in relation to an employee, means a day on which, in accordance with his contract of employment, he is normally required to work, "available day", in relation to an employee, means a working day beginning at or after the time of expiry which is a day on which he is not taking part in a strike of employees of the employer, and "available day within

the proposed period of extension" means an available day which begins before the end of that period.   [359]

111 Payments equivalent to redundancy rebates in respect of civil servants, etc

(1) The provisions of this section shall have effect with respect to employment of any of the following descriptions, that is to say—

    (a) any such employment as is mentioned in paragraph (a), paragraph (b) . . . of subsection (1) of section 99 (whether as originally enacted or as modified by any order under section 149(1));

    (b) any employment remunerated out of the revenue of the Duchy of Lancaster or the Duchy of Cornwall;

    (c) any employment remunerated out of the Queen's Civil List;

    (d) any employment remunerated out of Her Majesty's Privy Purse.

(2) Where the Secretary of State is satisfied that a payment has been, or will be, made in respect of the termination of any person's employment of any description specified in subsection (1), and that the payment has been, or will be, so made to or in respect of him—

    (a) in accordance with the Superannuation Act 1965, as that Act continues to have effect by virtue of section 23(1) of the Superannuation Act 1972,

    (b) in accordance with any provision of a scheme made under section 1 of the Superannuation Act 1972, or

    (c) in accordance with any such arrangements as are mentioned in subsection (3),

the Secretary of State shall pay the appropriate sum out of the fund to the appropriate fund or authority.

(3) The arrangements referred to in paragraph (c) of subsection (2) are any arrangements made with the approval of the Minister for the Civil Service for securing that payments by way of compensation for loss of any such employment as is mentioned in subsection (1) will be made—

    (a) in circumstances which in the opinion of the Minister for the Civil Service correspond (subject to the appropriate modifications) to those in which a right to a redundancy payment would have accrued if section 81 had applied, and

    (b) on a scale which in the opinion of the Minister for the Civil Service, taking into account any sums which are payable as mentioned in subsection (2)(a) or (b) to or in respect of the person losing the employment in question, corresponds (subject to the appropriate modifications) to that on which a redundancy payment would have been payable if section 81 had applied.

(4) For the purposes of subsection (2) the appropriate sum is the sum appearing to the Secretary of State to be equal to the amount of the redundancy rebate which would have been payable under section 104 if such a right as is mentioned in paragraph (a) of subsection (3) had accrued, and such a redundancy payment as is mentioned in paragraph (b) of subsection (3) had been payable and had been paid.

(5) Any accounts prepared by the Secretary of State under section 103(2) shall show as a separate item the aggregate amount of sums paid under subsection (2) during the period to which the accounts relate.

(6) In this section "the appropriate fund or authority"—

    (a) in relation to employment of any description falling within paragraph 7 of subsection (1) of section 39 of the Superannuation Act 1965 (whether as originally enacted or as modified by any order under that section), means the fund out of which, or the body out of whose revenues, the employment is remunerated;

(b) in relation to any employment remunerated out of the revenues of the Duchy of Lancaster, means the Chancellor of the Duchy, and, in relation to any employment remunerated out of the revenues of the Duchy of Cornwall, means such person as the Duke of Cornwall, or the possessor for the time being of the Duchy of Cornwall, appoints;

(c) in relation to any employment remunerated out of the Queen's Civil List or out of Her Majesty's Privy Purse, means the Civil List or the Privy Purse, as the case may be; and

(d) in any other case, means the Consolidated Fund.   [360]

NOTES

Sub-s (1): words omitted from para (a) repealed by the National Health Service and Community Care Act 1990, s 66(2).

112 References to tribunal relating to equivalent payments

(1) This section applies to any such payment as is mentioned in subsection (3) of section 111 which is payable in accordance with any such arrangements as are mentioned in that subsection.

(2) Where the terms and conditions (whether constituting a contract of employment or not) on which any person is employed in any such employment as is mentioned in subsection (1) of section 111 include provision—

(a) for the making of any payment to which this section applies, and

(b) for referring to a tribunal any such question as is mentioned in the following provisions of this subsection,

any question as to the right of any person to such a payment in respect of that employment, or as to the amount of such a payment shall be referred to and determined by an industrial tribunal.   [361]

113 *(Repealed by the Wages Act 1986, ss 28, 32(2), (3), Sch 5, Pt I, Sch 6, para 10(2).)*

114 Meaning of "Government of overseas territory"

In this Part "overseas territory" means any territory or country outside the United Kingdom; and any reference to the Government of an overseas territory includes a reference to a Government constituted for two or more overseas territories and to any authority established for the purpose of providing or administering services which are common to, or relate to matters of common interest to, two or more such territories.   [362]

115 Application of Part VI to employment not under contract of employment

(1) This section applies to employment of any description which—

(a) is not employment under a contract of service or of apprenticeship, and

(b) is not employment of any description falling within paragraphs (a) to (d) of section 111(1), but is employment such that secondary Class 1 contributions are payable under Part I of the Social Security Act 1975 in respect of persons engaged therein.

(2) The Secretary of State may by regulations under this section provide that, subject to such exceptions and modifications as may be prescribed by the regulations, this Part and the provisions of this Act supplementary thereto shall have effect in relation to any such employment of a description to which this section applies as may be so prescribed as if—

  (a) it were employment under a contract of employment, and
  (b) any person engaged in employment of that description were an employee, and
  (c) such person as may be determined by or under the regulations were his employer.

(3) Without prejudice to the generality of subsection (2), regulations made under this section may provide that section 105 shall apply to persons engaged in any such employment of a description to which this section applies as may be prescribed by the regulations, as if those persons were employees to whom that section applies.

[363]

116 Provision for treating termination of certain employment by statute as equivalent to dismissal

(1) The Secretary of State may by regulations under this section provide that, subject to such exceptions and modifications as may be prescribed by the regulations, the provisions of this Part shall have effect in relation to any person who, by virtue of any statutory provisions,—

  (a) is transferred to, and becomes a member of, a body specified in those provisions, but
  (b) at a time so specified ceases to be a member of that body unless before that time certain conditions so specified have been fulfilled,

as if the cessation of his membership of that body by virtue of those provisions were dismissal by his employer by reason of redundancy.

(2) The power conferred by subsection (1) shall be exercisable whether membership of the body in question constitutes employment within the meaning of section 153 or not; and, where that membership does not constitute such employment, that power may be exercised in addition to any power exercisable by virtue of section 115.

[364]

117 Employees paid by person other than employer

(1) This section applies to any employee whose remuneration is, by virtue of any statutory provision, payable to him by a person other than his employer.

(2) For the purposes of the operation, in relation to employees to whom this section applies, of the provisions of this Part and Schedule 13 specified in column 1 of Schedule 8, any reference to the employer which is specified in column 2 of Schedule 8 shall be construed as a reference to the person responsible for paying the remuneration.

  [(2A), (2B) . . .]

(3) In relation to employees to whom this section applies, section 119 shall have effect as if—

(a) any reference in subsection (1) or subsection (2) of that section to a notice required or authorised to be given by or to an employer included a reference to a notice which, by virtue of subsection (2), is required or authorised to be given by or to the person responsible for paying the remuneration;

(b) in relation to a notice required or authorised to be given to that person, any reference to the employer in paragraph (a) or paragraph (b) of subsection (2) of that section were a reference to that person; and

(c) the reference to the employer in subsection (5) of that section included a reference to that person.

(4) In this section and in Schedule 8, "the person responsible for paying the remuneration" means the person by whom the remuneration is payable as mentioned in subsection (1).   [365]

NOTES

Sub-ss (2A), (2B): inserted by the Wages Act 1986, s 27(4); repealed with savings by the Employment Act 1989, s 29(4), (6), Sch 7, Pt II, Sch 9.

118 Statutory compensation schemes

(1) This section applies to any statutory provision which was in force immediately before 6th December 1965, whereby the holders of such situations, places or employments as are specified in that provision are, or may become, entitled to compensation for loss of employment, or for loss or diminution of emoluments or of pension rights, in consequence of the operation of any other statutory provision referred to therein.

(2) The Secretary of State may make provision by regulations for securing that where apart from this section a person is entitled to compensation under a statutory provision to which this section applies, and the circumstances are such that he is also entitled to a redundancy payment, the amount of the redundancy payment shall be set off against the compensation to which he would be entitled apart from this section; and any statutory provision to which any such regulations apply shall have effect subject to the regulations.   [366]

119 Provisions as to notices

(1) Any notice which under this Part is required or authorised to be given by an employer to an employee may be given by being delivered to the employee, or left for him at his usual or last-known place of residence, or sent by post addressed to him at that place.

(2) Any notice which under this Part is required or authorised to be given by an employee to an employer may be given either by the employee himself or by a person authorised by him to act on his behalf, and, whether given by or on behalf of the employee,—

(a) may be given by being delivered to the employer, or sent by post addressed to him at the place where the employee is or was employed by him, or

(b) if arrangements in that behalf have been made by the employer, may be given by being delivered to a person designated by the employer in pursuance of the arrangements, or left for such a person at a place so designated, or sent by post to such a person at an address so designated.

(3) In the preceding provisions of this section, any reference to the delivery of a notice shall, in relation to a notice which is not required by this Part to be in writing, be construed as including a reference to the oral communication of the notice.

(4) Any notice which, in accordance with any provision of this section, is left for a person at a place referred to in that provision shall, unless the contrary is proved, be presumed to have been received by him on the day on which it was left there.

(5) Nothing in subsection (1) or subsection (2) shall be construed as affecting the capacity of an employer to act by a servant or agent for the purposes of any provision of this Part, including either of those subsections.   **[367]**

120 Offences

(1) Where an offence under this Part committed by a body corporate is proved to have been committed with the consent or connivance of, or to be attributable to any neglect on the part of, any director, manager, secretary or other similar officer of the body corporate or any person who was purporting to act in any such capacity, he as well as the body corporate shall be guilty of that offence and shall be liable to be proceeded against and punished accordingly.

(2) In this section "director", in relation to a body corporate established by or under any enactment for the purpose of carrying on under national ownership any industry or part of an industry or undertaking, being a body corporate whose affairs are managed by its members, means a member of that body corporate.   **[368]**

PART VII
INSOLVENCY OF EMPLOYER

121 *(Repealed by the Insolvency Act 1985, s 235(3), Sch 10, Pt IV, and the Bankruptcy (Scotland) Act 1985, s 75(2), Sch 8. See now the Insolvency Act 1986, s 386, Sch 6, paras 9–11, 13–16, below, paras [461]–[462].)*

122 Employee's rights on insolvency of employer

(1) If on an application made to him in writing by an employee the Secretary of State is satisfied—
  (a) that the employer of that employee has become insolvent; and
  [(aa) that the employment of the employee has been terminated; and]
  (b) that on the relevant date the employee was entitled to be paid the whole or part of any debt to which this section applies,

the Secretary of State shall, subject to the provisions of this section, pay the employee out of [the National Insurance Fund] the amount to which in the opinion of the Secretary of State the employee is entitled in respect of that debt.

  [(2) In this section "the relevant date"—
  (a) in relation to arrears of pay (not being remuneration under a protective award made under [section 189 of the Trade Union and Labour Relations (Consolidation) Act 1992]) and to holiday pay, means the date on which the employer became insolvent;
  (b) in relation to such an award and to a basic award of compensation for unfair dismissal, means whichever is the latest of—
    (i) the date on which the employer became insolvent;
    (ii) the date of the termination of the employee's employment; and
    (iii) the date on which the award was made;
  (c) in relation to any other debt to which this section applies, means whichever

is the later of the dates mentioned in sub-paragraphs (i) and (ii) of paragraph (b).]

(3) This section applies to the following debts:—

[(a) any arrears of pay in respect of one or more (but not more than eight) weeks;]

(b) any amount which the employer is liable to pay the employee for the period of notice required by section 49(1) or (2) or for any failure of the employer to give the period of notice required by section 49(1);

[(c) any holiday pay—

   (i) in respect of a period or periods of holiday not exceeding six weeks in all; and

   (ii) to which the employee became entitled during the twelve months ending with the relevant date;]

(d) any basic award of compensation for unfair dismissal (within the meaning of section 72);

(e) any reasonable sum by way of reimbursement of the whole or part of any fee or premium paid by an apprentice or articled clerk.

[(4) For the purposes of this section, the following amounts shall be treated as arrears of pay, namely—

(a) a guarantee payment;

(b) remuneration on suspension on medical grounds under section 19;

(c) any payment for time off under [section 31(3) or 31A(4) or under section 169 of the Trade Union and Labour Relations (Consolidation) Act 1992];

[(ca) remuneration on suspension on maternity grounds under section 47;]

(d) remuneration under a protective award made under [section 189 of that Act];

(e) . . .

(5) The total amount payable to an employee in respect of any debt mentioned in subsection (3), where the amount of that debt is referable to a period of time, shall not exceed [£205.00] in respect of any one week or, in respect of a shorter period, an amount bearing the same proportion to [£205.00] as that shorter period bears to a week.

(6) The Secretary of State may vary the limit referred to in subsection (5) after a review under section 148, by order made in accordance with that section.

(7) A sum shall be taken to be reasonable for the purposes of subsection (3)(e) in a case where a trustee in bankruptcy or liquidator has been or is required to be appointed if it is admitted to be reasonable by the trustee in bankruptcy or liquidator under [section [348 of the Insolvency Act 1986] (effect of bankruptcy on apprenticeships etc), whether as originally enacted or as applied to the winding up of a company by rules under [section 411] of that Act].

(8) Subsection (7) shall not apply to Scotland, but in Scotland a sum shall be taken to be reasonable for the purposes of subsection (3)(e) in a case where a trustee in bankruptcy or liquidator has been or is required to be appointed if it is [accepted] by the trustee in bankruptcy or the liquidator for the purposes of the bankruptcy or winding-up.

(9) The provisions of subsections (10) and (11) shall apply in a case where one of the following officers (hereafter in this section referred to as the "relevant officer") has been or is required to be appointed in connection with the employer's insolvency, that is to say, a trustee in bankruptcy, a liquidator, [an administrator,] a receiver or manager, or a trustee under a composition or arrangement between the employer and his creditors or under a trust deed for his creditors executed by the employer; and in

this subsection ["trustee", in relation to a composition or arrangement, includes the supervisor of a [voluntary arrangement proposed for the purposes of, and approved under, Part I or VIII of the Insolvency Act 1986]].

(10) Subject to subsection (11), the Secretary of State shall not in such a case make any payment under this section in respect of any debt until he has received a statement from the relevant officer of the amount of that debt which appears to have been owed to the employee on the relevant date and to remain unpaid; and the relevant officer shall, on request by the Secretary of State, provide him, as soon as reasonably practicable, with such a statement.

[(11) If the Secretary of State is satisfied that he does not require such a statement in order to determine the amount of the debt that was owed to the employee on the relevant date and remains unpaid, he may make a payment under this section in respect of the debt without having received such a statement.]   **[369]**

NOTES
  Sub-s (1): para (aa) added by the Insolvency Act 1985, s 218(2); other words in square brackets substituted by the Employment Act 1990, s 16(1), Sch 2, para 1(4).
  Sub-s (2): substituted by the Insolvency Act 1985, s 218(3); in para (a) words in square brackets substituted by the Trade Union and Labour Relations (Consolidation) Act 1992, s 300(2), Sch 2, para 18(2).
  Sub-s (3): paras (a), (c) substituted by the Employment Act 1982, s 21(2), Sch 3, Pt I, para 4.
  Sub-s (4): substituted by the Insolvency Act 1985, s 218(4); in paras (c), (d) words in square brackets substituted by the Trade Union and Labour Relations (Consolidation) Act 1992, s 300(2), Sch 2, para 18(3); para (ca) inserted by the Trade Union Reform and Employment Rights Act 1993, s 49(2), Sch 8, para 18, as from a day to be appointed; para (e) repealed by the Social Security Act 1986, s 86(2), Sch 11.
  Sub-s (5): sums in square brackets substituted by SI 1992/312, art 2, as from 1 April 1992. There was no annual increase in 1993. Previous sums were £198 (from 1 April 1991: SI 1991/1464) and £184 (from 1 April 1990: SI 1990/384).
  Sub-s (7): words in outer square brackets substituted by the Insolvency Act 1985, s 218(5); words in square brackets therein substituted by the Insolvency Act 1986, ss 437, 439(2), Schs 11, 14.
  Sub-s (8): amended by the Bankruptcy (Scotland) Act 1985, s 75(1), Sch 7, para 14(2).
  Sub-s (9): first words in square brackets added by the Insolvency Act 1985, s 218(6); second words in square brackets substituted by the Insolvency Act 1985, s 218(6), words in square brackets therein substituted by the Insolvency Act 1986, ss 437, 439(2), Schs 11, 14.
  Sub-s (11): substituted by the Employment Act 1989, ss 18(2), 29(6), Sch 9.
  See further: the Dock Work Act 1989, Sch 2, para 7.

123 Payment of unpaid contributions to occupational pension scheme

(1) If, on application made to him in writing by the person competent to act in respect of an occupational pension scheme [or a personal pension scheme], the Secretary of State is satisfied that an employer has become insolvent and that at the time that he did so there remained unpaid relevant contributions falling to be paid by him to the scheme, the Secretary of State shall, subject to the provisions of this section, pay into the resources of the scheme out of [the National Insurance Fund] the sum which in his opinion is payable in respect of the unpaid relevant contributions.

(2) In this section "relevant contributions" means contributions falling to be paid by an employer [to an occupational pension scheme or a personal pension scheme], either on his own account or on behalf of an employee; and for the purposes of this section a contribution of any amount shall not be treated as falling to be paid on behalf of an employee unless a sum equal to that amount has been deducted from the pay of the employee by way of a contribution from him.

(3) The sum payable under this section is respect of unpaid contributions of an employer on his own account to an occupational pension scheme [or a personal pension scheme] shall be the least of the following amounts—

  (a) the balance of relevant contributions remaining unpaid on the date when he became insolvent and payable by the employer on his own account to the scheme in respect of the twelve months immediately preceding that date;

(b) the amount certified by an actuary to be necessary for the purpose of meeting the liability of the scheme on dissolution to pay the benefits provided by the scheme to or in respect of the employees of the employer;

(c) an amount equal to ten per cent of the total amount of remuneration paid or payable to those employees in respect of the twelve months immediately preceding the date on which the employer became insolvent.

(4) For the purposes of subsection (3)(c), "remuneration" includes holiday pay, [statutory sick pay, statutory maternity pay under Part V of the Social Security Act [1986 or Part XII of the Social Security Contributions and Benefits Act 1992], *maternity pay under Part III of this Act*] and any such payment as if referred to in [section 122(4)].

(5) Any sum payable under this section in respect of unpaid contributions on behalf of an employee shall not exceed the amount deducted from the pay of the employee in respect of the employee's contributions to the . . . scheme during the twelve months immediately preceding the date on which the employer became insolvent.

(6) The provisions of subsections (7) to (9) shall apply in a case where one of the following officers (hereafter in this section referred to as the "relevant officer") has been or is required to be appointed in connection with the employer's insolvency, that is to say, a trustee in bankruptcy, a liquidator, [an administrator] a receiver or manager, or a trustee under a composition or arrangement between the employer and his creditors or under a trust deed for his creditors executed by the employer; and in this subsection ["trustee", in relation to a composition or arrangement, includes the supervisor of a [voluntary arrangement proposed for the purposes of, and approved under, Part I or VIII of the Insolvency Act 1986]].

(7) Subject to subsection (9), the Secretary of State shall not in such a case make any payment under this section in respect of unpaid relevant contributions until he has received a statement from the relevant officer of the amount of relevant contributions which appear to have been unpaid on the date on which the employer became insolvent and to remain unpaid; and the relevant officer shall, on request by the Secretary of State provide him, as soon as reasonably practicable, with such a statement.

(8) Subject to subsection (9), an amount shall be taken to be payable, paid or deducted as mentioned in subsection (3)(a) or (c) or subsection (5), only if it is so certified by the relevant officer.

[(9) If the Secretary of State is satisfied—

(a) that he does not require a statement under subsection (7) in order to determine the amount of relevant contributions that was unpaid on the date on which the employer became insolvent and remains unpaid, or

(b) that he does not require a certificate under subsection (8) in order to determine the amounts payable, paid or deducted as mentioned in subsections (3)(a) and (c) and (5),

he may make a payment under this section in respect of the contributions in question without having received such a statement or (as the case may be) such a certificate.]   [370]

NOTES

Sub-s (1): first words in square brackets inserted by the Social Security Act 1986, s 86, Sch 10, Pt I, para 31; final words in square brackets substituted by the Employment Act 1990, s 16(1), Sch 2, para 1(4).

Sub-s (2): words in square brackets substituted by the Social Security Act 1986, s 86, Sch 10, Pt I, para 31.

Sub-s (3): words in square brackets inserted by the Social Security Act 1986, s 86, Sch 10, Pt I, para 31.

Sub-s (4): first words in square brackets substituted by the Social Security Act 1986, s 86, Sch 10, Pt IV, para 76, words in square brackets therein substituted by the Social Security (Consequential Provisions) Act 1992, s 4, Sch 2, para 49; final words in square brackets substituted with savings by the Insolvency Act 1985, s 235, Sch 8, para 31, for savings see the Insolvency Act 1986, s 437, Sch 11; words in italics repealed by the Trade Union Reform and Employment Rights Act 1993, s 51, Sch 10, as from 30 August 1993 (SI 1993/1908, below, para [**1435**]).

Sub-s (5): words omitted repealed by the Social Security Act 1986, s 86, Sch 11.

Sub-s (6): first words in square brackets added and words in second (outer) pair of square brackets substituted with savings by the Insolvency Act 1985, s 235, Sch 8, para 31, for savings see the Insolvency Act 1986, s 437, Sch 11; words in third (inner) pair of square brackets substituted with savings by the Insolvency Act 1986, ss 437, 439(2), Schs 11, 14.

Sub-s (9): substituted with savings by the Employment Act 1989, ss 18(3), 29(6), Sch 9.

124 Complaint to industrial tribunal

(1) A person who has applied for a payment under section 122 may, within the period of three months beginning with the date on which the decision of the Secretary of State on that application was communicated to him or, if that is not reasonably practicable, within such further period as is reasonable, present a complaint to an industrial tribunal that—

  (a) the Secretary of State has failed to make any such payment; or

  (b) any such payment made by the Secretary of State is less than the amount which should have been paid.

(2) Any persons who are competent to act in respect of an occupational pension scheme [or a personal pension scheme] and who have applied for a payment to be made under section 123 into the resources of the scheme may, within the period of three months beginning with the date on which the decision of the Secretary of State on that application was communicated to them, or, if that is not reasonably practicable, within such further period as is reasonable, present a complaint to an industrial tribunal that—

  (a) the Secretary of State has failed to make any such payment; or

  (b) any such payment made by him is less than the amount which should have been paid.

(3) Where an industrial tribunal finds that the Secretary of State ought to make a payment under section 122 or 123, it shall make a declaration to that effect and shall also declare the amount of any such payment which it finds the Secretary of State ought to make.   **[371]**

NOTES

Sub-s (2): words in square brackets added by the Social Security Act 1986, s 86, Sch 10, Pt I, para 31.

125 Transfer to Secretary of State of rights and remedies

(1) Where, in pursuance of section 122, the Secretary of State makes any payment to an employee in respect of any debt to which that section applies—

  (a) any rights and remedies of the employee in respect of that debt (or, if the Secretary of State has paid only part of it, in respect of that part) shall, on the making of the payment, become rights and remedies of the Secretary of State; and

  (b) any decision of an industrial tribunal requiring an employer to pay that debt to the employee shall have the effect that the debt or, as the case may be, that part of it which the Secretary of State has paid, is to be paid to the Secretary of State.

[(2) Where a debt or any part of a debt in respect of which the Secretary of State has made a payment in pursuance of section 122 constitutes—

(a) a preferential debt within the meaning of the Insolvency Act 1986 for the purposes of any provision of that Act (including any such provision as applied by any order made under that Act) or any provision of the Companies Act 1985; or

(b) a preferred debt within the meaning of the Bankruptcy (Scotland) Act 1985 for the purposes of any provision of that Act (including any provision as applied by section 11A of the Judicial Factors (Scotland) Act 1889),

then, without prejudice to the generality of subsection (1) above, there shall be included among the rights and remedies which become rights and remedies of the Secretary of State in accordance with that subsection any right arising under any such provision by reason of the status of the debt or that part of it as a preferential or preferred debt.

(2A) In computing for the purposes of any provision mentioned in subsection (2)(a) or (b) above the aggregate amount payable in priority to other creditors of the employer in respect of—

(a) any claim of the Secretary of State to be so paid by virtue of subsection (2) above; and

(b) any claim by the employee to be so paid made in his own right,

any claim falling within paragraph (a) above shall be treated as if it were a claim of the employee; but the Secretary of State shall be entitled, as against the employee, to be so paid in respect of any such claim of his (up to the full amount of the claim) before any payment is made to the employee in respect of any claim falling within paragraph (b) above.]

(3) Where in pursuance of section 123 the Secretary of State makes any payment into the resources of an occupational pension scheme [or a personal pension scheme] in respect of any contributions to the scheme, any rights and remedies in respect of those contributions belonging to the persons competent to act in respect of the scheme shall, on the making of the payment, become rights and remedies of the Secretary of State.

[(3A) Where the Secretary of State makes any such payment as is mentioned in subsection (3) above and the sum (or any part of the sum) falling to be paid by the employer on account of the contributions in respect of which the payment is made constitutes—

(a) a preferential debt within the meaning of the Insolvency Act 1986 for the purposes of any provision mentioned in subsection (2)(a) above; or

(b) a preferred debt within the meaning of the Bankruptcy (Scotland) Act 1985 for the purposes of any provision mentioned in subsection (2)(b) above,

then, without prejudice to the generality of subsection (3) above, there shall be included among the rights and remedies which become rights and remedies of the Secretary of State in accordance with that subsection any right arising under any such provision by reason of the status of that sum (or that part of it) as a preferential or preferred debt.

(3B) In computing for the purposes of any provision referred to in subsection (3A)(a) or (b) above the aggregate amount payable in priority to other creditors of the employer in respect of—

(a) any claim of the Secretary of State to be so paid by virtue of subsection (3A) above; and

(b) any claim by the persons competent to act in respect of the scheme, any claim falling within paragraph (a) above shall be treated as if it were a claim of those persons; but the Secretary of State shall be entitled, as against those persons, to be so paid in respect of any such claim of his (up to the full amount of the claim) before any payment is made to them in respect of any claim falling within paragraph (b) above.]

(4) Any sum recovered by the Secretary of State in exercising any right or pursuing any remedy which is his by virtue of this section shall be paid into [the National Insurance Fund].   **[372]**

NOTES
Sub-ss (2), (2A): substituted for sub-s (2) as originally enacted by the Employment Act 1989, ss 19(2), 29(6), Sch 9.
Sub-s (3): words in square brackets added by the Social Security Act 1986, s 86, Sch 10, Pt I, para 31.
Sub-ss (3A), (3B): inserted with savings by the Employment Act 1989, ss 19(2), 29(6), Sch 9.
Sub-s (4): words in square brackets substituted by the Employment Act 1990, s 16(1), Sch 2, para 1(4).

126 Power of Secretary of State to obtain information in connection with applications

(1) Where an application is made to the Secretary of State under section 122 or 123 in respect of a debt owed, or contributions to an occupational pension scheme [or a personal pension scheme] falling to be made, by an employer, the Secretary of State may require—

(a) the employer to provide him with such information as the Secretary of State may reasonably require for the purpose of determining whether the application is well-founded; and

(b) any person having the custody or control of any relevant records or other documents to produce for examination on behalf of the Secretary of State any such document in that person's custody or under his control which is of such a description as the Secretary of State may require.

(2) Any such requirement shall be made by notice in writing given to the person on whom the requirement is imposed and may be varied or revoked by a subsequent notice so given.

(3) If a person refuses or wilfully neglects to furnish any information or produce any document which he has been required to furnish or produce by a notice under this section he shall be liable on summary conviction to a fine not exceeding [level 3 on the standard scale].

(4) If a person, in purporting to comply with a requirement of a notice under this section, knowingly or recklessly makes any false statement he shall be liable on summary conviction to a fine not exceeding [level 5 on the standard scale].   **[373]**

NOTES
Sub-s (1): words in square brackets added by the Social Security Act 1986, s 86, Sch 10, Pt I, para 31.
Sub-ss (3), (4): maximum fine increased and converted to a level on the standard scale by the Criminal Justice Act 1982, ss 37, 38, 46.

127 Interpretation of ss 122 to 126

(1) For the purposes of sections 122 to 126, an employer shall be taken to be insolvent if, but only if, in England and Wales,—

[(a) he has been adjudged bankrupt or has made a composition or arrangement with his creditors;

(b) he has died and his estate falls to be administered in accordance with an order under section [421 of the Insolvency Act 1986]; or]

(c) where the employer is a company, a winding up order [or an administration order] is made or a resolution for voluntary winding up is passed with respect to it, or a receiver or manager of its undertaking is duly appointed, or possession is taken, by or on behalf of the holders of any debentures secured by a floating charge, of any property of the company comprised in or subject to the charge [or a [voluntary arrangement proposed for the purposes of Part I of the Insolvency Act 1986 is approved under that Part]].

(2) For the purposes of sections 122 to 126, an employer shall be taken to be insolvent if, but only if, in Scotland—

(a) [sequestration of his estate is awarded] or he executes a trust deed for his creditors or enters into a composition contract;

(b) he has died and a judicial factor appointed under section [11A of the Judicial Factors (Scotland) Act 1889] is required by that section to divide his insolvent estate among his creditors;

(c) where the employer is a company, a winding-up order [or an administration order] is made or a resolution for voluntary winding up is passed with respect to it or a receiver of its undertaking is duly appointed [or a [voluntary arrangement proposed for the purposes of Part I of the Insolvency Act 1986 is approved under that Part]].

(3) In sections 122 to 126—

"holiday pay" means—

(a) pay in respect of a holiday actually taken; or

(b) any accrued holiday pay which under the employee's contract of employment would in the ordinary course have become payable to him in respect of the period of a holiday if his employment with the employer had continued until he became entitled to a holiday;

"occupational pension scheme" means any scheme or arrangement which provides or is capable of providing, in relation to employees in any description of employment, benefits (in the form of pensions or otherwise) payable to or in respect of any such employees on the termination of their employment or on their death or retirement;

["personal pension scheme" means any scheme or arrangement which is comprised in one or more instruments or agreements and which has, or is capable of having, effect so as to provide benefits, in the form of pensions or otherwise, payable on death or retirement to or in respect of employees who have made arrangements with the trustees or managers of the scheme for them to become members of the scheme;]

and any reference in those sections to the resources of . . . a scheme is a reference to the funds out of which the benefits provided by the scheme are from time to time payable.   [374]

NOTES

Sub-s (1): paras (a), (b) substituted and in para (c) first words in square brackets and words in second (outer) pair of square brackets added by the Insolvency Act 1985, s 235, Sch 8, para 31; in para (b) words in square brackets and in para (c) words in third (inner) pair of square brackets substituted with savings by the Insolvency Act 1986, ss 437, 439(2), Schs 11, 14.

Sub-s (2): para (a) amended by the Employment Act 1989, s 29(3), Sch 6, para 23; para (b) amended by the Bankruptcy (Scotland) Act 1985, s 75(1), Sch 7, para 14(4); para (c) amended by the Insolvency Act 1985, s 235(1), Sch 8, para 31(5)(b), and the Insolvency Act 1986, s 439(2), Sch 14.

Sub-s (3): definition "personal pension scheme" added and words omitted repealed by the Social Security Act 1986, s 86, Sch 10, Pt I, para 31, Sch 11.

PART VIII

RESOLUTION OF DISPUTES RELATING TO EMPLOYMENT

Industrial tribunals

128 Industrial tribunals

(1) The Secretary of State may by regulations make provision for the establishment of tribunals, to be known as industrial tribunals, to exercise the jurisdiction conferred on them by or under this Act or any other Act, whether passed before or after this Act.

(2) Regulations made wholly or partly under section 12 of the Industrial Training Act 1964 and in force immediately before the date on which this section comes into force shall, so far as so made, continue to have effect as if they had been made under subsection (1), and tribunals established in accordance with such regulations shall continue to be known as industrial tribunals.

[(2A) Subject to the following provisions of this section, proceedings before an industrial tribunal shall be heard by—

   (a) the person who, in accordance with regulations made under subsection (1), is the chairman, and

   (b) two other members, or (with the consent of the parties) one other member, selected as the other members (or member) in accordance with regulations so made.

(2B) Subject to subsection (2F), the proceedings to which subsection (2C) applies shall be heard by the person specified in subsection (2A)(a) alone.

(2C) This subsection applies to—

   (a) proceedings on an application under section 77, 78A or 79 of this Act or under section 161, 165 or 166 of the Trade Union and Labour Relations (Consolidation) Act 1992,

   (b) proceedings on a complaint under section 124 of this Act or under section 5 of the Wages Act 1986,

   (c) proceedings in respect of which an industrial tribunal has jurisdiction by virtue of an order under section 131,

   (d) proceedings in which the parties have given their written consent to the proceedings being heard in accordance with subsection (2B) (whether or not they have subsequently withdrawn it),

   (e) proceedings in which the person bringing the proceedings has given written notice withdrawing the case, and

   (f) proceedings in which the person (or, where more than one, each of the persons) against whom the proceedings are brought does not, or has ceased to, contest the case.

(2D) The Secretary of State may by order amend the provisions of sub-section (2C).

(2E) No order shall be made under subsection (2D) unless a draft of the order has been laid before Parliament and approved by a resolution of each House of Parliament.

(2F) Proceedings to which subsection (2C) applies shall be heard in accordance with subsection (2A) if a person who, in accordance with regulations made under subsection (1), may be the chairman of an industrial tribunal, having regard to—

   (a) whether there is a likelihood of a dispute arising on the facts which makes it desirable for the proceedings to be heard in accordance with subsection (2A),

(b) whether there is a likelihood of an issue of law arising which would make it desirable for the proceedings to be heard in accordance with subsection (2B),

(c) any views of any of the parties as to whether or not the proceedings ought to be heard in accordance with either of those subsections, and

(d) whether there are other proceedings which might be heard concurrently but which are not proceedings to which subsection (2C) applies,

decides (at any stage of the proceedings) that the proceedings are to be heard in accordance with subsection (2A).]

(3) Schedule 9, which makes provision, amongst other things, with respect to proceedings before industrial tribunals, shall have effect.

(4) Complaints, references [applications] and appeals to industrial tribunals shall be made in accordance with regulations made under *paragraph 1 of* Schedule 9.

[(5) Regulations made under Schedule 9 may provide that in such circumstances as the regulations may specify any act required or authorised by the regulations to be done by an industrial tribunal may be done by the person specified in subsection (2A)(a) alone.

(6) Where a Minister of the Crown so directs in relation to any proceedings on grounds of national security, the proceedings shall be heard and determined, and any act required or authorised by regulations made under Schedule 9 to be done by an industrial tribunal in relation to the proceedings shall be done, by the President of Industrial Tribunals (England and Wales) appointed in accordance with regulations made under subsection (1), or the President of Industrial Tribunals (Scotland) so appointed, alone.]   **[375]**

NOTES

Sub-ss (2A)–(2F): inserted by the Trade Union Reform and Employment Rights Act 1993, s 36(1), (2), as from a day to be appointed.

Sub-s (4): words in square brackets added by the Employment Act 1980, s 20, Sch 1, para 16; words in italics repealed by the Trade Union Reform and Employment Rights Act 1993, s 51, Sch 10, as from a day to be appointed.

Sub-ss (5), (6): added by the Trade Union Reform and Employment Rights Act 1993, s 36(1), (3), as from a day to be appointed.

129 Remedy for infringement of certain rights under this Act

The remedy of an employee for infringement of any of the rights conferred on him by sections 8 and 53 and Parts II, III, V and VII shall, if provision is made for a complaint or for the reference of a question to an industrial tribunal, be by way of such complaint or reference and not otherwise.   **[376]**

130 Jurisdiction of referees to be exercised by tribunals

(1) There shall be referred to and determined by an industrial tribunal any question which by any statutory provision is directed (in whatsoever terms) to be determined by a referee or board of referees constituted under any of the statutory provisions specified in Schedule 10 or which is so directed to be determined in the absence of agreement to the contrary.

(2) The transfer of any jurisdiction by this section shall not affect the principles on which any question is to be determined or the persons on whom the determination

is binding, or any provision which requires particular matters to be expressly dealt with or embodied in the determination, or which relates to evidence.   **[377]**

131 Power to confer jurisdiction on industrial tribunals in respect of damages, etc, for breach of contract of employment

(1) The appropriate Minister may by order provide that on any claim to which this section applies or any such claim of a description specified in the order, being in either case a claim satisfying the relevant condition or conditions mentioned in subsection (3), proceedings for the recovery of damages or any other sum, except damages or a sum due in respect of personal injuries, may be brought before an industrial tribunal.

(2) Subject to subsection (3), this section applies to any of the following claims, that is to say—

    (a) a claim for damages for breach of a contract of employment or any other contract connected with employment;

    (b) a claim for a sum due under such a contract;

    (c) a claim for the recovery of a sum in pursuance of any enactment relating to the terms or performance of such a contract;

being in each case a claim such that a court in England and Wales or Scotland, as the case may be, would under the law for the time being in force have jurisdiction to hear and determine an action in respect of the claim.

(3) An order under this section may make provision with respect to any such claim only if it satisfies either of the following conditions, that is to say—

    (a) it arises or is outstanding on the termination of the employee's employment; or

    (b) it arises in circumstances which also give rise to proceedings already or simultaneously brought before an industrial tribunal otherwise than by virtue of this section;

or, if the order so provides, it satisfies both those conditions.

(4) Where on proceedings under this section an industrial tribunal finds that the whole or part of a sum claimed in the proceedings is due, the tribunal shall order the respondent to the proceedings to pay the amount which it finds due.

[(4A) An order under this section may provide that an industrial tribunal shall not in proceedings in respect of a claim, or a number of claims relating to the same contract, order the payment of an amount exceeding such sum as may be specified in the order as the maximum amount which a tribunal may order to be paid in relation to a claim or in relation to a contract.]

(5) Without prejudice to section 154(3), an order under this section may include provisions—

    (a) as to the manner in which and time within which proceedings are to be brought by virtue of this section; and

    (b) modifying any other enactment.

[(5A) An order under this section may make different provision in relation to proceedings in respect of different descriptions of claims.]

(6) Any jurisdiction conferred on an industrial tribunal by virtue of this section in respect of any claim shall be exercisable concurrently with any court in England

and Wales or in Scotland, as the case may be, which has jurisdiction to hear and determine an action in respect of the claim.

(7) In this section—

"appropriate Minister", as respects a claim in respect of which an action could be heard and determined in England and Wales, means the Lord Chancellor and, as respects a claim in respect of which an action could be heard and determined by a court in Scotland, means the *Secretary of State* [Lord Advocate];

"personal injuries" includes any disease and any impairment of a person's physical or mental condition;

and any reference to breach of a contract includes a reference to breach of—

(a) a term implied in a contract by or under any enactment or otherwise;

(b) a term of a contract as modified by or under any enactment or otherwise; and

(c) a term which, although not contained in a contract, is incorporated in the contract by another term of the contract.

(8) No order shall be made under this section unless a draft of the order has been laid before Parliament and approved by resolution of each House of Parliament.

[378]

NOTES

Sub-s (1): substituted by the Trade Union Reform and Employment Rights Act 1993, s 38(a), as from 30 August 1993 (SI 1993/1908, below, para [**1435**]), as follows—

"(1) The appropriate Minister may by order provide that proceedings in respect of—

(a) any claim to which this section applies, or

(b) any such claim of a description specified in the order,

may, subject to such exceptions (if any) as may be specified in the order, be brought before an industrial tribunal.".

Sub-s (3): substituted by the Trade Union Reform and Employment Rights Act 1993, s 38(b), as from 30 August 1993 (SI 1993/1908), as follows—

"(3) This section does not apply to a claim for damages, or for a sum due, in respect of personal injuries.".

Sub-ss (4A), (5A): inserted by the Trade Union Reform and Employment Rights Act 1993, s 38(c), (d), as from 30 August 1993 (SI 1993/1908).

Sub-s (7): words in italics substituted by words in square brackets immediately following, by the Trade Union Reform and Employment Rights Act 1993, s 38(e), as from 30 August 1993 (SI 1993/1908).

No order had been made under this section at the date of going to press but on 1 July 1993 the Secretary of State for Employment announced his intention that such an order would be made by 30 November 1993.

Recoupment of certain benefits

132 Recoupment of unemployment benefit and supplementary benefit

(1) This section applies to payments which are the subject of proceedings before industrial tribunals, and which are—

(a) payments of wages or compensation for loss of wages; or

(b) payments, by employers to employees, under Part II . . . or V or section [47 or] 53 . . .; or

[(bb) payments by employers to employees under sections 146 to 151 or 168 to 173 of the Trade Union and Labour Relations (Consolidation) Act 1992, or in pursuance of an award under section 192 of that Act;]

(c) payments, by employers to employees, of a nature similar to, or for a purpose corresponding to the purpose of, such payments as are mentioned in paragraph (b) [or (bb)];

and to payments of remuneration in pursuance of a protective award under [section 189 of the Trade Union and Labour Relations (Consolidation) Act 1992].

(2) The Secretary of State may by regulations make provision with respect to payments to which this section applies for all or any of the following purposes—

    (a) enabling the Secretary of State to recover from an employer, by way of total or partial recoupment of unemployment benefit or [income support], a sum not exceeding the amount of the prescribed element of the monetary award or, in the case of a protective award, the amount of the remuneration;

    (b) requiring or authorising the tribunal to order the payment of such a sum, by way of total or partial recoupment of either benefit, to the Secretary of State instead of to the employee;

    (c) requiring the tribunal to order the payment to the employee of only the excess of the prescribed element of the monetary award over the amount of any unemployment benefit or [income support] shown to the tribunal to have been paid to the employee, and enabling the Secretary of State to recover from the employer, by way of total or partial recoupment of the benefit, a sum not exceeding that amount.

(3) Without prejudice to subsection (2), regulations under that subsection may—

    (a) be so framed as to apply to all payments to which this section applies or one or more classes of those payments, and so as to apply both to unemployment benefit and [income support] or only to one of those benefits;

    (b) confer powers and impose duties on industrial tribunals, on [a benefit officer within the meaning of the Supplementary Benefits Act 1976] and on insurance officers and other persons;

    (c) impose, on an employer to whom a monetary award or protective award relates, a duty to furnish particulars connected with the award and to suspend payments in pursuance of the award during any period prescribed by the regulations;

    (d) provide for an employer who pays a sum to the Secretary of State in pursuance of this section to be relieved from any liability to pay the sum to another person;

    (e) confer on an employee [a right of appeal to a social security appeal tribunal against any decision of an adjudication officer as to the total or partial recoupment of income support in pursuance of the regulations;]

    (f) provide for the proof in proceedings before industrial tribunals (whether by certificate or in any other manner) of any amount of unemployment benefit or [income support] paid to an employee; and

    (g) make different provision for different cases.

(4) Where in pursuance of any regulations under subsection (2) a sum has been recovered by or paid to the Secretary of State by way of total or partial recoupment of unemployment benefit or [income support, no sum shall be recoverable under [Part III or V of the Social Security Administration Act 1992], and no abatement, payment or reduction shall be made by reference to the income support recouped.]

(5) Any amount found to have been duly recovered by or paid to the Secretary of State in pursuance of regulations under subsection (2) by way of total or partial recoupment of unemployment benefit shall be paid into the National Insurance Fund.

(6) In this Section—

    "monetary award" means the amount which is awarded, or ordered to be paid, to the employee by the tribunal or would be so awarded or ordered apart from any provision of regulations under this section;

    "the prescribed element", in relation to any monetary award, means so much of that award as is attributable to such matters as may be prescribed by regulations under subsection (2);

. . .

"unemployment benefit" means unemployment benefit under [the Social Security Contributions and Benefits Act 1992].   [379]

NOTES

Sub-s (1): in para (b) first words omitted repealed by the Social Security Act 1986, s 86, Sch 11, second words omitted repealed by the Trade Union and Labour Relations (Consolidation) Act 1992, s 300(1), (2), Sch 1, Sch 2, para 19(a); words in square brackets inserted by the Trade Union Reform and Employment Rights Act 1993, s 49(2), Sch 8, para 19, as from a day to be appointed; para (bb) inserted by the Trade Union and Labour Relations (Consolidation) Act 1992, s 300(2), Sch 2, para 19(b); in para (c) words in square brackets added, and words in square brackets in closing words substituted, by the Trade Union and Labour Relations (Consolidation) Act 1992, s 300(2), Sch 2, para 19(c), (d).

Sub-s (2): words in square brackets substituted by the Social Security Act 1986, s 86, Sch 10, Pt II, para 50.

Sub-s (3): words in square brackets in para (a) substituted by the Social Security Act 1986, s 86, Sch 10, Pt II, para 50; words in square brackets in paras (b), (e), (f) and first and second words in square brackets in para (e) substituted by the Social Security Act 1980, s 20, Sch 4, para 13(1).

Sub-s (4): first words in square brackets substituted by the Social Security Act 1986, s 86, Sch 10, Pt II, para 50; words in square brackets therein substituted by the Social Security (Consequential Provisions) Act 1992, s 4, Sch 2, para 50(1).

Sub-s (6): definition "supplementary benefit" repealed by the Social Security Act 1986, s 86, Sch 11; in definition "unemployment benefit" words in square brackets substituted by the Social Security (Consequential Provisions) Act 1992, s 4, Sch 2, para 50(2).

Conciliation officers

133 General provisions as to conciliation officers

(1) The provisions of subsections (2) to (6) shall have effect in relation to industrial tribunal proceedings, or claims which could be the subject of tribunal proceedings,—

   (a) arising out of a contravention, or alleged contravention, of any of the following provisions of this Act, that is to say, sections 8, 12, 19, [22A,]. . . 29, 31, [31A,] [46, 47,] . . . and 53; or

   (b) arising out of a contravention, or alleged contravention, . . . of a provision of any other Act specified by an order under subsection (7) as one to which this paragraph applies; or

   (c) which are proceedings *or claims* in respect of which an industrial tribunal has jurisdiction by virtue of an order under section 131; or

   [(d) . . .].

   [(e) arising out of a contravention, or alleged contravention, of section 1(1) or (2) or section 2(1) or 3(4) of the Wages Act 1986] [; or

   (f) . . .]

   [(g) . . .]

(2) Where a complaint has been presented to an industrial tribunal, and a copy of it has been sent to a conciliation officer, it shall be the duty of the conciliation officer—

   (a) if he is requested to do so by the complainant and by the person against whom the complaint is presented, or

   (b) if, in the absence of any such request, the conciliation officer considers that he could act under this subsection with a reasonable prospect of success,

to endeavour to promote a settlement of the complaint without its being determined by an industrial tribunal.

(3) Where at any time—

   (a) a person claims that action has been taken in respect of which a complaint could be presented by him to an industrial tribunal, but

(b) before any complaint relating to that action has been presented by him,

a request is made to a conciliation officer (whether by that person or by the person against whom the complaint could be made) to make his services available to them, the conciliation officer shall act in accordance with subsection (2) as if a complaint has been presented to an industrial tribunal.

(4) Subsections (2) and (3) shall apply, with appropriate modifications, to the presentation of a claim and the reference of a question to an industrial tribunal as they apply to the presentation of a complaint.

(5) In proceeding under subsection (2) or (3) a conciliation officer shall, where appropriate, have regard to the desirability of encouraging the use of other procedures available for the settlement of grievances.

(6) Anything communicated to a conciliation officer in connection with the performance of his functions under this section shall not be admissible in evidence in any proceedings before an industrial tribunal, except with the consent of the person who communicated it to that officer.

(7) The Secretary of State may by order—

    (a) direct that further provisions of this Act be added to the list in subsection (1)(a);

    (b) specify a provision of any other Act as one to which subsection (1)(b) applies.   **[380]**

NOTES

Sub-s (1): in para (a) first figures omitted repealed by the Trade Union and Labour Relations (Consolidation) Act 1992, s 300(1), Sch 1, and final figure omitted repealed by the Social Security Act 1986, s 86(2), Sch 11; figure "31A" inserted by the Employment Act 1980, s 20, Sch 1, para 17, and figures "22A" and "46, 47" inserted by the Trade Union Reform and Employment Rights Act 1993, s 49(2), Sch 8, para 20, partly as from a day to be appointed (SI 1993/1908); in para (b), words omitted repealed by the Trade Union and Labour Relations (Consolidation) Act 1992, s 300(1), Sch 1; in para (c), words in italics repealed by the Trade Union Reform and Employment Rights Act 1993, s 51, Sch 10, as from a day to be appointed; para (d) added by the Employment Act 1980, s 20, Sch 1, para 17, repealed by the Trade Union and Labour Relations (Consolidation) Act 1992, s 300(1), Sch 1; para (e) added by the Wages Act 1986, s 32(1), Sch 4, para 9; para (f) added by the Employment Act 1988, s 33, Sch 3, Pt I, para 2(3), repealed by the Trade Union and Labour Relations (Consolidation) Act 1992, s 300(1), Sch 1; para (g) added by the Employment Act 1990, s 3(5), Sch 1, Pt I, para 4, repealed by the Trade Union and Labour Relations (Consolidation) Act 1992, s 300(1), Sch 1.

134 Functions of conciliation officers on complaint under s 67

(1) Where a complaint has been presented to an industrial tribunal under section 67 by a person (in this section referred to as the complainant) and a copy of it has been sent to a conciliation officer, it shall be the duty of the conciliation officer—

    (a) if he is requested to do so by the complainant and by the employer against whom it was presented, or

    (b) if, in the absence of any such request, the conciliation officer considers that he could act under this section with a reasonable prospect of success,

to endeavour to promote a settlement of the complaint without its being determined by an industrial tribunal.

(2) For the purpose of promoting such a settlement, in a case where the complainant has ceased to be employed by the employer against whom the complaint was made,—

    (a) the conciliation officer shall in particular seek to promote the reinstatement or re-engagement of the complainant by the employer, or by a successor of the employer or by an associated employer, on terms appearing to the conciliation officer to be equitable; but

(b) where the complainant does not wish to be reinstated or re-engaged, or where reinstatement or re-engagement is not practicable, and the parties desire the conciliation officer to act under this section, he shall seek to promote agreement between them as to a sum by way of compensation to be paid by the employer to the complainant.

[(3) Where—

(a) a person claims that action has been taken in respect of which a complaint could be presented by him under section 67, and

(b) before any complaint relating to that action has been so presented, a request is made to a conciliation officer (whether by that person or by the employer) to make his services available to them,

the conciliation officer shall act in accordance with subsections (1) and (2) above as if a complaint had been presented.]

(4) In proceeding under subsections (1) to (3), a conciliation officer shall where appropriate have regard to the desirability of encouraging the use of other procedures available for the settlement of grievances.

(5) Anything communicated to a conciliation officer in connection with the performance of his functions under this section shall not be admissible in evidence in any proceedings before an industrial tribunal, except with the consent of the person who communicated it to that officer.   **[381]**

NOTES

Sub-s (3): substituted by the Employment Act 1980, s 20, Sch 1, para 18.

Employment Appeal Tribunal

135 Employment Appeal Tribunal

(1) The Employment Appeal Tribunal established under section 87 of the Employment Protection Act 1975 shall continue in existence by that name . . .

(2) The Employment Appeal Tribunal (in this Act referred to as "the Appeal Tribunal") shall consist of—

(a) such number of judges as may be nominated from time to time by the Lord Chancellor from among the judges (other than the Lord Chancellor) of the High Court and the Court of Appeal;

(b) at least one judge of the Court of Session nominated from time to time by the Lord President of that Court; and

(c) such number of other members as may be appointed from time to time by Her Majesty on the joint recommendation of the Lord Chancellor and the Secretary of State.

(3) The members of the Appeal Tribunal appointed under subsection (2)(c) shall be persons who appear to the Lord Chancellor and the Secretary of State to have special knowledge or experience of industrial relations, either as representatives of employers or as representatives of workers (within the meaning of [the Trade Union and Labour Relations (Consolidation) Act 1992]).

(4) The Lord Chancellor shall, after consultation with the Lord President of the Court of Session, appoint one of the judges nominated under subsection (2) to be President of the Appeal Tribunal.

(5) No judge shall be nominated a member of the Appeal Tribunal except with his consent.

(6) The provisions of Schedule 11 shall have effect with respect to the Appeal Tribunal and proceedings before the Tribunal.   **[382]**

NOTES
Sub-s (1): words omitted repealed by the Employment Act 1980, s 20, Sch 2.
Sub-s (3): words in square brackets substituted by the Trade Union and Labour Relations (Consolidation) Act 1992, s 300(2), Sch 2, para 20.

136 Appeals to Tribunal from industrial tribunals and Certification Officer

(1) An appeal shall lie to the Appeal Tribunal on a question of law arising from any decision of, or arising in any proceedings before, an industrial tribunal under, or by virtue of, the following Acts—

    (a) the Equal Pay Act 1970;
    (b) the Sex Discrimination Act 1975;
    (c) . . .;
    (d) the Race Relations Act 1976;
    (e) this Act.
    [(f) the Wages Act 1986]
    [(g) . . .]

(2), (3) . . .

(4) Without prejudice to section 13 of the Administration of Justice Act 1960 (appeal in case of contempt of court), an appeal shall lie on any question of law from any decision or order of the Appeal Tribunal with the leave of the Tribunal or of the Court of Appeal or, as the case may be, the Court of Session,—

    (a) in the case of proceedings in England and Wales, to the Court of Appeal;
    (b) in the case of proceedings in Scotland, to the Court of Session.

(5) No appeal shall lie except to the Appeal Tribunal from any decision of an industrial tribunal under the Acts listed in subsection (1) . . .   **[383]**

NOTES
Sub-s (1): para (c) repealed by the Trade Union and Labour Relations (Consolidation) Act 1992, s 300(1), Sch 1; para (f) added by the Wages Act 1986, s 32(1), Sch 4, para 10; para (g) added by the Employment Act 1990, s 3(5), Sch 1, Pt I, para 8, repealed by the Trade Union and Labour Relations (Consolidation) Act 1992, s 300(1), Sch 1.
Sub-ss (2), (3): repealed by the Trade Union and Labour Relations (Consolidation) Act 1992, s 300(1), Sch 1.
Sub-s (5): words omitted repealed by the Trade Union and Labour Relations (Consolidation) Act 1992, s 300(1), Sch 1.

[136A Restriction of vexatious proceedings

(1) If, on an application made by the Attorney General or the Lord Advocate under this section, the Appeal Tribunal is satisfied that any person has habitually and persistently and without any reasonable ground—

    (a) instituted vexatious proceedings, whether in an industrial tribunal or before the Appeal Tribunal, and whether against the same person or against different persons; or
    (b) made vexatious applications in any proceedings, whether in an industrial tribunal or before the Appeal Tribunal,

the Appeal Tribunal may, after hearing that person or giving him an opportunity of being heard, make a restriction of proceedings order.

(2) A "restriction of proceedings order" is an order that—

    (a) no proceedings shall without the leave of the Appeal Tribunal be instituted in any industrial tribunal or before the Appeal Tribunal by the person against whom the order is made;

(b) any proceedings instituted by him in any industrial tribunal or before the Appeal Tribunal before the making of the order shall not be continued by him without the leave of the Appeal Tribunal; and

(c) no application (other than one for leave under this section) shall be made by him in any proceedings in any industrial tribunal or in the Appeal Tribunal without the leave of the Appeal Tribunal.

(3) A restriction of proceedings order may provide that it is to cease to have effect at the end of a specified period, but shall otherwise remain in force indefinitely.

(4) Leave for the institution or continuance of, or for the making of an application in, any proceedings in an industrial tribunal or before the Appeal Tribunal by a person who is the subject of a restricted proceedings order shall not be given unless the Appeal Tribunal is satisfied that the proceedings or application are not an abuse of the process of the tribunal in question and that there are reasonable grounds for the proceedings or application.

(5) No appeal shall lie from a decision of the Appeal Tribunal refusing leave for the institution or continuance of, or for the making of an application in, proceedings by a person who is the subject of a restriction of proceedings order.

(6) A copy of a restriction of proceedings order shall be published in the London Gazette and in the Edinburgh Gazette.]   **[383A]**

NOTE

Inserted by the Trade Union Reform and Employment Rights Act 1993, s 42, as from a day to be appointed.

PART IX
MISCELLANEOUS AND SUPPLEMENTAL

Extension of employment protection legislation

137 Power to extend employment protection legislation

(1) Her Majesty may by Order in Council provide that—

(a) the provisions of this Act; and

(b) any legislation (that is to say any enactment of the Parliament of Northern Ireland and any provision made by or under a Measure of the Northern Ireland Assembly) for the time being in force in Northern Ireland which makes provision for purposes corresponding to any of the purposes of this Act,

shall, to such extent and for such purposes as may be specified in the Order, apply (with or without modification) to or in relation to any person in employment to which this section applies.

(2) This section applies to employment for the purposes of any activities—

(a) in the territorial waters of the United Kingdom; or

(b) connected with the exploration of the sea bed or subsoil or the exploitation of their natural resources in any area designated by order under section 1(7) of the Continental Shelf Act 1964; or

(c) connected with the exploration or exploitation, in a foreign sector of the continental shelf, of a cross-boundary petroleum field.

(3) An Order in Council under subsection (1)—

(a) may make different provision for different cases;

(b) may provide that all or any of the enactments referred to in subsection (1), as applied by such an Order, shall apply to individuals whether or not they are British subjects and to bodies corporate whether or not they are incorporated under the law of any part of the United Kingdom (notwithstanding that the application may affect their activities outside the United Kingdom);

(c) may make provision for conferring jurisdiction on any court or class of court specified in the Order, or on industrial tribunals, in respect of offences, causes of action or other matters arising in connection with employment to which this section applies;

(d) without prejudice to the generality of subsection (1) or of paragraph (a), may provide that the enactments referred to in subsection (1), as applied by the Order, shall apply in relation to any person in employment for the purposes of such activities as are referred to in subsection (2) in any part of the areas specified in paragraphs (a) and (b) of that subsection;

(e) may exclude from the operation of section 3 of the Territorial Waters Jurisdiction Act 1878 (consents required for prosecutions) proceedings for offences under the enactments referred to in subsection (1) in connection with employment to which this section applies;

(f) may provide that such proceedings shall not be brought without such consent as may be required by the Order;

(g) may, without prejudice to the generality of the power under subsection (1) to modify the enactments referred to in that subsection in their application for the purposes of this section, modify or exclude the operation of sections 141 and 144 or paragraph 14 of Schedule 13 or of any corresponding provision in any such Northern Irish legislation as is referred to in subsection (1)(b).

(4) Any jurisdiction conferred on any court or tribunal under this section shall be without prejudice to jurisdiction exercisable apart from this section by that or any other court or tribunal.

(5) In subsection (2) above—

"cross-boundary petroleum field" means a petroleum field that extends across the boundary between a designated area and a foreign sector of the continental shelf;

"foreign sector of the continental shelf" means an area which is outside the territorial waters of any State and within which rights are exercisable by a State other than the United Kingdom with respect to the sea bed and subsoil and their natural resources;

"petroleum field" means a geological structure identified as an oil or gas field by the Order in Council concerned. [384]

NOTES

Sub-s (2): substituted by the Oil and Gas (Enterprise) Act 1982, s 37, Sch 3, para 40 (as substituted by the Trade Union and Labour Relations (Consolidation) Act 1992, s 300(2), Sch 2, para 29(1), (2)), as from a day to be appointed, as follows—

"(2) This section applies to employment for the purposes of—

(a) any activities in the territorial waters of the United Kingdom, and

(b) any such activities as are mentioned in section 23(2) of the Oil and Gas (Enterprise) Act 1982 in waters within subsection (6)(b) or (c) of that section.".

Sub-s (5): repealed by the Oil and Gas (Enterprise) Act 1982, s 37, Sch 3, para 40, Sch 4, as from a day to be appointed.

The powers under this section have been exercised by the Employment Protection (Offshore Employment) Order 1976, SI 1976/766, as amended by SI 1977/588, SI 1981/208.

Crown employment

138 Application of Act to Crown employment

(1) Subject to the following provisions of this section, Parts I *(so far as it relates to itemised pay statements)*, II, III . . ., V, VIII and this Part and section 53 shall have effect in relation to Crown employment and to persons in Crown employment as they have effect in relation to other employment and to other employees.

(2) In this section, *subject to subsections (3) to (5)*, "Crown employment" means employment under or for the purposes of a government department or any officer or body exercising on behalf of the Crown functions conferred by any enactment.

(3) This section does not apply to service as a member of the naval, military or air forces of the Crown . . ., but does apply to employment by any association established for the purposes of [Part VI of the Reserve Forces Act 1980].

(4) *For the purposes of this section, Crown employment does not include any employment* [Part I (so far as it relates to itemised pay statements), Part II (except sections 22A to 22C and 31A), section 53 (apart from subsection (2A)), Part V (except so far as relating to a dismissal which is regarded as unfair by reason of section 57A, 59(1)(a) or 60) and Part VIII and this Part (so far as relating to any of those provisions) shall not have effect in relation to any Crown employment] in respect of which there is in force a certificate issued by or on behalf of a Minister of the Crown certifying that employment of a description specified in the certificate, or the employment of a particular person so specified, is (or, at a time specified in the certificate, was) required to be excepted from this section for the purpose of safeguarding national security; and any document purporting to be a certificate so issued shall be received in evidence and shall, unless the contrary is proved, be deemed to be such a certificate.

(5) . . .

(6) For the purposes of the application of the provisions of this Act in relation to employment by any such body as is referred to in subsection (5), any reference to redundancy shall be construed as a reference to the existence of such circumstances as, in accordance with any arrangements for the time being in force as mentioned in section 111(3), are treated as equivalent to redundancy in relation to such employment.

(7) For the purposes of the application of the provisions of this Act in relation to Crown employment in accordance with subsection (1)—

(a) any reference to an employee shall be construed as a reference to a person in Crown employment;

(b) any reference to a contract of employment shall be construed as a reference to the terms of employment of a person in Crown employment;

(c) any reference to dismissal shall be construed as a reference to the termination of Crown employment;

(d) any reference to redundancy shall be construed as a reference to the existence of such circumstances as, in accordance with any arrangements for the time being in force as mentioned in section 111(3), are treated as equivalent to redundancy in relation to Crown employment;

(e) the reference in paragraph 1(5)(c) of Schedule 9 to a person's undertaking or any undertaking in which he works shall be construed as a reference to the national interest; and

(f) any other reference to an undertaking shall be construed, in relation to a Minister of the Crown, as a reference to his functions or (as the context may require) to the department of which he is in charge and, in relation to a government department, officer or body, shall be construed as a reference to the functions of the department, officer or body or (as the context may require) to the department, officer or body.

(8) Where the terms of employment of a person in Crown employment restrict his right to take part in—

(a) certain political activities; or

(b) activities which may conflict with his official functions,

nothing in section 29 shall require him to be allowed time off work for public duties connected with any such activities.   **[385]**

NOTES

Sub-s (1): words in italics repealed by the Trade Union Reform and Employment Rights Act 1993, ss 49(1), 51, Sch 7, para 3(a), Sch 10, as from a day to be appointed; words omitted repealed by the Social Security Act 1986, s 86, Sch 11.

Sub-s (2): words in italics repealed by the Trade Union Reform and Employment Rights Act 1993, s 51, Sch 10, as from a day to be appointed.

Sub-s (3): substituted by the Trade Union Reform and Employment Rights Act 1993, s 31(1), as from a day to be appointed, as follows—

"(3) This section applies to service as a member of the naval, military or air forces of the Crown but only in accordance with section 138A and it applies also to employment by any association established for the purposes of Part VI of the Reserve Forces Act 1980.".

Sub-s (4): words in italics substituted by words in square brackets immediately following, by the Trade Union Reform and Employment Rights Act 1993, s 49(1), Sch 7, para 3(b) as from a day to be appointed.

Sub-s (5): repealed by the National Health Service and Community Care Act 1990, s 66(2), Sch 10.

[138A Application of Act to armed forces

(1) The provisions of this Act which apply, by virtue of section 138, to service as a member of the naval, military or air forces of the Crown are—

Part I;

in Part II, sections 19 to 22 and 31A;

Part III;

in Part IV, section 53;

Part V, except sections 57A and 80;

Part VIII; and

this Part.

(2) Her Majesty may, by Order in Council,—

(a) amend subsection (1) above by making additions to, or omissions from, the provisions for the time being specified in that subsection by an Order under this subsection; and

(b) make any provision apply to service as a member of the naval, military or air forces of the Crown subject to such exceptions and modifications as may be specified in the Order.

(3) Subject to subsection (5) below, modifications made under subsection (2) above may include provision precluding the making of a complaint or reference to any industrial tribunal unless the person aggrieved has availed himself of the service procedures for the redress of complaints applicable to him.

(4) Where modifications include the provision authorised by subsection (3) above the Order in Council shall also include provision designed to secure that the service procedures for the redress of complaints result in a determination, or what is to be treated under the Order as a determination, in sufficient time to enable a complaint or reference to be made to an industrial tribunal.

(5) No provision shall be made by virtue of subsection (3) above which has the effect of substituting, for any period specified as the normal period for a complaint or reference on any matter to an industrial tribunal, a period longer than six months.

(6) No recommendation shall be made to Her Majesty to make an Order in Council under subsection (2) above unless a draft of the Order has been laid before Parliament and approved by a resolution of each House of Parliament.

(7) In this section—

"the normal period for a complaint or reference", in relation to any matter within the jurisdiction of an industrial tribunal, means the period specified in the relevant enactment as the period within which the complaint or reference must be made, disregarding any provision permitting an extension of that period at the discretion of the tribunal; and

"the service procedures for the redress of complaints" means the procedures, excluding those which relate to the making of a report on a complaint to Her Majesty, referred to in sections 180 and 181 of the. Army Act 1955, sections 180 and 181 of the Air Force Act 1955 and section 130 of the Naval Discipline Act 1957.] [385A]

NOTE

Inserted by the Trade Union Reform and Employment Rights Act 1993, s 31(2), as from a day to be appointed.

House of Commons staff

139 Provisions as to House of Commons staff

(1) The provisions of Parts I *(so far as it relates to itemised pay statements)*, II, III . . ., V and VIII, and this Part and section 53 shall apply to relevant members of House of Commons staff as they apply to persons in Crown employment within the meaning of section 138 and accordingly for the purposes of the application of those provisions in relation to any such members—

(a) any reference to an employee shall be construed as a reference to any such member;

(b) any reference to a contract of employment shall be construed as including a reference to the terms of employment of any such member;

(c) any reference to dismissal shall be construed as including a reference to the termination of any such member's employment;

(d) the reference in paragraph 1(5)(c) of Schedule 9 to a person's undertaking or any undertaking in which he works shall be construed as a reference to the national interest or, if the case so requires, the interests of the House of Commons; and

(e) any other reference to an undertaking shall be construed as a reference to the House of Commons.

(2) Nothing in any rule of law or the law or practice of Parliament shall prevent a relevant member of the House of Commons staff from bringing a civil employment claim before the court or from bringing before an industrial tribunal proceedings of any description which could be brought before such a tribunal by any person who is not such a member.

(3) In this section—

"relevant member of the House of Commons staff" means—

(a) any person appointed by the House of Commons Commission (in this section referred to as the Commission) or employed in the refreshment department; and

(b) any member of Mr Speaker's personal staff;

"civil employment claim" means a claim arising out of or relating to a contract of employment or any other contract connected with employment, or a claim in tort arising in connection with a person's employment; and

"the court" means the High Court or the county court.

(4) It is hereby declared that for the purposes of the enactments applied by subsection (1) and of Part VI (where applicable to relevant members of House of Commons staff) and for the purposes of any civil employment claim—

(a) the Commission is the employer of staff appointed by the Commission; and

(b) Mr. Speaker is the employer of his personal staff and of any person employed in the refreshment department and not falling within paragraph (a);

but the foregoing provision shall have effect subject to subsection (5).

(5) The Commission or, as the case may be, Mr Speaker may designate for all or any of the purposes mentioned in subsection (4)—

(a) any description of staff other than Mr Speaker's personal staff; and

(b) in relation to staff so designated, any person;

and where a person is so designated he, instead of the Commission or Mr. Speaker, shall be deemed for the purposes to which the designation relates to be the employer of the persons in relation to whom he is so designated.

(6) Where any proceedings are brought by virtue of this section against the Commission or Mr Speaker or any person designated under subsection (5), the person against whom the proceedings are brought may apply to the court or the industrial tribunal, as the case may be, to have some other person against whom the proceedings could at the time of the application be properly brought substituted for him as a party to those proceedings.

(7) For the purposes mentioned in subsection (4) a person's employment in or for the purposes of the House of Commons shall not, provided he continues to be employed in such employment, be treated as terminated by reason only of a change (whether effected before or after the passing of the House of Commons (Administration) Act 1978, and whether effected by virtue of that Act or otherwise) in his employer and (provided he so continues) his first appointment to such employment shall be deemed after the change to have been made by his employer for the time being, and accordingly—

(a) he shall be treated for the purposes so mentioned as being continuously employed by that employer from the commencement of such employment until its termination; and

(b) anything done by or in relation to his employer for the time being in respect of such employment before the change shall be so treated as having been done by or in relation to the person who is his employer for the time being after the change.

(8) In subsection (7) "employer for the time being", in relation to a person who has ceased to be employed in or for the purposes of the House of Commons, means the person who was his employer immediately before he ceased to be so employed, except that where some other person would have been his employer for the time being if he had not ceased to be so employed, it means that other person.

(9) If the House of Commons resolves at any time that any provision of subsections (3) to (6) should be amended in its application to any member of the staff

of that House, Her Majesty may by Order in Council amend that provision accordingly.   **[386]**

NOTES

Sub-s (1): words in italics repealed by the Trade Union Reform and Employment Rights Act 1993, s 51, Sch 10, as from a day to be appointed; words omitted repealed by the Social Security Act 1986, s 86, Sch 11.

[House of Lords staff

139A Provisions as to House of Lords staff

(1) The provisions of Parts I, II, III, V and VIII, and this Part and section 53 shall apply in relation to employment as a relevant member of the House of Lords staff as they apply to other employment.

(2) Nothing in any rule of law or the law or practice of Parliament shall prevent a relevant member of the House of Lords staff from bringing a civil employment claim before the court or from bringing before an industrial tribunal proceedings of any description which could be brought before such a tribunal by a person who is not such a member.

(3) For the purposes of the application of the enactments applied by subsection (1) in relation to a relevant member of the House of Lords staff—

(a) the reference in paragraph 1(5)(c) of Schedule 9 to a person's undertaking or any undertaking in which he works shall be construed as a reference to the national interest or, if the case so requires, the interests of the House of Lords; and

(b) any other reference to an undertaking shall be construed as a reference to the House of Lords.

(4) Where the terms of his contract of employment restrict the right of a relevant member of the House of Lords staff to take part in—

(a) certain political activities, or

(b) activities which may conflict with his official functions,

nothing in section 29 shall require him to be allowed time off work for public duties connected with any such activities.

(5) In this section—

"relevant member of the House of Lords staff" means any person who is employed under a contract of employment with the Corporate Officer of the House of Lords;

"civil employment claim" means a claim arising out of or relating to a contract of employment or any other contract connected with employment, or a claim in tort arising in connection with a person's employment; and

"the court" means the High Court or the county court.

(6) For the purposes of the application of the enactments applied by subsection (1) and of any civil employment claim in relation to a person continuously employed in or for the purposes of the House of Lords up to the time when he became so employed under a contract of employment with the Corporate Officer of the House of Lords, his employment shall not be treated as having been terminated by reason only of a change in his employer before or at that time.]   **[386A]**

NOTE

This section and the cross-heading immediately preceding it inserted by the Trade Union Reform and Employment Rights Act 1993, s 49(1), Sch 7, para 11, as from a day to be appointed.

Contracting out of provisions of Act

140 Restrictions on contracting out

(1) Except as provided by the following provisions of this section, any provision in an agreement (whether a contract of employment or not) shall be void in so far as it purports—

    (a) to exclude or limit the operation of any provision of this Act or;

    (b) to preclude any person from presenting a complaint to, or bringing any proceedings under this Act before, an industrial tribunal.

(2) Subsection (1) shall not apply—

    (a) to any provision in a collective agreement excluding rights under section 12 if an order under section 18 is for the time being in force in respect of it;

    (b) . . .

    (c) to any provision in a dismissal procedures agreement excluding rights under section 54 if that provision is not to have effect unless an order under section 65 is for the time being in force in respect of it;

    (d) to any agreement to refrain from presenting a complaint under section 67, where in compliance with a request under section 134(3) a conciliation officer has taken action in accordance with that subsection;

    (e) to any agreement to refrain from proceeding with a complaint presented under section 67 where a conciliation officer has taken action in accordance with section 134(1) and (2);

    (f) to any provision in an agreement if an order under section 96 is for the time being in force in respect of it;

    [(fa) to any agreement to refrain from instituting or continuing any proceedings before an industrial tribunal where the tribunal has jurisdiction in respect of the proceedings by virtue of an order under section 131;]

    [(fb) to any agreement to refrain from instituting or continuing any proceedings specified in section 133(1) (except (c)) or 134(1) before an industrial tribunal if the conditions regulating compromise agreements under this Act are satisfied in relation to the agreement.]

    (g) to any agreement to refrain from instituting or continuing any proceedings before an industrial tribunal where a conciliation officer has taken action in accordance with section 133(2) or (3);

    (h) to any provision of an agreement relating to dismissal from employment such as is mentioned in section 142(1) or (2).

[(3) The conditions regulating compromise agreements under this Act are that—

    (a) the agreement must be in writing;

    (b) the agreement must relate to the particular complaint;

    (c) the employee must have received independent legal advice from a qualified lawyer as to the terms and effect of the proposed agreement and in particular its effect on his ability to pursue his rights before an industrial tribunal;

    (d) there must be in force, when the adviser gives the advice, a policy of insurance covering the risk of a claim by the employee in respect of loss arising in consequence of the advice;

    (e) the agreement must identify the adviser; and

    (f) the agreement must state that the conditions regulating compromise agreements under this Act are satisfied.

(4) In subsection (3)—

"independent", in relation to legal advice to the employee, means that it is given by a lawyer who is not acting in the matter for the employer or an associated employer; and

"qualified lawyer" means—

    (a) as respects proceedings in England and Wales—

        (i) a barrister, whether in practice as such or employed to give legal advice, or

        (ii) a solicitor of the Supreme Court who holds a practising certificate;

    (b) as respects proceedings in Scotland—

        (i) an advocate, whether in practice as such or employed to give legal advice, or

        (ii) a solicitor who holds a practising certificate.]   **[387]**

NOTES

Sub-s (2): para (b) repealed by the Employment Act 1980, s 20, Sch 1, para 20, Sch 2; para (fa) inserted by the Trade Union Reform and Employment Rights Act 1993, s 49(2), Sch 8, para 21, as from 30 August 1993 (SI 1993/1908); para (fb) inserted by *ibid*, s 39(1)(a), as from 30 August 1993 (SI 1993/1908).

Sub-ss (3), (4): added by the Trade Union Reform and Employment Rights Act 1993, s 39(1)(b), as from 30 August 1993 (SI 1993/1908).

Excluded classes of employment

141 Employment outside Great Britain

(1) Sections 1 to 4 and 49 to 51 do not apply in relation to employment during any period when the employee is engaged in work wholly or mainly outside Great Britain *unless the employee ordinarily works in Great Britain and the work outside Great Britain is for the same employer.*

(2) Sections 8 and 53 and Parts II, III [and V] do not apply to employment where under his contract of employment the employee ordinarily works outside Great Britain.

[(2A) Part VII does not apply to employment where under his contract of employment the employee ordinarily works outside the territory of the Member States of the European Communities.]

(3) An employee shall not be entitled to a redundancy payment if on the relevant date he is outside Great Britain, unless under his contract of employment he ordinarily worked in Great Britain.

(4) An employee who under his contract of employment ordinarily works outside Great Britain shall not be entitled to a redundancy payment unless on the relevant date he is in Great Britain in accordance with instructions given to him by his employer.

(5) For the purpose of subsection (2), a person employed to work on board a ship registered in the United Kingdom (not being a ship registered at a port outside Great Britain) shall, unless—

    (a) the employment is wholly outside Great Britain, or

    (b) he is not ordinarily resident in Great Britain,

be regarded as a person who under his contract ordinarily works in Great Britain.

[388]

NOTES
Sub-s (1): words in italics substituted by the Trade Union Reform and Employment Rights Act 1993,
s 49(2), Sch 8, para 22, as from a day to be appointed, as follows—
"unless—
   (a)   the employee ordinarily works in Great Britain and the work outside Great Britain is for the
          same employer, or
   (b)   the law which governs his contract of employment is the law of England and Wales or of
          Scotland".
Sub-s (2): words in square brackets substituted by the Insolvency of Employer (Excluded Classes)
Regulations 1983, SI 1983/624, reg 3(1). These regulations give effect to EC Directive 80/987 (below,
paras [2153]–[2157]) so far as not previously implemented.
Sub-s (2A): added by SI 1983/624, reg 3(2).

---

142 Contracts for a fixed term

(1) Section 54 does not apply to dismissal from employment under a contract for a
fixed term of [one year] or more, where the dismissal consists only of the expiry of
that term without its being renewed, if before the term so expires the employee has
agreed in writing to exclude any claim in respect of rights under that section in relation
to that contract.

(2) An employee employed under a contract of employment for a fixed term of
two years or more entered into after 5th December 1965 shall not be entitled to a
redundancy payment in respect of the expiry of that term without its being renewed
(whether by the employer or by an associated employer of his), if before the term so
expires he has agreed in writing to exclude any right to a redundancy payment in that
event.

(3) Such an agreement as is mentioned in subsection (1) or (2) may be contained
either in the contract itself or in a separate agreement.

(4) Where an agreement under subsection (2) is made during the currency of a
fixed term, and that term is renewed, the agreement under that subsection shall not
be construed as applying to the term as renewed, but without prejudice to the making
of a further agreement under that subsection in relation to the term so renewed.
[389]

NOTE
Sub-s (1): words in square brackets substituted by the Employment Act 1980, s 8(2).

---

143 *(Repealed by the Employment Act 1982, s 21(3), Sch 4.)*

144 Mariners

(1) Sections 1 to 6 and 49 to 51 do not apply to—
   (a)   a person employed as a master of or a seaman on a sea-going British ship
          having a gross registered tonnage of eighty tons or more, including a
          person ordinarily employed as a seaman who is employed in or about such
          a ship in port by the owner or charterer of the ship to do work of a kind
          ordinarily done by a seaman on such a ship while it is in port, or
   (b)   a person employed as a skipper of or a seaman on a fishing boat for the
          time being [registered under Part II of the Merchant Shipping Act 1988]
          [under the Merchant Shipping (Registration, etc) Act 1993].

(2) Sections 8 and 53 and Parts II, III and V to VII do not apply to employment
as master or as a member of the crew of a fishing vessel where the employee is
remunerated only by a share in the profits or gross earnings of the vessel.

(3) Section 141(3) and (4) do not apply to an employee, and section 142(2) does not apply to a contract of employment, if the employee is employed as a master or seaman in a British ship and is ordinarily resident in Great Britain.

(4) Sections 8, 29, 31, 122 and 123 do not apply to employment as a merchant seaman.

(5) Employment as a merchant seaman does not include employment in the fishing industry or employment on board a ship otherwise than by the owner, manager or charterer of that ship except employment as a radio officer, but, save as aforesaid, it includes employment as master or a member of the crew of any ship and as a trainee undergoing training for the sea service, and employment in or about a ship in port by the owner, manager or charterer of the ship to do work of the kind ordinarily done by a merchant seaman on a ship while it is in port. **[390]**

NOTE
Sub-s (1): first words in square brackets substituted by the Merchant Shipping Act 1988, s 57(4), Sch 6 and further substituted by words in second square brackets by the Merchant Shipping (Registration, etc) Act 1993, s 8(1), Sch 2, para 11, as from a day to be appointed; substituted by the Trade Union Reform and Employment Rights Act 1993, s 49(2), Sch 8, para 23, as from a day to be appointed, as follows—
"(1) Sections 1 to 4 and 49 to 51 do not apply to a person employed as a seaman in a ship registered in the United Kingdom under a crew agreement the provisions and form of which are of a kind approved by the Secretary of State.".

145 *(Repealed by the Dock Work Act 1989, s 7(1), Sch 1, Pt I.)*

146 Miscellaneous classes of employment

(1) . . .

(2) Parts II, III [and V] and sections 8, 9, 53 and 86 do not apply to employment under a contract of employment in police service or to persons engaged in such employment.

(3) In subsection (2), "police service" means service—

    (a) as a member of any constabulary maintained by virtue of any enactment, or

    (b) in any other capacity by virtue of which a person has the powers or privileges of a constable.

(4) Subject to subsection (5), (6) and (7), the following provisions of this Act (which confer rights which do not depend upon an employee having a qualifying period of continuous employment) do not apply to employment under a contract which normally involves employment for less than sixteen hours weekly, that is to say, sections [*1, 4,*] 8, . . . and 29.

[(4A) Subject to subsection (4B), subsection (4) shall have effect as respects section 8 subject to the following modifications, namely—

    (a) the substitution of a reference to eight hours weekly for the reference to sixteen hours weekly, and

    (b) the omission of the words "Subject to subsections (5), (6) and (7)".

(4B) Subsection (4A) shall not apply in relation to employment if, at the relevant date, the number of employees employed by the employer, added to the number employed by any associated employer, is less than twenty.

(4C) For the purposes of subsection (4B) "relevant date" means the date on which any payment of wages or salary is made to an employee in respect of which he would, apart from subsection (4B), have the right to an itemised pay statement.]

(5) If the employee's relations with his employer cease to be governed by a contract which normally involves work for sixteen hours or more weekly and become governed by a contract which normally involves employment for eight hours or more, but less than sixteen hours, weekly, the employee shall nevertheless for a period of twenty-six weeks, computed in accordance with subsection (6), be treated for the purposes of subsection (4) as if his contract normally involved employment for sixteen hours or more weekly.

(6) In computing the said period of twenty-six weeks no account shall be taken of any week—

    (a) during which the employee is in fact employed for sixteen hours or more;

    (b) during which the employee takes part in a strike (as defined by paragraph 24 of Schedule 13) or is absent from work because of a lock-out (as so defined) by his employer; or

    (c) during which there is no contract of employment but which, by virtue of paragraph 9(1) of Schedule 13, counts in computing a period of continuous employment.

(7) An employee whose relations with his employer are governed by a contract of employment which normally involves employment for eight hours or more, but less than sixteen hours, weekly shall nevertheless, if he has been continuously employed for a period of five years or more be treated for the purposes of subsection (4) as if his contract normally involved employment for sixteen hours or more weekly.

[(8) References in subsections (4) to (7) to weeks are to weeks within the meaning of Schedule 13.]   **[391]**

NOTES

    Sub-s (1): repealed by the Employment Act 1982, s 21, Sch 3, Pt I, para 6, Sch 4.

    Sub-s (2): words in square brackets substituted by the Insolvency of Employer (Excluded Classes) Regulations 1983, SI 1983/624, reg 3(3).

    Sub-s (4): figures in square brackets inserted by the Employment Act 1982, s 20, Sch 2, para 8(5)(a); figures omitted repealed by the Trade Union and Labour Relations (Consolidation) Act 1992, s 300(1), Sch 1; figures in italics repealed by the Trade Union Reform and Employment Rights Act 1993, s 51, Sch 10, as from a day to be appointed.

    Sub-ss (4A)–(4C): inserted by the Trade Union Reform and Employment Rights Act 1993, s 27, as from a day to be appointed.

    Sub-s (8): added by the Employment Act 1982, s 20, Sch 2, para 8(5)(b).

[146A National Security

(1) Where in the opinion of any Minister of the Crown the disclosure of any information would be contrary to the interests of national security—

    (a) nothing in any of the provisions to which this section applies shall require any person to disclose the information, and

    (b) no person shall disclose the information in any proceedings in any court or tribunal relating to any of those provisions.

(2) This section applies to—

    (a) Part I so far as it relates to employment particulars,

    (b) sections 22A to 22C and section 31A,

    (c) Part III,

    (d) section 53(2A),

    (e) Part V so far as relating to a dismissal which is regarded as unfair by reason of section 57A, 59(1)(a) or 60, and

    (f) Part VIII and this Part so far as relating to any of the provisions in paragraphs (a) to (e).]   **[391A]**

NOTE
Inserted by the Trade Union Reform and Employment Rights Act 1993, s 49(1), Sch 7, para 5, as from
a day to be appointed.

147 *(Repealed by the Employment Act 1982, s 21(3), Sch 4.)*

Supplementary provisions

148 Review of limits

(1) The Secretary of State shall in each calendar year review—

    (a) the limits referred to in section 15;

    (b) the limit referred to in section 122(5); and

    (c) the limits imposed by paragraph 8(1) of Schedule 14 on the amount of a week's pay for the purposes of those provisions;

and shall determine whether any of those limits should be varied.

(2) In making a review under this section the Secretary of State shall consider—

    (a) the general level of earnings obtaining in Great Britain at the time of the review;

    (b) the national economic situation as a whole; and

    (c) such other matters as he thinks relevant.

(3) If on a review under this section the Secretary of State determines that, having regard to the considerations mentioned in subsection (2), any of those limits should be varied, he shall prepare and lay before each House of Parliament the draft of an order giving effect to his decision.

(4) Where a draft of an order under this section is approved by resolution of each House of Parliament the Secretary of State shall make an order in the form of the draft.

(5) If, following the completion of an annual review under this section, the Secretary of State determines that any of the limits referred to in subsection (1) shall not be varied, he shall lay before each House of Parliament a report containing a statement of his reasons for that determination.

(6) The Secretary of State may at any time, in addition to the annual review provided for in subsection (1), conduct a further review of the limits mentioned in subsection (1) so as to determine whether any of those limits should be varied, and subsections (2) to (4) shall apply to such a review as if it were a review under subsection (1). [392]

NOTE
    The powers under this section have been exercised by annual Employment Protection (Variation of Limits) Orders the effect of which is noted at ss 15 and 122 above and Sch 14 below. No order was made for 1993.

149 General power to amend Act

(1) Subject to the following provisions of this section, the Secretary of State may by order—

    (a) provide that any enactment contained in this Act which is specified in the order shall not apply to persons or to employments of such classes as may be prescribed in the order;

(b) provide that any such enactment shall apply to persons or employments of such classes as may be prescribed in the order subject, except in relation to section 54 (but without prejudice to paragraph (a)), to such exceptions and modifications as may be so prescribed;

(c) vary, or exclude the operation of, any of the following provisions of this Act, that is to say, sections [13(2), 20(2), 49(4A), [53(2)],] 64(1), [*64A(1)*], 99, 141(2) and (5), . . ., 144(1), (2), (4) and (5), . . . and 146 . . . (4) to (7);

(d) . . .

(2) Subsection (1) does not apply to the following provisions of this Act, namely, sections . . . 52, 55, 57, [57A,] . . ., 59, 62, 63, 65, 66, 67, [73(6C) and (6D),] [. . ., 75,] [75A(7) and (8),] 80, 103 to 120, 128, 134, 141(1) [,142(1) and 151] and Schedules 3, 9 and 13, and, in addition, paragraph (b) of subsection (1) does not apply to section 1 to 6 and 49 to 51 . . .

[(2A) The Secretary of State may by order provide that, subject to any such modifications and exceptions as may be prescribed in the order, sections 22A to 22C (and any other provisions of this Act so far as relating to those sections) shall apply to such descriptions of persons other than employees as may be prescribed in the order as they apply to employees (but as if references to their employer were references to such person as may be so prescribed).]

(3) The provisions of this section are without prejudice to any other power of the Secretary of State to amend, vary or repeal any provision of this Act or to extend or restrict its operation in relation to any person or employment.

(4) No order under *subsection (1)* [this section, other than one to which subsection (5) applies] shall be made unless a draft of the order has been laid before Parliament and approved by a resolution of each House of Parliament.

[(5) This subsection applies to an order under subsection (1)(b) which specifies only provisions contained in Part VI.]   **[393]**

NOTES

Sub-s (1): in para (c), first figures in square brackets added by the Employment Act 1982, s 20, Sch 2, para 9(1)(a), figure in square brackets therein added with savings by the Employment Act 1989, ss 15(2), 29(6), Sch 9, final figure in square brackets added by the Employment Act 1980, s 20, Sch 1, para 21; second figures omitted repealed by the Dock Work Act 1989, s 7(1), Sch 1, Pt I, other figures omitted repealed by the Employment Act 1982, s 21(3), Sch 4; figures in italics repealed by the Trade Union Reform and Employment Rights Act 1993, s 51, Sch 10, as from 30 August 1993 (SI 1993/1908, below, para [**1435**]); para (d) repealed by the National Health Service and Community Care Act 1990, s 66(2), Sch 10.

Sub-s (2): first and final figures omitted repealed and figures in square brackets added, by the Employment Act 1982, ss 20, 21, Sch 2, para 9(1)(b), Sch 3, Pt II, para 25, Sch 4; other figures omitted (which were added in part by the Employment Act 1980, s 20, Sch 1, para 21) repealed by the Trade Union and Labour Relations (Consolidation) Act 1992, s 300(1), Sch 1; figures "57A,", "73(6C) and (6D),", "75A(7) and (8)," inserted by the Trade Union Reform and Employment Rights Act 1993, s 49(2), Sch 8, para 24, as from 30 August 1993 (SI 1993/1908).

Sub-s (2A): inserted by the Trade Union Reform and Employment Rights Act 1993, s 49(1), Sch 7, para 13, as from 30 August 1993 (SI 1993/1908).

Sub-s (4): words in italics substituted by words in square brackets immediately following, by the Trade Union Reform and Employment Rights Act 1993, s 49(1), Sch 7, para 16(a), as from 30 August 1993 (SI 1993/1908).

Sub-s (5): added by the Trade Union Reform and Employment Rights Act 1993, s 49(1), Sch 7, para 16(b), as from 30 August 1993 (SI 1993/1908).

Orders under this section are the Redundancy Payments (Local Government) (Modification) Order 1983, SI 1983/1160, as amended by SI 1985/1872, SI 1988/907, SI 1989/532, SI 1990/826, SI 1991/818; the Employment Protection (Employment in Aided Schools) Order 1981, SI 1981/847 (disapplying ss 56A and 64A in certain circumstances); and orders amending s 64 above (see note to that section for details).

150 Death of employee or employer

Schedule 12 shall have effect for the purpose of supplementing and modifying the provisions of Part I (so far as it relates to itemised pay statements), section 53 and Parts II, III and V to VII as respects the death of an employee or employer.   **[394]**

[151 Computation of period of continuous employment

(1) References in any provision of this Act to a period of continuous employment are, except where provision is expressly made to the contrary, to a period computed in accordance with the provisions of this section and Schedule 13; and in any such provision which refers to a period of continuous employment expressed in months or years a month means a calendar month and a year means a year of twelve calendar months.

(2) In computing an employee's period of continuous employment any question arising as to—

(a) whether the employee's employment is of a kind counting towards a period of continuous employment, or

(b) whether periods (consecutive or otherwise) are to be treated as forming a single period of continuous employment,

shall be determined in accordance with Schedule 13 (that is to say, week by week), but the length of an employee's period of employment shall be computed in months and years of twelve months in accordance with the following rules.

(3) Subject to the following provisions of this section, an employee's period of continuous employment for the purposes of any provision of this Act begins with the day on which he starts work and ends with the day by reference to which the length of his period of continuous employment falls to be ascertained for the purposes of the provision in question.

(4) For the purposes of section 81 and Schedule 4 an employee's period of continuous employment shall be treated as beginning on his eighteenth birthday if that date is later than the starting date referred to in subsection (3).

(5) If an employee's period of continuous employment includes one or more periods which, by virtue of any provision of Schedule 13, do not count in computing the length of the period but do not break continuity, the beginning of the period shall be treated as postponed by the number of days falling within that intervening period or, as the case may be, by the aggregate number of days falling within those periods.

(6) The number of days falling within such an intervening period is—

(a) in the case of a period to which paragraph 14(3) of Schedule 13 applies, seven days for each week within that sub-paragraph;

(b) in the case of a period to which paragraph 15(2) or (4) of that Schedule applies, the number of days between the last working day before the strike or lock-out and the day on which work was resumed;

(c) in the case of a period to which paragraph 16(1) of that Schedule applies, the number of days between the employee's last day of employment before service under Part I of the National Service Act 1948 and the day on which he resumed employment in accordance with Part II of that Act.]   **[395]**

NOTE

Substituted with savings by the Employment Act 1982, s 20, Sch 2, para 7(1).

152 Calculation of normal working hours and a week's pay

Schedule 14 shall have effect for the purposes of this Act for calculating the normal working hours and the amount of a week's pay of any employee.   **[396]**

153 Interpretation

(1) In this Act, except so far as the context otherwise requires—

"act" and "action" each includes omission and references to doing an act or taking action shall be construed accordingly;

"business" includes a trade or profession and includes any activity carried on by a body of persons, whether corporate or unincorporate;

["childbirth" means the birth of a living child or the birth of a child whether living or dead after twenty-four weeks of pregnancy;]

. . .

"collective agreement" has the meaning given by [section 178(1) and (2) of the Trade Union and Labour Relations (Consolidation) Act 1992];

"confinement" means the birth of a living child or the birth of a child whether living or dead after twenty-eight weeks of pregnancy;

"contract of employment" means a contract of service or apprenticeship, whether express or implied, and (if it is express) whether it is oral or in writing;

"dismissal procedures agreement" means an agreement in writing with respect to procedures relating to dismissal made by or on behalf of one or more independent trade unions and one or more employers or employers' associations;

"effective date of termination" has the meaning given by section 55(4) [to (6)];

"employee" means an individual who has entered into or works under (or, where the employment has ceased, worked under) a contract of employment;

"employer", in relation to an employee, means the person by whom the employee is (or, in a case where the employment has ceased, was) employed;

"employers' association" has the same meaning as it has for the purposes of [the Trade Union and Labour Relations (Consolidation) Act 1992];

["employer's payment" has the meaning given by section 106(1A) and (1B);]

"employment", except for purposes of sections 111 to 115, means employment under a contract of employment;

["expected week of childbirth" means the week, beginning with midnight between Saturday and Sunday, in which it is expected that childbirth will occur;]

"expected week of confinement" means the week, beginning with midnight between Saturday and Sunday, in which it is expected that confinement will take place;

"government department", except in section 138 and paragraph 19 of Schedule 13, includes a Minister of the Crown;

"guarantee payment" has the meaning given by section 12(1);

. . .

"independent trade union" means a trade union which—

(a) is not under the domination or control of an employer or a group of employers or of one or more employers' associations; and

(b) is not liable to interference by an employer or any such group or association (arising out of the provision of financial or material support or by any other means whatsoever) tending towards such control;

and, in relation to a trade union, "independent" and "independence" shall be construed accordingly;

"job", in relation to an employee, means the nature of the work which he is employed to do in accordance with his contract and the capacity and place in which he is so employed;

["maternity leave period" shall be construed in accordance with sections 34 and 35;]
. . .
"notice of intention to claim" has the meaning given by section 88;

"notified day of return" *has the meaning given by section 47(1) and (8)* [shall be construed in accordance with section 43(3) and (4)];

["notified leave date" shall be construed in accordance with section 36;]

"official", in relation to a trade union, has [the same meaning as in the Trade Union and Labour Relations (Consolidation) Act 1992];

"original contract of employment", in relation to an employee who is absent from work wholly or partly because of pregnancy or confinement, means the contract under which she worked immediately before the beginning of her absence or, if she entered into that contract during her pregnancy by virtue of section 60(2) or otherwise by reason of her pregnancy, the contract under which she was employed immediately before she entered into the later contract or, if there was more than one later contract, the first of the later contracts;

"position", in relation to an employee, means the following matters taken as a whole, that is to say, his status as an employee, the nature of his work and his terms and conditions of employment;
. . .
"redundancy payment" has the meaning given by section 81(1);

"redundancy rebate" has the meaning given by section 104;

"relevant date", for the purposes of the provisions of this Act which relate to redundancy payments, has the meaning given by section 90;

"renewal" includes extension, and any reference to renewing a contract or a fixed term shall be construed accordingly;

"statutory provision" means a provision, whether of a general or a special nature, contained in, or in any document made or issued under, any Act, whether of a general or special nature;

["successor", in relation to the employer of an employee, means (subject to subsection (4A) below) a person who in consequence of a change occurring (whether by virtue of a sale or other disposition or by operation of law) in the ownership of the undertaking or of part of the undertaking for the purposes of which the employee was employed, has become the owner of the undertaking or of that part of it, as the case may be;]

"trade dispute" has the meaning given by [section 244 of the Trade Union and Labour Relations (Consolidation) Act 1992];

"trade union" has the meaning given by [section 1 of the Trade Union and Labour Relations (Consolidation) Act 1992]
. . .
"week" means, in relation to an employee whose remuneration is calculated weekly by a week ending with a day other than Saturday, a week ending with that other day, and in relation to any other employee, a week ending with Saturday.

(2) References in this Act to dismissal by reason of redundancy, and to cognate expressions, shall be construed in accordance with section 81.

(3) In sections 33, 47, 56, 61 and 86 and Schedule 2, except where the context otherwise requires, "to return to work" means to return to work in accordance with section 45(1), and cognate expressions shall be construed accordingly.

(4) For the purposes of this Act, any two employers are to be treated as associated if one is a company of which the other (directly or indirectly) has control, or if both are companies of which a third person (directly or indirectly) has control; and the expression "associated employer" shall be construed accordingly.

[(4A) The definition of "successor" in subsection (1) above has effect (subject to the necessary modifications) in relation to a case where—

(a) the person by whom an undertaking or part of an undertaking is owned immediately before a change is one of the persons by whom (whether as partners, trustees or otherwise) it is owned immediately after the change, or

(b) the persons by whom an undertaking or part of an undertaking is owned immediately before a change (whether as partners, trustees or otherwise) include the persons by whom, or include one or more of the persons by whom, it is owned immediately after the change,

as it has effect where the previous owner and the new owner are wholly different persons.]

(5) *For* [Subject to section 14(1)(b), for] the purposes of this Act it is immaterial whether the law which (apart from this Act) governs any person's employment is the law of the United Kingdom, or of a part of the United Kingdom, or not.

(6) In this Act, except where otherwise indicated—

(a) a reference to a numbered Part, section or Schedule is a reference to the Part or section of, or the Schedule to, this Act so numbered, and

(b) a reference in a section to a numbered subsection is a reference to the subsection of that section so numbered, and

(c) a reference in a section, subsection or Schedule to a numbered paragraph is a reference to the paragraph of that section, subsection or Schedule so numbered, and

(d) a reference to any provision of an Act (including this Act) includes a Schedule incorporated in the Act by that provision.

(7) Except so far as the context otherwise requires, any reference in this Act to an enactment shall be construed as a reference to that enactment as amended or extended by or under any other enactment, including this Act.   **[397]**

NOTES

Sub-s (1): definition "certified midwife" repealed by the Nurses, Midwives and Health Visitors Act 1979, s 23(5), Sch 8; in definitions "collective agreement", "employers' association", "official", "trade dispute" and "trade union" words in square brackets substituted, and definition "successor" substituted, by the Trade Union and Labour Relations (Consolidation) Act 1992, s 300(2), Sch 2, para 21(1), (2); in definition "effective date of termination" words in square brackets substituted by the Employment Act 1982, s 21, Sch 3, Pt II, para 26; definition "employer's payment" substituted by the Employment Act 1989, s 29(3), Sch 6, para 24; definition "inadmissible reason" repealed by the Employment Act 1982, s 21, Sch 4; definitions "maternity pay", "Maternity Pay Fund" and "maternity pay rebate" repealed by the Social Security Act 1986, s 86(2), Sch 11; definition "Redundancy fund" repealed by the Employment Act 1990, s 16(2), Sch 3; definition "redundancy rebate" repealed by the Employment Act 1989, s 29(4), Sch 7, Pt II; in definition "trade union" words omitted repealed by the Employment Act 1988, s 33, Sch 4; definitions "childbirth", "expected week of childbirth", "maternity leave period" and "notified leave date" inserted, in definition "notified day of return" words in italics substituted by words in square brackets immediately following, and definitions "confinement", "expected week of confinement" and "original contract of employment" repealed, by the Trade Union Reform and Employment Rights Act 1993, ss 49(2), 51, Sch 8, para 25(a), Sch 10, as from a day to be appointed.

Sub-s (3): repealed by the Trade Union Reform and Employment Rights Act 1993, s 51, Sch 10, as from a day to be appointed.

Sub-s (4A): added by the Trade Union and Labour Relations (Consolidation) Act 1992, s 300(2), Sch 2, para 21(1), (3).

Sub-s (5): words in italics substituted by words in square brackets immediately following, by the Trade Union Reform and Employment Rights Act 1993, s 49(2), Sch 8, para 25(b), as from a day to be appointed.

154 Orders, rules and regulations

(1) Any power conferred by any provision of this Act to make an order (other than an Order in Council . . .) or to make rules or regulations shall be exercisable by statutory instrument.

(2) Any statutory instrument made under any power conferred by this Act to make an Order in Council or other order or to make rules or regulations, except—

(a) an instrument required to be laid before Parliament in draft; and
(b) an order under section 18,

shall be subject to annulment in pursuance of a resolution of either House of Parliament.

(3) Any power conferred by this Act which is exercisable by statutory instrument shall include power to make such incidental, supplementary or transitional provisions as appear to the authority exercising the power to be necessary or expedient.

(4) An order made by statutory instrument under any provision of this Act may be revoked or varied by a subsequent order made under that provision.

This subsection does not apply to an order under [section 65, 66 or 96].   **[398]**

NOTES
Sub-ss (1), (4): words omitted from sub-s(1) repealed and words in square brackets in sub-s(4) substituted by the Employment Act 1980, s 20, Sch 1, para 22, Sch 2.

155 Offences by bodies corporate

(1) Where an offence under section . . . 126 committed by a body corporate is proved to have been committed with the consent or connivance of, or to be attributable to any neglect on the part of, any director, manager, secretary or other similar officer of the body corporate, or any person who was purporting to act in any such capacity, he as well as the body corporate shall be guilty of that offence and shall be liable to be proceeded against and punished accordingly.

(2) Where the affairs of a body corporate are managed by its members, subsection (1) shall apply in relation to the acts and defaults of a member in connection with his functions of management as if he were a director of the body corporate.   **[399]**

NOTES
Sub-s (1): words omitted repealed by the Social Security Act 1986, s 86, Sch 11.

156 Payments into the Consolidated Fund

(1) . . .

(2) There shall be paid out of [the National Insurance Fund] into the Consolidated Fund sums equal to the amount of any expenses incurred—

(a) by the Secretary of State in consequence of Part VI, except expenses incurred in the payment of sums in accordance with any such arrangements as are mentioned in section 111(3);
(b) by the Secretary of State (or by persons acting on his behalf) in exercising his functions under section 122 to 126.

(3) There shall be paid out of [the National Insurance Fund] into the Consolidated Fund such sums as the Secretary of State may estimate in accordance with directions given by the Treasury to be the amount of any expenses incurred by any government department other than the Secretary of State in consequence of the provisions of sections 103 to 109.   **[400]**

NOTES
Sub-s (1): repealed by the Social Security Act 1986, s 86, Sch 11.
Sub-ss (2), (3): words in square brackets substituted by the Employment Act 1990, s 16(1), Sch 2, para 1(5).

157, 158 *(Provide for matters connected with the application of the provisions of this Act to Northern Ireland and the Isle of Man and are omitted.)*

159 Transitional provisions, savings, consequential amendments and repeals

(1) The transitional provisions and savings in Schedule 15 shall have effect but nothing in that Schedule shall be construed as prejudicing section 38 of the Interpretation Act 1889 (effect of repeals).

(2), (3) ...   **[401]**

NOTE
Sub-ss (2), (3): provide for the amendment and repeal of other Acts.

[402]

160 Citation, commencement and extent

(1) This Act may be cited as the Employment Protection (Consolidation) Act 1978.

(2) This Act, except section 139(2) to (9) and the repeals in section 122 of the Employment Protection Act 1975 provided for in Schedule 17 to this Act, shall come into force on 1st November 1978, and section 139(2) to (9) and those repeals shall come into force on 1st January 1979.

(3) This Act, except sections 137 and 157 and paragraphs 12 and 28 of Schedule 16, shall not extend to Northern Ireland.

SCHEDULES

SCHEDULE 1

Section 19

PROVISIONS LEADING TO SUSPENSION ON MEDICAL GROUNDS

1.–16.	...	...	
[17.	The Control of Lead at Work Regulations 1980	SI 1980/1248	Reg 16]
[18.	The Ionising Radiations Regulations 1985	SI 1985/1333	Reg 16]
[19.	The Control of Substances Hazardous to Health Regulations 1988	SI 1988/1657	Reg 11]

[403]

SCHEDULE 2

Section 33

SUPPLEMENTARY PROVISIONS RELATING TO MATERNITY

PART I
UNFAIR DISMISSAL

Introductory

1 References in this Part to provisions of this Act relating to unfair dismissal are references to those provisions as they apply by virtue of section 56.   [**404**]

Adaptation of unfair dismissal provisions

2 (1) Section 57 shall have effect as if for subsection (3) there were substituted the following subsection:—

"(3) Where the employer has fulfilled the requirements of subsection (1), then, [subject to *sections 59 to 61* [sections 57A to 61], and to sections 152, 153 and 238 of the Trade Union and Labour Relations (Consolidation) Act 1992 (provisions as to dismissal on ground of trade union membership or activities or in connection with industrial action)], the determination of the question whether the dismissal was fair or unfair, having regard to the reason shown by the employer, shall depend on whether [in the circumstances (including the size and administrative resources of the employer's undertaking) the employer would have been acting reasonably or unreasonably in treating it as a sufficient reason for dismissing the employee if she had not been absent from work; and that question shall be determined in accordance with equity and the substantial merits of the case].".

(2) If in the circumstances described in *section 45(3)* [section 41(1)] no offer is made of such alternative employment as is referred to in that subsection, then the dismissal which by virtue of section 56 is treated as taking place shall, notwithstanding anything in section 57 . . ., be treated as an unfair dismissal for the purposes of Part V of this Act.

(3) The following references shall be construed as references to the notified day of return, that is to say—

(a) references in Part V of this Act to the effective date of termination;
(b) references in sections 69 and 70 to the date of termination of employment.

(4) The following provisions of this Act shall not apply, that is to say, sections 55, . . ., 64(1), 65, 66, 73(5) and (6), 141(2), 142(1), [and 144(2)], paragraph 11(1) of Schedule 13, paragraphs 7(1)(f) to (i) and (2) and 8(3) of Schedule 14 and paragraph 10 of Schedule 15.

(5) For the purposes of Part II of Schedule 14 as it applies for the calculation of a week's pay for the purposes of section 71 or 73, the calculation date is the last day on which the employee worked under *the original contract of employment* [her contract of employment immediately before the beginning of her maternity leave period].

Sch 8, para 26(a)(i), as from 30 August 1993 (SI 1993/1908); in sub-para (2) words omitted repealed by the Trade Union and Labour Relations (Consolidation) Act 1992, s 300(1), Sch 1; and words in italics substituted by words in square brackets immediately following by the Trade Union Reform and Employment Rights Act 1993, s 49(2), Sch 8, para 26(a)(ii), as from a day to be appointed; in sub-para (4), words omitted repealed by the Trade Union and Labour Relations (Consolidation) Act 1992, s 300(1), Sch 1; and words in square brackets substituted by the Dock Work Act 1989, s 7(4); in sub-para (5), words in italics substituted by words in square brackets immediately following by the Trade Union Reform and Employment Rights Act 1993, s 49(2), Sch 8, para 26(a)(iii), as from a day to be appointed.

PART II
REDUNDANCY PAYMENTS

Introductory

3 References in this Part to provisions of this Act relating to redundancy are references to those provisions as they apply by virtue of section 86. **[405]**

Adaptation of redundancy payments provisions

4 (1) References in Part VI of this Act shall be adapted as follows, that is to say—

(a) references to the relevant date, wherever they occur, shall be construed, except where the context otherwise requires, as references to the notified day of return;

(b) references in sections 82(4) and 84(1) to a renewal or re-engagement taking effect immediately on the ending of employment under the previous contract or after an interval of not more than four weeks thereafter, shall be construed as references to a renewal or re-engagement taking effect on the notified day of return or not more than four weeks after that day; and

(c) references in section 84(3) to the provisions of the previous contract shall be construed as references to the provisions of the original contract of employment.

(2) Nothing in section 86 shall prevent an employee from being treated, by reason of the operation of section 84(1), as not having been dismissed for the purposes of Part VI of this Act.

(3) The following provisions of this Act shall not apply, that is to say, sections 81(1)(b), 82(1) and (2), 83(1) and (2), 85, 87 to 89, 90(3), 92, 93, 96, 110, 144(2) . . . and 150, paragraph 4 of Schedule 4, Schedule 12 and paragraphs 7(1)(j) and (k) and 8(4) of Schedule 14.

(4) For the purposes of Part II of Schedule 14 as it applies for the calculation of a week's pay for the purposes of Schedule 4, the calculation date is the last day on which the employee worked under *the original contract of employment* [her contract of employment immediately before the beginning of her maternity leave period]. **[405A]**

Prior redundancy

5 If, in proceedings arising out of a failure to permit an employee to return to work [in accordance with section 42], the employer shows—

(a) that the reason for the failure is that the employee is redundant; and

(b) that the employee was dismissed or, had she continued to be employed by him, would have been dismissed, by reason of redundancy *during her absence on a day earlier than the notified day of return and falling after the beginning of the eleventh week before the expected week of confinement* [on a day falling after the commencement of her maternity leave period and before the notified day of return],

then, for the purposes of Part VI of this Act the employee—

(i) shall not be treated as having been dismissed with effect from the notified day of return; but

(ii) shall, if she would not otherwise be so treated, be treated as having been continuously employed until that earlier day and as having been dismissed by reason of redundancy with effect from that day. **[405B]**

NOTES

Para 4: sub-para (1)(c) substituted by the Trade Union Reform and Employment Rights Act 1993, s 49(2), Sch 8, para 26(b)(i), as from a day to be appointed, as follows—
"(c) the reference in section 84(3) to the provisions of the previous contract shall be construed as a reference to the provisions of the contract under which the employee worked immediately before the beginning of her maternity leave period.";
figures omitted from sub-para (3) repealed by the Employment Act 1982, s 21, Sch 4; words in italics in sub-para (4) substituted by words in square brackets immediately following by the Trade Union Reform and Employment Rights Act 1993, s 49(2), Sch 8, para 26(b)(ii), as from a day to be appointed.

Para 5: words in square brackets inserted, and words in italics substituted by words in square brackets immediately following by the Trade Union Reform and Employment Rights Act 1993, s 49(2), Sch 8, para 26(c), as from a day to be appointed.

PART III

GENERAL

Dismissal during period of absence

6 *(1) This paragraph applies to the dismissal of an employee who is under this Act entitled to return to work and whose contract of employment continues to subsist during the period of her absence but who is dismissed by her employer during that period after the beginning of the eleventh week before the expected week of confinement.*

(2) For the purposes of sub-paragraph (1), an employee shall not be taken to be dismissed *during the period of her absence* [after her maternity leave period] if the dismissal occurs in the course of the employee's attempting to return to work in accordance with her contract in circumstances in which *section 48* [section 44] applies.

(3) In the application of Part V of this Act to a dismissal to which this paragraph applies, the following provisions shall not apply, that is to say, sections . . ., 64, 65, 66, 141(2), [and 144(2)].

(4) Any such dismissal shall not affect the employee's right to return to work, but—
   (a) compensation in any unfair dismissal proceedings arising out of that dismissal shall be assessed without regard to the employee's right to return; and
   (b) that right shall be exercisable only on her repaying any redundancy payment or compensation for unfair dismissal paid in respect of that dismissal, if the employer requests such repayment.   [406]

Power to amend or modify

7 (1) The Secretary of State may by order amend the provisions of this Schedule and *section 48* [section 44] or modify the application of those provisions to any description of case.

(2) No order under this paragraph shall be made unless a draft of the order has been laid before Parliament and approved by a resolution of each House of Parliament.   [406]

NOTE

Para 6: sub-para (1) substituted by the Trade Union Reform and Employment Rights Act 1993, s 49(2), Sch 8, para 26(d)(i), as from a day to be appointed, as follows—
"(1) This paragraph applies where an employee has the right to return to work under section 39 and either her maternity leave period ends by reason of dismissal or she is dismissed after her maternity leave period.";
in sub-para (2), words in italics substituted by the words in square brackets immediately following in each case, by the Trade Union Reform and Employment Rights Act 1993, s 49(2), Sch 8, para 26(d)(ii), as from a day to be appointed; words omitted repealed by the Trade Union and Labour Relations (Consolidation) Act 1992, s 300(1), Sch 1; words in square brackets substituted by the Dock Work Act 1989, s 7(4).

Para 7: words in italics substituted by words in square brackets immediately following, by the Trade Union Reform and Employment Rights Act 1993, s 49(2), Sch 8, para 26(e), as from a day to be appointed.

SCHEDULE 3

Section 50

RIGHTS OF EMPLOYEE IN PERIOD OF NOTICE

Preliminary

1 In this Schedule the "period of notice" means the period of notice required by section 49(1) or, as the case may be, section 49(2).

Employments for which there are normal working hours

2 (1) If an employee has normal working hours under the contract of employment in force during the period of notice, and if during any part of those normal working hours—

(a) the employee is ready and willing to work but no work is provided for him by his employer; or

(b) the employee is incapable of work because of sickness or injury; or

[(ba) the employee is absent from work wholly or partly because of pregnancy or childbirth; or]

(c) the employee is absent from work in accordance with the terms of his employment relating to holidays,

then the employer shall be liable to pay the employee for the part of normal working hours covered by paragraphs (a), (b) [, (ba)] and (c) a sum not less than the amount of remuneration for that part of normal working hours calculated at the average hourly rate of remuneration produced by dividing a week's pay by the number of normal working hours.

(2) Any payments made to the employee by his employer in respect of the relevant part of the period of notice whether by way of sick pay [statutory sick pay], [maternity pay, statutory maternity pay,] holiday pay or otherwise, shall go towards meeting the employer's liability under this paragraph.

(3) Where notice was given by the employee, the employer's liability under this paragraph shall not arise unless and until the employee leaves the service of the employer in pursuance of the notice.

Employments for which there are no normal working hours

3 (1) If an employee does not have normal working hours under the contract of employment in force in the period of notice the employer shall be liable to pay the employee for each week of the period of notice a sum not less than a week's pay.

(2) Subject to sub-paragraph (3), the employer's obligation under this paragraph shall be conditional on the employee being ready and willing to do work of a reasonable nature and amount to earn a week's pay.

(3) Sub-paragraph (2) shall not apply—

(a) in respect of any period during which the employee is incapable of work because of sickness or injury, or

[(aa) in respect of any period during which the employee is absent from work wholly or partly because of pregnancy or childbirth, or]

(b) in respect of any period during which the employee is absent from work in accordance with the terms of his employment relating to holidays,

and any payment made to an employee by his employer in respect of such a period, whether by way of sick pay [statutory sick pay], [maternity pay, statutory maternity pay,] holiday pay or otherwise, shall be taken into account for the purposes of this paragraph as if it were remuneration paid by the employer in respect of that period.

(4) Where the notice was given by the employee, the employer's liability under this paragraph shall not arise unless and until the employee leaves the service of the employer in pursuance of the notice.

Sickness or industrial injury benefit

4 (1) The following provisions of this paragraph shall have effect where the arrangements in force relating to the employment are such that—

(a) payments by way of sick pay are made by the employer to employees to whom the arrangements apply, in cases where any such employees are incapable of work because of sickness or injury, and

(b) in calculating any payment so made to any such employee an amount representing, or treated as representing, sickness benefit or industrial injury benefit is taken into account, whether by way of deduction or by way of calculating the payment as a supplement to that amount.

(2) If during any part of the period of notice the employee is incapable of work because of sickness or injury, and—

(a) one or more payments, by way of sick pay are made to him by the employer in respect of that part of the period of notice, and

(b) in calculating any such payment such an amount as is referred to in sub-paragraph (1)(b) is taken into account as therein mentioned,

then for the purposes of this Schedule the amount so taken into account shall be treated as having been paid by the employer to the employee by way of sick pay in respect of that part of that period, and shall go towards meeting the liability of the employer under paragraph 2 or paragraph 3 accordingly.

Absence on leave granted at request of employee

5 The employer shall not be liable under the foregoing provisions of this Schedule to make any payment in respect of a period during which the employee is absent from work with the leave of the employer granted at the request of the employee (including any period of time off taken in accordance with [section 29, 31 or 31A of this Act or section 168 or 170 of the Trade Union and Labour Relations (Consolidation) Act 1992].

Notice given before a strike

6 No payment shall be due under this Schedule in consequence of a notice to terminate a contract given by an employee if, after the notice is given and on or before the termination of the contract, the employee takes part in a strike of employees of the employer.

In this paragraph "strike" has the meaning given by paragraph 24 of Schedule 13.

Termination of employment during period of notice

7 (1) If, during the period of notice, the employer breaks the contract of employment, payments received under this Schedule in respect of the part of the period after the breach shall go towards mitigating the damages recoverable by the employee for loss of earnings in the part of the period of notice.

(2) If, during the period of notice, the employee breaks the contract and the employer rightfully treats the breach as terminating the contract, no payment shall be due to the employee under this Schedule in respect of the part of the period of notice falling after the termination of the contract.　　　　　　　　　　　　　　　　　　　　　　　　　　　　　　　　**[407]**

NOTES

Paras 2, 3: words "statutory sick pay" inserted by the Social Security and Housing Benefits Act 1982, s 10, Sch 2, para 12; paras 2(1)(ba), 3(3)(aa) and other words in square brackets inserted by the Trade Union Reform and Employment Rights Act 1993, s 49(2), Sch 8, para 27, as from a day to be appointed.

Para 5: words in square brackets substituted by the Trade Union and Labour Relations (Consolidation) Act 1992, s 300(2), Sch 2, para 23.

SCHEDULE 4

Section 81

CALCULATION OF REDUNDANCY PAYMENTS

1 The amount of a redundancy payment to which an employee is entitled in any case shall, subject to the following provisions of this Schedule, be calculated by reference to the period, ending with the relevant date, during which he has been continuously employed.

2 Subject to paragraphs 3 and 4, the amount of the redundancy payment shall be calculated by reference to the period specified in paragraph 1 by starting at the end of that period and reckoning backwards the number of years of employment falling within that period, and allowing—

    (a)   one and a half weeks' pay for each such year of employment . . . in which the employee was not below the age of forty-one;

    (b)   one week's pay for each such year of employment (not falling within the preceding sub-paragraph) . . . in which the employee was not below the age of twenty-two; and

    (c)   half a week's pay for each such year of employment not falling within either of the preceding sub-paragraphs.

3 Where, in reckoning the number of years of employment in accordance with paragraph 2, twenty years of employment have been reckoned, no account shall be taken of any year of employment earlier than those twenty years.

4 (1) Where in the case of an employee the relevant date is after the specified anniversary, the amount of the redundancy payment, calculated in accordance with the preceding provisions of this Schedule, shall be reduced by the appropriate fraction.

(2) In this paragraph ["the specified anniversary", in relation to an employee, means the sixty-fourth anniversary of the day of his birth,] and "the appropriate fraction" means the fraction of which—

    (a)   the numerator is the number of whole months, reckoned from the specified anniversary, in the period beginning with that anniversary and ending with the relevant date, and

    (b)   the denominator is twelve.

5 For the purposes of any provision contained in Part VI whereby an industrial tribunal may determine that an employer shall be liable to pay to an employee either—

    (a)   the whole of the redundancy payment to which the employee would have been entitled apart from another provision therein mentioned, or

    (b)   such part of that redundancy payment as the tribunal thinks fit,

the preceding provisions of this Schedule shall apply as if in those provisions any reference to the amount of a redundancy payment were a reference to the amount of the redundancy payment to which the employee would have been so entitled.

6 The preceding provisions of this Schedule shall have effect without prejudice to the operation of any regulations made under section 98 whereby the amount of a redundancy payment, or part of a redundancy payment, may be reduced.

7 . . .   **[408]**

NOTES

    Para 2: words omitted repealed by the Employment Act 1982, ss 20, 21(3), Sch 2, para 6(5)(a), Sch 4.

    Para 4: words in square brackets substituted with savings by the Employment Act 1989, ss 16(2), 29(6), Sch 9.

    Para 7: repealed by the Employment Act 1982, ss 20, 21(3), Sch 2, para 6(5)(b), Sch 4.

    Modified by the Land Authority for Wales (Compensation for Premature Retirement) Regulations 1984, SI 1984/2048; the Local Government Reorganisation (Compensation) Regulations 1986, SI 1986/151, regs 3, 4, Sch 1, Pt II; and the Education (Reorganisation in Inner London) (Compensation) Regulations 1989, SI 1989/1139, regs 3(6), 4(4), (6), (8), Schedule, Pt III.

(Sch 5 repealed by the National Health Service and Community Care Act 1990, s 66(2), Sch 10; Sch 6 repealed by the Employment Act 1989, s 17(b), 29(4), Sch 7, Pt II.)

SCHEDULE 7

Section 106

CALCULATION OF PAYMENTS TO EMPLOYEES OUT OF REDUNDANCY FUND

1 (1) Where the employer's payment is a redundancy payment, the sum referred to in section 106(2) is a sum equal to the amount of that payment.

(2) Where, in a case falling within [section 106(1B)], the employer's payment is part of a redundancy payment, the sum referred to in section 106(2) is a sum equal to the amount of that part of the payment.

[**2** (1) Where the employer's payment is not a redundancy payment or part of a redundancy payment, the sum referred to in section 106(2) is a sum equal to—

    (a) the amount of the employer's payment, or

    (b) the amount of the relevant redundancy payment,

whichever is less.

(2) The reference in sub-paragraph (1)(b) to the amount of the relevant redundancy payment is a reference to the amount of the redundancy payment which the employer would have been liable to pay to the employee if—

    (a) the order in force in respect of the agreement as mentioned in section 106(1A)(b) had not been made;

    (b) the circumstances in which the employer's payment is payable had been such that the employer was liable to pay a redundancy payment to the employee in those circumstances;

    (c) the relevant date, in relation to any such redundancy payment, had been the date on which the termination of the employee's contract of employment is treated for the purposes of the agreement as having taken effect; and

    (d) in so far as the provisions of the agreement which relate to the following matters, that is to say—

        (i) the circumstances in which the continuity of an employee's period of employment is to be treated as broken, and

        (ii) the weeks which are to count in computing a period of employment,

    are inconsistent with the provisions of Schedule 13 as to those matters, those provisions of the agreement were substituted for those provisions of that Schedule.

(3) In sub-paragraph (2) "the agreement" means the agreement falling within section 106(1A)(b) by reference to which the employer's payment is payable.] **[409]**

NOTE

Para 1 amended and para 2 substituted by the Employment Act 1989, s 29(3), Sch 6, para 25(3).

SCHEDULE 8

Section 117

EMPLOYEES PAID BY VIRTUE OF STATUTORY PROVISION BY PERSON OTHER THAN EMPLOYER

Provision of Act	*Reference to be construed as reference to the person responsible for paying the remuneration*
Section 81(1)	The second reference to the employer.
Section 85(3)	The reference to the employer in paragraph(b).
Section 85(4)	The last reference to the employer.
Section 88(4)	The reference to the employer.
Section 89(1)	The first reference to the employer.
Section 89(4) and (5)	The references to the employer.
Section 92(3)	The second reference to the employer.
Section 98(3)	The reference to the employer.
Section 101(1)	The reference to the employer
Section 102	The references to the employer.
. . .	
Section 106	The references to the employer.
Section 107(1)	The reference to the employer.

Section 108(1)......................................The references to the employer.
Section 110(2)......................................The third reference to the employer.
Section 110(5) and (6) ....The reference to the employer.
Schedule 13, paragraph 12(3) ....The references to the employer.

[410]

NOTE

Reference to s 104 and s 108(2), (4) and (5) repealed by the Employment Act 1989, s 29(4), (6), Sch 7, Pt II, Sch 9.

SCHEDULE 9

Section 128

INDUSTRIAL TRIBUNALS

Regulations as to tribunal procedure

1 (1) The Secretary of State may by regulations (in this Schedule referred to as "the regulations") make such provision as appears to him to be necessary or expedient with respect to proceedings before industrial tribunals.

(2) The regulations may in particular include provision—

(a) for determining by which tribunal any appeal, question or complaint is to be determined;

(b) for enabling an industrial tribunal to hear and determine proceedings brought by virtue of section 131 concurrently with proceedings brought before the tribunal otherwise than by virtue of that section;

(c) for treating the Secretary of State (either generally or in such circumstances as may be prescribed by the regulations) as a party to any proceedings before an industrial tribunal, where he would not otherwise be a party to them, and entitling him to appear and to be heard accordingly;

(d) for requiring persons to attend to give evidence and produce documents, and for authorising the administration of oaths to witnesses;

[(e) for enabling an industrial tribunal, on the application of any party to proceedings before it or of its own motion, to order—

(i) in England and Wales, such discovery or inspection of documents, or the furnishing of such further particulars, as might be ordered by a county court on an application by a party to proceedings before it; or

(ii) in Scotland, such recovery or inspection of documents as might be ordered by the sheriff;]

(f) for prescribing the procedure to be followed on any appeal, reference or complaint or other proceedings before an industrial tribunal, including provisions as to the persons entitled to appear and to be heard on behalf of parties to such proceedings, and provisions for enabling an industrial tribunal to review its decisions, and revoke or vary its orders and awards, in such circumstances as may be determined in accordance with the regulations;

(g) for the appointment of one or more assessors for the purposes of any proceedings before an industrial tribunal, where the proceedings are brought under an enactment which provides for one or more assessors to be appointed;

[(ga) for authorising an industrial tribunal to require persons to furnish information and produce documents to a person required for the purposes of section 2A(1)(b) of the Equal Pay Act 1970 to prepare a report;]

(h) for the award of costs or expenses, including any allowances payable under paragraph 10 other than allowances payable to members of industrial tribunals or assessors;

(i) for taxing or otherwise settling any such costs or expenses (and, in particular, in England and Wales, for enabling such costs to be taxed in the county court); and

(j) for the registration and proof of decisions, orders and awards of industrial tribunals.

(3) In relation to proceedings on complaints under section 67 or any other enactment in relation to which there is provision for conciliation, the regulations shall include provision—

(a) for requiring a copy of any such complaint, and a copy of any notice relating to it which is lodged by or on behalf of the employer against whom the complaint is made, to be sent to a conciliation officer;

(b)   for securing that the complainant and the employer against whom the complaint is made are notified that the services of a conciliation officer are available to them; and

(c)   for postponing the hearing of any such complaint for such period as may be determined in accordance with the regulations for the purpose of giving an opportunity for the complaint to be settled by way of conciliation and withdrawn.

(4)   In relation to proceedings under section 67—

(a)   where the employee has expressed a wish to be reinstated or re-engaged which has been communicated to the employer at least seven days before the hearing of the complaint; or

(b)   where the proceedings arise out of the employer's failure to permit the employee to return to work after an absence due to pregnancy or *confinement* [childbirth].

regulations shall include provision for requiring the employer to pay the costs or expenses of any postponement or adjournment of the hearing caused by his failure, without a special reason, to adduce reasonable evidence as to the availability of the job from which the complainant was dismissed, or, as the case may be, which she held before her absence, or of comparable or suitable employment.

[(4A)   Without prejudice to sub-paragraph (5) or paragraph 2, a Minister of the Crown may on grounds of national security direct an industrial tribunal to sit in private when hearing or determining any proceedings specified in the direction.]

(5)   Without prejudice to paragraph 2, the regulations may enable an industrial tribunal to sit in private for the purpose of hearing evidence which in the opinion of the tribunal relates to matters of such a nature that it would be against the interests of national security to allow the evidence to be given in public or of hearing evidence from any person which in the opinion of the tribunal is likely to consist of—

(a)   information which he could not disclose without contravening a prohibition imposed by or under any enactment; or

(b)   any information which has been communicated to him in confidence, or which he has otherwise obtained in consequence of the confidence reposed in him by another person; or

(c)   information the disclosure of which would, for reasons other than its effect on negotiations with respect to any of the matters mentioned in section 29(1) of the Trade Union and Labour Relations Act 1974 (matters to which trade disputes relate) cause substantial injury to any undertaking of his or in which he works.

[(5A)   The regulations may include provision—

(a)   for cases involving allegations of the commission of sexual offences, for securing that the registration or other making available of documents or decisions shall be so effected as to prevent the identification of any person affected by or making the allegation;

(b)   for cases involving allegations of sexual misconduct, enabling an industrial tribunal, on the application of any party to proceedings before it or of its own motion, to make a restricted reporting order having effect (if not revoked earlier) until the promulgation of the decision of the tribunal.

In this sub-paragraph—

"identifying matter", in relation to a person, means any matter likely to lead members of the public to identify him as a person affected by, or as the person making, the allegation;

"restricted reporting order" means an order prohibiting the publication in Great Britain of identifying matter in a written publication available to the public or its inclusion in a relevant programme for reception in Great Britain;

"sexual misconduct" means the commission of a sexual offence, sexual harassment or other adverse conduct (of whatever nature) related to sex, and conduct is related to sex whether the relationship with sex lies in the character of the conduct or in its having reference to the sex or sexual orientation of the person at whom the conduct is directed;

"sexual offence" means any offence to which section 141A(2) of the Criminal Procedure (Scotland) Act 1975, section 4 of the Sexual Offences (Amendment) Act 1976 or the Sexual Offences (Amendment) Act 1992 applies (offences under the Sexual Offences Act 1956, the Sexual Offences (Scotland) Act 1976 and certain other enactments);

and "written publication" and "relevant programme" have the same meaning as in that Act of 1992.]

(6) The regulations may include provision authorising or requiring an industrial tribunal, in circumstances specified in the regulations, to send [(subject to any regulations under sub-paragraph (5A)(a))] notice or a copy of any document so specified relating to any proceedings before the tribunal, or of any decision, order or award of the tribunal, to any government department or other person or body so specified.

(7) Any person who without reasonable excuse fails to comply with any requirement imposed by the regulations by virtue of sub-paragraph (2)(d) [or (ga)] or any requirement with respect to the discovery, recovery or inspection of documents so imposed by virtue of sub-paragraph (2)(e) shall be liable on summary conviction to a fine not exceeding [level 3 on the standard scale].

[(8) If any identifying matter is published or included in a relevant programme in contravention of a restricted reporting order the following persons shall be guilty of an offence and liable on summary conviction to a fine not exceeding level 5 on the standard scale—

(a) in the case of publication in a newspaper or periodical, any proprietor, any editor and any publisher of the newspaper or periodical;

(b) in the case of publication in any other form, the person publishing the matter; and

(c) in the case of matter included in a relevant programme—
   (i) any body corporate engaged in providing the service in which the programme is included; and
   (ii) any person having functions in relation to the programme corresponding to those of an editor of a newspaper.

Expressions used in this sub-paragraph and in sub-paragraph (5A) have the same meaning in this sub-paragraph as in that sub-paragraph.

(9) Where a person is charged with an offence under sub-paragraph (8) it shall be a defence to prove that at the time of the alleged offence he was not aware, and neither suspected nor had reason to suspect, that the publication or programme in question was of, or (as the case may be) included, the matter in question.

(10) Where an offence under sub-paragraph (8) committed by a body corporate is proved to have been committed with the consent or connivance of, or to be attributable to any neglect on the part of—

(a) a director, manager, secretary or other similar officer of the body corporate, or

(b) a person purporting to act in any such capacity,

he as well as the body corporate shall be guilty of the offence and liable to be proceeded against and punished accordingly.

(11) In relation to a body corporate whose affairs are managed by its members "director", in sub-paragraph (10), means a member of the body corporate.]

[**1A** (1) The regulations may include provision—

(a) *for authorising a preliminary consideration of proceedings before an industrial tribunal ("a pre-hearing review") to be carried out—*
   (i) *by such person as may be determined by or in accordance with the regulations, or*
   (ii) *if so determined in accordance with the regulations, by the tribunal itself; and*

(b) for enabling such powers to be exercised in connection with a pre-hearing review as may be prescribed by the regulations.

(2) The regulations may in particular include provision—

(a) for authorising any *person or* tribunal carrying out a pre-hearing review under the regulations to make, in circumstances specified in the regulations, an order requiring a party to the proceedings in question, if he wishes to continue to participate in those proceedings, to pay a deposit of an amount not exceeding £150;

(b) for prescribing—
  (i) the manner in which the amount of any such deposit is to be determined in any particular case,
  (ii) the consequences of non-payment of any such deposit, and
  (iii) the circumstances in which any such deposit, or any part of it, may be refunded to the party who paid it, or be paid over to another party to the proceedings.

(3) The Secretary of State may from time to time by order substitute for the sum specified in sub-paragraph (2)(a) such other sum as is specified in the order.]

[**1B** The regulations may also include provision for authorising an industrial tribunal to hear and determine any issue relating to the entitlement of any party to proceedings to bring or contest the proceedings in advance of the hearing and determination of the proceedings by that or any other industrial tribunal.]

National security

2—(1) If on a complaint [under—

(a) section 146 of the Trade Union and Labour Relations (Consolidation) Act 1992 (action short of dismissal on grounds related to union membership or activities), or

(b) section 67 of this Act (unfair dismissal),]

it is shown that the action complained of was taken for the purpose of safe-guarding national security, the industrial tribunal shall dismiss the complaint.

(2) *A certificate* [Except where the complaint is that a dismissal is unfair by reason of section 57A, 59(1)(a) or 60, a certificate] purporting to be signed by or on behalf of a Minister of the Crown, and certifying that the action specified in the certificate was taken for the purpose of safeguarding national security, shall for the purposes of sub-paragraph (1) be conclusive evidence of that fact.

Payment of certain sums into Redundancy Fund

3 . . .

Exclusion of Arbitration Act 1950

4 The Arbitration Act 1950 shall not apply to any proceedings before an industrial tribunal.

Presumption as to dismissal for redundancy

5 Where in accordance with the regulations an industrial tribunal determines in the same proceedings—

(a) a question referred to it under sections 81 to 102, and
(b) a complaint presented under section 67,

section 91(2) shall not have effect for the purposes of the proceedings in so far as they relate to the complaint under section 67.

Right of appearance

6 Any person may appear before an industrial tribunal in person or be represented by counsel or by a solicitor or by a representative of a trade union or an employers' association or by any other person whom he desires to represent him.

[Interest on sums awarded

6A—(1) The Secretary of State may by order made with the approval of the Treasury provide that sums payable in pursuance of decisions of industrial tribunals shall carry interest at such rate and between such times as may be prescribed by the order.

(2) Any interest due by virtue of such an order shall be recoverable as a sum payable in pursuance of the decision.

(3) The power conferred by sub-paragraph (1) includes power—

(a) to specify cases or circumstances in which interest shall not be payable;

(b) to provide that interest shall be payable only on sums exceeding a specified amount or falling between specified amounts;

(c) to make provision for the manner in which and the periods by reference to which interest is to be calculated and paid;

(d) to provide that any enactment shall or shall not apply in relation to interest payable by virtue of an order under sub-paragraph (1) or shall apply to it with such modifications as may be specified in the order;   •

(e) to make provision for cases where sums are payable in pursuance of decisions or awards made on appeal from industrial tribunals;

(f) to make such incidental or supplemental provision as the Secretary of State considers necessary.

(4) Without prejudice to the generality of sub-paragraph (3), an order under sub-paragraph (1) may provide that the rate of interest shall be the rate specified in section 17 of the Judgments Act 1838 as that enactment has effect from time to time.]

Recovery of sums awarded

7 (1) Any sum payable in pursuance of a decision of an industrial tribunal in England and Wales which has been registered in accordance with the regulations shall, if a county court so orders, be recoverable by execution issued from the county court or otherwise as if it were payable under an order of that court.

[(2) Any order for the payment of any sum made by an industrial tribunal in Scotland (or any copy of such an order certified by the Secretary of the Tribunals may be enforced in like manner as an extract registered decree arbitral bearing a warrant for execution issued by the Sheriff Court of any Sheriffdom in Scotland.]

(3) In this paragraph any reference to a decision or order of an industrial tribunal—

(a) does not include a decision or order which, on being reviewed, has been revoked by the tribunal, and

(b) in relation to a decision or order which, on being reviewed, has been varied by the tribunal, shall be construed as a reference to the decision or order as so varied.

Constitution of tribunals for certain cases

8 *An industrial tribunal hearing an application under [section 161, 165 or 166 of the Trade Union and Labour Relations (Consolidation) Act 1992 (application for interim relief or arising out of order for interim relief)] may consist of a President of Industrial Tribunals, the chairman of the tribunal or a member of a panel of chairmen of such tribunals for the time being nominated by a President to hear such applications.*

Remuneration for presidents and full-time chairmen of industrial tribunals

9 The Secretary of State may pay such remuneration as he may with the consent of the Minister for the Civil Service determine to the President of the Industrial Tribunals (England and Wales), the President of the Industrial Tribunals (Scotland) and any person who is a member on a full-time basis of a panel of chairmen of tribunals which is appointed in accordance with regulations under subsection (1) of section 128.

Remuneration etc for members of industrial tribunals and for assessors and other persons

10 The Secretary of State may pay to members of industrial tribunals and to any assessors appointed for the purposes of proceedings before industrial tribunals [and to any persons required for the purposes of section 2A(1)(b) of the Equal Pay Act 1970 to prepare reports] such fees and allowances as he may with the consent of the Minister for the Civil Service determine and may pay to any other persons such allowances as he may with the consent of that Minister determine for the purposes of, or in connection with, their attendance at industrial tribunals. **[411]**

Pensions for full-time presidents or chairmen of industrial tribunals

11 . . .

NOTES

Para 1: in sub-para (2), sub-para (e) substituted by the Employment Act 1989, s 29(3), Sch 6, para 26; sub-para (ga) added by SI 1983/1794; in sub-para (4), word in italics substituted by word in square brackets immediately following by the Trade Union Reform and Employment Rights Act 1993, s 49(2), Sch 8, para 28(a), as from a day to be appointed; sub-para (4A) inserted by *ibid* s 49(1), Sch 7, para 6(a), as from a day to be appointed; sub-para (5A) and words in square brackets in sub-para (6) inserted, and sub-paras (8)–(11) added, by *ibid* s 40, as from 30 August 1993 (SI 1993/1908); in sub-para (7) first words in square brackets substituted by SI 1983/1794, second words in square brackets substituted by the Criminal Justice Act 1982, ss 37, 38, 46.

Para 1A: inserted by the Employment Act 1989, s 20; sub-para (1)(a) substituted by the Trade Union Reform and Employment Rights Act 1993, s 49(2), Sch 8, para 28(b), as from a day to be appointed, as follows—

"(a) for authorising the carrying out by an industrial tribunal of a preliminary consideration of any proceedings before it ("a pre-hearing review"); and";

words in italics in sub-para (2) repealed by *ibid*, s 51, Sch 10, as from a day to be appointed.

Para 1B: inserted by the Trade Union Reform and Employment Rights Act 1993, s 49(2), Sch 8, para 28(c), as from a day to be appointed.

Para 2: words in square brackets in sub-para (1) substituted by the Trade Union and Labour Relations (Consolidation) Act 1992, s 300(2), Sch 2, para 24(1), (2); words in italics in sub-para (2) substituted by words in square brackets immediately following by the Trade Union Reform and Employment Rights Act 1993, s 49(1), Sch 7, para 6(b), as from a day to be appointed.

Para 3: repealed by the Employment Act 1990, s 16(2), Sch 3.

Para 6A: inserted by the Employment Act 1982, s 21, Sch 3, Pt I, para 7.

Para 7: sub-para (2) substituted by the Employment Act 1980, s 20, Sch 1, para 27.

Para 8: repealed by the Trade Union Reform and Employment Rights Act 1993, s 51, Sch 10, as from a day to be appointed; words in square brackets substituted by the Trade Union and Labour Relations Act 1992, s 300(2), Sch 2, para 24(1), (3).

Para 10: words in square brackets inserted by SI 1983/1794.

Para 11: repealed by the Judicial Pensions Act 1981, s 36, Sch 4.

The principal regulations under this Schedule are the Industrial Tribunals (Rules of Procedure) Regulations 1985, SI 1985/16 (below, paras [**1211**]–[**1238**]); the Industrial Tribunals (Rules of Procedure) (Scotland) Regulations 1985, SI 1985/17 (below, paras [**1239**]–[**1266**]); and the Industrial Tribunals (Interest) Order 1990, SI 1990/479 (below, paras [**1372**]–[**1383**]). No separate regulations have been made under para 1A up to 1 September 1993.

SCHEDULE 10

Section 130

STATUTORY PROVISIONS RELATING TO REFEREES AND BOARDS OF REFEREES

1 Regulations under section 37 of the Coal Industry Nationalisation Act 1946.

2 Regulations under section 67 of the National Insurance Act 1946.

3 Regulations under section 68 of the National Health Service Act 1946, and orders under section 11(9) or section 31(5) of that Act.

4 Regulations under section 67 of the National Health Service (Scotland) Act 1947.

5 Regulations under Schedule 5 to the Fire Services Act 1947.

6 Regulations under section 101 of the Transport Act 1947.

7 ...

8 Regulations under section 140 of the Local Government Act 1948, and such regulations as applied by any local Act, whether passed before or after this Act.

9 Regulations under subsection (1) or subsection (2) of section 60 of the National Assistance Act 1948.

10 Rules under section 3 of the Superannuation (Miscellaneous Provisions) Act 1948.

11 Subsections (3) and (5) of section 58 of the Gas Act 1948, and regulations under section 60 of that Act.

12 Subsection (4) of section 6 of the Commonwealth Telegraphs Act 1949 and regulations under that section.

13 Regulations under section 25 of the Prevention of Damage by Pests Act 1949.

14 Regulations under section 42 of the Justices of the Peace Act 1949.

15 Regulations under section 27 or section 28 of the Transport Act 1953.

16 Regulations under section 24 of the Iron and Steel Act 1953.

17 ...

18 Orders under section 23 of the Local Government Act 1958 and regulations under section 60 of that Act.

19 Regulations under section 1 of the Water Officers Compensation Act 1960.

20 Regulations under section 18(6) of the Land Drainage Act 1961.

21 Subsection (6) of section 74 of the Transport Act 1962 and orders under that section, regulations under section 81 of that Act, and paragraph 17(3) of Schedule 7 to that Act.

22 Orders under section 84 of the London Government Act 1963 and regulations under section 85 of that Act.

23 Regulations under section 106 of the Water Resources Act 1963.   **[412]**

NOTE

Paras 7, 17: repealed by the Electricity Act 1989, s 112(4), Sch 18.

SCHEDULE 11

Section 135

EMPLOYMENT APPEAL TRIBUNAL

PART I
PROVISIONS AS TO MEMBERSHIP, PROCEEDINGS AND POWERS

Tenure of office of appointed members of Appeal Tribunal

1 Subject to paragraphs 2 and 3, a member of the Appeal Tribunal appointed by Her Majesty under section 135(2)(c) (in this Schedule referred to as an "appointed member") shall hold and vacate office as such a member in accordance with the terms of his appointment.

2 An appointed member

[(a)] may at any time resign his membership by notice in writing addressed to the Lord Chancellor and the Secretary of State [; and

(b) shall vacate his office on the day on which he attains the age of 70;

but paragraph (b) is subject to section 26(4) to (6) of the Judicial Pensions and Retirement Act 1993 (power to authorise continuance in office up to the age of 75)].

3 (1) If the Lord Chancellor, after consultation with the Secretary of State, is satisfied that an appointed member—

(a) has been absent from sittings of the Appeal Tribunal for a period longer than six consecutive months without the permission of the President of the Tribunal; or

(b) has become bankrupt or made an arrangement with his creditors; or

(c) is incapacitated by physical or mental illness; or

(d) is otherwise unable or unfit to discharge the functions of a member;

the Lord Chancellor may declare his office as a member to be vacant and shall notify the declaration in such manner as the Lord Chancellor thinks fit; and thereupon the office shall become vacant.

(2) In the application of this paragraph to Scotland for the references in sub-paragraph (1)(b) to a member's having become bankrupt and to a member's having made an arrangement with his creditors there shall be substituted respectively, references to a member's estate having been sequestrated and to a member's having made a trust deed for behoof of his creditors or a composition contract.

Temporary membership of Appeal Tribunal

4 At any time when the office of President of the Appeal Tribunal is vacant, or the person holding that office is temporarily absent or otherwise unable to act as President of the Tribunal, the Lord Chancellor may nominate another judge nominated under section 135(2)(a) to act temporarily in his place.

5 At any time when a judge of the Appeal Tribunal nominated by the Lord Chancellor is temporarily absent or otherwise unable to act as a judge of that Tribunal, the Lord Chancellor may nominate another person who is qualified to be nominated under section 135(2)(a) to act temporarily in his place.

6 At any time when a judge of the Appeal Tribunal nominated by the Lord President of the Court of Session is temporarily absent or otherwise unable to act as a judge of the Appeal Tribunal, the Lord President may nominate another judge of the Court of Session to act temporarily in his place.

7 At any time when an appointed member is temporarily absent or otherwise unable to act as a member of the Appeal Tribunal, the Lord Chancellor and the Secretary of State may jointly appoint a person appearing to them to have the qualifications for appointment as such a member to act temporarily in his place.

8 (1) At any time when it appears to the Lord Chancellor that it is expedient to do so in order to facilitate in England and Wales the disposal of business in the Appeal Tribunal, he may appoint a qualified person to be a temporary additional judge of the Tribunal during such period or on such occasions as the Lord Chancellor thinks fit.

(2) In this paragraph "qualified person" means a person qualified for appointment as a puisne judge of the High Court under section [10 of the Supreme Court Act 1981] or any person who has held office as a judge of the Court of Appeal or of the High Court.

9 A person appointed to act temporarily in place of the President or any other member of the Appeal Tribunal shall, when so acting, have all the functions of the person in whose place he acts.

10 A person appointed to be a temporary additional judge of the Appeal Tribunal shall have all the functions of a judge nominated under section 135(2)(a).

11 No judge shall be nominated under paragraph 5 or 6 except with his consent.

Organisation and sittings of Appeal Tribunal

12 The Appeal Tribunal shall be a superior court of record and shall have an official seal which shall be judicially noticed.

13 The Appeal Tribunal shall have a central office in London.

14 The Appeal Tribunal may sit at any time and in any place in Great Britain.

15 The Appeal Tribunal may sit, in accordance with directions given by the President of the Tribunal, either as a single tribunal or in two or more divisions concurrently.

16 *With the consent of the parties to any proceedings before the Appeal Tribunal, the proceedings may be heard by a judge and one appointed member, but, in default of such consent, any proceedings before the Tribunal shall be heard by a judge and either two or four appointed members, so that in either case there are equal numbers of persons whose experience is as representatives of employers and whose experience is as representatives of workers.*

Rules

17 (1) The Lord Chancellor, after consultation with the Lord President of the Court of Session, shall make rules with respect to proceedings before the Appeal Tribunal.

(2) Subject to those rules, the Tribunal shall have power to regulate its own procedure.

18 Without prejudice to the generality of paragraph 17 the rules may include provision—
- (a) with respect to the manner in which an appeal may be brought and the time within which it may be brought;
- [(aa) with respect to the manner in which *an application to the Appeal Tribunal under [section 67 or 176 of the Trade Union and Labour Relations (Consolidation) Act 1992] may be made* [any application to the Appeal Tribunal may be made;]]
- (b) for requiring persons to attend to give evidence and produce documents, and for authorising the administration of oaths to witnesses;
- (c) *enabling the Appeal Tribunal to sit in private for the purpose of hearing evidence to hear which an industrial tribunal may sit in private by virtue of paragraph 1 of Schedule 9;*
- [(d) for the registration and proof of any award made on an application to the Appeal Tribunal under [section 67 or 176 of the Trade Union and Labour Relations (Consolidation) Act 1992];]
- [(e) for interlocutory *proceedings* [matters arising on any appeal or application to the Appeal Tribunal] to be dealt with otherwise than in accordance with paragraph 16].

[**18A** (1) Without prejudice to the generality of paragraph 17 the rules may, as respects proceedings to which this paragraph applies, include provision—
- (a) for cases involving allegations of the commission of sexual offences, for securing that the registration or other making available of documents or decisions shall be so effected as to prevent the identification of any person affected by or making the allegation; and
- (b) for cases involving allegations of sexual misconduct, enabling the Appeal Tribunal, on the application of any party to the proceedings before it or of its own motion, to make a restricted reporting order having effect (if not revoked earlier) until the promulgation of the decision of the Appeal Tribunal.

(2) This paragraph applies to—
- (a) proceedings on an appeal against a decision of an industrial tribunal to make, or not to make, a restricted reporting order; and
- (b) proceedings on an appeal against any interlocutory decision of an industrial tribunal in proceedings in which the industrial tribunal has made a restricted reporting order which it has not revoked.

(3) If any identifying matter is published or included in a relevant programme in contravention of a restricted reporting order the following persons shall be guilty of an offence and liable on summary conviction to a fine not exceeding level 5 on the standard scale—
- (a) in the case of publication in a newspaper or periodical, any proprietor, any editor and any publisher of the newspaper or periodical;
- (b) in the case of publication in any other form, the person publishing the matter; and
- (c) in the case of matter included in a relevant programme—
  - (i) any body corporate engaged in providing the service in which the programme is included; and

(ii) any person having functions in relation to the programme corresponding to those of an editor of a newspaper.

(4) Where a person is charged with an offence under sub-paragraph (3) it shall be a defence to prove that at the time of the alleged offence he was not aware, and neither suspected nor had reason to suspect, that the publication or programme in question was of, or (as the case may be) included, the matter in question.

(5) Where an offence under sub-paragraph (3) committed by a body corporate is proved to have been committed with the consent or connivance of, or to be attributable to any neglect on the part of—

(a) a director, manager, secretary or other similar officer of the body corporate, or
(b) a person purporting to act in any such capacity,

he as well as the body corporate shall be guilty of the offence and liable to be proceeded against and punished accordingly.

(6) In relation to a body corporate whose affairs are managed by its members "director", in sub-paragraph (5), means a member of the body corporate.

(7) In this paragraph—

"identifying matter", in relation to a person, means any matter likely to lead members of the public to identify him as a person affected by, or as the person making, the allegation;

"restricted reporting order" means an order prohibiting the publication in Great Britain of identifying matter in a written publication available to the public or its inclusion in a relevant programme for reception in Great Britain;

"sexual misconduct" means the commission of a sexual offence, sexual harassment or other adverse conduct (of whatever nature) related to sex, and conduct is related to sex whether the relationship with sex lies in the character of the conduct or in its having reference to the sex or sexual orientation of the person at whom the conduct is directed;

"sexual offence" means any offence to which section 141A(2) of the Criminal Procedure (Scotland) Act 1975, section 4 of the Sexual Offences (Amendment) Act 1976 or the Sexual Offences (Amendment) Act 1992 applies (offences under the Sexual Offences Act 1956, the Sexual Offences (Scotland) Act 1976 and certain other enactments);

and "written publication" and "relevant programme" have the same meaning as in that Act of 1992.]

19 (1) Without prejudice to the generality of paragraph 17 the rules may empower the Appeal Tribunal to order a party to any proceedings before the Tribunal to pay to any other party to the proceedings the whole or part of the costs or expenses incurred by that other party in connection with the proceedings, where in the opinion of the Tribunal—

(a) the proceedings were unnecessary, improper or vexatious, or
(b) there has been unreasonable delay or other unreasonable conduct in bringing or conducting the proceedings.

(2) Except as provided by sub-paragraph (1), the rules shall not enable the Appeal Tribunal to order the payment of costs or expenses by any party to proceedings before the Tribunal.

20 Any person may appear before the Appeal Tribunal in person or be represented by counsel or by a solicitor or by a representative of a trade union or an employers' association or by any other person whom he desires to represent him.

Powers of Tribunal

21 (1) For the purpose of disposing of an appeal the Appeal Tribunal may exercise any powers of the body or officer from whom the appeal was brought or may remit the case to that body or officer.

(2) Any decision or award of the Appeal Tribunal on an appeal shall have the same effect and may be enforced in the same manner as a decision or award of a body or officer from whom the appeal was brought.

[21A (1) Any sum payable in England and Wales in pursuance of an award of the Appeal Tribunal under [section 67 or 176 of the Trade Union and Labour Relations (Consolidation) Act 1992] which has been registered in accordance with the rules shall, if a county court so orders, be recoverable by execution issued from the county court or otherwise as if it were payable under an order of that court.

(2) Any order by the Appeal Tribunal for the payment in Scotland of any sum in pursuance of such an award (or any copy of such an order certified by the Secretary of the Tribunals) may be enforced in like manner as an extract registered decree arbitral bearing a warrant for execution issued by the Sheriff Court of any Sheriffdom in Scotland.]

[(3) Any sum payable in pursuance of an award of the Appeal Tribunal under [section 67 or 176 of the Trade Union and Labour Relations (Consolidation) Act 1992] shall be treated as if it were a sum payable in pursuance of a decision of an industrial tribunal for the purposes of paragraph 6A of Schedule 9 (interest on industrial tribunal awards).]

22 (1) The Appeal Tribunal shall, in relation to the attendance and examination of witnesses, the production and inspection of documents and all other matters incidental to its jurisdiction, have the like powers, rights, privileges and authority—

    (a) in England and Wales, as the High Court,
    (b) in Scotland, as the Court of Session.

(2) No person shall be punished for contempt of the Tribunal except by, or with the consent of, a judge.

23 (1) . . .

(2) A magistrates' court shall not remit the whole or any part of a fine imposed by the Appeal Tribunal except with the consent of a judge who is a member of the Tribunal.

(3) This paragraph does not extend to Scotland.

Staff

24 The Secretary of State may appoint such officers and servants of the Appeal Tribunal as he may determine, subject to the approval of the Minister for the Civil Service as to numbers and as to terms and conditions of service.   **[413]**

NOTES

Para 2: para (a) prospectively numbered as such with savings, and para (b) added with savings, by the Judicial Pensions and Retirement Act 1993, s 26, Sch 6, para 30, as from a day to be appointed; for savings see s 27, Sch 7 thereof.

Para 8: words in square brackets in sub-para (2) substituted by the Supreme Court Act 1981, s 152(1), Sch 5.

Para 16: substituted by the Trade Union Reform and Employment Rights Act 1993, s 37, as from a day to be appointed, as follows—

"16(1) Subject to sub-paragraphs (2) to (4), proceedings before the Appeal Tribunal shall be heard by a judge and either two or four appointed members, so that in either case there is an equal number of persons whose knowledge or experience of industrial relations is as representatives of employers and whose knowledge or experience of industrial relations is as representatives of workers.

(2) With the consent of the parties proceedings before the Appeal Tribunal may be heard by a judge and one appointed member or by a judge and three appointed members.

(3) Proceedings on an appeal on a question arising from any decision of, or arising in any proceedings before, an industrial tribunal consisting of the person specified in section 128(2A)(a) alone shall be heard by a judge alone unless a judge directs that the proceedings shall be heard in accordance with sub-paragraphs (1) and (2).

(4) Where a Minister of the Crown so directs in relation to any proceedings on grounds of national security, the proceedings shall be heard by the President of the Appeal Tribunal alone.".

Para 18: sub-paras (aa), (d) inserted and added by the Employment Act 1980, s 20, Sch 1, para 28, words in square brackets therein substituted by the Trade Union and Labour Relations (Consolidation) Act 1992, s 300(2), Sch 2, para 25(a); words in italics in sub-para (aa) substituted by words in square brackets immediately following by the Trade Union Reform and Employment Rights Act 1993, s 49(2),

Sch 8, para 29, as from 30 August 1993 (SI 1993/1908); sub-para (c) substituted by *ibid* s 49(1), Sch 7, para 7, from the same date, as follows—
   "(c) for requiring or enabling the Appeal Tribunal to sit in private in circumstances in which an industrial tribunal is required or empowered to sit in private by virtue of paragraph 1 of Schedule 9;";
sub-para (e) added by the Employment Act 1982, s 21, Sch 3, Pt I, para 8; word in italics therein substituted by words in square brackets immediately following by the Trade Union Reform and Employment Rights Act 1993, s 49(2), Sch 8, para 30, as from a day to be appointed.
   Para 18A: inserted by the Trade Union Reform and Employment Rights Act 1993, s 41, as from 30 August (SI 1993/1908)
   Para 21A: inserted by the Employment Act 1980, s 20, Sch 1, para 29; in sub-para (1) words in square brackets substituted by the Trade Union and Labour Relations (Consolidation) Act 1992, s 300(2), Sch 2, para 25(b); sub-para (3) added by the Employment Act 1982, s 21, Sch 3, Pt I, para 9, and words in square brackets therein substituted by the Trade Union and Labour Relations (Consolidation) Act 1992, s 300(2), Sch 2, para 25.
   Para 23: sub-para (1) repealed by the Contempt of Court Act 1981, s 16(6).

PART II
SUPPLEMENTARY

Remuneration and allowances

25 The Secretary of State shall pay the appointed members of the Appeal Tribunal, the persons appointed to act temporarily as appointed members, and the officers and servants of the Tribunal such remuneration and such travelling and other allowances as he may with the approval of the Minister for the Civil Service determine.

26 A person appointed to be a temporary additional judge of the Appeal Tribunal shall be paid such remuneration and allowances as the Lord Chancellor may, with the approval of the Minister for the Civil Service, determine.

Pensions, etc

27 If the Secretary of State determines, with the approval of the Minister for the Civil Service, that this paragraph shall apply in the case of an appointed member, the Secretary of State shall pay such pension, allowance or gratuity to or in respect of that member on his retirement or death or make that member such payments towards the provision of such a pension, allowance or gratuity as the Secretary of State may with the like approval determine.

28 Where a person ceases to be an appointed member otherwise than on his retirement or death and it appears to the Secretary of State that there are special circumstances which make it right for him to receive compensation, the Secretary of State may make him a payment of such amount as the Secretary of State may, with the approval of the Minister for the Civil Service, determine.   [414]

SCHEDULE 12

Section 150

DEATH OF EMPLOYEE OR EMPLOYER

PART I
GENERAL

Introductory

1 In this Schedule "the relevant provisions" means Part I (so far as it relates to itemised pay statements), section 53 and Parts II, III, V, VI and VII of this Act and this Schedule.

Institution or continuance of tribunal proceedings

2 Where an employee or employer has died, tribunal proceedings arising under any of the relevant provisions may be instituted or continued by a personal representative of the deceased employee or, as the case may be, defended by a personal representative of the deceased employer.

3 (1) If there is no personal representative of a deceased employee, tribunal proceedings arising under any of the relevant provisions (or proceedings to enforce a tribunal award made in any such proceedings) may be instituted or continued on behalf of the estate of the deceased employee by such other person as the industrial tribunal may appoint being either—

   (a) a person authorised by the employee to act in connection with the proceedings before the employee's death; or

   (b) the widower, widow, child, father, mother, brother or sister of the deceased employee,

and references in this Schedule to a personal representative shall be construed as including such a person.

   (2) In such a case any award made by the industrial tribunal shall be in such terms and shall be enforceable in such manner as may be provided by regulations made by the Secretary of State.

4 (1) Subject to any specific provision of this Schedule to the contrary, in relation to an employee or employer who has died—

   (a) any reference in the relevant provisions to the doing of anything by or in relation to an employee or employer shall be construed as including a reference to the doing of that thing by or in relation to any personal representative of the deceased employee or employer; and

   (b) any reference in the said provisions to a thing required or authorised to be done by or in relation to an employee or employer shall be construed as including a reference to any thing which, in accordance with any such provision as modified by this Schedule (including sub-paragraph (a)), is required or authorised to be done by or in relation to any personal representative of the deceased employee or employer.

   (2) Nothing in this paragraph shall prevent references in the relevant provisions to a successor of an employer from including a personal representative of a deceased employer.

Rights and liabilities accruing after death

5 Any right arising under any of the relevant provisions as modified by this Schedule shall, if it had not accrued before the death of the employee in question, nevertheless devolve as if it had so accrued.

6 Where by virtue of any of the relevant provisions as modified by this Schedule a personal representative of a deceased employer is liable to pay any amount and that liability had not accrued before the death of the employer, it shall be treated for all purposes as if it were a liability of the deceased employer which had accrued immediately before the death.   **[415]**

PART II
UNFAIR DISMISSAL

Introductory

7 In this Part of this Schedule "the unfair dismissal provisions" means Part V of this Act and this Schedule.

Death during notice period

8 Where an employer has given notice to an employee to terminate his contract of employment and before that termination the employee or the employer dies, the unfair dismissal provisions shall apply as if the contract had been duly terminated by the employer by notice expiring on the date of the death.

[**9** Where—

    (a) the employee's contract of employment has been terminated; and

    (b) by virtue of subsection (5) or (6) of section 55 a date later than the effective date of termination as defined in subsection (4) of that section is to be treated as the effective date of termination for the purposes of certain of the unfair dismissal provisions; and

    (c) before that later date the employer or the employee dies;

subsection (5) or, as the case may be, (6) shall have effect as if the notice referred to in that section as required by section 49 would have expired on the date of the death.]

Remedies for unfair dismissal

10 Where an employee has died, then, unless an order for reinstatement or re-engagement has already been made, section 69 shall not apply; and accordingly if the industrial tribunal finds that the grounds of the complaint are well-founded the case shall be treated as falling within section 68(2) as a case in which no order is made under section 69.

11 If an order for reinstatement or re-engagement has been made and the employee dies before the order is complied with—

    (a) if the employer has before the death refused to reinstate or re-engage the employee in accordance with the order, section 71(2) and (3) shall apply and an award shall be made under section 71(2)(b) unless the employer satisfies the tribunal that it was not practicable at the time of the refusal to comply with the order;

    (b) if there has been no such refusal, section 71(1) shall apply if the employer fails to comply with any ancillary terms of the order which remain capable of fulfilment after the employee's death as it would apply to such a failure to comply fully with the terms of an order where the employee had been reinstated or re-engaged. **[416]**

NOTES

Para 9: substituted by the Employment Act 1982, s 21, Sch 3, Pt II, para 28.

PART III
REDUNDANCY PAYMENTS: DEATH OF EMPLOYER

Introductory

12 The provisions of this Part shall have effect in relation to an employee where his employer (in this Part referred to as "the deceased employer") dies.

13 *Section 94 shall not apply to any change whereby the ownership of the business, for the purposes of which the employee was employed by the deceased employer, passes to a personal representative of the deceased employer.*

Dismissal

14 Where by virtue of subsection (1) of section 93 the death of the deceased employer is to be treated for the purposes of Part VI of this Act as a termination by him of the contract of employment, section 84 shall have effect subject to the following modifications:—

    (a) for subsection (1) there shall be substituted the following subsection—

        "(1) If an employee's contract of employment is renewed, or he is re-engaged under a new contract of employment, by a personal representative of the deceased employer and the renewal or re-engagement takes effect not later than eight weeks after the death of the deceased employer, then, subject to subsections (3) and (6), the employee shall not be regarded as having been dismissed by reason of the ending of his employment under the previous contract.";

    (b) in subsection (2), paragraph (a) shall be omitted and in paragraph (b) for the words "four weeks" there shall be substituted the words "eight weeks";

    (c) in subsections (5) and (6), references to the employer shall be construed as references to the personal representative of the deceased employer.

15 Where by reason of the death of the deceased employer the employee is treated for the purposes of Part VI of this Act as having been dismissed by him, section 82 shall have effect subject to the following modifications—

(a) for subsection (3) there shall be substituted the following subsection—

"(3) If a personal representative of the deceased employer makes an employee an offer (whether in writing or not) to renew his contract of employment, or to re-engage him under a new contract of employment, so that the renewal or re-engagement would take effect not later than eight weeks after the death of the deceased employer the provisions of subsections (5) and (6) shall have effect.";

(b) in subsection (4), paragraph (a) shall be omitted and in paragraph (b) for the words "four weeks" there shall be substituted the words "eight weeks";

(c) in subsection (5), the reference to the employer shall be construed as a reference to the personal representative of the deceased employer.

16 For the purposes of section 82 as modified by paragraph 15—

(a) an offer shall not be treated as one whereby the provisions of the contract as renewed, or of the new contract, as the case may be, would differ from the corresponding provisions of the contract as in force immediately before the death of the deceased employer by reason only that the personal representative would be substituted as the employer for the deceased employer, and

(b) no account shall be taken of that substitution in determining whether the refusal of the offer was unreasonable, or, as the case may be, whether the employee acted reasonably in terminating the renewed, or new, employment during the trial period referred to in section 84.

Lay-off and short-time

17 Where the employee has before the death of the deceased employer been laid off or kept on short-time for one or more weeks, but has not given to the deceased employer notice of intention to claim, then if after the death of the deceased employer—

(a) his contract of employment is renewed, or he is re-engaged under a new contract by a personal representative of the deceased employer, and

(b) after the renewal or re-engagement, he is laid off or kept on short-time for one or more weeks by the personal representative of the deceased employer,

the provisions of sections 88 and 89 shall apply as if the week in which the deceased employer died and the first week of the employee's employment by the personal representative were consecutive weeks, and any reference in those sections to four weeks or thirteen weeks shall be construed accordingly.

18 The provisions of paragraph 19 or (as the case may be) paragraph 20 shall have effect where the employee has given to the deceased employer notice of intention to claim, and—

(a) the deceased employer has died before the end of the next four weeks after the service of that notice, and

(b) the employee has not terminated the contract of employment by notice expiring before the death of the deceased employer.

19 If in the circumstances specified in paragraph 18 the employee's contract of employment is not renewed by a personal representative of the deceased employer before the end of the next four weeks after the service of the notice of intention to claim, and he is not re-engaged under a new contract by such a personal representative before the end of those four weeks, section 88(1) and (2) and (in relation to subsection (1) of that section) section 89(2) and (3) shall apply as if—

(a) the deceased employer had not died, and

(b) the employee had terminated the contract of employment by a week's notice (or, if under the contract he is required to give more than a week's notice to terminate the contract, he had terminated it by the minimum notice which he is so required to give) expiring at the end of those four weeks,

but sections 88(3) and (4) and 89(1) and (4) shall not apply.

20 (1) The provisions of this paragraph shall have effect where, in the circumstances specified in paragraph 18, the employee's contract of employment is renewed by a personal representative of the deceased employer before the end of the next four weeks after the service of the notice of intention to claim, or he is re-engaged under a new contract by such a personal representative before the end of those four weeks, and—

(a) he was laid off or kept on short-time by the deceased employer for one or more of those weeks, and

(b) he is laid off or kept on short-time by the personal representative for the week, or for the next two or more weeks, following the renewal or re-engagement.

(2) Where the conditions specified in sub-paragraph (1) are fulfilled, sections 88 and 89 shall apply as if—

(a) all the weeks for which the employee was laid off or kept on short-time as mentioned in sub-paragraph (1) were consecutive weeks during which he was employed (but laid off or kept on short-time) by the same employer, and

(b) each of the periods specified in paragraphs (a) and (b) of subsection (5) of section 89 were extended by any week or weeks any part of which was after the death of the deceased employer and before the date on which the renewal or re-engagement took effect.

Continuity of period of employment

21 For the purposes of the application, in accordance with section 100(1), of any provisions of Part VI of this Act in relation to an employee who was employed as a domestic servant in a private household, any reference to a personal representative in—

(a) this Part of this Schedule, or

(b) paragraph 17 of Schedule 13,

shall be construed as including a reference to any person to whom, otherwise than in pursuance of a sale or other disposition for valuable consideration, the management of the household has passed in consequence of the death of the deceased employer.   **[417]**

NOTE

Para 13: repealed by the Trade Union Reform and Employment Rights Act 1993, s 51, Sch 10, as from 30 August 1993 (SI 1993/1908).

PART IV
REDUNDANCY PAYMENTS: DEATH OF EMPLOYEE

22 (1) Where an employer has given notice to an employee to terminate his contract of employment, and before that notice expires the employee dies, the provisions of Part VI of this Act shall apply as if the contract had been duly terminated by the employer by notice expiring on the date of the employee's death.

(2) Where the employee's contract of employment has been terminated by the employer and by virtue of section 90(3) a date later than the relevant date as defined by subsection (1) of that section is to be treated as the relevant date for the purposes of certain provisions of Part VI of this Act, and before that later date the employee dies, section 90(3) shall have effect as if the notice referred to in that subsection as required to be given by an employer would have expired on the employee's death.

23 (1) Where an employer has given notice to an employee to terminate his contract of employment, and has offered to renew his contract of employment, or to re-engage him under a new contract, then if—

(a) the employee dies without having either accepted or refused the offer, and

(b) the offer has not been withdrawn before his death,

section 82 shall apply as if for the words "the employee unreasonably refuses" there were substituted the words "it would have been unreasonable on the part of the employee to refuse".

(2) Where an employee's contract of employment has been renewed, or he has been re-engaged under a new contract of employment, and during the trial period the employee dies without having terminated or having given notice to terminate the contract, subsection (6) of

that section shall apply as if for the words from "and during the trial period" to "terminated" there were substituted the words "and it would have been unreasonable for the employee, during the trial period referred to in section 84, to terminate or give notice to terminate the contract".

24 Where an employee's contract of employment has been renewed, or he has been re-engaged under a new contract of employment, and during the trial period he gives notice to terminate the contract but dies before the expiry of that notice, sections 82(6) and 84(6)(a) shall have effect as if the notice had expired and the contract had thereby been terminated on the date of the employee's death.

25 (1) Where, in the circumstances specified in paragraphs (a) and (b) of subsection (1) of section 85, the employee dies before the notice given by him under paragraph (b) of that subsection is due to expire and before the employer has given him notice under subsection (3) of that section, subsection (4) of that section shall apply as if the employer had given him such notice and he had not complied with it.

(2) Where, in the said circumstances, the employee dies before his notice given under section 85(1)(b) is due to expire but after the employer has given him notice under subsection (3) of section 85, subsections (3) and (4) of that section shall apply as if the circumstances were that the employee had not died, but did not comply with the last-mentioned notice.

26 (1) Where an employee has given notice of intention to claim and dies before he has given notice to terminate his contract of employment and before the period allowed for the purposes of subsection (2)(a) of section 88 has expired, the said subsection (2)(a) shall not apply.

(2) Where an employee, who has given notice of intention to claim, dies within seven days after the service of that notice, and before the employer has given a counter-notice, the provisions of sections 88 and 89 shall apply as if the employer had given a counter-notice within those seven days.

(3) In this paragraph "counter-notice" has the same meaning as in section 89(1).

27 (1) In relation to the making of a claim by a personal representative of a deceased employee who dies before the end of the period of six months beginning with the relevant date, subsection (1) of section 101 shall apply with the substitution for the words "six months", of the words "one year".

(2) In relation to the making of a claim by a personal representative of a deceased employee who dies after the end of the period of six months beginning with the relevant date and before the end of the following period of six months, subsection (2) of section 101 shall apply with the substitution for the words "six months", of the words "one year".

28 In relation to any case where, under any provision contained in Part VI of this Act as modified by this Schedule, an industrial tribunal has power to determine that an employer shall be liable to pay to a personal representative of a deceased employee either—

(a) the whole of a redundancy payment to which he would have been entitled apart from another provision therein mentioned, or

(b) such part of such a redundancy payment as the tribunal thinks fit,

any reference in paragraph 5 to a right shall be construed as including a reference to any right to receive the whole or part of a redundancy payment if the tribunal determines that the employer shall be liable to pay it.   **[418]**

SCHEDULE 13

Section 151

COMPUTATION OF PERIOD OF EMPLOYMENT

[Preliminary

1 (1) Except so far as otherwise provided by the following provisions of this Schedule, a week which does not count under paragraphs 3 to 12 breaks the continuity of the period of employment.

(2) The provisions of this Schedule apply, subject to paragraph 14, to a period of employment notwithstanding that during that period the employee was engaged in work wholly or mainly outside Great Britain, or was excluded by or under this Act from any right conferred by this Act.

(3) A person's employment during any period shall, unless the contrary is shown, be presumed to have been continuous.]

2 . . .

Normal working weeks

3 Any week in which the employee is employed for sixteen hours or more shall count in computing a period of employment.

Employment governed by contract

4 Any week during the whole or part of which the employee's relations with the employer are governed by a contract of employment which normally involves employment for sixteen hours or more weekly shall count in computing a period of employment.

5 (1) If the employee's relations with his employer cease to be governed by a contract which normally involves work for sixteen hours or more weekly and become governed by a contract which normally involves employment for eight hours or more, but less than sixteen hours, weekly and, but for that change, the later weeks would count in computing a period of employment, or would not break the continuity of a period of employment, then those later weeks shall count in computing a period of employment or, as the case may be, shall not break the continuity of a period of employment, notwithstanding that change.

(2) Not more than twenty-six weeks shall count under this paragraph between any two periods falling under paragraph 4, and in computing the said figure of twenty-six weeks no account shall be taken of any week which counts in computing a period of employment, or does not break the continuity of a period of employment, otherwise than by virtue of this paragraph.

6 (1) An employee whose relations with his employer are governed, or have been from time to time governed, by a contract of employment which normally involves employment for eight hours or more, but less than sixteen hours, weekly shall nevertheless, if he satisfies the condition referred to in sub-paragraph (2), be treated for the purposes of this Schedule (apart from this paragraph) as if his contract normally involved employment for sixteen hours or more weekly, and had at all times at which there was a contract during the period of employment of five years or more referred to in sub-paragraph (2) normally involved employment for sixteen hours or more weekly.

(2) Sub-paragraph (1) shall apply if the employee, on the date by reference to which the length of any period of employment falls to be ascertained in accordance with the provisions of this Schedule, has been continuously employed within the meaning of sub-paragraph (3) for a period of five years or more.

(3) In computing for the purposes of sub-paragraph (2) an employee's period of employment, the provisions of this Schedule (apart from this paragraph) shall apply but as if, in paragraphs 3 and 4, for the words "sixteen hours" wherever they occur, there were substituted the words "eight hours".

7 (1) If an employee has, at any time during the relevant period of employment, been continuously employed for a period which qualifies him for any right which requires a qualifying period of continuous employment computed in accordance with this Schedule, then he shall be regarded for the purposes of qualifying for that right as continuing to satisfy that requirement until the condition referred to in sub-paragraph (3) occurs.

(2) In this paragraph the relevant period of employment means the period of employment ending on the date by reference to which the length of any period of employment falls to be ascertained which would be continuous (in accordance with the provisions of this Schedule)

if at all relevant times the employee's relations with the employer had been governed by a contract of employment which normally involved employment for sixteen hours or more weekly.

(3) The condition which defeats the operation of sub-paragraph (1) is that in a week subsequent to the time at which the employee qualified as referred to in that sub-paragraph—

    (a) his relations with his employer are governed by a contract of employment which normally involves employment for less than eight hours weekly; and

    (b) he is employed in that week for less than sixteen hours.

(4) If, in a case in which an employee is entitled to any right by virtue of sub-paragraph (1), it is necessary for the purpose of ascertaining the amount of his entitlement to determine for what period he has been continuously employed, he shall be regarded for that purpose as having been continuously employed throughout the relevant period.

[Power to amend paragraphs 3 to 7 by order

8 (1) The Secretary of State may by order—

    (a) amend paragraphs 3 to 7 so as to substitute for each of the references to sixteen hours a reference to such other number of hours less than sixteen as may be specified in the order; and

    (b) amend paragraphs 6 and 7 so as to substitute for each of the references to eight hours a reference to such other number of hours less than eight as may be specified in the order.

(2) No order under this paragraph shall be made unless a draft of the order has been laid before Parliament and approved by a resolution of each House of Parliament.

(3) The provisions of any order under this paragraph shall apply to periods before the order takes effect as they apply to later periods.]

Periods in which there is no contract of employment

9 (1) If in any week the employee is, for the whole or part of the week—

    (a) incapable of work in consequence of sickness or injury, or

    (b) absent from work on account of a temporary cessation of work, or

    (c) absent from work in circumstances such that, by arrangement or custom, he is regarded as continuing in the employment of his employer for all or any purposes, or

    (d) absent from work wholly or partly because of pregnancy or *confinement* [childbirth],

that week shall, notwithstanding that it does not fall under paragraph 3, 4 or 5, count as a period of employment.

(2) Not more than twenty-six weeks shall count under paragraph (a) or, subject to paragraph 10, under paragraph (d) of sub-paragraph (1) between any periods falling under paragraph 3, 4 or 5.

Maternity

10 If an employee returns to work in accordance with [*section 45(1)* [section 39] or in pursuance of an offer made in the circumstances described in section 56A(2)] after a period of absence from work wholly or partly occasioned by pregnancy or *confinement* [childbirth], every week during that period shall count in computing a period of employment, notwithstanding that it does not fall under paragraph 3, 4 or 5.

Intervals in employment where section 55(5) or 84(1) or 90(3) applies

11 (1) In ascertaining, for the purposes of section 64(1)(a), [*64A(1)*] and of section 73(3), the period for which an employee has been continuously employed, where by virtue of section 55(5) [or, as the case may be, (6)] a date is treated as the effective date of termination which is later than the effective date of termination as defined by section 55(4), the period of the interval between those two dates shall count as a period of employment notwithstanding that it does not otherwise count under the Schedule.

(2) Where by virtue of section 84(1) an employee is treated as not having been dismissed by reason of a renewal or re-engagement taking effect after an interval, then, in determining for the purposes of section 81(1) or Schedule 4 whether he has been continuously employed for the requisite period, the period of that interval shall count as a period of employment except in so far as it is to be disregarded under paragraphs 12 to 14 (notwithstanding that it does not otherwise count under this Schedule).

(3) Where by virtue of section 90(3) a date is to be treated as the relevant date for the purposes of section 81(4) which is later than the relevant date as defined by section 90(1), then in determining for the purposes of section 81(1) or Schedule 4 whether the employee has been continuously employed for the requisite period, the period of the interval between those two dates shall count as a period of employment except in so far as it is to be disregarded under paragraphs 12 to 14 (notwithstanding that it does not otherwise count under this Schedule).

Payment of previous redundancy payment or equivalent payment

12 (1) Where the conditions mentioned in sub-paragraph (2)(a) or (2)(b) are fulfilled in relation to a person, then in determining, for the purposes of section 81(1) or Schedule 4, whether at any subsequent time he has been continuously employed for the requisite period, or for what period he has been continuously employed, the continuity of the period of employment shall be treated as having been broken—

(a) in so far as the employment was under a contract of employment, at the date which was the relevant date in relation to the payment mentioned in sub-paragraph (2)(a) or, as the case may be, sub-paragraph (2)(b); or

(b) in so far as the employment was otherwise than under a contract of employment, at the date which would have been the relevant date in relation to that payment had the employment been under a contract of employment,

and accordingly no account shall be taken of any time before that date.

(2) Sub-paragraph (1) has effect—

(a) where—

(i) a redundancy payment is paid to an employee, whether in respect of dismissal or in respect of lay-off or short-time; and

(ii) the contract of employment under which he was employed (in this section referred to as "the previous contract") is renewed, whether by the same or another employer, or he is re-engaged under a new contract of employment, whether by the same or another employer; and

(iii) the circumstances of the renewal or re-engagement are such that, in determining for the purposes of section 81(1) or Schedule 4 whether at any subsequent time he has been continuously employed for the requisite period, or for what period he has been continuously employed, the continuity of his period of employment would, apart from this paragraph, be treated as not having been broken by the termination of the previous contract and the renewal or re-engagement; or

(b) where—

(i) a payment has been made, whether in respect of the termination of any person's employment or in respect of lay-off or short-time, either in accordance with any provisions of a scheme under section 1 of the Superannuation Act 1972 or in accordance with any such arrangements as are mentioned in section 111(3); and

(ii) he commences new, or renewed, employment; and

(iii) the circumstances of the commencement of the new, or renewed, employment are such that, in determining for the purposes of section 81(1) or Schedule 4 whether at any subsequent time he has been continuously employed for the requisite period, or for what period he has been continuously employed, the continuity of his period of employment would, apart from this paragraph, be treated as not having been broken by the termination of the previous employment and the commencement of the new, or renewed, employment.

(3) For the purposes of this paragraph, a redundancy payment shall be treated as having been paid if—

(a) the whole of the payment has been paid to the employee by the employer, or, in a case where a tribunal has determined that the employer is liable to pay part (but not the whole) of the redundancy payment, that part of the redundancy payment has been paid in full to the employee by the employer, or

(b) the Secretary of State has paid a sum to the employee in respect of the redundancy payment under section 106.

Certain weeks of employment to be disregarded for purposes of Schedule 4

13 ...

Redundancy payments: employment wholly or partly abroad

14 (1) In computing in relation to an employee the period specified in section 81(4) or the period specified in paragraph 1 of Schedule 4, a week of employment shall not count if—

(a) the employee was employed outside Great Britain during the whole or part of that week, and

(b) he was not during that week, or during the corresponding contribution week,—

[(ia) where the week is a week of employment beginning after 1st July 1992, an employed earner for the purposes of the Social Security Contributions and Benefits Act 1992 in respect of whom a secondary Class I contribution was payable under that Act; or]

(i) where the week is a week of employment after 1st June 1976 [and not falling within sub-paragraph (ia) above], an employed earner for the purposes of the Social Security Act 1975 in respect of whom a secondary Class 1 contribution was payable under that Act; or

(ii) where the week is a week of employment after 6th April 1975 and before 1st June 1976, an employed earner for the purposes of the Social Security Act 1975; or

(iii) where the week is a week of employment before 6th April 1975, an employee in respect of whom an employer's contribution was payable in respect of the corresponding contribution week;

whether or not the contribution mentioned in paragraph (i) or (iii) of this sub-paragraph was in fact paid.

(2) For the purposes of the application of sub-paragraph (1) to a week of employment where the corresponding contribution week began before 5th July 1948, an employer's contribution shall be treated as payable as mentioned in sub-paragraph (1) if such a contribution would have been so payable if the statutory provisions relating to national insurance which were in force on 5th July 1948 had been in force in that contribution week.

(3) Where by virtue of sub-paragraph (1) a week of employment does not count in computing such a period as is mentioned in that sub-paragraph, the continuity of that period shall not be broken by reason only that that week of employment does not count in computing that period.

(4) Any question arising under this paragraph whether—

(a) an employer's contribution was or would have been payable, as mentioned in sub-paragraph (1) or (2), or

(b) a person was an employed earner for the purposes of the Social Security Act 1975 [or the Social Security Contributions and Benefits Act 1992] and if so whether a secondary Class 1 contribution was payable in respect of him under that Act,

shall be determined by the Secretary of State: and any legislation (including regulations) as to the determination of questions which under that Act the Secretary of State is empowered to determine (including provisions as to the reference of questions for decision, or as to appeals, to the High Court or the Court of Session) shall apply to the determination of any question by the Secretary of State under this paragraph.

(5) In this paragraph "employer's contribution" has the same meaning as in the National Insurance Act 1965, and "corresponding contribution week", in relation to a week of employment, means a contribution week (within the meaning of the said Act of 1965) of which so much as falls within the period beginning with midnight between Sunday and Monday and ending with Saturday also falls within that week of employment.

(6) The provisions of this paragraph shall not apply in relation to a person who is employed as a master or seaman in a British ship and is ordinarily resident in Great Britain.

Industrial disputes

15 (1) A week shall not count under paragraph 3, 4, 5, 9 or 10 if in that week, or any part of that week, the employee takes part in a strike.

(2) The continuity of an employee's period of employment is not broken by a week which does not count under this Schedule, and which begins after 5th July 1964 if in that week, or any part of that week, the employee takes part in a strike.

(3) Sub-paragraph (2) applies whether or not the week would, apart from sub-paragraph (1), have counted under this Schedule.

(4) The continuity of the period of employment is not broken by a week which begins after 5th July 1964 and which does not count under this Schedule, if in that week, or any part of that week, the employee is absent from work because of a lock-out by the employer.

Reinstatement after service with the armed forces, etc

16 (1) If a person who is entitled to apply to his former employer under [the Reserve Forces (Safeguard of Employment) Act 1985] enters the employment of that employer not later than the end of the six month period mentioned in [section 1(4)(b)] of that Act, his previous period of employment with that employer (or if there was more than one such period, the last of those periods) and the period of employment beginning in the said period of six months shall be treated as continuous.

(2) . . .

Change of employer

17 (1) Subject to this paragraph and [paragraphs 18 and 18A], the foregoing provisions of this Schedule relate only to employment by the one employer.

(2) If a trade or business or an undertaking (whether or not it be an undertaking established by or under an Act of Parliament) is transferred from one person to another, the period of employment of an employee in the trade or business or undertaking at the time of the transfer shall count as a period of employment with the transferee, and the transfer shall not break the continuity of the period of employment.

(3) If by or under an Act of Parliament, whether public or local and whether passed before or after this Act, a contract of employment between any body corporate and an employee is modified and some other body corporate is substituted as the employer, the employee's period of employment at the time when the modification takes effect shall count as a period of employment with the second-mentioned body corporate, and the change of employer shall not break the continuity of the period of employment.

(4) If on the death of an employer the employee is taken into the employment of the personal representatives or trustees of the deceased, the employee's period of employment at the time of the death shall count as a period of employment with the employer's personal representatives or trustees, and the death shall not break the continuity of the period of employment.

(5) If there is a change in the partners, personal representatives or trustees who employ any person, the employee's period of employment at the time of the change shall count as a period of employment with the partners, personal representatives or trustees after the change, and the change shall not break the continuity of the period of employment.

18 If an employee of an employer is taken into the employment of another employer who, at the time when the employee enters his employment is an associated employer of the first-mentioned employer, the employee's period of employment at that time shall count as a period of employment with the second-mentioned employer and the change of employer shall not break the continuity of the period of employment.

[**18A** (1) If an employee of one of the employers described in sub-paragraph (2) is taken into the employment of another of those employers, his period of employment at the time of the change of employer shall count as a period of employment with the second employer and the change shall not break the continuity of the period of employment.

(2) The employers referred to in sub-paragraph (1) are the governors of the schools maintained by a local education authority and that authority.]

Crown employment

19 (1) Subject to the following provisions of this paragraph, the provisions of this Schedule shall have effect (for the purpose of computing an employee's period of employment, but not for any other purpose) in relation to Crown employment and to persons in Crown employment as they have effect in relation to other employment and to other employees, and accordingly, except where the context otherwise requires, references to an employer shall be construed as including a reference to the Crown.

(2) In this paragraph, subject to sub-paragraph (3), "Crown employment" means employment under or for the purposes of a government department or any officer or body exercising on behalf of the Crown functions conferred by any enactment.

(3) This paragraph does not apply to service as a member of the naval, military or air forces of the Crown . . ., but does apply to employment by any association established for the purposes of [Part VI of the Reserve Forces Act 1980].

(4) In so far as a person in Crown employment is employed otherwise than under a contract of employment, references in this Schedule to an employee's relations with his employer being governed by a contract of employment which normally involves employment for a certain number of hours weekly shall be modified accordingly.

(5) The reference in paragraph 17(2) to an undertaking shall be construed as including a reference to any function of (as the case may require) a Minister of the Crown, a government department, or any other officer or body performing functions on behalf of the Crown.

Reinstatement or re-engagement of dismissed employee

20 (1) Regulations made by the Secretary of State may make provision—

   (a) for preserving the continuity of a person's period of employment for the purposes of this Schedule or for the purposes of this Schedule as applied by or under any other enactment specified in the regulations, or
   (b) for modifying or excluding the operation of paragraph 12 subject to the recovery of any such payment as is mentioned in sub-paragraph (2) of that paragraph,

in cases where, in consequence of action to which sub-paragraph (2) applies, a dismissed employee is reinstated or re-engaged by his employer or by a successor or associated employer of that employer.

(2) This sub-paragraph applies to any action taken in relation to the dismissal of an employee which consists—

   (a) of the presentation by him of a *complaint under section 67,* [relevant complaint of dismissal] or
   (b) of his making a claim in accordance with a dismissal procedures agreement designated by an order under section 65, or

(c) of any action taken by a conciliation officer under *section 134(3)* [his relevant conciliation powers or].

[(d) of the making of a relevant compromise contract.]

[(3) In sub-paragraph (2)—

"relevant complaint of dismissal" means a complaint under section 67 of this Act, a complaint under section 63 of the Sex Discrimination Act 1975 arising out of a dismissal or a complaint under section 54 of the Race Relations Act 1976 arising out of a dismissal;

"relevant conciliation powers" means section 134(3) of this Act, section 64(2) of the Sex Discrimination Act 1975 or section 55(2) of the Race Relations Act 1976; and

"relevant compromise contract" means an agreement or contract authorised by section 140(2)(fa) or (fb) of this Act, section 77(4)(aa) of the Sex Discrimination Act 1975 or section 72(4)(aa) of the Race Relations Act 1976.]

Employment before the commencement of Act

21 Save as otherwise expressly provided, the provisions of this Schedule apply to periods before it comes into force as they apply to later periods.

22 If, in any week beginning before 6th July 1964, the employee was, for the whole or any part of the week, absent from work—

(a) because he was taking part in a strike, or

(b) because of a lock-out by the employer,

the week shall count as a period of employment.

23 Without prejudice to the foregoing provisions of this Schedule, any week which counted as a period of employment in the computation of a period of employment in accordance with the Contracts of Employment Act 1972 whether for the purposes of that Act, the Redundancy Payments Act 1965, the Trade Union and Labour Relations Act 1974 or the Employment Protection Act 1975, shall count as a period of employment for the purposes of this Act, and any week which did not break the continuity of a person's employment for the purposes of those Acts shall not break the continuity of a period of employment for the purposes of this Act.

Interpretation

24 (1) In this Schedule, unless the context otherwise requires,—

"lock-out" means the closing of a place of employment, or the suspension of work, or the refusal by an employer to continue to employ any number of persons employed by him in consequence of a dispute, done with a view to compelling those persons, or to aid another employer in compelling persons employed by him, to accept terms or conditions of or affecting employment;

"strike" means the cessation of work by a body of persons employed acting in combination, or a concerted refusal or a refusal under a common understanding of any number of persons employed to continue to work for an employer in consequence of a dispute, done as a means of compelling their employer or any person or body of persons employed, or to aid other employees in compelling their employer or any person or body of persons employed, to accept or not to accept terms or conditions of or affecting employment;

"week" means a week ending with Saturday.

(2) For the purposes of this Schedule the hours of employment of an employee who is required by the terms of his employment to live on the premises where he works shall be the hours during which he is on duty or during which his services may be required. **[419]**

NOTES

Para 1: substituted with savings for the original paras 1, 2 by the Employment Act 1982, s 20, Sch 2, para 7(2). Note that there is now no para 2.

Para 8: substituted with savings by the Employment Act 1982, s 20, Sch 2, para 7(3).

Para 9: word in italics substituted by word in square brackets immediately following by the Trade Union Reform and Employment Rights Act 1993, s 49(2), Sch 8, para 31(a), as from day to be appointed.

Para 10: words in square brackets substituted by the Employment Act 1980, s 20, Sch 1, para 31; words in italics substituted respectively by words in square brackets immediately following by the Trade Union Reform and Employment Rights Act 1993, s 49(2), Sch 8, para 31(b), as from a day to be appointed.

Para 11: words in first pair of square brackets inserted by the Employment Act 1980, s 20, Sch 1, para 32; words in second pair of square brackets inserted by the Employment Act 1982, s 21, Sch 3, Pt II, para 29; figure in italics repealed by the Trade Union Reform and Employment Rights Act 1993, s 51, Sch 10, as from 30 August 1993 (SI 1993/1908).

Para 13: repealed by the Employment Act 1982, s 21(3), Sch 4.

Para 14: sub-para (1)(b)(ia), and words in sub-paras (1)(b)(i), (4)(b), inserted by the Social Security (Consequential Provisions) Act 1992, s 4, Sch 2, para 51.

Para 16: words in square brackets in sub-para (1) substituted, and sub-para (2) repealed, by the Reserve Forces (Safeguard of Employment) Act 1985, s 21, Sch 4, Sch 5.

Para 17: words in square brackets in sub-para (1) substituted by the Employment Act 1982, s 21, Sch 3, Pt I, para 2(2).

Para 18A: inserted by the Employment Act 1982, s 21, Sch 3, Pt I, para 2(3).

Para 19: words omitted repealed by the Armed Forces Act 1981, s 28, Sch 5, Pt I; words in square brackets substituted by the Reserve Forces Act 1980, s 157, Sch 9, para 17.

Para 20: words in italics substituted respectively by words in square brackets immediately following and sub-paras (2)(d), (3) are added, by the Trade Union Reform and Employment Rights Act 1993, s 49(1), Sch 7, para 14, as from 30 August 1993 (SI 1993/1908).

SCHEDULE 14

Section 152

CALCULATION OF NORMAL WORKING HOURS AND A WEEK'S PAY

PART I
NORMAL WORKING HOURS

1 For the purposes of this Schedule the cases where there are normal working hours include cases where the employee is entitled to overtime pay when employed for more than a fixed number of hours in a week or other period, and, subject to paragraph 2, in those cases that fixed number of hours shall be the normal working hours.

2 If in such a case—

(a) the contract of employment fixes the number, or the minimum number, of hours of employment in the said week or other period (whether or not it also provides for the reduction of that number or minimum in certain circumstances), and

(b) that number or minimum number of hours exceeds the number of hours without overtime,

that number or minimum number of hours (and not the number of hours without overtime) shall be the normal working hours.   **[420]**

PART II
A WEEK'S PAY

Employments for which there are normal working hours

3 (1) This paragraph and paragraph 4 shall apply if there are normal working hours for an employee when employed under the contract of employment in force on the calculation date.

(2) Subject to paragraph 4, if an employee's remuneration for employment in normal working hours, whether by the hour or week or other period, does not vary with the amount of work done in the period, the amount of a week's pay shall be the amount which is payable by the employer under the contract of employment in force on the calculation date if the employee works throughout his normal working hours in a week.

(3) Subject to paragraph 4, if sub-paragraph (2) does not apply, the amount of a week's pay shall be the amount of remuneration for the number of normal working hours in a week calculated at the average hourly rate of remuneration payable by the employer to the employee in respect of the period of twelve weeks—

(a) where the calculation date is the last day of a week, ending with that week;

(b) in any other case, ending with the last complete week before the calculation date.

(4) References in this paragraph to remuneration varying with the amount of work done include references to remuneration which may include any commission or similar payment which varies in amount.

4 (1) This paragraph shall apply if there are normal working hours for an employee when employed under the contract of employment in force on the calculation date, and he is required under that contract to work during those hours on days of the week or at times of the day which differ from week to week or over a longer period so that the remuneration payable for, or apportionable to, any week varies according to the incidence of the said days or times.

(2) The amount of a week's pay shall be the amount of remuneration for the average weekly number of normal working hours (calculated in accordance with sub-paragraph (3)) at the average hourly rate of remuneration (calculated in accordance with sub-paragraph (4)).

(3) The average number of weekly hours shall be calculated by dividing by twelve the total number of the employee's normal working hours during the period of twelve weeks—

    (a) where the calculation date is the last day of a week, ending with that week;

    (b) in any other case, ending with the last complete week before the calculation date.

(4) The average hourly rate of remuneration shall be the average hourly rate of remuneration payable by the employer to the employee in respect of the period of twelve weeks—

    (a) where the calculation date is the last day of a week, ending with that week;

    (b) in any other case, ending with the last complete week before the calculation date.

5 (1) For the purpose of paragraphs 3 and 4, in arriving at the average hourly rate of remuneration only the hours when the employee was working, and only the remuneration payable for, or apportionable to, those hours of work, shall be brought in; and if for any of the twelve weeks mentioned in either of those paragraphs no such remuneration was payable by the employer to the employee, account shall be taken of remuneration in earlier weeks so as to bring the number of weeks of which account is taken up to twelve.

(2) Where, in arriving at the said hourly rate of remuneration, account has to be taken of remuneration payable for, or apportionable to, work done in hours other than normal working hours, and the amount of that remuneration was greater than it would have been if the work had been done in normal working hours, account shall be taken of that remuneration as if—

    (a) the work had been done in normal working hours; and

    (b) the amount of that remuneration had been reduced accordingly.

(3) For the purpose of the application of sub-paragraph (2) to a case falling within paragraph 2, sub-paragraph (2) shall be construed as if for the words "had been done in normal working hours", in each place where those words occur, there were substituted the words "had been done in normal working hours falling within the number of hours without overtime".

Employments for which there are no normal working hours

6 (1) This paragraph shall apply if there are no normal working hours for an employee when employed under the contract of employment in force on the calculation date.

(2) The amount of a week's pay shall be the amount of the employee's average weekly remuneration in the period of twelve weeks—

    (a) where the calculation date is the last day of a week, ending with that week;

    (b) in any other case, ending with the last complete week before the calculation date.

(3) In arriving at the said average weekly rate of remuneration no account shall be taken of a week in which no remuneration was payable by the employer to the employee and remuneration in earlier weeks shall be brought in so as to bring the number of weeks of which account is taken up to twelve.

The calculation date

7 (1) For the purposes of this Part, the calculation date is,—

    (a) where the calculation is for the purposes of section 14, the day in respect of which the guarantee payment is payable, or, where an employee's contract has been varied, or a new contract entered into, in connection with a period of short-time working, the last day on which the original contract was in force;

(b)   where the calculation is for the purposes of section 21, the day before that on which the suspension referred to in section 19(1) begins;

(c)   where the calculation is for the purposes of section 31, the day on which the employer's notice was given;

[(cc)   where the calculation is for the purposes of section 31A, the day of the appointment concerned;]

(d)   ...

(e)   where the calculation is for the purposes of Schedule 3, the day immediately preceding the first day of the period of notice required by section 49(1) or, as the case may be, section 49(2);

[(ea)   where the calculation is for the purposes of section 47, the day before the suspension referred to in section 45(1) begins or where that day falls within an employee's maternity leave period or within the further period up to the day on which an employee exercises her right to return to work under section 39, the day before the beginning of the maternity leave period;]

(f)   where the calculation is for the purposes of section 53 or 71(2)(b) and the dismissal was with notice, the date on which the employer's notice was given;

(g)   where the calculation is for the purposes of section 53 or 71(2)(b) but sub-paragraph (f) does not apply, the effective date of termination;

(h)   where the calculation is for the purposes of section 73 and by virtue of section 55(5) [or, as the case may be, (6)] a date is to be treated as the effective date of termination for the purposes of section 73(3) which is later than the effective date of termination as defined by section 55(4), the effective date of termination as defined by section 55(4);

(i)   where the calculation is for the purposes of section 73 but [neither subsection (5) nor subsection (6) of section 55 applies] in relation to the date of termination, the date on which notice would have been given had the conditions referred to in sub-paragraph (2) been fulfilled (whether those conditions were in fact fulfilled or not);

[(ia)   where the calculation is for the purposes of section 75A and the dismissal was with notice, the date on which the employer's notice was given;

(ib)   where the calculation is for the purposes of section 75A but sub-paragraph (ia) does not apply, the effective date of termination;]

(j)   where the calculation is for the purposes of section 87(2), the day immediately preceding the first of the four or, as the case may be, the six weeks referred to in section 88(1);

(k)   where the calculation is for the purposes of Schedule 4 and by virtue of section 90(3) a date is to be treated as the relevant date for the purposes of certain provisions of this Act which is later than the relevant date as defined by section 90(1), the relevant date as defined by section 90(1);

(l)   where the calculation is for the purposes of Schedule 4 but sub-paragraph (k) does not apply, the date on which notice would have been given had the conditions referred to in sub-paragraph (2) been fulfilled (whether those conditions were in fact fulfilled or not).

(2) The conditions referred to in sub-paragraphs (1)(i) and (l) are that the contract was terminable by notice and was terminated by the employer giving such notice as is required to terminate that contract by section 49 and that the notice expired on the effective date of termination or on the relevant date, as the case may be.

Maximum amount of week's pay for certain purposes

8 (1) Notwithstanding the preceding provisions of this Schedule, the amount of a week's pay for the purpose of calculating—

(a)   an additional award of compensation (within the meaning of section 71(2)(b)) shall not exceed [£205.00];

(b)   a basic award of compensation (within the meaning of section 72) shall not exceed [£205.00];

(c)   a redundancy payment shall not exceed [£205.00].

(2) The Secretary of State may after a review under section 148 vary the limit referred to in sub-paragraph (1)(a) or (b) or (c) by an order made in accordance with that section.

(3) Without prejudice to the generality of the power to make transitional provision in an order under section 148, such an order may provide that it shall apply in the case of a dismissal in relation to which the effective date of termination for the purposes of this sub-paragraph, as defined by section 55(5) [or, as the case may be, (6)], falls after the order comes into operation, notwithstanding that the effective date of termination, as defined by section 55(4), for the purposes of other provisions of this Act falls before the order comes into operation.

(4) Without prejudice to the generality of the power to make transitional provision in an order under section 148, such an order may provide that it shall apply in the case of a dismissal in relation to which the relevant date for the purposes of this sub-paragraph falls after the order comes into operation, notwithstanding that the relevant date for the purposes of other provisions of this Act falls before the order comes into operation.

Supplemental

9 In any case in which an employee has not been employed for a sufficient period to enable a calculation to be made under any of the foregoing provisions of this Part, the amount of a week's pay shall be an amount which fairly represents a week's pay; and in determining that amount the tribunal shall apply as nearly as may be such of the foregoing provisions of this Part as it considers appropriate, and may have regard to such of the following considerations as it thinks fit, that is to say—

(a) any remuneration received by the employee in respect of the employment in question;

(b) the amount offered to the employee as remuneration in respect of the employment in question;

(c) the remuneration received by other persons engaged in relevant comparable employment with the same employer;

(d) the remuneration received by other persons engaged in relevant comparable employment with other employers.

10 In arriving at an average hourly rate or average weekly rate of remuneration under this Part account shall be taken of work for a former employer within the period for which the average is to be taken if, by virtue of Schedule 13, a period of employment with the former employer counts as part of the employee's continuous period of employment with the later employer.

11 Where under this Part account is to be taken of remuneration or other payments for a period which does not coincide with the periods for which the remuneration or other payments are calculated, then the remuneration or other payments shall be apportioned in such manner as may be just.

12 The Secretary of State may by regulations provide that in prescribed cases the amount of a week's pay shall be calculated in such manner as the regulations may prescribe. **[421]**

NOTES

Para 7: in sub-para (1) sub-para (cc) inserted by the Employment Act 1980, s 20, Sch 1, para 33; sub-para (d) repealed by the Social Security Act 1986, s 86, Sch 11; paras (ea), (ia), (ib) inserted by the Trade Union Reform and Employment Rights Act 1993, s 49(2), Sch 8, para 32, partly (insertion of paras (ia), (ib)) as from 30 August 1993 (SI 1993/1908) in sub-para (h), words in square brackets inserted by the Employment Act 1982, s 21, Sch 3, Pt II, para 30(1), (2)(a); words in square brackets in sub-para (i) substituted by the Employment Act 1982, s 21, Sch 3, Pt II, para 30(1), (2)(b).

Para 8: in sub-para (1) sums in square brackets substituted by SI 1992/312, art 2, with effect from 1 April 1992. There was no further increase in 1993. Previous maxima were £198 from 1 April 1991 (SI 1991/1464) and £184 from 1 April 1990 (SI 1990/384); words in square brackets in sub-para (3) inserted by the Employment Act 1982, s 21, Sch 3, Pt II, para 30(1), (3).

Modified by the Land Authority for Wales (Compensation for Premature Retirement) Regulations 1984, SI 1984/2048, the Local Government Reorganisation (Compensation) Regulations 1986, SI 1986/151, regs 3, 4, 5, Sch 1, Pt II; and the Education (Reorganisation in Inner London) (Compensation) Regulations 1989, SI 1989/1139, regs 3(6), 4(4), (6), (8), Schedule, Pt III.

SCHEDULE 15

Section 159

TRANSITIONAL PROVISIONS AND SAVINGS

General

1 So far as anything done or treated as done under or for the purposes of any enactment repealed by this Act could have been done under a corresponding provision of this Act it shall not be invalidated by the repeal but shall have effect as if done under or for the purposes of that provision.

2 Where any period of time specified in an enactment repealed by this Act is current immediately before the corresponding provision of this Act comes into force, this Act shall have effect as if the corresponding provision had been in force when that period began to run.

3 Nothing in this Act shall affect the enactments repealed by this Act in their operation in relation to offences committed before the commencement of this Act.

4 Any reference in an enactment or document, whether express or implied, to—

    (a)   an enactment which is re-enacted in a corresponding provision of this Act;

    (b)   an enactment replaced or amended by a provision of the Employment Protection Act 1975 which is re-enacted in a corresponding provision of this Act;

    (c)   an enactment in the Industrial Relations Act 1971 which was re-enacted with or without amendment in a corresponding provision in Schedule 1 to the Trade Union and Labour Relations Act 1974 and that corresponding provision is re-enacted by a corresponding provision of this Act;

shall, except so far as the context otherwise requires, be construed as, or as including, a reference to the corresponding provision of this Act.

5 Paragraphs 1 to 4 have effect subject to the following provisions of this Schedule.

Guarantee payments

6 . . .

Maternity pay

7 . . .

Termination of employment

8 Sections 49 and 50 apply in relation to any contract made before the commencement of this Act.

Unfair dismissal

9 . . .

10 (1) Section 54 does not apply to a dismissal from employment under a contract for a fixed term of two years or more, where the contract was made before 28th February 1972 and is not a contract of apprenticeship, and the dismissal consists only of the expiry of that term without its being renewed.

(2) Sub-paragraph (1) in its application to an employee treated as unfairly dismissed by virtue of subsection (1) or (2) of section 60 shall have effect as if for the reference to 28th February 1972 there were substituted a reference to 1st June 1976.

Redundancy

11 . . .

12 Section 81 shall not apply to an employee who immediately before the relevant date (within the meaning of section 90) is employed under a contract of employment for a fixed term of two years or more, if that contract was made before 6th December 1965 and is not a contract of apprenticeship.

13, 14 . . .

Insolvency

15 (1) Subject to sub-paragraph (2), the provisions of sections 122 and 123 shall apply in relation to an employer who becomes insolvent (within the meaning of section 127) after 19th April 1976, and shall in such a case apply to any debts mentioned in section 122 and to any unpaid relevant contribution (within the meaning of section 123), whether falling due before or after that date.

(2) Section 122 shall have effect in relation to any case where the employer became insolvent before 1st February 1978 as if for each reference to £100 there were substituted a reference to £80.

Calculation of a week's pay

16 . . .

Computation of period of continuous employment

17 For the purposes of the computation of a period of continuous employment falling to be made before 1st February 1977—

    (a)   paragraphs 3 and 4 of Schedule 13 shall have effect as if for the word "sixteen" there were substituted the word "twenty-one", and

    (b)   paragraphs 5, 6 and 7 of that Schedule shall not apply.

Legal proceedings

18 Notwithstanding the repeal of any enactment by this Act, the Employment Appeal Tribunal and the industrial tribunals may continue to exercise the jurisdiction conferred on them by or under any enactment which is repealed by this Act with respect to matters arising out of or in connection with the repealed enactments.

House of Commons staff

19 . . .   [422]

NOTES

Paras 6, 9, 11, 13, 16, 19: repealed by the Statute Law (Repeals) Act 1989.

Para 7: repealed by the Social Security Act 1986, s 86, Sch 11.

Para 10: sub-para (2) repealed by the Trade Union Reform and Employment Rights Act 1993, s 51, Sch 10, as from a day to be appointed.

Para 13: repealed with savings by the Employment Act 1989, s 29(4), (6), Sch 7, Pt II, Sch 9, and by the Statute Law (Repeals) Act 1989.

Para 14: repealed by the Health and Social Services and Social Security Adjudications Act 1983, s 30, Sch 10.

(Schs 16, 17 (consequential amendments, repeals) omitted.)

EMPLOYMENT (CONTINENTAL SHELF) ACT 1978
(1978 c 46)

An Act to make provision for the application of certain enactments to employment connected with the exploration or exploitation of areas of the continental shelf adjacent to areas designated under the Continental Shelf Act 1964.

[31 July 1978]

1 Powers to apply employment legislation

(1) ...

(2) In relation to employment concerned with the exploration or exploitation of a cross-boundary petroleum field, the powers to make Orders in Council under—

    (a)   section 10(5) of the Sex Discrimination Act 1975, and
    (b)   section 8(5) of the Race Relations Act 1976,

in respect of designated areas shall be exercisable also in respect of foreign sectors of the continental shelf.   **[423]**

NOTES
    Sub-s (1): repealed by the Trade Union and Labour Relations (Consolidation) Act 1992, s 300(1), Sch 1.
    Sub-s (2): repealed by the Oil and Gas (Enterprise) Act 1982, s 37(2), Sch 4, as from a day to be appointed.

2 Interpretation

In section 1 above—

    "cross-boundary petroleum field" means a petroleum field that extends across the boundary between a designated area and a foreign sector of the continental shelf;
    "designated area" means an area designated under section 1(7) of the Continental Shelf Act 1964;
    "foreign sector of the continental shelf" means an area which is outside the territorial waters of any State and within which rights are exercisable by a State other than the United Kingdom with respect to the sea bed and subsoil and their natural resources;
    "petroleum field" means a geological structure identified as an oil or gas field by the Order in Council concerned.   **[424]**

NOTE
    Repealed by the Oil and Gas (Enterprise) Act 1982, s 37(2), Sch 4, as from a day to be appointed.

3 Short title

This Act may be cited as the Employment (Continental Shelf) Act 1978.   **[425]**

NOTE
    Repealed by the Oil and Gas (Enterprise) Act 1982, s 37(2), Sch 4, as from a day to be appointed.

EMPLOYMENT ACT 1980 (NOTE)
(1980 c 42)

GENERAL NOTE
    Almost all of this Act has either been repealed (ss 1–5, 11, 16–19) or amends other legislation (which is printed as amended elsewhere in this work) (ss 6–10, 12–15). The only surviving provisions deal with

commencement, extension to Northern Ireland, and consequential amendments and repeals (ss 20, 21, Schs 1, 2) and are omitted.

Ss 1–5, 16, 19 are consolidated in the Trade Union and Labour Relations (Consolidation) Act 1992: see Destination Table below, para [982A] for details.

[425A]

SOCIAL SECURITY AND HOUSING BENEFITS ACT 1982
(NOTE)
(1982 c 24)

GENERAL NOTE

Relevant parts of this Act (ie those dealing with Statutory Sick Pay) have been repealed and re-enacted in the Social Security Contributions and Benefits Act 1992, Pt XI (below, paras [613]–[625]).

[425B]

EMPLOYMENT ACT 1982
(1982 c 46)

ARRANGEMENT OF SECTIONS

An Act to provide for compensation out of public funds for certain past cases of dismissal for failure to conform to the requirements of a union membership agreement; to amend the law relating to workers, employers, trade unions and employers' associations; to make provision with respect to awards by industrial tribunals and awards by, and the procedure of, the Employment Appeal Tribunal; and for connected purposes

[28 October 1982]

1–19 (*S 1 repealed by the Companies Consolidation (Consequential Provisions) Act 1985, Sch 2; ss 2–19 repealed by the Trade Union and Labour Relations (Consolidation) Act 1992, s 300(1), Sch 1. For those provisions consolidated in the 1992 Act, see Destination Table below, para* [982A].)

Periods of continuous employment

20 Change of basis of computation of period of continuous employment

(1) The amendments set out in Schedule 2 shall have effect for the following purposes—

    (a) amending enactments which confer rights by reference to the length of an employee's period of continuous employment so as to substitute for

periods expressed in weeks or years of fifty-two weeks corresponding periods expressed in months or years of twelve months;
  (b) modifying the computation of an employee's period of continuous employment under Schedule 13 to the 1978 Act so as to provide for computing the length of the period in months and years of twelve months;
  (c) making minor and consequential amendments in connection with the purposes mentioned in paragraphs (a) and (b).

(2) The amendments set out in Schedule 2 shall not apply—
  (a) where the date by reference to which the length of an employee's period of continuous employment falls to be ascertained ("the qualification date") is before the commencement of this section, or
  (b) where the result would be to deprive a person of any right or entitlement which he would have had if the qualification date had fallen immediately before the commencement of this section.

(3) Subject to subsection (2), the amendments set out in Schedule 2 shall, so far as they relate to the computation of the length of a period of continuous employment, apply to periods before the commencement of this section as they apply to later periods.

(4) Nothing in this section shall affect—
  (a) any order made before the commencement of this section under section 18, 65 or 96 of the 1978 Act or any corresponding earlier enactment (exclusion of certain sections where equivalent protection afforded by collective agreement or wages order); or
  (b) the operation of any agreement or wages order to which such an order relates or the operation of any provision of the 1978 Act in relation to such an agreement or wages order.   **[425C]**

Supplemental

21 Interpretation, minor and consequential amendments and repeals

(1) In this Act "the 1978 Act" means the Employment Protection (Consolidation) Act 1978.

(2), (3) ...   **[425D]**

NOTE
  Sub-ss (2), (3): enact Schs 3, 4 (minor and consequential amendments and repeals).

22 Short title, commencement and extent

(1) This Act may be cited as the Employment Act 1982.

(2)–(5) ...   **[425E]**

NOTES
  Sub-ss (2), (3): commencement provisions; omitted.
  Sub-ss (4), (5): repealed by the Trade Union and Labour Relations (Consolidation) Act 1992, s 300(1), Sch 1.

(Sch 1 repealed by the Trade Union and Labour Relations (Consolidation) Act 1992, s 300(1), Sch 1; Schs 2–4 (amendments to the Employment Protection (Consolidation) Act 1978, consequential amendments and repeals) omitted.)

DATA PROTECTION ACT 1984
(1984 c 35)

ARRANGEMENT OF SECTIONS

An Act to regulate the use of automatically processed information relating to individuals and the provision of services in respect of such information

[12 July 1984]

NOTE

   This Act is reproduced in edited form to give those sections of most direct relevance to employment law and those sections that bear on their interpretation.

PART I

PRELIMINARY

1 Definition of "data" and related expressions

(1) The following provisions shall have effect for the interpretation of this Act.

(2) "Data" means information recorded in a form in which it can be processed by equipment operating automatically in response to instructions given for that purpose.

(3) "Personal data" means data consisting of information which relates to a living individual who can be identified from that information (or from that and other information in the possession of the data user), including any expression of opinion about the individual but not any indication of the intentions of the data user in respect of that individual.

(4) "Data subject" means an individual who is the subject of personal data.

(5) "Data user" means a person who holds data, and a person "holds" data if—

   (a) the data form part of a collection of data processed or intended to be processed by or on behalf of that person as mentioned in subsection (2) above; and

   (b) that person (either alone or jointly or in common with other persons) controls the contents and use of the data comprised in the collection; and

   (c) the data are in the form in which they have been or are intended to be processed as mentioned in paragraph (a) above or (though not for the time being in that form) in a form into which they have been converted after being so processed and with a view to being further so processed on a subsequent occasion.

(6) A person carries on a "computer bureau" if he provides other persons with services in respect of data, and a person provides such service if—

   (a) as agent for other persons he causes data held by them to be processed as mentioned in subsection (2) above; or

   (b) he allows other persons the use of equipment in his possession for the processing as mentioned in that subsection of data held by them.

(7) "Processing", in relation to data, means amending, augmenting, deleting or re-arranging the data or extracting the information constituting the data and, in the case of personal data, means performing any of those operations by reference to the data subject.

(8) Subsection (7) above shall not be construed as applying to any operation performed only for the purpose of preparing the text of documents.

(9) "Disclosing", in relation to data, includes disclosing information extracted from the data; and where the identification of the individual who is the subject of personal data depends partly on the information constituting the data and partly on other information in the possession of the data user, the data shall not be regarded as disclosed or transferred unless the other information is also disclosed or transferred.

[426]

2 The data protection principles

(1) Subject to subsection (3) below, references in this Act to the data protection principles are to the principles set out in Part I of Schedule 1 to this Act; and those principles shall be interpreted in accordance with Part II of that Schedule.

(2) The first seven principles apply to personal data held by data users and the eighth applies both to such data and to personal data in respect of which services are provided by persons carrying on computer bureaux.

(3) The Secretary of State may by order modify or supplement those principles for the purpose of providing additional safeguards in relation to personal data consisting of information as to—

 (a) the racial origin of the data subject;

 (b) his political opinions or religious or other beliefs;

 (c) his physical or mental health or his sexual life; or

 (d) his criminal convictions;

and references in this Act to the data protection principles include, except where the context otherwise requires, references to any modified or additional principle having effect by virtue of an order under this subsection.

(4) An order under subsection (3) above may modify a principle either by modifying the principle itself or by modifying its interpretation; and where an order under that subsection modifies a principle or provides for an additional principle it may contain provisions for the interpretation of the modified or additional principle.

(5) An order under subsection (3) above modifying the third data protection principle may, to such extent as the Secretary of State thinks appropriate, exclude or modify in relation to that principle any exemption from the non-disclosure provisions which is contained in Part IV of this Act; and the exemptions from those provisions contained in that Part shall accordingly have effect subject to any order made by virtue of this subsection.

(6) An order under subsection (3) above may make different provision in relation to data consisting of information of different descriptions.   **[427]**

NOTE

No order had been made under this section at the date of going to press.

3 The Registrar and the Tribunal

(1) For the purposes of this Act there shall be—

 (a) an officer known as the Data Protection Registrar (in this Act referred to as "the Registrar"); and

 (b) a tribunal known as the Data Protection Tribunal (in this Act referred to as "the Tribunal").

(2) The Registrar shall be appointed by Her Majesty by Letters Patent.

(3) The Tribunal shall consist of—

 (a) a chairman appointed by the Lord Chancellor after consultation with the Lord Advocate;

 (b) such number of deputy chairmen appointed as aforesaid as the Lord Chancellor may determine; and

 (c) such number of other members appointed by the Secretary of State as he may determine.

(4) The members of the Tribunal appointed under subsection (3)(a) and (b) above shall be—

    [(a) persons who have a 7 year general qualification, within the meaning of section 71 of the Courts and Legal Services Act 1990;

    (b) advocates or solicitors in Scotland of at least 7 years' standing; or

    (c) members of the Bar of Northern Ireland or solicitors of the Supreme Court of Northern Ireland of at least 7 years' standing.]

(5) The members of the Tribunal appointed under subsection (3)(c) above shall be—

    (a) persons to represent the interests of data users; and

    (b) persons to represent the interests of data subjects.

(6) Schedule 2 to this Act shall have effect in relation to the Registrar and the Tribunal.   **[428]**

NOTE

Sub-s (4): words in square brackets substituted by the Courts and Legal Services Act 1990, s 71(2), Sch 10, para 58.

PART II

REGISTRATION AND SUPERVISION OF DATA USERS AND COMPUTER BUREAUX

Registration

4 Registration of data users and computer bureaux

(1) The Registrar shall maintain a register of data users who hold, and of persons carrying on computer bureaux who provide services in respect of, personal data and shall make an entry in the register in pursuance of each application for registration accepted by him under this Part of this Act.

(2) Each entry shall state whether it is in respect of a data user, of a person carrying on a computer bureau or of a data user who also carries on such a bureau.

(3) Subject to the provisions of this section, an entry in respect of a data user shall consist of the following particulars—

    (a) the name and address of the data user;

    (b) a description of the personal data to be held by him and of the purpose or purposes for which the data are to be held or used;

    (c) a description of the source or sources from which he intends or may wish to obtain the data or the information to be contained in the data;

    (d) a description of any person or persons to whom he intends or may wish to disclose the data;

    (e) the names or a description of any countries or territories outside the United Kingdom to which he intends or may wish directly or indirectly to transfer the data; and

    (f) one or more addresses for the receipt of requests from data subjects for access to the data.

(4) Subject to the provisions of this section, an entry in respect of a person carrying on a computer bureau shall consist of that person's name and address.

(5) Subject to the provisions of this section, an entry in respect of a data user who also carries on a computer bureau shall consist of his name and address and, as respects the personal data to be held by him, the particulars specified in subsection (3)(b) to (f) above.

(6) In the case of a registered company the address referred to in subsections (3)(a), (4) and (5) above is that of its registered office, and the particulars to be included in the entry shall include the company's number in the register of companies.

(7) In the case of a person (other than a registered company) carrying on a business the address referred to in subsections (3)(a), (4) and (5) above is that of his principal place of business.

(8) The Secretary of State may by order vary the particulars to be included in entries made in the register.							**[429]**

5 Prohibition of unregistered holding etc of personal data

(1) A person shall not hold personal data unless an entry in respect of that person as a data user, or as a data user who also carries on a computer bureau, is for the time being contained in the register.

(2) A person in respect of whom such an entry is contained in the register shall not—

  (a) hold personal data of any description other than that specified in the entry;
  (b) hold any such data, or use any such data held by him, for any purpose other than the purpose or purposes described in the entry;
  (c) obtain such data, or information to be contained in such data, to be held by him from any source which is not described in the entry;
  (d) disclose such data held by him to any person who is not described in the entry; or
  (e) directly or indirectly transfer such data held by him to any country or territory outside the United Kingdom other than one named or described in the entry.

(3) A servant or agent of a person to whom subsection (2) above applies shall, as respects personal data held by that person, be subject to the same restrictions on the use, disclosure or transfer of the data as those to which that person is subject under paragraphs (b), (d) and (e) of that subsection and, as respects personal data to be held by that person, to the same restrictions as those to which he is subject under paragraph (c) of that subsection.

(4) A person shall not, in carrying on a computer bureau, provide services in respect of personal data unless an entry in respect of that person as a person carrying on such a bureau, or as a data user who also carries on such a bureau, is for the time being contained in the register.

(5) Any person who contravenes subsection (1) above or knowingly or recklessly contravenes any of the other provisions of this section shall be guilty of an offence.
							[430]

NOTES

  See further, as to transitional provision relating to the holding of personal data transferred to a body corporate established under that Act: the Further and Higher Education Act 1992, s 86.

6–8 (*(Application for and duration of restrictions) omitted.*)

9 Inspection etc. of registered particulars

(1) The Registrar shall provide facilities for making the information contained in the entries in the register available for inspection (in visible and legible form) by members of the public at all reasonable hours and free of charge.

(2) The Registrar shall, on payment of such fee, if any, as may be prescribed, supply any member of the public with a duly certified copy in writing of the particulars contained in the entry made in the register in pursuance of any application for registration.   [431]

NOTES
  The Data Protection (Fees) Regulations 1986, SI 1986/1899, prescribes a fee for copies of entries of £2 per entry.

10–20 ((*Enforcement, de-registration, transfer prohibition notices, appeals, miscellaneous and penalties) omitted.*))

PART III
RIGHTS OF DATA SUBJECTS

21 Rights of access to personal data

(1) Subject to the provisions of this section, an individual shall be entitled—

  (a) to be informed by any data user whether the data held by him include personal data of which that individual is the data subject; and

  (b) to be supplied by any data user with a copy of the information constituting any such personal data held by him;

and where any of the information referred to in paragraph (b) above is expressed in terms which are not intelligible without explanation the information shall be accompanied by an explanation of those terms.

(2) A data user shall not be obliged to supply any information under subsection (1) above except in response to a request in writing and on payment of such fee (not exceeding the prescribed maximum) as he may require; but a request for information under both paragraphs of that subsection shall be treated as a single request and a request for information under paragraph (a) shall, in the absence of any indication to the contrary, be treated as extending also to information under paragraph (b).

(3) In the case of a data user having separate entries in the register in respect of data held for different purposes a separate request must be made and a separate fee paid under this section in respect of the data to which each entry relates.

(4) A data user shall not be obliged to comply with a request under this section—

  (a) unless he is supplied with such information as he may reasonably require in order to satisfy himself as to the identity of the person making the request and to locate the information which he seeks; and

  (b) if he cannot comply with the request without disclosing information relating to another individual who can be identified from that information, unless he is satisfied that the other individual has consented to the disclosure of the information to the person making the request.

(5) In paragraph (b) of subsection (4) above the reference to information relating to another individual includes a reference to information identifying that individual as the source of the information sought by the request; and that paragraph shall not be construed as excusing a data user from supplying so much of the information

sought by the request as can by supplied without disclosing the identity of the other individual concerned, whether by the omission of names or other identifying particulars or otherwise.

(6) A data user shall comply with a request under this section within forty days of receiving the request or, if later, receiving the information referred to in paragraph (a) of subsection (4) above and, in a case where it is required, the consent referred to in paragraph (b) of that subsection.

(7) The information to be supplied pursuant to a request under this section shall be supplied by reference to the data in question at the time when the request is received except that it may take account of any amendment or deletion made between that time and the time when the information is supplied, being an amendment or deletion that would have been made regardless of the receipt of the request.

(8) If a court is satisfied on the application of any person who has made a request under the foregoing provisions of this section that the data user in question has failed to comply with the request in contravention of those provisions, the court may order him to comply with the request; but a court shall not make an order under this subsection if it considers that it would in all the circumstances be unreasonable to do so, whether because of the frequency with which the applicant has made requests to the data user under those provisions or for any other reason.

(9) The Secretary of State may by order provide for enabling a request under this section to be made on behalf of any individual who is incapable by reason of mental disorder of managing his own affairs.

[432]

NOTE

The Data Protection (Subject Access) Fees Regulations 1987, SI 1987/1507, prescribe a maximum fee of £10 in respect of each request made under this section.

22 Compensation for inaccuracy

(1) An individual who is the subject of personal data held by a data user and who suffers damage by reason of the inaccuracy of the data shall be entitled to compensation from the data user for that damage and for any distress which the individual has suffered by reason of the inaccuracy.

(2) In the case of data which accurately record information received or obtained by the data user from the data subject or a third party, subsection (1) above does not apply if the following requirements have been complied with—

(a) the data indicate that the information was received or obtained as aforesaid or the information has not been extracted from the data except in a form which includes an indication to that effect; and

(b) if the data subject has notified the data user that he regards the information as incorrect or misleading, an indication to that effect has been included in the data or the information has not been extracted from the data except in a form which includes an indication to that effect.

(3) In proceedings brought against any person by virtue of this section it shall be a defence to prove that he had taken such care as in all the circumstances was reasonably required to ensure the accuracy of the data at the material time.

(4) Data are inaccurate for the purposes of this section if incorrect or misleading as to any matter of fact.

[433]

23 Compensation for loss or unauthorised disclosure

(1) An individual who is the subject of personal data held by a data user or in respect of which services are provided by a person carrying on a computer bureau and who suffers damage by reason of—

  (a) the loss of the data;

  (b) the destruction of the data without the authority of the data user or, as the case may be, of the person carrying on the bureau,; or

  (c) subject to subsection (2) below, the disclosure of the data, or access having been obtained to the data, without such authority as aforesaid,

shall be entitled to compensation from the data user or, as the case may be, the person carrying on the bureau for that damage and for any distress which the individual has suffered by reason of the loss, destruction, disclosure or access.

(2) In the case of a registered data user, subsection (1)(c) above does not apply to disclosure to, or access by, any person falling within a description specified pursuant to section 4(3)(d) above in an entry in the register relating to that data user.

(3) In proceedings brought against any person by virtue of this section it shall be a defence to prove that he had taken such care as in all the circumstances was reasonably required to prevent the loss, destruction, disclosure or access in question.

[434]

24 Rectification and erasure

(1) If a court is satisfied on the application of a data subject that personal data held by a data user of which the applicant is the subject are inaccurate within the meaning of section 22 above, the court may order the rectification or erasure of the data and of any data held by the data user and containing an expression of opinion which appears to the court to be based on the inaccurate data.

(2) Subsection (1) above applies whether or not the data accurately record information received or obtained by the data user from the data subject or a third party but where the data accurately record such information, then—

  (a) if the requirements mentioned in section 22(2) above have been complied with, the court may, instead of making an order under subsection (1) above, make an order requiring the data to be supplemented by such statement of the true facts relating to the matters dealt with by the data as the court may approve; and

  (b) if all or any of those requirements have not been complied with, the court may, instead of making an order under that subsection, make such order as it thinks fit for securing compliance with those requirements with or without a further order requiring the data to be supplemented by such a statement as is mentioned in paragraph (a) above.

(3) If a court is satisfied on the application of a data subject—

  (a) that he has suffered damage by reason of the disclosure of personal data, or of access having been obtained to personal data, in circumstances entitling him to compensation under section 23 above; and

  (b) that there is a substantial risk of further disclosure of or access to the data without such authority as is mentioned in that section,

the court may order the erasure of the data; but, in the case of data in respect of which services were being provided by a person carrying on a computer bureau, the court shall not make such an order unless such steps as are reasonably practicable have been taken for notifying the person for whom those services were provided and giving him an opportunity to be heard. [435]

25 Jurisdiction and procedure

(1) The jurisdiction conferred by sections 21 and 24 above shall be exercisable by the High Court or a county court or, in Scotland, by the Court of Session or the sheriff.

(2) For the purpose of determining any question whether an applicant under subsection (8) of section 21 above is entitled to the information which he seeks (including any question whether any relevant data are exempt from that section by virtue of Part IV of this Act) a court may require the information constituting any data held by the data user to be made available for its own inspection but shall not, pending the determination of that question in the applicant's favour, require the information sought by the applicant to be disclosed to him or his representatives whether by discovery (or, in Scotland, recovery) or otherwise. [436]

PART IV

EXEMPTIONS

26 Preliminary

(1) References in any provision of Part II or III of this Act to personal data do not include references to data which by virtue of this Part of this Act are exempt from that provision.

(2) In this Part of this Act "the subject access provisions" means—
  (a) section 21 above; and
  (b) any provision of Part II of this Act conferring a power on the Registrar to the extent to which it is exercisable by reference to paragraph (a) of the seventh data protection principle.

(3) In this Part of this Act "the non-disclosure provisions" means—
  (a) sections 5(2)(d) and 15 above; and
  (b) any provision of Part II of this Act conferring a power on the Registrar to the extent to which it is exercisable by reference to any data protection principle inconsistent with the disclosure in question.

(4) Except as provided by this Part of this Act the subject access provisions shall apply notwithstanding any enactment or rule of law prohibiting or restricting the disclosure, or authorising the withholding, of information. [437]

27 National security

(1) Personal data are exempt from the provisions of Part II of this Act and of sections 21 to 24 above if the exemption is required for the purpose of safeguarding national security.

(2) Any question whether the exemption mentioned in subsection (1) above is or at any time was required for the purpose there mentioned in respect of any personal data shall be determined by a Minister of the Crown; and a certificate signed by a Minister of the Crown certifying that the exemption is or at any time was so required shall be conclusive evidence of that fact.

(3) Personal data which are not exempt under subsection (1) above are exempt from the non-disclosure provisions in any case in which the disclosure of the data is for the purpose of safeguarding national security.

(4) For the purposes of subsection (3) above a certificate signed by a Minister of the Crown certifying that personal data are or have been disclosed for the purpose mentioned in that subsection shall be conclusive evidence of that fact.

(5) A document purporting to be such a certificate as is mentioned in this section shall be received in evidence and deemed to be such a certificate unless the contrary is proved.

(6) The powers conferred by this section on a Minister of the Crown shall not be exercisable except by a Minister who is a member of the Cabinet or by the Attorney General or the Lord Advocate.   **[438]**

28–31 ((*Crime and taxation, health and social work, regulation of financial services, and judicial appointments and legal professional privilege) omitted.*)

32 Payrolls and accounts

(1) Subject to subsection (2) below, personal data held by a data user only for one or more of the following purposes—

    (a) calculating amounts payable by way of remuneration or pensions in respect of service in any employment or office or making payments of, or of sums deducted from, such remuneration or pensions; or

    (b) keeping accounts relating to any business or other activity carried on by the data user or keeping records of purchases, sales or other transactions for the purpose of ensuring that the requisite payments are made by or to him in respect of those transactions or for the purpose of making financial or management forecasts to assist him in the conduct of any such business or activity,

are exempt from the provisions of Part II of this Act and of sections 21 to 24 above.

(2) It shall be a condition of the exemption of any data under this section that the data are not used for any purpose other than the purpose or purposes for which they are held and are not disclosed except as permitted by subsections (3) and (4) below; but the exemption shall not be lost by any use or disclosure in breach of that condition if the data user shows that he had taken such care to prevent it as in all the circumstances was reasonably required.

(3) Data held only for one or more of the purposes mentioned in subsection (1)(a) above may be disclosed—

    (a) to any person, other than the data user, by whom the remuneration or pensions in question are payable;

    (b) for the purpose of obtaining actuarial advice;

    (c) for the purpose of giving information as to the persons in any employment or office for use in medical research into the health of, or injuries suffered by, persons engaged in particular occupations or working in particular places or areas;

    (d) if the data subject (or a person acting on his behalf) has requested or consented to the disclosure of the data either generally or in the circumstances in which the disclosure in question is made; or

(e) if the person making the disclosure has reasonable grounds for believing that the disclosure falls within paragraph (d) above.

(4) Data held for any of the purposes mentioned in subsection (1) above may be disclosed—

(a) for the purpose of audit or where the disclosure is for the purpose only of giving information about the data user's financial affairs; or

(b) in any case in which disclosure would be permitted by any other provision of this Part of this Act if subsection (2) above were included among the non-disclosure provisions.

(5) In this section "remuneration" includes remuneration in kind and "pensions" includes gratuities or similar benefits.   [439]

33 Domestic or other limited purposes

(1) Personal data held by an individual and concerned only with the management of his personal, family or household affairs or held by him only for recreational purposes are exempt from the provisions of Part II of this Act and of sections 21 to 24 above.

(2) Subject to subsections (3) and (4) below—

(a) personal data held by an unincorporated members' club and relating only to the members of the club; and

(b) personal data held by a data user only for the purpose of distributing, or recording the distribution of, articles or information to the data subjects and consisting only of their names, addresses or other particulars necessary for effecting the distribution,

are exempt from the provisions of Part II of this Act and of sections 21 to 24 above.

(3) Neither paragraph (a) nor paragraph (b) of subsection (2) above applies to personal data relating to any data subject unless he has been asked by the club or data user whether he objects to the data relating to him being held as mentioned in that paragraph and has not objected.

(4) It shall be a condition of the exemption of any data under paragraph (b) of subsection (2) above that the data are not used for any purpose other than that for which they are held and of the exemption of any data under either paragraph of that subsection that the data are not disclosed except as permitted by subsection (5) below; but the first exemption shall not be lost by any use, and neither exemption shall be lost by any disclosure, in breach of that condition if the data user shows that he had taken such care to prevent it as in all the circumstances was reasonably required.

(5) Data to which subsection (4) above applies may be disclosed—

(a) if the data subject (or a person acting on his behalf) has requested or consented to the disclosure of the data either generally or in the circumstances in which the disclosure in question is made;

(b) if the person making the disclosure has reasonable grounds for believing that the disclosure falls within paragraph (a) above; or

(c) in any case in which disclosure would be permitted by any other provision of this Part of this Act if subsection (4) above were included among the non-disclosure provisions.

(6) Personal data held only for—

(a) preparing statistics; or

(b) carrying out research,

are exempt from the subject access provisions; but it shall be a condition of that exemption that the data are not used or disclosed for any other purpose and that the resulting statistics or the results of the research are not made available in a form which identifies the data subjects or any of them. **[440]**

34 Other exemptions

(1) Personal data held by any person are exempt from the provisions of Part II of this Act and of sections 21 to 24 above if the data consist of information which that person is required by or under any enactment to make available to the public, whether by publishing it, making it available for inspection or otherwise and whether gratuitously or on payment of a fee.

(2) The Secretary of State may by order exempt from the subject access provisions personal data consisting of information the disclosure of which is prohibited or restricted by or under any enactment if he considers that the prohibition or restriction ought to prevail over those provisions in the interests of the data subject or of any other individual.

(3) Where all the personal data relating to a data subject held by a data user (or all such data in respect of which a data user has a separate entry in the register) consist of information in respect of which the data subject is entitled to make a request to the data user under section 158 of the Consumer Credit Act 1974 (files of credit reference agencies)—

    (a) the data are exempt from the subject access provisions; and

    (b) any request in respect of the data under section 21 above shall be treated for all purposes as if it were a request under the said section 158.

(4) Personal data are exempt from the subject access provisions if the data are kept only for the purpose of replacing other data in the event of the latter being lost, destroyed or impaired.

(5) Personal data are exempt from the non-disclosure provisions in any case in which the disclosure is—

    (a) required by or under any enactment, by any rule of law or by the order of a court; or

    (b) made for the purpose of obtaining legal advice or for the purposes of, or in the course of, legal proceedings in which the person making the disclosure is a party or a witness.

(6) Personal data are exempt from the non-disclosure provisions in any case in which—

    (a) the disclosure is to the data subject or a person acting on his behalf; or

    (b) the data subject or any such person has requested or consented to the particular disclosure in question; or

    (c) the disclosure is by a data user or a person carrying on a computer bureau to his servant or agent for the purpose of enabling the servant or agent to perform his functions as such; or

    (d) the person making the disclosure has reasonable grounds for believing that the disclosure falls within any of the foregoing paragraphs of this subsection.

(7) Section 4(3)(d) above does not apply to any disclosure falling within paragraph (a), (b) or (c) of subsection (6) above; and that subsection shall apply to the restriction on disclosure in section 33(6) above as it applies to the non-disclosure provisions.

(8) Personal data are exempt from the non-disclosure provisions in any case in which the disclosure is urgently required for preventing injury or other damage to the health of any person or persons; and in proceedings against any person for contravening a provision mentioned in section 26(3)(a) above it shall be a defence to prove that he had reasonable grounds for believing that the disclosure in question was urgently required for that purpose.

(9) A person need not comply with a notice, request or order under the subject access provisions if compliance would expose him to proceedings for any offence other than an offence under this Act; and information disclosed by any person in compliance with such a notice, request or order shall not be admissible against him in proceedings for an offence under this Act. **[441]**

NOTE
Order under this section: Data Protection Miscellaneous Subject Access Exemption Order 1987, SI 1987/1906.

35, 35A (*(Examination marks, information about human embryos) omitted.*)

PART V
GENERAL

36–40 (*(General provisions, including data held outside the United Kingdom, and regulations, rules and orders) omitted.*)

41 General interpretation

In addition to the provisions of sections 1 and 2 above, the following provisions shall have effect for the interpretation of this Act—

"business" includes any trade or profession;
"data equipment" means equipment for the automatic processing of data or for recording information so that it can be automatically processed;
"data material" means any document or other material used in connection with data equipment;
"a de-registration notice" means a notice under section 11 above;
"enactment" includes an enactment passed after this Act;
"an enforcement notice" means a notice under section 10 above;
"the European Convention" means the Convention for the Protection of Individuals with regard to Automatic Processing of Personal Data which was opened for signature on 28th January 1981;
"government department" includes a Northern Ireland department and any body or authority exercising statutory functions on behalf of the Crown;
"prescribed" means prescribed by regulations made by the Secretary of State;
"the Registrar" means the Data Protection Registrar;
"the register", except where the reference is to the register of companies, means the register maintained under section 4 above and (except where the reference is to a registered company, to the registered office of a company or to registered post) references to registration shall be construed accordingly;
"registered company" means a company registered under the enactments relating to companies for the time being in force in any part of the United Kingdom;

"a transfer prohibition notice" means a notice under section 12 above;
"the Tribunal" means the Data Protection Tribunal.   **[442]**

42 Commencement and transitional provisions

(1) No application for registration shall be made until such day as the Secretary of State may by order appoint, and sections 5 and 15 above shall not apply until the end of the period of six months beginning with that day.

(2) Until the end of the period of two years beginning with the day appointed under subsection (1) above the Registrar shall not have power—

    (a) to refuse an application made in accordance with section 6 above except on the ground mentioned in section 7(2)(a) above; or

    (b) to serve an enforcement notice imposing requirements to be complied with, a de-registration notice expiring, or a transfer prohibition notice imposing a prohibition taking effect, before the end of that period.

(3) Where the Registrar proposes to serve any person with an enforcement notice before the end of the period mentioned in subsection (2) above he shall, in determining the time by which the requirements of the notice are to be complied with, have regard to the probable cost to that person of complying with those requirements.

(4) Section 21 above and paragraph 1(b) of Schedule 4 to this Act shall not apply until the end of the period mentioned in subsection (2) above.

(5) Section 22 above shall not apply to damage suffered before the end of the period mentioned in subsection (1) above and in deciding whether to refuse an application or serve a notice under Part II of this Act the Registrar shall treat the provision about accuracy in the fifth data protection principle as inapplicable until the end of that period and as inapplicable thereafter to data shown to have been held by the data user in question since before the end of that period.

(6) Sections 23 and 24(3) above shall not apply to damage suffered before the end of the period of two months beginning with the date on which this Act is passed.

(7) Section 24(1) and (2) above shall not apply before the end of the period mentioned in subsection (1) above.   **[443]**

43 Short title and extent

(1) This Act may be cited as the Data Protection Act 1984.

(2) This Act extends to Northern Ireland.

(3) Her Majesty may by Order in Council direct that this Act shall extend to any of the Channel Islands with such exceptions and modifications as may be specified in the Order.   **[444]**

SCHEDULES

SCHEDULE 1

Section 2(1)

THE DATA PROTECTION PRINCIPLES

PART I
THE PRINCIPLES

Personal data held by data users

1 The information to be contained in personal data shall be obtained, and personal data shall be processed, fairly and lawfully.

2 Personal data shall be held only for one or more specified and lawful purposes.

3 Personal data held for any purpose or purposes shall not be used or disclosed in any manner incompatible with that purpose or those purposes.

4 Personal data held for any purpose or purposes shall be adequate, relevant and not excessive in relation to that purpose or those purposes.

5 Personal data shall be accurate and, where necessary, kept up to date.

6 Personal data held for any purposes shall not be kept for longer than is necessary for that purpose or those purposes.

7 An individual shall be entitled—

    (a) at reasonable intervals and without undue delay or expense—

        (i) to be informed by any data user whether he holds personal data of which that individual is the subject; and

        (ii) to access to any such data held by a data user; and

    (b) where appropriate, to have such data corrected or erased.

Personal data held by data users or in respect of which services are provided by persons carrying on computer bureaux

8 Appropriate security measures shall be taken against unauthorised access to, or alteration, disclosure or destruction of, personal data and against accidental loss or destruction of personal data. **[445]**

PART II
INTERPRETATION

The first principle

1 (1) Subject to sub-paragraph (2) below, in determining whether information was obtained fairly regard shall be had to the method by which it was obtained, including in particular whether any person from whom it was obtained was deceived or misled as to the purpose or purposes for which it is to be held, used or disclosed.

    (2) Information shall in any event be treated as obtained fairly if it is obtained from a person who—

    (a) is authorised by or under any enactment to supply it; or

    (b) is required to supply it by or under any enactment or by any convention or other instrument imposing an international obligation on the United Kingdom;

and in determining whether information was obtained fairly there shall be disregarded any disclosure of the information which is authorised or required by or under any enactment or required by any such convention or other instrument as aforesaid.

The second principle

2 Personal data shall not be treated as held for a specified purpose unless that purpose is described in particulars registered under this Act in relation to the data.

The third principle

3 Personal data shall not be treated as used or disclosed in contravention of this principle unless—

    (a)   used otherwise than for a purpose of a description registered under this Act in relation to the data; or

    (b)   disclosed otherwise than to a person of a description so registered.

The fifth principle

4 Any question whether or not personal data are accurate shall be determined as for the purposes of section 22 of this Act but, in the case of such data as are mentioned in subsection (2) of that section, this principle shall not be regarded as having been contravened by reason of any inaccuracy in the information there mentioned if the requirements specified in that subsection have been complied with.

The seventh principle

5 (1) Paragraph (a) of this principle shall not be construed as conferring any rights inconsistent with section 21 of this Act.

    (2) In determining whether access to personal data is sought at reasonable intervals regard shall be had to the nature of the data, the purpose for which the data are held and the frequency with which the data are altered.

    (3) The correction or erasure of personal data is appropriate only where necessary for ensuring compliance with the other data protection principles.

The eighth principle

6 Regard shall be had—

    (a)   to the nature of the personal data and the harm that would result from such access, alteration, disclosure, loss or destruction as are mentioned in this principle; and

    (b)   to the place where the personal data are stored, to security measures programmed into the relevant equipment and to measures taken for ensuring the reliability of staff having access to the data.

Use for historical, statistical or research purposes

7 Where personal data are held for historical, statistical or research purposes and not used in such a way that damage or distress is, or is likely to be, caused to any data subject—

    (a)   the information contained in the data shall not be regarded for the purposes of the first principle as obtained unfairly by reason only that its use for any such purpose was not disclosed when it was obtained; and

    (b)   the data may, notwithstanding the sixth principle, be kept indefinitely.   **[446]**

(Schs 2–4 (the Data Protection Register and the Data Protection Tribunal; appeal proceedings; powers of entry and inspection) omitted.)

TRADE UNION ACT 1984 (NOTE)

(1984 c 49)

GENERAL NOTE

This Act was repealed in its entirety by the Trade Union and Labour Relations (Consolidation) Act 1992, s 300(1), Sch 1; see the Destination Table, below, para [982A], for details.

[446A]

COMPANIES ACT 1985

(1985 c 6)

ARRANGEMENT OF SECTIONS

PART IX
A COMPANY'S MANAGEMENT; DIRECTORS AND SECRETARIES; THEIR QUALIFICATIONS, DUTIES AND RESPONSIBILITIES

Removal of directors

Other provisions about directors and officers

PART X
ENFORCEMENT OF FAIR DEALING BY DIRECTORS

Restrictions on directors taking financial advantage

PART XXV
MISCELLANEOUS AND SUPPLEMENTARY PROVISIONS

SCHEDULES
Schedule 7—Matters to be Dealt With in Directors' Report

An Act to consolidate the greater part of the Companies Acts

[11 March 1985]

GENERAL NOTE

Only a small part of this Act is directly relevant to employment law, and accordingly only those sections of most relevance have been included in this work. For reasons of space the subject matter of sections omitted is not annotated. The derivation of sections is given as this Act consolidates the Companies Act 1948 and subsequent company legislation.

PART IX

A COMPANY'S MANAGEMENT; DIRECTORS AND SECRETARIES; THEIR QUALIFICATIONS, DUTIES AND RESPONSIBILITIES

Removal of directors

03 Resolution to remove director

1) A company may by ordinary resolution remove a director before the expiration of his period of office, notwithstanding anything in its articles or in any agreement between it and him.

(2) Special notice is required of a resolution to remove a director under this section or to appoint somebody instead of a director so removed at the meeting at which he is removed.

(3) A vacancy created by the removal of a director under this section, if not filled at the meeting at which he is removed, may be filled as a casual vacancy.

(4) A person appointed director in place of a person removed under this section is treated, for the purpose of determining the time at which he or any other director is to retire, as if he had become director on the day on which the person in whose place he is appointed was last appointed a director.

(5) This section is not to be taken as depriving a person removed under it of compensation or damages payable to him in respect of the termination of his appointment as director or of any appointment terminating with that as director, or as derogating from any power to remove a director which may exist apart from this section.   **[447]**

NOTE

This section derived from the Companies Act 1948, s 184(1), (2), (4)–(6).

04 Director's right to protest removal

1) On receipt of notice of an intended resolution to remove a director under section 03, the company shall forthwith send a copy of the notice to the director concerned; and he (whether or not a member of the company) is entitled to be heard on the resolution at the meeting.

(2) Where notice is given of an intended resolution to remove a director under that section, and the director concerned makes with respect to it representations in writing to the company (not exceeding a reasonable length) and requests their notification to members of the company, the company shall, unless the representations are received by it too late for it to do so—

(a) in any notice of the resolution given to members of the company state the fact of the representations having been made; and

(b) send a copy of the representations to every member of the company to whom notice of the meeting is sent (whether before or after receipt of the representations by the company).

(3) If a copy of the representations is not sent as required by subsection (2) because received too late or because of the company's default, the director may (without prejudice to his right to be heard orally) require that the representations shall be read out at the meeting.

(4) But copies of the representations need not be sent out and the representation need not be read out at the meeting if, on the application either of the company or of any other person who claims to be aggrieved, the court is satisfied that the right conferred by this section are being abused to secure needless publicity for defamator matter.

(5) The court may order the company's costs on an application under this section to be paid in whole or in part by the director, notwithstanding that he is not a part to the application. **[448**

NOTE
This section derived from the Companies Act 1948, s 184(2), (3).

Other provisions about directors and officers

309 Directors to have regard to interests of employees

(1) The matters to which the directors of a company are to have regard in the performance of their functions include the interests of the company's employees i general, as well as the interests of its members.

(2) Accordingly, the duty imposed by this section on the directors is owed b them to the company (and the company alone) and is enforceable in the same way a any other fiduciary duty owed to a company by its directors.

(3) This section applies to shadow directors as it does to directors. **[449**

NOTE
This section derived from the Companies Act 1980, ss 46, 63(1).

PART X
ENFORCEMENT OF FAIR DEALING BY DIRECTORS

Restrictions on directors taking financial advantage

312 Payment to director for loss of office, etc

It is not lawful for a company to make to a director of the company any payment by way of compensation for loss of office, or as consideration for or in connection with his retirement from office, without particulars of the proposed payment (including its amount) being disclosed to members of the company and the proposal being approved by the company. **[450**

NOTE
This section derived from the Companies Act 1948, s 191.
Extended, with modifications, to members of the committee of management of friendly societies, b the Friendly Societies Act 1992, s 27, Sch 11, para 8(1).

316 Provisions supplementing ss 312 to 315

(1), (2) . . .

(3) References in sections 312 to 315 to payments made to a director by way o compensation for loss of office or as consideration for or in connection with hi

retirement from office, do not include any bona fide payment by way of damages for breach of contract or by way of pension in respect of past services.

"Pension" here includes any superannuation allowance, superannuation gratuity or similar payment.

(4) . . . **[451]**

NOTE
This section derived from the Companies Act 1948, s 194.
Sub-ss (1), (2), (4): outside the scope of this work.

318 Directors' service contracts to be open to inspection

(1) Subject to the following provisions, every company shall keep at an appropriate place—

    (a) in the case of each director whose contract of service with the company is in writing, a copy of that contract;

    (b) in the case of each director whose contract of service with the company is not in writing, a written memorandum setting out its terms; and

    (c) in the case of each director who is employed under a contract of service with a subsidiary of the company, a copy of that contract or, if it is not in writing, a written memorandum setting out its terms.

(2) All copies and memoranda kept by a company in pursuance of subsection (1) shall be kept at the same place.

(3) The following are appropriate places for the purposes of subsection (1)—

    (a) the company's registered office;

    (b) the place where its register of members is kept (if other than its registered office);

    (c) its principal place of business, provided that is situated in that part of Great Britain in which the company is registered.

(4) Every company shall send notice in the prescribed form to the registrar of companies of the place where copies and memoranda are kept in compliance with subsection (1), and of any change in that place, save in a case in which they have at all times been kept at the company's registered office.

(5) Subsection (1) does not apply to a director's contract of service with the company or with a subsidiary of it if that contract required him to work wholly or mainly outside the United Kingdom; but the company shall keep a memorandum—

    (a) in the case of a contract of service with the company, giving the director's name and setting out the provisions of the contract relating to its duration;

    (b) in the case of a contract of service with a subsidiary, giving the director's name and the name and place of incorporation of the subsidiary, and setting out the provisions of the contract relating to its duration,

at the same place as copies and memoranda are kept by the company in pursuance of subsection (1).

(6) A shadow director is treated for purposes of this section as a director.

(7) Every copy and memorandum required by subsection (1) or (5) to be kept shall . . . be open to inspection of any member of the company without charge.

(8) If—

    (a) default is made in complying with subsection (1) or (5), or

    (b) an inspection required under subsection (7) is refused, or

(c) default is made for 14 days in complying with subsection (4),

the company and every officer of it who is in default is liable to a fine and, for continued contravention, to a daily default fine.

(9) In the case of a refusal of an inspection required under subsection (7) of a copy or memorandum, the court may by order compel an immediate inspection of it.

(10) Subsections (1) and (5) apply to a variation of a director's contract of service as they apply to the contract.

(11) This section does not require that there be kept a copy of, or memorandum setting out the terms of, a contract (or its variation) at a time when the unexpired portion of the term for which the contract is to be in force is less than 12 months, or at a time at which the contract can, within the next ensuing 12 months, be terminated by the company without payment of compensation.   [452]

NOTE

This section derived from the Companies Act 1967, s 26, the Companies Act 1976, Sch 1, and the Companies Act 1980, ss 61, 63(4).

Sub-s (7): words omitted repealed by the Companies Act 1989, ss 143(7), 212, Sch 24.

319 Director's contract of employment for more than 5 years

(1) This section applies in respect of any term of an agreement whereby a director's employment with the company of which he is a director or, where he is the director of a holding company, his employment within the group is to continue, or may be continued, otherwise than at the instance of the company (whether under the original agreement or under a new agreement entered into in pursuance of it), for a period of more than 5 years during which the employment—

(a) cannot be terminated by the company by notice; or

(b) can be so terminated only in specified circumstances.

(2) In any case where—

(a) a person is or is to be employed with a company under an agreement which cannot be terminated by the company by notice or can be so terminated only in specified circumstances; and

(b) more than 6 months before the expiration of the period for which he is or is to be so employed, the company enters into a further agreement (otherwise than in pursuance of a right conferred by or under the original agreement on the other party to it) under which he is to be employed with the company or, where he is a director of a holding company, within the group,

this section applies as if to the period for which he is to be employed under that further agreement there were added a further period equal to the unexpired period of the original agreement.

(3) A company shall not incorporate in an agreement such a term as is mentioned in subsection (1), unless the term is first approved by a resolution of the company in general meeting and, in the case of a director of a holding company, by a resolution of that company in general meeting.

(4) No approval is required to be given under this section by any body corporate unless it is a company within the meaning of this Act, or is registered under section 680, or if it is a wholly-owned subsidiary of any body corporate, wherever incorporated.

(5) A resolution of a company approving such a term as is mentioned in subsection (1) shall not be passed at a general meeting of the company unless a written memorandum setting out the proposed agreement incorporating the term is available for inspection by members of the company both—

    (a) at the company's registered office for not less than 15 days ending with the date of the meeting; and

    (b) at the meeting itself.

(6) A term incorporated in an agreement in contravention of this section is, to the extent that it contravenes the section, void; and that agreement and, in a case where subsection (2) applies, the original agreement are deemed to contain a term entitling the company to terminate it at any time by the giving of reasonable notice.

(7) In this section—

    (a) "employment" includes employment under a contract for services; and

    (b) "group", in relation to a director of a holding company, means the group which consists of that company and its subsidiaries;

and for purposes of this section a shadow director is treated as a director.   **[453]**

NOTE

This section derived from the Companies Act 1980, ss 47, 63(1).

PART XXV
MISCELLANEOUS AND SUPPLEMENTARY PROVISIONS

719 Power of company to provide for employees on cessation or transfer of business

(1) The powers of a company include (if they would not otherwise do so apart from this section) power to make the following provision for the benefit of persons employed or formerly employed by the company or any of its subsidiaries, that is to say, provision in connection with the cessation or the transfer to any person of the whole or part of the undertaking of the company or that subsidiary.

(2) The power conferred by subsection (1) is exercisable notwithstanding that its exercise is not in the best interests of the company.

(3) The power which a company may exercise by virtue only of subsection (1) shall only be exercised by the company if sanctioned—

    (a) in a case not falling within paragraph (b) or (c) below, by an ordinary resolution of the company, or

    (b) if so authorised by the memorandum or articles, a resolution of the directors, or

    (c) if the memorandum or articles require the exercise of the power to be sanctioned by a resolution of the company of some other description for which more than a simple majority of the members voting is necessary, with the sanction of a resolution of that description;

and in any case after compliance with any other requirements of the memorandum or articles applicable to its exercise.

(4) Any payment which may be made by a company under this section may, if made before the commencement of any winding up of the company, be made out of profits of the company which are available for dividend.   **[454]**

NOTE

This section derived from the Companies Act 1980, ss 74(1)–(3), (6)(a).

See further the Insolvency Act 1986, s 187, and the Companies Act 1989, s 144(4), Sch 18, para 36.

SCHEDULES

SCHEDULE 7

Section 235

MATTERS TO BE DEALT WITH IN DIRECTORS' REPORT

PART III

DISCLOSURE CONCERNING EMPLOYMENT, ETC, OF DISABLED PERSONS

9 (1) This Part of this Schedule applies to the directors' report where the average number of persons employed by the company in each week during the financial year exceeded 250.

(2) That average number is the quotient derived by dividing, by the number of weeks in the financial year, the number derived by ascertaining, in relation to each of those weeks, the number of persons who, under contracts of service, were employed in the week (whether throughout it or not) by the company, and adding up the numbers ascertained.

(3) The directors' report shall in that case contain a statement describing such policy as the company has applied during the financial year—

    (a) for giving full and fair consideration to applications for employment by the company made by disabled persons, having regard to their particular aptitudes and abilities,

    (b) for continuing the employment of, and for arranging appropriate training for employees of the company who have become disabled persons during the period when they were employed by the company, and

    (c) otherwise for the training, career development and promotion of disabled persons employed by the company.

(4) In this Part—

    (a) "employment" means employment other than employment to work wholly or mainly outside the United Kingdom, and "employed" and "employee" shall be construed accordingly; and

    (b) "disabled person" means the same as in the Disabled Persons (Employment) Act 1944.   [455

NOTE

Para 9 derived from SI 1980/1160.

PART IV

HEALTH, SAFETY AND WELFARE AT WORK OF COMPANY'S EMPLOYEES

10 (1) In the case of companies of such classes as may be prescribed by regulations made by the Secretary of State, the directors' report shall contain such information as may be so prescribed about the arrangements in force in the financial year for securing the health, safety and welfare at work of employees of the company and its subsidiaries, and for protecting other persons against risks to health or safety arising out of or in connection with the activities at work of those employees.

(2) Regulations under this Part may—

    (a) make different provision in relation to companies of different classes,

    (b) enable any requirements of the regulations to be dispensed with or modified in particular cases by any specified person or by any person authorised in that behalf by a specified authority,

    (c) contain such transitional provisions as the Secretary of State thinks necessary or expedient in connection with any provision made by the regulations.

(3) The power to make regulations under this paragraph is exercisable by statutory instrument subject to annulment in pursuance of a resolution of either House of Parliament.

(4) Any expression used in sub-paragraph (1) above and in Part I of the Health and Safety at Work etc. Act 1974 has the same meaning here as it has in that Part of that Act; section 1(3) of that Act applies for interpreting that sub-paragraph; and in sub-paragraph (2) "specified" means specified in regulations made under that sub-paragraph.   [456]

NOTE

Para 10 derived from the Companies Act 1967, ss 16(1)(g), (5)–(7), and the Health and Safety at Work etc Act 1974, s 79(3).

PART V

EMPLOYEE INVOLVEMENT

11 (1) This Part of this Schedule applies to the directors' report where the average number of persons employed by the company in each week during the financial year exceeded 250.

(2) That average number is the quotient derived by dividing by the number of weeks in the financial year the number derived by ascertaining, in relation to each of those weeks, the number of persons who, under contracts of service, were employed in the week (whether throughout it or not) by the company, and adding up the numbers ascertained.

(3) The directors' report shall in that case contain a statement describing the action that has been taken during the financial year to introduce, maintain or develop arrangements aimed at—

(a) providing employees systematically with information on matters of concern to them as employees,

(b) consulting employees or their representatives on a regular basis so that the views of employees can be taken into account in making decisions which are likely to affect their interests,

(c) encouraging the involvement of employees in the company's performance through an employees' share scheme or by some other means,

(d) achieving a common awareness on the part of all employees of the financial and economic factors affecting the performance of the company.

(4) In sub-paragraph (3) "employee" does not include a person employed to work wholly or mainly outside the United Kingdom; and for the purposes of sub-paragraph (2) no regard is to be had to such a person. **[457]**

NOTE

Para 11 derived from the Companies Act 1967, s 16(1)(h), (1A), (8), and the Employment Act 1982, s 1.

INSOLVENCY ACT 1986

(1986 c 45)

ARRANGEMENT OF SECTIONS

THE FIRST GROUP OF PARTS

COMPANY INSOLVENCY; COMPANIES WINDING UP

PART II

ADMINISTRATION ORDERS

Administrators

PART III
RECEIVERSHIP

CHAPTER I
RECEIVERS AND MANAGERS (ENGLAND AND WALES)

THE THIRD GROUP OF PARTS

MISCELLANEOUS MATTERS BEARING ON BOTH COMPANY AND INDIVIDUAL
INSOLVENCY; GENERAL INTERPRETATION; FINAL PROVISIONS

Part XII
PREFERENTIAL DEBTS IN COMPANY AND INDIVIDUAL INSOLVENCY

An Act to consolidate the enactments relating to company insolvency and winding up (including the winding up of companies that are not insolvent, and of unregistered companies); enactments relating to the insolvency and bankruptcy of individuals; and other enactments bearing on those two subject matters, including the functions and qualification of insolvency practitioners, the public administration of insolvency, the penalisation and redress of malpractice and wrongdoing, and the avoidance of certain transactions at an undervalue

[25 July 1986]

GENERAL NOTE
   Most of this Act covers matters outside the scope of this work, and only those provisions most directly relevant to employment law are printed. For reasons of space the subject matter of sections not printed is not annotated. All provisions of the Act printed here extend to Scotland.

THE FIRST GROUP OF PARTS

COMPANY INSOLVENCY; COMPANIES WINDING UP

PART II
ADMINISTRATION ORDERS

Administrators

19 Vacation of office

(1) The administrator of a company may at any time be removed from office by order of the court and may, in the prescribed circumstances, resign his office by giving notice of his resignation to the court.

(2) The administrator shall vacate office if—

(a) he ceases to be qualified to act as an insolvency practitioner in relation to the company, or

(b) the administration order is discharged.

(3) Where at any time a person ceases to be administrator, the next two subsections apply.

(4) His remuneration and any expenses properly incurred by him shall be charged on and paid out of any property of the company which is in his custody or under his control at that time in priority to any security to which section 15(1) then applies.

(5) Any sums payable in respect of debts or liabilities incurred, while he was administrator, under contracts entered into or contracts of employment adopted by him or a predecessor of his in the carrying out of his or the predecessor's functions shall be charged on and paid out of any such property as is mentioned in subsection (4) in priority to any charge arising under that subsection.

For this purpose, the administrator is not to be taken to have adopted a contract of employment by reason of anything done or omitted to be done within 14 days after his appointment.   **[458]**

PART III
RECEIVERSHIP

CHAPTER I
RECEIVERS AND MANAGERS (ENGLAND AND WALES)

Receivers and managers appointed out of court

37 Liability for contracts, etc

(1) A receiver or manager appointed under powers conferred in an instrument (other than an administrative receiver) is, to the same extent as if he had been appointed by order of the court—

(a) personally liable on any contract entered into by him in the performance of his functions (except in so far as the contract otherwise provides) and on any contract of employment adopted by him in the performance of those functions, and

(b) entitled in respect of that liability to indemnity out of the assets.

(2) For the purposes of subsection (1)(a), the receiver or manager is not to be taken to have adopted a contract of employment by reason of anything done or omitted to be done within 14 days after his appointment.

(3) Subsection (1) does not limit any right to indemnity which the receiver or manager would have apart from it, nor limit his liability on contracts entered into without authority, nor confer any right to indemnity in respect of that liability.

(4) Where at any time the receiver or manager so appointed vacates office—

(a) his remuneration and any expenses properly incurred by him, and
(b) any indemnity to which he is entitled out of the assets of the company,

shall be charged on and paid out of any property of the company which is in his custody or under his control at that time in priority to any charge or other security held by the person by or on whose behalf he was appointed.　　　**[459]**

Administrative receivers: general

44 Agency and liability for contracts

(1) The administrative receiver of a company—

(a) is deemed to be the company's agent, unless and until the company goes into liquidation;
(b) is personally liable on any contract entered into by him in the carrying out of his functions (except in so far as the contract otherwise provides) and on any contract of employment adopted by him in the carrying out of those functions; and
(c) is entitled in respect of that liability to an indemnity out of the assets of the company.

(2) For the purposes of subsection (1)(b) the administrative receiver is not to be taken to have adopted a contract of employment by reason of anything done or omitted to be done within 14 days after his appointment.

(3) This section does not limit any right to indemnity which the administrative receiver would have apart from it, nor limit his liability on contracts entered into or adopted without authority, nor confer any right to indemnity in respect of that liability.

[460]

THE THIRD GROUP OF PARTS

MISCELLANEOUS MATTERS BEARING ON BOTH COMPANY AND INDIVIDUAL INSOLVENCY; GENERAL INTERPRETATION; FINAL PROVISIONS

PART XII
PREFERENTIAL DEBTS IN COMPANY AND INDIVIDUAL INSOLVENCY

386 Categories of preferential debts

(1) A reference in this Act to the preferential debts of a company or an individual is to the debts listed in Schedule 6 to this Act (money owed to the Inland Revenue for

income tax deducted at source; VAT, car tax, betting and gaming duties [, beer duty]; social security and pension scheme contributions; remuneration etc. of employees [; levies on coal and steel production]); and references to preferential creditors are to be read accordingly.

(2) In that Schedule "the debtor" means the company or the individual concerned.

(3) Schedule 6 is to be read with Schedule 3 to the Social Security Pensions Act 1975 (occupational pension scheme contributions).   **[461]**

NOTES
   Sub-s (1): first words in square brackets inserted by the Finance Act 1991, s 7, Sch 2, para 21A (as amended by the Finance (No 2) Act 1992, s 9); other amendment in square brackets made by SI 1987/2093, reg 2; further amended prospectively by the Finance Act 1993, s 36(1).
   Modified by the Building Societies Act 1986, s 90, Sch 15, Pt I.

SCHEDULES

SCHEDULE 6

Section 386

THE CATEGORIES OF PREFERENTIAL DEBTS

Category 1: Debts due to Inland Revenue

1 Sums due at the relevant date from the debtor on account of deductions of income tax from emoluments paid during the period of 12 months next before that date.

   The deductions here referred to are those which the debtor was liable to make under section [203 of the Income and Corporation Taxes Act 1988] (pay as you earn), less the amount of the repayments of income tax which the debtor was liable to make during that period.

2 Sums due at the relevant date from the debtor in respect of such deductions as are required to be made by the debtor for that period under section [559 of the Income and Corporation Taxes Act 1988] (sub-contractors in the construction industry).

3–5, 5A . . .

Category 3: Social security contributions

6 All sums which on the relevant date are due from the debtor on account of Class 1 or Class 2 contributions under the [Social Security Contributions and Benefits Act 1992] or the Social Security (Northern Ireland) Act 1975 and which became due from the debtor in the 12 months next before the relevant date.

7 . . .

Category 4: Contributions to occupational pension schemes, etc

8 Any sum which is owed by the debtor and is a sum to which Schedule 3 to the Social Security Pensions Act 1975 applies (contributions to occupational pension schemes and state scheme premiums).

Category 5: Remuneration, etc, of employees

9 So much of any amount which—
   (a) is owed by the debtor to a person who is or has been an employee of the debtor, and
   (b) is payable by way of remuneration in respect of the whole or any part of the period of 4 months next before the relevant date,

as does not exceed so much as may be prescribed by order made by the Secretary of State.

10 An amount owed by way of accrued holiday remuneration, in respect of any period of employment before the relevant date, to a person whose employment by the debtor has been terminated, whether before, on or after that date.

11 So much of any sum owed in respect of money advanced for the purpose as has been applied for the payment of a debt which, if it had not been paid, would have been a debt falling within paragraph 9 or 10.

12 So much of any amount which—

(a) is ordered (whether before or after the relevant date) to be paid by the debtor under the Reserve Forces (Safeguard of Employment) Act 1985, and

(b) is so ordered in respect of a default made by the debtor before that date in the discharge of his obligations under that Act,

as does no exceed such amount as may be prescribed by order made by the Secretary of State.

Interpretation for Category 5

13 (1) For the purposes of paragraphs 9 to 12, a sum is payable by the debtor to a person by way of remuneration in respect of any period if—

(a) it is paid as wages or salary (whether payable for time or for piece work or earned wholly or partly by way of commission) in respect of services rendered to the debtor in that period, or

(b) it is an amount falling within the following sub-paragraph and is payable by the debtor in respect of that period.

(2) An amount falls within this sub-paragraph if it is—

(a) a guarantee payment under section 12(1) of the Employment Protection (Consolidation) Act 1978 (employee without work to do for a day or part of a day);

(b) remuneration on suspension on medical grounds under section 19 of that Act [or remuneration on suspension on maternity grounds under section 47 of that Act];

(c) any payment for time off under [section 31(3) or 31A(4) of that Act (looking for work, etc; ante-natal care) or under section 169 of the Trade Union and Labour Relations (Consolidation) Act 1992 (trade union duties)]; or

(d) remuneration under a protective award made by an industrial tribunal under [section 189 of the latter Act] (redundancy dismissal with compensation).

14 (1) This paragraph relates to a case in which a person's employment has been terminated by or in consequence of his employer going into liquidation or being adjudged bankrupt or (his employer being a company not in liquidation) by or in consequence of—

(a) a receiver being appointed as mentioned in section 40 of this Act (debenture-holders secured by floating charge), or

(b) the appointment of a receiver under section 53(6) or 54(5) of this Act (Scottish company with property subject to floating charge), or

(c) the taking of possession by debenture-holders (so secured), as mentioned in section 196 of the Companies Act.

(2) For the purposes of paragraphs 9 to 12, holiday remuneration is deemed to have accrued to that person in respect of any period of employment if, by virtue of his contract of employment or of any enactment that remuneration would have accrued in respect of that period if his employment had continued until he became entitled to be allowed the holiday.

(3) The reference in sub-paragraph (2) to any enactment includes an order or direction made under an enactment.

15 Without prejudice to paragraphs 13 and 14—

(a) any remuneration payable by the debtor to a person in respect of a period of holiday or of absence from work through sickness or other good cause is deemed to be wages or (as the case may be) salary in respect of services rendered to the debtor in that period, and

(b) references here and in those paragraphs to remuneration in respect of a period of holiday include any sums which, if they had been paid, would have been treated for the purposes of the enactments to social security as earnings in respect of that period.

[*Category 6: Levies on coal and steel production*

15A ...]

Orders

16 An order under paragraph 9 or 12—

(a) may contain such transitional provisions as may appear to the Secretary of State necessary or expedient;

(b) shall be made by statutory instrument subject to annulment in pursuance of a resolution of either House of Parliament. **[462]**

NOTES

Paras 1, 2: words in square brackets substituted by the Income and Corporation Taxes Act 1988, s 844, Sch 29.

Paras 3–5, 5A: outside the scope of this work

Para 6: words in square brackets substituted by the Social Security (Consequential Provisions) Act 1992, s 4, Sch 2, para 73.

Para 7: outside the scope of this work

Para 13: words in square brackets in sub-para (2) substituted by the Trade Union and Labour Relations (Consolidation) Act 1992, s 300(2), Sch 2, para 33; words in square brackets in para (b) inserted by the Trade Union Reform and Employment Rights Act 1993, s 49(2), Sch 8, para 35, as from a day to be appointed.

Para 15A: outside the scope of this work.

No orders had been made under paras 9 or 12 up to 1 September 1993.

WAGES ACT 1986

(1986 c 48)

ARRANGEMENT OF SECTIONS

PART I
PROTECTION OF WORKERS IN RELATION TO THE PAYMENT OF WAGES

SCHEDULES
Schedule 1—Enactments Repealed by Section 11 [480]

An Act to make fresh provision with respect to the protection of workers in relation to the payment of wages; to make further provision with respect to wages councils; to restrict redundancy rebates to employers with less than ten employees and to abolish certain similar payments; and for connected purposes

[25 July 1986]

GENERAL NOTE

Part I of this Act, which is printed in full, commenced on 1 January 1987, except where a later date of commencement is indicated.

Part II of the Act (wages councils) is repealed in its entirety with effect from 30 August 1993 by the Trade Union Reform and Employment Rights Act 1993, s 35 (see SI 1993/1908, below, para [**1435**]. There are limited savings in relation to continuing liability for pre-commencement contraventions of the Act, and powers of inspectors and maintenance of records in relation to the pre-commencement period (Sch 9 to the 1993 Act, below, para [**1000N–1000Z**]). However for reasons of space the repealed sections are omitted, and Pt III is printed as (consequentially) amended by Sch 8 to the 1993 Act. In effect this Act is printed as in force on 30 August 1993.

PART I

PROTECTION OF WORKERS IN RELATION TO THE PAYMENT OF WAGES

1 General restrictions on deductions made, or payments received, by employers

(1) An employer shall not make any deduction from any wages of any worker employed by him unless the deduction satisfies one of the following conditions, namely—

(a) it is required or authorised to be made by virtue of any statutory provision or any relevant provision of the worker's contract; or

(b) the worker has previously signified in writing his agreement or consent to the making of it.

(2) An employer shall not receive any payment from any worker employed by him unless the payment satisfies one of the conditions set out in paragraphs (a) and (b) of subsection (1).

(3) In this section "relevant provision", in relation to a worker's contract, means any provision of the contract comprised—

(a) in one or more written terms of the contract of which the employer has given the worker a copy on any occasion prior to the employer making the deduction in question, or (where subsection (1)(a) applies for the purposes of subsection (2)) prior to his receiving the payment in question, or

(b) in one or more terms of the contract (whether express or implied and, if express, whether oral or in writing) whose existence and effect, or (as the case may be) combined effect, in relation to the worker the employer has notified to the worker in writing on any such occasion.

(4) For the purposes of this section—

(a) any relevant provision of a worker's contract having effect by virtue of any variation of the contract, or

(b) any agreement or consent signified by a worker as mentioned in subsection (1)(b), shall not operate to authorise the making of any deduction, or the receipt of any payment, on account of any conduct of the worker, or any other event occurring, before the variation took effect or (as the case may be) the agreement or consent was signified.

(5) Nothing in this section applies—

   (a) to any deduction from a worker's wages made by his employer, or any payment received from a worker by his employer, where the purpose of the deduction or payment is the reimbursement of the employer in respect of—

      (i) any overpayment of wages, or

      (ii) any overpayment in respect of expenses incurred by the worker in carrying out his employment,

     made (for any reason) by the employer to the worker;

   (b) to any deduction from a worker's wages made by his employer, or any payment received from a worker by his employer, in consequence of any disciplinary proceedings if those proceedings were held by virtue of any statutory provision;

   (c) to any deduction from a worker's wages made by his employer in pursuance of any requirement imposed on the employer by any statutory provision to deduct and pay over to a public authority amounts determined by that authority as being due to it from the worker, if the deduction is made in accordance with the relevant determination of that authority;

   (d) to any deduction from a worker's wages made by his employer in pursuance of any arrangements which have been established—

      (i) in accordance with any relevant provision of his contract to whose inclusion in the contract the worker has signified his agreement or consent in writing, or

      (ii) otherwise with the prior agreement or consent of the worker signified in writing,

     and under which the employer is to deduct and pay over to a third person amounts notified to the employer by that person as being due to him from the worker, if the deduction is made in accordance with the relevant notification by that person;

   (e) to any deduction from a worker's wages made by his employer, or any payment received from a worker by his employer, where the worker has taken part in a strike or other industrial action and the deduction is made, or the payment has been required, by the employer on account of the worker's having taken part in that strike or other action; or

   (f) to any deduction from a worker's wages made by his employer with his prior agreement or consent signified in writing, or any payment received from a worker by his employer, where the purpose of the deduction or payment is the satisfaction (whether wholly or in part) of an order of a court or tribunal requiring the payment of any amount by the worker to the employer.

(6) This section is without prejudice to any other statutory provision by virtue of which any sum payable to a worker by his employer but not falling within the definition of "wages" in section 7 is not to be subject to any deduction at the instance of the employer; . . .   **[463]**

NOTE

   Sub-s (6): words omitted, originally added by the Employment Act 1988, s 33, Sch 3, Pt I, para 6, repealed by the Trade Union and Labour Relations (Consolidation) Act 1992, s 300(1), Sch 1.

2 Deductions from wages of workers in retail employment on account of cash shortages etc

(1) Where (in accordance with section 1(1)) the employer of a worker in retail employment makes, on account of one or more cash shortages or stock deficiencies, any deduction or deductions from any wages payable to the worker on a pay day, the amount or aggregate amount of the deduction or deductions shall not exceed one-tenth of the gross amount of the wages payable to the worker on that day.

(2) In this Part—

"cash shortage" means a deficit arising in relation to amounts received in connection with retail transactions;

"pay day", in relation to a worker, means a day on which wages are payable to the worker;

"retail employment", in relation to a worker, means employment involving (whether on a regular basis or not)—

(a) the carrying out by the worker of retail transactions directly with members of the public or with fellow workers or other individuals in their personal capacities, or

(b) the collection by the worker of amounts payable in connection with retail transactions carried out by other persons directly with members of the public or with fellow workers or other individuals in their personal capacities;

"retail transaction" means the sale or supply of goods, or the supply of services (including financial services); and

"stock deficiency" means a stock deficiency arising in the course of retail transactions.

(3) Where the employer of a worker in retail employment makes a deduction from the worker's wages on account of a cash shortage or stock deficiency, the employer shall not be treated as making the deduction in accordance with section 1(1) unless (in addition to the requirements of that provision being satisfied with respect to the deduction)—

(a) the deduction is made, or

(b) in the case of a deduction which is one of a series of deductions relating to the shortage or deficiency, the first deduction in the series was made,

not later than the end of the period of 12 months beginning with the date when the employer established the existence of the shortage or deficiency or (if earlier) the date when he ought reasonably to have done so.

(4) This subsection applies where—

(a) by virtue of any agreement between a worker in retail employment and his employer, the amount of the worker's wages or any part of them is or may be determined by reference to the incidence of cash shortages or stock deficiencies, and

(b) the gross amount of the wages payable to the worker on any pay day is, on account of any such shortages or deficiencies, less than the gross amount of the wages that would have been payable to him on that day if there had been no such shortages or deficiencies.

(5) In a case where subsection (4) applies—

(a) the amount representing the difference between the two amounts referred to in paragraph (b) of that subsection ("the relevant amount") shall be treated for the purposes of this Part as a deduction from the wages payable to the worker on that day made by the employer on account of the cash shortages or stock deficiencies in question, and

(b) the second of the amounts so referred to shall be treated for the purposes of this Part (except subsection (4)) as the gross amount of the wages payable to him on that day;

and section 1(1) and (if the requirements of that provision and subsection (3) above are satisfied) subsection (1) above shall have effect in relation to the relevant amount accordingly. **[464]**

3 Payments by workers in retail employment on account of cash shortages etc

(1) Where the employer of a worker in retail employment receives from the worker any payment on account of a cash shortage or stock deficiency the employer shall not be treated as receiving the payment in accordance with section 1(2) unless (in addition to the requirements of that provision being satisfied with respect to the payment) he has previously—

(a) notified the worker in writing of the worker's total liability to him in respect of that shortage or deficiency; and

(b) required the worker to make the payment by means of a demand for payment made in accordance with this section.

(2) Any demand for payment made by the employer of a worker in retail employment in respect of a cash shortage or stock deficiency—

(a) shall be made in writing, and

(b) shall be made on one of the worker's pay days.

(3) A demand for payment in respect of a particular cash shortage or stock deficiency, or (in the case of a series of such demands) the first such demand, shall not be made—

(a) earlier than the first day of the worker following the date when he is notified of his total liability in respect of the shortage or deficiency in pursuance of subsection (1)(a) or, where he is so notified on a pay day, earlier than that day, or

(b) later than the end of the period of 12 months beginning with the date when the employer established the existence of the shortage or deficiency or (if earlier) the date when he ought reasonably to have done so.

(4) Where the employer of a worker in retail employment makes on any pay day one or more demands for payment in accordance with this section, the amount or aggregate amount required to be paid by the worker in pursuance of the demand or demands shall not exceed—

(a) one-tenth of the gross amount of the wages payable to the worker on that day, or

(b) where one or more deductions falling within section 2(1) are made by the employer from those wages, such amount as represents the balance of that one-tenth after subtracting the amount or aggregate amount of the deduction or deductions.

(5) Once any amount has been required to be paid by means of a demand for payment made in accordance with this section on any pay day, that amount shall not be taken into account under subsection (4) as it applies to any subsequent pay day, notwithstanding that the employer is obliged to make further requests for it to be paid.

(6) For the purposes of this Part a demand for payment shall be treated as made by the employer on one of the worker's pay days if it is given to the worker, or posted to, or left at, his last known address—

(a) on that pay day, or

(b) in the case of a pay day which is not a working day of the employer's business, on the first such working day following that pay day. **[465]**

4 Provisions supplementary to ss 2 and 3

(1) In this section "final instalment of wages", in relation to a worker, means—

(a) the amount of wages payable to the worker which consists of or includes an amount payable by way of contractual remuneration in respect of the last of the periods for which he is employed under his contract prior to its termination for any reason (but excluding any wages referable to any earlier such period), or

(b) where an amount in lieu of notice is paid to the worker later than the amount referred to in paragraph (a), the amount so paid,

in each case whether amount in question is paid before or after the termination of the worker's contract.

(2) Section 2(1) shall not operate to restrict the amount of any deductions that may (in accordance with section 1(1)) be made by the employer of a worker in retail employment from the worker's final instalment of wages.

(3) Nothing in section 3 shall apply to any payment falling within subsection (1) of that section that is made on or after the day on which any such worker's final instalment of wages is paid, but (notwithstanding that the requirements of section 1(2) would otherwise be satisfied with respect to it) his employer shall not be treated as receiving any such payment in accordance with section 1(2) if the payment was first required to be made after the end of the period referred to in section 3(3)(b).

(4) Legal proceedings by the employer of a worker in retail employment for the recovery from the worker of any amount in respect of a cash shortage or stock deficiency shall not be instituted by the employer after the end of the period referred to in section 3(3)(b) unless the employer has within that period made a demand for payment in respect of that amount in accordance with section 3.

(5) Where in any legal proceedings the court finds that the employer of a worker in retail employment is (in accordance with section 1(2), as it applies apart from section 3(1)) entitled to recover an amount from the worker in respect of a cash shortage or stock deficiency, the court shall, in ordering the payment by the worker to the employer of that amount, make such provision as appears to the court to be necessary to ensure that it is paid by the worker at a rate not exceeding that at which it could be recovered from him by the employer in accordance with section 3.

This subsection does not apply to any amount which is to be paid by a worker on or after the day on which his final instalment of wages is paid.

(6) References in this Part to a deduction made from any wages of a worker in retail employment, or to a payment received from such a worker by his employer, on account of a cash shortage or stock deficiency include references to a deduction or payment so made or received on account of—

(a) any dishonesty or other conduct on the part of the worker which resulted in any such shortage or deficiency, or

(b) any other event in respect of which he (whether together with any other workers or not) has any contractual liability and which so resulted,

in each case whether the amount of the deduction or payment is designed to reflect the exact amount of the shortage or deficiency or not; and references in this Part to the recovery from a worker of an amount in respect of a cash shortage or stock deficiency accordingly include references to the recovery from him of an amount in respect of any such conduct or event as is mentioned in paragraph (a) or (b). **[466]**

5 Complaints to industrial tribunals in respect of unauthorised deductions etc

(1) A worker may present a complaint to an industrial tribunal—

    (a) that his employer has made a deduction from his wages in contravention of section 1(1) (including a deduction made in contravention of that provision as it applies by virtue of section 2(3)), or

    (b) that his employer has received from him a payment in contravention of section 1(2) (including a payment received in contravention of that provision as it applies by virtue of section 3(1)), or

    (c) that his employer has recovered from his wages by means of one or more deductions falling within section 2(1) an amount or aggregate amount exceeding the limit applying to the deduction or deductions under that provision, or

    (d) that his employer has received from him in pursuance of one or more demands for payment made (in accordance with section 3) on a particular pay day, a payment or payments of an amount or aggregate amount exceeding the limit applying to the demand or demands under section 3(4).

(2) An industrial tribunal shall not entertain a complaint under this section unless it is presented within the period of three months beginning with—

    (a) in the case of a complaint relating to a deduction by the employer, the date of payment of the wages from which the deduction was made, or

    (b) in the case of a complaint relating to a payment received by the employer, the date when the payment was received,

or within such further period as the tribunal considers reasonable in a case where it is satisfied that it was not reasonably practicable for the complaint to be presented within the relevant period of three months.

(3) Where a complaint is brought in respect of—

    (a) a series of deductions or payments, or

    (b) a number of payments falling within subsection (1)(d) and made in pursuance of demands for payment subject to the same limit under section 3(4) but received by the employer on different dates,

subsection (2) shall be read as referring to the last deduction or payment in the series or to the last of the payments so received (as the case may require).

    [(3A) . . .]

(4) Where a tribunal finds that a complaint under this section is well-founded, it shall make a declaration to that effect; and (subject to subsections (5) and (6))—

    (a) in the case of a complaint under subsection (1)(a) or (b), the tribunal shall order the employer to pay to the worker the amount of any deduction, or to repay to him the amount of any payment, made or received in contravention of section 1; and

    (b) in the case of a complaint under subsection (1)(c) or (d), the tribunal shall order the employer to pay or (as the case may be) repay to the worker any amount recovered or received from him in excess of any such limit as is mentioned in that provision.

(5) Where, in the case of any complaint under subsection (1)(a) or (b), a tribunal finds that, although neither of the conditions set out in section 1(1)(a) and (b) was satisfied with respect to the whole amount of a deduction or payment, one of those

conditions was satisfied with respect to any lesser amount, the amount of the deduction or payment shall for the purposes of subsection (4)(a) be treated as reduced by the amount with respect to which that condition was satisfied.

(6) An employer shall not under subsection (4)(a) or (b) be ordered by a tribunal to pay or repay to a worker any amount in respect of a deduction or payment, or (as the case may be) in respect of any combination of deductions or payments, in so far as it appears to the tribunal that he has already paid or repaid any such amount to the worker.

(7) Where a tribunal has under subsection (4)(a) or (b) ordered an employer to pay or repay to a worker any amount in respect of a particular deduction or payment falling within subsection (1)(a) to (d) ("the relevant amount") the amount which the employer shall be entitled to recover (by whatever means) in respect of the matter in respect of which the deduction or payment was originally made or received shall be treated as reduced by the relevant amount.

(8) Where a tribunal has under subsection (4)(b) ordered an employer to pay or repay to a worker any amount in respect of any combination of deductions or payments falling within subsection (1)(c) or (d) ("the relevant amount") the aggregate amount which the employer shall be entitled to recover (by whatever means) in respect of the cash shortages or stock deficiencies in respect of which the deductions or payments were originally made or required to be made shall be treated as reduced by the relevant amount. **[467]**

NOTE
Sub-s (3A): inserted by the Employment Act 1988, s 33, Sch 3, Pt I, para 6, and repealed by the Trade Union and Labour Relations (Consolidation) Act 1992, s 300(1), Sch 1.

6 Supplementary provisions relating to complaints

(1) The remedy of a worker in respect of any contravention of section 1(1) or (2) or section 2(1) or 3(4) shall be by way of a complaint under section 5 and not otherwise.

(2) Section 5 shall not affect the jurisdiction of an industrial tribunal to entertain a reference under section 11 of the 1978 Act in relation to any deduction from the wages of a worker, but the aggregate of any amounts ordered by an industrial tribunal to be paid under section 11(8)(b) of that Act and under subsection (4) of section 5 of this Act (whether on the same or different occasions) in respect of a particular deduction shall not exceed the amount of the deduction.

(3) Any provision in an agreement shall be void in so far as it purports to exclude or limit the operation of any provision of this Part, or to preclude any person from presenting a complaint under section 5; but this subsection shall not apply to

[(a)]an agreement to refrain from presenting or continuing with a complaint where a conciliation officer has taken action in accordance with section 133(2) or (3) of the 1978 Act [; or

(b) an agreement to refrain from presenting or continuing with a complaint if the conditions regulating compromise agreements under this Part of this Act are satisfied in relation to the agreement].

[(4) The conditions regulating compromise agreements under this Part of this Act are that—

(a) the agreement must be in writing;

(b) the agreement must relate to the particular complaint;

(c) the worker must have received independent legal advice from a qualified lawyer as to the terms and effect of the proposed agreement and in particular its effect on his ability to pursue his complaint before an industrial tribunal;

(d) there must be in force, when the adviser gives the advice, a policy of insurance covering the risk of a claim by the worker in respect of loss arising in consequence of the advice;

(e) the agreement must identify the adviser; and

(f) the agreement must state that the conditions regulating compromise agreements under this Part of this Act are satisfied.

(5) In subsection (4)—

"independent", in relation to legal advice to the worker, means that it is given by a lawyer who is not acting in the matter for the employer or for a person who is connected with the employer; and

"qualified lawyer" means—

(a) as respects proceedings in England and Wales—

(i) a barrister, whether in practice as such or employed to give legal advice, or

(ii) a solicitor of the Supreme Court who holds a practising certificate;

(b) as respects proceedings in Scotland—

(i) an advocate, whether in practice as such or employed to give legal advice, or

(ii) a solicitor who holds a practising certificate.

(6) For the purposes of subsection (5) any two persons are to be treated as "connected" if one is a company of which the other (directly or indirectly) has control, or if both are companies of which a third person (directly or indirectly) has control.]

[468]

NOTE
Sub-s (3): words in square brackets inserted by the Trade Union Reform and Employment Rights Act 1993, s 39(2), Sch 6, para 3(a), as from 30 August 1993 (SI 1993/1908, below, para **[1435]**).
Sub-ss (4)–(6): added by the Trade Union Reform and Employment Rights Act 1993, s 39(2), Sch 6, para 3(b), as from 30 August 1993 (SI 1993/1908, below, para **[1435]**).

7 Meaning of "wages"

(1) In this Part "wages", in relation to a worker, means any sums payable to the worker by his employer in connection with his employment, including—

(a) any fee, bonus, commission, holiday pay or other emolument referable to his employment, whether payable under his contract or otherwise;

(b) any sum payable in pursuance of an order for reinstatement or re-engagement under section 69 of the 1978 Act;

(c) any sum payable by way of pay in pursuance of an order under [section 164 of the Trade Union and Labour Relations (Consolidation) Act 1992] for the continuation of a contract of employment;

(d) any of the payments referred to in paragraphs (a) to (d) of section 122(4) of [the Employment Protection (Consolidation) Act 1978] (guarantee payments and other statutory payments in lieu of wages);

(e) statutory sick pay under Part I of the Social Security and Housing Benefits Act 1982 [or Part XI of the Social Security Contributions and Benefits Act 1992]; and

(f) in the case of a female worker, [statutory maternity pay under the Social Security Act 1986], [or Part XII of the Social Security Contributions and Benefits Act 1992,]

but excluding any payments falling within subsection (2).

(2) Those payments are—

(a) any payment by way of an advance under an agreement for a loan or by way of an advance of wages (but without prejudice to the application of section 1(1) to any deduction made from the worker's wages in respect of any such advance);

(b) any payment in respect of expenses incurred by the worker in carrying out his employment;

(c) any payment by way of a pension, allowance or gratuity in connection with the worker's retirement or as compensation for loss of office;

(d) any payment referable to the worker's redundancy;

(e) any payment to the worker otherwise than in his capacity as a worker.

(3) Where any payment in the nature of a non-contractual bonus is (for any reason) made to a worker by his employer, then, for the purposes of this Part, the amount of the payment shall—

(a) be treated as wages of the worker, and

(b) be treated as payable to him as such on the day on which the payment is made.

(4) For the purposes of this Part any monetary value attaching to any payment or benefit in kind furnished to a worker by his employer shall not be treated as wages of the worker except in the case of any voucher, stamp or similar document which is—

(a) of a fixed value expressed in monetary terms, and

(b) capable of being exchanged (whether on its own or together with other vouchers, stamps or documents, and whether immediately or only after a time) for money, goods or services (or for any combination of two or more of those things). **[469]**

NOTES

Sub-s (1): in paras (c), (d) words in square brackets substituted by the Trade Union and Labour Relations (Consolidation) Act 1992, s 300(2), Sch 2, para 34; in para (e) words in square brackets added by the Social Security (Consequential Provisions) Act 1992, s 3, Sch 2, para 74(a); in para (f) first words in square brackets substituted by the Social Security Act 1986, s 86, Sch 10, Pt IV, para 81, second words in square brackets added by the Social Security (Consequential Provisions) Act 1992, s 3, Sch 2, para 74(b).

8 General interpretation of Part I

(1) In this Part—

"the 1978 Act" means the Employment Protection (Consolidation) Act 1978;

"cash shortage" has the meaning given by section 2(2);

"employer", in relation to a worker, means the person by whom the worker is (or, where the employment has ceased, was) employed;

"employment", in relation to a worker, means employment under his contract and 'employed", in relation to a worker, accordingly means employed under his contract;

"gross amount", in relation to any wages payable to a worker, means the total amount of those wages before deductions of whatever nature;

"pay day", "retail employment" and "retail transaction" have the meaning given by section 2(2);

"statutory provision" means a provision contained in or having effect under any enactment;

"stock deficiency" has the meaning given by section 2(2);

"wages" shall be construed in accordance with section 7;

"worker" means an individual who has entered into or works under (or, where the employment has ceased, worked under) one of the contracts referred to in subsection (2) and any reference to a worker's contract shall be construed accordingly.

(2) Those contracts are—

    (a) a contract of service;

    (b) a contract of apprenticeship; and

    (c) any other contract whereby the individual undertakes to do or perform personally any work or services for another party to the contract whose status is not by virtue of the contract that of a client or customer of any profession or business undertaking carried on by the individual,

in each case whether such a contract is express or implied and, if express, whether it is oral or in writing.

(3) Where the total amount of any wages that are paid on any occasion by an employer to any worker employed by him is less than the total amount of the wages that are properly payable by him to the worker on that occasion (after deductions) then, except in so far as the deficiency is attributable to an error of computation, the amount of the deficiency shall be treated for the purposes of this Part as a deduction made by the employer from the worker's wages on that occasion.

(4) In subsection (3) the reference to an error of computation is a reference to an error of any description on the part of the employer affecting the computation by him of the gross amount of the wages that are properly payable by him to the worker on that occasion.

(5) Any reference in this Part to an employer receiving a payment from a worker employed by him is a reference to his receiving such a payment in his capacity as the worker's employer. [470]

9 Crown employment

(1) Subject to subsection (4), this Part shall apply to Crown employment.

(2) In this section "Crown employment" means employment under or for the purposes of a government department or any officer or body exercising on behalf of the Crown functions conferred by any statutory provision.

(3) Without prejudice to the generality of subsection (2), "Crown employment" includes employment by any of the bodies specified in Schedule 5 to the 1978 Act (National Health Service employers.)

(4) This Part does not apply to service as a member of the naval, military or air forces of the Crown, but does apply to employment by any association established for the purposes of Part VI of the Reserve Forces Act 1980.

(5) For the purposes of the application of this Part to Crown employment in accordance with subsection (1)—

    (a) any reference to a worker shall be construed as a reference to a person in Crown employment;

    (b) any reference to a worker's contract shall be construed as a reference to the terms of employment of a person in Crown employment;

    (c) any reference to the termination of a worker's contract shall be construed as a reference to the termination of his Crown employment; and

    (d) any reference to redundancy shall be construed as a reference to the existence of such circumstances as, in accordance with any arrangements for the time being in force as mentioned in section 111(3) of the 1978 Act (payments equivalent to redundancy payments in respect of civil servants etc.), are treated as equivalent to redundancy in relation to Crown employment.   **[471]**

NOTE

Sub-s (3): repealed by the Trade Union Reform and Employment Rights Act 1993, s 51, Sch 10, as from 30 August 1993 (SI 1993/1908, below, para **[1435]**).

10 Power to extend provisions to employment outside United Kingdom

(1) Section 137 of the 1978 Act (power to extend employment legislation to employment for purposes of activities in territorial waters etc.) shall apply in relation to this Part as it applies in relation to the enactments referred to in subsection (1) of that section, but as if—

    (a) any reference to employment were a reference to employment within the meaning of this Part; and

    (b) subsection (3)(g) of that section were omitted.

(2) Any Order in Council made by virtue of subsection (1) above may modify or exclude the operation of any provision of section 30 of this Act (as it applies to this Part) in relation to persons to whom the Order applies.   **[472]**

11 Repeal of Truck Acts 1831 to 1940 etc

The enactments listed in Schedule 1 to this Act (which impose restrictions in relation to the payment of wages to manual and other workers and make other provision in connection with the payment of wages to such persons) shall cease to have effect.

[473]

12–26 (*(Pt II) repealed by the Trade Union Reform and Employment Rights Act 1993, ss 35, 51, Sch 10, as from 30 August 1993 (SI 1993/1908).*)

PART III

REDUNDANCY REBATES, ETC

27 (*Repealed by the Employment Act 1989, s 29(4), Sch 7, Pt II.*)

28 Abolition of payments equivalent to redundancy rebates

No payment shall be made by the Secretary of State under—

    (a) section 111(2) of the Employment Protection (Consolidation) Act 1978 (payments equivalent to redundancy rebates in respect of civil servants, etc.), or

    (b) section 113(1) of that Act (similar payments in respect of employees of foreign governments),

in respect of any termination of employment occurring after the commencement of this section.   **[474–475]**

29 ((*Power to make corresponding provision for Northern Ireland) omitted.*)

PART IV

GENERAL

30 Excluded employments

(1) *Parts I and II do* [Part I does] not apply to employment where under his contract the person employed ordinarily works outside Great Britain.

(2) For the purposes of subsection (1) a person employed to work on board a ship registered in the United Kingdom (not being a ship registered at a port outside Great Britain) shall, unless—

(a) the employment is wholly outside Great Britain, or

(b) he is not ordinarily resident in Great Britain,

be regarded as a person who under his contract ordinarily works in Great Britain.

(3) *Parts I and II do* [Part I does] not, however, apply to a person employed under a crew agreement within the meaning of the Merchant Shipping Act 1970. **[476]**

NOTE

Sub-ss (1), (3), words in italics substituted in each case by words in square brackets immediately following, by the Trade Union Reform and Employment Rights Act 1993, s 49(2), Sch 8, para 36, as from 30 August 1993 (SI 1993/1908, below, para **[1435]**).

31 Financial provisions

There shall be paid out of money provided by Parliament—

. . .

(c) any increase attributable to this Act in the sums payable out of money so provided under any other Act. **[477]**

NOTE

Paras (a), (b) repealed by the Trade Union Reform and Employment Rights Act 1993, s 51, Sch 10, as from 30 August 1993 (SI 1993/1908, below, para **[1435]**).

32 Amendments, repeals, transitional provisions and savings

(1) The enactments mentioned in Schedule 4 shall have effect subject to the minor and consequential amendments there specified.

(2) The enactments mentioned in Schedule 5 are hereby repealed to the extent specified in the third column of that Schedule.

(3) The transitional provisions and savings contained in Schedule 6 shall have effect; but nothing in that Schedule shall be taken as prejudicing the operation of sections 16 and 17 of the Interpretation Act 1978 (which relate to repeals). **[478]**

33 Short title, commencement and extent

(1) This Act may be cited as the Wages Act 1986.

(2)–(7) . . . **[479]**

NOTE

Sub-ss (2)–(7), which deal with commencement and application to Northern Ireland, are omitted.

SCHEDULES

SCHEDULE 1
Section 11

ENACTMENTS REPEALED BY SECTION 11

The Truck Act 1831 (c 37).
The Hosiery Manufacture (Wages) Act 1874 (c 48).
The Payment of Wages in Public-houses Prohibition Act 1883 (c 31).
Sections 12 and 13 of the Stannaries Act 1887 (c 43).
The Truck Amendment Act 1887 (c 46).
Sections 12 to 14 of the Coal Mines Regulation Act 1887 (c 58).
The Coal Mines (Check Weigher) Act 1894 (c 52).
The Truck Act 1896 (c 44).
The Shop Clubs Act 1902 (c 21).
The Coal Mines (Weighing of Minerals) Act 1905 (c 9).
The Checkweighing in Various Industries Act 1919 (c 51).
The Truck Act 1940 (c 38).
Section 51(2) of the Mines and Quarries Act 1954 (c 70).
The Payment of Wages Act 1960 (c 37).
Sections 135 and 135A of the Factories Act 1961 (c 34).   [480]

(Schs 2, 3 repealed by the Trade Union Reform and Employment Rights Act 1993, s 51, Sch 10, as from 30 August 1993 (SI 1993/1908); Schs 4–6 (minor and consequential amendments, repeals and transitional provisions) omitted.)

SOCIAL SECURITY ACT 1986 (NOTE)
(1986 c 50)

GENERAL NOTE
The relevant provisions of this Act) effect on social security benefits of trade disputes, and statutory maternity pay) were repealed and consolidated by the Social Security Contributions and Benefits Act 1992, below, paras **[609]**–**[636]**.

[481]

SEX DISCRIMINATION ACT 1986
(1986 c 59)

ARRANGEMENT OF SECTIONS

An Act to amend the Sex Discrimination Act 1975 and sections 64 and 73 of the Employment Protection (Consolidation) Act 1978; to make provision with respect to requirements to discriminate in relation to employment which are contained in public entertainment licences; to provide for the removal of certain

restrictions applying to the working hours and other working conditions of women; and to repeal the Baking Industry (Hours of Work) Act 1954
[7 November 1986]

1, 2 *(S 1 repeals the Sex Discrimination Act 1975, s 6(3), and amends ss 7(2), 11(1) of that Act; s 2 amends ss 6, 11, 82 of the 1975 Act and the Equal Pay Act 1970, s 6.)*

3 Age of retirement etc: unfair dismissal

(1), (2) . . .

(3) Subsection (2) above shall not affect any award for the unfair dismissal of an employee in relation to whom the effective date of termination (within the meaning of Part V of the said Act of 1978) was before the coming into force of that subsection.
[482]

NOTES
Sub-ss (1), (2): amend the Employment Protection (Consolidation) Act 1978, ss 64, 73.
The date of coming into force of sub-s (2) was 7 November 1987; see s 10(3) below.

4 *(Amends the Sex Discrimination Act 1975, s 47.)*

5 Discrimination required by public entertainment licences

(1) [Without prejudice to the generality of section 1(1) of the Employment Act 1989,] nothing in—

    (a) any licence granted (whether before or after the coming into force of this section) under Schedule 1 to the Local Government (Miscellaneous Provisions) Act 1982 or Schedule 12 to the London Government Act 1963 (public entertainment licences); or

    (b) any regulations made for the purpose of prescribing the terms, conditions or restrictions on or subject to which any such licence is deemed to be granted,

shall have effect, at any time after the coming into force of this section, so as to require any person to do any act which . . . is rendered unlawful by Part II of the 1975 Act (discrimination in relation to employment) or by so much of Part IV of the 1975 Act as relates to acts rendered unlawful by the said Part II.

    (2) In this section "act" has the same meaning as in the 1975 Act.   **[483]**

NOTES
Sub-s (1): words in square brackets added and words omitted repealed by the Employment Act 1989, s 29(3), (4), Sch 6, para 30(a), (b), Sch 7, Pt II.

6 Collective agreements and rules of undertakings

(1) Without prejudice to the generality of section 77 of the 1975 Act (which makes provision with respect to the validity and revision of contracts), that section shall apply, as it applies in relation to the term of a contract, to the following, namely—

    (a) any term of a collective agreement, including an agreement which was not intended, or is presumed not to have been intended, to be a legally enforceable contract;

(b) any rule made by an employer for application to all or any of the persons who are employed by him or who apply to be, or are, considered by him for employment;

(c) any rule made by an organisation, authority or body to which subsection (2) below applies for application to all or any of its members or prospective members or to all or any of the persons on whom it has conferred authorisations or qualifications or who are seeking the authorisations or qualifications which it has power to confer;

and that section shall so apply whether the agreement was entered into, or the rule made, before or after the coming into force of this section.

(2) This subsection applies to—

(a) any organisation of workers;

(b) any organisation of employers;

(c) any organisation whose members carry on a particular profession or trade for the purposes of which the organisation exists;

(d) any authority or body which can confer an authorisation or qualification which is needed for, or facilitates, engagement in a particular profession or trade.

(3) For the purposes of the said section 77 a term or rule shall be deemed to provide for the doing of an act which would be rendered unlawful by the 1975 Act if—

(a) it provides for the inclusion in any contract of employment of any term which by virtue of an equality clause would fall either to be modified or to be supplemented by an additional term; and

(b) that clause would not be prevented from operating in relation to that contract by section 1(3) of the Equal Pay Act 1970 (material factors justifying discrimination).

(4) Nothing in the said section 77 shall affect the operation of any term or rule in so far as it provides for the doing of a particular act in circumstances where the doing of that act would not be, or be deemed by virtue of subsection (3) above to be, rendered unlawful by the 1975 Act.

[(4A) A person to whom this subsection applies may present a complaint to an industrial tribunal that a term or rule is void by virtue of subsection (1) of the said section 77 if he has reason to believe—

(a) that the term or rule may at some future time have effect in relation to him, and

(b) where he alleges that it is void by virtue of paragraph (c) of that subsection, that—

(i) an act for the doing of which it provides may at some such time be done in relation to him, and

(ii) the act would be, or be deemed by virtue of subsection (3) above to be, rendered unlawful by the 1975 Act if done in relation to him in present circumstances.

(4B) In the case of a complaint about—

(a) a term of a collective agreement made by or on behalf of—

(i) an employer,

(ii) an organisation of employers of which an employer is a member, or

(iii) an association of such organisations of one of which an employer is a member, or

(b) a rule made by an employer,

subsection (4A) applies to any person who is, or is genuinely and actively seeking to become, one of his employees.

(4C) In the case of a complaint about a rule made by an organisation, authority or body to which subsection (2) above applies, subsection (4A) applies to any person—

(a) who is, or is genuinely and actively seeking to become, a member of the organisation, authority or body,

(b) on whom the organisation, authority or body has conferred an authorisation or qualification, or

(c) who is genuinely and actively seeking an authorisation or qualification which the organisation, authority or body has power to confer.

(4D) When an industrial tribunal finds that a complaint presented to it under subsection (4A) above is well-founded the tribunal shall make an order declaring that the term or rule is void.]

(5) The avoidance by virtue of the said section 77 of any term or rule which provides for any person to be discriminated against shall be without prejudice to the following rights except in so far as they enable any person to require another person to be treated less favourably than himself, namely—

(a) such of the rights of the person to be discriminated against; and

(b) such of the rights of any person who will be treated more favourably in direct or indirect consequence of the discrimination,

as are conferred by or in respect of a contract made or modified wholly or partly in pursuance of, or by reference to, that term or rule.

(6) In this section "collective agreement" means any agreement relating to one or more of the matters mentioned in [section 178(2) of the Trade Union and Labour Relations (Consolidation) Act 1992] (meaning of trade dispute), being an agreement made by or on behalf of one or more employers or one or more organisations of employers or associations of such organisations with one or more organisations of workers or associations of such organisations.

(7) Any expression used in this section and in the 1975 Act has the same meaning in this section as in that Act, and this section shall have effect as if the terms of any service to which Parts II and IV of that Act apply by virtue of subsection (2) of section 85 of that Act (Crown application) were terms of a contract of employment and, in relation to the terms of any such service, as if service for the purposes of any person mentioned in that subsection were employment by that person.   **[484]**

NOTES

Sub-ss (4A)–(4D): inserted by the Trade Union Reform and Employment Rights Act 1993, s 32, as from a day to be appointed.

Sub-s (6): words in square brackets substituted by the Trade Union and Labour Relations (Consolidation) Act 1992, s 300(2), Sch 2, para 36.

1975 Act: Sex Discrimination Act 1975.

7 *(Repealed by the Employment Act 1989, s 29(4), Sch 7, Pt II.)*

8 Repeal of Baking Industry (Hours of Work) Act 1954

The Baking Industry (Hours of Work) Act 1954 (which imposes restrictions on the hours for which a bakery worker may do work in relation to which restrictions on the working hours of women are removed by virtue of section 7 above) shall cease to have effect.   **[485]**

9 Consequential amendment, repeals and saving

(1) ...

(2) The enactments mentioned in the Schedule to this Act (which include enactments that are no longer of practical effect) are hereby repealed to the extent specified in the third column of that Schedule.

(3) Neither the repeal by this Act of section 3 of the Equal Pay Act 1970 (collective agreements and pay structures) nor the amendment made by subsection (1) above shall affect—

    (a) the continuing effect, after the coming into force of that repeal, of any declaration made under that section before the coming into force of that repeal; or

    (b) the operation, at any time after the coming into force of that repeal, of section 5(1) of that Act in so far as it refers to the rules which apply under subsection (4) of the said section 3.   **[485A]**

NOTES
Sub-s (1): amends the Equal Pay Act 1970, s 6.

10 Short title, commencement and extent

(1) This Act may be cited as the Sex Discrimination Act 1986.

(2) Sections 1, 6 and 9(1) and (3) above and Part II of the Schedule to this Act shall come into force at the end of the period of three months beginning with the day on which this Act is passed.

(3) Subject to subsection (4) below, sections 2, 3 ... and 8 above and Part III of the Schedule to this Act shall come into force on such day as the Secretary of State may by order made by statutory instrument appoint, and different days may be so appointed for different provisions or for different purposes.

(4) Except in so far as they come into force at an earlier time under subsection (3) above, sections 2 and 3 above shall come into force at the end of the period of twelve months beginning with the day on which this Act is passed.

(5) This Act does not extend to Northern Ireland ...   **[486]**

NOTE
Sub-ss (3), (5): figures and words omitted repealed by the Employment Act 1989, s 29(4), Sch 7, Pt II.

(Schedule (repeals) omitted.)

PUBLIC ORDER ACT 1986

(1986 c 64)

ARRANGEMENT OF SECTIONS

PART II
PROCESSIONS AND ASSEMBLIES

An Act to abolish the common law offences of riot, rout, unlawful assembly and affray and certain statutory offences relating to public order; to create new offences relating to public order; to control public processions and assemblies; to control the stirring up of racial hatred; to provide for the exclusion of certain offenders from sporting events; to create a new offence relating to the contamination of or interference with goods; to confer power to direct certain trespassers to leave land; to amend section 7 of the Conspiracy and Protection of Property Act 1875, section 1 of the Prevention of Crime Act 1953, Part V of the Criminal Justice (Scotland) Act 1980 and the Sporting Events (Control of Alcohol etc.) Act 1985; to repeal certain obsolete or unnecessary enactments; and for connected purposes

[7 November 1986]

NOTE
Only Part II of this Act is reproduced here as relevant to employment law. Ss 11, 13 do not extend to Scotland; ss 12, 14–16 do. Note also s 40(4), (5) which provide—
"(4) Nothing in this Act affects the common law powers in England and Wales to deal with or prevent a breach of the peace.
(5) As respects Scotland, nothing in this Act affects any power of a constable under any rule of law."

1–10 *((Pt I) Outside the scope of this work.)*

PART II

PROCESSIONS AND ASSEMBLIES

11 Advance notice of public processions

(1) Written notice shall be given in accordance with this section of any proposal to hold a public procession intended—

(a) to demonstrate support for or opposition to the views or actions of any person or body of persons,

(b) to publicise a cause or campaign, or

(c) to mark or commemorate an event,

unless it is not reasonably practicable to give any advance notice of the procession.

(2) Subsection (1) does not apply where the procession is one commonly or customarily held in the police area (or areas) in which it is proposed to be held or is a funeral procession organised by a funeral director acting in the normal course of his business.

(3) The notice must specify the date when it is intended to hold the procession, the time when it is intended to start it, its proposed route, and the name and address of the person (or of one of the persons) proposing to organise it.

(4) Notice must be delivered to a police station—

(a) in the police area in which it is proposed the procession will start, or

(b) where it is proposed the procession will start in Scotland and cross into England, in the first police area in England on the proposed route.

(5) If delivered not less than 6 clear days before the date when the procession is intended to be held, the notice may be delivered by post by the recorded delivery service; but section 7 of the Interpretation Act 1978 (under which a document sent

by post is deemed to have been served when posted and to have been delivered in the ordinary course of post) does not apply.

(6) If not delivered in accordance with subsection (5), the notice must be delivered by hand not less than 6 clear days before the date when the procession is intended to be held or, if that is not reasonably practicable, as soon as delivery is reasonably practicable.

(7) Where a public procession is held, each of the persons organising it is guilty of an offence if—

(a) the requirements of this section as to notice have not been satisfied, or
(b) the date when it is held, the time when it starts, or its route, differs from the date, time or route specified in the notice.

(8) It is a defence for the accused to prove that he did not know of, and neither suspected nor had reason to suspect, the failure to satisfy the requirements or (as the case may be) the difference of date, time or route.

(9) To the extent that an alleged offence turns on a difference of date, time or route, it is a defence for the accused to prove that the difference arose from circumstances beyond his control or from something done with the agreement of a police officer or by his direction.

(10) A person guilty of an offence under subsection (7) is liable on summary conviction to a fine not exceeding level 3 on the standard scale. **[487]**

NOTE

This section does not apply to Scotland.

12 Imposing conditions on public processions

(1) If the senior police officer, having regard to the time or place at which and the circumstances in which any public procession is being held or is intended to be held and to its route or proposed route, reasonably believes that—

(a) it may result in serious public disorder, serious damage to property or serious disruption to the life of the community, or
(b) the purpose of the persons organising it is the intimidation of others with a view to compelling them not to do an act they have a right to do, or to do an act they have a right not to do,

he may give directions imposing on the persons organising or taking part in the procession such conditions as appear to him necessary to prevent such disorder, damage, disruption or intimidation, including conditions as to the route of the procession or prohibiting it from entering any public place specified in the directions.

(2) In subsection (1) "the senior police officer" means—

(a) in relation to a procession being held, or to a procession intended to be held in a case where persons are assembling with a view to taking part in it, the most senior in rank of the police officers present at the scene, and
(b) in relation to a procession intended to be held in a case where paragraph (a) does not apply, the chief officer of police.

(3) A direction given by a chief officer of police by virtue of subsection (2)(b) shall be given in writing.

(4) A person who organises a public procession and knowingly fails to comply with a condition imposed under this section is guilty of an offence, but it is a defence for him to prove that the failure arose from circumstances beyond his control.

(5) A person who takes part in a public procession and knowingly fails to comply with a condition imposed under this section is guilty of an offence, but it is a defence for him to prove that the failure arose from circumstances beyond his control.

(6) A person who incites another to commit an offence under subsection (5) is guilty of an offence.

(7) A constable in uniform may arrest without warrant anyone he reasonably suspects is committing an offence under subsection (4), (5) or (6).

(8) A person guilty of an offence under subsection (4) is liable on summary conviction to imprisonment for a term not exceeding 3 months or a fine not exceeding level 4 on the standard scale or both.

(9) A person guilty of an offence under subsection (5) is liable on summary conviction to a fine not exceeding level 3 on the standard scale.

(10) A person guilty of an offence under subsection (6) is liable on summary conviction to imprisonment for a term not exceeding 3 months or a fine not exceeding level 4 on the standard scale or both, notwithstanding section 45(3) of the Magistrates' Courts Act 1980 (inciter liable to same penalty as incited).

(11) In Scotland this section applies only in relation to a procession being held, and to a procession intended to be held in a case where persons are assembling with a view to taking part in it.   **[488]**

13 Prohibiting public processions

(1) If at any time the chief officer of police reasonably believes that, because of particular circumstances existing in any district or part of a district, the powers under section 12 will not be sufficient to prevent the holding of public processions in that district or part from resulting in serious public disorder, he shall apply to the council of the district for an order prohibiting for such period not exceeding 3 months as may be specified in the application the holding of all public processions (or of any class of public procession so specified) in the district or part concerned.

(2) On receiving such an application, a council may with the consent of the Secretary of State make an order either in the terms of the application or with such modifications as may be approved by the Secretary of State.

(3) Subsection (1) does not apply in the City of London or the metropolitan police district.

(4) If at any time the Commissioner of Police for the City of London or the Commissioner of Police of the Metropolis reasonably believes that, because of particular circumstances existing in his police area or part of it, the powers under section 12 will not be sufficient to prevent the holding of public processions in that area or part from resulting in serious public disorder, he may with the consent of the Secretary of State make an order prohibiting for such period not exceeding 3 months as may be specified in the order the holding of all public processions (or of any class of public procession so specified) in the area or part concerned.

(5) An order made under this section may be revoked or varied by a subsequent order made in the same way, that is, in accordance with subsections (1) and (2) or subsection (4), as the case may be.

(6) Any order under this section shall, if not made in writing, be recorded in writing as soon as practicable after being made.

(7) A person who organises a public procession the holding of which he knows is prohibited by virtue of an order under this section is guilty of an offence.

(8) A person who takes part in a public procession the holding of which he knows is prohibited by virtue of an order under this section is guilty of an offence.

(9) A person who incites another to commit an offence under subsection (8) is guilty of an offence.

(10) A constable in uniform may arrest without warrant anyone he reasonably suspects is committing an offence under subsection (7), (8) or (9).

(11) A person guilty of an offence under subsection (7) is liable on summary conviction to imprisonment for a term not exceeding 3 months or a fine not exceeding level 4 on the standard scale or both.

(12) A person guilty of an offence under subsection (8) is liable on summary conviction to a fine not exceeding level 3 on the standard scale.

(13) A person guilty of an offence under subsection (9) is liable on summary conviction to imprisonment for a term not exceeding 3 months or a fine not exceeding level 4 on the standard scale or both, notwithstanding section 45(3) of the Magistrates' Courts Act 1980.   **[489]**

NOTE
This section does not apply to Scotland.

14 Imposing conditions on public assemblies

(1) If the senior police officer, having regard to the time or place at which and the circumstances in which any public assembly is being held or is intended to be held, reasonably believes that—

    (a) it may result in serious public disorder, serious damage to property or serious disruption to the life of the community, or

    (b) the purpose of the persons organising it is the intimidation of others with a view to compelling them not to do an act they have a right to do, or to do an act they have a right not to do,

he may give directions imposing on the persons organising or taking part in the assembly such conditions as to the place at which the assembly may be (or continue to be) held, its maximum duration, or the maximum number of persons who may constitute it, as appear to him necessary to prevent such disorder, damage, disruption or intimidation.

(2) In subsection (1) "the senior police officer" means—

    (a) in relation to an assembly being held, the most senior in rank of the police officers present at the scene, and

    (b) in relation to an assembly intended to be held, the chief officer of police.

(3) A direction given by a chief officer of police by virtue of subsection (2)(b) shall be given in writing.

(4) A person who organises a public assembly and knowingly fails to comply with a condition imposed under this section is guilty of an offence, but it is a defence for him to prove that the failure arose from circumstances beyond his control.

(5) A person who takes part in a public assembly and knowingly fails to comply with a condition imposed under this section is guilty of an offence, but it is a defence for him to prove that the failure arose from circumstances beyond his control.

(6) A person who incites another to commit an offence under subsection (5) is guilty of an offence.

(7) A constable in uniform may arrest without warrant anyone he reasonably suspects is committing an offence under subsection (4), (5) or (6).

(8) A person guilty of an offence under subsection (4) is liable on summary conviction to imprisonment for a term not exceeding 3 months or a fine not exceeding level 4 on the standard scale or both.

(9) A person guilty of an offence under subsection (5) is liable on summary conviction to a fine not exceeding level 3 on the standard scale.

(10) A person guilty of an offence under subsection (6) is liable on summary conviction to imprisonment for a term not exceeding 3 months or a fine not exceeding level 4 on the standard scale or both, notwithstanding section 45(3) of the Magistrates' Courts Act 1980.   **[490]**

15 Delegation

(1) The chief officer of police may delegate, to such extent and subject to such conditions as he may specify, any of his functions under sections 12 to 14 to a deputy or assistant chief constable; and references in those sections to the person delegating shall be construed accordingly.

(2) Subsection (1) shall have effect in the City of London and the metropolitan police district as if "a deputy or assistant chief constable" read "an assistant commissioner of police".   **[491]**

16 Interpretation

In this Part—

"the City of London" means the City as defined for the purposes of the Acts relating to the City of London police;

"the metropolitan police district" means that district as defined in section 76 of the London Government Act 1963;

"public assembly" means an assembly of 20 or more persons in a public place which is wholly or partly open to the air;

"public place"means—

  (a) any highway, or in Scotland any road within the meaning of the Roads (Scotland) Act 1984, and

  (b) any place to which at the material time the public or any section of the public has access, on payment or otherwise, as of right or by virtue of express or implied permission;

"public procession" means a procession in a public place.

          [492]

(Pts III–V, Schedules, outside the scope of this work.)

INCOME AND CORPORATION TAXES ACT 1988

(1988 c 1)

ARRANGEMENT OF SECTIONS

PART V
PROVISIONS RELATING TO THE SCHEDULE E CHARGE

CHAPTER I
SUPPLEMENTARY CHARGING PROVISIONS OF GENERAL APPLICATION

Payments on retirement, sick pay etc

CHAPTER II
EMPLOYEES EARNING £8,500 OR MORE AND DIRECTORS

Expenses

Benefits in kind

General supplementary provisions

CHAPTER III
PROFIT-RELATED PAY

Preliminary

The Relief

CHAPTER IV
OTHER EXEMPTIONS AND RELIEFS

Other expenses, subscriptions etc

CHAPTER V
ASSESSMENT, COLLECTION, RECOVERY AND APPEALS

PART XIV
PENSION SCHEMES, SOCIAL SECURITY BENEFITS, LIFE ANNUITIES ETC

CHAPTER I
RETIREMENT BENEFIT SCHEMES

Approval of schemes

Tax reliefs

SCHEDULES

An Act to consolidate certain of the enactments relating to income tax and corporation tax, including certain enactments relating also to capital gains tax; and to repeal as obsolete section 339(1) of the Income and Corporation Taxes Act 1970 and paragraphs 3 and 4 of Schedule 11 to the Finance Act 1980

[9 February 1988]

GENERAL NOTE

Most of the provisions of this Act are outside the scope of this work, and only those most relevant to employment law are printed. These include the operation of the PAYE system and liability to Schedule E taxation; taxation of expenses and benefits under PAYE including benefits in kind under the regime for "higher paid employees" and Directors, taxation of termination payments and the tax treatment of profit related pay, share options, payroll deduction of charitable donations and contributions to approved pension schemes.

The subject matter of sections and Schedules omitted is not annotated. The Act applies from the tax year 1988–89 (see s 843) but is a consolidation of earlier legislation. Commencement and derivations are not annotated except where this Act has been subsequently amended. Extensive amendments to the taxation of employee benefits are made by the Finance Act 1993. Where these apply from the assessment year 1993–94 and relate to provisions reproduced here, the amendments are incorporated. However for reasons of space the new tax regimes so introduced in respect of company vans (ss 159AA, 159AB, Sch 6A) and heavier commercial vehicles (s 159AC) and removal expenses met by employers (ss 191A, 191B, Sch 11A), and tax relief for employees on benefits consisting of the provision of recreational facilities (s 197G) and counselling services in connection with loss of employment (ss 589A, 589B) are omitted. Other amendments made by the Finance Act 1993 and which first come into force from the assessment year 1994–5 have also been omitted for reasons of space: the principal omission is the new regime for the taxation of company cars by reference to original value (1993 Act, s 75, Sch 3, prospectively amending ss 157, 168, inserting new ss 168A–168G and substituting Sch 6).

PART V

PROVISIONS RELATING TO THE SCHEDULE E CHARGE

CHAPTER I

SUPPLEMENTARY CHARGING PROVISIONS OF GENERAL APPLICATION

Payments on retirement, sick pay etc

148 Payments on retirement or removal from office or employment

(1) Subject to the provisions of this section and section 188, tax shall be charged under Schedule E in respect of any payment to which this section applies which is made to the holder or past holder of any office or employment, or to his executors or administrators, whether made by the person under whom he holds or held the office or employment or by any other person.

(2) This section applies to any payment (not otherwise chargeable to tax) which is made, whether in pursuance of any legal obligation or not, either directly or indirectly in consideration or in consequence of, or otherwise in connection with, the termination of the holding of the office or employment or any change in its functions or emoluments, including any payment in commutation of annual or periodical payments (whether chargeable to tax or not) which would otherwise have been so made.

(3) For the purposes of this section and section 188, any payment made to the spouse or any relative or dependant of a person who holds or has held an office or employment, or made on behalf of or to the order of that person, shall be treated as made to that person, and any valuable consideration other than money shall be treated as a payment of money equal to the value of that consideration at the date when it is given.

(4) Any payment which is chargeable to tax by virtue of this section shall be treated as income received on the following date, that is to say—

(a) in the case of a payment in commutation of annual or other periodical payments, the date on which the commutation is effected; and

(b) in the case of any other payment, the date of the termination or change in respect of which the payment is made;

and shall be treated as emoluments of the holder or past holder of the office or employment assessable to tax under Schedule E; and any such payment shall be treated for all the purposes of the Income Tax Acts as earned income.

(5) In the case of the death of any person who, if he had not died, would have been chargeable to tax in respect of any such payment, the tax which would have

been so chargeable shall be assessed and charged upon his executors or administrators and shall be a debt due from and payable out of his estate.

(6) This section shall not apply to any payment made in pursuance of an obligation incurred before 6th April 1960.

(7) Where any payment chargeable to tax under this section is made to any person in any year of assessment, it shall be the duty of the person by whom it is made to deliver particulars thereof in writing to the inspector not later than 30 days after the end of that year. **[493]**

149 Sick pay

(1) Where a person holding an employment is absent from work for any period by reason of sickness or disability, any sums which—

(a) are paid to, or to the order or for the benefit of, that person (or a member of his family or household) in respect of any such absence from work; and

(b) are, by reason of his employment, paid as a result of any arrangements entered into by his employer,

shall be chargeable to income tax under Schedule E as emoluments of the employment . . . if, apart from this section, they would not be so chargeable . . .

(2) Where the funds for making payments under any arrangements are attributable partly to contributions made by the employer and partly to contributions made by the persons employed by him, subsection (1) above shall apply only to such part of the sums paid as a result of the arrangements as it is just and reasonable to regard as attributable to the employer's contributions.

(3) In this section "employment" means an office or employment the emoluments of which fall to be assessed under Schedule E and related expressions shall be construed accordingly; and the reference to a person's family or household is to his spouse, his sons and daughters and their spouses, his parents and his dependants. **[494]**

NOTE
Sub-s (1): words omitted repealed, in relation to the year 1989-90 and subsequent years of assessment, by the Finance Act 1989, s 42(3), (6), 187, Sch 17, Pt IV.

150 Job release scheme allowances, maternity pay and statutory sick pay

The following payments shall be charged to income tax under Schedule E by virtue of this section if they would not otherwise be, that is to say—

(a) allowances paid under a scheme of the kind described in the Job Release Act 1977, being a scheme which provides for the payment of allowances for periods beginning earlier than one year before the date on which the recipient attains pensionable age, as defined in that Act;

(b) maternity pay (whether paid during the subsistence of a contract of employment or not) within the meaning of section 33 of the Employment Protection (Consolidation) Act 1978 or, in Northern Ireland, Article 15 of the Industrial Relations (No 2) (Northern Ireland) Order 1976;

(c) payments of statutory sick pay within the meaning of section 1 of the Social Security and Housing Benefits Act 1982 or, in Northern Ireland, Article 3 of the Social Security (Northern Ireland) Order 1982; and

(d) payments of statutory maternity pay under Part V of the Social Security

Act 1986 or, in Northern Ireland, under Part VI of the Social Security
(Northern Ireland) Order 1986.   **[495]**

NOTE
There is no reference to maternity pay in s 33 of the Employment Protection (Consolidation) Act 1978,
the reference thereto having been repealed by the Social Security Act 1986, s 86(2), Sch 11. S 33 is itself
prospectively repealed and substituted (by a section which again makes no reference to maternity pay) by
the Trade Union Reform and Employment Rights Act 1993, s 23, but there is no consequential amendment
of this section.

References to the Acts of 1982 and 1986 in paras (c) and (d) respectively are to be construed also as
references to the equivalent provisions (ie Pts XI and XII respectively) of the Social Security Contributions
and Benefits Act 1992, by virtue of the Social Security (Consequential Provisions) Act 1992, s 2(4).

CHAPTER II
[EMPLOYEES EARNING £8,500 OR MORE AND DIRECTORS]

Expenses

153 Payments in respect of expenses

(1) Subject to the provisions of this Chapter, where in any year a person is employed
in [employment to which this Chapter applies] and by reason of his employment there
are paid to him in respect of expenses any sums which, apart from this section, are
not chargeable to tax as his income, those sums are to be treated as emoluments of
the employment and accordingly chargeable to income tax under Schedule E.

(2) Subsection (1) above is without prejudice to any claim for deductions under
section 198, 201 or 332(3).

(3) The reference in subsection (1) above to sums paid in respect of expenses
includes any sums put at the employee's disposal by reason of his employment and
paid away by him.   **[496]**

NOTES
Chapter heading: words in square brackets substituted by the Finance Act 1989, s 53(2)(a).
Sub-s (1): words in square brackets substituted by the Finance Act 1989, s 53(2)(b).

Benefits in kind

154 General charging provision

(1) Subject to section 163, where in any year a person is employed in [employment
to which this Chapter applies] and—

   (a) by reason of his employment there is provided for him, or for others being
       members of his family or household, any benefit to which this section
       applies; and
   (b) the cost of providing the benefit is not (apart from this section) chargeable
       to tax as his income,

there is to be treated as emoluments of the employment, and accordingly chargeable
to income tax under Schedule E, an amount equal to whatever is the cash equivalent
of the benefit.

(2) The benefits to which this section applies are accommodation (other than
living accommodation), entertainment, domestic or other services, and other benefits

and facilities of whatsoever nature (whether or not similar to any of those mentioned above in this subsection), excluding however—

(a) any benefit consisting of the right to receive, or the prospect of receiving, any sums which would be chargeable to tax under section 149; and

(b) any benefit chargeable under section 157, 158, [159AA,] [159A,] 160 or 162;

and subject to the exceptions provided for by [sections 155 and 155A].

(3) For the purposes of this section and sections 155 and 156, the persons providing a benefit are those at whose cost the provision is made.   **[497]**

NOTES
Sub-s (1): words in square brackets substituted by the Finance Act 1989, s 53(2)(b).
Sub-s (2): first figure in square brackets in para (b) inserted, in relation to the year 1993–94 and subsequent years of assessment, by the Finance Act 1993, s 73, Sch 4, para 2; second figure in square brackets inserted, in relation to the year 1991–92 and subsequent years of assessment, by the Finance Act 1991, s 30(1), (3); words in final pair of square brackets substituted, in relation to the year 1990–91 and subsequent years of assessment, by the Finance Act 1990, s 21(2), (3).

155 Exceptions from the general charge

(1) Where the benefit of a car [or van] is taxable under section 157 [or 159AA], section 154 does not apply to any benefit in connection with the car [or van] other than a benefit in connection with the provision of a driver for the car [or van].

[(1A) Section 154 does not apply to a benefit consisting in the provision for the employee of a car parking space at or near his place of work.]

(2) Section 154 does not apply where the benefit consists in provision for the employee, in premises occupied by the employer or others providing it, of accommodation, supplies or services used by the employee solely in performing the duties of his employment.

(3) Where living accommodation is provided by reason of a person's employment—

(a) alterations and additions to the premises concerned which are of a structural nature, and

(b) repairs to the premises of a kind which, if the premises were let under a lease to which section 11 of the Landlord and Tenant Act 1985 (repairing obligations) applies, would be the obligation of the lessor under the covenants implied by subsection (1) of that section,

are not benefits to which section 154 applies.

(4) Section 154 does not apply to a benefit consisting in the provision by the employee's employer for the employee himself, or for the spouse, children or dependants of the employee, of any pension, annuity, lump sum, gratuity or other like benefit to be given on the employee's death or retirement.

(5) Section 154 does not apply to a benefit consisting in the provision by the employee's employer of meals in any canteen in which meals are provided for the staff generally.

(6) Section 154 does not apply where the benefit consists—

(a) in providing the employee with medical treatment outside the United Kingdom (including providing for him to be an in-patient) in a case where the need for the treatment arises while the employee is outside the United Kingdom for the purpose of performing the duties of his employment; or

(b) in providing insurance for the employee against the cost of such treatment in such a case;

and for the purpose of this subsection, medical treatment includes all forms of treatment for, and all procedures for diagnosing, any physical or mental ailment, infirmity or defect.

[(7) Section 154 does not apply to a benefit consisting in the provision of entertainment (including hospitality of any kind) for the employee, or for members of his family or household, if—

(a) the person providing the benefit is neither his employer nor a person connected with his employer;

(b) neither his employer nor a person connected with his employer has directly or indirectly procured its provision; and

(c) it is not provided either in recognition of particular services which have been performed by the employee in the course of his employment or in anticipation of particular services which are to be so performed by him;

and section 839 shall apply for determining whether persons are connected for the purposes of this subsection.] **[498]**

NOTES
Sub-s (1): words in square brackets inserted, with effect from 1993–94 and subsequent years of assessment, by the Finance Act 1993, s 73, Sch 4, para 3.
Sub-ss (1A), (7): inserted or added by the Finance Act 1988, ss 46(3), 49(1), with effect for the year 1988–89 and subsequent years of assessment.

[155A Care for children

(1) Where a benefit consists in the provision for the employee of care for a child, section 154 does not apply to the benefit to the extent that it is provided in qualifying circumstances.

(2) For the purposes of subsection (1) above the benefit is provided in qualifying circumstances if—

(a) the child falls within subsection (3) below,
(b) the care is provided on premises which are not domestic premises,
(c) the condition set out in subsection (4) below or the condition set out in subsection (5) below (or each of them) is fulfilled, and
(d) in a case where the registration requirement applies, it is met.

(3) The child falls within this subsection if—

(a) he is a child for whom the employee has parental responsibility,
(b) he is resident with the employee, or
(c) he is a child of the employee and maintained at his expense.

(4) The condition is that the care is provided on premises which are made available by the employer alone.

(5) The condition is that—

(a) the care is provided under arrangements made by persons who include the employer,
(b) the care is provided on premises which are made available by one or more of those persons, and
(c) under the arrangements the employer is wholly or partly responsible for financing and managing the provision of the care.

(6) The registration requirement applies where—

(a) the premises on which the care is provided are required to be registered under section 1 of the Nurseries and Child-Minders Regulation Act 1948 or section 11 of the Children and Young Persons Act (Northern Ireland) 1968, or

    (b) any person providing the care is required to be registered under section 71 of the Children Act 1989 with respect to the premises on which it is provided;

and the requirement is met if the premises are so registered or (as the case may be) the person is so registered.

(7) In subsection (3)(c) above the reference to a child of the employee includes a reference to a stepchild of his.

(8) In this section—

    "care" means any form of care or supervised activity, whether or not provided on a regular basis, but excluding supervised activity provided primarily for educational purposes;

    "child" means a person under the age of eighteen;

    "domestic premises" means any premises wholly or mainly used as a private dwelling;

    "parental responsibility" has the meaning given in section 3(1) of the Children Act 1989.]   **[499]**

NOTES

Commencement: 6 April 1990 (Finance Act 1990, s 21(3)).

Inserted, in relation to the year 1990-91 and subsequent years of assessment, by the Finance Act 1990, s 21(1), (3).

156   Cash equivalents of benefits charged under section 154

(1) The cash equivalent of any benefit chargeable to tax under section 154 is an amount equal to the cost of the benefit, less so much (if any) of it as is made good by the employee to those providing the benefit.

(2) Subject to the following subsections, the cost of a benefit is the amount of any expense incurred in or in connection with its provision, and (here and in those subsections) includes a proper proportion of any expense relating partly to the benefit and partly to other matters.

(3) Where the benefit consists in the transfer of an asset by any person, and since that person acquired or produced the asset it has been used or has depreciated, the cost of the benefit is deemed to be the market value of the asset at the time of transfer.

(4) Where the asset referred to in subsection (3) above is not a car and before the transfer a person (whether or not the transferee) has been chargeable to tax in respect of the asset in accordance with subsection (5) below, the amount which under subsection (3) above is deemed to be the cost of the benefit shall (if apart from this subsection it would be less) be deemed to be—

    (a) the market value of the asset at the time when it was first applied (by those providing the benefit in question) for the provision of any benefit for a person, or for members of his family or household, by reason of his employment, less

    (b) the aggregate of the amounts taken into account as the cost of the benefit in charging tax in accordance with subsection (5) below in the year or years up to and including that in which the transfer takes place.

(5) Where the benefit consists in an asset being placed at the employee's disposal, or at the disposal of others being members of his family or household, for his or their use (without any transfer of the property in the asset), or of its being used wholly or

partly for his or their purposes, then the cost of the benefit in any year is deemed to be—

(a) the annual value of the use of the asset ascertained under subsection (6) below; plus

(b) the total of any expense incurred in or in connection with the provision of the benefit excluding—

    (i) the expense of acquiring or producing it incurred by the person to whom the asset belongs; and

    (ii) any rent or hire charge payable for the asset by those providing the benefit.

(6) Subject to subsection (7) below, the annual value of the use of the asset, for the purposes of subsection (5) above—

(a) in the case of land, is its annual value determined in accordance with section 837; and

(b) in any other case is 20 per cent of its market value at the time when it was first applied (by those providing the benefit in question) in the provision of any benefit for a person, or for members of his family or household, by reason of his employment.

(7) Where there is payable, by those providing the benefit, any sum by way of rent or hire-charge for the asset, the annual amount of which is equal to, or greater than, the annual value of the use of the asset as ascertained under subsection (6) above, that amount shall be substituted for the annual value in subsection (5)(a) above.

(8) From the cash equivalent there are deductible in each case under section 198, 201 or 332(3) such amounts (if any) as would have been so deductible if the cost of the benefit had been incurred by the employee out of his emoluments.

(9) In the case of assets first applied before 6th April 1980 by those providing the benefit in question in the provision of any benefit for a person, or for members of his family or household, by reason of his employment—

(a) subsection (4) above shall not have effect; and

(b) in subsection (6)(b) above for the words "20 per cent" there shall be substituted the words "10 per cent".   [500]

157 Cars available for private use

(1) Where in any year in the case of a person employed in [employment to which this Chapter applies], a car is made available (without any transfer of the property in it) either to himself or to others being members of his family or household, and—

(a) it is so made available by reason of his employment and it is in that year available for his or their private use; and

(b) the benefit of the car is not (apart from this section) chargeable to tax as the employee's income,

there is to be treated as emoluments of the employment, and accordingly chargeable to income tax under Schedule E, an amount equal to whatever is the cash equivalent of that benefit in that year.

(2) Subject to the provisions of this section, the cash equivalent of that benefit is to be ascertained—

(a) from Tables A and B in Part I of Schedule 6, in the case of cars with an original market value of up to £19,250; and

(b) from Table C in that Part in the case of cars with an original market value of more than that amount;

the equivalent in each case being shown in the second or third column of the applicable Table by reference to the age of the car at the end of the relevant year of assessment.

(3) Where in any year the benefit of a car is chargeable to tax under this section as the employee's income he shall not be taxable—

 (a) under Schedule E in respect of the discharge of any liability of his in connection with the car;

 (b) under section 141 or 142 in respect of any non-cash voucher or credit-token to the extent that it is used by him—

  (i) for obtaining money which is spent on goods or services in connection with the car; or

  (ii) for obtaining such goods or services;

 (c) under section 153 in respect of any payment made to him in respect of expenses incurred by him in connection with the car.

(4) The Treasury may by order taking effect from the beginning of any year beginning after it is made—

 (a) increase or further increase the money sum specified in subsection (2)(a) above;

 (b) with or without such an increase, substitute for any of the three Tables a different Table of cash equivalents;

 (c) increase or further increase the money sum specified in paragraph 1(1) of Part II of Schedule 6.

(5) Part II of Schedule 6 has effect—

 (a) with respect to the application of the Tables in Part I; and

 (b) for the reduction of the cash equivalent under this section in cases where the car has not been available for the whole of the relevant year, or the use of it has been preponderantly business use, or the employee makes any payment for the use of it.   **[501]**

NOTE

 Sub-s (1): words in square brackets substituted by the Finance Act 1989, s 53(2)(b).

 Sub-s (2) will be substituted and sub-ss (4), (5) repealed, by the Finance Act 1993, s 72, Sch 3, para 2, with effect from 1994–95 and subsequent years of assessment.

158 Car fuel

(1) Where in any year in the case of a person employed in [employment to which this Chapter applies] fuel is provided by reason of his employment for a car which is made available as mentioned in section 157, an amount equal to whatever is the cash equivalent of that benefit in that year shall be treated as emoluments of the employment and, accordingly, shall be chargeable to income tax under Schedule E.

[(2) Subject to the provisions of this section, the cash equivalent of that benefit shall be ascertained from—

 (a) Table A below where the car has an internal combustion engine with one or more reciprocating pistons and is not a diesel car;

 (b) Table AB below where the car has an internal combustion engine with one or more reciprocating pistons and is a diesel car;

 (c) Table B below where the car does not have an internal combustion engine with one or more reciprocating pistons.

[TABLE A

Cylinder capacity of car in cubic centimetres	Cash equivalent
1,400 or less	£600
More than 1,400 but not more than 2,000	£760
More than 2,000	£1,130

TABLE AB

Cylinder capacity of car in cubic centimetres	Cash equivalent
2,000 or less	£550
More than 2,000	£710

TABLE B

Original market value of car	Cash equivalent
Less than £6,000	£600
£6,000 or more but less than £8,500	£760
£8,500 or more	£1,130]

(2A) For the purposes of subsection (2) above a diesel car is a car which uses heavy oil as fuel; and "heavy oil" here means heavy oil as defined by section 1(4) of the Hydrocarbon Oil Duties Act 1979.

(2B) For the purposes of Tables A and AB in subsection (2) above a car's cylinder capacity is the capacity of its engine calculated as for the purposes of the Vehicles (Excise) Act 1971.]

(3) Without prejudice to the generality of subsection (1) above, fuel is provided for a car if—

(a) any liability in respect of the provision of fuel for the car is discharged;
(b) a non-cash voucher or a credit-token is used to obtain fuel for the car or money which is spent on such fuel;
(c) any sum is paid in respect of expenses incurred in providing fuel for the car.

In this subsection "non-cash voucher" and "credit-token" have the meanings given by section 141(7) and 142(4) respectively.

(4) The Treasury may by order taking effect from the beginning of any year beginning after it is made substitute a different Table for [any] of the Tables in subsection (2) above.

(5) Where paragraph 2 . . . of Part II of Schedule 6 applies to reduce the cash equivalent of the benefit of the car for which the fuel is provided, the same reduction shall be made to the cash equivalent of the benefit of the fuel ascertained under subsection (2) above.

(6) If in the relevant year—

(a) the employee is required to make good to the person providing the fuel the whole of the expense incurred by him in or in connection with the provision of fuel for his private use and he does so; or
(b) the fuel is made available only for business travel;

the cash equivalent is nil. **[502]**

159 Pooled cars

(1) This section applies to any car in the case of which the inspector is satisfied (whether on a claim under this section or otherwise) that it has for any year been included in a car pool for the use of the employees of one or more employers.

(2) A car is to be treated as having been so included for a year if—

(a) in that year it was made available to, and actually used by, more than one of those employees and, in the case of each of them, it was made available to him by reason of his employment but it was not in that year ordinarily used by one of them to the exclusion of the others; and

(b) in the case of each of them any private use of the car made by him in that year was merely incidental to his other use of it in the year; and

(c) it was in that year not normally kept overnight on or in the vicinity of any residential premises where any of the employees was residing, except while being kept overnight on premises occupied by the person making the car available to them.

(3) Where this section applies to a car, then for the year in question the car is to be treated under sections 154 and 157 as not having been available for the private use of any of the employees.

(4) A claim under this section in respect of a car for any year may be made by any one of the employees mentioned in subsection (2)(a) above (referred to below as "the employees concerned") or by the employer on behalf of all of them.

(5) On an appeal against the decision of the inspector on a claim under this section all the employees concerned may take part in the proceedings, and the determination of the body of Commissioners or county court appealed to shall be binding on all those employees, whether or not they have taken part in the proceedings.

(6) Where an appeal against the decision of the inspector on a claim under this section has been determined, no appeal against the inspector's decision on any other such claim in respect of the same car and the same year shall be entertained. **[503]**

59AA, 159AB, 159AC (*Outside the scope of this work.*)

[159A Mobile telephones

(1) Where in any year in the case of a person employed in employment to which this Chapter applies a mobile telephone is made available (without any transfer of the property in it) either to that person or to others who are members of his family or household, and—

(a) it is so made available by reason of his employment and it is in that year available for his or their private use, and

(b) the benefit of the mobile telephone is not (apart from this section) chargeable to tax as the employee's income,

there is to be treated as emoluments of the employment, and accordingly chargeable to income tax under Schedule E, an amount equal to whatever is the cash equivalent of that benefit in that year.

(2) The cash equivalent of a benefit taxable under this section in any year shall be £200 for each mobile telephone made available in that year, but subject to the following provisions of this section.

(3) If for any year—

(a) there is no private use of the mobile telephone, or
(b) the employee is required to, and does, make good to the person providing the benefit the full cost of any private use of the mobile telephone,

then the cash equivalent of the benefit for that year is nil.

(4) If the mobile telephone is unavailable for any part of a year, the cash equivalent of the benefit for that year shall be reduced by an amount which bears to that specified in subsection (2) above for that year the proportion which the number of days in the year on which the mobile telephone is unavailable bears to 365.

(5) For the purposes of subsection (4) above, a mobile telephone is to be regarded as "unavailable" on any day if, and only if—

(a) it is not made available as mentioned in subsection (1) above until after that day, or
(b) it ceases to be so available before that day, or
(c) it is incapable of being used at all throughout a period of not less than 30 consecutive days of which that day is one.

(6) Where different mobile telephones are made available on different days in a year, the employee shall be treated for the purposes of this section as if the same mobile telephone (or, in a case where two or more mobile telephones are made available concurrently, the same mobile telephones) had been made available on each of those days.

(7) The Treasury may by order taking effect from the beginning of any year commencing after the making of the order increase or further increase the amount specified in subsection (2) above.

(8) For the purposes of this section—

(a) "mobile telephone" means wireless telegraphy apparatus designed or adapted for the purpose of transmitting and receiving spoken messages so as to provide a telephone which is connected to a public telecommunication system (within the meaning of the Telecommunications Act 1984) but which is not physically connected to a land-line and—

(i) includes any such apparatus provided in connection with a car [or van], notwithstanding that the car is made available as mentioned in section 157 [or 159AA], but
[(ia) includes any such apparatus provided in connection with a heavier commercial vehicle (within the meaning given by section 159AC) notwithstanding that the vehicle is made available as mentioned in that section;]
(ii) does not include a cordless telephone or a telepoint telephone, whether or not provided in connection with a car [or van] [or heavier commercial vehicle];

(b) "cordless telephone" means wireless telegraphy apparatus—

(i) designed or adapted for the purpose of transmitting and receiving spoken messages so as to provide a wireless extension to a telephone, and

(ii) used only as such an extension to a telephone that is physically connected to a land-line;

(c) "telepoint telephone" means wireless telegraphy apparatus used for the purpose of a short-range radio communications service utilising frequencies between 864 and 868 megahertz (inclusive);

(d) "private use", in relation to a mobile telephone, means any use of the telephone to make calls, other than calls made wholly, exclusively and necessarily in the performance of the duties of the employment;

(e) "full cost", in relation to any private use of a mobile telephone, means the aggregate of—

(i) the cost of any telephone calls which constitute private use of the mobile telephone; and

(ii) any other cost of the benefit provided, determined in accordance with the provisions of section 156(2) and (5) to (7) as they would apply if the benefit were chargeable to tax under section 154;

(f) an employee who accepts a call on the footing that the cost of the call will be charged to the person providing the benefit shall be treated as if the employee had made the call.]　　　　　　　　　　　　　　　　　　**[504]**

NOTE

Inserted by the Finance Act 1991, s 30(2), (3), with effect for the year 1991-92 and subsequent years of assessment.

Sub-s (8): words in square brackets inserted, with effect for 1993–94 and subsequent years of assessment, by the Finance Act 1993, ss 73, 74(2), Sch 4, para 5.

160 Beneficial loan arrangements

(1) Where in the case of a person employed in [employment to which this Chapter applies] there is outstanding for the whole or part of a year a loan (whether to the employee himself or a relative of his) of which the benefit is obtained by reason of his employment and—

(a) no interest is paid on the loan for that year; or

(b) the amount of interest paid on it for the year is less than interest at the official rate,

there is to be treated as emoluments of the employment, and accordingly chargeable to income tax under Schedule E, an amount equal to whatever is the cash equivalent of the benefit of the loan for that year.

(2) Where in the case of a person employed in [employment to which this Chapter applies]—

(a) there is in any year released or written off the whole or part of a loan (whether to the employee himself or a relative of his, and whether or not such a loan as is mentioned in subsection (1) above), and

(b) the benefit of that loan was obtained by reason of his employment,

then there is to be treated as emoluments of the employment, and accordingly chargeable to income tax under Schedule E, an amount equal to that which is released or written off.

[(3) Where—

(a) there was outstanding, at any time when a person was in employment to which this Chapter applies, the whole or part of a loan to him (or a relative of his) the benefit of which was obtained by reason of his employment, and

(b) that employment has terminated, or ceased to be employment to which this Chapter applies,

subsection (2) above applies as if the employment had not terminated or, as the case may be, had not ceased to be employment to which this Chapter applies.]

(4) Part I of Schedule 7 has effect as to what is meant by the benefit of a loan obtained by reason of a person's employment; the cash equivalent of the benefit is to be ascertained in accordance with Part II of that Schedule; and Part III of that Schedule has effect for excluding from the operation of subsection (1) above loans on which interest is eligible for relief under subsection (1) of section 353 or which would be so eligible apart from subsection (2) of that section [but that Part of that Schedule is subject to Part IV of that Schedule, which makes provision in connection with the restriction to tax at the basic rate of certain reliefs in respect of loans to which Part III of that Schedule has effect; and Part V of that Schedule has effect for the interpretation of the Schedule.]

[(4A) Where an assessment for any year in respect of a loan has been made or determined on the footing that the whole or part of the interest payable on the loan for that year was not in fact paid, but it is subsequently paid, then, on a claim in that behalf, the cash equivalent for that year shall be recalculated so as to take that payment into account and the assessment shall be adjusted accordingly.]

(5) In this section, sections 161 and 162 and Schedule 7—

(a) "loan" includes any form of credit;
(b) references to a loan include references to any other loan applied directly or indirectly towards the replacement of the first-mentioned loan;
(c) references to making a loan include arranging, guaranteeing or in any way facilitating a loan (related expressions being construed accordingly); and
(d) references to the official rate of interest are to the [rate applicable under section 178 of the Finance Act 1989].

(6) For the purposes of this section and section 161, a person is a relative of another person if he or she is—

(a) the spouse of that other; or
(b) a parent or remoter forebear, child or remoter issue, or brother or sister of that other or of the spouse of that other; or
(c) the spouse of a person falling within paragraph (b) above.

(7) Subject to section 161, this section applies to loans whether made before or after this Act is passed. [505]

NOTES

Sub-ss (1), (2): words in square brackets substituted by the Finance Act 1989, s 53(2)(b).
Sub-s (3): substituted by the Finance Act 1989, s 53(2)(c).
Sub-s (4): words in square brackets added, in relation to the year 1991-92 and subsequent years of assessment, by the Finance Act 1991, s 27(6), Sch 6, para 1.
Sub-s (4A): inserted, in relation to the year 1991-92 and subsequent years of assessment, by the Finance Act 1991, s 27(6), Sch 6, para 1.
Sub-s (5): words in square brackets in para (d) substituted, in relation to periods beginning on or after 18 August 1989, by the Finance Act 1989, s 179(1)(g), (4).

161 Exceptions from section 160

(1) There is no charge to tax under section 160(1) if the cash equivalent does not exceed [£300] or (for a year in which there are two or more loans outstanding) the total of all the cash equivalents does not exceed that amount.

(2) Where the amount of interest paid on a loan for the year in which it is made is not less than interest at the official rate applying for that year for the purposes of section 160 and the loan is made—

(a) for a fixed and unvariable period; and

(b) at a fixed and unvariable rate of interest,

subsection (1) of that section shall not apply to the loan in any subsequent year by reason only of an increase in the official rate since the year in which the loan was made.

(3) Where a loan was made at any time before 6th April 1978—

(a) for a fixed and unvariable period; and

(b) at a fixed and unvariable rate of interest,

section 160(1) shall not apply to the loan if it is shown that the rate of interest is not less than such rate as could have been expected to apply to a loan on the same terms (other than as to the rate of interest) made at that time between persons not connected with each other (within the meaning of section 839) dealing at arm's length.

(4) If the employee shows that he derived no benefit from a loan made to a relative of his, section 160(1) and (2) above shall not apply to that loan.

(5) Section 160(2) does not apply where the amount released or written off is chargeable to income tax as income of the employee apart from that section, except—

(a) where it is chargeable only by virtue of section 148; or

(b) to the extent that the amount exceeds the sums previously falling to be treated as the employee's income under section 677.

(6) On the employee's death—

(a) a loan within subsection (1) of section 160 ceases to be outstanding for the purposes of the operation of that subsection; and

(b) no charge arises under subsection (2) of that section by reference to any release or writing-off which takes effect on or after the death.

(7) Section 160(2) does not apply to benefits received in pursuance of arrangements made at any time with a view to protecting the holder of shares acquired before 6th April 1976 from a fall in their market value.   **[506]**

NOTE

Sub-s (1): figure in square brackets substituted, in relation to the year 1991-92 and subsequent years of assessment, by the Finance Act 1991, s 31.

General supplementary provisions

[167 Employment to which this Chapter applies

(1) This Chapter applies—

(a) to employment as a director of a company (but subject to subsection (5) below), and

(b) to employment with emoluments at the rate of £8,500 a year or more.

(2) For this purpose emoluments are to be calculated—

(a) on the basis that they include all such amounts as come, or would but for section 157(3) come, into charge under this Chapter or section 141, 142, 143 or 145, and

(b) without any deduction under section 198, 201 or 332(3).

[(2A) Where, by virtue of paragraph 15 of Schedule 7, the amount, or the total of the amounts, treated under section 160 as emoluments of a person exceeds what it would have been apart from that paragraph, then, for the purposes of subsection (2)(a) above there shall, instead of that excess, be brought into account an amount equal to the difference between—

(a)   the amount by which his total income for the purposes of excess liability exceeds the basic rate limit; and

(b)   what the amount referred to in paragraph (a) above would have been, apart from paragraph 15 of Schedule 7;

and in this subsection "excess liability" means the excess of liability to income tax over what it would be if all income tax [not chargeable at the lower rate] [by virtue of section 1(2)(aa) were charged at the basic rate, or (so far as applicable in accordance with section 207A) the lower rate], to the exclusion of any higher rate.]

(3) Where a person is employed in two or more employments by the same employer and either—

(a)   the total of the emoluments of those employments (applying this section) is at the rate of £8,500 a year or more, or

(b)   this Chapter applies (apart from this subsection) to one or more of those employments,

this Chapter shall apply to all the employments.

(4) All employees of a partnership or body over which an individual or another partnership or body has control are to be treated for the purposes of this section (but not for any other purpose) as if the employment were an employment by the individual or by that other partnership or body as the case may be.

(5) This Chapter shall not apply to a person's employment by reason only of its being employment as a director of a company (without prejudice to its application by virtue of subsection (1)(b) or (3) above) if he has no material interest in the company and either—

(a)   his employment is as a full-time working director; or

(b)   the company is non-profit making (meaning that neither does it carry on a trade nor do its functions consist wholly or mainly in the holding of investments or other property) or is established for charitable purposes only.]   [507]

NOTES

Substituted by the Finance Act 1989, s 53(1).

Sub-s (2A): inserted, in relation to the year 1991-92 and subsequent years of assessment, by the Finance Act 1991, s 27(6), Sch 6, para 2; words in outer square brackets therein inserted, in relation to the year 1992-93 and subsequent years of assessment, by the Finance (No 2) Act 1992, s 19(3), (7); words in inner square brackets substituted by the Finance Act 1993, s 79(1), Sch 6 para 1 in relation to the year 1993–94 and subsequent years of assessment.

168 Other interpretative provisions

(1) The following provisions of this section apply for the interpretation of expressions used in this Chapter.

(2) Subject to section 165(6)(b), "employment" means an office or employment the emoluments of which fall to be assessed under Schedule E; and related expressions shall be construed accordingly.

(3) For the purposes of this Chapter—

(a)   all sums paid to an employee by his employer in respect of expenses, and

(b)   all such provision as is mentioned in this Chapter which is made for an employee, or for members of his family or household, by his employer, are deemed to be paid to or made for him or them by reason of his employment, except any such payment or provision made by the employer, being an individual, as can be shown to have been made in the normal course of his domestic, family or personal relationships.

(4) References to members of a person's family or household are to his spouse, his sons and daughters and their spouses, his parents and his servants, dependants and guests.

(5) As respects cars, the following definitions apply—

  (a) "car" means any mechanically propelled road vehicle except—

    (i) a vehicle of a construction primarily suited for the conveyance of goods or burden of any description,

    (ii) a vehicle of a type not commonly used as a private vehicle and unsuitable to be so used,

    (iii) a motor cycle as defined in section 190(4) of the Road Traffic Act 1972, and

    (iv) an invalid carriage as defined in section 190(5) of that Act;

  (b) the age of a car at any time is the interval between the date of its first registration and that time;

  (c) "business travel" means travelling which a person is necessarily obliged to do in the performance of the duties of his employment;

  (d) the date of a car's first registration is the date on which it was first registered—

    (i) in Great Britain, under the Vehicles (Excise) Act 1971 or corresponding earlier legislation; or

    (ii) elsewhere, under the corresponding legislation of any country or territory;

  (e) the original market value of a car is the inclusive price which it might reasonably have been expected to fetch if sold in the United Kingdom singly in a retail sale in the open market immediately before the date of its first registration ("inclusive price" meaning the price inclusive of customs or excise duty, of any tax chargeable as if it were a duty of customs, and of value added tax and car tax); and

  (f) "private use", in relation to a car made available to any person, or to others being members of his family or household, means any use otherwise than for his business travel.

[(5A) As respects vans, the following definitions apply—

  (a) "van" means a mechanically-propelled road vehicle which is—

    (i) of a construction primarily suited for the conveyance of goods or burden of any description, and

    (ii) of a design weight not exceeding 3,500 kilograms,

and which is not a motor cycle as defined in section 185(1) of the Road Traffic Act 1988;

  (b) the age of a van at any time is the interval between the date of its first registration and that time;

  (c) "business travel" means travelling which a person is necessarily obliged to do in the performance of the duties of his employment;

  (d) the date of a van's first registration is the date on which it was first registered under the Vehicles (Excise) Act 1971 or under corresponding legislation of any country or territory;

  (e) "design weight" means the weight which a vehicle is designed or adapted not to exceed when in normal use and travelling on a road laden; and

(f) "private use", in relation to a van made available to any person, or to others being members of his family or household, means any use otherwise than for his business travel.]

(6) For the purposes of this Chapter—

(a) a car made available in any year to an employee, or to others being members of his family or household, by reason of his employment is deemed to be available in that year for his or their private use unless the terms on which the car is made available prohibit such use and no such use is made of the car in that year;

(b) a car made available to an employee, or to others being members of his family or household, by his employer is deemed to be made available to him or them by reason of his employment (unless the employer is an individual and it can be shown that the car was made so available in the normal course of his domestic, family or personal relationships)[;

(c) a van made available in any year to an employee, or to others being members of his family or household, by reason of his employment is deemed to be available in that year for his or their private use unless the terms on which the van is made available prohibit such use and no such use is made of the van in that year;

(d) a van made available to an employee, or to others being members of his family or household, by his employer is deemed to be made available to him or them by reason of his employment (unless the employer is an individual and it can be shown that the van was made so available in the normal course of his domestic, family or personal relationships)].

(7) For the purposes of section 156, the market value of an asset at any time is the price which it might reasonably have been expected to fetch on a sale in the open market at that time.

(8) Subject to subsection (9) below, "director" means—

(a) in relation to a company whose affairs are managed by a board of directors or similar body, a member of that board or similar body;

(b) in relation to a company whose affairs are managed by a single director or similar person, that director or person; and

(c) in relation to a company whose affairs are managed by the members themselves, a member of the company,

and includes any person in accordance with whose directions or instructions the directors of the company (as defined above) are accustomed to act.

(9) A person is not under subsection (8) above to be deemed to be a person in accordance with whose directions or instructions the directors of the company are accustomed to act by reason only that the directors act on advice given by him in a professional capacity.

(10) "Full-time working director" means a director who is required to devote substantially the whole of his time to the service of the company in a managerial or technical capacity.

(11) A person shall be treated as having a material interest [in a company if he, either on his own or with one or more associates, or if any associate of his with or without such other associates,—

(a) is the beneficial owner of, or able, directly or through the medium of other companies, or by any other indirect means to control, more than 5 per cent. of the ordinary share capital of the company, or

(b) in the case of a close company, possesses, or is entitled to acquire, such rights as would, in the event of the winding-up of the company or in any other circumstances, give an entitlement to receive more than 5 per cent of the assets which would then be available for distribution among the participators.]

In this subsection "associate" has the same meaning as in section 417(3), except that for this purpose "relative" in that subsection has the meaning given by section 160(6) [, and "participator" has the meaning given by section 417(1)].

(12) "Control", in relation to a body corporate or partnership, has the meaning given to it by section 840; and the definition of "control" in that section applies (with the necessary modifications) in relation to an unincorporated association as it applies in relation to a body corporate.

(13) "Year" means year of assessment (except where the expression is used with reference to the age of a car).   **[508]**

NOTES

Sub-s (5) will be amended by the Finance Act 1993, s 72, Sch 3, para 3, for the year 1994–95 and subsequent years of assessment.

Sub-s (5A): inserted, for 1993–94 and subsequent years of assessment, by the Finance Act 1993, s 73, Sch 4, para 6.

Sub-s (6): paras (c), (d) inserted, for 1993–94 and subsequent years of assessment, by the Finance Act 1993, s 73, Sch 4, para 6.

Sub-s (11): words in square brackets substituted or added, in relation to accounting periods beginning after 31 March 1989, by the Finance Act 1989, s 107, Sch 12, Pt II, para 8.

New ss 168A–168G (taxation of car benefits) will be inserted by the Finance Act 1993, s 72, Sch 3, para 4, for the year 1994–95 and subsequent years of assessment.

CHAPTER III
PROFIT-RELATED PAY

Preliminary

169 Interpretation

(1) In this Chapter—

"employment" means an office or employment whose emoluments fall to be assessed under Schedule E, and related expressions have corresponding meanings;

"employment unit" means an undertaking, or that part of an undertaking, to which a profit-related pay scheme relates;

"pay" (except in the expression "profit-related pay") means emoluments paid under deduction of tax pursuant to section 203, reduced by any amounts included in them by virtue of Chapter II of Part V;

"profit period" means an accounting period by reference to which any profit-related pay is calculated;

"profit-related pay" means emoluments from an employment which are paid in accordance with a profit-related pay scheme;

"profit-related pay scheme" means a scheme providing for the payment of emoluments calculated by reference to profits;

"profits", or "losses", in relation to a profit period, means the amount shown in the account prepared for that period in accordance with the relevant profit-related pay scheme as the profit, or as the case may be the loss, on ordinary activities after taxation;

"registered scheme" means a profit-related pay scheme registered under this Chapter;

"scheme employer" means the person on whose application a profit-related pay scheme is or may be registered under this Chapter.

(2) References in this Chapter to the employees to whom a profit-related pay scheme relates are references to the employees who will receive any payments of profit-related pay under the scheme.   **[509]**

170 (*Repealed by the Finance Act 1989, ss 42, 187, Sch 17, Pt IV.*)

The relief

171 Relief from tax

(1) [The whole] of any profit-related pay to which this section applies shall be exempt from income tax.

(2) This section applies to any profit-related pay paid to an employee by reference to a profit period and in accordance with a registered scheme, but only so far as it does not exceed the lower of the two limits specified in the following provisions of this section.

(3) The first of the limits referred to in subsection (2) above is one fifth of the aggregate of—

  (a) the pay (but not any profit-related pay) paid to the employee in the profit period in respect of his employment in the employment unit concerned (or, if the employee is eligible to receive profit-related pay by reference to part only of the period, so much of his pay, but not any profit-related pay, as is paid in that part); and

  (b) the profit-related pay paid to him by reference to that period in respect of that employment.

(4) The second of the limits referred to in subsection (2) above is [£4,000] (or, if the profit period is less than 12 months, or the employee is eligible to receive profit-related pay by reference to part only of the profit period, a proportionately reduced amount).   **[510]**

NOTES
Sub-s (1): words in square brackets substituted, in relation to profit-related pay paid by reference to profit periods beginning on or after 1 April 1991, by the Finance Act 1991, s 37.
Sub-s (4): figure in square brackets substituted, in relation to profit-related pay paid by reference to profit periods beginning on or after 1 April 1989, by the Finance Act 1989, s 61, Sch 4, paras 1, 2.

172 Exceptions from tax

(1) Profit-related pay shall not be exempt from income tax by virtue of section 171 if—

  (a) it is paid to an employee in respect of his employment in an employment unit during a time when he also has another employment; and

  (b) he receives in respect of that other employment during that time profit-related pay which is exempt from income tax by virtue of that section.

(2) Subject to subsection (3) below, profit-related pay in respect of which no secondary Class 1 contributions under Part I of the Social Security Act 1975 or Part I of the Social Security (Northern Ireland) Act 1975 are payable shall not be exempt from income tax by virtue of section 171.

(3) Subsection (2) above shall not apply to profit-related pay in respect of which no Class 1 contributions are payable only because the employee's earnings are below the lower earnings limit for such contributions.   **[511]**

CHAPTER IV
OTHER EXEMPTIONS AND RELIEFS

Retirement benefits etc

188 Exemptions from section 148

(1) Tax shall not be charged by virtue of section 148 in respect of the following payments, that is to say—

(a) any payment made in connection with the termination of the holding of an office or employment by the death of the holder, or made on account of injury to or disability of the holder of an office or employment;

(b) any sum chargeable to tax under section 313;

(c) a benefit provided in pursuance of a retirement benefits scheme within the meaning of Chapter II of Part IX of the 1970 Act or Chapter I of Part XIV of this Act or of an agreement as described in section 220(2) of the 1970 Act, where under section 220 of that Act or section 595 of this Act the holder of the office or employment was chargeable to tax in respect of sums paid, or treated as paid, with a view to the provision of the benefit;

(d) a benefit paid in pursuance of any such scheme or fund as was described in section 221(1) and (2) of the 1970 Act or as is described in section 596(1);

(e) any terminal grant, gratuity or other lump sum paid under any Royal Warrant, Queen's Order, or Order in Council relating to members of Her Majesty's forces, and any payment made in commutation of annual or other periodical payments authorised by any such Warrant or Order;

(f) a payment of benefit under any superannuation scheme administered by the government of an overseas territory within the Commonwealth, or of compensation for loss of career, interruption of service or disturbance made in connection with any change in the constitution of any such overseas territory to persons who, before the change, were employed in the public services of that territory;

and references in paragraph (f) above to an overseas territory, to the government of such a territory, and to employment in the public service of such a territory shall be construed as if they occurred in the Overseas Development and Co-operation Act 1980, and sections 10(2) and 13(1) and (2) of that Act (which relate to the construction of such references) shall apply accordingly.

(2) Subsection (1)(d) above shall not apply to any compensation paid for loss of office or employment or for loss or diminution of emoluments unless the loss or diminution is due to ill-health; but this subsection shall not be taken to apply to any payment properly regarded as a benefit earned by past service.

(3) Tax shall not be charged by virtue of section 148 in respect of any payment in the case of which the following conditions are satisfied—

(a) that the payment is in respect of an office or employment in which the holder's service included foreign service; and

(b) that the foreign service comprised either—

(i) in any case, three-quarters of the whole period of service down to the relevant date, or

(ii) where the period of service down to the relevant date exceeded ten years, the whole of the last ten years, or

(iii) where the period of service down to the relevant date exceeded 20 years, one-half of that period, including any ten of the last 20 years.

(4) Tax shall not be charged by virtue of section 148 in respect of a payment of an amount not exceeding [£30,000] ("the exempt sum") and, subject to subsection (5) below, in the case of a payment which exceeds that amount shall be charged only in respect of the excess.

(5) Where two or more payments in respect of which tax is chargeable by virtue of section 148, or would be so chargeable apart from subsection (4) above, are made to or in respect of the same person in respect of the same office or employment, or in respect of different offices or employments held under the same employer or under associated employers, subsection (4) above shall apply as if those payments were a single payment of an amount equal to that aggregate amount; and the amount of any one payment chargeable to tax shall be ascertained as follows, that is to say—

(a) where the payments are treated as income of different chargeable periods, the exempt sum shall be deducted from a payment treated as income of an earlier period before any payment treated as income of a later period; and
(b) subject to that, the exempt sum shall be deducted rateably from the payments according to their respective amounts.

(6) The person chargeable to tax by virtue of section 148 in respect of any payment may make a claim for such relief in respect of the payment as is applicable thereto under Schedule 11.

(7) For the purposes of this section and Schedule 11 offices or employments in respect of which payments to which section 148 applies are made shall be treated as held under associated employers if, on the date which is the relevant date in relation to any of those payments, one of those employers is under the control of the other or of a third person who controls or is under the control of the other on that or any other such date.

In this subsection "control" has the meaning given by section 840.

(8) In this section—

(a) "the relevant date" and "foreign service" have the same meaning as in Schedule 11; and
(b) references to an employer or to a person controlling or controlled by an employer include references to his successors. [512–515]

NOTE
Sub-s (4): sum in square brackets substituted with savings by the Finance Act 1988, s 74(1), (3), in relation to a payment treated by s 148(4) of this Act as income received on or after 6 April 1988.

189 Lump sum benefits on retirement

A lump sum paid to a person [(whether on his retirement from an office or employment or otherwise)] shall not be chargeable to income tax under Schedule E if—

(a) it is paid in pursuance of any such scheme or fund as was described in section 221(1) and (2) of the 1970 Act or as is described in section 596(1) and is neither a payment of compensation to which section 188(2) applies nor a payment chargeable to tax under section 600; or
(b) it is a benefit paid in pursuance of any such scheme or arrangement as was referred to in section 220 of the 1970 Act or a retirement benefits scheme within the meaning of section 611 of this Act and the person to whom it is paid was chargeable to tax under section 220 of the 1970 Act or section 595 of this Act in respect of sums paid, or treated as paid, with a view to the provision of the benefit; or
(c) it is paid under approved personal pension arrangements (within the meaning of Chapter IV of Part XIV). [516]

NOTE

Words in square brackets substituted with retrospective effect by the Finance Act 1988, s 57.

Other expenses, subscriptions etc

198 Relief for necessary expenses

(1) If the holder of an office or employment is necessarily obliged to incur and defray out of the emoluments of that office or employment the expenses of travelling in the performance of the duties of the office or employment, or of keeping and maintaining a horse to enable him to perform those duties, or otherwise to expend money wholly, exclusively and necessarily in the performance of those duties, there may be deducted from the emoluments to be assessed the expenses so necessarily incurred and defrayed.

(2) Subject to subsection (3) below, where the emoluments for any duties do not fall within Case I or II of Schedule E, then in relation to those or any other emoluments of the office or employment, subsection (1) above and [Part II of the 1990 Act] (capital allowances in respect of machinery and plant) shall apply as if the performance of those duties did not belong to that office or employment.

(3) There may be deducted from any emoluments chargeable under Case III of Schedule E the amount of—

(a) any expenses defrayed out of those emoluments, and

(b) any other expenses defrayed in the United Kingdom in the chargeable period or in an earlier chargeable period in which the holder of the office or employment has been resident in the United Kingdom,

being in either case expenses for which a deduction might have been made under subsection (1) above from emoluments of the office or employment if they had been chargeable under Case I of Schedule E for the chargeable period in which the expenses were incurred; but a deduction shall not be made twice, whether under this subsection or otherwise, in respect of the same expenses from emoluments of the office or employment.

(4) No deduction shall be made under this section in respect of expenditure incurred by a Member of the House of Commons in, or in connection with, the provision or use of residential or overnight accommodation to enable him to perform his duties as such a Member in or about the Palace of Westminster or his constituency.

[517]

NOTE

Sub-s (2): words in square brackets substituted, in relation to chargeable periods ending after 5 April 1990, by the Capital Allowances Act 1990, s 164, Sch 1, para 8(1), (10) (the "1990 Act" in the amended subsection).

202 Donations to charity: payroll deduction scheme

(1) This section applies where an individual ("the employee") is entitled to receive payments from which income tax falls to be deducted by virtue of section 203 and regulations under that section, and the person liable to make the payments ("the employer") withholds sums from them.

(2) If the conditions mentioned in subsections (3) to (7) below are fulfilled the sums shall, in assessing tax under Schedule E, be allowed to be deducted as expenses incurred in the year of assessment in which they are withheld.

(3) The sums must be withheld in accordance with a scheme which is (or is of a kind) approved by the Board at the time they are withheld and which either contains provisions falling within subsection (4)(a) below, or contains provisions falling within subsection (4)(a) below and provisions falling within subsection (4)(b) below.

(4) The provisions are that—

  (a) the employer is to pay sums withheld to a person ("the agent") who is approved by the Board at the time they are withheld, and the agent is to pay them to a charity or charities;

  (b) the employer is to pay sums withheld directly to a charity which (or charities each of which) is at the time the sums are withheld approved by the Board as an agent for the purpose of paying sums to other charities.

(5) The sums must be withheld in accordance with a request by the employee that they be paid to a charity or charities in accordance with a scheme approved (or of a kind approved) by the Board.

(6) The sums must constitute gifts by the employee to the charity or charities concerned, must not be paid by the employee under a covenant, and must fulfil any conditions set out in the terms of the scheme concerned.

(7) The sums must not in any year of assessment exceed [£900] in the case of any employee (however many offices or employments he holds or has held).

(8) The circumstances in which the Board may grant or withdraw approval of schemes (or kinds of schemes) or of agents shall be such as are prescribed by the Treasury by regulations; and the circumstances so prescribed (whether relating to the terms of schemes or the qualifications of agents or otherwise) shall be such as the Treasury think fit.

(9) The Treasury may by regulations make provision—

  (a) that a participating employer or agent shall comply with any notice which is served on him by the Board and which requires him within a prescribed period to make available for the Board's inspection documents of a prescribed kind or records of a prescribed kind;

  (b) that a participating employer or agent shall in prescribed circumstances furnish to the Board information of a prescribed kind;

  (c) for, and with respect to, appeals to the Special Commissioners against the Board's refusal to grant, or their withdrawal of, approval of any scheme (or any kind of scheme) or agent;

  (d) generally for giving effect to subsections (1) to (7) above.

In this subsection "prescribed" means prescribed by the regulations.

(10) For the purposes of subsection (9) above a person is a participating employer or agent if he is an employer or agent who participates, or has at any time participated, in a scheme under this section.

(11) In this section "charity" has the same meaning as in section 506. **[518]**

NOTE

Sub-s (7): sum in square brackets substituted, in relation to the year 1993-94 and subsequent years of assessment, by the Finance Act 1993, s 68. The previous sum (applicable to the years of assessment 1990–91 to 1992–93) was £600: Finance Act 1990, s 24.

CHAPTER V
ASSESSMENT, COLLECTION, RECOVERY AND APPEALS

[202A Assessment on receipts basis

(1) As regards any particular year of assessment—

    (a) income tax shall be charged under Cases I and II of Schedule E on the full amount of the emoluments received in the year in respect of the office or employment concerned;

    (b) income tax shall be charged under Case III of Schedule E on the full amount of the emoluments received in the United Kingdom in the year in respect of the office or employment concerned.

(2) Subsection (1) above applies—

    (a) whether the emoluments are for that year or for some other year of assessment;

    (b) whether or not the office or employment concerned is held at the time the emoluments are received or (as the case may be) received in the United Kingdom.

(3) Where subsection (1) above applies in the case of emoluments received, or (as the case may be) received in the United Kingdom, after the death of the person who held the office or employment concerned, the charge shall be a charge on his executors or administrators; and accordingly income tax—

    (a) shall be assessed and charged on the executors or administrators, and

    (b) shall be a debt due from and payable out of the deceased's estate.

(4) Section 202B shall have effect for the purposes of subsection (1)(a) above.]

[519]

NOTE
    Inserted with savings, with s 202B, by the Finance Act 1989, s 37, where the year of assessment in sub-s (1) above is 1989-90 or a subsequent year of assessment, even if the emoluments concerned are for a year of assessment before 1989-90; for savings see s 37(3) thereof.

[202B Receipts basis: meaning of receipt

(1) For the purposes of section 202A(1)(a) emoluments shall be treated as received at the time found in accordance with the following rules (taking the earlier or earliest time in a case where more than one rule applies)—

    (a) the time when payment is made of or on account of the emoluments;

    (b) the time when a person becomes entitled to payment of or on account of the emoluments;

    (c) in a case where the emoluments are from an office or employment with a company, the holder of the office or employment is a director of the company and sums on account of the emoluments are credited in the company's accounts or records, the time when sums on account of the emoluments are so credited;

    (d) in a case where the emoluments are from an office or employment with a company, the holder of the office or employment is a director of the company and the amount of the emoluments for a period is determined before the period ends, the time when the period ends;

    (e) in a case where the emoluments are from an office or employment with a company, the holder of the office or employment is a director of the company and the amount of the emoluments for a period is not known until the amount is determined after the period has ended, the time when the amount is determined.

(2) Subsection (1)(c), (d) or (e) above applies whether or not the office or employment concerned is that of director.

(3) Paragraph (c), (d) or (e) of subsection (1) above applies if the holder of the office or employment is a director of the company at any time in the year of assessment in which the time mentioned in the paragraph concerned falls.

(4) For the purposes of the rule in subsection (1)(c) above, any fetter on the right to draw the sums is to be disregarded.

(5) In subsection (1) above "director" means—

(a) in relation to a company whose affairs are managed by a board of directors or similar body, a member of that board or similar body,

(b) in relation to a company whose affairs are managed by a single director or similar person, that director or person, and

(c) in relation to a company whose affairs are managed by the members themselves, a member of the company.

(6) In subsection (1) above "director", in relation to a company, also includes any person in accordance with whose directions or instructions the company's directors (as defined in subsection (5) above) are accustomed to act; and for this purpose a person is not to be deemed to be a person in accordance with whose directions or instructions the company's directors are accustomed to act by reason only that the directors act on advice given by him in a professional capacity.

(7) Subsections (1) to (6) above shall have effect subject to subsections (8) to (11) below.

(8) In a case where section 141(1)(a), 142(1)(a), 143(1)(a) or 148(4) treats a person as receiving or being paid an emolument or emoluments at a particular time, for the purposes of section 202A(1)(a) the emolument or emoluments shall be treated as received at that time; and in such a case subsections (1) to (6) above shall not apply.

(9) In a case where section 145(1) treats a person as receiving emoluments, for the purposes of section 202A(1)(a) the emoluments shall be treated as received in the period referred to in section 145(1); and in such a case subsections (1) to (6) above shall not apply.

(10) In a case where section 154(1), 157(1), 158(1), 160(1), 160(2), 162(6) or 164(1) treats an amount as emoluments, for the purposes of section 202A(1)(a) the emoluments shall be treated as received in the year referred to in section 154(1) or the other provision concerned; and in such a case subsections (1) to (6) above shall not apply.

(11) In a case where—

(a) emoluments take the form of a benefit not consisting of money, and

(b) subsection (8), (9) or (10) above does not apply,

for the purposes of section 202A(1)(a) the emoluments shall be treated as received at the time when the benefit is provided; and in such a case subsections (1) to (6) above shall not apply.] **[520]**

NOTE

Inserted with savings, with s 202A, by the Finance Act 1989, s 37, where the year of assessment in s 202A(1) above is 1989-90 or a subsequent year of assessment, even if the emoluments concerned are for a year of assessment before 1989-90; for savings see s 37(3) thereof.

203 Pay as you earn

(1) On the making of any payment of, or on account of, any income assessable to income tax under Schedule E, income tax shall, subject to and in accordance with regulations made by the Board under this section, be deducted or repaid by the person making the payment, notwithstanding that when the payment is made no assessment has been made in respect of the income and notwithstanding that the income is in whole or in part income for some year of assessment other than the year during which the payment is made.

(2) The Board shall make regulations with respect to the assessment, charge, collection and recovery of income tax in respect of all income assessable thereto under Schedule E, and those regulations may, in particular, include provision—

(a) for requiring any person making any payment of, or on account of, any such income, when he makes the payment, to make a deduction or repayment of income tax calculated by reference to tax tables prepared by the Board, and for rendering persons who are required to make any such deduction or repayment accountable to, or, as the case may be, entitled to repayment from, the Board;

(b) for the production to and inspection by persons authorised by the Board of wages sheets and other documents and records for the purpose of satisfying themselves that income tax has been and is being deducted, repaid and accounted for in accordance with the regulations;

(c) for the collection and recovery, whether by deduction from any such income paid in any later year or otherwise, of income tax in respect of any such income which has not been deducted or otherwise recovered during the year;

[(d) for requiring the payment of interest on sums due to the Board which are not paid by the due date, for determining the date (being not less than 14 days after the end of the year of assessment in respect of which the sums are due) from which such interest is to be calculated and for enabling the repayment or remission of such interest;

(dd) for requiring the payment of interest on sums due from the Board and for determining the date (being not less than one year after the end of the year of assessment in respect of which the sums are due) from which such interest is to be calculated;]

(e) for the assessment and charge of income tax by the inspector in respect of income to which this section applies; and

(f) for appeals with respect to matters arising under the regulations which would otherwise not be the subject of an appeal;

and any such regulations shall have effect notwithstanding anything in the Income Tax Acts.

(3) The deductions of income tax required to be made by regulations under subsection (2)(a) above may be required to be made at the basic rate or other rates in such cases or classes of cases as may be provided for by the regulations.

[(3A) Regulations under this section may include provision for income tax in respect of any of a person's income for the year 1989–90 or any earlier year of assessment to be collected and recovered (whether by deduction from income assessable under Schedule E or otherwise) from the person's spouse if—

(a) the income was income to which section 279 applied, and

(b) the tax has not been deducted or otherwise recovered before 6th April 1990.]

(4) . . .

(5) Regulations under this section shall not affect any right of appeal to the General or Special Commissioners which a person would have apart from the regulations.

(6) The tax tables referred to in subsection (2)(a) above shall be constructed with a view to securing that so far as possible—

(a) the total income tax payable in respect of any income assessable under Schedule E for any year of assessment is deducted from such income paid during that year; and

(b) the income tax deductible or repayable on the occasion of any payment of, or on account of, any such income is such that the total net income tax deducted since the beginning of the year of assessment bears to the total income tax payable for the year the same proportion that the part of the year which ends with the date of the payment bears to the whole year.

(7) In subsection (6) above references to the total income tax payable for the year shall be construed as references to the total income tax estimated to be payable for the year in respect of the income in question, subject to a provisional deduction for allowances and reliefs, and subject also, if necessary, to an adjustment for amounts overpaid or remaining unpaid on account of income tax in respect of income assessable under Schedule E for any previous year.

(8) For the purpose of estimating the total income tax payable as mentioned in subsection (6)(a) above, it may be assumed in relation to any payment of, or on account of, income assessable under Schedule E that the income paid in the part of the year of assessment which ends with the making of the payment will bear to the income for the whole of that year the same proportion as that part of the year bears to the whole year.

[(9) Interest required to be paid by regulations under subsection (2) above shall be paid without any deduction of income tax and shall not be taken into account in computing any income, profits or losses for any tax purposes.]   [521]

NOTES

Sub-s (2): paras (d), (dd) substituted for original para (d) by the Finance Act 1988, s 128(1).
Sub-s (3A): inserted by the Finance Act 1988, s 35, Sch 3, Pt I, paras 1, 4.
Sub-s (4): repealed by the Finance Act 1989, ss 45(3), 187(1), Sch 17, Pt IV.
Sub-s (9): added by the Finance Act 1988, s 128(2).

[203A PAYE: meaning of payment

(1) For the purposes of section 203 and regulations under it a payment of, or on account of, any income assessable to income tax under Schedule E shall be treated as made at the time found in accordance with the following rules (taking the earlier or earliest time in a case where more than one rule applies)—

(a) the time when the payment is actually made;

(b) the time when a person becomes entitled to the payment;

(c) in a case where the income is income from an office or employment with a company, the holder of the office or employment is a director of the company and sums on account of the income are credited in the company's accounts or records, the time when sums on account of the income are so credited;

(d) in a case where the income is income from an office or employment with a company, the holder of the office or employment is a director of the company and the amount of the income for a period is determined before the period ends, the time when the period ends;

(e) in a case where the income is income from an office or employment with a company, the holder of the office or employment is a director of the company and the amount of the income for a period is not known until the amount is determined after the period has ended, the time when the amount is determined.

(2) Subsection (1)(c), (d) or (e) above applies whether or not the office or employment concerned is that of director.

(3) Paragraph (c), (d) or (e) of subsection (1) above applies if the holder of the office or employment is a director of the company at any time in the year of assessment in which the time mentioned in the paragraph concerned falls.

(4) For the purposes of the rule in subsection (1)(c) above, any fetter on the right to draw the sums is to be disregarded.

(5) Subsections (5) and (6) of section 202B shall apply for the purposes of subsection (1) above as they apply for the purposes of section 202B(1).]   **[522]**

NOTE
Inserted by the Finance Act 1989, s 45.

204 PAYE repayments

Without prejudice to the generality of section 203, regulations under that section may provide that no repayment of income tax shall be made under that section to any person if at any time—

   (a) he has claimed unemployment benefit in respect of a period including that time; or
   (b) he has claimed a payment of income support under the Social Security Act 1986 or the Social Security (Northern Ireland) Order 1986 in respect of a period including that time and his right to that income support is subject to the condition specified in section 20(3)(d)(i) of that Act or, in Northern Ireland, Article 21(3)(d)(i) of that Order (availability for employment); or
   (c) he is disqualified at the time from receiving unemployment benefit by virtue of section 19 of the Social Security Act 1975 or of section 19 of the Social Security (Northern Ireland) Act 1975 (loss of employment due to stoppage of work) or would be so disqualified if he otherwise satisfied the conditions for entitlement;

and such regulations may make different provision with respect to persons falling within paragraph (c) above from that made with respect to other persons.   **[523]**

PART XIV

PENSION SCHEMES, SOCIAL SECURITY BENEFITS, LIFE ANNUITIES ETC

CHAPTER I
RETIREMENT BENEFIT SCHEMES

Approval of schemes

590 Conditions for approval of retirement benefit schemes

(1) Subject to section 591, the Board shall not approve any retirement benefits scheme for the purposes of this Chapter unless the scheme satisfies all of the conditions set out in subsection (2) below.

(2) The conditions are—

(a) that the scheme is bona fide established for the sole purpose of providing relevant benefits in respect of service as an employee, being benefits payable to, or to the widow, [widower,] children or dependants or personal representatives of, the employee;

(b) that the scheme is recognised by the employer and employees to whom it relates, and that every employee who is, or has a right to be, a member of the scheme has been given written particulars of all essential features of the scheme which concern him;

(c) that there is a person resident in the United Kingdom who will be responsible for the discharge of all duties imposed on the administrator of the scheme under this Chapter;

(d) that the employer is a contributor to the scheme;

(e) that the scheme is established in connection with some trade or undertaking carried on in the United Kingdom by a person resident in the United Kingdom;

(f) that in no circumstances, whether during the subsistence of the scheme or later, can any amount be paid by way of repayment of an employee's contributions under the scheme.

(3) Subject to subsection (1) above, the Board shall approve a retirement benefits scheme for the purposes of this Chapter if the scheme satisfies all the conditions of this subsection, that is to say—

(a) that any benefit for an employee is a pension on retirement at a specified age not earlier than 60 [and not later than 75], which does not exceed one-sixtieth of the employee's final remuneration for each year of service up to a maximum of 40;

(b) that any benefit for any widow [or widower] of an employee is a pension payable on his death after retirement such that the amount payable to the widow [or widower] by way of pension does not exceed two-thirds of any pension or pensions payable to the employee;

(c) that no other benefits are payable under the scheme;

(d) that no pension is capable in whole or in part of surrender, commutation or assignment, except in so far as the scheme allows an employee on retirement to obtain, by commutation of his pension, a lump sum or sums not exceeding in all three-eightieths of his final remuneration . . . for each year of service up to a maximum of 40;

[(e) that, in the case of any employee who is a member of the scheme by virtue of two or more relevant associated employments, the amount payable by way of pension in respect of service in any one of them may not, when aggregated with any amount payable by way of pension in respect of service in the other or others, exceed the relevant amount;

(f) that, in the case of any employee who is a member of the scheme by virtue of two or more relevant associated employments, the amount payable by way of commuted pension in respect of service in any one of them may not, when aggregated with any amount payable by way of commuted pension in respect of service in the other or others, exceed the relevant amount;

(g) that, in the case of any employee in relation to whom the scheme is connected with another scheme which is (or other schemes each of which is) an approved scheme, the amount payable by way of pension under the scheme may not, when aggregated with any amount payable by way of pension under the other scheme or schemes, exceed the relevant amount;

(h) that, in the case of any employee in relation to whom the scheme is connected with another scheme which is (or other schemes each of which is) an approved scheme, the amount payable by way of commuted pension may not, when aggregated with any amount payable by way of commuted pension under the other scheme or schemes, exceed the relevant amount.]

(4) The conditions set out in subsections (2) and (3) above are in this Chapter referred to as "the prescribed conditions".

[(4A) In subsection (3)(c) above "benefits" does not include any benefits for whose payment the scheme makes provision in pursuance of any obligation imposed by legislation relating to social security.]

(5), (6) . . .

[(7) Subsections (8) to (10) below apply where the Board are considering whether a retirement benefits scheme satisfies or continues to satisfy the prescribed conditions.

(8) For the purpose of determining whether the scheme, so far as it relates to a particular class or description of employees, satisfies or continues to satisfy the prescribed conditions, that scheme shall be considered in conjunction with—

   (a) any other retirement benefits scheme (or schemes) which relates (or relate) to employees of that class or description and which is (or are) approved for the purposes of this Chapter,
   (b) any other retirement benefits scheme (or schemes) which relates (or relate) to employees of that class or description and which is (or are) at the same time before the Board in order for them to decide whether to give approval for the purposes of this Chapter,
   (c) any section 608 scheme or schemes relating to employees of that class or description, and
   (d) any relevant statutory scheme or schemes relating to employees of that class or description.

(9) If those conditions are satisfied in the case of both or all of those schemes taken together, they shall be taken to be satisfied in the case of the scheme mentioned in subsection (7) above (as well as the other or others).

(10) If those conditions are not satisfied in the case of both or all of those schemes taken together, they shall not be taken to be satisfied in the case of the scheme mentioned in subsection (7) above.

(11) The reference in subsection (8)(c) above to a section 608 scheme is a reference to a fund to which section 608 applies.]   **[524]**

NOTES

Sub-s (2): in para (a) word in square brackets inserted by the Finance Act 1988, s 35, Sch 3, Pt I, paras 1, 18, with effect on and after 6 April 1990.

Sub-s (3): in para (a) words in square brackets substituted, in relation to a scheme not approved by the Board before 25 July 1991, by the Finance Act 1991, s 34(1), (2), (4); in para (b) words in square brackets inserted by the Finance Act 1988, s 35, Sch 3, Pt I, paras 1, 18, with effect on and after 6 April 1990; words omitted from para (d) repealed with savings, and paras (e)-(h) substituted, in relation to a scheme not approved by the Board before 27 July 1989, by the Finance Act 1989, ss 75, 187(1), Sch 6, Pt I, paras 1, 3(1)-(3), 18(2), Sch 17, Pt IV; for savings see Sch 6, para 18(2) thereof.

Sub-s (4A): inserted, in relation to a scheme not approved by the Board before 25 July 1991, by the Finance Act 1991, s 34(1), (3), (4).

Sub-ss (5), (6): repealed, with retrospective effect, by the Finance Act 1991, ss 36(2), (3), 123, Sch 19, Pt V.

Sub-ss (7)-(11): substituted for original sub-s (7), in relation to determinations made on or after 27 July 1989, by the Finance Act 1989, s 75, Sch 6, Pt I, paras 1, 3(4), 18(3).

[590A   Section 590: supplementary provisions

(1) For the purposes of section 590(3)(e) and (f) two or more employments are relevant associated employments if they are employments in the case of which—

    (a) there is a period during which the employee has held both or all of them,

    (b) the period counts under the scheme in the case of both or all of them as a period in respect of which benefits are payable, and

    (c) the period is one during which both or all of the employers in question are associated.

(2) For the purposes of section 590(3)(g) and (h) the scheme is connected with another scheme in relation to an employee if—

    (a) there is a period during which he has been the employee of two persons who are associated employers,

    (b) the period counts under both schemes as a period in respect of which benefits are payable, and

    (c) the period counts under one scheme by virtue of service with one employer and under the other scheme by virtue of service with the other employer.

(3) For the purposes of subsections (1) and (2) above, employers are associated if (directly or indirectly) one is controlled by the other or if both are controlled by a third person.

(4) In subsection (3) above the reference to control, in relation to a body corporate, shall be construed—

    (a) where the body corporate is a close company, in accordance with section 416, and

    (b) where it is not, in accordance with section 840.]   [525]

NOTE

    Inserted, with ss 590B, 590C, in relation to a scheme not approved by the Board before 27 July 1989, by the Finance Act 1989, s 75, Sch 6, Pt I, paras 1, 4, 18(2).

[590B   Section 590: further supplementary provisions

(1) For the purposes of section 590(3)(e) the relevant amount, in relation to an employee, shall be found by applying the following formula—

$$\frac{A \times C}{60}$$

(2) For the purposes of section 590(3)(f) the relevant amount, in relation to an employee, shall be found by applying the following formula—

$$\frac{3 \times A \times C}{80}$$

(3) For the purposes of section 590(3)(g) the relevant amount, in relation to an employee, shall be found by applying the following formula—

$$\frac{B \times C}{60}$$

(4) For the purposes of section 590(3)(h) the relevant amount, in relation to an employee, shall be found by applying the following formula—

$$\frac{3 \times B \times C}{80}$$

(5) For the purposes of this section A is the aggregate number of years service (expressing parts of a year as a fraction), subject to a maximum of 40, which, in the

case of the employee, count for the purposes of the scheme at the time the benefits in respect of service in the employment become payable.

(6) But where the same year (or part of a year) counts for the purposes of the scheme by virtue of more than one of the relevant associated employments it shall be counted only once in calculating the aggregate number of years service for the purposes of subsection (5) above.

(7) For the purposes of this section B is the aggregate number of years service (expressing parts of a year as a fraction), subject to a maximum of 40, which, in the case of the employee, count for the purposes of any of the following—

(a) the scheme, and
(b) the other scheme or schemes with which the scheme is connected in relation to him,

at the time the benefits become payable.

(8) But where the same year (or part of a year) counts for the purposes of more than one scheme it shall be counted only once in calculating the aggregate number of years service for the purpose of subsection (7) above.

(9) For the purposes of this section C is the permitted maximum in relation to the year of assessment in which the benefits in question become payable, that is, the figure found for that year by virtue of subsections (10) and (11) below.

(10) For the years 1988–89 and 1989–90 the figure is £60,000.

(11) For any subsequent year of assessment the figure is the figure found for that year, for the purposes of section 590C, by virtue of section 590C(4) and (5).] **[526]**

NOTE

Inserted, in relation to a scheme not approved by the Board before 27 July 1989, by the Finance Act 1989, s 75, Sch 6, paras 4, 18(2); sub-s(11) will be amended by the Finance Act 1993, s 107(6) for 1994–95 and subsequent years of assessment.

[590C Earnings cap

(1) In arriving at an employee's final remuneration for the purposes of section 590(3)(a) or (d), any excess of what would be his final remuneration (apart from this section) over the permitted maximum for the year of assessment in which his participation in the scheme ceases shall be disregarded.

(2) In subsection (1) above "the permitted maximum", in relation to a year of assessment, means the figure found for that year by virtue of subsections (3) and (4) below.

(3) For the years 1988–89 and 1989–90 the figure is £60,000.

(4) For any subsequent year of assessment the figure is also £60,000, subject to subsection (5) below.

(5) If the retail prices index for the month of December preceding a year of assessment falling within subsection (4) above is higher than it was for the previous December, the figure for that year shall be an amount arrived at by—

(a) increasing the figure for the previous year of assessment by the same percentage as the percentage increase in the retail prices index, and
(b) if the result is not a multiple of £600, rounding it up to the nearest amount which is such a multiple.

(6) The Treasury shall in the year of assessment 1989–90, and in each subsequent year of assessment, make an order specifying the figure which is by virtue of this section the figure for the following year of assessment.] **[527]**

NOTE
Inserted, in relation to a scheme not approved by the Board before 27 July 1989, by the Finance Act 1989, s 75, Sch 6, paras 4, 18(2).

Orders under this section: SI 1990/679 (specifying £64,800 for the assessment year 1990–1); SI 1991/734 (specifying £71,400 for the assessment year 1991–2); SI 1992/624 (specifying £75,000 for the assessment year 1992–93); and SI 1993/757 (specifying £77,400 for the assessment year 1993–94). However this increase is overridden by the Finance Act 1993, s 106, which continues the cap at £75,000 for 1993–94.

Further amendments to this section will be made by the Finance Act 1993, s 107(4), (5) for 1994–95 and subsequent years of assessment.

Tax reliefs

592 Exempt approved schemes

(1) This section has effect as respects—

   (a) any approved scheme which is shown to the satisfaction of the Board to be established under irrevocable trusts; or

   (b) any other approved scheme as respects which the Board, having regard to any special circumstances, direct that this section shall apply;

and any scheme which is for the time being within paragraph (a) or (b) above is in this Chapter referred to as an "exempt approved scheme".

(2)–(6A) . . .

(7) Any contribution paid under the scheme by an employee shall, in assessing tax under Schedule E, be allowed to be deducted as an expense incurred in the year of assessment in which the contribution is paid.

(8) [Subject to subsection (8A) below,] the amount allowed to be deducted by virtue of subsection (7) above in respect of contributions paid by an employee in a year of assessment (whether under a single scheme or under two or more schemes) shall not exceed 15 per cent, or such higher percentage as the Board may in a particular case prescribe, of his remuneration for that year.

[(8A) Where an employee's remuneration for a year of assessment includes remuneration in respect of more than one employment, the amount allowed to be deducted by virtue of subsection (7) above in respect of contributions paid by the employee in that year by virtue of any employment (whether under a single scheme or under two or more schemes) shall not exceed 15 per cent, or such higher percentage as the Board may in a particular case prescribe, of his remuneration for the year in respect of that employment.

(8B) In arriving at an employee's remuneration for a year of assessment for the purposes of subsection (8) or (8A) above, any excess of what would be his remuneration (apart from this subsection) over the permitted maximum for that year shall be disregarded.

(8C) In subsection (8B) above "permitted maximum", in relation to a year of assessment, means the figure found for that year by virtue of subsections (8D) and (8E) below.

(8D) For the year 1989–90 the figure is £60,000.

(8E) For any subsequent year of assessment the figure is the figure found for that year, for the purposes of section 590C, by virtue of section 590C(4) and (5).]

(9)–(12) . . .

NOTES

Sub-ss (2)–(6A), (9)–(12) (taxation of employer's contributions and pension fund income) omitted.

Sub-s (8): words in square brackets inserted, in relation to the year 1989-90 and subsequent years of assessment, by the Finance Act 1989, s 75, Sch 6, Pt I, paras 1, 5(1), (2), 18(4).

Sub-s (8A): inserted, in relation to the year 1989-90 and subsequent years of assessment by the Finance Act 1989, s 75, Sch 6, Pt I, paras 5(1), (3), 18(4).

Sub-ss (8B)-(8E): inserted, in relation to the year 1989-90 and subsequent years of assessment, by the Finance Act 1989, s 75, Sch 6, Pt I, paras 5(1), (4), 18(4), except as regards a person's remuneration in respect of an office or employment in such circumstances as the Board may by regulations provide; sub-s(8E) will be amended by the Finance Act 1993, s 107(6) for 1994–95 and subsequent years of assessment.

SCHEDULES

SCHEDULE 6

Section 157

TAXATION OF DIRECTORS AND OTHERS IN RESPECT OF CARS

[PART I
TABLES OF FLAT RATE CASH EQUIVALENTS

[TABLE A
Cars with an original market value up to £19,250 and having a cylinder capacity

Cylinder capacity of car in cubic centimetres	Age of car at end of relevant year of assessment	
	Under 4 years	4 years or more
1,400 or less	£2,310	£1,580
More than 1,400, but not more than 2,000	£2,990	£2,030
More than 2,000	£4,800	£3,220

TABLE B
Cars with an original market value up to £19,250 and not having a cylinder capacity

Original market value of car	Age of car at end of relevant year of assessment	
	Under 4 years	4 years or more
Less than £6,000	£2,310	£1,580
£6,000 or more, but less than £8,500	£2,990	£2,030
£8,500 or more, but not more than £19,250	£4,800	£3,220

TABLE C
Cars with an original market value of more than £19,250

Original market value of car	Age of car at end of relevant year of assessment	
	Under 4 years	4 years or more
More than £19,250, but not more than £29,000	£6,210	£4,180
More than £29,000	£10,040	£6,660]]

[529–530]

NOTES

This Part was substituted by the Finance Act 1993, s 70, for the year 1993–94 and subsequent years of assessment. For the corresponding figures for years of assessment 1991–92 and 1992–93 respectively, see Finance Act 1991, s 29 and SI 1992/731, art 2.

See further the note at the end of Pt II of this Schedule.

PART II
SUPPLEMENTARY PROVISIONS

Application of Tables A and B

1 (1) In the case of cars with an original market value of £19,250 or less, Table A applies to those having an internal combustion engine with one or more reciprocating pistons, and Table B applies to other cars.

(2) A car's cylinder capacity is the cylinder capacity of its engine calculated as for the purposes of the Vehicles (Excise) Act 1971 or the Vehicles (Excise) Act (Northern Ireland) 1972.

Reduction for periods when car not available for use

2 (1) If, for any part of the relevant year, the car was unavailable, the cash equivalent is to be reduced by an amount which bears to the full amount of the equivalent (ascertained under Part I of this Schedule) the same proportion as the number of days in the year on which the car was unavailable bears to 365.

(2) The car is to be treated as being unavailable on any day if—

    (a)   it was not made available to the employee until after that day, or it had ceased before that day to be available to him; or

    (b)   it was incapable of being used at all throughout a period of not less than 30 consecutive days of which that day was one.

Car used preponderantly for business purposes

3 (1) The cash equivalent derived from Table A, B or C is to be reduced (or, where paragraph 2 above applies, further reduced) by half if it is shown to the inspector's satisfaction that the employee was required by the nature of his employment to make and made use of the car preponderantly for business travel, which means that such travel must have amounted to at least 18,000 miles in the relevant year.

(2) In relation to a car which for part of the year was unavailable in the sense of paragraph 2 above, the figure of 18,000 is proportionately reduced.

Reduction for employee paying for use of car

4 If in the relevant year the employee was required, as a condition of the car being available for his private use, to pay any amount of money (whether by way of deduction from his emoluments or otherwise) for that use, the cash equivalent—

    (a)   is to be reduced (or, if already reduced under the foregoing paragraphs, further reduced) by the amount so paid by the employee in or in respect of the year; or

    (b)   if that amount exceeds the equivalent shown in the applicable Table in Part I of this Schedule, is nil.

Cars with insubstantial business use and additional cars

5 (1) The cash equivalent derived from Table A, B or C is to be increased by half if in the relevant year—

    (a)   the car was not used for the employee's business travel; or

    (b)   its use for such travel did not amount to more than 2,500 miles.

(2) In relation to a car which for part of the year was unavailable in the sense of paragraph 2 above, the figure of 2,500 is proportionately reduced.

(3) Without prejudice to sub-paragraph (1) above, if in any year a person is taxable under section 157 in respect of two or more cars which are made available concurrently, there shall be increased by half the cash equivalent derived from Table A, B or C in respect of each of

those cars other than the one which in the period for which they are concurrently available is used to the greatest extent for the employee's business travel.

(4) In paragraphs 2 to 4 above references to the cash equivalent which is to be reduced shall be construed as references to the cash equivalent after any increase under this paragraph.

[531]

NOTE

This Schedule will be substituted in its entirety by the Finance Act 1993, s 72, Sch 3, para 5, for 1994–95 and subsequent years of assessment.

SCHEDULE 11

Section 188

RELIEF AS RESPECTS TAX ON PAYMENTS ON RETIREMENT OR REMOVAL FROM OFFICE OR EMPLOYMENT

PART I

GENERAL PROVISIONS

Preliminary

1 Relief shall be allowed in accordance with the following provisions of this Schedule in respect of tax chargeable by virtue of section 148, where a claim is made under section 188(6).

2 (1) A person shall not be entitled to relief under this Schedule in so far as such relief, together with any personal relief allowed to him, would reduce the amount of income on which he is chargeable below the amount of income tax on which he is entitled to charge against any other person, or to deduct, retain or satisfy out of any payment which he is liable to make to any other person.

(2) In sub-paragraph (1) above "personal relief" means relief under Chapter I of Part VII.

Relief by reduction of sums chargeable

3 In computing the charge to tax in respect of a payment chargeable to tax under section 148, being a payment made in respect of an office or employment in which the service of the holder includes foreign service, there shall be deducted from the payment a sum which bears to the amount which would be chargeable to tax apart from this paragraph the same proportion as the length of the foreign service bears to the length of the service before the relevant date.

4–7 ...

Supplemental

8 Any reference in this Schedule to the emoluments of an office or employment is a reference to those emoluments exclusive of any payment chargeable to tax under section 148; and in calculating for any purpose of this Schedule the amount of such emoluments—

(a) there shall be included any balancing charge to which the holder of the office or employment is liable under [Part II of the 1990 Act], and

(b) there shall be deducted any allowances under [Part II of the 1990 Act], and any allowances for expenses under section 198 or 201, to which he is entitled,

and any such charges or allowances for a chargeable period shall, for the purpose of ascertaining the amount of the emoluments for any year of service, be treated as accruing from day to day, and shall be apportioned in respect of time accordingly.

9 In this Schedule "the relevant date" means, in relation to a payment not being a payment in commutation of annual or other periodical payments, the date of the termination or change in respect of which it is made and, in relation to a payment in commutation of annual or other periodical payments, the date of the termination or change in respect of which those payments would have been made.

10 In this Schedule, "foreign service", in relation to an office or employment, means—
(a) service before the year 1974–75 such that tax was not chargeable in respect of the emoluments of the office or employment—
  (i) in the case of the year 1956–57 or any subsequent chargeable period, under Case I of Schedule E;
  (ii) in the case of any preceding year of assessment, under Schedule E; or
(b) service after the year 1973–74 such that the emoluments from the office or employment were not chargeable under Case I of Schedule E (or would not have been so chargeable, had there been any) or that a deduction equal to their whole amount was or would have been allowable under paragraph 1 of Schedule 2 to the Finance Act 1974, paragraph 1 of Schedule 7 to the Finance Act 1977 or section 193(1) in charging them.

11 Any reference in this Schedule to the amount of tax to which a person is or would be chargeable is a reference to the amount of tax to which he is or would be chargeable either by assessment or by deduction. **[532–533]**

NOTES
Paras 4-7: repealed by the Finance Act 1988, ss 74(2), 148, Sch 14, Pt IV, in relation to any payment treated by s 148(4) of this Act as income received on or after 6 April 1988, unless a notice is given in relation to it in accordance with para 12 of this Schedule.
Para 8: words in square brackets substituted, in relation to chargeable periods ending after 5 April 1990, by the Capital Allowances Act 1990, s 164, Sch 1, para 8(1), (39); for savings see s 164(3) thereof.

(*Pt II (payments in pursuance of pre-10 March 1981 obligations) omitted.*)

LOCAL GOVERNMENT ACT 1988
(1988 c 9)

ARRANGEMENT OF SECTIONS

PART II
PUBLIC SUPPLY OR WORKS CONTRACTS

An Act to secure that local and other public authorities undertake certain activities only if they can do so competitively; to regulate certain functions of local and other public authorities in connection with public supply or works contracts; to authorise and regulate the provision of financial assistance by local authorities for certain housing purposes; to prohibit the promotion of homosexuality by local authorities; to make provision about local authorities' publicity, local government administration, the powers of auditors, land held by public bodies, direct labour organisations, arrangements under the Employment and Training Act 1973, the Commission for Local Authority Accounts in Scotland, the auditing of accounts of local authorities in Scotland, and dog registration, dog licences and stray dogs; and for connected purposes

[24 March 1988]

GENERAL NOTE
Only the provisions of Part II of this Act, which places restrictions on "contractual compliance", together with the associated Sch 2, are reproduced. This Act applies to England and Wales and to Scotland, but not to Northern Ireland: s 42(2). All provisions printed here come into force on 6 April 1988: s 23.

1–16 (*(Pt 1) outside the scope of this work.*)

PART II
PUBLIC SUPPLY OR WORKS CONTRACTS

17 Local and other public authority contracts: exclusion of non-commercial considerations

(1) It is the duty of every public authority to which this section applies, in exercising, in relation to its public supply or works contracts, any proposed or any subsisting such contract, as the case may be, any function regulated by this section to exercise that function without reference to matters which are non-commercial matters for the purposes of this section.

(2) The public authorities to which this section applies are those specified in Schedule 2 to this Act.

(3) The contracts which are public supply or works contracts for the purposes of this section are contracts for the supply of goods or materials, for the supply of services or for the execution of works; but this section does not apply in relation to contracts entered into before the commencement of this section.

(4) The functions regulated by this section are—

(a) the inclusion of persons in or the exclusion of persons from—

    (i) any list of persons approved for the purposes of public supply or works contracts with the authority, or

    (ii) any list of persons from whom tenders for such contracts may be invited;

(b) in relation to a proposed public supply or works contract with the authority—

    (i) the inclusion of persons in or the exclusion of persons from the group of persons from whom tenders are invited,

    (ii) the accepting or not accepting the submission of tenders for the contract,

    (iii) the selecting the person with whom to enter into the contract, or

    (iv) the giving or withholding approval for, or the selecting or nominating, persons to be sub-contractors for the purposes of the contract; and

(c) in relation to a subsisting public supply or works contract with the authority—

    (i) the giving or withholding approval for, or the selecting or nominating, persons to be sub-contractors for the purposes of the contract, or

    (ii) the termination of the contract.

(5) The following matters are non-commercial matters as regards the public supply or works contracts of a public authority, any proposed or any subsisting such contract, as the case may be, that is to say—

(a) the terms and conditions of employment by contractors of their workers or the composition of, the arrangements for the promotion, transfer or training of or the other opportunities afforded to, their workforces;

(b) whether the terms on which contractors contract with their sub-contractors

constitute, in the case of contracts with individuals, contracts for the provision by them as self-employed persons of their services only;
(c) any involvement of the business activities or interests of contractors with irrelevant fields of Government policy;
(d) the conduct of contractors or workers in industrial disputes between them or any involvement of the business activities of contractors in industrial disputes between other persons;
(e) the country or territory of origin of supplies to, or the location in any country or territory of the business activities or interests of, contractors;
(f) any political, industrial or sectarian affiliations or interests of contractors or their directors, partners or employees;
(g) financial support or lack of financial support by contractors for any institution to or from which the authority gives or withholds support;
(h) use or non-use by contractors of technical or professional services provided by the authority under the Building Act 1984 or the Building (Scotland) Act 1959.

(6) The matters specified in subsection (5) above include matters which have occurred in the past as well as matters which subsist when the function in question falls to be exercised.

(7) Where any matter referable to a contractor would, as a matter specified in subsection (5) above, be a non-commercial matter in relation to him, the corresponding matter referable to—
(a) a supplier or customer of the contractor;
(b) a sub-contractor of the contractor or his supplier or customer;
(c) an associated body of the contractor or his supplier or customer; or
(d) a sub-contractor of an associated body of the contractor or his supplier or customer;

is also, in relation to the contractor, a non-commercial matter for the purposes of this section.

(8) In this section—
"approved list" means such a list as is mentioned in subsection (4)(a) above;
"associated body", in relation to a contractor, means any company which (within the meaning of the Companies Act 1985) is the contractor's holding company or subsidiary or is a subsidiary of the contractor's holding company;
"business" includes any trade or profession;
"business activities" and "business interests", in relation to a contractor or other person, mean respectively any activities comprised in, or any investments employed in or attributable to, the carrying on of his business and "activity" includes receiving the benefit of the performance of any contract;
"contractor", except in relation to a subsisting contract, means a "potential contractor", that is to say—
(a) in relation to functions as respects an approved list, any person who is or seeks to be included in the list; and
(b) in relation to functions as respects a proposed public supply or works contract, any person who is or seeks to be included in the group of persons from whom tenders are invited or who seeks to submit a tender for or enter into the proposed contract, as the case may be;
"exclusion" includes removal;
"Government policy" falls within "irrelevant fields" for the purposes of this section if it concerns matters of defence or foreign or Commonwealth policy and "involve", as regards business activities and any such field of

policy, includes the supply of goods or materials or services to, or the execution of works for, any authority or person having functions or carrying on business in that field and, as regards business interests and any such field of policy, includes investment in any authority or person whose business activities are so involved;

"industrial dispute" has, as regards a dispute in Great Britain, the same meaning as trade dispute in [Part V of the Trade Union and Labour Relations (Consolidation) Act 1992] and "involve", as regards business activities and an industrial dispute, includes the supply of goods, materials or services to or by, or the execution of works for or by, any party to the dispute, any other person affected by the dispute, or any authority concerned with the enforcement of law and order in relation to the dispute;

"political, industrial or sectarian affiliations or interests" means actual or potential membership of, or actual or potential support for, respectively, any political party, any employers' association or trade union or any society, fraternity or other association;

"suppliers or customers" and "sub-contractors" includes prospective suppliers or customers and sub-contractors; and "supplier", in relation to a contractor, includes any person who, in the course of business, supplies him with services or facilities of any description for the purposes of his business;

and "employers' association" and "trade union" have, as regards bodies constituted under the law of England and Wales or Scotland, the same meaning as in the [Trade Union and Labour Relations (Consolidation) Act 1992].

(9) This section is subject to section 18 below.   **[534]**

NOTE

Sub-s (8): words in square brackets substituted by the Trade Union and Labour Relations (Consolidation) Act 1992, s 300(2), Sch 2, para 38.

18 Race relations matters

(1) Except to the extent permitted by subsection (2) below, section 71 of the Race Relations Act 1976 (local authorities to have regard to need to eliminate unlawful racial discrimination and promote equality of opportunity, and good relations, between persons of different racial groups) shall not require or authorise a local authority to exercise any function regulated by section 17 above by reference to a non-commercial matter.

(2) Subject to subsection (3) below, nothing in section 17 above shall preclude a local authority from—

(a) asking approved questions seeking information or undertakings relating to workforce matters and considering the responses to them, or

(b) including in a draft contract or draft tender for a contract terms or provisions relating to workforce matters and considering the responses to them,

if, as the case may be, consideration of the information, the giving of the undertaking or the inclusion of the term is reasonably necessary to secure compliance with the said section 71.

(3) Subsection (2) above does not apply to the function of terminating a subsisting contract and, in relation to functions as respects approved lists or proposed contracts, does not authorise questions in other than written form.

(4) Where it is permissible under subsection (2) above to ask a question it is also permissible to make, if it is in writing, an approved request for evidence in support of an answer to the question.

(5) The Secretary of State may specify—

(a) questions which are to be approved questions for the purposes of this section; and

(b) descriptions of evidence which, in relation to approved questions, are to be approved descriptions of evidence for those purposes;

and the powers conferred by this subsection shall be exercised in writing.

(6) Any specification under subsection (5) above may include such consequential or transitional provisions as appear to the Secretary of State to be necessary or expedient.

(7) In this section—

"approved question" means a question for the time being specified by the Secretary of State under subsection (5) above;

"approved request for evidence" means a request for evidence of a description for the time being specified by the Secretary of State under that subsection in relation to an approved question;

"workforce matters" means matters falling within paragraph (a), but no other paragraph, of subsection (5) of section 17 above;

and any expression used in this section and section 17 above has the same meaning in this section as in that section. **[535]**

NOTE

The Secretary of State has specified the following "approved questions and descriptions of evidence under s 18(5)" (issued as Annex B to Department of the Environment Circular 8/1988, 6 April 1988):

"LOCAL GOVERNMENT ACT 1988—SECTION 18(5)

Specification of questions and descriptions of evidence

The Secretary of State for the Environment, as respects England, and the Secretary of State for Wales, as respects Wales, in exercise of the powers conferred on them by s 18(5) of the Local Government Act 1988 hereby specify the following questions and description of evidence—

1. *Is it your policy as an employer to comply with your statutory obligations under the Race Relations Act 1976 and, accordingly, your practice not to treat one person less favourably than others because of their colour, race, nationality or ethnic origin in relation to decisions to recruit, train or promote employees?*

2. *In the last three years, has any finding of unlawful racial discrimination been made against your organisation by any court or industrial tribunal?*

3. *In the last three years, has your organisation been the subject of formal investigation by the Commission for Racial Equality on grounds of alleged unlawful discrimination?*

If the answer to question 2 is in the affirmative or, in relation to question 3, the Commission made a finding adverse to your organisation,

4. *What steps did you take in consequence of that finding?*

5. *Is your policy on race relations set out—*

    (a) in instructions to those concerned with recruitment, training and promotion;

    (b) in documents available to employees, recognised trade unions or other representative groups of employees;

    (c) in recruitment advertisements or other literature?

6. *Do you observe as far as possible the Commission for Racial Equality's Code of Practice for Employment, as approved by Parliament in 1983, which gives practical guidance to employers and others on the elimination of racial discrimination and the promotion of equality of opportunity in employment, including the steps that can be taken to encourage members of the ethnic minorities to apply for jobs or take up training opportunities?*

Description of evidence

In relation to question 5: examples of the instructions, documents, recruitment advertisements or other literature.".

19 Provisions supplementary to or consequential on section 17

(1) The Secretary of State may, by order made by statutory instrument, specify as a non-commercial matter for the purposes of section 17 above, any other matter which appears to him to be irrelevant to the commercial purposes of public supply or works contracts of any description.

(2) The power conferred by subsection (1) above includes power to apply section 17(6) and (7) above to any matter specified in the order and to amend any definition in section 17(8) above of an expression used in any paragraph of section 17(5) above without making any other provision.

(3) An order under subsection (1) above may include such consequential and transitional provisions as appear to the Secretary of State to be necessary or expedient.

(4) No order under subsection (1) above shall be made unless a draft of it has been laid before and approved by a resolution of each House of Parliament.

(5) Section 17 above applies to a public authority where, in exercising functions regulated by that section, the authority is, as well as where it is not, acting on behalf of a Minister of the Crown.

(6) Where a public authority makes arrangements under section 101 of the Local Government Act 1972 or in relation to Scotland section 56 of the Local Government (Scotland) Act 1973 for the exercise by another public authority of any function regulated by section 17 above, section 17 shall apply to that other public authority in exercising that function as if it were exercising the function in relation to its own public supply or works contracts, any proposed or any subsisting such contract, as the case may be.

(7) The duty imposed by section 17(1) above does not create a criminal offence but—

    (a) in proceedings for judicial review, the persons who have a sufficient interest or, in Scotland, title and interest in the matter shall include any potential contractor or, in the case of a contract which has been made, former potential contractor (or, in any case, any body representing contractors), as such; and

    (b) a failure to comply with it is actionable by any person who, in consequence, suffers loss or damage.

(8) In any action under section 17(1) above by a person who has submitted a tender for a proposed public supply or works contract arising out of the exercise of functions in relation to the proposed contract the damages shall be limited to damages in respect of expenditure reasonably incurred by him for the purpose of submitting the tender.

(9) Nothing in section 17 above or subsection (1) above implies that the exercise of any function regulated by that section may not be impugned, in proceedings for judicial review, on the ground that it was exercised by reference to other matters than those which are non-commercial matters for the purposes of that section.

(10) If a public authority, in relation to public supply or works contracts or any proposed such contract, as the case may be—

    (a) asks a question of any potential contractor relating to any non-commercial matter other than a question consideration of the answer to which is permitted by section 18 above, or

    (b) submits to any potential contractor a draft contract or draft tender for a contract which includes terms or provisions relating to any non-commercial matter other than a term or provision the inclusion of which in the contract is permitted by section 18 above,

the authority shall be treated, for the purposes of section 17 above, as exercising functions regulated by that section by reference to non-commercial matters.

(11) In consequence of section 17 above, the following provisions (which require local authorities to secure the insertion of fair wages clauses in all housing contracts), namely—

    (a)   section 52(a) of the Housing Act 1985, and

    (b)   section 337 of the Housing (Scotland) Act 1987,

shall cease to have effect.

(12) Expressions used in this section and section 17 above have the same meaning in this section as in that section.   **[536]**

20 Duty of public authorities to give reasons for certain decisions within section 17

(1) Where a public authority exercises a function regulated by section 17 above by making, in relation to any person, a decision to which this section applies, it shall be the duty of the authority forthwith to notify that person of the decision and, if that person so requests in writing within the period of 15 days beginning with the date of the notice, to furnish him with a written statement of the reasons for the decision.

(2) This section applies to the following decisions in relation to any person, namely—

    (a)   in relation to an approved list, a decision to exclude him from the list,

    (b)   in relation to a proposed public supply or works contract—

        (i) where he has asked to be invited to tender for the contract, a decision not to invite him to tender,

        (ii) a decision not to accept the submission by him of a tender for the contract,

        (iii) where he has submitted a tender for the contract, a decision not to enter into the contract with him, or

        (iv) a decision to withhold approval for, or to select or nominate, persons to be sub-contractors for the purposes of the contract, or

    (c)   in relation to a subsisting public supply or works contract with him—

        (i) a decision to withhold approval for, or to select or nominate, persons to be sub-contractors for the purposes of the contract, or

        (ii) a decision to terminate the contract.

(3) A statement of reasons under subsection (1) above shall be sent to the person requesting it within the period of 15 days beginning with the date of the request.

(4) The Secretary of State may by order amend subsection (1) or (3) above so as to substitute for the period specified in that subsection such other period as he thinks fit and such an order may make different amendments of subsections (1) and (3).

(5) The power to make an order under subsection (4) above is exercisable by statutory instrument which shall be subject to annulment in pursuance of a resolution of either House of Parliament.

(6) Expressions used in this section and section 17 above have the same meaning in this section as in that section.   **[537]**

21 Transitional duty of public authorities as regards existing lists

(1) Subject to subsection (3) below, it is the duty of a public authority which, at the commencement of this section, maintains an approved list—

    (a) to consider whether persons have been included in or excluded from the list by reference to non-commercial matters, and

    (b) if it appears to the authority that that is the case to compile the list afresh in accordance with subsections (4) to (6) below.

(2) Persons shall be treated by a public authority as having been excluded from a list by reference to non-commercial matters if, in relation to the list, the authority has—

    (a) circulated to potential contractors questionnaires including questions relating to non-commercial matters, or

    (b) notified potential contractors of its intention to have regard to non-commercial matters, or

    (c) issued statements of policy framed by reference to non-commercial matters.

(3) Inclusion or exclusion by a local authority from its list by reference to a non-commercial matter does not give rise to the duty to compile the list afresh under subsection (1) above if that matter falls within paragraph (a) (but no other paragraph) of section 17(5) above and the local authority's action was reasonably necessary to secure compliance with section 71 of the Race Relations Act 1976.

(4) The duty of an authority to compile afresh an approved list shall be discharged as follows—

    (a) the authority shall publish notice of its intention to compile the list afresh and (by the notice) invite persons to apply within a specified period to be included in the list; and

    (b) at the end of that period the authority shall proceed to compile the list afresh from among the applicants in accordance with the duty imposed by section 17 above.

(5) Publication by an authority of the notice required by subsection (4) above shall be effected by causing the notice to be published—

    (a) in at least one newspaper circulating in the authority's area or, if the extent of the authority's functions so require, in at least one national newspaper; and

    (b) in at least one newspaper or journal circulating among such persons as undertake contracts of the description to which the list relates.

(6) The period specified in the notice under subsection (4) above as the period within which applications are to be made shall not be shorter than the period of 28 days beginning with the date of publication of the notice.

(7) The duty imposed by this section shall be discharged by a public authority as soon as is reasonably practicable after the commencement of this section and in any event within the period of three months.

(8) This section does not create a criminal offence but paragraph (a) of section 19(7) above applies for the purposes of the duty imposed by this section as it applies for the purposes of the duty imposed by section 17(1) above.

(9) Expressions used in this section and section 17 above have the same meaning in this section as in that section. **[538]**

22 Exclusion of charges for inclusion in approved list

(1) A public authority which maintains an approved list shall not require a person to pay any sum as a condition of his inclusion or continued inclusion in the list or of his being considered for such inclusion.

(2) Subsection (1) above does not create an offence but a contravention of it is actionable by the person seeking to be included or retained in the list.

(3) Expressions used in this section and section 17 above have the same meaning in this section as in that section. **[539]**

23 Commencement

Sections 17 to 22 above shall come into force at the end of the period of 14 days beginning with the day on which this Act is passed. **[540]**

24–42 (*Outside the scope of this work.*)

SCHEDULES

(*Sch 1 outside the scope of this work.*)

SCHEDULE 2

Section 17(2)

PUBLIC SUPPLY OR WORKS CONTRACTS: THE PUBLIC AUTHORITIES

Public authorities

A local authority.

An urban development corporation established by an order under section 135 of the Local Government, Planning and Land Act 1980.

A development corporation established for the purposes of a new town.

The Commission for the New Towns.

A police authority constituted under section 2 of the Police Act 1964 or as mentioned in section 3(1) of that Act, or established by section 24 or 25 of the Local Government Act 1985.

A fire authority constituted by a combination scheme and a metropolitan county fire and civil defence authority.

The London Fire and Civil Defence Authority.

A metropolitan county passenger transport authority.

An authority established by an order under section 10(1) of the Local Government Act 1985 (waste disposal).

A joint education committee established by an order under paragraph 3 of Part II of Schedule 1 to the Education Act 1944 . . .

A water development board in Scotland.

. . .

The Broads Authority.

The Lake District Special Planning Board.

The Peak Park Joint Planning Board.

A Passenger Transport Executive, that is to say, any body constituted as such an Executive for a passenger transport area for the purposes of Part II of the Transport Act 1968.

A probation and after-care committee, that is to say, any body constituted as such a committee for a probation and after-care area by paragraph 2(1) of Schedule 3 to the Powers of Criminal Courts Act 1973.

A joint committee discharging under section 101 of the Local Government Act 1972 functions of local authorities (within the meaning of that section).

Interpretation

In the application of this Schedule to England and Wales, "local authority" means—
  (a) a county council, a district council, a London borough council, a parish council, a community council or the Council of the Isles of Scilly;
  (b) the Common Council of the City of London in its capacity as local authority or police authority;
and includes a residuary body established by Part VII of the Local Government Act 1985.

In the application of this Schedule to Scotland—
  (a) "local authority" means a regional, islands or district council or any joint board or joint committee within the meaning of the Local Government (Scotland) Act 1973; and
  (b) "water development board" has the same meaning as in section 109(1) of the Water (Scotland) Act 1980. **[541–542]**

NOTE
First words omitted repealed by the Education Reform Act 1988, s 237(2), Sch 13, Pt I; second words omitted repealed by the Housing (Scotland) Act 1988, ss 1, 3, 72(3), Sch 2, para 17, Sch 10.

(Schs 3–7 outside the scope of this work.)

EMPLOYMENT ACT 1988
(1988 c 19)

ARRANGEMENT OF SECTIONS

PART II
EMPLOYMENT AND TRAINING

PART III
MISCELLANEOUS AND SUPPLEMENTAL

Supplemental

An Act to make provision with respect to trade unions, their members and their property, to things done for the purpose of enforcing membership of a trade union, to trade union ballots and elections and to proceedings involving trade unions; to provide for the Manpower Services Commission to be known as the

Training Commission; to amend the law with respect to the constitution and functions of that Commission and with respect to persons to whom facilities for work-experience and training for employment are made available; to enable additional members to be appointed to industrial training boards and to the Agricultural Training Board; and to provide that the terms on which certain persons hold office or employment under the Crown are to be treated for certain purposes as contained in contracts of employment

[26 May 1988]

GENERAL NOTE

Most of this Act has been repealed by and re-enacted in the Trade Union and Labour Relations (Consolidation) Act 1992. The provisions so affected are ss 1–23, 30, Sch 1 and parts of Sch 3. For details of the re-enacted provisions see Destination Table, below, para **[982A]**. Some other provisions are omitted for reasons given below.

1–23 *((Pt I) Repealed by the Trade Union and Labour Relations (Consolidation) Act 1992, s 300(1), Sch 1.)*

PART II

EMPLOYMENT AND TRAINING

24, 25 *(S 24 repealed by the Employment Act 1989, s 29(4), Sch 7, Pt I; s 25 substitutes the Employment and Training Act 1973, ss 2, 3.)*

26 Status of trainees etc

(1) Where it appears to the Secretary of State that provision has been made under section 2 of the 1973 Act [, or under section 2(3) [or section 14A] of the Enterprise and New Towns (Scotland) Act 1990,] for persons using facilities provided in pursuance of arrangements under [*the said section 2, or as the case may be the said section 2(3)* [any of those three sections],] to receive payments from any person in connection with their use of those facilities, the Secretary of State may by order provide—

(a) that those persons are, for the purposes and in the cases specified or described in or determined under the order, to be treated in respect of their use of those facilities as being or as not being employed;

(b) that where those persons are treated as being employed they are to be treated as being the employees of the persons so specified, described or determined and of no others;

(c) that where those persons are treated as not being employed they are to be treated as being trained, or are to be treated in such other manner as may be so specified, described or determined; and

(d) that those payments are to be treated for the purposes of such enactments and subordinate legislation as may be so specified, described or determined in such manner as may be so specified, described or determined.

(2) The power to make an order under this section shall be exercisable by statutory instrument subject to annulment in pursuance of a resolution of either House of Parliament; and such an order may—

(a) modify any enactment or subordinate legislation;

(b) make different provision for different purposes and for different cases; and

(c) contain such incidental, consequential and transitional provision as appears to the Secretary of State to be appropriate.

(3) The consent of the Treasury shall be required for the making of any order under this section which contains provision for the manner in which any payment is to be treated for the purposes of the Income Tax Acts.

(4) In this section—

"enactment" includes an enactment contained in this Act or in any Act passed after this Act; and

"subordinate legislation" has the same meaning as in the Interpretation Act 1978. **[543]**

NOTES
Sub-s (1): first words in square brackets inserted, second (italicised) words in square brackets substituted, by the Enterprise and New Towns (Scotland) Act 1990, s 38(1), Sch 4, para 16; words "or section 14A" in square brackets inserted, and for the words in italics there are substituted the words in inner square brackets immediately following, by the Trade Union Reform and Employment Rights Act 1993, s 49(2), Sch 8, para 38, as from 30 August 1993 (SI 1993/1908).
Order under this section: Social Security (Employment Training: Payments) Order 1988, SI 1988/1409.

27–29 (*S 27 repealed by the Social Security (Consequential Provisions) Act 1992, s 3(1), Sch 1; s 28 amends the Employment and Training Act 1973; s 29 (membership of training boards) omitted.*)

PART III

MISCELLANEOUS AND SUPPLEMENTAL

30 (*Repealed by the Trade Union and Labour Relations (Consolidation) Act 1992, s 300(1), Sch 1.*)

Supplemental

31 Financial provisions

There shall be paid out of money provided by Parliament any increases attributable to this Act in the sums payable under any other Act out of money so provided. **[544]**

32 Interpretation

(1) In this Act, except in so far as the context otherwise requires—

. . .

"the 1973 Act" means the Employment and Training Act 1973;

. . .

"modifications" includes additions, alterations and omissions, and cognate expressions shall be construed accordingly;

. . .

(2) . . . **[545]**

NOTES
Sub-s (1): words omitted repealed by the Trade Union and Labour Relations (Consolidation) Act 1992, s 300(1), Sch 1.
Sub-s (2): repealed by the Trade Union and Labour Relations (Consolidation) Act 1992, s 300(1), Sch 1.

33 (*(Minor and consequential amendments and repeals) omitted.*)

34 Short title, commencement and extent

(1) This Act may be cited as the Employment Act 1988.

(2)–(6) . . .   **[546]**

NOTES
    Sub-ss (2), (3): repealed by the Trade Union and Labour Relations (Consolidation) Act 1992, s 300(1), Sch 1.
    Sub-ss (4)–(6): (application and extension to Northern Ireland) omitted.

(*Sch 1, Sch 3, Pt I repealed by the Trade Union and Labour Relations (Consolidation) Act 1992, s 300(1), Sch 1; Sch 2 repealed in part by the Employment Act 1989, s 29(4), Sch 7, Pt I, remainder amends the Employment and Training Act 1973, ss 11, 12; Sch 3, Pt II (minor and consequential amendments), Sch 4 (repeals) omitted.*)

ACCESS TO MEDICAL REPORTS ACT 1988
(1988 c 28)

ARRANGEMENT OF SECTIONS

An Act to establish a right of access by individuals to reports relating to themselves provided by medical practitioners for employment or insurance purposes and to make provision for related matters

[29 July 1988]

1 Right of access

It shall be the right of an individual to have access, in accordance with the provisions of this Act, to any medical report relating to the individual which is to be, or has been, supplied by a medical practitioner for employment purposes or insurance purposes.

                                                                                 [547]

NOTES
    Commencement: 1 January 1989 (s 10(2), (3)).

2 Interpretation

(1) In this Act—

    "the applicant" means the person referred to in section 3(1) below;
    "care" includes examination, investigation or diagnosis for the purposes of, or in connection with, any form of medical treatment;

"employment purposes", in the case of any individual, means the purposes in relation to the individual of any person by whom he is or has been, or is seeking to be, employed (whether under a contract of service or otherwise);

"health professional" has the same meaning as in the Data Protection (Subject Access Modification) (Health) Order 1987;

"insurance purposes", in the case of any individual, means the purposes in relation to the individual of any person carrying on an insurance business with whom the individual has entered into, or is seeking to enter into, a contract of insurance, and "insurance business" and "contract of insurance" have the same meaning as in the Insurance Companies Act 1982;

"medical practitioner" means a person registered under the Medical Act 1983;

"medical report", in the case of an individual, means a report relating to the physical or mental health of the individual prepared by a medical practitioner who is or has been responsible for the clinical care of the individual.

(2) Any reference in this Act to the supply of a medical report for employment or insurance purposes shall be construed—

(a) as a reference to the supply of such a report for employment or insurance purposes which are purposes of the person who is seeking to be supplied with it; or

(b) (in the case of a report that has already been supplied) as a reference to the supply of such a report for employment or insurance purposes which, at the time of its being supplied, were purposes of the person to whom it was supplied. [548]

NOTES
Commencement: 1 January 1989 (s 10(2), (3)).
As from a date to be appointed, the reference to the Data Protection (Subject Access Modification) (Health) Order 1987 is to be read as a reference to that Order as amended by the Osteopaths Act 1993 s 38(3): *ibid* s 38(4).

3 Consent to applications for medical reports for employment or insurance purposes

(1) A person shall not apply to a medical practitioner for a medical report relating to any individual to be supplied to him for employment or insurance purposes unless—

(a) that person ("the applicant") has notified the individual that he proposes to make the application; and

(b) the individual has notified the applicant that he consents to the making of the application.

(2) Any notification given under subsection (1)(a) above must inform the individual of his right to withhold his consent to the making of the application, and of the following rights under this Act, namely—

(a) the rights arising under sections 4(1) to (3) and 6(2) below with respect to access to the report before or after it is supplied,

(b) the right to withhold consent under subsection (1) of section 5 below, and

(c) the right to request the amendment of the report under subsection (2) of that section,

as well as of the effect of section 7 below. [549]

NOTES
Commencement: 1 January 1989 (s 10(2), (3)).

4 Access to reports before they are supplied

(1) An individual who gives his consent under section 3 above to the making of an application shall be entitled, when giving his consent, to state that he wishes to have access to the report to be supplied in response to the application before it is so supplied; and, if he does so, the applicant shall—

    (a) notify the medical practitioner of that fact at the time when the application is made, and

    (b) at the same time notify the individual of the making of the application;

and each such notification shall contain a statement of the effect of subsection (2) below.

(2) Where a medical practitioner is notified by the applicant under subsection (1) above that the individual in question wishes to have access to the report before it is supplied, the practitioner shall not supply the report unless—

    (a) he has given the individual access to it and any requirements of section 5 below have been complied with, or

    (b) the period of 21 days beginning with the date of the making of the application has elapsed without his having received any communication from the individual concerning arrangements for the individual to have access to it.

(3) Where a medical practitioner—

    (a) receives an application for a medical report to be supplied for employment or insurance purposes without being notified by the applicant as mentioned in subsection (1) above, but

    (b) before supplying the report receives a notification from the individual that he wishes to have access to the report before it is supplied,

the practitioner shall not supply the report unless—

    (i) he has given the individual access to it and any requirements of section 5 below have been complied with, or

    (ii) the period of 21 days beginning with the date of that notification has elapsed without his having received (either with that notification or otherwise) any communication from the individual concerning arrangements for the individual to have access to it.

(4) References in this section and section 5 below to giving an individual access to a medical report are references to—

    (a) making the report or a copy of it available for his inspection; or

    (b) supplying him with a copy of it;

and where a copy is supplied at the request, or otherwise with the consent, of the individual the practitioner may charge a reasonable fee to cover the costs of supplying it.   **[550]**

NOTES

Commencement: 1 January 1989 (s 10(2), (3)).

5 Consent to supplying of report and correction of errors

(1) Where an individual has been given access to a report under section 4 above the report shall not be supplied in response to the application in question unless the individual has notified the medical practitioner that he consents to its being so supplied.

(2) The individual shall be entitled, before giving his consent under subsection (1) above, to request the medical practitioner to amend any part of the report which the individual considers to be incorrect or misleading; and, if the individual does so, the practitioner—

    (a) if he is to any extent prepared to accede to the individual's request, shall amend the report accordingly;

    (b) if he is to any extent not prepared to accede to it but the individual requests him to attach to the report a statement of the individual's views in respect of any part of the report which he is declining to amend, shall attach such a statement to the report.

(3) Any request made by an individual under subsection (2) above shall be made in writing.   **[551]**

NOTES
    Commencement: 1 January 1989 (s 10(2), (3)).

6 Retention of reports

(1) A copy of any medical report which a medical practitioner has supplied for employment or insurance purposes shall be retained by him for at least six months from the date on which it was supplied.

(2) A medical practitioner shall, if so requested by an individual, give the individual access to any medical report relating to him which the practitioner has supplied for employment or insurance purposes in the previous six months.

(3) The reference in subsection (2) above to giving an individual access to a medical report is a reference to—

    (a) making a copy of the report available for his inspection; or

    (b) supplying him with a copy of it;

and where a copy is supplied at the request, or otherwise with the consent, of the individual the practitioner may charge a reasonable fee to cover the costs of supplying it.   **[552]**

NOTES
    Commencement: 1 January 1989 (s 10(2), (3)).

7 Exemptions

(1) A medical practitioner shall not be obliged to give an individual access, in accordance with the provisions of section 4(4) or 6(3) above, to any part of a medical report whose disclosure would in the opinion of the practitioner be likely to cause serious harm to the physical or mental health of the individual or others or would indicate the intentions of the practitioner in respect of the individual.

(2) A medical practitioner shall not be obliged to give an individual access, in accordance with those provisions, to any part of a medical report whose disclosure would be likely to reveal information about another person, or to reveal the identity of another person who has supplied information to the practitioner about the individual, unless—

    (a) that person has consented; or

    (b) that person is a health professional who has been involved in the care of the individual and the information relates to or has been provided by the professional in that capacity.

(3) Where it appears to a medical practitioner that subsection (1) or (2) above is applicable to any part (but not the whole) of a medical report—

(a) he shall notify the individual of that fact; and
(b) references in the preceding sections of this Act to the individual being given access to the report shall be construed as references to his being given access to the remainder of it;

and other references to the report in sections 4(4), 5(2) and 6(3) above shall similarly be construed as references to the remainder of the report.

(4) Where it appears to a medical practitioner that subsection (1) or (2) above is applicable to the whole of a medical report—

(a) he shall notify the individual of that fact; but
(b) he shall not supply the report unless he is notified by the individual that the individual consents to its being supplied;

and accordingly, if he is so notified by the individual, the restrictions imposed by section 4(2) and (3) above on the supply of the report shall not have effect in relation to it.   [553]

NOTES
Commencement: 1 January 1989 (s 10(2), (3)).

8 Application to the court

(1) If a court is satisfied on the application of an individual that any person, in connection with a medical report relating to that individual, has failed or is likely to fail to comply with any requirement of this Act, the court may order that person to comply with that requirement.

(2) The jurisdiction conferred by this section shall be exercisable by a county court or, in Scotland, by the sheriff.   [554]

NOTES
Commencement: 1 January 1989 (s 10(2), (3)).

9 Notifications under this Act

Any notification required or authorised to be given under this Act—

(a) shall be given in writing; and
(b) may be given by post.   [555]

NOTES
Commencement: 1 January 1989 (s 10(2), (3)).

10 Short title, commencement and extent

(1) This Act may be cited as the Access to Medical Reports Act 1988.

(2) This Act shall come into force on 1st January 1989.

(3) Nothing in this Act applies to a medical report prepared before the coming into force of this Act.

(4) This Act does not extend to Northern Ireland.   [556]

NOTES
Commencement: 1 January 1989 (s 10(2), (3)).

EDUCATION REFORM ACT 1988

(1988 c 40)

ARRANGEMENT OF SECTIONS

PART I
SCHOOLS

CHAPTER III
FINANCE AND STAFF

Financial delegation: appointment and dismissal of staff

PART IV
MISCELLANEOUS AND GENERAL

Miscellaneous provisions

Supplementary

SCHEDULES
Schedule 3—Appointment and dismissal of school staff, etc, during financial delegation

[564–565]

An Act to amend the law relating to education

[29 July 1988]

GENERAL NOTE

Most of the provisions of this Act relate to education; those reproduced are confined to provisions of employment law in the context of local management of schools and restrictions on the employment powers of local education authorities. Those provisions omitted are not annotated. All substantive provisions reproduced apply only to England and Wales and came into force on 29 July 1988.

PART I

SCHOOLS

CHAPTER III

FINANCE AND STAFF

Financial delegation: appointment and dismissal of staff

44 Staff employed by the local education authority

(1) This section applies to a county, controlled or special agreement school at any time when it has a delegated budget.

(2) None of the following shall have effect in relation to a school to which this section for the time being applies—

   (a) sections 34 and 35 of the 1986 Act (determination of staff complement for schools by local education authority and general provisions about appointment and dismissal of staff);

   (b) any provision made by the articles of government in accordance with any of sections 36 to 41 of that Act (procedure for appointments, suspensions and dismissals); and

   (c) any provision of section 40 of that Act (appointment and dismissal of clerk to the governing body) other than subsection (5).

(3) Subject to the following provisions of this section—

   (a) the appointment, suspension and dismissal of staff at a school to which this section for the time being applies and the determination of their duties, grading and remuneration; and

   (b) the application in relation to such staff of—

   (i) any disciplinary rules and procedures; and

   (ii) any procedures for affording to them opportunities for seeking redress of any grievances relating to their employment;

shall be subject to Schedule 3 to this Act.

(4) Within the period of five years beginning with the date on which the financial year begins in which any county, controlled or special agreement school first has a delegated budget under a scheme, it shall be the duty of the local education authority concerned to amend the articles of government of the school so as to include a statement indicating that provisions made by the articles in accordance with any of sections 36 to 41 of the 1986 Act (specifying those provisions) are superseded by this section and Schedule 3 to this Act during any period when the school has a delegated budget.

(5) This section is subject to the provisions of sections 27 and 28 of the 1944 Act (which relate to religious education).   [557]

NOTES

Commencement: 29 July 1988: s 236.

This section does not extend to Scotland.

45 Staff at aided schools

(1) This section applies to an aided school at any time when it has a delegated budget.

(2) None of the following shall have effect in relation to a school to which this section for the time being applies—

    (a) section 22(4) of the 1944 Act (power of local education authority to give directions to governors of aided school as to number and conditions of service of school maintenance staff); and

    (b) any provision of the articles of government conferring any functions on a local education authority with respect to the number of teachers or other staff to be employed at the school or the appointment or dismissal of such teachers or other staff (including any such provision required by section 24(2) of that Act).

(3) Subject to any provision of the articles of government of any such school other than any provision for the time being excluded by subsection (2) above from applying to the school, the governing body of the school shall have (if they would not otherwise do so apart from any provision of the articles so excluded) power to appoint, suspend and dismiss staff as they think fit.

(4) Subsection (6) below applies if in the case of any such school—

    (a) the governing body of the school agree with the local education authority to accord advisory rights to the chief education officer of the authority in relation to the appointment or dismissal of teachers at the school; or

    (b) in default of such agreement the Secretary of State determines that it would be appropriate in the case of the school that such rights should be accorded to the chief education officer of the authority.

(5) Advisory rights accorded by an agreement or determination under subsection (4) above in the case of any school may relate to the appointment or dismissal, or both to the appointment and the dismissal, either of head teachers and deputy head teachers alone or of all teachers at the school.

(6) During any period while an agreement or determination under subsection (4) above is effective in the case of any school, the chief education officer of the authority, or an officer of the authority nominated by him, shall be entitled to attend all proceedings of the governing body relating to any action to which the advisory rights accorded to him extend (including interviews) for the purpose of giving advice to the governing body.

(7) The agreement of a governing body for the purposes of subsection (4)(a) above shall be given in writing and may only be withdrawn by notice in writing to the local education authority.

(8) A determination by the Secretary of State for the purposes of subsection (4)(b) above may be withdrawn at any time (without prejudice to a further determination for those purposes).

(9) The governing body of a school to which this section for the time being applies shall, on dismissing any member of the staff of the school employed by them, notify the local education authority in writing of the reasons for the dismissal.

(10) Where any member of the staff at any such school is employed by the local education authority, paragraphs 8 to 10 of Schedule 3 to this Act shall have effect in relation to his dismissal or withdrawal from the school as they have effect in relation to the dismissal or withdrawal from a school to which section 44 of this Act applies of a person employed to work at the school.

(11) Within the period of five years beginning with the date on which the

financial year begins in which any aided school first has a delegated budget under a scheme, it shall be the duty of the local education authority concerned to amend the articles of government of the school so as to include a statement indicating that provisions of the articles of a kind mentioned in subsection (2)(b) above (specifying those provisions) are superseded by this section during any period when the school has a delegated budget. **[558]**

NOTES
Commencement: 29 July 1988: s 236.
This section does not extend to Scotland.

46 Staff: further provisions

(1) ...

(2) Subject to subsection (3) below, it shall be for the governing body of any such school to determine—

(a) whether any payment should be made by the local education authority concerned in respect of the dismissal, or for the purpose of securing the resignation, of any member of the staff of the school; and

(b) the amount of any such payment.

(3) Subsection (2) above does not apply in relation to any payment which the authority are required to make—

(a) by virtue of any contract other than one made in contemplation of the impending dismissal or resignation of the member of staff concerned; or

(b) under any statutory provision.

(4) The local education authority concerned—

(a) shall take such steps as may be required for giving effect to any determination of the governing body of any such school under subsection (2) above; and

(b) shall not make, or agree to make, any payment to which that subsection applies in respect of the dismissal, or for the purpose of securing the resignation, of any member of the staff of any such school otherwise than in accordance with any such determination.

(5) Costs incurred by the local education authority concerned in respect of the dismissal or premature retirement, or for the purpose of securing the resignation, of any member of the staff of any such school shall not be met from the school's budget share for any financial year except in so far as the authority have good reason for deducting those costs, or any part of those costs, from that share.

(6) The fact that the authority have a policy precluding dismissal of their employees by reason of redundancy is not to be regarded as a good reason for the purposes of subsection (5) above. **[559]**

NOTES
Commencement: 29 July 1988: s 236.
Sub-s (1): repealed by the School Teachers' Pay and Conditions Act 1991, s 6(3), Sch 2.
This section does not extend to Scotland.

47 Community Schools

(1) This section applies to any school to which section 44 or 45 of this Act for the time being applies which is a community school.

(2) For the purposes of this section, a school is a community school if—

(a) activities other than school activities ("non-school activities") are carried on on the school premises; and

(b) all non-school activities which are so carried on are carried on under the management or control of the governing body of the school.

(3) A scheme may provide for applying sections 44(3), 45(10) and 46 of and Schedule 3 to this Act in relation to persons employed to work—

(a) partly for the purposes of school activities and partly for the purposes of non-school activities carried on on the premises of a school to which this section applies; or

(b) solely for the purposes of non-school activities so carried on;

as if all activities so carried on were school activities. [560]

NOTES
Commencement: 29 July 1988: s 236.
This section does not extend to Scotland.

PART IV
MISCELLANEOUS AND GENERAL

Miscellaneous provisions

221 Avoidance of certain contractual terms

(1) This section applies to any contract made after 20th November 1987 between—

(a) a local education authority in their capacity as such an authority;

(b) the governing body of an aided or grant-maintained school; or

(c) ...

and any person employed by them, not being a contract made in contemplation of the employee's pending dismissal by reason of redundancy.

(2) In so far as a contract to which this section applies provides that the employee—

(a) shall not be dismissed by reason of redundancy; or

(b) if he is so dismissed, shall be paid a sum in excess of the sum which the employer is liable to pay him under section 81 of the Employment Protection (Consolidation) Act 1978,

the contract shall be void and of no effect.

(3) In this section—

"governing body, in relation to an institution, includes a body corporate established for the purpose of conducting that institution;

... [561]

NOTES
Sub-s (1): para (c) repealed by the Further and Higher Education Act 1992, s 93, Sch 8, Part I, para 52, Sch 9.
Sub-s (3): definition "relevant institution" repealed by the Further and Higher Education Act 1992, s 93, Sch 8, Part I, para 52, Sch 9.
This section does not extend to Scotland.

222 Application of employment law during financial delegation

(1) The Secretary of State may by order make such modifications in any enactment relating to employment and, in particular, in any enactment—

(a) conferring powers or imposing duties on employers;

(b) conferring rights on employees; or

(c) otherwise regulating the relations between employers and employees;

as he considers necessary or expedient in consequence of the operation of any of the
provisions of this Act mentioned in subsection (2) below.

(2) Those provisions are—

(a) sections 44(2) and (3) and 45(10), section 46(1), (2) and (4), Schedule 3,
paragraph 4 of Schedule 4 and section 48 so far as relating to that
paragraph; and

(b) . . .

(3) Before making any order under section, the Secretary of State shall consult—

(a) such associations of local authorities;

(b) such bodies representing the interests of governors of voluntary schools;
and

(c) such organisations representing staff in schools required to be covered by
schemes under section 33 of this Act . . . ;

as appear to him to be concerned.　　　　　　　　　　　　　　　　　　　　[562]

NOTES

Sub-ss (2), (3): words omitted repealed by the Further and Higher Education Act 1992, s 93, Sch 8,
Part I, para 53, Sch 9

This section does not extend to Scotland.

Order under this section: Education (Modification of Enactments Relating to Employment) Order
1989, SI 1989/901.

Supplementary

235 General interpretation

(1) In this Act, except where the context otherwise requires—

"the 1944 Act" means the Education Act 1944;

"the 1980 Act" means the Education Act 1980;

"the 1981 Act" means the Education Act 1981;

"the 1986 Act" means the Education (No. 2) Act 1986;

"contract of employment", "employee" and "employer" have the same
meaning as in the Employment Protection (Consolidation) Act 1978, and
"employed" means employed under a contract of employment;

"financial year" means a period of twelve months ending with 31st March;

"functions" includes powers and duties;

"higher education" has the meaning given by section 120(1);

"land" includes buildings and other structures, land covered with water, and
any interest in land;

"liability" includes obligation;

"local authority" means a county council, a district council, a London borough
council or the Common Council of the City of London;

"modifications" includes additions, alterations and omissions and "modify"
shall be construed accordingly;

"statutory provision" means a provision of an enactment or a statutory
instrument;

"transfer date" has the meaning given by section 74(9), 123(2), 130(8) or
228(10) as the context may require;

"university" includes a university college and any college, or institution in the
nature of a college, in a university.

(2) . . .

(3) For the purposes of this Act—

(a) a person employed by a local education authority is to be regarded as employed to work at a school or other institution if his employment with the authority for the time being involves work at that school or institution; and

(b) subject to section 75(2) of this Act, a person employed by such an authority is to be regarded as employed to work solely at a school or other institution if his only employment with the authority (disregarding any employment under a separate contract with the authority) is for the time being at that school or institution.

(4)–(7) . . .

(8) Where an expression is given for the purposes of any provision of this Act a meaning different from that given to it for the purposes of the 1944 Act, the meaning given for the purposes of the 1944 Act shall not apply for the purposes of that provision. **[563]**

NOTES

Commencement: 29 July 1988: s 236.

Sub-ss (2), (4)–(7): (not relating to matters covered by the substantive provisions printed here) omitted.

SCHEDULES

(Schs 1, 2 outside the scope of this work.)

SCHEDULE 3

Section 44

APPOINTMENT AND DISMISSAL OF SCHOOL STAFF, ETC, DURING FINANCIAL DELEGATION

Appointment of head teacher and deputy head teacher

1 (1) This paragraph applies in relation to any appointment to fill a vacancy in the post of head teacher or deputy head teacher of a school to which section 44 of this Act for the time being applies.

(2) References in this Schedule to a vacancy in any post include a prospective vacancy in the post.

(3) The governing body shall notify the local education authority of the vacancy in writing before taking any of the steps mentioned below.

(4) Where the vacancy is in the post of head teacher and either the post has not been filled, or it appears to the governing body that the post will not be filled, by an appointment made in accordance with the following provisions of this paragraph before the date on which it falls vacant—

(a) the governing body shall recommend a person for appointment as acting head teacher; and

(b) the authority shall appoint the person recommended unless he does not meet any staff qualification requirements which are applicable in relation to his appointment.

(5) Where the vacancy is in the post of deputy head teacher and either the post has not been filled, or it appears to the governing body that the post will not be filled, by an appointment made in accordance with the following provisions of this paragraph before the date on which it falls vacant—

(a) the governing body may recommend a person for appointment as acting deputy head teacher; and

(b) the authority shall appoint the person recommended unless he does not meet any staff qualification requirements which are applicable in relation to his appointment.

(6) References in this Schedule to staff qualification requirements are references to any requirements with respect to—

    (a) qualifications;

    (b) health and physical capacity; or

    (c) fitness and educational grounds or in any other respect;

of teachers and other persons employed in work which brings them regularly into contact with persons who have not attained the age of nineteen years which for the time being apply under regulations made under section 27 of the 1980 Act (school and further education regulations).

(7) Before recommending any person for appointment as head teacher or deputy head teacher, the governing body shall advertise the vacancy in such publications circulating throughout England and Wales as they consider appropriate.

(8) The governing body shall appoint a selection panel consisting of at least three of their members to perform the functions conferred on the panel under this paragraph.

(9) The selection panel shall—

    (a) interview such applicants for the post as they think fit;

    (b) where they consider that it is appropriate to do so, recommend to the governing body for appointment one of the applicants interviewed by them; and

    (c) if their recommendation is approved by the governing body, recommend the applicant in question to the authority for appointment.

(10) If the selection panel are unable to agree on a person to recommend to the governing body or the governing body do not approve their recommendation, the governing body—

    (a) may, if they think fit, re-advertise the vacancy in the manner required by sub-paragraph (7) above; and

    (b) whether or not they re-advertise the vacancy, may require the panel to repeat the steps mentioned in sub-paragraph (9) above.

(11) The authority shall appoint the person recommended by the panel for appointment as head teacher or (as the case may be) as deputy head teacher unless he does not meet any staff qualification requirements which are applicable in relation to his appointment.

(12) Where the authority decline to appoint a person recommended by the governing body for appointment as acting head teacher, the governing body shall recommend another person for appointment.

(13) Where the authority decline to appoint a person recommended by a selection panel appointed under sub-paragraph (8) above for appointment as head teacher or deputy head teacher, sub-paragraph (10) above shall apply as it applies in the cases there mentioned.

Appointment of other teachers

2 (1) Subject to sub-paragraph (2) below, sub-paragraphs (4) to (11) below apply in relation to any appointment to fill a vacancy in any teaching post (whether full-time or part-time) at a school to which section 44 of this Act for the time being applies, other than a post to which paragraph 1 above applies.

(2) Sub-paragraphs (4) to (11) below do not apply in relation to a temporary appointment to fill such a vacancy for a period not exceeding four months or where it appears to the governing body that the period for which the person appointed will hold the post in question will not exceed four months.

(3) Where it appears to the governing body in the case of any post that it would be appropriate to make such an appointment as is mentioned in sub-paragraph (2) above—

    (a) they may recommend a person for appointment to the post on such terms as to the duration of the appointment as they may specify; and

    (b) the local education authority shall appoint the person recommended on the terms specified unless he does not meet any staff qualification requirements which are applicable in relation to his appointment.

(4) Before taking any of the steps mentioned below, the governing body shall—

(a) determine a specification for the post in consultation with the head teacher; and
(b) send a copy of the specification to the authority.

(5) The authority may nominate for consideration for appointment to the post any person who appears to them to be qualified to fill the post and who either—

(a) is at the time of his nomination an employee of theirs or has been appointed to take up employment with them at a future date; or
(b) is at the time of his nomination employed by the governing body of an aided school maintained by the authority;

subject, in a case within paragraph (b) above, to the consent of the governing body of the school concerned.

(6) The governing body may advertise the vacancy at any time after they have sent a copy of the specification for the post to the authority in accordance with sub-paragraph (4) above, and shall do so unless either—

(a) they accept for appointment to the post a person nominated by the authority under sub-paragraph (5) above; or
(b) they decide to recommend to the authority for appointment to the post a person who is already employed to work at the school.

(7) Where the governing body advertise the vacancy, they shall do so in a manner likely in their opinion to bring it to the notice of persons (including employees of the authority) who are qualified to fill the post.

(8) Where the governing body advertise the vacancy, they shall—

(a) interview such applicants for the post and such of the persons (if any) nominated by the authority under sub-paragraph (5) above as they think fit; and
(b) where they consider it is appropriate to do so—
    (i) recommend to the authority for appointment one of the applicants interviewed by them; or
    (ii) notify the authority that they accept for appointment any person so nominated;
    as the case may require.

(9) If the governing body are unable to agree on a person to recommend or accept for appointment, they may repeat the steps mentioned in paragraphs (a) and (b) of sub-paragraph (8) above, with or without first re-advertising the vacancy in accordance with sub-paragraph (7) above.

(10) The authority shall appoint the person recommended or accepted for appointment to the post by the governing body unless (in the case of a person other than one nominated by the authority) he does not meet any staff qualification requirements which are applicable in relation to his appointment.

(11) Where the authority decline to appoint a person recommended by the governing body for appointment the governing body shall repeat such of the steps mentioned in paragraphs (a) and (b) of sub-paragraph (8) above as they think fit, with or without first re-advertising the vacancy in accordance with sub-paragraph (7) above.

(12) The governing body may delegate any of their functions under this paragraph, in relation to the filling of a particular vacancy or a vacancy of a kind specified by them, to—

(a) one or more governors;
(b) the head teacher; or
(c) one or more governors and the head teacher acting together.

Appointments: advice of chief education officer and head teacher

3 (1) The chief education officer of the local education authority concerned shall be entitled to attend, for the purpose of giving advice, all proceedings—

(a) of the governing body;
(b) of any selection panel appointed under paragraph 1 above; or
(c) of any persons to whom any functions of the governing body under paragraph 2 above are delegated;

relating to appointments to which paragraph 1 or (as the case may be) paragraph 2 above applies (including in each case any interviews).

(2) The chief education officer shall also be under a duty—

(a) to offer such advice as he considers appropriate with respect to the appointment of a head teacher, a deputy head teacher, an acting head teacher or an acting deputy head teacher or any matter arising in connection with any such appointment; and

(b) to give such advice as he considers appropriate with respect to any appointment to which paragraph 2 above applies if requested to do so by the governing body.

(3) Each of the following, that is to say—

(a) the governing body;

(b) any selection panel appointed under paragraph 1 above; and

(c) any persons to whom any functions of the governing body under paragraph 2 above are delegated;

shall consider any advice given by the chief education officer with respect to any matter it falls to them to determine relating to any appointment before determining that matter, whether or not the advice was given at their request.

(4) Except in relation to the appointment of a head teacher—

(a) sub-paragraph (1) above shall apply in relation to the head teacher (if not otherwise entitled to be present at the proceedings there mentioned) as it applies in relation to the chief education officer; and

(b) sub-paragraph (3) above shall apply in relation to advice given by the head teacher as it applies in relation to advice given by the chief education officer.

Appointment of non-teaching staff

4 (1) Where the governing body of any school to which section 44 of this Act for the time being applies wish to appoint a person to work in a non-teaching post at the school, they may recommend a person to the local education authority concerned for appointment to the post.

(2) Such a recommendation shall be in writing and shall specify—

(a) the duties to be performed by the person appointed (including, where the post is part-time, his hours of work);

(b) the grade (on the scale of grades currently applicable in relation to employment with the authority) which the governing body consider appropriate for the post; and

(c) where the authority have any discretion with respect to the remuneration to be paid to a person appointed to the post, the determination of any matter to which that discretion applies which the governing body consider appropriate in the case of the person recommended for appointment.

(3) Before selecting a person to recommend for appointment to such a post and determining in relation to any such recommendation any matters mentioned in sub-paragraph (2) above, the governing body shall consult—

(a) the head teacher (where he would not otherwise be involved in the decision); and

(b) in any case where the post involves or, in the case of a new post, it is proposed that it should involve, work at the school for sixteen hours a week or more, the chief education officer of the authority.

(4) The authority shall appoint a person recommended for appointment to a non-teaching post at such a school by the governing body on such terms as to give effect, so far as relates to any matter mentioned in sub-paragraph (2) above, to the governing body's recommendation with respect to that matter unless he does not meet any staff qualification requirements which are applicable in relation to his appointment.

(5) For the purposes of sub-paragraph (2)(c) above, the authority are to be regarded as having a discretion with respect to the remuneration to be paid to a person appointed to any such post if any provisions regulating the rates of remuneration or allowances payable to persons in the authority's employment either—

(a) do not apply in relation to that appointment; or

(b) leave to the authority any degree of discretion with respect to rate of remuneration or allowances in the case of that appointment.

5 ...

Discipline

6 (1) The regulation of conduct and discipline in relation to the staff of any school to which section 44 of this Act for the time being applies, and any procedures for affording to members of the staff opportunities for seeking redress of any grievances relating to their employment, shall be under the control of the governing body.

(2) The governing body of any such school shall establish—

(a) disciplinary rules and procedures; and
(b) procedures such as are mentioned in sub-paragraph (1) above;

and shall take such steps as appear to them to be appropriate for making them known to the staff at the school.

(3) Where the implementation of any determination made by the governing body in the exercise of their control over the conduct and discipline of the staff of any such school requires any action which—

(a) is not within the functions exercisable by the governing body by virtue of this Act; or
(b) is within the power of the local education authority concerned;

it shall be the duty of the authority to take that action at the request of the governing body.

Suspension

7 (1) In the case of any school to which section 44 of this Act for the time being applies, the governing body and the head teacher shall both have power to suspend any person employed to work at the school where, in the opinion of the governing body or (as the case may be) of the head teacher, his exclusion from the school is required.

(2) The governing body or head teacher, when exercising that power, shall immediately inform the local education authority concerned and the head teacher or (as the case may be) the governing body.

(3) Any suspension under this paragraph may only be ended by the governing body; and the governing body shall, on ending such a suspension, immediately inform the local education authority concerned and the head teacher.

(4) In this paragraph "suspend" means suspend without loss of emoluments.

Dismissal, etc.

8 (1) Where the governing body of any school to which section 44 of this Act for the time being applies determine—

(a) that any person employed to work at the school should cease to work there; or
(b) that the clerk to the governing body should be dismissed;

they shall notify the local education authority concerned in writing of their determination and the reasons for it.

(2) If in a case within sub-paragraph (1)(a) above—

(a) the person concerned is employed to work solely at the school; and
(b) he does not resign;

the authority shall, before the end of the period of fourteen days beginning with the date on which the notification under sub-paragraph (1) above is given in relation to him, either give him such notice terminating his contract of employment with the authority as is required under that contract or terminate that contract without notice if the circumstances are such that they are entitled to do so by reason of his conduct.

(3) If in a case within sub-paragraph (1)(a) above the person concerned is not employed to work solely at the school the authority shall require him to cease to work at the school.

(4) In any case within sub-paragraph (3) above no part of the costs incurred by the authority in respect of the emoluments of the person concerned, so far as relates to any period falling after the expiration of his contractual notice period, shall be met from the school's budget share.

(5) In relation to any such person, the reference in sub-paragraph (4) above to his contractual notice period is a reference to the period of notice that would have been required under his contract of employment with the authority for termination of that contract if such notice had been given on the date on which the notification under sub-paragraph (1) above was given in relation to him.

(6) In a case within sub-paragraph (1)(b) above the authority shall dismiss the clerk to the governing body on receipt of the notification from the governing body.

(7) The governing body of such a school shall make arrangements for affording to any person in respect of whom they propose to make any determination under sub-paragraph (1) above an opportunity of making representations with respect to the action they propose to take, including (if he so wishes) oral representations to such person or persons as the governing body may appoint for the purpose, and shall have regard to any representations made by him.

(8) The governing body of such a school shall also make arrangements for affording to any person in respect of whom they have made such a determination an opportunity of appealing against it before they notify the authority of the determination.

(9) The head teacher (except where he is the person concerned) and the chief education officer of the authority shall be entitled to attend, for the purpose of giving advice, all proceedings of the governing body relating to any determination under sub-paragraph (1) above; and the governing body shall consider any advice given by a person entitled to attend such proceedings under this sub-paragraph before making any such determination.

9 (1) Subject to sub-paragraph (2) below, a local education authority shall not dismiss a person employed by the authority to work solely at a school to which section 44 of this Act for the time being applies except as provided by paragraph 8 above.

(2) Sub-paragraph (1) above shall not apply in any case where the dismissal of the person in question is required under any regulations made under section 27 of the 1980 Act.

School meal staff

10 Nothing in paragraphs 4 and 6 to 9 above shall apply in relation to the appointment of a person to work at a school to which section 44 of this Act for the time being applies, or in relation to a person so employed, where—

    (a)   the person concerned is to be, or is, employed to work solely in connection with the provision of meals; and

    (b)   no allowance is made for expenditure on or in connection with the provision of meals in determining the school's budget share.

Interpretation

11 (1) References in this Schedule to a vacancy in any post shall be read in accordance with paragraph 1(2) above.

(2) References in this Schedule to staff qualification requirements shall be read in accordance with paragraph 1(6) above.

(3) References in this Schedule to the chief education officer of a local education authority include references to any officer of the authority nominated by the chief education officer.

                                                                       [564–565]

NOTES

Commencement: 29 July 1988: s 236.
Para 5: repealed by the Education (Schools) Act 1992, s 21(8), Sch 5.
This Schedule does not extend to Scotland.

SOCIAL SECURITY ACT 1989
(1989 c 24)

An Act to amend the law relating to social security and occupational and personal pension schemes; to make provision with respect to certain employment-related benefit schemes; to provide for the recovery, out of certain compensation payments, of amounts determined by reference to payments of benefit; to make fresh provision with respect to the constitution and functions of war pensions committees; and for connected purposes

[21 July 1989]

GENERAL NOTE

Only s 23 and Sch 5, which implement Council Directive 86/378/EEC, are printed here. The Directive itself requires implementation by 1 January 1993 and the Government's initial announced intention was to bring these provisions into force on that date. In late 1992 it announced a postponement pending the resolution of the *Coloroll* litigation and no further implementation date had been announced as at 1st September 1993.

1–22 (*Outside the scope of this work.*)

Occupational and personal pensions etc

23 Equal treatment for men and women

Schedule 5 to this Act shall have effect for the purpose of implementing the directive of the Council of the European Communities, dated 24th July 1986, relating to the principle of equal treatment for men and women in occupational social security schemes, and of making additional, supplemental and consequential provision.

[566]

NOTES

Commencement: to be appointed by order under s 33(2).
Council Directive: 86/378/EEC.

24–33 (*Outside the scope of this work.*)

SCHEDULES

(*Schs 1–4 outside the scope of this work.*)

SCHEDULE 5

Section 23

EMPLOYMENT-RELATED SCHEMES FOR PENSIONS OR OTHER BENEFITS: EQUAL TREATMENT FOR MEN AND WOMEN

PART I
COMPLIANCE BY SCHEMES

Schemes to comply with the principle of equal treatment

1 Every employment-related benefit scheme shall comply with the principle of equal treatment.

The principle

2 (1) The principle of equal treatment is that persons of the one sex shall not, on the basis of sex, be treated less favourably than persons of the other sex in any respect relating to an employment-related benefit scheme.

(2) Sub-paragraphs (3) to (6) below have effect, where applicable, for the purpose of determining whether a scheme complies with the principle of equal treatment.

(3) Where any provision of the scheme imposes on both male and female members a requirement or condition—

(a) which is such that the proportion of persons of the one sex ("the sex affected") who can comply with it is considerably smaller than the proportion of persons of the other sex who can do so, and

(b) which is not justifiable irrespective of the sex of the members,

the imposition of that requirement or condition shall be regarded as less favourable treatment of persons of the sex affected.

(4) No account shall be taken of—

(a) any difference, on the basis of the sex of members, in the levels of contributions—

(i) *which members are required to make, to the extent that the difference is justifiable on actuarial grounds, or*

(ii) which the employer makes, to the extent that the difference is for the purpose of removing or limiting differences, as between men and women, in the amount or value of money purchase benefits;

(b) any difference, on the basis of sex, in the amount or value of money purchase benefits, to the extent that the difference is justifiable on actuarial grounds;

(c) any special treatment for the benefit of women in connection with pregnancy or childbirth;

(d) any permitted age-related differences;

(e) any difference of treatment in relation to benefits for a deceased member's surviving husband, wife or other dependants;

(f) any difference of treatment in relation to any optional provisions available; or

(g) any provisions of a scheme to the extent that they have been specially arranged for the benefit of one particular member of the scheme;

but where the scheme includes any unfair maternity provisions, it shall to that extent be regarded as according less favourable treatment to women on the basis of sex.

(5) Where the scheme treats persons of the one sex differently according to their marital or family status, that treatment is to be compared with the scheme's treatment of persons of the other sex who have the same status.

(6) The principle of equal treatment applies in relation to members' dependants as it applies in relation to members.

(7) If any question arises whether a condition or requirement falling within sub-paragraph (3)(a) above is or is not justifiable irrespective of the sex of the members, it shall be for those who assert that it is so justifiable to prove that fact.

(8) In this paragraph—

"money purchase benefits" has the meaning given by section 84(1) of the 1986 Act, but with the substitution for references to a personal or occupational pension scheme of references to an employment-related benefit scheme;

"optional provisions available" means those provisions of a scheme—

(a) which apply only in the case of members who elect for them to do so; and

(b) whose purpose is to secure for those members—

(i) benefits in addition to those otherwise provided under the scheme; or

(ii) a choice with respect to the date on which benefits under the scheme are to commence; or

(iii) a choice between any two or more benefits;

"permitted age-related difference" means any difference, on the basis of sex, in the age—

(a) at which a service-related benefit in respect of old age or retirement commences; or

(b) at which, in consequence of the commencement of such a benefit, any other service-related benefit either ceases to be payable or becomes payable at a reduced rate calculated by reference to the amount of the benefit so commencing.

(9) For the purposes of this paragraph—

(a) any reference to a person's family status is a reference to his having an unmarried partner or any dependants; and

(b) a person "has an unmarried partner" if that person and some other person to whom he is not married live together as husband and wife.

Non-compliance: compulsory levelling up

3 (1) To the extent that any provision of an employment-related benefit scheme does not comply with the principle of equal treatment, it shall be overridden by this Schedule and the more favourable treatment accorded to persons of the one sex shall also be accorded to persons of the other sex.

(2) Where more favourable treatment is accorded to any persons by virtue of sub-paragraph (1) above, that sub-paragraph requires them, in accordance with the principle of equal treatment—

(a) to pay contributions at a level appropriate to the treatment so accorded; and

(b) to bear any other burden which is an incident of that treatment;

but persons of either sex may instead elect to receive the less favourable treatment and, in accordance with the principle of equal treatment, pay contributions at the level appropriate to that treatment and bear the other burdens incidental to it.

(3) Where any provision of a scheme is overridden by sub-paragraph (1) above, nothing in this Schedule shall affect any rights accrued or obligations incurred during the period before the date on which that provision is so overridden.

(4) Sub-paragraph (1) above is without prejudice to the exercise, in compliance with the principle of equal treatment, of any power to amend the scheme.

Modification of schemes by the Occupational Pensions Board

4 (1) On an application made to them in respect of an employment-related benefit scheme, other than a public service scheme, by persons competent to make such an application, the Occupational Pensions Board (the "Board") may make an order modifying, or authorising the modification of, the scheme, for the purpose—

(a) of making provision implementing the principle of equal treatment otherwise than as provided by sub-paragraph (1) of paragraph 3 above; or

(b) of reflecting in the rules of the scheme any changes consequential upon the operation of that sub-paragraph.

(2) In relation to any employment-related benefit scheme, the persons competent to make an application to the Board under this paragraph are—

(a) the trustees or managers of the scheme;

(b) any person other than the trustees or managers who has power to alter the rules of the scheme;

(c) any person who is an employer of persons in service in an employment to which the scheme applies; and

(d) such other persons as regulations may specify, in relation to any category of schemes into which the scheme falls, as being proper persons to make an application for the purposes of this paragraph in respect of a scheme of that category.

(3) The Board shall not entertain an application for an order by them under this paragraph unless they are satisfied that the modification of the scheme in question—

(a) cannot be achieved otherwise than by means of such an order; or

(b) can only be achieved in accordance with a procedure which is liable to be unduly complex or protracted, or involves the obtaining of consents which cannot be obtained, or can only be obtained with undue delay or difficulty.

(4) Subject to sub-paragraph (3) above, the Board may on an application under this paragraph make (with the consent of the applicants) an order under sub-paragraph (1) above and may exercise their powers under this paragraph from time to time; and the extent of their powers under this paragraph is not limited, in relation to any purposes for which they are exercisable, to the minimum necessary to achieve those purposes.

(5) An order of the Board under sub-paragraph (1) above authorising the modification of a scheme shall be framed so as to confer the power of modification on such persons as the Board think proper (including persons who were not parties to the application made to the Board) and shall include such directions as the Board think appropriate indicating the modifications which they consider to be desirable.

Unfair maternity provisions

5 (1) In this Schedule "unfair maternity provisions", in relation to an employment-related benefit scheme, means any provision—

(a) which relates to continuing membership of, or the accrual of rights under, the scheme during any period of paid maternity absence in the case of any woman who is (or who, immediately before the commencement of such a period, was) an employed earner and which treats such a woman otherwise than in accordance with the normal employment requirement; or

(b) which requires the amount of any benefit payable under the scheme to or in respect of any such woman, to the extent that it falls to be determined by reference to her earnings during a period which included a period of paid maternity absence, to be determined otherwise than in accordance with the normal employment requirement.

(2) In the case of any unfair maternity provision—

(a) the more favourable treatment required by paragraph 3(1) above is treatment no less favourable than would be accorded to the women [members] in accordance with the normal employment requirement;

(b) paragraph 3(2) above does not authorise the making of any such election as is there mentioned; and

(c) paragraph 4(1)(a) above does not authorise the making of any modification which does not satisfy the requirements of paragraph (a) above;

but, in respect of a period of paid maternity absence, a woman shall only be required to pay contributions on the amount of contractual remuneration or statutory maternity pay actually paid to or for her in respect of that period.

(3) In this paragraph—

(a) "period of paid maternity absence" means any period—

(i) throughout which a woman is absent from work due to pregnancy or confinement; and

(ii) for which her employer (or, if she is no longer in his employment, her former employer) pays her any contractual remuneration or statutory maternity pay;

(b) "the normal employment requirement" is the requirement that any period of paid maternity absence shall be treated as if it were a period throughout which the woman in question works normally and receives the remuneration likely to be paid for doing so.

Unfair family leave provisions

6 (1) Where an employment-related benefit scheme includes any unfair family leave provisions (irrespective of any differences on the basis of sex in the treatment accorded to members under those provisions), then—

(a) the scheme shall be regarded to that extent as not complying with the principle of equal treatment; and

(b)   subject to sub-paragraph (3) below, this Schedule shall apply accordingly.

(2) In this Schedule "unfair family leave provisions" means any provision—

   (a)   which relates to continuing membership of, or the accrual of rights under, the scheme during any period of paid family leave in the case of any member who is an employed earner and which treats such a member otherwise than in accordance with the normal leave requirement; or

   (b)   which requires the amount of any benefit payable under the scheme to or in respect of any such member to the extent that it falls to be determined by reference to earnings during a period which included a period of paid family leave, to be determined otherwise than in accordance with the normal leave requirement.

(3) In the case of any unfair family leave provision—

   (a)   the more favourable treatment required by paragraph 3(1) above is treatment no less favourable than would be accorded to the members in accordance with the normal leave requirement;

   (b)   paragraph 3(2) above does not authorise the making of any such election as is there mentioned; and

   (c)   paragraph 4(1)(a) above does not authorise the making of any modification which does not satisfy the requirements of paragraph (a) above;

but, in respect of a period of paid family leave, a member shall only be required to pay contributions on the amount of contractual remuneration actually paid to or for him in respect of that period.

(4) In this paragraph—

   (a)   "period of paid family leave" means any period—

      (i)   throughout which a member is absent from work for family reasons; and

      (ii)   for which the employer pays him any contractual remuneration;

   (b)   "the normal leave requirement" is the requirement that any period of paid family leave shall be treated as if it were a period throughout which the member in question works normally but only receives the remuneration in fact paid to him for that period.

Meaning of "employment-related benefit scheme" etc

7 In this Schedule—

   (a)   "employment-related benefit scheme" means any scheme or arrangement which is comprised in one or more instruments or agreements and which has, or is capable of having, effect in relation to one or more descriptions or categories of employments so as to provide service-related benefits to or in respect of employed or self-employed earners—

      (i)   who have qualifying service in an employment of any such description or category, or

      (ii)   who have made arrangements with the trustees or managers of the scheme to enable them to become members of the scheme,

   but does not include a limited scheme;

   (b)   "limited scheme" means—

      (i)   any personal scheme for employed earners to which the employer does not contribute;

      (ii)   any scheme which has only one member, other than a personal scheme for an employed earner to which his employer contributes;

      (iii)   any contract of insurance which is made for the benefit of employed earners only and to which the employer is not a party;

   (c)   "personal scheme" means any scheme or arrangement which falls within paragraph (a) above by virtue of sub-paragraph (ii) of that paragraph (or which would so fall apart from paragraph (b) above);

   (d)   "public service scheme" has the meaning given by section 51(3)(b) of the 1973 Act;

   (e)   "service-related benefits" means benefits, in the form of pensions or otherwise, payable in money or money's worth in respect of—

(i) termination of service;
(ii) retirement, old age or death;
(iii) interruptions of service by reason of sickness or invalidity;
(iv) accidents, injuries or diseases connected with employment;
(v) unemployment; or
(vi) expenses incurred in connection with children or other dependants;

and includes, in the case of a member who is an employed earner, any other benefit so payable to or in respect of the member in consequence of his employment.

Extension of ban on compulsory membership

8 Section 15(1) of the 1986 Act (which renders void any provision making membership of a pension scheme compulsory for an employed earner) shall apply in relation to a self-employed earner as it applies in relation to an employed earner, but with the substitution for references to a personal pension scheme of references to an employment-related benefit scheme which would be such a pension scheme if self-employed earners were regarded as employed earners.

Jurisdiction

9 (1) The court, on the application of any person interested, shall have jurisdiction to determine any question arising as to—

(a) whether any provision of an employment-related benefit scheme does or does not comply with the principle of equal treatment; or

(b) whether, and with what effect, any such provision is overridden by paragraph 3 above.

(2) In sub-paragraph (1) above "the court" means—

(a) in England and Wales, the High Court or a county court; and

(b) in Scotland, the Court of Session or the sheriff court.

(3) An application under sub-paragraph (1) above may be commenced in a county court notwithstanding—

(a) any financial limit otherwise imposed on the jurisdiction of such a court; or

(b) that the only relief claimed is a declaration or an injunction.

Interpretation

10 Expressions other than "benefit" which are used in this Part of this Schedule and in the principal Act have the same meaning in this Part of this Schedule as they have in that Act.

Supplemental

11 In consequence of the foregoing provisions of this Schedule—

(a) sections 53 to 56 of the Pensions Act (equal access to schemes for men and women) and

(b) section 64(3)(dd) of the 1973 Act (functions of the Occupational Pensions Board relating to equal access),

shall cease to have effect.

Future repeal of actuarial provisions

12 The Secretary of State may by order repeal paragraph 2(4)(a)(i) above; and if and to the extent that he has not done so before 30th July 1999 it shall cease to have effect on that date.

[567]

NOTES

Commencement: to be appointed by order under s 33(2).

Para 2: sub-para (4)(a)(i) prospectively repealed by para 12 (qv).

Para 5: in sub-para (2)(a) word in square brackets inserted by the Social Security Act 1990, s 21(1), Sch 6, para 29, as from a day to be appointed.

Para 11: repeals the Social Security Pensions Act 1975, ss 53–56 and the Social Security Act 1973,
s 64(3)(dd).
The 1986 Act: Social Security Act 1986.
The 1973 Act: Social Security Act 1973.
Pensions Act: Social Security Pensions Act 1975.

*(Sch 5, Pt II amends the Equal Pay Act 1970, s 6, the Sex Discrimination Act 1975,
ss 4, 6, and the Employment Protection (Consolidation) Act 1978, s 45; Schs 6–9
outside the scope of this work.)*

EMPLOYMENT ACT 1989

(1989 c 38)

ARRANGEMENT OF SECTIONS

An Act to amend the Sex Discrimination Act 1975 in pursuance of the Directive of the Council of the European Communities, dated 9th February 1976, (No 76/207/EEC) on the implementation of the principle of equal treatment for men and women as regards access to employment, vocational training and promotion, and working conditions; to repeal or amend prohibitions or requirements relating to the employment of young persons and other categories of employees; to make other amendments of the law relating to employment and training; to repeal section 1(1)(a) of the Celluloid and Cinematograph Film Act 1922; to dissolve the Training Commission; to make further provision with respect to industrial training boards; to make provision with respect to the transfer of staff employed in the Skills Training Agency; and for connected purposes

[16 November 1989]

GENERAL NOTE

The following provisions are omitted: ss 21 (repeal of requirement to notify storage of celluloid film), 22–26 (dissolution of training commission and consequential provisions), 27 (extension to Northern Ireland), Schs 4, 5 (dissolution of training commission), 6–8 (consequential amendments, repeals and revocations).

Overriding of provisions requiring discrimination as respects employment or training

1 Overriding of statutory requirements which conflict with certain provisions of 1975 Act

(1) Any provision of—

    (a) an Act passed before the Sex Discrimination Act 1975, or

    (b) an instrument approved or made by or under such an Act (including one approved or made after the passing of the 1975 Act),

shall be of no effect in so far as it imposes a requirement to do an act which would be rendered unlawful by any of the provisions of that Act referred to in subsection (2).

(2) Those provisions are—

    (a) Part II (discrimination as respects employment);

    (b) Part III (discrimination as respects education etc.) so far as it applies to vocational training; and

    (c) Part IV (other unlawful acts) so far as it has effect in relation to the provisions mentioned in paragraphs (a) and (b) above.

(3) Where in any legal proceedings (of whatever nature) there falls to be determined the question whether subsection (1) operates to negative the effect of any provision in so far as it requires the application by any person of a requirement or condition falling within subsection (1)(b)(i) of section 1 or 3 of the 1975 Act (indirect discrimination on grounds of sex or marital status)—

    (a) it shall be for any party to the proceedings who claims that subsection (1) does not so operate in relation to that provision to show the requirement or condition in question to be justifiable as mentioned in subsection (1)(b)(ii) of that section; and

    (b) the said subsection (1)(b)(ii) shall accordingly have effect in relation to the requirement or condition as if the reference to the person applying it were a reference to any such party to the proceedings.

(4) Where an Act passed after the 1975 Act, whether before or after the passing of this Act, re-enacts (with or without modification) a provision of an Act passed before the 1975 Act, that provision as re-enacted shall be treated for the purposes of subsection (1) as if it continued to be contained in an Act passed before the 1975 Act.

[568]

NOTE
Commencement: 16 January 1990 (s 30(3)).

2 Power of Secretary of State to repeal statutory provisions requiring discrimination as respects employment or training

(1) Where it appears to the Secretary of State that a relevant provision, namely any provision of—

    (a) an Act passed before this Act, or

    (b) an instrument approved or made by or under such an Act (including one approved or made after the passing of this Act),

requires the doing of an act which would (within the meaning of the 1975 Act) constitute an act of discrimination in circumstances relevant for the purposes of any of the provisions of that Act falling within section 1(2) above, he may by order make such provision (whether by amending, repealing or revoking the relevant provision or otherwise) as he considers appropriate for removing any such requirement.

(2) Subsection (1) shall have effect in relation to a provision to which section 1(1) above applies as if the reference to a relevant provision requiring the doing of an act were a reference to its so requiring but for the operation of section 1(1).

(3) Any order under this section which makes any amendment, repeal or revocation of a relevant provision within the meaning of subsection (1) may (without prejudice to the generality of section 28(5) below) amend or repeal any provision of this Act by virtue of which acts done in pursuance of the relevant provision are not to be unlawful for the purposes of provisions of the 1975 Act.

(4) Where an Act passed after this Act re-enacts (with or without modification) a provision of an Act passed before this Act, that provision as re-enacted shall be treated for the purposes of subsection (1) as if it continued to be contained in an Act passed before this Act.   [569]

NOTE
Commencement: 16 January 1990 (s 30(3)).

Circumstances where Discrimination as respects Employment or Training is Permissible

3 (*Amends the Sex Discrimination Act 1975, s 7, substitutes ss 51, 51A for the original s 51 thereof, and inserts s 52A thereof.*)

4 Exemption for discrimination under certain provisions concerned with the protection of women at work

(1) Without prejudice to the operation of section 51 of the 1975 Act (as substituted by section 3(3) above), nothing in—

    (a) Part II of that Act,

    (b) Part III of that Act so far as it applies to vocational training, or

    (c) Part IV of that Act so far as it has effect in relation to the provisions mentioned in paragraphs (a) and (b) above,

shall render unlawful any act done by a person in relation to a woman if it was necessary for that person to do that act in order to comply with any requirement of any of the provisions specified in Schedule 1 to this Act (which are concerned with the protection of women at work).

(2) Each of the last two entries in that Schedule shall be construed as including a reference to any provision or provisions for the time being having effect in place of the provision or provisions specified in that entry.

(3) In this section "woman" means a female person of any age.   **[570]**

NOTE
Commencement: 16 January 1990 (s 30(3)).

5 Exemption for discrimination in connection with certain educational appointments

(1) Nothing in Parts II to IV of the 1975 Act shall render unlawful any act done by a person in connection with the employment of another person as the head teacher or principal of any educational establishment if it was necessary for that person to do that act in order to comply with any requirement of any instrument relating to the establishment that its head teacher or principal should be a member of a particular religious order.

(2) Nothing in—

(a) Part II of the 1975 Act, or

(b) Part IV of that Act so far as it has effect in relation to Part II,

shall render unlawful any act done by a person in connection with the employment of another person as a professor in any university if the professorship in question is, in accordance with any Act or instrument relating to the university, either a canon professorship or one to which a canonry is annexed.

(3) Nothing in the provisions of the 1975 Act referred to in subsection (2)(a) or (b) shall render unlawful any act done by a person in connection with the employment of another person as the head, a fellow or any other member of the academic staff of any college, or institution in the nature of a college, in a university if it was necessary for that person to do that act in order to comply with any requirement of any instrument relating to the college or institution that the holder of the position in question should be a woman.

(4) Subsection (3) shall not apply in relation to instruments taking effect after the commencement of that subsection; and section 6(b) of the Interpretation Act 1978 (words importing the feminine gender to include the masculine) shall not apply to that subsection.

(5) The Secretary of State may by order provide that any provision of subsections (1) to (3) shall not have effect in relation to—

(a) any educational establishment or university specified in the order; or

(b) any class or description of educational establishments so specified.

(6) In this section "educational establishment" means—

(a) any school within the meaning of the Education Act 1944 or the Education (Scotland) Act 1980;

(b) any college, or institution in the nature of a college, in a university; or

[(ba) any institution designated by order under section 28 of the Further and Higher Education Act 1992]

[(c) any institution designated by order made or having effect as if made under section 129 of the Education Reform Act 1988.]

(7) Nothing in this section shall be construed as prejudicing the operation of section 19 of the 1975 Act (exemption for discrimination in relation to employment of ministers of religion).   **[571]**

NOTES
Commencement: 16 January 1990 (s 30(3)).
Sub-s (6): para (ba) inserted, and para (c) substituted, by the Further and Higher Education Act 1992,
s 93, Sch 8, Pt II, para 93.

6 Power of Secretary of State to exempt particular acts of discrimination required by or under statute

(1) The Secretary of State may by order make such provision as he considers appropriate—

   (a) for disapplying subsection (1) of section 1 above in the case of any provision to which it appears to him that that subsection would otherwise apply;

   (b) for rendering lawful under any of the provisions of the 1975 Act falling within section 1(2) above acts done in order to comply with any requirement—

      (i) of a provision whose effect is preserved by virtue of paragraph (a) above, or

      (ii) of an instrument approved or made by or under an Act passed after the 1975 Act but before this Act (including one approved or made after the passing of this Act).

(2) Where an Act passed after this Act re-enacts (with or without modification) a provision of an Act passed as mentioned in sub-paragraph (ii) of subsection (1)(b), that provision as re-enacted shall be treated for the purposes of that sub-paragraph as if it continued to be contained in an Act passed as mentioned in that sub-paragraph.

[572]

NOTES
Commencement: 16 January 1990 (s 30(3)).
Order under this section: the Sex Discrimination Act 1975 (Exemption of Police Federation
Constitutional and Electoral Arrangements) Order 1989, SI 1989/2420.

Discrimination as respects training

7 (*Substitutes the Sex Discrimination Act 1975, s 14, substitutes the Race Relations Act 1976, s 13 and amends s 37 of the 1976 Act.*)

8 Power to exempt discrimination in favour of lone parents in connection with training

(1) The Secretary of State may by order provide with respect to—

   (a) any specified arrangements made under section 2 of the Employment and Training Act 1973 (functions of the Secretary of State as respects employment and training) [or under section 2(3) of the Enterprise and New Towns (Scotland) Act 1990 (arrangements by Scottish Enterprise and Highlands and Islands Enterprise in connection with training etc)], or

   (b) any specified class or description of training for employment provided otherwise than in pursuance of [either of those sections], or

   (c) any specified scheme set up under section 1 of the Employment Subsidies Act 1978 (schemes for financing employment),

that this section shall apply to such special treatment afforded to or in respect of lone parents in connection with their participation in those arrangements, or in that training or scheme, as is specified or referred to in the order.

(2) Where this section applies to any treatment afforded to or in respect of lone parents, neither the treatment so afforded nor any act done in the implementation of any such treatment shall be regarded for the purposes of the 1975 Act as giving rise to any discrimination falling within section 3 of that Act (discrimination against married persons for purposes of Part II of that Act).

(3) An order under subsection (1) above may specify or refer to special treatment afforded as mentioned in that subsection—

(a) whether it is afforded by the making of any payment or by the fixing of special conditions for participation in the arrangements, training or scheme in question, or otherwise, and

(b) whether it is afforded by the Secretary of State or by some other person;

and, without prejudice to the generality of paragraph (b) of that subsection, any class or description of training for employment specified in such an order by virtue of that paragraph may be framed by reference to the person, or the class or description of persons, by whom the training is provided.

(4) In this section—

(a) "employment" and "training" have the same meaning as in the Employment and Training Act 1973; and

(b) "lone parent" has the same meaning as it has for the purposes of any regulations made in pursuance of section 20(1)(a) of the Social Security Act 1986 (income support). **[573]**

NOTES

Commencement: 16 November 1989 (s 30(2)).

Sub-s (1): words in square brackets in para (a) inserted, and words in square brackets in para (b) substituted, by the Enterprise and New Towns (Scotland) Act 1990, s 38(1), Sch 4, para 18.

Order under this section: Sex Discrimination Act (Exemption of Special Treatment for Lone Parents) Orders 1989, 1991, SI 1989/2140, SI 1991/2813.

Removal of restrictions and other requirements relating to employment

9 Repeal or modification of provisions requiring different treatment of different categories of employees

(1) In sections 42(1), 43 and 44 of the Mines and Quarries Act 1954 (under which winding and rope haulage apparatus and conveyors are to be operated by or under the supervision of competent male persons who have attained the ages there specified), the word "male" shall be omitted wherever occurring.

(2) In section 93 of that Act (prohibition on heavy work by any woman or young person), the words "woman or young" shall be omitted in both places where they occur.

(3) Section 124(1) of that Act (prohibition on employment of woman in job requiring a significant proportion of the employee's time to be spent underground) shall cease to have effect.

(4) In section 20 of the Factories Act 1961 (prohibition on cleaning of machinery by any woman or young person), the words "woman or" shall be omitted in both places where they occur.

(5) In section 17 of the Offices, Shops and Railway Premises Act 1963 (fencing of exposed parts of machinery)—

(a) subsection (3),

(b) in subsection (4), the words from ", except when any" onwards, and

    (c) subsection (5),

shall cease to have effect.

    (6) In Schedule 2 to this Act—

      (a) the provisions of subordinate legislation listed in Part I (which require different treatment of different categories of employees) shall cease to have effect; and

      (b) the provisions of such legislation mentioned in Part II shall have effect subject to the amendments there specified (which assimilate the treatment of different categories of employees).   **[574]**

NOTES
    Commencement: sub-ss (1), (2), (4)–(6): 16 January 1990 (s 30(3)); sub-s (3): 26 February 1990 (SI 1990/189).

10 Removal of restrictions relating to employment of young persons

    (1) The following enactments, namely—

      (a) the enactments listed in Part I of Schedule 3 (which impose prohibitions or requirements with respect to the hours of employment and holidays of young persons and with respect to related matters), and

      (b) the enactments listed in Part II of that Schedule (which impose other prohibitions or requirements for, or in connection with, regulating the employment of young persons),

shall cease to have effect.

    (2) The enactments mentioned in Part III of Schedule 3 shall have effect subject to the amendments there specified (which include amendments by virtue of which certain occupations, instead of being restricted to persons who are 16 or older, are restricted to persons over school-leaving age).

    (3) If the Secretary of State considers it appropriate to do so, he may by order—

      (a) repeal or amend any statutory provision in consequence of subsection (1) or (2);

      (b) repeal any statutory provision relating to the employment of persons, or any class of persons, who have not attained the age of 18 or (as the case may be) some specified lower age of not less than 16;

      (c) amend any statutory provision falling within paragraph (b) and framed by reference to a specified age expressed as a number of years so that it is instead framed by reference to school-leaving age;

      (d) repeal any statutory provision appearing to the Secretary of State to be unnecessary in view of any other such provision, being a provision relating to the employment of persons under school-leaving age.

    (4) Nothing in any order under subsection (3) (apart from a repeal effected by virtue of paragraph (d) of that subsection) shall affect any statutory provision relating to the employment of persons under school-leaving age.

    (5) Any reference in subsection (3)(d) or (4) to a statutory provision relating to the employment of persons under school-leaving age shall be construed, in relation to a statutory provision which relates to both—

      (a) the employment of such persons, and

      (b) the employment of persons over that age,

as a reference to so much of that provision as relates to the employment of persons under that age.

(6) In this section—

"school-leaving age" means—

    (a) in relation to England and Wales, the upper limit of compulsory school age for the purposes of the Education Act 1944;

    (b) in relation to Scotland, the upper limit of school age for the purposes of the Education (Scotland) Act 1980; and

    (c) in relation to Northern Ireland, the upper limit of compulsory school age for the purposes of the Education and Libraries (Northern Ireland) Order 1986; and

"statutory provision" means a provision of an Act or of subordinate legislation (and references to the repeal of a statutory provision shall be construed accordingly).   [575]

NOTES

Commencement: sub-s (1)(a), those parts of sub-s (1)(b) not mentioned below, sub-s (2): 16 January 1990 (s 30(3)); sub-s (1)(b) in relation to the repeal made by Sch 3, Pt II, to the Employment of Women, Young Persons and Children Act 1920: 26 February 1990 (SI 1990/189); sub-s (1)(b) in relation to the repeal made by Sch 3, Pt II, of s 119A of the Factories Act 1961: to be appointed; sub-ss (3)–(6): 16 November 1989 (s 30(2)).

Order under this section: Employment Act 1989 Amendment and Revocation Order 1989, SI 1989/2311.

11 Exemption of Sikhs from requirements as to wearing of safety helmets on construction sites

(1) Any requirement to wear a safety helmet which (apart from this section) would, by virtue of any statutory provision or rule of law, be imposed on a Sikh who is on a construction site shall not apply to him at any time when he is wearing a turban.

(2) Accordingly, where—

    (a) a Sikh who is on a construction site is for the time being wearing a turban, and

    (b) (apart from this section) any associated requirement would, by virtue of any statutory provision or rule of law, be imposed—

        (i) on the Sikh, or

        (ii) on any other person,

    in connection with the wearing by the Sikh of a safety helmet,

that requirement shall not apply to the Sikh or (as the case may be) to that other person.

(3) In subsection (2) "associated requirement" means any requirement (other than one falling within subsection (1)) which is related to or connected with the wearing, provision or maintenance of safety helmets.

(4) It is hereby declared that, where a person does not comply with any requirement, being a requirement which for the time being does not apply to him by virtue of subsection (1) or (2)—

    (a) he shall not be liable in tort to any person in respect of any injury, loss or damage caused by his failure to comply with that requirement; and

    (b) in Scotland no action for reparation shall be brought against him by any person in respect of any such injury, loss or damage.

(5) If a Sikh who is on a construction site—

    (a) does not comply with any requirement to wear a safety helmet, being a requirement which for the time being does not apply to him by virtue of subsection (1), and

(b) in consequence of any act or omission of some other person sustains any injury, loss or damage which is to any extent attributable to the fact that he is not wearing a safety helmet in compliance with the requirement,

that other person shall, if liable to the Sikh in tort (or, in Scotland, in an action for reparation), be so liable only to the extent that injury, loss or damage would have been sustained by the Sikh even if he had been wearing a safety helmet in compliance with the requirement.

(6) Where—

(a) the act or omission referred to in subsection (5) causes the death of the Sikh, and

(b) the Sikh would have sustained some injury (other than loss of life) in consequence of the act or omission even if he had been wearing a safety helmet in compliance with the requirement in question,

the amount of any damages which, by virtue of that subsection, are recoverable in tort (or, in Scotland, in an action for reparation) in respect of that injury shall not exceed the amount of any damages which would (apart from that subsection) be so recoverable in respect of the Sikh's death.

(7) In this section—

"building operations" and "works of engineering construction" have the same meaning as in the Factories Act 1961;

"construction site" means any place where any building operations or works of engineering construction are being undertaken;

"injury" includes loss of life, any impairment of a person's physical or mental condition and any disease;

"safety helmet" means any form of protective headgear; and

"statutory provision" means a provision of an Act or of subordinate legislation.

(8) In this section—

(a) any reference to a Sikh is a reference to a follower of the Sikh religion; and

(b) any reference to a Sikh being on a construction site is a reference to his being there whether while at work or otherwise.

(9) This section shall have effect in relation to any relevant construction site within the territorial sea adjacent to Great Britain as it has effect in relation to any construction site within Great Britain.

(10) In subsection (9) "relevant construction site" means any construction site where there are being undertaken any building operations or works of engineering construction which are activities falling within Article 7(a) of the Health and Safety at Work etc Act 1974 (Application outside Great Britain) Order 1989.   **[576]**

NOTE

Commencement: 16 November 1989 (s 30(2)).

12 Protection of Sikhs from racial discrimination in connection with requirements as to wearing of safety helmets

(1) Where—

(a) any person applies to a Sikh any requirement or condition relating to the wearing by him of a safety helmet while he is on a construction site, and

(b) at the time when he so applies the requirement or condition that person has no reasonable grounds for believing that the Sikh would not wear a turban at all times when on such a site, then, for the purpose of determining whether the application of the requirement or condition to the Sikh constitutes an act of discrimination falling within section 1(1)(b) of the Race Relations Act 1976 (indirect racial discrimination), the requirement or condition shall be taken to be one which cannot be shown to be justifiable as mentioned in sub-paragraph (ii) of that provision.

(2) Any special treatment afforded to a Sikh in consequence of section 11(1) or (2) above shall not be regarded for the purposes of the Race Relations Act 1976 as giving rise, in relation to any other person, to any discrimination falling within section 1 of that Act.

(3) Subsections (7) to (10) of section 11 above shall apply for the purposes of this section as they apply for the purposes of that section.   **[577]**

NOTE

Commencement: 16 November 1989 (s 30(2)).

13–26 (*Ss 13–20 repeal, substitute, insert or amend the Employment Protection (Consolidation) Act 1978, ss 2, 2A, 4, 5, 27, 53, 149, 82, 104, 104A, 122, 125, 139, Schs 4, 6, 9; s 14 repealed by the Trade Union and Labour Relations (Consolidation) Act 1992, s 300(1), Sch 1; s 21 repeals the Celluloid and Cinematograph Film Act 1922, s 1(1)(a); ss 22 (dissolution of Training Commission), 23–25 (Industrial Training Boards), 26 (Skills Training Agency) omitted.*)

General

27 ((*Power to legislate for Northern Ireland) omitted.*)

28 Orders

(1) Any power to make an order under this Act shall be exercisable by statutory instrument.

(2) The Secretary of State shall consult the Equal Opportunities Commission before making—

  (a) an order under section 2 which makes any amendment or repeal of any provision of an Act, or

  (b) an order under section 6.

(3) An order of one of the following descriptions, namely—

  (a) such an order under section 2 as is mentioned in subsection (2)(a), or

  (b) an order under section 6(1)(a) which preserves the effect of any provision of an Act,

shall not be made unless a draft of it has been laid before and approved by resolution of each House of Parliament.

(4) Any statutory instrument containing an order under this Act other than—

  (a) an order to which subsection (3) applies,

  (b) an order under section 26, or

  (c) an order under section 30,

shall be subject to annulment in pursuance of a resolution of either House of Parliament.

(5) An order under this Act may contain such consequential or transitional provisions or savings as appear to the Secretary of State to be necessary or expedient. **[578]**

NOTE
Commencement: 16 November 1989 (s 30(2)).

29 Interpretation, minor and consequential amendments, repeals, etc

(1) In this Act—

"the 1975 Act" means the Sex Discrimination Act 1975;
"the 1978 Act" means the Employment Protection (Consolidation) Act 1978;
"act" includes a deliberate omission;
"subordinate legislation" has the same meaning as in the Interpretation Act 1978;
"vocational training" includes advanced vocational training and retraining.

(2) Any reference in this Act to vocational training shall be construed as including a reference to vocational guidance.

(3) The enactments mentioned in Schedule 6 shall have effect subject to the minor and consequential amendments specified in that Schedule.

(4) The enactments mentioned in Schedule 7 (which include some spent provisions) are hereby repealed to the extent specified in the third column of that Schedule.

(5) The instruments mentioned in Schedule 8 are hereby revoked to the extent specified in the third column of that Schedule.

(6) The transitional provisions and savings contained in Schedule 9 shall have effect. **[579]**

NOTE
Commencement: Sub-ss (1), (2), (6): 16 November 1989 (s 30(2)); sub-ss (3), (4): see SI 1990/189; otherwise not in force; sub-s (5): 16 January 1990 (s 30(3)).

30 Short title, commencement and extent

(1) This Act may be cited as the Employment Act 1989.

(2) The following provisions shall come into force on the day on which this Act is passed, namely—

    (a) section 8;
    (b) section 10(3) to (6);
    (c) sections 11 and 12;
    (d) section 22 and Schedules 4 and 5;
    (e) sections 23 to 28;
    (f) section 29(1) and (2);
    (g) paragraphs 9 to 15, 17 and 27 to 29 of Schedule 6 and section 29(3) so far as relating thereto;
    (h) Part I of Schedule 7 and section 29(4) so far as relating thereto;
    (i) section 29(6) and Schedule 9; and
    (j) this section.

(3) The following provisions shall come into force at the end of the period of two months beginning with the day on which this Act is passed, namely—

    (a) sections 1 to 6 and Schedule 1;
    (b) section 7;

(c) section 9(1), (2) and (4) to (6) and Schedule 2;
(d) section 10(1) and Parts I and II of Schedule 3 except so far as they repeal section 1(3) of, and Part II of the Schedule to, the Employment of Women, Young Persons, and Children Act 1920 and section 119A of the Factories Act 1961;
(e) section 10(2) and Part III of Schedule 3;
(f) sections 16 to 19;
(g) section 21;
(h) paragraphs 3 to 5, 7, 8, 16, 20 to 25 and 30 of Schedule 6 and section 29(3) so far as relating thereto;
(i) Part II of Schedule 7 and section 29(4) so far as relating thereto; and
(j) section 29(5) and Schedule 8.

(4) The remainder of this Act shall come into force on such day as the Secretary of State may appoint by order, and different days may be appointed for different provisions or for different purposes.

(5) With the exception of the provisions mentioned in subsection (6), this Act does not extend to Northern Ireland.

(6) Those provisions are—
(a) sections 10(1) and (2) and 29(3) and (4) and Schedules 3, 6 and 7 so far as they amend or repeal any enactment which extends to Northern Ireland (other than an enactment contained in the Celluloid and Cinematograph Film Act 1922);
(b) section 10(6);
(c) paragraph 2 of Schedule 5 and section 22(5) so far as relating thereto;
(d) section 27 (which extends only to Northern Ireland); and
(e) this section.   **[580]**

NOTE
Commencement: 16 November 1989 (sub-s (2)(j)).

SCHEDULES

SCHEDULE 1
Section 4

PROVISIONS CONCERNED WITH PROTECTION OF WOMEN AT WORK

Enactments

Section 61 of the Factory and Workshop Act 1901, as set out in Schedule 5 to the Factories Act 1961.

Section 205 of the Public Health Act 1936.

Sections 74, 128 and 131 of the Factories Act 1961.

Statutory instruments

Regulation 3 of the Regulations dated 21st January 1907 (Manufacture of paints and colours).

Regulation 10 of the Regulations dated 12th August 1911 (Smelting of materials containing lead, the manufacture of red or orange lead, and the manufacture of flaked litharge).

Regulation 1 of the Indiarubber Regulations 1922.

Regulation 1(ii) of the Electric Accumulator Regulations 1925.

Regulation 6(1)(i) to (vi) of the Pottery (Health and Welfare) Special Regulations 1950.

Parts IV and V of Schedule 1 to the Ionising Radiations Regulations 1985.

Article 20(8) of the Air Navigation Order 1985 so far as relating to pregnancy.

Other instruments

Paragraph 118 of the Approved Code of Practice relating to the Control of Lead at Work Regulations 1980 (approved under section 16 of the Health and Safety at Work etc Act 1974).

The following provisions of the medical standards contained in Merchant Shipping Notice No M 1331 (issued for the purposes of Regulation 7 of the Merchant Shipping (Medical Examination) Regulations 1983), namely—

    (a) Part X so far as relating to gynaecological conditions, and

    (b) Part XI.   **[581]**

NOTE
    Commencement: 16 January 1990 (s 30(3)(a)).

SCHEDULE 2

Section 9

REVOCATION ETC OF SUBORDINATE LEGISLATION REQUIRING DIFFERENT REATMENT OF CERTAIN EMPLOYEES

PART I

PROVISIONS REVOKED

Article 2 of the Order dated 5th October 1917 (Tin or terne plate factories).

The Woollen and Worsted Textiles (Lifting of Heavy Weights) Regulations 1926.

Article 1(d) of the Cement Works Welfare Order 1930.

Regulation 4 of the Jute (Safety, Health and Welfare) Regulations 1948.

Regulations 6(1)(x), 6(2), 6(5), 6(6) and 18(7) of the Pottery (Health and Welfare) Special Regulations 1950.   **[582]**

NOTE
    Commencement: 16 January 1990 (s 30(3)(c)).

(*Pt II amends SR & O 1905/1103, regs 4, 12, SI 1956/1776, Schedule, SI 1956/1778, Sch 1 and SI 1958/2110, reg 13.*)

SCHEDULE 3

Section 10

REMOVAL OF RESTRICTIONS RELATING TO EMPLOYMENT OF YOUNG PERSONS

PART I

REPEALS RELATING TO RESTRICTIONS TO EMPLOYMENT OF YOUNG PERSONS

Section 1(3) of, and Part II of the Schedule to, the Employment of Women, Young Persons, and Children Act 1920 (employment of young persons in industrial undertakings at night).

Section 19 of the Children and Young Persons Act 1933 (power of local authority to make byelaws with respect to employment of persons under 18 other than children).

Section 29 of the Children and Young Persons (Scotland) Act 1937 (power of education authority to make byelaws with respect to employment of persons under 18 other than children).

Part I of the Young Persons (Employment) Act 1938 (hours of employment and holidays of young persons in certain occupations).

The following provisions of the Shops Act 1950—

section 18 (special provisions as to half-holidays for young persons);
section 20 and Part II of Schedule 3 (special provisions as to meal times for young persons);
sections 24 to 36 (hours of employment of young persons);
section 68 (option to apply either the Act or the Young Persons (Employment) Act 1938 in certain cases); and
section 72 (enforcement by local authorities under Children and Young Persons Act 1933).

The following provisions of the Mines and Quarries Act 1954—

sections 125 to 128 (hours of employment of young persons);
section 130 (special exception for emergencies); and
section 132 (supplemental provisions).

The following provisions of the Factories Act 1961—

sections 86 to 94 (hours of employment and holidays of young persons);
sections 96 to 109 and 112 to 115 (suspension of, and exceptions from, provisions as to hours of employment etc);
section 116 (regulation of employment of young persons in certain occupations);
section 138(1)(d) (posting of notices); and
section 140(1)(d) (general registers).   [583]

NOTES

Commencement: except first repeal: 16 January 1990 (s 30(3)(d)); first repeal: 26 February 1990 (SI 1990/189).

PART II

REPEALS RELATING TO OTHER REQUIREMENTS

The following provisions of the Mines and Quarries Act 1954—

section 124(2) (restriction on male young persons being employed below ground); and
section 131 (register of women and young persons employed).

The following provisions of the Factories Act 1961—

section 11(1)(a)(iii) (power to require medical supervision);
section 73(1) (prohibition on employment of female young persons where certain processes are carried on); and
section 119A (duty of factory occupier to give notice of employment of young persons).

[584]

NOTES

Commencement: all except repeal of Factories Act 1961, s 119A: 16 January 1990 (s 30(3)(d)); repeal of Factories Act 1961, s 119A: to be appointed.

(Pt III amends the Employment of Women, Young Persons and Children Act 1920, the Children and Young Persons Act 1933, the Children and Young Persons (Scotland) Act 1937, the Factories Act 1961; Schs 4, 5 (dissolution of Training Commission), 6–8 (minor and consequential amendments, repeals and revocations) omitted.)

SCHEDULE 9

Section 29(6)

TRANSITIONAL PROVISIONS AND SAVINGS

Sex discrimination

1 Nothing in section 3 of this Act shall render unlawful any act done by any person if—

(a)   it was done before the commencement of that section, or
(b)   it was done before the commencement of section 9(3) of this Act and it was

necessary for him to do it in order to comply with section 124(1) of the Mines and Quarries Act 1954.

Time off for trade union duties

2 ...

Redundancy payments: assimilation of age limits

3 (1) The amendments made by section 16 of this Act shall not have effect in relation to an employee in whose case the relevant date (as defined in sub-paragraph (2)) falls before the commencement of that section.

(2) In sub-paragraph (1) "the relevant date" means the date which for the purposes of section 81(4) of the 1978 Act is the relevant date in the case of the employee by virtue of any provision of section 90 of that Act.

Redundancy rebates

4 (1) Nothing in this Act shall affect the continued operation of any provision of the 1978 Act for the purposes of, or in connection with, the payment of a redundancy rebate under section 104 of that Act in a case where—

   (a)   a claim for the rebate has been made in accordance with regulations under section 104(5) before the commencement of section 17 of this Act, or

   (b)   notwithstanding that such a claim has not been so made, the rebate is in respect of any payment falling within section 104(1)(a) or (b) in relation to which the relevant date (as defined in sub-paragraph (2)) falls before the commencement of section 17.

(2) In sub-paragraph (1)(b) "the relevant date"—

   (a)   in the case of a payment falling within section 104(1)(a), means the date which for the purposes of section 81(4) of the 1978 Act is the relevant date in relation to that payment by virtue of any provision of section 90 of that Act, and

   (b)   in the case of a payment falling within section 104(1)(b), means the date on which the termination of the employee's contract of employment is treated as having taken effect for the purposes of the agreement referred to in that provision.

Insolvency payments

5 The amendments made by section 19 of this Act shall not have effect in relation to any payment made in pursuance of section 122 or 123 of the 1978 Act in a case where the employer became insolvent before the commencement of section 19 of this Act.

Appointments to industrial training boards

6 ...   **[585]**

NOTES
Commencement: 16 November 1989 (s 30(2)).
Para 2: repealed by the Trade Union and Labour Relations (Consolidation) Act 1992, s 300(1), Sch 1.
Para 6 (appointments to Industrial Training Boards) omitted.

NATIONAL HEALTH SERVICE AND COMMUNITY CARE ACT 1990

(1990 c 19)

An Act to make further provision about health authorities and other bodies consti-tuted in accordance with the National Health Service Act 1977; to provide for the establishment of National Health Service trusts; to make further provision about the financing of the practices of medical practitioners; to amend Part VII of the Local Government (Scotland) Act 1973 and Part III of the Local Government Finance Act 1982; to amend the National Health Service Act 1977 and the National Health Service (Scotland) Act 1978; to amend Part VIII of the Mental Health (Scotland) Act 1984; to make further provision concerning the provision of accommodation and other welfare services by local authorities and the powers of the Secretary of State as respects the social services functions of such authorities; to make provision for and in connection with the establishment of a Clinical Standards Advisory Group; to repeal the Health Services Act 1976; and for connected purposes

[29 June 1990]

GENERAL NOTE
Only those provisions which deal with transfer of staff on the creation of NHS trusts are reproduced here. Those sections came into force on 5 July 1990 (SI 1990/1329) and do not extend to Scotland.

PART I

THE NATIONAL HEALTH SERVICE: ENGLAND AND WALES

National Health Service trusts

6 Transfer of staff to NHS trusts

(1) Subject to subsection (5) below, this section applies to any person who, immediately before an NHS trust's operational date—

    (a) is employed by a health authority to work solely at, or for the purposes of, a hospital or other establishment or facility which is to become the responsibility of the trust; or

    (b) is employed by a health authority to work at, or for the purposes of, such a hospital, establishment or facility and is designated for the purposes of this section by a scheme made by the health authority specified as mentioned in paragraph 3(1)(f) of Schedule 2 to this Act.

(2) A scheme under this section shall not have effect unless approved by the Secretary of State.

(3) Subject to section 7 below, the contract of employment between a person to whom this section applies and the health authority by whom he is employed shall have effect from the operational date as if originally made between him and the NHS trust.

(4) Without prejudice to subsection (3) above—

    (a) all the health authority's rights, powers, duties and liabilities under or in connection with a contract to which that subsection applies shall by virtue of this section be transferred to the NHS trust on its operational date; and

    (b) anything done before that date by or in relation to the health authority in respect of that contract or the employee shall be deemed from that date to have been done by or in relation to the NHS trust.

(5) In any case where—

    (a) an order under section 5(1) above provides for the establishment of an NHS trust with effect from a date earlier than the operational date of the trust, and

    (b) on or after that earlier date but before its operational date the NHS trust makes an offer of employment by the trust to a person who at that time is employed by a health authority to work (whether solely or otherwise) at,

or for the purposes of, the hospital or other establishment or facility which
is to become the responsibility of the trust, and

(c) as a result of the acceptance of the offer, the person to whom it was made
becomes an employee of the NHS trust,

subsections (3) and (4) above shall have effect in relation to that person's contract of
employment as if he were a person to whom this section applies and any reference
in those subsections to the operational date of the trust were a reference to the date
on which he takes up employment with the trust.

(6) Subsections (3) and (4) above are without prejudice to any right of an
employee to terminate his contract of employment if a substantial change is made to
his detriment in his working conditions; but no such right shall arise by reason only
of the change in employer effected by this section.

(7) A scheme under this section may designate a person either individually or as
a member of a class or description of employees.   **[586]**

NOTES
Commencement: 5 July 1990 (SI 1990/1329).
This section does not extend to Scotland.

7 Supplementary provisions as to transfer of staff

(1) In the case of a person who falls within section 6(1)(b) above, a scheme under
that section may provide that, with effect from the NHS trust's operational date, his
contract of employment (in this section referred to as "his original contract") shall be
treated in accordance with the scheme as divided so as to constitute—

(a) a contract of employment with the NHS trust: and
(b) a contract of employment with the health authority by whom he was
employed before that date (in this section referred to as "the transferor
authority").

(2) Where a scheme makes provision as mentioned in subsection (1) above,—

(a) the scheme shall secure that the benefits to the employee under the two
contracts referred to in that subsection, when taken together, are not less
favourable than the benefits under his original contract;

(b) section 6 above shall apply in relation to the contract referred to in
subsection (1)(a) above as if it were a contract transferred under that
section from the transferor authority to the NHS trust;

(c) so far as necessary to preserve any rights and obligations, the contract
referred to in subsection (1)(b) above shall be regarded as a continuation
of the employee's original contract; and

(d) for the purposes of section 146 of and Schedule 13 to the Employment
Protection (Consolidation) Act 1978, the number of hours normally
worked, or, as the case may be, the hours for which the employee is
employed in any week under either of those contracts shall be taken to be
the total of the hours normally worked or, as the case may be, for which
he is employed under the two contracts taken together.

(3) Where, as a result of the provisions of section 6 above, by virtue of his
employment during any period after the operational date of the NHS trust,—

(a) an employee has contractual rights against an NHS trust to benefits in the
event of his redundancy, and

(b) he also has statutory rights against the trust under Part VI of the Employment Protection (Consolidation) Act 1978 (redundancy payments),

any benefits provided to him by virtue of the contractual rights referred to in paragraph (a) above shall be taken as satisfying his entitlement to benefits under the said Part VI.   **[587]**

NOTES
Commencement: 5 July 1990 (SI 1990/1329).
This section does not extend to Scotland.

CONTRACTS (APPLICABLE LAW) ACT 1990

(1990 c 36)

ARRANGEMENT OF SECTIONS

An Act to make provision as to the law applicable to contractual obligations in the case of conflict of laws

[26 July 1990]

NOTE
This Act is included for its provisions as to the applicable law of contracts of employment only, and other provisions of the Act and of the Rome Convention are omitted. So far as relevant, the Act came into force on 1 April 1991.

1 Meaning of "the Conventions"

In this Act—

(a) "the Rome Convention" means the Convention on the law applicable to contractual obligations opened for signature in Rome on 19th June 1980 and signed by the United Kingdom on 7th December 1981;

(b) "the Luxembourg Convention" means the Convention on the accession of the Hellenic Republic to the Rome Convention signed by the United Kingdom in Luxembourg on 10th April 1984; and

(c) "the Brussels Protocol" means the first Protocol on the interpretation of the Rome Convention by the European Court signed by the United Kingdom in Brussels on 19th December 1988;

and the Rome Convention, the Luxembourg Convention and the Brussels Protocol are together referred to as "the Conventions".   **[588]**

NOTE
Commencement: 1 April 1991 (SI 1991/707).

2 Conventions to have force of law

(1) Subject to subsections (2) and (3) below, the Conventions shall have the force of law in the United Kingdom.

[(1A) The provisions of Schedule 3A to the Insurance Companies Act 1982 (law applicable to certain contracts of insurance) are the internal law for the purposes of Article 1(3) of the Rome Convention.]

(2) Articles 7(1) and 10(1)(e) of the Rome Convention shall not have the force of law in the United Kingdom.

(3) Notwithstanding Article 19(2) of the Rome Convention, the Conventions shall apply in the case of conflicts between the laws of different parts of the United Kingdom.

(4) For ease of reference there are set out in Schedules 1, 2 and 3 to this Act respectively the English texts of—

    (a) the Rome Convention;

    (b) the Luxembourg Convention; and

    (c) the Brussels Protocol.   **[589]**

NOTES
Commencement: 1 April 1991 (sub-s (1) (in so far as relates to the Rome Convention and the Luxembourg Convention), sub-ss (2)–(4)) (SI 1991/707); remainder not yet in force.
Sub-s (1A): inserted by the Insurance Companies (Amendment) Regulations 1993, SI 1993/174, reg 9.

3 Interpretation of Conventions

(1) Any question as to the meaning or effect of any provision of the Conventions shall, if not referred to the European Court in accordance with the Brussels Protocol, be determined in accordance with the principles laid down by, and any relevant decision of, the European Court.

(2) Judicial notice shall be taken of any decision of, or expression of opinion by, the European Court on any such question.

(3) Without prejudice to any practice of the courts as to the matters which may be considered apart from this subsection—

    (a) the report on the Rome Convention by Professor Mario Giuliano and Professor Paul Lagarde which is reproduced in the Official Journal of the Communities of 31st October 1980 may be considered in ascertaining the meaning or effect of any provision of that Convention; and

    (b) any report on the Brussels Protocol which is reproduced in the Official Journal of the Communities may be considered in ascertaining the meaning or effect of any provision of that Protocol.   **[590–595]**

NOTE
Commencement: 1 April 1991 (sub-s (3)(a)) (SI 1991/707); remainder not yet in force.

4–9 (*Ss 4–9 omitted. By s 6, this Act binds the Crown.*)

SCHEDULES

SCHEDULE 1

Section 2

THE ROME CONVENTION

The High Contracting Parties to the Treaty establishing the European Economic Community,

Anxious to continue in the field of private international law the work of unification of law which has already been done within the Community, in particular in the field of jurisdiction and enforcement of judgments,

Wishing to establish uniform rules concerning the law applicable to contractual obligations,

Have agreed as follows:

TITLE I
SCOPE OF THE CONVENTION

Article 1

Scope of the Convention

1 The rules of this Convention shall apply to contractual obligations in any situation involving a choice between the laws of different countries.

2–4 ...

Article 2

Application of law of non-contracting States

Any law specified by this Convention shall be applied whether or not it is the law of a Contracting State.

TITLE II
UNIFORM RULES

Article 3

Freedom of choice

1 A contract shall be governed by the law chosen by the parties. The choice must be express or demonstrated with reasonable certainty by the terms of the contract or the circumstances of the case. By their choice the parties can select the law applicable to the whole or a part only of the contract.

2 The parties may at any time agree to subject the contract to a law other than that which previously governed it, whether as a result of an earlier choice under this Article or of other provisions of this Convention. Any variation by the parties of the law to be applied made after the conclusion of the contract shall not prejudice its formal validity under Article 9 or adversely affect the rights of third parties.

3 The fact that the parties have chosen a foreign law, whether or not accompanied by the choice of a foreign tribunal, shall not, where all the other elements relevant to the situation at the time of the choice are connected with one country only, prejudice the application of rules of the law of that country which cannot be derogated from by contract, hereinafter called "mandatory rules".

4 The existence and validity of the consent of the parties as to the choice of the applicable law shall be determined in accordance with the provisions of Articles 8, 9 and 11.

Article 4

Applicable law in the absence of choice

1 To the extent that the law applicable to the contract has not been chosen in accordance with Article 3, the contract shall be governed by the law of the country with which it is most closely connected. Nevertheless, a severable part of the contract which has a closer connection with another country may by way of exception be governed by the law of that other country.

2 Subject to the provisions of paragraph 5 of this Article, it shall be presumed that the contract is most closely connected with the country where the party who is to effect the performance which is characteristic of the contract has, at the time of conclusion of the contract, his habitual residence, or, in the case of a body corporate or unincorporate, its central administration. However, if the contract is entered into in the course of that party's trade or profession, that country shall be the country in which the principal place of business is situated or, where under the terms of the contract the performance is to be effected through a place of business other than the principal place of business, the country in which that other place of business is situated.

3, 4 . . .

5 Paragraph 2 shall not apply if the characteristic performance cannot be determined, and the presumptions in paragraphs 2, 3 and 4 shall be disregarded if it appears from the circumstances as a whole that the contract is more closely connected with another country.

(*Article 5 omitted.*)

Article 6

Individual employment contracts

1 Notwithstanding the provisions of Article 3, in a contract of employment a choice of law made by the parties shall not have the result of depriving the employee of the protection afforded to him by the mandatory rules of the law which would be applicable under paragraph 2 in the absence of choice.

2 Notwithstanding the provisions of Article 4, a contract of employment shall, in the absence of choice in accordance with Article 3, be governed:

(a) by the law of the country in which the employee habitually carries out his work in performance of the contract, even if he is temporarily employed in another country; or

(b) if the employee does not habitually carry out his work in any one country, by the law of the country in which the place of business through which he was engaged is situated;

unless it appears from the circumstances as a whole that the contract is more closely connected with another country, in which case the contract shall be governed by the law of that country.

Article 7

Mandatory rules

1 When applying under this Convention the law of a country, effect may be given to the mandatory rules of the law of another country with which the situation has a close connection, if and in so far as, under the law of the latter country, those rules must be applied whatever the law applicable to the contract. In considering whether to give effect to these mandatory rules, regard shall be had to their nature and purpose and to the consequences of their application or non-application.

2 Nothing in this Convention shall restrict the application of the rules of the law of the forum in a situation where they are mandatory irrespective of the law otherwise applicable to the contract.

(*Article 8 omitted.*)

Article 9

Formal validity

1 A contract concluded between persons who are in the same country is formally valid if it satisfies the formal requirements of the law which governs it under this Convention or of the law of the country where it is concluded.

2 A contract concluded between persons who are in different countries is formally valid if it satisfies the formal requirements of the law which governs it under this Convention or of the law of one of those countries.

3–6 . . .

Article 10

Scope of the applicable law

1 The law applicable to a contract by virtue of Articles 3 to 6 and 12 of this Convention shall govern in particular:

(a) interpretation;
(b) performance;
(c) within the limits of the powers conferred on the court by its procedural law, the consequences of breach, including the assessment of damages in so far as it is governed by rules of law;
(d) the various ways of extinguishing obligations, and prescription and limitation of actions;
(e) the consequences of nullity of the contract.

2 In relation to the manner of performance and the steps to be taken in the event of defective performance regard shall be had to the law of the country in which performance takes place.

(Articles 11–13 omitted.)

Article 14

Burden of proof, etc.

1 The law governing the contract under this Convention applies to the extent that it contains, in the law of contract, rules which raise presumptions of law or determine the burden of proof.

2 A contract or an act intended to have legal effect may be proved by any mode of proof recognised by the law of the forum or by any of the laws referred to in Article 9 under which that contract or act is formally valid, provided that such mode of proof can be administered by the forum.

(Articles 15, 16 omitted.)

Article 17

No retrospective effect

This Convention shall apply in a Contracting State to contracts made after the date on which this Convention has entered into force with respect to that State.

Article 18

Uniform interpretation

In the interpretation and application of the preceding uniform rules, regard shall be had to their international character and to the desirability of achieving uniformity in their interpretation and application.

Article 19

States with more than one legal system

1 Where a State comprises several territorial units each of which has its own rules of law in respect of contractual obligations, each territorial unit shall be considered as a country for the purposes of identifying the law applicable under this Convention.

2 A State within which different territorial units have their own rules of law in respect of contractual obligations shall not be bound to apply this Convention to conflicts solely between the laws of such units.

(Articles 20–22 omitted.)

TITLE III
FINAL PROVISIONS

(Articles 23–26 omitted.)

Article 27

1 This Convention shall apply to the European territories of the Contracting States, including Greenland, and to the entire territory of the French Republic.

2 Notwithstanding paragraph 1:
  (a) this Convention shall not apply to the Faroe Islands, unless the Kingdom of Denmark makes a declaration to the contrary;
  (b) this Convention shall not apply to any European territory situated outside the United Kingdom for the international relations of which the United Kingdom is responsible, unless the United Kingdom makes a declaration to the contrary in respect of any such territory;
  (c) this Convention shall apply to the Netherlands Antilles, if the Kingdom of the Netherlands makes a declaration to that effect.

3, 4 ...

(*Articles 28–33, Protocol omitted.*)   **[596]**

NOTE
Commencement: 1 April 1991 (SI 1991/707).

(*Schs 2–4 outside the scope of this work.*)

EMPLOYMENT ACT 1990
(1990 c 38)

ARRANGEMENT OF SECTIONS

Miscellaneous

An Act make it unlawful to refuse employment, or any service of an employment agency, on grounds related to trade union membership; to amend the law relating to industrial action and ballots; to make further provision with respect to the Commissioner for the Rights of Trade Union Members; to confer a power to revise or revoke Codes of Practice; to provide for the merger of the Redundancy Fund with the National Insurance Fund; to amend the Education (Work Experience) Act 1973; and for connected purposes

[1 November 1990]

1–11 (*Repealed by the Trade Union and Labour Relations (Consolidation) Act 1992, s 300(1), Sch 1.*)

Miscellaneous

12 (*Repealed by the Trade Union and Labour Relations (Consolidation) Act 1992, s 300(1), Sch 1.*)

13 Merger of Redundancy Fund with National Insurance Fund, &c

(1) The assets and liabilities of the Redundancy Fund shall become assets and liabilities of the National Insurance Fund and the Redundancy Fund shall cease to exist.

(2) The Secretary of State shall prepare an account (in such form as the Treasury may direct) showing the final state of the Redundancy Fund, and shall send a copy of it to the Comptroller and Auditor General who shall examine, certify and report on the account and lay copies of it and of his report before each House of Parliament.

(3) References to the Redundancy Fund in subordinate legislation (within the meaning of the Interpretation Act 1978) shall be construed as references to the National Insurance Fund.

(4) Section 105 of the Employment Protection (Consolidation) Act 1978 (power to make repayments where contributions paid in respect of certain employees not entitled to redundancy payment) shall cease to have effect. **[597]**

NOTES
Commencement: 1 February 1991 (SI 1990/2378).

14 (*(Amendment of the Education (Work Experience) Act 1973, s 1(4)) omitted.*)

General

15 Financial provision

There shall be paid out of money provided by Parliament any increase attributable to this Act in the sums so payable under any other Act. **[598]**

NOTES
Commencement: 1 November 1990 (s 18(2)).

16 Consequential amendments and repeals

(1) The enactments mentioned in Schedule 2 have effect with the amendments specified there, which are consequential on the provisions of this Act.

(2) The enactments mentioned in Schedule 3 are repealed to the extent specified there. **[599]**

NOTES
Commencement: 1 January 1991; 1 February 1991 (SI 1990/2378).

17 (*(Extension to Northern Ireland) omitted.*)

18 Short title and commencement

(1) This Act may be cited as the Employment Act 1990.

(2) The following provisions of this Act come into force on Royal Assent—

. . .

section 14 (period during which children may be employed for work experience), and

sections 15 and 17 and this section (general ancillary provisions).

(3) The other provisions of this Act come into force on such day as the Secretary of State may appoint by order made by statutory instrument and different days may be appointed for different provisions.

(4) An order bringing into force any provision may contain such transitional provisions and savings as appear to the Secretary of State to be appropriate.

[600–601]

NOTES
Commencement: 1 November 1990 (sub-s (2)).
Sub-s (2): words omitted repealed by the Trade Union and Labour Relations (Consolidation) Act 1992, s 300(1), Sch 1.

(*Sch 1 repealed by the Trade Union and Labour Relations (Consolidation) Act 1992, s 300(1), Sch 1; Schs 2, 3 (consequential amendments, repeals) omitted.*)

SCHOOL TEACHERS' PAY AND CONDITIONS ACT 1991

(1991 c 49)

ARRANGEMENT OF SECTIONS

An Act to make provision with respect to the remuneration and other conditions of employment of school teachers; and for connected purposes [25 July 1991]

1 Establishment of review body to consider statutory conditions of employment of school teachers

(1) The Prime Minister shall appoint a body (in this Act referred to as "the review body") to examine and report on such matters relating to the statutory conditions of employment of school teachers in England and Wales as may from time to time be referred to the review body by the Secretary of State.

(2) In this Act "statutory conditions of employment", in relation to any school teachers, means their remuneration and such of their other conditions of employment as relate to their professional duties and working time.

(3) Schedule 1 to this Act shall have effect with respect to the constitution and proceedings of the review body.

(4) With respect to matters referred to the review body by him, the Secretary of State may give directions to the review body as to considerations to which they are to have regard and as to the time within which they are to report; and any such directions may be varied or revoked by further directions under this section.

(5) Where a matter has been referred to the review body, they shall give notice of the matter and of any relevant direction—

(a) to such associations of local education authorities as appear to them to be concerned and to any local education authority with whom consultation appears to them to be desirable,

(b) to such bodies representing the interests of governors of voluntary schools and, subject to subsection (6) below, grant-maintained schools as appear to them to be concerned, and

(c) to such bodies representing school teachers as appear to them to be concerned,

and shall afford every such association, authority and other body and, where subsection (6) below applies, the persons referred to in that subsection a reasonable opportunity of submitting evidence and representations with respect to the issues arising.

(6) If, in a case where the review body are required to give notice as mentioned in subsection (5) above, it appears to them that there is neither a body which represents nor bodies which collectively represent the interests of those governors of grant-maintained schools who appear to the review body to be concerned, then, so far as concerns the interests of those governors, it shall be a sufficient compliance with the duty of the review body under paragraph (b) of that subsection if the notice is given to such persons, being governors of grant-maintained schools, as appear to the review body to be appropriate to be representative of all the governors concerned.

(7) Where a matter has been referred to the review body, their report shall contain their recommendations on that matter and such other advice relating to that matter as they think fit.

(8) The review body shall send any report made by them under this section to the Prime Minister and to the Secretary of State and, upon receiving a report, the Secretary of State shall arrange for it to be published. [602]

NOTE
Commencement: 22 August 1991 (SI 1991/1874).
This section does not extend to Scotland.

2 Orders relating to statutory conditions of employment

(1) Where, following the reference of any matters to them under section 1 above, the review body have made a report, the Secretary of State may, after consulting—

(a) such associations of local education authorities as appear to him to be concerned and any local education authority with whom consultation appears to him to be desirable,

(b) such bodies representing the interests of governors of voluntary schools and, subject to subsection (2) below, grant-maintained schools as appear to him to be concerned, and

(c) such bodies representing school teachers as appear to him to be concerned,

make provision by order giving effect to the recommendations of the review body, with or without modification, or making such other provision with respect to the matters referred to the review body as he thinks fit.

(2) If, in any case where the Secretary of State is required to consult as mentioned in subsection (1) above, it appears to him that there is neither a body which represents nor bodies which collectively represent the interests of those governors of grant-maintained schools who appear to him to be concerned, then, so far as concerns the interests of those governors, it shall be a sufficient compliance with his duty under

paragraph (b) of that subsection if he consults such persons, being governors of grant-maintained schools, as appear to him to be appropriate to be representative of all the governors concerned.

(3) An order under this section is in the following provisions of this Act referred to as a "pay and conditions order", and such an order shall either—

    (a) contain the provision to be made; or

    (b) refer to provisions set out in a document published by Her Majesty's Stationary Office and direct that those provisions shall have effect or, as the case may be, be amended in accordance with the order.

(4) A pay and conditions order may, in particular, as regards the statutory conditions of employment of school teachers do all or any of the following—

    (a) confer discretion on the local education authority or, in the case of a grant-maintained school, on the governing body of the school with respect to any matter and provide for the exercise of any such discretion, in relation to a school which has a delegated budget, by the governing body of the school;

    (b) make provision as to the aggregate amount of allowances payable to teachers in a school;

    (c) set lower and upper limits on the number or proportion of teachers in a school to be paid on specified scales or who are at any specified time to be paid any specified allowance;

    (d) provide for the designation of schools in relation to which special provisions apply;

    (e) provide for the determination of any questions arising as to the interpretation or application of the provisions set out or referred to in the order;

    (f) make provision which is retrospective, but not so as to require the reduction of a teacher's remuneration in respect of a past period or so as to alter for any past period any other statutory condition of employment to the detriment of a teacher;

    (g) provide that, to the extent specified in the order, matters may be settled by agreement between, or in a manner agreed between, teachers and local education authorities;

    (h) provide, in the case of grant-maintained schools, that, to the extent specified in the order, matters may be settled by agreement between, or in a manner agreed between, teachers in such schools and the governing bodies of such schools.

(5) Without prejudice to his power to make a pay and conditions order by virtue of subsection (1) above, after consulting the associations, authorities and other bodies referred to in paragraphs (a) to (c) of subsection (1) above and, where appropriate, such persons as are referred to in subsection (2) above, the Secretary of State may make a pay and conditions order by virtue of this subsection if—

    (a) it appears to the Secretary of State, following consultation with the chairman (or, in his absence, the deputy chairman) of the review body, that the provision proposed to be made by the order is not of so significant a nature that the matter to which it relates should be referred to the review body under section 1 above; and

    (b) it appears to the Secretary of State to be expedient to make the provision in question.

(6) Subject to section 3 below and to any amendment or revocation by a later pay and conditions order, the effect of a pay and conditions order is that,—

    (a) so far as it relates to remuneration, the remuneration of school teachers to whom the order applies shall be determined, and paid to school teachers by local education authorities or, in the case of school teachers in grant-maintained schools, by the governing bodies of such schools, in accordance with the scales and other provisions set out or referred to in the order; and

(b) so far as it relates to other statutory conditions of employment, the provisions set out or referred to in the order shall have effect as terms of the contracts of employment of school teachers to whom the order applies.

(7) Subject to section 3 below, so far as concerns his statutory conditions of employment, the contract of employment of a school teacher shall contain no terms other than those which have effect by virtue of a pay and conditions order.

(8) Without prejudice to section 14 of the Interpretation Act 1978 (power to make an order implies a power, exercisable in the same manner etc, to revoke or amend a previous order made under that power) a pay and conditions order made by virtue of subsection (1) above may revoke or amend, or may be revoked or amended by, a pay and conditions order made by virtue of subsection (5) above.

(9) A pay and conditions order shall be made by statutory instrument and,—

(a) if the order gives effect without any material modification to recommendations of the review body or is made by virtue of subsection (5) above, the order shall contain a statement that it does so or, as the case may be, is so made; and

(b) in any other case, the statutory instrument by which the order is made shall be subject to annulment in pursuance of a resolution of either House of Parliament. **[603]**

NOTES
Commencement: sub-ss (1)–(6), (8): 6 March 1992 (SI 1992/532); sub-s (7): 4 December 1992 (SI 1992/3070); sub-s (9): 30 March 1992 (SI 1992/988).
This section does not extend to Scotland.

3 Special provisions as to grant-maintained schools

(1) A pay and conditions order shall not apply to the statutory conditions of employment of the school teachers in a grant-maintained school the governing body of which—

(a) have, by notice to the Secretary of State, made an application for exemption; and

(b) pursuant to that application are for the time being exempted from subsections (6) and (7) of section 2 above by virtue of an order under subsection (4) below.

(2) Before making an application under subsection (1) above, the governing body of the grant-maintained school concerned shall consult the school teachers employed by them with respect to the proposed application.

(3) A notice of application under subsection (1) above shall specify a date, at least three months after the date of the notice, with effect from which the governing body of the grant-maintained school concerned intend to make their own provision as to the statutory conditions of employment of the school teachers employed by them.

(4) On receipt of a notice of application under subsection (1) above the Secretary of State shall, by statutory instrument, make an order—

(a) naming the school; and

(b) specifying, as the date with effect from which, by virtue of the order, subsections (6) and (7) of section 2 above are not to apply, the date specified in the notice of application or such other date as may be agreed between the governing body and the Secretary of State.   **[604]**

NOTE
Commencement: 6 March 1992 (SI 1992/532).
This section does not extend to Scotland.

4 Financial provisions

There shall be paid out of money provided by Parliament any expenses of the Secretary of State under this Act and any increase attributable to this Act in the sums so payable under any other Act.   **[605]**

NOTE
Commencement: 22 August 1991 (SI 1991/1874).
This section does not extend to Scotland.

5 Interpretation, orders and application of provisions of Education Act 1944

(1) In this Act—

"contract of employment", in relation to a school teacher, means the contract, whether a contract of service or for services, under which he performs his duties as teacher;

"pay and conditions order" has the meaning given by section 2(3) above;

"the review body" has the meaning given by section 1(1) above;

"school teacher" means, subject to subsection (2) below, a teacher employed by—

(a)   a local education authority, or

(b)   the governing body of a voluntary or grant-maintained school,

in the provision of primary or secondary education;

"school which has a delegated budget" has the same meaning as in Chapter III of Part I of the Education Reform Act 1988; and

"statutory conditions of employment" has (subject to subsection (3) below) the meaning given by section 1(2) above;

and other expressions used in this Act have the same meaning as in the Education Act 1944.

(2) A person employed as a teacher in an establishment maintained by a local authority in the exercise of a social services function is not a school teacher for the purposes of this Act.

(3) For the purposes of this Act, the Secretary of State may by order made by statutory instrument provide that, with effect from the date on which the order comes into force or such later date as may be specified in or determined under the order,—

(a)   any payment or other benefit specified in the order is, or as the case may be is not, to be regarded as remuneration; or

(b)   any matter is, or as the case may be is not, to be regarded as falling within the professional duties or working time of school teachers.

(4) An order under any provision of this Act may—

(a)   make different provision for different cases, including different provision for different areas; and

(b)   contain such incidental, supplemental or transitional provisions as the Secretary of State thinks fit.

(5) In sections 68 and 99(1) of the Education Act 1944 (powers of Secretary of State in relation to functions of certain bodies under that Act), any reference to that Act includes a reference to this Act.   **[606]**

NOTE
Commencement: 22 August 1991 (SI 1991/1874).
This section does not extend to Scotland.
Orders under this section: the School Teachers' Remuneration, Professional Duties and Working Time Order 1992, SI 1992/3069; the Education (School Teachers' Pay and Conditions) Order 1993, SI 1993/962.

6 Citation, repeals, extent and commencement

(1) This Act may be cited as the School Teachers' Pay and Conditions Act 1991.

(2) This Act and the Education Acts 1944 to 1988 may be cited together as the Education Acts 1944 to 1991.

(3) This Act has effect in place of the Teachers' Pay and Conditions Act 1987 and, accordingly, the enactments in Schedule 2 to this Act are hereby repealed to the extent specified in the third column of that Schedule.

(4) This Act, except paragraph 5 of Schedule 1 to this Act (House of Commons disqualification), extends to England and Wales only; and that paragraph extends to the whole of the United Kingdom.

(5) This Act shall come into force on such day as the Secretary of State may by order made by statutory instrument appoint, and, without prejudice to section 5(4) above, different days may be so appointed for different provisions and for different purposes.   **[607]**

NOTES
Commencement: Sub-ss (1), (2), (4), (5): 22 August 1991 (SI 1991/1874).
Sub-s (3): 6 March 1992 (SI 1992/532).

SCHEDULES

SCHEDULE 1

Section 1

THE REVIEW BODY

Membership

1 (1) The review body shall consist of not less than five and not more than nine members, who may be appointed as full-time or part-time members.

(2) Members shall hold and vacate office in accordance with their terms of appointment, subject to the following provisions.

(3) A member may resign his membership by notice in writing to the Prime Minister.

(4) The Prime Minister may by notice in writing to the member concerned remove from office a member who—

    (a) has become bankrupt or made an arrangement with his creditors,
    (b) is incapacitated by physical or mental illness, or
    (c) has been absent from two or more consecutive meetings of the review body otherwise than for a reason approved by them,

or who is in the opinion of the Prime Minister otherwise unable or unfit to perform his duties as member.

Chairman and deputy chairman

2 (1) The Prime Minister shall appoint one of the members of the review body to be chairman and may appoint one of them to be deputy chairman.

(2) The persons so appointed shall hold and vacate those offices in accordance with their terms of appointment, subject to the following provisions.

(3) The chairman or deputy chairman may resign his office by notice in writing to the Prime Minister.

(4) If the chairman or deputy chairman ceases to be a member of the review body, he also ceases to be chairman or deputy chairman.

Financial provisions

3 (1) The Secretary of State may pay the chairman, deputy chairman and members of the review body such remuneration, and such allowances in respect of expenses properly incurred by them in the performance of their duties, as he may determine.

(2) The Secretary of State may determine to pay in respect of a person's office as chairman, deputy chairman or member of the review body—

    (a)   such pension, allowance or gratuity to or in respect of that person on his retirement or death, or

    (b)   such contributions or other payment towards the provision of such a pension, allowance or gratuity,

as the Secretary of State may determine.

(3) Where a person ceases to be a member of the review body otherwise than on the expiry of his term of office and it appears to the Secretary of State that there are special circumstances which make it right for him to receive compensation, the Secretary of State may determine to make a payment to him by way of compensation of such amount as the Secretary of State may determine.

(4) As soon as may be after making a determination under sub-paragraph (2) or sub-paragraph (3) above the Secretary of State shall lay before each House of Parliament a statement of the amount payable in pursuance of the determination.

(5) The consent of the Treasury is required for any determination of the Secretary of State under this paragraph.

Proceedings

4 (1) The quorum of the review body and the arrangements relating to their meetings shall be such as the review body may determine.

(2) The validity of proceedings of the review body is not affected by any vacancy among the members or any defect in the appointment of any member.

House of Commons disqualification

5 ...   **[608]**

NOTES
Commencement: 22 August 1991 (SI 1991/1874).
Para 5: amends the House of Commons Disqualification Act 1975, Sch 1, Part III.

(Sch 2 (repeals) omitted.)

SOCIAL SECURITY CONTRIBUTIONS AND BENEFITS ACT 1992

(1992 c 4)

ARRANGEMENT OF SECTIONS

An Act to consolidate certain enactments relating to social security contributions and benefits with amendments to give effect to recommendations of the Law Commission and the Scottish Law Commission

[13 February 1992]

GENERAL NOTE
This consolidating Act re-enacts the statutory provisions as to Statutory Sick Pay (Pt XI) and Statutory Maternity Pay (Pt XII) previously in the Social Security and Housing Benefits Act 1982 and the Social Security Act 1986 respectively. These are reproduced here, together with associated Schedules and selected sections dealing with aspects of unemployment benefit and income support of most relevance to employment law. Other provisions not printed here are not annotated.

The numerous sets of regulations made with respect to Statutory Sick Pay and Statutory Maternity Pay under the 1982 and 1986 Acts largely continue in force and the major regulations are reproduced in section 2 of this work:

Statutory Sick Pay (General) Regulations 1982, SI 1982/894, below, para **[1150]**.

Statutory Sick Pay (Compensation of Employers) and Miscellaneous Provisions Regulations 1983, SI 1983/376, below, para **[1177]**.

Statutory Sick Pay (Medical Evidence) Regulations 1985, SI 1985/1604, below, para **[1267]**.

Statutory Maternity Pay (General) Regulations 1986, SI 1986/1960, below, para **[1290]**.

Statutory Maternity Pay (Compensation of Employers) Regulations 1987, SI 1987/91, below, para **[1330]**.

Statutory Sick Pay (Medical Evidence) Regulations 1987, SI 1987/235, below, para **[1336]**.

Statutory Sick Pay (Small Employers' Relief) Regulations 1991, SI 1991/428 (as amended by SI 1992/797), below, para **[1384]**.

PART II
CONTRIBUTORY BENEFITS

Unemployment benefit

27 Interruption of employment in connection with trade dispute

(1) Subject to the following provisions of this section—

(a) an employed earner who has lost employment as an employed earner by reason of a stoppage of work due to a trade dispute at his place of employment is disqualified for receiving unemployment benefit for any day during the stoppage unless he proves that he is not directly interested in the dispute; and

(b) an employed earner who has withdrawn his labour in furtherance of a trade dispute, but does not fall within paragraph (a) above, is disqualified for receiving unemployment benefit for any day on which his labour remains withdrawn.

(2) A person disqualified under subsection (1)(a) above for receiving unemployment benefit shall cease to be so disqualified if he proves that during the stoppage—

(a) he has become bona fide employed elsewhere; or

(b) his employment has been terminated by reason of redundancy within the meaning of section 81(2) of the Employment Protection (Consolidation) Act 1978; or

(c) he has bona fide resumed employment with his employer but has subsequently left for a reason other than the trade dispute.

(3) In this Act—

(a) "place of employment" in relation to any person, means the factory, workshop, farm or other premises or place at which he was employed, so however that, where separate branches of work which are commonly carried on as separate businesses in separate premises or at separate places are in any case carried on in separate departments on the same premises or at the same place, each of those departments shall for the purposes of this paragraph be deemed to be a separate factory or workshop or farm or separate premises or a separate place, as the case may be;

(b) "trade dispute" means any dispute between employers and employees, or between employees and employees, which is connected with the employment or non-employment or the terms of employment or the conditions of employment of any persons, whether employees in the employment of the employer with whom the dispute arises, or not. **[609]**

NOTES

Commencement: 1 July 1992 (s 177(4)).

This section derived from the Social Security Act 1975, s 19, as amended by the Social Security Act 1986, s 44(1).

28 Unemployment benefit—other disqualifications etc

(1) Subject to section 29 below a person shall be disqualified for receiving unemployment benefit for such period not exceeding 26 weeks as may be determined in accordance with Part II of the Administration Act if—

(a) he has lost his employment as an employed earner through his misconduct, or has voluntarily left such employment without just cause;

(b) after a situation in any employment has been properly notified to him as vacant or about to become vacant, he has without good cause refused or failed to apply for that situation or refused to accept that situation when offered to him;

(c) he has without good cause neglected to avail himself of a reasonable opportunity of employment;

(d) he has without good cause refused or failed to carry out any official recommendations given to him with a view to assisting him to find employment, being recommendations which were reasonable having regard to his circumstances and to the means of obtaining that employment usually adopted in the district in which he resides;

(e) he has lost his place on an approved training scheme through his misconduct, or has voluntarily left such a place without good cause;

(f) after a place on an approved training scheme has been properly notified to him as vacant or about to become vacant, he has without good cause refused or failed to apply for that place or refused to accept that place when offered to him; or

(g) he has without good cause neglected to avail himself of a reasonable opportunity of a place on an approved training scheme.

(2) The Secretary of State may by order substitute a shorter period for the period for the time being mentioned in subsection (1) above.

(3) Regulations may also provide for imposing, in the case of any prescribed category of persons—

(a) additional conditions with respect to the receipt of unemployment benefit; and

(b) restrictions on the rate and duration of unemployment benefit,

if, having regard to special circumstances, it appears to the Secretary of State necessary to do so for the purpose of preventing inequalities, or injustice to the general body of employed earners, or of earners generally, as the case may be.

(4) For the purposes of this section a person who has been dismissed by his employer by reason of redundancy within the meaning of section 81(2) of the Employment Protection (Consolidation) Act 1978 after volunteering or agreeing so to be dismissed shall not be deemed to have left his employment voluntarily.

(5) For the purposes of subsection (1) above regulations may—

(a) prescribe matters which are or are not to be taken into account in determining whether a person does or does not have good cause for any act or omission; or

(b) prescribe circumstances in which a person is or is not to be regarded as having or not having good cause for any act or omission;

but, subject to any such regulations, in determining for the purposes of that subsection whether a person does or does not have good cause for any act or omission, there shall be disregarded any matter relating to the level of remuneration in the employment in question.

(6) For the purposes of this section—

(a) "properly notified", in subsection (1)(b) and (f) above, means notified by the Secretary of State, a local education authority or some other recognised agency, or by or on behalf of an employer;

(b) "official recommendations", in subsection (1)(d) above, means recommendations in writing made by an officer of a local education authority or the Secretary of State;

(c) "approved training scheme", in subsection (1)(e), (f) and (g) above, means a scheme under which persons—

(i) are trained for employment; or

(ii) acquire work-experience for the purpose of becoming or keeping fit for entry to or return to regular employment,

and which is approved by the Secretary of State for the purposes of this section;

(d) "local education authority", in relation to Scotland, means an education authority, that is to say, a regional or islands council; and

(e) "week" means any period of 7 days.   **[610]**

NOTES

Commencement: 1 July 1992 (s 177(4)).

Sub-s (1) derived from the Social Security Act 1975, s 20(1) as amended by the Employment Act 1988, ss 27(1), (2), 33(2), Sch 4, the Social Security Act 1989, s 12(1) and the Unemployment Benefit (Disqualification Period) Order 1988, SI 1988/487, art 2; sub-s (2) derived from the Social Security Act 1975, s 20(1A) as added and amended by the Social Security Act 1986, ss 12(2), (6), 31(2), s 43(3)(a), Sch 9; sub-s (3) derived from the Social Security Act 1975, s 20(3); sub-s (4) derived from the Social Security Act 1975, s 20(3A) as added by the Social Security Act 1985, s 10; sub-s (5) derived from the Social Security Act 1975, s 20(4) as substituted by the Social Security Act 1989, s 12(3); sub-s (6) derived from the Education (Scotland) Act 1962, s 145(16), the Local Government (Scotland) Act 1973, s 129, Sch 11, para 12, and from the Social Security Act 1975, s 20(5) as amended by the Employment Act 1988, s 27(3).

PART VII
INCOME-RELATED BENEFITS

Income support

126 Trade disputes

(1) This section applies to a person, other than a child or a person of a prescribed description—

    (a) who is disqualified under section 27 above for receiving unemployment benefit; or

    (b) who would be so disqualified if otherwise entitled to that benefit,

except during any period shown by the person to be a period of incapacity for work by reason of disease or bodily or mental disablement or to be within the maternity period.

(2) In subsection (1) above "the maternity period" means the period commencing at the beginning of the 6th week before the expected week of confinement and ending at the end of the 7th week after the week in which confinement takes place.

(3) For the purpose of calculating income support—

    (a) so long as this section applies to a person who is not a member of a family, the applicable amount shall be disregarded;

    (b) so long as it applies to a person who is a member of a family but is not a member of a married or unmarried couple, the portion of the applicable amount which is included in respect of him shall be disregarded;

    (c) so long as it applies to one of the members of a married or unmarried couple—

        (i) if the applicable amount consists only of an amount in respect of them, it shall be reduced to one half; and

        (ii) if it includes other amounts, the portion of it which is included in respect of them shall be reduced to one-half and any further portion of it which is included in respect of the member of the couple to whom this section applies shall be disregarded;

    (d) so long as it applies to both the members of a married or unmarried couple—

        (i) if neither of them is responsible for a child or person of a prescribed description who is a member of the same household, the applicable amount shall be disregarded; and

        (ii) in any other case, the portion of the applicable amount which is included in respect of them and any further portion of it which is included in respect of either of them shall be disregarded.

(4) Where a reduction under subsection (3)(c) above would not produce a sum which is a multiple of 5p, the reduction shall be to the nearest lower sum which is such a multiple.

(5) Where this section applies to a person for any period, then, except so far as regulations provide otherwise—

    (a) in calculating the entitlement to income support of that person or a member of his family the following shall be treated as his income and shall not be disregarded—

        (i) any payment which he or a member of his family receives or is entitled to obtain by reason of the person to whom this section applies being without employment for that period; and

(ii) without prejudice to the generality of sub-paragraph (i) above, any amount which becomes or would on an application duly made become available to him in that period by way of repayment of income tax deducted from his emoluments in pursuance of section 203 of the Income and Corporation Taxes Act 1988 (PAYE); and

(b) any payment by way of income support for that period or any part of it which apart from this paragraph would be made to him, or to a person whose applicable amount is aggregated with his—

(i) shall not be made if the weekly rate of payment is equal to or less than the relevant sum; or

(ii) if it is more than the relevant sum, shall be at a weekly rate equal to the difference.

(6) In respect of any period less than a week, subsection (5) above shall have effect subject to such modifications as may be prescribed.

(7) Subject to subsection (8) below, "the relevant sum" for the purposes of subsection (5) above shall be [£23.50].

(8) If an order under section 150 of the Administration Act (annual up-rating) has the effect of increasing payments of income support, from the time when the order comes into force there shall be substituted, in subsection (5)(b) above, for the references to the sum for the time being mentioned in it references to a sum arrived at by—

(a) increasing that sum by the percentage by which the personal allowance under paragraph 1(1) of Part I of Schedule 2 to the Income Support (General) Regulations 1987 for a single person aged not less than 25 has been increased by the order; and

(b) if the sum as so increased is not a multiple of 50p, disregarding the remainder if it is 25p and, if it is not, rounding it up or down to the nearest 50p,

and the order shall state the substituted sum.   **[611]**

NOTES

Commencement: 1 July 1992 (s 177(4)).

Sub-ss (1)–(4) derived from the Social Security Act 1986, s 23(1)–(4); sub-s (5) derived from the Social Security Act 1986, s 23(5) as amended by the Income and Corporation Taxes Act 1988, s 844, Sch 29, para 32, Table and amended by the Social Security Benefits Up-rating (No 2) Order 1991, SI 1991/2910, art 15; sub-s (6) derived from the Social Security Act 1986, s 23(5A) as added by the Social Security 1988, s 16, Sch 4, para 24(1); sub-s (7) derived from the Social Security Act 1986, s 23(6) as substituted by the Social Security Act 1990, s 21(1), Sch 6, para 17(2); sub-s (8) derived from the Social Security Act 1986, s 23(7) as amended by the Social Security Act 1990, s 21(1), Sch 6, para 17(3).

Sub-s (7): figure in square brackets substituted by the Social Security Benefits Up-Rating Order 1993, SI 1993/350, art 18, as from the beginning of the first benefit week to commence for the beneficiary on or after 12 April 1993. The previous sum was £22.50.

127 Effect of return to work

If a person returns to work with the same employer after a period during which section 126 above applies to him, and whether or not his return is before the end of any stoppage of work in relation to which he is or would be disqualified for receiving unemployment benefit—

(a) that section shall cease to apply to him at the commencement of the day on which he returns to work; and

(b) until the end of the period of 15 days beginning with that day, section 124(1) above shall have effect in relation to him as if the following paragraph were substituted for paragraph (c)—

"(c) in the case of a member of a married or unmarried couple, the other member is not engaged in remunerative work; and"; and

(c) any sum paid by way of income support for that period of 15 days to him or, where he is a member of a married or unmarried couple, to the other member of that couple, shall be recoverable in accordance with the regulations from the person to whom it was paid or from any prescribed person or, where the person to whom it was paid is a member of a married or unmarried couple, from the other member of the couple. **[612]**

NOTES
Commencement: 1 July 1992 (s 177(4)).
This section derived from the Social Security Act 1986, s 23A as added by the Social Security Act 1988, s 16, Sch 4, para 25 and amended by the Social Security Act 1989, s 31(1), Sch 8, para 16.

PART XI

STATUTORY SICK PAY

Employer's liability

151 Employer's liability

(1) Where an employee has a day of incapacity for work in relation to his contract of service with an employer, that employer shall, if the conditions set out in sections 152 to 154 below are satisfied, be liable to make him, in accordance with the following provisions of this Part of this Act, a payment (to be known as "statutory sick pay") in respect of that day.

(2) Any agreement shall be void to the extent that it purports—

(a) to exclude, limit or otherwise modify any provision of this Part of this Act, or

(b) to require an employee to contribute (whether directly or indirectly) towards any costs incurred by his employer under this Part of this Act.

(3) For the avoidance of doubt, any agreement between an employer and an employee authorising any deductions from statutory sick pay which the employer is liable to pay to the employee in respect of any period shall not be void by virtue of subsection (2)(a) above if the employer—

(a) is authorised by that or another agreement to make the same deductions from any contractual remuneration which he is liable to pay in respect of the same period, or

(b) would be so authorised if he were liable to pay contractual remuneration in respect of that period.

(4) For the purposes of this Part of this Act a day shall not be treated as a day of incapacity for work in relation to any contract of service unless on that day the employee concerned is, or is deemed in accordance with regulations to be, incapable by reason of some specific disease or bodily or mental disablement of doing work which he can reasonably be expected to do under that contract.

(5) In any case where an employee has more than one contract of service with the same employer the provisions of this Part of this Act shall, except in such cases as may be prescribed and subject to the following provisions of this Part of this Act, have effect as if the employer were a different employer in relation to each contract of service.

(6) Circumstances may be prescribed in which, notwithstanding the provisions of subsections (1) to (5) above, the liability to make payments of statutory sick pay is to be a liability of the Secretary of State. **[613]**

NOTES
Commencement: 1 July 1992 (s 177(4)).
Sub-ss (1), (2), (4), (5) derived from the Social Security and Housing Benefits Act 1982, s 1(1), (2), (3), (4); sub-s (3) derived from the Social Security and Housing Benefits Act 1982, s 23A(1) as added by the Health and Social Security Act 1984, s 21, Sch 7, para 8; sub-s (6) derived from the Social Security and Housing Benefits Act 1982, s 1(5) as added by the Social Security Act 1986, s 68.

The qualifying conditions

152 Period of incapacity for work

(1) The first condition is that the day in question forms part of a period of incapacity for work.

(2) In this Part of this Act "period of incapacity for work" means any period of four or more consecutive days, each of which is a day of incapacity for work in relation to the contract of service in question.

(3) Any two periods of incapacity for work which are separated by a period of not more than 8 weeks shall be treated as a single period of incapacity for work.

(4) The Secretary of State may by regulations direct that a larger number of weeks specified in the regulations shall be substituted for the number of weeks for the time being specified in subsection (3) above.

(5) No day of the week shall be disregarded in calculating any period of consecutive days for the purposes of this section.

(6) A day may be a day of incapacity for work in relation to a contract of service, and so form part of a period of incapacity for work, notwithstanding that—

(a) it falls before the making of the contract or after the contract expires or is brought to an end; or

(b) it is not a day on which the employee concerned would be required by that contract to be available for work.   **[614]**

NOTES
Commencement: 1 July 1992 (s 177(4)).
Sub-ss (1), (2), (5), (6) derived from the Social Security and Housing Benefits Act 1982, s 2(1), (2), (4), (5); sub-s (3) derived from the Social Security and Housing Benefits Act 1982, s 2(3) as amended by the Statutory Sick Pay (General) Regulations 1982, SI 1982/894, reg 2A as added by the Statutory Sick Pay (General) Amendment Regulations 1986, SI 1986/477, reg 2; sub-s (4) derived from the Social Security and Housing Benefits Act 1982, s 2(3A) as added by the Social Security Act 1985, s 18(4).

153 Period of entitlement

(1) The second condition is that the day in question falls within a period which is, as between the employee and his employer, a period of entitlement.

(2) For the purposes of this Part of this Act a period of entitlement, as between an employee and his employer, is a period beginning with the commencement of a period of incapacity for work and ending with whichever of the following first occurs—

(a) the termination of that period of incapacity for work;

(b) the day on which the employee reaches, as against the employer concerned, his maximum entitlement to statutory sick pay (determined in accordance with section 155 below);

(c) the day on which the employee's contract of service with the employer concerned expires or is brought to an end;

(d) in the case of an employee who is, or has been, pregnant, the day immediately preceding the beginning of the disqualifying period.

(3) Schedule 11 to this Act has effect for the purpose of specifying circumstances in which a period of entitlement does not arise in relation to a particular period of incapacity for work.

(4) A period of entitlement as between an employee and an employer of his may also be, or form part of, a period of entitlement as between him and another employer of his.

(5) The Secretary of State may by regulations—

(a) specify circumstances in which, for the purpose of determining whether an employee's maximum entitlement to statutory sick pay has been reached in a period of entitlement as between him and an employer of his, days falling within a previous period of entitlement as between the employee and any person who is or has in the past been an employer of his are to be counted; and

(b) direct that in prescribed circumstances an employer shall provide a person who is about to leave his employment, or who has been employed by him in the past, with a statement in the prescribed form containing such information as may be prescribed in relation to any entitlement of the employee to statutory sick pay.

(6) Regulations may provide, in relation to prescribed cases, for a period of entitlement to end otherwise than in accordance with subsection (2) above.

(7) In a case where the employee's contract of service first takes effect on a day which falls within a period of incapacity for work, the period of entitlement begins with that day.

(8) In a case where the employee's contract of service first takes effect between two periods of incapacity for work which by virtue of section 152(3) above are treated as one, the period of entitlement begins with the first day of the second of those periods.

(9) In any case where, otherwise than by virtue of section 6(1)(b) above, an employee's earnings under a contract of service in respect of the day on which the contract takes effect do not attract a liability to pay secondary Class 1 contributions, subsections (7) and (8) above shall have effect as if for any reference to the contract first taking effect there were substituted a reference to the first day in respect of which the employee's earnings attract such a liability.

(10) Regulations shall make provision as to an employer's liability under this Part of this Act to pay statutory sick pay to an employee in any case where the employer's contract of service with that employee has been brought to an end by the employer solely, or mainly, for the purpose of avoiding liability for statutory sick pay.

(11) Subsection (2)(d) above does not apply in relation to an employee who has been pregnant if her pregnancy terminated, before the beginning of the disqualifying period, otherwise than by confinement.

(12) In this section—

"confinement" is to be construed in accordance with section 171(1) below;
"disqualifying period" means—

(a) in relation to a woman entitled to statutory maternity pay, the maternity pay period; and

(b) in relation to a woman entitled to maternity allowance, the maternity allowance period;

"maternity allowance period" has the meaning assigned to it by section 35(2) above, and

"maternity pay period" has the meaning assigned to it by section 165(1) below.

[615]

NOTES
Commencement: 1 July 1992 (s 177(4)).
Sub-ss (1)–(4), (6), (7), (10), (11) derived from the Social Security and Housing Benefits Act 1982, s 3(1)–(4), (5), (6), (7), (8); sub-s (5) derived from the Social Security and Housing Benefits Act 1982, s 3(4A) as added by the Social Security Act 1985, s 18(5); sub-ss (8), (9) derived from the Social Security and Housing Benefits Act 1982, s 3(6A), (6B), as added by the Social Security Act 1985, s 21, Sch 4, para 4; sub-s (12) derived from the Social Security and Housing Benefits Act 1982, s 3(9) as substituted by the Social Security Act 1986, s 86(1), Sch 10, Part IV, para 77.

154 Qualifying days

(1) The third condition is that the day in question is a qualifying day.

(2) The days which are for the purposes of this Part of this Act to be qualifying days as between an employee and an employer of his (that is to say, those days of the week on which he is required by his contract of service with that employer to be available for work or which are chosen to reflect the terms of that contract) shall be such day or days as may, subject to regulations, be agreed between the employee and his employer or, failing such agreement, determined in accordance with regulations.

(3) In any case where qualifying days are determined by agreement between an employee and his employer there shall, in each week (beginning with Sunday), be at least one qualifying day.

(4) A day which is a qualifying day as between an employee and an employer of his may also be a qualifying day as between him and another employer of his.

[616]

NOTES
Commencement: 1 July 1992 (s 177(4)).
This section derived from the Social Security and Housing Benefits Act 1982, s 4 as amended by the Health and Social Security Act 1984, s 21, Sch 7, para 7.

Limitations on entitlement, etc

155 Limitations on entitlement

(1) Statutory sick pay shall not be payable for the first three qualifying days in any period of entitlement.

(2) An employee shall not be entitled, as against any one employer, to an aggregate amount of statutory sick pay in respect of any one period of entitlement which exceeds his maximum entitlement.

(3) The maximum entitlement as against any one employer is reached on the day on which the amount to which the employee has become entitled by way of statutory sick pay during the period of entitlement in question first reaches or passes the entitlement limit.

(4) The entitlement limit is an amount equal to 28 times the appropriate weekly rate set out in section 157 below.

(5) Regulations may make provision for calculating the entitlement limit in any case where an employee's entitlement to statutory sick pay is calculated by reference to different weekly rates in the same period of entitlement.   **[617]**

NOTES
Commencement: 1 July 1992 (s 177(4)).
This section derived from the Social Security and Housing Benefits Act 1982, s 5 as amended by the Social Security Act 1985, ss 18(1), (2)(a)–(c), 29(2), Sch 6.

156 Notification of incapacity for work

(1) Regulations shall prescribe the manner in which, and the time within which, notice of any day of incapacity for work is to be given by or on behalf of an employee to his employer.

(2) An employer who would, apart from this section, be liable to pay an amount of statutory sick pay to an employee in respect of a qualifying day (the "day in question") shall be entitled to withhold payment of that amount if—

    (a) the day in question is one in respect of which he has not been duly notified in accordance with regulations under subsection (1) above; or

    (b) he has not been so notified in respect of any of the first three qualifying days in a period of entitlement (a "waiting day") and the day in question is the first qualifying day in that period of entitlement in respect of which the employer is not entitled to withhold payment—

        (i) by virtue of paragraph (a) above; or

        (ii) in respect of an earlier waiting day by virtue of this paragraph.

(3) Where an employer withholds any amount of statutory sick pay under this section—

    (a) the period of entitlement in question shall not be affected; and

    (b) for the purposes of calculating his maximum entitlement in accordance with section 155 above the employee shall not be taken to have become entitled to the amount so withheld. **[618]**

NOTES
Commencement: 1 July 1992 (s 177(4)).
This section derived from the Social Security and Housing Benefits Act 1982, s 6.

Rates of payment, etc

157 Rates of payment

(1) Statutory sick pay shall be payable by an employer at the weekly rate of—

    [(a) £52.50, in a case where the employee's normal weekly earnings under his contract of service with that employer are not less than £195.00; or

    (b) £46.95, in any other case.]

(2) The Secretary of State may by order—

    (a) substitute alternative provisions for the paragraphs of subsection (1) above; and

    (b) make such consequential amendments as appear to him to be required of any provision contained in this Part of this Act.

(3) The amount of statutory sick pay payable by any one employer in respect of any day shall be the weekly rate applicable on that day divided by the number of days which are, in the week (beginning with Sunday) in which that day falls, qualifying days as between that employer and the employee concerned. **[619]**

NOTES
Commencement: 1 July 1992 (s 177(4)).
Sub-s (1) derived from the Social Security and Housing Benefits Act 1982, s 7(1) as amended by the Statutory Sick Pay (Rate of Payment) (No 2) Order 1991, SI 1991/2911, art 2; sub-s (2) derived from the

Social Security and Housing Benefits Act 1982, s 7(1A) as added by the Social Security Act 1986, s 67(1) and amended by the Social Security Act 1990, s 21(1), Sch 6, para 15(1); sub-s (3) derived from the Social Security and Housing Benefits Act 1982, s 7(2).

Sub-s (1): para (a) substituted with savings and para (b) substituted, by SI 1993/350, art 2; for savings see art 3 thereof. The previous amounts were £190 (for £195) and £45.30 (for £46.95).

158 Recovery by employers of amounts paid by way of statutory sick pay

(1) Regulations shall make provision—

  (a) entitling, except in prescribed circumstances, any employer who has made one or more payments of statutory sick pay in a prescribed period to recover an amount equal to the sum of—

    (i) the aggregate of such of those payments as qualify for small employers' relief; and

    (ii) an amount equal to 80 per cent of the aggregate of such of those payments as do not so qualify,

  by making one or more deductions from his contributions payments; and

  (b) for the payment, in prescribed circumstances, by or on behalf of the Secretary of State of sums to employers who are unable so to recover the whole, or any part, of the amounts which they are entitled to recover by virtue of paragraph (a) above.

(2) For the purposes of this section, a payment of statutory sick pay which an employer is liable to make to an employee for any day which forms part of a period of incapacity for work qualifies for small employers' relief if—

  (a) on that day the employer is a small employer who has been liable to pay statutory sick pay in respect of that employee for earlier days forming part of that period of incapacity for work; and

  (b) the aggregate amount of those payments exceeds the entitlement threshold, that is to say, an amount equal to W x R, where—

    W is a prescribed number of weeks; and

    R is the appropriate weekly rate set out in section 157 above;

and regulations may make provision for calculating the entitlement threshold in any case where the employee's entitlement to statutory sick pay is calculated by reference to different weekly rates in the same period of incapacity for work.

(3) For the purposes of this section, "small employer" shall have the meaning assigned to it by regulations, and, without prejudice to the generality of the foregoing, any such regulations—

  (a) may define that expression by reference to the amount of an employer's contributions payments for any prescribed period; and

  (b) if they do so, may in that connection make provision for the amount of those payments for that prescribed period—

    (i) to be determined without regard to any deductions that may be made from them under this section or under any other enactment or instrument; and

    (ii) in prescribed circumstances, to be adjusted, estimated or otherwise attributed to him by reference to their amount in any other prescribed period.

(4) In this section "contributions payments", in relation to an employer, means any payments which the employer is required, by or under any enactment, to make in discharge of any liability in respect of primary or secondary Class 1 contributions.

(5) Regulations under this section may, in particular,—

(a) provide for any deduction made in accordance with the regulations to be disregarded for prescribed purposes; and

(b) provide for the rounding up or down of any fraction of a penny which would otherwise result from calculating the amount which an employer is entitled to recover for any period by virtue of subsection (1)(a) above.

(6) Where, in accordance with any provision of regulations made under this section, an amount has been deducted from an employer's contributions payments, the amount so deducted shall (except in such cases as may be prescribed) be treated for the purposes of any provision made by or under any enactment in relation to primary or secondary Class 1 contributions as having been—

(a) paid (on such date as may be determined in accordance with the regulations); and

(b) received by the Secretary of State,

towards discharging the liability mentioned in subsection (4) above.

(7) Any day of incapacity for work falling before 6th April 1991 shall be left out of account for the purposes of subsection (2) above.   **[620]**

NOTES
Commencement: 1 July 1992 (s 177(4)).
Sub-s (1) derived from the Social Security and Housing Benefits Act 1982, s 9(1) as amended by the Statutory Sick Pay Act 1991, s 1(1); sub-ss (2), (3) derived from the Social Security and Housing Benefits Act 1982, s 9(1B), (1D), as added by the Statutory Sick Pay Act 1991, s 2(1); sub-s (4) derived from the Social Security and Housing Benefits Act 1982, s 9(2) as amended by the Statutory Sick Pay Act 1991 s 2(2); sub-s (5) derived from the Social Security and Housing Benefits Act 1982, s 9(3)(b), (c) as amended by the Statutory Sick Pay Act 1991, s 1(3); sub-s (6) derived from the Social Security and Housing Benefits Act 1982, s 9(6); sub-s (7) derived from the Statutory Sick Pay Act 1991, s 2(5).
Regs under sub-s (1): the Statutory Sick Pay (Compensation of Employers) and Miscellaneous Provisions Order 1983, SI 1983/376, below, para [**1177**]; under sub-s (2): the Statutory Sick Pay (Small Employers' Relief) Regulations 1991, SI 1991/428, below, para [**1384**].

159 Power to substitute provisions for s 158(2)

(1) If the Secretary of State by order so provides for any tax year, the following subsections shall have effect for that tax year in substitution for section 158(2) above—

"(2A) For the purposes of this section, a payment of statutory sick pay which an employer is liable to make to an employee for any day in a tax year qualifies for small employers' relief if—

(a) on that day the employer is a small employer who has been liable to make payments of statutory sick pay for earlier days in that tax year in respect of any employees of his; and

(b) the aggregate of any such payments for those earlier days exceeds a prescribed sum.

(2B) In any case where—

(a) an employer is liable to make two or more payments of statutory sick pay for the same day in a tax year; and

(b) by virtue of the condition in subsection (2A)(b) above, none of those payments would qualify for small employers' relief; but

(c) that condition would have been fulfilled in relation to a proportion of the aggregate amount of those payments, had he been liable—

(i) to pay as statutory sick pay for an earlier day in that tax year, instead of for the day in question, the smallest part of that aggregate that would enable that condition to be fulfilled; and

(ii) to pay the remainder as statutory sick pay for the day in question, he shall be treated for the purposes of subsection (2A) above as if he had been liable to make payments of statutory sick pay as mentioned in paragraph (c) above instead of as mentioned in paragraph (a) above.

(2C)   If, in a case not falling within subsection (2B) above—

  (a)   an employer is liable to make a single payment of statutory sick pay for a day in a tax year; and

  (b)   by virtue of the condition in subsection (2A)(b) above, that payment would not qualify for small employers' relief; but

  (c)   that condition would have been fulfilled in relation to a proportion of that payment, had he been liable—

     (i)   to pay as statutory sick pay for an earlier day in that tax year, instead of for the day in question, the smallest part of that payment that would enable that condition to be fulfilled; and

     (ii)   to pay the remainder as statutory sick pay for the day in question,

he shall be treated for the purposes of subsection (2A) above as if he had been liable to make payments of statutory sick pay as mentioned in paragraph (c) above instead of the payment mentioned in paragraph (a) above.".

(2)   Without prejudice to section 175(4) below, the Secretary of State may by regulations make such transitional or consequential provision or savings as he considers necessary or expedient in connection with the coming into force of an order under subsection (1) above or the expiry or revocation of any such order and the consequent revival of section 158(2) above.   **[621]**

NOTES
   Commencement: 1 July 1992 (s 177(4)).
   This section derived from the Social Security and Housing Benefits Act 1982 Act, s 9(1C) as added by the Statutory Sick Pay Act 1991, s 2(1).
   No order had been made under this section at the date of going to press.

Miscellaneous

160   Relationship with benefits and other payments, etc

Schedule 12 to this Act has effect with respect to the relationship between statutory sick pay and certain benefits and payments.   **[622]**

NOTE
   Commencement: 1 July 1992 (s 177(4)).

161   Crown employment—Part XI

(1)   Subject to subsection (2) below, the provisions of this Part of this Act apply in relation to persons employed by or under the Crown as they apply in relation to persons employed otherwise than by or under the Crown.

(2)   The provisions of this Part of this Act do not apply in relation to persons serving as members of Her Majesty's forces, in their capacity as such.

(3)   For the purposes of this section Her Majesty's forces shall be taken to consist of such establishments and organisations as may be prescribed, being establishments and organisations in which persons serve under the control of the Defence Council.
     [623]

NOTES
Commencement: 1 July 1992 (s 177(4)).
Sub-ss (1), (2) derived from the Social Security and Housing Benefits Act 1982, s 27(1), (2); sub-s (3) derived from the Social Security and Housing Benefits Act 1982, s 27(3) as added by the Social Security Act 1989, s 26, Sch 7, para 23.

162 Special classes of persons

(1) The Secretary of State may make regulations modifying this Part of this Act in such manner as he thinks proper in their application to any person who is, has been or is to be—

    (a) employed on board any ship, vessel, hovercraft or aircraft;

    (b) outside Great Britain at any prescribed time or in any prescribed circumstances; or

    (c) in prescribed employment in connection with continental shelf operations, as defined in section 120(2) above.

(2) Regulations under subsection (1) above may in particular provide—

    (a) for any provision of this Part of this Act to apply to any such person, notwithstanding that it would not otherwise apply;

    (b) for any such provision not to apply to any such person, notwithstanding that it would otherwise apply;

    (c) for excepting any such person from the application of any such provision where he neither is domiciled nor has a place of residence in any part of Great Britain;

    (d) for the taking of evidence, for the purposes of the determination of any question arising under any such provision, in a country or territory outside Great Britain, by a British consular official or such other person as may be determined in accordance with the regulations. **[624]**

NOTES
Commencement: 1 July 1992 (s 177(4)).
This section derived from the Social Security and Housing Benefits Act 1982, s 22 as amended by the Oil and Gas (Enterprise) Act 1982, s 37(1), Sch 3, para 44 and from Law Commission Recommendation No 4, Cmnd 1726.

163 Interpretation of Part XI and supplementary provisions

(1) In this Part of this Act—

    "contract of service" (except in paragraph (a) of the definition below of "employee") includes any arrangement providing for the terms of appointment of an employee;

    "employee" means a person who is—

        (a) gainfully employed in Great Britain either under a contract of service or in an office (including elective office) with emoluments chargeable to income tax under Schedule E; and

        (b) over the age of 16;

    but subject to regulations, which may provide for cases where any such person is not to be treated as an employee for the purposes of this Part of this Act and for cases where any person who would not otherwise be an employee for those purposes is to be treated as an employee for those purposes;

    "employer", in relation to an employee and a contract of service of his, means a person who under section 6 above is, or but for subsection (1)(b) of that section would be, liable to pay secondary Class 1 contributions in relation to any earnings of the employee under the contract;

"period of entitlement" has the meaning given by section 153 above;
"period of incapacity for work" has the meaning given by section 152 above;
"period of interruption of employment" has the same meaning as it has in the
    provisions of this Act relating to unemployment benefit, sickness benefit
    and invalidity benefit by virtue of section 57(1)(d) above;
"prescribed" means prescribed by regulations;
"qualifying day" has the meaning given by section 154 above;
"week" means any period of 7 days.

(2) For the purposes of this Part of this Act an employee's normal weekly earnings shall, subject to subsection (4) below, be taken to be the average weekly earnings which in the relevant period have been paid to him or paid for his benefit under his contract of service with the employer in question.

(3) For the purposes of subsection (2) above, the expressions "earnings" and "relevant period" shall have the meaning given to them by regulations.

(4) In such cases as may be prescribed an employee's normal weekly earnings shall be calculated in accordance with regulations.

(5) Without prejudice to any other power to make regulations under this Part of this Act, regulations may specify cases in which, for the purposes of this Part of this Act or such of its provisions as may be prescribed—

(a) two or more employers are to be treated as one;
(b) two or more contracts of service in respect of which the same person is an employee are to be treated as one.

(6) Where, in consequence of the establishment of one or more National Health Service trusts under Part I of the National Health Service and Community Care Act 1990 or the National Health Service (Scotland) Act 1978, a person's contract of employment is treated by a scheme under that Part or Act as divided so as to constitute two or more contracts, regulations may make provision enabling him to elect for all of those contracts to be treated as one contract for the purposes of this Part of this Act or of such provisions of this Part of this Act as may be prescribed; and any such regulations may prescribe—

(a) the conditions that must be satisfied if a person is to be entitled to make such an election;
(b) the manner in which, and the time within which, such an election is to be made;
(c) the persons to whom, and the manner in which, notice of such an election is to be given;
(d) the information which a person who makes such an election is to provide, and the persons to whom, and the time within which, he is to provide it;
(e) the time for which such an election is to have effect;
(f) which one of the person's employers under the two or more contracts is to be regarded for the purposes of statutory sick pay as his employer under the one contract;

and the powers conferred by this subsection are without prejudice to any other power to make regulations under this Part of this Act.

(7) Regulations may provide for periods of work which begin on one day and finish on the following day to be treated, for the purposes of this Part of this Act, as falling solely within one or other of those days.   **[625]**

NOTES
Commencement: 1 July 1992 (s 177(4)).
Sub-s (1) derived from the Social Security and Housing Benefits Act 1982, s 26(1) as amended by the Social Security Act 1985, s 21, Sch 4, para 6; sub-s (2) derived from the Social Security and Housing

Benefits Act 1982, s 26(2) as amended by the Social Security Act 1985, s 21, Sch 4, para 7; sub-ss (3)–(5), (7) derived from the Social Security and Housing Benefits Act 1982, s 26(3)–(5), (6); sub-s (6) derived from the Social Security and Housing Benefits Act 1982, s 26(5A) as added by the Social Security Act 1990, s 21(1), Sch 6, para 16.

Regulations under this section: Statutory Sick Pay (National Health Service Employees) Regulations 1991, SI 1991/589.

PART XII

STATUTORY MATERNITY PAY

164 Statutory maternity pay—entitlement and liability to pay

(1) Where a woman who is or has been an employee satisfies the conditions set out in this section, she shall be entitled, in accordance with the following provisions of this Part of this Act, to payments to be known as "statutory maternity pay".

(2) The conditions mentioned in subsection (1) above are—

(a) that she has been in employed earner's employment with an employer for a continuous period of at least 26 weeks ending with the week immediately preceding the 14th week before the expected week of confinement but has ceased to work for him, wholly or partly because of pregnancy or confinement;

(b) that her normal weekly earnings for the period of 8 weeks ending with the week immediately preceding the 14th week before the expected week of confinement are not less than the lower earnings limit in force under section 5(1)(a) above immediately before the commencement of the 14th week before the expected week of confinement; and

(c) that she has become pregnant and has reached, or been confined before reaching, the commencement of the 11th week before the expected week of confinement.

(3) The liability to make payments of statutory maternity pay to a woman is a liability of any person of whom she has been an employee as mentioned in subsection (2)(a) above.

(4) Except in such cases as may be prescribed, a woman shall be entitled to payments of statutory maternity pay only if—

(a) she gives the person who will be liable to pay it notice that she is going to be absent from work with him, wholly or partly because of pregnancy or confinement; and

(b) the notice is given at least 21 days before her absence from work is due to begin or, if that is not reasonably practicable, as soon as is reasonably practicable.

(5) The notice shall be in writing if the person who is liable to pay the woman statutory maternity pay so requests.

(6) Any agreement shall be void to the extent that it purports—

(a) to exclude, limit or otherwise modify any provision of this Part of this Act; or

(b) to require an employee or former employee to contribute (whether directly or indirectly) towards any costs incurred by her employer or former employer under this Part of this Act.

(7) For the avoidance of doubt, any agreement between an employer and an employee authorising any deductions from statutory maternity pay which the employer is liable to pay to the employee in respect of any period shall not be void by virtue of subsection (6)(a) above if the employer—

(a) is authorised by that or another agreement to make the same deductions from any contractual remuneration which he is liable to pay in respect of the same period, or

(b) would be so authorised if he were liable to pay contractual remuneration in respect of that period.

(8) Regulations shall make provision as to a former employer's liability to pay statutory maternity pay to a woman in any case where the former employer's contract of service with her has been brought to an end by the former employer solely, or mainly, for the purpose of avoiding liability for statutory maternity pay.

(9) The Secretary of State may by regulations—

(a) specify circumstances in which, notwithstanding subsections (1) to (8) above, there is to be no liability to pay statutory maternity pay in respect of a week;

(b) specify circumstances in which, notwithstanding subsections (1) to (8) above, the liability to make payments of statutory maternity pay is to be a liability of his;

(c) specify in what circumstances employment is to be treated as continuous for the purposes of this Part of this Act;

(d) provide that a woman is to be treated as being employed for a continuous period of at least 26 weeks where—

(i) she has been employed by the same employer for at least 26 weeks under two or more separate contracts of service; and

(ii) those contracts were not continuous;

(e) provide that any of the provisions specified in subsection (10) below shall have effect subject to prescribed modifications—

(i) where a woman has been dismissed from her employment;

(ii) where a woman is confined before the beginning of the 14th week before the expected week of confinement; and

(iii) in such other cases as may be prescribed;

(f) provide for amounts earned by a woman under separate contracts of service with the same employer to be aggregated for the purposes of this Part of this Act; and

(g) provide that—

(i) the amount of a woman's earnings for any period, or

(ii) the amount of her earnings to be treated as comprised in any payment made to her or for her benefit,

shall be calculated or estimated in such manner and on such basis as may be prescribed and that for that purpose payments of a particular class or description made or falling to be made to or by a woman shall, to such extent as may be prescribed, be disregarded or, as the case may be, be deducted from the amount of her earnings.

(10) The provisions mentioned in subsection (9)(e) above are—

(a) subsection (2)(a) and (b) above; and

(b) section 166(2), (4) and (5) below.   **[626]**

NOTES

Commencement: 1 July 1992 (s 177(4)).

Sub-ss (1)–(5), (8) derived from the Social Security Act 1986, s 46(1)–(5), (7); sub-ss (6), (7) derived from the Social Security and Housing Benefits Act 1982, s 23A(1) as added by the Health and Social Security Act 1984, s 21, Sch 7, para 8, and from the Social Security Act 1986, s 46(6); sub-s (9) derived from the Social Security Act 1986, s 46(8) as amended by the Social Security Act 1988, s 16, Sch 4, para 16(1); sub-s (10) derived from the Social Security Act 1986, s 46(9) as added by the Social Security Act 1988 s 16, Sch 4, para 16(2).

165 The maternity pay period

(1) Statutory maternity pay shall be payable, subject to the provisions of this Part of this Act, in respect of each week during a prescribed period ("the maternity pay period") of a duration not exceeding 18 weeks.

(2) Subject to subsections (3) and (7) below, the first week of the maternity pay period shall be the 11th week before the expected week of confinement.

(3) Cases may be prescribed in which the first week of the period is to be a prescribed week later than the 11th week before the expected week of confinement, but not later than the 6th week before the expected week of confinement.

(4) Statutory maternity pay shall not be payable to a woman by a person in respect of any week during any part of which she works under a contract of service with him.

(5) It is immaterial for the purposes of subsection (4) above whether the work referred to in that subsection is work under a contract of service which existed immediately before the maternity pay period or a contract of service which did not so exist.

(6) Except in such cases as may be prescribed, statutory maternity pay shall not be payable to a woman in respect of any week after she has been confined and during any part of which she works for any employer who is not liable to pay her statutory maternity pay.

(7) Regulations may provide that this section shall have effect subject to prescribed modifications in relation—

    (a) to cases in which a woman has been confined before the 11th week before the expected week of confinement; and

    (b) to cases in which—

        (i) a woman is confined during the period beginning with the 11th week, and ending with the 7th week, before the expected week of confinement; and

        (ii) the maternity pay period has not then commenced for her.   **[627]**

NOTES

Commencement: 1 July 1992 (s 177(4)).

This section derived from the Social Security Act 1986, s 47 as amended by the Social Security Act 1989, s 26, Sch 7, para 25.

166 Rates of payment

(1) There shall be two rates of statutory maternity pay, in this Act referred to as "the higher rate" and "the lower rate".

(2) The higher rate is a weekly rate equivalent to nine-tenths of a woman's normal weekly earnings for the period of 8 weeks immediately preceding the 14th week before the expected week of confinement or the weekly rate prescribed under subsection (3) below, whichever is the higher.

(3) The lower rate is such weekly rate as may be prescribed.

(4) Subject to the following provisions of this section, statutory maternity pay shall be payable at the higher rate to a woman who for a continuous period of at least 2 years ending with the week immediately preceding the 14th week before the expected week of confinement has been an employee in employed earner's employment of any person liable to pay it to her, and shall be so paid by any such person in respect of the first 6 weeks in respect of which it is payable.

(5) Statutory maternity pay shall not be payable at the higher rate to a woman whose relations with the person liable to pay it are or were governed by a contract of service which normally involves or involved employment for less than 16 hours weekly unless during a continuous period of at least 5 years ending with the week immediately preceding the 14th week before the expected week of confinement her contract of service normally involved employment for 8 hours or more weekly.

(6) The Secretary of State may by regulations make provision as to when a contract of service is to be treated for the purposes of subsection (5) above as normally involving or having involved employment—

(a) for less than 16 hours weekly; or

(b) for 8 hours or more weekly,

or as not normally involving or having involved such employment.

(7) Statutory maternity pay shall be payable to a woman at the lower rate if she is entitled to statutory maternity pay but is not entitled to payment at the higher rate.

(8) If a woman is entitled to statutory maternity pay at the higher rate, she shall be entitled to it at the lower rate in respect of the portion of the maternity pay period after the end of the 6 week period mentioned in subsection (4) above.   **[628]**

NOTES

Commencement: 1 July 1992 (s 177(4)).

This section derived from the Social Security Act 1986, s 48 as amended by the Social Security Act 1988, s 16, Sch 4, para 17.

The rate currently prescribed, as from 6 April 1993, is £47.95: SI 1993/350, art 10. Previously, from 6 April 1992, it was £46.30: SI 1991/2910, and from 6 April 1991 it was £44.50: SI 1991/503.

167 Recovery of amounts paid by way of statutory maternity pay

(1) Regulations shall make provision—

(a) entitling, except in prescribed circumstances, any person who has made a payment of statutory maternity pay to recover the amount so paid by making one or more deductions from his contributions payments;

(b) for the payment, in prescribed circumstances, by the Secretary of State or by the Commissioners of Inland Revenue on behalf of the Secretary of State, of sums to persons who are unable so to recover the whole, or any part, of any payments of statutory maternity pay which they have made;

(c) giving any person who has made a payment of statutory maternity pay a right, except in prescribed circumstances, to an amount, determined in such manner as may be prescribed —

(i) by reference to secondary Class 1 contributions paid in respect of statutory maternity pay; or

(ii) by reference to secondary Class 1 contributions paid in respect of statutory sick pay; or

(iii) by reference to the aggregate of secondary Class 1 contributions paid in respect of statutory maternity pay and secondary Class 1 contributions paid in respect of statutory sick pay;

(d) providing for the recovery, in prescribed circumstances, of the whole or any part of any such amount from contributions payments;

(e) for the payment in prescribed circumstances, by the Secretary of State or by the Commissioners of Inland Revenue on behalf of the Secretary of State, of the whole or any part of any such amount.

(2) In this section "contributions payments", in relation to an employer, means any payments which the employer is required, by or under any enactment, to make in discharge of any liability in respect of primary or secondary Class 1 contributions.

(3) Regulations under subsection (1) above may, in particular, provide for any deduction made in accordance with the regulations to be disregarded for prescribed purposes.

(4) Where, in accordance with any provision of regulations made under this section, an amount has been deducted from an employer's contributions payments, the amount so deducted shall (except in such cases as may be prescribed) be treated for the purposes of any provision made by or under any enactment in relation to primary or secondary Class 1 contributions as having been—

(a) paid (on such date as may be determined in accordance with the regulations); and

(b) received by the Secretary of State,

towards discharging the employer's liability in respect of such contributions.

[629]

NOTES

Commencement: 1 July 1992 (s 177(4)).

Sub-ss (1), (3), (4) derived from the Social Security Act 1986, s 49, Sch 4, Part I, paras 1, 2, 5; sub-s (2) derived from Law Commission Recommendation No 5, Cmnd 1726.

168 Relationship with benefits and other payments etc

Schedule 13 to this Act has effect with respect to the relationship between statutory maternity pay and certain benefits and payments.   [630]

NOTE

Commencement: 1 July 1992 (s 177(4)).

169 Crown employment—Part XII

The provisions of this Part of this Act apply in relation to women employed by or under the Crown as they apply in relation to women employed otherwise than by or under the Crown.   [631]

NOTES

Commencement: 1 July 1992 (s 177(4)).

This section derived from the Social Security Act 1986, s 79(4).

170 Special classes of person

(1) The Secretary of State may make regulations modifying this Part of this Act in such manner as he thinks proper in their application to any person who is, has been or is to be—

(a) employed on board any ship, vessel, hovercraft or aircraft;

(b) outside Great Britain at any prescribed time or in any prescribed circumstances; or

(c) in prescribed employment in connection with continental shelf operations, as defined in section 120(2) above.

(2) Regulations under subsection (1) above may in particular provide—

(a) for any provision of this Part of this Act to apply to any such person, notwithstanding that it would not otherwise apply;

(b) for any such provision not to apply to any such person, notwithstanding that it would otherwise apply;

(c) for excepting any such person from the application of any such provision where he neither is domiciled nor has a place of residence in any part of Great Britain;

(d) for the taking of evidence, for the purposes of the determination of any question arising under any such provision, in a country or territory outside Great Britain, by a British consular official or such other person as may be determined in accordance with the regulations.   **[632]**

NOTES
Commencement: 1 July 1992 (s 177(4)).
This section derived from the Social Security Act 1986, s 80 and Law Commission Recommendation No 4, Cmnd 1726.

171 Interpretation of Part XII and supplementary provisions

(1) In this Part of this Act—

"confinement" means—

(a) labour resulting in the issue of a living child, or
(b) labour after [24 weeks] of pregnancy resulting in the issue of a child whether alive or dead,

and "confined" shall be construed accordingly; and where a woman's labour begun on one day results in the issue of a child on another day she shall be taken to be confined on the day of the issue of the child or, if labour results in the issue of twins or a greater number of children, she shall be taken to be confined on the day of the issue of the last of them;

"dismissed" is to be construed in accordance with section 55(2) to (7) of the Employment Protection (Consolidation) Act 1978;

"employee" means a woman who is—

(a) gainfully employed in Great Britain either under a contract of service or in an office (including elective office) with emoluments chargeable to income tax under Schedule E; and
(b) over the age of 16;

but subject to regulations which may provide for cases where any such woman is not to be treated as an employee for the purposes of this Part of this Act and for cases where a woman who would not otherwise be an employee for those purposes is to be treated as an employee for those purposes;

"employer", in relation to a woman who is an employee, means a person who under section 6 above is, or but for subsection (1)(b) of that section would be, liable to pay secondary Class 1 contributions in relation to any of her earnings;

"maternity pay period" has the meaning assigned to it by section 165(1) above;

"modifications" includes additions, omissions and amendments, and related expressions shall be construed accordingly;

"prescribed" means specified in or determined in accordance with regulations;

"week" means a period of 7 days beginning with Sunday or such other period as may be prescribed in relation to any particular case or class of cases.

(2) Without prejudice to any other power to make regulations under this Part of this Act, regulations may specify cases in which, for the purposes of this Part of this Act or of such provisions of this Part of this Act as may be prescribed—

(a) two or more employers are to be treated as one;
(b) two or more contracts of service in respect of which the same woman is an employee are to be treated as one.

(3) Where, in consequence of the establishment of one or more National Health Service trusts under Part I of the National Health Service and Community Care Act 1990 or the National Health Service (Scotland) Act 1978, a woman's contract of employment is treated by a scheme under that Part or Act as divided so as to constitute

two or more contracts, regulations may make provision enabling her to elect for all of those contracts to be treated as one contract for the purposes of this Part of this Act or of such provisions of this Part of this Act as may be prescribed; and any such regulations may prescribe—

    (a) the conditions that must be satisfied if a woman is to be entitled to make such an election;

    (b) the manner in which, and the time within which, such an election is to be made;

    (c) the persons to whom, and the manner in which, notice of such an election is to be given;

    (d) the information which a woman who makes such an election is to provide, and the persons to whom, and the time within which, she is to provide it;

    (e) the time for which such an election is to have effect;

    (f) which one of the woman's employers under the two or more contracts is to be regarded for the purposes of statutory maternity pay as her employer under the one contract;

and the powers conferred by this subsection are without prejudice to any other power to make regulations under this Part of this Act.

(4) For the purposes of this Part of this Act a woman's normal weekly earnings shall, subject to subsection (6) below, be taken to be the average weekly earnings which in the relevant period have been paid to her or paid for her benefit under the contract of service with the employer in question.

(5) For the purposes of subsection (4) above "earnings" and "relevant period" shall have the meanings given to them by regulations.

(6) In such cases as may be prescribed a woman's normal weekly earnings shall be calculated in accordance with regulations.   [633]

NOTES
   Commencement: 1 July 1992 (s 177(4)).
   Sub-s (1) derived from the Social Security Act 1986, s 50(1) as amended by the Social Security Act 1988, s 16, Sch 4, para 18 and the Social Security Act 1989, ss 26, 31(2), Sch 7, para 26, Sch 9, and from the Social Security Act 1986, s 84(1); sub-ss (2), (4)–(6) derived from the Social Security Act 1986, s 50(2), (3)–(5); sub-s (3) derived from the Social Security Act 1986, s 50(2A) as added by the Social Security Act 1990, s 21(1), Sch 6, para 22.
   Sub-s (1): in definition "confinement" words in square brackets substituted by the Still-Birth (Definition) Act 1992, ss 2(1), 4(2).

SCHEDULES

SCHEDULE 11

Section 153(3)

CIRCUMSTANCES IN WHICH PERIODS OF ENTITLEMENT TO STATUTORY SICK PAY DO NOT ARISE

1 A period of entitlement does not arise in relation to a particular period of incapacity for work in any of the circumstances set out in paragraph 2 below or in such other circumstances as may be prescribed.

   2 The circumstances are that—

    (a) at the relevant date the employee is over pensionable age;

    (b) the employee's contract of service was entered into for a specified period of not more than three months;

    (c) at the relevant date the employee's normal weekly earnings are less than the lower earnings limit then in force under section 5(1)(a) above;

(d) the employee had—

    (i) in the period of 57 days ending immediately before the relevant date, at least one day which formed part of a period of interruption of employment; and

    (ii) at any time during that period of interruption of employment, an invalidity pension day (whether or not the day referred to in paragraph (i) above);

(e) in the period of 57 days ending immediately before the relevant date the employee had at least one day on which—

    (i) he was entitled to sickness benefit (or on which he would have been so entitled if he had satisfied the contribution conditions for sickness benefit mentioned in section 31(2)(a) above), or

    (ii) she was entitled to a maternity allowance;

(f) the employee has done no work for his employer under his contract of service;

(g) on the relevant date there is, within the meaning of section 27 above, a stoppage of work due to a trade dispute at the employee's place of employment;

(h) the employee is, or has been, pregnant and the relevant date falls within the disqualifying period (within the meaning of section 153(12) above).

3 In this Schedule "relevant date" means the date on which a period of entitlement would begin in accordance with section 153 above if this Schedule did not prevent it arising.

4 (1) Paragraph 2(b) above does not apply in any case where—

(a) at the relevant date the contract of service has become a contract for a period exceeding three months; or

(b) the contract of service (the "current contract") was preceded by a contract of service entered into by the employee with the same employer (the "previous contract") and—

    (i) the interval between the date on which the previous contract ceased to have effect and that on which the current contract came into force was not more than 8 weeks; and

    (ii) the aggregate of the period for which the previous contract had effect and the period specified in the current contract (or, where that period has been extended, the specified period as so extended) exceeds 13 weeks.

(2) For the purposes of sub-paragraph (1)(b)(ii) above, in any case where the employee entered into more than one contract of service with the same employer before the current contract, any of those contracts which came into effect not more than 8 weeks after the date on which an earlier one of them ceased to have effect shall be treated as one with the earlier contract.

5 (1) In paragraph 2(d) above "invalidity pension day" means a day—

(a) for which the employee in question was entitled to an invalidity pension, a non-contributory invalidity pension (under section 36 of the 1975 Act) or a severe disablement allowance; or

(b) for which he was not so entitled but which was the last day of the invalidity pension qualifying period.

(2) In sub-paragraph (1)(b) above the "invalidity pension qualifying period" means the period mentioned in section 33(1) or, as the case may be, 40(3) or 41(2) above as falling within the period of interruption of employment referred to in whichever of those provisions is applicable.

6 For the purposes of paragraph 2(f) above, if an employee enters into a contract of service which is to take effect not more than 8 weeks after the date on which a previous contract of service entered into by him with the same employer ceased to have effect, the two contracts shall be treated as one.

7 Paragraph 2(g) above does not apply in the case of an employee who proves that at no time on or before the relevant date did he have a direct interest in the trade dispute in question.

8 Paragraph 2(h) above does not apply in relation to an employee who has been pregnant if her pregnancy terminated, before the beginning of the disqualifying period, otherwise than by confinement (as defined for the purposes of statutory maternity pay in section 171(1) above).

NOTES
Commencement: 1 July 1992 (s 177(4)).
This Schedule derived from the Social Security and Housing Benefits Act 1982, Sch 1 as amended by the Social Security Act 1985, ss 18(2)(d), 29(2), Sch 6, the Social Security Act 1989, s 31(1), (2), Sch 8, para 14, Sch 9 and the Health and Social Security Act 1984, s 11(2), Sch 4, Part I, para 15(b).

SCHEDULE 12

Section 160

RELATIONSHIPS OF STATUTORY SICK PAY WITH BENEFITS AND OTHER PAYMENTS, ETC

The general principle

1 Any day which—

    (a)   is a day of incapacity for work in relation to any contract of service; and

    (b)   falls within a period of entitlement (whether or not it is also a qualifying day),

shall not be treated for the purposes of this Act as a day of incapacity for work for the purposes of determining whether a period is a period of interruption of employment.

Contractual remuneration

2 (1) Subject to sub-paragraphs (2) and (3) below, any entitlement to statutory sick pay shall not affect any right of an employee in relation to remuneration under any contract of service ("contractual remuneration").

(2) Subject to sub-paragraph (3) below—

    (a)   any contractual remuneration paid to an employee by an employer of his in respect of a day of incapacity for work shall go towards discharging any liability of that employer to pay statutory sick pay to that employee in respect of that day; and

    (b)   any statutory sick pay paid by an employer to an employee of his in respect of a day of incapacity for work shall go towards discharging any liability of that employer to pay contractual remuneration to that employee in respect of that day.

(3) Regulations may make provision as to payments which are, and those which are not, to be treated as contractual remuneration for the purposes of sub-paragraph (1) or (2) above.

Sickness benefit

3 (1) This paragraph applies in any case where—

    (a)   a period of entitlement as between an employee and an employer of his comes to an end; and

    (b)   the first day immediately following the day on which the period of entitlement came to an end—

        (i)   is a day of incapacity for work in relation to that employee; and

        (ii) is not prevented by paragraph 1 above from being treated as a day of incapacity for work for the purposes of determining whether a period is a period of interruption of employment.

(2) In a case to which this paragraph applies, the day of incapacity for work mentioned in sub-paragraph (1)(b) above shall, except in prescribed cases, be or as the case may be form part of a period of interruption of employment notwithstanding section 57(1)(d)(ii) above.

(3) Where each of the first two consecutive days, or the first three consecutive days, following the day on which the period of entitlement came to an end is a day falling within sub-paragraphs (i) and (ii) of sub-paragraph (1)(b) above, sub-paragraph (2) above shall have effect in relation to the second day or, as the case may be, the second and third days, as it has effect in relation to the first day.

(4) Any day which is, by virtue of section 57(1)(e) above to be disregarded in computing any period of consecutive days for the purposes of Part II of this Act shall be disregarded in

determining, for the purposes of this paragraph, whether a day is the first day following the end of a period of entitlement or, as the case may be, the second or third consecutive such day.

4 (1) This paragraph applies in any case where—

    (a)   a period of entitlement as between an employee and an employer of his comes to an end; and

    (b)   that employee has a day of incapacity for work which—

        (i)   is, or forms part of, a period of interruption of employment; and

        (ii)   falls within the period of 57 days immediately following the day on which the period of entitlement came to an end.

(2) In a case to which this paragraph applies, section 31(4) above shall not apply in relation to a day of incapacity for work of a kind mentioned in sub-paragraph (1)(b) above or to any later day in the period of interruption of employment concerned.

Invalidity pension for widows and widowers

5 Paragraph 1 above does not apply for the purpose of determining whether the conditions specified in section 40(3) or 41(2) above are satisfied.

Unemployability supplement

6 Paragraph 1 above does not apply in relation to paragraph 3 of Schedule 7 to this Act and accordingly the references in paragraph 3 of that Schedule to a period of interruption of employment shall be construed as if the provisions re-enacted in this Part of this Act had not been enacted.   **[635]**

NOTES

    Commencement: 1 July 1992 (s 177(4)).

    This Schedule derived from the Social Security and Housing Benefits Act 1982, Sch 2 as amended by the Social Security Act 1985, s 18(6).

SCHEDULE 13

Section 168

RELATIONSHIP OF STATUTORY MATERNITY PAY WITH BENEFITS AND OTHER PAYMENTS, ETC

The general principle

1 Except as may be prescribed, a day which falls within the maternity pay period shall not be treated for the purposes of this Act as a day of unemployment or of incapacity for work for the purpose of determining whether it forms part of a period of interruption of employment.

Invalidity

2 (1) Regulations may provide that in prescribed circumstances a day which falls within the maternity pay period shall be treated as a day of incapacity for work for the purpose of determining entitlement to an invalidity pension.

(2) Regulations may provide that an amount equal to a woman's statutory maternity pay for a period shall be deducted from invalidity benefit in respect of the same period and a woman shall be entitled to invalidity benefit only if there is a balance after the deduction and, if there is such a balance, at a weekly rate equal to it.

Contractual remuneration

3(1) Subject to sub-paragraphs (2) and (3) below, any entitlement to statutory maternity pay shall not affect any right of a woman in relation to remuneration under any contract of service ("contractual remuneration").

(2) Subject to sub-paragraph (3) below—

(a) any contractual remuneration paid to a woman by an employer of hers in respect of a week in the maternity pay period shall go towards discharging any liability of that employer to pay statutory maternity pay to her in respect of that week; and

(b) any statutory maternity pay paid by an employer to a woman who is an employee of his in respect of a week in the maternity pay period shall go towards discharging any liability of that employer to pay contractual remuneration to her in respect of that week.

(3) Regulations may make provision as to payments which are, and those which are not, to be treated as contractual remuneration for the purposes of sub-paragraphs (1) and (2) above.

[636]

NOTES
Commencement: 1 July 1992 (s 177(4)).
Para 1 derived from the Social Security Act 1986, Sch 4, para 11 as amended by the Social Security Act 1988, s 16, Sch 4, para 19(1); para 2 derived from the Social Security Act 1986, Sch 4, para 11A as added by the Social Security Act 1988, s 16, Sch 4, para 19(2); para 3 derived from the Social Security Act 1988, Sch 4, para 12.

FURTHER AND HIGHER EDUCATION ACT 1992
(1992 c 13)

ARRANGEMENT OF SECTIONS

PART I
FURTHER EDUCATION

CHAPTER II
INSTITUTIONS WITHIN THE FURTHER EDUCATION SECTOR

An Act to make new provision about further and higher education

[6 March 1992]

NOTE
The only sections of this substantial Act reproduced here are those dealing with the employment law consequences of the creation of Further Education Corporations. Sections omitted are not annotated.

PART I
FURTHER EDUCATION

CHAPTER II
INSTITUTIONS WITHIN THE FURTHER EDUCATION SECTOR

Transfer of property, etc, to further education corporations

26 Transfer of staff to further education corporations

(1) This section applies to any person who immediately before the operative date in relation to a further education corporation established to conduct an institution which, on the date the corporation was established, was maintained by a local education authority or was a grant-maintained school—

    (a) is employed by the transferor to work solely at the institution the corporation is established to conduct, or

    (b) is employed by the transferor to work at that institution and is designated for the purposes of this section by an order made by the Secretary of State.

(2) A contract of employment between a person to whom this section applies and the transferor shall have effect from the operative date as if originally made between that person and the corporation.

(3) Without prejudice to subsection (2) above—

    (a) all the transferor's rights, powers, duties and liabilities under or in connection with a contract to which that subsection applies shall by virtue of this section be transferred to the corporation on the operative date, and

    (b) anything done before that date by or in relation to the transferor in respect of that contract or the employee shall be deemed from that date to have been done by or in relation to the corporation.

(4) Subsections (2) and (3) above are without prejudice to any right of an employee to terminate his contract of employment if a substantial change is made to his detriment in his working conditions, but no such right shall arise by reason only of the change in employer effected by this section.

(5) An order under this section may designate a person either individually or as a member of a class or description of employees.

(6) References in this section, in relation to a further education corporation, to the transferor are—

    (a) in relation to a corporation established to conduct an institution which, on the date on which it was established, was maintained by a local education authority, that authority,

    (b) in relation to a corporation established to conduct an institution which, on that date, was a voluntary aided or special agreement school, the governing body of the school, and

    (c) in relation to a corporation established to conduct an institution which, on that date, was a grant-maintained school, the governing body of the school.

(7) For the purposes of this section—

    (a) a person employed by the transferor is to be regarded as employed to work at an institution if his employment with the transferor for the time being involves work at that institution, and

    (b) subject to subsection (8) below, a person employed by the transferor is to be regarded as employed to work solely at an institution if his only employment with the transferor (disregarding any employment under a separate contract with the transferor) is for the time being at that institution.

(8) A person employed by the transferor in connection with the provision of meals shall not be regarded for the purposes of subsection (7)(b) above as employed to work solely at an institution unless the meals are provided solely for consumption by persons at the institution.

(9) This section is subject to section 48 of this Act.   **[637]**

NOTES
Commencement: 30 September 1992 (SI 1992/831).
Order under this section: SI 1993/465, SI 1993/612.

Property, rights and liabilities: general

43 Remuneration of employees

(1) Where, in consequence of a determination by the local education authority or any other person of the rate of remuneration of any employees, the rate of remuneration of any relevant employees would, apart from this section, be increased as from a date (referred to in this section as the "proposed date of increase") falling after 1st September 1992, the authority—

    (a) shall notify the Secretary of State in writing of the determination and the proposed date of increase, and

    (b) shall not pay any relevant employee at the new rate unless the increase is authorised under this section by the Secretary of State.

(2) In this section "relevant employees" means persons who are employed at institutions which are relevant institutions by virtue of section 39(2)(a) or (b) of this Act.

(3) This section does not apply to remuneration determined in accordance with the scales and other provisions set out or referred to in a pay and conditions order (within the meaning of the School Teachers' Pay and Conditions Act 1991).

(4) Where the Secretary of State receives a notification under subsection (1) above, he shall, before the end of the period of four weeks beginning with the day on which he received the notification, either—

    (a) authorise the increase resulting from the determination so far as it relates to relevant employees, or

    (b) afford to the authority, and to such persons appearing to him to be representative of relevant employees affected by the determination as he considers appropriate, an opportunity of making representations to him in respect of the determination.

(5) After considering any representations made to him under subsection (4)(b) above, the Secretary of State shall—

    (a) authorise the increase resulting from the determination, or

    (b) refuse to authorise the increase,

so far as it relates to relevant employees.

(6) The Secretary of State shall give written notification of any decision under subsection (4)(a) or (5) above to the local education authority and, in the case of subsection (5) above, to any other persons who made representations to him under subsection (4)(b) above.

(7) Subsection (8) below applies where—

    (a) by virtue of this section a relevant employee is not paid at the new rate on the proposed date of increase, but

(b) the Secretary of State authorises the increase after that date.

(8) Where this subsection applies, the employee concerned shall, for the purpose of determining the terms of any contract affected by section 26 of this Act, be regarded as having been entitled under his contract of employment to be paid by the local education authority at the new rate as from the proposed date of increase.   **[638]**

NOTE
Commencement: 6 May 1992 (SI 1992/831).

Miscellaneous

48 Statutory conditions of employment

(1) This section applies where—

   (a) an educational institution at which a school teacher is employed by a local education authority, or by the governing body of a voluntary or grant-maintained school, becomes an institution within the further education sector, and

   (b) immediately before the operative date, any of the terms and conditions of his employment have effect by virtue of a pay and conditions order.

(2) As from the operative date the person's contract of employment shall have effect—

   (a) in relation to him and to the governing body of the institution as it had effect immediately before that date in relation to school teachers and to local education authorities or governing bodies of voluntary or grant-maintained schools, and

   (b) as if the contract required any remuneration determined in accordance with the scales and other provisions set out or referred to in the relevant pay and conditions order to be paid to him by the governing body of the institution.

(3) Nothing in this section affects any right to vary the terms of any contract of employment.

(4) In this section—

   (a) "pay and conditions order" and "school teacher" have the same meaning as in the School Teachers' Pay and Conditions Act 1991, and

   (b) "relevant pay and conditions order", in relation to any person, means the pay and conditions order having effect in relation to him immediately before the operative date or, if that order is no longer in force, the pay and conditions order which would have had effect in relation to him if the institution at which he is employed had not become an institution within the further education sector.   **[639]**

NOTE
Commencement: 1 April 1993 (SI 1992/831).

49 Avoidance of certain contractual terms

(1) This section applies to any contract made between the governing body of an institution within the further education sector and any person employed by them, not being a contract made in contemplation of the employee's pending dismissal by reason of redundancy.

   (2) In so far as a contract to which this section applies provides that the employee—

   (a) shall not be dismissed by reason of redundancy, or

(b) if he is so dismissed, shall be paid a sum in excess of the sum which the employer is liable to pay to him under section 81 of the Employment Protection (Consolidation) Act 1978,

the contract shall be void and of no effect. **[640]**

NOTE
Commencement: 1 April 1993 (SI 1992/831).

OFFSHORE SAFETY ACT 1992

(1992 c 15)

ARRANGEMENT OF SECTIONS

An Act to extend the application of Part I of the Health and Safety at Work etc Act 1974; to increase the penalties for certain offences under that Part; to confer powers for preserving the security of supplies of petroleum and petroleum products; and for connected purposes

[6 March 1992]

1 Application of Part I of 1974 Act for offshore purposes

(1) The general purposes of Part I of the Health and Safety at Work etc Act 1974 ("the 1974 Act") shall include—

(a) securing the safety, health and welfare of persons on offshore installations or engaged on pipe-line works;

(b) securing the safety of such installations and preventing accidents on or near them;

(c) securing the proper construction and safe operation of pipe-lines and preventing damage to them; and

(d) securing the safe dismantling, removal and disposal of offshore installations and pipe-lines;

and that Part shall have effect as if the provisions mentioned in subsection (3) below were existing statutory provisions within the meaning of that Part and, in the case of the enactments there mentioned, were specified in the third column of Schedule 1 to that Act.

(2) Without prejudice to the generality of subsection (1) of section 15 of the 1974 Act (health and safety regulations), regulations under that section may—

(a) repeal or modify any of the provisions mentioned in subsection (3) below; and

(b) make any provision which, but for any such repeal or modification, could be made by regulations or orders made under any enactment there mentioned.

(3) The provisions referred to in subsections (1) and (2) above are—

(a) the Mineral Workings (Offshore Installations) Act 1971;

(b) sections 26, 27 and 32 (safety, inspectors and regulations) of the Petroleum and Submarine Pipe-lines Act 1975;

(c) in the Petroleum Act 1987, section 11(2)(a) (regulations) so far as relating to safety requirements and sections 21 to 24 (safety zones); and

(d) the provisions of any regulations or orders made or having effect under any enactment mentioned in the foregoing paragraphs.

(4) In this section—

"offshore installation" means any installation which is an offshore installation within the meaning of the Mineral Workings (Offshore Installations) Act 1971, or is to be taken to be an installation for the purposes of sections 21 to 23 of the Petroleum Act 1987;

"pipe-line" and "pipe-line works" have the same meanings as in section 26(1) of the Petroleum and Submarine Pipe-lines Act 1975.

(5) The provisions mentioned in subsection (3) above and the definitions in subsection (4) above shall have effect as if any reference in—

(a) section 1(4) of the Mineral Workings (Offshore Installations) Act 1971;

(b) section 20(2) of the Petroleum and Submarine Pipe-lines Act 1975; or

(c) section 16(1) or 21(7) of the Petroleum Act 1987,

to tidal waters and parts of the sea in or adjacent to the United Kingdom, or to the territorial sea adjacent to the United Kingdom, were a reference to tidal waters and parts of the sea in or adjacent to Great Britain, or to the territorial sea adjacent to Great Britain.   [641]

NOTE
Commencement: 6 March 1992 (the date of Royal Assent).

2 Application of Part I for other purposes

(1) The general purposes of Part I of the 1974 Act shall include—

(a) securing the proper construction and safe operation of pipe-lines and preventing damage to them;

(b) securing that, in the event of the accidental escape or ignition of anything in a pipe-line, immediate notice of the event is given to persons who will or may have to discharge duties or take steps in consequence of the happening of the event; and

(c) protecting the public from personal injury, fire, explosions and other dangers arising from the transmission, distribution, supply or use of gas;

and that Part shall have effect as if the provisions mentioned in subsection (3) below were existing statutory provisions within the meaning of that Part and, in the case of the enactments there mentioned, were specified in the third column of Schedule 1 to that Act.

(2) Without prejudice to the generality of subsection (1) of section 15 of the 1974 Act (health and safety regulations), regulations under that section may—

(a) repeal or modify any of the provisions mentioned in subsection (3) below; and

(b) make any provision which, but for any such repeal or modification, could be made by regulations made under any enactment mentioned in paragraph (b) of that subsection.

(3) The provisions referred to in subsections (1) and (2) above are—

(a) sections 27 to 32 and 37 (avoidance of damage to pipe-lines and notification of accidents etc) of the Pipe-lines Act 1962;

(b) in the Gas Act 1986, section 16 (standards of quality) so far as relating to standards affecting safety and section 47(3) and (4) (provision which may be made by regulations) so far as relating to regulations under section 16 so far as so relating; and

(c) the provisions of any regulations made or having effect under any enactment mentioned in paragraph (b) above.

(4) In this section—

"gas" means any substance which is or (if it were in a gaseous state) would be gas within the meaning of Part I of the Gas Act 1986;

"pipe-line" has the same meaning as in the Pipe-lines Act 1962.   [642]

NOTE
Commencement: Sub-ss (1), (2), (3)(a), (4): 6 March 1992 (the date of Royal Assent): sub-ss (3)(b), (c): to be appointed (s 7(3)).

3 (*S 3 (consequential provisions), which repeals various statutory provisions and makes provision in relation to licensing functions outside the scope of this work, is omitted.*)

4 Increased penalties under Part I

(1)–(5) . . .

(6) This section does not affect the punishment for any offence committed before the commencement of this section.   [643]

NOTE
Commencement: 6 March 1992 (the date of Royal Assent).

5, 6 (*Ss 5 (which empowers the Secretary of State to issue directions for preserving the security of offshore installations etc), 6 (extension to Northern Ireland) omitted.*)

7 Short title, repeals, commencement and extent

(1) This Act may be cited as the Offshore Safety Act 1992.

(2) The enactments mentioned in Schedule 2 to this Act are hereby repealed to the extent specified in the third column of that Schedule.

(3) The following provisions of this Act, namely—

(a) section 2(3)(b) and (c);

(b) section 3(1)(a) and (e), (2) and (3)(b); and

(c) subsection (2) above so far as relating to the repeal in the Continental Shelf Act 1964 and the second repeal in the Gas Act 1986,

shall not come into force until such day as the Secretary of State may by order made by statutory instrument appoint, and different days may be appointed for different provisions or for different purposes.

(4) This Act, except section 6 above, does not extend to Northern Ireland.

                                                                         [644]

NOTE
Commencement: 6 March 1992.

(*Schs 1 (model clauses), 2 (repeals) omitted.*)

TRADE UNION AND LABOUR RELATIONS (CONSOLIDATION) ACT 1992

(1992 c 52)

ARRANGEMENT OF SECTIONS

PART I
TRADE UNIONS

CHAPTER I
INTRODUCTORY

Meaning of "trade union"

CHAPTER V
RIGHTS OF TRADE UNION MEMBERS

Right to a ballot before industrial action

Right not to be denied access to the courts

Right not to be unjustifiably disciplined

Right to require employer to stop deduction of union dues

Right not to suffer deduction of unauthorised or excessive union subscriptions

Right to terminate membership of union

Supplementary

CHAPTER VI
APPLICATION OF FUNDS FOR POLITICAL OBJECTS

Restriction on use of funds for certain political objects

Political resolution

CHAPTER VII
AMALGAMATIONS AND SIMILAR MATTERS

PART III
RIGHTS IN RELATION TO UNION MEMBERSHIP AND ACTIVITIES

PART IV
INDUSTRIAL RELATIONS

CHAPTER I
COLLECTIVE BARGAINING

Introductory

CHAPTER II
PROCEDURE FOR HANDLING REDUNDANCIES

Duty of employer to consult trade union representatives

CHAPTER III
CODES OF PRACTICE

Codes of Practice issued by ACAS

An Act to consolidate the enactments relating to collective labour relations, that is to say, to trade unions, employers' associations, industrial relations and industrial action

[16 July 1992]

GENERAL NOTE

This Act consolidates the legislation relating to trade unions and industrial relations. It came into force on 16 October 1992; for dates of commencement of the provisions consolidated, reference should be made to the provisions themselves and relevant commencement orders. The derivation of each section is given at the end of the section. A Destination Table, indicating the provisions consolidated and where they may be found in the new Act, is printed after the Act itself and its Schedules.

The Act is printed in full except for Northern Ireland and repealing and amending provisions (ss 300(1), (2), 302(2), (3), Schs 1, 2, Sch 3, para 12). The Act is further and substantially amended, prospectively, by the Trade Union Reform and Employment Rights Act 1993: details are given in each affected section.

PART I

TRADE UNIONS

CHAPTER I

INTRODUCTORY

Meaning of "trade union"

1 Meaning of "trade union"

In this Act a "trade union" means an organisation (whether temporary or permanent)—

   (a) which consists wholly or mainly of workers of one or more descriptions and whose principal purposes include the regulation of relations between workers of that description or those descriptions and employers or employers' associations; or

   (b) which consists wholly or mainly of—

      (i) constituent or affiliated organisations which fulfil the conditions in paragraph (a) (or themselves consist wholly or mainly of constituent or affiliated organisations which fulfil those conditions), or

      (ii) representatives of such constituent or affiliated organisations,

   and whose principal purposes include the regulation of relations between workers and employers or between workers and employers' associations, or the regulation of relations between its constituent or affiliated organisations.

[645]

NOTES

Commencement: 16 October 1992.

This section contains provisions formerly in the Trade Union Act 1913, s 2(1), as substituted by the Trade Union and Labour Relations Act 1974, s 25(1), Sch 3, para 2(1), (2); the Trade Union (Amalgamations, etc) Act 1964, s 9(1) (definition "trade union"), as substituted by s 25(1) of, Sch 3, para 10(1), (8) to, the 1974 Act; s 28(1) of the 1974 Act; the Employment Protection Act 1975, s 126(1) (definition "trade union"); the Employment Act 1980, s 3(9), as added by the Employment Act 1988, s 18(2); the Trade Union Act 1984, ss 9(1) (definition "trade union"), 10(5) (definition "trade union"); s 32(1) (definition "trade union") of the 1988 Act; the Employment Act 1990, ss 3(1), 7(5) (definition "trade union"), 8(7) (definition "trade union"), 10(4)(a) (definition "trade union"); and deriving from the Employment Protection (Consolidation) Act 1978, s 153(1) (definition "trade union").

The list of trade unions

2 The list of trade unions

(1) The Certification Officer shall keep a list of trade unions containing the names of—

  (a) the organisations whose names were, immediately before the commencement of this Act, duly entered in the list of trade unions kept by him under section 8 of the Trade Union and Labour Relations Act 1974, and

  (b) the names of the organisations entitled to have their names entered in the list in accordance with this Part.

(2) The Certification Officer shall keep copies of the list of trade unions, as for the time being in force, available for public inspection at all reasonable hours free of charge.

(3) A copy of the list shall be included in his annual report.

(4) The fact that the name of an organisation is included in the list of trade unions is evidence (in Scotland, sufficient evidence) that the organisation is a trade union.

(5) On the application of an organisation whose name is included in the list, the Certification Officer shall issue it with a certificate to that effect.

(6) A document purporting to be such a certificate is evidence (in Scotland, sufficient evidence) that the name of the organisation is entered in the list.   [646]

NOTES
Commencement: 16 October 1992.
Sub-s (1) contains provisions formerly in the Trade Union and Labour Relations Act 1974, s 8(1), (2) (both in part), as amended (in both cases) and as repealed in part (in the case of sub-s (1)) by the Employment Protection Act 1975, s 125(1), (3), Sch 16, Pt III, para 1, Sch 18. Sub-ss (2), (3) contain provisions formerly in s 8(9) (in part) of the 1974 Act, as amended by s 125(1) of, Sch 16, Pt III, paras 1, 4 to, the 1975 Act. Sub-ss (4)–(6) contain provisions formerly in the 1974 Act, s 8(10) (in part), as amended and repealed in part by, s 125(1), (3) of, Sch 16, Pt III, paras 1, 5, Sch 18 to, the 1975 Act.

3 Application to have name entered on list

(1) An organisation of workers, whenever formed, whose name is not entered in the list of trade unions may apply to the Certification Officer to have its name entered in the list.

(2) The application shall be made in such form and manner as the Certification Officer may require and shall be accompanied by—

  (a) a copy of the rules of the organisation,
  (b) a list of its officers,
  (c) the address of its head or main office, and
  (d) the name under which it is or is to be known,

and by the prescribed fee.

(3) If the Certification Officer is satisfied—

  (a) that the organisation is a trade union,
  (b) that subsection (2) has been complied with, and
  (c) that entry of the name in the list is not prohibited by subsection (4),

he shall enter the name of the organisation in the list of trade unions.

(4) The Certification Officer shall not enter the name of an organisation in the list of trade unions if the name is the same as that under which another organisation—

    (a) was on 30th September 1971 registered as a trade union under the Trade Union Acts 1871 to 1964,

    (b) was at any time registered as a trade union or employers' association under the Industrial Relations Act 1971, or

    (c) is for the time being entered in the list of trade unions or in the list of employers' associations kept under Part II of this Act,

or if the name is one so nearly resembling any such name as to be likely to deceive the public.   **[647]**

NOTES
Commencement: 16 October 1992.
Sub-ss (1), (3) contain provisions formerly in the Trade Union and Labour Relations Act 1974, s 8(3) (in part), as amended by the Employment Protection Act 1975, s 125(1), Sch 16, Pt III, para 1. Sub-s (2) contains provisions formerly in s 8(4) (in part) of the 1974 Act, as amended by s 125(1) of, Sch 16, Pt III, para 1 to, the 1975 Act. Sub-s (4) contains provisions formerly in s 8(5) (in part) of the 1974 Act, as amended by s 125(1) of, Sch 16, Pt III, para 1 to, the 1975 Act.
Prescribed fee: £291 (see SI 1993/936).

4 Removal of name from the list

(1) If it appears to the Certification Officer, on application made to him or otherwise, that an organisation whose name is entered in the list of trade unions is not a trade union, he may remove its name from the list.

(2) He shall not do so without giving the organisation notice of his intention and considering any representations made to him by the organisation within such period (of not less than 28 days beginning with the date of the notice) as may be specified in the notice.

(3) The Certification Officer shall remove the name of an organisation from the list of trade unions if—

    (a) he is requested by the organisation to do so, or

    (b) he is satisfied that the organisation has ceased to exist.   **[648]**

NOTES
Commencement: 16 October 1992.
Sub-ss (1), (2) contain provisions formerly in the Trade Union and Labour Relations Act 1974, s 8(6) (in part), as amended by the Employment Protection Act 1975, s 125(1), Sch 16, Pt III, para 1, and as repealed in part by the Trade Union and Labour Relations (Amendment) Act 1976, s 1. Sub-s (3) contains provisions formerly in s 8(6A) (in part) of the 1974 Act, as inserted by s 125(1) of, Sch 16, Pt III, para 2 to, the 1975 Act.

Certification as independent trade union

5 Meaning of "independent trade union"

In this Act an "independent trade union" means a trade union which—

    (a) is not under the domination or control of an employer or group of employers or of one or more employers' associations, and

    (b) is not liable to interference by an employer or any such group or association (arising out of the provision of financial or material support or by any other means whatsoever) tending towards such control;

and references to "independence", in relation to a trade union, shall be construed accordingly.   **[649]**

NOTES

Commencement: 16 October 1992.

This section contains provisions formerly in the Trade Union and Labour Relations Act 1974, s 30(1) (definition "independent trade union"), as amended by the Employment Protection Act 1975, s 125(1), Sch 16, Pt III, para 7(3); in s 126(1) (in part) (definitions "independent trade union", "independence") of the 1975 Act; and deriving from the Employment Protection (Consolidation) Act 1978, s 153(1) (definition "independent trade union").

6 Application for certificate of independence

(1) A trade union whose name is entered on the list of trade unions may apply to the Certification Officer for a certificate that it is independent.

The application shall be made in such form and manner as the Certification Officer may require and shall be accompanied by the prescribed fee.

(2) The Certification Officer shall maintain a record showing details of all applications made to him under this section and shall keep it available for public inspection (free of charge) at all reasonable hours.

(3) If an application is made by a trade union whose name is not entered on the list of trade unions, the Certification Officer shall refuse a certificate of independence and shall enter that refusal on the record.

(4) In any other case, he shall not come to a decision on the application before the end of the period of one month after it has been entered on the record; and before coming to his decision he shall make such enquiries as he thinks fit and shall take into account any relevant information submitted to him by any person.

(5) He shall then decide whether the applicant trade union is independent and shall enter his decision and the date of his decision on the record.

(6) If he decides that the trade union is independent he shall issue a certificate accordingly; and if he decides that it is not, he shall give reasons for his decision.

[650]

NOTES

Commencement: 16 October 1992.

Sub-s (1) contains provisions formerly in the Employment Protection Act 1975, s 8(1), (2). Sub-s (2) contains provisions formerly in s 8(3) of the 1975 Act. Sub-s (3) contains provisions formerly in s 8(4) of the 1975 Act. Sub-s (4) contains provisions formerly in s 8(6) of the 1975 Act. Sub-s (5) contains provisions formerly in s 8(5)(a), (b) of the 1975 Act. Sub-s (6) contains provisions formerly in s 8(5)(c) of the 1975 Act.

Prescribed fee: £436 (see SI 1993/936).

7 Withdrawal or cancellation of certificate

(1) The Certification Officer may withdraw a trade union's certificate of independence if he is of the opinion that the union is no longer independent.

(2) Where he proposes to do so he shall notify the trade union and enter notice of the proposal in the record.

(3) He shall not come to a decision on the proposal before the end of the period of one month after notice of it was entered on the record; and before coming to his decision he shall make such enquiries as he thinks fit and shall take into account any relevant information submitted to him by any person.

(4) He shall then decide whether the trade union is independent and shall enter his decision and the date of his decision on the record.

(5) He shall confirm or withdraw the certificate accordingly; and if he decides to withdraw it, he shall give reasons for his decision.

(6) Where the name of an organisation is removed from the list of trade unions, the Certification Officer shall cancel any certificate of independence in force in respect of that organisation by entering on the record the fact that the organisation's name has been removed from that list and that the certificate is accordingly cancelled.
[651]

NOTES
Commencement: 16 October 1992.
Sub-s (1) contains provisions formerly in the Employment Protection Act 1975, s 8(7). Sub-s (2) contains provisions formerly in s 8(8)(a) of the 1975 Act, and in s 8(3), (5)(b) of that Act, as applied by s 8(8)(b) thereof. Sub-s (3) contains provisions formerly in s 8(6) of the 1975 Act, as so applied. Sub-s (4) contains provisions formerly in s 8(5)(a), (b) of the 1975 Act, as so applied. Sub-s (5) contains provisions formerly in s 8(8)(c) of the 1975 Act, and in s 8(5)(c) thereof, as so applied. Sub-s (6) contains provisions formerly in, s 8(10) of the 1975 Act.

8 Conclusive effect of Certification Officer's decision

(1) A certificate of independence which is in force is conclusive evidence for all purposes that a trade union is independent; and a refusal, withdrawal or cancellation of a certificate of independence, entered on the record, is conclusive evidence for all purposes that a trade union is not independent.

(2) A document purporting to be a certificate of independence and to be signed by the Certification Officer, or by a person authorised to act on his behalf, shall be taken to be such a certificate unless the contrary is proved.

(3) A document purporting to be a certified copy of an entry on the record and to be signed by the Certification Officer, or by a person authorised to act on his behalf, shall be taken to be a true copy of such an entry unless the contrary is proved.

(4) If in any proceedings before a court, the Employment Appeal Tribunal, the Central Arbitration Committee, ACAS or an industrial tribunal a question arises whether a trade union is independent and there is no certificate of independence in force and no refusal, withdrawal or cancellation of a certificate recorded in relation to that trade union—
   (a) that question shall not be decided in those proceedings, and
   (b) the proceedings shall instead be stayed or sisted until a certificate of independence has been issued or refused by the Certification Officer.

(5) The body before whom the proceedings are stayed or sisted may refer the question of the independence of the trade union to the Certificate Officer who shall proceed in accordance with section 6 as on an application by that trade union. **[652]**

NOTES
Commencement: 16 October 1992.
Sub-ss (1)–(3) contain provisions formerly in the Employment Protection Act 1975, s 8(11). Sub-s (4) contains provisions formerly in s 8(12)(a) of the 1975 Act. Sub-s (5) contains provisions formerly in s 8(12)(b) of the 1975 Act.

Supplementary

9 Appeal against decision of Certification Officer

(1) An organisation aggrieved by the refusal of the Certification Officer to enter its name in the list of trade unions, or by a decision of his to remove its name from the list, may appeal to the Employment Appeal Tribunal.

(2) A trade union aggrieved by the refusal of the Certification Officer to issue it with a certificate of independence, or by a decision of his to withdraw its certificate, may appeal to the Employment Appeal Tribunal.

(3) If on appeal the Tribunal is satisfied that the organisation's name should be or remain entered in the list or, as the case may be, that the certificate should be issued or should not be withdrawn, it shall declare that fact and give directions to the Certification Officer accordingly.

(4) The rights of appeal conferred by this section extend to any question of fact or law arising in the proceedings before, or arising from the decision of, the Certification Officer.   **[653]**

NOTES
Commencement: 16 October 1992.
Sub-s (1) contains provisions formerly in the Trade Union and Labour Relations Act 1974, s 8(7) (in part), as substituted by the Employment Protection Act 1975, s 125(1), Sch 16, Pt III, para 3, and as amended by the Employment Protection (Consolidation) Act 1978, s 159(2), Sch 16, para 18. Sub-s (2) contains provisions formerly in s 8(9) (in part) of the 1975 Act, as amended by s 152(9) of, Sch 16, para 23(1), (3) to, the 1978 Act. Sub-s (3) contains provisions formerly in s 8(7) (in part) of the 1974 Act, as substituted by s 125(1) of, Sch 16, Pt III, para 3 to, the 1975 Act, and as amended by s 159(2) of, Sch 16, para 18 to, the 1978 Act, and in s 8(9) (in part) of the 1975 Act, as amended by s 159(2) of, Sch 16, para 23(1), (3) to, the 1978 Act. Sub-s (4) contains provisions formerly in s 136(3) (in part) of the 1978 Act.

CHAPTER II
STATUS AND PROPERTY OF TRADE UNIONS

General

10 Quasi-corporate status of trade unions

(1) A trade union is not a body corporate but—

    (a) it is capable of making contracts;

    (b) it is capable of suing and being sued in its own name, whether in proceedings relating to property or founded on contract or tort or any other cause of action; and

    (c) proceedings for an offence alleged to have been committed by it or on its behalf may be brought against it in its own name.

(2) A trade union shall not be treated as if it were a body corporate except to the extent authorised by the provisions of this Part.

(3) A trade union shall not be registered—

    (a) as a company under the Companies Act 1985, or

    (b) under the Friendly Societies Act 1974 or the Industrial and Provident Societies Act 1965;

and any such registration of a trade union (whenever effected) is void.   **[654]**

NOTES
Commencement: 16 October 1992.
Sub-ss (1), (2) contain provisions formerly in the Trade Union and Labour Relations Act 1974, s 2(1)(a), (c), (d) (all in part), as repealed in part (in the case of s 2(1)(c)) by the Employment Act 1982, s 21(3), Sch 4. Sub-s (3) contains provisions formerly in s 2(2) (in part) of the 1974 Act (as amended by the Companies Consolidation (Consequential Provisions) Act 1985, s 30, Sch 2), and in s 2(3) of the 1974 Act, as read with the Interpretation Act 1978, s 17(2)(a).

11 Exclusion of common law rules as to restraint of trade

(1) The purposes of a trade union are not, by reason only that they are in restraint of trade, unlawful so as—

    (a) to make any member of the trade union liable to criminal proceedings for conspiracy or otherwise, or

    (b) to make any agreement or trust void or voidable.

(2) No rule of a trade union is unlawful or unenforceable by reason only that it is in restraint of trade.   **[655]**

NOTES
Commencement: 16 October 1992.
This section contains provisions formerly in the Trade Union and Labour Relations Act 1974, s 2(5) (in part).

Property of trade union

12 Property to be vested in trustees

(1) All property belonging to a trade union shall be vested in trustees in trust for it.

(2) A judgment, order or award made in proceedings of any description brought against a trade union is enforceable, by way of execution, diligence, punishment for contempt or otherwise, against any property held in trust for it to the same extent and in the same manner as if it were a body corporate.

(3) Subsection (2) has effect subject to section 23 (restriction on enforcement of awards against certain property).   **[656]**

NOTES
Commencement: 16 October 1992.
Sub-s (1) contains provisions formerly in the Trade Union and Labour Relations Act 1974, s 2(1)(b) (in part). Sub-s (2) contains provisions formerly in s 2(1)(e) (in part) of the 1974 Act. Sub-s (3) is a drafting provision.

13 Vesting of property in new trustees

(1) The provisions of this section apply in relation to the appointment or discharge of trustees in whom any property is vested in trust for a trade union whose name is entered in the list of trade unions.

(2) In the following sections as they apply to such trustees references to a deed shall be construed as references to an instrument in writing—

    (a) section 39 of the Trustee Act 1925 and section 38 of the Trustee Act (Northern Ireland) 1958 (retirement of trustee without a new appointment), and

    (b) section 40 of the Trustee Act 1925 and section 39 of the Trustee Act (Northern Ireland) 1958 (vesting of trust property in new or continuing trustees).

(3) Where such a trustee is appointed or discharged by a resolution taken by or on behalf of the union, the written record of the resolution shall be treated for the purposes of those sections as an instrument in writing appointing or discharging the trustee.

(4) In section 40 of the Trustee Act 1925 and section 39 of the Trustee Act (Northern Ireland) 1958 as they apply to such trustees, paragraphs (a) and (c) of subsection (4) (which exclude certain property from the section) shall be omitted.

[657]

NOTES
Commencement: 16 October 1992.
Sub-ss (1), (2), (4) contain provisions formerly in the Trade Union and Labour Relations Act 1974,
s 4(1), (2) (both in part). Sub-s (3) contains provisions formerly in s 4(3) (in part) of the 1974 Act.

14 Transfer of securities held in trust for trade union

(1) In this section—

"instrument of appointment" means an instrument in writing appointing a new trustee of a trade union whose name is entered in the list of trade unions, and

"instrument of discharge" means an instrument in writing discharging a trustee of such a trade union;

and for the purposes of this section where a trustee is appointed or discharged by a resolution taken by or on behalf of such a trade union, the written record of the resolution shall be treated as an instrument in writing appointing or discharging the trustee.

(2) Where by any enactment or instrument the transfer of securities of any description is required to be effected or recorded by means of entries in a register, then if—

(a) there is produced to the person authorised or required to keep the register a copy of an instrument of appointment or discharge which contains or has attached to it a list identifying the securities of that description held in trust for the union at the date of the appointment or discharge, and

(b) it appears to that person that any of the securities so identified are included in the register kept by him,

he shall make such entries as may be necessary to give effect to the instrument of appointment or discharge.

This subsection has effect notwithstanding anything in any enactment or instrument regulating the keeping of the register.

(3) A document which purports to be a copy of an instrument of appointment or discharge containing or having attached to it such a list, and to be certified in accordance with the following subsection to be a copy of such an instrument, shall be taken to be a copy of such an instrument unless the contrary is proved.

(4) The certificate shall be given by the president and general secretary of the union and, in the case of an instrument to which a list of securities is attached, shall appear both on the instrument and on the list.

(5) Nothing done for the purposes of or in pursuance of this section shall be taken to affect any person with notice of any trust or to impose on any person a duty to inquire into any matter.

(6) In relation to a Scottish trust, references in this section to the appointment and discharge of a trustee shall be construed as including references to, respectively, the assumption and resignation of a trustee; and references to an instrument appointing or discharging a trustee shall be construed accordingly.   **[658]**

NOTES
Commencement: 16 October 1992.
Sub-s (1) contains provisions formerly in the Trade Union and Labour Relations Act 1974, s 4(3) (in part). Sub-s (2) contains provisions formerly in s 4(4) (in part) of the 1974 Act, as amended by the Companies Consolidation (Consequential Provisions) Act 1985, s 30, Sch 2. Sub-s (3) contains provisions formerly in s 4(5) of the 1974 Act. Sub-s (4) contains provisions formerly in s 4(6) (in part) of the 1974 Act. Sub-s (5) contains provisions formerly in s 4(7) of the 1974 Act. Sub-s (6) contains provisions formerly in s 4(8) (in part) of the 1974 Act.

15 Prohibition on use of funds to indemnify unlawful conduct

(1) It is unlawful for property of a trade union to be applied in or towards—

    (a) the payment for an individual of a penalty which has been or may be imposed on him for an offence or for contempt of court,

    (b) the securing of any such payment, or

    (c) the provision of anything for indemnifying an individual in respect of such a penalty.

(2) Where any property of a trade union is so applied for the benefit of an individual on whom a penalty has been or may be imposed, then—

    (a) in the case of a payment, an amount equal to the payment is recoverable by the union from him, and

    (b) in any other case, he is liable to account to the union for the value of the property applied.

(3) If a trade union fails to bring or continue proceedings which it is entitled by bring by virtue of subsection (2), a member of the union who claims that the failure is unreasonable may apply to the court on that ground for an order authorising him to bring or continue the proceedings on the union's behalf and at the union's expense.

(4) In this section "penalty", in relation to an offence, includes an order to pay compensation and an order for the forfeiture of any property; and references to the imposition of a penalty for an offence shall be construed accordingly.

(5) The Secretary of State may by order designate offences in relation to which the provisions of this section do not apply.

Any such order shall be made by statutory instrument which shall be subject to annulment in pursuance of a resolution of either House of Parliament.

(6) This section does not affect—

    (a) any other enactment, any rule of law or any provision of the rules of a trade union which makes it unlawful for the property of a trade union to be applied in a particular way; or

    (b) any other remedy available to a trade union, the trustees of its property or any of its members in respect of an unlawful application of the union's property.

(7) In this section "member", in relation to a trade union consisting wholly or partly of, or of representatives of, constituent or affiliated organisations, includes a member of any of the constituent or affiliated organisations.   **[659]**

NOTES

Commencement: 16 October 1992.

Sub-ss (1)–(3) contain provisions formerly in the Employment Act 1988, s 8(1)–(3). Sub-s (4) contains provisions formerly in s 8(4) (in part) of the 1988 Act. Sub-s (5) contains provisions formerly in s 8(4), (5) (in part) of the 1988 Act. Sub-s (6) contains provisions formerly in s 8(6) of the 1988 Act. Sub-s (7) contains provisions formerly in s 32(1) (definition "member") of the 1988 Act.

Up to 1 September 1993, no order had been made under this section.

16 Remedy against trustees for unlawful use of union property

(1) A member of a trade union who claims that the trustees of the union's property—

    (a) have so carried out their functions, or are proposing so to carry out their functions, as to cause or permit an unlawful application of the union's property, or

    (b) have complied, or are proposing to comply, with an unlawful direction which has been or may be given, or purportedly given, to them under the rules of the union, may apply to the court for an order under this section.

(2) In a case relating to property which has already been unlawfully applied, or to an unlawful direction that has already been complied with, an application under this section may be made only by a person who was a member of the union at the time when the property was applied or, as the case may be, the direction complied with.

(3) Where the court is satisfied that the claim is well-founded, it shall make such order as it considers appropriate.

The court may in particular—

(a) require the trustees (if necessary, on behalf of the union) to take all such steps as may be specified in the order for protecting or recovering the property of the union;

(b) appoint a receiver of, or in Scotland a judicial factor on, the property of the union;

(c) remove one or more of the trustees.

(4) Where the court makes an order under this section in a case in which—

(a) property of the union has been applied in contravention of an order of any court, or in compliance with a direction given in contravention of such an order, or

(b) the trustees were proposing to apply property in contravention of such an order or to comply with any such direction,

the court shall by its order remove all the trustees except any trustee who satisfies the court that there is a good reason for allowing him to remain a trustee.

(5) Without prejudice to any other power of the court, the court may on an application for an order under this section grant such interlocutory relief (in Scotland, such interim order) as it considers appropriate.

(6) This section does not affect any other remedy available in respect of a breach of trust by the trustees of a trade union's property.

(7) In this section "member", in relation to a trade union consisting wholly or partly of, or of representatives of, constituent or affiliated organisations, includes a member of any of the constituent or affiliated organisations.   **[660]**

NOTES

Commencement: 16 October 1992.

Sub-ss (1)–(4) contain provisions formerly in the Employment Act 1988, s 9(1)–(4). Sub-s (5) contains provisions formerly in s 23 (in part) of the 1988 Act. Sub-s (6) contains provisions formerly in s 9(5) of the 1988 Act. Sub-s (7) contains provisions formerly in s 32(1) (definition "member") of the 1988 Act.

17 Nomination by members of trade unions

(1) The Secretary of State may make provision by regulations for enabling members of trade unions who are not under 16 years of age to nominate a person or persons to become entitled, on the death of the person making the nomination, to the whole or part of any money payable on his death out of the funds of the trade union.

(2) The regulations may include provision as to the manner in which nominations may be made and as to the manner in which nominations may be varied or revoked.

(3) The regulations may provide that, subject to such exceptions as may be prescribed, no nomination made by a member of a trade union shall be valid if at the date of the nomination the person nominated is an officer or employee of the trade

union or is otherwise connected with the trade union in such manner as may be prescribed by the regulations.

(4) The regulations may include such incidental, transitional or supplementary provisions as the Secretary of State may consider appropriate.

(5) They may, in particular, include provision for securing, to such extent and subject to such conditions as may be prescribed in the regulations, that nominations made under the Trade Union Act 1871 Amendment Act 1876 have effect as if made under the regulations and may be varied or revoked accordingly.

(6) Regulations under this section shall be made by statutory instrument which shall be subject to annulment in pursuance of a resolution of either House of Parliament.   **[661]**

NOTES
Commencement: 16 October 1992.
Sub-s (1) contains provisions formerly in the Trade Union and Labour Relations Act 1974, Sch 1, para 31(1)(a). Sub-ss (2), (3) contain provisions formerly in Sch 1, para 31(2) to the 1974 Act. Sub-ss (4), (5) contain provisions formerly in Sch 1, para 31(3) to the 1974 Act. Sub-s (6) contains provisions formerly in s 26(2), (3) of the 1974 Act.
Regulations under this section: Trade Union (Nominations) Regulations 1977, SI 1977/789.

18 Payments out of union funds on death of member

(1) The Secretary of State may make provision by regulations for enabling money payable out of the funds of a trade union on the death of a member, to an amount not exceeding £5,000, to be paid or distributed on his death without letters of administration, probate of any will or confirmation.

(2) The regulations may include such incidental, transitional and supplementary provisions as the Secretary of State may consider appropriate.

(3) Regulations under this section shall be made by statutory instrument which shall be subject to annulment in pursuance of a resolution of either House of Parliament.

(4) The Treasury may by order under section 6(1) of the Administration of Estates (Small Payments) Act 1965 direct that subsection (1) above shall have effect with the substitution for the reference to £5,000 of a reference to such higher amount as may be specified in the order.   **[662]**

NOTES
Commencement: 16 October 1992.
Sub-s (1) contains provisions formerly in the Trade Union and Labour Relations Act 1974, Sch 1, para 31(1)(b), as amended by the Administration of Estates (Small Payments) (Increase of Limits) Order 1984, SI 1984/539. Sub-s (2) contains provisions formerly in Sch 1, para 31(3) (in part) to the 1974 Act. Sub-s (3) contains provisions formerly in s 26(2), (3) of the 1974 Act. Sub-s (4) contains provisions formerly in Sch 1, para 31(4) of the 1974 Act, as substituted by the Employment Protection Act 1975, s 125(1), Sch 16, Pt III, para 32.
Regulations under this section: Trade Union (Nominations) Regulations 1977, SI 1977/789.

19 Application of certain provisions relating to industrial assurance or friendly societies

(1) The following provisions apply to a trade union as to an industrial assurance company—

(a) section 6(1) of the Industrial Assurance and Friendly Societies Act 1948 (prohibition on insuring money to be paid on death of child under ten);
(b) sections 63 to 66 of the Friendly Societies Act 1896 and section 4(2) of the Industrial Assurance Act 1923 (conditions on which payments to be made),

so far as they apply to cases excepted from that prohibition by paragraph (c) of the proviso to section 6(1) (children not ordinarily resident in United Kingdom or the Isle of Man).

(2) A trade union which contravenes section 6(1) of the Industrial Assurance and Friendly Societies Act 1948 commits an offence and is liable on summary conviction to a fine not exceeding level 3 on the standard scale.

The provisions of the Friendly Societies Act 1974 as to offences under that Act apply to an offence under this subsection.

(3) Section 52 of the Friendly Societies Act 1974 (charitable subscriptions and contributions to other registered societies) extends to a trade union, or branch of a trade union, as regards contributing to the funds and taking part in the government of a medical society, that is, a society for the purpose of relief in sickness by providing medical attendance and medicine.

A trade union, or branch of a trade union, shall not withdraw from contributing to the funds of such a society except on three months' notice to the society and on payment of all contributions accrued or accruing due to the date of the expiry of the notice.
[663]

NOTES
Commencement: 16 October 1992.
Sub-s (1) contains provisions formerly in the Industrial Assurance and Friendly Societies Act 1948, s 6(1), (2) (both in part), as repealed in part (in the case of sub-s (1)) by the Companies Act 1967, s 129, Sch 7 and by the Friendly Societies Act 1974, s 116(4), Sch 11, as amended (in that case) by the Trade Union and Labour Relations Act 1974, s 25(1), Sch 3, para 5(1), (2), and as repealed in part (in the case of sub-s (2)) by the Friendly Societies Act 1974, s 116(4), Sch 11. Sub-s (2) contains provisions formerly in s 16(4) of the 1948 Act, as amended and repealed in part by the Friendly Societies Act 1974, s 116(1), (4), Sch 9, para 12, Sch 11, as amended by the Trade Union and Labour Relations Act 1974, s 25(1), Sch 3, para 5(1), (3), and as affected by the Criminal Justice Act 1982, ss 38, 46. Sub-s (3) contains provisions formerly in the Friendly Societies Act 1896, s 26(2), (3), as amended and repealed in part by the Friendly Societies Act 1974, s 116(1), (4), Sch 9, para 1, Sch 11.
Sub-s (1): substituted by the Friendly Societies Act 1992, s 120(1), Sch 21, para 17, as from a day to be appointed, as follows—
"(1) Section 99 of the Friendly Societies Act 1992 (insurance of lives of children under 10) applies to a trade union as to an industrial assurance company.".
Sub-s (2): repealed by the Friendly Societies Act 1992, s 120(2), Sch 22, Pt I, as from a day to be appointed.

Liability of trade unions in proceedings in tort

20 Liability of trade union in certain proceedings in tort

(1) Where proceedings in tort are brought against a trade union—

(a) on the ground that an act—

(i) induces another person to break a contract or interferes or induces another person to interfere with its performance, or
(ii) consists in threatening that a contract (whether one to which the union is a party or not) will be broken or its performance interfered with, or that the union will induce another person to break a contract or interfere with its performance, or

(b) in respect of an agreement or combination by two or more persons to do or to procure the doing of an act which, if it were done without any such agreement or combination, would be actionable in tort on such a ground,

then, for the purpose of determining in those proceedings whether the union is liable in respect of the act in question, that act shall be taken to have been done by the union if, but only if, it is to be taken to have been authorised or endorsed by the trade union in accordance with the following provisions.

(2) An act shall be taken to have been authorised or endorsed by a trade union if it was done, or was authorised or endorsed—

(a) by any person empowered by the rules to do, authorise or endorse acts of the kind in question, or

(b) by the principal executive committee or the president or general secretary, or

(c) by any other committee of the union or any other official of the union (whether employed by it or not).

(3) For the purposes of paragraph (c) of subsection (2)—

(a) any group of persons constituted in accordance with the rules of the union is a committee of the union; and

(b) an act shall be taken to have been done, authorised or endorsed by an official if it was done, authorised or endorsed by, or by any member of, any group of persons of which he was at the material time a member, the purposes of which included organising or co-ordinating industrial action.

(4) The provisions of paragraphs (b) and (c) of subsection (2) apply notwithstanding anything in the rules of the union, or in any contract or rule of law, but subject to the provisions of section 21 (repudiation by union of certain acts).

(5) Where for the purposes of any proceedings an act is by virtue of this section taken to have been done by a trade union, nothing in this section shall affect the liability of any other person, in those or any other proceedings, in respect of that act.

(6) In proceedings arising out of an act which is by virtue of this section taken to have been done by a trade union, the power of the court to grant an injunction or interdict includes power to require the union to take such steps as the court considers appropriate for ensuring—

(a) that there is no, or no further, inducement of persons to take part or to continue to take part in industrial action, and

(b) that no person engages in any conduct after the granting of the injunction or interdict by virtue of having been induced before it was granted to take part or to continue to take part in industrial action.

The provisions of subsections (2) to (4) above apply in relation to proceedings for failure to comply with any such injunction or interdict as they apply in relation to the original proceedings.

(7) In this section "rules", in relation to a trade union, means the written rules of the union and any other written provision forming part of the contract between a member and the other members.   **[664]**

NOTES

Commencement: 16 October 1992.

Sub-s (1) contains provisions formerly in the Employment Act 1982, s 15(2), as amended by the Employment Act 1990, s 6(1), (2). Sub-ss (2)–(4) contain provisions formerly in s 15(3)–(3B) of the 1982 Act, as substituted by s 6(1), (3) of the 1990 Act. Sub-s (5) contains provisions formerly in s 15(8) of the 1982 Act. Sub-s (6) contains provisions formerly in s 15(9) of the 1982 Act, as added by s 6(1), (8) of the 1990 Act. Sub-s (7) contains provisions formerly in s 15(7) (definition "rules" (in part)) of the 1982 Act.

21 Repudiation by union of certain acts

(1) An act shall not be taken to have been authorised or endorsed by a trade union by virtue only of paragraph (c) of section 20(2) if it was repudiated by the executive,

president or general secretary as soon as reasonably practicable after coming to the knowledge of any of them.

(2) Where an act is repudiated—

    (a) written notice of the repudiation must be given to the committee or official in question, without delay, and

    (b) the union must do its best to give individual written notice of the fact and date of repudiation, without delay—

        (i) to every member of the union who the union has reason to believe is taking part, or might otherwise take part, in industrial action as a result of the act, and

        (ii) to the employer of every such member.

(3) The notice given to members in accordance with paragraph (b)(i) of subsection (2) must contain the following statement—

'Your union has repudiated the call (or calls) for industrial action to which this notice relates and will give no support to unofficial industrial action taken in response to it (or them). If you are dismissed while taking unofficial industrial action, you will have no right to complain of unfair dismissal.'

(4) If subsection (2) or (3) is not complied with, the repudiation shall be treated as ineffective.

(5) An act shall not be treated as repudiated if at any time after the union concerned purported to repudiate it the executive, president or general secretary has behaved in a manner which is inconsistent with the purported repudiation.

(6) The executive, president or general secretary shall be treated as so behaving if, on a request made to any of them within *six months* [three months] of the purported repudiation by a person who—

    (a) is a party to a commercial contract whose performance has been or may be interfered with as a result of the act in question, and

    (b) has not been given written notice by the union of the repudiation,

it is not forthwith confirmed in writing that the act has been repudiated.

(7) In this section "commercial contract" means any contract other than—

    (a) a contract of employment, or

    (b) any other contract under which a person agrees personally to do work or perform services for another. **[665]**

NOTES

Commencement: 16 October 1992.

Sub-s (1) contains provisions formerly in the Employment Act 1982, s 15(4), as substituted by the Employment Act 1990, s 6(1), (4). Sub-ss (2)–(4) contain provisions formerly in s 15(5)–(5B) of the 1982 Act, as substituted by s 6(1), (5) of the 1990 Act. Sub-s (5) contains provisions formerly in s 15(6) of the 1982 Act, as repealed in part by s 16(2) of, Sch 3 to, the 1990 Act. Sub-s (6) contains provisions formerly in s 15(6A) of the 1982 Act, as inserted by s 6(1), (6) of the 1990 Act. Sub-s (7) contains provisions formerly in s 15(7) (in part) (definition "commercial contract", as inserted by s 6(1), (7) of the 1990 Act) of the 1982 Act.

Sub-s (6): words in italics substituted by words in square brackets immediately following by the Trade Union Reform and Employment Rights Act 1993, s 49(1), Sch 7, para 17, as from 30 August 1993 (SI 1993/1908, below, para [1435]).

22 Limit on damages awarded against trade unions in actions in tort

(1) This section applies to any proceedings in tort brought against a trade union, except—

    (a) proceedings for personal injury as a result of negligence, nuisance or breach of duty;

(b) proceedings for breach of duty in connection with the ownership, occupation, possession, control or use of property;

(c) proceedings brought by virtue of Part I of the Consumer Protection Act 1987 (product liability).

(2) In any proceedings in tort to which this section applies the amount which may be awarded against the union by way of damages shall not exceed the following limit—

Number of members of union	Maximum award of damages
Less than 5,000	£10,000
5,000 or more but less than 25,000	£50,000
25,000 or more but less than 100,000	£125,000
100,000 or more	£250,000

(3) The Secretary of State may by order amend subsection (2) so as to vary any of the sums specified; and the order may make such transitional provision as the Secretary of State considers appropriate.

(4) Any such order shall be made by statutory instrument which shall be subject to annulment in pursuance of a resolution of either House of Parliament.

(5) In this section—

"breach of duty" means breach of a duty imposed by any rule of law or by or under any enactment;

"personal injury" includes any disease and any impairment of a person's physical or mental condition; and

"property" means any property, whether real or personal (or in Scotland, heritable or moveable).   **[666]**

NOTES

Commencement: 16 October 1992.

Sub-s (1) contains provisions formerly in the Employment Act 1982, s 16(1), (2) (both in part), as amended, in the case of sub-s (2), by the Consumer Protection Act 1987, s 48(1), Sch 4, para 8. Sub-s (2) contains provisions formerly in s 16(1) (in part), (3) of the 1982 Act. Sub-s (3) contains provisions formerly in s 16(4), (5)(b) of the 1982 Act. Sub-s (4) contains provisions formerly in s 16(5)(a) of the 1982 Act. Sub-s (5) contains provisions formerly in s 16(2)(b) (in part), (6) of the 1982 Act.

Up to 1 September 1993 no order had been made under this section.

Restriction on enforcement against certain property

23 Restriction on enforcement of awards against certain property

(1) Where in any proceedings an amount is awarded by way of damages, costs or expenses—

(a) against a trade union,

(b) against trustees in whom property is vested in trust for a trade union, in their capacity as such (and otherwise than in respect of a breach of trust on their part), or

(c) against members or officials of a trade union on behalf of themselves and all of the members of the union,

no part of that amount is recoverable by enforcement against any protected property.

(2) The following is protected property—

(a) property belonging to the trustees otherwise than in their capacity as such;

(b) property belonging to any member of the union otherwise than jointly or in common with the other members;

(c) property belonging to an official of the union who is neither a member nor a trustee;

(d) property comprised in the union's political fund where that fund—

(i) is subject to rules of the union which prevent property which is or has been comprised in the fund from being used for financing strikes or other industrial action, and

(ii) was so subject at the time when the act in respect of which the proceedings are brought was done;

(e) property comprised in a separate fund maintained in accordance with the rules of the union for the purpose only of providing provident benefits.

(3) For this purpose "provident benefits" includes—

(a) any payment expressly authorised by the rules of the union which is made—

(i) to a member during sickness or incapacity from personal injury or while out of work, or

(ii) to an aged member by way of superannuation, or

(iii) to a member who has met with an accident or has lost his tools by fire or theft;

(b) a payment in discharge or aid of funeral expenses on the death of a member or the wife of a member or as provision for the children of a deceased member.   **[667]**

NOTES
Commencement: 16 October 1992.
Sub-s (1) contains provisions formerly in the Employment Act 1982, s 17(1) (in part). Sub-s (2) contains provisions formerly in s 17(2) (in part), (3) (definitions "political fund" and "provident benefits fund") of the 1982 Act. Sub-s (3) contains provisions formerly in s 17(3) (definition "provident benefits") of the 1982 Act.

CHAPTER III
TRADE UNION ADMINISTRATION

Register of members' names and addresses

24 Duty to maintain register of members' names and addresses

(1) A trade union shall compile and maintain a register of the names and addresses of its members, and shall secure, so far as is reasonably practicable, that the entries in the register are accurate and are kept up-to-date.

(2) The register may be kept by means of a computer.

(3) A trade union shall—

(a) allow any member, upon reasonable notice, to ascertain from the register, free of charge and at any reasonable time, whether there is an entry on it relating to him; and

(b) if requested to do so by any member, supply him as soon as reasonably practicable, either free of charge or on payment of a reasonable fee, with a copy of any entry on the register relating to him.

(4) Any duty falling upon a branch under this section by reason of its being a trade union shall be treated as having been discharged to the extent to which the union of which it is a branch has discharged the duty instead.

(5) For the purposes of this section a member's address means either his home address or another address which he has requested the union in writing to treat as his postal address.

(6) The remedy for failure to comply with the requirements of this section is by way of application under section 25 (to the Certification Officer) or section 26 (to the court).

The making of an application to the Certification Officer does not prevent the applicant, or any other person, from making an application to the court in respect of the same matter.   **[668]**

NOTES
Commencement: 16 October 1992.
Sub-s (1) contains provisions formerly in the Trade Union Act 1984, s 4(1). Sub-s (2) contains provisions formerly in s 4(2) of the 1984 Act. Sub-s (3) contains provisions formerly in s 4(2A) of the 1984 Act, as inserted by the Employment Act 1988, s 33(1), Sch 3, Pt I, para 5(3). Sub-s (4) contains provisions formerly in s 4(3) of the 1984 Act. Sub-s (5) contains provisions formerly in s 9(1) (in part) (definition "proper address") of the 1984 Act. Sub-s (6) contains provisions formerly in ss 5(10), 6(3) (both in part) of the 1984 Act (as amended, in the case of s 5(10), by s 33(1) of, and Sch 3, Pt I, para 5(4)(a) to, the 1988 Act).
Sub-s (4): repealed by the Trade Union Reform and Employment Rights Act 1993, s 51, Sch 10, as from 30 August 1993 (SI 1993/1908, below, para **[1435]**).

[24A Securing confidentiality of register during ballots

(1)   This section applies in relation to a ballot of the members of a trade union on—

(a)   an election under Chapter IV for a position to which that Chapter applies,
(b)   a political resolution under Chapter VI, and
(c)   a resolution to approve an instrument of amalgamation or transfer under Chapter VII.

(2) Where this section applies in relation to a ballot the trade union shall impose the duty of confidentiality in relation to the register of members' names and addresses on the scrutineer appointed by the union for the purposes of the ballot and on any person appointed by the union as the independent person for the purposes of the ballot.

(3) The duty of confidentiality in relation to the register of members' names and addresses is, when imposed on a scrutineer or on an independent person, a duty—

(a)   not to disclose any name or address in the register except in permitted circumstances; and
(b)   to take all reasonable steps to secure that there is no disclosure of any such name or address by any other person except in permitted circumstances;

and any reference in this Act to "the duty of confidentiality" is a reference to the duty prescribed in this subsection.

(4) The circumstances in which disclosure of a member's name and address is permitted are—

(a)   where the member consents;
(b)   where it is requested by the Certification Officer for the purposes of the discharge of any of his functions or it is required for the purposes of the discharge of any of the functions of an inspector appointed by him;
(c)   where it is required for the purposes of the discharge of any of the functions of the scrutineer or independent person, as the case may be, under the terms of his appointment;
(d)   where it is required for the purposes of the investigation of crime or of criminal proceedings.

(5) Any provision of this Part which incorporates the duty of confidentiality as respects the register into the appointment of a scrutineer or an independent person has the effect of imposing that duty on the scrutineer or independent person as a duty owed by him to the trade union.

(6) The remedy for failure to comply with the requirements of this section is by way of application under section 25 (to the Certification Officer) or section 26 (to the court).

The making of an application to the Certification Officer does not prevent the applicant, or any other person, from making an application to the court in respect of the same matter.]   **[669]**

NOTE
    Inserted by the Trade Union Reform and Employment Rights Act 1993, s 6, as from 30 August 1993 (SI 1993/1908, below, para **[1435]**).

25 Remedy for failure: application to Certification Officer

(1) A member of a trade union who claims that the union has failed to comply with any of the requirements of section 24 [or 24A] (duties with respect to register of members' names and addresses) may apply to the Certification Officer for a declaration to that effect.

(2) On an application being made to him, the Certification Officer shall—
  (a) make such enquiries as he thinks fit, and
  (b) where he considers it appropriate, give the applicant and the trade union an opportunity to be heard,
and may make or refuse the declaration asked for.

(3) If he makes a declaration he shall specify in it the provisions with which the trade union has failed to comply.

(4) Where he makes a declaration and is satisfied that steps have been taken by the union with a view to remedying the declared failure, or securing that a failure of the same or any similar kind does not occur in future, or that the union has agreed to take such steps, he shall specify those steps in the declaration.

(5) Whether he makes or refuses a declaration, he shall give reasons for his decision in writing; and the reasons may be accompanied by written observations on any matter arising from, or connected with, the proceedings.

(6) In exercising his functions under this section the Certification Officer shall ensure that, so far as is reasonably practicable, an application made to him is determined within six months of being made.

(7) Where he requests a person to furnish information to him in connection with enquiries made by him under this section, he shall specify the date by which that information is to be furnished and, unless he considers that it would be inappropriate to do so, shall proceed with his determination of the application notwithstanding that the information has not been furnished to him by the specified date.

[(8) The Certification Officer shall not entertain an application for a declaration as respects an alleged failure to comply with the requirements of section 24A in relation to a ballot to which that section applies unless the application is made before the end of the period of one year beginning with the last day on which votes could be cast in the ballot.]   **[670]**

NOTES
Commencement: 16 October 1992.
Sub-s (1) contains provisions formerly in the Trade Union Act 1984, s 5(1) (in part), as amended by
the Employment Act 1988, s 33(1), Sch 3, Pt I, para 5(4)(a). Sub-s (2) contains provisions formerly in
ss 5(3) (in part), 6(5) of the 1984 Act. Sub-s (3) contains provisions formerly in s 5(4) (in part) of the 1984
Act. Sub-s (4) contains provisions formerly in s 6(1) (in part) of the 1984 Act. Sub-s (5) contains provisions
formerly in s 6(2) (in part) of the 1984 Act. Sub-s (6) contains provisions formerly in s 6(7) (in part) of
the 1984 Act. Sub-s (7) contains provisions formerly in s 6(8) (in part) of the 1984 Act.
Sub-s (1): words in square brackets inserted by the Trade Union Reform and Employment Rights Act
1993, s 49(2), Sch 8, para 40(a), as from 30 August 1993 (SI 1993/1908, below, para **[1435]**).
Sub-s (8): added by the Trade Union Reform and Employment Rights Act 1993, s 49(1), Sch 8, para
40(b), as from 30 August 1993 (SI 1993/1908, below, para **[1435]**).

26 Remedy for failure: application to court

(1) A member of a trade union who claims that the union has failed to comply with
any of the requirements of section 24 [or 24A] (duties with respect to register of
members' names and addresses) may apply to the court for a declaration to that effect.

(2) If an application in respect of the same matter has been made to the
Certification Officer, the court shall have due regard to any declaration, reasons or
observations of his which are brought to its notice.

(3) If the court makes a declaration it shall specify in it the provisions with which
the trade union has failed to comply.

(4) Where the court makes a declaration it shall also, unless it considers that to
do so would be inappropriate, make an enforcement order, that is, an order imposing
on the union one or both of the following requirements—

    (a) to take such steps to remedy the declared failure, within such period, as
          may be specified in the order;

    (b) to abstain from such acts as may be so specified with a view to securing
          that a failure of the same or a similar kind does not occur in future.

(5) Where an enforcement order has been made, any person who is a member of
the union and was a member at the time it was made, is entitled to enforce obedience
to the order as if he had made the application on which the order was made.

(6) Without prejudice to any other power of the court, the court may on an
application under this section grant such interlocutory relief (in Scotland, such interim
order) as it considers appropriate.

[(7) The court shall not entertain an application for a declaration as respects an
alleged failure to comply with the requirements of section 24A in relation to a ballot
to which that section applies unless the application is made before the end of the
period of one year beginning with the last day on which votes could be cast in the
ballot.]   **[671]**

NOTES
Commencement: 16 October 1992.
Sub-s (1) contains provisions formerly in the Trade Union Act 1984, s 5(1) (in part), as amended by
the Employment Act 1988, s 33(1), Sch 3, Pt I, para 5(4)(a). Sub-s (2) contains provisions formerly in
s 6(4) (in part) of the 1984 Act. Sub-s (3) contains provisions formerly in s 5(4) (in part) of the 1984 Act.
Sub-s (4) contains provisions formerly in s 5(5), (6), (7)(b), (c), (9) (all in part) of the 1984 Act. Sub-s (5)
contains provisions formerly in s 5(11), (12) (both in part) of the 1984 Act. Sub-s (6) contains provisions
formerly in s 23 (in part) of the 1988 Act.
Sub-s (1): words in square brackets inserted by the Trade Union Reform and Employment Rights Act
1993, s 49(2), Sch 8, para 41(a), as from 30 August 1993 (SI 1993/1908, below, para **[1435]**).
Sub-s (7): added by the Trade Union Reform and Employment Rights Act 1993, s 49(2), Sch 8, para
41(b), as from 30 August 1993 (SI 1993/1908, below, para **[1435]**).

Duty to supply copy of rules

27 Duty to supply copy of rules

A trade union shall at the request of any person supply him with a copy of its rules either free of charge or on payment of a reasonable charge.   **[672]**

NOTES
Commencement: 16 October 1992.
This section contains provisions formerly in the Trade Union and Labour Relations Act 1974, s 11(4) (in part).

Accounting records

28 Duty to keep accounting records

(1) A trade union shall—

> (a) cause to be kept proper accounting records with respect to its transactions and its assets and liabilities, and
> (b) establish and maintain a satisfactory system of control of its accounting records, its cash holdings and all its receipts and remittances.

(2) Proper accounting records shall not be taken to be kept with respect to the matters mentioned in subsection (1)(a) unless there are kept such records as are necessary to give a true and fair view of the state of the affairs of the trade union and to explain its transactions.   **[673]**

NOTES
Commencement: 16 October 1992.
Sub-s (1) contains provisions formerly in the Trade Union and Labour Relations Act 1974, s 10(1), (2) (both in part). Sub-s (2) contains provisions formerly in s 10(3) (in part) of that Act.

29 Duty to keep records available for inspection

(1) A trade union shall keep available for inspection from their creation until the end of the period of six years beginning with the 1st January following the end of the period to which they relate such of the records of the union, or of any branch or section of the union, as are, or purport to be, records required to be kept by the union under section 28.

This does not apply to records relating to periods before 1st January 1988.

(2) In section 30 (right of member to access to accounting records)—

> (a) references to a union's accounting records are to any such records as are mentioned in subsection (1) above, and
> (b) references to records available for inspection are to records which the union is required by that subsection to keep available for inspection.

(3) The expiry of the period mentioned in subsection (1) above does not affect the duty of a trade union to comply with a request for access made under section 30 before the end of that period.   **[674]**

NOTES
Commencement: 16 October 1992.
Sub-s (1) contains provisions formerly in the Employment Act 1988, s 6(1), (9)(a) (in part). Sub-s (2) contains provisions formerly in s 6(9)(a) (in part) of the 1988 Act, and contains drafting provisions. Sub-s (3) contains provisions formerly in s 6(2) (in part) of the 1988 Act.

30 Right of access to accounting records

(1) A member of a trade union has a right to request access to any accounting records of the union which are available for inspection and relate to periods including a time when he was a member of the union.

In the case of records relating to a branch or section of the union, it is immaterial whether he was a member of that branch or section.

(2) Where such access is requested the union shall—

(a) make arrangements with the member for him to be allowed to inspect the records requested before the end of the period of twenty-eight days beginning with the day the request was made,

(b) allow him and any accountant accompanying him for the purpose to inspect the records at the time and place arranged, and

(c) secure that at the time of the inspection he is allowed to take, or is supplied with, any copies of, or of extracts from, records inspected by him which he requires.

(3) The inspection shall be at a reasonable hour and at the place where the records are normally kept, unless the parties to the arrangements agree otherwise.

(4) An "accountant" means a person who is eligible for appointment as a company auditor under section 25 of the Companies Act 1989.

(5) The union need not allow the member to be accompanied by an accountant if the accountant fails to enter into such agreement as the union may reasonably require for protecting the confidentiality of the records.

(6) Where a member who makes a request for access to a union's accounting records is informed by the union, before any arrangements are made in pursuance of the request—

(a) of the union's intention to charge for allowing him to inspect the records to which the request relates, for allowing him to take copies of, or extracts from, those records or for supplying any such copies, and

(b) of the principles in accordance with which its charges will be determined,

then, where the union complies with the request, he is liable to pay the union on demand such amount, not exceeding the reasonable administrative expenses incurred by the union in complying with the request, as is determined in accordance with those principles.

(7) In this section "member", in relation to a trade union consisting wholly or partly of, or of representatives of, constituent or affiliated organisations, includes a member of any of the constituent or affiliated organisations.   **[675]**

NOTES

Commencement: 16 October 1992.

Sub-s (1) contains provisions formerly in the Employment Act 1988, s 6(2) (in part), (10). Sub-ss (2), (3) contain provisions formerly in s 6(3), (4), respectively of the 1988 Act. Sub-s (4) contains provisions formerly in the Trade Union and Labour Relations Act 1974, Sch 2, para 6 (in part), as amended by the Companies Consolidation (Consequential Provisions) Act 1985, s 30, Sch 2, and as read with the Interpretation Act 1978, s 17(2)(a), and in s 6(9)(c) of the 1988 Act. Sub-ss (5), (6) contain provisions formerly in s 6(5), (6), respectively, of the 1988 Act. Sub-s (7) contains provisions formerly in s 32(1) (definition "member") of the 1988 Act.

31 Remedy for failure to comply with request for access

(1) A person who claims that a trade union has failed in any respect to comply with a request made by him under section 30 may apply to the court.

(2) Where the court is satisfied that the claim is well-founded, it shall make such order as it considers appropriate for ensuring that that person—

   (a) is allowed to inspect the records requested,
   (b) is allowed to be accompanied by an accountant when making the inspection of those records, and
   (c) is allowed to take, or is supplied with, such copies of, or of extracts from, the records as he may require.

(3) Without prejudice to any other power of the court, the court may on an application under this section grant such interlocutory relief (in Scotland, such interim order) as it considers appropriate.   **[676]**

NOTES
   Commencement: 16 October 1992.
   Sub-ss (1), (2) contain provisions formerly in the Employment Act 1988, s 6(7). Sub-s (3) contains provisions formerly in s 23 (in part) of the 1988 Act.

Annual return, accounts and audit

32 Annual return

(1) A trade union shall send to the Certification Officer as respects each calendar year a return relating to its affairs.

(2) The annual return shall be in such form and be signed by such persons as the Certification Officer may require and shall be sent to him before 1st June in the calendar year following that to which it relates.

(3) The annual return shall contain—

   (a) the following accounts—

      (i) revenue accounts indicating the income and expenditure of the trade union for the period to which the return relates,
      (ii) a balance sheet as at the end of that period, and
      (iii) such other accounts as the Certification Officer may require,

   each of which must give a true and fair view of the matters to which it relates,

   [(aa) details of the salary paid to and other benefits provided to or in respect of—

      (i) each member of the executive,
      (ii) the president, and
      (iii) the general secretary,

   by the trade union during the period to which the return relates,]
   (b) a copy of the report made by the auditor or auditors of the trade union on those accounts and such other documents relating to those accounts and such further particulars as the Certification Officer may require, *and*
   (c) a copy of the rules of the trade union as in force at the end of the period to which the return relates [, and
   (d) in the case of a trade union required to maintain a register by section 24, a statement of the number of names on the register as at the end of the period to which the return relates and the number of those names which were not accompanied by an address which is a member's address for the purposes of that section;]

and shall have attached to it a note of all the changes in the officers of the union and of any change in the address of the head or main office of the union during the period to which the return relates.

(4) The Certification Officer may, if in any particular case he considers it appropriate to do so—

    (a) direct that the period for which a return is to be sent to him shall be a period other than the calendar year last preceding the date on which the return is sent;

    (b) direct that the date before which a return is to be sent to him shall be such date (whether before or after 1st June) as may be specified in the direction.

(5) A trade union shall at the request of any person supply him with a copy of its most recent return either free of charge or on payment of a reasonable charge.

(6) The Certification Officer shall at all reasonable hours keep available for public inspection either free of charge or on payment of a reasonable charge, copies of all annual returns sent to him under this section.

[(7) For the purposes of this section and section 32A "member of the executive" includes any person who, under the rules or practice of the union, may attend and speak at some or all of the meetings of the executive, otherwise than for the purpose of providing the committee with factual information or with technical or professional advice with respect to matters taken into account by the executive in carrying out its functions.]   **[677]**

NOTES
Commencement: 16 October 1992.
Sub-s (1) contains provisions formerly in the Trade Union and Labour Relations Act 1974, s 11(1), (2) (both in part), as amended, in the case of s 11(2), by the Employment Protection Act 1975, s 125(1), Sch 16, Pt III, para 1. Sub-s (2) contains provisions formerly in Sch 2, Pt I, para 1(1), (2) (both in part) to the 1974 Act, as so amended. Sub-s (3) contains provisions formerly in Sch 2, Pt I, paras 2–4 (all in part) to the 1974 Act, as amended, in the case of para 2(c), by s 125(1) of, Sch 16, Pt III, para 1 to, the 1975 Act. Sub-s (4) contains provisions formerly in Sch 2, Pt I, para 5 (in part) to the 1974 Act, as amended by s 125(1) of, Sch 16, Pt III, para 1 to, the 1975 Act. Sub-s (5) contains provisions formerly in s 11(4) (in part) of the 1974 Act. Sub-s (6) contains provisions formerly in s 11(5) (in part) of the 1974 Act, as amended by s 125(1) of, Sch 16, Pt III, para 1 to, the 1975 Act.
Sub-s (3): para (aa) inserted, word "and" at the end of para (b) repealed, and para (d) and the word "and" at the end of para (c) added, by the Trade Union Reform and Employment Rights Act 1993, ss 8, 51, Sch 10, as from 1 January 1994 (SI 1993/1908, below, para **[1435]**).
Sub-s (7): added by the Trade Union Reform and Employment Rights Act 1993, s 49(2), Sch 8, para 42, as from 1 January 1994 (SI 1993/1908, below, para **[1435]**).

[32A   Statement to members following annual return

(1) A trade union shall take all reasonable steps to secure that, not later than the end of the period of eight weeks beginning with the day on which the annual return of the union is sent to the Certification Officer, all the members of the union are provided with the statement required by this section by any of the methods allowed by subsection (2).

    (2) Those methods are—

    (a) the sending of individual copies of the statement to members; or

    (b) any other means (whether by including the statement in a publication of the union or otherwise) which it is the practice of the union to use when information of general interest to all its members needs to be provided to them.

    (3) The statement required by this section shall specify—

    (a) the total income and expenditure of the trade union for the period to which the return relates,

    (b) how much of the income of the union for that period consisted of payments in respect of membership,

    (c) the total income and expenditure for that period of any political fund of the union, and

    (d) the salary paid to and other benefits provided to or in respect of—

        (i) each member of the executive,

        (ii) the president, and

        (iii) the general secretary,

by the trade union during that period.

(4) The requirement imposed by this section is not satisfied if the statement specifies anything inconsistent with the contents of the return.

(5) The statement—

    (a) shall also set out in full the report made by the auditor or auditors of the union on the accounts contained in the return and state the name and address of that auditor or of each of those auditors, and

    (b) may include any other matter which the union considers may give a member significant assistance in making an informed judgment about the financial activities of the union in the period to which the return relates.

(6) The statement—

    (a) shall also include the following statement—

"A member who is concerned that some irregularity may be occurring, or have occurred, in the conduct of the financial affairs of the union may take steps with a view to investigating further, obtaining clarification and, if necessary, securing regularisation of that conduct.

The member may raise any such concern with such one or more of the following as it seems appropriate to raise it with: the officials of the union, the trustees of the property of the union, the auditor or auditors of the union, the Certification Officer (who is an independent officer appointed by the Secretary of State) and the police.

Where a member believes that the financial affairs of the union have been or are being conducted in breach of the law or in breach of rules of the union and contemplates bringing civil proceedings against the union or responsible officials or trustees, he may apply for material assistance from the Commissioner for the Rights of Trade Union Members and should, in any case, consider obtaining independent legal advice."; and

    (b) may include such other details of the steps which a member may take for the purpose mentioned in the statement set out above as the trade union considers appropriate.

(7) A trade union shall send to the Certification Officer a copy of the statement which is provided to its members in pursuance of this section as soon as is reasonably practicable after it is so provided.

(8) Where the same form of statement is not provided to all the members of a trade union, the union shall send to the Certification Officer in accordance with subsection (7) a copy of each form of statement provided to any of them.

(9) If at any time during the period of two years beginning with the day referred to in subsection (1) any member of the traded union requests a copy of the statement required by this section, the union shall, as soon as practicable, furnish him with such a copy free of charge.]   **[678]**

NOTE
Inserted by the Trade Union Reform and Employment Rights Act 1993, s 9, as from 1 January 1994 (SI 1993/1908, below, para **[1435]**).

33 Duty to appoint auditors

(1) A trade union shall in respect of each accounting period appoint an auditor or auditors to audit the accounts contained in its annual return.

(2) An "accounting period" means any period in relation to which it is required to send a return to the Certification Officer.   **[679]**

NOTES
Commencement: 16 October 1992.
Sub-s (1) contains provisions formerly in the Trade Union and Labour Relations Act 1974, s 11(3) (in part). Sub-s (2) contains provisions formerly in Sch 2, Pt I, para 22 (in part) to the 1974 Act, as amended by the Employment Protection Act 1975, s 125(1), Sch 16, Pt III, para 1.

34 Eligibility for appointment as auditor

(1) A person is not qualified to be the auditor or one of the auditors of a trade union unless he is eligible for appointment as a company auditor under section 25 of the Companies Act 1989.

(2) Two or more persons who are not so qualified may act as auditors of a trade union in respect of an accounting period if—

   (a) the receipts and payments in respect of the union's last preceding accounting period did not in the aggregate exceed £5,000,
   (b) the number of its members at the end of that period did not exceed 500, and
   (c) the value of its assets at the end of that period did not in the aggregate exceed £5,000.

(3) Where by virtue of subsection (2) persons who are not qualified as mentioned in subsection (1) act as auditors of a trade union in respect of an accounting period, the Certification Officer may (during that period or after it comes to an end) direct the union to appoint a person who is so qualified to audit its accounts for that period.

(4) The Secretary of State may by regulations—

   (a) substitute for any sum or number specified in subsection (2) such sum or number as may be specified in the regulations; and
   (b) prescribe what receipts and payments are to be taken into account for the purposes of that subsection.

Any such regulations shall be made by statutory instrument which shall be subject to annulment in pursuance of a resolution of either House of Parliament.

(5) None of the following shall act as auditor of a trade union—

   (a) an officer or employee of the trade union or of any of its branches or sections;
   (b) a person who is a partner of, or in the employment of, or who employs, such an officer or employee;
   (c) a body corporate.

References in this subsection to an officer shall be construed as not including an auditor.   **[680]**

NOTES

Commencement: 16 October 1992.

Sub-s (1) contains provisions formerly in the Trade Union and Labour Relations Act 1974, Sch 2, Pt I, para 6 (in part), as amended by the Companies Consolidation (Consequential Provisions) Act 1985, s 30, Sch 2, and as read with the Interpretation Act 1978, s 17(2)(a). Sub-s (2) contains provisions formerly in Sch 2, Pt I, para 9(1) (in part) to the 1974 Act. Sub-s (3) contains provisions formerly in Sch 2, Pt I, para 9(2) (in part) to the 1974 Act, as amended by the Employment Protection Act 1975, s 125(1), Sch 16, Pt III, para 1. Sub-s (4) contains provisions formerly in s 26(2), (3) of, Sch 2, Pt I, para 9(3) (in part) to, the 1974 Act. Sub-s (5) contains provisions formerly in Sch 2, Pt I, para 10 (in part) to the 1974 Act.

Sub-s (5): words in italics repealed by the Trade Union Reform and Employment Rights Act 1993, s 49(1), Sch 7, para 18, as from 30 August 1993 (SI 1993/1908, below, para **[1435]**).

35 Appointment and removal of auditors

(1) The rules of every trade union shall contain provision for the appointment and removal of auditors.

But the following provisions have effect notwithstanding anything in the rules.

(2) An auditor of a trade union shall not be removed from office except by resolution passed at a general meeting of its members or of delegates of its members.

(3) An auditor duly appointed to audit the accounts of a trade union shall be re-appointed as auditor for the following accounting period, unless—

- (a) a resolution has been passed at a general meeting of the trade union appointing somebody instead of him or providing expressly that he shall not be re-appointed, or
- (b) he has given notice to the trade union in writing of his unwillingness to be re-appointed, or
- (c) he is ineligible for re-appointment, or
- (d) he has ceased to act as auditor by reason of incapacity.

(4) Where notice has been given of an intended resolution to appoint somebody in place of a retiring auditor but the resolution cannot be proceeded with at the meeting because of the death or incapacity of that person, or because he is ineligible for the appointment, the retiring auditor need not automatically be re-appointed.

(5) The references above to a person being ineligible for appointment as auditor of a trade union are to his not being qualified for the appointment in accordance with *subsections (1) to (6)* [subsections (1) to (4)] of section 34 or being precluded by *subsection (7)* [subsection (5)] of that section from acting as its auditor.

(6) The Secretary of State may make provision by regulations as to the procedure to be followed when it is intended to move a resolution—

- (a) appointing another auditor in place of a retiring auditor, or
- (b) providing expressly that a retiring auditor shall not be reappointed,

and as to the rights of auditors and members of the trade union in relation to such a motion.

Any such regulations shall be made by statutory instrument which shall be subject to annulment in pursuance of a resolution of either House of Parliament.

(7) Where regulations under subsection (6)—

- (a) require copies of any representations made by a retiring auditor to be sent out, or
- (b) require any such representations to be read out at a meeting,

the court, on the application of the trade union or of any other person, may dispense with the requirement if satisfied that the rights conferred on the retiring auditor by the regulations are being abused to secure needless publicity for defamatory matter.

(8) On such an application the court may order the costs or expenses of the trade union to be paid, in whole or in part, by the retiring auditor, whether he is a party to the application or not.   **[681]**

NOTES
Commencement: 16 October 1992.
Sub-s (1) contains provisions formerly in the Trade Union and Labour Relations Act 1974, Sch 2, Pt I, paras 11–13 (all in part). Sub-s (2) contains provisions formerly in Sch 2, Pt I, para 12 (in part) to the 1974 Act. Sub-ss (3)–(5) contain provisions formerly in Sch 2, Pt I, para 13(1) (in part), (2) (in part), (3) (in part), respectively, to the 1974 Act. Sub-s (6) contains provisions formerly in s 26(2), (3) of, Sch 2, Pt I, para 14 (in part) to, the 1974 Act. Sub-ss (7), (8) contain provisions formerly in Sch 2, Pt I, para 15(1) (in part), (2) (in part), respectively, to the 1974 Act.
Sub-s (5): words in italics substituted respectively by words in square brackets immediately following, by the Trade Union Reform and Employment Rights Act 1993, s 49(1), Sch 7, para 19, as from 30 August 1993 (SI 1993/1908, below, para **[1435]**).

36 Auditor's report

(1) The auditor or auditors of a trade union shall make a report to it on the accounts audited by him or them and contained in its annual return.

(2) The report shall state whether, in the opinion of the auditor or auditors, the accounts give a true and fair view of the matters to which they relate.

(3) It is the duty of the auditor or auditors in preparing their report to carry out such investigations as will enable them to form an opinion as to—

   (a)   whether the trade union has kept proper accounting records in accordance with the requirements of section 28,
   (b)   whether it has maintained a satisfactory system of control over its transactions in accordance with the requirements of that section, and
   (c)   whether the accounts to which the report relates agree with the accounting records.

(4) If in the opinion of the auditor or auditors the trade union has failed to comply with section 28, or if the accounts do not agree with the accounting records, the auditor or auditors shall state that fact in the report.   **[682]**

NOTES
Commencement: 16 October 1992.
Sub-s (1) contains provisions formerly in the Trade Union and Labour Relations Act 1974, Sch 2, Pt I, para 18 (in part). Sub-s (2) contains provisions formerly in Sch 2, Pt I, para 19 (in part) to the 1974 Act. Sub-ss (3), (4) contain provisions formerly in Sch 2, Pt I, para 20 (in part) to the 1974 Act.

37 Rights of auditors

(1) Every auditor of a trade union—

   (a)   has a right of access at all times to its accounting records and to all other documents relating to its affairs, and
   (b)   is entitled to require from its officers, or the officers of any of its branches or sections, such information and explanations as he thinks necessary for the performance of his duties as auditor.

(2) If an auditor fails to obtain all the information and explanations which, to the best of his knowledge and belief, are necessary for the purposes of an audit, he shall state that fact in his report.

(3) Every auditor of a trade union is entitled—

(a) to attend any general meeting of its members, or of delegates of its members, and to receive all notices of and other communications relating to any general meeting which any such member or delegate is entitled to receive, and

(b) to be heard at any meeting which he attends on any part of the business of the meeting which concerns him as auditor.   **[683]**

NOTES
Commencement: 16 October 1992.
Sub-s (1) contains provisions formerly in the Trade Union and Labour Relations Act 1974, Sch 2, Pt I, para 16 (in part). Sub-s (2) contains provisions formerly in Sch 2, Pt I, para 21 (in part) to the 1974 Act. Sub-s (3) contains provisions formerly in Sch 2, Pt I, para 17 (in part) to the 1974 Act.

[Investigation of financial affairs

37A Power of Certification Officer to require production of documents etc

(1) The Certification Officer may at any time, if he thinks there is good reason to do so, give directions to a trade union, or a branch or section of a trade union, requiring it to produce such relevant documents as may be specified in the directions; and the documents shall be produced at such time and place as may be so specified.

(2) The Certification Officer may at any time, if he thinks there is good reason to do so, authorise a member of his staff or any other person, on producing (if so required) evidence of his authority, to require a trade union, or a branch or section of a trade union, to produce forthwith to the member of staff or other person such relevant documents as the member of staff or other person may specify.

(3) Where the Certification Officer, or a member of his staff or any other person, has power to require the production of documents by virtue of subsection (1) or (2), the Certification Officer, member of staff or other person has the like power to require production of those documents from any person who appears to the Certification Officer, member of staff or other person to be in possession of them.

(4) Where such a person claims a lien on documents produced by him, the production is without prejudice to the lien.

(5) The power under this section to require the production of documents includes power—

(a) if the documents are produced—

(i) to take copies of them or extracts from them, and

(ii) to require the person by whom they are produced, or any person who is or has been an official or agent of the trade union, to provide an explanation of any of them; and

(b) if the documents are not produced, to require the person who was required to produce them to state, to the best of his knowledge and belief, where they are.

(6) In subsections (1) and (2) "relevant documents", in relation to a trade union or a branch or section of a trade union, means accounting documents, and documents of any other description, which may be relevant in considering the financial affairs of the trade union.

(7) A person shall not be excused from providing an explanation or making a statement in compliance with a requirement imposed under subsection (5) on the ground that to do so would tend to expose him to proceedings for an offence; but an

explanation so provided or statement so made may only be used in evidence against the person by whom it is made or provided—

(a) on a prosecution for an offence under section 45(9) (false explanations and statements), or

(b) on a prosecution for some other offence where in giving evidence the person makes a statement inconsistent with it.]   **[684]**

NOTE

This section, the cross-heading immediately preceding it, and ss 37B–37E below, are inserted by the Trade Union Reform and Employment Rights Act 1993, s 10, as from 30 August 1993 (SI 1993/1908, below, para **[1435]**).

[37B Investigations by inspectors

(1) The Certification Officer may appoint one or more members of his staff or other persons as an inspector or inspectors to investigate the financial affairs of a trade union and to report on them in such manner as he may direct.

(2) The Certification Officer may only make such an appointment if it appears to him that there are circumstances suggesting—

(a) that the financial affairs of the trade union are being or have been conducted for a fraudulent or unlawful purpose,

(b) that persons concerned with the management of those financial affairs have, in connection with that management, been guilty of fraud, misfeasance or other misconduct,

(c) that the trade union has failed to comply with any duty imposed on it by this Act in relation to its financial affairs, or

(d) that a rule of the union relating to its financial affairs has not been complied with.

(3) Where an inspector is, or inspectors are, appointed under this section it is the duty of all persons who are or have been officials or agents of the trade union—

(a) to produce to the inspector or inspectors all relevant documents which are in their possession,

(b) to attend before the inspector or inspectors when required to do so, and

(c) otherwise to give the inspector or inspectors all assistance in connection with the investigation which they are reasonably able to give.

(4) Where any person (whether or not within subsection (3)) appears to the inspector or inspectors to be in possession of information relating to a matter which he considers, or they consider, to be relevant to the investigation, the inspector or inspectors may require him—

(a) to produce to the inspector or inspectors any relevant documents relating to that matter,

(b) to attend before the inspector or inspectors, and

(c) otherwise to give the inspector or inspectors all assistance in connection with the investigation which he is reasonably able to give;

and it is the duty of the person to comply with the requirement.

(5) In subsections (3) and (4) "relevant documents", in relation to an investigation of the financial affairs of a trade union, means accounting documents, and documents of any other description, which may be relevant to the investigation.

(6) A person shall not be excused from providing an explanation or making a statement in compliance with subsection (3) or a requirement imposed under subsection (4) on the ground that to do so would tend to expose him to proceedings

for an offence; but an explanation so provided or statement so made may only be used in evidence against the person by whom it is provided or made—

    (a) on a prosecution for an offence under section 45(9) (false explanations and statements), or

    (b) on a prosecution for some other offence where in giving evidence the person makes a statement inconsistent with it.]   **[685]**

NOTE

This section, s 37A and the cross-heading immediately preceding it, and ss 37C–37E, are inserted by the Trade Union Reform and Employment Rights Act 1993, s 10, as from 30 August 1993 (SI 1993/1908, below, para **[1435]**).

[37C Inspectors' reports etc

(1) An inspector or inspectors appointed under section 37B—

    (a) may, and if so directed by the Certification Officer shall, make interim reports, and

    (b) on the conclusion of their investigation shall make a final report,

to the Certification Officer.

(2) Any report under subsection (1) shall be written or printed, as the Certification Officer directs.

(3) An inspector or inspectors appointed under section 37B may at any time, and if so directed by the Certification Officer shall, inform the Certification Officer of any matters coming to his or their knowledge as a result of the investigation.

(4) The Certification Officer may direct an inspector or inspectors appointed under section 37B to take no further steps in the investigation, or to take only such further steps as are specified in the direction, if—

    (a) it appears to the Certification Officer that matters have come to light in the course of the investigation which suggest that a criminal offence has been committed and those matters have been referred to the appropriate prosecuting authority, or

    (b) it appears to the Certification Officer appropriate to do so in any other circumstances.

(5) Where an investigation is the subject of a direction under subsection (4), the inspector or inspectors shall make a final report to the Certification Officer only where the Certification Officer directs him or them to do so at the time of the direction under that subsection or subsequently.

(6) The Certification Officer shall publish a final report made to him under this section.

(7) The Certification Officer shall furnish a copy of such a report free of charge—

    (a) to the trade union which is the subject of the report,

    (b) to any auditor of that trade union or of any branch or section of the union, if he requests a copy before the end of the period of three years beginning with the day on which the report is published, and

    (c) to any member of the trade union if—

        (i) he has complained to the Certification Officer that there are circumstances suggesting any of the states of affairs specified in section 37B(2)(a) to (d),

       (ii) the Certification Officer considers that the report contains findings which are relevant to the complaint, and

      (iii) the member requests a copy before the end of the period of three years beginning with the day on which the report is published.

(8) A copy of any report under this section, certified by the Certification Officer to be a true copy, is admissible in any legal proceedings as evidence of the opinion of the inspector or inspectors in relation to any matter contained in the report; and a document purporting to be a certificate of the Certification Officer under this subsection shall be received in evidence and be deemed to be such a certificate unless the contrary is proved.]   **[686]**

NOTE
This section, s 37A and the cross-heading immediately preceding it, and ss 37B, 37D, 37E, are inserted by the Trade Union Reform and Employment Rights Act 1993, s 10, as from 30 August 1993 (SI 1993/1908, below, para **[1435]**).

[37D Expenses of investigations

(1) The expenses of an investigation under section 37B shall be defrayed in the first instance by the Certification Officer.

(2) For the purposes of this section there shall be treated as expenses of an investigation, in particular, such reasonable sums as the Certification Officer may determine in respect of general staff costs and overheads.

(3) A person who is convicted on a prosecution instituted as a result of the investigation may in the same proceedings be ordered to pay the expenses of the investigation to such extent as may be specified in the order.]   **[687]**

NOTE
This section, s 37A and the cross-heading immediately preceding it, and ss 37B, 37C, 37E, are inserted by the Trade Union Reform and Employment Rights Act 1993, s 10, as from 30 August 1993 (SI 1993/1908, below, para **[1435]**).

[37E Sections 37A and 37B: supplementary

(1) Where—

(a) a report of the auditor or auditors of a trade union, or a branch or section of a trade union, on the accounts audited by him or them and contained in the annual return of the union, or branch or section—

(i) does not state without qualification that the accounts give a true and fair view of the matters to which they relate, or

(ii) includes a statement in compliance with section 36(4), or

(b) a member of a trade union has complained to the Certification Officer that there are circumstances suggesting any of the states of affairs specified in section 37B(2)(a) to (d),

the Certification Officer shall consider whether it is appropriate for him to exercise any of the powers conferred on him by sections 37A and 37B.

(2) If in a case where a member of a trade union has complained as mentioned in subsection (1)(b) the Certification Officer decides not to exercise any of the powers conferred by those sections he shall, as soon as reasonably practicable after making a decision not to do so, notify the member of his decision and, if he thinks fit, of the reasons for it.

(3) Nothing in section 37A or 37B—

(a) requires or authorises anyone to require the disclosure by a person of information which he would in an action in the High Court or the Court of Session be entitled to refuse to disclose on grounds of legal professional privilege except, if he is a lawyer, the name and address of his client, or

(b) requires or authorises anyone to require the production by a person of a document which he would in such an action be entitled to refuse to produce on such grounds.

(4) Nothing in section 37A or 37B requires or authorises anyone to require the disclosure of information or the production of documents in respect of which the person to whom the requirement would relate owes an obligation of confidence by virtue of carrying on the business of banking unless—

    (a) the person to whom the obligation is owed is the trade union, or any branch or section of the union, concerned or a trustee of any fund concerned, or

    (b) the person to whom the obligation of confidence is owed consents to the disclosure or production.

(5) In sections 37A and 37B and this section—

    (a) references to documents include information recorded in any form, and

    (b) in relation to information recorded otherwise than in legible form, references to its production are to the production of a copy of the information in legible form.]   **[688]**

NOTE

This section, s 37A and the cross-heading immediately preceding it, and ss 37B–37D, are inserted by the Trade Union Reform and Employment Rights Act 1993, s 10, as from 30 August 1993 (SI 1993/1908, below, para **[1435]**).

Members' superannuation schemes

38 Members' superannuation schemes: separate fund to be maintained

(1) In the following provisions a "members' superannuation scheme" means any scheme or arrangement made by or on behalf of a trade union (including a scheme or arrangement shown in the rules of the union) in so far as it provides—

    (a) for benefits to be paid by way of pension (including any widows' or children's pensions or dependants' pensions) to or in respect of members or former members of the trade union, and

    (b) for those benefits to be so paid either out of the funds of the union or under an insurance scheme maintained out of those funds.

(2) A trade union shall not maintain a members' superannuation scheme unless it maintains a separate fund for the payment of benefits in accordance with the scheme.

A "separate fund" means a fund separate from the general funds of the trade union.
                                                                              [689]

NOTES

Commencement: 16 October 1992.

Sub-s (1) contains provisions formerly in the Trade Union and Labour Relations Act 1974, Sch 2, Pt II, para 36(a) (in part). Sub-s (2) contains provisions formerly in Sch 2, Pt II, paras 34, 35, 36(c) (all in part) to the 1974 Act.

39 Examination of proposals for new scheme

(1) A trade union shall not begin to maintain a members' superannuation scheme unless, before the date on which the scheme begins to be maintained—

    (a) the proposals for the scheme have been examined by an appropriately qualified actuary, and

    (b) a copy of a report made to the trade union by the actuary on the results of his examination of the proposals, signed by the actuary, has been sent to the Certification Officer.

(2) The actuary's report shall state—

    (a) whether in his opinion the premium or contribution rates will be adequate,

    (b) whether the accounting or funding arrangements are suitable, and

(c) whether in his opinion the fund for the payment of benefits will be adequate.

(3) A copy of the actuary's report shall, on the application of any of the union's members, be supplied to him free of charge.   **[690]**

NOTES
Commencement: 16 October 1992.
Sub-s (1) contains provisions formerly in the Trade Union and Labour Relations Act 1974, Sch 2, Pt II, para 27(a), (b) (both in part), as amended, in the case of sub-para (b), by the Employment Protection Act 1975, s 125(1), Sch 16, Pt III, para 1. Sub-s (2) contains provisions formerly in Sch 2, Pt II, para 25 to the 1974 Act, as applied by para 27 thereof. Sub-s (3) contains provisions formerly in Sch 2, Pt II, para 28 (in part) to the 1974 Act.

40 Periodical re-examination of existing schemes

(1) Where a trade union maintains a members' superannuation scheme, it shall arrange for the scheme to be examined periodically by an appropriately qualified actuary and for a report to be made to it by the actuary on the result of his examination.

(2) The examination shall be of the scheme as it has effect at such date as the trade union may determine, not being more than five years after the date by reference to which the last examination or, as the case may be, the examination of the proposals for the scheme was carried out.

(3) The examination shall include a valuation (as at the date by reference to which the examination is carried out) of the assets comprised in the fund maintained for the payment of benefits and of the liabilities falling to be discharged out of it.

(4) The actuary's report shall state—
  (a) whether in his opinion the premium or contribution rates are adequate,
  (b) whether the accounting or funding arrangements are suitable, and
  (c) whether in his opinion the fund for the payment of benefits is adequate.

(5) A copy of the report, signed by the actuary, shall be sent to the Certification Officer.

(6) The trade union shall make such arrangements as will enable the report to be sent to the Certification Officer within a year of the date by reference to which the examination was carried out.

(7) A copy of the actuary's report shall, on the application of any of the union's members, be supplied to him free of charge.   **[691]**

NOTES
Commencement: 16 October 1992.
Sub-s (1) contains provisions formerly in the Trade Union and Labour Relations Act 1974, Sch 2, Pt II, para 32(1) (in part). Sub-s (2) contains provisions formerly in Sch 2, Pt II, para 32(2) (in part) to the 1974 Act. Sub-s (3) contains provisions formerly in Sch 2, Pt II, para 24 (in part) to the 1974 Act, as applied by para 33 thereof. Sub-s (4) contains provisions formerly in Sch 2, Pt II, para 25 (in part) to the 1974 Act, as so applied. Sub-ss (5), (6) contain provisions formerly in Sch 2, Pt II, para 26 (in part) to the 1974 Act, as amended by the Employment Protection Act 1975, s 125(1), Sch 16, Pt III, para 1, as so applied. Sub-s (7) contains provisions formerly in Sch 2, Pt II, para 28 (in part) to the 1974 Act, as so applied.

41 Powers of the Certification Officer

(1) The Certification Officer may, on the application of a trade union—
  (a) exempt a members' superannuation scheme which the union proposes to maintain from the requirements of section 39 (examination of proposals for new scheme), or
  (b) exempt a members' superannuation scheme which the union maintains

from the requirements of section 40 (periodical re–examination of scheme),

if he is satisfied that, by reason of the small number of members to which the scheme is applicable or for any other special reasons, it is unnecessary for the scheme to be examined in accordance with those provisions.

(2) An exemption may be revoked if it appears to the Certification Officer that the circumstances by reason of which it was granted have ceased to exist.

(3) Where an exemption is revoked under subsection (1)(b), the date as at which the next periodical examination is to be carried out under section 40 shall be such as the Certification Officer may direct.

(4) The Certification Officer may in any case direct that section 40 (periodical re-examination of schemes) shall apply to a trade union with the substitution for the reference to five years of a reference to such shorter period as may be specified in the direction. **[692]**

NOTES
Commencement: 16 October 1992.
Sub-s (1) contains provisions formerly in the Trade Union and Labour Relations Act 1974, Sch 2, Pt II, paras 30, 33A (both in part), as amended, in the case of para 30, by the Employment Protection Act 1975, s 125(1), Sch 16, Pt III, para 1, and as added, in the case of para 33A, by the Employment Act 1980, s 202, Sch 1, para 3. Sub-s (2) contains provisions formerly in Sch 2, Pt II, paras 31, 33B (both in part) to the 1974 Act, as amended, in the case of para 31, by the Employment Protection Act 1975, s 125(1), Sch 16, Pt III, para 1, and as added, in the case of para 33B, by the Employment Act 1980, s 202, Sch 1, para 3. Sub-s (3) contains provisions formerly in Sch 2, Pt II, para 33B (in part) to the 1974 Act, as added by the Employment Act 1980, s 202, Sch 1, para 3. Sub-s (4) contains provisions formerly in Sch 2, Pt II, para 32(3) (in part) to the 1974 Act, as amended by the Employment Protection Act 1975, s 125(1), Sch 16, Pt III, para 1.

42 Meaning of "appropriately qualified actuary"

In sections 39 and 40 an "appropriately qualified actuary" means a person who is either—

    (a) a Fellow of the Institute of Actuaries, or

    (b) a Fellow of the Faculty of Actuaries,

or is approved by the Certification Officer on the application of the trade union as a person having actuarial knowledge. **[693]**

NOTES
Commencement: 16 October 1992.
This section contains provisions formerly in the Trade Union and Labour Relations Act 1974, Sch 2, Pt II, para 36(b) (in part), as amended by the Employment Protection Act 1975, s 125(1), Sch 16, Pt III, para 1.

Supplementary

43 Newly-formed trade unions

(1) The following provisions of this Chapter do not apply to a trade union which has been in existence for less than twelve months—

    (a) section 27 (duty to supply copy of rules),

    (b) sections 32 to 37 (annual return, [statement for members,] accounts and audit), *and*

  [(ba) sections 37A to 37E (investigation of financial affairs), and]

    (c) sections 38 to 42 (members' superannuation schemes).

(2) Sections 24 to 26 (register of members' names and addresses) do not apply to a trade union until more than one year has elapsed since its formation (by amalgamation or otherwise).

For this purpose the date of formation of a trade union formed otherwise than by amalgamation shall be taken to be the date on which the first members of the executive of the union are first appointed or elected.   **[694]**

NOTES
Commencement: 16 October 1992.
Sub-s (1) contains provisions formerly in the Trade Union and Labour Relations Act 1974, s 11(1) (in part). Sub-s (2) contains provisions formerly in the Trade Union Act 1984, s 7(4)–(7) (in part).
Sub-s (1): words in square brackets inserted, the word "and" in italics repealed, and para (ba) inserted, by the Trade Union Reform and Employment Rights Act 1993, ss 49(2), 51, Sch 8, para 43, Sch 10, as from 1 January 1994 (para (b)) and 30 August 1993 (para (ba) and repeal) (SI 1993/1908, below, para **[1435]**).

44   Discharge of duties in case of union having branches or sections

(1) The following provisions apply where a trade union consists of or includes branches or sections.

(2) Any duty falling upon the union in relation to a branch or section under the provisions of—

> section 28 (duty to keep accounting records),
>
> *sections 32 to 37* [sections 32 and 33 to 37] (annual return, accounts and audit),
>
> or
>
> sections 38 to 42 (members' superannuation schemes),

shall be treated as discharged to the extent to which a branch or section discharges it instead of the union.

(3) In sections 29 to 31 (right of member to access to accounting records) references to a branch or section do not include a branch or section which is itself a trade union.

(4) Any duty falling upon a branch or section by reason of its being a trade union under—

> section 24 (register of members' names and addresses),
>
> section 28 (duty to keep accounting records),
>
> *sections 32 to 37* [sections 32 and 33 to 37] (annual return, accounts and audit),
>
> or
>
> sections 38 to 42 (members' superannuation schemes),

shall be treated as discharged to the extent to which the union of which it is a branch or section discharges the duty instead of it.

[(5) Where the duty falling on a trade union under section 32 to send to the Certification Officer a return relating to its affairs is treated as discharged by the union by virtue of subsection (2) or (4) of this section, the duties imposed by section 32A in relation to the return shall be treated as duties of the branch or section of the union, or the trade union of which it is a branch or section, by which that duty is in fact discharged.]   **[695]**

NOTES
Commencement: 16 October 1992.
Sub-ss (1), (2) contain provisions formerly in the Trade Union and Labour Relations Act 1974, ss 10(4), 11(8) (both in part). Sub-s (3) is a drafting provision. Sub-s (4) contains provisions formerly in ss 10(4), 11(8) (both in part) of the 1974 Act, and in the Trade Union Act 1984, s 4(3).
Sub-ss (2), (4): words in italics substituted in each case by words in square brackets immediately following by the Trade Union Reform and Employment Rights Act 1993, s 49(2), Sch 8, para 44(a), as from 1 January 1994 (SI 1993/1908, below, para **[1435]**).
Sub-s (5): added by the Trade Union Reform and Employment Rights Act 1993, s 49(2), Sch 8, para 44(b), as from 1 January 1994 (SI 1993/1908, below, para **[1435]**).

45 Offences

(1) If a trade union refuses or wilfully neglects to perform a duty imposed on it by or under any of the provisions of—

    section 27 (duty to supply copy of rules),
    sections 28 to 30 (accounting records),
    sections 32 to 37 (annual return, [statement for members,] accounts and audit), or
    sections 38 to 42 (members' superannuation schemes),

it commits an offence.

(2) The offence shall be deemed to have been also committed by—

    (a) every officer of the trade union who is bound by the rules of the union to discharge on its behalf the duty breach of which constitutes the offence, or

    (b) if there is no such officer, every member of the general committee of management of the union.

(3) In any proceedings brought against an officer or member by virtue of subsection (2) in respect of a breach of duty, it is a defence for him to prove that he had reasonable cause to believe, and did believe, that some other person who was competent to discharge that duty was authorised to discharge it instead of him and had discharged it or would do so.

(4) A person who wilfully alters or causes to be altered a document which is required for the purposes of any of the provisions mentioned in subsection (1), with intent to falsify the document or to enable a trade union to evade any of those provisions, commits an offence.

(5) A person guilty of an offence under this section is liable on summary conviction—

    (a) in the case of an offence under subsection (1), to a fine not exceeding level 3 on the standard scale;

    (b) in the case of an offence under subsection (4), to a fine not exceeding level 5 on the standard scale.   **[696]**

NOTES

Commencement: 16 October 1992.

Sub-ss (1)–(4) contain provisions formerly in the Trade Union and Labour Relations Act 1974, s 12(1)–(4) (in part), and in the Employment Act 1988, s 6(8) (in part). Sub-s (5) contains provisions formerly in s 12(5) (in part) of the 1974 Act, as affected by the Criminal Justice Act 1982, ss 38, 46, and in s 6(8) (in part) of the 1988 Act.

Sub-s (1): words in square brackets inserted by the Trade Union Reform and Employment Rights Act 1993, s 49(2), Sch 8, para 45, as from 1 January 1994 (SI 1993/1908, below, para **[1435]**).

Sub-s (5): substituted by new sub-ss (5)–(9) by the Trade Union Reform and Employment Rights Act 1993, s 11(1), as from 30 August 1993 (SI 1993/1908), as follows—

"(5) If a person contravenes any duty, or requirement imposed, under section 37A (power of Certification officer to require production of documents etc.) or 37B (investigations by inspectors) he commits an offence.

(6) In any proceedings brought against a person in respect of a contravention of a requirement imposed under section 37A(3) or 37B(4) to produce documents it is a defence for him to prove—

    (a) that the documents were not in his possession, and
    (b) that it was not reasonably practicable for him to comply with the requirement.

(7) If an official or agent of a trade union—

    (a) destroys, mutilates or falsifies, or is privy to the destruction, mutilation or falsification of, a document relating to the financial affairs of the trade union, or
    (b) makes, or is privy to the making of, a false entry in any such document,

he commits an offence unless he proves that he had no intention to conceal the financial affairs of the trade union or to defeat the law.

(8) If such a person fraudulently—

    (a) parts with, alters or deletes anything in any such document, or

    (b)   is privy to the fraudulent parting with, fraudulent alteration of or fraudulent deletion in, any such document,
he commits an offence.
    (9) If a person in purported compliance with a duty, or requirement imposed, under section 37A or 37B to provide an explanation or make a statement—
    (a) provides or makes an explanation or statement which he knows to be false in a material particular, or
    (b) recklessly provides or makes an explanation or statement which is false in a material particular,
he commits an offence.".

[45A Penalties and prosecution time limits

(1) A person guilty of an offence under section 45 is liable on summary conviction—

    (a) in the case of an offence under subsection (1) or (5), to a fine not exceeding level 5 on the standard scale;

    (b) in the case of an offence under subsection (4), (7), (8) or (9), to imprisonment for a term not exceeding six months or to a fine not exceeding level 5 on the standard scale or to both.

(2) Proceedings for an offence under section 45(1) relating to the duty imposed by section 32 (duty to send annual return to Certification Officer) may be commenced at any time before the end of the period of three years beginning with the date when the offence was committed.

(3) Proceedings for any other offence under section 45(1) may be commenced—

    (a) at any time before the end of the period of six months beginning with the date when the offence was committed, or

    (b) at any time after the end of that period but before the end of the period of twelve months beginning with the date when evidence sufficient in the opinion of the Certification Officer or, in Scotland, the procurator fiscal, to justify the proceedings came to his knowledge;

but no proceedings may be commenced by virtue of paragraph (b) after the end of the period of three years beginning with the date when the offence was committed.

(4) For the purposes of subsection (3)(b), a certificate signed by or on behalf of the Certification Officer or the procurator fiscal which states the date on which evidence sufficient in his opinion to justify the proceedings came to his knowledge shall be conclusive evidence of that fact.

(5) A certificate stating that matter and purporting to be so signed shall be deemed to be so signed unless the contrary is proved.

(6) For the purposes of this section—

    (a) in England and Wales, proceedings are commenced when an information is laid, and

    (b) in Scotland, subsection (3) of section 331 of the Criminal Procedure (Scotland) Act 1975 (date of commencement of proceedings) applies as it applies for the purposes of that section.]   **[697]**

NOTE
    Inserted by the Trade Union Reform and Employment Rights Act 1993, s 11(2), as from 30 August 1993 (SI 1993/1908, below, para **[1435]**).

[45B Duty to secure positions not held by certain offenders

(1) A trade union shall secure that a person does not at any time hold a position in the union to which this section applies if—

(a) within the period of five years immediately preceding that time he has been convicted of an offence under subsection (1) or (5) of section 45, or

(b) within the period of ten years immediately preceding that time he has been convicted of an offence under subsection (4), (7), (8) or (9) of that section.

(2) Subject to subsection (4), the positions to which this section applies are—

(a) member of the executive,

(b) any position by virtue of which a person is a member of the executive,

(c) president, and

(d) general secretary.

(3) For the purposes of subsection (2)(a) "member of the executive" includes any person who, under the rules or practice of the union, may attend and speak at some or all of the meetings of the executive, otherwise than for the purpose of providing the committee with factual information or with technical or professional advice with respect to matters taken into account by the executive in carrying out its functions.

(4) This section does not apply to the position of president or general secretary if the holder of that position—

(a) is not, in respect of that position, either a voting member of the executive or an employee of the union,

(b) holds that position for a period which under the rules of the union cannot end more than thirteen months after he took it up, and

(c) has not held either position at any time in the period of twelve months ending with the day before he took up that position.

(5) In subsection (4)(a) "a voting member of the executive" means a person entitled in his own right to attend meetings of the executive and to vote on matters on which votes are taken by the executive (whether or not he is entitled to attend all such meetings or to vote on all such matters or in all circumstances).]   **[698]**

NOTE

Inserted together with s 45C below by the Trade Union Reform and Employment Rights Act 1993, s 12, as from 30 August 1993 (SI 1993/1908, below, para **[1435]**).

[45C Remedies and enforcement

(1) A member of a trade union who claims that the union has failed to comply with the requirement of section 45B may apply to the Certification Officer or to the court for a declaration to that effect.

(2) On an application being made to him, the Certification Officer—

(a) shall, where he considers it appropriate, give the applicant and the trade union an opportunity to be heard,

(b) shall ensure that, so far as is reasonably practicable, the application is determined within six months of being made,

(c) may make or refuse the declaration asked for, and

(d) shall, whether he makes or refuses the declaration, give reasons for his decision in writing.

(3) Where an application is made to the Certification Officer, the person who made that application, or any other person, is not prevented from making an application to the court in respect of the same matter.

(4) If, after an application is made to the Certification Officer, an application in respect of the same matter is made to the court, the court shall have due regard to any declaration which has been made by the Certification Officer.

(5) Where the court makes a declaration it shall also, unless it considers that it would be inappropriate, make an order imposing on the trade union a requirement to take within such period as may be specified in the order such steps to remedy the declared failure as may be so specified.

(6) Where an order has been made, any person who is a member of the trade union and was a member at the time the order was made is entitled to enforce the order as if he had made the application on which the order was made.]   **[699]**

NOTE
Inserted together with s 45B above by the Trade Union Reform and Employment Rights Act 1993, s 12, as from 30 August 1993 (SI 1993/1908).

CHAPTER IV
ELECTIONS FOR CERTAIN POSITIONS

Duty to hold elections

46 Duty to hold elections for certain positions

(1) A trade union shall secure—

(a) that every person who holds a position in the union to which this Chapter applies does so by virtue of having been elected to it at an election satisfying the requirements of this Chapter, and

(b) that no person continues to hold such a position for more than five years without being re-elected at such an election.

(2) The positions to which this Chapter applies (subject as mentioned below) are—

(a) member of the executive,

(b) any position by virtue of which a person is a member of the executive,

(c) president, and

(d) general secretary;

and the requirements referred to above are those set out in sections 47 to 52 below.

(3) In this Chapter "member of the executive" includes any person who, under the rules or practice of the union, may attend and speak at some or all of the meetings of the executive, otherwise than for the purpose of providing the committee with factual information or with technical or professional advice with respect to matters taken into account by the executive in carrying out its functions.

(4) This Chapter does not apply to the position of president or general secretary if the holder of that position—

(a) is not, in respect of that position, either a voting member of the executive or an employee of the union,

(b) holds that position for a period which under the rules of the union cannot end more than 13 months after he took it up, and

(c) has not held either position at any time in the period of twelve months ending with the day before he took up that position.

(5) A "voting member of the executive" means a person entitled in his own right to attend meetings of the executive and to vote on matters on which votes are taken by the executive (whether or not he is entitled to attend all such meetings or to vote on all such matters or in all circumstances).

(6) The provisions of this Chapter apply notwithstanding anything in the rules or practice of the union; and the terms and conditions on which a person is employed by the union shall be disregarded in so far as they would prevent the union from complying with the provisions of this Chapter.   **[700]**

NOTES

Commencement: 16 October 1992.

Sub-ss (1), (2) contain provisions formerly in the Trade Union Act 1984, s 1(1), (2), (6B) (all in part), as amended, in the case of s 1(1), and as repealed in part, in the case of s 1(1), (2), and as inserted, in the case of s 1(6B), by the Employment Act 1988, ss 12(1), 33, Sch 3, Pt I, para 5(1), Sch 4. Sub-s (3) contains provisions formerly in s 1(6A) (in part) of the 1984 Act, as inserted by s 12(1) of the 1988 Act. Sub-s (4) contains provisions formerly in s 1(6C) of the 1984 Act, as inserted by s 12(1) of the 1988 Act. Sub-s (5) contains provisions formerly in s 1(7) of the 1984 Act. Sub-s (6) contains provisions formerly in s 1(1), (4), (6B) (all in part) of the 1984 Act, as inserted, in the case of s 1(6B), by s 12(1) of, Sch 3, Pt I, para 5(1) to, the 1988 Act.

Requirements to be satisfied with respect to elections

47 Candidates

(1) No member of the trade union shall be unreasonably excluded from standing as a candidate.

(2) No candidate shall be required, directly or indirectly, to be a member of a political party.

(3) A member of a trade union shall not be taken to be unreasonably excluded from standing as a candidate if he is excluded on the ground that he belongs to a class of which all the members are excluded by the rules of the union.

But a rule which provides for such a class to be determined by reference to whom the union chooses to exclude shall be disregarded.   **[701]**

NOTES

Commencement: 16 October 1992.

Sub-s (1) contains provisions formerly in the Trade Union Act 1984, s 2(9). Sub-s (2) contains provisions formerly in s 2(10) of the 1984 Act. Sub-s (3) contains provisions formerly in s 2(11), (12) of the 1984 Act.

48 Election addresses

(1) The trade union shall—

    (a) provide every candidate with an opportunity of preparing an election address in his own words and of submitting it to the union to be distributed to the persons accorded entitlement to vote in the election; and

    (b) secure that, so far as reasonably practicable, copies of every election address submitted to it in time are distributed to each of those persons by post along with the voting papers for the election.

(2) The trade union may determine the time by which an election address must be submitted to it for distribution; but the time so determined must not be earlier than the latest time at which a person may become a candidate in the election.

(3) The trade union may provide that election addresses submitted to it for distribution—

    (a) must not exceed such length, not being less than one hundred words, as may be determined by the union, and

    (b) may, as regards photographs and other matter not in words, incorporate only such matter as the union may determine.

(4) The trade union shall secure that no modification of an election address submitted to it is made by any person in any copy of the address to be distributed except—

(a) at the request or with the consent of the candidate, or

(b) where the modification is necessarily incidental to the method adopted for producing that copy.

(5) The trade union shall secure that the same method of producing copies is applied in the same way to every election address submitted and, so far as reasonably practicable, that no such facility or information as would enable a candidate to gain any benefit from—

(a) the method by which copies of the election addresses are produced, or

(b) the modifications which are necessarily incidental to that method,

is provided to any candidate without being provided equally to all the others.

(6) The trade union shall, so far as reasonably practicable, secure that the same facilities and restrictions with respect to the preparation, submission, length or modification of an election address, and with respect to the incorporation of photographs or other matter not in words, are provided or applied equally to each of the candidates.

(7) The arrangements made by the trade union for the production of the copies to be so distributed must be such as to secure that none of the candidates is required to bear any of the expense of producing the copies.

(8) No-one other than the candidate himself shall incur any civil or criminal liability in respect of the publication of a candidate's election address or of any copy required to be made for the purposes of this section.   **[702]**

NOTES

Commencement: 16 October 1992.

Sub-s (1) contains provisions formerly in the Employment Act 1988, s 13(2)(a), (b) (in part). Sub-s (2) contains provisions formerly in s 13(2)(b) (in part), (4) of the 1988 Act. Sub-s (3) contains provisions formerly in s 13(3) of the 1988 Act. Sub-ss (4)–(6) contain provisions formerly in s 13(2)(d), (e), (f) of the 1988 Act. Sub-s (7) contains provisions formerly in s 13(2)(c) of the 1988 Act. Sub-s (8) contains provisions formerly in s 13(5) of the 1988 Act.

49 Appointment of independent scrutineer

(1) The trade union shall, before the election is held, appoint a qualified independent person ("the scrutineer") to carry out—

(a) the functions in relation to the election which are required under this section to be contained in his appointment; and

(b) such additional functions in relation to the election as may be specified in his appointment.

(2) A person is a qualified independent person in relation to an election if—

(a) he satisfies such conditions as may be specified for the purposes of this section by order of the Secretary of State or is himself so specified; and

(b) the trade union has no grounds for believing either that he will carry out any functions conferred on him in relation to the election otherwise than competently or that his independence in relation to the union, or in relation to the election, might reasonably be called into question.

An order under paragraph (a) shall be made by statutory instrument which shall be subject to annulment in pursuance of a resolution of either House of Parliament.

(3) The scrutineer's appointment shall require him—

    (a) to be the person who supervises the production *and distribution of the voting papers* and to whom the voting papers are returned by those voting;

[(aa) to—

        (i) inspect the register of names and addresses of the members of the trade union, or

      (ii) examine the copy of the register as at the relevant date which is supplied to him in accordance with subsection (5A)(a),

whenever it appears to him appropriate to do so and, in particular, when the conditions specified in subsection (3A) are satisfied;]

    (b) to take such steps as appear to him to be appropriate for the purpose of enabling him to make his report (see section 52);

    (c) to make his report to the trade union as soon as reasonably practicable after the last date for the return of voting papers; and

    (d) to retain custody of all voting papers returned for the purposes of the election [and the copy of the register supplied to him in accordance with subsection (5A)(a)]—

        (i) until the end of the period of one year beginning with the announcement by the union of the result of the election; and

      (ii) if within that period an application is made under section 54 (complaint of failure to comply with election requirements), until the Certification Officer or the court authorises him to dispose of the papers [or copy].

[(3A) The conditions referred to in subsection (3)(aa) are—

    (a) that a request that the scrutineer inspect the register or examine the copy is made to him during the appropriate period by a member of the trade union or candidate who suspects that the register is not, or at the relevant date was not, accurate and up-to-date, and

    (b) that the scrutineer does not consider that the suspicion of the member or candidate is ill-founded.

(3B) In subsection (3A) "the appropriate period" means the period—

    (a) beginning with the first day on which a person may become a candidate in the election or, if later, the day on which the scrutineer is appointed, and

    (b) ending with the day before the day on which the scrutineer makes his report to the trade union.

(3C) The duty of confidentiality as respects the register is incorporated in the scrutineer's appointment.]

(4) The trade union shall ensure that nothing in the terms of the scrutineer's appointment (including any additional functions specified in the appointment) is such as to make it reasonable for any person to call the scrutineer's independence in relation to the union into question.

(5) The trade union shall, before the scrutineer begins to carry out his functions, either—

    (a) send a notice stating the name of the scrutineer to every member of the union to whom it is reasonably practicable to send such a notice, or

    (b) take all such other steps for notifying members of the name of the scrutineer as it is the practice of the union to take when matters of general interest to all its members need to be brought to their attention.

[(5A) The trade union shall—

    (a) supply to the scrutineer as soon as is reasonably practicable after the relevant date a copy of the register of names and addresses of its members as at that date, and

(b) comply with any request made by the scrutineer to inspect the register.

(5B)   Where the register is kept by means of a computer the duty imposed on the trade union by subsection (5A)(a) is either to supply a legible printed copy or (if the scrutineer prefers) to supply a copy of the computer data and allow the scrutineer use of the computer to read it at any time during the period when he is required to retain custody of the copy.]

(6)   The trade union shall ensure that the scrutineer duly carries out his functions and that there is no interference with his carrying out of those functions which would make it reasonable for any person to call the scrutineer's independence in relation to the union into question.

(7)   The trade union shall comply with all reasonable requests made by the scrutineer for the purposes of, or in connection with, the carrying out of his functions.

[(8)   In this section "the relevant date" means—

(a) where the trade union has rules determining who is entitled to vote in the election by reference to membership on a particular date, that date, and

(b) otherwise, the date, or the last date, on which voting papers are distributed for the purposes of the election.]   **[703]**

NOTES

Commencement: 16 October 1992.

Sub-s (1) contains provisions formerly in the Employment Act 1988, s 15(2)(a) (in part). Sub-ss (2), (3) contain provisions formerly in s 15(3), (4) (both in part) of the 1988 Act. Sub-s (4) contains provisions formerly in s 15(2)(b) (in part) of the 1988 Act. Sub-s (5) contains provisions formerly in s 15(2)(bb) (in part) of the 1988 Act, as inserted by the Employment Act 1990, s 5(5). Sub-ss (6), (7) contain provisions formerly in s 15(2)(c), (d) (both in part) of the 1988 Act.

Sub-s (3): for the words in italics in para (a) there are substituted the words "of the voting papers and (unless he is appointed under section 51A to undertake the distribution of the voting papers) their distribution", and para (aa) and the two sets of words in square brackets in para (d) are inserted, by the Trade Union Reform and Employment Rights Act 1993, ss 1(1)(a), (b), 49(2), Sch 8, para 46, as from 30 August 1993 (SI 1993/1908, para **[1435]**).

Sub-ss (3A)–(3C), (5A), (5B): inserted by the Trade Union Reform and Employment Rights Act 1993, s 1(1)(c), (d), as from 30 August 1993 (SI 1993/1908, para **[1435]**).

Sub-s (8): added by the Trade Union Reform and Employment Rights Act 1993, s 1(1)(e), as from 30 August 1993 (SI 1993/1908, para **[1435]**).

Orders under this section: Trade Union Ballots and Elections (Independent Scrutineer Qualifications) Order 1988, SI 1988/2117, as amended by SI 1989/31 (revoked and replaced by SI 1993/1909, see below, para **[1443]**).

50 Entitlement to vote

(1)   Subject to the provisions of this section, entitlement to vote shall be accorded equally to all members of the trade union.

(2)   The rules of the union may exclude entitlement to vote in the case of all members belonging to one of the following classes, or to a class falling within one of the following—

(a) members who are not in employment;

(b) members who are in arrears in respect of any subscription or contribution due to the union;

(c) members who are apprentices, trainees or students or new members of the union.

(3)   The rules of the union may restrict entitlement to vote to members who fall within—

(a) a class determined by reference to a trade or occupation,

(b) a class determined by reference to a geographical area, or

(c) a class which is by virtue of the rules of the union treated as a separate section within the union, or to members who fall within a class determined by reference to any combination of the factors mentioned in paragraphs (a), (b) and (c).

The reference in paragraph (c) to a section of a trade union includes a part of the union which is itself a trade union.

(4) Entitlement may not be restricted in accordance with subsection (3) if the effect is that any member of the union is denied entitlement to vote at all elections held for the purposes of this Chapter otherwise than by virtue of belonging to a class excluded in accordance with subsection (2).   **[704]**

NOTES
Commencement: 16 October 1992.
Sub-ss (1), (2) contain provisions formerly in the Trade Union Act 1984, s 2(1), (2). Sub-s (3) contains provisions formerly in ss 2(3), (4)(a), 9(1) (definition "section") of the 1984 Act. Sub-s (4) contains provisions formerly in s 2(4)(b) of the 1984 Act.

51 Voting

(1) The method of voting must be by the marking of a voting paper by the person voting.

(2) Each voting paper must—

    (a) state the name of the independent scrutineer and clearly specify the address to which, and the date by which, it is to be returned,

    (b) be given one of a series of consecutive whole numbers every one of which is used in giving a different number in that series to each voting paper printed or otherwise produced for the purposes of the election, and

    (c) be marked with its number.

(3) Every person who is entitled to vote at the election must—

    (a) be allowed to vote without interference from, or constraint imposed by, the union or any of its members, officials or employees, and

    (b) so far as is reasonably practicable, be enabled to do so without incurring any direct cost to himself.

(4) So far as is reasonably practicable, every person who is entitled to vote at the election must—

    (a) have sent to him by post, at his home address or another address which he has requested the trade union in writing to treat as his postal address, a voting paper which either lists the candidates at the election or is accompanied by a separate list of those candidates; and

    (b) be given a convenient opportunity to vote by post.

(5) The ballot shall be conducted so as to secure that—

    (a) so far as is reasonably practicable, those voting do so in secret, and

    (b) the votes given at the election are fairly and accurately counted.

For the purposes of paragraph (b) an inaccuracy in counting shall be disregarded if it is accidental and on a scale which could not affect the result of the election.

(6) The ballot shall be so conducted as to secure that the result of the election is determined solely by counting the number of votes cast directly for each candidate.

(7) Nothing in subsection (6) shall be taken to prevent the system of voting used for the election being the single transferable vote, that is, a vote capable of being given so as to indicate the voter's order of preference for the candidates and of being transferred to the next choice—

    (a) when it is not required to give a prior choice the necessary quota of votes, or

(b) when, owing to the deficiency in the number of votes given for a prior choice, that choice is eliminated from the list of candidates.   **[705]**

NOTES
Commencement: 16 October 1992.
Sub-s (1) contains provisions formerly in the Trade Union Act 1984, s 2(5) (in part). Sub-s (2) contains provisions formerly in s 2(5)(a)–(c) of the 1984 Act, as added by the Employment Act 1988, s 33(1), Sch 3, Pt I, para 5(2)(a), and as amended, in the case of para (a), by the Employment Act 1990, s 5(4). Sub-s (3) contains provisions formerly in s 2(6) of the 1984 Act. Sub-s (4) contains provisions formerly in ss 2(7), 9(1) (definition "proper address") of the 1984 Act. Sub-s (5) contains provisions formerly in s 2(8)(a), (c) of the 1984 Act. Sub-s (6) contains provisions formerly in s 2(8)(b) (in part) of the 1984 Act. Sub-s (7) contains provisions formerly in ss 2(8)(b) (in part), 9(1) (definition "single transferable vote") of the 1984 Act.

[51A Counting of votes etc by independent person

(1) The trade union shall ensure that—

(a) the storage and distribution of the voting papers for the purposes of the election, and

(b) the counting of the votes cast in the election,

are undertaken by one or more independent persons appointed by the union.

(2) A person is an independent person in relation to an election if—

(a) he is the scrutineer, or

(b) he is a person other than the scrutineer and the trade union has no grounds for believing either that he will carry out any functions conferred on him in relation to the election otherwise than competently or that his independence in relation to the union, or in relation to the election, might reasonably be called into question.

(3) An appointment under this section shall require the person appointed to carry out his functions so as to minimise the risk of any contravention of requirements imposed by or under any enactment or the occurrence of any unfairness or malpractice.

(4) The duty of confidentiality as respects the register is incorporated in an appointment under this section.

(5) Where the person appointed to undertake the counting of votes is not the scrutineer, his appointment shall require him to send the voting papers back to the scrutineer as soon as reasonably practicable after the counting has been completed.

(6) The trade union—

(a) shall ensure that nothing in the terms of an appointment under this section is such as to make it reasonable for any person to call into question the independence of the person appointed in relation to the union,

(b) shall ensure that a person appointed under this section duly carries out his functions and that there is no interference with his carrying out of those functions which would make it reasonable for any person to call into question the independence of the person appointed in relation to the union, and

(c) shall comply with all reasonable requests made by a person appointed under this section for the purposes of, or in connection with, the carrying out of his functions.]

[706]

NOTE
Inserted by the Trade Union Reform and Employment Rights Act 1993, s 2(1), as from 30 August 1993 (SI 1993/1908, below, para **[1435]**).

52 Scrutineer's report

(1) The scrutineer's report on the election shall state—

    (a) the number of voting papers distributed for the purposes of the election,

    (b) the number of voting papers returned to the scrutineer,

    (c) the number of valid votes cast in the election for each candidate, *and*

    (d) the number of spoiled or otherwise invalid voting papers returned [, and

    (e) the name of the person (or of each of the persons) appointed under section 51A or, if no person was so appointed, that fact.]

(2) The report shall also state whether the scrutineer is satisfied—

    (a) that there are no reasonable grounds for believing that there was any contravention of a requirement imposed by or under any enactment in relation to the election,

    (b) that the arrangements made [(whether by him or any other person)] with respect to the production, storage, distribution, return or other handling of the voting papers used in the election, and the arrangements for the counting of the votes, included all such security arrangements as were reasonably practicable for the purpose of minimising the risk that any unfairness or malpractice might occur, and

    (c) that he has been able to carry out his functions without such interference as would make it reasonable for any person to call his independence in relation to the union into question;

and if he is not satisfied as to any of those matters, the report shall give particulars of his reasons for not being satisfied as to that matter.

[(2A) The report shall also state—

    (a) whether the scrutineer—

        (i) has inspected the register of names and addresses of the members of the trade union, or

        (ii) has examined the copy of the register as at the relevant date which is supplied to him in accordance with section 49(5A)(a),

    (b) if he has, whether in the case of each inspection or examination he was acting on a request by a member of the trade union or candidate or at his own instance,

    (c) whether he declined to act on any such request, and

    (d) whether any inspection of the register, or any examination of the copy of the register, has revealed any matter which he considers should be drawn to the attention of the trade union in order to assist it in securing that the register is accurate and up-to-date,

but shall not state the name of any member or candidate who has requested such an inspection or examination.]

[(2B) Where one or more persons other than the scrutineer are appointed under section 51A, the statement included in the scrutineer's report in accordance with subsection (2)(b) shall also indicate—

    (a) whether he is satisfied with the performance of the person, or each of the persons, so appointed, and

    (b) if he is not satisfied with the performance of the person, or any of them, particulars of his reasons for not being so satisfied.]

(3) The trade union shall not publish the result of the election until it has received the scrutineer's report.

(4) The trade union shall within the period of three months after it receives the report either—

(a) send a copy of the report to every member of the union to whom it is reasonably practicable to send such a copy; or

(b) take all such other steps for notifying the contents of the report to the members of the union (whether by publishing the report or otherwise) as it is the practice of the union to take when matters of general interest to all its members need to be brought to their attention.

(5) Any such copy or notification shall be accompanied by a statement that the union will, on request, supply any member of the union with a copy of the report, either free of charge or on payment of such reasonable fee as may be specified in the notification.

(6) The trade union shall so supply any member of the union who makes such a request and pays the fee (if any) notified to him.   **[707]**

NOTES
Commencement: 16 October 1992.
Sub-s (1) contains provisions formerly in the Employment Act 1988, s 15(5)(a), (b), (c), (d) (all in part). Sub-s (2) contains provisions formerly in s 15(5)(e), (f), (6) (all in part) of the 1988 Act. Sub-ss (3)–(6) contain provisions formerly in s 15(7) (in part) of the 1988 Act.
Sub-s (1): at the end of para (c), the word "and" in italics is repealed, and the word "and" at the end of para (d), and para (e), are added, by the Trade Union Reform and Employment Rights Act 1993, ss 2(2)(a), 51, Sch 10, as from 30 August 1993 (SI 1993/1908, below, para **[1435]**).
Sub-s (2): words in square brackets in para (b) inserted by the Trade Union Reform and Employment Rights Act 1993, s 2(2)(b), as from 30 August 1993 (SI 1993/1908, below, para **[1435]**).
Sub-s (2A): inserted by the Trade Union Reform and Employment Rights Act 1993, s 1(2), as from 30 August 1993 (SI 1993/1908, below, para **[1435]**).
Sub-s (2B): inserted by the Trade Union Reform and Employment Rights Act 1993, s 2(2)(c), as from 30 August 1993 (SI 1993/1908, below, para **[1435]**).

53 Uncontested elections

Nothing in this Chapter shall be taken to require a ballot to be held at an uncontested election.   **[708]**

NOTES
Commencement: 16 October 1992.
This section contains provisions formerly in the Trade Union Act 1984, s 2(14).

Remedy for failure to comply with requirements

54 Remedy for failure to comply with requirements: general

(1) The remedy for a failure on the part of a trade union to comply with the requirements of this Chapter is by way of application under section 55 (to the Certification Officer) or section 56 (to the court).

The making of an application to the Certification Officer does not prevent the applicant, or any other person, from making an application to the court in respect of the same matter.

(2) An application under those sections may be made—

(a) by a person who is a member of the trade union (provided, where the election has been held, he was also a member at the time when it was held), or

(b) by a person who is or was a candidate at the election;

and the references in those sections to a person having a sufficient interest are to such a person.

(3) No such application may be made after the end of the period of one year beginning with the day on which the union announced the result of the election.

[709]

NOTES

Commencement: 16 October 1992.

Sub-s (1) contains provisions formerly in the Trade Union Act 1984, ss 5(1) (in part), (10) (in part), 6(3) (in part), as amended, in the case of s 5(1), (10), by the Employment Act 1988, s 33(1), Sch 3, Pt I, para 5(4)(a). Sub-s (2) contains provisions formerly in ss 5(1)(a) (in part), (b), (12A) (in part) of the 1984 Act, as inserted, in the case of s 5(12A), by s 33(1) of, Sch 3, Pt I, para 5(4)(c) to, the 1988 Act. Sub-s (3) contains provisions formerly in s 5(2) of the 1984 Act.

55 Application to Certification Officer

(1) A person having a sufficient interest (see section 54(2)) who claims that a trade union has failed to comply with any of the requirements of this Chapter may apply to the Certification Officer for a declaration to that effect.

(2) On an application being made to him, the Certification Officer shall—

(a) make such enquiries as he thinks fit, and
(b) where he considers it appropriate, give the applicant and the trade union an opportunity to be heard,

and may make or refuse the declaration asked for.

(3) If he makes a declaration he shall specify in it the provisions with which the trade union has failed to comply.

(4) Where he makes a declaration and is satisfied that steps have been taken by the union with a view to remedying the declared failure, or securing that a failure of the same or any similar kind does not occur in future, or that the union has agreed to take such steps, he shall specify those steps in the declaration.

(5) Whether he makes or refuses a declaration, he shall give reasons for his decision in writing; and the reasons may be accompanied by written observations on any matter arising from, or connected with, the proceedings.

(6) In exercising his functions under this section the Certification Officer shall ensure that, so far as is reasonably practicable, an application made to him is determined within six months of being made.

(7) Where he requests a person to furnish information to him in connection with enquiries made by him under this section, he shall specify the date by which that information is to be furnished and, unless he considers that it would be inappropriate to do so, shall proceed with his determination of the application notwithstanding that the information has not been furnished to him by the specified date.   **[710]**

NOTES

Commencement: 16 October 1992.

Sub-s (1) contains provisions formerly in the Trade Union Act 1984, s 5(1) (in part). Sub-s (2) contains provisions formerly in ss 5(3) (in part), 6(5) of the 1984 Act. Sub-s (3) contains provisions formerly in s 5(4) (in part) of the 1984 Act. Sub-ss (4), (5) contain provisions formerly in s 6(1), (2) (both in part) of the 1984 Act. Sub-ss (6), (7) contain provisions formerly in s 6(7), (8) (both in part) of the 1984 Act.

56 Application to court

(1) A person having a sufficient interest (see section 54(2)) who claims that a trade union has failed to comply with any of the requirements of this Chapter may apply to the court for a declaration to that effect.

(2) If an application in respect of the same matter has been made to the Certification Officer, the court shall have due regard to any declaration, reasons or observations of his which are brought to its notice.

(3) If the court makes the declaration asked for, it shall specify in the declaration the provisions with which the trade union has failed to comply.

(4) Where the court makes a declaration it shall also, unless it considers that to do so would be inappropriate, make an enforcement order, that is, an order imposing on the union one or more of the following requirements—

(a) to secure the holding of an election in accordance with the order;
(b) to take such other steps to remedy the declared failure as may be specified in the order;
(c) to abstain from such acts as may be so specified with a view to securing that a failure of the same or a similar kind does not occur in future.

The court shall in an order imposing any such requirement as is mentioned in paragraph (a) or (b) specify the period within which the union is to comply with the requirements of the order.

(5) Where the court makes an order requiring the union to hold a fresh election, the court shall (unless it considers that it would be inappropriate to do so in the particular circumstances of the case) require the election to be conducted in accordance with the requirements of this Chapter and such other provisions as may be made by the order.

(6) Where an enforcement order has been made—

(a) any person who is a member of the union and was a member at the time the order was made, or
(b) any person who is or was a candidate in the election in question,

is entitled to enforce obedience to the order as if he had made the application on which the order was made.

(7) Without prejudice to any other power of the court, the court may on an application under this section grant such interlocutory relief (in Scotland, such interim order) as it considers appropriate.   [711]

NOTES

Commencement: 16 October 1992.

Sub-s (1) contains provisions formerly in the Trade Union Act 1984, s 5(1) (in part), as amended by the Employment Act 1988, s 33(1), Sch 3, Pt I, para 5(4)(a). Sub-s (2) contains provisions formerly in s 6(4) (in part) of the 1984 Act. Sub-s (3) contains provisions formerly in s 5(4) (in part) of the 1984 Act. Sub-s (4) contains provisions formerly in s 5(5)–(7), (9) (all in part) of the 1984 Act. Sub-s (5) contains provisions formerly in s 5(8) (in part) of the 1984 Act, as amended by s 33(1) of, Sch 3, Pt I, para 5(4)(b) to, the 1988 Act. Sub-s (6) contains provisions formerly in s 5(11), (12), (12A) (all in part) of the 1984 Act, as inserted, in the case of s 5(12A), by s 33(1) of, Sch 3, Pt I, para 5(4)(c) to, the 1988 Act. Sub-s (7) contains provisions formerly in s 23 (in part) of the 1988 Act.

Supplementary

57 Exemption of newly-formed trade unions, &c

(1) The provisions of this Chapter do not apply to a trade union until more than one year has elapsed since its formation (by amalgamation or otherwise).

For this purpose the date of formation of a trade union formed otherwise than by amalgamation shall be taken to be the date on which the first members of the executive of the union are first appointed or elected.

(2) Where a trade union is formed by amalgamation, the provisions of this Chapter do not apply in relation to a person who—

(a) by virtue of an election held a position to which this Chapter applies in one of the amalgamating unions immediately before the amalgamation, and

(b) becomes the holder of a position to which this Chapter applies in the amalgamated union in accordance with the instrument of transfer,

until after the end of the period for which he would have been entitled in accordance with this Chapter to continue to hold the first-mentioned position without being re-elected.

(3) Where a trade union transfers its engagements to another trade union, the provisions of this Chapter do not apply in relation to a person who—

(a) held a position to which this Chapter applies in the transferring union immediately before the transfer, and

(b) becomes the holder of a position to which this Chapter applies in the transferee union in accordance with the instrument of transfer,

until after the end of the period of one year beginning with the date of the transfer or, if he held the first-mentioned position by virtue of an election, any longer period for which he would have been entitled in accordance with this Chapter to continue to hold that position without being re-elected.   **[712]**

NOTES
Commencement: 16 October 1992.
Sub-s (1) contains provisions formerly in the Trade Union Act 1984, s 7(4)–(7) (in part). Sub-s (2) contains provisions formerly in the Employment Act 1988, s 12(2) (in part). Sub-s (3) contains provisions formerly in s 7(8) of the 1984 Act, and in s 12(2) (in part) of the 1988 Act.

58 Exemption of certain persons nearing retirement

(1) Section 46(1)(b) (requirement of re-election) does not apply to a person holding a position to which this Chapter applies if the following conditions are satisfied.

(2) The conditions are that—

(a) he holds the position by virtue of having been elected at an election in relation to which the requirements of this Chapter were satisfied,

(b) he is a full-time employee of the union by virtue of the position,

(c) he will reach retirement age within five years,

(d) he is entitled under the rules of the union to continue as the holder of the position until retirement age without standing for re-election,

(e) he has been a full-time employee of the union for a period (which need not be continuous) of at least ten years, and

(f) the period between the day on which the election referred to in paragraph (a) took place and the day immediately preceding that on which paragraph (c) is first satisfied does not exceed five years.

(3) For the purposes of this section "retirement age", in relation to any person, means the earlier of—

(a) the age fixed by, or in accordance with, the rules of the union for him to retire from the position in question, or

(b) the age which is for the time being pensionable age for the purpose of Parts I to VI of the Social Security (Contributions and Benefits) Act 1992. **[713]**

NOTES
Commencement: 16 October 1992.
Sub-s (1) contains provisions formerly in the Trade Union Act 1984, s 8(1), as repealed in part by the Employment Act 1988, s 33, Sch 3, Pt I, para 5(5)(a), Sch 4. Sub-s (2) contains provisions formerly in s 8(2) of the 1984 Act, as amended by s 33(1) of, Sch 3, Pt I, para 5(5)(b) to, the 1988 Act. Sub-s (3) contains provisions formerly in s 8(3) of the 1988 Act, as read with the Interpretation Act 1978, s 17(2)(a).

59 Period for giving effect to election

Where a person holds a position to which this Chapter applies immediately before an election at which he is not re-elected to that position, nothing in this Chapter shall be taken to require the union to prevent him from continuing to hold that position for such period (not exceeding six months) as may reasonably be required for effect to be given to the result of the election.   **[714]**

NOTES

Commencement: 16 October 1992.

This section contains provisions formerly in the Trade Union Act 1984, s 1(3), as repealed in part by the Employment Act 1988, s 33(2), Sch 4.

60 Overseas members

(1) A trade union which has overseas members may choose whether or not to accord any of those members entitlement to vote at an election for a position to which this Chapter applies.

(2) An "overseas member" means a member of the union (other than a merchant seaman or offshore worker) who is outside Great Britain throughout the period during which votes may be cast.

For this purpose—

"merchant seaman" means a person whose employment, or the greater part of it, is carried out on board sea-going ships; and
"offshore worker" means a person in offshore employment, other than one who is in such employment in an area where the law of Northern Ireland applies.

(3) Where the union chooses to accord an overseas member entitlement to vote, section 51 (requirements as to voting) applies in relation to him; but nothing in section 47 (candidates) or section 50 (entitlement to vote) applies in relation to an overseas member or in relation to a vote cast by such a member.   **[715]**

NOTES

Commencement: 16 October 1992.

Sub-s (1) contains provisions formerly in the Trade Union Act 1984, s 2(13) (in part). Sub-s (2) contains provisions formerly in s 9(1) (definitions "merchant seaman", "offshore worker", "overseas member") of the 1984 Act. Sub-s (3) contains provisions formerly in s 2(13) (in part) of the 1984 Act, as amended by the Employment Act 1988, s 33(1), Sch 3, Pt I, para 5(2)(b).

61 Other supplementary provisions

(1) For the purposes of this Chapter the date on which a contested election is held shall be taken, in the case of an election in which votes may be cast on more than one day, to be the last of those days.

(2) Nothing in this Chapter affects the validity of anything done by a person holding a position to which this Chapter applies.   **[716]**

NOTES

Commencement: 16 October 1992.

Sub-s (1) contains provisions formerly in the Trade Union Act 1984, s 9(2). Sub-s (2) contains provisions formerly in s 1(6) of the 1984 Act.

CHAPTER V
RIGHTS OF TRADE UNION MEMBERS

Right to a ballot before industrial action

62 Right to ballot before industrial action

(1) A member of a trade union who claims that members of the union, including himself, are likely to be or have been induced by the union to take part or to continue to take part in industrial action which does not have the support of a ballot may apply to the court for an order under this section.

[In this section "the relevant time" means the time when the application is made.]

(2) For this purpose industrial action shall be regarded as having the support of a ballot only if—

    (a) the union has held a ballot in respect of the action in relation to which the requirements of sections 227 to 232 were satisfied and in which the applicant was accorded entitlement to vote,

    (b) the majority voting in the ballot answered "Yes" to the question applicable in accordance with section 229(2) to industrial action of the kind which the applicant has been or is likely to be induced to take part in, and

    (c) the requirements of section 233 (calling of industrial action with support of ballot) are satisfied.

(3) Where on an application under this section the court is satisfied that the claim is well-founded, it shall make such order as it considers appropriate for requiring the union to take steps for ensuring—

    (a) that there is no, or no further, inducement of members of the union to take part or to continue to take part in the industrial action to which the application relates, and

    (b) that no member engages in conduct after the making of the order by virtue of having been induced before the making of the order to take part or continue to take part in the action.

(4) Without prejudice to any other power of the court, the court may on an application under this section grant such interlocutory relief (in Scotland, such interim order) as it considers appropriate.

(5) For the purposes of this section an act shall be taken to be done by a trade union if it is authorised or endorsed by the union; and the provisions of section 20(2) to (4) apply for the purpose of determining whether an act is to be taken to be so authorised or endorsed.

Those provisions also apply in relation to proceedings for failure to comply with an order under this section as they apply in relation to the original proceedings.

(6) In this section—

"inducement" includes an inducement which is or would be ineffective, whether because of the member's unwillingness to be influenced by it or for any other reason; and

"industrial action" means a strike or other industrial action by persons employed under contracts of employment.

(7) Where a person holds any office or employment under the Crown on terms which do not constitute a contract of employment between that person and the Crown,

those terms shall nevertheless be deemed to constitute such a contract for the purposes of this section.

(8) References in this section to a contract of employment include any contract under which one person personally does work or performs services for another; and related expressions shall be construed accordingly.

(9) Nothing in this section shall be construed as requiring a trade union to hold separate ballots for the purposes of this section and sections 226 to 234 (requirement of ballot before action by trade union).   **[717]**

NOTES
Commencement: 16 October 1992.
Sub-s (1) contains provisions formerly in the Employment Act 1988, s 1(1), as amended by the Employment Act 1990, s 16(1), Sch 2, para 3(1), (2). Sub-s (2) contains provisions formerly in s 1(5) of the 1988 Act, as amended by s 16(1) of, Sch 2, para 3(1), (5) to, the 1990 Act. Sub-s (3) contains provisions formerly in s 1(2) of the 1988 Act, as amended and repealed in part by s 16 of, Sch 2, para 3(1), (3), Sch 3 to, the 1990 Act. Sub-s (4) contains provisions formerly in s 23 (in part) of the 1988 Act. Sub-s (5) contains provisions formerly in s 1(3) of the 1988 Act, as substituted by s 16(1) of, Sch 2, para 3(1), (4) to, the 1990 Act. Sub-s (6) contains provisions formerly in s 1(6), (7) (definition "industrial action") of the 1988 Act. Sub-s (7) contains provisions formerly in s 30(1) (in part) of the 1988 Act. Sub-s (8) contains provisions formerly in s 5(1) (in part) of the 1990 Act. Sub-s (9) contains provisions formerly in s 1(8) of the 1988 Act.
Sub-s (1): words in square brackets added by the Trade Union Reform and Employment Rights Act 1993, s 49(2), Sch 8, para 47(a), as from 30 August 1993 (SI 1993/1908, below, para **[1435]**).
Sub-s (2): paras (a)–(c) substituted by the Trade Union Reform and Employment Rights Act 1993, s 49(2), Sch 8, para 47(b), as from 30 August 1993 (SI 1993/1908, below, para **[1435]**), as follows—

"(a) the union has held a ballot in respect of the action—

    (i) in relation to which the requirements of section 226B so far as applicable before and during the holding of the ballot were satisfied,

    (ii) in relation to which the requirements of sections 227 to 231 were satisfied, and

    (iii) in which the majority voting in the ballot answered "Yes" to the question applicable in accordance with section 229(2) to industrial action of the kind which the applicant has been or is likely to be induced to take part in;

(b) such of the requirements of the following sections as have fallen to be satisfied at the relevant time have been satisfied, namely—

    (i) section 226B so far as applicable after the holding of the ballot, and

    (ii) section 231B; and

(c) the requirements of section 233 (calling of industrial action with support of ballot) are satisfied.

Any reference in this subsection to a requirement of a provision which is disapplied or modified by section 232 has effect subject to that section.".

Right not to be denied access to the courts

63 Right not to be denied access to the courts

(1) This section applies where a matter is under the rules of a trade union required or allowed to be submitted for determination or conciliation in accordance with the rules of the union, but a provision of the rules purporting to provide for that to be a person's only remedy has no effect (or would have no effect if there were one).

(2) Notwithstanding anything in the rules of the union or in the practice of any court, if a member or former member of the union begins proceedings in a court with respect to a matter to which this section applies, then if—

    (a) he has previously made a valid application to the union for the matter to be submitted for determination or conciliation in accordance with the union's rules, and

    (b) the court proceedings are begun after the end of the period of six months beginning with the day on which the union received the application,

the rules requiring or allowing the matter to be so submitted, and the fact that any relevant steps remain to be taken under the rules, shall be regarded for all purposes as irrelevant to any question whether the court proceedings should be dismissed, stayed or sisted, or adjourned.

(3) An application shall be deemed to be valid for the purposes of subsection (2)(a) unless the union informed the applicant, before the end of the period of 28 days beginning with the date on which the union received the application, of the respects in which the application contravened the requirements of the rules.

(4) If the court is satisfied that any delay in the taking of relevant steps under the rules is attributable to unreasonable conduct of the person who commenced the proceedings, it may treat the period specified in subsection (2)(b) as extended by such further period as it considers appropriate.

(5) In this section—

(a) references to the rules of a trade union include any arbitration or other agreement entered into in pursuance of a requirement imposed by or under the rules; and

(b) references to the relevant steps under the rules, in relation to any matter, include any steps falling to be taken in accordance with the rules for the purposes of or in connection with the determination or conciliation of the matter, or any appeal, review or reconsideration of any determination or award.

(6) This section does not affect any enactment or rule of law by virtue of which a court would apart from this section disregard any such rules of a trade union or any such fact as is mentioned in subsection (2).   **[718]**

NOTES

Commencement: 16 October 1992.

Sub-s (1) contains provisions formerly in the Employment Act 1988, s 2(4). Sub-s (2) contains provisions formerly in s 2(1) of the 1988 Act. Sub-s (3) contains provisions formerly in s 2(3) of the 1988 Act. Sub-s (4) contains provisions formerly in s 2(2) of the 1988 Act. Sub-ss (5), (6) contain provisions formerly in s 2(5), (6) of the 1988 Act.

Right not to be unjustifiably disciplined

64 Right not to be unjustifiably disciplined

(1) An individual who is or has been a member of a trade union has the right not to be unjustifiably disciplined by the union.

(2) For this purpose an individual is "disciplined" by a trade union if a determination is made, or purportedly made, under the rules of the union or by an official of the union or a number of persons including an official that—

(a) he should be expelled from the union or a branch or section of the union,

(b) he should pay a sum to the union, to a branch or section of the union or to any other person;

(c) sums tendered by him in respect of an obligation to pay subscriptions or other sums to the union, or to a branch or section of the union, should be treated as unpaid or paid for a different purpose,

(d) he should be deprived to any extent of, or of access to, any benefits, services or facilities which would otherwise be provided or made available to him by virtue of his membership of the union, or a branch or section of the union,

(e) another trade union, or a branch or section of it, should be encouraged or advised not to accept him as a member, or

(f) he should be subjected to some other detriment;

and whether an individual is "unjustifiably disciplined" shall be determined in accordance with section 65.

(3) Where a determination made in infringement of an individual's right under this section requires the payment of a sum or the performance of an obligation, no person is entitled in any proceedings to rely on that determination for the purpose of recovering the sum or enforcing the obligation.

(4) Subject to that, the remedies for infringement of the right conferred by this section are as provided by sections 66 and 67, and not otherwise.

(5) The right not to be unjustifiably disciplined is in addition to (and not in substitution for) any right which exists apart from this section; *and nothing* [and, subject to section 66(4), nothing] in this section or sections 65 to 67 affects any remedy for infringement of any such right.

[719]

NOTES
Commencement: 16 October 1992.
Sub-s (1) contains provisions formerly in the Employment Act 1988, s 3(1). Sub-s (2) contains provisions formerly in s 3(5) of the 1988 Act, and contains a drafting provision. Sub-s (3) contains provisions formerly in s 3(8) of the 1988 Act. Sub-ss (4), (5) contain provisions formerly in s 3(7) of the 1988 Act.
Sub-s (5): words in italics substituted by words in square brackets immediately following, by the Trade Union Reform and Employment Rights Act 1993, s 49(2), Sch 8, para 48, as from 30 November 1993 (SI 1993/1908, below, para **[1435]**).

65 Meaning of "unjustifiably disciplined"

(1) An individual is unjustifiably disciplined by a trade union if the actual or supposed conduct which constitutes the reason, or one of the reasons, for disciplining him is—

  (a) conduct to which this section applies, or
  (b) something which is believed by the union to amount to such conduct;

but subject to subsection (6) (cases of bad faith in relation to assertion of wrongdoing).

(2) This section applies to conduct which consists in—

  (a) failing to participate in or support a strike or other industrial action (whether by members of the union or by others), or indicating opposition to or a lack of support for such action;
  (b) failing to contravene, for a purpose connected with such a strike or other industrial action, a requirement imposed on him by or under a contract of employment;
  (c) asserting (whether by bringing proceedings or otherwise) that the union, any official or representative of it or a trustee of its property has contravened, or is proposing to contravene, a requirement which is, or is thought to be, imposed by or under the rules of the union or any other agreement or by or under any enactment (whenever passed) or any rule of law;
  (d) encouraging or assisting a person
      (i) to perform an obligation imposed on him by a contract of employment, or
      (ii) to make or attempt to vindicate any such assertion as is mentioned in paragraph (c); *or*
  (e) contravening a requirement imposed by or in consequence of a determination which infringes the individual's or another individual's right not to be unjustifiably disciplined
  [(f) failing to agree, or withdrawing agreement, to the making from his wages

(in accordance with arrangements between his employer and the union) of deductions representing payments to the union in respect of his membership,

   (g) resigning or proposing to resign from the union or from another union, becoming or proposing to become a member of another union, refusing to become a member of another union, or being a member of another union,

   (h) working with, or proposing to work with, individuals who are not members of the union or who are or are not members of another union,

   (i) working for, or proposing to work for, an employer who employs or who has employed individuals who are not members of the union or who are or are not members of another union, or

   (j) requiring the union to do an act which the union is, by any provision of this Act, required to do on the requisition of a member].

(3) This section applies to conduct which involves the Commissioner for the Rights of Trade Union Members or the Certification Officer being consulted or asked to provide advice or assistance with respect to any matter whatever, or which involves any person being consulted or asked to provide advice or assistance with respect to a matter which forms, or might form, the subject-matter of any such assertion as is mentioned in subsection (2)(c) above.

(4) This section also applies to conduct which consists in proposing to engage in, or doing anything preparatory or incidental to, conduct falling within subsection (2) or (3).

(5) This section does not apply to an act, omission or statement comprised in conduct falling within subsection (2), (3) or (4) above if it is shown that the act, omission or statement is one in respect of which individuals would be disciplined by the union irrespective of whether their acts, omissions or statements were in connection with conduct within subsection (2) or (3) above.

(6) An individual is not unjustifiably disciplined if it is shown—

   (a) that the reason for disciplining him, or one of them, is that he made such an assertion as is mentioned in subsection (2)(c), or encouraged or assisted another person to make or attempt to vindicate such an assertion,

   (b) that the assertion was false, and

   (c) that he made the assertion, or encouraged or assisted another person to make or attempt to vindicate it, in the belief that it was false or otherwise in bad faith,

and that there was no other reason for disciplining him or that the only other reasons were reasons in respect of which he does not fall to be treated as unjustifiably disciplined.

(7) In this section—

"conduct" includes statements, acts and omissions;

"contract of employment", in relation to an individual, includes any agreement between that individual and a person for whom he works or normally works [, "employer" includes such a person and related expressions shall be construed accordingly;] *and*

"representative", in relation to a union, means a person acting or purporting to act—

   (a) in his capacity as a member of the union, or

   (b) on the instructions or advice of a person acting or purporting to act in that capacity or in the capacity of an official of the union;

["require" (on the part of an individual) includes request or apply for, and "requisition" shall be construed accordingly; and "wages" shall be construed in accordance with the definitions of "contract of employment", "employer" and related expressions.]

(8) Where a person holds any office or employment under the Crown on terms which do not constitute a contract of employment between him and the Crown, those terms shall nevertheless be deemed to constitute such a contract for the purposes of this section.   **[720]**

NOTES

Commencement: 16 October 1992.

Sub-s (1) contains provisions formerly in the Employment Act 1988, s 3(2), and contains a drafting provision. Sub-s (2) contains provisions formerly in s 3(3)(a), (b) (in part), (c), (d) (in part), (f) of the 1988 Act. Sub-s (3) contains provisions formerly in ss 3(3)(e), 32(1) (definition "the Commissioner") of the 1988 Act. Sub-s (4) contains provisions formerly in s 3(3)(g) of the 1988 Act. Sub-s (5) contains provisions formerly in s 3(3) (closing words) of the 1988 Act. Sub-s (6) contains provisions formerly in s 3(4) of the 1988 Act. Sub-s (7) contains provisions formerly in ss 3(3)(b) (in part), (d) (in part), (6) (in part), 32(1) (definition "conduct") of the 1988 Act. Sub-s (8) contains provisions formerly in s 30(1) (in part) of the 1988 Act.

Sub-s (2): word "or" in italics at the end of para (d) repealed, and paras (f)–(j) added by the Trade Union Reform and Employment Rights Act 1993, ss 16(1), 51, Sch 10, as from 30 August 1993 (SI 1993/1908, below, para **[1435]**).

Sub-s (7): words in square brackets in definition "contract of employment", and definitions "require" and "wages" (and the word "and" preceding it), are added, and the word "and" in italics at end of definition "contract of employment" is repealed, by the Trade Union Reform and Employment Rights Act 1993, ss 16(2), 49(2), 51, Sch 8, para 49, Sch 10, as from 30 August 1993 (SI 1993/1908, below, para **[1435]**).

66 Complaint of infringement of right

(1) An individual who claims that he has been unjustifiably disciplined by a trade union may present a complaint against the union to an industrial tribunal.

(2) The tribunal shall not entertain such a complaint unless it is presented—

(a) before the end of the period of three months beginning with the date of the making of the determination claimed to infringe the right, or

(b) where the tribunal is satisfied—

(i) that it was not reasonably practicable for the complaint to be presented before the end of that period, or

(ii) that any delay in making the complaint is wholly or partly attributable to a reasonable attempt to appeal against the determination or to have it reconsidered or reviewed,

within such further period as the tribunal considers reasonable.

(3) Where the tribunal finds the complaint well-founded, it shall make a declaration to that effect.

(4) Where an individual who is, or is seeking to be, in employment to which section 174 applies (employment subject to union membership agreement) is refused membership of, or is expelled from, a union in pursuance of a determination which infringes his right not to be unjustifiably disciplined, he may not present a complaint under this section but the refusal or expulsion shall be regarded as unreasonable for the purposes of that section.   **[721]**

NOTES

Commencement: 16 October 1992.

Sub-s (1) contains provisions formerly in the Employment Act 1988, s 4(1). Sub-s (2) contains provisions formerly in s 4(2), (3) of the 1988 Act. Sub-s (3) contains provisions formerly in s 4(4) of the 1988 Act. Sub-s (4) contains provisions formerly in s 4(6) of the 1988 Act.

Sub-s (4): substituted by the Trade Union Reform and Employment Rights Act 1993, s 49(2), Sch 8, para 50, as from 30 November 1993 (SI 1993/1908, below, para **[1435]**), as follows—

"(4) Where a complaint relating to an expulsion which is presented under this section is declared to be well-founded, no complaint in respect of the expulsion shall be presented or proceeded with under section 174 (right not to be excluded or expelled from trade union).".

67 Further remedies for infringement of right

(1) An individual whose complaint under section 66 has been declared to be well-founded may make an application for one or both of the following—

    (a) an award of compensation to be paid to him by the union;

    (b) an order that the union pay him an amount equal to any sum which he has paid in pursuance of any such determination as is mentioned in section 64(2)(b).

(2) An application under this section shall be made to the Employment Appeal Tribunal if, when it is made—

    (a) the determination infringing the applicant's right not to be unjustifiably disciplined has not been revoked, or

    (b) the union has failed to take all the steps necessary for securing the reversal of anything done for the purpose of giving effect to the determination;

and in any other case it shall be made to an industrial tribunal.

(3) An application under this section shall not be entertained if made before the end of the period of four weeks beginning with the date of the declaration or after the end of the period of six months beginning with that date.

(4) Where the Employment Appeal Tribunal or industrial tribunal is satisfied that it would be required by virtue of subsection (2) to dismiss the application, it may instead transfer it to the tribunal to which it should have been made; and an application so transferred shall be proceeded with as if it had been made in accordance with that subsection when originally made.

(5) The amount of compensation awarded shall, subject to the following provisions, be such as the Employment Appeal Tribunal or industrial tribunal considers just and equitable in all the circumstances.

(6) In determining the amount of compensation to be awarded, the same rule shall be applied concerning the duty of a person to mitigate his loss as applies to damages recoverable under the common law in England and Wales or Scotland.

(7) Where the Employment Appeal Tribunal or industrial tribunal finds that the infringement complained of was to any extent caused or contributed to by the action of the applicant, it shall reduce the amount of the compensation by such proportion as it considers just and equitable having regard to that finding.

(8) The amount of compensation *awarded against a trade union on an application under this section* [calculated in accordance with subsections (5) to (7)] shall not exceed the aggregate of—

    (a) an amount equal to 30 times the limit for the time being imposed by paragraph 8(1)(b) of Schedule 14 to the Employment Protection (Consolidation) Act 1978 (maximum amount of a week's pay for basic award in unfair dismissal cases), and

    (b) an amount equal to the limit for the time being imposed by section 75 of that Act (maximum compensatory award in such cases);

and, in the case of an award by the Employment Appeal Tribunal, shall not be less than the amount for the time being specified in section *156(1) of this Act (minimum basic award in certain cases of unfair dismissal)* [176(6) of this Act (minimum award by Employment Appeal Tribunal in cases of exclusion or expulsion from union)].

(9) A reduction or increase required to be made by virtue of the limits in subsection (8) shall be made before a reduction made—

    (a) by virtue of subsection (6) or (7), or

(b) *on account of sums already paid by the union by way of compensation in respect of the determination to which the application relates or in respect of anything done for the purpose of giving effect to the determination;*

and, accordingly, where the case so requires, the reductions mentioned in paragraphs (a) and (b) shall be applied to the maximum or minimum award under subsection (8).
[722]

NOTES
Commencement: 16 October 1992.
This section contains provisions formerly in the Employment Act 1988, s 5(1)–(9).
Sub-s (8): words in italics substituted in each case by words in square brackets immediately following by the Trade Union Reform and Employment Rights Act 1993, s 49(2), Sch 8, para 51(a), as from 30 November 1993 (SI 1993/1908, below, para **[1435]**).
Sub-s (9): repealed by the Trade Union Reform and Employment Rights Act 1993, ss 49(2), 51, Sch 8, para 51(b), Sch 10 as from 30 November 1993 (SI 1993/1908, below, para **[1435]**).

Right to require employer to stop deduction of union dues

68 Right to require employer to stop deductions of union dues

(1) If a person certifies to his employer—

(a) *that notice given by him to a trade union for the purpose of terminating his membership has expired or will expire on a particular date, or*

(b) *that his membership of a trade union to the knowledge of the union has been or will be terminated from a particular date,*

the employer shall ensure that no amount representing a payment to the union in respect of his membership of the union after that date is deducted from emoluments payable to him.

(2) The employer's duty under subsection (1) applies from the first day, following the giving of the certificate, on which it is reasonably practicable for him to comply with that subsection.

(3) If a person who has given a certificate under subsection (1) notifies his employer that the certificate is withdrawn, the employer's duty under that subsection does not apply in relation to emoluments paid after the notification.

(4) A deduction made in contravention of this section shall be treated for the purposes of Part I of the Wages Act 1986 as a deduction in contravention of section 1(1) of that Act notwithstanding anything in any contract between the employee and employer, or in any agreement or consent signified by the employee.   **[723]**

NOTES
Commencement: 16 October 1992.
Sub-s (1) contains provisions formerly in the Employment Act 1988, s 7(1). Sub-ss (2), (3) contain provisions formerly in s 7(2) of the 1988 Act. Sub-s (4) contains provisions formerly in s 7(3) of the 1988 Act.
This section and the cross-heading preceding it are substituted by new ss 68, 68A, and a new cross-heading, by the Trade Union Reform and Employment Rights Act 1993, s 15, as from 30 August 1993 (SI 1993/1908, below, para **[1435]**), as follows—
   "Right not to suffer deduction of unauthorised or excessive union subscriptions
   68 Right not to suffer deduction of unauthorised or excessive subscriptions

   (1) Where arrangements ("subscription deduction arrangements") exist between the employer of a worker and a trade union relating to the making from workers' wages of deductions representing payments to the union in respect of the workers' membership of the union ("subscription deductions"), the employer shall ensure—

      (a) that no subscription deduction is made from wages payable to the worker on any day ("the relevant day") unless it is an authorised deduction, and
      (b) that the amount of any subscription deduction which is so made does not exceed the permitted amount.

      (2) For the purposes of subsection (1)(a) a subscription deduction is an authorised deduction in relation to the relevant day if—

(a) a document containing the worker's authorisation of the making from his wages of subscription deductions has been signed and dated by the worker, and

(b) the authorisation is current on that day.

(3) For the purposes of subsection (2)(b) an authorisation is current on the relevant day if that day falls within the period of three years beginning with the day on which the worker signs and dates the document containing the authorisation and subsection (4) does not apply.

(4) This subsection applies if a document containing the worker's withdrawal of the authorisation has been received by the employer in time for it to be reasonably practicable for him to secure that no subscription deduction is made from wages payable to the worker on the relevant day.

(5) For the purposes of subsection (1)(b) the permitted amount in relation to the relevant day is—

(a) the amount of the subscription deduction which falls to be made from wages payable to the worker on that day in accordance with the subscription deduction arrangements, or

(b) if there is a relevant increase in the amount of subscription deductions and appropriate notice has not been given by the employer to the worker at least one month before that day, the amount referred to in paragraph (a) less the amount of the increase.

(6) So much of the increase referred to in subsection (5)(b) is relevant as is not attributable solely to an increase in the wages payable on the relevant day.

(7) In subsection (5)(b) "appropriate notice" means, subject to subsection (8) below, notice in writing stating—

(a) the amount of the increase and the increased amount of the subscription deductions, and

(b) that the worker may at any time withdraw his authorisation of the making of subscription deductions by giving notice in writing to the employer.

(8) Where the relevant increase is attributable to an increase in any percentage by reference to which the worker's subscription deductions are calculated, subsection (7) above shall have effect with the substitution, in paragraph (a), for the reference to the amount of the increase and the increased amount of the deductions of a reference to the percentage before and the percentage after the increase.

(9) A worker's authorisation of the making of subscription deductions from his wages shall not give rise to any obligation on the part of the employer to the worker to maintain or continue to maintain subscription deduction arrangements.

(10) Where arrangements, whether included in subscription deduction arrangements or not, exist between the parties to subscription deduction arrangements for the making from workers' wages of deductions representing payments to the union which are additional to subscription deductions, the amount of the deductions representing such additional payments shall be treated for the purposes of this section (where they would otherwise not be so treated) as part of the subscription deductions.

(11) In this section and section 68A "employer", "wages" and "worker" have the same meanings as in Part I of the Wages Act 1986.   **[724]**

68A Complaint of infringement of rights

(1) A worker may present a complaint to an industrial tribunal that his employer has made a deduction from his wages in contravention of section 68—

(a) within the period of three months beginning with the date of the payment of the wages from which the deduction, or (if the complaint relates to more than one deduction) the last of the deductions, was made, or

(b) where the tribunal is satisfied that it was not reasonably practicable for the complaint to be presented within that period, within such further period as the tribunal considers reasonable.

(2) Where a tribunal finds that a complaint under this section is well-founded, it shall make a declaration to that effect and shall order the employer to pay to the worker—

(a) in the case of a contravention of paragraph (a) of subsection (1) of section 68, the whole amount of the deduction, and

(b) in the case of a contravention of paragraph (b) of that subsection, the amount by which the deduction exceeded the amount permitted to be deducted by that paragraph,

less any such part of the amount as has already been paid to the worker by the employer.

(3) Where the making of a deduction from the wages of a worker both contravenes section 68(1) and involves one or more of the contraventions specified in subsection (4) of this section, the aggregate amount which may be ordered by an industrial tribunal or court (whether on the same occasion or on different occasions) to be paid in respect of the contraventions shall not exceed the amount, or (where different amounts may be ordered to be paid in respect of different contraventions) the greatest amount, which may be ordered to be paid in respect of any one of them.

(4) The contraventions referred to in subsection (3) are—

(a) a contravention of the requirement not to make a deduction without having given the particulars required by section 8 (itemised pay statements) or 9(1) (standing statements of fixed deductions) of the Employment Protection (Consolidation) Act 1978,

(b) a contravention of section 1(1) of the Wages Act 1986 (requirement not to make
     unauthorised deductions), and
(c) a contravention of section 86(1) or 90(1) of this Act (requirements not to make deductions
     of political fund contributions in certain circumstances).".   **[725]**

Right to terminate membership of union

69 Right to terminate membership of union

In every contract of membership of a trade union, whether made before or after the
passing of this Act, a term conferring a right on the member, on giving reasonable
notice and complying with any reasonable conditions, to terminate his membership
of the union shall be implied.   **[726]**

NOTES
Commencement: 16 October 1992.
This section contains provisions formerly in the Trade Union and Labour Relations Act 1974, s 7, as
substituted by the Trade Union and Labour Relations (Amendment) Act 1976, s 3(1).

Supplementary

70 Membership of constituent or affiliated organisation

In this Chapter "member", in relation to a trade union consisting wholly or partly of,
or of representatives of, constituent or affiliated organisations, includes a member of
any of the constituent or affiliated organisations.   **[727]**

NOTES
Commencement: 16 October 1992.
This section contains provisions formerly in the Employment Act 1988, s 32(1) (definition "member").

CHAPTER VI
APPLICATION OF FUNDS FOR POLITICAL OBJECTS

Restriction on use of funds for certain political objects

71 Restriction on use of funds for certain political objects

(1) The funds of a trade union shall not be applied in the furtherance of the political
objects to which this Chapter applies unless—

(a) there is in force in accordance with this Chapter a resolution (a "political
     resolution") approving the furtherance of those objects as an object of the
     union (see sections 73 to 81), and
(b) there are in force rules of the union as to—

  (i) the making of payments in furtherance of those objects out of a
       separate fund, and
  (ii) the exemption of any member of the union objecting to contribute to
       that fund,

which comply with this Chapter (see sections 82, 84 and 85) and have been
approved by the Certification Officer.

(2) This applies whether the funds are so applied directly, or in conjunction with
another trade union, association or body, or otherwise indirectly.   **[728]**

NOTES
Commencement: 16 October 1992.
This section contains provisions formerly in the Trade Union Act 1913, s 3(1) (in part), as amended
and repealed in part by the Trade Union and Labour Relations Act 1974, s 25, Sch 3, para 2(1), (3), (4),
Sch 5, and the Employment Protection Act 1975, s 125, Sch 16, Pt IV, para 2(1), (2).

72 Political objects to which restriction applies

(1) The political objects to which this Chapter applies are the expenditure of money—

  (a) on any contribution to the funds of, or on the payment of expenses incurred directly or indirectly by, a political party;

  (b) on the provision of any service or property for use by or on behalf of any political party;

  (c) in connection with the registration of electors, the candidature of any person, the selection of any candidate or the holding of any ballot by the union in connection with any election to a political office;

  (d) on the maintenance of any holder of a political office;

  (e) on the holding of any conference or meeting by or on behalf of a political party or of any other meeting the main purpose of which is the transaction of business in connection with a political party;

  (f) on the production, publication or distribution of any literature, document, film, sound recording or advertisement the main purpose of which is to persuade people to vote for a political party or candidate or to persuade them not to vote for a political party or candidate.

(2) Where a person attends a conference or meeting as a delegate or otherwise as a participator in the proceedings, any expenditure incurred in connection with his attendance as such shall, for the purposes of subsection (1)(e), be taken to be expenditure incurred on the holding of the conference or meeting.

(3) In determining for the purposes of subsection (1) whether a trade union has incurred expenditure of a kind mentioned in that subsection, no account shall be taken of the ordinary administrative expenses of the union.

(4) In this section—

  "candidate" means a candidate for election to a political office and includes a prospective candidate;

  "contribution", in relation to the funds of a political party, includes any fee payable for affiliation to, or membership of, the party and any loan made to the party;

  "electors" means electors at an election to a political office;

  "film" includes any record, however made, of a sequence of visual images, which is capable of being used as a means of showing that sequence as a moving picture;

  "local authority" means a local authority within the meaning of section 270 of the Local Government Act 1972 or section 235 of the Local Government (Scotland) Act 1973; and

  "political office" means the office of member of Parliament, member of the European Parliament or member of a local authority or any position within a political party.   [729]

NOTES

Commencement: 16 October 1992.

Sub-ss (1)–(3) contain provisions formerly in the Trade Union Act 1913, s 3(3), (3A), (3B), as substituted by the Trade Union Act 1984, s 17(1). Sub-s (4) contains provisions formerly in s 3(3C) of the 1913 Act, as so substituted, and as read with the European Communities (Amendment) Act 1986, s 3.

Political resolution

73 Passing and effect of political resolution

(1) A political resolution must be passed by a majority of those voting on a ballot of the members of the trade union held in accordance with this Chapter.

(2) A political resolution so passed shall take effect as if it were a rule of the union and may be rescinded in the same manner and subject to the same provisions as such a rule.

(3) If not previously rescinded, a political resolution shall cease to have effect at the end of the period of ten years beginning with the date of the ballot on which it was passed.

(4) Where before the end of that period a ballot is held on a new political resolution, then—

(a) if the new resolution is passed, the old resolution shall be treated as rescinded, and

(b) if it is not passed, the old resolution shall cease to have effect at the end of the period of two weeks beginning with the date of the ballot.   **[730]**

NOTES

Commencement: 16 October 1992.

Sub-s (1) contains provisions formerly in the Trade Union Act 1913, s 3(1) (in part). Sub-s (2) contains provisions formerly in s 3(4) of the 1913 Act, as amended by the Trade Union and Labour Relations Act 1974, s 25(1), Sch 3, para 2(1), (3). Sub-s (3) contains provisions formerly in the Trade Union Act 1984, s 12(2)(a). Sub-s (4) contains provisions formerly in s 12(2)(b), (4) of the 1984 Act.

74 Approval of political ballot rules

(1) A ballot on a political resolution must be held in accordance with rules of the trade union (its "political ballot rules") approved by the Certification Officer.

(2) Fresh approval is required for the purposes of each ballot which it is proposed to hold, notwithstanding that the rules have been approved for the purposes of an earlier ballot.

(3) The Certification Officer shall not approve a union's political ballot rules unless he is satisfied that the requirements set out in—

section 75 (appointment of independent scrutineer),
section 76 (entitlement to vote),
section 77 (voting), *and*
[section 77A (counting of votes etc. by independent person), and]
section 78 (scrutineer's report),

would be satisfied in relation to a ballot held by the union in accordance with the rules.   **[731]**

NOTES

Commencement: 16 October 1992.

Sub-ss (1), (3) contain provisions formerly in the Trade Union Act 1913, s 4(1), as repealed in part by the Trade Union and Labour Relations Act 1974, s 25, Sch 3, para 2(1), (3), (4), Sch 5, as amended by the Employment Protection Act 1975, s 125, Sch 16, Pt IV, para 2(1), (2), by the Trade Union Act 1984, s 13(1), and by the Employment Act 1988, s 33(1), Sch 3, Pt I, para 1(1)(a), and contain provisions formerly in s 15(1)(a) of the 1988 Act. Sub-s (2) contains provisions formerly in the Trade Union Act 1984, s 13(3).

Sub-s (3): word "and" in italics repealed, and words in square brackets inserted, by the Trade Union Reform and Employment Rights Act 1993, ss 3, 51, Sch 1, para 1, Sch 10, as from 30 August 1993 (SI 1993/1908, below, para **[1435]**).

75 Appointment of independent scrutineer

(1) The trade union shall, before the ballot is held, appoint a qualified independent person ("the scrutineer") to carry out—

    (a) the functions in relation to the ballot which are required under this section to be contained in his appointment; and

    (b) such additional functions in relation to the ballot as may be specified in his appointment.

(2) A person is a qualified independent person in relation to a ballot if—

    (a) he satisfies such conditions as may be specified for the purposes of this section by order of the Secretary of State or is himself so specified; and

    (b) the trade union has no grounds for believing either that he will carry out any functions conferred on him in relation to the ballot otherwise than competently or that his independence in relation to the union, or in relation to the ballot, might reasonably be called into question.

An order under paragraph (a) shall be made by statutory instrument which shall be subject to annulment in pursuance of a resolution of either House of Parliament.

(3) The scrutineer's appointment shall require him—

    (a) to be the person who supervises the production *and distribution of the voting papers* [of the voting papers and (unless he is appointed under section 77A to undertake the distribution of the voting papers) their distribution] and to whom the voting papers are returned by those voting;

    [(aa) to—

        (i) inspect the register of names and addresses of the members of the trade union, or

        (ii) examine the copy of the register as at the relevant date which is supplied to him in accordance with subsection (5A)(a),

    whenever it appears to him appropriate to do so and, in particular, when the conditions specified in subsection (3A) are satisfied;]

    (b) to take such steps as appear to him to be appropriate for the purpose of enabling him to make his report (see section 78);

    (c) to make his report to the trade union as soon as reasonably practicable after the last date for the return of voting papers; and

    (d) to retain custody of all voting papers returned for the purposes of the ballot [and the copy of the register supplied to him in accordance with subsection (5A)(a)]—

        (i) until the end of the period of one year beginning with the announcement by the union of the result of the ballot; and

        (ii) if within that period an application is made under section 79 (complaint of failure to comply with ballot rules), until the Certification Officer or the court authorises him to dispose of the papers [or copy].

    [(3A) The conditions referred to in subsection (3)(aa) are—

    (a) that a request that the scrutineer inspect the register or examine the copy is made to him during the appropriate period by a member of the trade union who suspects that the register is not, or at the relevant date was not, accurate and up-to-date, and

    (b) that the scrutineer does not consider that the member's suspicion is ill-founded.

    (3B) In subsection (3A) "the appropriate period" means the period—

    (a) beginning with the day on which the scrutineer is appointed, and

    (b) ending with the day before the day on which the scrutineer makes his report to the trade union.

(3C)   The duty of confidentiality as respects the register is incorporated in the scrutineer's appointment.]

(4)   The trade union shall ensure that nothing in the terms of the scrutineer's appointment (including any additional functions specified in the appointment) is such as to make it reasonable for any person to call the scrutineer's independence in relation to the union into question.

(5)   The trade union shall, before the scrutineer begins to carry out his functions, either—

(a)   send a notice stating the name of the scrutineer to every member of the union to whom it is reasonably practicable to send such a notice, or

(b)   take all such other steps for notifying members of the name of the scrutineer as it is the practice of the union to take when matters of general interest to all its members need to be brought to their attention.

[(5A)   The trade union shall—

(a)   supply to the scrutineer as soon as is reasonably practicable after the relevant date a copy of the register of names and addresses of its members as at that date, and

(b)   comply with any request made by the scrutineer to inspect the register.

(5B)   Where the register is kept by means of a computer the duty imposed on the trade union by subsection (5A)(a) is either to supply a legible printed copy or (if the scrutineer prefers) to supply a copy of the computer data and allow the scrutineer use of the computer to read it at any time during the period when he is required to retain custody of the copy.]

(6)   The trade union shall ensure that the scrutineer duly carries out his functions and that there is no interference with his carrying out of those functions which would make it reasonable for any person to call the scrutineer's independence in relation to the union into question.

(7)   The trade union shall comply with all reasonable requests made by the scrutineer for the purposes of, or in connection with, the carrying out of his functions.

[(8)   In this section "the relevant date" means—

(a)   where the trade union has rules determining who is entitled to vote in the ballot by reference to membership on a particular date, that date, and

(b)   otherwise, the date, or the last date, on which voting papers are distributed for the purposes of the ballot.]   **[732]**

NOTES
Commencement: 16 October 1992.
Sub-s (1) contains provisions formerly in the Employment Act 1988, s 15(2)(a) (in part). Sub-ss (2), (3) contain provisions formerly in s 15(3), (4) (both in part) of the 1988 Act. Sub-s (4) contains provisions formerly in s 15(2)(b) (in part) of the 1988 Act. Sub-s (5) contains provisions formerly in s 15(2)(bb) (in part) of the 1988 Act, as inserted by the Employment Act 1990, s 5(5). Sub-ss (6), (7) contain provisions formerly in s 15(2)(c), (d) (both in part) of the 1988 Act.
Sub-s (3): words in italics in para (a) substituted by words in square brackets immediately following, and para (aa) and the two sets of words in square brackets in para (d) are inserted, by the Trade Union Reform and Employment Rights Act 1993, s 3, Sch 1, para 2(a)–(c), as from 30 August 1993 (SI 1993/1908, below, para **[1435]**).
Sub-ss (3A)–(3C), (5A), (5B): inserted by the Trade Union Reform and Employment Rights Act 1993, s 3, Sch 1, para 2(d), (e), as from 30 August 1993 (SI 1993/1908, below, para **[1435]**).
Sub-s (8): added by the Trade Union Reform and Employment Rights Act 1993, s 3, Sch 1, para 2(f), as from 30 August 1993 (SI 1993/1908, below, para **[1435]**).
Order under this section: Trade Union Ballots and Elections (Independent Scrutineer Qualifications) Order 1993, SI 1993/1909, below, para **[1443]**.

76 Entitlement to vote

Entitlement to vote in the ballot shall be accorded equally to all members of the trade union. **[733]**

NOTES
Commencement: 16 October 1992.
This section contains provisions formerly in the Trade Union Act 1913, s 4(1A), as inserted by the Trade Union Act 1984, s 13(2).

77 Voting

(1) The method of voting must be by the marking of a voting paper by the person voting.

(2) Each voting paper must—

    (a) state the name of the independent scrutineer and clearly specify the address to which, and the date by which, it is to be returned, and

    (b) be given one of a series of consecutive whole numbers every one of which is used in giving a different number in that series to each voting paper printed or otherwise produced for the purposes of the ballot, and

    (c) be marked with its number.

(3) Every person who is entitled to vote in the ballot must—

    (a) be allowed to vote without interference from, or constraint imposed by, the union or any of its members, officials or employees, and

    (b) so far as is reasonably practicable, be enabled to do so without incurring any direct cost to himself.

(4) So far as is reasonably practicable, every person who is entitled to vote in the ballot must—

    (a) have a voting paper sent to him by post at his home address or another address which he has requested the trade union in writing to treat as his postal address, and

    (b) be given a convenient opportunity to vote by post.

(5) The ballot shall be conducted so as to secure that—

    (a) so far as is reasonably practicable, those voting do so in secret, and

    (b) the votes given in the ballot are fairly and accurately counted.

For the purposes of paragraph (b) an inaccuracy in counting shall be disregarded if it is accidental and on a scale which could not affect the result of the ballot. **[734]**

NOTES
Commencement: 16 October 1992.
Sub-ss (1), (2) contain provisions formerly in the Trade Union Act 1913, s 4(1B), as inserted by the Trade Union Act 1984, s 13(2), and as amended by the Employment Act 1988, s 33, Sch 3, Pt I, para 1(1)(b), and by the Employment Act 1990, s 5(4). Sub-s (3) contains provisions formerly in s 4(1C) of the 1913 Act, as inserted by s 13(2) of the 1984 Act. Sub-s (4) contains provisions formerly in s 4(1D) of the 1913 Act, as inserted by s 13(2) of the 1984 Act, and as substituted by s 14(1) of the 1988 Act. Sub-s (5) contains provisions formerly in s 4(1E) of the 1913 Act, as inserted by s 13(2) of the 1984 Act.

[77A Counting of votes etc by independent person

(1) The trade union shall ensure that—

    (a) the storage and distribution of the voting papers for the purposes of the ballot, and

    (b) the counting of the votes cast in the ballot,

are undertaken by one or more independent persons appointed by the union.

(2) A person is an independent person in relation to a ballot if—

(a) he is the scrutineer, or

(b) he is a person other than the scrutineer and the trade union has no grounds for believing either that he will carry out any functions conferred on him in relation to the ballot otherwise than competently or that his independence in relation to the union, or in relation to the ballot, might reasonably be called into question.

(3) An appointment under this section shall require the person appointed to carry out his functions so as to minimise the risk of any contravention of requirements imposed by or under any enactment or the occurrence of any unfairness or malpractice.

(4) The duty of confidentiality as respects the register is incorporated in an appointment under this section.

(5) Where the person appointed to undertake the counting of votes is not the scrutineer, his appointment shall require him to send the voting papers back to the scrutineer as soon as reasonably practicable after the counting has been completed.

(6) The trade union—

(a) shall ensure that nothing in the terms of an appointment under this section is such as to make it reasonable for any person to call into question the independence of the person appointed in relation to the union,

(b) shall ensure that a person appointed under this section duly carries out his functions and that there is no interference with his carrying out of those functions which would make it reasonable for any person to call into question the independence of the person appointed in relation to the union, and

(c) shall comply with all reasonable requests made by a person appointed under this section for the purposes of, or in connection with, the carrying out of his functions.]   **[735]**

NOTE
Inserted by the Trade Union Reform and Employment Rights Act 1993, s 3, Sch 1, para 3, as from 30 August 1993 (SI 1993/1908).

78 Scrutineer's report

(1) The scrutineer's report on the ballot shall state—

(a) the number of voting papers distributed for the purposes of the ballot,

(b) the number of voting papers returned to the scrutineer,

(c) the number of valid votes cast in the ballot for and against the resolution, *and*

(d) the number of spoiled or otherwise invalid voting papers returned [; and

(e) the name of the person (or of each of the persons) appointed under section 77A or, if no person was so appointed, that fact.]

(2) The report shall also state whether the scrutineer is satisfied—

(a) that there are no reasonable grounds for believing that there was any contravention of a requirement imposed by or under any enactment in relation to the ballot,

(b) that the arrangements made [(whether by him or any other person)] with respect to the production, storage, distribution, return or other handling of the voting papers used in the ballot, and the arrangements for the counting of the votes, included all such security arrangements as were reasonably practicable for the purpose of minimising the risk that any unfairness or malpractice might occur, and

(c) that he has been able to carry out his functions without such interference as would make it reasonable for any person to call his independence in relation to the union into question;

and if he is not satisfied as to any of those matters, the report shall give particulars of his reasons for not being satisfied as to that matter.

[(2A) The report shall also state—

    (a) whether the scrutineer—

        (i) has inspected the register of names and addresses of the members of the trade union, or

        (ii) has examined the copy of the register as at the relevant date which is supplied to him in accordance with section 75(5A)(a),

    (b) if he has, whether in the case of each inspection or examination he was acting on a request by a member of the trade union or at his own instance,

    (c) whether he declined to act on any such request, and

    (d) whether any inspection of the register, or any examination of the copy of the register, has revealed any matter which he considers should be drawn to the attention of the trade union in order to assist it in securing that the register is accurate and up-to-date,

but shall not state the name of any member who has requested such an inspection or examination.

(2B) Where one or more persons other than the scrutineer are appointed under section 77A, the statement included in the scrutineer's report in accordance with subsection (2)(b) shall also indicate—

    (a) whether he is satisfied with the performance of the person, or each of the persons, so appointed, and

    (b) if he is not satisfied with the performance of the person, or any of them, particulars of his reasons for not being so satisfied.]

(3) The trade union shall not publish the result of the ballot until it has received the scrutineer's report.

(4) The trade union shall within the period of three months after it receives the report—

    (a) send a copy of the report to every member of the union to whom it is reasonably practicable to send such a copy; or

    (b) take all such other steps for notifying the contents of the report to the members of the union (whether by publishing the report or otherwise) as it is the practice of the union to take when matters of general interest to all its members need to be brought to their attention.

(5) Any such copy or notification shall be accompanied by a statement that the union will, on request, supply any member of the union with a copy of the report, either free of charge or on payment of such reasonable fee as may be specified in the notification.

(6) The trade union shall so supply any member of the union who makes such a request and pays the fee (if any) notified to him.   **[736]**

NOTES

Commencement: 16 October 1992.

Sub-s (1) contains provisions formerly in the Employment Act 1988, s 15(5)(a)–(d) (all in part). Sub-s (2) contains provisions formerly in s 15(5)(e), (f), (6) (all in part) of the 1988 Act. Sub-ss (3)–(6) contain provisions formerly in s 15(7) (in part) of the 1988 Act.

Sub-s (1): word "and" in italics at the end of para (c) repealed, and para (e) and the words "and" at the end of para (d) added, by the Trade Union Reform and Employment Rights Act 1993, ss 3, 51, Sch 1, para 4(a), Sch 10, as from 30 August 1993 (SI 1993/1908, below, para **[1435]**).

Sub-s (2): words in square brackets inserted by the Trade Union Reform and Employment Rights Act 1993, s 3, Sch 1, para 4(b), as from 30 August 1993 (SI 1993/1908, below, para **[1435]**).

Sub-ss (2A), (2B): inserted by the Trade Union Reform and Employment Rights Act 1993, s 3, Sch 1, para 4(c), as from 30 August 1993 (SI 1993/1908, below, para **[1435]**).

79 Remedy for failure to comply with ballot rules: general

(1) The remedy for—

(a) the taking by a trade union of a ballot on a political resolution otherwise than in accordance with political ballot rules approved by the Certification Officer, or

(b) the failure of a trade union, in relation to a proposed ballot on a political resolution, to comply with the political ballot rules so approved,

is by way of application under section 80 (to the Certification Officer) or 81 (to the court).

The making of an application to the Certification Officer does not prevent the applicant, or any other person, from making an application to the court in respect of the same matter.

(2) An application under those sections may be made only by a person who is a member of the trade union and, where the ballot has been held, was a member at the time when it was held.

References in those sections to a person having a sufficient interest are to such a person.

(3) No such application may be made after the end of the period of one year beginning with the day on which the union announced the result of the ballot. **[737]**

NOTES

Commencement: 16 October 1992.

Sub-s (1) contains provisions formerly in the Employment Act 1988, s 16(1) (in part), and in the Trade Union Act 1984, ss 5(10), 6(3) (as amended, in the case of s 5(10), by s 33(1) of, Sch 3, Pt I, para 5(4)(a) to, the 1988 Act), as applied by s 16(4) of the 1988 Act. Sub-s (2) contains provisions formerly in s 16(2) of the 1988 Act, and contains a drafting provision. Sub-s (3) contains provisions formerly in s 16(3) of the 1988 Act.

80 Application to Certification Officer

(1) A person having a sufficient interest (see section 79(2)) who claims that a trade union—

(a) has held a ballot on a political resolution otherwise than in accordance with political ballot rules approved by the Certification Officer, or

(b) has failed in relation to a proposed ballot on a political resolution to comply with political ballot rules so approved,

may apply to the Certification Officer for a declaration to that effect.

(2) On an application being made to him, the Certification Officer shall—

(a) make such enquiries as he thinks fit, and

(b) where he considers it appropriate, give the applicant and the trade union an opportunity to be heard,

and may make or refuse the declaration asked for.

(3) If he makes a declaration he shall specify in it the provisions with which the trade union has failed to comply.

(4) Where he makes a declaration and is satisfied that steps have been taken by the union with a view to remedying the declared failure, or securing that a failure of the same or any similar kind does not occur in future, or that the union has agreed to take such steps, he shall in making the declaration specify those steps.

(5) Whether he makes or refuses a declaration, he shall give reasons for his decision in writing; and the reasons may be accompanied by written observations on any matter arising from, or connected with, the proceedings.

(6) In exercising his functions under this section the Certification Officer shall ensure that, so far as is reasonably practicable, an application made to him is determined within six months of being made.

(7) Where he requests a person to furnish information to him in connection with enquiries made by him under this section, he shall specify the date by which that information is to be furnished and shall, unless he considers that it would be inappropriate to do so, proceed with his determination of the application notwithstanding that the information has not been furnished to him by the specified date.   **[738]**

NOTES

Commencement: 16 October 1992.

Sub-s (1) contains provisions formerly in the Employment Act 1988, s 16(1) (in part). Sub-s (2) contains provisions formerly in the Trade Union Act 1984, ss 5(3), 6(5), as applied by s 16(4) of the 1988 Act. Sub-s (3) contains provisions formerly in s 5(4) of the 1984 Act, as so applied. Sub-ss (4), (5) contain provisions formerly in s 6(1), (2) of the 1984 Act, as so applied. Sub-ss (6), (7) contain provisions formerly in s 6(7), (8) of the 1984 Act, as so applied.

81 Application to court

(1) A person having a sufficient interest (see section 79(2)) who claims that a trade union—

   (a) has held a ballot on a political resolution otherwise than in accordance with political ballot rules approved by the Certification Officer, or

   (b) has failed in relation to a proposed ballot on a political resolution to comply with political ballot rules so approved,

may apply to the court for a declaration to that effect.

(2) If an application in respect of the same matter has been made to the Certification Officer, the court shall have due regard to any declaration, reasons or observations of his which are brought to its notice.

(3) If the court makes the declaration asked for, it shall specify in the declaration the provisions with which the trade union has failed to comply.

(4) Where the court makes a declaration it shall also, unless it considers that to do so would be inappropriate, make an enforcement order, that is, an order imposing on the union one or more of the following requirements—

   (a) to secure the holding of a ballot in accordance with the order;

   (b) to take such other steps to remedy the declared failure as may be specified in the order;

   (c) to abstain from such acts as may be so specified with a view to securing that a failure of the same or a similar kind does not occur in future.

The court shall in an order imposing any such requirement as is mentioned in paragraph (a) or (b) specify the period within which the union must comply with the requirements of the order.

(5) Where the court makes an order requiring the union to hold a fresh ballot, the

court shall (unless it considers that it would be inappropriate to do so in the particular circumstances of the case) require the ballot to be conducted in accordance with the union's political ballot rules and such other provisions as may be made by the order.

(6) Where an enforcement order has been made, any person who is a member of the union and was a member at the time the order was made is entitled to enforce obedience to the order as if he had made the application on which the order was made.

(7) Without prejudice to any other power of the court, the court may on an application under this section grant such interlocutory relief (in Scotland, such interim order) as it considers appropriate.   **[739]**

NOTES

Commencement: 16 October 1992.

Sub-s (1) contains provisions formerly in the Employment Act 1988, s 16(1) (in part). Sub-s (2) contains provisions formerly in the Trade Union Act 1984, s 6(3) (in part), (4), as applied by s 16(4) of the 1988 Act. Sub-s (3) contains provisions formerly in s 5(4) of the 1984 Act, as so applied. Sub-s (4) contains provisions formerly in s 5(5)–(7), (9) of the 1984 Act, as so applied. Sub-s (5) contains provisions formerly in s 5(8) of the 1984 Act, as amended by s 33(1) of, Sch 3, Pt I, para 5(4)(b) to, the 1988 Act, as so applied. Sub-s (6) contains provisions formerly in s 5(11), (12) of the 1984 Act, as so applied. Sub-s (7) contains provisions formerly in s 23 (in part) of the 1988 Act.

The political fund

82 Rules as to political fund

(1) The trade union's rules must provide—

  (a) that payments in the furtherance of the political objects to which this Chapter applies shall be made out of a separate fund (the "political fund" of the union);

  (b) that a member of the union who gives notice in accordance with section 84 that he objects to contributing to the political fund shall be exempt from any obligation to contribute to it;

  (c) that a member shall not by reason of being so exempt—
      (i) be excluded from any benefits of the union, or
      (ii) be placed in any respect either directly or indirectly under a disability or at a disadvantage as compared with other members of the union (except in relation to the control or management of the political fund); and

  (d) that contribution to the political fund shall not be made a condition for admission to the union.

(2) A member of a trade union who claims that he is aggrieved by a breach of any rule made in pursuance of this section may complain to the Certification Officer.

(3) Where, after giving the member and a representative of the union an opportunity of being heard, the Certification Officer considers that a breach has been committed, he may make such order for remedying the breach as he thinks just under the circumstances.

(4) Any such order, on being recorded in the county court or, in Scotland, the sheriff court, may be enforced in the same way as an order of that court.   **[740]**

NOTES

Commencement: 16 October 1992.

Sub-s (1) contains provisions formerly in the Trade Union Act 1913, s 3(1) (in part), as amended by the Trade Union and Labour Relations Act 1974, s 25(1), Sch 3, para 2(1), (3). Sub-ss (2)–(4) contain provisions formerly in s 3(2) of the 1913 Act, as amended by s 25(1) of, Sch 3, para 2(1), (3) to, the 1974 Act and as amended and repealed in part by the Employment Protection Act 1975, s 125, Sch 16, Pt IV, para 2(1), (2), Sch 18.

83 Assets and liabilities of political fund

(1) There may be added to a union's political fund only—

    (a) sums representing contributions made to the fund by members of the union or by any person other than the union itself, and

    (b) property which accrues to the fund in the course of administering the assets of the fund.

(2) The rules of the union shall not be taken to require any member to contribute to the political fund at a time when there is no political resolution in force in relation to the union.

(3) No liability of a union's political fund shall be discharged out of any other fund of the union.

This subsection applies notwithstanding any term or condition on which the liability was incurred or that an asset of the other fund has been charged in connection with the liability.

[741]

NOTES

Commencement: 16 October 1992.

Sub-s (1) contains provisions formerly in the Trade Union Act 1984, s 14(1), (2)(a). Sub-s (2) contains provisions formerly in s 14(2)(b) of the 1984 Act. Sub-s (3) contains provisions formerly in s 14(3), (4) of the 1984 Act.

84 Notice of objection to contributing to political fund

(1) A member of a trade union may give notice in the following form, or in a form to the like effect, that he objects to contribute to the political fund:—

Name of Trade Union

POLITICAL FUND (EXEMPTION NOTICE)

I give notice that I object to contributing to the Political Fund of the Union, and am in consequence exempt, in manner provided by Chapter VI of Part I of the Trade Union and Labour Relations (Consolidation) Act 1992, from contributing to that fund.

A.B.

Address

day of   19

---

(2) On the adoption of a political resolution, notice shall be given to members of the union acquainting them—

    (a) that each member has a right to be exempted from contributing to the union's political fund, and

    (b) that a form of exemption notice can be obtained by or on behalf of a member either by application at or by post from—

        (i) the head office or any branch office of the union, or

        (ii) the office of the Certification Officer.

(3) The notice to members shall be given in accordance with rules of the union approved for the purpose by the Certification Officer, who shall have regard in each case to the existing practice and character of the union.

(4) On giving an exemption notice in accordance with this section, a member shall be exempt from contributing to the union's political fund—

    (a) where the notice is given within one month of the giving of notice to members under subsection (2) following the passing of a political resolution on a ballot held at a time when no such resolution is in force, as from the date on which the exemption notice is given;

    (b) in any other case, as from the 1st January next after the exemption notice is given.

(5) An exemption notice continues to have effect until it is withdrawn.   **[742]**

NOTES
Commencement: 16 October 1992.
Sub-s (1) contains provisions formerly in the Trade Union Act 1913, s 5(1) (in part), Schedule, as amended by the Trade Union and Labour Relations Act 1974, s 25(1), Sch 3, para 2(1), (3). Sub-ss (2), (3) contain provisions formerly in s 5(1) (in part) of the 1913 Act, as so amended, and as amended by the Employment Protection Act 1975, s 125(1), Sch 16, Pt IV, para 2(1), (2). Sub-ss (4), (5) contain provisions formerly in s 5(2) of the 1913 Act, as so amended, and in the Trade Union Act 1984, s 13(9), (10) (definition "new resolution").

85 Manner of giving effect to exemptions

(1) Effect may be given to the exemption of members from contributing to the political fund of a union either—

    (a) by a separate levy of contributions to that fund from the members who are not exempt, or

    (b) by relieving members who are exempt from the payment of the whole or part of any periodical contribution required from members towards the expenses of the union.

(2) In the latter case, the rules shall provide—

    (a) that relief shall be given as far as possible to all members who are exempt on the occasion of the same periodical payment, and

    (b) for enabling each member of the union to know what portion (if any) of any periodical contribution payable by him is a contribution to the political fund.   **[743]**

NOTES
Commencement: 16 October 1992.
This section contains provisions formerly in the Trade Union Act 1913, s 6, as amended by the Trade Union and Labour Relations Act 1974, s 25(1), Sch 3, para 2(1), (3), and as repealed in part by the Trade Union Act 1984, s 14(5).

Duties of employer who deducts union contributions

86 Certificate of exemption or objection to contributing to political fund

(1) If a member of a trade union which has a political fund certifies in writing to his employer that, or to the effect that—

    (a) he is exempt from the obligation to contribute to the fund, or

    (b) he has, in accordance with section 84, notified the union in writing of his objection to contributing to the fund,

the employer shall ensure that no amount representing a contribution to the political fund is deducted by him from emoluments payable to the member.

(2) The employer's duty under subsection (1) applies from the first day, following the giving of the certificate, on which it is reasonably practicable for him to comply with that subsection, until the certificate is withdrawn.

(3) An employer may not refuse to deduct any union dues from emoluments payable to a person who has given a certificate under this section if he continues to deduct union dues from emoluments payable to other members of the union, unless his refusal is not attributable to the giving of the certificate or otherwise connected with the duty imposed by subsection (1).   **[744]**

NOTES
Commencement: 16 October 1992.
Sub-ss (1), (2) contain provisions formerly in the Trade Union Act 1984, s 18(1), (2). Sub-s (3) contains provisions formerly in s 18(3) (in part) of the 1984 Act.

87 Application to court in respect of employer's failure

(1) A person who claims his employer has failed to comply with section 86 in deducting or refusing to deduct any amount from emoluments payable to him may apply to the county court or, in Scotland, the sheriff court.

(2) If the court is satisfied that there has been such a failure it shall make a declaration to that effect.

(3) The court may, if it considers it appropriate to do so in order to prevent a repetition of the failure, make an order requiring the employer to take, within a specified time, the steps specified in the order in relation to emoluments payable by him to the applicant.

(4) Where in proceedings arising out of section 86(3) (refusal to deduct union dues) the question arises whether the employer's refusal to deduct an amount was attributable to the certificate having been given or was otherwise connected with the duty under section 86(1), it is for the employer to satisfy the court that it was not.   **[745]**

NOTES
Commencement: 16 October 1992.
Sub-ss (1), (2) contain provisions formerly in the Trade Union Act 1984, s 18(4), (6). Sub-s (3) contains provisions formerly in s 18(5) of the 1984 Act. Sub-s (4) contains provisions formerly in s 18(3) (in part) of the 1984 Act.

88 Application of provisions of Wages Act 1986

(1) The following provisions apply where a certificate has been given by a worker to his employer for the purposes of section 86.

(2) Nothing in the worker's contract, or in any agreement or consent signified by him, shall be taken for the purposes of section 1 of the Wages Act 1986 (general restriction on deductions from wages) as authorising the making of deductions in contravention of the obligation imposed on the employer in consequence of the giving of the certificate.

(3) No complaint under section 5 of the Wages Act 1986 (complaint to industrial tribunal in respect of unauthorised deduction) shall be presented in respect of a deduction made in contravention of the obligation imposed on the employer in consequence of the giving of the certificate unless a declaration has been made under section 87(2), either before or after the date of payment of the wages from which the deduction was made, that the employer has failed to comply with that obligation.

(4) Section 5(2) of the Wages Act 1986 (time limit for presenting complaint) shall be read in relation to a complaint in respect of such a deduction, or of a series of deductions of which such a deduction is the last, as referring, if it is later, to the

date of the declaration instead of to the date of payment of the wages from which the
deduction was made.   **[746]**

NOTES
Commencement: 16 October 1992.
Sub-s (1) is a drafting provision. Sub-s (2) contains provisions formerly in the Wages Act 1986, s 1(6)
(in part), as amended by the Employment Act 1988, s 33(1), Sch 3, Pt I, para 6(1), (3). Sub-ss (3), (4)
contain provisions formerly in s 5(3A) of the 1986 Act, as inserted by s 33(1) of, Sch 3, Pt I, para 6(2),
(3) to, the 1988 Act.

Position where political resolution ceases to have effect

89 Administration of political fund where no resolution in force

(1) The following provisions have effect with respect to the political fund of a trade
union where there ceases to be any political resolution in force in relation to the union.

(2) If the resolution ceases to have effect by reason of a ballot being held on
which a new political resolution is not passed, the union may continue to make
payments out of the fund as if the resolution had continued in force for six months
beginning with the date of the ballot.

But no payment shall be made which causes the fund to be in deficit or increases
a deficit in it.

(3) There may be added to the fund only—

   (a) contributions to the fund paid to the union (or to a person on its behalf)
       before the resolution ceased to have effect, and
   (b) property which accrues to the fund in the course of administering the assets
       of the fund.

(4) The union may, notwithstanding any of its rules or any trusts on which the
fund is held, transfer the whole or part of the fund to such other fund of the union as
it thinks fit.

(5) If a new political resolution is subsequently passed, no property held
immediately before the date of the ballot by or on behalf of the union otherwise than
in its political fund, and no sums representing such property, may be added to the
fund.   **[747]**

NOTES
Commencement: 16 October 1992.
Sub-s (1) contains provisions formerly in the Trade Union Act 1984, s 15(10), and is in part a drafting
provision. Sub-s (2) contains provisions formerly in s 15(1), (2) of the 1984 Act. Sub-s (3) contains
provisions formerly in ss 14(2)(a), 15(5) of the 1984 Act. Sub-s (4) contains provisions formerly in
s 14(2)(c) of the 1984 Act. Sub-s (5) contains provisions formerly in the 1984 Act, s 15(9).

90 Discontinuance of contributions to political fund

(1) Where there ceases to be any political resolution in force in relation to a trade
union, the union shall take such steps as are necessary to ensure that the collection
of contributions to its political fund is discontinued as soon as is reasonably
practicable.

(2) The union may, notwithstanding any of its rules, pay into any of its other
funds any such contribution which is received by it after the resolution ceases to have
effect.

(3) If the union continues to collect contributions, it shall refund to a member who applies for a refund the contributions made by him collected after the resolution ceased to have effect.

(4) A member of a trade union who claims that the union has failed to comply with subsection (1) may apply to the court for a declaration to that effect.

(5) Where the court is satisfied that the complaint is well-founded, it may, if it considers it appropriate to do so in order to secure that the collection of contributions to the political fund is discontinued, make an order requiring the union to take, within such time as may be specified in the order, such steps as may be so specified.

Such an order may be enforced by a person who is a member of the union and was a member at the time the order was made as if he had made the application.

(6) The remedy for failure to comply with subsection (1) is in accordance with subsections (4) and (5), and not otherwise; but this does not affect any right to recover sums payable to a person under subsection (3). **[748]**

NOTES
Commencement: 16 October 1992.
Sub-ss (1), (2) contain provisions formerly in the Trade Union Act 1984, s 15(3). Sub-s (3) contains provisions formerly in s 15(4) of the 1984 Act. Sub-s (4) contains provisions formerly in s 16(1) of the 1984 Act. Sub-s (5) contains provisions formerly in s 16(2)–(4) of the 1984 Act. Sub-s (6) contains provisions formerly in s 16(5) of the 1984 Act.

91 Rules to cease to have effect

(1) If there ceases to be any political resolution in force in relation to a trade union, the rules of the union made for the purpose of complying with this Chapter also cease to have effect, except so far as they are required to enable the political fund to be administered at a time when there is no such resolution in force.

(2) If the resolution ceases to have effect by reason of a ballot being held on which a new political resolution is not passed, the rules cease to have effect at the end of the period of six months beginning with the date of the ballot.

In any other case the rules cease to have effect when the resolution ceases to have effect.

(3) Nothing in this section affects the operation of section 82(2) (complaint to Certification Officer in respect of breach of rules) in relation to a breach of a rule occurring before the rule in question ceased to have effect.

(4) No member of a trade union who has at any time been exempt from the obligation to contribute to its political fund shall by reason of his having been exempt—

    (a) be excluded from any benefits of the union, or

    (b) be placed in any respect either directly or indirectly under a disability or at a disadvantage as compared with other members (except in relation to the control or management of the political fund). **[749]**

NOTES
Commencement: 16 October 1992.
Sub-ss (1), (2) contain provisions formerly in the Trade Union Act 1984, s 15(6), (7)(a), (10). Sub-s (3) contains provisions formerly in s 15(7)(b) of the 1984 Act. Sub-s (4) contains provisions formerly in s 15(8) of the 1984 Act.

Supplementary

92 Manner of making union rules

If the Certification Officer is satisfied, and certifies, that rules of a trade union made for any of the purposes of this Chapter and requiring approval by him have been approved—

    (a) by a majority of the members of the union voting for the purpose, or

    (b) by a majority of delegates of the union at a meeting called for the purpose,

the rules shall have effect as rules of the union notwithstanding that the rules of the union as to the alteration of rules or the making of new rules have not been complied with.   **[750]**

NOTES
Commencement: 16 October 1992.
This section contains provisions formerly in the Trade Union Act 1913, s 4(2), as amended and repealed in part by the Trade Union and Labour Relations Act 1974, s 25, Sch 3, para 2(1), (3), (4), Sch 5, and as amended by the Employment Protection Act 1975, s 125, Sch 16, Pt IV, para 2(1), (2).

93 Effect of amalgamation

(1) Where on an amalgamation of two or more trade unions—

    (a) there is in force in relation to each of the amalgamating unions a political resolution and such rules as are required by this Chapter, and

    (b) the rules of the amalgamated union in force immediately after the amalgamation include such rules as are required by this Chapter,

the amalgamated union shall be treated for the purposes of this Chapter as having passed a political resolution.

(2) That resolution shall be treated as having been passed on the date of the earliest of the ballots on which the resolutions in force immediately before the amalgamation with respect to the amalgamating unions were passed.

(3) Where one of the amalgamating unions is a Northern Ireland union, the references above to the requirements of this Chapter shall be construed as references to the requirements of the corresponding provisions of the law of Northern Ireland.
     [751]

NOTES
Commencement: 16 October 1992.
Sub-s (1) contains provisions formerly in the Trade Union (Amalgamations, etc) Act 1964, s 5(4), as amended by the Trade Union and Labour Relations Act 1974, s 25(1), Sch 3, para 10(1), (2). Sub-s (2) contains provisions formerly in the Trade Union Act 1984, s 12(5). Sub-s (3) is a drafting provision.

94 Overseas members of trade unions

(1) Where a political resolution is in force in relation to the union—

    (a) rules made by the union for the purpose of complying with section 74 (political ballot rules) in relation to a proposed ballot may provide for overseas members of the union not to be accorded entitlement to vote in the ballot, and

    (b) rules made by the union for the purpose of complying with section 84 (notice of right to object to contribute to political fund to be given where resolution passed) may provide for notice not to be given by the union to its overseas members.

(2) Accordingly, where provision is made in accordance with subsection (1)(a), the Certification Officer shall not on that ground withhold his approval of the rules; and where provision is made in accordance with subsection (1)(b), section 84(2) (duty to give notice) shall not be taken to require notice to be given to overseas members.

(3) An "overseas member" means a member of the trade union (other than a merchant seaman or offshore worker) who is outside Great Britain throughout the period during which votes may be cast.

For this purpose—

"merchant seaman" means a person whose employment, or the greater part of it, is carried out on board sea-going ships; and

"offshore worker" means a person in offshore employment, other than one who is in such employment in an area where the law of Northern Ireland applies.

[752]

NOTES
Commencement: 16 October 1992.
Sub-ss (1), (2) contain provisions formerly in the Trade Union Act 1984, s 13(7), (8). Sub-s (3) contains provisions formerly in ss 9(1) (definition "overseas member"), 13(10) (definition "overseas member") of the 1984 Act.

95 Appeals from Certification Officer

An appeal lies to the Employment Appeal Tribunal on any question of law arising in proceedings before or arising from any decision of the Certification Officer under this Chapter.   **[753]**

NOTES
Commencement: 16 October 1992.
This section contains provisions formerly in the Trade Union Act 1913, s 5A, as inserted by the Employment Protection Act 1975, s 125, Sch 16, Pt IV, para 2(1), (3), and as amended by the Employment Protection (Consolidation) Act 1978, s 159(2), Sch 16, para 2, and in s 136(2)(a) of the 1978 Act.

96 Meaning of "date of the ballot"

In this Chapter the "date of the ballot" means, in the case of a ballot in which votes may be cast on more than one day, the last of those days.   **[754]**

NOTES
Commencement: 16 October 1992.
This section contains provisions formerly in the Trade Union Act 1984, s 19(2) (definition "date of the ballot").

CHAPTER VII
AMALGAMATIONS AND SIMILAR MATTERS

Amalgamation or transfer of engagements

97 Amalgamation or transfer of engagements

(1) Two or more trade unions may amalgamate and become one trade union, with or without a division or dissolution of the funds of any one or more of the amalgamating unions, but shall not do so unless—

(a) the instrument of amalgamation is approved in accordance with section 98, and

(b) the requirements of *sections 99 and 100 (notice to members and passing of resolution)* [section 99 (notice to members) and section 100 (resolution to be passed by required majority in ballot held in accordance with sections

100A to 100E)] are complied with in respect of each of the amalgamating unions.

(2) A trade union may transfer its engagements to another trade union which undertakes to fulfil those engagements, but shall not do so unless—

    (a)   the instrument of transfer is approved in accordance with section 98, and

    (b)   the requirements of *sections 99 and 100 (notice to members and passing of resolution)* [section 99 (notice to members) and section 100 (resolution to be passed by required majority in ballot held in accordance with sections 100A to 100E)] are complied with in respect of the transferor union.

(3) An amalgamation or transfer of engagements does not prejudice any right of any creditor of any trade union party to the amalgamation or transfer.

(4) The above provisions apply to every amalgamation or transfer of engagements notwithstanding anything in the rules of any of the trade unions concerned.   **[755]**

NOTES
Commencement: 16 October 1992.
Sub-ss (1), (2) contain provisions formerly in the Trade Unions (Amalgamations, etc) Act 1964, s 1(1)(a), (b) (both in part), as amended by the Trade Union and Labour Relations Act 1974, s 25(1), Sch 3, para 10(1), (2), and by the Employment Protection Act 1975, s 125(1), Sch 16, Pt IV, para 10(1), (2). Sub-s (3) contains provisions formerly in s 1(6) of the 1964 Act, as amended by s 25(1) of, Sch 3, para 10(1), (2) to, the 1974 Act. Sub-s (4) contains provisions formerly in s 2(1) of the 1964 Act, as so amended.
Sub-ss (1), (2): words in italics substituted by words in square brackets immediately following by the Trade Union Reform and Employment Rights Act 1993, s 49(2), Sch 8, para 52, as from 30 August 1993 (SI 1993/1908, below, para **[1435]**).

98 Approval of instrument of amalgamation or transfer

(1) The instrument of amalgamation or transfer must be approved by the Certification Officer and shall be submitted to him for approval before *the resolution to approve it is voted on by members of any amalgamating union or, as the case may be, of the transferor union* [a ballot of the members of any amalgamating union, or (as the case may be) of the transferor union, is held on the resolution to approve the instrument].

(2) The instrument must comply with the requirements of any regulations in force under this Chapter and the Certification Officer shall approve it if he is satisfied that it does so.   **[756]**

NOTES
Commencement: 16 October 1992.
Sub-s (1) contains provisions formerly in the Trade Union (Amalgamations, etc) Act 1964, s 1(1)(a), (b), (4)(a) (all in part), as amended by the Employment Protection Act 1975, s 125(1), Sch 16, Pt IV, para 10(1), (2). Sub-s (2) contains provisions formerly in s 1(3) (closing words) (in part), (4)(a) of the 1964 Act, in the case of s 1(4)(a), as so amended.
Sub-s (1): words in italics substituted by words in square brackets immediately following by the Trade Union Reform and Employment Rights Act 1993, s 49(2), Sch 8, para 53, as from 30 August 1993 (SI 1993/1908, below, para **[1435]**).

99 Notice to be given to members

(1) The trade union shall take all reasonable steps to secure *that, not less than seven days before voting begins on the resolution to approve the instrument of amalgamation or transfer, every member of the union is supplied with* [that every voting paper which is supplied for voting in the ballot on the resolution to approve the instrument of amalgamation or transfer is accompanied by] a notice in writing approved for the purpose by the Certification Officer.

(2) The notice shall be in writing and shall either—

(a) set out in full the instrument of amalgamation or transfer to which the resolution relates, or

(b) give an account of it sufficient to enable those receiving the notice to form a reasonable judgment of the main effects of the proposed amalgamation or transfer.

(3) If the notice does not set out the instrument in full it shall state where copies of the instrument may be inspected by those receiving the notice.

[(3A) The notice shall not contain any statement making a recommendation or expressing an opinion about the proposed amalgamation or transfer.]

(4) The notice shall also comply with the requirements of any regulations in force under this Chapter.

(5) The notice proposed to be supplied to members of the union under this section shall be submitted to the Certification Officer for approval; and he shall approve it if he is satisfied that it meets the requirements of this section.   **[757]**

NOTES

Commencement: 16 October 1992.

Sub-s (1) contains provisions formerly in the Trade Union (Amalgamations, etc) 1964, s 1(2)(d), as amended by the Trade Union and Labour Relations Act 1974, s 25(1), Sch 3, para 10(1), (2), and by the Employment Act 1975, s 125(1), Sch 16, Pt IV, para 10(1), (2). Sub-ss (2), (3) contain provisions formerly in s 1(3)(a), (b) of the 1964 Act. Sub-s (4) contains provisions formerly in s 1(3) (closing words) (in part) of the 1964 Act. Sub-s (5) contains provisions formerly in s 1(4)(b) of the 1964 Act, as amended by s 25(1) of, Sch 3, para 10(1), (2) to, the 1974 Act and by s 125(1) of, Sch 16, Pt V, para 10(1), (2) to, the 1975 Act.

Sub-s (1): words in italics substituted by words in square brackets immediately following by the Trade Union Reform and Employment Rights Act 1993, s 49(2), Sch 8, para 54, as from 30 August 1993 (SI 1993/1908, below, para **[1435]**).

Sub-s (3A): inserted by the Trade Union Reform and Employment Rights Act 1993, s 5, as from 30 August 1993 (SI 1993/1908, below, para **[1435]**).

100 Resolution approving instrument of amalgamation or transfer

(1) A resolution approving the instrument of amalgamation or transfer must be passed on a vote taken in a manner which satisfies the following conditions—

   (a) every member of the union must be entitled to vote on the resolution;

   (b) every member of the union must be allowed to vote without interference or constraint and must, so far as is reasonably possible, be given a fair opportunity of voting;

   (c) the method of voting must involve the marking of a voting paper by the person voting.

(2) The committee of management or other governing body of the union may arrange for the vote to be taken in any manner which that body thinks fit.

This subsection does not apply if the rules of the trade union expressly provide that it is not to apply in relation to that union.

(3) A simple majority of the votes recorded is sufficient to pass the resolution, whether the vote is taken under arrangements made under subsection (2) or under the rules of the union.

This subsection does not apply if the rules of the trade union expressly provide that it is not to apply in relation to that union.

(4) The provisions of subsections (2) and (3) have effect, where they apply, notwithstanding anything in the rules of the trade union and, in particular, notwithstanding anything in those rules which would require the resolution—

   (a) to be passed by a majority greater than a simple majority, or

> *(b)* to be voted on by not less than a specified proportion of the members of the union.   **[758]**

NOTES
Commencement: 16 October 1992.

Sub-s (1) contains provisions formerly in the Trade Union (Amalgamations, etc) Act 1964, ss 1(1) (in part), (2)(a)–(c), as amended by the Trade Union and Labour Relations Act 1974, s 25(1), Sch 3, para 10(1), (2), and, in the case of s 1(1), by the Employment Protection Act 1975, s 125(1), Sch 16, Pt IV, para 10(1), (2). Sub-s (2) contains provisions formerly in s 2(2) of the 1964 Act, as amended by s 25(1) of, Sch 3, para 10(1), (2) to, the 1974 Act. Sub-ss (3), (4) contain provisions formerly in s 2(3) of the 1964 Act, as so amended.

Substituted by new ss 100–100E, which are printed below (paras **[759]**–**[764]**), by the Trade Union Reform and Employment Rights Act 1993, s 4, as from 30 August 1993 (SI 1993/1908, below, para **[1435]**).

[100 Requirement of ballot on resolution

(1) A resolution approving the instrument of amalgamation or transfer must be passed on a ballot of the members of the trade union held in accordance with sections 100A to 100E.

(2) A simple majority of those voting is sufficient to pass such a resolution unless the rules of the trade union expressly require it to be approved by a greater majority or by a specified proportion of the members of the union.]   **[759]**

NOTE
This section substituted, together with ss 100A–100E, for the original s 100, by the Trade Union Reform and Employment Rights Act 1993, s 4, as from 30 August 1993 (SI 1993/1908, below, para **[1435]**).

[100A Appointment of independent scrutineer

(1) The trade union shall, before the ballot is held, appoint a qualified independent person ("the scrutineer") to carry out—

>   (a) the functions in relation to the ballot which are required under this section to be contained in his appointment; and
>   (b) such additional functions in relation to the ballot as may be specified in his appointment.

(2) A person is a qualified independent person in relation to a ballot if—

>   (a) he satisfies such conditions as may be specified for the purposes of this section by order of the Secretary of State or is himself so specified; and
>   (b) the trade union has no grounds for believing either that he will carry out any functions conferred on him in relation to the ballot otherwise than competently or that his independence in relation to the union, or in relation to the ballot, might reasonably be called into question.

An order under paragraph (a) shall be made by statutory instrument which shall be subject to annulment in pursuance of a resolution of either House of Parliament.

(3) The scrutineer's appointment shall require him—

>   (a) to be the person who supervises the production of the voting papers and (unless he is appointed under section 100D to undertake the distribution of the voting papers) their distribution and to whom the voting papers are returned by those voting;
>   (b) to—
>   (i) inspect the register of names and addresses of the members of the trade union, or
>   (ii) examine the copy of the register as at the relevant date which is supplied to him in accordance with subsection (9)(a),

whenever it appears to him appropriate to do so and, in particular, when the conditions specified in subsection (4) are satisfied;

(c) to take such steps as appear to him to be appropriate for the purpose of enabling him to make his report (see section 100E);

(d) to make his report to the trade union as soon as reasonably practicable after the last date for the return of voting papers; and

(e) to retain custody of all voting papers returned for the purposes of the ballot and the copy of the register supplied to him in accordance with subsection (9)(a)—

   (i) until the end of the period of one year beginning with the announcement by the union of the result of the ballot; and

   (ii) if within that period a complaint is made under section 103 (complaint as regards passing of resolution), until the Certification Officer or Employment Appeal Tribunal authorises him to dispose of the papers or copy.

(4) The conditions referred to in subsection (3)(b) are—

(a) that a request that the scrutineer inspect the register or examine the copy is made to him during the appropriate period by a member of the trade union who suspects that the register is not, or at the relevant date was not, accurate and up-to-date, and

(b) that the scrutineer does not consider that the member's suspicion is ill-founded.

(5) In subsection (4) "the appropriate period" means the period—

(a) beginning with the day on which the scrutineer is appointed, and

(b) ending with the day before the day on which the scrutineer makes his report to the trade union.

(6) The duty of confidentiality as respects the register is incorporated in the scrutineer's appointment.

(7) The trade union shall ensure that nothing in the terms of the scrutineer's appointment (including any additional functions specified in the appointment) is such as to make it reasonable for any person to call the scrutineer's independence in relation to the union into question.

(8) The trade union shall, before the scrutineer begins to carry out his functions, either—

(a) send a notice stating the name of the scrutineer to every member of the union to whom it is reasonably practicable to send such a notice, or

(b) take all such other steps for notifying members of the name of the scrutineer as it is the practice of the union to take when matters of general interest to all its members need to be brought to their attention.

(9) The trade union shall—

(a) supply to the scrutineer as soon as is reasonably practicable after the relevant date a copy of the register of names and addresses of its members as at that date, and

(b) comply with any request made by the scrutineer to inspect the register.

(10) Where the register is kept by means of a computer the duty imposed on the trade union by subsection (9)(a) is either to supply a legible printed copy or (if the scrutineer prefers) to supply a copy of the computer data and allow the scrutineer use of the computer to read it at any time during the period when he is required to retain custody of the copy.

(11) The trade union shall ensure that the scrutineer duly carries out his functions and that there is no interference with his carrying out of those functions which would make it reasonable for any person to call the scrutineer's independence in relation to the union into question.

(12) The trade union shall comply with all reasonable requests made by the scrutineer for the purposes of, or in connection with, the carrying out of his functions.

(13) In this section "the relevant date" means—

    (a) where the trade union has rules determining who is entitled to vote in the ballot by reference to membership on a particular date, that date, and

    (b) otherwise, the date, or the last date, on which voting papers are distributed for the purposes of the ballot.]   **[760]**

NOTE
    This section substituted, together with ss 100, 100B–100E, for the original s 100, by the Trade Union Reform and Employment Rights Act 1993, s 4, as from 30 August 1993 (SI 1993/1908, below, para **[1435]**).
    Order under this section: Trade Union Ballots and Elections (Independent Scrutineer Qualifications) Order 1993, SI 1993/1909, below, para **[1443]**.

[100B Entitlement to vote

Entitlement to vote in the ballot shall be accorded equally to all members of the trade union.]   **[761]**

NOTE
    This section substituted, together with ss 100, 100A, 100C–100E, for the original s 100, by the Trade Union Reform and Employment Rights Act 1993, s 4, as from 30 August 1993 (SI 1993/1908, below, para **[1435]**).

[100C Voting

(1) The method of voting must be by the marking of a voting paper by the person voting.

(2) Each voting paper must—

    (a) state the name of the independent scrutineer and clearly specify the address to which, and the date by which, it is to be returned, and

    (b) be given one of a series of consecutive whole numbers every one of which is used in giving a different number in that series to each voting paper printed or otherwise produced for the purposes of the ballot, and

    (c) be marked with its number.

(3) Every person who is entitled to vote in the ballot must—

    (a) be allowed to vote without interference or constraint, and

    (b) so far as is reasonably practicable, be enabled to do so without incurring any direct cost to himself.

(4) So far as is reasonably practicable, every person who is entitled to vote in the ballot must—

    (a) have a voting paper sent to him by post at his home address or another address which he has requested the trade union in writing to treat as his postal address, and

    (b) be given a convenient opportunity to vote by post.

(5) No voting paper which is sent to a person for voting shall have enclosed with it any other document except—

    (a) the notice which, under section 99(1), is to accompany the voting paper,

    (b) an addressed envelope, and

    (c) a document containing instructions for the return of the voting paper,

without any other statement.

(6) The ballot shall be conducted so as to secure that—

    (a) so far as is reasonably practicable, those voting do so in secret, and

    (b) the votes given in the ballot are fairly and accurately counted.

For the purposes of paragraph (b) an inaccuracy in counting shall be disregarded if it is accidental and on a scale which could not affect the result of the ballot.]

[762]

NOTE

This section substituted, together with ss 100, 100A, 100B, 100D, 100E, for the original s 100, by the Trade Union Reform and Employment Rights Act 1993, s 4, as from 30 August 1993 (SI 1993/1908, below, para **[1435]**).

[100D Counting of votes etc by independent person

(1) The trade union shall ensure that—

    (a) the storage and distribution of the voting papers for the purposes of the ballot, and

    (b) the counting of the votes cast in the ballot,

are undertaken by one or more independent persons appointed by the trade union.

(2) A person is an independent person in relation to a ballot if—

    (a) he is the scrutineer, or

    (b) he is a person other than the scrutineer and the trade union has no grounds for believing either that he will carry out any functions conferred on him in relation to the ballot otherwise than competently or that his independence in relation to the union, or in relation to the ballot, might reasonably be called into question.

(3) An appointment under this section shall require the person appointed to carry out his functions so as to minimise the risk of any contravention of requirements imposed by or under any enactment or the occurrence of any unfairness or malpractice.

(4) The duty of confidentiality as respects the register is incorporated in the scrutineer's appointment.

(5) Where the person appointed to undertake the counting of votes is not the scrutineer, his appointment shall require him to send the voting papers back to the scrutineer as soon as reasonably practicable after the counting has been completed.

(6) The trade union—

    (a) shall ensure that nothing in the terms of an appointment under this section is such as to make it reasonable for any person to call into question the independence of the person appointed in relation to the union,

    (b) shall ensure that a person appointed under this section duly carries out his functions and that there is no interference with his carrying out of those functions which would make it reasonable for any person to call into question the independence of the person appointed in relation to the union, and

    (c) shall comply with all reasonable requests made by a person appointed under this section for the purposes of, or in connection with, the carrying out of his functions.]

[763]

NOTE

This section substituted, together with ss 100, 100A–100C, 100E, for the original s 100, by the Trade Union Reform and Employment Rights Act 1993, s 4, as from 30 August 1993 (SI 1993/1908, below, para **[1435]**).

[100E Scrutineer's report

(1) The scrutineer's report on the ballot shall state—

    (a) the number of voting papers distributed for the purposes of the ballot,

    (b) the number of voting papers returned to the scrutineer,

    (c) the number of valid votes cast in the ballot for and against the resolution,

    (d) the number of spoiled or otherwise invalid voting papers returned, and

    (e) the name of the person (or of each of the persons) appointed under section 100D or, if no person was so appointed, that fact.

(2) The report shall also state whether the scrutineer is satisfied—

    (a) that there are no reasonable grounds for believing that there was any contravention of a requirement imposed by or under any enactment in relation to the ballot,

    (b) that the arrangements made (whether by him or any other person) with respect to the production, storage, distribution, return or other handling of the voting papers used in the ballot, and the arrangements for the counting of the votes, included all such security arrangements as were reasonably practicable for the purpose of minimising the risk that any unfairness or malpractice might occur, and

    (c) that he has been able to carry out his functions without any such interference as would make it reasonable for any person to call his independence in relation to the union into question;

and if he is not satisfied as to any of those matters, the report shall give particulars of his reasons for not being satisfied as to that matter.

(3) The report shall also state—

    (a) whether the scrutineer—

        (i) has inspected the register of names and addresses of the members of the trade union, or

        (ii) has examined the copy of the register as at the relevant date which is supplied to him in accordance with section 100A(9)(a),

    (b) if he has, whether in the case of each inspection or examination he was acting on a request by a member of the trade union or at his own instance,

    (c) whether he declined to act on any such request, and

    (d) whether any inspection of the register, or any examination of the copy of the register, has revealed any matter which he considers should be drawn to the attention of the trade union in order to assist it in securing that the register is accurate and up-to-date,

but shall not state the name of any member who has requested such an inspection or examination.

(4) Where one or more persons other than the scrutineer are appointed under section 100D, the statement included in the scrutineer's report in accordance with subsection (2)(b) shall also indicate—

    (a) whether he is satisfied with the performance of the person, or each of the persons, so appointed, and

    (b) if he is not satisfied with the performance of the person, or any of them, particulars of his reasons for not being so satisfied.

(5) The trade union shall not publish the result of the ballot until it has received the scrutineer's report.

(6) The trade union shall within the period of three months after it receives the report—

(a) send a copy of the report to every member of the union to whom it is reasonably practicable to send such a copy; or

(b) take all such other steps for notifying the contents of the report to the members of the union (whether by publishing the report or otherwise) as it is the practice of the union to take when matters of general interest to all its members need to be brought to their attention.

(7) Any such copy or notification shall be accompanied by a statement that the union will, on request, supply any member of the trade union with a copy of the report, either free of charge or on payment of such reasonable fee as may be specified in the notification.

(8) The trade union shall so supply any member of the union who makes such a request and pays the fee (if any) notified to him.] **[764]**

NOTE

This section substituted, together with ss 100, 100A–100D, for the original s 100, by the Trade Union Reform and Employment Rights Act 1993, s 4, as from 30 August 1993 (SI 1993/1908, below, para **[1435]**).

101 Registration of instrument of amalgamation or transfer

(1) An instrument of amalgamation or transfer shall not take effect before it has been registered by the Certification Officer under this Chapter.

(2) It shall not be so registered before the end of the period of six weeks beginning with the date on which an application for its registration is sent to the Certification Officer.

[(3) An application for registration of an instrument of amalgamation or transfer shall not be sent to the Certification Officer until section 100E(6) has been complied with in relation to the scrutineer's report on the ballot held on the resolution to approve the instrument.] **[765]**

NOTES

Commencement: 16 October 1992.

This section contains provisions formerly in the Trade Union (Amalgamations, etc) Act 1964, s 1(5), as amended by the Employment Protection Act 1975, s 125(1), Sch 16, Pt IV, para 10(1), (2).

Sub-s (3): added by the Trade Union Reform and Employment Rights Act 1993, s 49(2), Sch 8, para 55, as from 30 August 1993 (SI 1993/1908, below, para **[1435]**).

102 Power to alter rules of transferee union for purposes of transfer

(1) Where a trade union proposes to transfer its engagements to another trade union and an alteration of the rules of the transferee union is necessary to give effect to provisions in the instrument of transfer, the committee of management or other governing body of that union may by memorandum in writing alter the rules of that union so far as is necessary to give effect to those provisions.

This subsection does not apply if the rules of the trade union expressly provide that this section is not to apply to that union.

(2) An alteration of the rules of a trade union under subsection (1) shall not take effect unless or until the instrument of transfer takes effect.

(3) The provisions of subsection (1) have effect, where they apply, notwithstanding anything in the rules of the union. **[766]**

NOTES

Commencement: 16 October 1992.

This section contains provisions formerly in the Trade Union (Amalgamations, etc) Act 1964, s 3, as amended by the Trade Union and Labour Relations Act 1974, s 25(1), Sch 3, para 10(1), (2).

103 Complaints as regards passing of resolution

(1) A member of a trade union which passes or purports to pass a resolution approving an instrument of amalgamation or transfer may complain to the Certification Officer on one or more of the following grounds—

    (a) that section 99 (notice to be given to members) was not complied with;

    (b) that the manner in which the vote on the resolution was taken did not satisfy the conditions specified in section 100(1);

    (c) where that vote was taken under arrangements made under section 100(2), that the manner in which it was taken was not in accordance with the arrangements;

    (d) where that vote was taken under provisions in the rules of the union, that the manner in which it was taken was not in accordance with those rules;

    (e) that the votes recorded did not have the effect of passing the resolution.

(2) Any complaint must be made before the end of the period of six weeks beginning with the date on which an application for registration of the instrument of amalgamation or transfer is sent to the Certification Officer.

Where a complaint is made, the Certification Officer shall not register the instrument before the complaint is finally determined or is withdrawn.

(3) If the Certification Officer, after giving the complainant and the trade union an opportunity of being heard, finds the complaint to be justified—

    (a) he shall make a declaration to that effect, and

    (b) he may make an order specifying the steps which must be taken before he will entertain any application to register the instrument of amalgamation or transfer;

and where he makes such an order, he shall not entertain any application to register the instrument unless he is satisfied that the steps specified in the order have been taken.

An order under this subsection may be varied by the Certification Officer by a further order.

(4) The Certification Officer shall furnish a statement, orally or in writing, of the reasons for his decision on a complaint under this section.

(5) The validity of a resolution approving an instrument of amalgamation or transfer shall not be questioned in any legal proceedings whatsoever (except proceedings before the Certification Officer under this section or proceedings arising out of such proceedings) on any ground on which a complaint could be, or could have been, made to the Certification Officer under this section.   **[767]**

NOTES

Commencement: 16 October 1992.

Sub-s (1) contains provisions formerly in the Trade Union (Amalgamations, etc) Act 1964, s 4(1), as amended by the Trade Union and Labour Relations Act 1974, s 25(1), Sch 3, para 10(1), (2), and by the Employment Protection Act 1975, s 125(1), Sch 16, Pt IV, para 10(1), (2). Sub-s (2) contains provisions formerly in s 4(2), (10) of the 1964 Act, as amended, in the case of s 4(2), by s 125(1) of, Sch 16, Pt IV, para 10(1), (2) to, the 1975 Act. Sub-s (3) contains provisions formerly in s 4(3), (5) of the 1964 Act, as amended by s 25(1) of, Sch 3, para 10(1), (2) to, the 1974 Act and by s 125(1) of, Sch 16, Pt IV, para 10(1), (2) to, the 1975 Act. Sub-s (4) contains provisions formerly in s 4(4) of the 1964 Act, as amended by s 125(1) of, Sch 16, Pt IV, para 10(1), (2) to, the 1975 Act. Sub-s (5) contains provisions formerly in s 4(7) of the 1964 Act, as amended by s 125(1) of, Sch 16, Pt IV, para 10(1), (2) to, the 1975 Act.

Sub-s (1): substituted by the Trade Union Reform and Employment Rights Act 1993, s 49(2), Sch 8, para 56, as from 30 August 1993 (SI 1993/1908, below, para **[1435]**), as follows—

"(1) A member of a trade union who claims that the union—

    (a) has failed to comply with any of the requirements of sections 99 to 100E, or

    (b) has, in connection with a resolution approving an instrument of amalgamation or transfer, failed to comply with any rule of the union relating to the passing of the resolution,

may complain to the Certification Officer.".

104 Appeal from decision of Certification Officer

An appeal lies to the Employment Appeal Tribunal, at the instance of the complainant or the trade union, on any question of law arising in any proceedings before, or arising from any decision of, the Certification Officer under section 103.   **[768]**

NOTES

Commencement: 16 October 1992.

This section contains provisions formerly in the Trade Union (Amalgamations, etc) Act 1964, s 4(8), as substituted by the Employment Protection Act 1975, s 125(1), Sch 16, Pt IV, para 10(1), (3), and as amended by the Employment Protection (Consolidation) Act 1978, s 159(2), Sch 16, para 5, and in s 136(2)(b) of the 1978 Act.

105 Transfer of property on amalgamation or transfer

(1) Where an instrument of amalgamation or transfer takes effect, the property held—

    (a) for the benefit of any of the amalgamating unions, or for the benefit of a branch of any of those unions, by the trustees of the union or branch, or

    (b) for the benefit of the transferor trade union, or for the benefit of a branch of the transferor trade union, by the trustees of the union or branch,

shall without any conveyance, assignment or assignation vest, on the instrument taking effect, or on the appointment of the appropriate trustees, whichever is the later, in the appropriate trustees.

(2) In the case of property to be held for the benefit of a branch of the amalgamated union, or of the transferee union, "the appropriate trustees" means the trustees of that branch, unless the rules of the amalgamated or transferee union provide that the property to be so held is to be held by the trustees of the union.

(3) In any other case "the appropriate trustees" means the trustees of the amalgamated or transferee union.

(4) This section does not apply

    (a) to property excepted from the operation of this section by the instrument of amalgamation or transfer, or

    (b) to stocks and securities in the public funds of the United Kingdom or Northern Ireland.   **[769]**

NOTES

Commencement: 16 October 1992.

Sub-s (1) contains provisions formerly in the Trade Union (Amalgamations, etc) Act 1964, s 5(1), as amended by the Trade Union and Labour Relations Act 1974, s 25(1), Sch 3, para 10(1), (2). Sub-ss (2), (3) contain provisions formerly in s 5(3)(a), (b) of the 1964 Act, as so amended. Sub-s (4) contains provisions formerly in s 5(2) of the 1964 Act.

106 Amalgamation or transfer involving Northern Ireland

(1) This Chapter has effect subject to the following modifications in the case of an amalgamation or transfer of engagements to which a trade union and a Northern Ireland union are party.

(2) The requirements of sections *98 to 100 (approval of instrument; notice to members; passing of resolution)* [98 to 100E and 101(3) (approval of instrument, notice to members and ballot on resolution)] do not apply in relation to the Northern Ireland union; but the Certification Officer shall not register the instrument under section 101 unless he is satisfied that it will be effective under the law of Northern Ireland.

(3) The instrument of amalgamation or transfer submitted to the Certification Officer for his approval under section 98 shall state which of the bodies concerned is a Northern Ireland union and, in the case of an amalgamation, whether the amalgamated body is to be a Northern Ireland union; and the Certification Officer shall withhold his approval if the instrument does not contain that information.

(4) Nothing in section 102 (alteration of rules) or *section 103* [sections 103 and 104] (complaint as to passing of resolution) applies in relation to the Northern Ireland union.

(5) Subject to the exceptions specified above, the provisions of this Chapter as to amalgamations or transfers of engagements apply in relation to the Northern Ireland union.   **[770]**

NOTES

Commencement: 16 October 1992.

Sub-s (1) contains provisions formerly in the Trade Union (Amalgamations, etc) Act 1964, s 10(2), as amended by the Trade Union and Labour Relations Act 1974, s 25(1), Sch 3, para 10(1), (2). Sub-s (2) contains provisions formerly in Sch 2, para 2(1) to the 1964 Act, as amended by s 25(1) of, Sch 3, para 10(1), (2) to, the 1974 Act, and by the Employment Protection Act 1975, s 125(1), Sch 16, Pt IV, para 10(1), (2). Sub-s (3) contains provisions formerly in Sch 2, para 4 to the 1964 Act, as amended by the Employment Protection Act 1975, s 125(1), Sch 16, Pt IV, para 10(1), (2), and by the Industrial Relations Act 1971, s 169, Sch 8. Sub-s (4) contains provisions formerly in Sch 2, paras 2(2), 3 to the 1964 Act. Sub-s (5) contains provisions formerly in Sch 2, para 1 to the 1964 Act, as amended by s 25(1) of, Sch 3, para 10(1), (2) to, the 1974 Act.

Sub-s (2): words in italics substituted by words in square brackets immediately following by the Trade Union Reform and Employment Rights Act 1993, s 49(2), Sch 8, para 57(a), as from 30 August 1993 (SI 1993/1908, below, para **[1435]**).

Sub-s (4): words in italics substituted by words in square brackets immediately following by the Trade Union Reform and Employment Rights Act 1993, s 49(2), Sch 8, para 57(b), as from 30 August 1993 (SI 1993/1908, below, para **[1435]**).

Change of name

107 Change of name of trade union

(1) A trade union may change its name by any method expressly provided for by its rules or, if its rules do not expressly provide for a method of doing so, by adopting in accordance with its rules an alteration of the provision in them which gives the union its name.

(2) If the name of the trade union is entered in the list of trade unions a change of name shall not take effect until approved by the Certification Officer.

(3) The Certification Officer shall not approve a change of name if it appears to him that the proposed new name—

    (a) is the same as one entered in the list as the name of another trade union, or

    (b) is the same as one entered in the list of employers' associations kept under Part II of this Act,

or is a name so nearly resembling such a name as to be likely to deceive the public.

(4) A change of name by a trade union does not affect any right or obligation of the union or any of its members; and any pending legal proceedings may be continued by or against the union, the trustees of the union or any other officer of the union who can sue or be sued on its behalf notwithstanding its change of name.   **[771]**

NOTES

Commencement: 16 October 1992.

Sub-s (1) contains provisions formerly in the Trade Union (Amalgamations, etc) Act 1964, s 6(1) (in part). Sub-ss (2), (3) contain provisions formerly in s 6(2) (in part) of the 1964 Act, as substituted by the Trade Union and Labour Relations Act 1974, s 25(1), Sch 3, para 10(1), (5), and as amended by the Employment Protection Act 1975, s 125(1), Sch 16, Pt IV, para 10(1), (2). Sub-s (4) contains provisions formerly in s 6(3) (in part) of the 1964 Act.

Supplementary

108 General powers to make regulations

(1) The Secretary of State may make regulations as respects—
    (a) applications to the Certification Officer under this Chapter,
    (b) the registration under this Chapter of any document or matter,
    (c) the inspection of documents kept by the Certification Officer under this Chapter,
    (d) the charging of fees in respect of such matters, and of such amounts, as may with the approval of the Treasury be prescribed by the regulations,
and generally for carrying this Chapter into effect.

(2) Provision may in particular be made—
    (a) requiring an application for the registration of an instrument of amalgamation or transfer, or of a change of name, to be accompanied by such statutory declarations or other documents as may be specified in the regulations;
    (b) as to the form or content of any document required by this Chapter, or by the regulations, to be sent or submitted to the Certification Officer and as to the manner in which any such document is to be signed or authenticated;
    (c) authorising the Certification Officer to require notice to be given or published in such manner as he may direct of the fact that an application for registration of an instrument of amalgamation or transfer has been or is to be made to him.

(3) Regulations under this section may make different provision for different circumstances.

(4) Regulations under this section shall be made by statutory instrument which shall be subject to annulment in pursuance of a resolution of either House of Parliament. **[772]**

NOTES
Commencement: 16 October 1992.
Sub-s (1) contains provisions formerly in the Trade Union (Amalgamations, etc) Act 1964, s 7(1), as amended by the Secretary of State for Employment and Productivity Order 1968, SI 1968/729, and as amended and repealed in part by the Employment Protection Act 1975, s 125(1), (3), Sch 16, Pt IV, para 10(1), (2), Sch 18. Sub-s (2) contains provisions formerly in s 7(2) of the 1964 Act, as amended by s 125(1) of, Sch 16, Pt IV, para 10(1), (2) to, the 1975 Act. Sub-ss (3), (4) contain provisions formerly in s 7(3) (in part), (4) of the 1964 Act.
Regulations under this section: Trade Union and Employers' Associations (Amalgamations, etc) Regulations 1975, SI 1975/536, as amended by SI 1975/1344, and the Certification Officer (Amendment of Fees) Regulations 1993, SI 1993/936.

CHAPTER VIII
ASSISTANCE FOR CERTAIN LEGAL PROCEEDINGS

109 Proceedings in relation to which assistance may be provided

(1) This Chapter applies to proceedings or prospective proceedings to the extent that they consist in, or arise out of—
    (a) an application to the court under section 15(3) (application for order authorising member to take or continue proceedings on behalf of trade union) or any other proceedings brought by virtue of that section;
    (b) an application to the court under section 16 (remedy against trustees for unlawful use of trade union property);

    (c)   an application to the court under section 26 (remedy for failure to maintain register of members [or secure confidentiality]);

    (d)   an application to the court under section 31 (remedy for failure to comply with request for access to trade union's accounting records);

    [(da) an application to the court under section 45C (remedy for failure to comply with duty to secure positions not held by certain offenders);]

    (e)   an application to the court under section 56 (remedy for failure to comply with requirements as to election for office);

    (f)   an application to the court under section 62 (application for order where industrial action does not have support of ballot);

    (g)   proceedings brought by virtue of section 71 (restriction on use of funds for political objects) with respect to the unlawful application of the funds of a trade union;

    (h)   an application to the court under section 81 (remedy for failure to comply with requirements as to political ballot).

(2) This Chapter applies to proceedings or prospective proceedings *in the High Court or the Court of Session (or on an appeal therefrom to the Court of Appeal or the House of Lords) to the extent that they arise out of* [to the extent that they consist in, or arise out of, proceedings in the High Court or the Court of Session with respect to] an alleged breach or threatened breach of the rules of a trade union relating to any of the following matters—

    (a)   the appointment or election of a person to, or the removal of a person from, any office;

    (b)   disciplinary proceedings by the union (including expulsion);

    (c)   the authorising or endorsing of industrial action;

    (d)   the balloting of members;

    (e)   the application of the union's funds or property;

    (f)   the imposition, collection or distribution of any levy for the purposes of industrial action;

    (g)   the constitution or proceedings of any committee, conference or other body.

The reference above to the rules of a trade union includes the rules of any branch or section of the trade union; and in paragraph (a) "office" includes any position by virtue of which a person is an official in relation to the trade union or is entitled to attend as a representative any meeting concerned with union business.

(3) This Chapter also applies to proceedings or prospective proceedings to the extent that they consist in, or arise out of such other proceedings against a trade union, an official of a trade union or the trustees of the property of a trade union as may be specified in an order made by the Secretary of State.

Any order shall be made by statutory instrument; and no such order shall be made unless a draft of it has been laid before and approved by resolution of each House of Parliament.   **[773]**

NOTES

Commencement: 16 October 1992.

Sub-s (1) contains provisions formerly in the Employment Act 1988, s 20(7)(a)–(d). Sub-s (2) contains provisions formerly in the Employment Act 1990, s 10(1)–(3), (4)(b). Sub-s (3) contains provisions formerly in s 20(7)(e), (8) of the 1988 Act.

Sub-s (1): words in square brackets in para (c), and para (da), inserted by the Trade Union Reform and Employment Rights Act 1993, s 49(3), Sch 8, para 58(a), as from 30 August 1993 (SI 1993/1908, below, para **[1435]**).

Sub-s (2): words in italics substituted by words in square brackets immediately following by the Trade Union Reform and Employment Rights Act 1993, s 49(3), Sch 8, para 58(b), as from 30 August 1993 (SI 1993/1908, below, para **[1435]**).

110 Application for assistance: its consideration

(1) An individual who is an actual or prospective party to proceedings to which this Chapter applies may apply *to the Commissioner* [to the Commissioner for the Rights of Trade Union Members (in this Chapter referred to as "the Commissioner")] for assistance in relation to the proceedings, and the Commissioner shall, as soon as reasonably practicable after receiving the application, consider it and decide whether and to what extent to grant it.

(2) The matters to which the Commissioner may have regard in determining whether, and to what extent, to grant an application include—

    (a) whether the case raises a question of principle,

    (b) whether it is unreasonable, having regard to the complexity of the case, to expect the applicant to deal with it unaided, and

    (c) whether, in the Commissioner's opinion, the case involves a matter of substantial public interest.

(3) In the case of an application made by virtue of section 109(1)(c), [*(f)*] [(e)] or (h) (failure to maintain register of members or to comply with requirements as to election *or ballot* [or political ballot]), if—

    (a) the Certification Officer has already made a declaration with respect to the subject-matter of the proceedings or prospective proceedings, and

    (b) it appears to the Commissioner that the applicant would (if assisted) have a reasonable prospect of securing the making of an enforcement order in the proceedings,

the Commissioner shall grant the application to the extent he considers necessary for securing that, so far as reasonably practicable, all the steps he considers appropriate (including, where appropriate, the holding of another ballot or election) are taken by the trade union for the purpose of remedying the declared failure and of ensuring that a failure of the same or a similar kind does not occur in future.

(4) The Commissioner shall not grant an application made by virtue of section 109(2) (proceedings arising out of breach of rules) unless it appears to him—

    (a) that the breach of rules in question affects, or may affect, members of the union other than the applicant, or

    (b) that similar breaches of the rules have been or may be committed in relation to other members of the union.

(5) If the Commissioner decides not to provide assistance, he shall, as soon as reasonably practicable after making the decision, notify the applicant of his decision and, if he thinks fit, of the reasons for it.   [774]

NOTES

Commencement: 16 October 1992.

Sub-s (1) contains provisions formerly in the Employment Act 1988, s 20(1). Sub-ss (2), (3) contain provisions formerly in s 20(4), (5) of the 1988 Act. Sub-s (4) contains provisions formerly in the Employment Act 1990, s 10(5). Sub-s (5) contains provisions formerly in s 20(2)(b) of the 1988 Act.

Sub-s (1): for the words in italics there are substituted the words in square brackets immediately following by the Trade Union Reform and Employment Rights Act 1993, s 49(3), Sch 8, para 59, as from 30 August 1993 (SI 1993/1908, below, para [1435]).

Sub-s (3): words in italics in each case substituted by words in square brackets immediately following by the Trade Union Reform and Employment Rights Act 1993, s 49(1), Sch 7, para 20, as from 30 August 1993 (SI 1993/1908, below, para [1435]).

111 Provision of assistance

(1) If the Commissioner decides to provide assistance, he shall, as soon as reasonably practicable after making the decision—

   (a) notify the applicant, stating the extent of the assistance to be provided, and

   (b) give him a choice, subject to any restrictions specified in the notification, as to the financial arrangements to be made in connection with the provision of the assistance.

(2) The assistance provided may include the making of arrangements for, or for the Commissioner to bear the costs of—

   (a) the giving of advice or assistance by a solicitor or counsel, and

   (b) the representation of the applicant, or the provision to him of such assistance as is usually given by a solicitor or counsel—

      (i) in steps preliminary or incidental to the proceedings, or

     (ii) in arriving at or giving effect to a compromise to avoid or bring an end to the proceedings.

(3) Where assistance is provided with respect to the conduct of proceedings, it shall include an agreement by the Commissioner to indemnify the applicant (subject only to any exceptions specified in the notification) in respect of liability to pay costs or expenses arising by virtue of any judgment or order of the court in the proceedings.

(4) Where the Commissioner provides assistance in relation to any proceedings, he shall do so on such terms, or make such other arrangements, as will secure that a person against whom the proceedings have been or are commenced is informed that assistance has been or is being provided by the Commissioner in relation to them.

(5) In England and Wales, the recovery of expenses incurred by the Commissioner in providing an applicant with assistance (as taxed or assessed in such manner as may be prescribed by rules of court) shall constitute a first charge for the benefit of the Commissioner—

   (a) on any costs which, by virtue of any judgment or order of the court, are payable to the applicant by any other person in respect of the matter in connection with which the assistance is provided, and

   (b) on any sum payable to the applicant under a compromise or settlement arrived at in connection with that matter to avoid or bring proceedings to an end.

(6) In Scotland, the recovery of such expenses (as taxed or assessed in such manner as may be prescribed by rules of court) shall be paid to the Commissioner, in priority to to other debts—

   (a) out of any expenses which, by virtue of any judgment or order of the court, are payable to the applicant by any other person in respect of the matter in connection with which the assistance is provided, and

   (b) out of any sum payable to the applicant under a compromise or settlement arrived at in connection with that matter to avoid or bring proceedings to an end.   **[775]**

NOTES

Commencement: 16 October 1992.

Sub-s (1) contains provisions formerly in the Employment Act 1988, s 20(2)(a). Sub-s (2) contains provisions formerly in s 20(3) (in part) of the 1988 Act. Sub-s (3) contains provisions formerly in s 21(3) of the 1988 Act. Sub-s (4) contains provisions formerly in s 21(2) of the 1988 Act. Sub-s (5) contains provisions formerly in s 21(4) of the 1988 Act. Sub-s (6) contains provisions formerly in s 21(5) of the 1988 Act.

Sub-s (3): substituted by the Trade Union Reform and Employment Rights Act 1993, s 49(3), Sch 8, para 60, as from 30 August 1993 (SI 1993/1908, below, para **[1435]**), as follows—

"(3) Where assistance is provided with respect to the conduct of proceedings—

   (a) it shall include an agreement by the Commissioner to indemnify the applicant (subject only to any exceptions specified in the notification) in respect of any liability to pay costs or expenses arising by virtue of any judgment or order of the court in the proceedings,

(b) it may include an agreement by the Commissioner to indemnify the applicant in respect of any liability to pay costs or expenses arising by virtue of any compromise or settlement arrived at in order to avoid the proceedings or bring the proceedings to an end, and

(c) it may include an agreement by the Commissioner to indemnify the applicant in respect of any liability to pay damages pursuant to an undertaking given on the grant of interlocutory relief (in Scotland, an interim order) to the applicant.".

112 Title of proceedings where assistance provided

(1) Where a person is receiving assistance in relation to proceedings, there shall, if he so wishes, be added after his name in the title of the proceedings the words "(assisted by the Commissioner for the Rights of Trade Union Members)".

(2) The addition of those words shall not be construed as making the Commissioner a party to the proceedings or as liable to be treated as a party for any purpose; and the omission of those words shall be treated as an irregularity only and shall not nullify the proceedings, any step taken in the proceedings or any document, judgment or order therein.   [776]

NOTES

Commencement: 16 October 1992.

This section contains provisions formerly in the Employment Act 1990, s 11(1), (2).

113 Recovery of sums paid in case of fraud

(1) Where the Commissioner grants an application to a person who for the purposes of the application—

(a) has made a statement which he knew to be false in a material particular, or

(b) has recklessly made a statement which was false in a material particular,

he is entitled to recover from that person any sums paid by him to that person, or to any other person, by way of assistance.

(2) This does not affect the power of the Commissioner to enter into any agreement he thinks fit as to the terms on which assistance is provided.   [777]

NOTES

Commencement: 16 October 1992.

This section contains provisions formerly in the Employment Act 1988, s 21(1).

114 Supplementary provisions

(1) Nothing in this Chapter affects the law and practice regulating the descriptions of persons who may appear in, conduct, defend and address the court in any proceedings.

(2) The power of the Commissioner to provide assistance to a prospective applicant to the court under section 26, 56 or 81 (under which applications may be made either to the court or to the Certification Officer, and in certain cases to both) does not entitle the Commissioner to provide assistance with the making of an application to the Certification Officer.

(3) In this Chapter "applicant", in relation to assistance under this Chapter, means the individual on whose application the assistance is provided.   [778]

NOTES

Commencement: 16 October 1992.

Sub-s (1) contains provisions formerly in the Employment Act 1988, s 20(3) (closing words). Sub-s (2) contains provisions formerly in s 20(6) of the 1988 Act. Sub-s (3) contains provisions formerly in s 21(6) of the 1988 Act.

CHAPTER IX
MISCELLANEOUS AND GENERAL PROVISIONS

Further provisions with respect to ballots

115 Payments towards expenditure in connection with secret ballots

(1) The Secretary of State may by regulations make a scheme providing for payments by the Certification Officer towards expenditure incurred by independent trade unions in respect of such ballots to which this section applies as may be prescribed by the scheme.

(2) This section applies to a ballot if the purpose of the question to be asked (or if there is more than one such question, the purpose of any of them) is—

   (a) to obtain a decision or ascertain the views of members of a trade union—
      (i) as to the acceptance or rejection of a proposal made by an employer in relation to the contractual terms and conditions upon which, or the other incidents of the relationship whereby, a person works or provides services for the employer, or
      (ii) as to the calling or ending of a strike or other industrial action;
   (b) to carry out an election—
      (i) provided for by the rules of a trade union, or
      (ii) required by section 46 (duty to hold elections for certain offices),

   or to elect a worker who is a member of a trade union to be a representative of other members also employed by his employer;

   (c) to amend the rules of a trade union;
   (d) to obtain a decision in accordance with Chapter VI on a political resolution within the meaning of that Chapter at a time when there is such a resolution in force in relation to the union;
   (e) to obtain a decision in accordance with Chapter VII on a resolution to approve an instrument of amalgamation or transfer;
   (f) any other purpose specified by order of the Secretary of State.

(3) The scheme may include provision for payments to be made towards expenditure incurred in respect of arrangements to hold a ballot which is not proceeded with but which would have been a ballot to which this section applies if it had been held.

(4) The circumstances in which and the conditions subject to which payments may be made under the scheme, and the amounts of the payments, shall be such as may be prescribed by the scheme; and the scheme shall include provision for restricting the cases in which payments are made to cases in which the ballot is so conducted as to secure, so far as reasonably practicable, that those voting do so in secret.

(5) Regulations or an order under this section shall be made by statutory instrument; and—

   (a) a statutory instrument containing regulations shall be subject to annulment in pursuance of a resolution of either House of Parliament; and
   (b) no order shall be made unless a draft of it has been laid before and approved by a resolution of each House of Parliament.   **[779]**

NOTES
Commencement: 16 October 1992.
   Sub-s (1) contains provisions formerly in the Employment Act 1980, s 1(1). Sub-s (2) contains provisions formerly in s 1(2)–(3A) of the 1980 Act, as amended, in the case of s 1(3)(b), as added, in the

case of s 1(3)(f), and as inserted, in the case of s 1(3A), by the Trade Union Act 1984, s 20(1)–(3), and in the Funds for Trade Union Ballots Order 1982, SI 1982/953, art 2. Sub-s (3) contains provisions formerly in s 1(4) of the 1980 Act. Sub-s (4) contains provisions formerly in s 1(5) of the 1980 Act, as repealed in part by s 20(1), (4) of the 1984 Act. Sub-s (5) contains provisions formerly in s 1(7) of the 1980 Act.

Repealed by the Trade Union Reform and Employment Rights Act 1993, ss 7(1), (4), 51, Sch 10, as from 1 April 1996 (SI 1993/1908, below, para **[1435]**).

Orders under this section: Funds for Trade Union Ballots Regulations 1984, SI 1984/1654, as amended by SI 1988/1123, SI 1988/2116; Funds for Trade Union Ballots Regulations (Revocation) Regulations 1993, SI 1993/233 (revoking the earlier regulations from 1 April 1996, with transitional provisions). The regulations are printed below, paras **[1188]**–**[1210]** and **[1427]**–**[1431]**.

116 Use of employer's premises for secret ballot

(1) Where an independent trade union which is recognised by an employer to any extent for the purposes of collective bargaining—

> *(a) proposes to hold a ballot to which this section applies, and*
> *(b) requests the employer to permit premises of his to be used for the purpose of giving workers employed by him who are members of the union a convenient opportunity of voting,*

the employer shall, so far as reasonably practicable, comply with that request.

(2) This section applies to a ballot if—

> *(a) as respects the purposes of the question (or one of the questions) to be voted upon, the ballot satisfies the requirements of a scheme under section 115, and*
> *(b) the proposals for the conduct of the ballot are such as to secure, so far as reasonably practicable, that those voting do so in secret.*

(3) Subsection (1) does not apply where—

> *(a) the ballot is one in which every person who is entitled to vote must be given a convenient opportunity to vote by post; or*
> *(b) at the time the request is made the number of workers employed by the employer, added to the number employed by any associated employer, does not exceed 20.*

(4) A trade union which claims that an employer has failed to comply with a request made by the union in accordance with subsection (1), which it was reasonably practicable for him to comply with, may present a complaint to an industrial tribunal.

(5) The tribunal shall not entertain a complaint unless it is presented to the tribunal—

> *(a) before the end of the period of three months beginning with the date of the failure, or*
> *(b) where the tribunal is satisfied that it was not reasonably practicable for the complaint to be presented before the end of that period, within such further period as the tribunal considers reasonable.*

(6) Where the tribunal finds that the complaint is well-founded, it shall make a declaration to that effect and may make an award of compensation to be paid by the employer to the union of such amount as it considers just and equitable in all the circumstances having regard to the employer's failure and to any expenses incurred by the union in consequence of the failure.

(7) The remedy of a union for failure to comply with a request under subsection (1) is by way of complaint to an industrial tribunal in accordance with this section, and not otherwise.

[780]

NOTES
Commencement: 16 October 1992.
Sub-s (1) contains provisions formerly in the Employment Act 1980, s 2(1) (in part), (3)(a). Sub-s (2) contains provisions formerly in s 2(2) of the 1980 Act, as repealed in part by the Trade Union Act 1984, s 20(1), (5). Sub-s (3)(a) contains provisions formerly in s 2(1) (the words added by the Employment Act 1988, s 33(1), Sch 3, Pt I, para 3(1)) of the 1980 Act. Sub-s (3)(b) contains provisions formerly in s 2(3)(b) of the 1980 Act. Sub-ss (4)–(6) contain provisions formerly in s 2(4)–(6) of the 1980 Act. Sub-s (7) contains provisions formerly in s 2(8) of the 1980 Act.
Repealed by the Trade Union Reform and Employment Rights Act 1993, s 7(1), (4), 51, Sch 10, as from 1 April 1996 (SI 1993/1908, below, para **[1435]**).

Exceptions and adaptations for certain bodies

117 Special register bodies

(1) In this section a "special register body" means an organisation whose name appeared in the special register maintained under section 84 of the Industrial Relations Act 1971 immediately before 16 September 1974, and which is a company registered under the Companies Act 1985 or is incorporated by charter or letters patent.

(2) The provisions of this Part apply to special register bodies as to other trade unions, subject to the following exceptions and adaptations.

(3) In Chapter II (status and property of trade unions)—

    (a) in section 10 (quasi-corporate status of trade unions)—

        (i) subsections (1) and (2) (prohibition on trade union being incorporated) do not apply, and

        (ii) subsection (3) (prohibition on registration under certain Acts) does not apply so far as it relates to registration as a company under the Companies Act 1985;

    (b) section 11 (exclusion of common law rules as to restraint of trade) applies to the purposes or rules of a special register body only so far as they relate to the regulation of relations between employers or employers' associations and workers;

    (c) sections 12 to 14 (vesting of property in trustees; transfer of securities) do not apply; and

    (d) in section 20 (liability of trade union in certain proceedings in tort) in subsection (7) the reference to the contract between a member and the other members shall be construed as a reference to the contract between a member and the body.

(4) Sections 33 to 35 (appointment and removal of auditors) do not apply to a special register body which is registered as a company under the Companies Act 1985; and sections 36 and 37 (rights and duties of auditors) apply to the auditors appointed by such a body under Chapter V of Part XI of that Act.

(5) *Chapter IV (elections for certain union position) only applies* [Sections 45B and 45C (disqualification) and Chapter IV (elections) apply only] to—

    (a) the position of voting member of the executive, and

    (b) any position by virtue of which a person is a voting member of the executive.

In this subsection "voting member of the executive" has the meaning given by section 46(5).   **[781]**

NOTES
Commencement: 16 October 1992.
Sub-s (1) contains provisions formerly in the Trade Union and Labour Relations Act 1974, s 30(1) (definition "special register body"), as amended by the Companies Consolidation (Consequential Provisions) Act 1985, s 30, Sch 2. Sub-s (2) is a drafting provision. Sub-s (3)(a)–(c) contain provisions

formerly in ss 2(1), (2), (5), 4(1)–(4), (6), (8) (all in part) of the 1974 Act (as repealed in part in the case of s 2(1)(c) by the Employment Act 1982, s 21(3), Sch 4, and as amended, in the case of ss 2(2), 4(4), by the Companies Consolidation (Consequential Provisions) Act 1985, s 30, Sch 2). Sub-s (3)(d) contains provisions formerly in s 15(2)–(3B), (7) (definition "rules"), (8), (9) of the 1982 Act (as amended in the case of s 15(2), as substituted in the case of s 15(3)–(3B), and as added in the case of s 15(9), by the Employment Act 1990, s 6(1)–(3), (8)). Sub-s (4) contains provisions formerly in s 11(9) (in part) of the 1974 Act, as added by the Companies Act 1989, s 124. Sub-s (5) contains provisions formerly in the Trade Union Act 1984, s 1(1), (2), (6A), (6B), (7) (all in part), as amended in the case of s 1(1), and as repealed in part in the case of s 1(1), (2), and as inserted, in the case of s 1(6A), (6B), by the Employment Act 1988, ss 12(1), 33, Sch 3, Pt I, para 5(1), Sch 4.

Sub-s (5): words in italics substituted by words in square brackets immediately following by the Trade Union Reform and Employment Rights Act 1993, s 49(3), Sch 8, para 61, as from 30 August 1993 (SI 1993/1908, below, para **[1435]**).

118 Federated trade unions

(1) In this section a "federated trade union" means a trade union which consists wholly or mainly of constituent or affiliated organisations, or representatives or such organisations, as described in paragraph (b) of the definition of "trade union" in section 1.

(2) The provisions of this Part apply to federated trade unions subject to the following exceptions and adaptations.

(3) For the purposes of section 22 (limit on amount of damages) as it applies to a federated trade union, the members of such of its constituent or affiliated organisations as have their head or main office in Great Britain shall be treated as members of the union.

(4) The following provisions of Chapter III (trade union administration) do not apply to a federated trade union which consists wholly or mainly of representatives of constituent or affiliated organisations—

    (a)   section 27 (duty to supply copy of rules),
    (b)   section 28 (duty to keep accounting records),
    (c)   sections 32 to 37 (annual return, [statement for members,] accounts and audit), *and*
    [(ca) sections 37A to 37E (investigation of financial affairs), and]
    (d)   sections 38 to 42 (members' superannuation schemes).

(5) Sections 29 to 31 (right of member to access to accounting records) do not apply to a federated trade union which has no members other than constituent or affiliated organisations or representatives of such organisations.

(6) Sections 24 to 26 (register of members' names and addresses) and Chapter IV (elections for certain trade union positions) do not apply to a federated trade union—

    (a)   if it has no individual members other than representatives of constituent or affiliated organisations, or
    (b)   if its individual members (other than such representatives) are all merchant seamen and a majority of them are ordinarily resident outside the United Kingdom.

For this purpose "merchant seaman" means a person whose employment, or the greater part of it, is carried out on board sea-going ships.

(7) The provisions of Chapter VI (application of funds for political objects) apply to a trade union which is in whole or part an association or combination of other unions as if the individual members of the component unions were members of that union and not of the component unions.

But nothing in that Chapter prevents a component union from collecting contributions on behalf of the association or combination from such of its members as are not exempt from the obligation to contribute to the political fund of the association or combination.   **[782]**

NOTES

Commencement: 16 October 1992.

Sub-ss (1), (2) are drafting provisions. Sub-s (3) contains provisions formerly in the Employment Act 1982, s 16(7). Sub-s (4) contains provisions formerly in the Trade Union and Labour Relations Act 1974, ss 10(1), 11(1) (both in part). Sub-s (5) contains provisions formerly in the Employment Act 1988, s 6(9)(b). Sub-s (6) contains provisions formerly in the Trade Union Act 1984, s 7(1)–(3), 9(1) (definition "merchant seaman"). Sub-s (7) contains provisions formerly in the Trade Union Act 1913, s 3(5) (in part).

Sub-s (4): words in square brackets in para (c), and para (ca), inserted, and word "and" in italics at the end of para (c) repealed, by the Trade Union Reform and Employment Rights Act 1993, ss 49(3), 51, Sch 8, para 62, Sch 10, as from 1 January 1994 (para (c)), 30 August 1993 (para (ca) and repeal) (SI 1993/1908, below, para **[1435]**).

Interpretation

119 Expressions relating to trade unions

In this Act, in relation to a trade union—

["agent" means a banker or solicitor of, or any person employed as an auditor by, the union or any blanch or section of the union;]

"branch or section", except where the context otherwise requires, includes a branch or section which is itself a trade union;

"executive" means the principal committee of the union exercising executive functions, by whatever name it is called;

["financial affairs" means affairs of the union relating to any fund which is applicable for the purposes of the union (including any fund of a branch or section of the union which is so applicable);]

"general secretary" means the official of the union who holds the office of general secretary or, where there is no such office, holds an office which is equivalent, or (except in section 14(4)) the nearest equivalent, to that of general secretary;

"officer" includes—

(a) any member of the governing body of the union, and

(b) any trustee of any fund applicable for the purposes of the union;

"official" means—

(a) an officer of the union or of a branch or section of the union, or

(b) a person elected or appointed in accordance with the rules of the union to be a representative of its members or of some of them,

and includes a person so elected or appointed who is an employee of the same employer as the members or one or more of the members whom he is to represent;

"president" means the official of the union who holds the office of president or, where there is no such office, who holds an office which is equivalent, or (except in section 14(4) or Chapter IV) the nearest equivalent, to that of president; and

"rules", except where the context otherwise requires, includes the rules of any branch or section of the union.   **[783]**

NOTES

Commencement: 16 October 1992.

This section contains provisions formerly in the Trade Union Act 1984, s 9(1) (definition "section"), and in the Employment Act 1988, s 32(1) (definition "branch or section"); in the Trade Union Act 1984, ss 1(5), 9(1), 19(2), and s 12(6) of the 1988 Act (definition "principal executive committee"); in s 1(6B)(b) (in part) of the 1984 Act, as inserted by s 12(1) of the 1988 Act; in the Trade Union and Labour Relations

Act 1974, s 30(1) (definition "officer", as inserted by the Employment Protection Act 1975, s 125(1), Sch 16, Pt III, para 7(5)); in s 30(1) of the 1974 Act, s 126(1) of the 1975 Act, deriving from the Employment Protection (Consolidation) Act 1978, s 153(1), and formerly in s 32(1) of the 1988 Act (definition "official"); in s 1(6B)(a) (in part) of the 1984 Act, as inserted by s 12(1) of the 1988 Act; and in s 32(1) of the 1988 Act (definition "rules").

Definitions "agent" and "financial affairs" inserted by the Trade Union Reform and Employment Rights Act 1993, s 49(3), Sch 8, para 63, as from 30 August 1993 (SI 1993/1908, below, para **[1435]**).

120   Northern Ireland unions

In this Part a "Northern Ireland union" means a trade union whose principal office is situated in Northern Ireland.   **[784]**

NOTES

Commencement: 16 October 1992.

This section contains provisions formerly in the Trade Union (Amalgamations, etc) Act 1964, s 10(5), (6), and in the Industrial Relations (Northern Ireland) Order 1992, SI 1992/807 (NI 5), arts 56(5), 81(5).

121   Meaning of "the court"

In this Part "the court" (except where the reference is expressed to be to the county court or sheriff court) means the High Court or the Court of Session.   **[785]**

NOTES

Commencement: 16 October 1992.

This is a drafting provision.

PART II

EMPLOYERS' ASSOCIATIONS

Introductory

122   Meaning of "employers' association"

(1) In this Act an "employers' association" means an organisation (whether temporary or permanent)—

    (a) which consists wholly or mainly of employers or individual owners of undertakings of one or more descriptions and whose principal purposes include the regulation of relations between employers of that description or those descriptions and workers or trade unions; or

    (b) which consists wholly or mainly of—

        (i) constituent or affiliated organisations which fulfil the conditions in paragraph (a) (or themselves consist wholly or mainly of constituent or affiliated organisations which fulfil those conditions), or

        (ii) representatives of such constituent or affiliated organisations,

and whose principal purposes include the regulation of relations between employers and workers or between employers and trade unions, or the regulation of relations between its constituent or affiliated organisations.

(2) References in this Act to employers' associations include combinations of employers and employers' associations.   **[786]**

NOTES

Commencement: 16 October 1992.

Sub-s (1) contains provisions formerly in the Trade Union Act 1913, s 2(1A), as inserted in part substitution for the original s 2(1) by the Trade Union and Labour Relations Act 1974, s 25(1), Sch 3, para 2(1), (2); in the Trade Union (Amalgamations, etc) Act 1964, s 9(1) (definition "employers' association"), as substituted by s 25(1) of, Sch 3, para 10(1), (8) to, the 1974 Act. Sub-s (2) contains provisions formerly in ss 28(2), 30(1) (definition "employers' association") of the 1974 Act.

The list of employers' associations

123 The list of employers' associations

(1) The Certification Officer shall keep a list of employers' associations containing the names of—

    (a) the organisations whose names were, immediately before the commencement of this Act, duly entered in the list of employers' associations kept by him under section 8 of the Trade Union and Labour Relations Act 1974, and

    (b) the names of the organisations entitled to have their names entered in the list in accordance with this Part.

(2) The Certification Officer shall keep copies of the list of employers' associations, as for the time being in force, available for public inspection at all reasonable hours free of charge.

(3) A copy of the list shall be included in his annual report.

(4) The fact that the name of an organisation is included in the list of employers' associations is evidence (in Scotland, sufficient evidence) that the organisation is an employers' association.

(5) On the application of an organisation whose name is included in the list, the Certification Officer shall issue it with a certificate to that effect.

(6) A document purporting to be such a certificate is evidence (in Scotland, sufficient evidence) that the name of the organisation is entered in the list.   **[787]**

NOTES

Commencement: 16 October 1992.

Sub-s (1) contains provisions formerly in the Trade Union and Labour Relations Act 1974, s 8(1), (2) (both in part), as amended (in both cases) and as repealed in part (in the case of sub-s (1)) by the Employment Protection Act 1975, s 125(1), (3), Sch 16, Pt III, para 1, Sch 18. Sub-ss (2), (3) contain provisions formerly in s 8(9) (in part) of the 1974 Act, as amended by s 125(1) of, Sch 16, Pt III, paras 1, 4 to, the 1975 Act. Sub-ss (4)–(6) contain provisions formerly in s 8(10) (in part) of the 1974 Act, as amended and repealed in part by s 125(1), (3) of, Sch 16, Pt III, paras 1, 5, Sch 18 to, the 1975 Act.

124 Application to have name entered in the list

(1) An organisation of employers, whenever formed, whose name is not entered in the list of employers' associations may apply to the Certification Officer to have its name entered in the list.

(2) The application shall be made in such form and manner as the Certification Officer may require and shall be accompanied by—

    (a) a copy of the rules of the organisation,

    (b) a list of its officers,

    (c) the address of its head or main office, and

    (d) the name under which it is or is to be known,

and by the prescribed fee.

(3) If the Certification Officer is satisfied—

    (a) that the organisation is an employers' association,

    (b) that subsection (2) has been complied with, and

    (c) that entry of the name in the list is not prohibited by subsection (4),

he shall enter the name of the organisation in the list of employers associations.

(4) The Certification Officer shall not enter the name of an organisation in the list of employers' associations if the name is the same as that under which another organisation—

(a) was on 30th September 1971 registered as a trade union under the Trade Union Acts 1871 to 1964,

(b) was at any time registered as an employers' association or trade union under the Industrial Relations Act 1971, or

(c) is for the time being entered in the list of employers' associations or in the list of trade unions kept under Chapter I of Part I of this Act,

or if the name is one so nearly resembling any such name as to be likely to deceive the public.   **[788]**

NOTES
Commencement: 16 October 1992.
Sub-ss (1), (3) contain provisions formerly in the Trade Union and Labour Relations Act 1974, s 8(3) (in part), as amended by the Employment Protection Act 1975, s 125(1), Sch 16, Pt III, para 1. Sub-s (2) contains provisions formerly in s 8(4) (in part) of the 1974 Act, as amended by s 125(1) of, Sch 16, Pt III, para 1 to, the 1975 Act. Sub-s (5) contains provisions formerly in s 8(5) (in part) of the 1974 Act, as amended by s 125(1) of, Sch 16, Pt III, para 1 to, the 1975 Act.
Prescribed fee: £291 (see SI 1993/936).

125 Removal of name from the list

(1) If it appears to the Certification Officer, on application made to him or otherwise, that an organisation whose name is entered in the list of employers' associations is not an employers' association, he may remove its name from the list.

(2) He shall not do so without giving the organisation notice of his intention and considering any representations made to him by the organisation within such period (of not less than 28 days beginning with the date of the notice) as may be specified in the notice.

(3) The Certification Officer shall remove the name of an organisation from the list of employers' associations if—

(a) he is requested by the organisation to do so, or

(b) he is satisfied that the organisation has ceased to exist.   **[789]**

NOTES
Commencement: 16 October 1992.
Sub-ss (1), (2) contain provisions formerly in the Trade Union and Labour Relations Act 1974, s 8(6) (in part), as amended by the Employment Protection Act 1975, s 125(1), Sch 16, Pt III, para 1, and as repealed in part by the Trade Union and Labour Relations (Amendment) Act 1976, s 1. Sub-s (3) contains provisions formerly in s 8(6A) (in part) of the 1974 Act, as inserted by s 125(1) of, Sch 16, Pt III, para 2 to, the 1975 Act.

126 Appeal against decision of Certification Officer

(1) An organisation aggrieved by the refusal of the Certification Officer to enter its name in the list of employers' associations, or by a decision of his to remove its name from the list, may appeal to the Employment Appeal Tribunal.

(2) If on appeal the Tribunal is satisfied that the organisation's name should be or remain entered in the list, it shall declare that fact and give directions to the Certification Officer accordingly.

(3) The right of appeal conferred by this section extend to any question of fact or law arising in the proceedings before, or arising from the decision of, the Certification Officer.   **[790]**

NOTES
Commencement: 16 October 1992.
Sub-ss (1), (2) contain provisions formerly in the Trade Union and Labour Relations Act 1974, s 8(7)
(in part), as substituted by the Employment Protection Act 1975, s 125(1), Sch 16, Pt III, para 3, and as
amended by the Employment Protection (Consolidation) Act 1978, s 159(2), Sch 16, para 18. Sub-s (3)
contains provisions formerly in s 136(3) (in part) of the 1978 Act.

Status and property of employers' associations

127 Corporate or quasi-corporate status of employers' associations

(1) An employers' association may be either a body corporate or an unincorporated
association.

(2) Where. an employers' association is unincorporated—

(a) it is capable of making contracts;

(b) it is capable of suing and being sued in its own name, whether in
proceedings relating to property or founded on contract or tort or any other
cause of action; and

(c) proceedings for an offence alleged to have been committed by it or on its
behalf may be brought against it in its own name.

(3) Nothing in section 716 of the Companies Act 1985 (associations of over 20
members to be incorporated or otherwise formed in special ways) shall be taken to
prevent the formation of an employers' association which is neither registered as a
company under that Act nor otherwise incorporated.   **[791]**

NOTES
Commencement: 16 October 1992.
Sub-s (1) contains provisions formerly in the Trade Union and Labour Relations Act 1974, s 3(1). Sub-
s (2) contains provisions formerly in s 3(2)(a), (c), (d) of the 1974 Act, as repealed in part, in the case of
para (c), by the Employment Act 1982, s 21(3), Sch 4. Sub-s (3) contains provisions formerly in s 3(4) of
the 1974 Act, as amended by the Companies Consolidation (Consequential Provisions) Act 1985, s 30,
Sch 2.

128 Exclusion of common law rules as to restraint of trade

(1) The purposes of an unincorporated employers' association and, so far as they
relate to the regulation of relations between employers and workers or trade unions,
the purposes of an employers' association which is a body corporate are not, by reason
only that they are in restraint of trade, unlawful so as—

(a) to make any member of the association liable to criminal proceedings for
conspiracy or otherwise, or

(b) to make any agreement or trust void or voidable.

(2) No rule of an unincorporated employers' association or, so far as it relates to
the regulation of relations between employers and workers or trade unions, of an
employers' association which is a body corporate, is unlawful or unenforceable by
reason only that it is in restraint of trade.   **[792]**

NOTES
Commencement: 16 October 1992.
This section contains provisions formerly in the Trade Union and Labour Relations Act 1974, s 3(5).

129 Property of unincorporated employers' associations, &c

(1) The following provisions of Chapter II of Part I of this Act apply to an
unincorporated employers' association as in relation to a trade union—

    (a) section 12(1) and (2) (property to be vested in trustees),
    (b) section 13 (vesting of property in new trustees), and
    (c) section 14 (transfer of securities held in trust for trade union).

    (2) In sections 13 and 14 as they apply by virtue of subsection (1) the reference to entry in the list of trade unions shall be construed as a reference to entry in the list of employers' associations.

    (3) Section 19 (application of certain provisions relating to industrial assurance or friendly societies) applies to any employers' association as in relation to a trade union.   **[793]**

NOTES
Commencement: 16 October 1992.
Sub-s (1) contains provisions formerly in the Trade Union and Labour Relations Act 1974, ss 3(2)(b), (e), 4(1)–(8) (in part), as amended, in the case of s 4(4), by the Companies Consolidation (Consequential Provisions) Act 1985, s 30, Sch 2. Sub-s (2) contains drafting provisions. Sub-s (3) contains provisions formerly in the Friendly Societies Act 1896, s 26(2), (3) (as amended and repealed in part by the Friendly Societies Act 1974, s 116(1), (4), Sch 9, para 1, Sch 11), in the Industrial Assurance and Friendly Societies Act 1948, s 6(1), (2) (both in part) (as repealed in part (in the case of sub-s (1)) by the Companies Act 1967, s 129, Sch 7 and by s 116(4) of, Sch 11 to, the 1974 Act, as amended (in that case) by the Trade Union and Labour Relations Act 1974, s 25(1), Sch 3, para 5(1), (2), and as repealed in part (in the case of sub-s (2)) by the Friendly Societies Act 1974, s 116(4), Sch 11), and in s 16(4) of the 1948 Act (as amended and repealed in part by the Friendly Societies Act 1974, s 116(1), (4), Sch 9, para 12, Sch 11, as amended by the Trade Union and Labour Relations Act 1974, s 25(1), Sch 3, para 5(1), (3), and as affected by the Criminal Justice Act 1982, ss 38, 46).

130 Restriction on enforcement of awards against certain property

(1) Where in any proceedings an amount is awarded by way of damages, costs or expenses—

    (a) against an employers' association,
    (b) against trustees in whom property is vested in trust for an employers' association, in their capacity as such (and otherwise than in respect of a breach of trust on their part), or
    (c) against members or officials of an employers' association on behalf of themselves and all of the members of the association,

no part of that amount is recoverable by enforcement against any protected property.

(2) The following is protected property—

    (a) property belonging to the trustees otherwise than in their capacity as such;
    (b) property belonging to any member of the association otherwise than jointly or in common with the other members;
    (c) property belonging to an official of the association who is neither a member nor a trustee.   **[794]**

NOTES
Commencement: 16 October 1992.
Sub-s (1) contains provisions formerly in the Employment Act 1982, s 17(1) (in part). Sub-s (2) contains provisions formerly in s 17(2)(a)–(c) (in part) of the 1982 Act.

Administration of employers' associations

131 Administrative provisions applying to employers' associations

(1) The following provisions of Chapter III of Part I of this Act apply to an employers' association as in relation to a trade union—

    section 27 (duty to supply copy of rules),
    section 28 (duty to keep accounting records),

sections 32 to 37 [section 32(1), (2), (3)(a), (b) and (c) and (4) to (6) and sections
     33 to 37] (annual return, accounts and audit),
[sections 37A to 37E (investigation of financial affairs),]
sections 38 to 42 (members' superannuation schemes),
section 43(1) (exemption for newly-formed organisations),
section 44(1),(2) and (4) (discharge of duties in case of organisation having
     branches or sections), and
section 45 [sections 45 and 45A] (offences).

   (2) Sections 33 to 35 (appointment and removal of auditors) do not apply to an
employers' association which is registered as a company under the Companies Act
1985; and sections 36 and 37 (rights and duties of auditors) apply to the auditors
appointed by such an association under Chapter V of Part XI of that Act.   **[795]**

NOTES
Commencement: 16 October 1992.
   Sub-s (1) contains provisions formerly in the Trade Union and Labour Relations Act 1974, ss 10,
11(1)–(5), (8), 12, 26(2), (3), Sch 2, paras 1–6, 9–22, 24–28, 30–33, 33A, 33B, 34–36 (all in part) (as
amended, in the case of s 11 (2), (5), Sch 2, paras 1, 2, 5, 9, 22, 26, 27, 30–32, 36, by the Employment
Protection Act 1975, s 125(1), Sch 16, Pt III, para 1, as affected, in the case of s 12(5), by the Criminal
Justice Act 1982, ss 38, 46, as amended, in the case of Sch 2, para 6, by the Companies Consolidation
(Consequential Provisions) Act 1985, s 30, Sch 2, and as read with (in that case) the Interpretation Act
1978, s 17(2)(a), and as added, in the case of Sch 2, paras 33A, 33B, by the Employment Act 1980, s 202,
Sch 1, para 3); in the Trade Union Act 1984, s 4(3), and in the Employment Act 1988, s 6(8). Sub-s (2)
contains provisions formerly in s 11(9) of the 1974 Act, as added by the Companies Act 1989, s 124.
   Sub-s (1): words in italics substituted in each case by words in square brackets immediately following
and other words in square brackets inserted, by the Trade Union Reform and Employment Rights Act
1993, s 49(2), Sch 8, para 64, as from 30 August 1993; 1 January 1994 (SI 1993/1908, below, para **[1435]**).

Application of funds for political objects

132 Application of funds for political objects

The provisions of Chapter VI of Part I of this Act (application of funds for political
objects) apply to an unincorporated employers' association as in relation to a trade
union.   **[796]**

NOTES
Commencement: 16 October 1992.
   This section contains provisions formerly in the Trade Union Act 1913, s 6A, as inserted by the Trade
Union and Labour Relations Act 1974, s 25, Sch 3, para 2(1), (5), in the Trade Union Act 1984, s 19(4),
and in the Employment Act 1988, ss 15(8), 16(5).

Amalgamations and similar matters

133 Amalgamations and transfers of engagements

*The provisions of Chapter VII of Part I of this Act (amalgamations and similar
matters), with the exception of section 107 (change of name: see section 134 below),
apply to unincorporated employers' associations as in relation to trade unions.*
                                                                            [797]

NOTES
Commencement: 16 October 1992.
   This section contains provisions formerly in the Trade Union (Amalgamations, etc) Act 1964, s 1(1A)
(in part), as substituted by the Trade Union and Labour Relations Act 1974, s 25(1), Sch 3, para 10(1), (3).
   Substituted by the Trade Union Reform and Employment Rights Act 1993, s 49(2), Sch 8, para 65, as
from 30 August 1993 (SI 1993/1908, below, para **[1435]**), as follows—
   "133 Amalgamations and transfers of engagements

      (1) Subject to subsection (2), the provisions of Chapter VII of Part I of this Act (amalgamations
   and similar matters) apply to unincorporated employers' associations as in relation to trade unions.

(2) In its application to such associations that Chapter shall have effect—

    (a) as if in section 99(1) for the words from "that every" to "accompanied by" there were substituted the words "that, not less than seven days before the ballot on the resolution to approve the instrument of amalgamation or transfer is held, every member is supplied with",

    (b) as if the requirements imposed by sections 100A to 100E consisted only of those specified in sections 100B and 100C(1) and (3)(a) together with the requirement that every member must, so far as is reasonably possible, be given a fair opportunity of voting, and

    (c) with the omission of sections 101(3) and 107.".

134 Change of name of employers' association

(1) An unincorporated employers' association may change its name by any method expressly provided for by its rules or, if its rules do not expressly provide for a method of doing so, by adopting in accordance with its rules an alteration of the provision in them which gives the association its name.

(2) If the name of an employers' association, whether incorporated or unincorporated, is entered in the list of employers' associations a change of name shall not take effect until approved by the Certification Officer.

(3) The Certification Officer shall not approve a change of name if it appears to him that the proposed new name—

    (a) is the same as one entered in the list as the name of another employers' association, or

    (b) is the same as one entered in the list of trade unions kept under Part I of this Act,

or is a name so nearly resembling such a name as to be likely to deceive the public.

(4) A change of name by an unincorporated employers' association does not affect any right or obligation of the association or any of its members; and any pending legal proceedings may be continued by or against the association, the trustees of the association or any other officer of the association who can sue or be sued on its behalf notwithstanding its change of name.

(5) The power conferred by section 108 (power to make regulations for carrying provisions into effect) applies in relation to this section as in relation to a provision of Chapter VII of Part I. **[798]**

NOTES

Commencement: 16 October 1992.

Sub-s (1) contains provisions formerly in the Trade Union (Amalgamations, etc) Act 1964, ss 1(1A), 6(1) (both in part), as substituted, in the case of s 1(1A), by the Trade Union and Labour Relations Act 1974, s 25(1), Sch 3, para 10(1), (3). Sub-ss (2), (3) contain provisions formerly in s 6(2) (in part) of the 1964 Act, as substituted by s 25(1) of, Sch 3, para 10(1), (5) to, the 1974 Act, and as amended by the Employment Protection Act 1975, s 125(1), Sch 16, Pt IV, para 10(1), (2). Sub-s (4) contains provisions formerly in ss 1(1A), 6(3) (both in part) of the 1964 Act, as substituted, in the case of s 1(1A), by s 25(1) of, Sch 3, para 10(1), (3) to, the 1974 Act. Sub-s (5) contains provisions formerly in s 7 (in part) of the 1964 Act, as amended by the Secretary of State for Employment and Productivity Order 1968, SI 1968/729, and as amended and repealed in part by s 125(1), (3) of, Sch 16, Pt IV, para 10(1), (2), Sch 18 to, the 1975 Act.

General

135 Federated employers' associations

(1) In this section a "federated employers' association" means an employers' association which consists wholly or mainly of constituent or affiliated organisations,

or representatives or such organisations, as described in paragraph (b) of the definition of "employers' association" in section 122.

(2) The provisions of Part I applied by this Part to employers' associations apply to federated employers' associations subject to the following exceptions and adaptations.

(3) The following provisions of Chapter III of Part I (administration) do not apply to a federated employers' association which consists wholly or mainly of representatives of constituent or affiliated organisations—

    (a) section 27 (duty to supply copy of rules),

    (b) section 28 (duty to keep accounting records),

    (c) *sections 32 to 37* [section 32(1), (2), (3)(a), (b) and (c) and (4) to (6) and sections 33 to 37] (annual return, accounts and audit), *and*

    [(ca) sections 37A to 37E (investigation of financial affairs), and]

    (d) sections 38 to 42 (members' superannuation schemes).

(4) The provisions of Chapter VI of Part I (application of funds for political objects) apply to a employers' association which is in whole or part an association or combination of other associations as if the individual members of the component associations were members of that association and not of the component associations.

But nothing in that Chapter prevents a component association from collecting contributions on behalf of the association or combination from such of its members as are not exempt from the obligation to contribute to the political fund of the association or combination.   **[799]**

NOTES

Commencement: 16 October 1992.

Sub-ss (1), (2) are drafting provisions. Sub-s (3) contains provisions formerly in the Trade Union and Labour Relations Act 1974, ss 10(1), 11(1) (both in part). Sub-s (4) contains provisions formerly in the Trade Union Act 1913, s 3(5) (in part).

Sub-s (3): words in italics at the beginning of para (c) substituted by words in square brackets immediately following; the word "and" in italics at the end of para (c) is repealed, and para (ca) is inserted, by the Trade Union Reform and Employment Rights Act 1993, ss 49(2), 51, Sch 8, para 66, Sch 10, as from 1 January 1994 (para (c)); 30 August 1993 (para (ca) and repeal) (SI 1993/1908, below, para **[1435]**).

136 Meaning of "officer" of employers' association

In this Act "officer", in relation to an employers' association, includes—

    (a) any member of the governing body of the association, and

    (b) any trustee of any fund applicable for the purposes of the association.

       [800]

NOTES

Commencement: 16 October 1992.

This section contains provisions formerly in the Trade Union and Labour Relations Act 1974, s 30(1) (definition "officer" (in part) as inserted by the Employment Protection Act 1975, s 125(1), Sch 16, Pt III, para 7(5)).

PART III

RIGHTS IN RELATION TO UNION MEMBERSHIP AND ACTIVITIES

Access to employment

137 Refusal of employment on grounds related to union membership

(1) It is unlawful to refuse a person employment—

    (a) because he is, or is not, a member of a trade union, or

   (b) because he is unwilling to accept a requirement—

      (i) to take steps to become or cease to be, or to remain or not to become, a member of a trade union, or

      (ii) to make payments or suffer deductions in the event of his not being a member of a trade union.

(2) A person who is thus unlawfully refused employment has a right of complaint to an industrial tribunal.

(3) Where an advertisement is published which indicates, or might reasonably be understood as indicating—

   (a) that employment to which the advertisement relates is open only to a person who is, or is not, a member of a trade union, or

   (b) that any such requirement as is mentioned in subsection (1)(b) will be imposed in relation to employment to which the advertisement relates,

a person who does not satisfy that condition or, as the case may be, is unwilling to accept that requirement, and who seeks and is refused employment to which the advertisement relates, shall be conclusively presumed to have been refused employment for that reason.

(4) Where there is an arrangement or practice under which employment is offered only to persons put forward or approved by a trade union, and the trade union puts forward or approves only persons who are members of the union, a person who is not a member of the union and who is refused employment in pursuance of the arrangement or practice shall be taken to have been refused employment because he is not a member of the trade union.

(5) A person shall be taken to be refused employment if he seeks employment of any description with a person and that person—

   (a) refuses or deliberately omits to entertain and process his application or enquiry, or

   (b) causes him to withdraw or cease to pursue his application or enquiry, or

   (c) refuses or deliberately omits to offer him employment of that description, or

   (d) makes him an offer of such employment the terms of which are such as no reasonable employer who wished to fill the post would offer and which is not accepted, or

   (e) makes him an offer of such employment but withdraws it or causes him not to accept it.

(6) Where a person is offered employment on terms which include a requirement that he is, or is not, a member of a trade union, or any such requirement as is mentioned in subsection (1)(b), and he does not accept the offer because he does not satisfy or, as the case may be, is unwilling to accept that requirement, he shall be treated as having been refused employment for that reason.

(7) Where a person may not be considered for appointment or election to an office in a trade union unless he is a member of the union, or of a particular branch or section of the union or of one of a number of particular branches or sections of the union, nothing in this section applies to anything done for the purpose of securing compliance with that condition although as holder of the office he would be employed by the union.

For this purpose an "office" means any position—

   (a) by virtue of which the holder is an official of the union, or

   (b) to which Chapter IV of Part I applies (duty to hold elections).

(8) The provisions of this section apply in relation to an employment agency acting, or purporting to act, on behalf of an employer as in relation to an employer.

[801]

NOTES
Commencement: 16 October 1992.
Sub-ss (1)–(6), (8) contain provisions formerly in the Employment Act 1990, s 1(1)–(6), (7). Sub-s (7) contains provisions formerly in s 3(2) of the 1990 Act.

138 Refusal of service of employment agency on grounds related to union membership

(1) It is unlawful for an employment agency to refuse a person any of its services—

    (a) because he is, or is not, a member of a trade union, or

    (b) because he is unwilling to accept a requirement to take steps to become or cease to be, or to remain or not to become, a member of a trade union.

(2) A person who is thus unlawfully refused any service of an employment agency has a right of complaint to an industrial tribunal.

(3) Where an advertisement is published which indicates, or might reasonably be understood as indicating—

    (a) that any service of an employment agency is available only to a person who is, or is not, a member of a trade union, or

    (b) that any such requirement as is mentioned in subsection (1)(b) will be imposed in relation to a service to which the advertisement relates,

a person who does not satisfy that condition or, as the case may be, is unwilling to accept that requirement, and who seeks to avail himself of and is refused that service, shall be conclusively presumed to have been refused it for that reason.

(4) A person shall be taken to be refused a service if he seeks to avail himself of it and the agency—

    (a) refuses or deliberately omits to make the service available to him, or

    (b) causes him not to avail himself of the service or to cease to avail himself of it, or

    (c) does not provide the same service, on the same terms, as is provided to others.

(5) Where a person is offered a service on terms which include a requirement that he is, or is not, a member of a trade union, or any such requirement as is mentioned in subsection (1)(b), and he does not accept the offer because he does not satisfy or, as the case may be, is unwilling to accept that requirement, he shall be treated as having been refused the service for that reason.   **[802]**

NOTES
Commencement: 16 October 1992.
Sub-ss (1)–(5) contain provisions formerly in the Employment Act 1990, s 2(1)–(5).

139 Time limit for proceedings

(1) An industrial tribunal shall not consider a complaint under section 137 or 138 unless it is presented to the tribunal—

    (a) before the end of the period of three months beginning with the date of the conduct to which the complaint relates, or

    (b) where the tribunal is satisfied that it was not reasonably practicable for the complaint to be presented before the end of that period, within such further period as the tribunal considers reasonable.

(2) The date of the conduct to which a complaint under section 137 relates shall be taken to be—

(a) in the case of an actual refusal, the date of the refusal;

(b) in the case of a deliberate omission—

(i) to entertain and process the complainant's application or enquiry, or

(ii) to offer employment,

the end of the period within which it was reasonable to expect the employer to act;

(c) in the case of conduct causing the complainant to withdraw or cease to pursue his application or enquiry, the date of that conduct;

(d) in a case where an offer was made but withdrawn, the date when it was withdrawn;

(e) in any other case where an offer was made but not accepted, the date on which it was made.

(3) The date of the conduct to which a complaint under section 138 relates shall be taken to be—

(a) in the case of an actual refusal, the date of the refusal;

(b) in the case of a deliberate omission to make a service available, the end of the period within which it was reasonable to expect the employment agency to act;

(c) in the case of conduct causing the complainant not to avail himself of a service or to cease to avail himself of it, the date of that conduct;

(d) in the case of failure to provide the same service, on the same terms, as is provided to others, the date or last date on which the service in fact provided was provided.   **[803]**

NOTES

Commencement: 16 October 1992.

Sub-ss (1)–(3) contain provisions formerly in the Employment Act 1990, Sch 1, Pt I, para 3(1)–(3).

140 Remedies

(1) Where the industrial tribunal finds that a complaint under section 137 or 138 is well-founded, it shall make a declaration to that effect and may make such of the following as it considers just and equitable—

(a) an order requiring the respondent to pay compensation to the complainant of such amount as the tribunal may determine;

(b) a recommendation that the respondent take within a specified period action appearing to the tribunal to be practicable for the purpose of obviating or reducing the adverse effect on the complainant of any conduct to which the complaint relates.

(2) Compensation shall be assessed on the same basis as damages for breach of statutory duty and may include compensation for injury to feelings.

(3) If the respondent fails without reasonable justification to comply with a recommendation to take action, the tribunal may increase its award of compensation or, if it has not made such an award, make one.

(4) The total amount of compensation shall not exceed the limit for the time being imposed by section 75 of the Employment Protection (Consolidation) Act 1978 (limit on compensation for unfair dismissal).   **[804]**

NOTES

Commencement: 16 October 1992.

Sub-ss (1)–(4) contain provisions formerly in the Employment Act 1990, Sch 1, Pt I, para 5(1)–(4).

141 Complaint against employer and employment agency

(1) Where a person has a right of complaint against a prospective employer and against an employment agency arising out of the same facts, he may present a complaint against either of them or against them jointly.

(2) If a complaint is brought against one only, he or the complainant may request the tribunal to join or sist the other as a party to the proceedings.

The request shall be granted if it is made before the hearing of the complaint begins, but may be refused if it is made after that time; and no such request may be made after the tribunal has made its decision as to whether the complaint is well-founded.

(3) Where a complaint is brought against an employer and an employment agency jointly, or where it is brought against one and the other is joined or sisted as a party to the proceedings, and the tribunal—

    (a) finds that the complaint is well-founded as against the employer and the agency, and

    (b) makes an award of compensation,

it may order that the compensation shall be paid by the one or the other, or partly by one and partly by the other, as the tribunal may consider just and equitable in the circumstances.   **[805]**

NOTES

Commencement: 16 October 1992.

Sub-ss (1)–(3) contain provisions formerly in the Employment Act 1990, Sch 1, Pt I, para 6(1)–(3).

142 Awards against third parties

(1) If in proceedings on a complaint under section 137 or 138 either the complainant or the respondent claims that the respondent was induced to act in the manner complained of by pressure which a trade union or other person exercised on him by calling, organising, procuring or financing a strike or other industrial action, or by threatening to do so, the complainant or the respondent may request the industrial tribunal to direct that the person who he claims exercised the pressure be joined or sisted as a party to the proceedings.

(2) The request shall be granted if it is made before the hearing of the complaint begins, but may be refused if it is made after that time; and no such request may be made after the tribunal has made its decision as to whether the complaint is well-founded.

(3) Where a person has been so joined or sisted as a party to the proceedings and the tribunal—

    (a) finds that the complaint is well-founded,

    (b) makes an award of compensation, and

    (c) also finds that the claim in subsection (1) above is well-founded,

it may order that the compensation shall be paid by the person joined instead of by the respondent, or partly by that person and partly by the respondent, as the tribunal may consider just and equitable in the circumstances.

(4) Where by virtue of section 141 (complaint against employer and employment agency) there is more than one respondent, the above provisions apply to either or both of them.   **[806]**

NOTES

Commencement: 16 October 1992.

Sub-ss (1)–(4) contain provisions formerly in the Employment Act 1990, Sch 1, Pt I, para 7(1)–(4).

143 Interpretation and other supplementary provisions

(1) In sections 137 to 143—

"advertisement" includes every form of advertisement or notice, whether to the public or not, and references to publishing an advertisement shall be construed accordingly;

"employment" means employment under a contract of employment, and related expressions shall be construed accordingly; and

"employment agency" means a person who, for profit or not, provides services for the purpose of finding employment for workers or supplying employers with workers, but subject to subsection (2) below.

(2) For the purposes of sections 137 to 143 as they apply to employment agencies—

(a) services other than those mentioned in the definition of "employment agency" above shall be disregarded, and

(b) a trade union shall not be regarded as an employment agency by reason of services provided by it only for, or in relation to, its members.

(3) References in sections 137 to 143 to being or not being a member of a trade union are to being or not being a member of any trade union, of a particular trade union or of one of a number of particular trade unions.

Any such reference includes a reference to being or not being a member of a particular branch or section of a trade union or of one of a number of particular branches or sections of a trade union.

(4) The remedy of a person for conduct which is unlawful by virtue of section 137 or 138 is by way of a complaint to an industrial tribunal in accordance with this Part, and not otherwise.

No other legal liability arises by reason that conduct is unlawful by virtue of either of those sections.   **[807]**

NOTES

Commencement: 16 October 1992.

Sub-s (1) contains provisions formerly in the Employment Act 1990, s 3(1) (in part). Sub-ss (2), (3) contain provisions formerly in s 3(3), (4) of the 1990 Act. Sub-s (4) contains provisions formerly in Sch 1, Pt I, para 2(1), (2) to the 1990 Act.

Contracts for supply of goods or services

144 Union membership requirement in contract for goods or services void

A term or condition of a contract for the supply of goods or services is void in so far as it purports to require that the whole, or some part, of the work done for the purposes of the contract is done only by persons who are, or are not, members of trade unions or of a particular trade union.   **[808]**

NOTES

Commencement: 16 October 1992.

This section contains provisions formerly in the Employment Act 1982, s 12(1).

145 Refusal to deal on union membership grounds prohibited

(1) A person shall not refuse to deal with a supplier or prospective supplier of goods or services on union membership grounds.

"Refuse to deal" and "union membership grounds" shall be construed as follows.

(2) A person refuses to deal with a person if, where he maintains (in whatever form) a list of approved suppliers of goods or services, or of persons from whom tenders for the supply of goods or services may be invited, he fails to include the name of that person in that list.

He does so on union membership grounds if the ground, or one of the grounds, for failing to include his name is that if that person were to enter into a contract with him for the supply of goods or services, work to be done for the purposes of the contract would, or would be likely to, be done by persons who were, or who were not, members of trade unions or of a particular trade union.

(3) A person refuses to deal with a person if, in relation to a proposed contract for the supply of goods or services—

    (a) he excludes that person from the group of persons from whom tenders for the supply of the goods or services are invited, or

    (b) he fails to permit that person to submit such a tender, or

    (c) he otherwise determines not to enter into a contract with that person for the supply of the goods or services.

He does so on union membership grounds if the ground, or one of the grounds, on which he does so is that if the proposed contract were entered into with that person, work to be done for the purposes of the contract would, or would be likely to, be done by persons who were, or who were not, members of trade unions or of a particular trade union.

(4) A person refuses to deal with a person if he terminates a contract with him for the supply of goods or services.

He does so on union membership grounds if the ground, or one of the grounds, on which he does so is that work done, or to be done, for the purposes of the contract has been, or is likely to be, done by persons who are or are not members of trade unions or of a particular trade union.

(5) The obligation to comply with this section is a duty owed to the person with whom there is a refusal to deal and to any other person who may be adversely affected by its contravention; and a breach of the duty is actionable accordingly (subject to the defences and other incidents applying to actions for breach of statutory duty).

[809]

NOTES

Commencement: 16 October 1992.

Sub-s (1) contains provisions formerly in the Employment Act 1982, s 12(2), (7) (in part), and contains drafting provisions. Sub-s (2) contains provisions formerly in s 12(2)(a), (4) of the 1982 Act. Sub-s (3) contains provisions formerly in s 12(2)(c), (3), (6) of the 1982 Act. Sub-s (4) contains provisions formerly in s 12(2)(b), (5) of the 1982 Act. Sub-s (5) contains provisions formerly in s 12(7) (in part) of the 1982 Act.

Action short of dismissal

146 Action short of dismissal on grounds related to union membership or activities

(1) An employee has the right not to have action short of dismissal taken against him as an individual by his employer for the purpose of—

    (a) preventing or deterring him from being or seeking to become a member of an independent trade union, or penalising him for doing so,

    (b) preventing or deterring him from taking part in the activities of an independent trade union at an appropriate time, or penalising him for doing so, or

   (c) compelling him to be or become a member of any trade union or of a particular trade union or of one of a number of particular trade unions.

(2) In subsection (1)(b) "an appropriate time" means—

   (a) a time outside the employee's working hours, or

   (b) a time within his working hours at which, in accordance with arrangements agreed with or consent given by his employer, it is permissible for him to take part in the activities of a trade union;

and for this purpose "working hours", in relation to an employee, means any time when, in accordance with his contract of employment, he is required to be at work.

(3) An employee also has the right not to have action short of dismissal taken against him for the purpose of enforcing a requirement (whether or not imposed by his contract of employment or in writing) that, in the event of his not being a member of any trade union or of a particular trade union or of one of a number of particular trade unions, he must make one or more payments.

(4) For the purposes of subsection (3) any deduction made by an employer from the remuneration payable to an employee in respect of his employment shall, if it is attributable to his not being a member of any trade union or of a particular trade union or of one of a number of particular trade unions, be treated as action short of dismissal taken against him for the purpose of enforcing a requirement of a kind mentioned in that subsection.

(5) An employee may present a complaint to an industrial tribunal on the ground that action has been taken against him by his employer in contravention of this section.
[810]

NOTES
Commencement: 16 October 1992.
Sub-s (1) contains provisions formerly in the Employment Protection (Consolidation) Act 1978, s 23(1), as repealed in part by the Employment Act 1980, ss 15(1), 20(3), Sch 2, and by the Employment Act 1988, s 33(b), Sch 4, and as amended by the Employment Act 1982, s 10(4). Sub-s (2) contains provisions formerly in s 23(2) of the 1978 Act. Sub-ss (3), (4) contain provisions formerly in s 23(1A), (1B) of the 1978 Act, as inserted by s 10(3) of the 1982 Act. Sub-s (5) contains provisions formerly in s 24(1) of the 1978 Act.

147 Time limit for proceedings

An industrial tribunal shall not consider a complaint under section 146 unless it is presented—

   (a) before the end of the period of three months beginning with the date of the action to which the complaint relates or, where that action is part of a series of similar actions, the last of those actions, or

   (b) where the tribunal is satisfied that it was not reasonably practicable for the complaint to be presented before the end of that period, within such further period as it considers reasonable.   **[811]**

NOTES
Commencement: 16 October 1992.
This section contains provisions formerly in the Employment Protection (Consolidation) Act 1978, s 24(2).

148 Consideration of complaint

(1) On a complaint under section 146 it shall be for the employer to show the purpose for which action was taken against the complainant.

(2) In determining any question whether action was taken by the employer or the purpose for which it was taken, no account shall be taken of any pressure which was exercised on him by calling, organising, procuring or financing a strike or other industrial action, or by threatening to do so; and that question shall be determined as if no such pressure had been exercised.

[(3) In determining what was the purpose for which action was taken by the employer against the complainant in a case where—

(a) there is evidence that the employer's purpose was to further a change in his relationship with all or any class of his employees, and

(b) there is also evidence that his purpose was one falling within section 146,

the tribunal shall regard the purpose mentioned in paragraph (a) (and not the purpose mentioned in paragraph (b)) as the purpose for which the employer took the action, unless it considers that the action was such as no reasonable employer would take having regard to the purpose mentioned in paragraph (a).

(4) Where the action which the tribunal determines to have been the action taken against the complainant was action taken in consequence of previous action by the employer paragraph (a) of subsection (3) is satisfied if the purpose mentioned in that paragraph was the purpose of the previous action.

(5) In subsection (3) "class", in relation to an employer and his employees, means those employed at a particular place of work, those employees of a particular grade, category or description or those of a particular grade, category or description employed at a particular place of work.]   **[812]**

NOTES

Commencement: 16 October 1992 (sub-ss (1), (2)).

Sub-ss (1), (2) contain provisions formerly in the Employment Protection (Consolidation) Act 1978, s 25(1), (2), as repealed in part, in the case of s 25(1), by the Employment Act 1980, ss 15(3), 20(3), Sch 2.

Sub-ss (3)–(5): added by the Trade Union Reform and Employment Rights Act 1993, s 13, as from 30 August 1993 (SI 1993/1908, below, para **[1435]**).

149 Remedies

(1) Where the industrial tribunal finds that a complaint under section 146 is well-founded, it shall make a declaration to that effect and may make an award of compensation to be paid by the employer to the complainant in respect of the action complained of.

(2) The amount of the compensation awarded shall be such as the tribunal considers just and equitable in all the circumstances having regard to the infringement complained of and to any loss sustained by the complainant which is attributable to the action which infringed his right.

(3) The loss shall be taken to include—

(a) any expenses reasonably incurred by the complainant in consequence of the action complained of, and

(b) loss of any benefit which he might reasonably be expected to have had but for that action.

(4) In ascertaining the loss, the tribunal shall apply the same rule concerning the duty of a person to mitigate his loss as applies to damages recoverable under the common law of England and Wales or Scotland.

(5) In determining the amount of compensation to be awarded no account shall be taken of any pressure which was exercised on the employer by calling, organising, procuring or financing a strike or other industrial action, or by threatening to do so; and that question shall be determined as if no such pressure had been exercised.

(6) Where the tribunal finds that the action complained of was to any extent caused or contributed to by action of the complainant, it shall reduce the amount of the compensation by such proportion as it considers just and equitable having regard to that finding.   **[813]**

NOTES
Commencement: 16 October 1992.
Sub-s (1) contains provisions formerly in the Employment Protection (Consolidation) Act 1978, s 24(3). Sub-ss (2)–(6) contain provisions formerly in s 26(1)–(5) of the 1978 Act.

150 Awards against third parties

(1) If in proceedings on a complaint under section 146—

  (a) the complaint is made on the ground that action has been taken against the complainant by his employer for the purpose of compelling him to be or become a member of any trade union or of a particular trade union or of one of a number of particular trade unions, and

  (b) either the complainant or the employer claims in proceedings before the tribunal that the employer was induced to take the action complained of by pressure which a trade union or other person exercised on him by calling, organising, procuring or financing a strike or other industrial action, or by threatening to do so,

the complainant or the employer may request the tribunal to direct that the person who he claims exercised the pressure be joined or sisted as a party to the proceedings.

(2) The request shall be granted if it is made before the hearing of the complaint begins, but may be refused if it is made after that time; and no such request may be made after the tribunal has made a declaration that the complaint is well-founded.

(3) Where a person has been so joined or sisted as a party to proceedings and the tribunal—

  (a) makes an award of compensation, and

  (b) finds that the claim mentioned in subsection (1)(b) is well-founded,

it may order that the compensation shall be paid by the person joined instead of by the employer, or partly by that person and partly by the employer, as the tribunal may consider just and equitable in the circumstances.   **[814]**

NOTES
Commencement: 16 October 1992.
Sub-ss (1)–(3) contain provisions formerly in the Employment Protection (Consolidation) Act 1978, s 26A(1)–(3), as substituted by the Employment Act 1982, s 11.

151 Interpretation and other supplementary provisions

(1) References in sections 146 to 150 to being, becoming or ceasing to remain a member of a trade union include references to being, becoming or ceasing to remain a member of a particular branch or section of that union and to being, becoming or

ceasing to remain a member of one of a number of particular branches or sections of that union; and references to taking part in the activities of a trade union shall be similarly construed.

(2) The remedy of an employee for infringement of the right conferred on him by section 146 is by way of a complaint to an industrial tribunal in accordance with this Part, and not otherwise.   **[815]**

NOTES

Commencement: 16 October 1992.

Sub-s (1) contains provisions formerly in the Employment Protection (Consolidation) Act 1978, s 23(7), as added by the Employment Act 1988, s 33(1), Sch 3, Pt I, para 2(1). Sub-s (2) contains provisions deriving from s 129 (in part) of the 1978 Act.

Dismissal

152 Dismissal on grounds related to union membership or activities

(1) For purposes of Part V of the Employment Protection (Consolidation) Act 1978 (unfair dismissal) the dismissal of an employee shall be regarded as unfair if the reason for it (or, if more than one, the principal reason) was that the employee—

    (a) was, or proposed to become, a member of an independent trade union, or

    (b) had taken part, or proposed to take part, in the activities of an independent trade union at an appropriate time, or

    (c) was not a member of any trade union, or of a particular trade union, or of one of a number of particular trade unions, or had refused, or proposed to refuse, to become or remain a member.

(2) In subsection (1)(b) "an appropriate time" means—

    (a) a time outside the employee's working hours, or

    (b) a time within his working hours at which, in accordance with arrangements agreed with or consent given by his employer, it is permissible for him to take part in the activities of a trade union;

and for this purpose "working hours", in relation to an employee, means any time when, in accordance with his contract of employment, he is required to be at work.

(3) Where the reason, or one of the reasons, for the dismissal was—

    (a) the employee's refusal, or proposed refusal, to comply with a requirement (whether or not imposed by his contract of employment or in writing) that, in the event of his not being a member of any trade union, or of a particular trade union, or of one of a number of particular trade unions, he must make one or more payments, or

    (b) his objection, or proposed objection, (however expressed) to the operation of a provision (whether or not forming part of his contract of employment or in writing) under which, in the event mentioned in paragraph (a), his employer is entitled to deduct one or more sums from the remuneration payable to him in respect of his employment,

the reason shall be treated as falling within subsection (1)(c).

(4) References in this section to being, becoming or ceasing to remain a member of a trade union include references to being, becoming or ceasing to remain a member of a particular branch or section of that union or of one of a number of particular branches or sections of that trade union; and references to taking part in the activities of a trade union shall be similarly construed.   **[816]**

NOTES
Commencement: 16 October 1992.
Sub-ss (1), (2) contain provisions formerly in the Employment Protection (Consolidation) Act 1978, s 58(1), (2), as substituted by the Employment Act 1982, s 3, and as repealed in part, in the case of s 58(1), by the Employment Act 1988, s 33(2), Sch 4. Sub-ss (3), (4) contain provisions formerly in s 58(13), (14) of the 1978 Act, as substituted by s 3 of the 1982 Act, as further substituted, in the case of s 58(14), and as amended, in the case of s 58(13), by s 33(1) of, Sch 3, Pt I, para 2(2) to, the 1988 Act.

153 Selection for redundancy on grounds related to union membership or activities

Where the reason or principal reason for the dismissal of an employee was that he was redundant, but it is shown—

(a) that the circumstances constituting the redundancy applied equally to one or more other employees in the same undertaking who held positions similar to that held by him and who have not been dismissed by the employer, and

(b) that the reason (or, if more than one, the principal reason) why he was selected for dismissal was one of those specified in section 152(1),

the dismissal shall be regarded as unfair for the purposes of Part V of the Employment Protection (Consolidation) Act 1978 (unfair dismissal).   **[817]**

NOTES
Commencement: 16 October 1992.
This section contains provisions formerly in the Employment Protection (Consolidation) Act 1978, s 59(a), and deriving from the introductory and closing words of that section, as amended by the Employment Act 1982, s 21(2), Sch 3, Pt II, para 17.

154 Exclusion of requirement as to qualifying period, &c

[(1)] *Sections* [Section] 64 *and 64A* of the Employment Protection (Consolidation) Act 1978 (qualifying period and upper age limit for unfair dismissal protection) *do* [does] not apply to the dismissal of an employee if it is shown that the reason principal reason for the dismissal *was one of those specified in section 152(1)* [or in a redundancy case, for selecting the employee for dismissal, was an inadmissible reason.]

[(2) For the purposes of this section—

"inadmissible", in relation to a reason, means that it is one of those specified in section 152(1); and

"a redundancy case" means a case where the reason or principal reason for the dismissal was that the employee was redundant but the equal application of the circumstances to non-dismissed employees required by section 153(a) is also shown.]   **[818]**

NOTES
Commencement: 16 October 1992.
This section contains provisions formerly in the Employment Protection (Consolidation) Act 1978, ss 64(3), 64A(2) (in part), as inserted, in the case of s 64A, by the Employment Act 1980, s 8, and as amended, in the case of both sections, by the Employment Act 1982, s 21(2), Sch 3, Pt II, paras 19, 20.
The original words of this section are renumbered sub-s (1), sub-s (2) is added, and in sub-s (1) the words in italics are substituted in each case by the words in square brackets immediately following, and the words "and 64A" are repealed by the Trade Union Reform and Employment Rights Act 1993, ss 49(1), (2), 51, Sch 7, para 1, Sch 8, para 67, Sch 10, as from 30 August 1993 (SI 1993/1908, below, para [1435]).

155 Matters to be disregarded in assessing contributory fault

(1) Where an industrial tribunal makes an award of compensation for unfair dismissal in a case where the dismissal is unfair by virtue of section 152 or 153, the tribunal shall disregard, in considering whether it would be just and equitable to reduce, or further reduce, the amount of any part of the award, any such conduct or action of the complainant as is specified below.

(2) Conduct or action of the complainant shall be disregarded in so far as it constitutes a breach or proposed breach of a requirement—

(a) to be or become a member of any trade union or of a particular trade union or of one of a number of particular trade unions,

(b) to cease to be, or refrain from becoming, a member of any trade union or of a particular trade union or of one of a number of particular trade unions, or

(c) not to take part in the activities of any trade union or of a particular trade union or of one of a number of particular trade unions.

For the purposes of this subsection a requirement means a requirement imposed on the complainant by or under an arrangement or contract of employment or other agreement.

(3) Conduct or action of the complainant shall be disregarded in so far as it constitutes a refusal, or proposed refusal, to comply with a requirement of a kind mentioned in section 152(3)(a) (payments in lieu of membership) or an objection, or proposed, objection, (however expressed) to the operation of a provision of a kind mentioned in section 152(3)(b) (deductions in lieu of membership).   **[819]**

NOTES
Commencement: 16 October 1992.
Sub-s (1) contains provisions formerly in the Employment Protection (Consolidation) Act 1978, s 72A(1), (2) (opening words), as inserted by the Employment Act 1982, s 6. Sub-s (2) contains provisions formerly in s 72A(2)(a), (3) of the 1978 Act, as so inserted. Sub-s (3) contains provisions formerly in s 72A(2)(b), (c) of the 1978 Act, as so inserted.

156 Minimum basic award

(1) Where a dismissal is unfair by virtue of section 152(1) or 153, the amount of the basic award of compensation, before any reduction is made under subsection (7A), (7B) or (9) of section 73 of the Employment Protection (Consolidation) Act 1978, shall be not less than £2,700.

(2) But where the dismissal is unfair by virtue of section 153, subsection (7B) of that section (reduction for contributory fault) applies in relation to so much of the basic award as is payable because of subsection (1) above.   **[820]**

NOTES
Commencement: 16 October 1992.
Sub-s (1) contains provisions formerly in the Employment Protection (Consolidation) Act 1978, s 73(4A), as inserted by the Employment Act 1982, s 4(1), and as amended by the Unfair Dismissal (Increase of Limits of Basic and Special Awards) Order 1992, SI 1992/313. Sub-s (2) derives from the original s 73(7C) of the 1978 Act, as inserted by s 4(2) of the 1982 Act.
Sum of £2,700 applies where the effective date of dismissal was on or after 1 April 1992 (see SI 1992/313): no order has been made under s 159 increasing the amount in 1993.

157 Special award of compensation

(1) Where an industrial tribunal makes an award of compensation for unfair dismissal in a case where the dismissal is unfair by virtue of section 152(1) or 153, then, unless—

    (a) the complaint does not request the tribunal to make an order for reinstatement or re-engagement, or

    (b) the case falls within section 73(2) of the Employment Protection (Consolidation) Act 1978 (cases where employer takes requisite steps to renew employment or re-engage employee),

the award shall include a special award calculated in accordance with section 158.

(2) Section 71(2)(b) of the Employment Protection (Consolidation) Act 1978 (additional award of compensation in case of failure to comply with an order for reinstatement or re-engagement) does not apply in a case where the dismissal is unfair by virtue of section 152(1) or 153.   **[821]**

NOTES

Commencement: 16 October 1992.

Sub-s (1) contains provisions deriving from the Employment Protection (Consolidation) Act 1978, s 72 (para (c) and closing words), as substituted by the Employment Act 1982, s 5(2). Sub-s (2) contains provisions deriving from the original s 71(2)(b) of the 1978 Act, as inserted by s 5(1) of the 1982 Act.

158 Amount of special award

(1) Subject to the following provisions of this section, the amount of the special award shall be one week's pay multiplied by 104, or £13,400, whichever is the greater, but shall not exceed £26,800.

(2) Where the award of compensation is made under section 71 (2)(a) of the Employment Protection (Consolidation) Act 1978 (compensation where employee not reinstated or re-engaged in accordance with order) then, unless the employer satisfies the tribunal that it was not practicable to comply with the order for reinstatement or re-engagement, the amount of the special award shall be increased to one week's pay multiplied by 156, or £20,100 whichever is the greater [, but subject to the following provisions of this section].

(3) In a case where the amount of the basic award is reduced under section 73(5) of the Employment Protection (Consolidation) Act 1978 (reduction where complainant aged over 64), the amount of the special award shall be reduced by the same fraction.

(4) Where the tribunal considers that any conduct of the complainant before the dismissal (or, where the dismissal was with notice, before the notice was given) was such that it would be just and equitable to reduce or further reduce the amount of the special award to any extent, the tribunal shall reduce or further reduce that amount accordingly.

(5) Where the tribunal finds that the complainant has unreasonably—

    (a) prevented an order for reinstatement or re-engagement from being complied with, or

    (b) refused an offer by the employer (made otherwise than in compliance with such an order) which if accepted would have the effect of reinstating the complainant in his employment in all respects as if he had not been dismissed,

the tribunal shall reduce or further reduce the amount of the special award to such extent as it considers just and equitable having regard to that finding.

(6) Where the employer has engaged a permanent replacement for the complainant, the tribunal shall not take that fact into account in determining for the purposes of subsection (2) whether it was practicable to comply with an order for reinstatement or re-engagement unless the employer shows that it was not practicable for his to arrange for the complainant's work to be done without engaging a permanent replacement.

[(7) Schedule 14 to the Employment Protection (Consolidation) Act 1978 (calculation of a week's pay) shall apply for the purposes of this section with the substitution, for paragraph 7, of the following:—

For the purposes of this Part in its application to section 158 of the Trade Union and Labour Relations (Consolidation) Act 1992, the calculation date is—

   (a) where the dismissal was with notice, the date on which the employer's notice was given;

   (b) where paragraph (a) does not apply, the effective date of termination.]

[822]

NOTES

Commencement: 16 October 1992.

Sub-ss (1)–(6) contain provisions formerly in the Employment Protection (Consolidation) Act 1978, s 75A(1)–(6), as inserted by the Employment Act 1982, s 5(3), and as amended, in the case of s 75A(1), (2), by the Unfair Dismissal (Increase of Limits of Basic and Special Awards) Order 1992, SI 1992/313.

Sub-s (2): words in square brackets added by the Trade Union Reform and Employment Rights Act 1993, s 49(2), Sch 8, para 68, as from 30 August 1993 (SI 1993/1908, below, para **[1435]**).

Sub-s (7): added by the Trade Union Reform and Employment Rights Act 1993, s 49(1), Sch 7, para 21, as from 30 August 1993 (SI 1993/1908, below, para **[1435]**).

The sums specified in this section apply as from 1 April 1992 (see SI 1992/313) and have not been increased in 1993.

159 Power to increase sums by order

(1) The Secretary of State may by order made by statutory instrument increase—

   (a) the sum mentioned in section 156(1) (minimum basic award), or

   (b) any of the sums specified in section 158(1) or (2) (limits on amount of special award).

(2) The order may contain such incidental, supplementary or transitional provisions as appear to the Secretary of State to be necessary or expedient.

(3) No order under this section shall be made unless a draft of the order has been laid before Parliament and approved by a resolution of each House of Parliament.

[823]

NOTES

Commencement: 16 October 1992.

Sub-ss (1), (3) contain provisions formerly in the Employment Protection (Consolidation) Act 1978, ss 73(4B), 75A(7), as inserted, in the case of s 73(4B), by the Employment Act 1982, s 4(1), and as inserted, in the case of s 75A(7), by s 5(3) of the 1982 Act, and also contains provisions deriving from s 154(1) (in part) of the 1978 Act. Sub-s (2) contains provisions deriving from s 154(3) of the 1978 Act.

Up to 1 September 1993, no order had been made under this section.

160 Awards against third parties

(1) If in proceedings before an industrial tribunal on a complaint of unfair dismissal either the employer or the complainant claims—

   (a) that the employer was induced to dismiss the complainant by pressure which a trade union or other person exercised on the employer by calling, organising, procuring or financing a strike or other industrial action, or by threatening to do so, and

(b) that the pressure was exercised because the complainant was not a member of any trade union or of a particular trade union or of one of a number of particular trade unions,

the employer or the complainant may request the tribunal to direct that the person who he claims exercised the pressure be joined or sisted as a party to the proceedings.

(2) The request shall be granted if it is made before the hearing of the complaint begins, but may be refused after that time; and no such request may be made after the tribunal has made an award of compensation for unfair dismissal or an order for reinstatement or re-engagement.

(3) Where a person has been so joined or sisted as a party to the proceedings and the tribunal—

(a) makes an award of compensation for unfair dismissal, and
(b) finds that the claim mentioned in subsection (1) is well-founded,

the tribunal may order that the compensation shall be paid by that person instead of the employer, or partly by that person and partly by the employer, as the tribunal may consider just and equitable.   **[824]**

NOTES
Commencement: 16 October 1992.
This section contains provisions formerly in the Employment Protection (Consolidation) Act 1978, s 76A, as originally inserted by the Employment Act 1980, s 10, and as substituted by the Employment Act 1982, s 7.

161 Application for interim relief

(1) An employee who presents a complaint of unfair dismissal alleging that the dismissal is unfair by virtue of section 152 may apply to the tribunal for interim relief.

(2) The tribunal shall not entertain an application for interim relief unless it is presented to the tribunal before the end of the period of seven days immediately following the effective date of termination (whether before, on or after that date).

(3) In a case where the employee relies on section 152(1)(a) or (b) the tribunal shall not entertain an application for interim relief unless before the end of that period there is also so presented a certificate in writing signed by an authorised official of the independent trade union of which the employee was or proposed to become a member stating—

(a) that on the date of the dismissal the employee was or proposed to become a member of the union, and
(b) that there appear to be reasonable grounds for supposing that the reason for his dismissal (or, if more than one, the principal reason) was one alleged in the complaint.

(4) An "authorised official" means an official of the trade union authorised by it to act for the purposes of this section.

(5) A document purporting to be an authorisation of an official by a trade union to act for the purposes of this section and to be signed on behalf of the union shall be taken to be such an authorisation unless the contrary is proved; and a document purporting to be a certificate signed by such an official shall be taken to be signed by him unless the contrary is proved.

(6) For the purposes of subsection (3) the date of dismissal shall be taken to be—

(a) where the employee's contract of employment was terminated by notice

(whether given by his employer or by him), the date on which the
employer's notice was given, and

(b) in any other case, the effective date of termination.   **[825]**

NOTES
Commencement: 16 October 1992.
Sub-s (1) contains provisions formerly in the Employment Protection (Consolidation) Act 1978,
s 77(1), as substituted by the Employment Act 1982, s 8(1). Sub-ss (2), (3) contain provisions formerly in
s 77(2)(a), (b) of the 1978 Act, as amended, in the case of s 77(2)(b), by s 21(2) of, Sch 3, Pt II, para 24(1)
to, the 1982 Act. Sub-ss (4), (6) contain provisions formerly in s 77(10) of the 1978 Act, as repealed in
part by s 21(3) of, Sch 4 to, the 1982 Act. Sub-s (5) contains provisions formerly in s 77(11) of the 1978
Act.

162 Application to be promptly determined

(1) An industrial tribunal shall determine an application for interim relief as soon as
practicable after receiving the application and, where appropriate, the requisite
certificate.

(2) The tribunal shall give to the employer, not later than seven days before the
hearing, a copy of the application and of any certificate, together with notice of the
date, time and place of the hearing.

(3) If a request under section 160 (awards against third parties) is made three
days or more before the date of the hearing, the tribunal shall also give to the person
to whom the request relates, as soon as reasonably practicable, a copy of the
application and of any certificate, together with notice of the date, time and place of
the hearing.

(4) The tribunal shall not exercise any power it has of postponing the hearing of
an application for interim relief except where it is satisfied that special circumstances
exist which justify it in doing so.   **[826]**

NOTES
Commencement: 16 October 1992.
Sub-ss (1)–(3) contain provisions formerly in the Employment Protection (Consolidation) Act 1978,
s 77(3), (3A), as amended by the Employment Act 1982, ss 8(2), 21(2), Sch 3, Pt II, para 24(2). Sub-s (4)
contains provisions formerly in s 77(4) of the 1978 Act.

163 Procedure on hearing of application and making of order

(1) If on hearing an application for interim relief it appears to the tribunal that it is
likely that on determining the complaint to which the application relates that it will
find that, by virtue of section 152, the complainant has been unfairly dismissed, the
following provisions apply.

(2) The tribunal shall announce its findings and explain to both parties (if present)
what powers the tribunal may exercise on the application and in what circumstances
it will exercise them, and shall ask the employer (if present) whether he is willing,
pending the determination or settlement of the complaint—

(a) to reinstate the employee, that is to say, to treat him in all respects as if he
had not been dismissed, or

(b) if not, to re-engage him in another job on terms and conditions not less
favourable than those which would have been applicable to him if he had
not been dismissed.

(3) For this purpose "terms and conditions not less favourable than those which
would have been applicable to him if he had not been dismissed" means as regards

seniority, pension rights and other similar rights that the period prior to the dismissal shall be regarded as continuous with his employment following the dismissal.

(4) If the employer states that he is willing to reinstate the employee, the tribunal shall make an order to that effect.

(5) If the employer states that he is willing to re-engage the employee in another job, and specifies the terms and conditions on which he is willing to do so, the tribunal shall ask the employee whether he is willing to accept the job on those terms and conditions; and—

>   (a)   if the employee is willing to accept the job on those terms and conditions, the tribunal shall make an order to that effect, and
>   (b)   if he is not, then, if the tribunal is of the opinion that the refusal is reasonable, the tribunal shall make an order for the continuation of his contract of employment, and otherwise the tribunal shall make no order.

(6) If on the hearing of an application for interim relief the employer fails to attend before the tribunal, or states that he is unwilling either to reinstate the employee or re-engage him as mentioned in subsection (2), the tribunal shall make an order for the continuation of the employee's contract of employment.   **[827]**

NOTES

Commencement: 16 October 1992.

Sub-ss (1), (2) contain provisions formerly in the Employment Protection (Consolidation) Act 1978, s 77(5), as amended by the Employment Act 1982, s 21(2), Sch 3, Pt II, para 24(3). Sub-ss (3)–(6) contain provisions formerly in s 77(6)–(9) of the 1978 Act.

164 Order for continuation of contract of employment

(1) An order under section 163 for the continuation of a contract of employment is an order that the contract of employment continue in force—

>   (a)   for the purposes of pay or *any benefit* [any other benefit] derived from the employment, seniority, pension rights and other similar matters, and
>   (b)   for the purpose of determining for any purpose the period for which the employee has been continuously employed,

from the date of its termination (whether before or after the making of the order) until the determination or settlement of the complaint.

(2) Where the tribunal makes such an order it shall specify in the order the amount which is to be paid by the employer to the employee by way of pay in respect of each normal pay period, or part of any such period, falling between the date of dismissal and the determination or settlement of the complaint.

(3) Subject as follows, the amount so specified shall be that which the employee could reasonably have been expected to earn during that period, or part, and shall be paid—

>   (a)   in the case of payment for any such period falling wholly or partly after the making of the order, on the normal pay day for that period, and
>   (b)   in the case of a payment for any past period, within such time as may be specified in the order.

(4) If an amount is payable in respect only of part of a normal pay period, the amount shall be calculated by reference to the whole period and reduced proportionately.

(5) Any payment made to an employee by an employer under his contract of employment, or by way of damages for breach of that contract, in respect of a normal pay period or part of any such period shall go towards discharging the employer's

liability in respect of that period under subsection (2); and conversely any payment under that subsection in respect of a period shall go towards discharging any liability of the employer under, or in respect of the breach of, the contract of employment in respect of that period.

(6) If an employee, on or after being dismissed by his employer, receives a lump sum which, or part of which, is in lieu of wages but is not referable to any normal pay period, the tribunal shall take the payment into account in determining the amount of pay to be payable in pursuance of any such order.

(7) For the purposes of this section the amount which an employee could reasonably have been expected to earn, his normal pay period and the normal pay day for each such period shall be determined as if he had not been dismissed. **[828]**

NOTES
Commencement: 16 October 1992.
Sub-s (1) contains provisions formerly in the Employment Protection (Consolidation) Act 1978, s 78(1). Sub-ss (2), (3) contain provisions formerly in s 78(2) of the 1978 Act. Sub-ss (4)–(7) contain provisions formerly in s 78(3)–(6) of the 1978 Act.
Sub-s (1): words in italics substituted by words in square brackets immediately following by the Trade Union Reform and Employment Rights Act 1993, s 49(2), Sch 8, para 69, as from 30 August 1993 (SI 1993/1908, below, para **[1435]**).

165 Application for variation or revocation of order

(1) At any time between the making of an order under section 163 and the determination or settlement of the complaint, the employer or the employee may apply to an industrial tribunal for the revocation or variation of the order on the ground of a relevant change of circumstances since the making of the order.

(2) Sections 161 to 163 apply in relation to such an application as in relation to an original application for interim relief, except that—

(a) no certificate need be presented to the tribunal under section 161(3), and

(b) in the case of an application by the employer, section 162(2) (service of copy of application and notice of hearing) has effect with the substitution of a reference to the employee for the reference to the employer.   **[829]**

NOTES
Commencement: 16 October 1992.
This section contains provisions formerly in the Employment Protection (Consolidation) Act 1978, s 79(1).

166 Consequences of failure to comply with order

(1) If on the application of an employee an industrial tribunal is satisfied that the employer has not complied with the terms of an order for the reinstatement or re-engagement of the employee under section 163(4) or *(5)(a)* [(5)], the tribunal shall—

(a) make an order for the continuation of the employee's contract of employment, and

(b) order the employer to pay the employee such compensation as the tribunal considers just and equitable in all the circumstances having regard—

(i) to the infringement of the employee's right to be reinstated or re-engaged in pursuance of the order, and

(ii) to any loss suffered by the employee in consequence of the non-compliance.

(2) Section 164 applies to an order under subsection (1)(a) as in relation to an order under section 163.

(3) If on the application of an employee an industrial tribunal is satisfied that the employer has not complied with the terms of an order for the continuation of a contract of employment, the following provisions apply.

(4) If the non-compliance consists of a failure to pay an amount by way of pay specified in the order, the tribunal shall determine the amount owed by the employer on the date of the determination.

If on that date the tribunal also determines the employee's complaint that he has been unfairly dismissed, it shall specify that amount separately from any other sum awarded to the employee.

(5) In any other case, the tribunal shall order the employer to pay the employee such compensation as the tribunal considers just and equitable in all the circumstances having regard to any loss suffered by the employee in consequence of the non-compliance.   **[830]**

NOTES
Commencement: 16 October 1992.
Sub-ss (1), (2) contain provisions formerly in the Employment Protection (Consolidation) Act 1978, s 79(2). Sub-ss (3)–(5) contain provisions formerly in s 79(3) of the 1978 Act.
Sub-s (1): "(5)(a)" substituted by "(5)" by the Trade Union Reform and Employment Rights Act 1993, s 49(1), Sch 7, para 22, as from 30 August 1993 (SI 1993/1908, below, para **[1435]**).

167 Interpretation and other supplementary provisions

(1) Part V of the Employment Protection (Consolidation) Act 1978 (unfair dismissal) has effect subject to the provisions of sections 152 to 166 above.

(2) Those sections shall be construed as one with that Part; and in those sections—

"complaint of unfair dismissal" means a complaint under section 67 of the Employment Protection (Consolidation) Act 1978;
"award of compensation for unfair dismissal" means an award of compensation for unfair dismissal under section 68(2) or 71(2)(a) of that Act; and
"order for reinstatement or re-engagement" means an order for reinstatement or re-engagement under section 69 of that Act.

(3) Nothing in those sections shall be construed as conferring a right to complain of unfair dismissal from employment of a description to which that Part does not otherwise apply.   **[831]**

NOTES
Commencement: 16 October 1992.
This section is a drafting provision.

Time off for trade union duties and activities

168 Time off for carrying out trade union duties

(1) An employer shall permit an employee of his who is an official of an independent trade union recognised by the employer to take time off during his working hours for the purpose of carrying out any duties of his, as such an official, concerned with—

(a) negotiations with the employer related to or connected with matters falling within section 178(2) (collective bargaining) in relation to which the trade union is recognised by the employer, or
(b) the performance on behalf of employees of the employer of functions related to or connected with matters falling within that provision which the employer has agreed may be so performed by the trade union.

(2) He shall also permit such an employee to take time off during his working hours for the purpose of undergoing training in aspects of industrial relations—

(a) relevant to the carrying out of such duties as are mentioned in subsection (1), and

(b) approved by the Trades Union Congress or by the independent trade union of which he is an official.

(3) The amount of time off which an employee is to be permitted to take under this section and the purposes for which, the occasions on which and any conditions subject to which time off may be so taken are those that are reasonable in all the circumstances having regard to any relevant provisions of a Code of Practice issued by ACAS.

(4) An employee may present a complaint to an industrial tribunal that his employer has failed to permit him to take time off as required by this section. **[832]**

NOTES
Commencement: 16 October 1992.
Sub-s (1) contains provisions formerly in the Employment Protection (Consolidation) Act 1978, s 27(1)(a), as amended by the Employment Act 1989, s 14(a). Sub-s (2) contains provisions formerly in s 27(1)(b) of the 1978 Act, as amended by s 14(b) of the 1989 Act. Sub-s (3) contains provisions formerly in s 27(2) of the 1978 Act. Sub-s (4) contains provisions formerly in s 27(7) (in part) of the 1978 Act.
The relevant code is ACAS Code of Practice 3: Time off for Trade Union Duties and Activities (1991): below, paras **[3108]**–**[3147]**.

169 Payment for time off under section 168

(1) An employer who permits an employee to take time off under section 168 shall pay him for the time taken off pursuant to the permission.

(2) Where the employee's remuneration for the work he would ordinarily have been doing during that time does not vary with the amount of work done, he shall be paid as if he had worked at that work for the whole of that time.

(3) Where the employee's remuneration for the work he would ordinarily have been doing during that time varies with the amount of work done, he shall be paid an amount calculated by reference to the average hourly earnings for that work.

The average hourly earnings shall be those of the employee concerned or, if no fair estimate can be made of those earnings, the average hourly earnings for work of that description of persons in comparable employment with the same employer or, if there are no such persons, a figure of average hourly earnings which is reasonable in the circumstances.

(4) A right to be paid an amount under this section does not affect any right of an employee in relation to remuneration under his contract of employment, but—

(a) any contractual remuneration paid to an employee in respect of a period of time off to which this section applies shall go towards discharging any liability of the employer under this section in respect of that period, and

(b) any payment under this section in respect of a period shall go towards discharging any liability of the employer to pay contractual remuneration in respect of that period.

(5) An employee may present a complaint to an industrial tribunal that his employer has failed to pay him in accordance with this section. **[833]**

NOTES
Commencement: 16 October 1992.
Sub-ss (1), (2) contain provisions formerly in the Employment Protection (Consolidation) Act 1978, s 27(3)(a). Sub-s (3) contains provisions formerly in s 27(3)(b), (4) of the 1978 Act. Sub-s (4) contains provisions formerly in s 27(5), (6) of the 1978 Act. Sub-s (5) contains provisions formerly in s 27(7) (in part) of the 1978 Act.

170 Time off for trade union activities

(1) An employer shall permit an employee of his who is a member of an independent trade union recognised by the employer in respect of that description of employee to take time off during his working hours for the purpose of taking part in—

    (a) any activities of the union, and

    (b) any activities in relation to which the employee is acting as a representative of the union.

(2) The right conferred by subsection (1) does not extent to activities which themselves consist of industrial action, whether or not in contemplation or furtherance of a trade dispute.

(3) The amount of time off which an employee is to be permitted to take under this section and the purposes for which, the occasions on which and any conditions subject to which time off may be so taken are those that are reasonable in all the circumstances having regard to any relevant provisions of a Code of Practice issued by ACAS.

(4) An employee may present a complaint to an industrial tribunal that his employer has failed to permit him to take time off as required by this section. **[834]**

NOTES
Commencement: 16 October 1992.
Sub-ss (1), (2) contain provisions formerly in the Employment Protection (Consolidation) Act 1978, s 28(1), (2). Sub-ss (3), (4) contain provisions formerly in s 28(3), (4) of the 1978 Act.
Sub-s (3): the code under this subsection is ACAS Code of Practice 3: Time off for Trade Union Duties and Activities (1991): below, paras **[3108]**–**[3147]**.

171 Time limit for proceedings

An industrial tribunal shall not consider a complaint under section 168, 169 or 170 unless it is presented to the tribunal—

    (a) within three months of the date when the failure occurred, or

    (b) where the tribunal is satisfied that it was not reasonably practicable for the complaint to be presented within that period, within such further period as the tribunal considers reasonable. **[835]**

NOTES
Commencement: 16 October 1992.
This section contains provisions deriving from the Employment Protection (Consolidation) Act 1978, s 30(1).

172 Remedies

(1) Where the tribunal finds a complaint under section 168 or 170 is well-founded, it shall make a declaration to that effect and may make an award of compensation to be paid by the employer to the employee.

(2) The amount of the compensation shall be such as the tribunal considers just and equitable in all the circumstances having regard to the employer's default in failing to permit time off to be taken by the employee and to any loss sustained by the employee which is attributable to the matters complained of.

(3) Where on a complaint under section 169 the tribunal finds that the employer has failed to pay the employee in accordance with that section, it shall order him to pay the amount which it finds to be due. **[836]**

NOTES
Commencement: 16 October 1992.
Sub-ss (1), (2) contain provisions deriving from the Employment Protection (Consolidation) Act 1978, s 30(2) (in part). Sub-s (3) contains provisions formerly in s 30(3) of the 1978 Act.

173 Interpretation and other supplementary provisions

(1) For the purposes of sections 168 and 170 the working hours of an employee shall be taken to be any time when in accordance with his contract of employment he is required to be at work.

(2) The remedy of an employee for infringement of the rights conferred on him by section 168, 169 or 170 is by way of complaint to an industrial tribunal in accordance with this Part, and not otherwise.   **[837]**

NOTES
Commencement: 16 October 1992.
Sub-s (1) contains provisions deriving from the Employment Protection (Consolidation) Act 1978, s 32(1) (in part), as substituted by the Employment Act 1989, s 29(3), Sch 6, para 19. Sub-s (2) contains provisions deriving from s 129 (in part) of the 1978 Act.

NOTE
Ss 174–177, and the cross-heading immediately preceding them, below, are substituted by new ss 174–177, and a new cross-heading, by the Trade Union Reform and Employment Rights Act 1993, s 14, as from 30 November 1993 (SI 1993/1908, below, para [1435]). The new sections and cross-heading are printed after the original (italicised) sections, beginning with para [842].

Exclusion or expulsion from trade union where employment subject to union membership agreement

174 Right not to be unreasonably excluded or expelled from union

(1) A person who is, or is seeking to be, in employment with respect to which it is the practice, in accordance with a union membership agreement, for the employee to belong to a specified trade union, or one of a number of specified trade unions, has the right—

    (a) not to have an application for membership of a specified trade union unreasonably refused, and

    (b) not to be unreasonably expelled from a specified union.

(2) A "union membership agreement" means an agreement or arrangement relating to employees of an identifiable class which—

    (a) is made by or on behalf of, or otherwise exists between one or more independent trade unions and one or more employers or employers' associations, and

    (b) has the effect in practice of requiring the employees of the class to which it relates (whether or not there is a condition to that effect in their contract of employment) to be or become members of the union or one of the unions which is or are parties to the agreement or arrangement or of another specified independent trade union.

Employees shall be treated as belonging to the same class if they have been identified as such by the parties to the agreement, and they may be so identified by reference to any characteristics or circumstances whatever.

(3) A trade union shall be treated as "specified" for the purposes of, or in relation to, a union membership agreement if it is specified in the agreement or is accepted by the parties to the agreement as being the equivalent of a union so specified.

(4) For the purposes of this section—

(a)   *an application for membership of a trade union which is neither granted nor rejected before the end of the period within which it might reasonably have been expected to be granted if it was to be granted, shall be treated as having been refused on the last day of that period, and*

(b)   *a person who under the rules of a trade union ceases to be a member of the union on the happening of an event specified in the rules shall be treated as having been expelled from the union.*

(5) A person who claims that an application by him for membership of a trade union has been unreasonably refused, or that he has been unreasonably expelled from a trade union, in contravention of this section, may present a complaint to an industrial tribunal.

(6) The question whether the trade union acted reasonably or unreasonably shall be determined in accordance with equity and the substantial merits of the case.

In particular, a union shall not be regarded as having acted reasonably only because it has acted in accordance with the requirements of its rules or unreasonably only because it has acted in contravention of them. **[838]**

NOTES
Commencement: 16 October 1992.
Sub-s (1) contains provisions formerly in the Employment Act 1980, s 4(1), (2). Sub-ss (2), (3) contain provisions formerly in the Trade Union and Labour Relations Act 1974, s 30(1) (definition "union membership agreement" (in part)), (5A), as amended, in the case of s 30(1), by the Trade Union and Labour Relations (Amendment) Act 1976, s 3(3), and as inserted, in the case of s 30(5A), by s 3(4) of the 1976 Act, and in s 4(10) (in part) of the 1980 Act. Sub-s (4) contains provisions formerly in s 4(9) of the 1980 Act. Sub-ss (5), (6) contain provisions formerly in s 4(4), (5) of the 1980 Act.

175 Time limit for proceedings

An industrial tribunal shall not entertain a complaint under section 174 unless it is presented to the tribunal—

(a)   *before the end of the period of six months beginning with the date of the refusal or expulsion, or*

(b)   *where the tribunal is satisfied that it was not reasonably practicable for the complaint to be presented before the end of that period, within such further period as the tribunal considers reasonable.* **[839]**

NOTES
Commencement: 16 October 1992.
This section contains provisions formerly in the Employment Act 1980, s 4(6).

176 Remedies

(1) Where the industrial tribunal finds a complaint under section 174 is well-founded, it shall make a declaration to that effect.

(2) A person whose complaint has been declared to be well-founded may make an application for an award of compensation to be paid to him by the union.

The application shall be made to an industrial tribunal if when it is made the applicant has been admitted or re-admitted to membership of the union, and otherwise to the Employment Appeal Tribunal.

(3) The application shall not be entertained if made—

(a)   *before the end of the period of four weeks beginning with the date of the declaration, or*

(b) after the end of the period of six months beginning with that date.

(4) The amount of compensation awarded by an industrial tribunal shall be such as it considers appropriate to compensate the applicant for the loss sustained by him in consequence of the refusal or expulsion complained of.

The amount of the compensation shall not exceed the aggregate of—

(a) an amount equal to thirty times the limit for the time being imposed by paragraph 8(1)(b) of Schedule 14 to the Employment Protection (Consolidation) Act 1978 (maximum amount of a week's pay for basic award in unfair dismissal cases), and

(b) an amount equal to the limit for the time being imposed by section 75 of that Act (maximum compensatory award in such cases).

(5) The amount of compensation awarded by the Employment Appeal Tribunal shall be such as it considers just and equitable in all the circumstances.

The amount of the compensation shall not exceed the aggregate of—

(a) the aggregate amount mentioned in subsection (4), and

(b) an amount equal to fifty-two times the limit for the time being imposed by paragraph 8(1)(a) of Schedule 14 to the Employment Protection (Consolidation) Act 1978 (maximum amount of a week's pay for additional award of compensation in unfair dismissal cases),

and shall not be less than the amount for the time being specified in section 156(1) (minimum basic award).

(6) In determining the amount of compensation to be awarded, the industrial tribunal or Employment Appeal Tribunal shall apply the same rule concerning the duty of a person to mitigate his loss as applies to damages recoverable under the common law of England and Wales or Scotland.

(7) Where the industrial tribunal or Employment Appeal Tribunal finds that the refusal or expulsion complained of was to any extent caused or contributed to by action of the applicant, it shall reduce the amount of compensation by such proportion as it considers just and equitable having regard to that finding.

(8) In determining the amount of compensation to be awarded, any reduction or increase under subsection (4) or (5) shall be made before—

(a) any reduction by virtue of subsection (6) or (7), or

(b) any reduction on account of sums already paid by the union by way of compensation in respect of the subject matter of the application;

and accordingly, where the case so required the reductions mentioned in paragraphs (a) and (b) shall be made to the maximum or, as the case may be, minimum award under subsection (4) or (5).   **[840]**

NOTES

Commencement: 16 October 1992.

Sub-s (1) contains provisions formerly in the Employment Act 1980, s 4(7). Sub-s (2) contains provisions formerly in s 5(1), (2) of the 1980 Act. Sub-s (3) contains provisions formerly in s 5(3) of the 1980 Act. Sub-s (4) contains provisions formerly in s 5(4)(a), (7) of the 1980 Act. Sub-s (5) contains provisions formerly in s 5(4)(b), (8) of the 1980 Act, as amended in the case of sub-s (8) by the Employment Act 1988, s 33(1), Sch 3, Pt I, para 3(2)(a). Sub-ss (6), (7) contain provisions formerly in s 5(5), (6) of the 1980 Act. Sub-s (8) contains provisions formerly in s 5(8A) of the 1980 Act, as inserted by s 33(1) of, and Sch 3, Pt I, para 3(2)(b) to, the 1988 Act.

177 Interpretation and other supplementary provisions

(1) References in section 174 to a trade union include a branch or section of a trade union.

(2) The remedy of a person for infringement of the rights conferred by section 174 is by way of a complaint to an industrial tribunal in accordance with this Part, and not otherwise.

(3) Those rights are in addition to, and not in substitution for, any right existing apart from that section.

[841]

NOTES
Commencement: 16 October 1992.
Sub-s (1) contains provisions formerly in the Trade Union and Labour Relations Act 1974, s 30(1) (definition "union membership agreement" (in part)), as amended by the Trade Union and Labour Relations (Amendment) Act 1976, s 3(3), and in the Employment Act 1980, s 4(10) (in part). Sub-ss (2), (3) contain provisions formerly in s 4(3) of the 1980 Act.

[Right to membership of trade union

174 Right not to be excluded or expelled from union

(1) An individual shall not be excluded or expelled from a trade union unless the exclusion or expulsion is permitted by this section.

(2) The exclusion or expulsion of an individual from a trade union is permitted by this section if (and only if)—

    (a) he does not satisfy, or no longer satisfies, an enforceable membership requirement contained in the rules of the union,

    (b) he does not qualify, or no longer qualifies, for membership of the union by reason of the union operating only in a particular part or particular parts of Great Britain,

    (c) in the case of a union whose purpose is the regulation of relations between its members and one particular employer or a number of particular employers who are associated, he is not, or is no longer, employed by that employer or one of those employers, or

    (d) the exclusion or expulsion is entirely attributable to his conduct.

(3) A requirement in relation to membership of a union is "enforceable" for the purposes of subsection (2)(a) if it restricts membership solely by reference to one or more of the following criteria—

    (a) employment in a specified trade, industry or profession,

    (b) occupational description (including grade, level or category of appointment), and

    (c) possession of specified trade, industrial or professional qualifications or work experience.

(4) For the purposes of subsection (2)(d) "conduct", in relation to an individual, does not include—

    (a) his being or ceasing to be, or having been or ceased to be—

        (i) a member of another trade union,

        (ii) employed by a particular employer or at a particular place, or

        (iii) a member of a political party, or

    (b) conduct to which section 65 (conduct for which an individual may not be disciplined by a trade union) applies or would apply if the references in that section to the trade union which is relevant for the purposes of that section were references to any trade union.

(5) An individual who claims that he has been excluded or expelled from a trade union in contravention of this section may present a complaint to an industrial tribunal.]   **[842]**

NOTE
    This section and the cross-heading preceding it, and ss 175–177 below, are substituted for the original ss 174–177, printed in italics above, by the Trade Union Reform and Employment Rights Act 1993, s 14, as from 30 November 1993 (SI 1993/1908, below, para **[1435]**).

[175 Time limit for proceedings

An industrial tribunal shall not entertain a complaint under section 174 unless it is presented—

    (a) before the end of the period of six months beginning with the date of the exclusion or expulsion, or

    (b) where the tribunal is satisfied that it was not reasonably practicable for the complaint to be presented before the end of that period, within such further period as the tribunal considers reasonable.]   **[843]**

NOTE
    This section, s 174 and the cross-heading preceding it, and ss 176, 177, are substituted for the original ss 174–177, printed in italics above, by the Trade Union Reform and Employment Rights Act 1993, s 14, as from 30 November 1993 (SI 1993/1908, below, para **[1435]**).

[176 Remedies

(1) Where the industrial tribunal finds a complaint under section 174 is well-founded, it shall make a declaration to that effect.

(2) An individual whose complaint has been declared to be well-founded may make an application for an award of compensation to be paid to him by the union.

The application shall be made to an industrial tribunal if when it is made the applicant has been admitted or readmitted to the union, and otherwise to the Employment Appeal Tribunal.

(3) The application shall not be entertained if made—

    (a) before the end of the period of four weeks beginning with the date of the declaration, or

    (b) after the end of the period of six months beginning with that date.

(4) The amount of compensation awarded shall, subject to the following provisions, be such as the industrial tribunal or the Employment Appeal Tribunal considers just and equitable in all the circumstances.

(5) Where the industrial tribunal or Employment Appeal Tribunal finds that the exclusion or expulsion complained of was to any extent caused or contributed to by the action of the applicant, it shall reduce the amount of the compensation by such proportion as it considers just and equitable having regard to that finding.

(6) The amount of compensation calculated in accordance with subsections (4) and (5) shall not exceed the aggregate of—

    (a) an amount equal to thirty times the limit for the time being imposed by paragraph 8(1)(b) of Schedule 14 to the Employment Protection (Consolidation) Act 1978 (maximum amount of a week's pay for basic award in unfair dismissal cases), and

(b)   an amount equal to the limit for the time being imposed by section 75 of that Act (maximum compensatory award in such cases);

and, in the case of an award by the Employment Appeal Tribunal, shall not be less than £5,000.

(7)   The Secretary of State may by order increase the sum specified in subsection (6).

(8)   An order under subsection (7)—

(a)   shall be made by statutory instrument which shall be subject to annulment in pursuance of a resolution of either House of Parliament, and

(b)   may contain such incidental, supplementary or transitional provisions as appear to the Secretary of State to be necessary or expedient.]   **[844]**

NOTE

This section, s 174 and the cross-heading preceding it, and ss 175, 177, are substituted for the original ss 174–177, printed in italics above, by the Trade Union Reform and Employment Rights Act 1993, s 14, as from 30 November 1993 (SI 1993/1908, below, para **[1435]**).

Up to 1 September 1993 no order had been made under this section.

[177   Interpretation and other supplementary provisions

(1)   For the purposes of section 174—

(a)   "trade union" does not include an organisation falling within paragraph (b) of section 1,

(b)   "conduct" includes statements, acts and omissions, and

(c)   "employment" includes any relationship whereby an individual personally does work or performs services for another person (related expressions being construed accordingly).

(2)   For the purposes of sections 174 to 176—

(a)   if an individual's application for membership of a trade union is neither granted nor rejected before the end of the period within which it might reasonably have been expected to be granted if it was to be granted, he shall be treated as having been excluded from the union on the last day of that period, and

(b)   an individual who under the rules of a trade union ceases to be a member of the union on the happening of an event specified in the rules shall be treated as having been expelled from the union.

(3)   The remedy of an individual for infringement of the rights conferred by section 174 is by way of a complaint to an industrial tribunal in accordance with that section, sections 175 and 176 and this section, and not otherwise.

(4)   Where a complaint relating to an expulsion which is presented under section 174 is declared to be well-founded, no complaint in respect of the expulsion shall be presented or proceeded with under section 66 (complaint of infringement of right not to be unjustifiably disciplined).

(5)   The rights conferred by section 174 are in addition to, and not in substitution for, any right which exists apart from that section; and, subject to subsection (4), nothing in that section, section 175 or 176 or this section affects any remedy for infringement of any such right.]   **[845]**

NOTE

This section, s 174 and the cross-heading preceding it, and ss 175, 176, are substituted for the original ss 174–177, printed in italics above, by the Trade Union Reform and Employment Rights Act 1993, s 14, as from 30 November 1993 (SI 1993/1908, below, para **[1435]**).

PART IV
INDUSTRIAL RELATIONS

CHAPTER I
COLLECTIVE BARGAINING

Introductory

178 Collective agreements and collective bargaining

(1) In this Act "collective agreement" means any agreement or arrangement made by or on behalf of one or more trade unions and one or more employers or employers' associations and relating to one or more of the matters specified below; and "collective bargaining" means negotiations relating to or connected with one or more of those matters.

(2) The matters referred to above are—

(a) terms and conditions of employment, or the physical conditions in which any workers are required to work;

(b) engagement or non-engagement, or termination or suspension of employment or the duties of employment, of one or more workers;

(c) allocation of work or the duties of employment between workers or groups of workers;

(d) matters of discipline;

(e) a worker's membership or non-membership of a trade union;

(f) facilities for officials of trade unions; and

(g) machinery for negotiation or consultation, and other procedures, relating to any of the above matters, including the recognition by employers or employers' associations of the right of a trade union to represent workers in such negotiation or consultation or in the carrying out of such procedures.

(3) In this Act "recognition", in relation to a trade union, means the recognition of the union by an employer, or two or more associated employers, to any extent, for the purpose of collective bargaining; and "recognised" and other related expressions shall be construed accordingly.   **[846]**

NOTES
Commencement: 16 October 1992.
Sub-ss (1), (2) contain provisions formerly in the Trade Union and Labour Relations Act 1974, s 29(1), as read with s 30(1) thereof (definition "collective agreement"); in the Employment Protection Act 1975, s 126(1) (definitions "collective agreement", "collective bargaining"), and deriving from the Employment Protection (Consolidation) Act 1978, s 153(1) (definition "collective agreement"). Sub-s (3) contains provisions formerly in s 126(1) of the 1975 Act (definition "recognition"), as amended by the Employment Act 1980, s 20(2), Sch 1, para 6, and deriving from s 32(2) of the 1978 Act, as substituted by the Employment Act 1989, s 29(3), Sch 6, para 19.

Enforceability of collective agreements

179 Whether agreement intended to be a legally enforceable contract

(1) A collective agreement shall be conclusively presumed not to have been intended by the parties to be a legally enforceable contract unless the agreement—

(a) is in writing, and

(b) contains a provision which (however expressed) states that the parties intend that the agreement shall be a legally enforceable contract.

(2) A collective agreement which does satisfy those conditions shall be conclusively presumed to have been intended by the parties to be a legally enforceable contract.

(3) If a collective agreement is in writing and contains a provision which (however expressed) states that the parties intend that one or more parts of the agreement specified in that provision, but not the whole of the agreement, shall be a legally enforceable contract, then—

    (a) the specified part or parts shall be conclusively presumed to have been intended by the parties to be a legally enforceable contract, and

    (b) the remainder of the agreement shall be conclusively presumed not to have been intended by the parties to be such a contract.

(4) A part of a collective agreement which by virtue of subsection (3)(b) is not a legally enforceable contract may be referred to for the purpose of interpreting a party of the agreement which is such a contract. **[847]**

NOTES

Commencement: 16 October 1992.

Sub-ss (1), (2) contain provisions formerly in the Trade Union and Labour Relations Act 1974, s 18(1), (2). Sub-ss (3), (4) contain provisions formerly in s 18(3) of the 1974 Act.

180 Effect of provisions restricting right to take industrial action

(1) Any terms of a collective agreement which prohibit or restrict the right of workers to engage in a strike or other industrial action, or have the effect of prohibiting or restricting that right, shall not form part of any contract between a worker and the person for whom he works unless the following conditions are met.

(2) The conditions are that the collective agreement—

    (a) is in writing,

    (b) contains a provision expressly stating that those terms shall or may be incorporated in such a contract,

    (c) is reasonably accessible at his place of work to the worker to whom it applies and is available for him to consult during working hours, and

    (d) is one where each trade union which is a party to the agreement is an independent trade union;

and that the contract with the worker expressly or impliedly incorporates those terms in the contract.

(3) The above provisions have effect notwithstanding anything in section 179 and notwithstanding any provision to the contrary in any agreement (including a collective agreement or a contract with any worker). **[848]**

NOTES

Commencement: 16 October 1992.

Sub-ss (1), (2) contain provisions formerly in the Trade Union and Labour Relations Act 1974, s 18(4). Sub-s (3) contains provisions formerly in s 18(5) of the 1974 Act.

Disclosure of information for purposes of collective bargaining

181 General duty of employers to disclose information

(1) An employer who recognises an independent trade union shall, for the purposes of all stages of collective bargaining about matters, and in relation to descriptions of workers, in respect of which the union is recognised by him, disclose to representatives of the union, on request, the information required by this section.

In this section and sections 182 to 185 "representative", in relation to a trade union, means an official or other person authorised by the union to carry on such collective bargaining.

(2) The information to be disclosed is all information relating to the employer's undertaking which is in his possession, or that of an associated employer, and is information—

(a) without which the trade union representatives would be to a material extent impeded in carrying on collective bargaining with him, and

(b) which it would be in accordance with good industrial relations practice that he should disclose to them for the purposes of collective bargaining.

(3) A request by trade union representatives for information under this section shall, if the employer so requests, be in writing or be confirmed in writing.

(4) In determining what would be in accordance with good industrial relations practice, regard shall be had to the relevant provisions of any Code of Practice issued by ACAS, but not so as to exclude any other evidence of what that practice is.

(5) Information which an employer is required by virtue of this section to disclose to trade union representatives shall, if they so request, be disclosed or confirmed in writing.   **[849]**

NOTES
Commencement: 16 October 1992.
Sub-ss (1), (2) contain provisions formerly in the Employment Protection Act 1975, s 17(1), (2)(a).
Sub-ss (3)–(5) contain provisions formerly in s 17(3)–(5) of the 1975 Act.
Sub-s (4): see further ACAS Code of Practice: Disclosure of Information to Trade Unions for Collective Bargaining Purposes, 1977, below, paras **[3021]**–**[3043]**.

182 Restrictions on general duty

(1) An employer is not required by section 181 to disclose information—

(a) the disclosure of which would be against the interests of national security, or

(b) which he could not disclose without contravening a prohibition imposed by or under an enactment, or

(c) which has been communicated to him in confidence, or which he has otherwise obtained in consequence of the confidence reposed in him by another person, or

(d) which relates specifically to an individual (unless that individual has consented to its being disclosed), or

(e) the disclosure of which would cause substantial injury to his undertaking for reasons other than its effect on collective bargaining, or

(f) obtained by him for the purpose of bringing, prosecuting or defending any legal proceedings.

In formulating the provisions of any Code of Practice relating to the disclosure of information, ACAS shall have regard to the provisions of this subsection.

(2) In the performance of his duty under section 181 an employer is not required—

(a) to produce, or allow inspection of, any document (other than a document prepared for the purpose of conveying or confirming the information) or to make a copy of or extracts from any document, or

(b) to compile or assemble any information where the compilation or assembly would involve an amount of work or expenditure out of reasonable proportion to the value of the information in the conduct of collective bargaining.

[850]

NOTES

Commencement: 16 October 1992.

Sub-ss (1), (2) contain provisions formerly in the Employment Protection Act 1975, s 18(1), (2).

183 Complaint of failure to disclose information

(1) A trade union may present a complaint to the Central Arbitration Committee that an employer has failed—

(a) to disclose to representatives of the union information which he was required to disclose to them by section 181, or

(b) to confirm such information in writing in accordance with that section.

The complaint must be in writing and in such form as the Committee may require.

(2) If on receipt of a complaint the Committee is of the opinion that it is reasonably likely to be settled by conciliation, it shall refer the complaint to ACAS and shall notify the trade union and employer accordingly, whereupon ACAS shall seek to promote a settlement of the matter.

If a complaint so referred is not settled or withdrawn and ACAS is of the opinion that further attempts at conciliation are unlikely to result in a settlement, it shall inform the Committee of its opinion.

(3) If the complaint is not referred to ACAS or, if it is so referred, on ACAS informing the Committee of its opinion that further attempts at conciliation are unlikely to result in a settlement, the Committee shall proceed to hear and determine the complaint and shall make a declaration stating whether it finds the complaint well-founded, wholly or in part, and stating the reasons for its findings.

(4) On the hearing of a complaint any person who the Committee considers has a proper interest in the complaint is entitled to be heard by the Committee, but a failure to accord a hearing to a person other than the trade union and employer directly concerned does not affect the validity of any decision of the Committee in those proceedings.

(5) If the Committee finds the complaint wholly or partly well founded, the declaration shall specify—

(a) the information in respect of which the Committee finds that the complaint is well founded,

(b) the date (or, if more than one, the earliest date) on which the employer refused or failed to disclose or, as the case may be, to confirm in writing, any of the information in question, and

(c) a period (not being less than one week from the date of the declaration) within which the employer ought to disclose that information, or, as the case may be, to confirm it in writing.

(6) On a hearing of a complaint under this section a certificate signed by or on behalf of a Minister of the Crown and certifying that a particular request for information could not be complied with except by disclosing information the disclosure of which would have been against the interests of national security shall be conclusive evidence of that fact.

A document which purports to be such a certificate shall be taken to be such a certificate unless the contrary is proved.

[851]

NOTES
Commencement: 16 October 1992.
Sub-s (1) contains provisions formerly in the Employment Protection Act 1975, s 19(1). Sub-s (2)
contains provisions formerly in s 19(2), (3) of the 1975 Act. Sub-ss (3)–(6) contain provisions formerly
in s 19(4)–(7) of the 1975 Act.

184 Further complaint of failure to comply with declaration

(1) After the expiration of the period specified in a declaration under section
183(5)(c) the trade union may present a further complaint to the Central Arbitration
Committee that the employer has failed to disclose or, as the case may be, to confirm
in writing to representatives of the union information specified in the declaration.

The complaint must be in writing and in such form as the Committee may require.

(2) On receipt of a further complaint the Committee shall proceed to hear and
determine the complaint and shall make a declaration stating whether they find the
complaint well-founded, wholly or in part, and stating the reasons for their finding.

(3) On the hearing of a further complaint any person who the Committee consider
has a proper interest in that complaint shall be entitled to be heard by the Committee,
but a failure to accord a hearing to a person other than the trade union and employer
directly concerned shall not affect the validity of any decision of the Committee in
those proceedings.

(4) If the Committee find the further complaint wholly or partly well-founded
the declaration shall specify the information in respect of which the Committee find
that that complaint is well-founded.   **[852]**

NOTES
Commencement: 16 October 1992.
Sub-ss (1)–(4) contain provisions formerly in the Employment Protection Act 1975, s 20(1)–(4).

185 Determination of claim and award

(1) On or after presenting a further complaint under section 184 the trade union may
present to the Central Arbitration Committee a claim, in writing, in respect of one or
more descriptions of employees (but not workers who are not employees) specified
in the claim that their contracts should include the terms and conditions specified in
the claim.

(2) The right to present a claim expires if the employer discloses or, as the case
may be, confirms in writing, to representatives of the trade union the information
specified in the declaration under section 183(5) or 184(4); and a claim presented
shall be treated as withdrawn if the employer does so before the Committee make an
award on the claim.

(3) If the Committee find, or have found, the further complaint wholly or partly
well-founded, they may, after hearing the parties, make an award that in respect of
any description of employees specified in the claim the employer shall, from a
specified date, observe either

(a) the terms and conditions specified in the claim; or
(b) other terms and conditions which the Committee consider appropriate.

The date specified may be earlier than that on which the award is made but not
earlier than the date specified in accordance with section 183(5)(b) in the declaration
made by the Committee on the original complaint.

(4) An award shall be made only in respect of a description of employees, and

shall comprise only terms and conditions relating to matters in respect of which the trade union making the claim is recognised by the employer.

(5) Terms and conditions which by an award under this section an employer is required to observe in respect of an employee have effect as part of the employee's contract of employment as from the date specified in the award, except in so far as they are superseded or varied—

    (a) by a subsequent award under this section,

    (b) by a collective agreement between the employer and the union for the time being representing that employee, or

    (c) by express or implied agreement between the employee and the employer so far as that agreement effects an improvement in terms and conditions having effect by virtue of the award.

(6) Where—

    (a) by virtue of any enactment, other than one contained in this section, providing for minimum remuneration or terms and conditions, a contract of employment is to have effect as modified by an award, order or other instrument under that enactment, and

    (b) by virtue of an award under this section any terms and conditions are to have effect as part of that contract,

that contract shall have effect in accordance with that award, order or other instrument or in accordance with the award under this section, whichever is the more favourable, in respect of any terms and conditions of that contract, to the employee.

(7) No award may be made under this section in respect of terms and conditions of employment which are fixed by virtue of any enactment. **[853]**

NOTES

Commencement: 16 October 1992.

Sub-ss (1), (2) contain provisions formerly in the Employment Protection Act 1975, s 21(1), (2). Sub-s (3) contains provisions formerly in s 21(3), (4) of the 1975 Act. Sub-s (4) contains provisions formerly in s 21(5)(a) of the 1975 Act. Sub-ss (5)–(7) contain provisions formerly in s 21(6)–(8) of the 1975 Act.

Prohibition of union recognition requirements

186 Recognition requirement in contract for goods or services void

A term or condition of a contract for the supply of goods or services is void in so far as it purports to require a party to the contract—

    (a) to recognise one or more trade unions (whether or not named in the contract) for the purpose of negotiating on behalf of workers, or any class of worker, employed by him, or

    (b) to negotiate or consult with, or with an official of, one or more trade unions (whether or not so named). **[854]**

NOTES

Commencement: 16 October 1992.

This section contains provisions formerly in the Employment Act 1982, s 13(1).

187 Refusal to deal on grounds of union exclusion prohibited

(1) A person shall not refuse to deal with a supplier or prospective supplier of goods or services if the ground or one of the grounds for his action is that the person against whom it is taken does not, or is not likely to—

    (a) recognise one or more trade unions for the purpose of negotiating on behalf of workers, or any class of worker, employed by him, or

(b) negotiate or consult with, or with an official of, one or more trade unions.

(2) A person refuses to deal with a person if—

    (a) where he maintains (in whatever form) a list of approved suppliers of goods or services, or of persons from whom tenders for the supply of goods or services may be invited, he fails to include the name of that person in that list; or

    (b) in relation to a proposed contract for the supply of goods or services—

        (i) he excludes that person from the group of persons from whom tenders for the supply of the goods or services are invited, or

        (ii) he fails to permit that person to submit such a tender; or

    (c) *he otherwise determines not to enter into a contract with that person for the supply of the goods or services.*

(3) The obligation to comply with this section is a duty owed to the person with whom there is a refusal to deal and to any other person who may be adversely affected by its contravention; and a breach of the duty is actionable accordingly (subject to the defences and other incidents applying to actions for breach of statutory duty).

[855]

NOTES

Commencement: 16 October 1992.

Sub-s (1) contains provisions formerly in the Employment Act 1982, s 13(1)–(3). Sub-s (2) contains provisions formerly in ss 12(2)(a)–(c), 13(2) of the 1982 Act. Sub-s (3) contains provisions formerly in s 13(4) of the 1982 Act.

Sub-s (2): the existing para (c), printed in italics, becomes sub-para (iii) of para (b), and after that provision there is added the word "or" and a new para (c), by the Trade Union Reform and Employment Rights Act 1993, s 49(1), Sch 7, para 23, as from 30 August 1993 (SI 1993/1908, below, para **[1435]**), as follows—

"(c)   he terminates a contract with that person for the supply of goods or services.".

CHAPTER II

PROCEDURE FOR HANDLING REDUNDANCIES

Duty of employer to consult trade union representatives

188 Duty of employer to consult trade union representatives

(1) An employer proposing to dismiss as redundant an employee of a description in respect of which an independent trade union is recognised by him shall consult representatives of the union about the dismissal in accordance with this section.

(2) The consultation must begin at the earliest opportunity, and in any event—

    (a) where the employer is proposing to dismiss as redundant 100 or more employees at one establishment within a period of 90 days or less, at least 90 days before the first of those dismissals takes effect;

    (b) where the employer is proposing to dismiss as redundant at least 10 but less than 100 employees at one establishment within a period of 30 days or less, at least 30 days before the first of those dismissals takes effect.

(3) In determining how many employees an employer is proposing to dismiss as redundant no account shall be taken of employees in respect of whose proposed dismissals consultation has already begun.

(4) For the purposes of the consultation the employer shall disclose in writing to the trade union representatives—

    (a) the reasons for his proposals,

(b) the numbers and descriptions of employees whom it is proposed to dismiss as redundant,

(c) the total number of employees of any such description employed by the employer at the establishment in question,

(d) the proposed method of selecting the employees who may be dismissed, *and*

(e) the proposed method of carrying out the dismissals, with due regard to any agreed procedure, including the period over which the dismissals are to take effect [and

(f) the proposed method of calculating the amount of any redundancy payments to be made (otherwise than in compliance with an obligation imposed by or by virtue of any enactment) to employees who may be dismissed].

(5) That information shall be delivered to the trade union representatives, or sent by post to an address notified by them to the employer, or sent by post to the union at the address of its head or main office.

(6) In the course of the consultation the employer shall—

(a) consider any representations made by the trade union representatives, and

(b) reply to those representations and, if he rejects any of those representations, state his reasons.

(7) If in any case there are special circumstances which render it not reasonably practicable for the employer to comply with a requirement of subsection (2), (4) or (6), the employer shall take all such steps towards compliance with that requirement as are reasonably practicable in those circumstances.

[Where the decision leading to the proposed dismissals is that of a person controlling the employer (directly or indirectly), a failure on the part of that person to provide information to the employer shall not constitute special circumstances rendering it not reasonably practicable for the employer to comply with such a requirement.]

(8) This section does not confer any rights on a trade union or an employee except as provided by sections 189 to 192 below.   **[856]**

NOTES

Commencement: 16 October 1992.

Sub-s (1) contains provisions formerly in the Employment Protection Act 1975, s 99(1). Sub-s (2) contains provisions formerly in s 99(3) of the 1975 Act, as amended by the Employment Protection (Handling of Redundancies) Variation Order 1979, SI 1979/958. Sub-ss (3)–(8) contain provisions formerly in s 99(4)–(9) of the 1975 Act.

Sub-s (4): word "and" in italics at the end of para (d) repealed, and word "and" at the end of para (e) and para (f) added, by the Trade Union Reform and Employment Rights Act 1993, ss 34(1), (2)(a), 51, Sch 10, as from 30 August 1993 (SI 1993/1908, below, para **[1435]**).

Sub-s (6): substituted by the Trade Union Reform and Employment Rights Act 1993, s 34(1), (2)(b), as from 30 August 1993 (SI 1993/1908, below, para **[1435]**), as follows—

"(6) The consultation required by this section shall include consultation about ways of—

(a) avoiding the dismissals,

(b) reducing the numbers of employees to be dismissed, and

(c) mitigating the consequences of the dismissals,

and shall be undertaken by the employer with a view to reaching agreement with the trade union representatives.".

Sub-s (7): proviso added by the Trade Union Reform and Employment Rights Act 1993, s 34(1), (2)(c), as from 30 August 1993 (SI 1993/1908, below, para **[1435]**).

For transitional provisions affecting the commencement of amendments under the 1993 Act, see SI 1993/1908, Art 3(12).

189 Complaint by trade union and protective award

(1) Where an employer has dismissed as redundant, or is proposing to dismiss as redundant, one or more employees of a description in respect of which an independent

trade union is recognised by him, and has not complied with the requirements of section 188, the union may present a complaint to an industrial tribunal on that ground.

(2) If the tribunal finds the complaint well-founded it shall make a declaration to that effect and may also make a protective award.

(3) A protective award is an award in respect of one or more descriptions of employees—

(a) who have been dismissed as redundant, or whom it is proposed to dismiss as redundant, and

(b) in respect of whose dismissal or proposed dismissal the employer has failed to comply with a requirement of section 188,

ordering the employer to pay remuneration for the protected period.

(4) The protected period—

(a) begins with the date on which the first of the dismissals to which the complaint relates takes effect, or the date of the award, whichever is the earlier, and

(b) is of such length as the tribunal determines to be just and equitable in all the circumstances having regard to the seriousness of the employer's default in complying with any requirement of section 188;

but shall not exceed 90 days in a case falling within section 188(2)(a), 30 days in a case falling within section 188(2)(b), or 28 days in any other case.

(5) An industrial tribunal shall not consider a complaint under this section unless it is presented to the tribunal—

(a) before the proposed dismissal takes effect, or

(b) before the end of the period of three months beginning with the date on which the dismissal takes effect, or

(c) where the tribunal is satisfied that it was not reasonably practicable for the complaint to be presented within the period of three months, within such further period as it considers reasonable.

(6) If on a complaint under this section a question arises—

(a) whether there were special circumstances which rendered it not reasonably practicable for the employer to comply with any requirement of section 188, or

(b) whether he took all such steps towards compliance with that requirement as were reasonably practicable in those circumstances,

it is for the employer to show that there were and that he did.   **[857]**

NOTES
Commencement: 16 October 1992.
Sub-s (1) contains provisions formerly in the Employment Protection Act 1975, s 101(1), (7). Sub-ss (2)–(5) contain provisions formerly in s 101(3)–(6) of the 1975 Act. Sub-s (6) contains provisions formerly in s 101(2) of the 1975 Act.

190 Entitlement under protective award

(1) Where an industrial tribunal has made a protective award, every employee of a description to which the award relates is entitled, subject to the following provisions and to section 191, to be paid remuneration by his employer for the protected period.

(2) The rate of remuneration payable is a week's pay for each week of the period; and remuneration in respect of a period less than one week shall be calculated by reducing proportionately the amount of a week's pay.

(3) Any payment made to an employee by an employer in respect of a period falling within a protected period—

(a) *under the employee's contract of employment, or*

(b) *by way of damages for breach of that contract,*

shall go towards discharging the employer's liability to pay remuneration under the protective award in respect of that first mentioned period.

Conversely, any payment of remuneration under a protective award in respect of any period shall go towards discharging any liability of the employer under, or in respect of any breach of, the contract of employment in respect of that period.

(4) An employee is not entitled to remuneration under a protective award in respect of a period during which he is employed by the employer unless he would be entitled to be paid by the employer in respect of that period—

(a) by virtue of his contract of employment, or

(b) by virtue of Schedule 3 to the Employment Protection (Consolidation) Act 1978 (rights of employee in period of notice),

if that period fell within the period of notice required to be given by section 49(1) of that Act.

(5) Schedule 14 to the Employment Protection (Consolidation) Act 1978 applies with respect to the calculation of a week's pay for the purposes of this section.

The calculation date for the purposes of Part II of that Schedule is the date on which the protective award was made or, in the case of an employee who was dismissed before the date on which the protective award was made, the date which by virtue of paragraph 7(1)(k) or (1) of that Schedule is the calculation date for the purpose of computing the amount of a redundancy payment in relation to that dismissal (whether or not the employee concerned is entitled to any such payment).

(6) If an employee of a description to which a protective award relates dies during the protected period, the award has effect in his case as if the protected period ended on his death.   [858]

NOTES
Commencement: 16 October 1992.
Sub-ss (1)–(4) contain provisions formerly in the Employment Protection Act 1975, s 102(1)–(4), as amended, in the case of s 102(4), by the Employment Protection (Consolidation) Act 1978, s 159(2), Sch 16, para 23(1), (4). Sub-s (5) contains provisions formerly in s 106(3) of the 1975 Act, as amended by s 159(2) of, Sch 16, para 23(1), (6) to, the 1978 Act. Sub-s (6) contains provisions formerly in Sch 12, Pt I, para 7 to the 1975 Act.
Sub-s (3): repealed by the Trade Union Reform and Employment Rights Act 1993, ss 34(1), (3), 51, Sch 10, as from 30 August 1993 (SI 1993/1908, below, para [**1435**]).
For transitional provisions affecting this repeal see SI 1993/1908, Art 3(12).

191 Termination of employment during protected period

(1) Where the employee is employed by the employer during the protected period and—

(a) he is fairly dismissed by his employer *for a reason other than redundancy,* or

(b) he unreasonably terminates the contract of employment,

then, subject to the following provisions, he is not entitled to remuneration under the protective award in respect of any period during which but for that dismissal or termination he would have been employed.

(2) If an employer makes an employee an offer (whether in writing or not and whether before or after the ending of his employment under the previous contract) to renew his contract of employment, or to re-engage him under a new contract, so that the renewal or re-engagement would take effect before or during the protected period, and either—

    (a) the provisions of the contract as renewed, or of the new contract, as to the capacity and place in which he would be employed, and as to the other terms and conditions of his employment, would not differ from the corresponding provisions of the previous contract, or

    (b) the offer constitutes an offer of suitable employment in relation to the employee,

the following subsections have effect.

(3) If the employee unreasonably refuses the offer, he is not entitled to remuneration under the protective award in respect of a period during which but for that refusal he would have been employed.

(4) If the employee's contract of employment is renewed, or he is re-engaged under a new contract of employment, in pursuance of such an offer as is referred to in subsection (2)(b), there shall be a trial period in relation to the contract as renewed, or the new contract (whether or not there has been a previous trial period under this section).

(5) The trial period begins with the ending of his employment under the previous contract and ends with the expiration of the period of four weeks beginning with the date on which he starts work under the contract as renewed, or the new contract, or such longer period as may be agreed in accordance with subsection (6) for the purpose of retraining the employee for employment under that contract.

(6) Any such agreement—

    (a) shall be made between the employer and the employee or his representative before the employee starts work under the contract as renewed or, as the case may be, the new contract,

    (b) shall be in writing,

    (c) shall specify the date of the end of the trial period, and

    (d) shall specify the terms and conditions of employment which will apply in the employee's case after the end of that period.

(7) If during the trial period—

    (a) the employee, for whatever reason, terminates the contract, or gives notice to terminate it and the contract is thereafter, in consequence, terminated, or

    (b) the employer, for a reason connected with or arising out of the change to the renewed, or new, employment, terminates the contract, or gives notice to terminate it and the contract is thereafter, in consequence, terminated,

the employee remains entitled under the protective award unless, in a case falling within paragraph (a), he acted unreasonably in terminating or giving notice to terminate the contract.   **[859]**

NOTES

Commencement: 16 October 1992.

Sub-ss (1)–(7) contain provisions formerly in the Employment Protection Act 1975, s 102(5)–(11).

Sub-s (1): for the words in italics in para (a) there are substituted the words "otherwise than as redundant" by the Trade Union Reform and Employment Rights Act 1993, s 49(2), Sch 8, para 70, as from 30 August 1993 (SI 1993/1908, below, para **[1435]**).

192 Complaint by employee to industrial tribunal

(1) An employee may present a complaint to an industrial tribunal on the ground that he is an employee of a description to which a protective award relates and that his employer has failed, wholly or in part, to pay him remuneration under the award.

(2) An industrial tribunal shall not entertain a complaint under this section unless it is presented to the tribunal—

(a) before the end of the period of three months beginning with the day (or, if the complaint relates to more than one day, the last of the days) in respect of which the complaint is made of failure to pay remuneration, or

(b) where the tribunal is satisfied that it was not reasonably practicable for the complaint to be presented within the period of three months, within such further period as it may consider reasonable.

(3) Where the tribunal finds a complaint under this section well founded it shall order the employer to pay the complainant the amount of remuneration which it finds is due to him.

(4) The remedy of an employee for infringement of his right to remuneration under a protective award is by way of complaint under this section, and not otherwise.

[860]

NOTES

Commencement: 16 October 1992.

Sub-ss (1)–(3) contain provisions formerly in the Employment Protection Act 1975, s 103(1)–(3). Sub-s (4) contains provisions formerly in s 108(1) (in part) of the 1975 Act.

Duty of employer to notify Secretary of State

193 Duty of employer to notify Secretary of State of certain redundancies

(1) An employer proposing to dismiss as redundant 100 or more employees at one establishment within a period of 90 days or less shall notify the Secretary of State, in writing, of his proposal at least 90 days before the first of those dismissals takes effect.

(2) An employer proposing to dismiss as redundant 10 or more employees at one establishment within a period of 30 days or less shall notify the Secretary of State, in writing, of his proposal at least 30 days before the first of those dismissals takes effect.

(3) In determining how many employees an employer is proposing to dismiss as redundant within the period mentioned in subsection (1) or (2), no account shall be taken of employees in respect of whose proposed dismissal notice has already been given to the Secretary of State.

(4) A notice under this section shall—

(a) be given to the Secretary of State by delivery to him or by sending it by post to him, at such address as the Secretary of State may direct in relation to the establishment where the employees proposed to be dismissed are employed,

(b) in a case where consultation with trade union representatives is required by section 188, identify the trade union concerned and state the date when consultation began, and

(c) be in such form and contain such particulars, in addition to those required by paragraph (b), as the Secretary of State may direct.

(5) After receiving a notice under this section from an employer the Secretary of State may by written notice require the employer to give him such further information as may be specified in the notice.

(6) Where a notice given under subsection (1) or subsection (2) relates to employees of a description in respect of which an independent trade union is recognised by the employer, the employer shall give a copy of the notice to representatives of that union.

The copy shall be delivered to them or sent by post to an address notified by them to the employer, or sent by post to the union at the address of its head or main office.

(7) If in any case there are special circumstances rendering it not reasonably practicable for the employer to comply with any of the requirements of subsections (1) to (6), he shall take all such steps towards compliance with that requirement as are reasonably practicable in the circumstances.

[Where the decision leading to the proposed dismissals is that of a person controlling the employer (directly or indirectly), a failure on the part of that person to provide information to the employer shall not constitute special circumstances rendering it not reasonably practicable for the employer to comply with any of those requirements.]   [861]

NOTES
Commencement: 16 October 1992.
Sub-ss (1), (2) contain provisions formerly in the Employment Protection Act 1975, s 100(1) (in part), as amended by the Employment Protection (Handling of Redundancies) Variation Order 1979, SI 1979/958. Sub-ss (3), (4) contain provisions formerly in s 100(2), (3) of the 1975 Act. Sub-s (5) contains provisions formerly in s 100(5) of the 1975 Act. Sub-s (6) contains provisions formerly in s 100(1) (in part), (4) of the 1975 Act. Sub-s (7) contains provisions formerly in s 100(6) of the 1975 Act.
Sub-s (7): proviso added by the Trade Union Reform and Employment Rights Act 1993, s 34(1), (4), as from 30 August 1993 (SI 1993/1908, below, para [**1435**]).
For transitional provisions as to this amendment see SI 1993/1908, Art 3(12).

194 Offence of failure to notify

(1) An employer who fails to give notice to the Secretary of State in accordance with section 193 commits an offence and is liable on summary conviction to a fine not exceeding level 5 on the standard scale.

(2) Proceedings in England or Wales for such an offence shall be instituted only by or with the consent of the Secretary of State or by an officer authorised for that purpose by special or general directions of the Secretary of State.

An officer so authorised may, although not of counsel or a solicitor, prosecute or conduct proceedings for such an offence before a magistrates' court.

(3) Where an offence under this section committed by a body corporate is proved to have been committed with the consent or connivance of, or to be attributable to neglect on the part of, any director, manager, secretary or other similar officer of the body corporate, or any person purporting to act in any such capacity, he as well as the body corporate is guilty of the offence and liable to be proceeded against and punished accordingly.

(4) Where the affairs of a body corporate are managed by its members, subsection (3) applies in relation to the acts and defaults of a member in connection with his functions of management as if he were a director of the body corporate.   [862]

NOTES
Commencement: 16 October 1992.
Sub-s (1) contains provisions formerly in the Employment Protection Act 1975, s 105(1), as affected by the Criminal Justice Act 1982, ss 38, 46. Sub-s (2) contains provisions formerly in s 105(2), (3) of the 1975 Act. Sub-ss (3), (4) contain provisions formerly in s 117(1), (2) of the 1975 Act.

Supplementary provisions

195 Meaning of "redundancy"

(1) In this Chapter, references to redundancy or to being redundant, in relation to an employee, are references to—

    (a) the fact that the employer has ceased, or intends to cease, to carry on the business for the purposes of which the employee is or was employed by him, or has ceased, or intends to cease, to carry on that business in the place where the employee is or was so employed, or

    (b) the fact that the requirements of that business for employees to carry out work of a particular kind, or for employees to carry out work of a particular kind in the place where he is or was so employed, have ceased or diminished or are expected to cease or diminish.

(2) In subsection (1)—

    "business" includes a trade or profession and includes any activity carried on by a body of persons, whether corporate or unincorporate; and

    "cease" means cease either permanently or temporarily and from whatever cause, and "diminish" has a corresponding meaning.

(3) For the purposes of any proceedings under this Chapter, the dismissal or proposed dismissal of an employee shall be presumed, unless the contrary is proved, to be by reason of redundancy.   **[863]**

NOTES
Commencement: 16 October 1992.
Sub-s (1) contains provisions formerly in the Employment Protection Act 1975, s 126(6). Sub-s (2) contains provisions formerly in s 126(1) (definition "business"), (7) of the 1975 Act. Sub-s (3) contains provisions formerly in s 106(2) of the 1975 Act.
Substituted by the Trade Union Reform and Employment Rights Act 1993, s 34(1), (5), as from 30 August 1993 (SI 1993/1908), as follows—
"195 Construction of references to dismissal as redundant etc

(1) In this Chapter references to dismissal as redundant are references to dismissal for a reason not related to the individual concerned or for a number of reasons all of which are not so related.

(2) For the purposes of any proceedings under this Chapter, where an employee is or is proposed to be dismissed it shall be presumed, unless the contrary is proved, that he is or is proposed to be dismissed as redundant.".
For transitional provisions as to this amendment see SI 1993/1908, Art 3(12).

196 Meaning of "trade union representative"

References in this Chapter to a trade union representative, in relation to an employer, are to an official or other person authorised by the trade union to carry on collective bargaining with that employer.   **[864]**

NOTES
Commencement: 16 October 1992.
This section contains provisions formerly in the Employment Protection Act 1975, s 99(2).

197 Power to vary provisions

(1) The Secretary of State may by order made by statutory instrument vary—

    (a) the provisions of sections 188(2) and 193(1) (requirements as to consultation and notification), and

    (b) the periods referred to at the end of section 189(4) (maximum protected period);

but no such order shall be made which has the effect of reducing to less than 30 days the periods referred to in sections 188(2) and 193(1) as the periods which must elapse before the first of the dismissals takes effect.

(2) No such order shall be made unless a draft of the order has been laid before Parliament and approved by a resolution of each House of Parliament.   **[865]**

NOTES
Commencement: 16 October 1992.
Sub-ss (1), (2) contain provisions formerly in the Employment Protection Act 1975, s 106(4), (5).

198 Power to adapt provisions in case of collective agreement

(1) This section applies where there is in force a collective agreement which establishes—

(a) arrangements for providing alternative employment for employees to whom the agreement relates if they are dismissed as redundant by an employer to whom it relates, or

(b) arrangements for *the handling of redundancies* [handling the dismissal of employees as redundant].

(2) On the application of all the parties to the agreement the Secretary of State may, if he is satisfied having regard to the provisions of the agreement that the arrangements are on the whole at least as favourable to those employees as the foregoing provisions of this Chapter, by order made by statutory instrument adapt, modify or exclude any of those provisions both in their application to all or any of those employees and in their application to any other employees of any such employer.

(3) The Secretary of State shall not make such an order unless the agreement—

(a) provides for procedures to be followed (whether by arbitration or otherwise) in cases where an employee to whom the agreement relates claims that any employer or other person to whom it relates has not complied with the provisions of the agreement, and

(b) provides that those procedures include a right to arbitration or adjudication by an independent referee or body in cases where (by reason of an equality of votes or otherwise) a decision cannot otherwise be reached,

or indicates that any such employee may present a complaint to an industrial tribunal that any such employer or other person has not complied with those provisions.

(4) An order under this section may confer on an industrial tribunal to whom a complaint is presented as mentioned in subsection (3) such powers and duties as the Secretary of State considers appropriate.

(5) An order under this section may be varied or revoked by a subsequent order thereunder either in pursuance of an application made by all or any of the parties to the agreement in question or without any such application.   **[866]**

NOTES
Commencement: 16 October 1992.
Sub-ss (1), (2) contain provisions formerly in the Employment Protection Act 1975, s 107(1). Sub-ss (3)–(5) contain provisions formerly in s 107(2)–(4) of the 1975 Act.
Sub-s (1): words in italics in para (b) substituted by words in square brackets immediately following by the Trade Union Reform and Employment Rights Act 1993, s 49(2), Sch 8, para 71, as from 30 August 1993 (SI 1993/1908, below, para **[1435]**).
Up to 1 September 1993 no orders had been made under this section or its predecessor.

Codes of Practice issued by ACAS

199 Issue of Codes of Practice by ACAS

(1) ACAS may issue Codes of Practice containing such practical guidance as it thinks fit for the purpose of promoting the improvement of industrial relations.

(2) In particular, ACAS shall in one or more Codes of Practice provide practical guidance on the following matters—

(a) the time off to be permitted by an employer to a trade union official in accordance with section 168 (time off for carrying out trade union duties);

(b) the time off to be permitted by an employer to a trade union member in accordance with section 170 (time off for trade union activities); and

(c) the information to be disclosed by employers to trade union representatives in accordance with sections 181 and 182 (disclosure of information for purposes of collective bargaining).

(3) The guidance mentioned in subsection (2)(a) shall include guidance on the circumstances in which a trade union official is to be permitted to take time off under section 168 in respect of duties connected with industrial action; and the guidance mentioned in subsection (2)(b) shall include guidance on the question whether, and the circumstances in which, a trade union member is to be permitted to take time off under section 170 for trade union activities connected with industrial action.

(4) ACAS may from time to time revise the whole or any part of a Code of Practice issued by it and issue that revised Code.   **[867]**

NOTES

Commencement: 16 October 1992.

Sub-s (1) contains provisions formerly in the Employment Protection Act 1975, s 6(1). Sub-ss (2), (3) contain provisions formerly in s 6(2) of the 1975 Act, as amended and repealed in part by the Employment Protection (Consolidation) Act 1978, s 159(2), Sch 16, para 23(1), (2). Sub-s (4) contains provisions formerly in s 6(10) (in part) of the 1975 Act.

Codes made under this section: Disciplinary Practice and Procedures in Employment (1977): Disclosure of Information to Trade Unions for Collective Bargaining Purposes (1977): Time off for Trade Union Duties and Activities (1991): printed below, paras **[3001]**–**[3020]**, **[3021]**–**[3043]** and **[3108]**–**[3147]** respectively.

200 Procedure for issue of Code by ACAS

(1) Where ACAS proposes to issue a Code of Practice, or a revised Code, it shall prepare and publish a draft of the Code, shall consider any representations made to it about the draft and may modify the draft accordingly.

(2) If ACAS determines to proceed with the draft, it shall transmit the draft to the Secretary of State who—

(a) if he approves of it, shall lay it before both Houses of Parliament, and

(b) if he does not approve of it, shall publish details of his reasons for withholding approval.

(3) A Code containing practical guidance on any of the matters referred to in section 199(2) shall not be issued unless the draft has been approved by a resolution of each House of Parliament; and if it is so approved, ACAS shall issue the Code in the form of the draft.

(4) In any other case the following procedure applies—

(a) if, within the period of 40 days beginning with the day on which the draft is laid before Parliament, (or, if copies are laid before the two Houses on different days, with the later of the two days) either House so resolves, no further proceedings shall be taken thereon, but without prejudice to the laying before Parliament of a new draft;

(b) if no such resolution is passed, ACAS shall issue the Code in the form of the draft.

In reckoning the period of 40 days no account shall be taken of any period during which Parliament is dissolved or prorogued or during which both Houses are adjourned for more than four days.

(5) A Code issued in accordance with this section shall come into effect on such day as the Secretary of State may appoint by order made by statutory instrument.

The order may contain such transitional provisions or savings as appear to him to be necessary or expedient.   **[868]**

NOTES
Commencement: 16 October 1992.
Sub-s (1) contains provisions formerly in the Employment Protection Act 1975, s 6(3), (10) (in part). Sub-ss (2), (3) contain provisions formerly in s 6(4), (5) (in part) of the 1975 Act. Sub-s (4) contains provisions formerly in s 6(6), (7), (8) (in part) of the 1975 Act. Sub-s (5) contains provisions formerly in s 6(5) (in part), (8) (in part), (9) of the 1975 Act.

201 Consequential revision of Code issued by ACAS

(1) A Code of Practice issued by ACAS may be revised by it in accordance with this section for the purpose of bringing it into conformity with subsequent statutory provisions by the making of consequential amendments and the omission of obsolete passages.

"Subsequent statutory provisions" means provisions made by or under an Act of Parliament and coming into force after the Code was issued (whether before or after the commencement of this Act).

(2) Where ACAS proposes to revise a Code under this section, it shall transmit a draft of the revised Code to the Secretary of State who—

(a) if he approves of it, shall lay the draft before each House of Parliament, and

(b) if he does not approve of it, shall publish details of his reasons for withholding approval.

(3) If within the period of 40 days beginning with the day on which the draft is laid before Parliament, (or, if copies are laid before the two Houses on different days, with the later of the two days) either House so resolves, no further proceedings shall be taken thereon, but without prejudice to the laying before Parliament of a new draft.

In reckoning the period of 40 days no account shall be taken of any period during which Parliament is dissolved or prorogued or during which both Houses are adjourned for more than four days.

(4) If no such resolution is passed ACAS shall issue the Code in the form of the draft and it shall come into effect on such day as the Secretary of State may appoint by order made by statutory instrument.

The order may contain such transitional provisions or savings as appear to the Secretary of State to be necessary or expedient.   **[869]**

NOTES
Commencement: 16 October 1992.
Sub-s (1) contains provisions formerly in the Employment Act 1990, s 12(1), (2)(b). Sub-ss (2), (3) contain provisions formerly in s 12(4), (5) (in part) of the 1990 Act. Sub-s (4) contains provisions formerly in s 12(6), (9) (both in part) of the 1990 Act.

202 Revocation of Code issued by ACAS

(1) A Code of Practice issued by ACAS may, at the request of ACAS, be revoked by the Secretary of State by order made by statutory instrument.

The order may contain such transitional provisions and savings as appear to him to be appropriate.

(2) If ACAS requests the Secretary of State to revoke a Code and he decides not to do so, he shall publish details of his reasons for his decision.

(3) An order shall not be made under this section unless a draft of it has been laid before and approved by resolution of each House of Parliament.   **[870]**

NOTES
Commencement: 16 October 1992.
Sub-s (1) contains provisions formerly in the Employment Act 1990, s 12(7)(a), (9) (in part). Sub-s (2) contains provisions formerly in s 12(8) of the 1990 Act. Sub-s (3) contains provisions formerly in s 12(7)(b) (in part) of the 1990 Act.

Codes of Practice issued by the Secretary of State

203 Issue of Codes of Practice by the Secretary of State

(1) The Secretary of State may issue Codes of Practice containing such practical guidance as he thinks fit for the purpose—

(a) of promoting the improvement of industrial relations, or
(b) of promoting what appear to him to be to be desirable practices in relation to the conduct by trade unions of ballots and elections.

(2) The Secretary of State may from time to time revise the whole or any part of a Code of Practice issued by him and issue that revised Code.   **[871]**

NOTES
Commencement: 16 October 1992.
Sub-s (1) contains provisions formerly in the Employment Act 1980, s 3(1), as amended by the Employment Act 1988, s 18(1). Sub-s (2) contains provisions formerly in s 3(6) (in part) of the 1980 Act.
Codes issued under this section: Picketing (revised 1992), below, paras [**3215**]–[**3278**], and Trade Union Ballots on Industrial Action (revised 1991), below, paras [**3148**]–[**3214**].

204 Procedure for issue of Code by Secretary of State

(1) When the Secretary of State proposes to issue a Code of Practice, or a revised Code, he shall after consultation with ACAS prepare and publish a draft of the Code, shall consider any representations made to him about the draft and may modify the draft accordingly.

(2) If he determines to proceed with the draft, he shall lay it before both Houses of Parliament and, if it is approved by resolution of each House, shall issue the Code in the form of the draft.

(3) A Code issued under this section shall come into effect on such day as the Secretary of State may by order appoint.

The order may contain such transitional provisions or savings as appear to him to be necessary or expedient.

(4) An order under subsection (3) shall be made by statutory instrument, which shall be subject to annulment in pursuance of a resolution of either House of Parliament.   **[872]**

NOTES
Commencement: 16 October 1992.
Sub-s (1) contains provisions formerly in the Employment Act 1980, s 3(2), (3), (6) (in part). Sub-s (2) contains provisions formerly in s 3(4) of the 1980 Act. Sub-ss (3), (4) contain provisions formerly in s 3(5) of the 1980 Act.

205 Consequential revision of Code issued by Secretary of State

(1) A Code of Practice issued by the Secretary of State may be revised by him in accordance with this section for the purpose of bringing it into conformity with subsequent statutory provisions by the making of consequential amendments and the omission of obsolete passages.

"Subsequent statutory provisions" means provisions made by or under an Act of Parliament and coming into force after the Code was issued (whether before or after the commencement of this Act).

(2) Where the Secretary of State proposes to revise a Code under this section, he shall lay a draft of the revised Code before each House of Parliament.

(3) If within the period of 40 days beginning with the day on which the draft is laid before Parliament, or, if copies are laid before the two Houses on different days, with the later of the two days, either House so resolves, no further proceedings shall be taken thereon, but without prejudice to the laying before Parliament of a new draft.

In reckoning the period of 40 days no account shall be taken of any period during which Parliament is dissolved or prorogued or during which both Houses are adjourned for more than four days.

(4) If no such resolution is passed the Secretary of State shall issue the Code in the form of the draft and it shall come into effect on such day as he may appoint by order made by statutory instrument.

The order may contain such transitional provisions and savings as appear to him to be appropriate.   **[873]**

NOTES
Commencement: 16 October 1992.
Sub-s (1) contains provisions formerly in the Employment Act 1990, s 12(1), (2)(a). Sub-s (2) contains provisions formerly in s 12(3) of the 1990 Act. Sub-s (3) contains provisions formerly in s 12(5) (in part) of the 1990 Act. Sub-s (4) contains provisions formerly in s 12(6), (9) (both in part) of the 1990 Act.

206 Revocation of Code issued by Secretary of State

(1) A Code of Practice issued by the Secretary of State may be revoked by him by order made by statutory instrument.

The order may contain such transitional provisions and savings as appear to him to be appropriate.

(2) An order shall not be made under this section unless a draft of it has been laid before and approved by resolution of each House of Parliament.   **[874]**

NOTES
Commencement: 16 October 1992.
Sub-ss (1), (2) contain provisions formerly in the Employment Act 1990, s 12(7), (9) (both in part).

Supplementary provisions

207 Effect of failure to comply with Code

(1) A failure on the part of any person to observe any provision of a Code of Practice issued under this Chapter shall not of itself render him liable to any proceedings.

(2) In any proceedings before an industrial tribunal or the Central Arbitration Committee any Code of Practice issued under this Chapter by ACAS shall be admissible in evidence, and any provision of the Code which appears to the tribunal or Committee to be relevant to any question arising in the proceedings shall be taken into account in determining that question.

(3) In any proceedings before a court or industrial tribunal or the Central Arbitration Committee any Code of Practice issued under this Chapter by the Secretary of State shall be admissible in evidence, and any provision of the Code which appears to the court, tribunal or Committee to be relevant to any question arising in the proceedings shall be taken into account in determining that question.   **[875]**

NOTES
Commencement: 16 October 1992.
This section contains provisions formerly in the Employment Protection Act 1975, s 6(11), and in the Employment Act 1980, s 3(8).

208 Provisions of earlier Code superseded by later

(1) If ACAS is of the opinion that the provisions of a Code of Practice to be issued by it under this Chapter will supersede the whole or part of a Code previously issued under this Chapter, by it or by the Secretary of State, it shall in the new Code state that on the day on which the new Code comes into effect the old Code or a specified part of it shall cease to have effect.

(2) If the Secretary of State is of the opinion that the provisions of a Code of Practice to be issued by him under this Chapter will supersede the whole or part of a Code previously issued under this Chapter by him or by ACAS, he shall in the new Code state that on the day on which the new Code comes into effect the old Code or a specified part of it shall cease to have effect.

(3) The above provisions do not affect any transitional provisions or savings made by the order bringing the new Code into effect.   **[876]**

NOTES
Commencement: 16 October 1992.
This section contains provisions formerly in the Employment Protection Act 1975, s 6(10A), as inserted by the Employment Act 1980, s 20(2), Sch 1, para 4, and in s 3(7) (in part) of the 1980 Act.

CHAPTER IV
GENERAL

Functions of ACAS

209 General duty to promote improvement of industrial relations

It is the general duty of ACAS to promote the improvement of industrial relations, *and in particular to encourage the extension of collective bargaining and the development and, where necessary, reform of collective bargaining machinery* [in particular, by exercising its functions in relation to the settlement of trade disputes under sections 210 and 212].   **[877]**

NOTES
Commencement: 16 October 1992.
This section contains provisions formerly in the Employment Protection Act 1975, s 1(2).
Words in italics substituted by words in square brackets immediately following by the Trade Union
Reform and Employment Rights Act 1993, ss 43(1), 51, Sch 10, as from 30 August 1993 (SI 1993/1908,
below, para **[1435]**).

210 Conciliation

(1) Where a trade dispute exists or is apprehended ACAS may, at the request of one or more parties to the dispute or otherwise, offer the parties to the dispute its assistance with a view to bringing about a settlement.

(2) The assistance may be by way of conciliation or by other means, and may include the appointment of a person other than an officer or servant of ACAS to offer assistance to the parties to the dispute with a view to bringing about a settlement.

(3) In exercising its functions under this section ACAS shall have regard to the desirability of encouraging the parties to a dispute to use any appropriate agreed procedures for negotiation or the settlement of disputes.   **[878]**

NOTES
Commencement: 16 October 1992.
Sub-ss (1)–(3) contain provisions formerly in the Employment Protection Act 1975, s 2(1)–(3).

211 Conciliation officers

(1) ACAS shall designate some of its officers to perform the functions of conciliation officers under any enactment (whenever passed) relating to matters which are or could be the subject of proceedings before an industrial tribunal.

(2) References in any such enactment to a conciliation officer are to an officer designated under this section.   **[879]**

NOTES
Commencement: 16 October 1992.
This section contains provisions formerly in the Employment Protection Act 1975, s 2(4).

212 Arbitration

(1) Where a trade dispute exists or is apprehended ACAS may, at the request of one or more of the parties to the dispute and with the consent of all the parties to the dispute, refer all or any of the matters to which the dispute relates for settlement to the arbitration of—

    (a) one or more persons appointed by ACAS for that purpose (not being officers or employees of ACAS), or

    (b) the Central Arbitration Committee.

(2) In exercising its functions under this section ACAS shall consider the likelihood of the dispute being settled by conciliation.

(3) Where there exist appropriate agreed procedures for negotiation or the settlement of disputes, ACAS shall not refer a matter for settlement to arbitration under this section unless—

    (a) those procedures have been used and have failed to result in a settlement, or

    (b) there is, in ACAS's opinion, a special reason which justifies arbitration under this section as an alternative to those procedures.

(4) Where a matter is referred to arbitration under subsection (1)(a)—

(a) if more than one arbitrator or arbiter is appointed, ACAS shall appoint one of them to act as chairman; and

(b) the award may be published if ACAS so decides and all the parties consent.

(5) Part I of the Arbitration Act 1950 (general provisions as to arbitration) does not apply to an arbitration under this section.   **[880]**

NOTES
Commencement: 16 October 1992.
Sub-s (1) contains provisions formerly in the Employment Protection Act 1975, s 3(1). Sub-ss (2), (3) contain provisions formerly in s 3(2) of the 1975 Act. Sub-s (4) contains provisions formerly in s 3(3), (4) of the 1975 Act. Sub-s (5) contains provisions formerly in s 3(5) of the 1975 Act.

213 Advice

(1) ACAS may give employers, employers' associations, workers and trade unions such advice as it thinks appropriate on matters concerned with industrial relations or employment policies.

The advice may be given on request or otherwise, and shall be without charge.

(2) The matters on which advice may be given include the following—

(a) the organisation of workers or employers for the purpose of collective bargaining;

(b) the recognition of trade unions by employers;

(c) machinery for the negotiation of terms and conditions of employment, and for joint consultation;

(d) procedures for avoiding and settling disputes and workers' grievances;

(e) questions relating to communication between employers and workers;

(f) facilities for officials of trade unions;

(g) procedures relating to the termination of employment;

(h) disciplinary matters;

(i) manpower planning, labour turnover and absenteeism;

(j) recruitment, retention, promotion and vocational training of workers;

(k) payment systems, including job evaluation and equal pay.

(3) ACAS may also publish general advice on matters concerned with industrial relations or employment policies, including any of the matters referred to above.
                                        [881]

NOTES
Commencement: 16 October 1992.
Sub-ss (1), (2) contain provisions formerly in the Employment Protection Act 1975, s 4(1). Sub-s (3) contains provisions formerly in s 4(2) of the 1975 Act.
Substituted by the Trade Union Reform and Employment Rights Act 1993, s 43(2), as from 30 August 1993 (SI 1993/1908, below, para [**1435**]), as follows—
"**213 Advice**
    (1) ACAS may, on request or otherwise, give employers, employers' associations, workers and trade unions such advice as it thinks appropriate on matters concerned with or affecting or likely to affect industrial relations.
    (2) ACAS may also publish general advice on matters concerned with or affecting or likely to affect industrial relations.".

214 Inquiry

(1) ACAS may, if it thinks fit, inquire into any question relating to industrial relations generally or to industrial relations in any particular industry or in any particular undertaking or part of an undertaking.

(2) The findings of an inquiry under this section, together with any advice given by ACAS in connection with those findings, may be published by ACAS if—

(a) it appears to ACAS that publication is desirable for the improvement of industrial relations, either generally or in relation to the specific question inquired into, and

(b) after sending a draft of the findings to all parties appearing to be concerned and taking account of their views, it thinks fit.   **[882]**

NOTES
Commencement: 16 October 1992.
Sub-ss (1), (2) contain provisions formerly in the Employment Protection Act 1975, s 5(1), (2).

Courts of inquiry

215 Inquiry and report by court of inquiry

(1) Where a trade dispute exists or is apprehended, the Secretary of State may inquire into the causes and circumstances of the dispute, and, if he thinks fit, appoint a court of inquiry and refer to it any matters appearing to him to be connected with or relevant to the dispute.

(2) The court shall inquire into the matters referred to it and report on them to the Secretary of State; and it may make interim reports if it thinks fit.

(3) Any report of the court, and any minority report, shall be laid before both Houses of Parliament as soon as possible.

(4) The Secretary of State may, before or after the report has been laid before Parliament, publish or cause to be published from time to time, in such manner as he thinks fit, any information obtained or conclusions arrived at by the court as the result or in the course of its inquiry.

(5) No report or publication made or authorised by the court or the Secretary of State shall include any information obtained by the court of inquiry in the course of its inquiry—

(a) as to any trade union, or

(b) as to any individual business (whether carried on by a person, firm, or company),

which is not available otherwise than through evidence given at the inquiry, except with the consent of the secretary of the trade union or of the person, firm, or company in question.

Nor shall any individual member of the court or any person concerned in the inquiry disclose such information without such consent.

(6) The Secretary of State shall from time to time present to Parliament a report of his proceedings under this section.   **[883]**

NOTES
Commencement: 16 October 1992.
Sub-s (1) contains provisions formerly in the Industrial Courts Act 1919, s 4(1) (in part), as repealed in part by the Employment Protection Act 1975, s 125(1), (3), Sch 16, Pt III, para 35, Pt IV, para 3(1), (2), Sch 18, and as amended by the Secretary of State for Employment and Productivity Order 1968, SI 1968/729, as read with the Secretary of State for Trade and Industry Order 1970, SI 1970/1537, art 3(1). Sub-s (2) contains provisions formerly in ss 4(1) (in part), 5(1) of the 1919 Act, as amended, in the case of s 4(1), by the 1968 Order. Sub-ss (3), (4) contain provisions formerly in s 5(2), (3) (in part) of the 1919 Act, as amended, in the case of s 5(3), by the 1968 Order. Sub-s (5) contains provisions formerly in s 5(3) (in part) of the 1919 Act, as amended by the 1968 Order. Sub-s (6) contains provisions formerly in s 13 of the 1919 Act, as amended by the 1968 Order.

216 Constitution and proceedings of court of inquiry

(1) A court of inquiry shall consist of—

(a) a chairman and such other persons as the Secretary of State thinks fit to appoint, or

(b) one person appointed by the Secretary of State,

as the Secretary of State thinks fit.

(2) A court may act notwithstanding any vacancy in its number.

(3) A court may conduct its inquiry in public or. in private, at its discretion.

(4) The Secretary of State may make rules regulating the procedure of a court of inquiry, including rules as to summoning of witnesses, quorum, and the appointment of committees and enabling the court to call for such documents as the court may determine to be relevant to the subject matter of the inquiry.

(5) A court of inquiry may, if and to such extent as may be authorised by rules under this section, by order require any person who appears to the court to have knowledge of the subject-matter of the inquiry—

(a) to supply (in writing or otherwise) such particulars in relation thereto as the court may require, and

(b) where necessary, to attend before the court and give evidence on oath;

and the court may administer or authorise any person to administer an oath for that purpose.

(6) Provision shall be made by rules under this section with respect to the cases in which persons may appear by counsel or solicitor in proceedings before a court of inquiry, and except as provided by those rules no person shall be entitled to appear in any such proceedings by counsel or solicitor. **[884]**

NOTES
Commencement: 16 October 1992.

Sub-ss (1), (2) contain provisions formerly in the Industrial Courts Act 1919, s 4(2), (3), as amended, in the case of s 4(2), by the Secretary of State for Employment and Productivity Order 1968, SI 1968/729, as read with the Secretary of State for Trade and Industry Order 1970, SI 1970/1537, art 3(1). Sub-s (3) contains provisions formerly in s 4(1) (in part) of the 1919 Act. Sub-ss (4), (5) contain provisions formerly in s 4(4), (5) of the 1919 Act, as amended, in the case of s 4(4), by the 1968 Order. Sub-s (6) contains provisions formerly in s 9 of the 1919 Act, as repealed in part by the Employment Protection Act 1975, s 125(1), (3), Sch 16, Pt III, para 35, Pt IV, para 3(1), (2), Sch 18.

Supplementary provisions

217 Exclusion of power of arbiter to state case to Court of Session

Section 3 of the Administration of Justice (Scotland) Act 1972 (power of arbiter to state case for opinion of Court of Session) does not apply to—

(a) any form of arbitration relating to a trade dispute, or

(b) any other arbitration arising from a collective agreement. **[885]**

NOTES
Commencement: 16 October 1992.

This section contains provisions formerly in the Administration of Justice (Scotland) Act 1972, s 3(3), as amended by the Employment Act 1982, s 21(2), Sch 3, para 11, and by the Employment Protection Act 1975, s 10(2).

218 Meaning of "trade dispute" in Part IV

(1) In this Part "trade dispute" means a dispute between employers and workers, or between workers and workers, which is connected with one or more of the following matters—

   (a) terms and conditions of employment, or the physical conditions in which any workers are required to work;

   (b) engagement or non-engagement, or termination or suspension of employment or the duties of employment, of one or more workers;

   (c) allocation of work or the duties of employment as between workers or groups of workers;

   (d) matters of discipline;

   (e) the membership or non-membership of a trade union on the part of a worker;

   (f) facilities for officials of trade unions; and

   (g) machinery for negotiation or consultation, and other procedures, relating to any of the foregoing matters, including the recognition by employers or employers' associations of the right of a trade union to represent workers in any such negotiation or consultation or in the carrying out of such procedures.

(2) A dispute between a Minister of the Crown and any workers shall, notwithstanding that he is not the employer of those workers, be treated for the purposes of this Part as a dispute between an employer and those workers if the dispute relates—

   (a) to matters which have been referred for consideration by a joint body on which, by virtue of any provision made by or under any enactment, that Minister is represented, or

   (b) to matters which cannot be settled without that Minister exercising a power conferred on him by or under an enactment.

(3) There is a trade dispute for the purpose of this Part even though it relates to matters occurring outside Great Britain.

(4) A dispute to which a trade union or employer's association is a party shall be treated for the purposes of this Part as a dispute to which workers or, as the case may be, employers are parties.

(5) In this section—

"employment" includes any relationship whereby one person personally does work or performs services for another; and

"worker", in relation to a dispute to which an employer is a party, includes any worker even if not employed by that employer.   **[886]**

NOTES

Commencement: 16 October 1992.

Sub-ss (1)–(5) contain provisions formerly in the Industrial Courts Act 1919, s 8 (definition "trade dispute"), as substituted by the Employment Act 1982, s 21(2), Sch 3, Pt II, para 10; and in the Employment Protection Act 1975, ss 126(1) (definition "trade dispute"), 126A(1)–(4), (6), as added, in the case of the definition "trade dispute" in s 126(1), by s 21(2) of, Sch 3, Pt II, para 13(1), (2) to, the 1982 Act, and as inserted, in the case of s 126A, by s 21(2) of, Sch 3, Pt II, para 13(1), (3) to, the 1982 Act.

PART V

INDUSTRIAL ACTION

Protection of acts in contemplation or furtherance of trade dispute

219 Protection from certain tort liabilities

(1) An act done by a person in contemplation or furtherance of a trade dispute is not actionable in tort on the ground only—

    (a) that it induces another person to break a contract or interferes or induces another person to interfere with its performance, or

    (b) that it consists in his threatening that a contract (whether one to which he is a party or not) will be broken or its performance interfered with, or that he will induce another person to break a contract or interfere with its performance.

(2) An agreement or combination by two or more persons to do or procure the doing of an act in contemplation or furtherance of a trade dispute is not actionable in tort if the act is one which if done without any such agreement or combination would not be actionable in tort.

(3) Nothing in subsections (1) and (2) prevents an act done in the course of picketing from being actionable in tort unless it is done in the course of attendance declared lawful by section 220 (peaceful picketing)

(4) Subsections (1) and (2) have effect subject to sections 222 to 225 (action excluded from protection) and *to section 226 (requirement of ballot before action by trade union); and in those sections "not protected" means excluded from the protection afforded by this section* [to sections 226 (requirement of ballot before action by trade union) and 234A (requirement of notice to employer of industrial action); and in those sections "not protected" means excluded from the protection afforded by this section or, where the expression is used with reference to a particular person, excluded from that protection as respects that person.]   **[887]**

NOTES

Commencement: 16 October 1992.

Sub-s (1) contains provisions formerly in the Trade Union and Labour Relations Act 1974, s 13(1), as substituted by the Trade Union and Labour Relations (Amendment) Act 1976, s 3(2). Sub-s (2) contains provisions formerly in s 13(4) of the 1974 Act. Sub-s (3) contains provisions formerly in s 16(2) of the Employment Act 1980. Sub-s (4) is a drafting provision.

Sub-s (4): words in italics substituted by words in square brackets immediately following by the Trade Union Reform and Employment Rights Act 1993, s 49(2), Sch 8, para 72, as from 30 August 1993 (SI 1993/1908, below, para **[1435]**).

220 Peaceful picketing

(1) It is lawful for a person in contemplation or furtherance of a trade dispute to attend—

    (a) at or near his own place of work, or

    (b) if he is an official of a trade union, at or near the place of work of a member of the union whom he is accompanying and whom he represents,

for the purpose only of peacefully obtaining or communicating information, or peacefully persuading any person to work or abstain from working.

(2) If a person works or normally works—

    (a) otherwise than at any one place, or

    (b) at a place the location of which is such that attendance there for a purpose mentioned in subsection (1) is impracticable, his place of work for the purposes of that subsection shall be any premises of his employer from which he works or from which his work is administered.

(3) In the case of a worker not in employment where—

(a) his last employment was terminated in connection with a trade dispute, or

(b) the termination of his employment was one of the circumstances giving rise to a trade dispute,

in relation to that dispute his former place of work shall be treated for the purposes of subsection (1) as being his place of work.

(4) A person who is an official of a trade union by virtue only of having been elected or appointed to be a representative of some of the members of the union shall be regarded for the purposes of subsection (1) as representing only those members; but otherwise an official of a union shall be regarded for those purposes as representing all its members.   **[888]**

NOTES

Commencement: 16 October 1992.

Sub-ss (1)–(4) contain provisions formerly in the Trade Union and Labour Relations Act 1974, s 15(1)–(4), as substituted by the Employment Act 1980, s 16(1), and as amended. in the case of s 16(3), by the Employment Act 1982, s 21(a), Sch 3, Pt II, para 12.

221 Restrictions on grant of injunctions and interdicts

(1) Where—

(a) an application for an injunction or interdict is made to a court in the absence of the party against whom it is sought or any in representative of his, and

(b) he claims, or in the opinion of the court would be likely to claim, that he acted in contemplation or furtherance of a trade dispute,

the court shall not grant the injunction or interdict unless satisfied that all steps which in the circumstances were reasonable have been taken with a view to securing that notice of the application and an opportunity of being heard with respect to the application have been given to him.

(2) Where—

(a) an application for an interlocutory injunction is made to a court pending the trial of an action, and

(b) the party against whom it is sought claims that he acted in contemplation or furtherance of a trade dispute,

the court shall, in exercising its discretion whether or not to grant the injunction, have regard to the likelihood of that party's succeeding at the trial of the action in establishing any matter which would afford a defence to the action under section 219 (protection from certain tort liabilities) or section 220 (peaceful picketing).

This subsection does not extend to Scotland.   **[889]**

NOTES

Commencement: 16 October 1992.

Sub-s (1) contains provisions formerly in the Trade Union and Labour Relations Act 1974, s 17(1), as renumbered by the Employment Protection Act 1975, s 125(1), Sch 16, Pt III, para 6. Sub-s (2) contains provisions formerly in s 17(2), (3) of the 1974 Act, as added by s 125(1) of, Sch 16, Pt III, para 6 to, the 1975 Act, and as repealed in part, in the case of s 17(2), by the Employment Act 1982, s 21(3), Sch 4.

Action excluded from protection

222 Action to enforce trade union membership

(1) An act is not protected if the reason, or one of the reasons, for which it is done is the fact or belief that a particular employer—

    (a) is employing, has employed or might employ a person who is not a member of a trade union, or

    (b) is failing, has failed or might fail to discriminate against such a person.

(2) For the purposes of subsection (1)(b) an employer discriminates against a person if, but only if, he ensures that his conduct in relation to—

    (a) persons, or persons of any description, employed by him, or who apply to be, or are, considered by him for employment, or

    (b) the provision of employment for such persons,

is different, in some or all cases, according to whether or not they are members of a trade union, and is more favourable to those who are.

(3) An act is not protected if it constitutes, or is one of a number of acts which together constitute, an inducement or attempted inducement of a person—

    (a) to incorporate in a contract to which that person is a party, or a proposed contract to which he intends to be a party, a term or condition which is or would be void by virtue of section 144 (union membership requirement in contract for goods or services), or

    (b) to contravene section 145 (refusal to deal with person on grounds relating to union membership).

(4) References in this section to an employer employing a person are to a person acting in the capacity of the person for whom a worker works or normally works.

(5) References in this section to not being a member of a trade union are to not being a member of any trade union, of a particular trade union or of one of a number of particular trade unions.

Any such reference includes a reference to not being a member of a particular branch or section of a trade union or of one of a number of particular branches or sections of a trade union. **[890]**

NOTES

Commencement: 16 October 1992.

Sub-ss (1), (2) contain provisions formerly in the Employment Act 1988, s 10(1), (2) (both in part). Sub-s (3) contains provisions formerly in the Employment Act 1982, s 14(1) (in part). Sub-s (4) contains provisions formerly in s 10(3)(a) of the 1988 Act. Sub-s (5) contains provisions formerly in s 10(1), (2) (both in part), (3)(b) of the 1988 Act.

223 Action taken because of dismissal for taking unofficial action

An act is not protected if the reason, or one of the reasons, for doing it is the fact or belief that an employer has dismissed one or more employees in circumstances such that by virtue of section 237 (dismissal in connection with unofficial action) they have no right to complain of unfair dismissal. **[891]**

NOTES

Commencement: 16 October 1992.

This section contains provisions formerly in the Employment Act 1990, s 9(2), (3).

224 Secondary action

(1) An act is not protected if one of the facts relied on for the purpose of establishing liability is that there has been secondary action which is not lawful picketing.

(2) There is secondary action in relation to a trade dispute when, and only when, a person—

(a) induces another to break a contract of employment or interferes or induces another to interfere with its performance, or

(b) threatens that a contract of employment under which he or another is employed will be broken or its performance interfered with, or that he will induce another to break a contract of employment or to interfere with its performance,

and the employer under the contract of employment is not the employer party to the dispute.

(3) Lawful picketing means acts done in the course of such attendance as is declared lawful by section 220 (peaceful picketing)—

(a) by a worker employed (or, in the case of a worker not in employment, last employed) by the employer party to the dispute, or

(b) by a trade union official whose attendance is lawful by virtue of subsection (1)(b) of that section.

(4) For the purposes of this section an employer shall not be treated as party to a dispute between another employer and workers of that employer; and where more than one employer is in dispute with his workers, the dispute between each employer and his workers shall be treated as a separate dispute.

In this subsection "worker" has the same meaning as in section 244 (meaning of "trade dispute").

(5) An act in contemplation or furtherance of a trade dispute which is primary action in relation to that dispute may not be relied on as secondary action in relation to another trade dispute.

Primary action means such action as is mentioned in paragraph (a) or (b) of subsection (2) where the employer under the contract of employment is the employer party to the dispute.

(6) In this section "contract of employment" includes any contract under which one person personally does work or performs services for another, and related expressions shall be construed accordingly.   **[892]**

NOTES
Commencement: 16 October 1992.
Sub-ss (1)–(6) contain provisions formerly in the Employment Act 1990, s 4(1)–(6).

225 Pressure to impose union recognition requirement

(1) An act is not protected if it constitutes, or is one of a number of acts which together constitute, an inducement or attempted inducement of a person—

(a) to incorporate in a contract to which that person is a party, or a proposed contract to which he intends to be a party, a term or condition which is or would be void by virtue of section 186 (recognition requirement in contract for goods or services), or

(b) to contravene section 187 (refusal to deal with person on grounds of union exclusion).

(2) An act is not protected if—

(a) it interferes with the supply (whether or not under a contract) of goods or services, or can reasonably be expected to have that effect, and

(b) one of the facts relied upon for the purpose of establishing liability is that a person has—

(i) induced another to break a contract of employment or interfered or induced another to interfere with its performance, or

(ii) threatened that a contract of employment under which he or another is employed will be broken or its performance interfered with, or that he will induce another to break a contract of employment or to interfere with its performance, and

(c) the reason, or one of the reasons, for doing the act is the fact or belief that the supplier (not being the employer under the contract of employment mentioned in paragraph (b)) does not, or might not—

(i) recognise one or more trade unions for the purpose of negotiating on behalf of workers, or any class of worker, employed by him, or

(ii) negotiate or consult with, or with an official of, one or more trade unions.   **[893]**

NOTES
Commencement: 16 October 1992.
Sub-s (1) contains provisions formerly in the Employment Act 1982, s 14(1) (in part). Sub-s (2) contains provisions formerly in s 14(2), (3) of the 1982 Act, as substituted, in the case of s 14(3), by the Employment Act 1988, s 33(1), Sch 3, Pt I, para 4.

Requirement of ballot before action by trade union

226 Requirement of ballot before action by trade union

(1) An act done by a trade union to induce a person to take part, or continue to take part, in industrial action *is not protected unless the industrial action has the support of a ballot.*

[In this section "the relevant time", in relation to an act by a trade union to induce a person to take part, or continue to take part, in industrial action, means the time at which proceedings are commenced in respect of the act.]

(2) Industrial action shall be regarded as having the support of a ballot only if—

(a) the union has held a ballot in respect of the action in relation to which the requirements of sections 227 to 232 were satisfied,

(b) the majority voting in that ballot answered "Yes" to the question applicable in accordance with section 229(2) to industrial action of the kind to which the act of inducement relates, and

(c) the requirements of section 233 (calling of industrial action with support of ballot) are satisfied.

(3) Where separate workplace ballots are held by virtue of *section 228(1), industrial action shall be regarded as having the support of a ballot if the above conditions are satisfied in relation* to the ballot for the place of work of the person induced to take part, or continue to take part, in the industrial action.

(4) For the purposes of this section an inducement, in relation to a person, includes an inducement which is or would be ineffective, whether because of his unwillingness to be influenced by it or for any other reason.   **[894]**

NOTES
Commencement: 16 October 1992.

Sub-s (1) contains provisions formerly in the Trade Union Act 1984, s 10(1), as substituted by the Employment Act 1990, s 16(1), Sch 2, para 2(1), (2). Sub-s (2) contains provisions formerly in s 10(3), (4), (4A) of the 1984 Act, as substituted, in the case of s 10(4), (4A), by the Employment Act 1988, s 33(1), Sch 3, Pt I, para 5(7), and as amended, in the case of s 10(3), (4), (4A), by s 16(1) of, Sch 2, para 2(1), (3), (5), (6) to, the 1990 Act. Sub-s (3) contains provisions formerly in s 10(3A) of the 1984 Act, as inserted by s 17(2) of the 1988 Act, and as amended by s 16(1) of, Sch 2, para 2(1), (4) to, the 1990 Act. Sub-s (4) contains provisions formerly in s 1(6) of the 1988 Act, as applied by s 11(11) (in part) of the 1984 Act, as amended, in the case of s 11(11), by s 33(1) of, Sch 3, Pt I, para 5(8)(f) to, the 1988 Act.

Sub-s (1): for the words in italics there is substituted the following, by the Trade Union Reform and Employment Rights Act 1993, s 18(1), as from 30 August 1993 (SI 1993/1908, below, para **[1435]**)—
"—

(a) is not protected unless the industrial action has the support of a ballot, and
(b) where section 226A falls to be complied with in relation to the person's employer, is not protected as respects the employer unless the trade union has complied with section 226A in relation to him.".

and the words in square brackets at the end of that subsection are added by s 49(2) of, Sch 8, para 73(a) to, the 1993 Act, as from 30 August 1993 (SI 1993/1908, below, para **[1435]**).

Sub-s (2): paras (a)–(c) substituted by the Trade Union Reform and Employment Rights Act 1993, s 49(2), Sch 8, para 73(b), as from 30 August 1993 (SI 1993/1908, below, para **[1435]**), as follows—
"(a) the union has held a ballot in respect of the action—

(i) in relation to which the requirements of section 226B so far as applicable before and during the holding of the ballot were satisfied,
(ii) in relation to which the requirements of sections 227 to 231A were satisfied, and
(iii) in which the majority voting in the ballot answered "Yes" to the question applicable in accordance with section 229(2) to industrial action of the kind to which the act of inducement relates;

(b) such of the requirements of the following sections as have fallen to be satisfied at the relevant time have been satisfied, namely—

(i) section 226B so far as applicable after the holding of the ballot, and
(ii) section 231B; and

(c) the requirements of section 233 (calling of industrial action with support of ballot) are satisfied.

Any reference in this subsection to a requirement of a provision which is disapplied or modified by section 232 has effect subject to that section.";

Sub-s (3): words in italics substituted by the Trade Union Reform and Employment Rights Act 1993, s 49(2), Sch 8, para 73(c), as from 30 August 1993 (SI 1993/1908, below, para **[1435]**), as follows—
"section 228(1)—

(a) industrial action shall be regarded as having the support of a ballot if the conditions specified in subsection (2) are satisfied, and
(b) the trade union shall be taken to have complied with the requirements relating to a ballot imposed by section 226A if those requirements are complied with,

in relation".

[226A Notice of ballot and sample voting paper for employers

(1) The trade union must take such steps as are reasonably necessary to ensure that—

(a) not later than the seventh day before the opening day of the ballot, the notice specified in subsection (2), and

(b) not later than the third day before the opening day of the ballot, the sample voting paper specified in subsection (3),

is received by every person who it is reasonable for the union to believe (at the latest time when steps could be taken to comply with paragraph (a)) will be the employer of persons who will be entitled to vote in the ballot.

(2) The notice referred to in paragraph (a) of subsection (1) is a notice in writing—

(a) stating that the union intends to hold the ballot,

(b) specifying the date which the union reasonably believes will be the opening day of the ballot, and

(c) describing (so that he can readily ascertain them) the employees of the employer who it is reasonable for the union to believe (at the time when the steps to comply with that paragraph are taken) will be entitled to vote in the ballot.

(3) The sample voting paper referred to in paragraph (b) of subsection (1) is—

(a) a sample of the form of voting paper which is to be sent to the employees who it is reasonable for the trade union to believe (at the time when the steps to comply with paragraph (a) of that subsection are taken) will be entitled to vote in the ballot, or

(b) where they are not all to be sent the same form of voting paper, a sample of each form of voting paper which is to be sent to any of them.

(4) In this section references to the opening day of the ballot are references to the first day when a voting paper is sent to any person entitled to vote in the ballot.

(5) This section, in its application to a ballot in which merchant seamen to whom section 230(2A) applies are entitled to vote, shall have effect with the substitution in subsection (3), for references to the voting paper which is to be sent to the employees, of references to the voting paper which is to be sent or otherwise provided to them.]

[895]

NOTE
Inserted by the Trade Union Reform and Employment Rights Act 1993, s 18(2), as from 30 August 1993 (SI 1993/1908, below, para **[1435]**).

[226B Appointment of scrutineer

(1) The trade union shall, before the ballot in respect of the industrial action is held, appoint a qualified person ("the scrutineer") whose terms of appointment shall require him to carry out in relation to the ballot the functions of—

(a) taking such steps as appear to him to be appropriate for the purpose of enabling him to make a report to the trade union (see section 231B); and

(b) making the report as soon as reasonably practicable after the date of the ballot and, in any event, not later than the end of the period of four weeks beginning with that date.

(2) A person is a qualified person in relation to a ballot if—

(a) he satisfies such conditions as may be specified for the purposes of this section by order of the Secretary of State or is himself so specified; and

(b) the trade union has no grounds for believing either that he will carry out the functions conferred on him under subsection (1) otherwise than competently or that his independence in relation to the union, or in relation to the ballot, might reasonably be called into question.

An order under paragraph (a) shall be made by statutory instrument which shall be subject to annulment in pursuance of a resolution of either House of Parliament.

(3) The trade union shall ensure that the scrutineer duly carries out the functions conferred on him under subsection (1) and that there is no interference with the carrying out of those functions from the union or any of its members, officials or employees.

(4) The trade union shall comply with all reasonable requests made by the scrutineer for the purposes of, or in connection with, the carrying out of those functions.]

[896]

NOTE
Inserted by the Trade Union Reform and Employment Rights Act 1993, s 20(1), as from 30 August 1993 (SI 1993/1908, below, para **[1435]**).
Order under this section: Trade Union Ballots and Elections (Independent Scrutineer Qualifications) Order 1993, SI 1993/1909, below, para **[1443]**.

[226C Exclusion for small ballots

Nothing in section 226B, section 229(1A)(a) or section 231B shall impose a requirement on a trade union unless—

    (a) the number of members entitled to vote in the ballot, or

    (b) where separate workplace ballots are held in accordance with section 228(1), the aggregate of the number of members entitled to vote in each of them,

exceeds 50.]   **[897]**

NOTE

Inserted by the Trade Union Reform and Employment Rights Act 1993, s 20(4), as from 30 August 1993 (SI 1993/1908, below, para **[1435]**).

227 Entitlement to vote in ballot

(1) Entitlement to vote in the ballot must be accorded equally to all the members of the trade union who it is reasonable at the time of the ballot for the union to believe will be induced to take part or, as the case may be, to continue to take part in the industrial action in question, and to no others.

(2) The requirement in subsection (1) shall be taken not to have been satisfied if any person who was a member of the trade union at the time when the ballot was held and was denied entitlement to vote in the ballot is induced by the union to take part or, as the case may be, to continue to take part in the industrial action.   **[898]**

NOTES

Commencement: 16 October 1992.

Sub-s (1) contains provisions formerly in the Trade Union Act 1984, s 11(1), as amended by the Employment Act 1988, s 33(1), Sch 3, Pt I, para 5(8)(a). Sub-s (2) contains provisions formerly in s 11(2) of the 1984 Act, as amended by s 33(1) of, Sch 3, Pt I, para 5(8)(b) to, the 1988 Act.

228 Separate workplace ballots

(1) Subject to the following provisions, where the members who it is reasonable at the time of the ballot for the union to believe will be induced to take part, or continue to take part, in the industrial action in question have different places of work, separate ballots shall be held for each place of work.

    In such a case entitlement to vote in the ballot for each place of work shall be accorded only to such of those members as the union reasonably believes to have that as their place of work.

(2) Subsection (1) does not apply if at the time of the ballot it is reasonable for the union to believe, and it does believe, that all the members who are accorded entitlement to vote in the ballot have the same place of work.

(3) Subsection (1) does not apply if at the time of the ballot it is reasonable for the union to believe, and it does believe, that there is in relation to each of the members of the union who is accorded entitlement to vote in the ballot some factor (whether or not the same factor) which—

    (a) relates to the terms or conditions of his employment or to the occupational description which is applicable to him in his employment,

    (b) is a factor which he has in common with one or more of the other members of the union who are accorded that entitlement, and

(c) in a case where there are individuals employed by the same employer as he is who are members of the union but are not accorded that entitlement, is not a factor—

(i) which he has in common with any of those individuals, or

(ii) which individuals employed by that employer have in common as a consequence of having the same place of work;

nor does that subsection apply if at the time of the ballot it is reasonable for the union to believe, and it does believe, that the above conditions would be satisfied if any overseas members accorded entitlement to vote in the ballot were disregarded.

[(4) In this section "place of work", in relation to any person who is employed, means the premises occupied by his employer at or from which that person works or, where he does not work at or from any such premises or works at or from more than one set of premises, the premises occupied by his employer with which his employment has the closest connection.]   **[899]**

NOTES

Commencement: 16 October 1992.

Sub-s (1) contains provisions formerly in the Trade Union Act 1984, s 11(1A), as inserted by the Employment Act 1988, s 17(1). Sub-s (2) contains provisions formerly in s 11(1B)(a) of the 1984 Act, as so inserted. Sub-s (3) contains provisions formerly in s 11(1B)(b), (c) of the 1984 Act, as so inserted.

Sub-s (4): added by the Trade Union Reform and Employment Rights Act 1993, s 49(1), Sch 7, para 24, as from 30 August 1993 (SI 1993/1908, below, para **[1435]**).

229 Voting paper

(1) The method of voting in a ballot must be by the marking of a voting paper by the person voting.

[(1A) Each voting paper must—

(a) state the name of the independent scrutineer,

(b) clearly specify the address to which, and the date by which, it is to be returned,

(c) be given one of a series of consecutive whole numbers every one of which is used in giving a different number in that series to each voting paper printed or otherwise produced for the purposes of the ballot, and

(d) be marked with its number.

This subsection, in its application to a ballot in which merchant seamen to whom section 230(2A) applies are entitled to vote, shall have effect with the substitution, for the reference to the address to which the voting paper is to be returned, of a reference to the ship to which the seamen belong.]

(2) The voting paper must contain at least one of the following questions—

(a) a question (however framed) which requires the person answering it to say, by answering "Yes" or "No", whether he is prepared to take part or, as the case may be, to continue to take part in a strike;

(b) a question (however framed) which requires the person answering it to say, by answering "Yes" or "No", whether he is prepared to take part or, as the case may be, to continue to take part in industrial action short of a strike.

(3) The voting paper must specify who, in the event of a vote in favour of industrial action, is authorised for the purposes of section 233 to call upon members to take part or continue to take part in the industrial action.

The person or description of persons so specified need not be authorised under the rules of the union but must be within section *20(3)* [20(2)] (persons for whose acts the union is taken to be responsible).

(4) The following statement must (without being qualified or commented upon by anything else on the voting paper) appear on every voting paper—

'If you take part in a strike or other industrial action, you may be in breach of your contract of employment.'.   **[900]**

NOTES
Commencement: 16 October 1992.
Sub-s (1) contains provisions formerly in the Trade Union Act 1984, s 11(3) (in part). Sub-s (2) contains provisions formerly in s 11(4) of the 1984 Act, as amended by the Employment Act 1988, s 33(1), Sch 3, Pt I, para 5(8)(d). Sub-s (3) contains provisions formerly in s 11(4A) of the 1984 Act, as inserted by the Employment Act 1990, s 7(1). Sub-s (4) contains provisions formerly in s 11(3) (in part) of the 1984 Act, as amended by s 33(1) of, Sch 3, Pt I, para 5(8)(c) to, the 1988 Act.
Sub-s (1A): inserted by the Trade Union Reform and Employment Rights Act 1993, s 20(2), as from 30 August 1993 (SI 1993/1908, below, para **[1435]**).
Sub-s (3): figure in italics substituted by figure in square brackets immediately following by the Trade Union Reform and Employment Rights Act 1993, s 49(1), Sch 7, para 25, as from 30 August 1993 (SI 1993/1908, below, para **[1435]**).

230 Conduct of ballot

(1) Every person who is entitled to vote in the ballot must—

(a) be allowed to vote without interference from, or constraint imposed by, the union or any of its members, officials or employees, and

(b) so far as is reasonably practicable, be enabled to do so without incurring any direct cost to himself.

(2) So far as is reasonably practicable, every person who is entitled to vote in the ballot must—

(a) be supplied with a voting paper, or

(b) have one made available to him immediately before, immediately after, or during his working hours, at his place of work or at a place which is more convenient for him.

(3) So far as reasonably practicable, every person who is entitled to vote in the ballot must be given either—

(a) a convenient opportunity to vote by post, or

(b) an opportunity to vote immediately before, immediately after, or during, his working hours at his place of work or at a place which is more convenient for him,

or, as alternatives, both of those opportunities.

No opportunity to vote shall be given except as mentioned above.

(4) A ballot shall be conducted so as to secure that—

(a) so far as is reasonably practicable, those voting do so in secret, and

(b) the votes given in the ballot are fairly and accurately counted.

For the purposes of paragraph (b) an inaccuracy in counting shall be disregarded if it is accidental and on a scale which could not affect the result of the ballot. **[901]**

NOTES
Commencement: 16 October 1992.
Sub-s (1) contains provisions formerly in the Trade Union Act 1984, s 11(5). Sub-s (2) contains provisions formerly in s 11(6)(a) of the 1984 Act. Sub-s (3) contains provisions formerly in s 11(6)(b) of the 1984 Act. Sub-s (4) contains provisions formerly in s 11(7) of the 1984 Act.
Sub-ss (2), (3): substituted by new sub-ss (2), (2A)–(2C), by the Trade Union Reform and Employment Rights Act 1993, s 17, as from 30 August 1993 (SI 1993/1908, below, para **[1435]**), as follows—
"(2) Except as regards persons falling within subsection (2A), so far as is reasonably practicable, every person who is entitled to vote in the ballot must—
(a) have a voting paper sent to him by post at his home address or any other address which he has requested the trade union in writing to treat as his postal address; and
(b) be given a convenient opportunity to vote by post.

(2A) Where a merchant seaman to whom this subsection applies is entitled to vote in the ballot he must, so far as is reasonably practicable—
  (a) have a voting paper made available to him while he is on board the ship or is at a place where the ship is; and
  (b) be given an opportunity to vote while he is on board the ship or is at a place where the ship is.

(2B) Subsection (2A) applies to a merchant seaman who the trade union reasonably believes will, throughout the period during which votes may be cast in the ballot, be employed in a ship either at sea or at a place outside Great Britain.

(2C) In subsections (2A) and (2B) "merchant seaman" means a person whose employment, or the greater part of it, is carried out on board sea-going ships.".

231 Information as to result of ballot

As soon as is reasonably practicable after the holding of the ballot, the trade union shall take such steps as are reasonably necessary to ensure that all persons entitled to vote in the ballot are informed of the number of—
  (a) votes cast in the ballot,
  (b) individuals answering "Yes" to the question, or as the case may be, to each question,
  (c) individuals answering "No" to the question, or, as the case may be, to each question, and
  (d) spoiled voting papers.   **[902]**

NOTES
Commencement: 16 October 1992.
This section contains provisions formerly in the Trade Union Act 1984, s 11(8), as amended by the Employment Act 1988, s 33(1), Sch 3, Pt I, para 5(8)(e).

[231A Employers to be informed of ballot result

(1) As soon as reasonably practicable after the holding of the ballot, the trade union shall take such steps as are reasonably necessary to ensure that every relevant employer is informed of the matters mentioned in section 231.

(2) In subsection (1) "relevant employer" means a person who it is reasonable for the trade union to believe (at the time when the steps are taken) was at the time of the ballot the employer of any persons entitled to vote.]   **[903]**

NOTE
Inserted by the Trade Union Reform and Employment Rights Act 1993, s 19, as from 30 August 1993 (SI 1993/1908, below, para **[1435]**).

[231B Scrutineer's report

(1) The scrutineer's report on the ballot shall state whether the scrutineer is satisfied—
  (a) that there are no reasonable grounds for believing that there was any contravention of a requirement imposed by or under any enactment in relation to the ballot,
  (b) that the arrangements made with respect to the production, storage, distribution, return or other handling of the voting papers used in the ballot, and the arrangements for the counting of the votes, included all such security arrangements as were reasonably practicable for the purpose of minimising the risk that any unfairness or malpractice might occur, and
  (c) that he has been able to carry out the functions conferred on him under section 226B(1) without any interference from the trade union or any of its members, officials or employees;

and if he is not satisfied as to any of those matters, the report shall give particulars of his reason for not being satisfied as to that matter.

(2) If at any time within six months from the date of the ballot—

(a) any person entitled to vote in the ballot, or

(b) the employer of any such person,

requests a copy of the scrutineer's report, the trade union must, as soon as practicable, provide him with one either free of charge or on payment of such reasonable fee as may be specified by the trade union.]   **[904]**

NOTE
Inserted by the Trade Union reform and Employment Rights Act 1993, s 20(3), as from 30 August 1993 (SI 1993/1908, below, para **[1435]**).

232 Balloting of overseas members

(1) A trade union which has overseas members may choose whether or not to accord any of those members entitlement to vote in a ballot; and nothing in section *227 to 230* [226B to 230 and 231B] applies in relation to an overseas member or a vote cast by such a member.

(2) Where overseas members have voted in the ballot, section 231 (information as to result of ballot) shall be read as requiring the information mentioned in that provision—

(a) to be provided to all those entitled to vote in the ballot other than overseas members, and

(b) to distinguish between overseas members and other members.

(3) An "overseas member" of a trade union means a member (other than a merchant seaman or offshore worker) who is outside Great Britain throughout the period during which votes may be cast.

For this purpose—

"merchant seaman" means a person whose employment, or the greater part of it, is carried out on board sea-going ships; and

"offshore worker" means a person in offshore employment, other than one who is in such employment in an area where the law of Northern Ireland applies.

(4) A member who throughout the period during which votes may be cast is in Northern Ireland shall not be treated as an overseas member—

(a) where the ballot is one to which section 228(1) or (2) applies (workplace ballots) and his place of work is in Great Britain, or

(b) where the ballot is one to which section 228(3) applies (general ballots) and relates to industrial action involving members both in Great Britain and in Northern Ireland.

(5) In relation to offshore employment the references in subsection (4) to Northern Ireland include any area where the law of Northern Ireland applies and the references to Great Britain include any area where the law of England and Wales or Scotland applies.   **[905]**

NOTES
Commencement: 16 October 1992.
Sub-ss (1), (2) contain provisions formerly in the Trade Union Act 1984, s 11(9), (10). Sub-s (3) contains provisions formerly in ss 9(1) (definitions "merchant seaman", "offshore worker", "overseas member"), 11(11) (definition "overseas member") of the 1984 Act. Sub-ss (4), (5) contain provisions formerly in the Employment Act 1990, s 5(2), (3).
Sub-s (1): words in italics substituted by words in square brackets immediately following by the Trade Union Reform and Employment Rights Act 1993, s 49(2), Sch 8, para 74(a), as from 30 August 1993 (SI 1993/1908, below, para **[1435]**).

Sub-s (2): substituted by the Trade Union Reform and Employment Rights Act 1993, s 49(2), Sch 8, para 74(b), as from 30 August 1993 (SI 1993/1908, below, para **[1435]**), as follows—
"(2) Where overseas members have voted in the ballot—
    (a) the references in sections 231 and 231A to persons entitled to vote in the ballot do not include overseas members, and
    (b) those sections shall be read as requiring the information mentioned in section 231 to distinguish between overseas members and other members.".

233 Calling of industrial action with support of ballot

(1) Industrial action shall not be regarded as having the support of a ballot unless it is called by a specified person and the conditions specified below are satisfied.

(2) A "specified person" means a person specified or of a description specified in the voting paper for the ballot in accordance with section 229(3).

(3) The conditions are that—

    (a) there must have been no call by the trade union to take part or continue to take part in industrial action to which the ballot relates, or any authorisation or endorsement by the union of any such industrial action, before the date of the ballot;

    (b) there must be a call for industrial action by a specified person, and industrial action to which it relates must take place, before the ballot ceases to be effective in accordance with section 234.

(4) For the purposes of this section a call shall be taken to have been made by a trade union if it was authorised or endorsed by the union; and the provisions of section 20(2) to (4) apply for the purpose of determining whether a call, or industrial action, is to be taken to have been so authorised or endorsed.   **[906]**

NOTES
Commencement: 16 October 1992.
Sub-s (1) contains provisions formerly in the Employment Act 1990, s 7(2). Sub-s (2) contains provisions formerly in s 7(5) (definition "specified person") of the 1990 Act. Sub-ss (3), (4) contain provisions formerly in s 7(3), (4) of the 1990 Act.

234 Period after which ballot ceases to be effective

(1) Subject to the following provisions, a ballot ceases to be effective for the purposes of section 233(3)(b) at the end of the period of four weeks beginning with the date of the ballot.

(2) Where for the whole or part of that period the calling or organising of industrial action is prohibited—

    (a) by virtue of a court order which subsequently lapses or is discharged, recalled or set aside, or

    (b) by virtue of an undertaking given to a court by any person from which he is subsequently released or by which he ceases to be bound,

the trade union may apply to the court for an order that the period during which the prohibition had effect shall not count towards the period referred to in subsection (1).

(3) The application must be made forthwith upon the prohibition ceasing to have effect—

    (a) to the court by virtue of whose decision it ceases to have effect, or

    (b) where an order lapses or an undertaking ceases to bind without any such decision, to the court by which the order was made or to which the undertaking was given;

and no application may be made after the end of the period of eight weeks beginning with the date of the ballot.

(4) The court shall not make an order if it appears to the court—

(a) that the result of the ballot no longer represents the views of the union members concerned, or

(b) that an event is likely to occur as a result of which those members would vote against industrial action if another ballot were to be held.

(5) No appeal lies from the decision of the court to make or refuse an order under this section.

(6) The period between the making of an application under this section and its determination does not count towards the period referred to in subsection (1).

But a ballot shall not by virtue of this subsection (together with any order of the court) be regarded as effective for the purposes of section 233(3)(b) after the end of the period of twelve weeks beginning with the date of the ballot.   **[907]**

NOTES
Commencement: 16 October 1992.
Sub-ss (1)–(6) contain provisions formerly in the Employment Act 1990, s 8(1)–(6).

[Requirement on trade union to give notice of industrial action

234A Notice to employers of industrial action

(1) An act done by a trade union to induce a person to take part, or continue to take part, in industrial action is not protected as respects his employer unless the union has taken or takes such steps as are reasonably necessary to ensure that the employer receives within the appropriate period a relevant notice covering the act.

(2) Subsection (1) imposes a requirement in the case of an employer only if it is reasonable for the union to believe, at the latest time when steps could be taken to ensure that he receives such a notice, that he is the employer of persons who will be or have been induced to take part, or continue to take part, in the industrial action.

(3) For the purposes of this section a relevant notice is a notice in writing which—

(a) describes (so that he can readily ascertain them) the employees of the employer who the union intends to induce or has induced to take part, or continue to take part, in the industrial action ("the affected employees"),

(b) states whether industrial action is intended to be continuous or discontinuous and specifies—

(i) where it is to be continuous, the intended date for any of the affected employees to begin to take part in the action,

(ii) where it is to be discontinuous, the intended dates for any of the affected employees to take part in the action, and

(c) states that it is given for the purposes of this section.

(4) For the purposes of subsection (1) the appropriate period is the period—

(a) beginning with the day when the union satisfies the requirement of section 231A in relation to the ballot in respect of the industrial action, and

(b) ending with the seventh day before the day, or before the first of the days, specified in the relevant notice.

(5) For the purposes of subsection (1) a relevant notice covers an act done by the union if the person induced is one of the affected employees and—

(a) where he is induced to take part or continue to take part in industrial action which the union intends to be continuous, if—

  (i) the notice states that the union intends the industrial action to be continuous, and

  (ii) there is no participation by him in the industrial action before the date specified in the notice in consequence of any inducement by the union not covered by a relevant notice; and

(b) where he is induced to take part or continue to take part in industrial action which the union intends to be discontinuous, if there is no participation by him in the industrial action on a day not so specified in consequence of any inducement by the union not covered by a relevant notice.

(6) For the purposes of this section—

(a) a union intends industrial action to be discontinuous if it intends it to take place only on some days on which there is an opportunity to take the action, and

(b) a union intends industrial action to be continuous if it intends it to be not so restricted.

(7) Where—

(a) continuous industrial action which has been authorised or endorsed by a union ceases to be so authorised or endorsed otherwise than to enable the union to comply with a court order or an undertaking given to a court, and

(b) the industrial action has at a later date again been authorised or endorsed by the union (whether as continuous or discontinuous action),

no relevant notice covering acts done to induce persons to take part in the earlier action shall operate to cover acts done to induce persons to take part in the action authorised or endorsed at the later date and this section shall apply in relation to an act to induce a person to take part, or continue to take part, in the industrial action after that date as if the references in subsection (3)(b)(i) to the industrial action were to the industrial action taking place after that date.

(8) The requirement imposed on a trade union by subsection (1) shall be treated as having been complied with if the steps were taken by other relevant persons or committees whose acts were authorised or endorsed by the union and references to the belief or intention of the union in subsection (2) or, as the case may be, subsections (3), (5) and (6) shall be construed as references to the belief or the intention of the person or committee taking the steps.

(9) The provisions of section 20(2) to (4) apply for the purpose of determining for the purposes of subsection (1) who are relevant persons or committees and whether the trade union is to be taken to have authorised or endorsed the steps the person or committee took and for the purposes of subsection (7) whether the trade union is to be taken to have authorised or endorsed the industrial action.]   **[908]**

NOTE

   This section, and the cross-heading preceding it, are inserted by the Trade Union Reform and Employment Rights Act 1993, s 21, as from 30 August 1993 (SI 1993/1908, below, para **[1435]**).

235 Construction of references to contract of employment

In sections 226 to *234* [234A] (requirement of ballot before action by trade union) references to a contract of employment include any contract under which one person personally does work or performs services for another; *and related expressions* [and "employer" and other related expressions] shall be construed accordingly.   **[909]**

NOTES
Commencement: 16 October 1992.
This section contains provisions formerly in the Employment Act 1990, s 5(1) (in part).
Number and words in italics substituted respectively by number and words in square brackets
immediately following by the Trade Union Reform and Employment Rights Act 1993, s 49(2), Sch 8, para
75, as from 30 August 1993 (SI 1993/1908, below, para **[1435]**).

[Industrial action affecting supply of goods or services to an individual

235A   Industrial action affecting supply of goods or services to an individual

(1) Where an individual claims that—

   (a) any trade union or other person has done, or is likely to do, an unlawful
act to induce any person to take part, or to continue to take part, in industrial
action, and

   (b) an effect, or a likely effect, of the industrial action is or will be to—

      (i) prevent or delay the supply of goods or services, or
      (ii) reduce the quality of goods or services supplied,

   to the individual making the claim,

he may apply to the High Court or the Court of Session for an order under this section.

(2) For the purposes of this section an act to induce any person to take part, or
to continue to take part, in industrial action is unlawful—

   (a) if it is actionable in tort by any one or more persons, or

   (b) (where it is or would be the act of a trade union) if it could form the basis
of an application by a member under section 62.

(3) In determining whether an individual may make an application under this
section it is immaterial whether or not the individual is entitled to be supplied with
the goods or services in question.

(4) Where on an application under this section the court is satisfied that the claim
is well-founded, it shall make such order as it considers appropriate for requiring the
person by whom the act of inducement has been, or is likely to be, done to take steps
for ensuring—

   (a) that no, or no further, act is done by him to induce any persons to take part
or to continue to take part in the industrial action, and

   (b) that no person engages in conduct after the making of the order by virtue
of having been induced by him before the making of the order to take part
or continue to take part in the industrial action.

(5) Without prejudice to any other power of the court, the court may on an
application under this section grant such interlocutory relief (in Scotland, such interim
order) as it considers appropriate.

(6) For the purposes of this section an act of inducement shall be taken to be done
by a trade union if it is authorised or endorsed by the union; and the provisions of
section 20(2) to (4) apply for the purposes of determining whether such an act is to
be taken to be so authorised or endorsed.

Those provisions also apply in relation to proceedings for failure to comply with
an order under this section as they apply in relation to the original proceedings.]

[910]

NOTE
   This section, the cross-heading preceding it, and ss 235B, 235C below, are inserted by the Trade Union
Reform and Employment Rights Act 1993, s 22, as from 30 August 1993 (SI 1993/1908, below, para
[1435]).

[235B Application for assistance for proceedings under section 235A

(1) An individual who is an actual or prospective party to proceedings to which this section applies may apply to the Commissioner for Protection Against Unlawful Industrial Action (in this section and section 235C referred to as "the Commissioner") for assistance in relation to the proceedings, and the Commissioner shall, as soon as reasonably practicable after receiving the application, consider it and decide whether and to what extent to grant it.

(2) This section applies to proceedings or prospective proceedings to the extent that they consist in, or arise out of, an application to the court under section 235A brought with respect to an act of a trade union; but the Secretary of State may by order provide that this section shall also apply to such proceedings brought with respect to an act of a person other than a trade union.

Any order shall be made by statutory instrument; and no such order shall be made unless a draft of it has been laid before and approved by a resolution of each House of Parliament.

(3) The matters to which the Commissioner may have regard in determining whether, and to what extent, to grant an application under this section include—

    (a) whether it is unreasonable, having regard to the complexity of the case, to expect the applicant to deal with it unaided, and

    (b) whether, in the Commissioner's opinion, the case involves a matter of substantial public interest or concern.

(4) If the Commissioner decides not to provide assistance, he shall, as soon as reasonably practicable after making the decision, notify the applicant of his decision and, if he thinks fit, of the reasons for it.

(5) If the Commissioner decides to provide assistance, he shall, as soon as reasonably practicable after making the decision—

    (a) notify the applicant, stating the extent of the assistance to be provided, and

    (b) give him a choice, subject to any restrictions specified in the notification, as to the financial arrangements to be made in connection with the provision of the assistance.

(6) The assistance provided may include the making of arrangements for, or for the Commissioner to bear the costs of—

    (a) the giving of advice or assistance by a solicitor or counsel, and

    (b) the representation of the applicant, or the provision to him of such assistance as is usually given by a solicitor or counsel—

        (i) in steps preliminary or incidental to the proceedings, or

        (ii) in arriving at or giving effect to a compromise to avoid or bring an end to the proceedings.]   **[911]**

NOTE

This section, s 235A and the cross-heading preceding it, and s 235C below, are inserted by the Trade Union Reform and Employment Rights Act 1993, s 22, as from 30 August 1993 (SI 1993/1908, below, para **[1435]**).

[235C Provisions supplementary to section 235B

(1) Where assistance is provided under section 235B with respect to the conduct of proceedings—

    (a) it shall include an agreement by the Commissioner to indemnify the applicant (subject only to any exceptions specified in the notification) in respect of any liability to pay costs or expenses arising by virtue of any judgment or order of the court in the proceedings,

(b) it may include an agreement by the Commissioner to indemnify the applicant in respect of any liability to pay costs or expenses arising by virtue of any compromise or settlement arrived at in respect of the matter in connection with which the assistance is provided in order to avoid or bring proceedings to an end, and

(c) it may include an agreement by the Commissioner to indemnify the applicant in respect of any liability to pay damages pursuant to an undertaking given on the grant of interlocutory relief (in Scotland, an interim order) to the applicant.

(2) Where the Commissioner provides assistance in relation to any proceedings, he shall do so on such terms, or make such other arrangements, as will secure that a person against whom the proceedings have been or are commenced is informed that assistance has been or is being provided by the Commissioner in relation to them.

(3) In England and Wales, the recovery of expenses incurred by the Commissioner in providing an applicant with assistance (as taxed or assessed in such manner as may be prescribed by rules of court) shall constitute a first charge for the benefit of the Commissioner—

(a) on any costs which, by virtue of any judgment or order of the court, are payable to the applicant by any other person in respect of the matter in connection with which the assistance is provided, and

(b) on any sum payable to the applicant under a compromise or settlement arrived at in connection with that matter to avoid or bring proceedings to an end.

(4) In Scotland, the recovery of such expenses (as taxed or assessed in such manner as may be prescribed by rules of court) shall be paid to the Commissioner, in priority to other debts—

(a) out of any expenses which, by virtue of any judgment or order of the court, are payable to the applicant by any other person in respect of the matter in connection with which the assistance is provided, and

(b) out of any sum payable to the applicant under a compromise or settlement arrived at in connection with that matter to avoid or bring proceedings to an end.

(5) Where a person is receiving assistance in relation to proceedings, there shall, if he so wishes, be added after his name in the title of the proceedings the words "(assisted by the Commissioner for Protection Against Unlawful Industrial Action)".

(6) The addition of those words shall not be construed as making the Commissioner a party to the proceedings or as liable to be treated as a party for any purpose; and the omission of those words shall be treated as an irregularity only and shall not nullify the proceedings, any step taken in the proceedings or any document, judgment or order therein.

(7) Where the Commissioner grants an application to a person who for the purposes of the application—

(a) has made a statement which he knew to be false in a material particular, or

(b) has recklessly made a statement which was false in a material particular,

he is entitled to recover from that person any sum paid by him to that person, or to any other person, by way of assistance; but nothing in this subsection affects the power of the Commissioner to enter into any agreement he thinks fit as to the terms on which assistance is provided.

(8) Nothing in section 235B or this section affects the law and practice regulating the description of persons who may appear in, conduct, defend and address the court in any proceedings.

(9) In section 235B and this section "applicant", in relation to assistance, means the individual on whose application the assistance is provided.]   **[912]**

NOTE
This section, s 235A and the cross-heading preceding it, and s 235B, are inserted by the Trade Union Reform and Employment Rights Act 1993, s 22, as from 30 August 1993 (SI 1993/1908, below, para **[1435]**).

No compulsion to work

236 No compulsion to work

No court shall, whether by way of—

   (a) an order for specific performance or specific implement of a contract of employment, or
   (b) an injunction or interdict restraining a breach or threatened breach of such a contract,

compel an employee to do any work or attend at any place for the doing of any work.   **[913]**

NOTES
Commencement: 16 October 1992.
This section contains provisions formerly in the Trade Union and Labour Relations Act 1974, s 16.

Loss of unfair dismissal protection

237 Dismissal of those taking part in unofficial industrial action

(1) An employee has no right to complain of unfair dismissal if at the time of dismissal he was taking part in an unofficial strike or other unofficial industrial action.

[(1A) Subsection (1) does not apply to the dismissal of the employee if it is shown that the reason (or, if more than one, the principal reason) for the dismissal or, in a redundancy case, for selecting the employee for dismissal was one of those specified in section 57A or 60 of the Employment Protection (Consolidation) Act 1978 (dismissal in health and safety cases and maternity cases).

In this subsection "redundancy case" has the meaning given in section 59 of that Act.]

(2) A strike or other industrial action is unofficial in relation to an employee unless—

   (a) he is a member of a trade union and the action is authorised or endorsed by that union, or
   (b) he is not a member of a trade union but there are among those taking part in the industrial action members of a trade union by which the action has been authorised or endorsed.

Provided that, a strike or other industrial action shall not be regarded as unofficial if none of those taking part in it are members of a trade union.

(3) The provisions of section 20(2) apply for the purpose of determining whether industrial action is to be taken to have been authorised or endorsed by a trade union.

(4) The question whether industrial action is to be so taken in any case shall be determined by reference to the facts as at the time of dismissal.

Provided that, where an act is repudiated as mentioned in section 21, industrial action shall not thereby be treated as unofficial before the end of the next working day after the day on which the repudiation takes place.

(5) In this section the "time of dismissal" means—

(a) where the employee's contract of employment is terminated by notice, when the notice is given,

(b) where the employee's contract of employment is terminated without notice, when the termination takes effect, and

(c) where the employee is employed under a contract for a fixed term which expires without being renewed under the same contract, when that term expires;

and a "working day" means any day which is not a Saturday or Sunday, Christmas Day, Good Friday or a bank holiday under the Banking and Financial Dealings Act 1971.

(6) For the purposes of this section membership of a trade union for purposes unconnected with the employment in question shall be disregarded; but an employee who was a member of a trade union when he began to take part in industrial action shall continue to be treated as a member for the purpose of determining whether that action is unofficial in relation to him or another notwithstanding that he may in fact have ceased to be a member.   **[914]**

NOTES

Commencement: 16 October 1992.

Sub-ss (1)–(6) contain provisions formerly in the Employment Protection (Consolidation) Act 1978, s 62A(1)–(6), as inserted by the Employment Act 1990, s 9(1).

Sub-s (1A): inserted by the Trade Union Reform and Employment Rights Act 1993, s 49(2), Sch 8, para 76, partly as from 30 August 1993 (SI 1993/1908, below, para **[1435]**).

238 Dismissals in connection with other industrial action

(1) This section applies in relation to an employee who has a right to complain of unfair dismissal (the "complainant") and who claims to have been unfairly dismissed, where at the date of the dismissal—

(a) the employer was conducting or instituting a lock-out, or

(b) the complainant was taking part in a strike or other industrial action.

(2) In such a case an industrial tribunal shall not determine whether the dismissal was fair or unfair unless it is shown—

(a) that one or more relevant employees of the same employer have not been dismissed, or

(b) that a relevant employee has before the expiry of the period of three months beginning with the date of his dismissal been offered re-engagement and that the complainant has not been offered re-engagement.

[(2A) Subsection (2) does not apply to the dismissal of the employee if it is shown that the reason (or, if more than one, the principal reason) for the dismissal or, in a redundancy case, for selecting the employee for dismissal was one of those specified in section 57A or 60 of the Employment Protection (Consolidation) Act 1978 (dismissal in health and safety cases and maternity cases).

In this subsection "redundancy case" has the meaning given in section 59 of that Act.]

(3) For this purpose "relevant employees" means—

(a) in relation to a lock-out, employees who were directly interested in the dispute in contemplation or furtherance of which the lock-out occurred, and

(b) in relation to a strike or other industrial action, those employees at the establishment of the employer at or from which the complainant works who at the date of his dismissal were taking part in the action.

Nothing in section 237 (dismissal of those taking part in unofficial industrial action) affects the question who are relevant employees for the purposes of this section.

(4) An offer of re-engagement means an offer (made either by the original employer or by a successor of that employer or an associated employer) to re-engage an employee, either in the job which he held immediately before the date of dismissal or in a different job which would be reasonably suitable in his case.

(5) In this section "date of dismissal" means—

(a) where the employee's contract of employment was terminated by notice, the date on which the employer's notice was given, and

(b) in any other case, the effective date of termination.   **[915]**

NOTES

Commencement: 16 October 1992.

Sub-s (1) contains provisions formerly in the Employment Protection (Consolidation) Act 1978, s 62(1), as amended by the Employment Act 1982, s 9(1), (4), and in s 62(5) (in part) of the 1978 Act, as added by the Employment Act 1990, s 16(1), Sch 2, para 1(1), (2). Sub-s (2) contains provisions formerly in s 62(2) of the 1978 Act, as amended by s 9(1), (2) of the 1982 Act. Sub-s (3) contains provisions formerly in s 62(4)(b) of the 1978 Act, as amended by ss 9(1), (3), 21(2) of, Sch 3, Pt II, para 18 to, the 1982 Act, and in s 62(5) (remainder) of the 1978 Act, as added by s 16(1) of, Sch 2, para 1(1), (2) to, the 1990 Act. Sub-s (4) contains provisions formerly in s 62(4)(c) of the 1978 Act. Sub-s (5) contains provisions formerly in s 62(4)(a) of the 1978 Act.

Sub-s (2A): inserted by the Trade Union Reform and Employment Rights Act 1993, s 49(2), Sch 8, para 77, partly as from 30 August 1993 (SI 1993/1908, below, para [**1435**]).

239 Supplementary provisions relating to unfair dismissal

(1) Sections 237 and 238 (loss of unfair dismissal protection in connection with industrial action) shall be construed as one with Part V of the Employment Protection (Consolidation) Act 1978 (unfair dismissal).

(2) In relation to a complaint to which section 238 applies, section 67(2) of that Act (time limit for complaint) does not apply, but an industrial tribunal shall not consider the complaint unless it is presented to the tribunal—

(a) before the end of the period of six months beginning with the date of the complainant's dismissal (as defined by section 238(5)), or

(b) where the tribunal is satisfied that it was not reasonably practicable for the complaint to be presented before the end of that period, within such further period as the tribunal considers reasonable.

(3) Where it is shown that the condition referred to in section 238(2)(b) is fulfilled (discriminatory re-engagement), the references in—

(a) sections 57 to 61 of the Employment Protection (Consolidation) Act 1978, and

(b) sections 152 and 153 of this Act,

to the reason or principal reason for which the complainant was dismissed shall be read as references to the reason or principal reason he has not been offered re-engagement.   **[916]**

NOTES

Commencement: 16 October 1992.

Sub-s (1) is a drafting provision. Sub-s (2) contains provisions formerly in the Employment Protection (Consolidation) Act 1978, s 67(3), as substituted by the Employment Act 1982, s 9(1), (5). Sub-s (3) contains provisions formerly in s 62(3) of the 1978 Act, as amended by s 9(1), (4) of the 1982 Act.

Criminal offences

240 Breach of contract involving injury to persons or property

(1) A person commits an offence who wilfully and maliciously breaks a contract of service or hiring, knowing or having reasonable cause to believe that the probable consequences of his so doing, either alone or in combination with others, will be—

    (a) to endanger human life or cause serious bodily injury, or

    (b) to expose valuable property, whether real or personal, to destruction or serious injury.

(2) Subsection (1) applies equally whether the offence is committed from malice conceived against the person endangered or injured or, as the case may be, the owner of the property destroyed or injured, or otherwise.

(3) A person guilty of an offence under this section is liable on summary conviction to imprisonment for a term not exceeding three months or to a fine not exceeding level 2 on the standard scale or both.

(4) This section does not apply to seamen.   **[917]**

NOTES

Commencement: 16 October 1992.

Sub-s (1) contains provisions formerly in the Conspiracy, and Protection of Property Act 1875, s 5 (in part), and in the Merchant Shipping Act 1970, s 42(1). Sub-s (2) contains provisions deriving from the Malicious Damage Act 1861, s 58, as applied by s 15 of the 1875 Act. Sub-s (3) contains provisions formerly in s 5 (in part) of the 1875 Act, as repealed in part by the Criminal Law Act 1977, s 65(5), Sch 13, and as affected by the Criminal Justice Act 1982, ss 38, 46, and contains provisions deriving from the Criminal Procedure (Scotland) Act 1975, s 289C(4), (5), (8). Sub-s (4) contains provisions formerly in s 16 of the 1875 Act, as substituted by s 100(1) of, Sch 3, para 1 to, the 1970 Act.

241 Intimidation or annoyance by violence or otherwise

(1) A person commits an offence who, with a view to compelling another person to abstain from doing or to do any act which that person has a legal right to do or abstain from doing, wrongfully and without legal authority—

    (a) uses violence to or intimidates that person or his wife or children, or injures his property,

    (b) persistently follows that person about from place to place,

    (c) hides any tools, clothes or other property owned or used by that person, or deprives him of or hinders him in the use thereof,

    (d) watches or besets the house or other place where that person resides, works, carries on business or happens to be, or the approach to any such house or place, or

    (e) follows that person with two or more other persons in a disorderly manner in or through any street or road.

(2) A person guilty of an offence under this section is liable on summary conviction to imprisonment for a term not exceeding six months or a fine not exceeding level 5 on the standard scale, or both.

(3) A constable may arrest without warrant anyone he reasonably suspects is committing an offence under this section. **[918]**

NOTES
Commencement: 16 October 1992.
This section contains provisions formerly in the Conspiracy, and Protection of Property Act 1875, s 7, as amended by the Public Order Act 1986, s 40(2), Sch 2, para 1.

242 Restriction of offence of conspiracy: England and Wales

(1) Where in pursuance of any such agreement as is mentioned in section 1(1) of the Criminal Law Act 1977 (which provides for the offence of conspiracy) the acts in question in relation to an offence are to be done in contemplation or furtherance of a trade dispute, the offence shall be disregarded for the purposes of that subsection if it is a summary offence which is not punishable with imprisonment.

(2) This section extends to England and Wales only. **[919]**

NOTES
Commencement: 16 October 1992.
Sub-s (1) contains provisions formerly in the Criminal Law Act 1977, s 1(3). Sub-s (2) is derived from s 65(10) (in part) of the 1977 Act.

243 Restriction of offence of conspiracy: Scotland

(1) An agreement or combination by two or more persons to do or procure to be done an act in contemplation or furtherance of a trade dispute is not indictable as a conspiracy if that act committed by one person would not be punishable as a crime.

(2) A crime for this purpose means an offence punishable on indictment, or an offence punishable on summary conviction, and for the commission of which the offender is liable under the statute making the offence punishable to be imprisoned either absolutely or at the discretion of the court as an alternative for some other punishment.

(3) Where a person is convicted of any such agreement or combination as is mentioned above to do or procure to be done an act which is punishable only on summary conviction, and is sentenced to imprisonment, the imprisonment shall not exceed three months or such longer time as may be prescribed by the statute for the punishment of the act when committed by one person.

(4) Nothing in this section—

(a) exempts from punishment a person guilty of a conspiracy for which a punishment is awarded by an Act of Parliament, or
(b) affects the law relating to riot, unlawful assembly, breach of the peace, or sedition or any offence against the State or the Sovereign.

(5) This section extends to Scotland only. **[920]**

NOTES
Commencement: 16 October 1992.
Sub-ss (1)–(4) contain provisions formerly in the Conspiracy, and Protection of Property Act 1875, s 3, as amended by the Trade Union and Labour Relations Act 1974, s 25, Sch 3, para 1. Sub-s (5) is a drafting provision.

Supplementary

244 Meaning of "trade dispute" in Part V

(1) In this Part a "trade dispute" means a dispute between workers and their employer which relates wholly or mainly to one or more of the following—

  (a) terms and conditions of employment, or the physical conditions in which any workers are required to work;
  (b) engagement or non-engagement, or termination or suspension of employment or the duties of employment, of one or more workers;
  (c) allocation of work or the duties of employment between workers or groups of workers;
  (d) matters of discipline;
  (e) a worker's membership or non-membership of a trade union;
  (f) facilities for officials of trade unions; and
  (g) machinery for negotiation or consultation, and other procedures, relating to any of the above matters, including the recognition by employers or employers' associations of the right of a trade union to represent workers in such negotiation or consultation or in the carrying out of such procedures.

(2) A dispute between a Minister of the Crown and any workers shall, notwithstanding that he is not the employer of those workers, be treated as a dispute between those workers and their employer if the dispute relates to matters which—

  (a) have been referred for consideration by a joint body on which, by virtue of provision made by or under any enactment, he is represented, or
  (b) cannot be settled without him exercising a power conferred on him by or under an enactment.

(3) There is a trade dispute even though it relates to matters occurring outside the United Kingdom, so long as the person or persons whose actions in the United Kingdom are said to be in contemplation or furtherance of a trade dispute relating to matters occurring outside the United Kingdom are likely to be affected in respect of one or more of the matters specified in subsection (1) by the outcome of the dispute.

(4) An act, threat or demand done or made by one person or organisation against another which, if resisted, would have led to a trade dispute with that other, shall be treated as being done or made in contemplation of a trade dispute with that other, notwithstanding that because that other submits to the act or threat or accedes to the demand no dispute arises.

(5) In this section—

"employment" includes any relationship whereby one person personally does work or performs services for another; and
"worker", in relation to a dispute with an employer, means—

  (a) a worker employed by that employer; or
  (b) a person who has ceased to be so employed if his employment was terminated in connection with the dispute or if the termination of his employment was one of the circumstances giving rise to the dispute.
[921]

NOTES
Commencement: 16 October 1992.
   Sub-s (1) contains provisions formerly in the Trade Union and Labour Relations Act 1974, s 29(1), as amended and repealed in part by the Employment Act 1982, s 18(1), (2). Sub-s (2) contains provisions formerly in s 29(2) of the 1974 Act, as amended by s 18(1), (3) of the 1982 Act. Sub-s (3) contains provisions formerly in s 29(3) of the 1974 Act, as repealed in part by the Trade Union and Labour Relations (Amendment) Act 1976, s 1, and as amended by s 18(1), (4) of the 1982 Act. Sub-s (4) contains provisions formerly in s 29(5) of the 1974 Act. Sub-s (5) contains provisions formerly in s 29(6) of the 1974 Act, as amended by s 18(1), (6) of the 1982 Act.

245 Crown employees and contracts

Where a person holds any office or employment under the Crown on terms which do not constitute a contract of employment between that person and the Crown, those terms shall nevertheless be deemed to constitute such a contract for the purposes of—

(a) the law relating to liability in tort of a person who commits an act which—
    (i) induces another person to break a contract, interferes with the performance of a contract or induces another person to interfere with its performance, or
    (ii) consists in a threat that a contract will be broken or its performance interfered with, or that any person will be induced to break a contract or interfere with its performance, and
(b) the provisions of this or any other Act which refer (whether in relation to contracts generally or only in relation to contracts of employment) to such an act.   **[922]**

NOTES

Commencement: 16 October 1992.

This section contains provisions formerly in the Employment Act 1988, s 30(1) (in part).

246 Minor definitions

In this Part—

"date of the ballot" means, in the case of a ballot in which votes may be cast on more than one day, the last of those days;

"place of work", in relation to any person who is employed, means the premises occupied by his employer at or from which that person works or, where he does not work at or from any such premises or works at or from more than one set of premises, the premises occupied by his employer with which his employment has the closest connection;

"strike" means any concerted stoppage of work;

"working hours", in relation to a person, means any time when under his contract of employment, or other contract personally to do work or perform services, he is required to be at work.   **[923]**

NOTES

Commencement: 16 October 1992.

This section contains provisions formerly in the Trade Union Act 1984, s 10(5) (definitions "the date of the ballot", "place of work"), as inserted, in the case of the definition "place of work", by the Employment Act 1988, s 17(3); in s 11(11) of the 1984 Act (definitions "strike", "working hours"); and in the Employment Act 1990, ss 7(5), 8(7) (both in part).

Definition "place of work" repealed by the Trade Union Reform and Employment Rights Act 1993, ss 49(1), 51, Sch 7, para 26, Sch 10, as from 30 August 1993 (SI 1993/1908, below, para [1435]).

PART VI

ADMINISTRATIVE PROVISIONS

ACAS

247 ACAS

(1) There shall continue to be a body called the Advisory, Conciliation and Arbitration Service (referred to in this Act as "ACAS").

(2) ACAS is a body corporate of which the corporators are the members of its Council.

(3) Its functions, and those of its officers and servants, shall be performed on behalf of the Crown, but not so as to make it subject to directions of any kind from any Minister of the Crown as to the manner in which it is to exercise its functions under any enactment.

(4) For the purposes of civil proceedings arising out of those functions the Crown Proceedings Act 1947 applies to ACAS as if it were a government department and the Crown Suits (Scotland) Act 1857 applies to it as if it were a public department.

(5) Nothing in section 9 of the Statistics of Trade Act 1947 (restriction on disclosure of information obtained under that Act) shall prevent or penalise the disclosure to ACAS, for the purposes of the exercise of any of its functions, of information obtained under that Act by a government department.

(6) ACAS shall maintain offices in such of the major centres of employment in Great Britain as it thinks fit for the purposes of discharging its functions under any enactment.   **[924]**

NOTES
Commencement: 16 October 1992.
Sub-s (1) contains provisions formerly in the Employment Protection Act 1975, s 1(1). Sub-s (2) contains provisions formerly in Sch 1, Pt I, para 1 (in part) to the 1975 Act. Sub-ss (3), (4) contain provisions formerly in Sch 1, Pt I, para 11(1), (2) to the 1975 Act. Sub-s (5) contains provisions formerly in Sch 1, Pt I, para 12 to the 1975 Act. Sub-s (6) contains provisions formerly in Sch 1, Pt I, para 9 to the 1975 Act.

248 The Council of ACAS

(1) ACAS shall be directed by a Council which, subject to the following provisions, shall consist of a chairman and nine ordinary members appointed by the Secretary of State.

(2) Before appointing those ordinary members of the Council, the Secretary of State shall—

(a) as to three of them, consult such organisations representing employers as he considers appropriate, and

(b) as to three of them, consult such organisations representing workers as he considers appropriate.

(3) The Secretary of State may, if he thinks fit, appoint a further two ordinary members of the Council (who shall be appointed so as to take office at the same time); and before making those appointments he shall—

(a) as to one of them, consult such organisations representing employers as he considers appropriate, and

(b) as to one of them, consult such organisations representing workers as he considers appropriate.

(4) The Secretary of State may appoint up to three deputy chairman who may be appointed from the ordinary members, or in addition to those members.

(5) The Council shall determine its own procedure, including the quorum necessary for its meetings.

(6) If the Secretary of State has not appointed a deputy chairman, the Council may choose a member to act as chairman in the absence or incapacity of the chairman.

(7) The validity of proceedings of the Council is not affected by any vacancy among the members of the Council or by any defect in the appointment of any of them.   **[925]**

NOTES

Commencement: 16 October 1992.

Sub-s (1) contains provisions formerly in the Employment Protection Act 1975, Sch 1, Pt I, paras 1, 2(1) (both in part). Sub-s (2) contains provisions formerly in Sch 1, Pt I, para 2(2) to the 1975 Act. Sub-s (3) contains provisions formerly in Sch 1, Pt I, para 2(4) to the 1975 Act. Sub-s (4) contains provisions formerly in Sch 1, Pt I, para 2(3) (in part) to the 1975 Act. Sub-ss (5), (6) contain provisions formerly in Sch 1, Pt I, para 4(1), (2) to the 1975 Act. Sub-s (7) contains provisions formerly in Sch 1, Pt I, para 5 to the 1975 Act.

249 Terms of appointment of members of Council

(1) The members of the Council shall hold and vacate office in accordance with their terms of appointment, subject to the following provisions.

(2) *Appointment as chairman shall be a full-time appointment.*

Appointment as [chairman, or as] deputy chairman, or as an ordinary member of the Council, may be a full-time or part-time appointment; and the Secretary of State may, with the consent of the member concerned, vary the terms of his appointment as to whether his appointment is full-time or part-time.

(3) A person shall not be appointed to the Council for a term exceeding five years, but previous membership does not affect eligibility for re-appointment.

(4) A member may at any time resign his membership, and the chairman or a deputy chairman may at any time resign his office as such, by notice in writing to the Secretary of State.

A deputy chairman appointed in addition to the ordinary members of the Council shall on resigning his office as deputy chairman cease to be a member of the Council.

(5) If the Secretary of State is satisfied that a member—

(a) has been absent from meetings of the Council for a period longer than six consecutive months without the permission of the Council, or

(b) has become bankrupt or made an arrangement with his creditors (or, in Scotland, has had his estate sequestrated or has made a trust deed for his creditors or has made and had accepted a composition contract), or

(c) is incapacitated by physical or mental illness, or

(d) is otherwise unable or unfit to discharge the functions of a member,

the Secretary of State may declare his office as a member to be vacant and shall notify the declaration in such manner as he thinks fit, whereupon the office shall become vacant.

If the chairman or a deputy chairman ceases to be a member of the Council, he shall also cease to be chairman or, as the case may be, a deputy chairman.   **[926]**

NOTES

Commencement: 16 October 1992.

Sub-s (1) contains provisions formerly in the Employment Protection Act 1975, Sch 1, Pt I, para 3(1). Sub-s (2) contains provisions formerly in Sch 1, Pt I, paras 2(1), (3) (both in part), 3(3), (4) to the 1975 Act. Sub-s (3) contains provisions formerly in Sch 1, Pt I, para 3(2) to the 1975 Act. Sub-s (4) contains provisions formerly in Sch 1, Pt I, para 3(5), (6) to the 1975 Act. Sub-s (5) contains provisions formerly in Sch 1, Pt I, para 3(7)–(9) to the 1975 Act, and deriving from the Bankruptcy (Scotland) Act 1985, s 75(10).

Sub-s (2): words in italics repealed, and words in square brackets inserted, by the Trade Union Reform and Employment Rights Act 1993, ss 43(3), 51, Sch 10, as from 30 August 1993 (SI 1993/1908, below, para **[1435]**).

250 Remuneration, &c of members of Council

(1) ACAS shall pay to the members of its Council such remuneration and travelling and other allowances as may be determined by the Secretary of State.

(2) The Secretary of State may pay, or make provision for payment, to or in respect of a member of the Council such pension, allowance or gratuity on death or retirement as he may determine.

(3) Where a person ceases to be the holder of the Council otherwise than on the expiry of his term of office and it appears to the Secretary of State that there are special circumstances which make it right for him to receive compensation, he may make him a payment of such amount he may determine.

(4) The approval of the Treasury is required for any determination by the Secretary of State under this section.   **[927]**

NOTES
Commencement: 16 October 1992.
Sub-s (1) contains provisions formerly in the Employment Protection Act 1975, Sch 1, Pt III, para 28(a) (in part). Sub-s (2) contains provisions formerly in Sch 1, Pt III, para 30 (in part) to the 1975 Act. Sub-s (3) contains provisions formerly in Sch 1, Pt III, para 31 (in part) to the 1975 Act. Sub-s (4) contains provisions formerly in Sch 1, Pt III, paras 28(a), 30, 31 (all in part) to the 1975 Act, as affected by the Transfer of Functions (Minister for the Civil Service and Treasury) Order 1981, SI 1981/1670.

251 Secretary, officers and staff of ACAS

(1) ACAS may, with the approval of the Secretary of State, appoint a secretary.

The consent of-the Secretary of State is required as to his terms and conditions of service.

(2) ACAS may appoint such other officers and staff as it may determine.

The consent of the Secretary of State is required as to their numbers, manner of appointment and terms and conditions of service.

(3) The Secretary of State shall not give his consent under subsection (1) or (2) without the approval of the Treasury.

(4) ACAS shall pay to the Treasury, at such times in each accounting year as may be determined by the Treasury, sums of such amounts as may be so determined as being equivalent to the increase in that year of such liabilities of his as are attributable to the provision of pensions, allowances or gratuities to or in respect of persons who are or have been in the service of ACAS in so far as that increase results from the service of those persons during that accounting year and to the expense to be incurred in administering those pensions, allowances or gratuities.

(5) The fixing of the common seal of ACAS shall be authenticated by the signature of the secretary of ACAS or some other person authorised by ACAS to act for that purpose.

A document purporting to be duly executed under the seal of ACAS shall be received in evidence and shall, unless the contrary is proved, be deemed to be so executed.   **[928]**

NOTES
Commencement: 16 October 1992.
Sub-s (1) contains provisions formerly in the Employment Protection Act 1975, Sch 1, Pt I, para 6 (in part). Sub-s (2) contains provisions formerly in Sch 1, Pt I, para 7 (in part) to the 1975 Act. Sub-s (3) contains provisions formerly in Sch 1, Pt I, paras 6, 7 (both in part) to the 1975 Act, as affected by the Transfer of Functions (Minister for the Civil Service and Treasury) Order 1981, SI 1981/1670. Sub-s (4) contains provisions formerly in Sch 1, Pt III, para 32 to the 1975 Act, as so affected. Sub-s (5) contains provisions formerly in Sch 1, Pt I, para 10 to the 1975 Act.

[251A Fees for exercise of functions by ACAS

(1) ACAS may, in any case in which it thinks it appropriate to do so, but subject to any directions under subsection (2) below, charge a fee for exercising a function in relation to any person.

(2) The Secretary of State may direct ACAS to charge fees, in accordance with the direction, for exercising any function specified in the direction, but the Secretary of State shall not give a direction under this subsection without consulting ACAS.

(3) A direction under subsection (2) above may require ACAS to charge fees in respect of the exercise of a function only in specified descriptions of case.

(4) A direction under subsection (2) above shall specify whether fees are to be charged in respect of the exercise of any specified function—

  (a) at the full economic cost level, or
  (b) at a level less than the full economic cost but not less than a specified proportion or percentage of the full economic cost.

(5) Where a direction requires fees to be charged at the full economic cost level ACAS shall fix the fee for the case at an amount estimated to be sufficient to cover the administrative costs of ACAS of exercising the function including an appropriate sum in respect of general staff costs and overheads.

(6) Where a direction requires fees to be charged at a level less than the full economic cost ACAS shall fix the fee for the case at such amount, not being less than the proportion or percentage of the full economic cost specified under subsection (4)(b) above, as it thinks appropriate (computing that cost in the same way as under subsection (5) above).

(7) No liability to pay a fee charged under this section shall arise on the part of any person unless ACAS has notified that person that a fee may or will be charged.

(8) For the purposes of this section—

  (a) a function is exercised "in relation to" a person who avails himself of the benefit of its exercise, whether or not he requested its exercise and whether the function is such as to be exercisable in relation to particular persons only or in relation to persons generally; and
  (b) where a function is exercised in relation to two or more persons the fee chargeable for its exercise shall be apportioned among them as ACAS thinks appropriate.]   **[929]**

NOTE
Inserted by the Trade Union reform and Employment Rights Act 1993, s 44, as from 30 August 1993 (SI 1993/1908, below, para **[1435]**).

252 General financial provisions

(1) The Secretary of State shall pay to ACAS such sums as are approved by the Treasury and as he considers appropriate for the purpose of enabling ACAS to perform its functions.

(2) ACAS may pay to—

  (a) persons appointed under section 210(2) (conciliation) who are not officers or servants of ACAS, and
  (b) arbitrators or arbiters appointed by ACAS under any enactment,

such fees and travelling and other allowances as may be determined by the Secretary of State with the approval of the Treasury.   **[930]**

NOTES
Commencement: 16 October 1992.
Sub-s (1) contains provisions formerly in the Employment Protection Act 1975, Sch 1, Pt III, para 33.
Sub-s (2) contains provisions formerly in Sch 1, Pt III, para 29 to the 1975 Act, as affected by the Transfer of Functions (Minister for the Civil Service and Treasury) Order 1981, SI 1981/1670.

253 Annual report and accounts

(1) ACAS shall as soon as practicable after the end of each calendar year make a report to the Secretary of State on its activities during that year.

The Secretary of State shall lay a copy of the report before each House of Parliament and arrange for it to be published.

(2) ACAS shall keep proper accounts and proper records in relation to the accounts and shall prepare in respect of each financial year a statement of accounts, in such form as the Secretary of State may, with the approval of the Treasury, direct.

(3) ACAS shall not later than 30th November following the end of the financial year to which the statement relates, send copies of the statement to the Secretary of State and to the Comptroller and Auditor General.

(4) The Comptroller and Auditor General shall examine, certify and report on each such statement and shall lay a copy of the statement and of his report before each House of Parliament.   **[931]**

NOTES
Commencement: 16 October 1992.
Sub-s (1) contains provisions formerly in the Employment Protection Act 1975, Sch 1, Pt I, para 13(1), (3) (both in part). Sub-s (2) contains provisions formerly in Sch 1, Pt III, paras 34, 35(1) (in part) to the 1975 Act. Sub-ss (3), (4) contain provisions formerly in Sch 1, Pt III, para 35(2) to the 1975 Act.

The Certification Officer

254 The Certification Officer

(1) There shall continue to be an officer called the Certification Officer.

(2) The Certification Officer shall be appointed by the Secretary of State after consultation with ACAS.

(3) The Certification Officer may appoint one or more assistant certification officers and shall appoint an assistant certification officer for Scotland.

(4) The Certification Officer may delegate to an assistant certification officer such functions as he thinks appropriate, and in particular may delegate to the assistant certification officer for Scotland such functions as he thinks appropriate in relation to organisations whose principal office is in Scotland.

References to the Certification Officer in enactments relating to his functions shall be construed accordingly.

(5) ACAS shall provide for the Certification Officer the requisite staff (from among the officers and servants of ACAS) and the requisite accommodation, equipment and other facilities.

[(5A) Subject to subsection (6), ACAS shall pay to the Certification Officer such sums as he may require for the performance of any of his functions.]

(6) The Secretary of State shall pay to the Certification Officer such sums as he may require for making payments under the scheme under section 115 (payments towards expenditure in connection with secret ballots).   **[932]**

NOTES
Commencement: 16 October 1992.
Sub-ss (1), (2) contain provisions formerly in the Employment Protection Act 1975, s 7(1). Sub-s (3) contains provisions formerly in s 7(4) of the 1975 Act. Sub-s (4) contains provisions formerly in the Trade Union (Amalgamations, etc) Act 1964, s 8, and in s 7(5), (6) of the 1975 Act. Sub-s (5) contains provisions formerly in Sch 1, Pt I, para 8 (in part) to the 1975 Act. Sub-s (6) contains provisions formerly in the Employment Act 1980, s 1(6).
Sub-s (5A): inserted by the Trade Union Reform and Employment Rights Act 1993, s 49(2), Sch 8, para 78, as from 30 August 1993 (SI 1993/1908, below, para **[1435]**).

255 Remuneration, &c of Certification Officer and assistants

(1) ACAS shall pay to the Certification Officer and any assistant certification officer such remuneration and travelling and other allowances as may be determined by the Secretary of State.

(2) The Secretary of State may pay, or make provision for payment, to or in respect of the Certification Officer and any assistant certification officer such pension, allowance or gratuity on death or retirement as he may determine.

(3) Where a person ceases to be the Certification Officer or an assistant certification officer otherwise than on the expiry of his term of office and it appears to the Secretary of State that there are special circumstances which make it right for him to receive compensation, he may make him a payment of such amount as he may determine.

(4) The approval of the Treasury is required for any determination by the Secretary of State under this section.   **[933]**

NOTES
Commencement: 16 October 1992.
Sub-s (1) contains provisions formerly in the Employment Protection Act 1975, Sch 1, Pt III, para 28(c) (in part). Sub-s (2) contains provisions formerly in Sch 1, Pt III, para 30 (in part) to the 1975 Act. Sub-s (3) contains provisions formerly in Sch 1, Pt III, para 31 (in part) to the 1975 Act. Sub-s (4) contains provisions formerly in Sch 1, Pt III, paras 28(c), 30, 31 (all in part) to the 1975 Act, as affected by the Transfer of Functions (Minister for the Civil Service and Treasury) Order 1981, SI 1981/1670.

256 Procedure before the Certification Officer

(1) Except in relation to matters as to which express provision is made by or under an enactment, the Certification Officer may regulate the procedure to be followed—

   (a) on any application or complaint made to him, or
   (b) where his approval is sought with respect to any matter.

(2) He shall, in particular, make such provision as he thinks appropriate for restricting the circumstances in which the identity of an individual who has made, or is proposing to make, any such application or complaint is disclosed to any person.

(3) The Secretary of State may, with the consent of the Treasury, make a scheme providing for the payment by the Certification Officer to persons of such sums as may be specified in or determined under the scheme in respect of expenses incurred by them for the purposes of, or in connection with, their attendance at hearings held by him in the course of carrying out his functions.

(4) ACAS shall pay to the Certification Officer such sums as he may require for the making of payments in pursuance of any such scheme.   **[934]**

NOTES
Commencement: 16 October 1992.
Sub-ss (1), (2) contain provisions formerly in the Employment Act 1988, s 22(1). Sub-s (3) contains provisions formerly in s 22(2) of the 1988 Act. Sub-s (4) contains provisions formerly in the Employment Protection Act 1975, Sch 1, Pt III, para 32A, as inserted by s 22(3) of the 1988 Act.
Sub-s (4): repealed by the Trade Union Reform and Employment Rights Act 1993, s 51, Sch 10, as from 30 August 1993 (SI 1993/1908, below, para **[1435]**).

257 Custody of documents submitted under earlier legislation

(1) The Certification Officer shall continue to have custody of the annual returns, accounts, copies of rules and other documents submitted for the purposes of—

    (a) the Trade Union Acts 1871 to 1964,
    (b) the Industrial Relations Act 1971, or
    (c) the Trade Union and Labour Relations Act 1974,

of which he took custody under section 9 of the Employment Protection Act 1975.

(2) He shall keep available for public inspection (either free of charge or on payment of a reasonable charge) at all reasonable hours such of those documents as were available for public inspection in pursuance of any of those Acts.   **[935]**

NOTES
Commencement: 16 October 1992.
Sub-ss (1), (2) contain provisions formerly in the Employment Protection Act 1975, s 9(1), (2).

258 Annual report and accounts

(1) The Certification Officer shall, as soon as practicable after the end of each calendar year, make a report of his activities during that year to ACAS and to the Secretary of State.

The Secretary of State shall lay a copy of the report before each House of Parliament and arrange for it to be published.

(2) The accounts prepared by ACAS in respect of any financial year shall show separately any sums disbursed to or on behalf of the Certification Officer in consequence of the provisions of this Part.   **[936]**

NOTES
Commencement: 16 October 1992.
Sub-s (1) contains provisions formerly in the Employment Protection Act 1975, Sch 1, Pt I, para 13(2), (3) (in part). Sub-s (2) contains provisions formerly in Sch 1, Pt III, para 35(1) (in part) to the 1975 Act.

Central Arbitration Committee

259 The Central Arbitration Committee

(1) There shall continue to be a body called the Central Arbitration Committee.

(2) The functions of the Committee shall be performed on behalf of the Crown, but not so as to make it subject to directions of any kind from any Minister of the Crown as to the manner in which it is to exercise its functions.

(3) ACAS shall provide for the Committee the requisite staff (from among the officers and servants of ACAS) and the requisite accommodation, equipment and other facilities.   **[937]**

NOTES
Commencement: 16 October 1992.
Sub-s (1) contains provisions formerly in the Employment Protection Act 1975, s 10(1). Sub-s (2) contains provisions formerly in Sch 1, Pt II, para 27 to the 1975 Act. Sub-s (3) contains provisions formerly in Sch 1, Pt I, para 8 (in part) to the 1975 Act.

260 The members of the Committee

(1) The Central Arbitration Committee shall consist of a chairman appointed by the Secretary of State after consultation with ACAS and other members appointed by the Secretary of State as follows.

(2) The members of the Committee apart from the chairman shall be appointed by the Secretary of State from persons nominated by ACAS as experienced in industrial relations, and shall include some persons whose experience is as representatives of employers and some whose experience is as representatives of workers.

(3) The Secretary of State may, after consultation with ACAS, appoint one or more deputy chairmen in addition to the existing members of the Committee.

(4) At any time when the chairman of the Committee is absent or otherwise incapable of acting, or there is a vacancy in the office of chairman, and the Committee has a deputy chairman or deputy chairmen—

    (a) the deputy chairman, if there is only one, or

    (b) if there is more than one, such of the deputy chairmen as they may agree
        or in default of agreement as the Secretary of State may direct,

may perform any of the functions of chairman of the Committee.

(5) At any time when every person who is chairman or deputy chairman is absent or otherwise incapable of acting, or there is no such person, such member of the Committee as the Secretary of State may direct may perform any of the functions of the chairman of the Committee.

(6) The validity of any proceedings of the Committee shall not be affected by any vacancy among the members of the Committee or by any defect in the appointment of a member of the Committee.   [938]

NOTES
Commencement: 16 October 1992.
Sub-ss (1)–(3) contain provisions formerly in the Employment Protection Act 1975, Sch 1, Pt I, para 14(1)–(3). Sub-ss (4), (5) contain provisions formerly in Sch 1, Pt II, para 16(1), (2) to the 1975 Act. Sub-s (6) contains provisions formerly in Sch 1, Pt II, para 21 to the 1975 Act.

261 Terms of appointment of members of Committee

(1) The members of the Central Arbitration Committee shall hold and vacate office in accordance with their terms of appointment, subject to the following provisions.

(2) A person shall not be appointed to the Committee for a term exceeding five years, but previous membership does not affect eligibility for re-appointment.

(3) The Secretary of State may, with the consent of the member concerned, vary the terms of his appointment as to whether he is a full-time or part-time member.

(4) A member may at any time resign his membership, and the chairman or a deputy chairman may at any time resign his office as such, by notice in writing to the Secretary of State.

(5) If the Secretary of State is satisfied that a member—

(a) has become bankrupt or made an arrangement with his creditors (or, in Scotland, has had his estate sequestrated or has made a trust deed for his creditors or has made and had accepted a composition contract), or

(b) is incapacitated by physical or mental illness, or

(c) is otherwise unable or unfit to discharge the functions of a member,

the Secretary of State may declare his office as a member to be vacant and shall notify the declaration in such manner as he thinks fit, whereupon the office shall become vacant.

(6) If the chairman or a deputy chairman ceases to be a member of the Committee, he shall also cease to be chairman or, as the case may be, a deputy chairman. **[939]**

NOTES

Commencement: 16 October 1992.

Sub-ss (1)–(4) contain provisions formerly in the Employment Protection Act 1975, Sch 1, Pt II, para 15(1)–(4). Sub-s (5) contains provisions formerly in Sch 1, Pt II, para 15(5), (6) to the 1975 Act, and deriving from the Bankruptcy (Scotland) Act 1985, s 75(10). Sub-s (6) contains provisions formerly in Sch 1, Pt II, para 15(7) to the 1975 Act.

262 Remuneration, &c of members of Committee

(1) ACAS shall pay to the members of the Central Arbitration Committee such remuneration and travelling and other allowances as may be determined by the Secretary of State.

(2) The Secretary of State may pay, or make provision for payment, to or in respect of a member of the Committee such pension, allowance or gratuity on death or retirement as he may determine.

(3) Where a person ceases to be the holder of the Committee otherwise than on the expiry of his term of office and it appears to the Secretary of State that there are special circumstances which make it right for him to receive compensation, he may make him a payment of such amount he may determine.

(4) The approval of the Treasury is required for any determination by the Secretary of State under this section.   **[940]**

NOTES

Commencement: 16 October 1992.

Sub-s (1) contains provisions formerly in the Employment Protection Act 1975, Sch 1, Pt III, para 28(b) (in part). Sub-s (2) contains provisions formerly in Sch 1, Pt III, para 30 (in part) to the 1975 Act. Sub-s (3) contains provisions formerly in Sch 1, Pt III, para 31 (in part) to the 1975 Act. Sub-s (4) contains provisions formerly in Sch 1, Pt III, paras 28(b), 30, 31 (all in part) to the 1975 Act, as affected by the Transfer of Functions (Minister for the Civil Service and Treasury) Order 1981, SI 1981/1670.

263 Proceedings of the Committee

(1) For the purpose of discharging its functions in any particular case the Central Arbitration Committee shall consist of the chairman and such other members as the chairman may direct:

Provided that, it may sit in two or more divisions constituted of such members as the chairman may direct, and in a division in which the chairman does not sit the functions of the chairman shall be performed by a deputy chairman.

(2) The Committee may, at the discretion of the chairman, where it appears expedient to do so, call in the aid of one or more assessors, and may settle the matter wholly or partly with their assistance.

(3) The Committee may at the discretion of the chairman sit in private where it appears expedient to do so.

(4) If in any case the Committee cannot reach a unanimous decision on its award, the chairman shall decide the matter acting with the full powers of an umpire or, in Scotland, an oversman.

(5) Subject to the above provisions, the Committee shall determine its own procedure.

(6) Part I of the Arbitration Act 1950 (general provisions as to arbitration) and section 3 of the Administration of Justice (Scotland) Act 1972 (power of arbiter to state case to Court of Session) do not apply to proceedings before the Committee.

[941]

NOTES
Commencement: 16 October 1992.
Sub-s (1) contains provisions formerly in the Employment Protection Act 1975, Sch 1, Pt II, para 17(1), (2). Sub-s (2) contains provisions formerly in Sch 1, Pt II, para 17(3) to the 1975 Act. Sub-ss (3)–(5) contain provisions formerly in Sch 1, Pt II, paras 18–20 to the 1975 Act. Sub-s (6) contains provisions deriving from the Administration of Justice (Scotland) Act 1972, s 3(3), and formerly in Sch 1, Pt II, para 26 to the 1975 Act.

264 Awards of the Committee

(1) The Central Arbitration Committee may correct in any award any clerical mistake or error arising from an accidental slip or omission.

(2) If a question arises as to the interpretation of an award of the Committee, any party may apply to the Committee for a decision; and the Committee shall decide the question after hearing the parties or, if the parties consent, without a hearing, and shall notify the parties.

(3) Decisions of the Committee in the exercise of any of its functions shall be published.   **[942]**

NOTES
Commencement: 16 October 1992.
Sub-ss (1)–(3) contain provisions formerly in the Employment Protection Act 1975, Sch 1, Pt II, paras 22–24.

265 Annual report and accounts

(1) ACAS shall, as soon as practicable after the end of each calendar year, make a report to the Secretary of State on the activities of the Central Arbitration Committee during that year.

For that purpose the Committee shall, as soon as practicable after the end of each calendar year, transmit to ACAS an account of its activities during that year.

(2) The accounts prepared by ACAS in respect of any financial year shall show separately any sums disbursed to or on behalf of the Committee in consequence of the provisions of this Part.   **[943]**

NOTES
Commencement: 16 October 1992.
Sub-s (1) contains provisions formerly in the Employment Protection Act 1975, Sch 1, Pt I, para 13(1) (in part), Pt II, para 25. Sub-s (2) contains provisions formerly in Sch 1, Pt III, para 35(1) (in part) to the 1975 Act.

The Commissioner for the Rights of Trade Union Members

266 The Commissioner

(1) There shall continue to be an officer called the Commissioner for the Rights of Trade Union Members (referred to in this Act as "the Commissioner") whose function is to provide assistance in accordance with Chapter VIII of Part I of this Act in connection with certain legal proceedings.

(2) The Commissioner shall be appointed by the Secretary of State.

(3) The Commissioner shall have an official seal for the authentication of documents required for the purposes of his functions.

(4) Anything authorised or required by or under this Act to be done by the Commissioner may be done by a member of his staff authorised by him for the purpose, whether generally or specifically.

An authorisation given for the purposes of this subsection continues to have effect during a vacancy in the office of Commissioner.

(5) Neither the Commissioner nor any member of his staff shall, in that capacity, be regarded as a servant or agent of the Crown or as enjoying any status, immunity or privilege of the Crown.   **[944]**

NOTES

Commencement: 16 October 1992.

Sub-ss (1), (2) contain provisions formerly in the Employment Act 1988, s 19(1). Sub-s (3) contains provisions formerly in Sch 1, para 11 to the 1988 Act. Sub-s (4) contains provisions formerly in Sch 1, para 4 to the 1988 Act. Sub-s (5) contains provisions formerly in s 19(3) of the 1988 Act.

This section and the cross-heading preceding it are substituted by the Trade Union Reform and Employment Rights Act 1993, s 49(2), Sch 8, para 79, as from 30 August 1993 (SI 1993/1908, below, para **[1435]**), as follows—

"The Commissioner for the Rights of Trade Union Members and the Commissioner for Protection Against Unlawful Industrial Action

266 The Commissioners

(1) There—

    (a)   shall continue to be an officer called the Commissioner for the Rights of Trade Union Members whose function is to provide assistance in accordance with Chapter VIII of Part I of this Act in connection with certain legal proceedings, and

    (b)   shall be an officer called the Commissioner for Protection Against Unlawful Industrial Action whose function is to provide assistance in accordance with sections 235B and 235C of this Act in connection with proceedings brought by virtue of section 235A.

(2) Each of the Commissioners shall be appointed by the Secretary of State.

(3) Each of the Commissioners shall have an official seal for the authentication of documents required for the purposes of his functions.

(4) Anything authorised or required by or under this Act to be done by either of the Commissioners may be done by a member of his staff authorised by him for that purpose, whether generally or specifically.

An authorisation given for the purposes of this subsection continues to have effect during a vacancy in the office of the Commissioner concerned.

(5) Neither of the Commissioners nor any member of the staff of either of the Commissioners shall, in that capacity, be regarded as a servant or agent of the Crown or as enjoying any status, immunity or privilege of the Crown.".

267 Terms of appointment of Commissioner

(1) *The Commissioner* [Each of the Commissioners] shall hold and vacate office in accordance with the terms of his appointment, subject to the following provisions.

(2) The appointment of a person to hold office as *the Commissioner* [one of the Commissioners] shall be for a term not exceeding five years; but previous appointment to that office does not affect eligibility for re-appointment.

(3) The Secretary of State may remove a person from *that office* [office as one of the Commissioners] if he is satisfied—

    (a) that that person has been adjudged bankrupt, his estate has been sequestrated or he has made a composition or arrangement with, or granted a trust deed for, his creditors,

    (b) that he is incapacitated by physical or mental illness, or

    (c) that he is otherwise unable or unfit to discharge *his functions as the Commissioner* [the functions of the office].   **[945]**

NOTES
Commencement: 16 October 1992.
Sub-s (1) contains provisions formerly in the Employment Act 1988, Sch 1, para 1(3). Sub-ss (2), (3) contain provisions formerly in Sch 1, para 1(1), (2) to the 1988 Act.
Sub-s (1): words in italics substituted by words in square brackets immediately following by the Trade Union Reform and Employment Rights Act 1993, s 49(2), Sch 8, para 80(a), as from 30 August 1993 (SI 1993/1908, below, para **[1435]**).
Sub-s (2): words in italics substituted by words in square brackets immediately following by the Trade Union Reform and Employment Rights Act 1993, s 49(2), Sch 8, para 80(b), as from 30 August 1993 (SI 1993/1908, below, para **[1435]**).
Sub-s (3): words in italics substituted in each case by words in square brackets immediately following by the Trade Union Reform and Employment Rights Act 1993, s 49(2), Sch 8, para 80(c), as from 30 August 1993 (SI 1993/1908, below, para **[1435]**).

268 Remuneration, pension, &c

(1) There shall be paid to *the Commissioner* [each of the Commissioners] such remuneration, and such travelling and other allowances, as the Secretary of State may determine.

(2) If the Secretary of State so determines in the case of *any holder of the office of Commissioner* [any person who holds office as one of the Commissioners], there shall be paid such pension, allowance or gratuity to or in respect of him on his retirement or death, or such contributions or payments towards provision for such a pension, allowance or gratuity as may be so determined.

(3) If, when a person ceases to hold office as *the Commissioner* [one of the Commissioners], the Secretary of State determines that there are special circumstances which make it right that he should receive compensation, there may be paid to him a sum by way of compensation of such amount as may be so determined.

(4) Payments required to be made under this section shall be made by the Secretary of State.

(5) The consent of the Treasury is required for the making of a determination under this section.   **[946]**

NOTES
Commencement: 16 October 1992.
Sub-ss (1)–(3) contain provisions formerly in the Employment Act 1988, Sch 1, para 2(1)–(3). Sub-s (4) contains provisions formerly in Sch 1, para 2(5) to the 1988 Act. Sub-s (5) contains provisions formerly in Sch 1, para 2(4) to the 1988 Act.
Sub-ss (1), (3): words in italics substituted in each case by words in square brackets immediately following by the Trade Union Reform and Employment Rights Act 1993, s 49(2), Sch 8, para 81(a), (c), as from 30 August 1993 (SI 1993/1908, below, para **[1435]**).
Sub-s (2): words in italics substituted by words in square brackets immediately following by the Trade Union Reform and Employment Rights Act 1993, s 49(2), Sch 8, para 81(b), as from 30 August 1993 (SI 1993/1908, below, para **[1435]**).

269 Staff of the Commissioner

(1) *The Commissioner* [Each of the Commissioners] may appoint such staff as he may determine, with the approval of the Secretary of State as to numbers and terms and conditions of service.

The consent of the Treasury is required for the giving of an approval under this subsection.

(2) Employment as a member of the staff of *the Commissioner* [one of the Commissioners] is one of the kinds of employment to which a superannuation scheme under section 1 of the Superannuation Act 1972 may apply.

(3) Where a person who is a participant in a scheme under section 1 of that Act by reference to his employment by *the Commissioner becomes the Commissioner* [one of the Commissioners becomes one of the Commissioners], the Treasury may determine that his service as *the Commissioner shall be treated for the purposes of the scheme as service as an employee of the Commissioner* [Commissioner shall be treated for the purposes of the scheme as service as an employee]; and his rights under the scheme shall not be affected by the preceding provisions of this Part.

(4) *The Commissioner is not* [Neither of the Commissioners is] required to effect insurance under the Employers' Liability (Compulsory Insurance) Act 1969. **[947]**

NOTES

Commencement: 16 October 1992.

Sub-s (1) contains provisions formerly in the Employment Act 1988, Sch 1, para 3. Sub-ss (2), (3) contain provisions formerly in Sch 1, para 5(1), (2) to the 1988 Act. Sub-s (4) contains provisions formerly in Sch 1, para 6 to the 1988 Act.

Sub-s (1): words in italics substituted by words in square brackets immediately following by the Trade Union Reform and Employment Rights Act 1993, s 49(2), Sch 8, para 82(a), as from 30 August 1993 (SI 1993/1908, below, para [1435]).

Sub-s (2): words in italics substituted in each case by words in square brackets immediately following by the Trade Union Reform and Employment Rights Act 1993, s 49(2), Sch 8, para 82(b), as from 30 August 1993 (SI 1993/1908, below, para [1435]).

Sub-s (3): words in italics substituted by the Trade Union Reform and Employment Rights Act 1993, s 49(2), Sch 8, para 82(c), as from 30 August 1993 (SI 1993/1908, below, para [1435]).

Sub-s (4): words in italics substituted by words in square brackets immediately following by the Trade Union Reform and Employment Rights Act 1993, s 49(2), Sch 8, para 82(d), as from 30 August 1993 (SI 1993/1908, para [1435]).

270 Financial provisions

(1) *The Commissioner* [Each of the Commissioners] may, with the approval of the Secretary of State, make such provision as he considers appropriate for the payment by him to those who apply for assistance of sums in respect of travelling and other expenses incurred by them in connection with their applications.

(2) The Secretary of State shall pay *to the Commissioner* [to each of the Commissioners] such sums as he may determine are required *by the Commissioner* [by him] for the purpose of carrying out his functions.

(3) The consent of the Treasury is required for the giving of an approval under subsection (1) or the making of a determination under subsection (2).   ·   **[948]**

NOTES

Commencement: 16 October 1992.

Sub-s (1) contains provisions formerly in the Employment Act 1988, Sch 1, para 7(1). Sub-s (2) contains provisions formerly in Sch 1, para 8(1) to the 1988 Act. Sub-s (3) contains provisions formerly in Sch 1, paras 7(2), 8(2) to the 1988 Act.

Sub-s (1): words in italics substituted by words in square brackets immediately following by the Trade Union Reform and Employment Rights Act 1993, s 49(2), Sch 8, para 83(a), as from 30 August 1993 (SI 1993/1908, below, para [1435]).

Sub-s (2): words in italics substituted in each case by words in square brackets immediately following, by the Trade Union Reform and Employment Rights Act 1993, s 49(2), Sch 8, para 83(b), as from 30 August 1993 (SI 1993/1908, below, para [1435]).

271 Annual report and accounts

(1) As soon as reasonably practicable after the end of a financial year *the Commissioner* [each of the Commissioners] shall prepare a report on his activities during that year and shall send a copy of it to the Secretary of State.

The Secretary of State shall lay a copy of the report before each House of Parliament.

(2) *The Commissioner* [Each of the Commissioners] shall keep proper accounts and proper records in relation to the accounts, and shall prepare in respect of each financial year a statement of accounts in such form as the Secretary of State may, with the approval of the Treasury, direct.

(3) *The Commissioner* [Each of the Commissioners] shall, not later than 30th November following the end of the financial year to which the statement relates, send copies of the statement to the Secretary of State and to the Comptroller and Auditor General.

(4) The Comptroller and Auditor General shall examine, certify and report on each such statement and shall lay a copy of the statement and of his report before each House of Parliament.   **[949]**

NOTES

Commencement: 16 October 1992.

Sub-s (1) contains provisions formerly in the Employment Act 1988, Sch 1, para 10. Sub-s (2) contains provisions formerly in Sch 1, para 9(1)(a), (b) to the 1988 Act. Sub-s (3) contains provisions formerly in Sch 1, para 9(1)(c) to the 1988 Act. Sub-s (4) contains provisions formerly in Sch 1, para 9(2) to the 1988 Act.

Sub-s (1): words in italics substituted by words in square brackets immediately following by the Trade Union Reform and Employment Rights Act 1993, s 49(2), Sch 8, para 84(a), as from 30 August 1993 (SI 1993/1908, below, para **[1435]**).

Sub-ss (2), (3): words in italics in both subsections substituted by words in square brackets immediately following by the Trade Union Reform and Employment Rights Act 1993, s 49(2), Sch 8, para 84(b), as from 30 August 1993 (SI 1993/1908, below, para **[1435]**).

Supplementary

272 Meaning of "financial year"

In this Part "financial year" means the twelve months ending with 31st March.
                                                                                                [950]

NOTES

Commencement: 16 October 1992.

This section contains provisions formerly in the Employment Protection Act 1975, Sch 1, Pt III, para 35(3), and in the Employment Act 1988, Sch 1, para 14.

PART VII

MISCELLANEOUS AND GENERAL

Crown employment, etc.

273 Crown employment

(1) The provisions of this Act have effect (except as mentioned below) in relation to Crown employment and persons in Crown employment as in relation to other employment and other workers or employees.

(2) The following provisions are excepted from subsection (1)—

section 87(3) (power of court to make order in respect of employer's failure to comply with duties as to union contributions);

sections 184 and 185 (remedy for failure to comply with declaration as to disclosure of information);

Chapter II of Part IV (procedure for handling redundancies).

(3) In this section "Crown employment" means employment under or for the purposes of a government department or any officer or body exercising on behalf of the Crown functions conferred by an enactment.

(4) For the purposes of the provisions of this Act as they apply in relation to Crown employment or persons in Crown employment—

(a) "employee" and "contract of employment" mean a person in Crown employment and the terms of employment of such a person (but subject to subsection (5) below);

(b) "dismissal" means the termination of Crown employment;

(c) *"redundancy" means the existence of such circumstances as, in accordance with any arrangements for the time being in force as mentioned in section 111(3) of the Employment Protection (Consolidation) Act 1978 are treated as equivalent to redundancy in relation to Crown employment;*

(d) the reference in 182(1)(e) (disclosure of information for collective bargaining: restrictions on general duty) to the employer's undertaking shall be construed as a reference to the national interest; and

(e) any other reference to an undertaking shall be construed, in relation to a Minister of the Crown, as a reference to his functions or (as the context may require) to the department of which he is in charge, and in relation to a government department, officer or body shall be construed as a reference to the functions of the department, officer or body or (as the context may require) to the department, officer or body.

(5) Sections 137 to 143 (rights in relation to trade union membership: access to employment) apply in relation to Crown employment otherwise than under a contract only where the terms of employment correspond to those of a contract of employment.

(6) This section has effect subject to section 274 (armed forces) and section 275 (exemption on grounds of national security).   **[951]**

NOTES

Commencement: 16 October 1992.

Sub-s (1) contains provisions formerly in the Industrial Courts Act 1919, s 10(1), as substituted by the Employment Protection Act 1975, s 125(1), Sch 16, Pt IV, para 3(1), (4); in the Trade Union and Labour Relations Act 1974, Sch 1, Pt IV, para 33(1); in the Employment Protection Act 1975, s 121(1) (in part), as repealed in part by the Employment Protection (Consolidation) Act 1978, s 159(3), Sch 17, and as amended and repealed in part by the Employment Act 1980, s 20(2), (3), Sch 1, para 5, Sch 2; in the Trade Union Act 1984, s 18(7) (in part); in the Employment Act 1988, s 30(3) (in part); in the Employment Act 1990, Sch 1, Pt II, para 11(1); and deriving from s 138(1) of the 1978 Act, as repealed in part by the Social Security Act 1986, s 86(2), Sch 11. Sub-s (2) contains provisions formerly in s 121(1) (in part) of the 1975 Act, as repealed in part by s 159(3) of, Sch 17 to, the 1978 Act, and as amended and repealed in part by s 20(2), (3) of, Sch 1, para 5, Sch 2 to, the 1980 Act, and in s 18(7) (in part) of the 1984 Act. Sub-s (3) contains provisions formerly in s 10(2) of the 1919 Act, as substituted by s 125(1) of, Sch 16, Pt IV, para 3(1), (4) to, the 1975 Act; in Sch 1, Pt IV, para 33(2) (in part) to the 1974 Act, as amended by s 125(1) of, Sch 16, Pt III, para 33 to, the 1975 Act; in s 121(2) of the 1975 Act; in s 30(3) (in part) of the 1988 Act; in Sch 1, Pt II, para 11(2) to the 1990 Act; and deriving from s 138(2) of the 1978 Act. Sub-s (4) contains provisions formerly in Sch 1, Pt IV, para 33(3) to the 1974 Act, as amended by s 125(1) of, Sch 16, Pt III, paras 33, 34 to, the 1975 Act, and as repealed in part by s 159(3) of, Sch 17 to, the 1978 Act; in s 121(7) of the 1975 Act, as amended by s 159(2) of, Sch 16, para 23(1), (11) to, the 1978 Act; and deriving from s 138(7) of the 1978 Act. Sub-s (5) contains provisions formerly in Sch 1, Pt II, para 13(a) to the 1990 Act. Sub-s (6) is a drafting provision.

Sub-s (4): para (c) repealed by the Trade Union Reform and Employment Rights Act 1993, s 51, Sch 10, as from 30 August 1993 (SI 1993/1908, below, para **[1435]**).

274 Armed forces

(1) Section 273 (application of Act to Crown employment) does not apply to service as a member of the naval, military or air forces of the Crown.

(2) But that section applies to employment by an association established for the purposes of Part VI of the Reserve Forces Act 1980 (territorial, auxiliary and reserve forces associations) as it applies to employment for the purposes of a government department.   [952]

NOTES
Commencement: 16 October 1992.
This section contains provisions formerly in the Industrial Courts Act 1919, s 10(3), as substituted by the Employment Protection Act 1975, s 125(1), Sch 16, Pt IV, para 3(1), (4), and as read with the Interpretation Act 1978, s 17(2)(a); in the Trade Union and Labour Relations Act 1974, Sch 1, Pt IV, paras 33(2) (in part), 33(4)(b), as amended (in the case of para 33(4)(b)) by the Reserve Forces Act 1980, s 157, Sch 9, para 15; in s 121(3) of the 1975 Act, as repealed in part by the Armed Forces Act 1981, s 28(2), Sch 5, Pt I, and as read with s 17(2)(a) of the 1978 Act; and in the Employment Act 1990, Sch 1, Pt II, para 11(3).

275 Exemption on grounds of national security

(1) Section 273 (application of Act to Crown employment) does not apply to employment in respect of which there is in force a certificate issued by or on behalf of a Minister of the Crown certifying that employment of a description specified in the certificate, or the employment of a particular person so specified, is (or, at a time specified in the certificate, was) required to be excepted from that section for the purpose of safeguarding national security.

(2) A document purporting to be such a certificate shall, unless the contrary is proved, be deemed to be such a certificate.   [953]

NOTES
Commencement: 16 October 1992.
This section contains provisions formerly in the Industrial Courts Act 1919, s 10(4), as substituted by the Employment Protection Act 1975, s 125(1), Sch 16, Pt IV, para 3(1), (4); in the Trade Union and Labour Relations Act 1974, Sch 1, Pt IV, para 33(5); in s 121(4) of the 1975 Act; in the Employment Act 1990, Sch 1, Pt II, para 11(4); and deriving from the Employment Protection (Consolidation) Act 1978, s 138(4).

276 Further provision as to Crown application

(1) Section 138 (refusal of service of employment agency on grounds related to union membership), and the other provisions of Part III applying in relation to that section, bind the Crown so far as they relate to the activities of an employment agency in relation to employment to which those provisions apply.

This does not affect the operation of those provisions in relation to Crown employment by virtue of section 273.

(2) Sections 144 and 145 (prohibition of union membership requirements) and sections 186 and 187 (prohibition of union recognition requirements) bind the Crown.
                                                                                                            [954]

NOTES
Commencement: 16 October 1992.
Sub-s (1) contains provisions formerly in the Employment Act 1990, Sch 1, Pt II, para 18. Sub-s (2) contains provisions formerly in the Employment Act 1988, s 30(2).

House of Lords and House of Commons staff

277 House of Lords staff

(1) *Sections 137 to 143 (rights in relation to trade union membership: access to employment)* [The provisions of this Act (except those specified below)] apply in relation to employment as a relevant member of the House of Lords staff as in relation to other employment.

[(1A) The following provisions are excepted from subsection (1)—

sections 184 and 185 (remedy for failure to comply with declaration as to disclosure of information),

Chapter II of Part IV (procedure for handling redundancies).]

(2) Nothing in any rule of law or the law or practice of Parliament prevents a person from bringing [a civil employment claim before the court or from bringing] before an industrial tribunal proceedings of any description *under those sections* which could be brought before such a tribunal in relation to other employment.

[(2A) For the purposes of the application of the other provisions of this Act as they apply by virtue of this section—

(a) the reference in section 182(1)(e) (disclosure of information for collective bargaining: restrictions) to a person's undertaking shall be construed as a reference to the national interest or, if the case so requires, the interests of the House of Lords; and

(b) any other reference to an undertaking shall be construed as a reference to the House of Lords.]

(3) A "relevant member of the House of Lords staff" means a member of the House of Lords staff appointed by the Clerk of the Parliaments or the Gentleman Usher of the Black Rod.

(4) In relation to employment as such a member references to employment include employment otherwise than under a contract if the terms of that employment correspond to those of a contract of employment; and related expressions shall be construed accordingly.

(5) For the purposes of sections 137 to 143 the holder for the time being of the office of Clerk of the Parliaments or Gentleman Usher of the Black Rod is the employer in relation to employment to which a person is appointed by the holder of that office; and anything done, before or after he took office, in relation to a person seeking such employment shall be treated as done by him.

(6) If the House of Lords resolves at any time that any provision of subsection (3) or (5) should be amended in its application to any employment as a member of the staff of that House, Her Majesty may by Order in Council amend that provision accordingly.

Any such Order—

(a) may contain such incidental, supplementary or transitional provisions as appear to Her Majesty to be appropriate, and

(b) shall be subject to annulment in pursuance of a resolution of either House of Parliament.   **[955]**

NOTES

Commencement: 16 October 1992.

Sub-ss (1), (2) contain provisions formerly in the Employment Act 1990, Sch 1, Pt II, para 12(1) (in part), (2). Sub-s (3) contains provisions formerly in Sch 1, Pt II, para 12(4) to the 1990 Act. Sub-s (4) contains provisions formerly in Sch 1, Pt II, para 13(b) (in part) to the 1990 Act. Sub-ss (5), (6) contain provisions formerly in Sch 1, Pt II, para 12(5), (6) to the 1990 Act.

Sub-s (1): words in italics substituted by words in square brackets immediately following by the Trade Union Reform and Employment Rights Act 1993, s 49(1), Sch 7, para 12(a), as from a day to be appointed.

Sub-s (1A): inserted by the Trade Union Reform and Employment Rights Act 1993, s 49(1), Sch 7, para 12(b), as from a day to be appointed.

Sub-s (2): words in square brackets inserted, and words in italics repealed, by the Trade Union Reform and Employment Rights Act 1993, ss 49(1), 51, Sch 7, para 12(c), Sch 10, as from a day to be appointed.

Sub-s (2A): inserted by the Trade Union Reform and Employment Rights Act 1993, s 49(1), Sch 7, para 12(d), as from a day to be appointed.

Sub-ss (3)–(6): substituted by a new sub-s (3) by the Trade Union Reform and Employment Rights Act 1993, s 49(1), Sch 7, para 12(e), as from a day to be appointed, as follows—

"(3) In this section—
    "relevant member of the House of Lords staff" means any person who is employed under a contract of employment with the Corporate Officer of the House of Lords;
    "civil employment claim" means a claim arising out of or relating to a contract of employment or any other contract connected with employment, or a claim in tort arising in connection with a person's employment; and
    "the court" means the High Court or a county court.".

278 House of Commons staff

(1) The provisions of this Act (except those specified below) apply in relation to employment as a relevant member of the House of Commons staff as in relation to other employment.

(2) The following provisions are excepted from subsection (1)—

sections 184 and 185 (remedy for failure to comply with declaration as to disclosure of information),

Chapter II of Part IV (procedure for handling redundancies).

[(2A) Nothing in any rule of law or the law or practice of Parliament prevents a relevant member of the House of Commons staff from bringing a civil employment claim before the court or from bringing before an industrial tribunal proceedings of any description which could be brought before such a tribunal by any person who is not such a member.]

(3) In this section "relevant member of the House of Commons staff" has the same meaning as in section 139 of the Employment Protection (Consolidation) Act 1978.

["civil employment claim" means a claim arising out of or relating to a contract of employment or any other contract connected with employment, or a claim in tort arising in connection with a person's employment; and

"the court" means the High Court or the county court.]

(4) For the purposes of the other provisions of this Act as they apply by virtue of this section—

(a) "employee" and "contract of employment" include a relevant member of the House of Commons staff and the terms of employment of any such member (but subject to subsection (5) below);

(b) "dismissal" includes the termination of any such member's employment;

(c) the reference in [section] 182(1)(e) (disclosure of information for collective bargaining: restrictions on general duty) to the employer's undertaking shall be construed as a reference to the national interest or, if the case so requires, the interests of the House of Commons; and

(d) any other reference to an undertaking shall be construed as a reference to the House of Commons.

(5) Sections 137 to 143 (access to employment) apply by virtue of this section in relation to employment otherwise than under a contract only where the terms of employment correspond to those of a contract of employment.

(6) Subsections (4) to (9) of section 139 of the Employment Protection (Consolidation) Act 1978 (person to be treated as employer of House of Commons staff) apply, with any necessary modifications, for the purposes of this section.

[956]

NOTES

Commencement: 16 October 1992.

Sub-ss (1), (2) contain provisions formerly in the Employment Protection Act 1975, s 122(1) (in part), as repealed in part by the Employment Protection (Consolidation) Act 1978, s 159(3), Sch 17; in the Employment Act 1990, Sch 1, Pt II, para 12(1) (in part); and deriving from s 139(1) of the 1978 Act, as repealed in part by the Social Security Act 1986, s 86(2), Sch 11. Sub-s (3) contains provisions formerly in s 122(4) (definition "relevant member of the House of Commons staff") of the 1975 Act, as substituted by the House of Commons (Administration) Act 1978, s 5(3), Sch 2, para 5(1), (3), and in Sch 1, Pt II, para 12(3) (in part) to the 1990 Act. Sub-s (4) contains provisions formerly in s 122(1) of the 1975 Act, as repealed in part by s 159(3) of, Sch 17 to, the 1978 Act, and as amended, in the case of s 122(1)(b), (c), by the House of Commons (Administration) Act 1978, s 5(3), Sch 2, para 5(1), (2); and in Sch 1, Pt II, para 12(3) (in part) to the 1990 Act. Sub-s (5) contains provisions formerly in Sch 1, Pt II, para 13(b) (in part) to the 1990 Act. Sub-s (6) contains provisions formerly in s 122(5)–(8) of the 1975 Act, as repealed in part (in the case of s 122(5)) by the Employment Protection (Consolidation) Act 1978, s 159(3), Sch 17, and as substituted (in the case of s 122(5), (6), (7), (7A), (7B)) and amended (in the case of s 122(8)) by the House of Commons (Administration) Act 1978, s 5(3), Sch 2, para 5(1), (3), (4); and in Sch 1, Pt II, para 12(3) (in part) to the 1990 Act.

Sub-s (2A): inserted by the Trade Union Reform and Employment Rights Act 1993, s 49(2), Sch 8, para 85(a), as from a day to be appointed.

Sub-s (3): definitions "civil employment claim" and "the court" inserted by the Trade Union Reform and Employment Rights Act 1993, s 49(2), Sch 8, para 85(b), as from a day to be appointed.

Sub-s (4): word in square brackets in para (c) inserted by the Trade Union Reform and Employment Rights Act 1993, s 49(1), Sch 7, para 27, as from 30 August 1993 (SI 1993/1908, below, para **[1435]**).

Health service practitioners

279 Health service practitioners

In this Act "worker" includes an individual regarded in his capacity as one who works or normally works or seeks to work as a person providing general medical services, general dental services, general ophthalmic services or pharmaceutical services in accordance with arrangements made—

(a) by a Family Health Services Authority under section 29, 35, 38 or 41 of the National Heath Service Act 1977, or

(b) by a Health Board under section 19, 25, 26, or 27 of the National Health Service (Scotland) Act 1978;

and "employer", in relation to such an individual, regarded in that capacity, means that authority or board.   **[957]**

NOTES

Commencement: 16 October 1992.

This section contains provisions formerly in the Trade Union and Labour Relations Act 1974, s 30(2), as amended by the National Health Service Act 1977, s 129, Sch 15, para 62, and by the Health Services Act 1980, ss 1, 2, Sch 1, Pt I, para 25; in the National Health Service (Scotland) Act 1978, Sch 16, para 39; and as read with the National Health Service and Community Care Act 1990, s 2(1)(b); and formerly in the Employment Protection Act 1975, s 126(1) (definition "worker").

Police service

280 Police service

(1) In this Act "employee" or "worker" does not include a person in police service; and the provisions of sections 137 and 138 (rights in relation to trade union membership: access to employment) do not apply in relation to police service.

(2) "Police service" means service as a member of any constabulary maintained by virtue of an enactment, or in any other capacity by virtue of which a person has the powers or privileges of a constable.   **[958]**

NOTES
Commencement: 16 October 1992.

Sub-s (1) contains provisions formerly in the Trade Union and Labour Relations Act 1974, s 30(1) (definitions "employee" (in part), "worker" (in part)); in the Employment Protection Act 1975, s 126(1) (definitions "employee" (in part), "worker" (in part)); in the Employment Act 1990, Sch 1, Pt II, para 14 (in part); and deriving from the Employment Protection (Consolidation) Act 1978, s 146(2) (in part). Sub-s (2) contains provisions formerly in s 30(1) (definition "police service") of the 1974 Act; in Sch 1, Pt II, para 14 (remainder) to the 1990 Act; and deriving from s 146(3) of the 1978 Act.

Excluded classes of employment

281 Part-time employment

(1) Sections 168 and 170 (time off for trade union duties and activities) do not apply to employment under a contract which normally involves employment for less than sixteen hours weekly.

(2) If the employee's relations with his employer cease to be governed by a contract which normally involve work for sixteen hours or more weekly and become governed by a contract which normally involves employment for eight hours or more, but less than sixteen hours, weekly, the employee shall nevertheless for a period of 26 weeks be treated for the purposes of this section as if his contract normally involved employment for sixteen hours or more weekly.

(3) In computing that period of 26 weeks no account shall be taken of any week—

(a) during which the employee is in fact employed for sixteen hours or more;
(b) during which the employee takes part in a strike (as defined by paragraph 24 of Schedule 13 to the Employment Protection (Consolidation) Act 1978); or
(c) during which there is no contract of employment but which by virtue of paragraph 9(1) of that Schedule counts in computing a period of continuous employment.

(4) An employee whose relations with his employer are governed by a contract of employment which normally involves employment for eight hours or more, but less than sixteen hours, weekly shall nevertheless, if he had been continuously employed for a period of five years or more be treated for the purposes of this section as if his contract normally involved employment for sixteen hours or more weekly.

(5) Section 151 of and Schedule 13 to the Employment Protection (Consolidation) Act 1978 (computation of period of continuous employment), and any provision modifying or supplementing that section or Schedule for the purposes of that Act, apply for the purposes of this section; and references in this section to weeks are to weeks within the meaning of that Schedule.

(6) An employee's normal working hours for the purposes of this section shall be calculated in accordance with Part I of Schedule 14 to that Act.   **[959]**

NOTES
Commencement: 16 October 1992.

Sub-s (1) contains provisions formerly in the Employment Protection (Consolidation) Act 1978, s 146(4) (in part). Sub-ss (2)–(4) contain provisions deriving from s 146(5)–(7) of the 1978 Act. Sub-s (5) contains provisions deriving from ss 146(8), 151 of the 1978 Act. Sub-s (6) contains provisions deriving from s 152 of the 1978 Act.

282 Short-term employment

(1) The provisions of Chapter II of Part IV (procedure for handling redundancies) do not apply to employment—

(a) under a contract for a fixed term of three months or less, or

(b) under a contract made in contemplation of the performance of a specific task which is not expected to last for more than three months,

where the employee has not been continuously employed for a period of more than three months.

(2) Section 151 of and Schedule 13 to the Employment Protection (Consolidation) Act 1978 (computation of period of continuous employment), and any provision modifying or supplementing that section or Schedule for the purposes of that Act, apply for the purposes of this section.   **[960]**

NOTES
Commencement: 16 October 1992.
This section contains provisions formerly in the Employment Protection Act 1975, s 119(7), as repealed in part by the Employment Protection (Consolidation) Act 1978, s 159(3), Sch 17, and as amended by the Employment Act 1982, s 20, Sch 2, para 6(1).

283 Mariners

(1) The provisions of Chapter II of Part IV (procedure for handling redundancies) do not apply to employment as a merchant seaman.

(2) For this purpose employment as a merchant seaman means employment as master or as a member of the crew of a sea-going ship, including an apprentice or trainee employed on any such ship and employment as a radio officer on such a ship.   **[961]**

NOTES
Commencement: 16 October 1992.
Sub-ss (1), (2) contain provisions formerly in the Employment Protection Act 1975, s 119(12), (14).
Repealed by the Trade Union reform and Employment Rights Act 1993, ss 34(1), (6), 51, Sch 10, as from 30 August 1993 (SI 1993/1908, below, para **[1435]**).
For transitional provisions as to the commencement of this repeal see SI 1993/1908, Art 3(12).

284 Share fishermen

The following provisions of this Act do not apply to employment as master or as member of the crew of a fishing vessel where the employee is remunerated only by a share in the profits or gross earnings of the vessel—

In Part III (rights in relation to trade union membership and activities)—
sections 137 to 143 (access to employment),
sections 146 to 151 (action short of dismissal), and
sections 168 to 173 (time off for trade union duties and activities);
In Part IV, Chapter II (procedure for handling redundancies).   **[962]**

NOTES
Commencement: 16 October 1992.
This section contains provisions formerly in the Employment Protection Act 1975, s 119(4), as repealed in part by the Employment Protection (Consolidation) Act 1978, s 159(3), Sch 17; in the Employment Act 1990, Sch 1, Pt II, para 16(3); and deriving from s 144(2) of the 1978 Act.

285 Employment outside Great Britain

(1) The following provisions of this Act do not apply to employment where under his contract of employment an employee works, or in the case of a prospective employee would ordinarily work, outside Great Britain

In Part III (rights in relation to trade union membership and activities)—

sections 137 to 143 (access to employment),
sections 146 to 151 (action short of dismissal), and
sections 168 to 173 (time off for trade union duties and activities);

In Part IV, Chapter II (procedure for handling redundancies).

(2) For the purposes of subsection (1) employment on board a ship registered in the United Kingdom shall be treated as employment where under his contract a person ordinarily works in Great Britain unless—

(a) the ship is registered at a port outside Great Britain, or
(b) the employment is wholly outside Great Britain, or
(c) the employee or, as the case may be, the person seeking employment or seeking to avail himself of a service of an employment agency, is not ordinarily resident in Great Britain.   [963]

NOTES
Commencement: 16 October 1992.
Sub-s (1) contains provisions formerly in the Employment Protection Act 1975, s 119(5), as repealed in part by the Employment Protection (Consolidation) Act 1978, s 159(3), Sch 17; in the Employment Act 1990, Sch 1, Pt II, para 15, and deriving from the Employment Protection (Consolidation) Act 1978, s 141(2). Sub-s (2) contains provisions formerly in s 119(6) of the 1975 Act; in Sch 1, Pt II, para 16(1), (2) to the 1990 Act, and deriving from s 141(5) of the 1978 Act.

286 Power to make further provision as to excluded classes of employment

(1) This section applies in relation to the following provisions—

In Part III (rights in relation to trade union membership and activities), sections 146 to 151 (action short of dismissal),
In Part IV, Chapter II (procedure for handling redundancies), and
In Part V (industrial action), section 237 (dismissal of those taking part in unofficial industrial action).

(2) The Secretary of State may by order made by statutory instrument provide that any of those provisions—

(a) shall not apply to persons or to employment of such classes as may be prescribed by the order, or
(b) shall apply to persons or employments of such classes as may be prescribed by the order subject to such exceptions and modifications as may be so prescribed,

and may vary or revoke any of the provisions of sections 281 to 285 above (excluded classes of employment) so far as they relate to any such provision.

(3) Any such order shall be made by statutory instrument and may contains such incidental, supplementary or transitional provisions as appear to the Secretary of State to be necessary or expedient.

(4) No such order shall be made unless a draft of the order has been laid before Parliament and approved by a resolution of each House of Parliament.   [964]

NOTES
Commencement: 16 October 1992.
Sub-ss (1), (2) contain provisions formerly in the Employment Protection Act 1975, s 119(15), and deriving from the Employment Protection (Consolidation) Act 1978, s 149(1), (2) (both in part). Sub-s (3) contains provisions formerly in s 123(3) of the 1975 Act, and deriving from s 154(3) of the 1978 Act. Sub-s (4) contains provisions formerly in s 119(16) of the 1975 Act; and deriving from s 149(4) of the 1978 Act.

Offshore employment

287 Offshore employment

(1) In this Act "offshore employment" means employment for the purposes of activities

    (a) in the territorial waters of the United Kingdom, or

    (b) connected with the exploration of the sea-bed or subsoil, or the exploitation of their natural resources, in the United Kingdom sector of the continental shelf, or

    (c) connected with the exploration or exploitation, in a foreign sector of the continental shelf, of a cross-boundary petroleum field.

  (2) Her Majesty may by Order in Council provide that—

    (a) the provisions of this Act, and

    (b) any Northern Ireland legislation making provision for purposes corresponding to any of the purposes of this Act,

apply, to such extent and for such purposes as may be specified in the Order and with or without modification, to or in relation to a person in offshore employment or, in relation to sections 137 to 143 (access to employment), a person seeking such employment.

  (3) An Order in Council under this section—

    (a) may make different provision for different cases;

    (b) may provide that the enactments to which this section applies, as applied, apply—

      (i) to individuals whether or not they are British subjects, and

      (ii) to bodies corporate whether or not they are incorporated under the law of a part of the United Kingdom,

and apply notwithstanding that the application may affect the activities of such an individual or body outside the United Kingdom;

    (c) may make provision for conferring jurisdiction on any court or class of court specified in the Order, or on industrial tribunals, in respect of offences, causes of action or other matters arising in connection with offshore employment;

    (d) may provide that the enactments to which this section applies apply in relation to a person in offshore employment in a part of the areas referred to in subsection (1)(a) and (b);

    (e) may exclude from the operation of section 3 of the Territorial Waters Jurisdiction Act 1878 (consents required for prosecutions) proceedings for offences under the enactments to which this section applies in connection with offshore employment;

    (f) may provide that such proceedings shall not be brought without such consent as may be required by the Order;

    (g) may modify or exclude any of sections 281 to 285 (excluded classes of employment) or any corresponding provision of Northern Ireland legislation.

  (4) Any jurisdiction conferred on a court or tribunal under this section is without prejudice to jurisdiction exercisable apart from this section, by that or any other court or tribunal.

  (5) In this section—

    "cross-boundary petroleum field" means a petroleum field that extends across

*the boundary between the United Kingdom sector of the continental shelf
and a foreign sector;*
*"foreign sector of the continental shelf" means an area outside the territorial
waters of any state, within which rights with respect to the sea-bed and
subsoil and their natural resources are exercisable by a state other than
the United Kingdom;*
*"petroleum field" means a geological structure identified as an oil or gas field
by the Order in Council concerned; and*
*"United Kingdom sector of the continental shelf" means the areas designated
under section 1(7) of the Continental Shelf Act 1964.*   **[965]**

NOTES
Commencement: 16 October 1992.
Sub-s (1) contains provisions formerly in the Employment Protection Act 1975, s 127(2); in the
Employment (Continental Shelf) Act 1978, s 1(1); deriving from the Employment Protection
(Consolidation) Act 1978, s 137(2), and contains drafting provisions. Sub-s (2) contains provisions
formerly in s 127(1)(e)–(g) of the 1975 Act, as inserted, in the case of s 127(1)(ff), by the Employment
Act 1980, s 20(2), Sch 1, para 7, and in the case of s 127(1)(fg), by the Employment Act 1982, s 21(2),
Sch 3, para 13(1), (4), and as repealed in part, in the case of s 127(1)(g), by s 20(3) of, Sch 2 to, the 1980
Act; in the Employment Act 1990, Sch 1, Pt II, para 17; and deriving from the Employment Protection
(Consolidation) Act 1978, s 137(1). Sub-s (3) contains provisions formerly in s 127(3) of the 1975 Act,
as repealed in part by the Employment Protection (Consolidation) Act 1978, s 159(3), Sch 17, and deriving
from the Employment Protection (Consolidation) Act 1978, s 137(3). Sub-s (4) contains provisions
formerly in s 127(4) of the 1975 Act, and deriving from the Employment Protection (Consolidation) Act
1978, s 137(4). Sub-s (5) contains provisions deriving from the Employment (Continental Shelf) Act 1978,
s 2, and from the Employment Protection (Consolidation) Act 1978, s 137(5), and also contains drafting
provisions.
Sub-s (1): prospectively substituted by the Oil and Gas (Enterprise) Act 1982, Sch 3, para 45, as added
by s 300(2) of, Sch 2, para 29(1), (3), (4) to, this Act, as follows—
"(1) In this Act "offshore employment" means employment for the purposes of—
    (a)   any activities in the territorial waters of the United Kingdom, and
    (b)   any such activities as are mentioned in section 23(2) of the Oil and Gas (Enterprise) Act 1982
           in waters within subsection (6)(b) or (c) of that section.".
Sub-s (5): prospectively repealed by the Oil and Gas (Enterprise) Act 1982, Sch 3, para 45, as added
by s 300(2) of, and Sch 2, para 29(1), (3), (4) to, this Act.
Orders under this section: the Employment Protection (Offshore Employment) Order 1976, SI
1976/766, as amended by SI 1977/588, SI 1984/1149.

Contracting out, &c

288 Restriction on contracting out

(1) Any provision in an agreement (whether a contract of employment or not) is void
in so far as it purports—

    (a) to exclude or limit the operation of any provision of this Act, or
    (b) to preclude a person from bringing—

        (i) proceedings before an industrial tribunal or the Central Arbitration
        Committee under any provision of this Act, or
        (ii) an application to the Employment Appeal Tribunal under section 67
        (remedy for infringement of right not to be unjustifiably disciplined)
        or section 176 (compensation for *unreasonable* exclusion or
        expulsion).

(2) Subsection (1) does not apply to an agreement to refrain from instituting or
continuing proceedings where a conciliation officer has taken action under—

    (a) section 133(2) or (3) of the Employment Protection (Consolidation) Act
    1978 (general provisions as to conciliation), or
    (b) section 134(1), (2) or (3) of that Act (conciliation in case of unfair
    dismissal).

[(2A) Subsection (1) does not apply to an agreement to refrain from instituting or continuing any proceedings, other than excepted proceedings, specified in section 290 before an industrial tribunal if the conditions regulating compromise agreements under this Act are satisfied in relation to the agreement.

(2B) The conditions regulating compromise agreements under this Act are that—

(a) the agreement must be in writing;

(b) the agreement must relate to the particular complaint;

(c) the complainant must have received independent legal advice from a qualified lawyer as to the terms and effect of the proposed agreement and in particular its effect on his ability to pursue his rights before an industrial tribunal;

(d) there must be in force, when the adviser gives the advice, a policy of insurance covering the risk of a claim by the complainant in respect of loss arising in consequence of the advice;

(e) the agreement must identify the adviser; and

(f) the agreement must state that the conditions regulating compromise agreements under this Act are satisfied.

(2C) The proceedings excepted from subsection (2A) are proceedings on a complaint of non-compliance with section 188.]

(3) Subsection (1) does not apply—

(a) to such an agreement as is referred to in section 185(5)(b) or (c) to the extent that it varies or supersedes an award under that section;

(b) to any provision in a collective agreement excluding rights under Chapter II of Part IV (procedure for handling redundancies), if an order under section 198 is in force in respect of it.

[(4) In subsection (2B)—

"independent", in relation to legal advice to the complainant means that it is given by a lawyer who is not acting for the other party or for a person who is connected with that other party; and

"qualified lawyer" means—

(a) as respects proceedings in England and Wales—

(i) a barrister, whether in practice as such or employed to give legal advice, or

(ii) a solicitor of the Supreme Court who holds a practising certificate;

(b) as respects proceedings in Scotland—

(i) an advocate, whether in practice as such or employed to give legal advice, or

(ii) a solicitor who holds a practising certificate.

(5) For the purposes of subsection (4) any two persons are to be treated as "connected" if one is a company of which the other (directly or indirectly) has control, or if both are companies of which a third person (directly or indirectly) has control.]

[966]

NOTES

Commencement: 16 October 1992.

Sub-s (1) contains provisions formerly in the Trade Union and Labour Relations Act 1974, Sch 1, Pt IV, para 32(1)(a), as repealed in part by the Employment Act 1980, s 20(3), Sch 2; in the Employment Protection Act 1975, s 118(1); in the Employment Act 1980, s 4(11) (in part); in the Employment Act 1988, s 4(7) (in part); in the Employment Act 1990, Sch 1, Pt II, para 10(1); and deriving from the Employment Protection (Consolidation) Act 1978, s 140(1). Sub-s (2) contains provisions formerly in s 4(11) (remainder) of the 1980 Act; in s 4(7) (in part) of the 1988 Act; in Sch 1, Pt II, para 10(2) to the 1990 Act; and deriving from s 140(2)(d), (e), (g) of the 1978 Act. Sub-s (3) contains provisions formerly in s 118(2)(a), (d) of the 1975 Act, as repealed in part, in the case of sub-s (2)(a), by s 159(3) of, Sch 17 to, the 1978 Act and, in the case of sub-s (2)(d), by s 20(3) of, Sch 2 to, the 1980 Act.

Sub-s (1): word in italics in para (b)(ii) repealed by the Trade Union Reform and Employment Rights Act 1993, s 51, Sch 10, as from 30 November 1993 (SI 1993/1908, below, para **[1435]**).

Sub-ss (2A)–(2C): inserted by the Trade Union Reform and Employment Rights Act 1993, s 39(2), Sch 6, para 4(a), as from 30 August 1993 (SI 1993/1908, below, para **[1435]**).

Sub-ss (4), (5): added by the Trade Union Reform and Employment Rights Act 1993, s 39(2), Sch 6, para 4(b), as from 30 August 1993 (SI 1993/1908, below, para **[1435]**).

289 Employment governed by foreign law

For the purposes of this Act it is immaterial whether the law which (apart from this Act) governs any person's employment is the law of the United Kingdom, or of a part of the United Kingdom, or not.   **[967]**

NOTE

Commencement: 16 October 1992.

This section contains provisions formerly in the Trade Union and Labour Relations Act 1974, s 30(6), in the Employment Protection Act 1975, s 126(8), and deriving from the Employment Protection (Consolidation) Act 1978, s 153(5).

Industrial tribunal proceedings

290 General provisions as to conciliation

The provisions of section 133(2) to (6) of the Employment Protection (Consolidation) Act 1978 (general provisions as to functions of conciliation officers) have effect in relation to industrial tribunal proceedings, and claims which could be the subject of industrial tribunal proceedings, arising out of a contravention or alleged contravention of any of the following provisions of this Act—

    (a)   section 64 (right of trade union member not to be unjustifiably disciplined);

   [(aa) section 68 (right not to suffer deduction of unauthorised or excessive union subscriptions);]

    (b)   section 137 or 138 (refusal of employment or service of employment agency on grounds related to union membership);

    (c)   section 146 (action short of dismissal on grounds related to union membership or activities);

    (d)   section 168, 169 or 170 (time off for trade union duties and activities);

    (e)   section 174 (*unreasonable* exclusion or expulsion from union *where employment subject to union membership agreement*);

    (f)   section 188 (failure to consult trade union representatives on proposed redundancies);

    (g)   section 190 (entitlement under protective award).   **[968]**

NOTES

Commencement: 16 October 1992.

This section contains provisions formerly in the Employment Protection (Consolidation) Act 1978, s 133(1)(a) (in part: references to ss 23, 27, 28 thereof), (b) (in part: references to the Employment Protection Act 1975, ss 99, 102), (d), (f), as amended, in the case of s 133(1)(a), (d), by the Employment Act 1980, s 20(2), Sch 1, para 17, and as inserted, in the case of s 133(1)(f), by the Employment Act 1988, s 33(1), Sch 3, Pt I, para 2(3); and in s 133(1)(g) of the 1978 Act, as added by the Employment Act 1990, Sch 1, Pt I, para 4.

Para (aa): inserted by the Trade Union Reform and Employment Rights Act 1993, s 49(2), Sch 8, para 86, as from 30 August 1993 (SI 1993/1908, below, para **[1435]**).

Para (e): words in italics repealed by the Trade Union Reform and Employment Rights Act 1993, s 51, Sch 10, as from 30 November 1993 (SI 1993/1908, below, para **[1435]**).

291 Right of appeal from industrial tribunal

(1) An appeal lies to the Employment Appeal Tribunal on any question of law or fact arising from a decision of, or arising in proceedings before, an industrial tribunal under section 174 (right not to be unreasonably excluded or expelled from trade union).

(2) An appeal lies to the Employment Appeal Tribunal on any question of law arising from a decision of, or arising in proceedings before, an industrial tribunal under *any other provision of* this Act.

(3) No other appeal lies from a decision of an industrial tribunal under this Act; and section 11 of the Tribunals and Inquiries Act 1992 (appeals from certain tribunals to High Court or Court of Session) does not apply to proceedings before an industrial tribunal under this Act.   **[969]**

NOTES

Commencement: 16 October 1992.

Sub-s (1) contains provisions formerly in the Employment Act 1980, s 4(8). Sub-s (2) contains provisions formerly in the Employment Protection (Consolidation) Act 1978, s 136(1)(c); in s 136(1)(g) of the 1978 Act, as added by the Employment Act 1990, s 3(5), Sch 1, Pt I, para 8; in ss 2(7), 5(9) of the 1980 Act; in ss 4(5), 5(10) of the Employment Act 1988; and deriving from s 136(1)(e) of the 1978 Act, as inserted by the Wages Act 1986, s 32(1), Sch 4, para 9. Sub-s (3) contains provisions formerly in s 136(5) (in part) of the 1978 Act, as amended by s 20(2) of, Sch 1, para 19 to, the 1980 Act, and by s 33(1) of, Sch 3, Pt I, para 2(4) to, the 1988 Act; and deriving from the Tribunals and Inquiries Act 1971, s 13(1A), as inserted by Sch 16, para 11 to the 1978 Act.

Sub-s (1): repealed by the Trade Union Reform and Employment Rights Act 1993, ss 49(2), 51, Sch 8, para 87(a), Sch 10, as from 30 November 1993 (SI 1993/1908, below, para **[1435]**).

Sub-s (2): words in italics repealed by the Trade Union Reform and Employment Rights Act 1993, ss 49(2), 51, Sch 8, para 87(b), Sch 10, as from 30 November 1993 (SI 1993/1908, below, para **[1435]**).

Other supplementary provisions

292 Death of employee or employer

(1) This section has effect in relation to the following provisions so far as they confer rights on employees or make provision in connection therewith—

(a) sections 146 to 151 (action short of dismissal taken on grounds related to union membership or activities);

(b) sections 168 to 173 (time off for trade union duties and activities);

(c) sections 188 to 198 (procedure for handling redundancies).

(2) Where the employee or employer dies, tribunal proceedings may be instituted or continued by a personal representative of the deceased employee or, as the case may be, defended by a personal representative of the deceased employer.

(3) If there is no personal representative of a deceased employee, tribunal proceedings or proceedings to enforce a tribunal award may be instituted or continued on behalf of his estate by such other person as the industrial tribunal may appoint, being either—

(a) a person authorised by the employee to act in connection with the proceedings before his death, or

(b) the widower, widow, child, father, mother, brother or sister of the employee.

In such a case any award made by the industrial tribunal shall be in such terms and shall be enforceable in such manner as may be prescribed.

(4) Any right arising under any of the provisions mentioned in subsection (1) which by virtue of this section accrues after the death of the employee in question shall devolve as if it had accrued before his death.

(5) Any liability arising under any of those provisions which by virtue of this section accrues after the death of the employer in question shall be treated for all purposes as if it had accrued immediately before his death.   **[970]**

NOTES

Commencement: 16 October 1992.

Sub-s (1) contains provisions formerly in the Employment Protection Act 1975, Sch 12, Pt I, para 1, as repealed in part by the Employment Protection (Consolidation) Act 1978, s 159(3), Sch 17, and deriving from Sch 12, Pt I, para 1 (in part) to the 1978 Act. Sub-s (2) contains provisions formerly in Sch 12, Pt I, para 2 to the 1975 Act, and deriving from Sch 12, Pt I, para 2 to the 1978 Act. Sub-s (3) contains provisions formerly in Sch 12, Pt I, para 3 to the 1975 Act, and deriving from Sch 12, Pt I, para 3(1) to the 1978 Act. Sub-s (4) contains provisions formerly in Sch 12, Pt I, para 5 to the 1975 Act, and deriving from Sch 12, Pt I, para 5 to the 1978 Act. Sub-s (5) contains provisions formerly in Sch 12, Pt I, para 6 to the 1975 Act, and deriving from Sch 12, Pt I, para 6 to the 1978 Act.

293 Regulations

(1) The Secretary of State may by regulations prescribe anything authorised or required to be prescribed for the purposes of this Act.

(2) The regulations may contain such incidental, supplementary or transitional provisions as appear to the Secretary of State to be necessary or expedient.

(3) Regulations under this section shall be made by statutory instrument which shall be subject to annulment in pursuance of a resolution of either House of Parliament.   **[971]**

NOTES

Commencement: 16 October 1992.

Sub-s (1) is a drafting provision. Sub-s (2) contains provisions formerly in the Employment Protection Act 1975, s 123(3), and deriving from the Employment Protection (Consolidation) Act 1978, s 154(3). Sub-s (3) contains provisions formerly in s 123(2) of the 1975 Act, and deriving from s 154(2) of the 1978 Act.

294 Reciprocal arrangements with Northern Ireland

(1) If provision is made by Northern Ireland legislation for purposes corresponding to the purposes of any provision of this Act re-enacting a provision of the Employment Protection Act 1975 or the Employment Protection (Consolidation) Act 1978, the Secretary of State may, with the consent of the Treasury, make reciprocal arrangements with the appropriate Northern Ireland authority for co-ordinating the relevant provisions of this Act with the corresponding Northern Ireland provisions so as to secure that they operate, to such extent as may be provided by the arrangements, as a single system.

(2) The Secretary of State may make regulations for giving effect to any such arrangements.

(3) The regulations may make different provision for different cases and may contain such supplementary, incidental and transitional provisions as appear to the Secretary of State to be necessary or expedient.

(4) The regulations may provide that the relevant provisions of this Act shall have effect in relation to persons affected by the arrangements subject to such

modifications and adaptations as may be specified in the regulations, including provisions—

(a) for securing that acts, omission and events having any effect for the purposes of the Northern Ireland legislation have a corresponding effect for the purposes of the relevant provisions of this Act (but not so as to confer a right to double payment in respect of the same act, omission or event, and

(b) for determining, in cases where rights accrue both under the relevant provisions of this Act and under the Northern Ireland legislation, which of these rights is available to the person concerned.

(5) In this section "the appropriate Northern Ireland authority" means such authority as is specified in that behalf in the Northern Ireland legislation.

(6) Regulations under this section shall be made by statutory instrument which shall be subject to annulment in pursuance of a resolution of either House of Parliament.   **[972]**

NOTES
Commencement: 16 October 1992.
Sub-s (1) contains provisions formerly in the Employment Protection Act 1975, s 128(1), as repealed in part by the Employment Protection (Consolidation) Act 1978, s 159(3), Sch 17, and deriving from the Employment Protection (Consolidation) Act 1978, s 157(1). Sub-s (2) contains provisions formerly in s 128(3) (in part) of the 1975 Act, and deriving from s 157(3) (in part) of the 1978 Act. Sub-s (3) contains provisions formerly in s 128(3) (in part) of the 1975 Act, and deriving from s 157(3) (in part) of the 1978 Act. Sub-s (4) contains provisions formerly in s 128(3) (in part) of the 1975 Act, as repealed in part by s 159(3) of, Sch 17 to, the 1978 Act, and deriving from s 157(3) (in part) of the 1978 Act. Sub-s (5) contains provisions formerly in s 128(4) of the 1975 Act, and deriving from s 157(4) of the 1978 Act. Sub-s (6) contains provisions formerly in s 123(1) (in part), (2) of the 1975 Act, and deriving from s 154(1) (in part), (2) of the 1978 Act.

Interpretation

295 Meaning of "employee" and related expressions

(1) In this Act—

"contract of employment" means a contract of service or of apprenticeship,

"employee" means an individual who has entered into or works under (or, where the employment has ceased, worked under) a contract of employment, and

"employer", in relation to an employee, means the person by whom the employee is (or, where the employment has ceased, was) employed.

(2) Subsection (1) has effect subject to section 235 and other provisions conferring a wider meaning on "contract of employment" or related expressions.   **[973]**

NOTES
Commencement: 16 October 1992.
Sub-s (1) contains provisions formerly in the Trade Union and Labour Relations Act 1974, s 30(1) (definitions "contract of employment", "employee", "employer" (para (a)), as inserted, in the case of the definition "employer", by the Employment Protection Act 1975, s 125(1), Sch 16, Pt III, para 7(2); in s 126(1) (definitions "employee", "employer") of the 1975 Act; in the Employment Act 1988, s 32(1) (definitions "contract of employment", "employer"); in the Employment Act 1990, s 3(1) (definition "contract of employment"); and deriving from the Employment Protection (Consolidation) Act 1978, s 153(1) (definitions "contract of employment", "employee", "employer"). Sub-s (2) contains drafting provisions.

296 Meaning of "worker" and related expressions

(1) In this Act "worker" means an individual who works, or normally works or seeks to work—

    (a) under a contract of employment, or

    (b) under any other contract whereby he undertakes to do or perform personally any work or services for another party to the contract who is not a professional client of his, or

    (c) in employment under or for the purposes of a government department (otherwise than as a member of the naval, military or air forces of the Crown) in so far as such employment does not fall within paragraph (a) or (b) above.

(2) In this Act "employer", in relation to a worker, means a person for whom one or more workers work, or halve worked or normally work or seek to work.

    [(3) This section has effect subject to section 68(11).]   **[974]**

NOTES

Commencement: 16 October 1992.

Sub-s (1) contains provisions formerly in the Industrial Courts Act 1919, s 8 (definition "worker"), as substituted by the Employment Act 1982, s 21(2), Sch 3, Pt II, para 10; in the Trade Union and Labour Relations Act 1974, s 30(1) (definition "worker"), as repealed in part by the Armed Forces Act 1981, s 28, Sch 5, Pt I; in the Employment Protection Act 1975, s 126(1) (definition "worker"); and in the Employment Act 1988, s 32(1) (definition "worker"). Sub-s (2) contains provisions formerly in s 30(1) (para (b) of the definition "employer") of the 1974 Act, as inserted by s 125(1) of, Sch 16, Pt III, para 7(2) to, the 1975 Act; in s 126(1) (definition "employer") of the 1975 Act; and in s 32(1) (definition "employer") of the 1988 Act.

Sub-s (3): added by the Trade Union Reform and Employment Rights Act 1993, s 49(2), Sch 8, para 88, as from 30 August 1993 (SI 1993/1908, below, para **[1435]**).

297 Associated employers

For the purposes of this Act any two employers shall be treated as associated if—

    (a) one is a company of which the other (directly or indirectly) has control, or

    (b) both are companies of which a third person (directly or indirectly) has control;

and "associated employer" shall be construed accordingly.   **[975]**

NOTES

Commencement: 16 October 1992.

This section contains provisions formerly in the Trade Union and Labour Relations Act 1974, s 30(5), and in the Employment Protection Act 1975, s 126(1) (definition "associated employer").

298 Minor definitions: general

In this Act, unless the context otherwise requires—

    "act" and "action" each includes omission, and references to doing an act or taking action shall be construed accordingly;

    "contravention" includes a failure to comply, and cognate expressions shall be construed accordingly;

    "dismiss", "dismissal" and "effective date of termination", in relation to an employee, shall be construed in accordance with section 55 of the Employment Protection (Consolidation) Act 1978;

    "post" means a postal service which—

        (a) is provided by the Post Office or under a licence granted under section 68 of the British Telecommunications Act 1981, or

        (b) does not by virtue of an order made under section 69 of that Act (suspension of postal privilege) infringe the exclusive privilege conferred on the Post Office by section 66(1) of that Act;

"tort", as respects Scotland, means delict, and cognate expressions shall be construed accordingly.   **[976]**

NOTES

Commencement: 16 October 1992.

This section contains provisions formerly in the Trade Union Act 1913, s 4(1F) (definition "post"), as inserted by the Trade Union Act 1984, s 13(2), and as repealed in part by the Employment Act 1988, s 33(2), Sch 4; in the Trade Union and Labour Relations Act 1974, s 30(1) (definitions "act", "action", "tort") as amended, in the case of the definition "tort", by the Employment Act 1982, s 19(2); in the Employment Protection Act 1975, s 126(1) (definition ""dismiss", "dismissal" and "effective date of termination""), as amended by the Employment Protection (Consolidation) Act 1978, s 159(2), Sch 16, para 23(1), (13); in the Employment Act 1980, s 2(9) (definition "post"), as amended by the Employment Act 1988, s 33(1), Sch 3, Pt I, para 3(1); in the Trade Union Act 1984, ss 9(1) (definition "post"), 11(11) (definition "post"); in ss 13(6) (definition "post"), 32(1) (definition "contravention") of the 1988 Act; and deriving from s 153(1) (definitions ""act" and "action"" and "effective date of termination") of the 1978 Act and s 16(3) (definition "tort") of the 1980 Act.

299   Index of defined expressions

In this Act the expressions listed below are defined by or otherwise fall to be construed in accordance with the provisions indicated—

ACAS	section 247(1)
act and action	section 298
advertisement (in sections 137 to 143)	section 143(1)
[agent (of trade union)	section 119]
appropriately qualified actuary (in sections 38 to 41)	section 42
associated employer	section 297
branch or section (of trade union)	section 119
collective agreement and collective bargaining	section 178(1)
the Commissioner	*section 266*
contract of employment	
—generally	section 295(1)
—in sections 226 to 234	section 235
—in relation to Crown employment	section 273(4)(a)
—in relation to House of Lords or House of Commons staff	section 277(4) and 278(4)(a)
contravention	section 298
the court (in Part I)	section 121
date of the ballot (in Part V)	section 246
dismiss and dismissal	
—generally	section 298
—in relation to Crown employment	section 273(4)(c)
—in relation to House of Commons staff	section 278(4)(b)
[the duty of confidentiality	section 24A(3)]
effective date of termination	section 298
employee	
—generally	section 295(1)
—in relation to Crown employment	section 273(4)(a)
—in relation to House of Commons staff	section 278(4)(a)
—excludes police service	section 280
employer	
—in relation to an employee	section 295(1)
—in relation to a worker	section 296(2)
—in relation to health service practitioners	section 279

employment and employment agency (in sections 137 to 143)	section 143(1)
executive (of trade union)	section 119
[financial affairs (of trade union)	section 119]
financial year (in Part VI)	section 72
general secretary	section 119
independent trade union (and related expressions)	section 5
list	
—of trade unions	section 2
—of employers' associations	section 123
Northern Ireland union (in Part I) not protected	
(in sections 222 to 226)	section 219(4)
officer	
—of trade union	section 119
—of employers' association	section 136
official (of trade union)	section 119
offshore employment	section 287
place of work (in Part V)	section 246
political fund	section 82(1)(a)
political resolution	section 82(1)(a)
post	section 298
prescribed	section 293(1)
president	section 119
recognised, recognition and related expressions	section 178(3)
redundancy (in Part IV, Chapter II)	
—generally	*section 195*
—in relation to Crown employment	*section 273(4)(d)*
representative (of trade union) (in Part IV, Chapter II)	section 196
rules (of trade union)	section 119
strike (in Part V)	section 246
tort (as respects Scotland)	section 298
trade dispute	
—in Part IV	section 218
—in Part V	section 244
trade union	section 1
undertaking (of employer)	
—in relation to Crown employment	section 273(4)(e) and (f)
—in relation to House of Commons staff	section 278(4)(c) and (d)
worker	
—generally	section 296(1)
—includes health service practitioners	section 279
—excludes police service	section 280
working hours (in Part V)	section 246

[977]

NOTE

Commencement: 16 October 1992.

This section is a drafting provision.

Definitions "agent (of trade union)", "the duty of confidentiality" and "financial affairs (of trade union)" inserted by the Trade Union Reform and Employment Rights Act 1993, s 49(2), Sch 8, para 89, as from 30 August 1993 (SI 1993/1908, below, para **[1435]**).

Italicised entries relating to "the Commissioner" and "redundancy" repealed by the Trade Union Reform and Employment Rights Act 1993, s 51, Sch 10, as from 30 August 1993 (SI 1993/1908, below, para **[1435]**).

Final provisions

300 Repeals, consequential amendments, transitional provisions and savings

(1), (2) . . .

(3) Schedule 3 contains transitional provisions and savings.   **[978]**

NOTE
Commencement: 16 October 1992.
Sub-ss (1), (2): introduce Schs 1, 2 (omitted).

301 Extent

(1) This Act extends to England and Wales and Scotland.   **[979]**

NOTES
Commencement: 16 October 1992.
Sub-ss (2), (3): (extension to Northern Ireland) omitted.

302 Commencement

This Act comes into force at the end of the period of three months beginning with the day on which it is passed.   **[980]**

NOTES
Commencement: 16 October 1992.

303 Short title

This Act may be cited as the Trade Union and Labour Relations (Consolidation) Act 1992.   **[981]**

NOTE
Commencement: 16 October 1992.

SCHEDULES

(Schs 1, 2 (repeals and consequential amendments) omitted.)

SCHEDULE 3

Section 300(3)

TRANSITIONAL PROVISIONS AND SAVINGS

Continuity of the law

1 (1) The repeal and re-enactment of provisions in this Act does not affect the continuity of the law.

(2) Anything done (including subordinate legislation made), or having effect as done, under a provision reproduced in this Act has effect as if done under the corresponding provision of this Act.

(3) References (express or implied) in this Act or any other enactment, instrument or document to a provision of this Act shall, so far as the context permits, be construed as including, in relation to times, circumstances and purposes before the commencement of this Act, a reference to corresponding earlier provisions.

(4) A reference (express or implied) in any enactment, instrument or other document to a provision reproduced in this Act shall be construed, so far as is required for continuing its effect, and subject to any express amendment made by this Act, as being, or as the case may required including, a reference to the corresponding provision of this Act.

General saving for old transitional provisions and savings

2 (1) The repeal by this Act of a transitional provision or saving relating to the coming into force of a provision reproduced in this Act does not affect the operation of the transitional provision or saving, in so far as it is not specifically reproduced in this Act but remains capable of having effect in relation to the corresponding provision of this Act.

(2) The repeal by this Act of an enactment previously repealed subject to savings does not affect the continued operation of those savings.

(3) The repeal by this Act of a saving on the previous repeal of an enactment does not affect the operation of the saving in so far as it is not specifically reproduced in this Act but remains capable of having effect.

Effect of repeal of 1946 Act

3 The repeal by this Act of the Trade Disputes and Trade Unions Act 1946 shall not be construed as reviving in any respect the effect of the Trade Disputes and Trade Unions Act 1927.

Pre-1974 references to registered trade unions or employers' associations

4 (1) Any reference in an enactment passed, or instrument made under an enactment, before 16th September 1974—

    (a)   to a trade union or employers' association registered under—
        (i) the Trade Union Acts 1871 to 1964, or
        (ii) the Industrial Relations Act 1971, or
    (b)   to an organisation of workers or an organisation of employers within the meaning of the Industrial Relations Act 1971,

shall be construed as a reference to a trade union or employers' association within the meaning of this Act.

(2) Subsection (1) does not apply to any enactment relating to income tax or corporation tax.

Enforceability of collective agreements

5 Section 179 of this Act (enforceability of collective agreements) does not apply to a collective agreement made on or after 1st December 1971 and before 16th September 1974.

Trade unions and employers' associations ceasing to be incorporated by virtue of 1974 Act

6 (1) The repeal by this Act of section 19 of the Trade Union and Labour Relations Act 1974 (transitional provisions for trade unions and employers' associations ceasing to be incorporated) does not affect—

    (a)   the title to property which by virtue of that section vested on 16th September 1974 in "the appropriate trustees" as defined by that section, or
    (b)   any liability, obligation or right affecting such property which by virtue of that section became a liability, obligation or right of those trustees.

(2) A certificate given by the persons who on that date were the president and general secretary of a trade union or employers' association, or occupied positions equivalent to that of president and general secretary, that the persons named in the certificate are the appropriate trustees of the union or association for the purposes of section 19(2) of the Trade Union and

Labour Relations Act 1974 is conclusive evidence that those persons were the appropriate trustees for those purposes.

(3) A document which purports to be such a certificate shall be taken to be such a certificate unless the contrary is proved.

References to former Industrial Arbitration Board

7 Any reference to the former Industrial Arbitration Board in relation to which section 10(2) of the Employment Protection Act 1975 applied immediately before the commencement of this Act shall continue to be construed as a reference to the Central Arbitration Committee.

Effect of political resolution passed before 1984 amendments

8 A resolution under section 3 of the Trade Union Act 1913, or rule made for the purposes of that section, in relation to which section 17(2) of the Trade Union Act 1984 applied immediately before the commencement of this Act shall continue to have effect as if for any reference to the political objects to which section 3 of the 1913 Act formerly applied there were substituted a reference to the objects to which that section applied as amended by the 1984 Act.

Persons elected to trade union office before 1988 amendments

9 (1) In relation to a person who was, within the period of five years ending with 25th July 1989, elected to a position to which the requirements of section 1 of the Trade Union Act 1984 were extended by virtue of section 12(1) of the Employment Act 1988—

    (a) the references in section 46(1)(a) and 58(2)(a) to satisfying the requirements of Chapter IV of Part I shall be disregarded, and

    (b) the period of five years mentioned in section 46(1)(b) shall be calculated from the date of that election.

(2) Sub-paragraph (1) does not apply if the only persons entitled to vote in the election were themselves persons holding positions to which Chapter IV of Part I would have applied had that Chapter been in force at the time.

10 In relation to a person who was elected to a position to which Chapter IV of Part I applies before 26th July 1989, the reference in section 58(2)(a) (exemption of persons nearing retirement) to satisfying the requirements of that Chapter—

    (a) shall not be construed as requiring compliance with any provision corresponding to a provision of section 13 or 15 of the Employment Act 1988 (additional requirements as to elections) which was not then in force, and

    (b) in relation to an election before the commencement of section 14(2) of that Act (postal ballots) shall be construed as requiring compliance with section 3 of the Trade Union Act 1984 (non-postal ballots).

Qualification to act as auditor of trade union or employers' association

11 (1) Nothing in section 34 (eligibility for appointment as auditor) affects the validity of any appointment as auditor of a trade union or employers' association made before 1st October 1991 (when section 389 of the Companies Act 1985 was repealed and replaced by the provisions of Part II of the Companies Act 1989).

(2) A person who is not qualified as mentioned in section 34(1) may act as auditor of a trade union in respect of an accounting period if—

    (a) the union was registered under the Trade Union Acts 1871 to 1964 on 30th September 1971,

    (b) he acted as its auditor in respect of the last period in relation to which it was required to make an annual return under section 16 of the Trade Union Act 1871,

    (c) he has acted as its auditor in respect of every accounting period since that period, and

    (d) he retains an authorisation formerly granted by the Board of Trade or the Secretary of State under section 16(1)(b) of the Companies Act 1948 (adequate knowledge and experience, or pre-1947 practice).

12 ...

Use of existing forms, &c.

13 Any document made, served or issued on or after the commencement of this Act which contains a reference to an enactment repealed by this Act shall be construed, except so far as a contrary intention appears, as referring or, as the context may require, including a reference to the corresponding provision of this Act.

Saving for power to vary or revoke

14 The power of the Secretary of State by further order to vary or revoke the Funds for Trade Union Ballots Order 1982 extends to so much of section 115(2)(a) as reproduces the effect of Article 2 of that order.   **[982]**

NOTES
    Commencement: 16 October 1992.
    Para 12 (provisions applying to Northern Ireland) omitted.

DESTINATION TABLE

This table shows in column (1) the enactments repealed by the Trade Union and Labour Relations (Consolidation) Act 1992, Sch 1, and in column (2) the provisions of that Act corresponding thereto.

In certain cases the enactment in column (1), though having a corresponding provision in column (2) is not, or not wholly, repealed as it is still required, or partly required, for the purposes of other legislation.

A "dash" in the right hand column means that the repealed provision to which it corresponds in the left hand column is spent, unnecessary or for some other reason not specifically reproduced.

The derivation notes to this Act and this destination table do not specifically take into account all of the effects of the Trade Union and Labour Relations Act 1974, Sch 3, paras 2(3), 10(2), (7). Those provisions negatived the amendments made by the Industrial Relations Act 1971, Sch 8, to the Trade Union Act 1913, ss 3–6, and to the Trade Union (Amalgamations, etc) Act 1964, ss 1–11, and revived s 8 of the 1964 Act.

(1)	(2)	(1)	(2)
Malicious Damage Act 1861 (c 97)	Trade Union and Labour Relations (Consolidation) Act 1992 (c 52)	Trade Union Act 1913 (c 30)	Trade Union and Labour Relations (Consolidation) Act 1992 (c 52)
s 58† ....s 240(2)		s 5A ....s 95	
		s 6................................s 85	
Conspiracy and Protection of Property Act 1875 (c 86)	Trade Union and Labour Relations (Consolidation) Act 1992 (c 52)	s 6A ....s 132	
		s 7 ....—	
		s 8 ....—	
		Schedule ....s 84(1)	
s 3 ....s 243		Industrial Courts Act 1919 (c 69)	Trade Union and Labour Relations (Consolidation) Act 1992 (c 52)
s 5 ....s 240(1), (3)			
s 7 ....s 241			
s 15 ....s 240(2)			
s 16 ....s 240(4)		ss 1–3 ....Rep 1975 c 71, s 125(3), Sch 18	
Friendly Societies Act 1896 (c 25)	Trade Union and Labour Relations (Consolidation) Act 1992 (c 52)	s 4(1) ....ss 215(1), (2), 216(3)	
		s 4(2), (3)......................s 216(1), (2)	
		s 4(4), (5) ....s 216(4), (5)	
		s 5(1), (2)......................s 215(2), (3)	
s 22(2) ....ss 19(3), 129(3)		s 5(3) ....s 215(4), (5)	
s 22(3) ....ss 19(3), 129(3)		s 6................................Rep 1927 c 42	
		s 7 ....—	
Trade Union Act 1913 (c 30)	Trade Union and Labour Relations (Consolidation) Act 1992 (c 52)	s 8 ....ss 218, 296(1)	
		s 9 ....s 216(6)	
		s 10(1) ....s 273(1)	
s 1(1) ....Rep 1971 c 72, ss 169, 170(5), Sch 9		s 10(2) ....s 273(3)	
		s 10(3) ....s 274	
s 1(2) ....Rep 1984 c 49, ss 17(3), 22(6)		s 10(4) ....s 275	
		ss 11, 12 ....Rep 1975 c 71, s 125(3), Sch 18	
s 2(1) ....s 1		s 13 ....s 215(6)	
s 2(1A) ....s 122(1)		s 14................................—	
s 2(2)–(5)........................Rep 1971 c 72, s 169, Sch 9		Schedule.......................Rep 1927 c 42	
s 3(1) ....ss 71, 73(1), 82(1)		Trade Disputes and Trade Unions Act 1946 (c 52)	Trade Union and Labour Relations (Consolidation) Act 1992 (c 52)
s 3(2) ....s 82(2)–(4)			
s 3(3)–(3C)......................s 72(1)–(4)			
s 3(4) ....s 73(2)			
s 3(5) ....ss 118(7), 135(4)		ss 1, 2 ....—	
s 4(1) ....s 74(1), (3)		Schedule.......................Rep 1973 c 39	
s 4(1A) ....s 76			
s 4(1B)............................s 77(1), (2)		Industrial Assurance and Friendly Societies Act 1948 (c 39)	Trade Union and Labour Relations (Consolidation) Act 1992 (c 52)
s 4(1C)–(1E)....................s 77(3)–(5)			
s 4(1F) ....s 298			
s 4(2) ....s 92			
s 5(1) ....s 84(1)–(3)			
s 5(2) ....s 84(4), (5)		s 6(1)* ....ss 19(1)(a), 129(3)	

† Not repealed　　　　　　*Repealed in part

(1)	(2)	(1)	(2)
Industrial Assurance and Friendly Societies Act 1948 (c 39)	Trade Union and Labour Relations (Consolidation) Act 1992 (c 52)	Trade Union (Amalgamations, etc) Act 1964 (c 24)	Trade Union and Labour Relations (Consolidation) Act 1992 (c 52)
s 6(2)*............ss 19(1)(b), 129(3)		para 4............s 106(3)	
s 16(4)............ss 19(2), 129(3)		Sch 3............Rep 1969 c 52	
s 23(1)(d)............—			

(1)	(2)	(1)	(2)
Trade Union (Amalgamations, etc) Act 1964 (c 24)	Trade Union and Labour Relations (Consolidation) Act 1992 (c 52)	Merchant Shipping Act 1970 (c 36)	Trade Union and Labour Relations (Consolidation) Act 1992 (c 52)
s 1(1)............ss 97(1), (2), 98(1), 100(1)		s 42(1)............s 240(1)	
s 1(1A)............ss 133, 134(1), (4)		Sch 3	
s 1(2)............ss 99(1), 100(1)		para 1............s 240(4)	
s 1(3)............ss 98(2), 99(2)–(4)		Tribunals and Inquiries Act 1971 (c 62)	Trade Union and Labour Relations (Consolidation) Act 1992 (c 52)
s 1(4)............ss 98, 99(5)			
s 1(5)............s 101			
s 1(6)............s 97(3)			
s 2(1)............s 97(4)		s 13(1A)†............s 291(3)	
s 2(2)............s 100(2)			
s 2(3)............s 100(3), (4)		Administration of Justice (Scotland) Act 1972 (c 59)	Trade Union and Labour Relations (Consolidation) Act 1992 (c 52)
s 3............s 102			
s 4(1)............s 103(1)			
s 4(2)............s 103(2)			
s 4(3)............s 103(3)		s 3(3)............ss 217, 263(6)	
s 4(4)............s 103(4)			
s 4(5)............s 103(3)		Friendly Societies Act 1974 (c 46)	Trade Union and Labour Relations (Consolidation) Act 1992 (c 52)
s 4(6)............Rep 1988 c 19, s 33(2), Sch 4			
s 4(7)............s 103(5)			
s 4(8)............s 104			
s 4(9)............—		Sch 9	
s 4(10)............s 103(2)		para 1............ss 19(3), 129(3)	
s 4(11)............Rep 1971 c 72, s 169, Sch 9		para 12............ss 19(2), 129(3)	
s 5(1)............s 105(1)			
s 5(2)............s 105(4)		Trade Union and Labour Relations 1974 (c 52)	Trade Union and Labour Relations (Consolidation) Act 1992 (c 52)
s 5(3)............s 105(2), (3)			
s 5(4)............s 93(1)			
s 6(1)............ss 107(1), 134(1)		s 1(1)............Rep 1986 c 12	
s 6(2)............ss 107(2), (3), 134(2), (3)		s 1(2)............—	
s 6(3)............ss 107(4), 134(4)		s 1(3)............Rep 1986 c 12	
s 7(1)............ss 108(1), 134(5)		s 1A............Rep 1980 c 42, ss 19, 20(3), Sch 2	
s 7(2)............ss 108(2), 134(5)			
s 7(3)............ss 108(3), 134(5)		s 2(1)............ss 10(1), (2), 12(1), (2), 117(3)	
s 7(4)............ss 108(4), 134(5)			
s 8............s 254(4)		s 2(2)............ss 10(3), 117(3)	
s 9(1)............ss 1, 122(1)		s 2(3)............s 10(3)	
s 9(2)............—		s 2(4)............—	
s 10(1)............—		s 2(5)............ss 11, 117(3)	
s 10(2)............s 106(1)		s 3(1)............s 127(1)	
s 10(3)............s 301(3)		s 3(2)............ss 127(2), 129(1)	
s 10(4)............Rep 1973 c 36, s 41(1), Sch 6, Pt I		s 3(3)............—	
		s 3(4)............s 127(3)	
s 10(5), (6)............s 120		s 3(5)............s 128	
s 11............—		s 4(1)............ss 13(1), (2), (4), 14(1), 117(3), 129(1)	
Sch 1............Rep 1988 c 19, s 33(2), Sch 4			
Sch 2		s 4(2)............ss 13(1), 14(1), 117(3), 129(1)	
para 1............s 106(5)			
para 2(1)............s 106(2)		s 4(3)............ss 13(3), 14(1), 117(3), 129(1)	
para 2(2)............s 106(4)			
para 3............s 106(4)			

† No repealed   *Repealed in part

(1)	(2)
Trade Union and Labour Relations 1974 (c 52)	Trade Union and Labour Relations (Consolidation) Act 1992 (c 52)
s 4(4)	ss 14(2), 117(3), 129(1)
s 4(5)	ss 14(3), 129(1)
s 4(6)	ss 14(4), 117(3), 129(1)
s 4(7)	ss 14(5), 129(1)
s 4(8)	ss 14(6), 117(3), 129(1)
ss 5, 6	Rep 1976 c 7, s 1
s 7	s 69
s 8(1)	ss 2(1), 123(1)
s 8(2)	ss 2(1), 123(1)
s 8(3)	ss 3(1), (3), 124(1), (3)
s 8(4)	ss 3(2), 124(2)
s 8(5)	ss 3(4), 124(4)
s 8(6)	ss 4(1), (2), 125(1), (2)
s 8(6A)	ss 4(3), 125(3)
s 8(7)	ss 9(1), (3), 126(1), (2)
s 8(8)	Rep 1975 c 71, s 125(3), Sch 18
s 8(9)	ss 2(2), (3), 123(2), (3)
s 8(10)	ss 2(4)–(6), 123(4)–(6)
s 9	—
s 10(1)	ss 28(1), 118(4), 131(1), 135(3)
s 10(2)	ss 28(1), 131(1)
s 10(3)	ss 28(2), 131(1)
s 10(4)	ss 44(1), (2), (4), 131(1)
s 11(1)	ss 32(1), 43(1), 118(4), 131(1), 135(3)
s 11(2)	ss 32(1), 131(1)
s 11(3)	ss 33(1), 131(1)
s 11(4)	ss 27, 32(5), 131(1)
s 11(5)	ss 32(6), 131(1)
s 11(6), (7)	—
s 11(8)	ss 44(1), (2), (4), 131(1)
s 11(9)	ss 117(4), 131(2)
s 12(1)	ss 45(1), 131(1)
s 12(2)	ss 45(2), 131(1)
s 12(3)	ss 45(3), 131(1)
s 12(4)	ss 45(4), 131(1)
s 12(5)	ss 45(5), 131(1)
s 13(1)	s 219(1)
s 13(2)	Rep 1982 c 46, ss 19(1), 21(3), Sch 4
s 13(3)	Rep 1980 c 42, ss 17(8), 20(3), Sch 2
s 13(4)	s 219(2)
s 14	Rep 1982 c 46, ss 15(1), 21(3), Sch 4
s 15	s 220
s 16	s 236
s 17(1)	s 221(1)
s 17(2), (3)	s 221(2)
s 18(1), (2)	s 179(1), (2)
s 18(3)	s 179(3), (4)
s 18(4)	s 180(1), (2)
s 18(5)	s 180(3)
s 19	—
ss 20–24	Rep 1986 c 12
s 25	—
s 26(1)	—
s 26(2)	ss 17(6), 18(3), 34(4), 35(6), 131(1)
s 26(3)	ss 17(6), 18(3), 34(4), 35(6), 131(1)

(1)	(2)
Trade Union and Labour Relations 1974 (c 52)	Trade Union and Labour Relations (Consolidation) Act 1992 (c 52)
s 26(4)	—
s 27	—
s 28(1)	s 1
s 28(2)	s 122(1)
s 29(1)	ss 178(1), (2), 244(1)
s 29(2), (3)	s 244(2), (3)
s 29(4)	Rep 1982 c 46, s 18(5)
s 29(5), (6)	s 244(4), (5)
s 29(7)	Rep 1977 c 45, s 65(5), Sch 13
s 30(1)	ss 5, 117(1), 119, 122(2), 136, 174(2), (3), 177(1), 178(1), (2), 280, 295(1), 296, 298
s 30(2)	s 279
s 30(3), (4)	—
s 30(5)	s 297
s 30(5A)	s 174(2)
s 30(6)	s 289
s 30(7)	—
s 31(1)–(4)	—
s 31(5)	s 301(2)(a)
Sch 1, Pts I–III	
paras 1–3	Rep 1975 c 71, s 125(3), Sch 18
paras 4–16	Rep 1978 c 44, s 159(3), Sch 17
para 17(1)	Rep 1978 c 44, s 159(3), Sch 17
para 17(2), (3)	Rep 1975 c 71, s 125(3), Sch 18
para 18	Rep 1978 c 44, s 159(3), Sch 17
para 19	Rep 1975 c 71, s 125(3), Sch 18
paras 20–25	Rep 1978 c 44, s 159(3), Sch 17
Sch 1, Pt IV	
paras 26, 27	Rep 1978 c 44, s 159(3), Sch 17
para 28	Rep 1976 c 74, s 79(5), Sch 5
para 29	Rep 1975 c 71, s 125(3), Sch 18
para 30	Rep 1978 c 44, s 159(3), Sch 17
para 31(1)(a)	s 17(1)
para 31(1)(b)	s 18(1)
para 31(2)	s 17(2), (3)
para 31(3)	ss 17(4), (5), 18(2)
para 31(4)	s 18(4)
para 32(1)(a)	s 288(1)
para 32(1)(b)	Rep 1978 c 44, s 159(3), Sch 17
para 32(2)	Rep 1980 c 42, s 20(2),(3), Sch 1, para 2, Sch 2
para 33(1)	s 273(1)
para 33(2)	ss 273(3), 274
para 33(3)	s 273(4)
para 33(4)(a)	—

(1)	(2)	(1)	(2)
Trade Union and Labour Relations 1974 (c 52)	Trade Union and Labour Relations (Consolidation) Act 1992 (c 52)	Trade Union and Labour Relations 1974 (c 52)	Trade Union and Labour Relations (Consolidation) Act 1992 (c 52)
para 33(4)(b) ....s 274		para 2(6)....................Rep 1975 c 71, s 125(3), Sch 18	
para 33(4A) ....Rep 1978 c 44, s 159(3), Sch 17		para 3.........................Rep 1975 c 71, s 125(3), Sch 18	
para 33(5)...................s 275		para 4.........................Rep 1980 c 42, s 20(3), Sch 2	
Sch 2, Pt I		para 5.........................ss 19(1), (2), 129(3)	
para 1(1)....................ss 32(2), 131(1)		para 6.........................Rep 1975 c 24, s 10(2), Sch 3; 1975 c 25, s 5(2), Sch 3, Pt I	
para 1(2)....................ss 32(2), 131(1)			
para 2.........................ss 32(3), 131(1)		para 7.........................—	
para 3.........................ss 32(3), 131(1)		para 8.........................Rep 1975 c 71, s 125(3), Sch 18	
para 4.........................ss 32(3), 131(1)			
para 5.........................ss 32(4), 131(1)		para 9.........................Rep 1979 c 12, s 31(3), Sch 7	
para 6.........................ss 30(4), 34(1), 131(1)			
paras 7, 8 ....—		para 10(1), (2) ....—	
para 9(1)....................ss 34(2), 131(1)		para 10(3)...................ss 133, 134(1), (4)	
para 9(2)....................ss 34(3), 131(1)		para 10(4)...................Rep 1975 c 71, s 125(3), Sch 18	
para 9(3)....................ss 34(4), 131(1)			
para 10.......................ss 34(5), 131(1)		para 10(5)...................ss 107(2), (3), 134(2), (3)	
para 11.......................ss 35(1), 131(1)		para 10(6)...................Rep 1975 c 71, s 125(3), Sch 18	
para 12.......................ss 35(1), (2), 131(1)			
para 13(1)..................ss 35(1), (3), 131(1)		para 10(7)...................s 254(4)	
para 13(2)..................ss 35(4), 131(1)		para 10(8)..................ss 1, 122(1)	
para 13(3)..................ss 35(5), 131(1)		paras 11, 12 ....—	
para 13(4)..................—		para 13.......................Rep 1980 c 25, s 4(3) Sch 5	
para 14.......................ss 35(6), 131(1)			
para 15(1)..................ss 35(7), 131(1)		para 14.......................—	
para 15(2)..................ss 35(8), 131(1)		para 15.......................Rep 1975 c 71, s 125(3), Sch 18	
para 16.......................ss 37(1), 131(1)			
para 17.......................ss 37(3), 131(1)		para 16.......................Rep 1978 c 44, s 159(3), Sch 17	
para 18.......................ss 36(1), 131(1)			
para 19.......................ss 36(2), 131(1)		para 17.......................ss 217, 263(6)	
para 20.......................ss 36(3), (4), 131(1)		Schs 4, 5 ....—	
para 21.......................ss 37(2), 131(1)			
para 22.......................ss 33(2), 131(1)			
Sch 2, Pt II		**Employment Protection Act 1975 (c 71)**	**Trade Union and Labour Relations (Consolidation) Act 1992 (c 52)**
para 23.......................—			
para 24.......................ss 40(3), 131(1)			
para 25.......................ss 39(2), 40(4), 131(1)			
para 26.......................ss 40(5), (6), 131(1)		s 1(1) ....s 247(1)	
para 27.......................ss 39(1), (2), 131(1)		s 1(2) ....s 209	
para 28.......................ss 39(3), 40(7), 131(1)		s 1(3)............................—	
para 29.......................—		s 2(1)–(3)......................s 210(1)–(3)	
para 30.......................ss 41(1), 131(1)		s 2(4) ....s 211	
para 31.......................ss 41(2), 131(1)		s 3(1) ....s 212(1)	
para 32(1)..................ss 40(1), 131(1)		s 3(2) ....s 212(2), (3)	
para 32(2)..................ss 40(2), 131(1)		s 3(3), (4)......................s 212(4)	
para 32(3)..................ss 41(4), 131(1)		s 3(5) ....s 212(5)	
para 33.......................ss 40(3)–(7), 131(1)		s 3(6) ....s 212(4)(a)	
para 33A....................ss 41(1), 131(1)		s 4(1) ....s 213(1), (2)	
para 33B....................ss 41(2), (3), 131(1)		s 4(2) ....s 213(3)	
para 34.......................ss 38(2), 131(1)		s 5 ....s 214	
para 35.......................ss 38(2), 131(1)		s 6(1) ....s 199(1)	
para 36(a) ....ss 38(1), 131(1)		s 6(2) ....s 199(2), (3)	
para 36(b)...................ss 42, 131(1)		s 6(3), (4)......................s 200(1), (2)	
para 36(c) ....ss 38(2), 131(1)		s 6(5) ....s 200(3), (5)	
Sch 3		s 6(6), (7)......................s 200(4)	
para 1.........................s 243(1)		s 6(8) ....s 200(4), (5)	
para 2(1)....................—		s 6(9) ....s 200(5)	
para 2(2)....................ss 1, 122(1)			
para 2(3)....................—			
para 2(4) ....s 92			
para 2(5)....................s 132			

(1)	(2)	(1)	(2)
Employment Protection Act 1975 (c 71)	Trade Union and Labour Relations (Consolidation) Act 1992 (c 52)	Employment Protection Act 1975 (c 71)	Trade Union and Labour Relations (Consolidation) Act 1992 (c 52)
s 6(10)	ss 199(4), 200(1)	s 106(1)	Rep 1980 c 42, s 20(3), Sch 2
s 6(10A)	s 208(1), (3)	s 106(2)	s 195(3)
s 6(11)	s 207(1), (2)	s 106(3)	s 190(5)
s 7(1)	s 254(1), (2)	s 106(4), (5)	s 197(1), (2)
s 7(2), (3)	—	s 107(1)	s 198(1), (2)
s 7(4)	s 254(3)	s 107(2)–(4)	s 198(3)–(5)
s 7(5), (6)	s 254(4)	s 108(1)	s 192(4)
s 8(1), (2)	s 6(1)	s 108(2)–(8)	Rep 1978 c 44, s 159(3), Sch 17
s 8(3)	ss 6(2), 7(2)	s 110	—
s 8(4)	s 6(3)	s 117(1), (2)	s 194(3), (4)
s 8(5)(a)	ss 6(5), 7(4)	s 118(1)	s 288(1)
s 8(5)(b)	ss 6(5), 7(2),(4)	s 118(2)(a)	s 288(3)
s 8(5)(c)	s 6(6), (5)	s 118(2)(b), (c)	Rep 1978 c 44, s 159(3), Sch 17
s 8(6)	ss 6(4), 7(3)	s 118(2)(d)	s 288(3)
s 8(7)	s 7(1)	s 119(1)	—
s 8(8)	s 7(2)–(5)	s 119(2)	Rep 1978 c 44, s 159(3), Sch 17
s 8(9)	s 9(2), (3)	s 119(3)	Rep 1989 c 13, s 7(1), Sch 1, Pt I
s 8(10)	s 7(6)	s 119(4)	s 284
s 8(11)	s 8(1)–(3)	s 119(5), (6)	s 285(1), (2)
s 8(12)(a)	s 8(4)	s 119(7)	s 282
s 8(12)(b)	s 8(5)	s 119(8)–(11)	Rep 1978 c 44, s 159(3), Sch 17
s 9	s 257	s 119(12)	s 283(1)
s 10(1)	s 259(1)	s 119(13)	—
s 10(2)	Cf Sch 3, para 7	s 119(14)	s 283(2)
s 10(3)	—	s 119(15)	s 286(1), (2)
s 17(1)	s 181(1), (2)	s 119(16)	s 286(4)
s 17(2)(a)	s 181(1), (2)	s 119(17)	Rep 1982 c 46, s 21(3), Sch 4
s 17(2)(b)	Rep 1980 c 42, s 20(3), Sch 2	s 121(1)	s 273(1), (2)
s 17(3)–(5)	s 181(3)–(5)	s 121(2)	s 273(3)
s 18	s 182	s 121(3), (4)	ss 274, 275
s 19(1)	s 183(1)	s 121(5), (6)	—
s 19(2), (3)	s 183(2)	s 121(7)	s 273(4)
s 19(4)–(7)	s 183(3)–(6)	s 121(8)	Rep 1978 c 44, s 159(3), Sch 17
s 20	s 184	s 122(1)	s 278(1), (2), (4)
s 21(1), (2)	s 185(1), (2)	s 122(2)	Sch 2, paras 3, 6, 7
s 21(3), (4)	s 185(3)	s 122(3)	Rep 1978 c 44, s 159(3), Sch 17
s 21(5)(a)	s 185(4)	s 122(4)	s 278(3)
s 21(5)(b)	Rep 1980 c 42, s 20(3), Sch 2	s 122(5)–(8)	s 278(6)
s 21(6)–(8)	s 185(5)–(7)	s 122(9)	Rep 1978 c 36, s 5(4), Sch 3
s 99(1)	s 188(1)	s 123(1)	s 294(6)
s 99(2)	s 196	s 123(2)	ss 293(3), 294(6)
s 99(3)–(9)	s 188(2)–(8)	s 123(3)	ss 286(3), 293(2)
s 100(1)	s 193(1), (2), (6)	s 123(4)	—
s 100(2), (3)	s 193(3), (4)	s 124(1)(b)	—
s 100(4)	s 193(6)	s 125(1)*	—
s 100(5), (6)	s 193(5), (7)	s 126(1)	ss 1, 5, 119, 178, 195(2), 218, 279, 280(1), 295(1), 296–298
s 101(1)	s 189(1)		
s 101(2)	s 189(6)	s 126(2)	—
s 101(3)–(6)	s 189(2)–(5)	s 126(3)	Rep 1978 c 44, s 159(3), Sch 17
s 101(7)	s 189(1)		
s 102(1)–(4)	s 190(1)–(4)	s 126(4)	—
s 102(5)–(11)	s 191(1)–(7)		
s 103(1)–(3)	s 192(1)–(3)		
s 104	Rep 1986 c 48, s 32(2), Sch 5, Pt I		
s 105(1)	s 194(1)		
s 105(2), (3)	s 194(2)		
s 105(4), (5)	Rep 1986 c 48, s 32(2), Sch 5, Pt I		

* Repealed in part

(1)	(2)	(1)	(2)
Employment Protection Act 1975 (c 71)	Trade Union and Labour Relations (Consolidation) Act 1992 (c 52)	Employment Protection Act 1975 (c 71)	Trade Union and Labour Relations (Consolidation) Act 1992 (c 52)

(1)	(2)
s 126(5) ....Rep 1978 c 44, s 159(3), Sch 17
s 126(6), (7)....................s 195(1), (2)
s 126(8) ....s 289
s 126(9) ....—
s 126A(1)–(4)..................s 218
s 126A(5) ....—
s 126A(6) ....s 218
s 127(1)(a)......................Rep 1979 c 12, s 31(3), Sch 7
s 127(1)(b)......................Sch 2, para 28
s 127(1)(bb)....................Sch 2, para 27
s 127(1)(c),(d) ....Rep 1978 c 44, s 159(3), Sch 17
s 127(1)(e)–(g) ....s 287(2)
s 127(2)–(4)....................s 287(1), (3), (4)
s 128(1) ....s 294(1)
s 128(2) ....Rep 1978 c 44, s 159(3), Sch 17
s 128(3) ....s 294(2)–(4)
s 128(4) ....s 294(5)
s 129(5)* ....—
s 129(6)* ....s 301(2)(c), (d)
Sch 1, Pt I
para 1..............................ss 247(2), 248(1)
para 2(1)..........................ss 248(1), 249(2)
para 2(2)..........................s 248(2)
para 2(3)..........................ss 248(4), 249(2)
para 2(4) ....s 248(3)
para 3(1)..........................s 249(1)
para 3(2)..........................s 249(3)
para 3(3), (4) ....s 249(2)
para 3(5), (6) ....s 249(4)
para 3(7)–(9) ....s 249(5)
para 4(1), (2) ....s 248(5), (6)
para 5..............................s 248(7)
para 6..............................s 251(1), (3)
para 7..............................s 251(2), (3)
para 8..............................ss 254(5), 259(3)
para 9..............................s 247(6)
para 10............................s 251(5)
para 11(1), (2) ....s 247(3), (4)
para 12............................s 247(5)
para 13(1)........................ss 253(1), 265(1)
para 13(2)........................s 258(1)
para 13(3)........................ss 253(1), 258(1)
Sch 1, Pt II
para 14(1)–(3) ....s 260(1)–(3)
para 15(1)–(5) ....s 261(1)–(5)
para 15(6)........................Bankruptcy (Scotland) Act 1985, s 75(10)
para 15(7)........................s 261(6)
para 16(1), (2) ....s 260(4), (5)
para 17(1), (2) ....s 263(1)
para 17(3)........................s 263(2)
paras 18–20................s 263(3)–(5)
para 21............................s 260(6)
paras 22–24................s 264(1)–(3)
para 25............................s 265(1)
para 26............................s 263(6)
para 27............................s 259(2)

(1)	(2)
Sch 1, Pt III
para 28(a) ....s 250(1), (4)
para 28(b) ....s 262(1), (4)
para 28(c) ....s 255(1), (4)
para 29......................s 252(2)
para 30......................ss 250(2), (4), 255(2), (4), 262(2), (4)
para 31......................ss 250(3), (4), 255(3), (4), 262(3), (4)
para 32......................s 251(4)
para 32A....................s 256(4)
para 33......................s 252(1)
para 34......................s 253(2)
para 35(1) ....ss 253(2), 258(2), 265(2)
para 35(2) ....s 253(3), (4)
para 35(3) ....s 272
Sch 12, Pt I
paras 1–3 ....s 292(1)–(3)
para 4........................—
paras 5, 6 ....s 292(4), (5)
para 7........................s 190(6)
Sch 12, Pt II..................Rep 1978 c 44, s 159(3), Sch 17
Sch 16, Pt III
para 1........................s 2(1), (2), (5), 3(1), (3), (4), 32(1)–(4), (6), 34(3), 39(1), 41(1), (2), (4), 42, 123(1), 124, 125(1), (2), 131(1)
para 2........................ss 4(3), 125(3)
para 3........................ss 9(1), (3),126(1), (2)
para 4........................ss 2(3), 123(2), (3)
para 5........................ss 2(4), 123(4)–(6)
para 6........................s 221
para 7(1) ....—
para 7(2) ....ss 295(1), 296(2)
para 7(3) ....s 5
para 7(4) ....—
para 7(5) ....ss 119, 136
paras 8–30.................Rep 1978 c 44, s 159(3), Sch 17
para 31......................—
para 32......................s 18(4)
para 33......................s 273(3), (4)
para 34......................Rep 1978 c 44, s 159(3), Sch 17
para 35......................—
Sch 16, Pt IV
para 2(1) ....—
para 2(2) ....ss 74(1), (3), 82(2)–(4), 84(2), (3), 92
para 2(3) ....s 95
para 2(4) ....—
para 3(1), (2) ....—
para 3(3) ....Rep 1982 c 46, s 21(3), Sch 4
para 3(4) ....ss 273(1), (3), 274, 275
para 7........................—
para 10(1) ....—
para 10(2) ....ss 99(1), (5), 100(1), 101, 103, 106(2), (3), 107(2), (3), 108(1), (2), 134(2), (3), (5)

* Repealed in part

(1)	(2)	(1)	(2)
Employment Protection Act 1975 (c 71)	Trade Union and Labour Relations (Consolidation) Act 1992 (c 52)	House of Commons (Administration) Act 1978 (c 36)	Trade Union and Labour Relations (Consolidation) Act 1992 (c 52)
para 10(3) ....s 104		Sch 2	
para 13(1) ....—		para 1*.....................—	
para 13(2), (3) ....Cf Sch 2, para 3(3)		para 5........................s 278(3), (4), (6)	
para 13(4), (5) ....Rep 1986 c 59, s 9(2), Schedule, Pt II			
para 13(6)–(11) ....Rep 1986 c 48, s 32(2), Sch 5, Pt II		Employment Protection (Consolidation) Act 1978 (c 44)	Trade Union and Labour Relations (Consolidation) Act 1992 (c 52)
para 16.......................Cf Sch 2, para 4(2), (3) Sch 17		s 23(1) ....s 146(1)	
paras 1–6 ....—		s 23(1A) ....s 146(3)	
		s 23(1B).........................s 146(4)	
Trade Union and Labour Relations (Amendment) Act 1976 (c 7)	Trade Union and Labour Relations (Consolidation) Act 1992 (c 52)	s 23(2) ....s 146(2)	
		s 23(2A), (2B) ....Rep 1988 c 19, ss 11(a), 33(2), Sch 4	
s 1....................................—		s 23(3)–(6)......................Rep 1980 c 42, ss 15(3), 20(3), Sch 2	
s 2....................................Rep 1980 c 42, s 20(3), Sch 2		s 23(7) ....s 151(1)	
s 3(1) ....s 69		s 24(1) ....s 146(5)	
s 3(2) ....s 219(1)		s 24(2) ....s 147	
s 3(3) ....ss 174(2), (3), 177(1)		s 24(3) ....s 149(1)	
s 3(4) ....s 174(2)		s 25(1)(a).......................s 148(1)	
s 3(5), (6) ....Rep 1978 c 44, s 159(3), Sch 17		s 25(1)(b).......................Rep 1980 c 42, ss 15(3), 20(3), Sch 2	
s 4....................................—		s 25(2) ....s 148(2)	
		s 26(1)–(5) ....s 149(2)–(6)	
Race Relations Act 1976 (c 74)	Trade Union and Labour Relations (Consolidation) Act 1992 (c 52)	s 26A(1)–(3) ....s 150(1)–(3)	
		s 27(1)(a).......................s 168(1)	
Sch 3		s 27(1)(b).......................s 168(2)	
para 1(1).......................—		s 27(2) ....s 168(3)	
para 1(2)–(4) ....Rep 1978 c 44, s 159(3), Sch 17		s 27(3)(a).......................s 169(1), (2)	
para 1(5) ....Sch 2, paras 3, 6, 7		s 27(3)(b), (4) ....s 169(3)	
		s 27(5), (6) ....s 169(4)	
Criminal Law Act 1977 (c 45)	Trade Union and Labour Relations (Consolidation) Act 1992 (c 52)	s 27(7) ....ss 168(4), 169(5)	
		s 28(1), (2) ....s 170(1), (2)	
		s 28(3), (4) ....s 170(3), (4)	
s 1(3) ....s 242(1)		s 30(1)† ....s 171	
s 5(11) ....—		s 30(2)† ....s 172(1), (2)	
s 63(2)*..........................passim		s 30(3) ....s 172(3)	
s 65(10)† ....s 242(2)		s 32(1)† ....ss 15(7), 16(7), 173(1)	
		s 32(2)† ....s 178(3)	
National Health Service Act 1977 (c 49)	Trade Union and Labour Relations (Consolidation) Act 1992 (c 52)	s 58(1), (2) ....s 152(1), (2)	
		s 58(3)–(12) ....Rep 1988 c 19, ss 11(b), 33(2), Sch 4	
		s 58(13), (14) ....s 152(3), (4)	
Sch 15		s 59*..............................s 153	
para 62.......................s 279		s 62(1), (2) ....s 238(1), (2)	
		s 62(3) ....s 239(3)	
National Health Service (Scotland) Act 1978 (c 29)	Trade Union and Labour Relations (Consolidation) Act 1992 (c 52)	s 62(4)(a).......................s 238(5)	
		s 62(4)(b).......................s 238(3)	
		s 62(4)(c).......................s 238(4)	
		s 62(5) ....s 238(1), (3)	
Sch 16		s 62A ....s 237	
para 39.......................s 279		s 64(1)* ....—	
		s 64(3) ....s 154	
		s 64A(2)* ....s 154	
		s 67(3) ....s 239(2)	
		s 71(2)(b)†.....................s 157(2)	
		s 72(c)†..........................s 157(1)	
		s 72A(1) ....s 155(1)	
		s 72A(2) ....s 155(1)–(3)	
		s 72A(3) ....s 155(2)	

† Not repealed   * Repealed in part

(1)	(2)	(1)	(2)
Employment Protection (Consolidation) Act 1978 (c 44)	Trade Union and Labour Relations (Consolidation) Act 1992 (c 52)	Employment Protection (Consolidation) Act 1978 (c 44)	Trade Union and Labour Relations (Consolidation) Act 1992 (c 52)
s 73(4A) ....s 156(1)		s 154(3)† ....ss 159(2), 286(3), 293(2), 294(2)–(4)	
s 73(4B).....................s 159(1), (3)			
s 73(7C)† ....s 156(2)		s 157(1)† ....s 294(1)	
s 75A(1)–(6) ....s 158(1)–(6)		s 157(3)† ....s 294(2), (4)	
s 75A(7) ....s 159(1), (3)		s 157(4)† ....s 294(5)	
s 76A(1)–(3) ....s 160(1)–(3)		s 160(3)† ....s 301(2)(c), (d)	
ss 76B, 76C ....Rep 1982 c 46, s 21(3), Sch 4		Sch 2, Pt I	
s 77(1) ....s 161(1)		para 2(2)* ....—	
s 77(2) ....s 161(2), (3)		para 2(4)* ....—	
s 77(3), (3A)..................s 162(1)–(3)		para 6(3)* ....—	
s 77(4) ....s 162(4)		Sch 12, Pt I	
s 77(5) ....s 163(1), (2)		para 1† ....s 292(1)	
s 77(6)–(9) ....s 163(3)–(6)		para 2† ....s 292(2)	
s 77(10) ....s 161(4), (6)		para 3† ....s 292(3)	
s 77(11) ....s 161(5)		para 5† ....s 292(4)	
s 78(1) ....s 164(1)		para 6† ....s 292(5)	
s 78(2) ....s 164(2), (3)		Sch 16	
s 78(3)–(6) ....s 164(4)–(7)		para 2.....................s 95	
s 79(1) ....s 165		para 5.....................s 104	
s 79(2) ....s 166(1), (2)		para 18..................ss 9(1), (3), 126(1), (2)	
s 79(3) ....s 166(3)–(5)		para 23(1) ....—	
s 129† ....ss 151(2), 173(2)		para 23(2) ....s 199(2), (3)	
s 132(1)(b)* ....Cf Sch 2, para 19		para 23(3) ....s 9(2), (3)	
s 133(1)(a)* ....s 290		para 23(4) ....s 190(4)	
s 133(1)(b)* ....s 290		para 23(6) ....s 190(5)	
s 133(1)(d), (f), (g) ......s 290		para 23(7) ....—	
s 136(1)(c), (e)†, (g).....s 291(2)		para 23(8) ....—	
s 136(2)(a)....................s 95		para 23(9) ....Rep 1982 c 46, s 21(3), Sch 4	
s 136(2)(b)....................s 104		para 23(10) ....—	
s 136(3) ....ss 9(4), 126(3)		para 23(11) ....s 273(4)	
s 136(5)* ....s 291(3)		para 23(13) ....s 298	
s 137(1)† ....s 287(2)			
s 137(2)† ....s 287(1)		Employment (Continental Shelf) Act 1978 (c 46)	Trade Union and Labour Relations (Consolidation) Act 1992 (c 52)
s 137(3)† ....s 287(3)			
s 137(4)† ....s 287(4)			
s 137(5)† ....s 287(5)			
s 138(1)† ....s 273(1)		s 1(1) ....s 287(1)	
s 138(2)† ....s 273(3)		s 2† ....s 287(5)	
s 138(4)† ....s 275			
s 138(7)† ....s 273(4)		Reserve Forces Act 1980 (c 9)	Trade Union and Labour Relations (Consolidation) Act 1992 (c 52)
s 139(1)† ....s 278(1), (2)			
s 140(1)† ....s 288(1)			
s 140(2)(d)†, (e)†, (g)†..s 288(2)			
s 141(2)† ....s 285(1)		Sch 9	
s 141(5)† ....s 285(2)		para 15.....................s 274	
s 144(2)† ....s 284			
s 146(2)† ....s 280(1)		Employment Act 1980 (c 42)	Trade Union and Labour Relations (Consolidation) Act 1992 (c 52)
s 146(3)† ....s 280(2)			
s 146(4)* ....s 281(1)			
s 146(5)–(7)† ....s 281(2)–(4)			
s 146(8)† ....s 281(5)		s 1(1) ....s 115(1)	
s 149(1)†, (2)* ....s 286(1), (2)		s 1(2), (3), (3A).............s 115(2)	
s 149(4)† ....s 286(4)		s 1(4) ....s 115(3)	
s 151† ....s 281(5)		s 1(5) ....s 115(4)	
s 152† ....s 281(6)		s 1(6) ....s 254(6)	
s 153(1)† ....ss 1, 5, 119, 178(1), (2), 295(1), 298		s 1(7) ....s 115(5)	
s 153(5)† ....s 289		s 1(8) ....—	
s 154(1)† ....ss 159(1), 294(6)		s 2(1) ....s 116(1), (3)(a)	
s 154(2)† ....ss 293(3), 294(6)			

† Not repealed   *Repealed in part

(1)	(2)	(1)	(2)
Employment Act 1980 (c 42)	Trade Union and Labour Relations (Consolidation) Act 1992 (c 52)	Agricultural Training Board Act 1982 (c 9)	Trade Union and Labour Relations (Consolidation) Act 1992 (c 52)
s 2(2) ....s 116(2)		s 11(3) ....Sch 2, para 27	
s 2(3) ....s 116(1), (3)			
s 2(4)–(6) ....s 116(4)–(6)		Industrial Training Act 1982 (c 10)	Trade Union and Labour Relations (Consolidation) Act 1992 (c 52)
s 2(7) ....s 291(2)			
s 2(8) ....s 116(7)			
s 2(9) ....s 298			
s 3(1) ....s 203(1)		Sch 3	
s 3(2), (3) ....s 204(1)		para 6........................Sch 2, para 28	
s 3(4) ....s 204(2)			
s 3(5) ....s 204(3), (4)		Oil and Gas Enterprise Act 1982 (c 23	Trade Union and Labour Relations (Consolidation) Act 1992 (c 52)
s 3(6) ....ss 203(2), 204(1)			
s 3(7) ....s 208(2), (3)			
s 3(8) ....s 207(1), (3)			
s 3(9) ....s 1		Sch 3	
s 4(1), (2) ....s 174(1)		para 25......................Cf Sch 2, para 29	
s 4(3) ....s 177(2), (3)			
s 4(4), (5) ....s 174(5), (6)		Employment Act 1982 (c 46)	Trade Union and Labour Relations (Consolidation) Act 1992 (c 52)
s 4(6) ....s 175			
s 4(7) ....s 176(1)			
s 4(8) ....s 291(1)			
s 4(9) ....s 174(4)		s 2...............................—	
s 4(10) ....ss 174(2), (3), 177(1)		s 3...............................s 152	
s 4(11) ....s 288(1), (2)		s 4(1) ....ss 156(1), 159(1), (3)	
s 5(1), (2) ....s 176(2)		s 4(2) ....s 156(2)	
s 5(3) ....s 176(3)		s 5(1) ....s 157(2)	
s 5(4)(a).........................s 176(4)		s 5(2) ....s 157(1)	
s 5(4)(b).........................s 176(5)		s 5(3) ....ss 158, 159(1), (3)	
s 5(5), (6) ....s 176(6), (7)		s 6...............................s 155	
s 5(7) ....s 176(4)		s 7...............................s 160	
s 5(8) ....s 176(5)		s 8(1) ....s 161(1)	
s 5(8A) ....s 176(8)		s 8(2) ....s 162(1)–(3)	
s 5(9) ....s 291(2)		s 9(1) ....—	
s 15(1) ....—		s 9(2) ....s 238(2)	
s 15(2) ....Rep 1988 c 19, s 33(2), Sch 4		s 9(3) ....s 238(3)	
		s 9(4) ....ss 238(1), 239(3)	
s 15(3) ....—		s 9(5) ....s 239(2)	
s 15(4) ....Rep 1982 c 46, s 21(3), Sch 4		s 10(1), (2) ....Rep 1988 c 19, s 33(2), Sch 4	
s 16(1) ....s 220		s 10(3) ....s 146(3), (4)	
s 16(2) ....s 219(3)		s 10(4) ....s 146(1)	
s 16(3) ....s 298		s 11...............................s 150	
s 19...............................—		s 12(1) ....s 144	
s 20(1)* ....—		s 12(2) ....ss 145(1)–(4), 187(2)	
Sch 1		s 12(3) ....s 145(3)	
para 2...........................—		s 12(4) ....s 145(2)	
para 3...........................ss 41(1)–(3), 131(1)		s 12(5) ....s 145(4)	
para 4...........................s 208(1), (3)		s 12(6) ....s 145(3)	
para 5...........................s 273(1), (2)		s 12(7) ....s 145(1), (5)	
para 6...........................s 178(3)		s 13(1) ....ss 186, 187(1)	
para 7...........................s 287(2)		s 13(2) ....s 187, (1), (2)	
para 17*.........................s 290		s 13(3) ....s 187(1)	
para 19.........................s 291(3)		s 13(4) ....s 187(3)	
para 21(b)........................—		s 14(1) ....ss 222(3), 225(1)	
para 24...........................—		s 14(2), (3) ....s 225(2)	
Health Services Act 1980 (c 53)	Trade Union and Labour Relations (Consolidation) Act 1992 (c 52)	s 15(1) ....—	
		s 15(2) ....ss 20(1), 117(3)	
		s 15(3) ....ss 20(2), 117(3)	
Sch 1, Pt I		s 15(3A).........................ss 20(3), 117(3)	
para 25......................s 279		s 15(3B).........................ss 20(4), 117(3)	

* Repealed in part

(1)	(2)	(1)	(2)
Employment Act 1982 (c 46)	Trade Union and Labour Relations (Consolidation) Act 1992 (c 52)	Trade Union Act 1984 (c 49)	Trade Union and Labour Relations (Consolidation) Act 1992 (c 52)

(1)	(2)	(1)	(2)
s 15(4)	s 21(1)	s 1(6B)	ss 46(1), (2), (6), 117(5), 119
s 15(5)	s 21(2)	s 1(6C)	s 46(4)
s 15(5A)	s 21(3)	s 1(7)	ss 46(5), 117(5)
s 15(5B)	s 21(4)	s 2(1), (2)	s 50(1), (2)
s 15(6)	s 21(5)	s 2(3), (4)(a)	s 50(3)
s 15(6A)	s 21(6)	s 2(4)(b)	s 50(4)
s 15(7)	ss 20(7), 21(7), 117(3)	s 2(5)	s 51(1), (2)
s 15(8), (9)	ss 20(5), (6), 117(3)	s 2(5)(a), (c)	s 51(2)
s 16(1)	s 22(1), (2)	s 2(6)	s 51(3)
s 16(2)	s 22(1), (5)	s 2(7)	s 51(4)
s 16(3)	s 22(2)	s 2(8)(a), (c)	s 51(5)
s 16(4)	s 22(3)	s 2(8)(b)	s 51(6), (7)
s 16(5)	s 22(3), (4)	s 2(9), (10)	s 47(1), (2)
s 16(6)	s 22(5)	s 2(11), (12)	s 47(3)
s 16(7)	s 118(3)	s 2(13)	s 60(1), (3)
s 17(1)	ss 23(1), 130(1)	s 2(14)	s 53
s 17(2)	ss 23(2), 130(2)	s 3	Rep 1988 c 19, ss 14(2), 33(2), Sch 4
s 17(3)	s 23(2), (3)	s 4(1), (2)	s 24(1), (2)
s 18(1)	—	s 4(2A)	s 24(3)
s 18(2)	ss 1, 244(1)	s 4(3)	ss 24(4), 44(4), 131(1)
s 18(3)	s 244(2)	s 5(1)	ss 25(1), 26(1), 54(1), (2), 55(1), 56(1)
s 18(4)	s 244(3)	s 5(2)	s 54(3)
s 18(5)	—	s 5(3)	ss 25(2), 55(2), 80(2)
s 18(6)	s 244(5)	s 5(4)	ss 25(3), 26(3), 55(3), 56(3), 80(3), 81(3)
s 18(7)	—	s 5(5)	ss 26(4), 56(4), 81(4)
s 19(1)	—	s 5(6)	ss 26(4), 56(4), 81(4)
s 19(2)	s 298	s 5(7)	ss 26(4), 56(4), 81(4)
s 22(4)	—	s 5(8)	ss 56(5), 81(5)
s 22(5)	s 301(2)(c), (d)	s 5(9)	ss 26(4), 56(4), 81(4)
Sch 1	—	s 5(10)	ss 24(6), 54(1), 79(1)
Sch 2		s 5(11), (12)	ss 26(5), 56(6), 81(6)
para 6(1)	s 282	s 5(12A)	ss 54(2), 56(6)
Sch 3, Pt II		s 5(13)	Cf s 121
para 10	ss 218, 296(1)	s 6(1)	ss 25(1), 55(4), 80(4)
para 11	s 298	s 6(2)	ss 25(5), 55(5), 80(5)
para 12	s 220(3)	s 6(3)	ss 24(6), 54(1), 79(1), 81(2)
para 13(1)	—	s 6(4)	ss 26(2), 56(2), 81(2)
para 13(2), (3)	s 218	s 6(5)	ss 25(2), 55(2), 80(2)
para 13(4)	s 287(2)	s 6(6)	Rep 1988 c 19, s 33(2), Sch 4
para 17	s 153	s 6(7)	ss 25(6), 55(6), 80(6)
para 18	s 238(3)	s 6(8)	ss 25(7), 55(7), 80(7)
para 19	s 154	s 7(1)–(3)	s 118(6)
para 20	s 154	s 7(4)	ss 43(2), 57(1)
para 24(1)	s 161(2), (3)	s 7(5)	ss 43(2), 57(1)
para 24(2)	s 162(1)	s 7(6)	ss 43(2), 57(1)
para 24(3)	s 163(1)	s 7(7)	ss 43(2), 57(1)
para 27(2)(a)	—	s 7(8)	s 57(3)
para 27(3)(a)	—	s 8(1)–(3)	s 58(1)–(3)
		s 8(4)	Cf Sch 3, para 9
Trade Union Act 1984 (c 49)	Trade Union and Labour Relations (Consolidation) Act 1992 (c 52)	s 8(5)	Cf Sch 3, para 10
		s 9(1)	ss 1, 24(5), 50(3), 51(4), (7), 60(2), 94(3), 118(6), 119, 232(3), 298
s 1(1)	ss 46(1), (2), (6), 117(5)		
s 1(2)	ss 46(1), (2), 117(5)		
s 1(3)	s 59		
s 1(4)	s 46(6)		
s 1(5)	s 119	s 9(2)	s 61(1)
s 1(6)	s 61(2)	s 9(3), (4)	Cf Sch 3, paras 9, 10
s 1(6A)	ss 46(3), 117(5)		

(1)	(2)	(1)	(2)
Trade Union Act 1984 (c 49)	Trade Union and Labour Relations (Consolidation) Act 1992 (c 52)	Trade Union Act 1984 (c 49)	Trade Union and Labour Relations (Consolidation) Act 1992 (c 52)
s 10(1)	s 226(1)	s 18(7)	s 273(1), (2)
s 10(2)	—	s 19(1)	—
s 10(3)	s 226(2)	s 19(2)	ss 96, 119
s 10(3A)	s 226(3)	s 19(3)	—
s 10(4), (4A)	s 226(2)	s 19(4)	s 132
s 10(5)	ss 1, 246	s 20(1)	—
s 11(1)	s 227(1)	s 20(2), (3)	s 115(2)
s 11(1A)	s 228(1)	s 20(4), (5)	—
s 11(1B)(a)	s 228(2)	s 21	—
s 11(1B)(b), (c)	s 228(3)	s 22(1)–(5)	—
s 11(2)	s 227(2)	s 22(6)	s 301(2)(b)
s 11(3)	s 229(1), (4)		
s 11(4)	s 229(2)	Companies Consolidation (Consequential Provisions) Act 1985	Trade Union and Labour Relations (Consolidation) Act 1992 (c 52)
s 11(4A)	s 229(3)		
s 11(5)	s 230(1)		
s 11(6)(a)	s 230(2)	Sch 2*	ss 10(3), 14(2), 30(4), 34(1), 117(1), (3), 127(3), 129(1), 131(1)
s 11(6)(b)	s 230(3)		
s 11(7)	s 230(4)		
s 11(8)	s 231	Wages Act 1986 (c 48)	Trade Union and Labour Relations (Consolidation) Act 1992 (c 52)
s 11(9), (10)	s 232(1), (2)		
s 11(11)	ss 226(4), 232(3), 246, 298		
s 12(1)	—	s 1(6)*	s 88(2)
s 12(2)(a)	s 73(3)	s 5(3A)	s 88(3), (4)
s 12(2)(b)	s 73(4)	Sch 4 para 9†	s 291(2)
s 12(3)	—		
s 12(4)	s 73(4)	Public Order Act 1986 (c 64)	Trade Union and Labour Relations (Consolidation) Act 1992 (c 52)
s 12(5)	s 93(2)		
s 13(1)	s 74(1), (3)		
s 13(2)	ss 76, 77(1)–(5), 298	Sch 2 para 1	s 241(2), (3)
s 13(3)	s 74(2)		
s 13(4)–(6)		Consumer Protection Act 1987 (c 43)	Trade Union and Labour Relations (Consolidation) Act 1992 (c 52)
s 13(7), (8)	s 94(1), (2)		
s 13(9)	s 84(4), (5)		
s 13(10)	ss 84(4), 94(3)	Sch 4 para 8	s 22(1)
s 14(1), (2)(a)	ss 83(1), 89(3)		
s 14(2)(b)	s 83(2)	Employment Act 1988 (c 19)	Trade Union and Labour Relations (Consolidation) Act 1992 (c 52)
s 14(2)(c)	s 89(4)		
s 14(3), (4)	s 83(3)		
s 14(5)		s 1(1)	s 62(1)
s 15(1), (2)	s 89(2)	s 1(2)	s 62(3)
s 15(3)	s 90(1), (2)	s 1(3)	s 62(5)
s 15(4)	s 90(3)	s 1(4)	—
s 15(5)	s 89(3)	s 1(5)	s 62(2)
s 15(6)	s 91(1), (2)	s 1(6)	ss 62(6), 226(4)
s 15(7)(a)	s 91(1)	s 1(7)	s 62(8)
s 15(7)(b)	s 91(3)	s 1(8)	s 62(9)
s 15(8)	s 91(4)	s 2(1)	s 63(2)
s 15(9)	s 89(5)	s 2(2)	s 63(4)
s 15(10)	ss 89(1), 91(1), (2)	s 2(3)	s 63(3)
s 15(11)	—		
s 16(1)	s 90(4)		
s 16(2)–(4)	s 90(5)		
s 16(5)	s 90(6)		
s 16(6)	Cf s 121		
s 17(1)	s 72		
s 17(2)	Sch 3, para 8		
s 17(3)	—		
s 18(1), (2)	s 86(1), (2)		
s 18(3)	ss 86(3), 87(4)		
s 18(4)	s 87(1)		
s 18(5)	s 87(3)		
s 18(6)	s 87(2)		

† Not repealed   * Repealed in part

(1)	(2)	(1)	(2)
Employment Act 1988 (c 19)	Trade Union and Labour Relations (Consolidation) Act 1992 (c 52)	Employment Act 1988 (c 19)	Trade Union and Labour Relations (Consolidation) Act 1992 (c 52)
s 2(4)	s 63(1)	s 15(2)(a)	ss 49(1), 75(1)
s 2(5), (6)	s 63(5), (6)	s 15(2)(b)	ss 49(4), 75(4)
s 3(1)	s 64(1)	s 15(2)(bb)	ss 49(5), 75(5)
s 3(2)	s 65(1)	s 15(2)(c)	ss 49(6), 75(6)
s 3(3)	s 65(2)–(5), (7)	s 15(2)(d)	ss 49(7), 75(7)
s 3(4)	s 65(6)	s 15(3)	ss 49(2), 75(2)
s 3(5)	s 64(2)	s 15(4)	ss 49(3), 75(3)
s 3(6)	s 65(7)	s 15(5)(a)	ss 52(1), 78(1)
s 3(7)	s 64(4), (5)	s 15(5)(b)	ss 52(1), 78(1)
s 3(8)	s 64(3)	s 15(5)(c)	ss 52(1), 78(1)
s 4(1)	s 66(1)	s 15(5)(d)	ss 52(1), 78(1)
s 4(2), (3)	s 66(2)	s 15(5)(e)	ss 52(2), 78(2)
s 4(4)	s 66(3)	s 15(5)(f)	ss 52(2), 78(2)
s 4(5)	s 291(2)	s 15(6)	ss 52(2), 78(2)
s 4(6)	s 66(4)	s 15(7)	ss 52(3)–(6), 78(3)–(6)
s 4(7)	s 288(1), (2)	s 15(8)	s 132
s 5(1)–(9)	s 67(1)–(9)	s 16(1)	ss 79(1), 80(1), 81(1)
s 5(10)	s 291(2)	s 16(2)	s 79(2)
s 6(1)	s 29(1)	s 16(3)	s 79(3)
s 6(2)	ss 29(3), 30(1)	s 16(4)	ss 79(1), 80(2)–(7), 81(2)–(6)
s 6(3), (4)	s 30(2), (3)		
s 6(5), (6)	s 30(5), (6)	s 16(5)	s 132
s 6(7)	s 31(1), (2)	s 17(1)	s 228
s 6(8)	ss 45, 131(1)	s 17(2)	s 226(3)
s 6(9)(a)	s 29(1), (2)	s 17(3)	s 246
s 6(9)(b)	s 118(5)	s 18(1)	s 203(1)
s 6(9)(c)	s 30(4)	s 18(2)	s 1
s 6(10)	s 30(1)	s 19(1)	s 266(1), (2)
s 7(1)	s 68(1)	s 19(2)	—
s 7(2)	s 68(2), (3)	s 19(3)	s 266(5)
s 7(3)	s 68(4)	s 20(1)	s 110(1)
s 8(1)–(3)	s 15(1)–(3)	s 20(2)(a)	s 111(1)
s 8(4)	s 15(4), (5)	s 20(2)(b)	s 110(5)
s 8(5)	s 15(5)	s 20(3)	ss 111(2), 114(1)
s 8(6)	s 15(6)	s 20(4), (5)	s 110(2), (3)
s 9(1)–(4)	s 16(1)–(4)	s 20(6)	s 114(2)
s 9(5)	s 16(6)	s 20(7)(a)–(d)	s 109(1)
s 10(1)	s 222(1), (5)	s 20(7)(e), (8)	s 109(3)
s 10(2)	s 222(1), (5)	s 21(1)	s 113
s 10(3)(a)	s 222(4)	s 21(2)	s 111(4)
s 10(3)(b)	s 222(5)	s 21(3)	s 111(3)
s 11	—	s 21(4), (5)	s 111(5), (6)
s 12(1)	ss 46(2)–(4), (6), 117(5), 119	s 21(6)	s 114(3)
		s 22(1)	s 256(1), (2)
s 12(2)	s 57(2), (3)	s 22(2)	s 256(3)
s 12(3), (4)	Cf Sch 3, para 9	s 22(3)	s 256(4)
s 12(5)	—	s 23	ss 16(5), 26(6), 31(3), 56(7), 62(4), 81(7)
s 12(6)	s 119, and cf Sch 3, para 9	s 30(1)	ss 62(7), 65(8), 245
s 13(1)	—	s 30(2)	s 276(2)
s 13(2)(a)	s 48(1)	s 30(3)	s 273(1), (3)
s 13(2)(b)	s 48(1), (2)	s 32(1)*	ss 1, 15(7), 16(7), 30(7), 65(3), (7), 70, 119, 121, 295(1), 296, 298
s 13(2)(c)	s 48(7)		
s 13(2)(d)–(f)	s 48(4)–(6)		
s 13(3)	s 48(3)	s 32(2)	—
s 13(4)	s 48(2)	s 34(2), (3)	—
s 13(5)	s 48(8)	s 34(6)*	s 301(2)(b)
s 13(6)	s 298	Sch 1	
s 14(1)	s 77(4)	para 1(1), (2)	s 267(2), (3)
s 14(2)	—	para 1(3)	s 267(1)
s 15(1)(a)	s 74(1), (3)	para 2(1)–(3)	s 268(1)–(3)
s 15(1)(b)	—	para 2(4)	s 268(5)

* Repealed in part

(1)	(2)	(1)	(2)
Employment Act 1988 (c 19)	Trade Union and Labour Relations (Consolidation) Act 1992 (c 52)	Employment Act 1989 (c 38)	Trade Union and Labour Relations (Consolidation) Act 1992 (c 52)
para 2(5) ....s 268(4)		Sch 9	
para 3.........................s 269(1)		para 2.........................—	
para 4.........................s 266(4)			
para 5(1), (2) ....s 269(2), (3)		Companies Act 1989 (c 40)	Trade Union and Labour Relations (Consolidation) Act 1992 (c 52)
para 6.........................s 269(4)			
para 7(1) ....s 270(1)			
para 7(2) ....s 270(3)		s 124............................ss 117(4), 131(2)	
para 8(1), (2) ....s 270(2), (3)			
para 9(1)(a), (b)........s 271(2)		National Health Service and Community Care Act 1990 (c 19)	Trade Union and Labour Relations (Consolidation) Act 1992 (c 52)
para 9(1)(c)...............s 271(3)			
para 9(2) ....s 271(4)			
para 10.......................s 271(1)		s 2(1)(b)†.......................s 279	
para 11.......................s 266(3)			
para 12.......................Cf Sch 2, para 1		Employment Act 1990 (c 38)	Trade Union and Labour Relations (Consolidation) Act 1992 (c 52)
para 13.......................Cf Sch 2, para 4(4)			
para 14.......................s 272			
Sch 3, Pt I			
para 1(1)(a)...............s 74(3)		s 1(1)–(6) ....s 137(1)–(6)	
para 1(1)(b) ....s 77(2)		s 1(7) ....s 137(8)	
para 1(2) ....—		s 2 ....s 138	
para 2(1) ....s 151(1)		s 3(1) ....ss 1, 143(1), 295(1)	
para 2(2) ....s 152(3), (4)		s 3(2) ....s 137(7)	
para 2(3) ....s 290		s 3(3), (4) ....s 143(2), (3)	
para 2(4) ....s 291(3)		s 3(5) ....—	
para 2(5) ....Cf Sch 2, para 25		s 4(1)–(6) ....s 224(1)–(6)	
para 3(1) ....ss 116(3), 298		s 4(7) ....—	
para 3(2) ....s 176(5), (8)		s 5(1) ....ss 62(8), 235	
para 4.......................s 225(2)		s 5(2), (3) ....s 232(4), (5)	
para 5(1) ....ss 46(1), (2), 117(5)		s 5(4) ....ss 51(2), 77(2)	
para 5(2)(a)...............s 51(2)		s 5(5) ....ss 49(5), 75(5)	
para 5(2)(b) ....s 60(3)		s 6(1) ....—	
para 5(3) ....s 24(3)		s 6(2) ....ss 20(1), 117(3)	
para 5(4)(a)...............ss 24(6), 25(1), 26(1), 54(1), 56(1), 79(1)		s 6(3) ....ss 20(2)–(4), 117(3)	
para 5(4)(b) ....ss 56(5), 81(5)		s 6(4) ....s 21(1)	
para 5(4)(c)...............ss 54(2), 56(6)		s 6(5) ....s 21(2)–(4)	
para 5(5)(a)...............—		s 6(6) ....s 21(6)	
para 5(5)(b) ....s 58(2)		s 6(7) ....s 21(7)	
para 5(5)(c)...............Cf Sch 3, para 9		s 6(8) ....ss 20(6), 117(3)	
para 5(5)(d) ....Cf Sch 3, para 10		s 7(1) ....s 229(3)	
para 5(6) ....—		s 7(2) ....s 233(1)	
para 5(7) ....s 226(2)		s 7(3), (4) ....s 233(3), (4)	
para 5(8)(a)...............s 227(1)		s 7(5) ....ss 1, 233(2), 246	
para 5(8)(b) ....s 227(2)		s 8(1)–(6) ....s 234(1)–(6)	
para 5(8)(c)...............s 229(4)		s 8(7) ....ss 1, 246	
para 5(8)(d) ....s 229(2)		s 9(1) ....s 237	
para 5(8)(e)...............s 231		s 9(2), (3) ....s 223	
para 5(8)(f)...............s 226(4)		s 10(1)–(3) ....s 109(2)	
para 5(9) ....s 301(2)(b)		s 10(4)(a)......................ss 1, 119	
para 6(1) ....s 88(2)		s 10(4)(b)......................s 109(2)	
para 6(2) ....s 88(3), (4)		s 10(5) ....s 110(4)	
para 6(3) ....—		s 10(6) ....—	
		s 11(1), (2) ....s 112	
Employment Act 1989 (c 38)	Trade Union and Labour Relations (Consolidation) Act 1992 (c 52)	s 11(3) ....—	
		s 12(1) ....ss 201(1), 205(1)	
s 14(a)..........................s 168(1)		s 12(2)(a)......................s 205(1)	
s 14(b) ....s 168(2)		s 12(2)(b)......................s 201(1)	
Sch 6		s 12(2)(c)........................—	
para 19.......................ss 173(1), 178(3)			

† Not repealed

(1)	(2)	(1)	(2)
Employment Act 1990 (c 38)	Trade Union and Labour Relations (Consolidation) Act 1992 (c 52)	Employment Act 1990 (c 38)	Trade Union and Labour Relations (Consolidation) Act 1992 (c 52)
s 12(3) ....s 205(2)		para 12(2)...................s 277(2)	
s 12(4) ....s 201(2)		para 12(3)..................s 278(3), (4), (6)	
s 12(5) ....ss 201(3), 205(3)		para 12(4)...................s 277(3)	
s 12(6) ....ss 201(4), 205(4)		para 12(5), (6) ....s 277(5), (6)	
s 12(7)(a)......................s 202(1)		para 13...................ss 273(5), 277(4), 278(5)	
s 12(7)(b)......................ss 202(3), 206(1)		para 14......................s 280	
s 12(8) ....s 202(2)		para 15......................s 285(1)	
s 12(9) ....ss 201(4), 202(1), 205(4), 206(2)		para 16(1), (2) ....s 285(2)	
s 18(1)* ....—		para 16(3)..................s 284	
Sch 1, Pt I		para 17......................s 287(2)	
para 1..........................—		para 18......................s 276(1)	
para 2..........................s 143(4)		Sch 2	
para 3..........................s 139		para 1(2)....................s 238(1), (3)	
para 4..........................s 290		para 2(1)....................—	
para 5..........................s 140		para 2(2)....................s 226(1)	
para 6..........................s 141		para 2(3)....................s 226(2)	
para 7..........................s 142		para 2(4)....................s 226(3)	
para 8..........................s 291(2)		para 2(5), (6) ....s 226(2)	
Sch 1, Pt II		para 2(7)....................—	
para 9..........................—		para 3(1)....................—	
para 10(1), (2) ....s 288(1),(2)		para 3(2)....................s 62(1)	
para 11(1)...................s 273(1)		para 3(3)....................s 62(3)	
para 11(2)...................s 273(3)		para 3(4)....................s 62(5)	
para 11(3)...................s 274		para 3(5)....................s 62(2)	
para 11(4)...................s 275			
para 12(1) ....ss 277(1), 278(1), (2)			

* Repealed in part

TRADE UNION REFORM AND EMPLOYMENT RIGHTS ACT 1993

(1993 c 19)

ARRANGEMENT OF SECTIONS

An Act to make further reforms of the law relating to trade unions and industrial relations; to make amendments of the law relating to employment rights and to abolish the right to statutory minimum remuneration; to amend the law relating to the constitution and jurisdiction of industrial tribunals and the Employment Appeal Tribunal; to amend section 56A of the Sex Discrimination Act 1975; to provide for the Secretary of State to have functions of securing the provision of careers services; to make further provision about employment and training functions of Scottish Enterprise and of Highlands and Islands Enterprise; and for connected purposes.

[1 July 1993]

GENERAL NOTE
This major Act covers a wide range of aspects of trade union and employment law. In the process it implements several EC Directives: 91/533 (proof of employment), 92/56 (amendments to collective redundancies) and in part 92/85 (maternity rights) and 89/391 (the "framework" health and safety Directive). It also aims to rectify incomplete previous implementation of Directives 75/129 (collective redundancies) and 77/187 (acquired rights).

Commencement. Sections 52–55 came into force on Royal Assent (1 July 1993). Section 7(1) comes into effect on 1 April 1996 (s 7(4)). The remainder of the Act is subject to commencement by Order.

The first (and as at 1 September 1993, only) Commencement Order is the Trade Union Reform and Employment Rights Act 1993 (Commencement No 1 and Transitional Provisions) Order 1993, SI 1993/1908, printed below, paras **[1435]–[1442]**. This Order contains important transitional provisions, as to which reference should be made to the Order. Under this Order much of the Act came into force on 30 August 1993, with other commencement dates of 30 November 1993 and 1 January 1994.

Principal provisions for which no commencement date has yet been appointed, together with an indication of expected commencement dates (based on Government statements) are as follows—

Ss 23–25 (maternity rights) and associated Schedules: October 1994.
S 26 (together with Sch 4: particulars of terms of employment): end of November 1993.
S 27 (itemised pay statements): end of November 1993.
S 31 (employment protection for armed forces): no date given.
S 32 (discriminatory agreements and rules): end of November 1993.
Ss 37, 42 (Employment Appeal Tribunal; vexatious litigants): end of November 1993.

References to commencement dates in the notes to sections and Schedules are to those appointed by the Commencement No 1 Order (except in relation to ss 7, 52–55).

Most of the Act enacts amendments to other statutes, principally the Employment Protection (Consolidation) Act 1978 and the Trade Union and Labour Relations (Consolidation) Act 1992. The text of amendments and new and substituted sections is printed at the appropriate point in those Acts. Only substantive parts of the 1993 Act are printed here, but cross-references are given under every section. Sections 45–47 (careers services and training in Scotland) and 54 (Northern Ireland) are omitted, as are Schs 7, 8, 10 (miscellaneous amendments, consequential amendments and repeals).

PART I

TRADE UNIONS ETC

Union elections and ballots

1 Election scrutineer to check register

(Amends ss 49, 52, of the Trade Union and Labour Relations (Consolidation) Act 1992, above, paras **[703]**, **[707]**.)   **[983]**

NOTE
Commencement: 30 August 1993.

2 Counting of election votes etc by independent person

(Inserts s 51A in the Trade Union and Labour Relations (Consolidation) Act 1992 (above, para **[706]**) *and further amends ibid s 52 (above, para* **[707]**).)   **[984]**

3 Political fund ballots

Schedule 1 to this Act (which makes in relation to political fund ballots provision corresponding to that made in relation to elections by sections 1 and 2 above) shall have effect. **[985]**

NOTE
Commencement: 30 August 1993.

4 Ballots for union amalgamations and transfers of engagements

(*Substitutes for s 100 of the Trade Union and Labour Relations (Consolidation) Act 1992 (above, para* **[758]**)*, new ss 100–100E (above, paras* **[759]**–**[764]**)*.*) **[986]**

NOTE
Commencement: 30 August 1993.

5 Ballots for union amalgamations and transfers of engagements: notice not to include influential material

(*Inserts new sub-s (3A) in s 99 of the Trade Union and Labour Relations (Consolidation) Act 1992, above, para* **[757]**.) **[987]**

NOTE
Commencement: 30 August 1993.

6 Confidentiality of trade union's register of member's names and addresses

(*Inserts new s 24A in the Trade Union and Labour Relations (Consolidation) Act 1992, above, para* **[669]**.) **[988]**

NOTE
Commencement: 30 August 1993.

7 Ballots: repeal of provisions for financial assistance and use of employers' premises

(1) Sections 115 and 116 of the 1992 Act (financial assistance towards expenditure on certain ballots and obligations of employers to make premises available) shall cease to have effect.

(2) No application under regulations under section 115 (whether made before or after its repeal) shall be entertained by the Certification Officer in relation to expenditure in respect of a ballot if the date of the ballot falls after 31 March 1996 or in respect of arrangements to hold a ballot which is not proceeded with if the date of the ballot would have fallen after that date; but, for the purposes of applications made after (as well as before) the repeal in relation to expenditure not excluded by this subsection, the regulations shall continue in force notwithstanding the repeal.

(3) In subsection (2) above, the "date of the ballot" means, in the case of a ballot in which votes may be cast on more than one day, the last of those days.

(4) Subsection (1) above shall come into force on 1 April 1996.   **[989]**

NOTE
Commencement: 1 April 1996 (sub-s (1)); to be appointed (remainder).

Financial affairs of unions etc

8 Annual return to contain additional information

(Amends s 32(3) of the Trade Union and Labour Relations (Consolidation) Act 1992, above, para **[677]***.)*   **[990]**

NOTE
Commencement: 1 January 1994.

9 Statement to members following annual return

(Inserts new s 32A in the Trade Union and Labour Relations (Consolidation) Act 1992, above, para [678]*.)*   **[991]**

NOTE
Commencement: 1 January 1994.

10 Investigation of financial affairs

(Inserts new ss 37A–E in the Trade Union and Labour Relations (Consolidation) Act 1992, above, paras **[984]**–**[688]***.)*   **[992]**

NOTE
Commencement: 30 August 1993.

11 Offences

(Amends s 45 of, and inserts new s 45A in the Trade Union and Labour Relations (Consolidation) Act 1992, above, paras **[696]**, **[697]***.)*   **[993]**

NOTE
Commencement: 30 August 1993.

12 Disqualification of offenders

(Inserts new ss 45B, 45C in the Trade Union and Labour Relations (Consolidation) Act 1992, above, paras **[698]**, **[699]***.)*   **[994]**

NOTE
Commencement: 30 August 1993.

Rights in relation to union membership

13 Action short of dismissal: non-infringing actions

(Amends s 148 of the Trade Union and Labour Relations (Consolidation) Act 1992, above, para **[812]***.)*   **[995]**

NOTE
Commencement: 30 August 1993.

14 Right not to be excluded or expelled

(*Substitutes new ss 174–177 in the Trade Union and Labour Relations (Consolidation) Act 1992, above, paras* **[838]–[841]** *(present sections) and* **[842]–[845]** *(prospectively substituted sections).*)   **[996]**

NOTE
Commencement: 30 November 1993.

15 Right not to suffer deduction of unauthorised or excessive subscriptions

(*Substitutes for section 68 of the Trade Union and Labour Relations (Consolidation) Act 1992 and the heading thereto (above, para* [723]) *new ss 68, 68A (above, paras* **[724], [725]**).)   **[997]**

NOTE
Commencement: 30 August 1993.

16 Extension of right not to be unjustifiably disciplined

(*Amends s 65 of the Trade Union and Labour Relations (Consolidation) Act 1992, above, para* **[720]**.)   **[998]**

NOTE
Commencement: 30 August 1993.

Industrial action

17 Requirement of postal ballot

(*Amends s 230 of the Trade Union and Labour Relations (Consolidation) Act 1992, above, para* **[901]**.)   **[999]**

NOTE
Commencement: 30 August 1993.

18 Notice of ballot and sample voting paper for employers

(*Amends s 226 of, and inserts s 226A in, the Trade Union and Labour Relations (Consolidation) Act 1992, above, paras* **[894], [895]**.)   **[999A]**

NOTE
Commencement: 30 August 1993.

19 Ballot result for employers

(*Inserts new s 231A in the Trade Union and Labour Relations (Consolidation) Act 1992, above, para* **[903]**.)   **[999B]**

NOTE
Commencement: 30 August 1993.

20 Scrutiny of ballots

(Inserts new ss 226B, 226C, 231B in, and a new sub-s (1A) in s 229 of, the Trade Union and Labour Relations (Consolidation) Act 1992, above, paras **[896]**, **[897]**, **[904]**, **[900]** *respectively.)*   **[999C]**

NOTE
Commencement: 30 August 1993.

21 Notice of industrial action for employers

(Inserts new s 234A in the Trade Union and Labour Relations (Consolidation) Act 1992, above, para **[908]**.*)*   **[999D]**

NOTE
Commencement: 30 August 1993.

22 Industrial action affecting supply of goods or services to an individual

(Inserts new ss 235A–C in the Trade Union and Labour Relations (Consolidation) Act 1992, above, paras **[910]**–**[912]**.*)*   **[999E]**

NOTE
Commencement: 30 August 1993.

PART II

EMPLOYMENT RIGHTS

Maternity

23 Right to maternity leave and right to return to work

(1) In the Employment Protection (Consolidation) Act 1978 (referred to in this Act as "the 1978 Act"), for Part III (maternity: right to return to work) there shall be substituted—

    (a) the sections 33 to 38A set out in subsection (2) below (which provide for a new right to maternity leave), and

    (b) the sections 39 to 44, together with the heading, set out in Schedule 2 to this Act (which continue in effect the right to return to work with amendments to take account of the new right).

    (2) ...   **[999F]**

NOTES
Commencement: to be appointed.
Sub-s (2): enacts new ss 33–38A of the Employment Protection (Consolidation) Act 1978. The existing s 33 is printed above at para **[301]**; ss 34–38 have been repealed. The new sections are printed above at paras **[305A]**–**[305H]**.

24 Dismissal rights

(Substitutes s 60, and amends ss 53, 59 and 64, of the Employment Protection (Consolidation) Act 1978. See above paras **[317]** *(s 60),* **[708]**, **[714]**, **[719]**.)

[999G]

NOTE
Commencement: 30 August 1993 (partly) remainder to be appointed.

---

25 Rights on suspension on maternity grounds

After section 44 of the 1978 Act (set out in Schedule 2 to this Act) there shall be inserted as provisions of Part III the sections 45 to 47, together with the heading, set out in Schedule 3 to this Act (which makes provision conferring rights on employees suspended from work on grounds of maternity). **[999H]**

NOTE
Commencement: to be appointed.

Employment particulars

26 Right to employment particulars

For sections 1 to 6 of the 1978 Act (particulars relating to employment) there shall be substituted the sections set out in Schedule 4 to this Act. **[999I]**

NOTE
Commencement: to be appointed.

---

27 Entitlement to itemised pay statement

(Inserts new sub-ss (4A)–(4C) in the Employment Protection (Consolidation) Act 1978, s 146, above, para [391].) **[999J]**

NOTE
Commencement: to be appointed.

Employment protection in health and safety cases

28 Rights to claim unfair dismissal and not to suffer detriment

Schedule 5 to this Act (which makes amendments of the 1978 Act for protecting employees against dismissal, and being subjected to other detriment in health and safety cases) shall have effect. **[999K]**

NOTE
Commencement: 30 August 1993.

Unfair dismissal: assertion of statutory right

29 Dismissal on ground of assertion of statutory right

(Inserts new s 60A in, and amends ss 59, 64 of the Employment Protection (Consolidation) Act 1978, above, paras **[317A], [316], [320]**.)   **[999L]**

NOTE
Commencement: 30 August 1993.

Reinstatement orders: compensation

30 Compensation for unfair dismissal when reinstatement or re-engagement ordered

(Amends ss 71, 74, 75 of the Employment Protection (Consolidation) Act 1978, above, paras **[328], [331], [332]**.)   **[999M]**

NOTE
Commencement: 30 August 1993.

Service in armed forces

31 Application of 1978 Act to service in armed forces

(Substitutes sub-s (3) in s 138 of, and inserts new s 138A in, the Employment Protection (Consolidation) Act 1978, above, paras **[385], [385A]**.)   **[999N]**

NOTE
Commencement: to be appointed.

Sex discrimination

32 Right to declaration of invalidity of discriminatory terms and rules

(Inserts new sub-ss (4A)–(4D) in s 6 of the Sex Discrimination Act 1986, above, para **[484]**.)   **[999O]**

NOTE
Commencement: to be appointed.

Transfer and redundancy rights

33 Amendments of transfer of undertakings regulations

(Amends the Transfer of Undertakings (Protection of Employment) Regulations 1981, SI 1981/1794, below, paras **[1137]–[1149]**.)   **[999P]**

NOTE
Commencement: 30 August 1993.

34 Redundancy consultation procedures

(Amends ss 188, 190, 193, substitutes s 195, and repeals s 283, of the Trade Union and Labour Relations (Consolidation) Act 1992 above, paras **[856]**, **[858]**, **[861]**, **[863]**, **[961]**.)

[999Q]

NOTE

Commencement: 30 August 1993 (see SI 1993/1908 for transitional provision).

PART III

OTHER EMPLOYMENT MATTERS

Abolition of right to statutory minimum remuneration

35 Repeal of Part II of Wages Act 1986

Part II of the Wages Act 1986 (which provides for statutory minimum remuneration for certain workers in accordance with wages orders made by wages councils) shall cease to have effect.

[999R]

NOTE

Commencement: 30 August 1993.

Constitution and jurisdiction of tribunals

36 Constitution of industrial tribunals

(Amends s 128 of the Employment Protection (Consolidation) Act 1978, above, para **[375]**.)

[999S]

NOTE

Commencement: 30 August 1993 (partly); remainder to be appointed.

37 Constitution of Employment Appeal Tribunal

(Substitutes Sch 11, Pt I, para 16 to the Employment Protection (Consolidation) Act 1978, above, para **[413]**.)

[999T]

NOTE

Commencement: to be appointed.

38 Extension of power to confer on industrial tribunals jurisdiction in respect of contracts of employment etc

(Amends s 131 of the Employment Protection (Consolidation) Act 1978, above, para **[378]**.)

[999U]

NOTE

Commencement: 30 August 1993.

39 Agreements not to take proceedings before industrial tribunal

(1) ...

(2) Schedule 6 to this Act shall have effect for making corresponding amendments in the Sex Discrimination Act 1975, the Race Relations Act 1976, the Wages Act 1986 and the Trade Union and Labour Relations (Consolidation) Act 1992.   **[999V]**

NOTES
Commencement: 30 August 1993.
Sub-s (1): amends s 140(2) of, and inserts sub-ss 140(3), (4) in, the Employment Protection (Consolidation) Act 1978, above, para [387].

40 Restriction of publicity in cases involving sexual misconduct: industrial tribunals

(*Amends Sch 9, para 1 to the Employment Protection (Consolidation) Act 1978, above, para* **[411]**.)   **[999W]**

NOTES
Commencement: 30 August 1993.

41 Restriction of publicity in cases involving sexual misconduct: Employment Appeal Tribunal

(*Inserts new para 18A in Sch 11, Pt I to the Employment Protection (Consolidation) Act 1978, above, para* **[413]**.)   **[999X]**

NOTES
Commencement: 30 August 1993.

42 Restriction of vexatious proceedings

(*Inserts new s 136A in the Employment Protection (Consolidation) Act 1978, above, para* **[383A]**.)   **[999Y]**

NOTES
Commencement: to be appointed.

ACAS

43 Functions of ACAS

(*Amends ss 209, 249(2), and substitutes s 213, of the Trade Union and Labour Relations (Consolidation) Act 1992. See respectively paras* **[877]**, **[926]**, **[881]** *above.*)   **[999Z]**

NOTES
Commencement: 30 August 1993.

44 Fees for exercise of functions by ACAS

(*Inserts new s 251A in the Trade Union and Labour Relations (Consolidation) Act 1992, above, para* **[929]**.)   **[1000]**

NOTES

Commencement: 30 August 1993.

45–47 (*Ss 45–47 (careers services and training etc in Scotland), which amend the Employment and Training Act 1973 and the Enterprise and New Towns (Scotland) Act 1990, are omitted.*)

PART IV

SUPPLEMENTARY

48 Interpretation

In this Act—

"the 1978 Act" means the Employment Protection (Consolidation) Act 1978, and

"the 1992 Act" means the Trade Union and Labour Relations (Consolidation) Act 1992.

[1000A]

NOTES

Commencement: 30 August 1993.

49 Miscellaneous and consequential amendments

(1) The enactments specified in Schedule 7 to this Act shall have effect subject to the amendments there specified (which are miscellaneous amendments).

(2) The enactments specified in Schedule 8 to this Act shall have effect subject to the amendments there specified (which are consequential amendments). **[1000B]**

NOTES

Commencement: 30 August 1993 (partly) 30 November 1993 (partly) 1 January 1994 (partly) remainder to be appointed.

50 Transitional provisions and savings

The transitional provisions and savings set out in Schedule 9 to this Act shall have effect.

[1000C]

NOTES

Commencement: 30 August 1993 (partly) remainder to be appointed.

51 Repeals and revocations

The enactments mentioned in Schedule 10 to this Act (which include enactments which are unnecessary) are repealed, and the Repeals and instruments mentioned in that Schedule are revoked, to the extent revocations. specified in the third column of that Schedule.

[1000D]

52 Commencement

Subject to any other commencement provision, the preceding sections of, and the Schedules to, this Act shall not come into force until such day as the Secretary of State may appoint by order made by statutory instrument; and different days may be appointed for different provisions and different purposes.   **[1000E]**

53 Financial provision

There shall be paid out of money provided by Parliament—
   (a)   any expenditure of the Secretary of State under this Act, and
   (b)   any increase attributable to this Act in the sums payable out of money so provided under any other Act.   **[1000F]**

NOTES
Commencement: 1 July 1993.

54   (*Provides for parallel legislation for Northern Ireland; omitted.*)

55 Short title

This Act may be cited as the Trade Union Reform and Employment Rights Act 1993.
     [1000G]

NOTES
Commencement: 1 July 1993.

SCHEDULES

SCHEDULE 1

Section 3

POLITICAL FUND BALLOTS
(*Amends ss 74, 75, 78 of, and inserts new s 77A in, the Trade Union and Labour Relations (Consolidation) Act 1992, above, paras* **[731]**, **[732]**, **[736]**, **[735]** *respectively.*)
     [1000H]

NOTES
Commencement: 30 August 1993.

SCHEDULE 2

Section 23

MATERNITY: THE RIGHT TO RETURN TO WORK
(*Inserts new ss 39–44 in the Employment Protection (Consolidation) Act 1978 (the previous sections having been repealed by the Social Security Act 1986) in substitution for ss 45–48, repealed by s 23(1) of this Act. For new ss 39–44, see above paras* **[305I]**–**[305N]**.)
     [1000I]

NOTES
Commencement: to be appointed.

SCHEDULE 3

Section 25

SUSPENSION FROM WORK ON MATERNITY GROUNDS

(Inserts new ss 45–47 in the Employment Protection (Consolidation) Act 1978 (the existing ss 45–47, inter alia, being repealed prospectively by s 23(1) of this Act). For the new ss 45–47, see above, paras [305O]–[305Q].) [1000J]

NOTES

Commencement: to be appointed.

SCHEDULE 4

Section 26

PROVISIONS SUBSTITUTED FOR SECTIONS 1 TO 6 OF 1978 ACT

(Substitutes ss 1–6 of the Employment Protection (Consolidation) Act 1978; see above, paras [274]–[280] *(existing ss 1, 2, 2A, 4, 5, 5A, 6) and paras* [280A]–[280F] *(substituted ss 1–6).)* [1000K]

NOTES

Commencement: to be appointed.

SCHEDULE 5

Section 28

EMPLOYMENT PROTECTION IN HEALTH AND SAFETY CASES

(Inserts new ss 22A–C, 57A, 75A, 77, 77A, 78, 78A, 79 in the Employment Protection (Consolidation) Act 1978 (the previous ss 77, 78, 79 having been repealed by the Trade Union and Labour Relations (Consolidation) Act 1992); for those sections as inserted, see above paras [295A]–[295C], [315A], [332A], [333A]–[333E]. *Also amends ss 57, 59, 64, 71–73 of the 1978 Act, above, paras* [315], [316], [320], [328]–[330].) [1000L]

NOTES

Commencement: 30 August 1993.

SCHEDULE 6

Section 39(2)

COMPROMISE CONTRACTS

(Amends s 77 of the Sex Discrimination Act 1975, above, para [162]; *s 72 of the Race Relations Act 1976, above, para* [232]; *s 6 of the Wages Act 1986, above, para* [468]; *and s 288 of the Trade Union and Labour Relations (Consolidation) Act 1992, above, para* [966].) [1000M]

NOTES

Commencement: 30 August 1993.

(Schs 7, 8, which make miscellaneous and consequential amendments, are omitted. Relevant provisions are shown as amended elsewhere in this book.)

SCHEDULE 9

Section 50

TRANSITIONAL PROVISIONS AND SAVINGS

General

1 (1) An order under section 52 of this Act may contain such transitional provisions and savings as appear to the Secretary of State to be appropriate.

(2) Nothing in the following provisions of this Schedule prejudices the generality of sub-paragraph (1) above.

(3) Nothing in this Schedule prejudices the operation of sections 16 and 17 of the Interpretation Act 1978 (effect of repeals).

Deduction of trade union subscriptions

2 For the purposes of section 68 of the 1992 Act (as substituted by section 15 of this Act) a deduction representing a payment to a trade union in respect of a worker's membership which is made in accordance with arrangements existing between his employer and the union immediately before the day on which section 15 comes into force under which deductions were made in his case before that day shall be treated as an authorised deduction where—

    (a)   the day on which the deduction is made falls before the end of the period of one year beginning with the day on which section 15 comes into force, and

    (b)   written notice from the worker stating that he does not wish such deductions to be made has not been received by the employer in time for it to be reasonably practicable for him to secure that the deduction is not made.

Employment particulars

3 (1) In this paragraph "existing employee" means an employee whose employment with his employer has begun before the day on which section 26 of this Act comes into force (whether or not the provisions of sections 1 to 6 of the 1978 Act applied to him before that day).

(2) Subject to the following provisions of this paragraph, the provisions substituted for sections 1 to 4 and 6 of the 1978 Act by section 26 of this Act shall not apply to any existing employee.

(3) Where an existing employee, at any time—

    (a)   on or after the day on which section 26 of this Act comes into force, and

    (b)   either before the end of his employment or within the period of three months beginning with the day on which his employment ends,

requests from his employer a statement under section 1 of the 1978 Act (as substituted by section 26), the employer shall (subject to section 5 and any other provision disapplying or having the effect of disapplying section 1) be treated as being required by section 1 to give him a written statement under that section, in accordance with the provisions of the 1978 Act as so substituted, not later than two months after the request is made; and section 4 of that Act (as so substituted) shall, subject as aforesaid, apply in relation to the existing employee after he makes the request.

(4) An employer shall not be required to give a statement under section 1 by virtue of sub-paragraph (3) above to an existing employee on more than one occasion by virtue of that sub-paragraph.

(5) Where—

    (a)   on or after the day on which section 26 of this Act comes into force there is in the case of any existing employee a change in any of the matters particulars of which would, had he been given a statement of particulars as at that day under section 1 of the 1978 Act (as substituted by that section), have been included or referred to in the statement, and

    (b)   he has not previously requested a statement under sub-paragraph (3) above,

subsections (1) and (5) of section 4 of the 1978 Act (as substituted by section 26 of this Act) shall be treated (subject to section 5 and any other provision disapplying or having the effect of disapplying section 4) as requiring his employer to give him a written statement containing particulars of the change at the time specified in subsection (1) of section 4; and subsections (3) and (6) of that section shall apply accordingly.

(6) Nothing in any enactment providing for the application of sections 1 to 4 of the 1978 Act to a person who comes or ceases to come within any of the exceptions from those sections

specified in that Act shall have effect in relation to an existing employee by reason of his coming or ceasing to come within that exception by virtue of any of the amendments of the 1978 Act made by this Act.

Transfers of undertakings

4 The amendments of the Transfer of Undertakings (Protection of Employment) Regulations 1981 made by section 33 of this Act shall not have effect in relation to any transfer of an undertaking taking place before the date on which that section comes into force; and, accordingly, the repeal by this Act of—

    (a) section 94 of the 1978 Act, and

    (b) section 23 of the Contracts of Employment and Redundancy Payments Act (Northern Ireland) 1965,

shall have effect only in relation to any change in the ownership of a business occurring on or after that date.

Wages Councils

5 (1) Notwithstanding the repeal of Part II of the Wages Act 1986 by section 35 of this Act, the provisions of that Part specified or referred to below shall continue to have effect, on and after the day appointed for the repeal ("the appointed day"), in accordance with the following provisions.

(2) Section 16 (effect and enforcement of wages orders under section 14) shall have effect in relation to a failure occurring or continuing on or after the appointed day to pay, with respect to any period ending before that day, an amount equal to or exceeding the statutory minimum remuneration as it has effect in relation to such a failure before the appointed day; and, subject to the following provisions, the other sections of Part II which relate to section 16 shall continue to have effect accordingly.

(3) Section 19(1) and (4) (obligation to keep records etc) shall have effect on and after the appointed day as if—

    (a) the reference to the provisions of Part II being complied with in relation to the payment of remuneration were a reference to their having been complied with in relation to payments of remuneration made—

        (i) before the appointed day, or

        (ii) on or after the appointed day with respect to any period ending before that day;

    (b) the reference to deductions or payments made were references to deductions or payments so made; and

    (c) in a case where the three-year retention period for records would end after the expiry of the period of six months beginning with the appointed day, the retention period were—

        (i) that period of six months, or

        (ii) if within that period of six months a court so orders, such longer period as is specified by the court;

and, subject to the following provisions, the other sections of Part II which relate to section 19 shall continue to have effect accordingly.

(4) Section 20 (wages inspectors) shall continue to have effect on and after the appointed day for the purposes of this paragraph; but—

    (a) the powers conferred by subsections (3) and (4) shall not be exercisable after the end of the period of six months beginning with the appointed day, and

    (b) subsection (6) shall not authorise the institution of proceedings by a wages inspector after the end of the period of six months beginning with the appointed day.

(5) Paragraph 4 of Schedule 3 shall continue to have effect on and after the appointed day in relation to orders under section 14 made before that day.   **[1000N]**

PART 2
STATUTORY INSTRUMENTS

STATUTORY INSTRUMENTS

para

INDUSTRIAL TRIBUNALS (ENGLAND AND WALES) REGULATIONS 1965

(SI 1965/1101)

NOTES
Made: 11 May 1965
Authority: Industrial Training Act 1964, s 12 (see now the Employment Protection (Consolidation) Act 1978, s 128, Sch 9).
Modified by the Solicitors' Incorporated Practices Order 1991, SI 1991/2684.
These Regulations govern the establishment and membership of Industrial Tribunals. Reg 6 and Schs 1, 2 prescribe the procedure in appeals against assessment to levies under the Industrial Training Act 1964. The Schedules are omitted for reasons of space. The Regulations apply to England and Wales only.

ARRANGEMENT OF REGULATIONS

1 Title and commencement

These Regulations may be cited as the Industrial Tribunals (England and Wales) Regulations 1965 and shall come into operation on 31st May 1965.   **[1001]**

2 Interpretation

(1) In these Regulations, unless the content otherwise requires:—

"the Act" means the Industrial Training Act 1964;
"appellant" means a person who has appealed to a tribunal under the provisions of a levy order made under section 4 of the Act;
"the Board" means in relation to an appeal the respondent industrial training board;
"the clerk to the tribunal" means the person appointed by [the Secretary, or an Assistant Secretary, of the Tribunals] to act in that capacity at one or more hearings;
"hearing" means a sitting of a tribunal duly constituted for the purpose of receiving evidence, hearing addresses and witnesses or doing anything lawfully requisite to enable the tribunal to reach a decision on an appeal;
"levy" means a levy imposed under the Act;
"the Minister" means the Minister of Labour;
"the Office of the Tribunals" means the Central Office of the Industrial Tribunals (England and Wales);
["the panel of chairmen" means the panel of persons, being barristers or solicitors of not less than seven years' standing, appointed by the Lord Chancellor in pursuance of Regulation 5(2) of these Regulations;]
"the President" means the President of the Industrial Tribunals (England and

Wales) or the person nominated by the Lord Chancellor to discharge for the time being the functions of the President;

"the Register of Appeals" means the Register of Industrial Levy Appeals and Decisions kept in pursuance of these Regulations;

"Rule" means a Rule of Procedure contained in [either Schedule] to these Regulations;

["the Secretary of the Tribunals" and "an Assistant Secretary of the Tribunals" mean respectively the persons for the time being acting as the Secretary or as an Assistant Secretary, of the Central Office of the Industrial Tribunals (England and Wales);]

"tribunal" means an industrial tribunal (England and Wales) established under these Regulations, and in relation to an appeal means the tribunal to which the appeal has been referred by the President [or by a member of the panel of chairmen for the time being nominated by the President.]

[(2) A form referred to by number in either Schedule to these Regulations means the form so numbered in the Appendix to that Schedule.]

(3) The Interpretation Act 1889 applies to the interpretation of these Regulations as it applies to the interpretation of an Act of Parliament.   **[1002]**

NOTES

Para (1): definition "the panel of chairmen" inserted, definitions "the Secretary of the Tribunals" and "an assistant Secretary of the Tribunals" substituted, and definitions "clerk to the tribunal", "Rule" and "tribunal" amended, by the Industrial Tribunals (England and Wales) (Amendment) Regulations 1967, SI 1967/301.

Para (2): substituted by SI 1967/301.

3 President of Industrial Tribunals

(1) There shall be a President of the Industrial Tribunals (England and Wales) who shall be appointed by the Lord Chancellor and shall be a [person who has a 7 year general qualification, within the meaning of section 71 of the Courts and Legal Services Act 1990].

[*(2) The President shall vacate his office at the end of the completed year of service in the course of which he attains the age of seventy-two years.*]

(3) The President may resign his office by notice in writing to the Lord Chancellor.

(4) If the Lord Chancellor is satisfied that the President is incapacitated by infirmity of mind or body from discharging the duties of his office, or if the President is adjudged bankrupt or makes a composition or arrangement with his creditors, the Lord Chancellor may revoke his appointment.

(5) The functions of the President under these Regulations may, if he is for any reason unable to act or during a vacancy in his office, be discharged by a person nominated for that purpose by the Lord Chancellor.   **[1003]**

NOTES

Para (1): words in square brackets substituted by the Courts and Legal Services Act 1990, s 71(2), Sch 10, para 27.

Para (2): substituted by the Industrial Tribunals (England and Wales) (Amendment) Regulations 1970, SI 1970/941, reg 3; further substituted by the Judicial Pensions and Retirement Act 1993, s 26, Sch 6, para 27(2) (subject to s 27 of, and Sch 7 to, the 1993 Act), as from a day to be appointed, as follows—

"(2) The President shall vacate his office on the day on which he attains the age of seventy years, but subject to section 26(4) to (6) of the Judicial Pensions and Retirement Act 1993 (Lord Chancellor's power to authorise continuance in office up to the age of 75).".

[4 Establishment of Tribunals

(1) Such number of tribunals shall be established in England and Wales for the determination of appeals by persons assessed to a levy as the President may from time to time determine.

(2) The tribunals shall sit at such times and in such places as may from time to time be determined by the President or, in relation to any area specified by him in England and Wales, by a member of the panel of chairmen nominated by him to act in that area.]   **[1004]**

NOTE
   Substituted by SI 1967/301, reg 3.

5 Membership of Tribunals

[(1) Subject to the provisions of paragraph (1A) of this Regulation, a tribunal shall consist of a chairman and two other members but, in the absence of any one member of a tribunal other than the chairman, an appeal may with the consent of the parties be heard in the absence of such member, and in that event the tribunal shall be deemed to be properly constituted.

(1A) A tribunal may consist of the President, the chairman of the tribunal or a member of the panel of chairmen for the time being nominated for the purpose by the President, for any of the following purposes, that is to say—

   (a) making an order dismissing the proceedings where the appellant or applicant has given written notice of the abandonment of his appeal or application;

   (b) making an order allowing the appeal where the Board has given written notice that the appeal is not contested;

   (c) deciding an appeal or application in accordance with the written agreement of the parties;

   (d) dealing with any interlocutory matter or application;

   (e) making an order for costs in connection with an order or decision mentioned in the foregoing sub-paragraphs of this paragraph.

(2) For each hearing the chairman shall be the President or a person selected from a panel of persons [who have a 7 year general qualification, within the meaning of section 71 of the Courts and Legal Services Act 1990,] appointed by the Lord Chancellor; such selection shall be made by the President or by a member of the said panel for the time being nominated by the President for the purpose, and that member may select himself.]

[(3) For each hearing the two members of a tribunal other than the chairman shall be selected by the President (or by a member of the panel of chairmen for the time being nominated by the President for the purpose), as to one member from a panel of persons appointed by the Secretary of State after consultation with any organisation or association of organisations representative of employers, and as to the other member from a panel of persons appointed by the Secretary of State after consultation with any organisation or association of organisations representative of employed persons.]

(4) The President [(or a member of the panel of chairmen for the time being nominated by the President for the purpose)] may at any time select from the appropriate panel another person in substitution for the chairman or other member of a tribunal previously selected . . . to hear an appeal.

(5) [Subject to paragraph (6)] members of panels constituted under these Regulations shall hold and vacate office under the terms of the instruments under which they are appointed, but may resign office by notice in writing in the case of a member of the panel of chairmen to the Lord Chancellor and in any other case to the Minister; and any such member who ceases to hold office shall be eligible for reappointment.

[(6) A member of a panel of chairmen appointed under paragraph (2) shall vacate his office on the day on which he attains the age of seventy years, but subject to section 26(4) to (6) of the Judicial Pensions and Retirement Act 1993 (Lord Chancellor's power to authorise continuance in office up to the age of 75).]   **[1005]**

NOTES
Paras (1), (1A): substituted for the original para (1) by SI 1967/301, reg 4.
Para (2): substituted by SI 1967/301, reg 4; words in square brackets substituted by the Courts and Legal Services Act 1990, s 71(2), Sch 10, para 27.
Para (3): substituted by the Industrial Tribunals (England and Wales) (Amendment) Regulations 1977, SI 1977/1473, reg 3.
Para (4): words in square brackets inserted, and words omitted revoked, by SI 1967/301, reg 4.
Para (5): words in square brackets inserted by the Judicial Pensions and Retirement Act 1993, s 26, Sch 6, para 27(3), as from a day to be appointed (subject to s 27 of, and Sch 7 to, the 1993 Act).
Para (6): added by the Judicial Pensions and Retirement Act 1993, s 26, Sch 6, para 27(3), as from a day to be appointed (subject to s 27 of, and Sch 7 to, the 1993 Act).

[6 Procedure as to levy appeals

The Rules of Procedure contained in Schedule 1 to these Regulations shall continue to have effect in relation to appeals by persons assessed to a levy under a levy order that came into operation before 13th March 1967, and the Rules of Procedure contained in Schedule 2 to these Regulations shall have effect in relation to appeals by persons assessed to a levy under a levy order coming into operation on or after that date.]   **[1006]**

NOTE
Substituted by SI 1967/301, reg 5.

[7 Proof of Decisions of Tribunals

The production in any proceedings in any court of a document purporting to be certified by the Secretary of the Tribunals to be a true copy of an entry of a decision in the Register of Appeals shall, unless the contrary is proved, be sufficient evidence of the document and of the facts stated therein.]   **[1007]**

NOTE
Added by SI 1967/301, reg 6.

(Schs 1, 2 not printed.)

INDUSTRIAL TRIBUNALS (SCOTLAND) REGULATIONS 1965
(SI 1965/1157)

NOTES
Made: 18 May 1965.
Authority: Industrial Training Act 1964, s 12 (see now the Employment Protection (Consolidation) Act 1978, s 128, Sch 9).
These Regulations govern the establishment and membership of Industrial Tribunals in Scotland, and apply to Scotland only. Schs 1, 2 prescribe rules of procedure in appeals against assessments to levies under the Industrial Training Act 1964. The Schedules are omitted for reasons of space.

ARRANGEMENT OF REGULATIONS

1 Title and commencement

These Regulations may be cited as the Industrial Tribunals (Scotland) Regulations 1965 and shall come into operation on 31st May 1965.   **[1008]**

2 Interpretation

(1) In these Regulations, unless the context otherwise requires:—

"the Act" means the Industrial Training Act 1964;

"appellant" means a person who has appealed to a tribunal under the provisions of a levy order made under section 4 of the Act;

"the Board" means in relation to an appeal the respondent industrial training board;

"the clerk to the tribunal" means the person appointed by [the Secretary, or an Assistant Secretary, of the Tribunals] to act in that capacity at one or more hearings;

"hearing" means a sitting of a tribunal duly constituted for the purpose of receiving evidence, hearing addresses and witnesses or doing anything lawfully requisite to enable the tribunal to reach a decision on an appeal;

"levy" means a levy imposed under the Act;

"the Lord President" means the Lord President of the Court of Session;

"the Minister" means the Minister of Labour;

"the Office of the Tribunals" means the Central Office of the Industrial Tribunals (Scotland);

["the panel of chairmen" means the panel of persons, being advocates or solicitors of not less than seven years' standing, appointed by the Lord President in pursuance of Regulation 5(2) of these Regulations;]

"the President" means the President of the Industrial Tribunals (Scotland) or the person nominated by the Lord President to discharge for the time being the functions of the President;

"the Register of Appeals " means the Register of Industrial Levy Appeals and Decisions kept in pursuance of these Regulations;

"Rule" means a Rule of Procedure contained in [either Schedule] to these Regulations;

["the Secretary of the Tribunals" and "an Assistant Secretary of the Tribunals" means respectively the persons for the time being acting as the Secretary, or as an Assistant Secretary, of the Central Office of the Industrial Tribunals (Scotland);]

"tribunal" means an industrial tribunal (Scotland) established under these Regulations, and in relation to an appeal means the tribunal to which the appeal has been referred by the President [or by a member of the panel of chairmen for the time being nominated by the President.]

[(2) A form referred to by number in either Schedule to these Regulations means the form so numbered in the Appendix to that Schedule.]

(3) The Interpretation Act 1889 applies to the interpretation of these Regulations as it applies to the interpretation of an Act of Parliament.   **[1009]**

NOTES

Para (1): words in square brackets substituted or inserted by the Industrial Tribunals (Scotland) (Amendment) Regulations 1967, SI 1967/302, reg 2(1).

Para (2): substituted by SI 1967/302, reg 2(2).

3 President of Industrial Tribunals

(1) There shall be a President of the Industrial Tribunals (Scotland) who shall be appointed by the Lord President and shall be an advocate or solicitor of not less than seven years' standing.

[(2) The President shall vacate his office at the end of the completed year of service in the course of which he attains the age of seventy-two years.]

(3) The President may resign his office by notice in writing to the Lord President.

(4) If the Lord President is satisfied that the President is incapacitated by infirmity of mind or body from discharging the duties of his office, or if the President has had his estate sequestrated or has made a trust deed for behalf of his creditors or a composition contract, the Lord President may revoke his appointment.

(5) The functions of the President under these Regulations may, if he is for any reason unable to act or during a vacancy in his office, be discharged by a person nominated for that purpose by the Lord President.   **[1010]**

NOTE

Para (2): substituted by the Industrial Tribunals (Scotland) (Amendment) Regulations 1972, SI 1972/638, reg 3.

[4 Establishment of tribunals

(1) Such number of tribunals shall be established in Scotland for the determination of appeals by persons assessed to a levy as the President may from time to time determine.

(2) The tribunals shall sit at such times and in such places as may from time to time be determined by the President or, in relation to any area specified by him in Scotland, by a member of the panel of chairmen nominated by him to act in that area.]   **[1011]**

NOTE

Substituted by SI 1967/302, reg 3.

5 Membership of Tribunals

[(1) Subject to the provisions of paragraph (1A) of this Regulation, a tribunal shall consist of a chairman and two other members but, in the absence of any one member of a tribunal other than the chairman, an appeal may with the consent of the parties be heard in the absence of such member, and in that event the tribunal shall be deemed to be properly constituted.

(1A)   A tribunal may consist of the President, the chairman of the tribunal or a member of the panel of chairmen for the time being nominated for the purpose by the President, for any of the following purposes, that is to say—

    (a)   making an order dismissing the proceedings where the appellant or applicant has given written notice of the abandonment of his appeal or application;

    (b)   making an order allowing the appeal where the Board has given written notice that the appeal is not contested;

    (c)   deciding an appeal or application in accordance with the written agreement of the parties;

    (d)   dealing with any interlocutory matter or application;

    (e)   making an order for expenses in connection with an order or decision mentioned in the foregoing sub-paragraphs of this paragraph.]

[(2)   For each hearing the chairman shall be the President or a person selected from a panel of persons (being advocates or solicitors of not less than seven years' standing) appointed by the Lord President; such selection shall be made by the President or by a member of the said panel for the time being nominated by the President for the purpose, and that member may select himself.]

[(3)   For each hearing the two members of a tribunal other than the chairman shall be selected by the President (or by a member of the panel of chairmen for the time being nominated by the President for the purpose), as to one member from a panel of persons appointed by the Secretary of State after consultation with any organisation or association of organisations representative of employers, and as to the other member from a panel of persons appointed by the Secretary of State after consultation with any organisation or association of organisations representative of employed persons.]

(4)   The President [(or a member of the panel of chairmen for the time being nominated by the President for the purpose)] may at any time select from the appropriate panel another person in substitution for the chairman or other member of a tribunal previously selected . . . to hear an appeal.

(5)   Members of panels constituted under these Regulations shall hold and vacate office under the terms of the instruments under which they are appointed, but may resign office by notice in writing in the case of a member of the panel of chairmen to the Lord President and in any other case to the Minister; and any such member who ceases to hold office shall be eligible for reappointment.   **[1012]**

NOTES

Paras (1), (1A): substituted for the original para (1) by SI 1967/302, reg 4(1).

Para (2): substituted by SI 1967/302, reg 4(2).

Para (3): substituted by the Industrial Tribunals (Scotland) (Amendment) Regulations 1977, SI 1977/1474, reg 3.

Para (4): words in square brackets inserted, and words omitted revoked, by SI 1967/302, reg 4(4).

[6   Procedure as to levy appeals

The Rules of Procedure contained in Schedule 1 to these Regulations shall continue to have effect in relation to appeals by persons assessed to a levy under a new levy order that came into operation before 13 March 1967, and the Rules of Procedure contained in Schedule 2 to these Regulations shall have effect in relation to appeals by persons assessed to a levy under a levy order coming into operation on or after that date.]   **[1013]**

NOTE

Substituted by SI 1967/302, reg 5.

[7 Proof of decisions of tribunals

The production in any proceedings in any court of a document purporting to be certified by the Secretary of the Tribunals to be a true copy of an entry of a decisions in the Register of Appeals shall, unless the contrary is proved, be sufficient evidence of the document and of the facts stated therein.] **[1013A]**

NOTE
    Inserted by SI 1967/302, reg 6.

(*Schs 1, 2, not printed.*)

REDUNDANCY PAYMENTS PENSIONS REGULATIONS 1965

(SI 1965/1932)

NOTES
    Made: 10 November 1965.
    Authority: Redundancy Payments Act 1965, s 14.
    These Regulations make provision under what is now the Employment Protection (Consolidation) Act 1978, s 98.

ARRANGEMENT OF REGULATIONS

1 Citation and commencement

These Regulations may be cited as the Redundancy Payments Pensions Regulations 1965 and shall come into operation on 6th December 1965. **[1014]**

2 Interpretation

(1) The Interpretation Act 1889 applies to the interpretation of these Regulations as it applies to the Interpretation of an Act of Parliament.

(2) In these Regulations, unless the context otherwise requires, the following expressions have the meanings hereby assigned to them respectively, that is to say—
    "the Act" means the Redundancy Payments Act 1965;
    "employee" has the meaning assigned to it in subsection (1) of section 25 of the Act and includes any person in respect of whom the Act has effect as if he were an employee within the meaning of that subsection;
    "employer" has the meaning assigned to it in subsection (1) of section 25 of the Act and includes any person in respect of whom the Act has effect as if he were an employer within the meaning of that subsection;
    "the Minister" means the Minister of Labour;

"pension" has the meaning assigned to it in Regulation 3 and includes any part of a pension;

"pensioned employee" means an employee who has a right or claim to a pension of a kind referred to in Regulation 4;

"tribunal" means a tribunal established under section 12 of the Industrial Training Act 1964;

"week" means a week ending with Saturday.   **[1015]**

3 Meaning of "pension"

(1) Subject to the provisions of this Regulation, in these Regulations "pension" means a periodical payment or lump sum by way of pension, gratuity or superannuation allowance as respects which the Minister is satisfied that it is to be paid in accordance with any scheme or arrangement having for its object or one of its objects to make provision in respect of persons serving in particular employments for providing them with retirement benefits and (except in the case of such a lump sum which had been paid to the employee) that—

(a) the scheme or arrangement is established by Act of Parliament or of the Parliament of Northern Ireland, or other instrument having the force of law; or

(b) the benefits under the scheme or arrangement are secured by an irrevocable trust which is subject to the laws of any part of Great Britain; or

(c) the benefits under the scheme or arrangement are secured by a contract of assurance or an annuity contract which is made with—

(i) an insurance company to which the Insurance Companies Act 1958 applies; or

(ii) a registered friendly society; or

(iii) an industrial and provident society registered under the Industrial and Provident Societies Act 1893; or

(d) the benefits under the scheme or arrangement are secured by any regulation or other instrument (not being a regulation or instrument having the force of law) made with the authority of a Minister of the Crown or with the consent of the Treasury for the purpose of authorising the payment to persons not employed in the Civil Service of the State of such pensions, gratuities or other like benefits as might have been granted to persons so employed; or

(e) the scheme or arrangement is established by an enactment or other instrument having the force of law in any part of the Commonwealth outside the United Kingdom;

and that the provision made to enable benefits to be paid (taking into account any additional resources which could and would be provided by the employer, or any person connected with the employer, to meet any deficiency) is adequate to ensure payment in full of the benefits aforesaid.

(2) If in any case the Minister is satisfied that benefits under the scheme or arrangement are wholly or mainly provided for the benefit of persons not resident in Great Britain he may if he thinks fit and subject to such conditions, if any, as he thinks proper, waive the requirement contained in sub-paragraph (b) of the foregoing paragraph in respect of a scheme or arrangement the benefits under which are secured by an irrevocable trust or the requirements of heads (i), (ii) or (iii) of sub-paragraph (c) thereof in the case of a scheme or arrangement the benefits under which are secured by a contract of assurance or an annuity contract.

(3) In these Regulations "pension" does not include—

(a) a payment to an employee which consists solely of a return of his own contributions, with or without interest;

(b) that part of a payment to an employee which is attributable solely to additional voluntary contributions by that employee made in accordance with the scheme or arrangement;

(c) a periodical payment or lump sum, in so far as that payment or lump sum represents such compensation as is mentioned in section 47(1) of the Act (which relates to statutory compensation schemes) and is payable under a statutory provision, whether made or passed before, on or after the appointed day.   **[1016]**

4 Application of Regulations

(1) These Regulations apply in any case where an employee who is entitled, or but for these Regulations, would be entitled to a redundancy payment from an employer has a right or claim to a pension for himself which—

(a) is to be paid by reference to the employee's last period of continuous employment with that employer;

(b) (i) if it is a lump sum is to be paid, or

(ii) if it is a periodical payment is to begin to accrue,

at the time when the employee leaves the employment with that employer or within 90 weeks thereafter; and

(c) in so far as it consists of periodical payments satisfies the conditions specified in the next following paragraph.

(2) The conditions referred to in the preceding paragraph are that the Minister is satisfied that the pension is payable for life and is not capable of being terminated or suspended except for—

(a) the operation of any provision for the termination or suspension of the pension—

(i) upon the commutation thereof; or

(ii) upon assignment, charge or other alienation (whether by operation of law or otherwise), or any attempt thereat; or

(iii) in case of mental disorder or inability to act (if there is provision enabling the pension in either of these circumstances to be paid or applied at discretion for the maintenance or support of the pensioner's spouse or of other persons dependent on him);

(b) the operation of any provision for the suspension of the pension during imprisonment or detention in legal custody or upon resumption of employment with the employer or of any other provision for the suspension of the pension during employment, being a provision contained in or made under any of the enactments specified in Schedule 5 to the National Insurance Act 1965, or in subsection (6) of section 62 of that Act (which relate to certain statutory superannuation schemes) or a provision of the Superannuation Acts 1934 to 1950, and any Act amending those Acts, as applied by any enactment or other instrument having the force of law or by any instrument referred to in sub-paragraphs (d) or (e) of Regulation 3(1) of these Regulations;

(c) the operation of section 2 of the Forfeiture Act 1870, (which provides, in certain cases of persons convicted of treason or felony, for the termination of a pension or superannuation allowance payable by the public or out of any public fund).   **[1017]**

5 Exclusion or reduction of redundancy payments

(1) An employer of a pensioned employee may, by notice in writing to that employee, claim to—

(a) exclude the right of the employee to the redundancy payment to which he would otherwise be entitled; or

(b) reduce the amount thereof,

in accordance with or to the extent permitted by Schedule 1 to these Regulations and in such a case the employee shall not be entitled to a redundancy payment or, as the case may be, shall be entitled only to the reduced amount thereof.

(2) The notice in writing referred to in paragraph (1) of this Regulation shall contain a written statement explaining how the right of the pensioned employee to the redundancy payment has been excluded or, as the case may be, how the amount of the redundancy payment has been reduced by reason of the pension and specifying the amount of any redundancy payment so reduced.

(3) The provisions of this Regulation are without prejudice to the right of an employee to apply to a tribunal to determine any question as to his right to a redundancy payment or as to the amount of such payment.   **[1018]**

6 Employees paid by person other than employer

(1) This Regulation applies to any employee whose remuneration is, by virtue of any statutory provision, payable to him by a person other than his employer.

(2) For the purposes of the operation, in relation to employees to whom this Regulation applies, of the provisions of these Regulations specified in column 1 of Schedule 2 to these Regulations, any reference to the employer which is specified in column 2 of that Schedule shall be construed as a reference to the person responsible for paying the remuneration.   **[1019]**

SCHEDULES

SCHEDULE 1

Regulation 5(1)

EXCLUSION OF OR REDUCTION IN THE AMOUNT OF A REDUNDANCY
PAYMENT BY REASON OF A PENSION

1 (1) An employer of a pensioned employee may exclude the right of that employee to the redundancy payment to which he would otherwise be entitled under the Act by reason of his employment with the employer if the pension to which he has a right or claim by reference to that employment amounts in the annual value thereof to at least one-third of the employee's annual pay and is one as respects which—

(a) in so far as it consists of periodical payments the employee has a right or claim for the payments to begin to accrue, and

(b) in so far as it consists of a lump sum the employee has a right or claim for it to be paid,

immediately the employee ceases to be employed by the employer.

(2) An employer of a pensioned employee may reduce by an amount, not exceeding the appropriate proportion, the amount of the redundancy payment to which that employee would otherwise be entitled under the Act by reason of his employment with the employer if the pension to which he has a right or claim by reference to that employment is one as respects which—

(a)   in so far as it consists of periodical payments the employee has a right or claim for the payments to begin to accrue, and

(b)   in so far as it consists of a lump sum the employee has a right or claim for it to be paid,

immediately the employee ceases to be employed by the employer.

2 In a case in which the preceding paragraph of this Schedule does not apply but in which a pensioned employee has a right or claim to a pension as respects which—

(a)   in so far as it consists of periodical payments the employee has a right or claim for the payments to begin to accrue, and

(b)   in so far as it consists of a lump sum the employee has a right or claim for it to be paid,

at some time (not exceeding 90 weeks) later than the time when the pensioned employee ceases to be employed by him, an employer of that employee may reduce the amount of the redundancy payment by an amount not exceeding the appropriate proportion:

Provided that to the reduced payment so ascertained there shall be added the weekly value of the pension for each week that is to elapse between the cessation of the pensioned employee's employment with the employer and the time when the pensioned employee has a right or claim for the pension to begin to accrue or, as the case may be, to be paid; so however that the total payment due to the pensioned employee under this paragraph shall not exceed the amount of the redundancy payment to which he would be entitled apart from these Regulations.

3 For the purposes of this Schedule—

"appropriate proportion" means the proportion which the annual value of the pension to the employee bears to one-third of that employee's annual pay;

"annual pay" means the amount of a week's pay of the employee, calculated in accordance with paragraph 5 of Schedule 1 to the Act, multiplied by 52, any fraction of a pound in the product being disregarded;

"annual value of the pension" means—

(a)   in the case of a pension to which the employee has a right or claim which consists of periodical payments—

(i)   where the pension is payable at intervals of seven days the amount of the first payment multiplied by 52, any fraction of a pound in the product being disregarded if the pension consists wholly of periodical payments;

(ii)   where the pension is payable at other than intervals of seven days the amount which would accrue during the 12 calendar months beginning with the day on which the pension begins to accrue and assuming that the value of the pension does not change, any fraction of a pound being disregarded if the pension consists wholly of periodical payments;

(b)   in the case of a pension to which the employee has a right or claim which consists of a lump sum, one-tenth of the amount of such lump sum, any fraction of a pound being disregarded if the pension consists wholly of a lump sum;

(c)   in the case of a pension to which the employee has a right or claim which consists partly of periodical payments and partly of a lump sum, the total annual value ascertained in accordance with sub-paragraph (a) and sub-paragraph (b) of this paragraph, any fraction of a pound in that total being disregarded;

"weekly value of the pension" means the amount, not exceeding one-third of one week's value of the employee (calculated in accordance with paragraph 5 of Schedule 1 to the Act), obtained by dividing the annual value of the pension by 52.   **[1020]**

SCHEDULE 2

Regulation 6

Provisions of Regulations	*Reference to be construed as reference to the person responsible for paying the remuneration*
Regulation 3(1).	The references to "employer".
Regulation 4(1).	The first reference to "employer".
Regulation 5(1).	The reference to "employer".
Schedule 1, paragraph 1(1).	The first reference to "employer".
Schedule 1, paragraph 1(2).	The first reference to "employer".
Schedule 1, paragraph 2.	The first reference to "employer".

[1021]

INDUSTRIAL TRIBUNALS (IMPROVEMENT AND PROHIBITION NOTICES APPEALS) REGULATIONS 1974

(SI 1974/1925)

NOTES
Made: 18 November 1974.
Authority: Trade Union and Labour Relations Act 1974, Sch 1, para 21 (now the Employment Protection (Consolidation) Act 1978, Sch 9, para 1(1)); Health and Safety at Work etc Act 1974, s 24(2).

ARRANGEMENT OF REGULATIONS

1 Citation and commencement

These Regulations may be cited as the Industrial Tribunals (Improvement and Prohibition Notices Appeals) Regulations 1974 and shall come into operation on 1st January 1975.   **[1022]**

2 Interpretation

(1) The Interpretation Act 1889 shall apply to the interpretation of these Regulations as it applies to the interpretation of an Act of Parliament.

(2) In these Regulations, unless the context otherwise requires, the following expressions have the meanings hereby assigned to them respectively, that is to say—

"appellant" means a person who has appealed to a tribunal under section 24 of the principal Act;

"the clerk to the tribunal" means the person appointed by the Secretary of the Tribunals or an Assistant Secretary to act in that capacity at one or more hearings;

"decision" in relation to a tribunal includes a direction under Rule 4 and any other order which is not an interlocutory order;

"hearing" means a sitting of a tribunal duly constituted for the purpose of receiving evidence, hearing addresses and witnesses or doing anything lawfully requisite to enable the tribunal to reach a decision on any question;

"improvement notice" means a notice under section 21 of the principal Act;

"inspector" means a person appointed under section 19(1) of the principal Act;

"nominated chairman" means a member of the panel of chairmen for the time being nominated by the President;

"the Office of the Tribunals" means the Central Office of the Industrial Tribunals (England and Wales);

"the panel of chairmen" means the panel of persons, being barristers or solicitors of not less than seven years' standing, appointed by the Lord Chancellor in pursuance of Regulation 5(2) of the Industrial Tribunal (England and Wales) Regulations 1965, as amended;

"party" means the appellant and the respondent;

"the President" means the President of the Industrial Tribunals (England and Wales) or the person nominated by the Lord Chancellor to discharge for the time being the functions of the President;

"the principal Act" means the Health and Safety at Work etc. Act 1974;

"prohibition notice" means a notice under section 22 of the principal Act;

"Regional Office of the Industrial Tribunals" means a regional office which has been established under the Office of the Tribunals for an area specified by the President;

"Register" means the Register kept in pursuance of the Industrial Tribunals (Labour Relations) Regulations 1974;

"respondent" means the inspector who issued the improvement notice or prohibition notice which is the subject of the appeal;

"Rule" means a Rule of Procedure contained in the Schedule to these Regulations;

"the Secretary of the Tribunals" and "an Assistant Secretary of the Tribunals" mean respectively the persons for the time being acting as the Secretary of the Office of the Tribunals and as the Assistant Secretary of a Regional Office of the Industrial Tribunals;

"tribunal" means an industrial tribunal (England and Wales) established in pursuance of the Industrial Tribunals (England and Wales) Regulations 1965, as amended, and in relation to any proceedings means the tribunal to which the proceedings have been referred by the President or by a nominated chairman.   **[1023]**

3 Proceedings of tribunals

The Rules of Procedure contained in the Schedule to these Regulations shall have effect in relation to appeals to a tribunal under section 24 of the principal Act against improvement notices or prohibition notices relating to matters arising in England or Wales.   **[1024]**

4 Proof of decisions of tribunals

The production in any proceedings in any court of a document purporting to be certified by the Secretary of the Tribunals to be a true copy of an entry of a decision in the Register shall, unless the contrary is proved, be sufficient evidence of the document and of the facts stated therein.   **[1025]**

SCHEDULE

Regulation 3

RULES OF PROCEDURE

1 Notice of Appeal

An appeal shall be commenced by the appellant sending to the Secretary of the Tribunals a notice of appeal which shall be in writing and shall set out:—

    (a)   the name of the appellant and his address for the service of documents;

    (b)   the date of the improvement notice or prohibition notice appealed against and the address of the premises or place concerned;

    (c)   the name and address of the respondent;

    (d)   particulars of the requirements or directions appealed against; and

    (e)   the grounds of the appeal.

2 Time limit for bringing appeal

(1) Subject to paragraph (2) of this Rule, the notice of appeal shall be sent to the Secretary of the Tribunals within 21 days from the date of the service on the appellant of the notice appealed against.

(2) A tribunal may extend the time mentioned above where it is satisfied on an application made in writing to the Secretary of the Tribunals either before or after the expiration of that time that it is not or was not reasonably practicable for an appeal to be brought within that time.

3 Action upon receipt of notice of appeal

Upon receiving a notice of appeal the Secretary of the Tribunals shall enter particulars of it in the Register and shall forthwith send a copy of it to the respondent and inform the parties in writing of the case number of the appeal entered in the Register (which shall thereafter constitute the title of the proceedings) and of the address to which notices and other communications to the Secretary of the Tribunals shall be sent.

4 Application for direction suspending the operation of a prohibition notice

(1) Where an appeal has been brought against a prohibition notice and an application is made to the tribunal by the appellant in pursuance of section 24(3)(b) of the principal Act for a direction suspending the operation of the notice until the appeal is finally disposed of or withdrawn, the application shall be sent in writing to the Secretary of the Tribunals and shall set out:—

    (a)   the case number of the appeal if known to the appellant or particulars sufficient to identify the appeal; and

    (b)   the grounds on which the application is made.

(2) Upon receiving the application, the Secretary of the Tribunals shall enter particulars of it against the entry in the Register relating to the appeal and shall forthwith send a copy of it to the respondent.

5 Power to require attendance of witnesses and production of documents etc.

(1) A tribunal may on the application of a party made either by notice to the Secretary of the Tribunals or at the hearing—

    (a)   require a party to furnish in writing to another party further particulars of the grounds on which he relies and of any facts and contentions relevant thereto;

    (b)   grant to a party such discovery or inspection of documents as might be granted by a county court; and

(c) require the attendance of any person as a witness or require the production of any document relating to the matter to be determined,

and may appoint the time at or within which or the place at which any act required in pursuance of this Rule is to be done.

(2) The tribunal shall not under paragraph (1) of this Rule require the production of any document certified by the Secretary of State as being a document of which the production would be against the interests of national security.

(3) A person on whom a requirement has been made under paragraph (1) of this Rule may apply to the tribunal either by notice to the Secretary of the Tribunals or at the hearing to vary or set aside the requirement.

(4) No such application to vary or set aside shall be entertained in a case where a time has been appointed under paragraph (1) of this Rule in relation to the requirement unless it is made before the time or, as the case may be, expiration of the time so appointed.

(5) Every document containing a requirement under paragraph (1)(b) or (c) of this Rule shall contain a reference to the fact that under paragraph 21(6) of Schedule 1 to the Trade Union and Labour Relations Act 1974 any person who without reasonable excuse fails to comply with any such requirement shall be liable on summary conviction to a fine not exceeding £100.

6 Time and place of hearing and appointment of assessor

(1) The President or a nominated chairman shall fix the date, time and place of the hearing of the appeal and of any application under Rule 4, and the Secretary of the Tribunals shall not less than 14 days (or such shorter time as may be agreed by him with the parties) before the date so fixed send to each party a notice of hearing which shall include information and guidance as to attendance at the hearing, witnesses and the bringing of documents (if any), representation by another person and written representations.

(2) Where the President or a nominated chairman so directs, the Secretary of the Tribunals shall also send notice of the hearing to such persons as may be directed, but the requirement as to the period of notice contained in the foregoing paragraph of this Rule shall not apply to any such notices.

(3) The President or a nominated chairman may, if he thinks fit, appoint in pursuance of section 24(4) of the principal Act a person or persons having special knowledge or experience in relation to the subject matter of the appeal to sit with the tribunal as assessor or assessors.

7 The hearing

(1) Any hearing of or in connection with an appeal shall take place in public unless the tribunal on the application of a party decides that a private hearing is appropriate for the purpose of hearing evidence which relates to matters of such a nature that it would be against the interests of national security to allow the evidence to be given in public or hearing evidence from any person which in the opinion of the tribunal is likely to consist of information the disclosure of which would be seriously prejudicial to the interests of the undertaking of the appellant or of any undertaking in which he works for reasons other than its effect on negotiations with respect to any of the matters mentioned in section 29(1) of the Trade Union and Labour Relations Act 1974.

(2) In cases to which the foregoing provisions of this Rule apply, a member of the Council on Tribunals in his capacity as such shall be entitled to attend the hearing.

8 Written representations

If a party shall desire to submit representations in writing for consideration by a tribunal at the hearing of the appeal, that party shall send such representations to the Secretary of the Tribunals not less than 7 days before the hearing and shall at the same time send a copy of it to the other party.

9 Right of appearance

At any hearing of or in connection with an appeal a party may appear before the tribunal in person or may be represented by counsel or by a solicitor or by any other person whom he desires to represent him, including in the case of the appellant a representative of a trade union or an employers' association.

10 Procedure at hearing

(1) At any hearing of or in connection with an appeal a party shall be entitled to make an opening statement, to give evidence on his own behalf, to call witnesses, to cross-examine any witnesses called by the other party and to address the tribunal.

(2) If a party shall fail to appear or to be represented at the time and place fixed for the hearing of an appeal, the tribunal may dispose of the appeal in the absence of that party or may adjourn the hearing to a later date: Provided that before disposing of an appeal in the absence of a party the tribunal shall consider any written representations submitted by that party in pursuance of Rule 8.

(3) A tribunal may require any witness to give evidence on oath or affirmation and for that purpose there may be administered an oath or affirmation in due form.

11 Decision of tribunal

(1) A decision of a tribunal may be taken by a majority thereof and, if the tribunal shall be constituted of two members only, the chairman shall have a second or casting vote.

(2) The decision of a tribunal shall be recorded in a document signed by the chairman which shall contain the reasons for the decision.

(3) The clerk to the tribunal shall transmit the document signed by the chairman to the Secretary of the Tribunals who shall as soon as may be enter it in the Register and shall send a copy of the entry to each of the parties.

(4) The specification of the reasons for the decision shall be omitted from the Register in any case in which evidence has been heard in private and the tribunal so directs and in that event a specification of the reasons shall be sent to the parties and to any superior court in any proceedings relating to such decision together with the copy of the entry.

(5) The Register shall be kept at the Office of the Tribunals and shall be open to the inspection of any person without charge at all reasonable hours.

(6) The chairman of a tribunal shall have power by certificate under his hand to correct in documents recording the tribunals' decisions clerical mistakes or errors arising therein from any accidental slip or omission.

(7) The clerk to the tribunal shall send a copy of any document so corrected and the certificate of the chairman to the Secretary of the Tribunals who shall as soon as may be make such correction as may be necessary in the Register and shall send a copy of the corrected entry or of the corrected specification of the reasons, as the case may be, to each of the parties.

(8) If any decision is—

  (a) corrected under paragraph (6) of this Rule; or
  (b) reviewed, revoked or varied under Rule 12; or
  (c) altered in any way by order of a superior court,

the Secretary of the Tribunals shall alter the entry in the Register to conform with any such certificate or order and shall send a copy of the new entry to each of the parties.

12 Review of tribunal's decision

(1) A tribunal shall have power on the application of a party to review and to revoke or vary by certificate under the chairman's hand any of its decisions in a case in which a county court has power to order a new trial on the grounds that—

> (a) the decision was wrongly made as a result of an error on the part of the tribunal staff; or
> (b) a party did not receive notice of the proceedings leading to the decision; or
> (c) the decision was made in the absence of a party; or
> (d) new evidence has become available since the making of the decision provided that its existence could not have been reasonably known of or foreseen; or
> (e) the interests of justice require such a review.

(2) An application for the purposes of paragraph (1) of this Rule may be made at the hearing. If the application is not made at the hearing, such application shall be made to the Secretary of the Tribunals within 14 days from the date of the entry of a decision in the Register and must be in writing stating the grounds in full.

(3) An application for the purposes of paragraph (1) of this Rule may be refused by the chairman of the tribunal which decided the case, by the President or by a nominated chairman if in his opinion it has no reasonable prospect of success and he shall state the reasons for his opinion.

(4) If such an application is not refused under paragraph (3) of this Rule, it shall be heard by the tribunal and if it is granted the tribunal shall either vary its decision or revoke its decision and order a re-hearing.

(5) The clerk to the tribunal shall send to the Secretary of the Tribunals the certificate of the chairman as to any revocation or variation of the tribunal's decision under this Rule. The Secretary of the Tribunals shall as soon as may be make such correction as may be necessary in the Register and shall send a copy of the entry to each of the parties.

13 Costs

(1) A tribunal may make an order that a party shall pay to another party either a specified sum in respect of the costs of or in connection with an appeal incurred by that other party or, in default of agreement, the taxed amount of those costs.

(2) Any costs required by an order under this Rule to be taxed may be taxed in the county court according to such of the scales prescribed by the county court rules for proceedings in the county court as shall be directed by the order.

14 Miscellaneous powers of tribunal

(1) Subject to the provisions of these Rules, a tribunal may regulate its own procedure.

(2) A tribunal may, if it thinks fit—

> (a) postpone the day or time fixed for, or adjourn, any hearing;
> (b) before granting an application under Rule 5 or 12 require the party making the application to give notice thereof to the other party;
> (c) either on the application of any person or of its own motion, direct any other person to be joined as a party to the appeal (giving such consequential directions as it considers necessary), but may do so only after having given to the person proposed to be joined a reasonable opportunity of making written or oral objection;
> (d) make any necessary amendments to the description of a party in the Register and in other documents relating to the appeal;
> (e) if the appellant shall at any time give notice of the abandonment of his appeal, dismiss the appeal;
> (f) if the parties agree in writing upon the terms of a decision to be made by the tribunal, decide accordingly.

(3) Any act, other than the hearing of an appeal or of an application for the purposes of Rule 4 or 12(1) or the granting of an extension of time under Rule 2(2), required or authorised by these Rules to be done by a tribunal may be done by, or on the direction of, the President, the chairman of the tribunal or a nominated chairman.

(4) Rule 13 shall apply to an order dismissing proceedings under paragraph (2) of this Rule.

(5) Where the President so directs, any function of the Secretary of the Tribunals may be performed by an Assistant Secretary of the Tribunals and a notice of appeal under Rule 1, an application under Rule 4, and any other notice or other document required by these Rules to be sent to the Secretary of the Tribunals may be sent either to the Secretary of the Tribunals or to an Assistant Secretary of the Tribunals in accordance with such direction.

15 Notices, etc.

(1) Any notice given under these Rules shall be in writing and all notices and documents required or authorised by these Rules to be sent or given to any person hereinafter mentioned may be sent by post (subject to paragraphs (3) and (4) of this Rule) or delivered to or at—

(a) in the case of a document directed to the Secretary of the Tribunals, the Office of the Tribunals or such other office as may be notified by the Secretary of the Tribunals to the parties;

(b) in the case of a document directed to a party, his address for service specified in the notice of appeal or in a notice under paragraph (2) of this Rule or (if no address for service is so specified), his last known address or place of business in the United Kingdom or, if the party is a corporation, the corporation's registered or principal office;

(c) in the case of a document directed to any person (other than a person specified in the foregoing provisions of this paragraph), his address or place of business in the United Kingdom, or if such a person is a corporation, the corporation's registered or principal office;

and if sent or given to the authorised representative of a party shall be deemed to have been sent or given to that party.

(2) A party may at any time by notice to the Secretary of the Tribunals and to the other party change his address for service under these Rules.

(3) Where a notice of appeal is not delivered, it shall be sent by the recorded delivery service.

(4) Where for any sufficient reason service of any document or notice cannot be effected in the manner prescribed under this Rule, the President or a nominated chairman may make an order for substituted service in such manner as he may deem fit and such service shall have the same effect as service in the manner prescribed under this Rule.

(5) In the case of an appeal to which the respondent is an inspector appointed otherwise than by the Health and Safety Executive, the Secretary of the Tribunals shall send to that Executive copies of the notice of appeal and the document recording the decision of the tribunal on the appeal.   **[1026]**

REHABILITATION OF OFFENDERS ACT 1974 (EXCEPTIONS) ORDER 1975

(SI 1975/1023)

NOTES
Made: 24 June 1975.
Authority: Rehabilitation of Offenders Act 1974, ss 4(4), 7(4).

ARRANGEMENT OF ARTICLES

1 This Order may be cited as the Rehabilitation of Offenders Act 1974 (Exceptions) Order 1975 and shall come into operation on 1st July 1975.   **[1027]**

2 [(1) In this Order, except where the context otherwise requires—

"the Act" means the Rehabilitation of Offenders Act 1974;
"the Building Societies Commission" means the Building Societies Commission established by section 1 of the Building Societies Act 1986;
"relevant offence" means—

(a) an offence involving fraud or other dishonesty; or
(b) an offence under legislation (whether or not of the United Kingdom) relating to building societies, companies (including insider dealing), industrial and provident societies, credit unions, friendly societies, insurance, banking or other financial services, insolvency, consumer credit or consumer protection;

the expressions "authorisation", "building society" and "officer" have the meanings respectively given to them by section 119(1) of the Building Societies Act 1986.

(2) Where, by virtue of this Order, the operation of any of the provisions of the Act is excluded in relation to spent convictions the exclusion shall be taken to extend to spent convictions for offences of every description unless the said provisions are excluded only in relation to spent convictions for relevant offences.]

(3) Part IV of Schedule 1 to this Order shall have effect for the interpretation of expressions used in that Schedule.

(4) In this Order a reference to any enactment shall be construed as a reference to that enactment as amended, extended or applied by or under any other enactment.

(5) The Interpretation Act 1889 shall apply to the interpretation of this Order as it applies to the interpretation of an Act of Parliament.   **[1028]**

NOTE
Paras (1), (2): substituted by the Rehabilitation of Offenders Act 1974 (Exceptions) (Amendment No 2) Order 1986, SI 1986/2268, art 2(1), Schedule, para 1.

3 None of the provisions of section 4(2) of the Act shall apply in relation to—

(a) any question asked by or on behalf of any person, in the course of the duties of his office or employment, in order to assess the suitability—

    (i) of the person to whom the question relates for admission to any of the professions specified in Part I of Schedule 1 to this Order; or

    (ii) of the person to whom the question relates for any office or employment specified in Part II of the said Schedule 1; or

    (iii) of the person to whom the question relates or of any other person to pursue any occupation specified in Part III of the said Schedule 1 or to pursue it subject to a particular condition or restriction; or

    (iv) of the person to whom the question relates or of any other person to hold a licence, certificate or permit of a kind specified in Schedule 2 to this Order or to hold it subject to a particular condition or restriction,

where the person questioned is informed at the time the question is asked that, by virtue of this Order, spent convictions are to be disclosed;

[(aa) any question asked by or on behalf of any person, in the course of the duties of his office or employment, in order to assess the suitability of another person for any office or employment specified in paragraph 14 of Part II of the said Schedule 1 or the suitability of another person to be concerned, otherwise than in the course of the duties of his office or employment, with such provision as is mentioned in that paragraph, if—

    (i) the question relates to that other person and the said provision would normally enable that other person to have access to the persons referred to in that paragraph; or

    (ii) the question relates to a person who lives in the same household as that other person and the said provision would normally take place in that household,

where the person questioned is informed at the time the question is asked that, by virtue of this Order, spent convictions are to be disclosed;]

[(ab) any question relating to a relevant offence which is put by or on behalf of the Building Societies Commission or a building society in order to assess the suitability of the person to whom the question relates to be a director or other officer of a building society, whether or not that individual is the person questioned and where the person questioned is informed at the time the question is asked that, by virtue of this Order, spent convictions for any relevant offence are to be disclosed;]

(b) any question asked by or on behalf of any person, in the course of his duties as a person employed in the service of the Crown, the United Kingdom Atomic Energy Authority, the Civil Aviation Authority or the Post Office Corporation, in order to assess, for the purpose of safeguarding national security, the suitability of the person to whom the question relates or of any other person for any office or employment where the person questioned is informed at the time the question is asked that, by virtue of this Order, spent convictions are to be disclosed for the purpose of safeguarding national security.   **[1029]**

NOTES

Para (aa): inserted by the Rehabilitation of Offenders Act 1974 (Exceptions) (Amendment) Order 1986, SI 1986/1249, art 2, Schedule.

Para (ab): inserted by SI 1986/2268, art 2(1), Schedule, para 2.

4 Paragraph (b) of section 4(3) of the Act shall not apply in relation to—

(a) the dismissal or exclusion of any person from any profession specified in Part I of Schedule 1 to this Order;

(b) any office, employment or occupation specified in Part II or Part III of the said Schedule 1;

(c) any action taken for the purpose of safeguarding national security;

[(d) any of the following, that is to say—

(i) the refusal by the Building Societies Commission to grant authorisation;

(ii) the revocation by the said Commission of a building society's authorisation;

(iii) the imposition by the said Commission of conditions on its authorisation;

(iv) the dismissal or exclusion by a building society of a person from a position as an officer in a building society,

by reason, or partly by reason, of a spent conviction of an individual for a relevant offence, or of any circumstances ancillary to such a conviction or of a failure (whether or not by that individual) to disclose such a conviction or any such circumstances.]

[1030]

NOTE
Para (d): added by SI 1986/2268, art 2(1), Schedule, para 3.

[5 (1) Section 4(1) of the Act shall not—

(a) apply in relation to any proceedings specified in Schedule 3 to this Order;

(b) apply in relation to any proceedings specified in paragraph (2) below to the extent that there falls to be determined therein any issue relating to a person's spent conviction for any relevant offence or to circumstances ancillary thereto;

(c) prevent, in any proceedings specified in paragraph (2) below, the admission or requirement of any evidence relating to a person's spent conviction for any relevant offence or to circumstances ancillary thereto.

(2) The proceedings referred to in paragraph (1) above are—

(a) any proceedings before the Building Societies Commission—

(i) on an application for authorisation;

(ii) for the revocation of authorisation, or

(iii) for the imposition of conditions on authorisations, as to the conditions imposed or as to their revocation; and

(b) any proceedings by way of appeal against, or review of, any decision taken by the said Commission following any proceedings falling within sub-paragraph (a) above.]

[1031]

NOTE
Substituted by SI 1986/2268, art 2(1), Schedule, para 4.

SCHEDULE 1

Article 2(3), 3, 4

EXCEPTED PROFESSIONS, OFFICES, EMPLOYMENTS AND OCCUPATIONS

PART I
PROFESSIONS

1 Medical practitioner.

2 Barrister (in England and Wales), advocate (in Scotland), solicitor.

3 Chartered accountant, certified accountant.

4 Dentist, dental hygienist, dental auxiliary.

5 Veterinary surgeon.

6 Nurse, midwife.

7 Ophthalmic optician, dispensing optician.

8 Pharmaceutical chemist.

9 Registered teacher (in Scotland).

10 Any profession to which the Professions Supplementary to Medicine Act 1960 applies and which is undertaken following registration under that Act.   **[1032]**

[**11** Registered osteopath.]

NOTE
Para 11 added by the Osteopaths Act 1993, s 39(2) as from a day to be appointed.

PART II
OFFICES AND EMPLOYMENTS

1 Judicial appointments.

2 The Director of Public Prosecutions and any employment in his office.

3 Procurators Fiscal and District Court Prosecutors, and any employment in the office of a Procurator Fiscal or District Court Prosecutor or in the Crown Office.

4 Justices' clerks and their assistants.

5 Clerks (including depute and assistant clerks) and officers of the High Court of Justiciary, the Court of Session and the district court, sheriff clerks (including sheriff clerks depute) and their clerks and assistants.

6 Constables, persons appointed as police cadets to undergo training with a view to becoming constables and persons employed for the purposes of, or to assist the constables of, a police force established under any enactment; naval, military and air force police.

7 Any employment which is concerned with the administration of, or is otherwise normally carried out wholly or partly within the precincts of, a prison, remand centre, [young offender institution] or young offenders institution, and members of boards of visitors appointed under section 6 of the Prison Act 1952 or of visiting committees appointed under section 7 of the Prisons (Scotland) Act 1952.

8 Traffic wardens appointed under section 81 of the Road Traffic Regulation Act 1967 or section 9 of the Police (Scotland) Act 1967.

9 Probation officers appointed under Schedule 3 to the Powers of Criminal Courts Act 1973.

10, 11 . . .

12 Any employment by a local authority in connection with the provision of social services or by any other body in connection with the provision by it of similar services, being employment which is of such a kind as to enable the holder to have access to any of the following classes of person in the course of his normal duties, namely—

    (a) persons . . . over the age of 65;
    (b) persons suffering from serious illness or mental disorder of any description;
    (c) persons addicted to alcohol or drugs;
    (d) persons who are blind, deaf or dumb;
    (e) other persons who are substantially and permanently handicapped by illness, injury or congenital deformity.

13 Any employment which is concerned with the provision of health services and which is of such a kind as to enable the holder to have access to persons in receipt of such services in the course of his normal duties.

[14 Any office or employment concerned with the provision to persons aged under 18 of accommodation, care, leisure and recreational facilities, schooling, social services, supervision or training, being an office or employment of such a kind as to enable the holder to have access in the course of his normal duties to such persons, and any other office or employment the normal duties of which are carried out wholly or partly on the premises where such provision takes place.]   **[1033]**

NOTES
Para 7: words in square brackets substituted by virtue of the Criminal Justice Act 1988, s 123(6), Sch 8, paras 1, 3(2).
Paras 10, 11: revoked by SI 1986/1249, art 2, Schedule.
Para 12: words omitted revoked by SI 1986/1249, art 2, Schedule.
Para 14: substituted for existing paras 14, 15, by SI 1986/1249, art 2, Schedule.

PART III
REGULATED OCCUPATIONS

1 Firearms dealer.

2 Any occupation in respect of which an application to the Gaming Board for Great Britain for a licence, certificate or registration is required by or under any enactment.

3 Director, controller or manager of an insurance company—

(a) in respect of which the Secretary of State's authorisation is required under section 3(1)(b) of the Insurance Companies Act 1974 for it to carry on insurance business; or

(b) to which Part II of that Act applies.

4 *Dealer in securities.*

5 *Manager or trustee under a unit trust scheme.*

6 Any occupation which is concerned with—

(a) the management of a place in respect of which the approval of the Secretary of State is required by section 1 of the Abortion Act 1967; or

(b) in England and Wales, carrying on a nursing home in respect of which registration is required by section 187 of the Public Health Act 1936 or section 14 of the Mental Health Act 1959; or

(c) in Scotland, carrying on a nursing home in respect of which registration is required under section 1 of the Nursing Homes Registration (Scotland) Act 1938 or a private hospital in respect of which registration is required under section 15 of the Mental Health (Scotland) Act 1960.

7 Any occupation which is concerned with carrying on an establishment in respect of which registration is required by section 37 of the National Assistance Act 1948 or section 61 of the Social Work (Scotland) Act 1968.

8 Any occupation in respect of which the holder, as occupier of premises on which explosives are kept, is required by any Order in Council made under section 43 of the Explosives Act 1875 to obtain from the police or a court of summary jurisdiction a certificate as to his fitness to keep the explosives.

NOTE
Paras 4, 5: revoked by SI 1986/2268, art 2(2)(a), as from a day to be appointed.

PART IV
INTERPRETATION

In this Schedule—

"certified accountant" means a member of the Association of Certified Accountants;
"chartered accountant" means a member of the Institute of Chartered Accountants in England and Wales or of the Institute of Chartered Accountants of Scotland;

"dealer in securities" means a person dealing in securities within the meaning of section 26(1) of the Prevention of Fraud (Investments) Act 1958;
"firearms dealer" has the meaning assigned to that expression by section 57(4) of the Firearms Act 1968;
"further education" has the meaning assigned to that expression by section 41 of the Education Act 1944 or, in Scotland, section 4 of the Education (Scotland) Act 1962;
"health services" means services provided under the National Health Service Acts 1946 to 1973 or the National Health Service (Scotland) Acts 1947 to 1973 and similar services provided otherwise than under the National Health Service;
"insurance company" has the meaning assigned to that expression by section 85 of the Insurance Companies Act 1974 and, in relation to an insurance company, "director" shall be construed in accordance with that section and "controller" and "manager" shall be construed in accordance with section 7 of that Act;
"judicial appointment" means an appointment to any office by virtue of which the holder has power (whether alone or with others) under any enactment or rule of law to determine any question affecting the rights, privileges, obligations or liabilities of any person;
"proprietor" and "independent school" have the meanings assigned to those expressions by section 114(1) of the Education Act 1944 or, in Scotland, section 145 of the Education (Scotland) Act 1962;
["registered osteopath" has the meaning given by section 41 of the Osteopaths Act 1993.]
"registered teacher" means a teacher registered under the Teaching Council (Scotland) Act 1965 and includes a provisionally registered teacher;
"school" has the meaning assigned to that expression by section 114(1) of the Education Act 1944 or, in Scotland, section 145 of the Education (Scotland) Act 1962;
"social services", in relation to a local authority, means—
    (a)   in England and Wales, services provided by the authority in discharging its social services functions within the meaning of the Local Authority Social Services Act 1970;
    (b)   in Scotland, services provided by the authority in discharging functions referred to in section 2(2) of the Social Work (Scotland) Act 1968;
"teacher" includes a warden of a community centre, leader of a youth club or similar institution, youth worker and, in Scotland, youth and community worker;
"unit trust scheme" has the meaning assigned to that expression by section 26(1) of the Prevention of Fraud (Investments) Act 1958 and, in relation thereto, "manager" and "trustee" shall be construed in accordance with section 26(3) of that Act.

[1035]

NOTE
Definitions of "dealer in securities" and "unit trust scheme" revoked by SI 1986/2268, art 2(2)(a), as from a day to be appointed; definition "registered osteopath" inserted by the Osteopaths Act 1993, s 39(4) as from a day to be appointed.

(Schs 2, 3 not printed.)

SEX DISCRIMINATION (FORMAL INVESTIGATIONS) REGULATIONS 1975

(SI 1975/1993)

NOTES
Made: 3 December 1975.
Authority: Sex Discrimination Act 1975, ss 58(3), 59(1), 67(2), 82(1).

ARRANGEMENT OF REGULATIONS

1 Citation and operation

These Regulations may be cited as the Sex Discrimination (Formal Investigations) Regulations 1975 and shall come into operation on 29th December 1975.   **[1036]**

2 Interpretation

(1) In these Regulations any reference to the Act is a reference to the Sex Discrimination Act 1975.

(2) Any reference to the Commission, in Regulations 4, 5 and 6 below, is a reference to the Equal Opportunities Commission except that, as respects any of the functions of the Commission in relation to a formal investigation which the Commission have delegated under section 57(3) of the Act, any such reference in Regulation 4 or 5 is a reference to the persons, being either Commissioners or Additional Commissioners, to whom those functions have been so delegated.

(3) The Interpretation Act 1889 shall apply for the interpretation of these Regulations as it applies for the interpretation of an Act of Parliament.   **[1037]**

3 Service of notices

Any reference to a person being served with a notice, in Regulations 4, 5 and 6 below, is a reference to service of the notice on him being effected—

    (a) by delivering it to him; or

    (b) by sending it by post to him at his usual or last-known residence or place of business; or

    (c) where the person is a body corporate or is a trade union or employers' association within the meaning of the Trade Union and Labour Relations Act 1974, by delivering it to the secretary or clerk of the body, union or association at its registered or principal office or by sending it by post to that secretary or clerk at that office; or

    (d) where the person is acting by a solicitor by delivering it at, or by sending it by post to, the solicitor's address for service.   **[1038]**

4 Notice of holding of formal investigation

(1) Where, in pursuance of section 58 of the Act, notice of the holding of a formal investigation falls to be given by the Commission to a person named in the terms of reference for the investigation, that person shall be served with a notice setting out the terms of reference.

(2) Where the terms of reference for a formal investigation are revised, paragraph (1) shall apply in relation to the revised investigation and terms of reference as it applied to the original.   **[1039]**

5 Requirement to furnish or give information or produce documents

Where, in pursuance of section 59(1) of the Act, the Commission require a person to furnish written information, give oral information or produce documents, that person shall be served with a notice in the form set out in Schedule 1 to these Regulations or a form to the like effect, with such variations as the circumstances may require.

[1040]

6 Non-discrimination notice

Where, in pursuance of section 67(2) of the Act, the Commission issue a non-discrimination notice, the person to whom it is directed shall be served with a notice in the form set out in Schedule 2 to these Regulations or a form to the like effect, with such variations as the circumstances may require.   **[1041]**

SCHEDULES

SCHEDULE 1

REQUIREMENT TO FURNISH WRITTEN INFORMATION OR GIVE ORAL
EVIDENCE AND PRODUCE DOCUMENTS
(Sex Discrimination Act 1975, s 59(1))

To A. B. of

For the purposes of the formal investigation being conducted by the Equal Opportunities Commission ("the Commission") the terms of reference of which [were given to you in a notice dated .. ..] [are set out in the Schedule hereto], you are hereby required, in pursuance of section 59(1) of the Sex Discrimination Act 1975 ("the Act") and subject to section 59(3) thereof, [to furnish such written information as is hereinafter described, namely, (*description of information*). The said information is to be furnished (*specify the time or times at which, and the manner and form in which, the information is to be furnished*).] [to attend at (*insert time*) on (*insert date*) at (*insert place*) and give oral information about (*or* give oral evidence about, and produce all documents in your possession or control relating to,) such matters as are hereinafter specified, namely (*specify matters*).]

Dated the .... day of .... 19 ......

This notice was issued by the [Commission] [Commissioners/Commissioners and Additional Commissioners to whom the Commission have, in pursuance of section 57(3) of the Act and in relation to the investigation, delegated their functions under section 59(1)(a) thereof].

[Service of this notice was authorised by an order made in pursuance of section 59(2)(a) of the Act and dated (*insert date*), a copy of which is attached.]

[Having regard to the terms of reference of the investigation and the provisions of section 59(2)(b)/section 69 of the Act, service of this notice does not require the consent of the Secretary of State.]

C.D.
[COMMISSIONER.]

[Chief Officer (*or other appropriate officer*) of the Commission.]

[1042]

[SCHEDULE
TERMS OF REFERENCE OF INVESTIGATION]
[SCHEDULE 2

NON-DISCRIMINATION NOTICE
(Sex Discrimination Act 1975, s 59(1))

To A. B. of

Whereas, in the course of a formal investigation, the Equal Opportunities Commission ("the Commission") have become satisfied that you were committing/had committed an act/acts to which section 67(2) of the Sex Discrimination Act 1975 ("the Act") applies, namely, (*insert particulars of act or acts*) [and are of the opinion that further such acts are likely to be committed unless changes are made in your practices or other arrangements as respects (*insert particulars*)].

Now, therefore, without prejudice to your other duties under the Act or the Equal Pay Act 1970, you are hereby required, in pursuance of section 67(2) of the Act, not to commit any such act as aforesaid or any other act which is [an unlawful discriminatory act by virtue of (*insert reference to relevant Part or provision of the Act*)] [a contravention of section 37 of the Act] [an act which is a contravention of section 38/39/40 of the Act by reference to Part II/Part III thereof] [an act in breach of a term of a contract under which a person is employed, being a term modified or included by virtue of an equality clause within the meaning of the Equal Pay Act 1970].

In so far as compliance with the aforesaid requirement involves changes in any of your practices or other arrangements, you are further required, in pursuance of the said section 67(2), to inform the Commission [as hereinafter provided] that you have effected those changes and what those changes are [and to take the following steps for the purpose of affording that information to other persons concerned, namely (*specify steps to be taken*)].

[You are further required, in pursuance of section 67(3) of the Act, to furnish the Commission as hereinafter provided with the following information, to enable them to verify your compliance with this notice, namely, (*insert description of information required*).]

[The information to be furnished by you to the Commission in pursuance of this notice shall be furnished as follows, namely, (*specify the time or times at which, and the manner and form in which, the information, or information of a particular description, is to be furnished*).]

Dated the .... day of .... 19 ......

This notice was issued by the Commission, the provisions of section 67(5) of the Act having been complied with.

C.D.
[COMMISSIONER].

[Chief Officer (*or other appropriate officer*) of the Commission.]

[1043]

NOTE
Sch 2: substituted by the Sex Discrimination (Formal Investigation) (Amendment) Regulations 1977, SI 1977/843.

SEX DISCRIMINATION (QUESTIONS AND REPLIES) ORDER 1975

(SI 1975/2048)

NOTES
Made: 5 December 1975.
Authority: Sex Discrimination Act 1975, ss 74, 81(4).

ARRANGEMENT OF ARTICLES

1 Citation and operation

This Order may be cited as the Sex Discrimination (Questions and Replies) Order 1975 and shall come into operation on 29th December 1975.   **[1044]**

2 Interpretation

(1) In this Order "the Act" means the Sex Discrimination Act 1975.

(2) In this Order any reference to a court is a reference to a county court in England or Wales or a sheriff court in Scotland and any reference to a tribunal is a reference to an industrial tribunal.

(3) The Interpretation Act 1889 shall apply to the interpretation of this Order as it applies to the interpretation of an Act of Parliament.   **[1045]**

3 Forms for asking and answering questions

The forms respectively set out in Schedules 1 and 2 to this Order or forms to the like effect with such variation as the circumstances may require are, respectively, hereby prescribed as forms—

- (a) by which a person aggrieved may question a respondent as mentioned in subsection (1)(a) of section 74 of the Act;
- (b) by which a respondent may if he so wishes reply to such questions as mentioned in subsection (1)(b) of that section.   **[1046]**

4 Period for service of questions—court cases

In proceedings before a court, a question shall only be admissible as evidence in pursuance of section 74(2)(a) of the Act—

- [(a) where it was served before those proceedings had been instituted, if it was so served during—
  - (i) the period of six months beginning when the act complained of was done, or
  - (ii) in a case to which section 66(5) of the Act applies, the period of eight months so beginning;]
- (b) where it was served when those proceedings had been instituted, if it was served with the leave of, and within a period specified by, the court.   **[1047]**

NOTE
Amended by the Sex Discrimination (Questions and Replies) (Amendment) Order 1977, SI 1977/844.

5 Period for service of questions—tribunal cases

In proceedings before a tribunal, a question shall only be admissible as evidence in pursuance of section 74(2)(a) of the Act—

- (a) where it was served before a complaint had been presented to a tribunal, if it was so served within the period of three months beginning when the act complained of was done;
- (b) where it was served when a complaint had been presented to a tribunal, either if it was so served within the period of twenty-one days beginning with the day on which the complaint was presented or if it was so served later with leave given, and within a period specified, by a direction of a tribunal.   **[1048]**

6 Manner of service of questions and replies

A question and any reply thereto may be served on the respondent or, as the case may be, on the person aggrieved—

(a) by delivering it to him; or

(b) by sending it by post to him at his usual or last-known residence or place of business; or

(c) where the person to be served is a body corporate or is a trade union or employers' association within the meaning of the Trade Union and Labour Relations Act 1974, by delivering it to the secretary or clerk of the body, union or association at its registered or principal office or by sending it by post to the secretary or clerk at that office; or

(d) where the person to be served is acting by a solicitor, by delivering it at, or by sending it by post to, the solicitor's address for service; or

(e) where the person to be served is the person aggrieved, by delivering the reply, or sending it by post, to him at his address for reply as stated by him in the document containing the questions.   **[1049]**

SCHEDULE 1

THE SEX DISCRIMINATION ACT 1975 s 74(1)(a)
QUESTIONNAIRE OF PERSON AGGRIEVED

To .... *(name of person to be questioned)* of ....
.... *(address)*

1—(1) I .... *(name of questioner)* of .... *(address)* consider that you may have discriminated against me contrary to the Sex Discrimination Act 1975.

(2) *(Give date, approximate time and a factual description of the treatment received and of the circumstances leading up to the treatment.)*

(3) I consider that this treatment may have been unlawful [because .... *(complete if you wish to give reasons, otherwise delete)*].

2 Do you agree that the statement in paragraph 1(2) above is an accurate description of what happened? If not, in what respect do you disagree or what is your version of what happened?

3 Do you accept that your treatment of me was unlawful discrimination by you against me?

If not—

(a) why not,

(b) for what reason did I receive the treatment accorded to me, and

(c) how far did my sex or marital status affect your treatment of me?

4 *(Any other questions you wish to ask.)*

5 My address for any reply you may wish to give to the questions raised above is [that set out in paragraph 1(1) above] [the following address ....].

....*(signature of questioner)*

.... *(date)*

N.B.—By virtue of section 74 of the Act this questionnaire and any reply are (subject to the provisions of the section) admissible in proceedings under the Act and a court or tribunal may draw any such inference as is just and equitable from a failure without reasonable excuse to reply within a reasonable period, or from an evasive or equivocal reply, including an inference that the person questioned has discriminated unlawfully.   **[1050]**

SCHEDULE 2
THE SEX DISCRIMINATION ACT 1975 s 74(1)(b)
REPLY BY RESPONDENT

To .... *(name of questioner)* of .... *(address)*

1 I .... *(name of person questioned)* of .... *(address)* hereby acknowledge receipt of the questionnaire signed by you and dated .... which was served on me on .... *(date)*.

2 [I agree that the statement in paragraph 1(2) of the questionnaire is an accurate description of what happened.]

[I disagree with the statement in paragraph 1(2) of the questionnaire in that ....
....................]

3 I accept/dispute that my treatment of you was unlawful discrimination by me against you.

[My reasons for so disputing are .... The reason why you received the treatment accorded to you and the answers to the other questions in paragraph 3 of the questionnaire are ....]

4 *(Replies to questions in paragraph 4 of the questionnaire.)*

[5. I have deleted (in whole or in part) the paragraph(s) numbered .... above, since I am unable/unwilling to reply to the relevant questions in the correspondingly numbered paragraph(s) of the questionnaire for the following reasons ....]

.... *(signature of person questioned)*

.... *(date)*

[1051]

LABOUR RELATIONS (CONTINUITY OF EMPLOYMENT) REGULATIONS 1976

(SI 1976/660)

NOTES

Made: 27 April 1976.
Authority: Trade Union and Labour Relations Act 1974, Sch 1, para 30(3) (now Employment Protection (Consolidation) Act 1978, Sch 13, para 20). Statutory references to legislation now consolidated into the 1978 Act ("EP(C)A 1978") have not been amended, but Sch 15, para 4 of that Act (see para **[422]** above) requires such references to be construed as references to the corresponding provisions of the 1978 Act. These references are therefore noted at the end of each Regulation.
These Regulations are revoked and replaced as from 4 October 1993 by the Employment Protection (Continuity of Employment) Regulations 1993, SI 1993/2165, below, para **[1451]**.

ARRANGEMENT OF REGULATIONS

1 Citation, commencement and revocation

(1) These Regulations may be cited as the Labour Relations (Continuity of Employment) Regulations 1976 and shall come into operation on 1st June 1976.

(2) As from that date the Industrial Relations (Continuity of Employment) Regulations 1972 shall cease to have effect.   **[1052]**

2 Interpretation

(1) The Interpretation Act 1889 shall apply to these Regulations as it applies to the interpretation of an Act of Parliament and as if these Regulations and the Regulations hereby revoked were Acts of Parliament.

(2) In these Regulations, unless the context otherwise requires—

"the 1965 Act" means the Redundancy Payments Act 1965;
"the 1974 Act" means the Trade Union and Labour Relations Act 1974;
"the 1975 Act" means the Employment Protection Act 1975; and
"the effective date of termination" has the same meaning as in paragraph 5(5) of Schedule 1 to the 1974 Act.   **[1053]**

NOTE
"Para 5(5)": now the EP(C)A 1978, s 55(4).

3 Application

These Regulations apply to any action taken in relation to the dismissal of an employee which consists—

   (a) of the presentation by him of a complaint under paragraph 17 of Schedule 1 to the 1974 Act, or
   (b) of his making a claim in accordance with a dismissals procedure agreement designated by an order under paragraph 13 of that Schedule, or
   (c) of any action taken by a conciliation officer under paragraph 26(4) of that Schedule.   **[1054]**

NOTES
"Para 17": now the EP(C)A 1978, s 67(1).
"Para 13": now the EP(C)A 1978, s 65(1)–(3).
"Para 26(4)": now the EP(C)A 1978, s 134(3).

4 Continuity of employment where employee re-engaged

(1) The provisions of this Regulation shall have effect to preserve the continuity of a person's period of employment for the purposes of Schedule 1 to the Contracts of Employment Act 1972 and for the purposes of that Schedule as applied by the 1965 Act, the 1974 Act and the 1975 Act.

(2) If in consequence of any action to which these Regulations apply a dismissed employee is reinstated or re-engaged by his employer or by a successor or associated employer of the employer the continuity of that employee's period of employment shall be preserved and, accordingly, any week falling within the interval beginning with the effective date of termination and ending with the date of reinstatement or re-engagement, as the case may be, shall count in the computation of the employee's period of continuous employment.   **[1055]**

NOTE
"Schedule 1": now the EP(C)A 1978, Sch 13.

5   Exclusion of operation of sections 24 and 24A of the 1965 Act where redundancy or equivalent payment repaid

(1) Where in consequence of any action to which these Regulations apply a dismissed employee is reinstated or re-engaged by his employer or by a successor or associated employer of the employer and the terms upon which he is so reinstated or re-engaged include provision for him to repay the amount of a redundancy payment or an equivalent payment paid in respect of the relevant dismissal, section 24 or 24A of the 1965 Act (which require the continuity of the period of employment to be treated as broken where a redundancy payment or an equivalent payment is paid and he is subsequently re-engaged) shall not apply if those provisions are complied with.

(2) For the purposes of this Regulation the cases in which a redundancy payment shall be treated as having been paid are cases mentioned in paragraphs (a) and (b) of section 24(3) of the 1965 Act.   **[1056]**

NOTE
"Ss 24, 24A": now the EP(C)A 1978, Sch 13, para 12.

SAFETY REPRESENTATIVES AND SAFETY COMMITTEES REGULATIONS 1977

(SI 1977/500)

NOTES
Made: 16 March 1977.
Authority: Health and Safety at Work etc Act 1974, ss 2(4), (7), 15(1), (3)(b), (5)(b), 80(1), (4), 82(3)(a). See also the Health and Safety Commission Codes of Practice: Safety Representatives and Safety Committees (1978) and Time off for the Training of Safety Representatives (1978) below, paras **[3044]** and **[3050]**.

ARRANGEMENT OF REGULATIONS

1   Citation and commencement

These Regulations may be cited as the Safety Representatives and Safety Committees Regulations 1977 and shall come into operation on 1st October 1978.   **[1057]**

2   Interpretation

(1) In these Regulations, unless the context otherwise requires—

"the 1974 Act" means the Health and Safety at Work etc Act 1974 as amended
by the 1975 Act;

"the 1975 Act" means the Employment Protection Act 1975;

"employee" has the meaning assigned by section 53(1) of the 1974 Act and
"employer" shall be construed accordingly;

"recognised trade union" means an independent trade union as defined in
section 30(1) of the Trade Union and Labour Relations Act 1974 which
the employer concerned recognises for the purpose of negotiations relating
to or connected with one or more of the matters specified in section 29(1)
of that Act in relation to persons employed by him or as to which the
Advisory, Conciliation and Arbitration Service has made a
recommendation for recognition under the 1975 Act which is operative
within the meaning of section 15 of that Act;

"safety representative" means a person appointed under Regulation 3(1) of
these Regulations to be a safety representative;

"welfare at work" means those aspects of welfare at work which are the subject
of health and safety regulations or of any of the existing statutory
provisions within the meaning of section 53(1) of the 1974 Act;

"workplace" in relation to a safety representative means any place or places
where the group or groups of employees he is appointed to represent are
likely to work or which they are likely to frequent in the course of their
employment or incidentally to it.

(2) The Interpretation Act 1889 shall apply to the interpretation of these
Regulations as it applies to the interpretation of an Act of Parliament.

(3) These Regulations shall not be construed as giving any person a right to
inspect any place, article, substance or document which is the subject of restrictions
on the grounds of national security unless he satisfies any test or requirement imposed
on those grounds by or on behalf of the Crown.   **[1058]**

3 Appointment of safety representatives

(1) For the purposes of section 2(4) of the 1974 Act, a recognised trade union may
appoint safety representatives from amongst the employees in all cases where one or
more employees are employed by an employer by whom it is recognised, except in
the case of employees employed in a mine within the meaning of section 180 of the
Mines and Quarries Act 1954 which is a coal mine.

(2) Where the employer has been notified in writing by or on behalf of a trade
union of the names of the persons appointed as safety representatives under this
Regulation and the group or groups of employees they represent, each such safety
representative shall have the functions set out in Regulation 4 below.

(3) A person shall cease to be a safety representative for the purposes of these
Regulations when—

(a) the trade union which appointed him notifies the employer in writing that
his appointment has been terminated; or

(b) he ceases to be employed at the workplace but if he was appointed to
represent employees at more than one workplace he shall not cease by
virtue of this sub-paragraph to be a safety representative so long as he
continues to be employed at any one of them; or

(c) he resigns.

(4) A person appointed under paragraph (1) above as a safety representative shall
so far as is reasonably practicable either have been employed by his employer

throughout the preceding two years or have had at least two years experience in similar employment.   **[1059]**

4 Functions of safety representatives

(1) In addition to his function under section 2(4) of the 1974 Act to represent the employees in consultations with the employer under section 2(6) of the 1974 Act (which requires every employer to consult safety representatives with a view to the making and maintenance of arrangements which will enable him and his employees to cooperate effectively in promoting and developing measures to ensure the health and safety at work of the employees and in checking the effectiveness of such measures), each safety representative shall have the following functions:—

  (a) to investigate potential hazards and dangerous occurrences at the workplace (whether or not they are drawn to his attention by the employees he represents) and to examine the causes of accidents at the workplace;
  (b) to investigate complaints by any employee he represents relating to that employee's health, safety or welfare at work;
  (c) to make representations to the employer on matters arising out of sub-paragraphs (a) and (b) above;
  (d) to make representations to the employer on general matters affecting the health, safety or welfare at work of the employees at the workplace;
  (e) to carry out inspections in accordance with Regulations 5, 6 and 7 below;
  (f) to represent the employees he was appointed to represent in consultations at the workplace with inspectors of the Health and Safety Executive and of any other enforcing authority;
  (g) to receive information from inspectors in accordance with section 28(8) of the 1974 Act; and
  (h) to attend meetings of safety committees where he attends in his capacity as a safety representative in connection with any of the above functions;

but, without prejudice to sections 7 and 8 of the 1974 Act, no function given to a safety representative by this paragraph shall be construed as imposing any duty on him.

  (2) An employer shall permit a safety representative to take such time off with pay during the employee's working hours as shall be necessary for the purposes of—

  (a) performing his functions under section 2(4) of the 1974 Act and paragraph (1)(a) to (h) above;
  (b) undergoing such training in aspects of those functions as may be reasonable in all the circumstances having regard to any relevant provisions of a code of practice relating to time off for training approved for the time being by the Health and Safety Commission under section 16 of the 1974 Act.

In this paragraph "with pay" means with pay in accordance with the Schedule to these Regulations.   **[1060]**

[4A Employer's duty to consult and provide facilities and assistance

(1) Without prejudice to the generality of section 2(6) of the Health and Safety at Work etc Act 1974, every employer shall consult safety representatives in good time with regard to–

  (a) the introduction of any measure at the workplace which may substantially affect the health and safety of the employees the safety representatives concerned represent;

(b) his arrangements for appointing or, as the case may be, nominating persons in accordance with regulations 6(1) and 7(1)(b) of the Management of Health and Safety at Work Regulations 1992;

(c) any health and safety information he is required to provide to the employees the safety representatives concerned represent by or under the relevant statutory provisions;

(d) the planning and organisation of any health and safety training he is required to provide to the employees the safety representatives concerned represent by or under the relevant statutory provisions; and

(e) the health and safety consequences for the employees the safety representatives concerned represent of the introduction (including the planning thereof) of new technologies into the workplace.

(2) Without prejudice to regulations 5 and 6 of these Regulations, every employer shall provide such facilities and assistance as safety representatives may reasonably require for the purpose of carrying out their functions under section 2(4) of the 1974 Act and under these Regulations.]   **[1061]**

NOTES

Commencement: 1 January 1993.

Inserted by the Management of Health and Safety at Work Regulations 1992, SI 1992/2051, reg 17, Schedule.

5 Inspections of the workplace

(1) Safety representatives shall be entitled to inspect the workplace or a part of it if they have given the employer or his representative reasonable notice in writing of their intention to do so and have not inspected it, or that part of it, as the case may be, in the previous three months; and may carry out more frequent inspections by agreement with the employer.

(2) Where there has been a substantial change in the conditions of work (whether because of the introduction of new machinery or otherwise) or new information has been published by the Health and Safety Commission or the Health and Safety Executive relevant to the hazards of the workplace since the last inspection under this Regulation, the safety representatives after consultation with the employer shall be entitled to carry out a further inspection of the part of the workplace concerned notwithstanding that three months have not elapsed since the last inspection.

(3) The employer shall provide such facilities and assistance as the safety representatives may reasonably require (including facilities for independent investigation by them and private discussion with the employees) for the purpose of carrying out an inspection under this Regulation, but nothing in this paragraph shall preclude the employer or his representative from being present in the workplace during the inspection.

(4) An inspection carried out under section 123 of the Mines and Quarries Act 1954 shall count as an inspection under this Regulation.   **[1062]**

6 Inspections following notifiable accidents, occurrences and diseases

(1) Where there has been a notifiable accident or dangerous occurrence in a workplace or a notifiable disease has been contracted there and—

(a) it is safe for an inspection to be carried out; and

(b) the interests of employees in the group or groups which safety representatives are appointed to represent might be involved.

those safety representatives may carry out an inspection of the part of the workplace concerned and so far as is necessary for the purpose of determining the cause they may inspect any other part of the workplace; where it is reasonably practicable to do so they shall notify the employer or his representative of their intention to carry out the inspection.

(2) The employer shall provide such facilities and assistance as the safety representatives may reasonably require (including facilities for independent investigation by them and private discussion with the employees) for the purpose of carrying out an inspection under this Regulation; but nothing in this paragraph shall preclude the employer or his representative from being present in the workplace during the inspection.

(3) In this Regulation "notifiable accident or dangerous occurrence" and "notifiable disease" mean any accident, dangerous occurrence or disease, as the case may be, notice of which is required to be given by virtue of any of the relevant statutory provisions within the meaning of section 53(1) of the 1974 Act.   **[1063]**

7 Inspection of documents and provision of information

(1) Safety representatives shall for the performance of their functions under section 2(4) of the 1974 Act and under Regulations, if they have given the employer reasonable notice, be entitled to inspect and take copies of any document relevant to the workplace or to the employees the safety representatives represent which the employer is required to keep by virtue of any relevant statutory provision within the meaning of section 53(1) of the 1974 Act except a document consisting of or relating to any health record of an identifiable individual.

(2) An employer shall make available to safety representatives the information, within the employer's knowledge, necessary to enable them to fulfil their functions except—

(a) any information the disclosure of which would be against the interests of national security; or

(b) any information which he could not disclose without contravening a prohibition imposed by or under an enactment; or

(c) any information relating specifically to an individual, unless he has consented to its being disclosed; or

(d) any information the disclosure of which would, for reasons other than its effect on health, safety or welfare at work, cause substantial injury to the employer's undertaking or, where the information was supplied to him by some other person, to the undertaking of that other person; or

(e) any information obtained by the employer for the purpose of bringing, prosecuting or defending any legal proceedings.

(3) Paragraph (2) above does not require an employer to produce or allow inspection of any document or part of a document which is not related to health, safety or welfare.   **[1064]**

8 Cases where safety representatives need not be employees

(1) In the cases mentioned in paragraph (2) below safety representatives appointed under Regulation 3(1) of these Regulations need not be employees of the employer concerned; and section 2(4) of the 1974 Act shall be modified accordingly.

(2) The said cases are those in which the employees in the group or groups the safety representatives are appointed to represent are members of the British Actors' Equity Association or of the Musicians' Union.

(3) Regulations 3(3)(b) and (4) and 4(2) of these Regulations shall not apply to safety representatives appointed by virtue of this Regulation and in the case of safety representatives to be so appointed Regulation 3(1) shall have effect as if the words "from amongst the employees" were omitted.   **[1065]**

9 Safety committees

(1) For the purposes of section 2(7) of the 1974 Act (which requires an employer in prescribed cases to establish a safety committee if requested to do so by safety representatives) the prescribed cases shall be any cases in which at least two safety representatives request the employer in writing to establish a safety committee.

(2) Where an employer is requested to establish a safety committee in a case prescribed in paragraph (1) above, he shall establish it in accordance with the following provisions—

    (a) he shall consult with the safety representatives who made the request and with the representatives of recognised trade unions whose members work in any workplace in respect of which he proposes that the committee should function;

    (b) the employer shall post a notice stating the composition of the committee and the workplace or workplaces to be covered by it in a place where it may be easily read by the employees;

    (c) the committee shall be established not later than three months after the request for it.   **[1066]**

10 Power of Health and Safety Commission to grant exemptions

The Health and Safety Commission may grant exemptions from any requirement imposed by these Regulations and any such exemption may be unconditional or subject to such conditions as the Commission may impose and may be with or without a limit of time.   **[1067]**

11 Provisions as to industrial tribunals

(1) A safety representative may, in accordance with the jurisdiction conferred on industrial tribunals by paragraph 16(2) of Schedule 1 to the Trade Union and Labour Relations Act 1974, present a complaint to an industrial tribunal that—

    (a) the employer has failed to permit him to take time off in accordance with Regulation 4(2) of these Regulations; or

    (b) the employer has failed to pay him in accordance with Regulation 4(2) of and the Schedule to these Regulations.

(2) An industrial tribunal shall not consider a complaint under paragraph (1) above unless it is presented within three months of the date when the failure occurred or within such further period as the tribunal considers reasonable in a case where it is satisfied that it was not reasonably practicable for the complaint to be presented within the period of three months.

(3) Where an industrial tribunal finds a complaint under paragraph (1)(a) above well-founded the tribunal shall make a declaration to that effect and may make an

award of compensation to be paid by the employer to the employee which shall be of such amount as the tribunal considers just and equitable in all the circumstances having regard to the employer's default in failing to permit time off to be taken by the employee and to any loss sustained by the employee which is attributable to the matters complained of.

(4) Where on a complaint under paragraph (1)(b) above an industrial tribunal finds that the employer has failed to pay the employee the whole or part of the amount required to be paid under paragraph (1)(b), the tribunal shall order the employer to pay the employee the amount which it finds due to him.

(5) ...   [1068]

NOTE
Para 5: amends the Trade Union and Labour Relations Act 1974, Sch 1, para 16.

SCHEDULE

Regulation 4(2)

PAY FOR TIME OFF ALLOWED TO SAFETY REPRESENTATIVES

1 Subject to paragraph 3 below, where a safety representative is permitted to take time off in accordance with Regulation 4(2) of these Regulations, his employer shall pay him—

(a) where the safety representative's remuneration for the work he would ordinarily have been doing during that time does not vary with the amount of work done, as if he had worked at that work for the whole of that time;

(b) where the safety representative's remuneration for that work varies with the amount of work done, an amount calculated by reference to the average hourly earnings for that work (ascertained in accordance with paragraph 2 below).

2 The average hourly earnings referred to in paragraph 1(b) above are the average hourly earnings of the safety representative concerned or, if no fair estimate can be made of those earnings, the average hourly earnings for work of that description of persons in comparable employment with the same employer or, if there are no such persons, a figure of average hourly earnings which is reasonable in the circumstances.

3 Any payment to a safety representative by an employer in respect of a period of time off—

(a) if it is a payment which discharges any liability which the employer may have under section 57 of the 1975 Act in respect of that period, shall also discharge his liability in respect of the same period under Regulation 4(2) of these Regulations;—

(b) if it is a payment under any contractual obligation, shall go towards discharging the employer's liability in respect of the same period under Regulation 4(2) of these Regulations;

(c) if it is a payment under Regulation 4(2) of these Regulations shall go towards discharging any liability of the employer to pay contractual remuneration in respect of the same period.   [1069]

EMPLOYMENT PROTECTION (RECOUPMENT OF UNEMPLOYMENT BENEFIT AND SUPPLEMENTARY BENEFIT) REGULATIONS 1977

(SI 1977/674)

NOTES
Made: 7 April 1977.
Authority: Employment Protection (Consolidation) Act 1978, s 132; Social Security Act 1975, s 114.
Although Supplementary Benefit was replaced by income support and references to the former in the text of these Regulations were amended by the Employment Protection (Recoupment of Unemployment Benefit and Supplementary Benefit) (Amendment) Regulations 1988, SI 1988/419, the title to these Regulations has not been amended.

PART I

INTRODUCTORY

1 Citation and commencement

These Regulations may be cited as the Employment Protection (Recoupment of
Unemployment Benefit and Supplementary Benefit) Regulations 1977 and shall
come into operation on 9th May 1977.   **[1070]**

2 Interpretation

(1) The Interpretation Act 1889 shall apply to the interpretation of these Regulations
as it applies to the interpretation of an Act of Parliament.

(2) In these Regulations, unless the context otherwise requires, the following
expressions have the meanings hereby assigned to them respectively, that is to say—

    (a) "the 1975 Act" means the Employment Protection Act 1975;

    [(aa) "the 1978 Act" means the Employment Protection (Consolidation) Act
        1978]

    (b) "employer" and "employee" have the same meanings as in the [1978 Act]
        and references to an employer and an employee in these Regulations are
        respectively references to those persons as parties to relevant proceedings
        before an industrial tribunal;

    (c) "monetary award" has the same meaning as in [section 132(6) of the 1978
        Act;]

    (d) "prescribed element" has the meaning assigned to it in Regulation 3 below
        and in the Schedule to these Regulations;

(e) "protected period" has the meaning assigned to it in section 101(5) of the 1975 Act;

(f) "protective award" means an award made by an industrial tribunal on a complaint presented by an appropriate trade union under section 101 of the 1975 Act;

(g) "recoupable benefit" means any unemployment benefit or [income support] as the case may be, which is recoupable under these Regulations;

(h) "recoupment notice" means a notice under these Regulations;

(i) "Secretary of the Tribunals" means the Secretary of the Central Office of the Industrial Tribunals (England and Wales) or, as the case may require, the Secretary of the Central Office of the Industrial Tribunals (Scotland), for the time being;

[(j) "Unemployment benefit" and "income support" have the same meaning as in the Social Security Act 1975 and the Social Security Act 1986 respectively and references to "benefit" include income support as the context may require;]

(k) any other expression used in Regulation 11 or 12 below to which a meaning is assigned by or under the [Social Security Acts 1975 to 1986], has that meaning.

(3) In the Schedule to these Regulations references to sections are references to sections of the [1978 Act unless otherwise indicated] and references in column 3 of the table to the conclusion of the tribunal proceedings are references to the conclusion of the proceedings mentioned in the corresponding entry in column 2.

(4) For the purposes of these Regulations (and in particular for the purposes of any calculations to be made by an industrial tribunal as respects the prescribed element) the conclusion of the tribunal proceedings shall be taken to occur—

(a) where the industrial tribunal at the hearing announces the effect of its decision to the parties, on the date on which that announcement is made;

(b) in any other case, on the date on which the decision of the tribunal is sent to the parties.

(5) References to parties in relevant industrial tribunal proceedings shall be taken to include references to persons appearing on behalf of parties in a representative capacity.

(6) References in these Regulations to anything done, or to be done, in, or in consequence of, any tribunal proceedings include references to anything done, or to be done, in, or in consequence of any such proceedings as are in the nature of a review, or re-hearing or a further hearing consequent on an appeal.   **[1071]**

NOTES
Paras (2), (3): words in square brackets substituted or inserted by the Employment Protection (Recoupment of Unemployment Benefit and Supplementary Benefit) (Amendment) Regulations 1988, SI 1988/419, reg 3(1), (2), subject to transitional provisions contained in reg 4.
    References to the Employment Protection Act 1975 are taken to include a reference to the Trade Union and Labour Relations (Consolidation) Act 1992 ("TULRA 1992"); see s 300(3) of, and Sch 3, para 1(4) to, that Act.
    "Section 101 of the 1975 Act": see TULRA 1992, s 189(2).

PART II
INDUSTRIAL TRIBUNAL PROCEEDINGS

3 Application to payments and proceedings

(1) Subject to paragraph (2) and Regulation 4 below these Regulations apply—

(a) to the payments described in column 1 of the table contained in the Schedule to these Regulations, being, in each case, payments which are the subject of industrial tribunal proceedings of the kind described in the corresponding entry in column 2 and the prescribed element in relation to each such payment is so much of the relevant monetary award as is attributable to the matter described in the corresponding entry in column 3; and

(b) to payments of remuneration in pursuance of a protective award.

(2) The payments to which these Regulations apply by virtue of paragraph (1)(a) above include payments in proceedings under section 103 of the 1975 Act and, accordingly, where an order is made on an employee's complaint under that section, the relevant protective award shall, as respects that employee and to the appropriate extent, be taken to be subsumed in the order made under section 103 so that the provisions of these Regulations relating to monetary awards shall apply to payments under that order to the exclusion of the provisions relating to protective awards, but without prejudice to anything done under the latter in connection with the relevant protective award before the making of the order under section 103.   **[1072]**

NOTE

"Section 103 of the 1975 Act": see now TULRA 1992, s 192.

4 *(Revoked by SI 1988/419, reg 3(3)).*

5 Duties of the industrial tribunals and of the Secretary of the Tribunals in respect of monetary awards

(1) Where these Regulations apply, no regard shall be had, in assessing the amount of a monetary award, to the amount of any [income support] or any unemployment benefit which may have been paid to or claimed by the employee for a period which coincides with any part of a period to which the prescribed element is attributable.

(2) Where the industrial tribunal in arriving at a monetary award makes a reduction on account of the employee's contributory fault or on account of any limit imposed by or under the [1975 Act or the 1978 Act], a proportionate reduction shall be made in arriving at the amount of the prescribed element.

(3) Subject to the following provisions of this Regulation it shall be the duty of the industrial tribunal to set out in any decision which includes a monetary award the following particulars—

(a) the monetary award;
(b) the amount of the prescribed element, if any;
(c) the dates of the period to which the prescribed element is attributable;
(d) the amount, if any, by which the monetary award exceeds the prescribed element.

(4) Where the industrial tribunal at the hearing announces to the parties the effect of a decision which includes a monetary award it shall inform those parties at the same time of the amount of any prescribed element included in the monetary award and shall explain the effect of Regulations 8 and 9 below in relation to the prescribed element.

(5) Where the industrial tribunal has made such an announcement as is described in paragraph (4) above the Secretary of the Tribunals shall forthwith notify the Secretary of State that the tribunal has decided to make a monetary award including a prescribed element and shall notify him of the particulars set out in paragraph (3) above.

(6) As soon as reasonably practicable after the Secretary of the Tribunals has sent a copy of a decision containing the particulars set out in paragraph (3) above to the parties he shall send a copy of that decision to the Secretary of State.

(7) In addition to containing the particulars required under paragraph (3) above, any such decision as is mentioned in that paragraph shall contain a statement explaining the effect of Regulations 8 and 9 below in relation to the prescribed element.

(8) The requirements of paragraphs (3) to (7) above do not apply where the tribunal is satisfied that in respect of each day falling within the period to which the prescribed element relates the employee has neither received nor claimed unemployment benefit or [income support].   **[1073]**

NOTE

Paras (1), (2), (8): words in square brackets substituted by SI 1988/419, reg 3(1), (4), subject to transitional provision contained in reg 4.

6 Duties of the industrial tribunals and of the Secretary of the Tribunals in respect of protective awards

(1) Where, on a complaint by an appropriate trade union under section 101 of the 1975 Act, an industrial tribunal—

(a) at the hearing announces to the parties the effect of a decision to make a protective award; or

(b) (where it has made no such announcement) sends a decision to make such an award to the parties;

the Secretary of the Tribunals shall forthwith notify the Secretary of State of the following particulars relating to the award—

(i) where the industrial tribunal has made such an announcement as is described in paragraph (1)(a) above, the date of the hearing or where it has made no such announcement, the date on which the decision was sent to the parties;

(ii) the location of the tribunal;

(iii) the name and address of the employer;

(iv) the description of the employees to whom the award relates; and

(v) the dates of the protected period.

(2)(a) Where an industrial tribunal makes such an announcement as is described in paragraph (1)(a) above in the presence of the employer or his representative it shall advise him of his duties under Regulation 7 below and shall explain the effect of Regulations 8 and 9 below in relation to remuneration under the protective award.

(b) Without prejudice to (a) above any decision of an industrial tribunal to make a protective award under section 101 of the 1975 Act shall contain a statement advising the employer of his duties under Regulation 7 below and an explanation of the effect of Regulations 8 and 9 below in relation to remuneration under the protective award.   **[1074]**

NOTE

"Section 101 of the 1975 Act": see now TULRA 1992, s 189(2).

7 Duties of the employer to give information about protective awards

(1) Where an industrial tribunal makes a protective award under section 101 of the 1975 Act against an employer, the employer shall give to the Secretary of State the following information in writing—

    (a) the name, address and national insurance number of every employee to whom the award relates; and

    (b) the date of termination (or proposed termination) of the employment of each such employee.

(2) Subject to paragraph (3) below the employer shall comply with paragraph (1) above within the period of ten days commencing on the day on which the industrial tribunal at the hearing announces to the parties the effect of a decision to make a protective award or (in a case where no such announcement is made) on the day on which the relevant decision is sent to the parties.

(3) Where, in any case, it is not reasonably practicable for the employer to comply with paragraph (1) above within the period applicable under paragraph (2) above he shall comply as soon as reasonably practicable after the expiration of that period.

[1075]

NOTE

"Section 101 of the 1975 Act": see now TULRA 1992, s 189(2).

PART III

RECOUPMENT OF BENEFIT

8 Postponement of Awards

(1) This Regulation shall have effect for the purpose of postponing relevant awards in order to enable the Secretary of State to initiate recoupment under Regulation 9 below.

(2) Accordingly—

    (a) so much of the monetary award as consists of the prescribed element;

    (b) payment of any remuneration to which an employee would otherwise be entitled under a protective award,

shall be treated as stayed (in Scotland, sisted) as respects the relevant employee until—

    (i) the Secretary of State has served a recoupment notice on the employer; or

    (ii) the Secretary of State has notified the employer in writing that he does not intend to serve a recoupment notice.

(3) The stay or sist under paragraph (2) above is without prejudice to the right of an employee under section 103 of the 1975 Act to present a complaint to an industrial tribunal of his employer's failure to pay remuneration under a protective award and Regulation 3(2) above has effect as respects any such complaint and as respects any order made under section 103(3) of that Act. **[1076]**

NOTE

"Section 103 of the 1975 Act": see now TULRA 1992, s 192; as to s 103(3) of the 1975 Act, see now s 192(3) of the 1992 Act.

9 Recoupment of Benefit

(1) Recoupment shall be initiated by the Secretary of State serving on the employer a recoupment notice claiming by way of total or partial recoupment of unemployment benefit or [income support] the appropriate amount, computed, as the case may require, under paragraph (2) or (3) below.

(2) In the case of monetary awards the appropriate amount shall be whichever is the less of the following two sums—

(a) the amount of the prescribed element (less any tax or social security contributions which fall to be deducted therefrom by the employer); or

(b) the amount paid as on account of unemployment benefit or [income support] to the employee for any period which coincides with any part of the period to which the prescribed element is attributable.

(3) In the case of remuneration under a protective award the appropriate amount shall be whichever is the less of the following two sums—

(a) the amount (less any tax or social security contributions which fall to be deducted therefrom by the employer) accrued due to the employee in respect of so much of the protected period as falls before the date on which the Secretary of State receives from the employer the information required under Regulation 7 above; or

(b) the amount paid as on account of unemployment benefit or [income support] to the employee for any period which coincides with any part of the protected period falling before the date described in (a) above.

(4) A recoupment notice shall be served on the employer by post or otherwise and copies shall likewise be sent to the employee and, if requested, to the Secretary of the Tribunals.

(5) The Secretary of State shall serve a recoupment notice on the employer, or notify the employer that he does not intend to serve such a notice, within the period applicable, as the case may require, under paragraph (6) or (7) below, or as soon as practicable thereafter.

(6) In the case of a monetary award the period shall be—

(a) in any case in which the tribunal at the hearing announces to the parties the effect of its decision as described in Regulation 5(4) above, the period ending 21 days after the conclusion of the hearing or the period ending 9 days after the decision has been sent to the parties, whichever is the later; or

(b) in any other case, the period ending 21 days after the decision has been sent to the parties.

(7) In the case of a protective award the period shall be the period ending 21 days after the Secretary of State has received from the employer the information required under Regulation 7 above.

(8) A recoupment notice served on an employer shall operate as an instruction to the employer to pay, by way of deduction out of the sum due under the award, the recoupable amount to the Secretary of State and it shall be the duty of the employer to comply with the notice. The employer's duty under this paragraph shall not affect his obligation to pay any balance that may be due to the employee under the relevant award.

(9) The duty imposed on the employer by service of the recoupment notice shall not be discharged by payment of the recoupable amount to the employee during the

postponement period or thereafter if a recoupment notice is served on the employer during the said period.

(10) Payment by the employer to the Secretary of State under this Regulation shall be a complete discharge in favour of the employer as against the employee in respect of any sum so paid but without prejudice to any rights of the employee under Regulations 11 and 12 below.

(11) The recoupable amount shall be recoverable by the Secretary of State from the employer as a debt. **[1077]**

NOTE

Paras (1)–(3): words in square brackets substituted by SI 1988/419, reg 3(1), subject to transitional provision contained in reg 4.

10 Order made in secondary proceedings

(1) In the application of any of the above provisions in the case of—

(a) proceedings for an award under section 103 of the Act; or

(b) proceedings in the nature of a review, a re-hearing or a further hearing consequent on an appeal,

it shall be the duty of the industrial tribunal or, as the case may require, the Secretary of State, to take appropriate account of anything done under or in consequence of these Regulations in relation to any award made in the original proceedings.

(2) For the purposes of this Regulation the original proceedings are—

(a) where paragraph (1)(a) above applies the proceedings under section 101 of the 1975 Act; or

(b) where paragraph (1)(b) above applies the proceedings in respect of which the re-hearing, the review or the further hearing consequent on an appeal takes place. **[1078]**

NOTES

"Section 103 of the 1975 Act": see now TULRA 1992, s 192.
"Section 101 of the 1975 Act": see now TULRA 1992, s 189.

PART IV

DETERMINATION AND REVIEW OF BENEFIT RECOUPED

11 Provisions relating to determination of amount paid on account of benefit

(1) Without prejudice to the right of the Secretary of State to recover from an employer the recoupable benefit, an employee on whom a copy of a recoupment notice has been served in accordance with Regulation 9 above may, within 21 days of the date on which such notice was served on him or within such further time as the Secretary of State may for special reasons allow, give notice in writing to the Secretary of State that he does not accept that the amount specified in the recoupment notice in respect of unemployment benefit or [income support] is correct.

(2) Where an employee has given notice in writing to the Secretary of State under paragraph (1) above that he does not accept that an amount specified in the recoupment notice is correct, then, if and to the extent that—

(a) an amount is specified in respect of unemployment benefit, the Secretary of State shall forthwith submit to an [adjudication officer] the question as to the amount of unemployment benefit paid in respect of the period to which the prescribed element is attributable or, as appropriate, in respect of so much of the protected period as falls before the date on which the employer complies with Regulation 7 above and any question so submitted shall be for determination by an [adjudication officer], a [Social Security Appeal Tribunal] and a Commissioner, in accordance with sections 99 to 104 of the Social Security Act 1975;

(b) an amount is specified in respect of [income support] the Secretary of State shall forthwith submit to [a] [adjudication officer] the question as to the amount of [income support] paid in respect of the period to which the prescribed element is attributable or, as appropriate, in respect of so much of the protected period as falls before the date on which the employer complies with Regulation 7 above and any question so submitted shall be determined by [a] [adjudication officer] and, if the employee is dissatisfied with such determination, Regulation 12(2) below shall apply.

[(2A) Notice of a determination under paragraph (2)(b) above shall be in writing and shall be served, by post or otherwise, on the employee and on the Secretary of State.]

(3) If any question is raised as to the amount of [income support] recoverable by recoupment, other than a question to which paragraph (2) above applies, the Secretary of State shall refer for review under Regulation 12 below the determination by which that benefit was awarded.

(4) Where—

(a) on the determination of a question submitted to an [adjudication officer] or to [a] [adjudication officer] under paragraph (2) above; or

(b) on the review under section 104 of the Social Security Act 1975 of a decision in pursuance of which a sum was paid on account of unemployment benefit; or

(c) on review under Regulation 12 below of a determination as to [income support],

the amount recovered by the Secretary of State from the employer under these Regulations exceeds the total amount paid by way of unemployment benefit or [income support] to the employee which would not have been paid if a decision on review under section 104 of the Social Security Act 1975 or a decision on review under Regulation 12 below, had been made in the first instance, the Secretary of State shall pay to the employee an amount equal to such excess.

(5) In any case where, after the Secretary of State has recovered from an employer any amount by way of recoupment of benefit, the decision given by the industrial tribunal in consequence of which such recoupment took place is set aside or varied on appeal or on a re-hearing by the industrial tribunal, the Secretary of State shall make such repayment to the employer or payment to the employee of the whole or part of the amount recovered as he is satisfied should properly be made having regard to the decision given on appeal or re-hearing. **[1079]**

NOTES

Para (1): words in square brackets substituted by SI 1988/419, reg 3(1), subject to transitional provisions contained in reg 4.

Para (2): words in fifth and eighth pairs of square brackets substituted by the Employment Protection (Recoupment of Unemployment Benefit and Supplementary Benefit) (Amendment) Regulations 1980, SI 1980/1608, reg 2(a); words in remaining pairs of square brackets substituted by SI 1988/419, reg 3(1), (5), (6), subject to transitional provisions contained in reg 4.

Para (2A): inserted by SI 1980/1608, reg 2(b).

Para (4): words in second pair of square brackets substituted by SI 1980/1608, reg 2(a); words in remaining pairs of square brackets substituted by SI 1988/419, reg 3(1), (5), subject to transitional provisions contained in reg 4.

"Sections 99 to 104 of the Social Security Act 1975": this is to be read as a reference to the corresponding provisions of the Social Security Administration Act 1992 (principally ss 21–23, 25–36, 69); see the Social Security (Consequential Provisions) Act 1992, s 2(4).

12 Review of determination relating to [income support]

(1) Where under Regulation 11(3) above a determination as to [income support] is referred for review, [a] [adjudication officer] shall determine whether any and if so how much benefit would have been payable in respect of the period to which the recoupment notice relates, or to such part thereof as affects [income support], on the assumption that—

    (a) before the amount of benefit had been determined, the employer had paid an amount, or had been paying amounts in aggregate, equal to the amount of the prescribed element or, as the case may be, equal to the amount of remuneration payable in pursuance of a protective award; and

    (b) where an amount is recovered by the Secretary of State from an employer in respect of unemployment benefit paid to the employee for the relevant period, such benefit had not been payable and had not been paid.

(2) An employee shall have the same rights of appeal to [a Social Security] Appeal Tribunal against any determination made on review under this Regulation or made under Regulation 11(2) above as has a person to whom [section 100(1) of the Social Security Act 1975] applies and any such appeal shall be heard and determined and any decision on the appeal shall have the same effect as if the appeal was an appeal under that subsection.

(3) Notice of a determination under this Regulation shall be in writing and shall be served, by post or otherwise, on the employee and on the Secretary of State.

[1080]

NOTES

Para (1): words in second pair of square brackets substituted by SI 1980/1608, reg 2(a); words in remaining pairs of square brackets substituted by SI 1988/419, reg 3(1), (5), subject to transitional provisions contained in reg 4.

Para (2): words in square brackets substituted by SI 1988/419, reg 3(8), subject to transitional provisions contained in reg 4.

"Section 100(1) of the Social Security Act 1975": see now Social Security Administration Act 1992, s 22(1) (see note to Reg 11 above).

[SCHEDULE

TABLE RELATING TO MONETARY AWARDS

Regulation 3

Column 1 PAYMENT	*Column 2* PROCEEDINGS	*Column 3* MATTER TO WHICH PRESCRIBED ELEMENT IS ATTRIBUTABLE
1. Guarantee payments under section 12.	1. Complaint under section 17.	1. Any amount found to be due to the complainant and ordered to be paid under section 17(3) for a period before the conclusion of the tribunal proceedings.
2. Payments under any collective agreement having regard to which the appropriate Minister has made an exemption order under section 18.	2. Complaint under section 18(4).	2. Any amount found to be due to the complainant and ordered to be paid under section 17(3), as applied by section 18(4), for a period before the conclusion of the tribunal proceedings
3. Payments of remuneration in respect of a period of suspension on medical grounds under section 19 and section 64(2).	3. Complaint under section 22.	3. Any amount found to be due to the complainant and ordered to be paid under section 22(3) for a period before the conclusion of the tribunal proceedings.
4. Payments under an order for reinstatement under section 69(2).	4. Complaint of unfair dismissal under section 67(1).	4. Any amount ordered to be paid under section 69(2)(a) in respect of arrears of pay for a period before the conclusion of the tribunal proceedings.
5. Payments under an order for re-engagement under section 71(5).	5. Complaint of unfair dismissal under section 67(1).	5. Any amount ordered to be paid under section 69(4)(d) in respect of arrears of pay for a period before the conclusion of the tribunal proceedings.
6. Payments under an award of compensation for unfair dismissal in cases falling under section 68(2) (cases where no order for reinstatement or re-engagement has been made).	6. Complaint of unfair dismissal under section 67(1).	6. Any amount ordered to be paid and calculated under section 74 in respect of compensation for loss of wages for a period before the conclusion of the tribunal proceedings.

Column 1 PAYMENT	Column 2 PROCEEDINGS	Column 3 MATTER TO WHICH PRESCRIBED ELEMENT IS ATTRIBUTABLE
7. Payments under an award of compensation for unfair dismissal under section 71(2) where reinstatement order not complied with.	7. Proceedings in respect of non-compliance with order.	7. Any amount ordered to be paid and calculated under section 74 in respect of compensation for loss of wages for a period before the conclusion of the tribunal proceedings.
8. Payments under an award of compensation for unfair dismissal under section 71(2) where re-engagement order not complied with.	8. Proceedings in respect of non-compliance with order.	8. Any amount ordered to be paid and calculated under section 74 in respect of compensation for loss of wages for a period before the conclusion of the tribunal proceedings.
9. Payments under an interim order for reinstatement under section 77(7).	9. Proceedings on an application for an order for interim relief under section 77(1).	9. Any amount found to be due to the complainant and ordered to be paid in respect of arrears of pay for the period between the date of termination of employment and the conclusion of the tribunal proceedings.
10. Payments under an interim order for re-engagement under 77(8)(a). section	10. Proceedings on an application for an order for interim relief under section 77(1).	10. Any amount found to be due to the complainant and ordered to be paid in respect of arrears of pay for the period between the date of termination of employment and the conclusion of the tribunal proceedings.
11. Payments under an order for the continuation of a contract of employment under section 77(8)(b) where employee reasonably refuses re-engagement.	11. Proceedings on an application for an order for interim relief under section 77(1).	11. Any amount found to be due to the complainant and ordered to be paid in respect of arrears of pay for the period between the date of termination of employment and the conclusion of the tribunal proceedings.

Column 1 PAYMENT	*Column 2* PROCEEDINGS	*Column 3* MATTER TO WHICH PRESCRIBED ELEMENT IS ATTRIBUTABLE
12. Payments under an order for the continuation of a contract of employment under section 77(9) where employer fails to attend or is unwilling to reinstate or re-engage.	12. Proceedings on an application for an order for interim relief under section 77(1).	12. Any amount found to be due to the complainant and ordered to be paid in respect of arrears of pay for the period between the date of termination of employment and the conclusion of the tribunal proceedings.
13. Payments under an order for the continuation of a contract of employment under section 79(2) where reinstatement or re-engagement order not complied with.	13. Proceedings in respect of non-compliance with order.	13. Any amount ordered to be paid to the employee by way of compensation under section 79(2)(b) for loss of wages for the period between the date of termination of employment and the conclusion of the tribunal proceedings.
14. Payments under an order for compensation under section 79(3) where order for the continuation of contract of employment not complied with.	14. Proceedings in respect of non-compliance with order.	14. Any amount ordered to be paid to the employee by way of compensation under section 79(3)(a) for loss of wages for the period between the date of termination of employment and the conclusion of the tribunal proceedings.
15. Payments under an order under section 103(3) of the 1975 Act on employer's default in respect of remuneration due to employee under protective award.	15. Complaint under section 103(1) of the 1975 Act.	15. Any amount ordered to be paid to the employee in respect of so much of the relevant protected period as falls before the date of the conclusion of the tribunal proceedings.]

[1081]

NOTES

Substituted by SI 1988/419, regs 3(9), 4.

Items 9–15: ss 77, 79 of the EP(C)A 1978 are now ss 164, 166 of TULRA 1992; s 103(3) of the 1975 Act is now s 192(3) of the 1992 Act.

RACE RELATIONS (FORMAL INVESTIGATIONS) REGULATIONS 1977

(SI 1977/841)

NOTES
Made: 13 May 1977.
Authority: Race Relations Act 1976, ss 49(3), 50(1), 58(2), 78(1).
Modified by the Solicitors' Incorporated Practices Order 1991, SI 1991/2684.

ARRANGEMENT OF REGULATIONS

1 Citation and operation

These Regulations may be cited as the Race Relations (Formal Investigations) Regulations 1977 and shall come into operation on 13th June 1977.   **[1082]**

2 Interpretation

(1) In these Regulations any reference to the Act is a reference to the Race Relations Act 1976.

(2) Any reference to the Commission, in Regulations 4, 5 and 6 below, is a reference to the Commission for Racial Equality except that, as respects any of the functions of the Commission in relation to a formal investigation which the Commission have delegated under section 48(3) of the Act, any such reference in Regulation 4 or 5 is a reference to the persons, being either Commissioners or additional Commissioners, to whom those functions have been so delegated.

(3) The Interpretation Act 1889 shall apply for the interpretation of these Regulations as it applies for the interpretation of an Act of Parliament.   **[1083]**

3 Service of notices

Any reference to a person being served with a notice, in Regulations 4, 5 and 6 below, is a reference to service of the notice on him being effected—

(a) by delivering it to him; or

(b) by sending it by post to him at his usual or last-known residence or place of business; or

(c) where the person is a body corporate or is a trade union or employers' association within the meaning of the Trade Union and Labour Relations Act 1974, by delivering it to the secretary or clerk of the body, union or

association at its registered or principal office or by sending it by post to that secretary or clerk at that office; or
(d) where the person is acting by a solicitor by delivering it at, or by sending it by post to, the solicitor's address for service.   **[1084]**

4 Notice of holding of formal investigation

(1) Where, in pursuance of section 49 of the Act, notice of the holding of a formal investigation falls to be given by the Commission to a person named in the terms of reference for the investigation, that person shall be served with a notice setting out the terms of reference.

(2) Where the terms of reference for a formal investigation are revised, paragraph (1) shall apply in relation to the revised investigation and terms of reference as it applied to the original.   **[1085]**

5 Requirement to furnish or give information or produce documents

Where, in pursuance of section 50(1) of the Act, the Commission require a person to furnish written information, give oral information or produce documents, that person shall be served with a notice in the form set out in Schedule 1 to these Regulations or a form to the like effect, with such variations as the circumstances may require.   **[1086]**

6 Non-discrimination notice

Where, in pursuance of section 58(2) of the Act, the Commission issue a non-discrimination notice, the person to whom it is directed shall be served with a notice in the form set out in Schedule 2 to these Regulations or a form to the like effect, with such variations as the circumstances may require.   **[1087]**

SCHEDULES

SCHEDULE 1

Regulation 5

REQUIREMENT TO FURNISH WRITTEN INFORMATION OR GIVE ORAL
EVIDENCE AND PRODUCE DOCUMENTS
(RACE RELATIONS ACT 1976, s 50(1))

To A.B. of

For the purposes of the formal investigation being conducted by the Commission for Racial Equality ("the Commission") the terms of reference of which [were given to you in a notice dated .. ..] [are set out in the Schedule hereto], you are hereby required in pursuance of section 50(1) of the Race Relations Act 1976 ("the Act") and subject to section 50(3) thereof, [to furnish such written information as is hereinafter described, namely, *(description of information)*. The said information is to be furnished *(specify the time or times at which, and the manner and form in which, the information is to be furnished)*.] [to attend at *(insert time)* on *(insert date)* at *(insert place)* and give oral information about *(or* give oral evidence about, and produce all documents in your possession or control relating to,) such matters as are hereinafter specified, namely *(specify matters)*.]

Dated the .... day of .... 19 ......

This notice was issued by the [Commission] [Commissioners/Commissioners and additional Commissioners to whom the Commission have, in pursuance of section 48(3) of the Act and in relation to the investigation, delegated their functions under section 50(1)(a) thereof].

[Service of this notice was authorised by an order made in pursuance of section 50(2)(a) of the Act and dated (*insert date*), a copy of which is attached.]

[Having regard to the terms of reference of the investigation and the provisions of section 50(2)(b)/section 60 of the Act, service of this notice does not require the consent of the Secretary of State.] **[1088]**

C.D.
[COMMISSIONER.]
[Chief Officer (or other appropriate officer) of the Commission.]

[SCHEDULE
TERMS OF REFERENCE OF INVESTIGATION]

SCHEDULE 2

Regulation 6

NON-DISCRIMINATION NOTICE
(RACE RELATIONS ACT 1976, s 58)

To A.B. of

Whereas, in the course of a formal investigation, the Commission for Racial Equality ("the Commission") have become satisfied that you were committing/had committed an act/acts to which section 58(2) of the Race Relations Act 1976 ("the Act") applies, namely, (*insert particulars of act or acts*) [and are of the opinion that further such acts are likely to be committed unless changes are made in your practices or other arrangements as respects (*insert particulars*)].

Now, therefore, without prejudice to your other duties under the Act, you are hereby required, in pursuance of section 58(2) of the Act, not to commit any such act as aforesaid or any other act which is [an unlawful discriminatory act by virtue of (*insert reference to relevant Part or provision of the Act*)] [a contravention of section 28 of the Act] [an act which is a contravention of section 29/30/31 of the Act by reference to Part II/Part III thereof].

In so far as compliance with the aforesaid requirement involves changes in any of your practices or other arrangements, you are further required, in pursuance of the said section 58(2), to inform the Commission [as hereinafter provided] that you have effected those changes and what those changes are [and to take the following steps for the purpose of affording that information to other persons concerned, namely, (specify steps to be taken)].

[You are further required, in pursuance of section 58(3) of the Act, to furnish the Commission as hereinafter provided with the following information, to enable them to verify your compliance with this notice, namely, (*insert description of information required*).]

[The information to be furnished by you to the Commission in pursuance of this notice shall be furnished as follows, namely, (*specify the time or times at which, and the manner and form in which, the information, or information of a particular description, is to be furnished*).]

Dated the .... day of .... 19 ....

This notice was issued by the Commission, the provisions of section 58(5) of the Act having been complied with.

C.D.
[COMMISSIONER.]
[Chief Officer (*or other appropriate officer*) of the Commission.]

[1089]

RACE RELATIONS (QUESTIONS AND REPLIES) ORDER 1977

(SI 1977/842)

NOTES
Made: 13 May 1977.
Authority: Race Relations Act 1976, ss 65, 74(3).
Modified by the Solicitors' Incorporated Practices Order 1991, SI 1991/2684.

ARRANGEMENT OF ARTICLES

1 Citation and operation

This Order may be cited as the Race Relations (Questions and Replies) Order 1977 and shall come into operation on 13th June 1977.   **[1090]**

2 Interpretation

(1) In this Order "the Act" means the Race Relations Act 1976.

(2) In this Order any reference to a court is a reference to a county court in England or Wales designated for the time being for the purposes of the Act by an order made by the Lord Chancellor under section 67(1) of the Act or a sheriff court in Scotland and any reference to a tribunal is a reference to an industrial tribunal.

(3) The Interpretation Act 1889 shall apply to the interpretation of this Order as it applies to the interpretation of an Act of Parliament.   **[1091]**

3 Forms for asking and answering questions

The forms respectively set out in Schedules 1 and 2 to this Order or forms to the like effect with such variation as the circumstances may require are, respectively, hereby prescribed as forms—

(a) by which a person aggrieved may question a respondent as mentioned in subsection (1)(a) of section 65 of the Act;

(b) by which a respondent may if he so wishes reply to such questions as mentioned in subsection (1)(b) of that section.   **[1092]**

4 Period for service of questions—court cases

In proceedings before a court, a question shall only be admissible as evidence in pursuance of section 65(2)(a) of the Act—

    (a) where it was served before those proceedings had been instituted, if it was so served during—

       (i) the period of six months beginning when the act complained of was done, or

       (ii) in a case to which section 57(5) of the Act applies, the period of eight months so beginning;

    (b) where it was served when those proceedings had been instituted, if it was served with the leave of, and within a period specified by, the court.

[1093]

5 Period for service of questions—tribunal cases

In proceedings before a tribunal, a question shall only be admissible as evidence in pursuance of section 65(2)(a) of the Act—

    (a) where it was served before a complaint had been presented to a tribunal, if it was so served within the period of three months beginning when the act complained of was done;

    (b) where it was served when a complaint had been presented to a tribunal, either if it was so served within the period of twenty-one days beginning with the day on which the complaint was presented or if it was so served later with leave given, and within a period specified, by a direction of a tribunal. **[1094]**

6 Manner of service of questions and replies

A question and any reply thereto may be served on the respondent or, as the case may be, on the person aggrieved—

    (a) by delivering it to him; or

    (b) by sending it by post to him at his usual or last-known residence or place of business; or

    (c) where the person to be served is a body corporate or is a trade union or employers' association within the meaning of the Trade Union and Labour Relations Act 1974, by delivering it to the secretary or clerk of the body, union or association at its registered or principal office or by sending it by post to the secretary or clerk at that office; or

    (d) where the person to be served is acting by a solicitor, by delivering it at, or by sending it by post to, the solicitor's address for service; or

    (e) where the person to be served is the person aggrieved, by delivering the reply, or sending it by post, to him at his address for reply as stated by him in the document containing the questions. **[1095]**

SCHEDULES

SCHEDULE 1

Article 3

THE RACE RELATIONS ACT 1976 s 65(1)(a)
QUESTIONNAIRE OF PERSON AGGRIEVED

To ....*(name of person to be questioned)*

of .... *(address)*

    1. (1) I .... *(name of questioner)* of .... *(address)* consider that you may have discriminated against me contrary to the Race Relations Act 1976.

(2) (*Give date, approximate time and a factual description of the treatment received and of the circumstances leading up to the treatment.*)

(3) I consider that this treatment may have been unlawful [because .... (*complete if you wish to give reasons, otherwise delete*)].

2. Do you agree that the statement in paragraph 1(2) above is an accurate description of what happened? If not, in what respect do you disagree or what is your version of what happened?

3. Do you accept that your treatment of me was unlawful discrimination by you against me? If not—

    (a)   why not,
    [(b) for what reason did I receive the treatment accorded to me, and
    (c)   how far did considerations of colour, race, nationality (including citizenship) or ethnic or national origins affect your treatment of me?

4. (*Any other questions you wish to ask.*)

5. My address for any reply you may wish to give to the questions raised above is [that set out in paragraph 1 (1) above] [the following address ....].

.... (*signature of person questioned*)

.... (*date*).

.N.B.—By virtue of section 65 of the Act this questionnaire and any reply are (subject to the provisions of the section) admissible in proceedings under the Act and a court or tribunal may draw any such inference as is just and equitable from a failure without reasonable excuse to reply within a reasonable period, or from an evasive or equivocal reply, including an inference that the person questioned has discriminated unlawfully.   **[1096]**

SCHEDULE 2

Article 3

THE RACE RELATIONS ACT 1976 s 65(1)(b)
REPLY BY RESPONDENT

To .... (*name of questioner*) of ....
.... (*address*).

1. I .... (*name of person questioned*) of .... (*address*) hereby acknowledge receipt of the questionnaire signed by you and dated .... which was served on me on .... (*date*).

2. [I agree that the statement in paragraph 1(2) of the questionnaire is an accurate description of what happened.] [I disagree with the statement in paragraph 1(2) of the questionnaire in that ....]

3. I accept/dispute that my treatment of you was unlawful discrimination by me against you.

[My reasons for so disputing are .... The reason why you received the treatment accorded to you and the answers to the other questions in paragraph 3 of the questionnaire are ....]

4. (*Replies to questions in paragraph 4 of the questionnaire.*)

[5. I have deleted (in whole or in part) the paragraph(s) numbered .... above, since I am unable/unwilling to reply to the relevant questions in the correspondingly numbered paragraph(s) of the questionnaire for the following reasons ....]

.... (*signature of person questioned*)

.... (*date*)
[1097]

INDUSTRIAL TRIBUNALS (NON-DISCRIMINATION NOTICES APPEALS) REGULATIONS 1977

(SI 1977/1094)

NOTES
Made: 29 June 1977.
Authority: Trade Union and Labour Relations Act 1974, Sch 1, para 21 (see now the Employment Protection (Consolidation) Act 1978, Sch 9, para 1(1)).

ARRANGEMENT OF REGULATIONS

1 Citation and commencement

(1) These Regulations may be cited as the Industrial Tribunals (Non-Discrimination Notices Appeals) Regulations 1977 and shall come into operation on 5th August 1977.

(2) *(Repeals SI 1975/2098, subject to a transitional provision.)*   **[1098]**

2 Interpretation

(1) The Interpretation Act 1889 shall apply to these Regulations as it applies to an Act of Parliament as if these Regulations and the Regulations hereby revoked were Acts of Parliament.

(2) In these Regulations, unless the context otherwise requires, the following expressions have the meanings hereby assigned to them respectively, that is to say—

"the 1974 Act" means the Trade Union and Labour Relations Act 1974 as amended by the Employment Protection Act 1975 and the Trade Union and Labour Relations (Amendment) Act 1976;

"the 1975 Act" means the Sex Discrimination Act 1975;

"the 1976 Act" means the Race Relations Act 1976;

"appellant" means a person who has appealed to a tribunal under section 68 of the 1975 Act or, as the case may be, under section 59 of the 1976 Act;

"the clerk to the tribunal" means the person appointed by the Secretary of the Tribunals or an Assistant Secretary to act in that capacity at one or more hearings;

"decision" in relation to a tribunal includes a direction under section 68(3) of the 1975 Act or, as the case may be, under section 59(3) of the 1976 Act and any other order which is not an interlocutory order;

"hearing" means a sitting of tribunal duly constituted for the purpose of receiving evidence, hearing addresses and witnesses or doing anything lawfully requisite to enable the tribunal to reach a decision on any question;

"non-discrimination notice" means a notice under section 67 of the 1975 Act, or as the case may be, under section 58 of the 1976 Act;

"nominated chairman" means a member of the panel of chairmen for the time being nominated by the President;

"the Office of the Tribunals" means the Central Office of the Industrial Tribunals (England and Wales);

"the panel of chairmen" means the panel of persons, being barristers or solicitors of not less than seven years' standing, appointed by the Lord Chancellor in pursuance of Regulation 5(2) of the Industrial Tribunals (England and Wales) Regulations 1965, as amended;

"party" means the appellant and the respondent;

"the President" means the President of the Industrial Tribunals (England and Wales) or the person nominated by the Lord Chancellor to discharge for the time being the functions of the President;

"Regional Office of the Industrial Tribunals" means a regional office which has been established under the Office of the Tribunals for an area specified by the President;

"Register" means the Register kept in pursuance of the Industrial Tribunals (Labour Relations) Regulations 1974;

"respondent" means the Equal Opportunities Commission established under section 53 of the 1975 Act or, as the case may be, the Commission for Racial Equality established under section 43 of the 1976 Act;

"Rules means a Rule of Procedure contained in the Schedule to these Regulations;

"the Secretary of the Tribunals" and "an Assistant Secretary of the Tribunals" means respectively the persons for the time being acting as the Secretary of the Office of the Tribunals and as the Assistant Secretary of a Regional Office of the Industrial Tribunals;

"tribunal" means an industrial tribunal (England and Wales) established in pursuance of the Industrial Tribunals (England and Wales) Regulation 1965, as amended, and in relation to any proceedings means the tribunal to which the proceedings have been referred by the President or by a nominated chairman.   **[1099]**

3 Proceedings of tribunals

The Rules of Procedure contained in the Schedule to these Regulations shall have effect in relation to appeals to a tribunal under section 68 of the 1975 Act and under section 59 of the 1976 Act against non-discrimination notices relating to matters arising in England and Wales.   **[1100]**

4 Proof of decision of tribunals

The production in any proceedings in any court of a document purporting to be certified by the Secretary of the Tribunals to be a true copy of an entry of a decision in the Register shall, unless the contrary is proved, be sufficient evidence of the document and of the facts stated therein.   **[1101]**

SCHEDULE

Regulation 3

RULES OF PROCEDURE

1 Notice of appeal

An appeal shall be commenced not later than six weeks after service of the non-discrimination notice, as specified in section 68(1) of the 1975 Act and in section 59(1) of the 1976 Act, by the appellant sending to the Secretary of the Tribunals a notice of appeal which shall be in writing and shall set out:—

(a) the name of the appellant and his address for the service of documents;
(b) the date of the non-discrimination notice appealed against;
(c) the name and address of the respondent;
(d) particulars of the requirements appealed against; and
(e) the grounds of the appeal.

2 Action upon receipt of notice of appeal

Upon receiving a notice of appeal the Secretary of the Tribunals shall enter particulars of it in the Register and shall forthwith send a copy of it to the respondent and inform the parties in writing of the case number of the appeal entered in the Register (which shall thereafter constitute the title of the proceedings) and of the address to which notices and other communications to the Secretary of the Tribunals shall be sent.

3 Power to require attendance of witnesses and production of documents, etc.

(1) A tribunal may on the application of a party made either by notice to the Secretary of the Tribunals or at the hearing—

(a) require a party to furnish in writing to another party further particulars of the grounds on which he relies and of any facts and contentions relevant thereto;
(b) grant to a party such discovery or inspection of documents as might be granted by a county court; and
(c) require the attendance of any person as a witness or require the production of any document relating to the matter to be determined,

and may appoint the time at or within which or the place at which any act required in pursuance of this Rule is to be done.

(2) The tribunal shall not under paragraph (1) of this Rule require the production of any document certified by the Secretary of State as being a document of which the production would be against the interests of national security.

(3) A person on whom a requirement has been made under paragraph (1) of this Rule may apply to the tribunal either by notice to the Secretary of the Tribunals or at the hearing to vary or set aside the requirement.

(4) No such application to vary or set aside shall be entertained in a case where a time has been appointed under paragraph (1) of this Rule in relation to the requirement unless it is made before the time or, as the case may be, expiration of the time so appointed.

(5) Every document containing a requirement under paragraph (1)(b) or (c) of this Rule shall contain a reference to the fact that under paragraph 21(6) of Part III of Schedule 1 to the 1974 Act any person who without reasonable excuse fails to comply with any such requirement shall be liable on summary conviction to a fine not exceeding £100.

NOTE

"1974 Act, Sch 1, Pt II, para 21(6)": replaced by the Employment Protection (Consolidation) Act 1978, Sch 9, para 1, which provides for a fine on summary conviction not exceeding level 3 on the standard scale.

4 Time and place of hearing

(1) The President or a nominated chairman shall fix the date, time and place of the hearing of the appeal and the Secretary of the Tribunals shall not less than 14 days (or such shorter time as may be agreed by him with the parties) before the date so fixed send to each party a notice of hearing which shall include information and guidance as to attendance at the hearing, witnesses and the bringing of documents (if any), representation by another person and written representations.

(2) Where the President or nominated chairman so directs, the Secretary of the Tribunals shall also send notice of the hearing to such persons as may be directed, but the requirements as to the period of notice contained in the foregoing paragraph of this rule shall not apply to any such notices.

5 The hearing

(1) Any hearing of or in connection with an appeal shall take place in public unless the tribunal on the application of a party decides that a private hearing is appropriate for the purpose of hearing evidence which relates to matters of such a nature that it would be against the interests of national security to allow the evidence to be given in public or hearing evidence from any person which in the opinion of the tribunal is likely to consist of information the disclosure of which would cause substantial injury to the undertaking of the appellant or of any undertaking in which he works for reasons other than its effect on negotiators with respect to any of the matters mentioned in section 29(1) of the 1974 Act.

(2) In cases to which the foregoing provisions of this Rule apply, a member of the Council on Tribunals in his capacity as such shall be entitled to attend the hearing.

6 Written representations

If a party shall desire to submit representations in writing for consideration by a tribunal at the hearing of the appeal, that party shall send such representations to the Secretary of the Tribunals not less than 7 days before the hearing and shall at the same time send a copy thereof to the other party.

7 Right of appearance

At any hearing of or in connection with an appeal a party may appear before the tribunal in person or may be represented by counsel or by a solicitor or by any other person whom he desires to represent him, including in the case of the appellant a representative of a trade union or an employer's association.

8 Procedure at hearing

(1) At any hearing of or in connection with an appeal a party shall be entitled to make an opening statement, to give evidence, to call witnesses, to cross-examine any witnesses called by the other party and to address the tribunal.

(2) If a party shall fail to appear or to be represented at the time and place fixed for the hearing of an appeal, the tribunal may dispose of the appeal in the absence of that party or may adjourn the hearing to a later date: Provided that before disposing of an appeal in the absence of a party the tribunal shall consider any written representations submitted by that party in pursuance of Rule 6.

(3) A tribunal may require any witness to give evidence on oath or affirmation and for that purpose there may be administered an oath or affirmation in due form.

9 Decision of tribunal

(1) A decision of a tribunal may be taken by a majority thereof and, if the tribunal shall be constituted of two members only, the chairman shall have a second or casting vote.

(2) The decision of a tribunal shall be recorded in a document signed by the chairman which shall contain the reasons for the decision.

(3) The clerk to the tribunal shall transmit the document signed by the chairman to the Secretary of the Tribunals who shall as soon as may be enter it in the Register and shall send a copy of the entry to each of the parties.

(4) The specification of the reasons for the decision shall be omitted from the Register in any case in which evidence has been heard in private and the tribunal so directs and in that event a specification of the reasons shall be sent to the parties and to any superior court in any proceedings relating to such decision together with the copy of the entry.

(5) The Register shall be kept at the Office of the Tribunals and shall be open to the inspection of any person without charge at all reasonable hours.

(6) The chairman of a tribunal shall have power by certificate under his hand to correct in documents recording the tribunal's decisions clerical mistakes or errors arising therein from any accidental slip or omission.

(7) The clerk to the tribunal shall send a copy of any document so corrected and the certificate of the chairman to the Secretary of the Tribunals who shall as soon as may be make such corrections as may be necessary in the Register and shall send a copy of the corrected entry or of the corrected specification of the reasons, as the case may be, to each of the parties.

(8) If any decision is—

    (a)   corrected under paragraph (6) of this Rule; or

    (b)   reviewed, revoked or varied under Rule 10; or

    (c)   altered in any way by order of a superior court,

the Secretary of the Tribunals shall alter the entry in the Register to conform with any such certificate or order and shall send a copy of the new entry to each of the parties.

10 Review of tribunal's decision

(1) A tribunal shall have power on the application of a party to review and to revoke or vary by certificate under the chairman's hand any of its decisions in a case in which a county court has power to order a new trial on the grounds that—

    (a)   the decision was wrongly made as a result of an error on the part of the tribunal staff; or

    (b)   a party did not receive notice of the proceedings leading to the decision; or

    (c)   the decision was made in the absence of a party; or

    (d)   new evidence has become available since the making of the decision provided that its existence could not have been reasonably known of or foreseen; or

    (e)   the interests of justice require such a review.

(2) An application for the purposes of paragraph (1) of this Rule may be made at the hearing. If the application is not made at the hearing, such application shall be made to the Secretary of the Tribunals at any time from the date of the hearing until 14 days after the date on which the decision was sent to the parties and must be in writing stating the grounds in full.

(3) An application for the purposes of paragraph (1) of this Rule may be refused by the chairman of the tribunal which decided the case, by the President or by a nominated chairman if his opinion it has no reasonable prospect of success and he shall state the reasons for his opinion.

(4) If such an application is not refused under paragraph (3) of this Rule, it shall be heard by the tribunal and if it is granted the tribunal shall either vary its decision or revoke its decision and order a re-hearing.

(5) The clerk to the tribunal shall send to the Secretary of the Tribunals the certificate of the chairman as to any revocation or variation of the tribunal's decision under this Rule. The Secretary of the Tribunals shall as soon as may be make such correction as may be necessary in the Register and shall send a copy of the entry to each of the parties.

11 Costs

(1) A tribunal may make an order that a party shall pay to another party either a specified sum in respect of the costs of or in connection with an appeal incurred by that other party or, in default of agreement, the taxed amount of those costs.

(2) Any costs required by an order under this Rule to be taxed may be taxed in the county court according to such of the scales prescribed by the county court rules for proceedings in the county court as shall be directed by the order.

12 Miscellaneous powers of tribunal

(1) Subject to the provision of these Rules, a tribunal may regulate its own procedure.

(2) A tribunal may, if it thinks fit—

- (a) postpone the day or time fixed for, or adjourn, any hearing;
- (b) before granting an application under Rule 3 or 10 require the party making the application to give notice thereof to the other party;
- (c) either on the application of any person or of its own motion, direct any other person to be joined as a party to the appeal (giving such consequential directions as it considers necessary), but may do so only after having given to the person proposed to be joined a reasonable opportunity of making written or oral objection;
- (d) make any necessary amendments to the description of a party in the Register and in other documents relating to the appeal;
- (e) if the appellant shall at any time give notice of the abandonment of his appeal, dismiss the appeal;
- (f) if the parties agree in writing upon the terms of a decision to be made by the tribunal, decide accordingly.

(3) Any act, other than the hearing of an appeal or of an application for the purposes of Rule 10(1), required or authorised by these Rules to be done by a tribunal may be done by, or on the direction of, the President, the chairman of the tribunal or a nominated chairman.

(4) Rule 11 shall apply to an order dismissing proceedings under paragraph (2) of this Rule.

(5) Any functions of the Secretary of the Tribunals may be performed by an Assistant Secretary of the Tribunals.

13 Notices, etc.

(1) Any notice given under these Rules shall be in writing and all notices and documents required or authorised by these Rules to be sent or given to any person hereinafter mentioned may be sent by post (subject to paragraphs (3) and (4) of this Rule) or delivered to or at—

- (a) in a case of a document directed to the Secretary of the Tribunals, the Office of the Tribunals or such other office as may be notified by the Secretary of the Tribunals to the parties;
- (b) in the case of a document directed to a party, his address for service specified in the notice of appeal or in a notice under paragraph (2) of this Rule or (if no address for service is so specified), his last known address or place of business in the United Kingdom or, if the party is a corporation, the corporation's registered or principal office;
- (c) in the case of a document directed to any person (other than a person specified in the foregoing provisions of this paragraph), his address or place of business in the United Kingdom, or if such a person is a corporation, the corporation's registered or principal office;

and if sent or given to the authorised representative of a party shall be deemed to have been sent or given to that party.

(2) A party may at any time by notice to the Secretary of the Tribunals and to the other party change his address for service under these Rules.

(3) Where a notice of appeal is not delivered, it shall be sent by the recorded delivery service.

(4) Where for any sufficient reason service of any document or notice cannot be effected in the manner prescribed under this Rule, the President or a nominated chairman may make an order for substituted service in such manner as he may deem fit and such service shall have the same effect as service in the manner prescribed under this Rule. **[1102]**

EMPLOYMENT APPEAL TRIBUNAL RULES 1980

(SI 1980/2035)

NOTES
Made: 18 December 1980.
Authority: Employment Protection (Consolidation) Act 1978, Sch 11, para 17.

ARRANGEMENT OF REGULATIONS

1 Citation and commencement

(1) These Rules may be cited as the Employment Appeal Tribunal Rules 1980 and shall come into operation on 1st February 1981.

(2) The Employment Appeal Tribunal Rules 1976 shall cease to have effect except in relation to appeals instituted before that date.   **[1103]**

2 Interpretation

In these Rules, unless the context otherwise requires—

"the Act" means the Employment Protection (Consolidation) Act 1978 and a section or Schedule referred to by number means the section or Schedule so numbered in the Act;

"the Appeal Tribunal" means the Employment Appeal Tribunal established under section 87 of the Employment Protection Act 1975 and continued in existence under section 135 of the Act and includes the President, a judge, a member or the Registrar acting on behalf of the Tribunal;

"judge" means a judge of the Appeal Tribunal nominated under section 135(2)(a) or (b) and includes a judge nominated under paragraph 5 or 6 and a judge appointed under paragraph 8 of Schedule 11 to act temporarily in the place of a judge of the Tribunal;

"member" means a member of the Appeal Tribunal appointed under section 135(2)(c) and includes a member appointed under paragraph 7 of Schedule 11 to act temporarily in the place of a member appointed under that section;

"the President" means the judge appointed under section 135(4) to be President of the Appeal Tribunal and includes a judge nominated under paragraph 4 of Schedule 11 to act temporarily in his place;

"the Registrar" means the person appointed to be Registrar of the Appeal Tribunal and includes any officer of the Tribunal authorised by the President to act on behalf of the Registrar;

"the Secretary of Industrial Tribunals" means the person acting for the time being as the Secretary of the Central Office of the Industrial Tribunals (England and Wales) or, as may be appropriate, of the Central Office of the Industrial Tribunals (Scotland);

"the Certification Officer" means the person appointed to be the Certification Officer under section 7(1) of the Employment Protection Act 1975;

"taxing officer" means any officer of the Appeal Tribunal authorised by the President to assess costs or expenses.   **[1104]**

3 Institution of appeal

[(1) Every appeal to the Appeal Tribunal shall be instituted by serving on the Tribunal the following documents:

   (a) a notice of appeal in, or substantially in, accordance with Form 1, 2 or 3 in the Schedule to these Rules;

   (b) a copy of the decision or order of an industrial tribunal or of the Certification Officer which is the subject of the appeal;

   (c) in the case of an appeal from an industrial tribunal, a copy of the full written reasons for the decision or order of that tribunal.

(1A) The period within which an appeal to the Appeal Tribunal may be instituted is 42 days from the date on which full written reasons for the decision or order of the industrial tribunal were sent to the appellant, or, in the case of an appeal from a decision of the Certification Officer, 42 days from the date on which the written record of that decision was so sent.]

(2) Where it appears to the Registrar that the grounds of appeal stated in the notice of appeal do not give the Appeal Tribunal jurisdiction to entertain the appeal, he shall notify the appellant accordingly informing him of the reasons for the opinion and, subject to paragraphs (3) and (5) of this rule, no further action shall be taken on the appeal.

(3) Where notification has been given under paragraph (2) of this rule, the appellant may serve a fresh notice of appeal within the time remaining under [paragraph (1A)] or within 28 days from the date on which the Registrar's notification was sent to him, whichever is the longer period.

(4) Where the appellant serves a fresh notice of appeal under paragraph (3) of this rule the Registrar shall consider such fresh notice of appeal with regard to jurisdiction as though it were an original notice of appeal lodged pursuant to [paragraphs (1) and (1A)] of this rule.

(5) Where an appellant expresses dissatisfaction in writing with the reasons given by the Registrar, under paragraph (2) of this rule, for his opinion that the grounds of appeal stated in a notice of appeal do not give the Appeal Tribunal jurisdiction to entertain the appeal, the Registrar shall place the papers before the President or a judge for his direction as to whether any further action should be taken on the appeal. **[1105]**

NOTES

Paras (1), (1A): substituted for the original para (1) by the Employment Appeal Tribunal (Amendment) Rules 1985, SI 1985/29.
Paras (3), (4): words in square brackets substituted by SI 1985/29.

4 Service of notice of appeal

On receipt of notice under rule 3, the Registrar shall seal the notice with the Appeal Tribunal's seal and shall serve a sealed copy on the appellant and on—

    (a) every person who, in accordance with rule 5, is a respondent to the appeal; and

    (b) the Secretary of Industrial Tribunals in the case of an appeal from an industrial tribunal; or

    (c) the Certification Officer in the case of an appeal from any of his decisions; or

    (d) the Secretary of State in the case of an appeal under section 36 or Part VI of the Act or Part IV of the Employment Protection Act 1975 to which he is not a respondent. **[1106]**

5 Respondents to appeals

The respondents to an appeal shall be—

    (a) in the case of an appeal from an industrial tribunal or from a decision of the Certification Officer under section 3 of the Trade Union Act 1913 or section 4 of the Trade Union (Amalgamations, etc) Act 1964, the parties (other than the appellant) to the proceedings before the industrial tribunal or the Certification Officer;

    (b) in the case of an appeal against a decision of the Certification Officer under section 4 or 5 of the Trade Union Act 1913, section 8 of the Trade Union and Labour Relations Act 1974 or [section 8 of the Employment Protection Act 1975], that Officer. **[1107]**

NOTE
Words in square brackets substituted by the Employment Appeal Tribunal (Amendment) Rules 1988,
SI 1988/2072, r 3.

6 Respondent's answer and notice of cross-appeal

(1) The Registrar shall, as soon as practicable, notify every respondent of the date appointed by the Appeal Tribunal by which any answer under this rule must be delivered.

(2) A respondent who wishes to resist an appeal shall, within the time appointed under paragraph (1) of this rule, deliver to the Appeal Tribunal an answer in writing in, or substantially in accordance with, Form 4 in the Schedule to these Rules, setting out the grounds on which he relies, so, however, that it shall be sufficient for a respondent to an appeal referred to in rule 5(a) who wishes to rely on any ground which is the same as a ground relied on by the industrial tribunal or the Certification Officer for making the decision or order appealed from to state that fact in his answer.

(3) A respondent who wishes to cross-appeal may do so by including in his answer a statement of the grounds of his cross-appeal, and in that event an appellant who wishes to resist the cross-appeal shall, within a time to be appointed by the Appeal Tribunal, deliver to the Tribunal a reply in writing setting out the grounds on which he relies.

(4) The Registrar shall serve a copy of every answer and reply to a cross-appeal on every party other than the party by whom it was delivered.

(5) Where the respondent does not wish to resist an appeal, the parties may deliver to the Appeal Tribunal an agreed draft of an order allowing the appeal and the Tribunal may, if it thinks it right to do so, make an order allowing the appeal in the terms agreed.   **[1108]**

7 Disposal of appeal

(1) The Registrar shall, as soon as practicable, give notice of the arrangements made by the Appeal Tribunal for hearing the appeal to—

    (a) every party to the proceedings; and
    (b) the Secretary of Industrial Tribunals in the case of an appeal from an industrial tribunal; or
    (c) the Certification Officer in the case of an appeal from one of his decisions; or
    (d) the Secretary of State in the case of an appeal under section 36 or Part VI of the Act or Part IV of the Employment Protection Act 1975 to which he is not a respondent.

(2) Any such notice shall state the date appointed by the Appeal Tribunal by which any interlocutory application must be made.   **[1109]**

[8 Application under section 5 of the Employment Act 1980 or under section 5 of the Employment Act 1988

Every application to the Appeal Tribunal for:

    (a) an award of compensation for unreasonable exclusion or expulsion from a trade union; or
    (b) one or both of the following, that is to say—

(i) an award of compensation for unjustifiable discipline;

(ii) an order that the union pay to the applicant an amount equal to any sum which he has paid in pursuance of a determination falling within subsection (5)(b) of section 3 of the Employment Act 1988;

shall be made in writing in, or substantially in, accordance with Form 5 in the Schedule to these Rules and shall be served on the Tribunal together with a copy of the decision or order declaring that the applicant's complaint against the trade union was well-founded.]   [1110]

NOTES

Commencement: 29 December 1988.
Substituted by SI 1988/2072, r 4.

9 If on receipt of an application under [rule 8(a)] it becomes clear that at the time the application was made the applicant had been admitted or re-admitted to membership of the union against which the complaint was made, the Registrar shall forward the application to the Central Office of Industrial Tribunals.   [1111]

NOTES

Words in square brackets substituted by SI 1988/2072, r 5.

10 Service of application

On receipt of an application under rule 8, the Registrar shall seal it with the Appeal Tribunal's seal and shall serve a sealed copy on the applicant and on the respondent trade union and the Secretary of Industrial Tribunals.   [1112]

[11 Appearance by respondent trade union

(1) Subject to paragraph (2) of this rule, a respondent trade union wishing to resist an application under rule 8 shall within 14 days of receiving the sealed copy of the application enter an appearance in, or substantially in, accordance with Form 6 in the Schedule to these Rules and setting out the grounds on which the union relies.

(2) Paragraph (1) above shall not require a respondent trade union to enter an appearance where the application is before the Appeal Tribunal by virtue of having been transferred there by an industrial tribunal and, prior to that transfer, the respondent had entered an appearance to the proceedings before the industrial tribunal.]   [1113]

NOTES

Commencement: 29 December 1988.
Substituted by SI 1988/2072, r 6.

12 On receipt of the notice of appearance the Registrar shall serve a copy of it on the applicant.   [1114]

13 Disposal of application

(1) The Registrar shall, as soon as practicable, give notice to the parties to the application of the arrangements made by the Appeal Tribunal for hearing the application.

(2) Any such notice shall state the date appointed by the Appeal Tribunal by which any interlocutory application must be made.　　　　　　**[1115]**

14 Joinder of parties

The Appeal Tribunal may, on the application of any person or of its own motion, direct that any person not already a party to the proceedings be added as a party, or that any party to proceedings shall cease to be a party, and in either case may give such consequential directions as it considers necessary.　　　　　　**[1116]**

15 Interlocutory applications

(1) An interlocutory application may be made to the Appeal Tribunal by giving notice in writing specifying the direction or order sought.

(2) On receipt of a notice under paragraph (1) of this rule, the Registrar shall serve a copy on every other party to the proceedings who appears to him to be concerned in the matter to which the notice relates and shall notify the applicant and every such party of the arrangements made by the Appeal Tribunal for disposing of the application.　　　　　　**[1117]**

16 Disposal of interlocutory applications

(1) Every interlocutory application made to the Appeal Tribunal shall be considered in the first place by the Registrar who will have regard to the just and economical disposal of the application and to the expense which may be incurred by the parties in attending an oral hearing.

(2) Every interlocutory application shall be disposed of by the Registrar except that any matter which he thinks should properly be decided by the President or a judge shall be referred by him to the President or a judge, who may dispose of it himself or refer it in whole or in part to the Appeal Tribunal as required to be constituted by paragraph 16 of Schedule 11 or refer it back to the Registrar with such directions as he thinks fit.　　　　　　**[1118]**

17 Appeals from Registrar

(1) Where an application is disposed of by the Registrar in pursuance of rule 16(2) any party aggrieved by his decision may appeal to a judge and in that case the judge may determine the appeal himself or refer it in whole or in part to the Appeal Tribunal as constituted by paragraph 16 of Schedule 11.

(2) Notice of appeal under paragraph (1) of this rule may be given to the Appeal Tribunal, either orally or in writing, within [five] days of the decision appealed from [; and] the Registrar shall notify every other party who appears to him to be concerned in the appeal and shall inform every such party and the appellant of the arrangements made by the Tribunal for disposing of the appeal.　　　　　　**[1119]**

NOTE

Para (2): word in first square brackets substituted, and word in second square brackets inserted, by SI 1988/2072, r 7.

18 Hearing of interlocutory applications

The Appeal Tribunal may sit either in private or in public for the hearing of any interlocutory application.   **[1120]**

19 Appointment for directions

(1) Where it appears to the Appeal Tribunal that the future conduct of any proceedings would thereby be facilitated, the Tribunal may (either of its own motion or on application) at any stage in the proceedings appoint a date for a meeting for directions as to their future conduct and thereupon the following provisions of this rule shall apply.

(2) The Registrar shall give to every party in the proceedings notice of the date appointed under paragraph (1) of this rule and any party applying for directions shall, if practicable, before that date give to the Appeal Tribunal particulars of any direction for which he asks.

(3) The Registrar shall take such steps as may be practicable to inform every party of any directions applied for by any other party.

(4) On the date appointed under paragraph (1) of this rule, the Appeal Tribunal shall consider every application for directions made by any party and any written representations relating to the application submitted to the Tribunal and shall give such directions as it thinks fit for the purpose of securing the just, expeditious and economical disposal of the proceedings, including, where appropriate, directions in pursuance of rule 30, for the purpose of ensuring that the parties are enabled to avail themselves of opportunities for conciliation.

(5) Without prejudice to the generality of paragraph (4) of this rule, the Appeal Tribunal may give such directions as it thinks fit as to—

    (a) the amendment of any notice, answer or other document;
    (b) the admission of any facts or documents;
    (c) the admission in evidence of any documents;
    (d) the mode in which evidence is to be given at the hearing;
    (e) the consolidation of the proceedings with any other proceedings pending before the Tribunal;
    (f) the place and date of the hearing.

(6) An application for further directions or for the variation of any directions already given may be made in accordance with rule 15.   **[1121]**

20 Appeal Tribunal's power to give directions

The Appeal Tribunal may either of its own motion or on application, at any stage of the proceedings, give any party directions as to any steps to be taken by him in relation to the proceedings.   **[1122]**

21 Default by parties

If a respondent to any proceedings fails to deliver an answer or, in the case of an application made under [section 5 of the Employment Act 1980 or section 5 of the Employment Act 1988], a notice of appearance within the time appointed under these Rules, or if any party fails to comply with an order or direction of the Appeal Tribunal, the Tribunal may order that he be debarred from taking any further part in the proceedings, or may make such other order as it thinks just. [1123]

NOTE

Words in square brackets substituted by SI 1988/2072, r 8.

22 Attendance of witnesses and production of documents

(1) The Appeal Tribunal may, on the application of any party, order any person to attend before the Tribunal as a witness or to produce any document.

(2) No person to whom an order is directed under paragraph (1) of this rule shall be treated as having failed to obey that order unless at the time at which the order was served on him there was tendered to him a sufficient sum of money to cover his costs of attending before the Appeal Tribunal. [1124]

23 Oaths

The Appeal Tribunal may, either of its own motion or on application, require any evidence to be given on oath. [1125]

24 Oral hearings

(1) Subject to paragraph (2) of this rule, an oral hearing at which any proceedings before the Appeal Tribunal are finally disposed of shall take place in public before such members of the Tribunal as (subject to paragraph 16 of Schedule 11) the President may nominate for the purpose.

(2) The Appeal Tribunal may sit in private to conduct proceedings which in the opinion of the Tribunal—

- (a) relate to matters of such a nature that it would be against the interests of national security to allow the proceedings to be conducted in public; or
- (b) in the course of which, evidence is likely to be given (wholly or in part) of information which—
  - (i) the person giving the evidence could not disclose without contravening a prohibition imposed by or under an enactment; or
  - (ii) has been communicated to that person in confidence or which he has otherwise obtained in consequence of the confidence reposed in him by another person; or
  - (iii) of information the disclosure of which would cause substantial injury to an undertaking of the person giving the evidence or any undertaking in which he works for reasons other than its effects on any negotiations with respect to any of the matters mentioned in section 29(1) of the Trade Union and Labour Relations Act 1974. [1126]

25 Drawing up, reasons for, and enforcement of orders

(1) Every order of the Appeal Tribunal shall be drawn up by the Registrar and a copy, sealed with the seal of the Tribunal, shall be served by the Registrar on every party to the proceedings to which it relates and—

    (a) in the case of an order disposing of an appeal from an industrial tribunal, on the Secretary of the Industrial Tribunals; or

    (b) in the case of an order disposing of an appeal from the Certification Officer, on that Officer.

(2) The Appeal Tribunal shall, on the application of any party made within 14 days after the making of an order finally disposing of any proceedings, give its reasons in writing for the order unless it was made after the delivery of a reasoned judgment.

(3) Subject to any order made by the Court of Appeal or Court of Session and to any directions given by the Appeal Tribunal, an appeal from the Tribunal shall not suspend the enforcement of any order made by it. **[1127]**

[25A Registration and proof of awards under section 5 of the Employment Act 1980 [or section 5 of the Employment Act 1988]

(1) This rule applies where an application has been made to the Appeal Tribunal under [section 5 of the Employment Act 1980 or under section 5 of the Employment Act 1988].

[(2) Without prejudice to rule 25, where the Appeal Tribunal makes an order in respect of an application to which this rule applies, and that order—

    (a) makes an award of compensation, or

    (b) is or includes an order of the kind referred to in rule 8(b)(ii),

or both, the Registrar shall as soon as may be enter a copy of the order, sealed with the seal of the Tribunal, into the Register.]

(3) The production in any proceedings in any court of a document, purporting to be certified by the Registrar of the Appeal Tribunal to be a true copy of an entry in the Register of an order to which this rule applies shall, unless the contrary is proved, be sufficient evidence of the document and of the facts stated therein.] **[1128]**

NOTES
Commencement: 29 December 1988 (para 2); 1 March 1985 (remainder).
Inserted by SI 1985/29, r 6.
Heading: words in square brackets added by SI 1988/2072, r 9(a).
Para (1): words in square brackets substituted by SI 1988/2072, r 9(b).
Para (2): substituted by SI 1988/2072, r 9(c).

26 Review of decisions and correction of errors

(1) The Appeal Tribunal may, either of its own motion or on application, review any order made by it and may, on such review, revoke or vary that order on the grounds that—

    (a) the order was wrongly made as the result of an error on the part of the Tribunal or its staff;

    (b) a party did not receive proper notice of the proceedings leading to the order; or

    (c) the interests of justice require such review.

(2) An application under paragraph (1) above shall be made within 14 days of the date of the order.

(3) A clerical mistake in any order arising from an accidental slip or omission may at any time be corrected by, or on the authority of, a judge or member. **[1129]**

27 Costs or expenses

(1) Where it appears to the Appeal Tribunal that any proceedings were unnecessary, improper or vexatious or that there has been unreasonable delay or other unreasonable conduct in bringing or conducting the proceedings the Tribunal may order the party at fault to pay any other party the whole or such part as it thinks fit of the costs or expenses incurred by that other party in connection with the proceedings.

(2) Where an order is made under paragraph (1) of this rule, the Appeal Tribunal may assess the sum to be paid, or may direct that it be assessed by the taxing officer, from whose decision an appeal shall lie to a judge.

(3) Rules 17 and 18 shall apply to an appeal under paragraph (2) of this rule as they apply to an appeal from the Registrar.

(4) The costs of an assisted person shall be taxed in accordance with Schedule 2 to the Legal Aid Act 1974 by a Taxing Master of the Supreme Court. **[1130]**

28 Service of documents

(1) Any notice or other document required or authorised by these Rules to be served on, or delivered to, any person may, be sent to him by post to his address for service or, where no address for service has been given, to his registered office, principal place of business, head or main office or last known address, as the case may be, and any notice or other document required or authorised to be served on, or delivered to, the Appeal Tribunal may be sent by post or delivered to the Registrar—

    (a) in the case of a notice instituting proceedings, at the central office of any other offices of the Tribunal; or

    (b) in any other case, at the office of the Tribunal in which the proceedings in question are being dealt with in accordance with rule 32(2).

(2) Any notice or other document required or authorised to be served on, or delivered to, an unincorporated body may be sent to its secretary, manager or other similar officer.

(3) Every document served by post shall be assumed, in the absence of evidence to the contrary, to have been delivered in the normal course of post.

(4) The Appeal Tribunal may inform itself in such manner as it thinks fit of the posting of any document by an officer of the Tribunal.

(5) The Appeal Tribunal may direct that service of any document be dispensed with or be effected otherwise than in the manner prescribed by these Rules. **[1131]**

29 Conciliation

Where at any stage of any proceedings it appears to the Appeal Tribunal that there is a reasonable prospect of agreement being reached between the parties, the Tribunal may take such steps as it thinks fit to enable the parties to avail themselves of any opportunities for conciliation, whether by adjourning any proceedings or otherwise. **[1132]**

30 Time

(1) The time prescribed by these Rules or by order of the Appeal Tribunal for doing any act may be extended (whether it has already expired or not) or abridged, and the date appointed for any purpose may be altered, by order of the Tribunal.

(2) Where the last day for the doing of any act falls on a day on which the appropriate office of the Tribunal is closed and by reason thereof the act cannot be done on that day, it may be done on the next day on which that office is open.

(3) An application for an extension of the time prescribed for the doing of an act, including the institution of an appeal under rule 3, shall be heard and determined as an interlocutory application under rule 16.   **[1133]**

31 Tribunal offices and allocation of business

(1) The central office and any other office of the Appeal Tribunal shall be open at such times as the President may direct.

(2) Any proceedings before the Tribunal may be dealt with at the central office or at such other office as the President may direct.   **[1134]**

32 Non-compliance with, and waiver of, rules

(1) Failure to comply with any requirements of these Rules shall not invalidate any proceedings unless the Appeal Tribunal otherwise directs.

(2) The Tribunal may, if it considers that to do so would lead to the more expeditious or economical disposal of any proceedings or would otherwise be desirable in the interests of justice, dispense with the taking of any step required or authorised by these Rules, or may direct that any such steps be taken in some manner other than that prescribed by these Rules.

[(3) The powers of the Tribunal under paragraph (2) extend to authorising the institution of an appeal notwithstanding that the period prescribed in rule 3(1A) may not have commenced.]   **[1135]**

NOTE
Para (3): added by SI 1985/29, r 4.

SCHEDULE

Rules 3, 6, 8, 11

FORMS 1–6

[FORM 1

Notice of Appeal from Decision of Industrial Tribunal

1. The appellant is (*name and address of appellant*).

2. Any communication relating to this appeal may be sent to the appellant at (*appellant's address for service, including telephone number, if any*).

3. The appellant appeals from (*here give particulars of the decision of the industrial tribunal from which the appeal is brought, including the date*).

4.   The parties to the proceedings before the industrial tribunal, other than the appellant, were *(names and addresses of other parties to the proceedings resulting in decision appealed from)*.

5.   A copy of the industrial tribunal's decision or order and of the full written reasons for that decision or order are attached to this notice.

6.   The grounds upon which this appeal is brought are that the industrial tribunal erred in law in that *(here set out in paragraphs the various grounds of appeal)*.

Date   Signed   ]

FORM 2

Notice of Appeal from Decision of Certification Officer

1.   The appellant is *(name and address of appellant)*.

2.   Any communication relating to this appeal may be sent to the appellant at *(appellant's address for service, including telephone number if any)*.

3.   The appellant appeals from: *(here give particulars of the order or decision of the Certification Officer from which the appeal is brought)*.

4.   The appellant's grounds of appeal are: *(here state the grounds of appeal)*.

5.   A copy of the Certification Officer's decision is attached to this notice.

Date   Signed

[FORM 3

Notice of Appeal from Decision of Industrial Tribunal under Section 4(8) of the Employment Act 1980

1.   The appellant is *(name and address of appellant)*.

2.   Any communication relating to this appeal may be sent to the appellant at *(appellant's address for service, including telephone number if any)*.

3.   The appellant appeals from: *(here give particulars of the decision of the industrial tribunal from which the appeal is brought)*.

4.   The appellant's grounds of appeal are: *(here state the grounds of appeal)*.

5.   Insofar as the appeal relates to the findings of fact by the industrial tribunal, the appellant states

    (a)   that the following findings of fact by the industrial tribunal were wrong:
    (b)   and that the industrial tribunal should have found the facts to be as follows:

6.   A copy of the industrial tribunal's decision or order and of the full written reasons for that decision or order are attached to this notice.

Date   Signed   ]

FORM 4

Respondent's Answer

1.   The respondent is *(name and address of respondent)*.

2.   Any communication relating to this appeal may be sent to the respondent at *(respondent's address for service, including telephone number, if any)*.

3.   The respondent intends to resist the appeal of *(here give the name of appellant)*. The grounds on which the respondent will rely are [the grounds relied upon by the industrial tribunal/Certification Officer for making the decision or order appealed from] [and] [the

following grounds]: (*here set out any grounds which differ from those relied upon by the industrial tribunal or Certification Officer, as the case may be*).

4.   The respondent cross-appeals from: (*here give particulars of the decision appealed from*).

5.   The respondent's grounds of appeal are: (*here state the grounds of appeal*).

Date   Signed

[FORM 5

Application to the Employment Appeal Tribunal for Compensation for Unreasonable Exclusion or Expulsion from a Trade Union or for Compensation or an Order in respect of unjustifiable discipline

1.   My name is

My address is

2.   Any communication relating to this application may be sent to me at (*state address for service, including telephone number if any*).

3.   My complaint against (*state the name and address of the trade union*) was declared to be well-founded by:
(*state tribunal or court*)
on
(*give date of decision or order*).

4.   (*Where the application relates to unreasonable exclusion or expulsion from a trade union*) I have not been admitted/re-admitted* to membership of the above-named trade union and hereby apply for compensation on the following grounds.
(*Where the application relates to unjustifiable discipline*) The determination constituting the infringement of my right under section 3 of the Employment Act 1988 has not been revoked./The trade union has failed to take all such steps as are necessary for securing the reversal of things done for the purpose of giving effect to that determination.*

(*Delete as appropriate)

Date   Signed

N.B.—A copy of the decision or order declaring the complaint against the trade union to be well-founded must be enclosed with this application.

FORM 6

Notice of appearance to Application to Employment Appeal Tribunal for Compensation for Unreasonable Exclusion or Expulsion from a Trade Union or for Compensation or an Order in respect of unjustifiable discipline

1.   The respondent trade union is (*name and address of union*).

2.   Any communication relating to this application may be sent to the respondent at (*respondent's address for service, including telephone number if any*).

3.   The respondent intends to resist the application of (*here give name of the applicant*). The grounds on which the respondent will rely are as follows:

4. (*Where the application relates to unreasonable exclusion or expulsion from the trade union, state whether or not the applicant has been admitted or re-admitted to membership on or before the date of the application.*)
(*Where the application relates to unjustifiable discipline, state whether—*

    (a)   the determination constituting the infringement of the applicant's right under section 3 of the Employment Act 1988 has been revoked; and
    (b)   the trade union has taken all such steps as are necessary for securing the reversal of anything done for the purpose of giving effect to that determination.*)

Date   Signed

                              Position in union.]   **[1136]**

NOTES
    Forms 1, 5, 6: substituted by SI 1988/2072, r 10.
    Form 3: substituted by SI 1985/29, r 5.

TRANSFER OF UNDERTAKINGS (PROTECTION OF EMPLOYMENT) REGULATIONS 1981

(SI 1981/1794)

NOTES
    Made: 14 December 1981.
    Authority: European Communities Act 1972, s 2.
    These Regulations implement Council Directive 77/187/EEC, post (see paras **[2121]**–**[2131]**); important amendments are made by the Trade Union Reform and Employment Rights Act 1993, s 33, as from 30 August 1993 (see SI 1993/1908, below, para **[1435]**). By Sch 9, para 4 to that Act, those amendments do not apply to a transfer of an undertaking taking place before that date.

ARRANGEMENT OF REGULATIONS

1 Citation, commencement and extent

(1) These Regulations may be cited as the Transfer of Undertakings (Protection of Employment) Regulations 1981.

(2) These Regulations, except Regulations 4 to 9 and 14, shall come into operation on 1st February 1982 and Regulations 4 to 9 and 14 shall come into operation on 1st May 1982.

(3) These Regulations, except Regulations 11(10) and 13(3) and (4), extend to Northern Ireland.   **[1137]**

NOTE
    Applied for certain purposes by the Ordinance Factories and Military Services Act 1984, s 4, Sch 2, and the Dockyard Services Act 1986, s 1(4).

2 Interpretation

(1) In these Regulations—

"collective agreement", "employers' association", and "trade union" have the
    same meanings respectively as in the 1974 Act or, in Northern Ireland, the
    1976 Order;

"collective bargaining" has the same meaning as it has in the 1975 Act or, in
    Northern Ireland, the 1976 Order;

"contract of employment" means any agreement between an employee and his
    employer determining the terms and conditions of his employment;

"employee" means any individual who works for another person whether under
    a contract of service or apprenticeship or otherwise but does not include
    anyone who provides services under a contract for services and references
    to a person's employer shall be construed accordingly;

"the 1974 Act", "the 1975 Act", "the 1978 Act" and "the 1976 Order" mean,
    respectively, the Trade Union and Labour Relations Act 1974, the
    Employment Protection Act 1975, the Employment Protection
    (Consolidation) Act 1978 and the Industrial Relations (Northern Ireland)
    Order 1976;

"recognised", in relation to a trade union, means recognised to any extent by
    an employer, or two or more associated employers, (within the meaning
    of the 1978 Act, or, in Northern Ireland, the 1976 Order), for the purpose
    of collective bargaining;

"relevant transfer" means a transfer to which these Regulations apply and
    "transferor" and "transferee" shall be construed accordingly; and

"undertaking" includes any trade or business *but does not include any
    undertaking or part of an undertaking which is not in the nature of a
    commercial venture.*

(2) References in these Regulations to the transfer of part of an undertaking are
references to a transfer of a part which is being transferred as a business and,
accordingly, do not include references to a transfer of a ship without more.

(3) For the purposes of these Regulations the representative of a trade union
recognised by an employer is an official or other person authorised to carry on
collective bargaining with that employer by that union.   **[1138]**

NOTE
Para (1): words omitted from definition "undertaking" repealed by the Trade Union Reform and
Employment Rights Act 1993, ss 33(1), (2), 51, Sch 10, as from 30 August 1993 (SI 1993/1908, below,
para **[1435]**). See further the Introductory Note to these Regulations.

3 A relevant transfer

(1) Subject to the provisions of these Regulations, these Regulations apply to a
transfer from one person to another of an undertaking situated immediately before
the transfer in the United Kingdom or a part of one which is so situated.

(2) Subject as aforesaid, these Regulations so apply whether the transfer is
effected by sale or by some other disposition or by operation of law.

(3) Subject as aforesaid, these Regulations so apply notwithstanding—

(a) that the transfer is governed or effected by the law of a country or territory
    outside the United Kingdom;

(b) that persons employed in the undertaking or part transferred ordinarily
    work outside the United Kingdom;

(c) that the employment of any of those persons is governed by any such law.

(4) It is hereby declared that a transfer of an undertaking or part of [one—

(a) may be effected by a series of two or more transactions; and

(b) may take place whether or not any property is transferred to the transferee by the transferor].

(5) Where, in consequence (whether directly or indirectly) of the transfer of an undertaking or part of one which was situated immediately before the transfer in the United Kingdom, a ship within the meaning of the Merchant Shipping Act 1894 registered in the United Kingdom ceases to be so registered, these Regulations shall not affect the right conferred by section 5 of the Merchant Shipping Act 1970 (right of seamen to be discharged when ship ceases to be registered in the United Kingdom) on a seaman employed in the ship.   **[1139]**

NOTE

Para (4): words in square brackets substituted by the Trade Union Reform and Employment Rights Act 1993, s 33(1), (3), as from 30 August 1993 (SI 1993/1908, below, para **[1435]**). The substituted words were as follows: "may be effected by a series of two or more transactions between the same parties, but in determining whether or not such a series constitutes a single transfer regard shall be had to the extent to which the undertaking or part was controlled by the transferor and transferee respectively before the last transaction, to the lapse of time between each of the transactions, to the intention of the parties and to all the other circumstances."

4 Transfers by receivers and liquidators

(1) Where the receiver of the property or part of the property of a company [or the administrator of a company appointed under Part II of the Insolvency Act 1986] or, in the case of a creditors' voluntary winding up, the liquidator of a company transfers the company's undertaking, or part of the company's undertaking, or part of the company's undertaking (the "relevant undertaking") to a wholly owned subsidiary of the company, the transfer shall for the purposes of these Regulations be deemed not to have been effected until immediately before—

(a) the transferee company ceases (otherwise than by reason of its being wound up) to be a wholly owned subsidiary of the transferor company; or

(b) the relevant undertaking is transferred by the transferee company to another person;

whichever first occurs, and, for the purposes of these Regulations, the transfer of the relevant undertaking shall be taken to have been effected immediately before that date by one transaction only.

(2) In this Regulation—

"creditors' voluntary winding up" has the same meaning as in the Companies Act 1948 or, in Northern Ireland, the Companies Act (Northern Ireland) 1960; and

"wholly owned subsidiary" has the same meaning as it has for the purposes of section 150 of the Companies Act 1948 and section 144 of the Companies Act (Northern Ireland) 1960.   **[1140]**

NOTE

Para (1): words in square brackets inserted by the Transfer of Undertakings (Protection of Employment) (Amendment) Regulations 1987, SI 1987/442, reg 2.

5 Effect of relevant transfer on contracts of employment, etc

(1) [Except where objection is made under paragraph (4A) below,] a relevant transfer shall not operate so as to terminate the contract of employment of any person employed by the transferor in the undertaking or part transferred but any such contract which would otherwise have been terminated by the transfer shall have effect after the transfer as if originally made between the person so employed and the transferee.

(2) Without prejudice to paragraph (1) above, [but subject to paragraph (4A) below,] on the completion of a relevant transfer—

(a) all the transferor's rights, powers, duties and liabilities under or in connection with any such contract shall be transferred by virtue of this Regulation to the transferee; and

(b) anything done before the transfer is completed by or in relation to the transferor in respect of that contract or a person employed in that undertaking or part shall be deemed to have been done by or in relation to the transferee.

(3) Any reference in paragraph (1) or (2) above to a person employed in an undertaking or part of one transferred by a relevant transfer is a reference to a person so employed immediately before the transfer, including, where the transfer is effected by a series of two or more transactions, a person so employed immediately before any of those transactions.

(4) Paragraph (2) above shall not transfer or otherwise affect the liability of any person to be prosecuted for, convicted of and sentenced for any offence.

[(4A) Paragraphs (1) and (2) above shall not operate to transfer his contract of employment and the rights, powers, duties and liabilities under or in connection with it if the employee informs the transferor or the transferee that he objects to becoming employed by the transferee.

(4B) Where an employee so objects the transfer of the undertaking or part in which he is employed shall operate so as to terminate his contract of employment with the transferor but he shall not be treated, for any purpose, as having been dismissed by the transferor.]

(5) [Paragraphs (1) and (4A) above are] without prejudice to any right of an employee arising apart from these Regulations to terminate his contract of employment without notice if a substantial change is made in his working conditions to his detriment; but no such right shall arise by reason only that, under that paragraph, the identity of his employer changes unless the employee shows that, in all the circumstances, the change is a significant change and is to his detriment.   **[1141]**

NOTES
Commencement: 30 August 1993 (para (4A), (4B)) (SI 1993/1908, below, para **[1435]**); 1 May 1982 (remainder).
Para (1): words in square brackets inserted by the Trade Union Reform and Employment Rights Act 1993, s 33(1), (4)(a), as from 30 August 1993 (SI 1993/1908, below, para **[1435]**).
Para (2): words in square brackets inserted by the Trade Union Reform and Employment Rights Act 1993, s 33(1), (4)(b), as from 30 August 1993 (SI 1993/1908, below, para **[1435]**).
Paras (4A), (4B): inserted by the Trade Union Reform and Employment Rights Act 1993, s 33(1), (4)(c), as from 30 August 1993 (SI 1993/1908, below, para **[1435]**).
Para (5): words in square brackets substituted by the Trade Union Reform and Employment Rights Act 1993, s 33(1), (4)(d), as from 30 August 1993 (SI 1993/1908, below, para **[1435]**).

6 Effect of relevant transfer on collective agreements

Where at the time of a relevant transfer there exists a collective agreement made by or on behalf of the transferor with a trade union recognised by the transferor in respect of any employee whose contract of employment is preserved by Regulation 5(1) above, then,—

(a) without prejudice to section 18 of the 1974 Act or Article 63 of the 1976 Order (collective agreements presumed to be unenforceable in specified circumstances) that agreement, in its application in relation to the employee, shall, after the transfer, have effect as if made by or on behalf of the transferee with that trade union, and accordingly anything done under or in connection with it, in its application as aforesaid, by or in relation to the transferor before the transfer, shall, after the transfer, be deemed to have been done by or in relation to the transferee; and

(b) any order made in respect of that agreement, in its application in relation to the employee, shall, after the transfer, have effect as if the transferee were a party to the agreement.   **[1142]**

NOTE
"Section 18 of the 1974 Act": see now TULRA 1992, ss 179, 180.

7 Exclusion of occupational pensions schemes

[(1)] Regulations 5 and 6 above shall not apply—

  (a) to so much of a contract of employment or collective agreement as relates to an occupational pension scheme within the meaning of the Social Security Pensions Act 1975 or the Social Security Pensions (Northern Ireland) Order 1975; or

  (b) to any rights, powers, duties or liabilities under or in connection with any such contract or subsisting by virtue of any such agreement and relating to such a scheme or otherwise arising in connection with that person's employment and relating to such a scheme.

[(2) For the purposes of paragraph (1) above any provisions of an occupational pension scheme which do not relate to benefits for old age, invalidity or survivors shall be treated as not being part of the scheme.]   **[1143]**

NOTES
Commencement: 30 August 1993 (para (2)) (SI 1993/1908, below, para **[1435]**); 1 May 1982 (remainder).
This Regulation is renumbered para (1), and para (2) is inserted, by the Trade Union Reform and Employment Rights Act 1993, s 33(1), (5), as from 30 August 1993 (SI 1993/1908, below, para **[1435]**).

8 Dismissal of employee because of relevant transfer

(1) Where either before or after a relevant transfer, any employee of the transferor or transferee is dismissed, that employee shall be treated for the purposes of Part V of the 1978 Act and Articles 20 to 41 of the 1976 Order (unfair dismissal) as unfairly dismissed if the transfer or a reason connected with it is the reason or principal reason for his dismissal.

(2) Where an economic, technical or organisational reason entailing changes in the workforce of either the transferor or the transferee before or after a relevant transfer is the reason or principal reason for dismissing an employee—

  (a) paragraph (1) above shall not apply to his dismissal; but

  (b) with prejudice to the application of section 57(3) of the 1978 Act or Article 22(10) of the 1976 Order (test of fair dismissal), the dismissal shall for the purposes of section 57(1)(b) of that Act and Article 22(1)(b) of that Order (substantial reason for dismissal) be regarded as having been for a substantial reason of a kind such as to justify the dismissal of an employee holding the position which that employee held.

(3) The provisions of this Regulation apply whether or not the employee in question is employed in the undertaking or part of the undertaking transferred or to be transferred.

(4) Paragraph (1) above shall not apply in relation to the dismissal of any employee which was required by reason of the application of section 5 of the Aliens Restriction (Amendment) Act 1919 to his employment.   **[1144]**

9 Effect of relevant transfer on trade union recognition

(1) This Regulation applies where after a relevant transfer the undertaking or part of the undertaking transferred maintains an identity distinct from the remainder of the transferee's undertaking.

(2) Where before such a transfer an independent trade union is recognised to any extent by the transferor in respect of employees of any description who in consequence of the transfer become employees of the transferee, then, after the transfer—

    (a) the union shall be deemed to have been recognised by the transferee to the same extent in respect of employees of that description so employed; and

    (b) any agreement for recognition may be varied or rescinded accordingly.

[1145]

10 Duty to inform and consult trade union representatives.

(1) In this Regulation and Regulation 11 below "an affected employee" means, in relation to a relevant transfer, any employee of the transferor or the transferee (whether or not employed in the undertaking or the part of the undertaking to be transferred) who may be affected by the transfer or may be affected by measures taken in connection with it; and references to the employer shall be construed accordingly.

(2) Long enough before a relevant transfer to enable consultations to take place between the employer of any affected employees of a description in respect of which an independent trade union is recognised by him and that union's representatives, the employer shall inform those representatives of—

    (a) the fact that the relevant transfer is to take place, when, approximately, it is to take place and the reasons for it; and

    (b) the legal, economic and social implications of the transfer for the affected employees; and

    (c) the measures which he envisages he will, in connection with the transfer, take in relation to those employees or, if he envisages that no measures will be so taken, that fact; and

    (d) if the employer is the transferor, the measures which the transferee envisages he will, in connection with the transfer, take in relation to such of those employees as, by virtue of Regulation 5 above, become employees of the transferee after the transfer or, if he envisages that no measures will be so taken, that fact.

(3) The transferee shall give the transferor such information at such a time as will enable the transferor to perform the duty imposed on him by virtue of paragraph (2)(d) above.

(4) The information which is to be given to the representatives of a trade union under this Regulation shall be delivered to them, or sent by post to an address notified by them to the employer, or sent by post to the union at the address of its head or main office.

(5) Where an employer of any affected employees envisages that he will, in connection with the transfer, be taking measures in relation to any such employees of a description in respect of which an independent trade union is recognised by him, he shall enter into consultations with the representatives of that union [with a view to seeking their agreement to measures to be taken].

(6) In the course of those consultations the employer shall—

    (a) consider any representations made by the trade union representatives; and

    (b) reply to those representations and, if he rejects any of those representations, state his reasons.

(7) If in any case there are special circumstances which render it not reasonably practicable for an employer to perform a duty imposed on him by any of the foregoing paragraphs, he shall take all such steps towards performing that duty as are reasonably practicable in the circumstances.   **[1146]**

NOTE

Para (5): words in square brackets inserted by the Trade Union Reform and Employment Rights Act 1993, s 33(1), (6), as from 30 August 1993 (SI 1993/1908, below, para **[1435]**).

11 Failure to inform or consult

(1) A complaint that an employer has failed to inform or consult a representative of a trade union in accordance with Regulation 10 above may be presented to an industrial tribunal by that union.

(2) If on a complaint under paragraph (1) above a question arises whether or not it was reasonably practicable for an employer to perform a particular duty or what steps he took towards performing it, it shall be for him to show—

(a) that there were special circumstances which rendered it not reasonably practicable for him to perform the duty; and

(b) that he took all such steps towards its performance as were reasonably practicable in those circumstances.

(3) On any such complaint against a transferor that he had failed to perform the duty imposed upon him by virtue of paragraph (2)(d) or, so far as relating thereto, paragraph (7) of Regulation 10 above, he may not show that it was not reasonably practicable for him to perform the duty in question for the reason that the transferee had failed to give him the requisite information at the requisite time in accordance with Regulation 10(3) above unless he gives the transferee notice of his intention to show that fact; and the giving of the notice shall make the transferee a party to the proceedings.

(4) Where the tribunal finds a complaint under paragraph (1) above well-founded it shall make a declaration to that effect and may—

(a) order the employer to pay appropriate compensation to such descriptions of affected employees as may be specified in the award; or

(b) if the complaint is that the transferor did not perform the duty mentioned in paragraph (3) above and the transferor (after giving due notice) shows the facts so mentioned, order the transferee to pay appropriate compensation to such descriptions of affected employees as may be specified in the award.

(5) An employee may present a complaint to an industrial tribunal on the ground that he is an employee of a description to which an order under paragraph (4) above relates and that the transferor or the transferee has failed, wholly or in part, to pay him compensation in pursuance of the order.

(6) Where the tribunal finds a complaint under paragraph (5) above well-founded it shall order the employer to pay the complainant the amount of compensation which it finds is due to him.

(7) Where an employer, in failing to perform a duty under Regulation 10 above, also fails to comply with the requirements of section 99 of the 1975 Act or Article 49 of the 1976 Order (duty of employer to consult trade union representatives on redundancy)—

(a) any compensation awarded to an employee under this Regulation shall go to reduce the amount of remuneration payable to him under a protective

award subsequently made under Part IV of that Act or Part IV of that Order and shall also go towards discharging any liability of the employer under, or in respect of a breach of, the contract of employment in respect of a period falling within the protected period under that award; and

(b) *conversely any remuneration so payable and any payment made to the employee by the employer under, or by way of damages for breach of, that contract in respect of a period falling within the protected period shall go to reduce the amount of any compensation which may be subsequently awarded under this Regulation;*

but this paragraph shall be without prejudice to section 102(3) of that Act and Article 52(3) of that Order (avoidance of duplication of contractual payments and remuneration under protective awards).

(8) An industrial tribunal shall not consider a complaint under paragraph (1) or (5) above unless it is presented to the tribunal before the end of the period of three months beginning with—

(a) the date on which the relevant transfer is completed, in the case of a complaint under paragraph (1);

(b) the date of the tribunal's order under paragraph (4) above, in the case of a complaint under paragraph (5);

or within such further period as the tribunal considers reasonable in a case where it is satisfied that it was not reasonably practicable for the complaint to be presented before the end of the period of three months.

(9) Section 129 of the 1978 Act (complaint to be sole remedy for breach of relevant rights) and section 133 of that Act (functions of conciliation officer) and Articles 58(2) and 62 of the 1976 Order (which make corresponding provision for Northern Ireland) shall apply to the rights conferred by this Regulation and to proceedings under this Regulation as they apply to the rights conferred by that Act or that Order and the industrial tribunal proceedings mentioned therein.

(10) An appeal shall lie and shall lie only to the Employment Appeal Tribunal on a question of law arising from any decision of, or arising in any proceedings before, an industrial tribunal under or by virtue of these Regulations; and section 13(1) of the Tribunals and Inquiries Act 1971 (appeal from certain tribunals to the High Court) shall not apply in relation to any such proceedings.

(11) In this Regulation "appropriate compensation" means such sum not exceeding *two weeks' pay* [four weeks' pay] for the employee in question as the tribunal considers just and equitable having regard to the seriousness of the failure of the employer to comply with his duty.

(12) Schedule 14 to the 1978 Act or, in Northern Ireland, Schedule 2 to the 1976 Order shall apply for calculating the amount of a week's pay for any employee for the purposes of paragraph (11) above; and, for the purposes of that calculation, the calculation date shall be—

(a) in the case of an employee who is dismissed by reason of redundancy (within the meaning of section 81 of the 1978 Act or, in Northern Ireland, section 11 of the Contracts of Employment and Redundancy Payments Act (Northern Ireland) 1965) the date which is the calculation date for the purposes of any entitlement of his to a redundancy payment (within the meaning of that section) or which would be that calculation date if he were so entitled;

(b) in the case of an employee who is dismissed for any other reason, the effective date of termination (within the meaning of section 55 of the 1978

Act or, in Northern Ireland, Article 21 of the 1976 Order) of his contract of employment;

(c) in any other case, the date of the transfer in question.　　　**[1147]**

NOTES
Para (7): repealed by the Trade Union Reform and Employment Rights Act 1993, ss 33(1), (7)(a), 51, Sch 10, as from 30 August 1993 (SI 1993/1908, below, para **[1435]**).
Para (11): words in square brackets substituted for the preceding words in italics by the Trade Union Reform and Employment Rights Act 1993, s 33(1), (7)(b), as from 30 August 1993 (SI 1993/1908, below, para **[1435]**).

12 Restriction on contracting out

Any provision of any agreement (whether a contract of employment or not) shall be void in so far as it purports to exclude or limit the operation of Regulation 5, 8 or 10 above or to preclude any person from presenting a complaint to an industrial tribunal under Regulation 11 above.　　　**[1148]**

13 Exclusion of employment abroad or as dock worker

(1) Regulations 8, 10 and 11 of these Regulations do not apply to employment where under his contract of employment the employee ordinarily works outside the United Kingdom.

(2) For the purposes of this Regulation a person employed to work on board a ship registered in the United Kingdom shall, unless—

(a) the employment is wholly outside the United Kingdom, or

(b) he is not ordinarily resident in the United Kingdom,

be regarded as a person who under his contract ordinarily works in the United Kingdom.

(3), (4) ...　　　**[1149]**

NOTE
Paras (3), (4): revoked by the Dock Work Act 1989, s 7(2).

14 (*Amends the Employment Protection (Consolidation) Act 1978, s 4(4), and equivalent Northern Ireland legislation.*)

STATUTORY SICK PAY (GENERAL) REGULATIONS 1982
(SI 1982/894)

NOTES
Made: 30 June 1982.
Authority: Social Security and Housing Benefits Act 1982, ss 1(3), (4), 3(5), (7), 4(2), 5(5), 6(1), 8(1)–(3), 17(4), 18(1), 20, 26(1), (3)–(5), Sch 1, para 1, Sch 2, paras 2(3), 3(2) (see now the Social Security Contributions and Benefits Act 1992, Pt XI).

ARRANGEMENT OF REGULATIONS

1 Citation, commencement and interpretation

(1) These regulations may be cited as the Statutory Sick Pay (General) Regulations 1982, and shall come into operation on 6th April 1983.

(2) In these regulations—

"the Act" means the Social Security and Housing Benefits Act 1982;
["the Contributions and Benefits Act" means the Social Security Contributions and Benefits Act 1992;]
"Part I" means Part I of the Act;

and other expressions, unless the context otherwise requires, have the same meanings as in Part I.

(3) Unless the context otherwise requires, any reference—

(a)   in these regulations to a numbered section or Schedule is a reference to the section or Schedule, as the case may be, of or to the Act bearing that number;

(b)   in these regulations to a numbered regulation is a reference to the regulation bearing that number in these regulations; and

(c)   in any of these regulations to a numbered paragraph is a reference to the paragraph bearing that number in that regulation.   **[1150]**

NOTE

Para (2): definition "the Contributions and Benefits Act" added by the Social Security (Miscellaneous Provisions) Amendment Regulations 1992, SI 1992/2595, reg 14.

2 Persons deemed incapable of work

(1) A person who is not incapable of work of which he can reasonably be expected to do under a particular contract of service may be deemed to be incapable of work of such a kind by reason of some specific disease or bodily or mental disablement for any day on which either—

(a)   (i) he is under medical care in respect of a disease or disablement as aforesaid,

(ii) it is stated by a registered medical practitioner that for precautionary or convalescent reasons consequential on such disease or disablement

he should abstain from work, or from work of such a kind, and
(iii) he does not work under that contract of service, or

(b) he is excluded from work, or from work of such a kind, on the certificate of a Medical Officer for Environmental Health and is under medical observation by reason of his being a carrier, or having been in contact with a case, of infectious disease.

(2) A person who at the commencement of any day is, or thereafter on that day becomes, incapable of work of such a kind by reason of some specific disease or bodily or mental disablement, and

(a) on that day, under that contract of service, does no work, or no work except during a shift which ends on that day having begun on the previous day; and

(b) does no work under that contract of service during a shift which begins on that day and ends on the next,

shall be deemed to be incapable of work of such a kind by reason of that disease or bodily or mental disablement throughout that day. **[1151]**

2A (Amends the Social Security and Housing Benefits Act 1982, s 2(3).)

3 Period of entitlement ending or not arising

(1) In a case where an employee is detained in legal custody or sentenced to a term of imprisonment (except where the sentence is suspended) on a day which in relation to him falls within a period of entitlement, that period shall end with that day.

(2) A period of entitlement shall not arise in relation to a period of incapacity for work where at any time on the first day of that period of incapacity for work the employee in question is in legal custody or sentenced to or undergoing a term of imprisonment (except where the sentence is suspended).

[(3) A period of entitlement as between an employee and his employer shall end after 3 years if it has not otherwise ended in accordance with section 3(2) of the 1982 Act or with regulations (other than this paragraph) made under section 3(5) of that Act.]

[(4) Where a period of entitlement is current as between an employee and her employer and the employee—

(a) is or was pregnant;
(b) has reached or been confined before reaching the day immediately preceding the 6th week before the expected week of confinement, and
(c) is not by virtue of that pregnancy or confinement entitled to statutory maternity pay under Part V of the Social Security Act 1986 or to maternity allowance under section 22 of the Social Security Act 1975,

the period of entitlement shall end on that day, or if earlier, on the day she was confined.

(5) Where an employee—

(a) has been confined or has reached the beginning of the 6th week before the expected week of her confinement, and
(b) is not either by virtue of or in expectation of that confinement entitled to statutory maternity pay under Part V of the Social Security Act 1986 or to maternity allowance under section 22 of the Social Security Act 1975,

a period of entitlement as between her and her employer shall not arise in relation to a period of incapacity for work where the first day in that period falls within 18 weeks of the beginning of the 6th week before her expected week of confinement, or if earlier, of the week in which she was confined.

(6) In paragraphs (4) and (5) "confinement" and "confined" have the same meanings as in section 50 of the Social Security Act 1986.] **[1152]**

NOTES

Para (3): inserted by the Statutory Sick Pay (General) Amendment Regulations 1986, SI 1986/477, reg 3.

Paras (4)–(6): added by the Statutory Sick Pay (General) Amendment (No 2) Regulations 1987, SI 1987/868, reg 2.

"Section 3(2) and (5) of the 1982 Act": see now the Social Security Contributions and Benefits Act 1992, s 153(2), (6), (7).

"Section 22 of the Social Security Act 1975": see now the Social Security Contributions and Benefits Act 1992, s 35.

"Part V of the Social Security Act 1986": see now the Social Security Contributions and Benefits Act 1992, Pt XII.

"Section 5 of the Social Security Act 1986": see now the Social Security Contributions and Benefits Act 1992, ss 35(6), 171.

[3A Maximum entitlement to Statutory Sick Pay in a period of entitlement

(1) For the purpose of determining whether an employee's maximum entitlement to statutory sick pay has been reached in a period of entitlement as between him and an employer of his, days falling within a previous period of entitlement as between the employee and any person who is or has in the past been an employer of his are, subject to paragraph (3), to be counted in the circumstances specified in paragraph (2).

(2) The circumstances specified for the purpose of paragraph (1) are—

(a) the period of entitlement as between the employee and his employer arose not more than 8 weeks after the last day in respect of which a person who is or has in the past been an employer of his was liable to make to him a payment of statutory sick pay; and either

(b) the employee has provided his employer with a statement issued in accordance with regulation 15A by a previous employer of his—

(i) on or before the seventh day after the first qualifying day in the period of entitlement, or

(ii) within such longer period as the employer may require,

so however that where an employee shows good cause for delay in providing the statement, he may provide it later than the time specified in heads (i) and (ii) above but not later than the ninety-first day after the first qualifying day in the period of entitlement; or

(c) the employer has himself issued such a statement to the employee.

(3) Where an employee provides his employer with more than one statement or the employer himself issued more than one statement such as is referred to in paragraph (2), the employer shall have regard to one only of those statements and if the number of weeks specified in the statements is not the same he shall have regard to the statement which specifies the greatest number of weeks.

(4) For the purposes of paragraph (2)(b) a statement enclosed in an envelope which is properly addressed and sent by prepaid post shall be deemed to have been provided on the day which it was posted.

(5) The employer shall return the statement to the employee where—

(a) a period of entitlement does not arise as between the employee and his employer, or

(b) the employee leaves his employment with the employer within eight weeks of its commencement, and the employer is not himself required to provide the employee with a statement in accordance with regulation 15A,

and in such cases regulation 13(2) shall not apply to him.]   **[1153]**

NOTE
  Inserted by SI 1986/477, reg 4.

4 Contract of service ended for the purpose of avoiding liability for statutory sick pay

(1) The provisions of this regulation apply in any case where an employer's contract of service with an employee is brought to an end by the employer solely or mainly for the purpose of avoiding liability for statutory sick pay.

(2) Where a period of entitlement is current on the day on which the contract is brought to an end, the employer shall be liable to pay statutory sick pay to the employee until the occurrence of an event which, if the contract had still been current, would have caused the period of entitlement to come to an end under section 3(2)(a), (b) or (d) or regulation 3(1) [of these regulations or regulation 10(2) of the Statutory Sick Pay (Mariners, Airmen and Persons Abroad) Regulations 1982], or (if earlier) until the date on which the contract would have expired.   **[1154]**

NOTE
  Para (2): words in square brackets inserted by the Statutory Sick Pay (Mariners, Airmen and Persons Abroad) Regulations 1982, SI 1982/1349, reg 10(3).

5 Qualifying days

(1) In this regulation "week" means a period of 7 consecutive days beginning with Sunday.

(2) Where an employee and an employer of his have not agreed which day or days in any week are or were qualifying days [or where in any week the only day or days are or were such as are referred to in paragraph (3)], the qualifying day or days in that week shall be—

(a) the day or days on which it is agreed between the employer and the employee that the employee is or was required to work (if not incapable) for that employer or, if it is so agreed that there is or was no such day,

(b) the Wednesday, or, if there is no such agreement between the employer and employee as mentioned in sub-paragraph (a),

(c) every day, except that or those (if any) on which it is agreed between the employer and the employee that none of that employer's employees are or were required to work (any agreement that all days are or were such days being ignored).

[(3) No effect shall be given to any agreement between an employee and his employer to treat as qualifying days—

(a) any day where the day is identified, whether expressly or otherwise, by reference to that or another day being a day of incapacity for work in relation to the employee's contract of service with an employer;

(b) any day identified, whether expressly or otherwise, by reference to a period of entitlement or to a period of incapacity for work.]   **[1155]**

NOTES
  Para (2): words in square brackets inserted by the Statutory Sick Pay (General) Amendment Regulations 1985, SI 1985/126, reg 2.
  Para (3): added by SI 1985/126, reg 2.

6 Calculation of entitlement limit

(1) Where an employee's entitlement to statutory sick pay is calculated by reference to different weekly rates in the same period of entitlement . . ., the entitlement limit shall be calculated in the manner described in paragraphs (2) and (3), or, as the case may be, (4) and (5); and where a number referred to in paragraph (2)(b) or (d) or (4)(a)(ii) or (d)(ii) is not a whole number [of thousandths, it shall be rounded up to the next thousandth].

(2) For the purpose of determining whether an employee has reached his maximum entitlement to statutory sick pay in respect of a period of entitlement, there shall be calculated—

    (a) the amount of statutory sick pay to which the employee became entitled during the part of the period of entitlement before the change in the weekly rate;

    (b) the number by which the weekly rate (before the change) must be multiplied in order to produce the amount mentioned in sub-paragraph (a);

    (c) the amount of statutory sick pay to which the employee has so far become entitled during the part of the period of entitlement after the change in the weekly rate; and

    (d) the number by which the weekly rate (after the change) must be multiplied in order to produce the amount mentioned in sub-paragraph (c);

    (e) the sum of the amounts mentioned in sub-paragraphs (a) and (c); and

    (f) the sum of the numbers mentioned in sub-paragraphs (b) and (d).

(3) When the sum mentioned in paragraph (2)(f) reaches [28], the sum mentioned in paragraph (2)(e) reaches the entitlement limit.

    (4), (5) . . . **[1156]**

NOTES

    Para (1): words omitted revoked by SI 1986/477, reg 9; words in square brackets substituted by the Statutory Sick Pay (General) Amendment Regulations 1984, SI 1984/385, reg 2.

    Para (3): number in square brackets substituted by SI 1986/477, reg 9.

    Paras (4), (5): revoked by SI 1986/477, reg 9.

7 Time and manner of notification of incapacity for work

(1) Subject to paragraph (2), notice of any day of incapacity for work shall be given by or on behalf of an employee to his employer—

    (a) in a case where the employer has decided on a time limit (not being one which requires the notice to be given earlier than . . . the first qualifying day in the period of incapacity for work which includes that day of incapacity for work [or by a specified time during that qualifying day]) and taken reasonable steps to make it known to the employee, within that time limit; and

    (b) in any other case, on or before the seventh day after that day of incapacity for work.

(2) Notice of any day of incapacity for work may be given later than as provided by paragraph (1) where there is good cause for giving it later, so however that it shall in any event be given on or before the 91st day after that day.

(3) A notice contained in a letter which is properly addressed and sent by prepaid post shall be deemed to have been given on the day on which it was posted.

(4) Notice of any day of incapacity for work shall be given by or on behalf of an employee to his employer—

(a) in a case where the employer has decided on a manner in which it is to be given (not being a manner which imposes a requirement such as is specified in paragraph (5)) and taken reasonable steps to make it known to the employee, in that manner; and

(b) in any other case, in any manner, so however that unless otherwise agreed between the employer and employee it shall be given in writing.

(5) The requirements mentioned in paragraph (4)(a) are that notice shall be given—

(a) personally;
(b) in the form of medical evidence;
(c) more than one in every 7 days during a period of entitlement;
(d) on a document supplied by the employer; or
(e) on a printed form.   **[1157]**

NOTE
    Para (1): words omitted revoked and words in square brackets inserted by SI 1984/385, reg 2.

8 Manner in which statutory sick pay may not be paid

Statutory sick pay may not be paid in kind or by way of the provision of board or lodging or of services or other facilities.   **[1158]**

9 Time limits for paying statutory sick pay

(1) In this regulation, "pay day" means a day on which it has been agreed, or it is the normal practice, between an employer and an employee of his, that payments by way of remuneration are to be made, or, where there is no such agreement or normal practice, the last day of a calendar month.

(2) In any case where—

(a) a decision has been made by an insurance officer, local tribunal or Commissioner in proceedings under Part I that an employee is entitled to an amount of statutory sick pay; and

(b) the time for bringing an appeal against the decision has expired and either—
    (i) no such appeal has been brought; or
    (ii) such an appeal has been brought and has been finally disposed of,

that amount of statutory sick pay is to be paid within the time specified in paragraph (3).

(3) Subject to paragraphs (4) and (5), the employer is required to pay the amount not later than the first pay day after—

(a) where an appeal has been brought, the day on which the employer receives notification that it has been finally disposed of;

(b) where leave to appeal has been refused and there remains no further opportunity to apply for leave, the day on which the employer receives notification of the refusal; and

(c) in any other case, the day on which the time for bringing an appeal expires.

(4) Subject to paragraph (5), where it is impracticable, in view of the employer's methods of accounting for and paying remuneration, for the requirement of payment referred to in paragraph (3) to be met by the pay day referred to in that paragraph, it shall be met not later than the next following pay day.

(5) Where the employer would not have remunerated the employee for his work on the day of incapacity for work in question (if it had not been a day of incapacity for work) as early as the pay day specified in paragraph (3) or (if it applies) paragraph (4), the requirement of payment shall be met on the first day on which the employee would have been remunerated for his work on that day. **[1159]**

[9A Liability of the Secretary of State for payments of statutory sick pay

(1) Notwithstanding the provisions of section 1 of the Act and subject to paragraph (4), where—

(a)   an adjudicating authority has determined that an employer is liable to make payments of statutory sick pay to an employee, and
(b)   the time for appealing against that determination has expired, and
(c)   no appeal against the determination has been lodged or leave to appeal against the determination is required and has been refused,

then for any day of incapacity for work in respect of which it was determined the employer was liable to make those payments, and for any further days of incapacity for work which fall within the same spell of incapacity for work and in respect of which the employer was liable to make payments of statutory sick pay to that employee, the liability to make payments of statutory sick pay in respect of those days shall, to the extent that payment has not been made by the employer, be that of the Secretary of State and not the employer.

(2) For the purposes of this regulation a spell of incapacity for work consists of consecutive days of incapacity for work with no day of the week disregarded.

(3) In paragraph (1) above "adjudicating authority" means, as the case may be, the Chief or other adjudication officer, a Social Security Appeal Tribunal or the Chief or any other Social Security Commissioner.

(4) This regulation shall not apply to any liability of an employer to make a payment of statutory sick pay where the day of incapacity for work in respect of which the liability arose falls within a period of entitlement which commenced before 6th April 1987.] **[1160]**

NOTE
Inserted by the Statutory Sick Pay (General) Amendment Regulations 1987, SI 1987/372, reg 2.

[9B Insolvency of employer

(1) Notwithstanding the provisions of section 1 of the Act and subject to paragraph (3), any liability arising under Part I of the Act to make a payment of statutory sick pay in respect of a day of incapacity for work in relation to an employee's contract of service with his employer shall be that of the Secretary of State and not that of the employer where the employer is insolvent on that day.

(2) For the purposes of paragraph (1) an employer shall be taken to be insolvent if, and only if—

(a)   in England and Wales—
  (i) he has been adjudged bankrupt or has made a composition or arrangement with his creditors;
  (ii) he has died and his estate falls to be administered in accordance with an order under section 421 of the Insolvency Act 1986; or
  (iii) where an employer is a company, a winding-up order or an administration order is made or a resolution for voluntary winding-up

is passed with respect to it, or a receiver or manager of its undertaking is duly appointed, or possession is taken by or on behalf of the holders of any debentures secured by a floating charge, or any property of the company comprised in or subject to the charge or a voluntary arrangement proposed for the purposes of Part I of the Insolvency Act 1986 is approved under that Part;

   (b) in Scotland—

      (i) an award of sequestration is made on his estate or he executes a trust deed for his creditors or enters into a composition contract;

     (ii) he has died and a judicial factor appointed under section 11A of the Judicial Factors (Scotland) Act 1889 is required by that section to divide his insolvent estate among his creditors; or

    (iii) where the employer is a company, a winding-up order or an administration order is made or a resolution for voluntary winding-up is passed with respect to it or a receiver of its undertaking is duly appointed or a voluntary arrangement proposed for the purposes of Part I of the Insolvency Act 1986 is approved under that Part.

(3) This regulation shall not apply where the employer became insolvent before 6th April 1987.]   **[1161]**

NOTE
Inserted by SI 1987/372, reg 2.

[9C Payments by the Secretary of State

Where the Secretary of State becomes liable in accordance with regulation 9A or 9B to make payments of statutory sick pay to a person, the first payment shall be made as soon as reasonably practicable after he becomes so liable, and payments thereafter shall be made at weekly intervals, by means of an instrument of payment or by such other means as appears to the Secretary of State to be appropriate in the circumstances of the particular case.]   **[1162]**

NOTE
Inserted by SI 1987/372, reg 2.

10 Persons unable to act

(1) Where in the case of any employee—

   (a) statutory sick pay is payable to him or he is alleged to be entitled to it;

   (b) he is unable for the time being to act; and

   (c) either—

      (i) no receiver has been appointed by the Court of Protection with power to receive statutory sick pay on his behalf, or

     (ii) in Scotland, his estate is not being administered by any tutor, curator or other guardian acting or appointed in terms of law,

the Secretary of State may, upon written application to him by a person who, if a natural person, is over the age of 18, appoint that person to exercise, on behalf of the employee, any right to which he may be entitled under Part I and to deal on his behalf with any sums payable to him.

(2) Where the Secretary of State has made an appointment under paragraph (1)—

   (a) he may at any time in his absolute discretion revoke it;

   (b) the person appointed may resign his office after having given one month's notice in writing to the Secretary of State of his intention to do so; and

   (c) the appointment shall terminate when the Secretary of State is notified that a receiver or other person to whom paragraph (1)(c) applies has been appointed.

(3) Anything required by Part I to be done by or to any employee who is unable to act may be done by or to the person appointed under this regulation to act on his behalf, and the receipt of the person so appointed shall be a good discharge to the employee's employer for any sum paid. **[1163]**

11 Rounding to avoid fractional amounts

Where any payment of statutory sick pay is made and the statutory sick pay due for the period for which the payment purports to be made includes a fraction of a penny, the payment shall be rounded up to the next whole number of pence. **[1164]**

12 Days not to be treated as, or as parts of, periods of interruption of employment

In a case to which paragraph 3 of Schedule 2 applies, the day of incapacity for work mentioned in sub-paragraph (1)(b) of that paragraph shall not be, or form part of, a period of interruption of employment where it is a day which, by virtue of section 17(1) or (2) of the Social Security Act 1975 or any regulations made thereunder, is not to be treated as a day of incapacity for work. **[1165]**

NOTE

"Section 17(1) or (2) of the Social Security Act 1975": see now the Social Security Contributions and Benefits Act 1992, s 57(1), (3).

13 Records to be maintained by employers

[(1)] Every employer shall maintain for 3 years after the end of each tax year a record, in relation to each employee of his, of—

  (a) any day in that tax year which was one of 4 or more consecutive days on which, according to information supplied by or on behalf of the employee, the employee was incapable by reason of some specific disease or bodily or mental disablement of doing work which he could reasonably be expected to do under any contract of service between him and the employer, whether or not he would normally have been expected to work on that day;

  (b) any day recorded under paragraph (a) for which the employer did not pay statutory sick pay to the employee;

  (c) the reason why he did not; and

  (d) the days which were qualifying days as between that employer and that employee in each period of entitlement which fell wholly or partly in that tax year.

[(2) Subject to the following provisions of this regulation, and to regulation 3A(5), where an employee has a period of incapacity for work in relation to his contract of service with his employer, then that employer shall retain any statement which

  (a) was provided by the employee, and

  (b) was issued to that employee in accordance with regulation 15A by a person who was his employer.

(3) An employer who issues a statement to an employee in accordance with regulation 15A shall retain a complete copy of that statement.

(4) Where the whole of the information contained on the written statement referred to in paragraph (2) or (3) above is also recorded in a form in which it can be processed by equipment operating automatically in response to instructions given for that purpose, the employer may retain that record instead of the written statement.

(5) The statement or, as the case may be, information retained by the employer in accordance with paragraphs (2) to (4) above shall be retained by him for 3 years after the end of the tax year to which the information relates.] **[1166]**

NOTE

Para (1): regulation numbered para (1), and paras (2)–(5) added, by SI 1986/477, reg 5.

14 Provision of information in connection with determination of questions

Any person claiming to be entitled to statutory sick pay, or any other person who is a party to proceedings arising under Part I, shall, if he receives notification from the Secretary of State that any information is required from him for the determination of any question arising in connection therewith, furnish that information to the Secretary of State within 10 days of receiving that notification. **[1167]**

15 Provision of information by employers to employees

(1) In a case which falls within paragraph (a), (b) or (c) of section 18(3) (provision of information by employers in connection with the making of claims for sickness and other benefits), the employer shall furnish to his employee, in writing on a form approved by the Secretary of State for the purpose, the information specified in paragraph (2), (3) or (4) below respectively within the time specified in the appropriate one of those paragraphs.

(2) In a case which falls within paragraph (a) (no period of entitlement arising in relation to a period of incapacity for work) of section 18(3)—

   (a) the information mentioned in paragraph (1) is a statement of all the reasons why, under the provisions of paragraph 1 of Schedule 1 and regulations made thereunder, a period of entitlement does not arise; and

   (b) it shall be furnished not more than 7 days after the day on which the employer is notified by or on behalf of the employee of the employee's incapacity for work on the fourth day of the period of incapacity for work.

(3) In a case which falls within paragraph (b) (period of entitlement ending but period of incapacity for work continuing) of section 18(3)—

   [(a) the information mentioned in paragraph (1) above is a statement informing the employee of—

     (i) the reason why the period of entitlement ended;

     (ii) the date of the first day in the period of entitlement or where the employer has taken into account days falling within a previous period of entitlement as between the employee and a person who is or was an employer of his, the date of the first day in that previous period of entitlement;

     (iii) the date of the last day in respect of which the employer is or was liable to make a payment of statutory sick pay to him;

     (iv) the number of qualifying days falling within the last week (beginning with Sunday) in the period of entitlement in which the employer is or was liable to make to him a payment of statutory sick pay; and either

     (v) where the period of entitlement ends otherwise than by virtue of section 3(2)(b) of the Act, the number of weeks (a week being 7 days beginning with Sunday) and days in respect of which the employer was liable to make a payment of statutory sick pay to him in that period of entitlement; or

(vi) where the period of entitlement ends otherwise than by virtue of section 3(2)(b) of the Act and where the employee provided the employer with a statement issued to him in accordance with regulation 15A by a person who is or was an employer of his, the number of weeks (a week being 7 days beginning with Sunday) and days in respect of which he and the previous employer were together liable to make a payment of statutory sick pay to him; and

(b) the statement shall be furnished not more than 7 days after the day on which the period of entitlement ended, or if earlier, on the day on which it is already required to be furnished under paragraph (4).]

(4) In a case which falls within paragraph (c) (period of entitlement expected to end before period of incapacity for work ends, on certain assumptions) of section 18(3)—

[(a) the information mentioned in paragraph (1) above is a statement informing the employee of

(i) the reason why the period of entitlement is expected to end;

(ii) the date of the first day in the period of entitlement or where the employer has taken into account days of incapacity for work in a previous period of entitlement as between the employee and a person who is or was an employer of his, the date of the first day in that previous period of entitlement;

(iii) the date of the last day in respect of which the employer is or was expected to be liable to make a payment of statutory sick pay to him;

(iv) the number of qualifying days falling within the last week (beginning with Sunday) in the period of entitlement in which the employer is or was expected to be liable to make to him a payment of statutory sick pay; and either

(v) where the period of entitlement is expected to end otherwise than by virtue of section 3(2)(b) of the Act, the number of weeks (a week being 7 days beginning with Sunday) and days in respect of which the employer will have been liable to make a payment of statutory sick pay to him in that period of entitlement; or

(vi) where the period of entitlement is expected to end otherwise than by virtue of section 3(2)(b) of the Act and where the employee provided the employer with a statement issued to him in accordance with regulation 15A by a person who is or was an employer of his, the number of weeks (a week being 7 days beginning with Sunday) and days in respect of which he and the previous employer were together liable to make a payment of statutory sick pay to him; and

(b) the statement shall be furnished—

(i) in a case where the period of entitlement is expected to end in accordance with section 3(2)(b) of the Act (maximum entitled to statutory sick pay), on or before the 42nd day before the period of entitlement is expected to end, or

(ii) in any other case, on or before the seventh day before the period of entitlement is expected to end,

or, if later, the seventh day after the first day on which the employer could have known that the circumstances mentioned in paragraph (c) of section 18(3) existed.]

(5) For the purposes of section 18(3)(c)(i) (period for which the period of incapacity for work is to be assumed to continue to run) the prescribed period shall be 14 days. **[1168]**

NOTE

Paras (3), (4): sub-paras (a), (b) substituted by SI 1986/477, reg 6.

[15A Statements relating to the payment of Statutory Sick Pay

(1) Subject to the provisions of this regulation, where

    (a) an employee is about to leave his employment with his employer, or has been employed by him in the past,

    (b) the period of entitlement as between the employee and that employer will come or has come to an end within the period of 8 weeks ending with the day on which the employee's contract of service with the employer concerned expires or is brought to an end, and

    [(c) the employer is or was liable to make a payment of statutory sick pay to the employee in respect of any week within that period, and for this purpose a week includes any days rounded up to a week in accordance with paragraph (4),]

the employer shall provide the employee with a statement in writing containing the information specified in paragraph (2) within 7 days of the employment ending.

(2) The information mentioned in paragraph (1) is—

    (a) the date of the first day of the period of entitlement;

    (b) the number of weeks (a week being 7 days beginning with Sunday) . . . in respect of which the employer was liable to make a payment of statutory sick pay to the employee in that period of entitlement;

    (c) the date of the last day in respect of which the employer was liable to make to the employee a payment of statutory sick pay;

    (d) the date the statement was made by the employer; and

    (e) the full name, address and, if there is one, telephone number of the employer making the statement.

(3) For the purposes of paragraph (2)(a) and (b) above, the period of entitlement includes any previous period of entitlement relevant for the purposes of regulation 3A (maximum entitlement to statutory sick pay in a period of entitlement).

(4) For the purposes of this regulation, where the total number of days in the period of entitlement in respect of which the employer is or was liable to make the employee a payment in respect of statutory sick pay amounts in aggregate to less than a complete week or number of weeks, then the number of weeks shall be determined by disregarding the remainder where it is 3 days or less and if it is not by rounding them up to a week.

(5) Where a question arises under Part I of the 1982 Act as to or in connection with entitlement to statutory sick pay, a written statement or, as the case may be, a revised written statement containing the information specified in paragraph (2) shall be provided by the employer to the employee within 7 days of the question being determined.

(6) A question is determined for the purpose of paragraph (5) when the time for appealing from a decision of an adjudication officer, a local tribunal or a Commissioner, as the case may be, has expired or leave to appeal has been refused.

(7) Where an employer does not have a record of an employee's place of residence and the employee does not attend his place of employment, the employer

shall retain all the information contained on the statement for 3 years after the end of the tax year to which the statement relates; so however that the employer shall issue a statement to the employee if within the period in which the information is so retained he provides the employer with the postal address of his place of residence or attends in person at his former place of employment.

(8) An employer may, at the request of a person who is or was employed by him, provide a second copy of the statement if he is satisfied that the person making the request has a need for it.] **[1169]**

NOTES
Inserted by SI 1986/477, reg 7.
Para (1): sub-para (c) substituted by SI 1987/868, reg 3(a).
Para (2): words omitted revoked by SI 1987/868, reg 3(b).

16 Meaning of "employee"

(1) In a case where, and in so far as, a person over the age of 16 is treated as an employed earner by virtue of the Social Security (Categorisation of Earners) Regulations 1978, he shall be treated as an employee for the purposes of Part I and in a case where, and in so far as, such a person is treated otherwise than as an employed earner by virtue of those regulations, he shall not be treated as an employee for the purposes of Part I.

[(1A) Any person who is in employed earner's employment within the meaning of the Social Security Act 1975 under a contract of apprenticeship shall be treated as an employee for the purposes of Part I.]

(2) A person who is in employed earner's employment within the meaning of the Social Security Act 1975 but whose employer—

    (a) does not fulfil the conditions prescribed in regulation 119(1)(b) of the Social Security (Contributions) Regulations 1979 as to residence or presence in Great Britain, or

    (b) is a person who, by reason of any international treaty to which the United Kingdom is a party or of any international convention binding the United Kingdom—

        (i) is exempt from the provisions of the Social Security Act 1975, or

        (ii) is a person against whom the provisions of that Act are not enforceable,

shall not be treated as an employee for the purposes of Part I. **[1170]**

NOTE
Para (1A): inserted by SI 1983/376, reg 5(2).

17 Meaning of "earnings"

(1) ...

[(2) For the purposes of section 163(2) of the Contributions and Benefits Act, the expression "earnings" refers to gross earnings and includes any remuneration or profit derived from a person's employment except any payment or amount which is excluded from the computation of a person's earnings under regulation 19 or 19B of the Social Security (Contributions) Regulations 1979.]

[(2A) ...]

(3) For the purposes of section 26(2) the expression "earnings" includes also—

(a) any sum payable by way of maternity pay or payable by the Secretary of State in pursuance of section 40 of the Employment Protection (Consolidation) Act 1978 in respect of maternity pay;

(b) any sum which is payable by the Secretary of State by virtue of section 122(3)(a) of that Act in respect of arrears of pay and which by virtue of section 42(1) of that Act is to go towards discharging a liability to pay maternity pay;

(c) any sum payable in respect of arrears of pay in pursuance of an order for re-instatement or re-engagement under that Act;

(d) any sum payable by way of pay in pursuance of an order under the Act for the continuation of a contract of employment;

(e) any sum payable by way of remuneration in pursuance of a protective award under the Employment Protection Act 1975;

(f) any sum payable to any employee under the Temporary Short-time Working Compensation Scheme administered under powers conferred by the Employment Subsidies Act 1978;

(g) any sum paid in satisfaction of any entitlement to statutory sick pay;

[(h) any sum payable by way of statutory maternity pay under Part V of the Social Security Act 1986, including sums payable in accordance with regulations made under section 46(8)(b) of that Act.]

(4), (5) ...   **[1171]**

NOTES

Commencement: 16 November 1992 (para (2)); 7 June 1987 (para (3)(h)); 6 April 1983 (para (3)(a)–(g)).

Paras (1), (4), (5): revoked by SI 1992/2595, reg 15.

Para (2): substituted by SI 1992/2595, reg 15.

Para (2A): inserted by the Statutory Sick Pay (Compensation of Employers) and Miscellaneous Provisions Regulations 1983, SI 1983/376, reg 5(3); revoked by SI 1992/2595, reg 15.

Para (3): sub-para (h) added by SI 1987/868, reg 4(b).

The reference in para (3), as originally enacted, to s 26(2) was to the Social Security Act 1975, s 26(2) (see now the Social Security Contributions and Benefits Act 1992, s 39(4), (5)).

"Employment Protection Act 1975": relevant provisions are now contained in the Trade Union and Labour Relations (Consolidation) Act 1992, ss 188 et seq.

"Part V of the Social Security Act 1986": see now the Social Security Contributions and Benefits Act 1992, Pt XII.

18 Payments to be treated or not to be treated as contractual remuneration

For the purposes of paragraph 2(1) and (2) of Schedule 2 to the Act, those things which are included within the expression "earnings" by regulation 17 (except paragraph (3)(g) thereof) shall be, and those things which are excluded from that expression by that regulation shall not be, treated as contractual remuneration.

[1172]

19 Normal weekly earnings

(1) For the purposes of section 26(2) and (4), an employee's normal weekly earnings shall be determined in accordance with the provisions of this regulation.

(2) In this regulation—

"the critical date" means the first day of the period of entitlement in relation to which a person's normal weekly earnings fall to be determined, or, in a case to which paragraph 2(c) of Schedule 1 applies, the relevant date within the meaning of Schedule 1;

"normal pay day" means a day on which the terms of an employee's contract of service require him to be paid, or the practice in his employment is for

him to be paid, if any payment is due to him; and
"day of payment" means a day on which the employee was paid.

(3) Subject to paragraph (4), the relevant period (referred to in section 26(2)) is the period between—

(a) the last normal pay day to fall before the critical date; and

(b) the last normal pay day to fall at least 8 weeks earlier than the normal pay day mentioned in sub-paragraph (a),

including the normal pay day mentioned in sub-paragraph (a) but excluding that first mentioned in sub-paragraph (b).

(4) In a case where an employee has no identifiable normal pay day, paragraph (3) shall have effect as if the words "day of payment" were substituted for the words "normal pay day" in each place where they occur.

(5) In a case where an employee has normal pay days at intervals of or approximating to one or more calendar months (including intervals of or approximating to a year) his normal weekly earnings shall be calculated by dividing his earnings in the relevant period by the number of calendar months in that period (or, if it is not a whole number, the nearest whole number), multiplying the result by 12 and dividing by 52.

(6) In a case to which paragraph (5) does not apply and the relevant period is not an exact number of weeks, the employee's normal weekly earnings shall be calculated by dividing his earnings in the relevant period by the number of days in the relevant period and multiplying the result by 7.

(7) In a case where the normal pay day mentioned in sub-paragraph (a) of paragraph (3) exists but that first mentioned in sub-paragraph (b) of that paragraph does not yet exist, the employee's normal weekly earnings shall be calculated as if the period for which all the earnings under his contract of service received by him before the critical date represented payment were the relevant period.

(8) In a case where neither of the normal pay days mentioned in paragraph (3) yet exists, the employee's normal weekly earnings shall be the remuneration to which he is entitled, in accordance with the terms of his contract of service, for, as the case may be—

(a) a week's work; or

(b) a number of calendar months' work, divided by that number of months, multiplied by 12 and divided by 52.   **[1173]**

20 Treatment of one or more employers as one

(1) In a case where the earnings paid to an employee in respect of 2 or more employments are aggregated and treated as a single payment of earnings under regulation 12(1) of the Social Security (Contributions) Regulations 1979, the employers of the employee in respect of those employments shall be treated as one for all purposes of Part I.

(2) Where 2 or more employers are treated as one under the provisions of paragraph (1), liability for the statutory sick pay payable by them to the employee shall be apportioned between them in such proportions as they may agree or, in default of agreement, in the proportions which the employee's earnings from each employment bear to the amount of the aggregated earnings.

(3) [Subject to paragraphs (4) and (5)] where a contract of service ("the current 'ract") was preceded by a contract of service entered into between the same

employer and employee ("the previous contract"), and the interval between the date on which the previous contract ceased to have effect and that on which the current contract came into force was not more than 8 weeks, then for the purposes of 'establishing the employee's maximum entitlement within the meaning of section 5 (limitation on entitlement to statutory sick pay in any one period of entitlement or tax year), the provisions of Part I shall not have effect as if the employer were a different employer in relation to each of those contracts of service.

[(4) Where a contract of service ("the current contract") was preceded by two or more contracts of service entered into between the same employer and employee ("the previous contracts") and the previous contracts—

(a) existed concurrently for at least part of their length, and
(b) the intervals between the dates on which each of the previous contracts ceased to have effect and that on which the current contract came into force was not more than 8 weeks,

then for the purposes of establishing the employee's maximum entitlement within the meaning of section 5 the provisions of Part I shall not have effect as if the employer were a different employer in relation to the current contract and whichever of the previous contracts was the contract by virtue of which the employer had become liable to pay the greatest proportion of statutory sick pay in respect of any tax year or period of entitlement.

(5) If, in any case to which paragraph (4) applies, the same proportion of the employer's liability for statutory sick pay becomes due under each of the previous contracts, then for the purpose of establishing the employee's maximum entitlement within the meaning of section 5, the provisions of Part I shall have effect in relation to only one of the previous contracts.]   **[1174]**

NOTES

Para (3): words in square brackets inserted by SI 1983/376, reg 3(4).
Paras (4), (5): added by SI 1983/376, reg 3(4).

21 Treatment of more than one contract of service as one

Where 2 or more contracts of service exist concurrently between one employer and one employee, they shall be treated as one for all purposes of Part I except where, by virtue of regulation 11 of the Social Security (Contributions) Regulations 1979, the earnings from those contracts of service are not aggregated for the purposes of earnings-related contributions.   **[1175]**

22 Penalties

Any person who without reasonable excuse contravenes or fails to comply with any provision of regulation 9, 13, 14 [15 or 15A] shall be guilty of an offence under Part I, and liable on summary conviction to a penalty not exceeding—

[(a) for any one offence, level 3 on the standard scale; or]
(b) for an offence of continuing any such [contravention or] failure after conviction, [£40] for each day on which it is so continued.   **[1176]**

NOTE

Words in first pair of square brackets substituted by SI 1986/477, reg 8; para (a) substituted and in para (b), words in square brackets added and sum in square brackets substituted, by the Social Security (Miscellaneous Provisions) Amendment Regulations 1992, SI 1992/247, reg 5.

STATUTORY SICK PAY (COMPENSATION OF EMPLOYERS) AND MISCELLANEOUS PROVISIONS REGULATIONS 1983

(SI 1983/376)

NOTES

Made: 11 March 1983.

Authority: Social Security and Housing Benefits Act 1982, ss 1(4), 9(1), (6), 26(1), (3), Sch 4, para 39 (see now the Social Security Contributions and Benefits Act 1992, Pt XI).

1 Citation, commencement and interpretation

(1) These regulations may be cited as the Statutory Sick Pay (Compensation of Employers) and Miscellaneous Provisions Regulations 1983, and shall come into operation on 6th April 1983.

(2) In these regulations—

"the Act" means the Social Security and Housing Benefits Act 1982;
"contributions payments" has the same meaning as in section 9 of the Act;
["income tax month" means the period beginning on the 6th day of any calendar month and ending on the 5th day of the following calendar month;]
"section 9(6)" means section 9(6) of the Act;
"regulation 2" and "regulation 3" mean regulations 2 and 3 respectively of these regulations;

and other expressions have the same meanings as in the Act.   **[1177]**

NOTE

Para (2): definition "income tax month" added by the Statutory Sick Pay Act 1991 (Consequential) Regulations 1991, SI 1991/694, reg 2(1).

2 Deductions from contributions payments

[(1) An employer who has made one or more payments of statutory sick pay in an income tax month may recover an amount equal to the sum of the aggregate of such of those payments as qualify for small employers' relief, and an amount equal to 80 per cent. of the aggregate of such of those payments as do not so qualify, by making one or more deductions from his contributions payments] except where and insofar as—

(a) the contributions payments relate to earnings paid before the beginning of the income tax month in which the payment of statutory sick pay was made;
(b) the contributions payments are made by him later than 6 years after the end of the tax year in which that payment was made;
(c) the amount of that payment has been repaid to him by or on behalf of the Secretary of State under regulation 3; or
(d) he has made a request in writing under regulation 3 that the amount of that payment be repaid to him, and he has not, or not yet, received notification by or on behalf of the Secretary of State that the request is refused.

[(2) Where any calculation of the amount specified in paragraph (1) above includes a fraction of a penny that amount shall be rounded up to the next whole number of pence.]   **[1178]**

NOTES

Commencement: 6 April 1983 (para (1)); 6 April 1991 (para (2)).

Para (1): words in square brackets substituted by SI 1991/694, reg 2(3)(a).
Para (2): added by SI 1991/694, reg 2(3)(b).

3 Payments to employers by or on behalf of the Secretary of State

[Where a sum has been paid by way of statutory sick pay by an employer, and

  (a) the employer has requested in writing the Secretary of State to repay him an amount, and

  (b) the Secretary of State is satisfied that either—

    (i) the total amount which the employer is or would otherwise be entitled to deduct under regulation 2 exceeds the total amount which the employer is liable to pay by way of primary and secondary Class 1 contributions in respect of earnings paid in an income tax month (disregarding any liability arising under the National Insurance Surcharge Act 1976), or

    (ii) the employer is not liable to pay any primary or secondary Class 1 contributions but would otherwise be entitled to deduct an amount under regulation 2,

the Secretary of State shall pay to the employer an amount in a case to which paragraph (b)(i) applies, equal to the amount of the excess, and in a case to which paragraph (b)(ii) applies, an amount equal to the amount he would otherwise be entitled to deduct under regulation 2.] **[1179]**

NOTE
Commencement: 6 April 1991.
Substituted by SI 1991/694, reg 2(4).

4 Date when certain contributions are to be treated as paid

Where an employer has made a deduction from a contributions payment under regulation 2 [of these regulations . . .], the date on which it is to be treated for the purposes of section 9(6) (amount deducted to be treated as paid and received towards discharging liability in respect of Class 1 contributions) as having been paid is—

  (a) in a case where the deduction did not extinguish the contributions payment, the date on which the remainder of the contributions payment, or, as the case may be, the first date on which any part of the remainder of the contributions payment, was paid; and

  (b) in a case where the deduction extinguished the contributions payment, the fourteenth day after the end of the income tax month during which there were paid the earnings in respect of which the contributions payment was payable. **[1180]**

NOTE
Words in square brackets added by the Statutory Sick Pay (Additional Compensation of Employers and Consequential Amendments) Regulations 1985, SI 1985/1411, reg 7; words omitted therefrom revoked by SI 1991/694, reg 2(5).

5 (*Amends SI 1982/894, regs 16, 17, 20 ante.*)

6 (*Contains transitional provisions.*)

REDUNDANCY PAYMENTS (LOCAL GOVERNMENT) (MODIFICATION) ORDER 1983
(SI 1983/1160)

NOTES
Made: 28 July 1983.
Authority: Employment Protection (Consolidation) Act 1978, ss 149(1)(b), 154(3), (4).

1 Citation, commencement and interpretation

(1) This Order may be cited as the Redundancy Payments (Local Government) (Modification) Order 1983 and shall come into operation on the fourteenth day after the day on which it is made.

(2) In this Order, unless the context otherwise requires—

   (a) "relevant event" means any event occurring on or after the coming into operation of this Order on the happening of which an employee may become entitled to a redundancy payment in accordance with the provisions of the 1978 Act [or, in relation to any person to whom this Order applies by reason of an amendment contained in the Redundancy Payments (Local Government) (Modification) (Amendment) Order 1985, any event occurring on or after the coming into operation of that Order on the happening of which an employee may become entitled to a redundancy payment in accordance with the provisions of the 1978 Act] [or, in relation to any person to whom this Order applies by reason of an amendment contained in the Redundancy Payments (Local Government) (Modification) (Amendment) Order 1988, any event occurring on or after the coming into force of that Order on the happening of which an employee may become entitled to a redundancy payment in accordance with the provisions of the 1978 Act] [or, in relation to any person to whom this Order applies by reason of an amendment contained in the Redundancy Payments (Local Government) (Modification) (Amendment) Order 1989, any event occurring on or after the coming into force of that Order on the happening of which an employee may become entitled to a redundancy payment in accordance with the provisions of the 1978 Act] [or, in relation to any person to whom this Order applies by reason of an amendment contained in the Redundancy Payments (Local Government) (Modification) (Amendment) Order 1990, any event occurring on or after the coming into force of that Order on the happening of which an employee may become entitled to a redundancy payment in accordance with the provisions of the 1978 Act] [or, in relation to any person to whom this Order applies by reason of an amendment contained in the Redundancy Payments (Local Government) (Modification) (Amendment) Order 1991, any event occurring on or after the coming into force of that Order on the happening of which an employee may become entitled to a redundancy payment in accordance with the provisions of the 1978 Act] [or, in relation to any person to whom this Order applies by reason of an amendment contained in the Education (Reorganisation in Inner London) (Redundancy Payments) (Amendment) Order 1990, any event occurring on or after the coming into force of that Order on the happening of which an employee may become entitled to a redundancy payment in accordance with the provisions of the 1978 Act] [or, in relation to any person to whom this Order applies by reason of an amendment contained in the Redundancy Payments (Local Government) (Modification) (Amendment) Order 1993, any event occurring on or after the coming into force of that Order on the happening of which an employee may become entitled to a redundancy payment in accordance with the provisions of the 1978 Act].

(b) "the 1978 Act" means the Employment Protection (Consolidation) Act 1978.   **[1181]**

NOTE

Para (2): in sub-para (a) words in first pair of square brackets added by the Redundancy Payments (Local Government) (Modification) (Amendment) Order 1985, SI 1985/1872, art 2(a); words in second pair of square brackets added by the Redundancy Payments (Local Government) (Modification) (Amendment) Order 1988, SI 1988/907, art 2(a); words in third pair of square brackets added by the Redundancy Payments (Local Government) (Modification) (Amendment) Order 1989, SI 1989/532, art 2(a); words in fourth pair of square brackets added by the Redundancy Payments (Local Government) (Modification) (Amendment) Order 1990, SI 1990/826, art 2(a); words in fifth pair of square brackets added by the Redundancy Payments (Local Government) (Modification) (Amendment) Order 1991, SI 1991/818, art 2(a); words in sixth pair of square brackets added by the Education (Reorganisation in Inner London) (Redundancy Payments) (Amendment) Order 1990, SI 1990/1432, art 3; words in final pair of square brackets added by the Redundancy Payments (Local Government) (Modification) (Amendment) Order 1993, SI 1993/784, art 2(a).

2 Application of order

This Order applies to any person who immediately before the occurrence of the relevant event is employed by an employer described in Schedule 1 to this Order, for the purposes of determining that person's entitlement to a redundancy payment under the 1978 Act and the amount of such payment.   **[1182]**

3 Application of certain redundancy payments provisions with modifications

In relation to any person to whom this Order applies the provisions of the 1978 Act mentioned in Schedule 2 to this Order shall have effect subject to the modifications specified in that Schedule.   **[1183]**

4 Transitional, supplementary and incidental provisions

(1) Any reference to the 1978 Act in any enactment shall have effect as a reference to that Act as modified by this Order in relation to persons to whom this Order applies.

(2) Any document which refers, whether specifically or by means of a general description, to an enactment which is modified by any provision of this Order shall, except so far as the context otherwise requires, be construed as referring or as including a reference, to that provision.

(3) [Subject to [paragraphs (4), (5), (6), [(7), (8), (9) and (10)]]] below] where a period of employment of a person to whom this Order applies falls to be computed in accordance with the provisions of the 1978 Act as modified by this Order, the provisions of this Order shall have effect in relation to any period whether falling wholly or partly before or after the coming into operation of this Order.

[(4) Where a period of employment of a person to whom this Order applies by reason of an amendment contained in the Redundancy Payments (Local Government) (Modification) (Amendment) Order 1985 falls to be computed in accordance with the provisions of the 1978 Act as modified by this Order, the provisions of this Order shall have effect in relation to any period whether falling wholly or partly before or after the coming into operation of that Order.]

[(5) Where a period of employment of a person to whom this Order applies by reason of an amendment contained in the Redundancy Payments (Local Government) (Modification) (Amendment) Order 1988 falls to be computed in accordance with the provisions of the 1978 Act as modified by this Order, the provisions of this Order shall have effect in relation to any period whether falling wholly or partly before or after the coming into force of that Order.]

[(6) Where a period of employment of a person to whom this Order applies by reason of an amendment contained in the Redundancy Payments (Local Government) (Modification) (Amendment) Order 1989 falls to be computed in accordance with the provisions of the 1978 Act as modified by this Order, the provisions of this Order shall have effect in relation to any period whether falling wholly or partly before or after the coming into force of that Order.]

[(7) Where a period of employment of a person to whom this Order applies by reason of an amendment contained in the Redundancy Payments (Local Government) (Modification) (Amendment) Order 1990 falls to be computed in accordance with the provisions of the 1978 Act as modified by this Order, the provisions of this Order shall have effect in relation to any period whether falling wholly or partly before or after the coming into force of that Order.]

[(8) Where a period of employment of a person to whom this Order applies by reason of an amendment contained in the Education (Reorganisation in Inner London) (Redundancy Payments) (Amendment) Order 1990 falls to be computed in accordance with the provisions of the 1978 Act as modified by this Order, the provisions of this Order shall have effect in relation to any period whether falling wholly or partly before or after the coming into force of that Order.]

[[(9)] Where a period of employment of a person to whom this Order applies by reason of an amendment contained in the Redundancy Payments (Local Government) (Modification) (Amendment) Order 1991 falls to be computed in accordance with the provisions of the 1978 Act as modified by this Order, the provisions of this Order shall have effect in relation to any period whether falling wholly or partly before or after the coming into force of that Order].

[(10) Where a period of employment of a person to whom this Order applies by reason of an amendment contained in the Redundancy Payments (Local Government) (Modification) (Amendment) Order 1993 falls to be computed in accordance with the provisions of the 1978 Act as modified by this Order, the provisions of this Order shall have effect in relation to any period whether falling wholly or partly before or after the coming into force of that Order.]   **[1184]**

NOTES

Commencement: 1 April 1993 (para (10)); 1 April 1991 (para (9)); 31 August 1990 (para (8)); 1 April 1990 (para (7)); 1 April 1989 (para (6)); 2 June 1988 (para (5)); 16 December 1985 (para (4)); 11 August 1983 (remainder).

Para (3): words in first (outer) pair of square brackets inserted by SI 1985/1872, art 2(b); words in square brackets therein substituted by SI 1990/1432, art 4; further words in square brackets therein substituted by SI 1993/784, art 2(b).

Para (4): added by SI 1985/1872, art 2(c).
Para (5): added by SI 1988/907, art 2(c).
Para (6): added by SI 1989/532, art 2(c).
Para (7): added by SI 1990/826, art 2(c).
Para (8): added by SI 1990/1432, art 5.
Para (9): added by SI 1991/818, art 2(c); renumbered (formerly para (8)) by SI 1993/784, art 2(c).
Para (10): added by SI 1993/784, art 2(d).

SCHEDULES

SCHEDULE 1

Article 2

EMPLOYMENT TO WHICH THIS ORDER APPLIES: EMPLOYERS IMMEDIATELY
BEFORE THE RELEVANT EVENT

1 A county council, the Greater London Council, a district council, a London borough council, the Common Council of the City of London, the Council of the Isles of Scilly.

2 A regional council, islands council or district council established by or under the Local Government (Scotland) Act 1973.

3 A joint board or joint body constituted by or under any enactment for the purpose of exercising the functions of two or more bodies described in paragraph 1 or 2 above, and any special planning board within the meaning of paragraph 3 of Schedule 17 to the Local Government Act 1972.

4 Any other authority or body, not specified in paragraph 1, 2 or 3 above, established by or under any enactment for the purpose of exercising the functions of, or advising, one or more of the bodies specified in paragraph 1, 2 or 3 above.

5 Any committee (including a joint committee) established by or under any enactment for the purpose of exercising the functions of, or advising, one or more of the bodies specified in paragraph 1, 2, 3 or 4 above.

6 Any two or more bodies described in paragraph 1, 2, 3, 4 or 5 above acting jointly or as a combined authority.

7 Any association which is representative of any two or more authorities described in paragraph 1 or 2 above.

8 Any committee established by one or more of the associations described in paragraph 7 above for the purpose of exercising the functions of, or advising, one or more of such associations.

9 An association which is representative of one or more of the associations described in paragraph 7 above and of another body or other bodies, and included in whose objects is the assembling and dissemination of information and advising with regard to conditions of service generally and in local government service.

10 An organisation which is representative of an association or associations described in paragraph 7 above and employee's organisations and among whose objects is the negotiation of pay and conditions of service in local government service.

11 . . .

12 A probation committee within the meaning of the Criminal Justice Act 1982.

13 A magistrates' courts committee or the Committee of Magistrates for the Inner London Area, within the meaning of the Justices of the Peace Act 1979.

14 The Commission for the New Towns.

15 The Housing Corporation.

16 A development corporation within the meaning of the New Towns Act 1981.

17 A development corporation established under section 2 of the New Towns (Scotland) Act 1968.

18 A Passenger Transport Executive established under section 9(1) of the Transport Act 1968.

19 An Urban Development Corporation established under section 135 of the Local Government Planning and Land Act 1980.

20 The English Industrial Estates Corporation established by section 8 of the Local Employment Act 1960.

21 The Welsh Development Agency.

22 The Development Board for Rural Wales.

23 The Scottish Development Agency.

24 The Scottish Special Housing Association.

25 A fire authority constituted by a combination scheme, or in Scotland an administration scheme, made under the Fire Services Act 1947.

26 A police authority, other than the Secretary of State, or a combined police authority within the meaning of the Police Act 1964 or the Police (Scotland) Act 1967, as amended by section 146 of the Local Government (Scotland) Act 1973.

27 The Central Scotland Water Development Board.

28 A river purification board established under section 135 of the Local Government (Scotland) Act 1973.

29 The governing body of a further education establishment for the time being mainly dependent for its maintenance on assistance from local education authorities, on grants under section 100(1)(b) of the Education Act 1944 or on such assistance and grants taken together.

30 The governing body of a voluntary school (within the meaning of section 9(2) of the Education Act 1944).

31 The proprietors (within the meaning of section 114(1) of the Education Act 1944) of a school for the time being recognised as a grammar school for the purposes of Regulation 4(1) of the Direct Grant Schools Regulations 1959, being a school—

    (a)   in relation to which, before 1st January 1976, the Secretary of State was satisfied as mentioned in Regulation 3(1) of the Direct Grant Grammar Schools (Cessation of Grant) Regulations 1975, and

    (b)   in the case of which grants are paid under the said Regulations of 1959 for the educational year (within the meaning of those Regulations) within which the relevant event falls either—

        (i) in respect of pupils admitted in that year, or

        (ii) if, on or after the coming into operation of this Order, Regulation 5 of the said Regulations of 1975 applies to the school by virtue of paragraph (3) thereof, in respect of any pupils.

32 The managers of a grant-aided school as defined in section 135(1) of the Education (Scotland) Act 1980.

33 The governing body of a central institution as defined in section 135(1) of the Education (Scotland) Act 1980 other than a college of agriculture.

34 The governing body of a College of Education as defined in section 135(1) of the Education (Scotland) Act 1980.

[**35** The managers, other than a local authority, of a school which before any direction made by the Secretary of State under paragraph 2(1) of Schedule 7 to the Social Work (Scotland) Act 1968 was a school which immediately before the commencement of Part III of the Social Work (Scotland) Act 1968 was approved under section 83 of the Children and Young Persons (Scotland) Act 1937 if the employee was employed by those managers at the date the direction became effective.]

36 A local valuation panel established under the General Rate Act 1967.

37 The Sports Council.

38 The Sports Council for Wales.

39 The Scottish Sports Council.

40 The Forth Road Bridge Joint Board.

41 The Tay Road Bridge Joint Board.

42 The Commission for Local Administration in England.

43 The Commission for Local Administration in Wales.

44 The Commissioner for Local Administration in Scotland.

45 The Commission for Local Authority Accounts in Scotland.

46 The Land Authority for Wales.

[47 The Inner London Education Authority, to be known as the Inner London Interim Education Authority until the abolition date as defined in section 1(2) of the Local Government Act 1985.

48 Any authority established by an order under section 10 of the Local Government Act 1985.

49 A metropolitan county police authority established by section 24 of the Local Government Act 1985.

50 The Northumbria Police Authority established by section 25 of the Local Government Act 1985, to be known as the Northumbria Interim Police Authority until the abolition date as defined in section 1(2) of the Local Government Act 1985.

51 A metropolitan county fire and civil defence authority established by section 26 of the Local Government Act 1985.

52 The London Fire and Civil Defence Authority.

53 A metropolitan county passenger transport authority established by section 28 of the Local Government Act 1985.

54 The London Residuary Body established by section 57(1)(a) of the Local Government Act 1985.

55 A residuary body established by section 57(1)(b) of the Local Government Act 1985.

56 The Board of Governors of the Museum of London.

57 In England a parish council, a common parish council, a parish meeting; in Wales, a community council.

58 The Scottish Council for Research in Education.

59 The Scottish Council for Educational Technology.]

[60 The National Advisory Body for Public Sector Higher Education.

61 The Further Education Staff College.

62 The Centre for Information on Language Teaching and Research.

63 The National Institute of Adult Continuing Education (England and Wales).

64 The Scottish Museums Council.

65 The Scottish Community Education Council.

66 The Scottish Vocational Education Council.

67 The Scottish Examination Board.

68 Newbattle Abbey College.

69 National Mobility Services Trust Limited.

70 The Board of Trustees of The National Museums and Galleries on Merseyside.

71 The South Yorkshire Pensions Authority.]

[72 A school maintained under Chapter IV of Part I of the Education Reform Act 1988 (grant maintained schools).

73 The Polytechnics and Colleges Funding Council as established by section 132 of the Education Reform Act 1988.

74 An institution falling within section 218(11) of the Education Reform Act 1988 (institutions within the Polytechnics and Colleges Funding Sector).

75 City Technology Colleges and City Colleges for the Technology of the Arts established with the agreement of the Secretary of State for Education and Science under section 105 of the Education Reform Act 1988.

76 Scottish Consultative Council on the Curriculum.

77 The Broads Authority, established under the Norfolk and Suffolk Broads Act 1988.

78 Countryside Commission for Scotland.]

[79 Scottish Homes, established under the Housing (Scotland) Act 1988.

80 The Edinburgh New Town Conservation Committee.

81 Corporate Colleges established under the Self-Governing Schools etc (Scotland) Act 1989.

82 The London Pension Fund Authority.

83 The Board of Management of a Self-Governing School as defined in section 80(1) of the Self-Governing Schools etc (Scotland) Act 1989.

84 The Horniman Public Museum and Public Park Trust.

85 The Geffrye Museum Trust.]

[86 The City Literary Institute.]

[87 The General Teaching Council for Scotland, established under the Teaching Council (Scotland) Act 1965.

88 Scottish Enterprise, established under the Enterprise and New Towns (Scotland) Act 1990.

89 The Local Government Management Board.]

[90 The Humberside Independent Care Association.

91 Quantum Care Limited.

92 A Further Education Funding Council established by section 1 of the Further and Higher Education Act 1992.

93 Further Education Corporations established under section 15 or 16 of the Further and Higher Education Act 1992 or in respect of which an order has been made under section 47 of that Act.

94 The governing body of an institution which is a designated institution for the purposes of Part I of the Further and Higher Education Act 1992 or in the case of such an institution conducted by a company, that company.

95 The Board of Management of a College of Further Education, which is managed by such a Board in terms of Part I of the Further and Higher Education (Scotland) Act 1992.

96 The governing body of a designated institution within the meaning of section 44(2) of the Further and Higher Education (Scotland) Act 1992.]   **[1185]**

NOTES
Commencement: 1 April 1993 (paras 90–96) 1 April 1991 (paras 87–89); 31 August 1990 (para 86); 1 April 1990 (paras 79–85); 1 April 1989 (paras 72–78); 2 June 1988 (paras 60–71); 16 December 1985 (paras 35, 47–49); 11 August 1983 (remainder).
Para 11: revoked by SI 1991/818, art 2(d).
Para 35: substituted by SI 1985/1872, art 2(d).
Paras 47-59: inserted by SI 1985/1872, art 2(e).
Paras 60-71: inserted by SI 1988/907, art 2(d).
Paras 72-78: inserted by SI 1989/532, art 2(d).
Paras 79-85: inserted by SI 1990/826, art 2(d).
Para 86: inserted by SI 1990/1432, art 6.
Paras 87-89: inserted (as paras 86–88) by SI 1991/818, art 2(e); substituted as paras 87–89 by SI 1993/784, art 2(e).
Paras 90–96: added by SI 1993/784, art 2(f).

SCHEDULE 2

Article 3

MODIFICATIONS TO CERTAIN REDUNDANCY PAYMENTS PROVISIONS OF THE 1978 ACT

1 Section 81 of the 1978 Act shall have effect as if:—

(a) in subsection (1) for the words "has been continuously employed for the requisite period" there were substituted the words "has been employed in relevant local government service for the requisite period" and for the words "Schedules 4, 13 and 14" there were substituted the words "Schedule 4, as modified by the Redundancy Payments (Local Government) (Modification) Order 1983, and Schedules 13 and 14";

(b) after subsection (4) there were inserted the following subsection:—

"(5) In this section and Schedule 4—

(a) "relevant local government service" means—

(i) continuous employment by an employer referred to in the Appendix to Schedule 2 to the Redundancy Payments (Local Government) (Modification) Order 1983, or

(ii) where immediately before the relevant event a person has been successively employed by two or more employers referred to in the Appendix to Schedule 2 to the said Order, such aggregate period of service with such employers as would be continuous employment if they were a single employer;

(b) "relevant event" means any event occurring on or after the coming into operation of the Redundancy Payments (Local Government) (Modification) Order 1983 on the happening of which an employee may become entitled to a redundancy payment in accordance with this Act.".

2 Section 82 of the 1978 Act shall have effect as if immediately after subsection (7) there were inserted:—

"(7A) Any reference in this section to re-engagement by the employer shall be construed as including a reference to re-engagement by any employer referred to in the Appendix to Schedule 2 to the Redundancy Payments (Local Government) (Modification) Order 1983 and any reference in this section to an offer by the employer shall be construed as including a reference to an offer made by any such employer.".

3 Section 84 of the 1978 Act shall have effect as if immediately after subsection (7) thereof there were inserted the following subsection:—

"(7A) Any reference in this section to re-engagement by the employer shall be construed as including a reference to re-engagement by any employer referred to in the Appendix to Schedule 2 to the Redundancy Payments (Local Government) (Modification) Order 1983 and any reference in this section to an offer made by the employer shall be construed as including a reference to an offer made by any such employer.".

4 Section 94(6) of the 1978 Act shall have effect as if for the words "Section 82(7) and 84(7)" there were substituted the words "Sections 82(7), 82(7A), 84(7) and 84(7A)".

5 Schedule 4 to the 1978 Act shall have effect as if for paragraph 1 there were substituted the following paragraph:—

"**1** The amount of a redundancy payment to which an employee is entitled in any case to which the Redundancy Payments (Local Government) (Modification) Order 1983 applies shall, subject to the following provisions of this Schedule, be calculated by reference to the period ending with the relevant date during which he has been employed in relevant local government service.".

6 Schedule 6 to the 1978 Act shall have effect as if in paragraph 1 for the words "Schedule 4" there were substituted the words "Schedule 4 as modified by the Redundancy Payments (Local Government) (Modification) Order 1983".

[1186]

APPENDIX

EMPLOYERS WITH WHICH EMPLOYMENT MAY CONSTITUTE RELEVANT LOCAL GOVERNMENT SERVICE

1 Any employer described in Schedule 1 whether or not in existence at the time of the relevant event.

2 The council of an administrative county, county borough, metropolitan borough or county district.

3 The council of a county, county of a city, large burgh, small burgh or district ceasing to exist after 15 May 1975.

4 Any joint board or joint body constituted by or under any enactment for the purpose of exercising the functions of two or more of the bodies described in paragraph 2 or 3 above.

5 Any other body, not specified in paragraph 2, 3 or 4 above, established by or under any enactment for the purpose of exercising the functions of, or advising, one or more of the bodies specified in paragraph 2, 3 or 4 above.

6 Any committee (including a joint committee) established by or under any enactment for the purpose of exercising the functions of, or advising, one or more of the bodies described in paragraph 2, 3, 4 or 5 above.

7 Any two or more bodies described in paragraph 2, 3, 4, 5 or 6 above acting jointly or as a combined authority.

8 Any association which was representative of any two or more bodies described in paragraph 2 or 3 above.

9 Any committee established by one or more of the associations described in paragraph 8 above for the purpose of exercising the functions of, or advising, one or more of such associations.

10 An organisation which was representative of an association or association described in paragraph 8 above and employees' organisations and among whose objects was to negotiate pay and conditions of service in local government service.

11 A local valuation panel constituted under the Local Government Act 1948.

12 A previous police authority for which Schedule 11 to the Police Act 1964 had effect or which was the police authority for an area or district which was before 1st April 1947 or after 31 March 1946 a separate police area or, in Scotland, a previous police authority for an area which was before 16 May 1975 a separate or combined police area.

13 The proprietors (within the meaning of section 114(1) of the Education Act 1944) of a school not falling within paragraph 31 of Schedule 1 which throughout the period of employment was recognised as a grammar school or, as the case may be, as a direct grant grammar school for the purposes of Regulation 4(1) of the Direct Grant Schools Regulations 1959, of Part IV of the Schools Grant Regulations 1951 or of Part IV of the Primary and Secondary Schools (Grant Conditions) Regulations 1945.

14 The managers of a school which during the period of employment was approved under section 83 of the Children and Young Persons (Scotland) Act 1937.

15 The managers of a school which during the period of employment was a grant-aided school within the meaning of section 143(1) of the Education (Scotland) Act 1946, section 145(22) of the Education (Scotland) Act 1962 or section 135(1) of the Education (Scotland) Act 1980.

16 The Secretary of State for Defence in relation only to employees in schools administered by the Service Children's Education Authority.

17 A regional water board established under section 5 of the Water (Scotland) Act 1967.

18 A river purification board established under section 2 of the Rivers (Prevention of Pollution) (Scotland) Act 1951.

19 The Scottish Industrial Estates Corporation (formerly the Industrial Estates Management Corporation for Scotland) established by section 8 of the Local Employment Act 1960.

20 The Welsh Industrial Estates Corporation (formerly the Industrial Estates Management Corporation for Wales) established by section 8 of the Local Employment Act 1960.

21 The Small Industries Council for Rural Areas of Scotland, being a company which was registered under the Companies Act and dissolved by section 15(5) of the Scottish Development Agency Act 1975.

22 A person or body of persons responsible for the management of an assisted community home within the meaning of section 36 of the Children and Young Persons Act 1969 or of an approved institution within the meaning of section 46 of that Act.

23 A development Corporation within the meaning of the New Towns Act 1946 or the New Towns Act 1965.

[**24** The managers of a school which during the period of employment was a school which immediately before the commencement of Part III of the Social Work (Scotland) Act 1968 was approved under section 83 of the Children and Young Persons (Scotland) Act 1937.]

[**25** The Scottish Technical Education Council.

26 The Scottish Business Education Council.

27 The Scottish Association for National Certificates and Diplomas.

28 The Scottish Council for Commercial, Administrative and Professional Education.

29 The Secretary of State for Education and Science, in relation only to teachers employed under contract in the European School established under Article 1 of the Statute of the European School and in schools designated as European Schools under Article 1 of the Protocol to that Statute.]

[**30** The Local Government Training Board.]   **[1187]**

NOTES
Para 24: inserted by SI 1985/1872, art 2(f).
Paras 25-29: inserted by SI 1988/907, art 2(e).
Para 30: added by SI 1991/818, art 2(f).

FUNDS FOR TRADE UNION BALLOTS REGULATIONS 1984
(SI 1984/1654)

NOTES

Made: 23 October 1984.

Authority: Employment Act 1980, s 1 (see now the Trade Union and Labour Relations (Consolidation) Act 1992, s 115).

These Regulations are prospectively revoked as from 1 April 1996 by the Funds for Trade Union Ballots Regulations (Revocation) Regulations 1993, SI 1993/233 (which contain transitional provisions as to the phasing out of payments); see paras [**1427**]–[**1431**] post.

ARRANGEMENT OF REGULATIONS

1 Citation, commencement and application

(1) These Regulations may be cited as the Funds for Trade Union Ballots Regulations 1984 and shall come into operation on 5th February 1985.

(2) ...   **[1188]**

NOTE

Prospectively revoked as from 1 April 1996 by SI 1993/233; see paras [**1427**]–[**1431**] post for transitional provisions.

Para (2): revoked by the Funds for Trade Union Ballots (Amendment) Regulations 1988, SI 1988/1123, reg 3(2).

2 *(Revoked by SI 1988/1123, reg 3(2).)*

3 Interpretation

In these Regulations—

"the 1913 Act" means the Trade Union Act 1913;

"the 1964 Act" means the Trade Union (Amalgamations, etc) Act 1964;

"the 1984 Act" means the Trade Union Act 1984;

. . . . . .
["the 1988 Act" means the Employment Act 1988];
. . . . . .
"the date of the ballot" means, in the case of a ballot in which votes may be cast on more than one day, the last of those days;
["overseas member" has the meaning given in section 9(1) of the 1984 Act, as read (in the case only of a ballot which includes a question the purpose of which falls within paragraph (a) of regulation 5 below) with section 5(2) and (3) of the Employment Act 1990;]
"the Scheme" means the scheme made by these Regulations;
["the scrutineer" means the person appointed by a trade union in relation to the ballot in question in accordance with section 15(2) of the 1988 Act;]
"strike" means any concerted stoppage of work;
["working hours" has the meaning given by section 11(11) of the 1984 Act, as read (in the case only of a ballot which includes a question the purpose of which falls within paragraph (a) of regulation 5 below) with section 5(1) of the Employment Act 1990;]
"merchant seaman", "offshore worker", . . . "post", "proper address", "section" [and], "single transferable vote" . . . have the same meanings respectively as in section 9(1) of the 1984 Act.   **[1189]**

NOTES
Prospectively revoked as from 1 April 1996 by SI 1993/233; see paras **[1427]**–**[1431]** post for transitional provisions.
Definition "the 1980 Regulations" revoked and definition "the 1988 Act" inserted by SI 1988/1123, regs 3(2), 4.
Definition "contract of employment" revoked by the Funds for Trade Union Ballots (Amendment) Regulations 1990, SI 1990/2379, reg 3(1)(a).
Definitions "overseas member" and "working hours" inserted by SI 1990/2379, reg 3(1)(c), (d), (2).
Definition "the scrutineer" inserted by SI 1988/2116, regs 3(1), 4
In definition "merchant seaman etc" words omitted revoked, and word "and" inserted, by SI 1990/2379, reg 3(1)(b).
Note that all of the Acts referred to in this Regulation are consolidated in the Trade Union and Labour Relations (Consolidation) Act 1992 ("TULRA 1992").

4 Scope of the Scheme

Subject to regulations 6 and 7 below, the Scheme applies to a ballot if—

(a) *the purpose of the question, or of each of the questions, to be voted upon falls within the purposes mentioned in regulation 5 below; or*
(b) *the purpose of one or more of the questions to be voted upon falls within those purposes and each other question to be voted upon relates to the same issue as a question the purpose of which falls within those purposes.*   **[1190]**

NOTE
Prospectively revoked as from 1 April 1996 by SI 1993/233; see paras **[1427]**–**[1431]** post for transitional provisions.

5 The purposes referred to in regulation 4 above are—

(a) *obtaining a decision or ascertaining the views of members of a trade union as to the calling or ending of a strike or other industrial action;*
(b) *carrying out an election—*
    (i) *in relation to which section 2 of the 1984 Act is required to be satisfied; or*
    (ii) *provided for by the rules of a trade union to the principal committee of the union exercising executive functions, by whatever name it is known; or*

(iii) *provided for by the rules of a trade union to the positions of president, chairman, secretary or treasurer of the union or to any position which the person elected will hold as an employee of the union.*

(c) *amending the rules of a trade union;*

(d) *obtaining a decision in accordance with the 1964 Act on a resolution to approve an instrument of amalgamation or transfer;*

(e) *obtaining a decision on a resolution for the purposes of section 3 of the 1913 Act;*

(f) *obtaining a decision or ascertaining the views of members of a trade union as the acceptance or rejection of a proposal made by an employer which relates in whole or in part to remuneration (whether in money or money's worth), hours of work, level of performance, holidays or pensions.*

[1191]

NOTES

Prospectively revoked as from 1 April 1996 by SI 1993/233; see paras **[1427]**–**[1431]** post for transitional provisions.

"Section 2 of the 1984 Act": see now TULRA 1992, ss 47, 50, 51, 53.

"1964 Act": see now TULRA 1992, Pt I, Chapter VII.

"Section 3 of the 1913 Act": see now TULRA 1992, ss 72, 73.

6 *Notwithstanding anything in regulations 4 and 5 above, the Scheme does not apply to a ballot if—*

(a) *the purpose of any question to be voted upon is the obtaining of a decision of the kind mentioned in paragraph (e) of regulation 5 above; and*

(b) *the ballot is held at a time when there is no resolution in force in respect of the trade union under section 3 of the 1913 Act.*   **[1192]**

NOTE

Prospectively revoked as from 1 April 1996 by SI 1993/233; see paras **[1427]**–**[1431]** post for transitional provisions.

7 *The Scheme applies only to ballots which are so conducted as to secure, so far as reasonably practicable, that those voting do so in secret.*   **[1193]**

NOTE

Prospectively revoked as from 1 April 1996 by SI 1993/233; see paras **[1427]**–**[1431]** post for transitional provisions.

8 Application for payments

(1) An independent trade union claiming to have incurred expenditure on a ballot to which the Scheme applies may apply to the Certification Officer within six months of the date of the ballot for payments in respect of that ballot.

[(1A) The Certification Officer may, if he thinks fit, accept an application under paragraph (1) above in respect of more than one ballot relating to the same question or to related questions and in any such case, for all purposes of these regulations, he shall proceed as if each ballot had been the subject of a separate application.]

[(1B) Notwithstanding anything in paragraph (1), above, no application shall be made in respect of a ballot containing a question the purpose of which falls within paragraphs (b)(i) or (e) of regulation 5, above, before the date on which the trade union publishes the result of the ballot in accordance with subsection (7) of section 15 of the 1988 Act.]

(2) An application under paragraph (1) above shall be made in such form [, shall contain such assurances] and shall be accompanied, or subsequently supported, by such other [assurances and] documents as the Certification Officer may require.

[(2A) Every application under paragraph (1) in respect of such a ballot as is mentioned in paragraph (1B), above, shall be accompanied by a copy of such report with respect to the ballot as is mentioned in subsection (5) of section 15 of the 1988 Act.]

(3) Where a ballot ("the first ballot") has been held and set aside (whether as the result of an enforcement order made under section 5(5) of the 1984 Act, or otherwise) and another ballot ("the second ballot") has been, or is to be, held in its place—

   (a) the Certification Officer (if he is aware of those circumstances) shall take no further action under these Regulations in relation to any application that has already been made under paragraph (1) above in respect of the first ballot; and

   (b) no application may be made under paragraph (1) above—

      (i) in respect of the first ballot; or

      (ii) in respect of the second ballot if a payment has been made under regulations 14 to 18 below in respect of the first ballot.   **[1194]**

NOTES

Prospectively revoked as from 1 April 1996 by SI 1993/233; see paras **[1427]–[1431]** post for transitional provisions.

Para (1A): inserted by SI 1988/1123, reg 5(1), in relation to ballots on or after 26 July 1988.

Paras (1B), (2A): inserted by the Funds for Trade Union Ballots (Amendment No 2) Regulations 1988, SI 1988/2116, regs 3, 5.

Para (2): words in square brackets inserted by SI 1988/1123, reg 5(2), in relation to ballots on or after 26 July 1988.

"Section 15 of the 1988 Act": see now TULRA 1992, ss 49, 52, 75, 78.

"Section 5(5) of the 1984 Act": see now TULRA 1992, s 26(4).

9 *(1) If the Certification Officer is satisfied that an application under paragraph (1) of regulation 8 above is in respect of a ballot to which the Scheme applies he shall proceed in accordance with the following regulations.*

   (2) Where the Certification Officer—

      (a) is aware of the institution of any legal proceedings relating to a ballot in respect of which an application has been made under paragraph (1) of regulation 8 above; and

      (b) considers that any issue relevant to his duties in relation to that application may be raised in those proceedings;

he shall take no further action under these Regulations in relation to that application until those proceedings have been finally determined.

   (3) For the purposes of paragraph (2) above, proceedings shall be taken to have been finally determined when any appeal in respect of such proceedings has been determined, withdrawn or abandoned or when the time for appealing has expired without an appeal having been brought.

   [(4) For the avoidance of doubt, in paragraph (2) above, "legal proceedings" includes proceedings before the Certification Officer under section 4 of the 1964 Act, under section 5 of the 1984 Act or under section 16 of the 1988 Act.]   **[1195]**

NOTES

Prospectively revoked as from 1 April 1996 by SI 1993/233; see paras **[1427]–[1431]** post for transitional provisions.

Para (4): added by SI 1988/1123, reg 6.
"Section 4 of the 1964 Act"; see now TULRA 1992, ss 103, 104.
"Section 5 of the 1984 Act": see now TULRA 1992, ss 25, 26, 54–56.
"Section 16 of the 1988 Act": see now TULRA 1992, ss 80(1), 81(1).

10 Conditions to be satisfied if payment is to be made

[(1) Except as provided by regulation 24 below, the Certification Officer shall not make any payments under regulations 14 to 18 below unless he considers that adequate assurances have been given by the trade union as to compliance with—

  (a) the conditions mentioned in regulation 11 below (which are applicable to all ballots); and

  (b) such of the conditions mentioned in regulation 12 below (which are applicable to specific questions asked in ballots) as are applicable to the question or questions asked in the ballot.

 (2) For the purposes of paragraph (1) above, the Certification Officer shall not consider adequate such assurances as have been given if, on consideration of any matter which has come to his notice, he is of the opinion that any of the conditions referred to in that paragraph has not been satisfied.]   **[1196]**

NOTES
Prospectively revoked as from 1 April 1996 by SI 1993/233; see paras **[1427]**–**[1431]** post for transitional provisions.
Substituted by SI 1988/1123, reg 7.

11 The conditions (applicable to all ballots) referred to in regulation [10(1)(a)] above are—

  (a) that the method of voting was by the marking of a voting paper by the person voting;

  (b) that every person who was entitled to vote in the ballot was—

   (i) allowed to vote without interference from, or constraint imposed by, the trade union or any of its members, officials or employees; and

   (ii) so far as was reasonably practicable, enabled to do so without incurring any direct cost to himself;

  (c) that, so far as was reasonably practicable, every person who was entitled to vote—

   (i) had sent to him, at his proper address and by post, a voting paper; and

   (ii) was given a convenient opportunity to vote by post;

  (d) where the votes on any question have been counted, that the decision not to count them was taken because of a change in circumstances occurring after the first day on which voting papers were made available or supplied to persons entitled to vote which materially affected the issue to which the question related;

  (e) where the votes on any question have been counted, that the ballot was conducted so as to secure that the votes given in the ballot were fairly and accurately counted (any inaccuracy in counting being disregarded for the purposes of this paragraph if it was accidental and on a scale which did not affect the result of the ballot);

  (f) that the ballot was conducted so as to secure that the result of the ballot was determined solely by counting the number of votes cast directly by those voting (this condition shall not be taken not to have been satisfied by reason only that the system of voting used was the single transferable vote).   **[1197]**

NOTES
Prospectively revoked as from 1 April 1996 by SI 1993/233; see paras **[1427]**–**[1431]** post for transitional provisions.
Words in square brackets substituted by SI 1988/1123, reg 8.

---

12 *The conditions (applicable to specific questions) referred to in regulation [10(1)(b)] above are—*

[(a) *in the case of a question the purpose of which falls within paragraph (a) of regulation 5 above and is concerned only with the ending of a strike or other industrial action—*

  (i) *that the ballot was conducted so as to secure, so far as reasonably practicable, that all the members participating in the action were entitled to vote; and*

  (ii) *that as soon as was reasonably practicable after the holding of the ballot the trade union took such steps as were reasonably necessary to ensure that all persons entitled to vote on that question were informed of the number of—*

  (A) *votes cast on that question;*
  (B) *individuals voting in favour of that question;*
  (C) *individuals voting against that question; and*
  (D) *spoiled ballot papers;]*

[(b) *in the case of a question the purpose of which falls within paragraph (a) of regulation 5 above, other than a question to which paragraph (a) of this regulation relates, that subsections (1), (1A), (1B), (2), (3), (4) [, (4A)] and (8) of section 11 of the 1984 Act have, within the meaning of that section, been satisfied in relation to the ballot;]*

(c) . . .

(d) *in the case of a question the purpose of which falls within paragraph (b) of regulation 5 above, that, subject to regulation 13(5) below, entitlement to vote at the election was accorded equally to all members of the trade union in question other than those mentioned in regulation 13(3) below;*

(e) *in the case of a question the purpose of which falls within paragraph (b) of regulation 5 above, that the voting papers either listed the candidates at the election or were accompanied by a separate list of those candidates;*

[(ea) *in the case of a question the purpose of which falls within paragraph (b)(i) of regulation 5 above, that the requirements of subsection (2) of section 13 of the 1988 Act have been satisfied in relation to that ballot;]*

[(eb) *in the case of a question the purpose of which falls within paragraphs (b)(i) or (e) of regulation 5, above, that the requirements of subsection (2) of section 15 of the 1988 Act have been satisfied in relation to that ballot;*

(ec) *in the case of a question the purpose of which falls within paragraphs (b)(i) or (e) of regulation 5, above, that each voting paper—*

  (i) *clearly specified the address to which, and the date by which, the voting paper was to be returned;*

  (ii) *was given one of a series of consecutive whole numbers every one of which was used in giving a different number in that series to each voting paper printed or otherwise produced for the purposes of the ballot; . . .*

  (iii) *was marked with its number; [and*
  (iv) *stated the name of the scrutineer.]]*

(f) *in the case of a question the purpose of which falls within paragraph (c) of regulation 5 above, that any requirements in the rules of the trade union as to entitlement to vote were complied with;*

(g) *in the case of a question the purpose of which falls within paragraph (d)*

of regulation 5 above, that entitlement to vote on that question was
accorded to members as required by the condition in section 1(2)(a) of the
1964 Act;

(h) in the case of a question the purpose of which falls within paragraph (e)
of regulation 5 above, that entitlement to vote on that question was
accorded equally to all members of the trade union;

(i) in the case of a question the purpose of which falls within paragraph (f) of
regulation 5 above, that only persons who were union members and were
affected by the proposal were entitled to vote on that question.   **[1198]**

NOTES
Prospectively revoked as from 1 April 1996 by SI 1993/233; see paras **[1427]**–**[1431]** post for
transitional provisions.
Words in first pair of square brackets substituted by SI 1988/1123, reg 9(1).
Para (a): substituted by SI 1988/1123, reg 9(2).
Para (b): substituted by SI 1988/1123, reg 9(3); number in square brackets therein inserted with savings
by the Funds for Trade Union Ballots (Amendment) Regulations 1990, SI 1990/2379, reg 4.
Para (c): revoked by SI 1988/1123, reg 9(4).
Para (ea): inserted by SI 1988/1123, reg 9(5).
Para (eb): inserted by SI 1988/2116, reg 6.
Para (ec): inserted by SI 1988/2116, reg 6; word omitted therefrom revoked, and word "and" and sub-
para (iv) thereof added, with savings, by SI 1990/2379, reg 5.
"Section 11 of the 1984 Act": see now TULRA 1992, ss 227(1), (2), 228, 229, 231.
"Sections 13(2) and 15(2) of the 1988 Act": see now TULRA 1992, ss 48(1), (2), (4)–(7) and ss 49,
75 respectively.
"Section 1(2)(a) of the 1964 Act": see now TULRA 1992, s 100(1).

13 (1) [In the case of a question the purpose of which falls within paragraphs (a)
or (f) of regulation 5 above], the Certification Officer shall proceed as if for sub-
paragraphs (i) and (ii) of paragraph (c) of regulation 11 above there were
substituted—

"(i) had made available to him—

(A) immediately before, immediately after, or during, his working
hours, and
(B) at his place of work or at a place which was more convenient for
him;

or was supplied with, a voting paper; and

(ii) was given a convenient opportunity to vote by post (but no other
opportunity to vote);".

(2) . . .

(3) The members referred to in regulation 12(d) above (in respect of whom the
condition therein need not have been satisfied) are those who belonged to a class—

(a) which was, or which fell within, one or other of the classes mentioned in
paragraph (4) of this regulation; and
(b) all the members of which were excluded by the rules of the union from
voting at the election.

(4) The classes are—

(a) members who are not in employment;
(b) members who are in arrears in respect of any subscription or contribution
due to the union;
(c) members who are apprentices, trainees or students or new members of the
union.

(5) Where the conditions mentioned in paragraph (6) of this regulation were
satisfied, the condition in regulation 12(d) above shall not be taken not to have been

satisfied by reason only that the trade union restricted entitlement to vote at the election to members of the union who fell within—

  (a) *a class determined by reference to any trade or occupation;*
  (b) *a class determined by reference to any geographical area;*
  (c) *a class which was by virtue of the rules of the union treated as a separate section within the union; or*
  (d) *a class determined by reference to any combination of the matters mentioned in paragraphs (a), (b) and (c) above.*

  (6) The conditions are that—

  (a) *entitlement to vote was restricted by the rules of the union;*
  (b) *no member of the union is denied entitlement to vote at all elections held for the purposes of Part I of the 1984 Act otherwise than by virtue of belonging to a class mentioned in paragraph (3) above.*   **[1199]**

NOTES
  Prospectively revoked as from 1 April 1996 by SI 1993/233; see paras **[1427]**–**[1431]** post for transitional provisions.
  Para (1): words in square brackets substituted by SI 1988/1123, reg 10(1).
  Para (2): revoked by SI 1988/1123, reg 10(2).

14 Payments towards stationery and printing expenditure

(1) The Certification Officer shall make a payment towards the expenditure incurred by the trade union on stationery and printing in respect of—

  (a) *voting papers, envelopes for sending out and returning voting papers and any additional envelopes used for the purpose of helping to secure the secrecy of the voting;*
  (b) *that part of any material enclosed with the voting papers which explains the matter to which the question to be voted upon relates or the procedure for voting.*

  (2) The amount of the payment referred to in paragraph (1) above shall, if the Certification Officer considers the expenditure incurred to have been reasonable, be the amount spent or, if he considers the expenditure incurred to have been unreasonable, the amount which he considers would have been reasonable. **[1200]**

NOTE
  Prospectively revoked as from 1 April 1996 by SI 1993/233; see paras **[1427]**–**[1431]** post for transitional provisions.

15 Payments towards postal costs

The Certification Officer shall make a payment towards the postal expenditure incurred by the trade union in sending by post to the persons entitled to vote the voting papers, envelopes and material referred to in regulation 14 above in respect of which a payment is payable. **[1201]**

NOTE
  Prospectively revoked as from 1 April 1996 by SI 1993/233; see paras **[1427]**–**[1431]** post for transitional provisions.

16 *The Certification Officer shall make a payment towards the postal expenditure incurred by the trade union in paying for the persons entitled to vote to return their voting papers by post.* **[1202]**

NOTE
  Prospectively revoked as from 1 April 1996 by SI 1993/233; see paras **[1427]**–**[1431]** post for transitional provisions.

17 Subject to regulation 18 below, the amount of the payments referred to in regulations 15 and 16 above shall be—

 (a) to the extent that second class post or a cheaper postal means was used, the amount spent on such use;

 (b) to the extent that a means more expensive than second class post was used, the amount which would have been spent if second class post had been used, or, if the Certification Officer considers the use of the more expensive means to have been reasonable in the circumstances, the amount spent on such use.

                         [1203]

NOTE

 Prospectively revoked as from 1 April 1996 by SI 1993/233; see paras **[1427]**–**[1431]** post for transitional provisions.

18 If the Certification Officer considers that additional postal expenditure has been incurred by the use of paper of a greater quantity or heavier quality than is reasonable, a payment made under regulation 15 or 16 above shall not include the amount of the additional postal expenditure so incurred.   **[1204]**

NOTE

 Prospectively revoked as from 1 April 1996 by SI 1993/233; see paras **[1427]**–**[1431]** post for transitional provisions.

19 Provisions as to payments

The Certification Officer shall not make any payments until the expiration of a period of six weeks beginning with whichever is the last of the following dates—

 (a) the date on which the results relating to the questions asked in the ballot in respect of which the votes were counted have been made available to the persons entitled to vote;

 (b) the date on which an application is made under regulation 8 above;

 (c) in the case of a ballot containing a question the purpose of which falls within paragraph (a) of regulation 5 above, the date on which the industrial action, in respect of which the question was asked, ended;

 [(ca) in the case of a ballot containing a question the purpose of which falls within paragraphs (b)(i) or (e) of regulation 5, above, with respect to which ballot the report mentioned in paragraph (2A) of regulation 8, above, indicates that the scrutineer was not satisfied as to one or more of the matters specified in subsection (6) of section 15 of the 1988 Act, the last date on which an application under section 5 of the 1984 Act, or, as the case may be, section 16 of the 1988 Act, could be made in respect of the ballot;]

 (d) in the case of a ballot containing a question the purpose of which falls within paragraph (d) of regulation 5 above, where the amalgamating or transferor trade union has passed a resolution approving the instrument of amalgamation or transfer and an application has been made to register the instrument or the Certification Officer has reason to believe that such an application will be made, the date of registration of the instrument or, if a complaint is made under section 4 of the 1964 Act and the Certification Officer makes an order under subsection (3) of that section specifying steps which must be taken before he will entertain any application to register the instrument, the date on which the order is made.   **[1205]**

NOTES

 Prospectively revoked as from 1 April 1996 by SI 1993/233; see paras **[1427]**–**[1431]** post for transitional provisions.

Para (ca): inserted by SI 1988/2116, regs 3, 7.
"Section 15(6) of the 1988 Act": see now TULRA 1992, aa 52(2), 78(1), (2).
"Section 5 of the 1984 Act": see now TULRA 1992, ss 24–26, 54–56.
"Section 16 of the 1988 Act": see now TULRA 1992, ss 79–81.
"Section 4 of the 1964 Act": see now TULRA 1992, ss 103, 104.

20 *All payments shall be made to the applicant trade union.*   **[1206]**

NOTE
   Prospectively revoked as from 1 April 1996 by SI 1993/233; see paras **[1427]**–**[1431]** post for
transitional provisions.

21 **Arrangements to hold ballots**

*(1) The Scheme applies to arrangements to hold a ballot which is not proceeded with
if voting papers have been made available or supplied to persons entitled to vote
before the decision not to proceed with the ballot is taken.*

   *(2) Where the Scheme applies by virtue of this regulation, these Regulations shall
have effect with such modifications as may be appropriate.*   **[1207]**

NOTE
   Prospectively revoked as from 1 April 1996 by SI 1993/233; see paras **[1427]**–**[1431]** post for
transitional provisions.

22 **Special provisions as to amalgamations and transfers of engagements**

*If an amalgamating or transferor trade union has passed a resolution approving an
instrument of amalgamation or transfer under section 1 of the 1964 Act which is
registered and, having incurred expenditure in respect of a ballot, has either made
an application under regulation 8 above before the date of registration of the
instrument, or, being eligible to make such an application, has not done so before
that date, and the amalgamated or transferee trade union is an independent trade
union, then—*

   *(a) with effect from the date of registration of the instrument the amalgamated
        or transferee trade union shall be treated for the purposes of the Scheme
        other than regulations 10 to 13 above as if, in a case where an application
        under regulation 8 has been made before that date, it were the applicant
        trade union and in that case and the case where no such application has
        been made it had incurred the expenditure in respect of the ballot;*
   *(b) an assurance . . . pursuant to regulation [10(1)] above shall be treated as
        being given by the amalgamating or transferor trade union if given by a
        person who was an officer of that union immediately before the date of
        registration of the instrument.*   **[1208]**

NOTES
   Prospectively revoked as from 1 April 1996 by SI 1993/233; see paras **[1427]**–**[1431]** post for
transitional provisions.
   Para (b): words omitted revoked, and number in square brackets substituted, by SI 1988/1123, reg 11.
   "Section 1 of the 1964 Act": see now TULRA 1992, ss 97–101.

23 **Special provisions as to section 2 of the Employment Act 1980**

*If on a complaint presented under section 2 of the Employment Act 1980 in respect
of a ballot an industrial tribunal has made an award of compensation to be paid to
a trade union and the Scheme applies to that ballot, the Certification Officer shall
on an application under regulation 8 above reduce the total of the payments made*

under regulations 14 to 18 above by so much of the award as he considers relates to the expenditure in respect of which payments are to be made under those regulations.

NOTES   **[1209]**

Prospectively revoked as from 1 April 1996 by SI 1993/233; see paras **[1427]**–**[1431]** post for transitional provisions.

"Section 2 of the Employment Act 1980": see now TULRA 1992, s 116.

24 Special provisions as to overseas members

(1) Paragraph (2) of this regulation does not apply in the case of a ballot containing a question the purpose of which falls within [paragraphs (b)(i), (d) or (e)] of regulation 5 above.

[(1A) In the case of a ballot containing a question the purpose of which falls within paragraph (b)(i) of regulation 5 above, no account shall be taken for the purposes of paragraph (d) of regulation 12 above of the treatment of any overseas member.

(1B) In the case of a ballot containing a question the purpose of which falls within paragraph (e) of regulation 5 above, no account shall be taken, for the purposes of paragraph (h) of regulation 12, of the treatment of overseas members if rules made by the trade union for the purpose of complying with section 4(1) of the 1913 Act in relation to the ballot provided for such members not to be accorded entitlement to vote in the ballot.]

[(2) Where the Certification Officer is of the opinion that any of the conditions mentioned in regulation 11 and 12 above has not been satisfied in respect of overseas members, or any overseas member, but he considers that in all other respects adequate assurances have been given by the trade union he may, subject to paragraph (3) below, make payments under regulation 14 to 18 above, notwithstanding regulation 10 above.]

(3) Where paragraph (2) above applies, no payment under regulations 14 to 18 above may include any amount in respect of expenditure incurred in relation to the overseas member or members mentioned in paragraph (2) above.   **[1210]**

NOTES

Prospectively revoked as from 1 April 1996 by SI 1993/233; see paras **[1427]**–**[1431]** post for transitional provisions.

Para (1): words in square brackets substituted by SI 1988/1123, reg 12(1).

Paras (1A), (1B): inserted by SI 1988/1123, reg 12(2).

Para (2): substituted by SI 1988/1123, reg 12(3).

"Section 4(1) of the 1913 Act": see now TULRA 1992, s 74(1).

INDUSTRIAL TRIBUNALS (RULES OF PROCEDURE) REGULATIONS 1985

(SI 1985/16)

NOTES

Made: 9 January 1985.

Authority: Employment Protection (Consolidation) Act 1978, s 128, Sch 9, para 1.

These Regulations apply to England and Wales only. The equivalent Scottish Regulations are SI 1985/17 post.

1 Citation, commencement and revocation

(1) These Regulations may be cited as the Industrial Tribunals (Rules of Procedure) Regulations 1985 (and the Rules of Procedure contained in Schedules 1 and 2 to these Regulations may be referred to as the Industrial Tribunals Rules of Procedure 1985 and the Industrial Tribunals Complementary Rules of Procedure 1985 respectively). They shall come into operation on 1st March 1985.

(2) The Industrial Tribunals (Rules of Procedure) Regulations 1980 and the Industrial Tribunals (Rules of Procedure) (Equal Value Amendment) Regulations 1983 shall cease to have effect on 1st March 1985 except in relation to proceedings instituted before that date.   **[1211]**

2 Interpretation

In these Regulations, unless the context otherwise requires, the following expressions have the meanings hereby assigned to them respectively, that is to say—

"the 1966 Act" means the Docks and Harbours Act 1966;
"the 1978 Act" means the Employment Protection (Consolidation) Act 1978;

"applicant" means a person who in pursuance of Rule 1 has presented an originating application to the Secretary of the Tribunals for a decision of a tribunal and includes:—

  (a) the Secretary of State, the Board or a licensing authority,
  (b) a claimant or complainant,
  (c) in the case of proceedings under section 51 of the 1966 Act, a person on whose behalf an originating application has been sent by a trade union, and
  (d) in relation to interlocutory applications under these Rules, a person who seeks any relief;

"the Board" means the National Dock Labour Board as reconstituted under the Dock Work Regulation Act 1976;

"the clerk to the tribunal" means the person appointed by the Secretary of the Tribunals or an Assistant Secretary to act in that capacity at one or more hearings;

"court" means a magistrates' court or the Crown Court;

"decision" in relation to a tribunal includes a declaration, an order (other than an interlocutory order), a recommendation or an award of the tribunal but does not include an opinion given pursuant to a pre-hearing assessment held under Rule 6;

"the Equal Pay Act" means the Equal Pay Act 1970;

"equal value claim" means a claim by an applicant which rests upon entitlement to the benefit of an equality clause by virtue of the operation of section 1(2)(c) of the Equal Pay Act;

"expert" means a member of the panel of independent experts within the meaning of section 2A(4) of the Equal Pay Act;

"hearing" means a sitting of a tribunal duly constituted for the purpose of receiving evidence, hearing addresses and witnesses or doing anything lawfully requisite to enable the tribunal to reach a decision on any question;

"licensing authority" means a body having the function of issuing licences under the 1966 Act;

"the Office of the Tribunals" means the Central Office of the Industrial Tribunals (England and Wales);

"the panel of chairmen" means the panel of persons, being barristers or solicitors of not less than seven years' standing, appointed by the Lord Chancellor in pursuance of Regulation 5(2) of the Industrial Tribunals (England and Wales) Regulations 1965;

"party" in relation to proceedings under section 51 of the 1966 Act means the applicant and the Board or the licensing authority with which or (as the case may be) any person with whom it appears to the applicant that he is in dispute about a question to which that section applies and, in a case where such a question is referred to a tribunal by a court, any party to the proceedings before the court in which the question arose;

"person entitled to appear" in relation to proceedings under section 51 of the 1966 Act means a party and any person who, under subsection (5) of that section, is entitled to appear and be heard before a tribunal in such proceedings;

"the President" means the President of the Industrial Tribunals (England and Wales) or the person nominated by the Lord Chancellor to discharge for the time being the functions of the President;

"the Race Relations Act" means the Race Relations Act 1976;

"Regional Chairman" means the chairman appointed by the President to take charge of the due administration of justice by tribunals in an area specified by the President, or a person nominated either by the President or the

Regional Chairman to discharge for the time being the functions of the Regional Chairman;

"Regional Office of the Industrial Tribunals" means a regional office which has been established under the Office of the Tribunals for an area specified by the President;

"Register" means the Register of Applications and Decisions kept in pursuance of these Regulations;

"report" means a report required by a tribunal to be prepared by an expert, pursuant to section 2A(1)(b) of the Equal Pay Act;

"respondent" means a party to the proceedings before a tribunal other than the applicant, and other than the Secretary of State in proceedings under Parts III and VI of the 1978 Act in which he is not cited as the person against whom relief is sought;

"Rule" means, in Schedule 1 to these Regulations, a Rule of Procedure contained in that Schedule, and, in Schedule 2 to these Regulations, a Rule of Procedure contained in Schedule 1 or Schedule 2 as appropriate;

"the Secretary of the Tribunals" and "an Assistant Secretary of the Tribunals" mean respectively the persons for the time being acting as the Secretary of the Office of the Tribunals and as the Assistant Secretary of a Regional Office of the Industrial Tribunals;

"the Sex Discrimination Act" means the Sex Discrimination Act 1975;

"tribunal" means an industrial tribunal (England and Wales) established in pursuance of the Industrial Tribunals (England and Wales) Regulations 1965 and in relation to any proceedings means the tribunal to which the proceedings have been referred by the President or a Regional Chairman.

[1212]

3 Proceedings of tribunals

(1) Except where separate Rules of Procedure made under the provisions of any enactment are applicable and subject to paragraph (2) of this Regulation, the Rules of Procedure contained in Schedule 1 to these Regulations shall have effect in relation to all proceedings before a tribunal where:—

    (a) the respondent or one of the respondents resides or carries on business in England or Wales; or

    (b) had the remedy been by way of action in the county court, the cause of action would have arisen wholly or in part in England or Wales; or

    (c) the proceedings are to determine a question which has been referred to the tribunal by a court in England or Wales; or

    (d) in proceedings under the 1966 Act they are in relation to a port in England or Wales.

(2) In any such proceedings before a tribunal involving an equal value claim the Rules of Procedure contained in Schedule 2 to these Regulations (including Rule 7A) shall replace Rules 4, 8, 9, 11, 12 and 17 in Schedule 1.   **[1213]**

4 Proof of decisions of tribunals

The production in any proceedings in any court of a document purporting to be certified by the Secretary of the Tribunals to be a true copy of an entry of a decision in the Register shall, unless the contrary is proved, be sufficient evidence of the document and of the facts stated therein.   **[1214]**

SCHEDULES

SCHEDULE 1

Regulation 3(1)

RULES OF PROCEDURE

1 Originating application

(1) Proceedings for the determination of any matter by a tribunal shall be instituted by the applicant (or, where applicable, by a court) presenting to the Secretary of the Tribunals an originating application, which shall be in writing and shall set out:—

    (a)   the name and address of the applicant; and

    (b)   the names and addresses of the person or persons against whom relief is sought or (where applicable) of the parties to the proceedings before the court; and

    (c)   the grounds, with particulars thereof, on which relief is sought, or in proceedings under section 51 of the 1966 Act the question for determination and (except where the question is referred by a court) the grounds on which relief is sought.

(2) Where the Secretary of the Tribunals is of the opinion that the originating application does not seek or on the facts stated therein cannot entitle the applicant to a relief which a tribunal has power to give, he may give notice to that effect to the applicant stating the reasons for his opinion and informing him that the application will not be registered unless he states in writing that he wishes to proceed with it.

(3) An application as respects which a notice has been given in pursuance of the preceding paragraph shall not be treated as having been received for the purposes of Rule 2 unless the applicant intimates in writing to the Secretary of the Tribunals that he wishes to proceed with it; and upon receipt of such an intimation the Secretary of the Tribunals shall proceed in accordance with that Rule.

2 Action upon receipt of originating application

Upon receiving an originating application the Secretary of the Tribunals shall enter particulars of it in the Register and shall forthwith send a copy of it to the respondent and inform the parties in writing of the case number of the originating application entered in the Register (which shall thereafter constitute the title of the proceedings) and of the address to which notices and other communications to the Secretary of the Tribunals shall be sent. Every copy of the originating application sent by the Secretary of the Tribunals under this Rule shall be accompanied by a written notice which shall include information, as appropriate to the case, about the means and time for entering an appearance, the consequences of failure to do so, and the right to receive a copy of the decision. The Secretary of the Tribunals shall also notify the parties that in all cases under the provisions of any enactment providing for conciliation the services of a conciliation officer are available to them.

3 Appearance by respondent

(1) A respondent shall within 14 days of receiving the copy originating application enter an appearance to the proceedings by presenting to the Secretary of the Tribunals a written notice of appearance setting out his full name and address and stating whether or not he intends to resist the application and, if so, setting out sufficient particulars to show on what grounds. Upon receipt of a notice of appearance the Secretary of the Tribunals shall forthwith send a copy of it to any other party.

(2) A respondent who has not entered an appearance shall not be entitled to take any part in the proceedings except—

    (i)   to apply under Rule 13(1) for an extension of the time appointed by this Rule for entering an appearance;

    (ii)   to make an application under Rule 4(1)(i);

    (iii) to make an application under Rule 10(2) in respect of Rule 10(1)(b);

    (iv) to be called as a witness by another person;

    (v) to be sent a copy of a document or corrected entry in pursuance of Rule 9(6), 9(10) or 10(5).

(3) A notice of appearance which is presented to the Secretary of the Tribunals after the time appointed by this Rule for entering appearances shall be deemed to include an application under Rule 13(1) (by the respondent who has presented the notice of appearance) for an extension of the time so appointed. Without prejudice to Rule 13(4), if the tribunal grants the application (which it may do notwithstanding that the grounds of the application are not stated) the Secretary of the Tribunals shall forthwith send a copy of the notice of appearance to any other party. The tribunal shall not refuse an extension of time under this Rule unless it has sent notice to the person wishing to enter an appearance giving him an opportunity to show cause why the extension should be granted. **[1217]**

4 Power to require further particulars and attendance of witnesses and to grant discovery

(1) A tribunal may—

    (a) subject to Rule 3(2), on the application of a party to the proceedings made either by notice to the Secretary of the Tribunals or at the hearing of the originating application, or

    (b) in relation to sub-paragraph (i) of this paragraph, if it thinks fit, of its own motion—

        (i) require a party to furnish in writing to the person specified by the tribunal further particulars of the grounds on which he or it relies and of any facts and contentions relevant thereto;

        (ii) grant to the person making the application such discovery or inspection (including the taking of copies) of documents as might be granted by a county court; and

        (iii) require the attendance of any person (including a party to the proceedings) as a witness, wherever such person may be within Great Britain, and may, if it does so require the attendance of a person, require him to produce any document relating to the matter to be determined;

and may appoint the time at or within which or the place at which any act required in pursuance of this Rule is to be done.

(2) A party on whom a requirement has been made under paragraph (1)(i) or (1)(ii) of this Rule on an *ex parte* application, or (in relation to a requirement under paragraph (1)(i)) on the tribunal's own motion, and a person on whom a requirement has been made under paragraph (1)(iii) may apply to the tribunal by notice to the Secretary of the Tribunals before the appointed time at or within which the requirement is to be complied with to vary or set aside the requirement. Notice of an application under this paragraph to vary or set aside a requirement shall be given to the parties (other than the party making the application) and, where appropriate, in proceedings which may involve payments out of the [National Insurance Fund] or Maternity Pay Fund, the Secretary of State if not a party.

(3) Every document containing a requirement under paragraph (1)(ii) or (1)(iii) of this Rule shall contain a reference to the fact that, under paragraph 1(7) of Schedule 9 to the 1978 Act, any person who without reasonable excuse fails to comply with any such requirement shall be liable on summary conviction to a fine, and the document shall state the amount of the current maximum fine.

(4) If the requirement under paragraph (1)(i) or (1)(ii) of this Rule is not complied with, a tribunal, before or at the hearing, may dismiss the whole or part of the originating application, or, as the case may be, strike out the whole or part of the notice of appearance, and, where appropriate, direct that a respondent shall be debarred from defending altogether: Provided that a tribunal shall not so dismiss or strike out or give such a direction unless it has sent notice to the party who has not complied with the requirement giving him an opportunity to show cause why such should not be done. **[1218]**

NOTE
Para (2): words in square brackets substituted by virtue of the Employment Act 1990, s 13(3).

5 Time and place of hearing and appointment of assessor

(1) The President or a Regional Chairman shall fix the date, time and place of the hearing of the originating application and the Secretary of the Tribunals shall (subject to Rule 3(2)) not less than 14 days (or such shorter time as may be agreed by him with the parties) before the date so fixed send to each party a notice of hearing which shall include information and guidance as to attendance at the hearing, witnesses and the bringing of documents (if any), representation by another person and written representations.

(2) In any proceedings under the 1966 Act in which the President or a Regional Chairman so directs, the Secretary of the Tribunals shall also take such of the following steps as may be so directed, namely—

(a) publish in one or more newspapers circulating in the locality in which the port in question is situated notice of the hearing;

(b) send notice of the hearing to such persons as may be directed;

(c) post notices of the hearing in a conspicuous place or conspicuous places in or near the port in question;

but the requirement as to the period of notice contained in paragraph (1) of this Rule shall not apply to any such notices.

(3) Where in the case of any proceedings it is provided for one or more assessors to be appointed, the President or a Regional Chairman may, if he thinks fit, appoint a person or persons having special knowledge or experience in relation to the subject matter of the originating application to sit with the tribunal as assessor or assessors.   **[1219]**

6 Pre-hearing assessment

(1) A tribunal may at any time before the hearing (either, subject to Rule 3(2), on the application of a party to the proceedings made by notice to the Secretary of the Tribunals or of its own motion) consider, by way of a pre-hearing assessment, the contents of the originating application and entry of appearance, any representations in writing which have been submitted and any oral argument advanced by or on behalf of a party.

(2) If, upon a pre-hearing assessment, the tribunal considers that the originating application or the contentions or any particular contention of a party appear or, as the case may be, appears to have no reasonable prospect of success, it may indicate that in its opinion, if the originating application shall not be withdrawn or the contentions or contention of the party shall be persisted in up to or at the hearing, the party in question may have an order for costs made against him at the hearing under the provisions of Rule 11. A pre-hearing assessment shall not take place unless the tribunal has sent notice to the parties to the proceedings giving them (and, where appropriate, in proceedings which may involve payments out of the [National Insurance Fund] or Maternity Pay Fund, the Secretary of State, if not a party) an opportunity to submit representations in writing and to advance oral argument at the pre-hearing assessment if they so wish.

(3) Any indication of opinion made in accordance with paragraph (2) of this Rule shall be recorded in a document signed by the chairman, a copy of which shall be sent to the parties to the proceedings and a copy of which shall be available to the tribunal at the hearing.

(4) Where a tribunal has indicated its opinion in accordance with paragraph (2) of this Rule no member thereof shall be a member of the tribunal at the hearing.   **[1220]**

NOTE
Para (2): words in square brackets substituted by virtue of the Employment Act 1990, s 13(3).

7 The hearing

(1) Any hearing of or in connection with an originating application shall take place in public unless in the opinion of the tribunal a private hearing is appropriate for the purpose of hearing evidence which relates to matters of such a nature that it would be against the interests of national security to allow the evidence to be given in public or hearing evidence from any person which in the opinion of the tribunal is likely to consist of—

(a) information which he could not disclose without contravening a prohibition imposed by or under any enactment; or

(b) any information which has been communicated to him in confidence, or which he has otherwise obtained in consequence of the confidence reposed in him by another person; or

(c) information the disclosure of which would cause substantial injury to any undertaking of his or any undertaking in which he works for reasons other than its effect on negotiations with respect to any of the matters mentioned in section 29(1) of the Trade Union and Labour Relations Act 1974.

(2) A member of the Council on Tribunals shall be entitled to attend any hearing taking place in private in his capacity as such member.

(3) Subject to Rule 3(2), if a party shall desire to submit representations in writing for consideration by a tribunal at the hearing of the originating application that party shall present such representations to the Secretary of the Tribunals not less than 7 days before the hearing and shall at the same time send a copy to the other party or parties.

(4) Where a party has failed to attend or be represented at the hearing (whether or not he has sent any representations in writing) the contents of his originating application or, as the case may be, of his entry of appearance may be treated by a tribunal as representations in writing.

(5) The Secretary of State if he so elects shall be entitled to apply under Rule 4(1), 13(1) and (2), 15 and 16(1) and to appear as if he were a party and be heard at any hearing of or in connection with an originating application in proceedings in which he is not a party which may involve payments out of the [National Insurance Fund] or Maternity Pay Fund.

(6) Subject to Rule 3(2), at any hearing of or in connection with an originating application a party and any person entitled to appear may appear before the tribunal and may be heard in person or be represented by counsel or by a solicitor or by a representative of a trade union or an employers' association or by any other person whom he desires to represent him.   **[1221]**

NOTE

Para (5): words in square brackets substituted by virtue of the Employment Act 1990, s 13(3).

8 Procedure at hearing

(1) The tribunal shall conduct the hearing in such manner as it considers most suitable to the clarification of the issues before it and generally to the just handling of the proceedings; it shall so far as appears to it appropriate seek to avoid formality in its proceedings and it shall not be bound by any enactment or rule of law relating to the admissibility of evidence in proceedings before the courts of law.

(2) Subject to paragraph (1) of this Rule, at the hearing of the originating application a party (unless disentitled by virtue of Rule 3(2)), the Secretary of State (if, not being a party, he elects to appear as provided in Rule 7(5)) and any other person entitled to appear shall be entitled to give evidence, to call witnesses, to question any witnesses and to address the tribunal.

(3) If a party shall fail to appear or to be represented at the time and place fixed for the hearing, the tribunal may, if that party is an applicant, dismiss or, in any case, dispose of the application in the absence of that party or may adjourn the hearing to a later date: Provided that before deciding to dismiss or disposing of any application in the absence of a party the tribunal shall consider any representations submitted by that party in pursuance of Rule 7(3).

(4) A tribunal may require any witness to give evidence on oath or affirmation and for that purpose there may be administered an oath or affirmation in due form.   **[1222]**

9 Decision of tribunal

(1) A decision of a tribunal may be taken by a majority thereof and, if the tribunal shall be constituted of two members only, the chairman shall have a second or casting vote.

(2) The decision of a tribunal, which may be given orally at the end of a hearing or reserved, shall be recorded in a document signed by the chairman.

(3) A tribunal shall give reasons, which may be in full or in summary form, for its decision.

(4) The reasons for the decision of the tribunal shall be recorded in a document signed by the chairman, which shall also contain a statement as to whether the reasons are in full or in summary form.

(5) Where:—

    (a) the proceedings before the tribunal involved the determination of an issue arising under or relating to section 51 of the 1966 Act, the Equal Pay Act, the Sex Discrimination Act, the Race Relations Act, sections 23, 58, 59(a) or 77 of the 1978 Act, or sections 4 or 5 of the Employment Act 1980; or

    (b) the reasons have been given in summary form and it appears at any time to the tribunal that the reasons should be given in full; or

    (c) a request that the reasons be given in full is made orally at the hearing by a party or by a person entitled to appear who did so appear; or

    (d) such a request is made in writing within 21 days of the date on which the document recording the reasons in summary form was sent to the parties;

the reasons shall be recorded in full in a document signed by the chairman.

(6) The clerk to the tribunal shall transmit any document referred to in paragraphs (2), (4) and (5) of this Rule to the Secretary of the Tribunals who shall as soon as may be enter it in the Register and shall send a copy of the entry to each of the parties and to the persons entitled to appear who did so appear and, where the originating application was sent to a tribunal by a court, to that court.

(7) Any document referred to in paragraphs (4) and (5) of this Rule shall be omitted from the Register in any case in which evidence has been heard in private and the tribunal so directs and in that event any such document shall be sent to the parties and to any superior court in any proceedings relating to such decision together with the copy of the entry.

(8) The Register shall be kept at the Office of the Tribunals and shall be open to the inspection of any person without charge at all reasonable hours.

(9) Clerical mistakes in any document referred to in paragraphs (2), (4) and (5) of this Rule, or errors arising in such a document from an accidental slip or omission, may at any time be corrected by the chairman by certificate under his hand.

(10) The clerk to the tribunal shall send a copy of any document so corrected and the certificate of the chairman to the Secretary of the Tribunals who shall as soon as may be make such correction as may be necessary in the Register and shall send a copy of any corrected entry or of any corrected document containing reasons for the tribunal's decision, as the case may be, to each of the parties and, in the case of a corrected entry, to the persons entitled to appear who did so appear and, where the originating application was sent to the tribunal by a court, to that court.

(11) If any decision is—

    (a) corrected under paragraph (9) of this Rule,

    (b) reviewed, revoked or varied under Rule 10, or

    (c) altered in any way by order of a superior court,

the Secretary of the Tribunals shall alter the entry in the Register to conform with any such certificate or order and shall send a copy of the new entry to each of the parties and to the persons entitled to appear who did so appear and, where the originating application was sent to the tribunal by a court, to that court.

(12) Where by this Rule a document is required to be signed by the chairman but by reason of death or incapacity the chairman is unable to sign such document it shall be signed by the other members of the tribunal, who shall certify that the chairman is unable to sign.   **[1223]**

10 Review of tribunal's decision

(1) A tribunal shall have power to review and to revoke or vary by certificate under the chairman's hand any decision on the grounds that—

    (a)   the decision was wrongly made as a result of an error on the part of the tribunal staff; or

    (b)   a party did not receive notice of the proceedings leading to the decision; or

    (c)   the decision was made in the absence of a party or person entitled to be heard; or

    (d)   new evidence has become available since the conclusion of the hearing to which the decision relates provided that its existence could not have been reasonably known of or foreseen; or

    (e)   the interests of justice require such a review.

(2) An application for the purposes of paragraph (1) of this Rule may be made at the hearing. If the application is not made at the hearing, such application shall be made to the Secretary of the Tribunals at any time from the date of the hearing until 14 days after the date on which the decision was sent to the parties and must be in writing stating the grounds in full.

(3) An application for the purposes of paragraph (1) of this Rule may be refused by the President or by the chairman of the tribunal which decided the case or by a Regional Chairman if in his opinion it has no reasonable prospect of success.

(4) If such an application is not refused under paragraph (3) of this Rule it shall be heard by the tribunal which decided the case, or

    (a)   where it is not practicable for it to be heard by that tribunal, or

    (b)   where the decision was made by a chairman acting alone under Rule 12(4),

by a tribunal appointed either by the President or a Regional Chairman, and if the application is granted the tribunal shall proceed to a review of the decision and, having reviewed it, may confirm, vary or revoke that decision, and if the tribunal revokes the decision it shall order a re-hearing before either the same or a differently constituted tribunal.

(5) The clerk to the tribunal shall send to the Secretary of the Tribunals the certificate of the chairman as to any revocation or variation of the tribunal's decision under this Rule. The Secretary of the Tribunals shall as soon as may be make such correction as may be necessary in the Register and shall send a copy of the entry to each of the parties and to the persons entitled to appear who did so appear and where the originating application was sent to a tribunal by a court, to that court.   **[1224]**

11 Costs

(1) Subject to paragraphs (2), (3) and (4) of this Rule, a tribunal shall not normally make an award in respect of the costs or expenses incurred by a party to the proceedings but where in its opinion a party (and if he is a respondent whether or not he has entered an appearance) has in bringing or conducting the proceedings acted frivolously, vexatiously or otherwise unreasonably the tribunal may make—

    (a)   an order that that party shall pay to another party (or to the Secretary of State if, not being a party, he has acted as provided in Rule 7(5)) either a specified sum in respect of the costs or expenses incurred by that other party (or, as the case may be, by the Secretary of State) or the whole or part of those costs or expenses as taxed (if not otherwise agreed);

    (b)   an order that that party shall pay to the Secretary of State the whole, or any part, of any allowances (other than allowances paid to members of tribunals or assessors) paid by the Secretary of State under paragraph 10 of Schedule 9 to the 1978 Act to any person for the purposes of, or in connection with, his attendance at the tribunal.

(2) Where the tribunal has on the application of a party to the proceedings postponed the day or time fixed for or adjourned the hearing, the tribunal may make orders against or, as the case may require, in favour of that party as at paragraph (1)(a) and (b) of this Rule as respects any costs or expenses incurred or any allowances paid as a result of the postponement or adjournment.

(3) Where, on a complaint of unfair dismissal in respect of which—

   (i) the applicant has expressed a wish to be reinstated or re-engaged which has been communicated to the respondent at least 7 days before the hearing of the complaint, or

   (ii) the proceedings arise out of the respondent's failure to permit the applicant to return to work after an absence due to pregnancy or confinement,

any postponement or adjournment of the hearing has been caused by the respondent's failure, without a special reason, to adduce reasonable evidence as to the availability of the job from which the applicant was dismissed, or, as the case may be, which she held before her absence, or of comparable or suitable employment, the tribunal shall make orders against that respondent as at paragraph (1)(a) and (b) of this Rule as respects any costs or expenses incurred or any allowances paid as a result of the postponement or adjournment.

(4) In any proceedings under the 1966 Act a tribunal may make—

   (a) an order that a party or any other person entitled to appear who did so appear, shall pay to another party or such person either a specified sum in respect of the costs or expenses incurred by that other party or person or the whole or part of those costs or expenses as taxed (if not otherwise agreed);

   (b) an order that a party, or any other person entitled to appear who did so appear, shall pay to the Secretary of State a specified sum in respect of the whole, or any part, of any allowances (other than allowances paid to members of tribunals) paid by the Secretary of State under paragraph 10 of Schedule 9 to the 1978 Act to any person for the purposes of, or in connection with, his attendance at the tribunal.

(5) Any costs required by an order under this Rule to be taxed may be taxed in the county court according to such of the scales prescribed by the county court rules for proceedings in the county court as shall be directed by the order.   **[1225]**

12 Miscellaneous powers of tribunal

(1) Subject to the provisions of these Rules, a tribunal may regulate its own procedure.

(2) A tribunal may, if it thinks fit—

   (a) extend the time appointed by or under these Rules for doing any act notwithstanding that the time appointed may have expired;

   (b) postpone the day or time fixed for, or adjourn, any hearing (particularly as respects cases under the provisions of any enactment providing for conciliation for the purpose of giving an opportunity for the complaint to be settled by way of conciliation and withdrawn);

   (c) if the applicant shall at any time give notice of the withdrawal of his originating application, dismiss the proceedings;

   (d) except in proceedings under the 1966 Act, if both or all the parties (and the Secretary of State, if, not being a party, he has acted as provided in Rule 7(5)) agree in writing upon the terms of a decision to be made by the tribunal, decide accordingly;

   (e) subject to the Proviso below, at any stage of the proceedings order to be struck out or amended any originating application or notice of appearance or anything in such application or notice of appearance on the grounds that it is scandalous, frivolous or vexatious;

   (f) subject to the Proviso below, on the application of the respondent, or of its own motion, order to be struck out any originating application for want of prosecution;

Provided that before making any order under (e) or (f) above the tribunal shall send notice to the party against whom it is proposed that any such order should be made giving him an opportunity to show cause why such an order should not be made.

(3) Subject to Rule 4(2), a tribunal may, if it thinks fit, before granting an application under Rule 4 or Rule 13 require the party (or, as the case may be, the Secretary of State) making the application to give notice of it to the other party or parties. The notice shall give particulars of the application and indicate the address to which and the time within which any objection to the application shall be made being an address and time specified for the purposes of the application by the tribunal.

(4) Any act other than the holding of a pre-hearing assessment under Rule 6, the hearing of an originating application or the making of an order under Rule 10(1), required or authorised by these Rules to be done by a tribunal may be done by, or on the direction of, the President or the chairman of the tribunal or any chairman being a member of the panel of chairmen.

(5) Rule 11 shall apply to an order dismissing proceedings under paragraph (2)(c) of this Rule.

(6) Any functions of the Secretary of the Tribunals other than that mentioned in Rule 1(2) may be performed by an Assistant Secretary of the Tribunals.   **[1226]**

13 Extension of time and directions

(1) An application to a tribunal for an extension of the time appointed by these Rules for doing any act may be made by a party either before or after the expiration of any time so appointed.

(2) Subject to Rule 3(2), a party may at any time apply to a tribunal for directions on any matter arising in connection with the proceedings.

(3) An application under the foregoing provisions of this Rule shall be made by presenting to the Secretary of the Tribunals a notice of application, which shall state the title of the proceedings and shall set out the grounds of the application.

(4) The Secretary of the Tribunals shall give notice to both or all the parties (subject to Rule 3(2)) of any extension of time granted under Rule 12(2)(a) or any directions given in pursuance of this Rule.   **[1227]**

14 Joinder and representative respondents

(1) A tribunal may at any time either upon the application of any person or, where appropriate, of its own motion, direct any person against whom any relief is sought to be joined as a party to the proceedings, and give such consequential directions as it considers necessary.

(2) A tribunal may likewise, either upon such application or of its own motion, order that any respondent named in the originating application or subsequently added, who shall appear to the tribunal not to have been, or to have ceased to be, directly interested in the subject of the originating application, be dismissed from the proceedings.

(3) Where there are numerous persons having the same interest in an originating application, one or more of them may be cited as the person or persons against whom relief is sought, or may be authorised by the tribunal, before or at the hearing, to defend on behalf of all the persons so interested.   **[1228]**

15 Consolidation of proceedings

Where there are pending before the industrial tribunals two or more originating applications, then, if at any time upon the application of a party or of its own motion it appears to a tribunal that—

    (a)   some common question of law or fact arises in both or all the originating applications, or

    (b)   the relief claimed therein is in respect of or arises out of the same set of facts, or

    (c)   for some other reason it is desirable to make an order under this Rule, the tribunal may order that some (as specified in the order) or all of the originating applications shall be considered together, and may give such consequential directions as may be necessary: Provided that the tribunal shall not make an order under this Rule without sending notice to all parties concerned giving them an opportunity to show cause why such an order should not be made.

[1229]

16 Transfer of proceedings

(1) Where there is pending before the industrial tribunals an originating application in respect of which it appears to the President or a Regional Chairman that the proceedings could be determined in an industrial tribunal (Scotland) established in pursuance of the Industrial Tribunals (Scotland) Regulations 1965 and that the originating application would more conveniently be determined by such a tribunal, the President or a Regional Chairman may, at any time upon the application of a party or of his own motion, with the consent of the President of the Industrial Tribunals (Scotland), direct that the said proceedings be transferred to the Office of the Industrial Tribunals (Scotland): Provided that no such direction shall be made unless notice has been sent to all parties concerned giving them an opportunity to show cause why such a direction should not be made.

(2) Where proceedings have been transferred to the Office of the Industrial Tribunals (England and Wales) under Rule 16(1) of the Industrial Tribunals (Rules of Procedure) (Scotland) Regulations 1985 they shall be treated as if in all respects they had been commenced by an originating application pursuant to Rule 1.

[1230]

17 Notices, etc

(1) Any notice given under these Rules shall be in writing.

(2) All notices and documents required by these Rules to be presented to the Secretary of the Tribunals may be presented at the Office of the Tribunals or such other office as may be notified by the Secretary of the Tribunals to the parties.

(3) All notices and documents required or authorised by these Rules to be sent or given to any person hereinafter mentioned may be sent by post (subject to paragraph (5) of this Rule) or delivered to or at—

    (a) in the case of a notice or document directed to the Secretary of State in proceedings to which he is not a party, the offices of the Department of Employment at Caxton House, Tothill Street, London SW1H 9NF, or such other office as may be notified by the Secretary of State;

    (b) in the case of a notice or document directed to the Board, the principal office of the Board;

    (c) in the case of a notice or document directed to a court, the office of the clerk of the court;

    (d) in the case of a notice or document directed to a party:—

        (i) his address for service specified in the originating application or in a notice of appearance or in a notice under paragraph (4) of this Rule; or

        (ii) if no address for service has been so specified, his last known address or place of business in the United Kingdom or, if the party is a corporation, the corporation's registered or principal office in the United Kingdom, or, in any case, such address or place outside the United Kingdom as the President or a Regional Chairman may allow;

    (e) in the case of a notice or document directed to any person (other than a person specified in the foregoing provisions of this paragraph), his address or place of business in the United Kingdom, or if such a person is a corporation, the corporation's registered or principal office in the United Kingdom;

and if sent or given to the authorised representative of a party shall be deemed to have been sent or given to that party.

(4) A party may at any time by notice to the Secretary of the Tribunals and to the other party or parties (and, where appropriate, to the appropriate conciliation officer) change his address for service under these Rules.

(5) The recorded delivery service shall be used instead of the ordinary post:—

(a) when a second set of documents or notices is to be sent to a respondent who has not entered an appearance under Rule 3(1);

(b) for service of an order made under Rule 4(1)(iii) requiring the attendance of a witness.

(6) Where for any sufficient reason service of any document or notice cannot be effected in the manner prescribed under this Rule, the President or a Regional Chairman may make an order for substituted service in such manner as he may deem fit and such service shall have the same effect as service in the manner prescribed under this Rule.

(7) In proceedings brought under the provisions of any enactment providing for conciliation the Secretary of the Tribunals shall send copies of all documents and notices to a conciliation officer who in the opinion of the Secretary is an appropriate officer to receive them.

(8) In proceedings which may involve payments out of the [National Insurance Fund] or Maternity Pay Fund, the Secretary of the Tribunals shall, where appropriate, send copies of all documents and notices to the Secretary of State notwithstanding the fact that he may not be a party to such proceedings.

(9) In proceedings under the Equal Pay Act, the Sex Discrimination Act or the Race Relations Act the Secretary of the Tribunals shall send to the Equal Opportunities Commission or, as the case may be, the Commission for Racial Equality copies of all documents sent to the parties under Rule 9(6), (10) and (11) and Rule 10(5).   **[1231]**

NOTE

Para (8): words in square brackets substituted by virtue of the Employment Act 1990, s 13(3).

SCHEDULE 2

Regulation 3(2)

COMPLEMENTARY RULES OF PROCEDURE

For use only in proceedings involving an equal value claim

4 Power to require further particulars and attendance of witnesses and to grant discovery

(1) A tribunal may—

(a) subject to Rule 3(2), on the application of a party to the proceedings made either by notice to the Secretary of the Tribunals or at the hearing of the originating application, or

(b) in relation to sub-paragraph (i) of this paragraph, if it thinks fit, of its own motion—

(i)   require a party to furnish in writing to the person specified by the tribunal further particulars of the grounds on which he or it relies and of any facts and contentions relevant thereto;

(ii) grant to the person making the application such discovery or inspection (including the taking of copies) of documents as might be granted by a county court; and

(iii) require the attendance of any person (including a party to the proceedings) as a witness, wherever such person may be within Great Britain, and may, if it does so require the attendance of a person, require him to produce any document relating to the matter to be determined;

and may appoint the time at or within which or the place at which any act required in pursuance of this Rule is to be done.

(1A)   Subject to paragraph (1B), a tribunal may, on the application of an expert who has been required by the tribunal to prepare a report,

    (a)   require any person who the tribunal is satisfied may have information which may be relevant to the question or matter on which the expert is required to report to furnish, in writing, such information as the tribunal may require;

    (b)   require any person to produce any documents which are in the possession, custody or power of that person and which the tribunal is satisfied may contain matter relevant to the question on which the expert is required to report;

and any information so required to be furnished or document so required to be produced shall be furnished or produced, at or within such time as the tribunal may appoint, to the Secretary of the Tribunals who shall send the information or document to the expert.

(1B)   A tribunal shall not make a requirement under paragraph (1A) of this Rule—

    (a)   of a conciliation officer who has acted in connection with the complaint under section 64 of the Sex Discrimination Act, or

    (b)   if it is satisfied that the person so required would have good grounds for refusing to comply with the requirement if it were a requirement made in connection with a hearing before the tribunal.

(2) A party on whom a requirement has been made under paragraph (1)(i) or (1)(ii) of this Rule on an *ex parte* application, or (in relation to a requirement under paragraph (1)(i)) on the tribunal's own motion, and a person on whom a requirement has been made under paragraph (1)(iii) may apply to the tribunal by notice to the Secretary of the Tribunals before the appointed time at or within which the requirement is to be complied with to vary or set aside the requirement. Notice of an application under this paragraph to vary or set aside a requirement shall be given to the parties (other than the party making the application) and, where appropriate, in proceedings which may involve payments out of the [National Insurance Fund] or Maternity Pay Fund, the Secretary of State if not a party.

(2A)   A person, whether or not a party to the proceedings, upon whom a requirement has been made under paragraph (1A) of this Rule, may apply to the tribunal by notice to the Secretary of the Tribunals before the appointed time at or within which the requirement is to be complied with to vary or set aside the requirement. Notice of such application shall be given to the parties and to the expert upon whose application the requirement was made.

(3) Every document containing a requirement under paragraph (1)(ii) or (1)(iii) or paragraph (1A) of this Rule shall contain a reference to the fact that, under paragraph 1(7) of Schedule 9 to the 1978 Act, any person who without reasonable excuse fails to comply with any such requirement shall be liable on summary conviction to a fine, and the document shall state the amount of the current maximum fine.

(4) If the requirement under paragraph (1)(i) or (1)(ii) of this Rule is not complied with, a tribunal, before or at the hearing, may dismiss the whole or part of the originating application, or, as the case may be, strike out the whole or part of the notice of appearance, and, where appropriate, direct that a respondent shall be debarred from defending altogether: Provided that a tribunal shall not so dismiss or strike out or give such a direction unless it has sent notice to the party who has not complied with the requirement giving him an opportunity to show cause why such should not be done.   **[1232]**

NOTE

Para (2): words in square brackets substituted by virtue of the Employment Act 1990, s 13(3).

7A Procedure relating to expert's report

(1) In any case involving an equal value claim where a dispute arises as to whether any work is of equal value to other work in terms of the demands made on the person employed on the work (for instance under such headings as effort, skill and decision) (in this Rule hereinafter referred to as "the question"), a tribunal shall, before considering the question, except in cases to which section 2A(1)(a) of the Equal Pay Act applies, require an expert to prepare a report with respect to the question and the requirement shall be made in accordance with paragraphs (2) and (3) of this Rule.

(2) The requirement shall be made in writing and shall set out—

    (a)   the name and address of each of the parties;

    (b)   the address of the establishment at which the applicant is (or, as the case may be, was) employed;

    (c)   the question; and

    (d)   the identity of the person with reference to whose work the question arises;

and a copy of the requirement shall be sent to each of the parties.

(3) The requirement shall stipulate that the expert shall—

    (a)   take account of all such information supplied and all such representations made to him as have a bearing on the question;

    (b)   before drawing up his report, produce and send to the parties a written summary of the said information and representations and invite the representations of the parties upon the material contained therein;

    (c)   make his report to the tribunal in a document which shall reproduce the summary and contain a brief account of any representations received from the parties upon it, any conclusion he may have reached upon the question and the reasons for that conclusion or, as the case may be, for his failure to reach such a conclusion;

    (d)   take no account of the difference of sex and at all times act fairly.

(4) Without prejudice to the generality of Rule 12(2)(b), where a tribunal requires an expert to prepare a report, it shall adjourn the hearing.

(5) If, on the application of one or more of the parties made not less than 42 days after a tribunal has notified an expert of the requirement to prepare a report, the tribunal forms the view that there has been or is likely to be undue delay in receiving that report, the tribunal may require the expert to provide in writing to the tribunal an explanation for the delay or information as to his progress and may, on consideration of any such explanation or information as may be provided and after seeking representations from the parties, revoke, by notice in writing to the expert, the requirement to prepare a report, and in such a case paragraph (1) of this Rule shall again apply.

(6) Where a tribunal has received the report of an expert, it shall forthwith send a copy of the report to each of the parties and shall fix a date for the hearing of the case to be resumed; provided that the date so fixed shall be at least 14 days after the date on which the report is sent to the parties.

(7) Upon the resuming of the hearing of the case in accordance with paragraph (6) of this Rule the report shall be admitted as evidence in the case unless the tribunal has exercised its power under paragraph (8) of this Rule not to admit the report.

(8) Where the tribunal, on the application of one or more of the parties or otherwise, forms the view—

    (a)   that the expert has not complied with a stipulation in paragraph (3) of this Rule, or

    (b)   that the conclusion contained in the report is one which, taking due account of the information supplied and representations made to the expert, could not reasonably have been reached, or

    (c)   that for some other material reason (other than disagreement with the conclusion that the applicant's work is or is not of equal value or with the reasoning leading to that conclusion) the report is unsatisfactory,

the tribunal may, if it thinks fit, determine not to admit the report, and in such a case paragraph (1) of this Rule shall again apply.

(9) In forming its view on the matters contained in paragraph (8)(a), (b) and (c) of this Rule, the tribunal shall take account of any representations of the parties thereon and may in that connection, subject to Rule 8(2A) and (2B), permit any party to give evidence upon, to call witnesses and to question any witness upon any matter relevant thereto.

(10) The tribunal may, at any time after it has received the report of an expert, require that expert (or, if that is impracticable, another expert) to explain any matter contained in his report or, having regard to such matters as may be set out in the requirement, to give further consideration to the question.

(11) The requirement in paragraph (10) of this Rule shall comply with paragraph (2) of this Rule and shall stipulate that the expert shall make his reply in writing to the tribunal, giving his explanation or, as the case may be, setting down any conclusion which may result from his further consideration and his reasons for that conclusion.

(12) Where the tribunal has received a reply from the expert under paragraph (11) of this Rule, it shall forthwith send a copy of the reply to each of the parties and shall allow the parties to make representations thereon, and the reply shall be treated as information furnished to the tribunal and be given such weight as the tribunal thinks fit.

(13) Where a tribunal has determined not to admit a report under paragraph (8), that report shall be treated for all purposes (other than the award of costs or expenses under Rule 11) connected with the proceedings as if it had not been received by the tribunal and no further account shall be taken of it, and the requirement on the expert to prepare a report shall lapse.
[1233]

8 Procedure at hearing

(1) Subject to paragraphs (2A), (2B), (2C), (2D) and (2E) of this Rule the tribunal shall conduct the hearing in such manner as it considers most suitable to the clarification of the issues before it and generally so far as appears to it appropriate seek to avoid formality in its proceedings and it shall not be bound by any enactment or rule of law relating to the admissibility of evidence in proceedings before the courts of law.

(2) Subject to paragraphs (1), (2A), (2B), (2C) and (2D) of this Rule, at the hearing of the originating application a party (unless disentitled by virtue of Rule 3(2)), the Secretary of State (if, not being a party, he elects to appear as provided in Rule 7(5)) and any other person entitled to appear shall be entitled to give evidence, to call witnesses, to question any witnesses and to address the tribunal.

(2A) The tribunal may, and shall upon the application of a party, require the attendance of an expert who has prepared a report in connection with an equal value claim in any hearing relating to that claim. Where an expert attends in compliance with such requirement any party may, subject to paragraph (1) of this Rule, cross-examine the expert on his report and on any other matter pertaining to the question on which the expert was required to report.

(2B) At any time after the tribunal has received the report of the expert, any party may, on giving reasonable notice of his intention to do so to the tribunal and to any other party to the claim, call one witness to give expert evidence on the question on which the tribunal has required the expert to prepare a report; and where such evidence is given, any other party may cross-examine the person giving that evidence upon it.

(2C) Except as provided in Rule 7A(9) or by paragraph (2D) of this Rule, no party may give evidence upon, or question any witness upon, any matter of fact upon which a conclusion in the report of the expert is based.

(2D) Subject to paragraphs (2A) and (2B) of this Rule, a tribunal may, notwithstanding paragraph (2C) of this Rule, permit a party to give evidence upon, to call witnesses and to question any witness upon any such matters of fact as are referred to in that paragraph if either—

    (a) the matter of fact is relevant to and is raised in connection with the issue contained in subsection (3) of section 1 of the Equal Pay Act (defence of genuine material factor) upon which the determination of the tribunal is being sought; or

    (b) the report of the expert contains no conclusion on the question of whether the applicant's work and the work of the person identified in the requirement of the tribunal under Rule 7A(2) are of equal value and the tribunal is satisfied that the absence of that conclusion is wholly or mainly due to the refusal or deliberate omission of a person required by the tribunal under Rule 4(1A) to furnish information or to produce documents to comply with that requirement.

(2E) A tribunal may, on the application of a party, if in the circumstances of the case, having regard to the considerations expressed in paragraph (1) of this Rule, it considers that it is appropriate so to proceed, hear evidence upon and permit the parties to address it upon the issue contained in subsection (3) of section 1 of the Equal Pay Act (defence of genuine material factor) before it requires an expert to prepare a report under Rule 7A. Where the tribunal so proceeds, it shall be without prejudice to further consideration of that issue after the tribunal has received the report.

(3) If a party shall fail to appear or to be represented at the time and place fixed for the hearing, the tribunal may, if that party is an applicant, dismiss or, in any case, dispose of the application in the absence of that party or may adjourn the hearing to a later date: Provided that before deciding to dismiss or disposing of any application in the absence of a party the tribunal shall consider any representations submitted by that party in pursuance of Rule 7(3).

(4) A tribunal may require any witness to give evidence on oath or affirmation and for that purpose there may be administered an oath or affirmation in due form.   **[1234]**

9 Decision of tribunal

(1) A decision of a tribunal may be taken by a majority thereof and, if the tribunal shall be constituted of two members only, the chairman shall have a second or casting vote.

(2) The decision of a tribunal, which may be given orally at the end of a hearing or reserved, shall be recorded in a document signed by the chairman.

(3) A tribunal shall give reasons for its decision.

(4) The reasons for the decision of the tribunal shall be recorded in full form in a document signed by the chairman.

(4A)   There shall be appended to the document referred to in paragraph (4) of this Rule a copy of the report (if any) of an expert received by the tribunal in the course of the proceedings.

[paragraph (5) is omitted because it has no relevance in proceedings involving an equal value claim]

(6) The clerk to the tribunal shall transmit any document referred to in paragraphs (2), (4) and (4A) of this Rule to the Secretary of the Tribunals who shall as soon as may be enter it in the Register and shall send a copy of the entry to each of the parties and to the persons entitled to appear who did so appear and, where the originating application was sent to a tribunal by a court, to that court.

(7) Any document referred to in paragraphs (4) and (4A) of this Rule shall be omitted from the Register in any case in which evidence has been heard in private and the tribunal so directs and in that event any such document shall be sent to the parties and to any superior court in any proceedings relating to such decision together with the copy of the entry.

(8) The Register shall be kept at the Office of the Tribunals and shall be open to the inspection of any person without charge at all reasonable hours.

(9) Clerical mistakes in any document referred to in paragraphs (2) and (4) of this Rule, or errors arising in such a document from an accidental slip or omission, may at any time be corrected by the chairman by certificate under his hand.

(10) The clerk to the tribunal shall send a copy of any document so corrected and the certificate of the chairman to the Secretary of the Tribunals who shall as soon as may be make such correction as may be necessary in the Register and shall send a copy of any corrected entry or of any corrected document containing reasons for the tribunal's decision, as the case may be, to each of the parties and, in the case of a corrected entry, to the persons entitled to appear who did so appear and, where the originating application was sent to the tribunal by a court, to that court.

(11) If any decision is—

    (a)   corrected under paragraph (9) of this Rule,
    (b)   reviewed, revoked or varied under Rule 10, or
    (c)   altered in any way by order of a superior court,

the Secretary of the Tribunals shall alter the entry in the Register to conform with any such certificate or order and shall send a copy of the new entry to each of the parties and to the persons entitled to appear who did so appear and, where the originating application was sent to the tribunal by a court, to that court.

(12) Where by this Rule a document is required to be signed by the chairman but by reason of death or incapacity the chairman is unable to sign such document it shall be signed by the other members of the tribunal, who shall certify that the chairman is unable to sign.   **[1235]**

11 Costs

(1) Subject to paragraphs (2) and (3) of this Rule, a tribunal shall not normally make an award in respect of the costs or expenses incurred by a party to the proceedings but where in its opinion a party (and if he is a respondent whether or not he has entered an appearance) has in bringing or conducting the proceedings acted frivolously, vexatiously or otherwise unreasonably the tribunal may make—

(a) an order that that party shall pay to another party (or to the Secretary of State, if, not being a party, he has acted as provided in Rule 7(5)) either a specified sum in respect of the costs or expenses incurred by that other party (or, as the case may be, by the Secretary of State) or the whole or part of those costs or expenses as taxed (if not otherwise agreed);

(b) an order that that party shall pay to the Secretary of State the whole, or any part, of any allowances (other than allowances paid to members of tribunals, experts or assessors) paid by the Secretary of State under paragraph 10 of Schedule 9 to the 1978 Act to any person for the purposes of, or in connection with, his attendance at the tribunal.

(1A)   For the purposes of paragraph (1)(a) of this Rule, the costs or expenses in respect of which a tribunal may make an order include costs or expenses incurred by the party in whose favour the order is to be made in or in connection with the investigations carried out by the expert in preparing his report.

(2) Where the tribunal has on the application of a party to the proceedings postponed the day or time fixed for or adjourned the hearing, the tribunal may make orders against or, as the case may require, in favour of that party as at paragraph (1)(a) and (b) of this Rule as respects any costs or expenses incurred or any allowances paid as a result of the postponement or adjournment.

(3) Where, on a complaint of unfair dismissal in respect of which—

(i) the applicant has expressed a wish to be reinstated or re-engaged which has been communicated to the respondent at least 7 days before the hearing of the complaint, or

(ii) the proceedings arise out of the respondent's failure to permit the applicant to return to work after an absence due to pregnancy or confinement,

any postponement or adjournment of the hearing has been caused by the respondent's failure, without a special reason, to adduce reasonable evidence as to the availability of the job from which the applicant was dismissed, or, as the case may be, which she held before her absence, or of comparable or suitable employment, the tribunal shall make orders against that respondent as at paragraph (1)(a) and (b) of this Rule as respects any costs or expenses incurred or any allowances paid as a result of the postponement or adjournment.

[paragraph (4) is omitted because it has no relevance in proceedings involving an equal value claim]

(5) Any costs required by an order under this Rule to be taxed may be taxed in the county court according to such of the scales prescribed by the county court rules for proceedings in the county court as shall be directed by the order.   **[1236]**

12 Miscellaneous powers of tribunal

(1) Subject to the provisions of these Rules, a tribunal may regulate its own procedure.

(2) A tribunal may, if it thinks fit—

(a) extend the time appointed by or under these Rules for doing any act notwithstanding that the time appointed may have expired;

(b) postpone the day or time fixed for, or adjourn, any hearing (particularly as respects cases under the provisions of any enactment providing for conciliation for the purpose of giving an opportunity for the complaint to be settled by way of conciliation and withdrawn);

(c) if the applicant shall at any time give notice of the withdrawal of his originating application, dismiss the proceedings;

(d) except in proceedings under the 1966 Act, if both or all the parties (and the Secretary of State, if, not being a party, he has acted as provided in Rule 7(5)) agree in writing upon the terms of a decision to be made by the tribunal, decide accordingly;

(e) subject to the Proviso below, at any stage of the proceedings order to be struck out or amended any originating application or notice of appearance or anything in such application or notice of appearance on the grounds that it is scandalous, frivolous or vexatious;

(f) subject to the Proviso below, on the application of the respondent, or of its own motion, order to be struck out any originating application for want of prosecution;

Provided that before making any order under (e) or (f) above the tribunal shall send notice to the party against whom it is proposed that any such order should be made giving him an opportunity to show cause why such an order should not be made.

(2A) Without prejudice to the generality of paragraph (2)(b) of this Rule, the tribunal shall, before proceeding to hear the parties on an equal value claim, invite them to apply for an adjournment for the purpose of seeking to reach a settlement of the claim and shall, if both or all the parties agree to such a course, grant an adjournment for that purpose.

(2B) If, after the tribunal has adjourned the hearing under rule 7A(4) but before the tribunal has received the report of the expert, the applicant gives notice under paragraph (2)(c) of this Rule, the tribunal shall forthwith notify the expert that the requirement to prepare a report has ceased. The notice shall be without prejudice to the operation of Rule 11(1A).

(3) Subject to Rule 4(2), and (2A), a tribunal may, if it thinks fit, before granting an application under Rule 4 or Rule 13 require the party (or, as the case may be, the Secretary of State or, in the case of an application under Rule 4(1A), the expert) making the application to give notice of it to the other party or parties (or, in the case of an application by an expert, the parties and any other person in respect of whom the tribunal is asked, in the application, to impose a requirement). The notice shall give particulars of the application and indicate the address to which and the time within which any objection to the application shall be made being an address and time specified for the purposes of the application by the tribunal.

(4) Any act other than the holding of a pre-hearing assessment under Rule 6, the hearing of an originating application, or the making of an order under Rule 10(1), required or authorised by these Rules to be done by a tribunal may be done by, or on the direction of, the President or the chairman of the tribunal or any chairman being a member of the panel of chairmen.

(5) Rule 11 shall apply to an order dismissing proceedings under paragraph (2)(c) of this Rule.

(6) Any functions of the Secretary of the Tribunals other than that mentioned in Rule 1(2) may be performed by an Assistant Secretary of the Tribunals.   **[1237]**

17 Notices etc

(1) Any notice given under these Rules shall be in writing.

(2) All notices and documents required by these Rules to be presented to the Secretary of

the Tribunals may be presented at the Office of the Tribunals or such other office as may be notified by the Secretary of the Tribunals to the parties.

(3) All notices and documents required or authorised by these Rules to be sent or given to any person hereinafter mentioned may be sent by post (subject to paragraph (5) of this Rule) or delivered to or at—

    (a) in the case of a notice or document directed to the Secretary of State in proceedings to which he is not a party, the offices of the Department of Employment at Caxton House, Tothill Street, London SW1H 9NF, or such other office as may be notified by the Secretary of State;

[sub-paragraph (b) is omitted because it has no relevance in proceedings involving an equal value claim]

    (c) in the case of a notice or document directed to a court, the office of the clerk of the court;

    (d) in the case of a notice or document directed to a party:—

        (i) his address for service specified in the originating application or in a notice of appearance or in a notice under paragraph (4) of this Rule; or

        (ii) if no address for service has been so specified, his last known address or place of business in the United Kingdom or, if the party is a corporation, the corporation's registered or principal office in the United Kingdom or, in any case, such address or place outside the United Kingdom as the President or a Regional Chairman may allow;

    (e) in the case of a notice or document directed to any person (other than a person specified in the foregoing provisions of this paragraph), his address or place of business in the United Kingdom, or if such a person is a corporation, the corporation's registered or principal office in the United Kingdom; and if sent or given to the authorised representative of a party shall be deemed to have been sent or given to that party.

(4) A party may at any time by notice to the Secretary of the Tribunals and to the other party or parties (and, where appropriate, to the appropriate conciliation officer and the appropriate expert) change his address for service under these Rules.

(5) The recorded delivery service shall be used instead of the ordinary post:—

    (a) when a second set of documents or notices is to be sent to a respondent who has not entered an appearance under Rule 3(1);

    (b) for service of an order made under Rule 4(1)(iii) or (1A).

(6) Where for any sufficient reason service of any document or notice cannot be effected in the manner prescribed under this Rule, the President or a Regional Chairman may make an order for substituted service in such manner as he may deem fit and such service shall have the same effect as service in the manner prescribed under this Rule.

(7) In proceedings brought under the provisions of any enactment providing for conciliation the Secretary of the Tribunals shall send copies of all documents and notices to a conciliation officer who in the opinion of the Secretary is an appropriate officer to receive them.

(8) In proceedings which may involve payments out of the [National Insurance Fund] or Maternity Pay Fund, the Secretary of the Tribunals shall, where appropriate, send copies of all documents and notices to the Secretary of State notwithstanding the fact that he may not be a party to such proceedings.

(9) In proceedings under the Equal Pay Act, the Sex Discrimination Act or the Race Relations Act the Secretary of the Tribunals shall send to the Equal Opportunities Commission or, as the case may be, the Commission for Racial Equality copies of all documents sent to the parties under Rule 9(6), (10) and (11) and Rule 10(5).   **[1238]**

NOTE

    Para (8): words in square brackets substituted by virtue of the Employment Act 1990, s 13(3).

INDUSTRIAL TRIBUNALS (RULES OF PROCEDURE) (SCOTLAND) REGULATIONS 1985

(SI 1985/17)

NOTES

Made: 9 January 1985.

Authority: Employment Protection (Consolidation) Act 1978, s 128, Sch 9, para 1.

These Regulations apply to Scotland only. For the equivalent Regulations applying to England and Wales, see SI 1985/16 ante.

ARRANGEMENT OF REGULATIONS AND RULES

1 Citation, commencement and revocation

(1) These Regulations may be cited as the Industrial Tribunals (Rules of Procedure) (Scotland) Regulations 1985 (and the Rules of Procedure contained in Schedules 1 and 2 to these Regulations may be referred to as the Industrial Tribunals Rules of Procedure (Scotland) 1985 and the Industrial Tribunals Complementary Rules of Procedure (Scotland) 1985 respectively). They shall come into operation on 1st March 1985.

(2) The Industrial Tribunals (Rules of Procedure) (Scotland) Regulations 1980 shall cease to have effect on 1st March 1985 except in relation to proceedings instituted before that date.   **[1239]**

2 Interpretation

In these Regulations, unless the context otherwise requires, the following expressions have the meanings hereby assigned to them respectively, that is to say—

"the 1966 Act" means the Docks and Harbours Act 1966;

"the 1978 Act" means the Employment Protection (Consolidation) Act 1978;

"applicant" means a person who in pursuance of Rule 1 has presented an originating application to the Secretary of the Tribunals for a decision of a tribunal and includes:—

   (a) the Secretary of State, the Board or a licensing authority,
   (b) a claimant or complainant,
   (c) in the case of proceedings under section 51 of the 1966 Act, a person on whose behalf an originating application has been sent by a trade union, and
   (d) in relation to interlocutory applications under these Rules, a person who seeks any relief;

"the Board" means the National Dock Labour Board as reconstituted under the Dock Work Regulation Act 1976;

"the clerk to the tribunal" means the person appointed by the Secretary of the Tribunals or an Assistant Secretary to act in that capacity at one or more hearings;

"decision" in relation to a tribunal includes a declaration, an order (other than an interlocutory order), a recommendation or an award of the tribunal but does not include an opinion given pursuant to a pre-hearing assessment held under Rule 6;

"the Equal Pay Act" means the Equal Pay Act 1970;

"equal value claim" means a claim by an applicant which rests upon entitlement to the benefit of an equality clause by virtue of the operation of section 1(2)(c) of the Equal Pay Act;

"expert" means a member of the panel of independent experts within the meaning of section 2A(4) of the Equal Pay Act;

"hearing" means a sitting of a tribunal duly constituted for the purpose of receiving evidence, hearing addresses and witnesses or doing anything lawfully requisite to enable the tribunal to reach a decision on any question;

"licensing authority" means a body having the function of issuing licences under the 1966 Act;

"the Office of the Tribunals" means the Central Office of the Industrial Tribunals (Scotland);

"the panel of chairmen" means the panel of persons, being advocates or solicitors of not less than seven years' standing, appointed by the Lord President of the Court of Session in pursuance of Regulation 5(2) of the Industrial Tribunals (Scotland) Regulations 1965;

"party" in relation to proceedings under section 51 of the 1966 Act means the applicant and the Board or the licensing authority with which or (as the case may be) any person with whom it appears to the applicant that he is in dispute about a question to which that section applies and, in a case where such a question is referred to a tribunal by a sheriff, any party to the proceedings before the court in which the question arose;

"person entitled to appear" in relation to proceedings under section 51 of the 1966 Act means a party and any person who, under subsection (5) of that section, is entitled to appear and be heard before a tribunal in such proceedings;

"the President" means the President of the Industrial Tribunals (Scotland) or the person nominated by the Lord President of the Court of Session to discharge for the time being the functions of the President;

"the Race Relations Act" means the Race Relations Act 1976;

"Regional Chairman" means a chairman appointed by the President to carry out such functions as the President may designate in connection with the due administration of justice by tribunals in Scotland, or a person nominated either by the President or a Regional Chairman to discharge for the time being the functions of a Regional Chairman;

"Register" means the Register of Applications and Decisions kept in pursuance of these Regulations;

"report" means a report required by a tribunal to be prepared by an expert, pursuant to section 2A(1)(b) of the Equal Pay Act;

"respondent" means a party to the proceedings before a tribunal other than the applicant, and other than the Secretary of State in proceedings under Parts III and VI of the 1978 Act in which he is not cited as the person against whom relief is sought;

"Rule" means, in Schedule 1 to these Regulations, a Rule of Procedure contained in that Schedule, and, in Schedule 2 to these Regulations, a Rule of Procedure contained in Schedule 1 or Schedule 2 as appropriate;

"the Secretary of the Tribunals" and "an Assistant Secretary of the Tribunals" mean respectively the persons for the time being acting as the Secretary, or as an Assistant Secretary, of the Office of the Tribunals;

"the Sex Discrimination Act" means the Sex Discrimination Act 1975;

"tribunal" means an industrial tribunal (Scotland) established in pursuance of the Industrial Tribunals (Scotland) Regulations 1965 and in relation to any proceedings means the tribunal to which the proceedings have been referred by the President or by a Regional Chairman.   **[1240]**

3 Proceedings of tribunals

(1) Except where separate Rules of Procedure made under the provisions of any enactment are applicable and subject to paragraph (2) of this Regulation, the Rules of Procedure contained in Schedule 1 to these Regulations shall have effect in relation to all proceedings before a tribunal where:—

(a) the respondent or one of the respondents resides or carries on business in Scotland; or

(b) the proceedings relate to a contract of employment the place of execution or performance of which is in Scotland; or

(c) the proceedings are to determine a question which has been referred to the tribunal by a sheriff in Scotland; or

(d) in proceedings under the 1966 Act they are in relation to a port in Scotland.

(2) In any such proceedings before a tribunal involving an equal value claim the Rules of Procedure contained in Schedule 2 to these Regulations (including Rule 7A) shall replace Rules 4, 8, 9, 11, 12 and 17 in Schedule 1.   **[1241]**

4 Proof of decisions of tribunals

The production in any proceedings in any court of a document purporting to be certified by the Secretary of the Tribunals to be a true copy of an entry of a decision in the Register shall, unless the contrary is proved, be sufficient evidence of the document and of the facts stated therein.

[1242]

SCHEDULE 1

Regulation 3(1)

RULES OF PROCEDURE

1 Originating application

(1) Proceedings for the determination of any matter by a tribunal shall be instituted by the applicant (or, where applicable, by a sheriff) presenting to the Secretary of the Tribunals an application, to be known as an originating application, which shall be in writing and shall set out:

    (a)   the name and address of the applicant; and

    (b)   the names and addresses of the person or persons against whom relief is sought or (where applicable) of the parties to the proceedings before a sheriff; and

    (c)   the grounds, with particulars thereof, on which relief is sought; or in proceedings under section 51 of the 1966 Act the question for determination and (except where the question is referred by a sheriff) the grounds on which relief is sought.

(2) Where the Secretary of the Tribunals is of the opinion that the originating application does not seek or on the facts stated therein cannot entitle the applicant to a relief which a tribunal has power to give, he may give notice to that effect to the applicant stating the reasons for his opinion and informing him that the application will not be registered unless he states in writing that he wishes to proceed with it.

(3) An application as respects which a notice has been given in pursuance of the preceding paragraph shall not be treated as having been received for the purposes of Rule 2 unless the applicant intimates in writing to the Secretary of the Tribunals that he wishes to proceed with it; and upon receipt of such an intimation the Secretary of the Tribunals shall proceed in accordance with that Rule.

[1243]

2 Action upon receipt of originating application

Upon receiving an originating application the Secretary of the Tribunals shall enter particulars of it in the Register and shall forthwith send a copy of it to the respondent and inform the parties in writing of the case number of the originating application entered in the Register (which shall thereafter constitute the title of the proceedings) and of the address to which notices and other communications to the Secretary of the Tribunals shall be sent. Every copy of the originating application sent by the Secretary of the Tribunals under this Rule shall be accompanied by a written notice which shall include information, as appropriate to the case, about the means and time for entering an appearance, the consequences of failure to do so, and the right to receive a copy of the decision. The Secretary of the Tribunals shall also notify the parties that in all cases under the provisions of any enactment providing for conciliation the services of a conciliation officer are available to them.

[1244]

3 Appearance by respondent

(1) A respondent shall within 14 days of receiving the copy originating application enter an appearance to the proceedings by presenting to the Secretary of the Tribunals a written notice of appearance setting out his full name and address and stating whether or not he intends to resist the application and, if so, setting out sufficient particulars to show on what grounds. Upon receipt of a notice of appearance the Secretary of the Tribunals shall forthwith send a copy of it to any other party.

(2) A respondent who has not entered an appearance shall not be entitled to take any part in the proceedings except—

    (i)   to apply under Rule 13(1) for an extension of the time appointed by this Rule for entering an appearance;

(ii) to make an application under Rule 4(1)(i);
(iii) to make an application under Rule 10(2) in respect of Rule 10(1)(b);
(iv) to be called as a witness by another person;
(v) to be sent a copy of a document or corrected entry in pursuance of Rule 9(6), 9(10) or 10(5).

(3) A notice of appearance which is presented to the Secretary of the Tribunals after the time appointed by this Rule for entering appearances shall be deemed to include an application under Rule 13(1) (by the respondent who has presented the notice of appearance) for an extension of the time so appointed. Without prejudice to Rule 13(4), if the tribunal grants the application (which it may do notwithstanding that the grounds of the application are not stated) the Secretary of the Tribunals shall forthwith send a copy of the notice of appearance to any other party. The tribunal shall not refuse an extension of time under this Rule unless it has sent notice to the person wishing to enter an appearance giving him an opportunity to show cause why the extension should be granted.   **[1245]**

4 Power to require further particulars and attendance of witnesses and to order recovery of documents

(1) A tribunal may—
  (a) subject to Rule 3(2), on the application of a party to the proceedings made either by notice to the Secretary of the Tribunals or at the hearing of the originating application, or
  (b) in relation to sub-paragraph (i) of this paragraph, if it thinks fit, of its own motion—
      (i) require a party to furnish in writing to the person specified by the tribunal further particulars of the grounds on which he or it relies and of any facts and contentions relevant thereto;
      (ii) grant to the person making the application such recovery or inspection of documents (including the taking of copies) as might be granted by a sheriff; and
      (iii) require the attendance of any person (including a party to the proceedings) as a witness, wherever such person may be within Great Britain, and may, if it does so require the attendance of a person, require him to produce any document relating to the matter to be determined; .

and may appoint the time at or within which or the place at which any act required in pursuance of this Rule is to be done.

(2) A party on whom a requirement has been made under paragraph (1)(i) or (1)(ii) of this Rule on an *ex parte* application, or (in relation to a requirement under paragraph (1)(i)) on the tribunal's own motion, and a person on whom a requirement has been made under paragraph (1)(iii) may apply to the tribunal by notice to the Secretary of the Tribunals before the appointed time at or within which the requirement is to be complied with to vary or set aside the requirement. Notice of an application under this paragraph to vary or set aside a requirement shall be given to the parties (other than the party making the application) and, where appropriate, in proceedings which may involve payments out of the [National Insurance Fund] or Maternity Pay Fund, the Secretary of State if not a party.

(3) Every document containing a requirement under paragraph (1)(ii) or (1)(iii) of this Rule shall contain a reference to the fact that, under paragraph 1(7) of Schedule 9 to the 1978 Act, any person who without reasonable excuse fails to comply with any such requirement shall be liable on summary conviction to a fine, and the document shall state the amount of the current maximum fine.

(4) If the requirement under paragraph (1)(i) or (1)(ii) of this Rule is not complied with, a tribunal, before or at the hearing, may dismiss the whole or part of the originating application, or, as the case may be, strike out the whole or part of the notice of appearance, and, where appropriate, direct that a respondent shall be debarred from defending altogether: Provided that a tribunal shall not so dismiss or strike out or give such a direction unless it has sent notice to the party who has not complied with the requirement giving him an opportunity to show cause why such should not be done.   **[1246]**

NOTE
Para (2): words in square brackets substituted by virtue of the Employment Act 1990, s 13(3).

5 Time and place of hearing and appointment of assessor

(1) The President or a Regional Chairman shall fix a date, time and place of the hearing of the originating application and the Secretary of the Tribunals shall (subject to Rule 3(2)) not less than 14 days (or such shorter time as may be agreed by him with the parties) before the date so fixed send to each party a notice of hearing which shall include information and guidance as to attendance at the hearing, witnesses and the bringing of documents (if any), representation by another person and written representations.

(2) In any proceedings under the 1966 Act in which the President or a Regional Chairman so directs, the Secretary of the Tribunals shall also take such of the following steps as may be so directed, namely—

  (a) publish in one or more newspapers circulating in the locality in which the port in question is situated notice of the hearing;
  (b) send notice of the hearing to such persons as may be directed;
  (c) post notices of the hearing in a conspicuous place or conspicuous places in or near the port in question;

but the requirement as to the period of notice contained in paragraph (1) of this Rule shall not apply to any such notices.

(3) Where in the case of any proceedings it is provided for one or more assessors to be appointed, the President or a Regional Chairman may, if he thinks fit, appoint a person or persons having special knowledge or experience in relation to the subject matter of the originating application to sit with the tribunal as assessor or assessors.   **[1247]**

6 Pre-hearing assessment

(1) A tribunal may at any time before the hearing (either, subject to Rule 3(2), on the application of a party to the proceedings made by notice to the Secretary of the Tribunals or of its own motion) consider, by way of a pre-hearing assessment, the contents of the originating application and entry of appearance, any representations in writing which have been submitted and any oral argument advanced by or on behalf of a party.

(2) If, upon a pre-hearing assessment, the tribunal considers that the originating application or the contentions or any particular contention of a party appear or, as the case may be, appears to have no reasonable prospect of success, it may indicate that in its opinion, if the originating application shall not be withdrawn or the contentions or contention of the party shall be persisted in up to or at the hearing, the party in question may have an order for expenses made against him at the hearing under the provisions of Rule 11. A pre-hearing assessment shall not take place unless the tribunal has sent notice to the parties to the proceedings giving them (and, where appropriate, in proceedings which may involve payments out of the [National Insurance Fund] or Maternity Pay Fund, the Secretary of State, if not a party) an opportunity to submit representations in writing and to advance oral argument at the pre-hearing assessment if they so wish.

(3) Any indication of opinion made in accordance with paragraph (2) of this Rule shall be recorded in a document signed by the chairman, a copy of which shall be sent to the parties to the proceedings and a copy of which shall be available to the tribunal at the hearing.

(4) Where a tribunal has indicated its opinion in accordance with paragraph (2) of this Rule no member thereof shall be a member of the tribunal at the hearing.   **[1248]**

NOTE
Para (2): words in square brackets substituted by virtue of the Employment Act 1990, s 13(3).

7 The hearing

(1) Any hearing of or in connection with an originating application shall take place in public unless in the opinion of the tribunal a private hearing is appropriate for the purpose of hearing

evidence which relates to matters of such a nature that it would be against the interests of national security to allow the evidence to be given in public or hearing evidence from any person which in the opinion of the tribunal is likely to consist of—

(a) information which he could not disclose without contravening a prohibition imposed by or under any enactment; or

(b) any information which has been communicated to him in confidence, or which he has otherwise obtained in consequence of the confidence reposed in him by another person; or

(c) information the disclosure of which would cause substantial injury to any undertaking in which he works for reasons other than its effect on negotiations with respect to any of the matters mentioned in section 29(1) of the Trade Union and Labour Relations Act 1974(a).(2) A member of the Council on Tribunals or of its Scottish Committee shall be entitled to attend any hearing taking place in private in his capacity as such member.

(2) A member of the Council on Tribunals or of its Scottish Committee shall be entitled to attend any hearing taking place in private in his capacity as such member,

(3) Subject to Rule 3(2), if a party shall desire to submit representations in writing for consideration by a tribunal at the hearing of the originating application that party shall present such representations to the Secretary of the Tribunals not less than 7 days before the hearing and shall at the same time send a copy to the other party or parties.

(4) Where a party has failed to attend or be represented at the hearing (whether or not he has sent any representations in writing) the contents of his originating application or, as the case may be, of his entry of appearance may be treated by a tribunal as representations in writing.

(5) The Secretary of State if he so elects shall be entitled to apply under Rule 4(1), 13(1) and (2), 15 and 16(1) and to appear as if he were a party and be heard at any hearing of or in connection with an originating application in which he is not a party in proceedings which may involve payments out of the [National Insurance Fund] or Maternity Pay Fund.

(6) Subject to Rule 3(2), at any hearing of or in connection with an originating application a party and any person entitled to appear may appear before the tribune and may be heard in person or be represented by counsel or by a solicitor or by a representative of a trade union or an employers' association or by any other person whom he desires to represent him.   **[1249]**

NOTE
Para (5): words in square brackets substituted by virtue of the Employment Act 1990, s 13(3).

8 Procedure at hearing

(1) The tribunal shall conduct the hearing in such manner as it considers most suitable to the clarification of the issues before it and generally to the just handling of the proceedings; it shall so far as appears to it appropriate seek to avoid formality in its proceedings and it shall not be bound by any enactment or rule of law relating to the admissibility of evidence in proceedings before the courts of law.

(2) Subject to paragraph (1) of this Rule, at the hearing of the originating application a party (unless disentitled by virtue of Rule 3(2)), the Secretary of State (if, not being a party, he elects to appear as provided in Rule 7(5)) and any other person entitled to appear shall be entitled to give evidence, to call witnesses, to question any witnesses and to address the tribunal.

(3) If a party shall fail to appear or to be represented at the time and place fixed for the hearing, the tribunal may, if that party is an applicant, dismiss or, in any case, dispose of the application in the absence of that party or may adjourn the hearing to a later date: Provided that before deciding to dismiss or disposing of any application in the absence of a party the tribunal shall consider any representations submitted by that party in pursuance of Rule 7(3).

(4) A tribunal may require any witness to give evidence on oath or affirmation and for that purpose there may be administered an oath or affirmation in due form.   **[1250]**

9 Decision of tribunal

(1) A decision of a tribunal may be taken by a majority thereof and, if the tribunal shall be constituted of two members only, the chairman shall have a second or casting vote.

(2) The decision of a tribunal, which may be given orally at the end of a hearing or reserved, shall be recorded in a document signed by the chairman.

(3) A tribunal shall give reasons, which may be in full or in summary form, for its decision.

(4) The reasons for the decision of the tribunal shall be recorded in a document signed by the chairman, which shall also contain a statement as to whether the reasons are in full or in summary form.

(5) Where:—

(a) the proceedings before the tribunal involved the determination of an issue arising under or relating to section 51 of the 1966 Act, the Equal Pay Act, the Sex Discrimination Act, the Race Relations Act, sections 23, 58, 59(a) or 77 of the 1978 Act, or sections 4 or 5 of the Employment Act 1980; or

(b) the reasons have been given in summary form and it appears at any time to the tribunal that the reasons should be given in full; or

(c) a request that the reasons be given in full is made orally at the hearing by a party or by a person entitled to appear who did so appear; or

(d) such a request is made in writing within 21 days of the date on which the document recording the reasons in summary form was sent to the parties;

the reasons shall be recorded in full in a document signed by the chairman.

(6) The clerk to the tribunal shall transmit any document referred to in paragraphs (2), (4) and (5) of this Rule to the Secretary of the Tribunals who shall as soon as may be enter it in the Register and shall send a copy of the entry to each of the parties and to the persons entitled to appear who did so appear and, where the originating application was sent to a tribunal by a sheriff, to that sheriff

(7) Any document referred to in paragraphs (4) and (5) of this Rule shall be omitted from the Register in any case in which evidence has been heard in private and the tribunal so directs and in that event any such document shall be sent to the parties and to any appellate court in any proceedings relating to such decision together with the copy of the entry.

(8) The Register shall be kept at the Office of the Tribunals and shall be open to the inspection of any person without charge at all reasonable hours.

(9) Clerical mistakes in any document referred to in paragraphs (2), (4) and (5) of this Rule, or errors arising in such a document from an accidental slip or omission may at any time be corrected by the chairman by certificate under his hand.

(10) The clerk to the tribunal shall send a copy of any document so corrected and the certificate of the chairman to the Secretary of the Tribunals who shall as soon as may be make such correction as may be necessary in the Register and shall send a copy of any corrected entry or of any corrected document containing reasons for the tribunal's decision, as the case may be, to each of the parties and, in the case of a corrected entry, to the persons entitled to appear who did so appear and, where the originating application was sent to the tribunal by a sheriff, to that sheriff

(11) If any decision is—

(a) corrected under paragraph (9) of this Rule,
(b) reviewed, revoked or varied under Rule 10, or
(c) altered in any way by order of an appellate court,

the Secretary of the Tribunals shall alter the entry in the Register to conform with any such certificate or order and shall send a copy of the new entry to each of the parties and to the persons entitled to appear who did so appear and, where the originating application was sent to the tribunal by a sheriff, to that sheriff.

(12) Where by this Rule a document is required to be signed by the chairman but by reason of death or incapacity the chairman is unable to sign such document it shall be signed by the other members of the tribunal, who shall certify that the chairman is unable to sign.   **[1251]**

10 Review of tribunal's decision

(1) A tribunal shall have power to review and to revoke or vary by certificate under the chairman's hand any decision on the grounds that—

- (a)   the decision was wrongly made as a result of an error on the part of the tribunal staff; or
- (b)   a party did not receive notice of the proceedings leading to the decision; or
- (c)   the decision was made in the absence of a party or person entitled to be heard; or
- (d)   new evidence has become available since the conclusion of the hearing to which the decision relates provided that its existence could not have been reasonably known of or foreseen; or
- (e)   the interests of justice require such a review.

(2) An application for the purposes of paragraph (1) of this Rule may be made at the hearing. If the application is not made at the hearing, such application shall be made to the Secretary of the Tribunals at any time from the date of the hearing until 14 days after the date on which the decision was sent to the parties and must be in writing stating the grounds in full.

(3) An application for the purposes of paragraph (1) of this Rule may be refused by the President or by the chairman of the tribunal which decided the case or by a Regional Chairman if in his opinion it has no reasonable prospect of success.

(4) If such an application is not refused under paragraph (3) of this Rule it shall be heard by the tribunal which decided the case, or

- (a)   where it is not practicable for it to be heard by that tribunal, or
- (b)   where the decision was made by a chairman acting alone under Rule 12(4),

by a tribunal appointed either by the President or a Regional Chairman, and if the application is granted the tribunal shall proceed to a review of the decision and, having reviewed it, may confirm, vary or revoke that decision, and if the tribunal revokes the decision it shall order a re-hearing before either the same or a differently constituted tribunal.

(5) The clerk to the tribunal shall send to the Secretary of the Tribunals the certificate of the chairman as to any revocation or variation of the tribunal's decision under this Rule. The Secretary of the Tribunals shall as soon as may be make such correction as may be necessary in the Register and shall send a copy of the entry to each of the parties and to the persons entitled to appear who did so appear and where the originating application was sent to a tribunal by a sheriff, to that sheriff.   **[1252]**

11 Expenses

(1) Subject to paragraphs (2), (3) and (4) of this Rule, a tribunal shall not normally make an award in respect of the expenses incurred by a party to the proceedings but where in its opinion a party (and if he is a respondent whether or not he has entered an appearance) has in bringing or conducting the proceedings acted frivolously, vexatiously or otherwise unreasonably the tribunal may make—

- (a)   an order that that party shall pay to another party (or to the Secretary of State if, not being a party, he has acted as provided in Rule 7(5)) a specified sum in respect of the expenses incurred by that other party (or, as the case may be, by the Secretary of State) or the whole or part of those expenses as taxed (if not otherwise agreed);
- (b)   an order that that party shall pay to the Secretary of State the whole, or any part, of any allowances (other than allowances paid to members of tribunals or assessors) paid by the Secretary of State under paragraph 10 of Schedule 9 to the 1978 Act to any person for the purposes of, or in connection with, his attendance at the tribunal.

(2) Where the tribunal has on the application of a party to the proceedings postponed the day or time fixed for or adjourned the hearing, the tribunal may make orders against or, as the case may require, in favour of that party as at paragraph (1)(a) and (b) of this Rule as respects any expenses incurred or any allowances paid as a result of the postponement or adjournment.

(3) Where, on a complaint of unfair dismissal in respect of which—

(i) the applicant has expressed a wish to be reinstated or re-engaged which has been communicated to the respondent at least 7 days before the hearing of the complaint, or

(ii) the proceedings arise out of the respondent's failure to permit the applicant to return to work after an absence due to pregnancy or confinement,

any postponement or adjournment of the hearing has been caused by the respondent's failure, without a special reason, to adduce reasonable evidence as to the availability of the job from which the applicant was dismissed, or, as the case may be, which she held before her absence, or of comparable or suitable employment, the tribunal shall make orders against that respondent as at paragraph (1)(a) and (b) of this Rule as respects any expenses incurred or any allowances paid as a result of the postponement or adjournment.

(4) In any proceedings under the 1966 Act a tribunal may make—

(a) an order that a party, or any other person entitled to appear who did so appear, shall pay to another party or such person either a specified sum in respect of the expenses incurred by that other party or person or the whole or part of those expenses as taxed (if not otherwise agreed);

(b) an order that a party, or any.other person entitled to appear who did so appear, shall pay to the Secretary of State a specified sum in respect of the whole, or any part, of any allowance (other than allowances paid to members of tribunals) paid by the Secretary of State under paragraph 10 of Schedule 9 to the 1978 Act to any person for the purposes of, or in connection with, his attendance at the tribunal.

(5) Any expenses required by an order under this Rule to be taxed may be taxed in the sheriff court according to such of the scales prescribed by the sheriff court rules for civil proceedings in the sheriff court as shall be directed by the order.   **[1253]**

12 Miscellaneous powers of tribunal

(1) Subject to the provisions of these Rules, a tribunal may regulate its own procedure.

(2) A tribunal may, if it thinks fit—

(a) extend the time appointed by or under these Rules for doing any act notwithstanding that the time appointed may have expired;

(b) postpone the day or time fixed for, or adjourn, any hearing (particularly as respects cases under the provisions of any enactment providing for conciliation for the purpose of giving an opportunity for the complaint to be settled by way of conciliation and withdrawn);

(c) if the applicant shall at any time give notice of the withdrawal of his originating application, dismiss the proceedings;

(d) except in proceedings under the 1966 Act, if both or all the parties (and the Secretary of State if, not being a party, he has acted as provided in Rule 7(5)) agree in writing upon the terms of a decision to be made by the tribunal, decide accordingly;

(e) subject to the Proviso below, at any stage of the proceedings order to be struck out or amended any originating application or notice of appearance or anything in such application or notice of appearance on the ground that it is vexatious;

(f) subject to the Proviso below, on the application of the respondent, or of its own motion, order to be struck out any application for excessive delay in proceeding with it;

Provided that before making any order under (e) or (f) above the tribunal shall send notice to the party against whom it is proposed that any such order should be made giving him an opportunity to show cause why such an order should not be made.

(3) Subject to Rule 4(2), a tribunal may, if it thinks fit, before granting an application under Rule 4 or Rule 13 require the party (or, as the case may be, the Secretary of State) making the application to give notice of it to the other party or parties. The notice shall give particulars of the application and indicate the address to which and the time within which any objection to the application shall be made being an address and time specified for the purposes of the application by the tribunal.

(4) Any act other than the holding of a pre-hearing assessment under Rule 6, the hearing of an originating application or the making of an order under Rule 10(1), required or authorised by these Rules to be done by a tribunal may be done by, or on the direction of, the President or the chairman of the tribunal or any chairman being a member of the panel of chairmen.

(5) Rule 11 shall apply to an order dismissing proceedings under paragraph (2)(c) of this Rule.

(6) Any functions of the Secretary of the Tribunals other than that mentioned in Rule 1(2) may be performed by an Assistant Secretary of the Tribunals.   **[1254]**

13 Extension of time and directions

(1) An application to a tribunal for an extension of the time appointed by these Rules for doing any act may be made by a party either before or after the expiration of any time so appointed.

(2) Subject to Rule 3(2), a party may at any time apply to a tribunal for directions on any matter arising in connection with the proceedings.

(3) An application under the foregoing provisions of this Rule shall be made by presenting to the Secretary of the Tribunals a notice of application, which shall state the title of the proceedings and shall set out the grounds of the application.

(4) The Secretary of the Tribunals shall give notice to both or all the parties (subject to Rule 3(2)) of any extension of time granted under Rule 12(2)(a) or any directions given in pursuance of this Rule.   **[1255]**

14 Additional and representative respondents

(1) A tribunal may at any time either upon the application of any person or, where appropriate, of its own motion, direct any person against whom any relief is sought to be sisted as a party, and give such consequential directions as it considers necessary.

(2) A tribunal may likewise, either upon such application or of its own motion, order that any respondent named in the originating application or subsequently added, who shall appear to the tribunal not to have been, or to have ceased to be, directly interested in the subject of the originating application, be dismissed from the proceedings.

(3) Where there are numerous persons having the same interest in an originating application, one or more of them may be cited as the person or persons against whom relief is sought or may be authorised by the tribunal, before or at the hearing, to defend on behalf of all the persons so interested.   **[1256]**

15 Consolidation of proceedings

Where there are pending before the industrial tribunals two or more originating applications, then, if at any time upon the application of a party or of its own motion it appears to a tribunal that—

  (a) some common question of law or fact arises in both or all of the originating applications, or

  (b) the relief claimed therein is in respect of or arises out of the same set of facts, or

  (c) for some other reason it is desirable to make an order under this Rule, the tribunal may order that some (as specified in the order) or all of the originating applications shall be considered together, and may give such consequential directions as may be necessary: Provided that the tribunal shall not make an order under this Rule without sending notice to all parties concerned giving them an opportunity to show cause why such an order should not be made.

[1257]

16 Transfer of proceedings

(1) Where there is pending before the industrial tribunals an originating application in respect of which it appears to the President or a Regional Chairman that the proceedings could be determined in an industrial tribunal (England and Wales) established in pursuance of the Industrial Tribunals (England and Wales) Regulations 1965 and that such application would more conveniently be determined by such a tribunal, the President or a Regional Chairman may, at any time upon the application of a party or of his own motion, with the consent of the President of the Industrial Tribunals (England and Wales), direct that the said proceedings be transferred to the Office of the Industrial Tribunals (England and Wales): Provided that no such directions shall be made unless notice has been sent to all parties concerned giving them an opportunity to show cause why such a direction should not be made.

(2) Where proceedings have been transferred to the Office of the Industrial Tribunals (Scotland) under Rule 16(1) of the Industrial Tribunals (Rules of Procedure) Regulations 1985 they shall be treated as if in all respects they had been commenced by an originating application.

[1258]

17 Notices, etc

(1) Any notice given under these Rules shall be in writing.

(2) All notices and documents required by these Rules to be presented to the Secretary of the Tribunals may be presented at the Office of the Tribunals or such other office as may be notified by the Secretary of the Tribunals to the parties.

(3) All notices and documents required or authorised by these Rules to be sent or given to any person hereinafter mentioned may be sent by post (subject to paragraph (5) of this Rule) or delivered to or at—

    (a) in the case of a notice or document directed to the Secretary of State in proceedings to which he is not a party, the offices of the Department of Employment at Pentland House, 41 Robb's Loan, Edinburgh EH14 1TW, or such other office as may be notified by the Secretary of State;

    (b) in the case of a notice or document directed to the Board, the principal office of the Board;

    (c) in the case of a notice or document directed to a sheriff, the office of the sheriff clerk;

    (d) in the case of a notice or document directed to a party:—

        (i) his address for service specified in the originating application or in a notice of appearance or in a notice under paragraph (4) of this Rule; or

        (ii) if no address for service has been so specified, his last known address or place of business in the United Kingdom or, if the party is a corporation, the corporation's registered or principal office in the United Kingdom or, in any case, such address or place outside the United Kingdom as the President or a Regional Chairman may allow;

    (e) in the case of a notice or document directed to any person (other than a person specified in the foregoing provisions of this paragraph), his address or place of business in the United Kingdom, or if such a person is a corporation, the corporation's registered or principal office in the United Kingdom;

and if sent or given to the authorised representative of a party shall be deemed to have been sent or given to that party.

(4) A party may at any time by notice to the Secretary of the Tribunals and to the other party or parties (and, where appropriate, to the appropriate conciliation officer) change his address for service under these Rules.

(5) The recorded delivery service shall be used instead of the ordinary post:—

   (a)   when a second set of documents or notices is to be sent to a respondent who has not entered an appearance under Rule 3(1);

   (b)   for service of an order made under Rule 4(1)(iii) requiring the attendance of a witness.

(6) Where for any sufficient reason service of any document or notice cannot be effected in the manner prescribed under this Rule, the President or a Regional Chairman may make an order for service in such manner as he may deem fit and such service shall have the same effect as service in the manner prescribed under this Rule.

(7) In proceedings brought under the provisions of any enactment providing for conciliation the Secretary of the Tribunals shall send copies of all documents and notices to a conciliation officer who in the opinion of the Secretary is an appropriate officer to receive them.

(8) In proceedings which may involve payments out of the [National Insurance Fund] or Maternity Pay Fund, the Secretary of the Tribunals shall, where appropriate, send copies of all documents and notices to the Secretary of State notwithstanding the fact that he may not be a party to such proceedings.

(9) In proceedings under the Equal Pay Act, the Sex Discrimination Act or the Race Relations Act the Secretary of the Tribunals shall send to the Equal Opportunities Commission or, as the case may be, the Commission for Racial Equality copies of all documents sent to the parties under Rule 9(6), (10) and (11) and Rule 10(5).   **[1259]**

NOTE

   Para (8): words in square brackets substituted by virtue of the Employment Act 1990, s 13(3).

SCHEDULE 2

Regulation 3(2)

COMPLEMENTARY RULES OF PROCEDURE

For use only in proceedings involving an equal value claim

4 Power to require further particulars and attendance of witnesses and to order recovery of documents

(1) A tribunal may—

   (a)   subject to Rule 3(2), on the application of a party to the proceedings made either by notice to the Secretary of the Tribunals or at the hearing of the originating application, or

   (b)   in relation to sub paragraph (i) of this paragraph, if it thinks fit, of its own motion—

      (i)   require a party to furnish in writing to the person specified by the tribunal further particulars of the grounds on which he or it relies and of any facts and contentions relevant thereto;

      (ii)   grant to the person making the application such recovery or inspection of documents (including the taking of copies) as might be granted by a sheriff; and

      (iii)   require the attendance of any person (including a party to the proceedings) as a witness, wherever such person may be within Great Britain, and may, if it does so require the attendance of a person, require him to produce any document relating to the matter to be determined;

and may appoint the time at or within which or the place at which any act required in pursuance of this Rule is to be done.

(1A) Subject to paragraph (1B), a tribunal may, on the application of an expert who has been required by the tribunal to prepare a report,

(a) require any person who the tribunal is satisfied may have information which may be relevant to the question or matter on which the expert is required to report to furnish, in writing, such information as the tribunal may require;

(b) require any person to produce any documents which are in the possession, custody or power of that person and which the tribunal is satisfied may contain matter relevant to the question on which the expert is required to report;

and any information so required to be furnished or document so required to be produced shall be furnished or produced, at or within such time as the tribunal may appoint, to the Secretary of the Tribunals who shall send the information or document to the expert.

(1B) A tribunal shall not make a requirement under paragraph (1A) of this Rule—

(a) of a conciliation officer who has acted in connection with the complaint under section 64 of the Sex Discrimination Act, or

(b) if it is satisfied that the person so required would have good grounds for refusing to comply with the requirement if it were a requirement made in connection with a hearing before the tribunal.

(2) A party on whom a requirement has been made under paragraph (1)(i) or (1)(ii) of this Rule on an *ex parte* application, or (in relation to a requirement under paragraph (1)(i)) on the tribunal's own motion, and a person on whom a requirement has been made under paragraph (1)(iii) may apply to the tribunal by notice to the Secretary of the Tribunals before the appointed time at or within which the requirement is to be complied with to vary or set aside the requirement. Notice of an application under this paragraph to vary or set aside a requirement shall be given to the parties (other than the party making the application) and, where appropriate, in proceedings which may involve payments out of the [National Insurance Fund] or Maternity Pay Fund, the Secretary of State if not a party.

(2A) A person, whether or not a party to the proceedings, upon whom a requirement has been made under paragraph (1A) of this Rule, may apply to the tribunal by notice to the Secretary of the Tribunals before the appointed time at or within which the requirement is to be complied with to vary or set aside the requirement. Notice of such application shall be given to the parties and to the expert upon whose application the requirement was made.

(3) Every document containing a requirement under paragraph (1)(ii) or (1)(iii) or paragraph (1A) of this Rule shall contain a reference to the fact that, under paragraph 1(7) of Schedule 9 to the 1978 Act, any person who without reasonable excuse fails to comply with any such requirement shall be liable on summary conviction to a fine, and the document shall state the amount of the current maximum fine.

(4) If the requirement under paragraph (1)(i) or (1)(ii) of this Rule is not complied with, a tribunal, before or at the hearing, may dismiss the whole or part of the originating application, or, as the case may be, strike out the whole or part of the notice of appearance, and, where appropriate, direct that a respondent shall be debarred from defending altogether: Provided that a tribunal shall not so dismiss or strike out or give such a direction unless it has sent notice to the party who has not complied with the requirement giving him an opportunity to show cause why such should not be done.   **[1260]**

NOTE

Para (2): words in square brackets substituted by virtue of the Employment Act 1990, s 13(3).

7A Procedure relating to expert's report

(1) In any case involving an equal value claim where a dispute arises as to whether any work is of equal value to other work in terms of the demands made on the person employed on the work (for instance under such headings as effort, skill and decision) (in this Rule hereinafter referred to as "the question"), a tribunal shall, before considering the question, except in cases to which section 2A(1)(a) of the Equal Pay Act applies, require an expert to prepare a report with respect to the question and the requirement shall be made in accordance with paragraphs (2) and (3) of this Rule.

(2) The requirement shall be made in writing and shall set out—
- (a) the name and address of each of the parties;
- (b) the address of the establishment at which the applicant is (or, as the case may be, was) employed;
- (c) the question; and
- (d) the identity of the person with reference to whose work the question arises;

and a copy of the requirement shall be sent to each of the parties.

(3) The requirement shall stipulate that the expert shall—
- (a) take account of all such information supplied and all such representations made to him as have a bearing on the question;
- (b) before drawing up his report, produce and send to the parties a written summary of the said information and representations and invite the representations of the parties upon the material contained therein;
- (c) make his report to the tribunal in a document which shall reproduce the summary and contain a brief account of any representations received from the parties upon it, any conclusion he may have reached upon the question and the reasons for that conclusion or, as the case may be, for his failure to reach such a conclusion;
- (d) take no account of the difference of sex and at all times act fairly.

(4) Without prejudice to the generality of Rule 12(2)(b), where a tribunal requires an expert to prepare a report, it shall adjourn the hearing.

(5) If, on the application of one or more of the parties made not less than 42 days after a tribunal has notified an expert of the requirement to prepare a report, the tribunal forms the view that there has been or is likely to be undue delay in receiving that report, the tribunal may require the expert to provide in writing to the tribunal an explanation for the delay or information as to his progress and may, on consideration of any such explanation or information as may be provided and after seeking representations from the parties, revoke, by notice in writing to the expert, the requirement to prepare a report, and in such a case paragraph (1) of this Rule shall again apply.

(6) Where a tribunal has received the report of an expert, it shall forthwith send a copy of the report to each of the parties and shall fix a date for the hearing of the case to be resumed, provided that the date so fixed shall be at least 14 days after the date on which the report is sent to the parties.

(7) Upon the resuming of the hearing of the case in accordance with paragraph (6) of this Rule the report shall be admitted as evidence in the case unless the tribunal has exercised its power under paragraph (8) of this Rule not to admit the report.

(8) Where the tribunal, on the application of one or more of the parties or otherwise, forms the view—
- (a) that the expert has not complied with a stipulation in paragraph (3) of this Rule, or
- (b) that the conclusion contained in the report is one which, taking due account of the information supplied and representations made to the expert, could not reasonably have been reached, or
- (c) that for some other material reason (other than disagreement with the conclusion that the applicant's work is or is not of equal value or with the reasoning leading to that conclusion) the report is unsatisfactory,

the tribunal may, if it thinks fit, determine not to admit the report, and in such a case paragraph (1) of this Rule shall again apply.

(9) In forming its view on the matters contained in paragraph (8)(a), (b) and (c) of this Rule, the tribunal shall take account of any representations of the parties thereon and may in that connection, subject to Rule 8(2A) and (2B), permit any party to give evidence upon, to call witnesses and to question any witness upon any matter relevant thereto.

(10) The tribunal may, at any time after it has received the report of an expert, require that expert (or, if that is impracticable, another expert) to explain any matter contained in his report or, having regard to such matters as may be set out in the requirement, to give further consideration to the question.

(11) The requirement in paragraph (10) of this Rule shall comply with paragraph (2) of this Rule and shall stipulate that the expert shall make his reply in writing to the tribunal, giving his explanation or, as the case may be, setting down any conclusion which may result from his further consideration and his reasons for that conclusion.

(12) Where the tribunal has received a reply from the expert under paragraph (11) of this Rule, it shall forthwith send a copy of the reply to each of the parties and shall allow the parties to make representations thereon, and the reply shall be treated as information furnished to the tribunal and be given such weight as the tribunal thinks fit.

(13) Where a tribunal has determined not to admit a report under paragraph (8), that report shall be treated for all purposes (other than the award of expenses under Rule 11) connected with the proceedings as if it had not been received by the tribunal and no further account shall be taken of it, and the requirement on the expert to prepare a report shall lapse. **[1261]**

8 Procedure at hearing

(1) Subject to paragraphs (2A), (2B), (2C), (2D) and (2E) of this Rule the tribunal shall conduct the hearing in such manner as it considers most suitable to the clarification of the issues before it and generally to the just handling of the proceedings; it shall so far as appears to it appropriate seek to avoid formality in its proceedings and it shall not be bound by any enactment or rule of law relating to the admissibility of evidence in proceedings before the courts of law.

(2) Subject to paragraphs (1), (2A), (2B), (2C) and (2D) of this Rule, at the hearing of the originating application a party (unless disentitled by virtue of Rule 3(2)), the Secretary of State (if, not being a party, he elects to appear as provided in Rule 7(5)) and any other person entitled to appear shall be entitled to give evidence, to call witnesses, to question any witnesses and to address the tribunal.

(2A) The tribunal may, and shall upon the application of a party, require the attendance of an expert who has prepared a report in connection with an equal value claim in any hearing relating to that claim. Where an expert attends in compliance with such requirement any party may, subject to paragraph (1) of this Rule, cross-examine the expert on his report and on any other matter pertaining to the question on which the expert was required to report

(2B) At any time after the tribunal has received the report of the expert, any party may, on giving reasonable notice of his intention to do so to the tribunal and to any other party to the claim, call one witness to give expert evidence on the question on which the tribunal has required the expert to prepare a report; and where such evidence is given, any other party may cross-examine the person giving that evidence upon it.

(2C) Except as provided in Rule 7A(9) or by paragraph (2D) of this Rule, no party may give evidence upon, or question any witness upon, any matter of fact upon which a conclusion in the report of the expert is based.

(2D) Subject to paragraphs (2A) and (2B) of this Rule, a tribunal may, notwithstanding paragraph (2C) of this Rule, permit a party to give evidence upon, to call witnesses and to question any witness upon any such matters of fact as are referred to in that paragraph if either—

(a) the matter of fact is relevant to and is raised in connection with the issue contained in subsection (3) of section 1 of the Equal Pay Act (defence of genuine material factor) upon which the determination of the tribunal is being sought; or

(b) the report of the expert contains no conclusion on the question of whether the applicant's work and the work of the person identified in the requirement of the tribunal under Rule 7A(2) are of equal value and the tribunal is satisfied that the absence of that conclusion is wholly or mainly due to the refusal or deliberate omission of a person required by the tribunal under Rule 4(1A) to furnish information or to produce documents to comply with that requirement.

(2E) A tribunal may, on the application of a party, if in the circumstances of the case, having regard to the considerations expressed in paragraph (1) of this Rule, it considers that it is appropriate so to proceed, hear evidence upon and permit the parties to address it upon the issue contained in subsection (3) of section 1 of the Equal Pay Act (defence of genuine material factor) before it requires an expert to prepare a report under Rule 7A. Where the tribunal so proceeds, it shall be without prejudice to further consideration of that issue after the tribunal has received the report.

(3) If a party shall fail to appear or to be represented at the time and place fixed for the hearing, the tribunal may, if that party is an applicant, dismiss or, in any case, dispose of the application in the absence of that party or may adjourn the hearing to a later date: Provided that before deciding to dismiss or disposing of any application in the absence of a party the tribunal shall consider any representations submitted by that party in pursuance of Rule 7(3).

(4) A tribunal may require any witness to give evidence on oath or affirmation and for that purpose there may be administered an oath or affirmation in due form.   **[1262]**

9 Decision of tribunal

(1) A decision of a tribunal may be taken by a majority thereof and, if the tribunal shall be constituted of two members only, the chairman shall have a second or casting vote.

(2) The decision of a tribunal, which may be given orally at the end of a hearing or reserved, shall be recorded in a document signed by the chairman.

(3) A tribunal shall give reasons for its decision.

(4) The reasons for the decision of the tribunal shall be recorded in full form in a document signed by the chairman.

(4A)   There shall be appended to the document referred to in paragraph (4) of this Rule a copy of the report (if any) of an expert received by the tribunal in the course of the proceedings.

[paragraph (5) is omitted because it has no relevance in proceedings involving an equal value claim]

(6) The clerk to the tribunal shall transmit any document referred to in paragraphs (2), (4) and (4A) of this Rule to the Secretary of the Tribunals who shall as soon as may be enter it in the Register and shall send a copy of the entry to each of the parties and to the persons entitled to appear who did so appear and, where the originating application was sent to a tribunal by a sheriff, to that sheriff.

(7) Any document referred to in paragraphs (4) and (4A) of this Rule shall be omitted from the Register in any case in which evidence has been heard in private and the tribunal so directs and in that event any such document shall be sent to the parties and to any appellate court in any proceedings relating to such decision together with the copy of the entry.

(8) The Register shall be kept at the Office of the Tribunals and shall be open to the inspection of any person without charge at all reasonable hours.

(9) Clerical mistakes in any document referred to in paragraphs (2) and (4) of this Rule, or errors arising in such a document from an accidental slip or omission, may at any time be corrected by the chairman by certificate under his hand.

(10) The clerk to the tribunal shall send a copy of any document so corrected and the certificate of the chairman to the Secretary of the Tribunals who shall as soon as may be make such correction as may be necessary in the Register and shall send a copy of any corrected entry or of any corrected document containing reasons for the tribunal's decision, as the case may be, to each of the parties and, in the case of a corrected entry, to the persons entitled to appear who did so appear and, where the originating application was sent to the tribunal by a sheriff, to that sheriff.

(11) If any decision is—

    (a) corrected under paragraph (9) of this Rule,
    (b) reviewed, revoked or varied under Rule 10, or
    (c) altered in any way by order of an appellate court,

the Secretary of the Tribunals shall alter the entry in the Register to conform with any such certificate or order and shall send a copy of the new entry to each of the parties and to the persons entitled to appear who did so appear and, where the originating application was sent to the tribunal by a sheriff, to that sheriff.

(12) Where by this Rule a document is required to be signed by the chairman but by reason of death or incapacity the chairman is unable to sign such document it shall be signed by the other members of the tribunal, who shall certify that the chairman is unable to sign.   **[1263]**

11 Expenses

(1) Subject to paragraphs (2) and (3) of this Rule, a tribunal shall not normally make an award in respect of the expenses incurred by a party to the proceedings but where in its opinion a party (and if he is a respondent whether or not he has entered an appearance) has in bringing or conducting the proceedings acted frivolously, vexatiously or otherwise unreasonably the tribunal may make—

    (a) an order that that party shall pay to another party (or to the Secretary of State if, not being a party, he has acted as provided in Rule 7(5)) a specified sum in respect of the expenses incurred by that other party (or, as the case may be, by the Secretary of State) or the whole or part of those expenses as taxed (if not otherwise agreed);

    (b) an order that that party shall pay to the Secretary of State the whole, or any part, of any allowances (other than allowances paid to members of tribunals, experts or assessors) paid by the Secretary of State under paragraph 10 of Schedule 9 to the 1978 Act to any person for the purposes of, or in connection with, his attendance at the tribunal.

(1A) For the purposes of paragraph (1)(a) of this Rule, the expenses in respect of which a tribunal may make an order include expenses incurred by the party in whose favour the order is to be made in or in connection with the investigations carried out by the expert in preparing his report.

(2) Where the tribunal has on the application of a party to the proceedings postponed the day or time for or adjourned the hearing, the tribunal may make orders against or, as the case may require, in favour of that party as at paragraph (1)(a) and (b) of this Rule as respects any expenses incurred or any allowances paid as a result of the postponement or adjournment.

(3) Where, on a complaint of unfair dismissal in respect of which—

    (i) the applicant has expressed a wish to be reinstated or re-engaged which has been communicated to the respondent at least 7 days before the hearing of the complaint, or

    (ii) the proceedings arise out of the respondent's failure to permit the applicant to return to work after an absence due to pregnancy or confinement,

any postponement or adjournment of the hearing has been caused by the respondent's failure, without a special reason, to adduce reasonable evidence as to the availability of the job from which the applicant was dismissed, or, as the case may be, which she held before her absence, or of comparable or suitable employment, the tribunal shall make orders against that respondent as at paragraph (1)(a) and (b) of this Rule as respects any expenses incurred or any allowances paid as a result of the postponement or adjournment.

[paragraph (4) is omitted because it has no relevance in proceedings involving an equal value claim]

(5) Any expenses required by an order under this Rule to be taxed may be taxed in the sheriff court according to such of the scales prescribed by the sheriff court rules for civil proceedings in the sheriff court as shall be directed by the order.   **[1264]**

12 Miscellaneous powers of tribunal

(1) Subject to the provisions of these Rules, a tribunal may regulate its own procedure.

(2) A tribunal may, if it thinks fit—

(a) extend the time appointed by or under these Rules for doing any act notwithstanding that the time appointed may have expired;

(b) postpone the day or time fixed for, or adjourn, any hearing (particularly as respects cases under the provisions of any enactment providing for conciliation for the purpose of giving an opportunity for the complaint to be settled by way of conciliation and withdrawn);

(c) if the applicant shall at any time give notice of the withdrawal of his originating application, dismiss the proceedings;

(d) except in proceedings under the 1966 Act, if both or all the parties (and the Secretary of State if, not being a party, he has acted as provided in Rule 7(5)) agree in writing upon the terms of a decision to be made by the tribunal, decide accordingly;

(e) subject to the proviso below, at any stage of the proceedings order to be struck out or amended any originating application or notice of appearance or anything in such application or notice of appearance on the ground that it is vexatious;

(f) subject to the proviso below, on the application of the respondent, or of its own motion, order to be struck out any application for excessive delay in proceeding with it;

Provided that before making any order under (e) or (f) above the tribunal shall send notice to the party against whom it is proposed that any such order should be made giving him an opportunity to show cause why such an order should not be made.

(2A)   Without prejudice to the generality of paragraph (2)(b) of this Rule, the tribunal shall, before proceeding to hear the parties on an equal value claim, invite them to apply for an adjournment for the purpose of seeking to reach a settlement of the claim and shall, if both or all the parties agree to such a course, grant an adjournment for that purpose.

(2B)   If, after the tribunal has adjourned the hearing under rule 7A(4) but before the tribunal has received the report of the expert, the applicant gives notice under paragraph (2)(c) of this Rule, the tribunal shall forthwith notify the expert that the requirement to prepare a report has ceased. The notice shall be without prejudice to the operation of Rule 11(1A).

(3) Subject to Rule 4(2), and (2A), a tribunal may, if it thinks fit, before granting an application under Rule 4 or Rule 13 require the party (or, as the case may be, the Secretary of State or, in the case of an application under Rule 4(1A), the expert) making the application to give notice of it to the other party or parties (or, in the case of an application by an expert, the parties and any other person in respect of whom the tribunal is asked, in the application, to impose a requirement). The notice shall give particulars of the application and indicate the address to which and the time within which any objection to the application shall be made being an address and time specified for the purposes of the application by the tribunal.

(4) Any act other than the holding of a pre-hearing assessment under Rule 6, the hearing of an originating application or the making of an order under Rule 10(1), required or authorised by these Rules to be done by a tribunal may be done by, or on the direction of, the President or the chairman of the tribunal or any chairman being a member of the panel of chairmen.

(5) Rule 11 shall apply to an order dismissing proceedings under paragraph (2)(c) of this Rule.

(6) Any functions of the Secretary of the Tribunals other than that mentioned in Rule 1(2) may be performed by an Assistant Secretary of the Tribunals.   **[1265]**

17 Notices, etc

(1) Any notice given under these Rules shall be in writing.

(2) All notices and documents required by these Rules to be presented to the Secretary of the Tribunals may be presented at the Office of the Tribunals or such other office as may be notified by the Secretary of the Tribunals to the parties.

(3) All notices and documents required or authorised by these Rules to be sent or given to any person hereinafter mentioned may be sent by post (subject to paragraph (5) of this Rule) or delivered to or at—

(a) in the case of a notice or document directed to the Secretary of State in proceedings to which he is not a party, the offices of the Department of Employment at Pentland House, 41 Robb's Loan, Edinburgh EH14 1TW, or such other office as may be notified by the Secretary of State;

[sub-paragraph (b) is omitted because it has no relevance in proceedings involving an equal value claim]

(c) in the case of a notice or document directed to a sheriff, the office of the sheriff clerk;

(d) in the case of a notice or document directed to a party:—

(i) his address for service specified in the originating application or in a notice of appearance or in a notice under paragraph (4) of this Rule; or

(ii) if no address for service has been so specified, his last known address or place of business in the United Kingdom or, if the party is a corporation, the corporation's registered or principal office in the United Kingdom or, in any case, such address or place outside the United Kingdom as the President or a Regional Chairman may allow;

(e) in the case of a notice or document directed to any person (other than a person specified in the foregoing provisions of this paragraph), his address or place of business in the United Kingdom, or if such a person is a corporation, the corporation's registered or principal office in the United Kingdom;

and if sent or given to the authorised representative of a party shall be deemed to have been sent or given to that party.

(4) A party may at any time by notice to the Secretary of the Tribunals and to the other party or parties (and, where appropriate, to the appropriate conciliation officer and the appropriate expert) change his address for service under these Rules.

(5) The recorded delivery service shall be used instead of the ordinary post:—

(a) when a second set of documents or notices is to be sent to a respondent who has not entered an appearance under Rule 3(1);

(b) for service of an order made under Rule 4(1)(iii) or (1A).

(6) Where for any sufficient reason service of any document or notice cannot be effected in the manner prescribed under this Rule, the President or a Regional Chairman may make an order for service in such manner as he may deem fit and such service shall have the same effect as service in the manner prescribed under this Rule.

(7) In proceedings brought under the provisions of any enactment providing for conciliation the Secretary of the Tribunals shall send copies of all documents and notices to a conciliation officer who in the opinion of the Secretary is an appropriate officer to receive them.

(8) In proceedings which may involve payments out of the Redundancy Fund or Maternity Pay Fund, the Secretary of the Tribunals shall, where appropriate, send copies of all documents and notices to the Secretary of State notwithstanding the fact that he may not be a party to such proceedings.

(9) In proceedings under the Equal Pay Act, the Sex Discrimination Act or the Race Relations Act the Secretary of the Tribunals shall send to the Equal Opportunities Commission or, as the case may be, the Commission for Racial Equality copies of all documents sent to the parties under Rule 9(6), (10) and (11) and Rule 10(5).　　　　　　**[1266]**

STATUTORY SICK PAY (MEDICAL EVIDENCE) REGULATIONS 1985

(SI 1985/1604)

NOTES
Made: 22 October 1985.
Authority: Social Security and Housing Benefits Act 1982, s 17(2A), (see now Social Security (Contributions and Benefits) Act 1992, Part XI).

ARRANGEMENT OF REGULATIONS

1 Citation, commencement and interpretation

(1) These regulations may be cited as the Statutory Sick Pay (Medical Evidence) Regulations 1985 and shall come into operation on 6th April 1986.

(2) In these regulations, unless the context otherwise requires—

"the 1982 Act" means the Social Security and Housing Benefits Act 1982;
"signature" means, in relation to a statement given in accordance with these regulations, the name by which the person giving that statement is usually known (any name other than the surname being either in full or otherwise indicated) written by that person in his own handwriting; and "signed" shall be construed accordingly.

(3) . . .   **[1267]**

NOTE
Para (3): revoked by the Social Security (Miscellaneous Provisions) Amendment Regulations 1992, SI 1992/247, reg 6(1), (2).

2 Medical information

[(1) Medical information required under section 17(2) of the 1982 Act relating to incapacity for work shall be provided either—

(a) in the form of a statement given by a doctor in accordance with the rules set out in Part I of Schedule 1 to these Regulations on the form set out in Part II of that Schedule; or
(b) where the doctor—
    (i) has not given a statement under sub-paragraph (a) of this paragraph since the patient was examined and wishes to give such a statement but more than one day has passed since the examination; or
    (ii) advises that the patient should refrain from work on the basis of a written report from another doctor,

by means of a special statement given in accordance with the rules set out in Part I of Schedule 1A to these Regulations on the form set out in Part II of that Schedule; or

    (c) by such other means as may be sufficient in the circumstances of any particular case.]

(2) An employee shall not be required under section 17(2) of the 1982 Act to provide medical information in respect of the first 7 days in any spell of incapacity for work; and for this purpose "spell of incapacity" means a continuous period of incapacity for work which is immediately preceded by a day on which the claimant either worked or was not incapable of work.   **[1268]**

NOTE

Para (1): substituted by SI 1992/247, reg 6(1), (2).

Note that the Social Security and Housing Benefits Act 1982, s 17(2), was repealed by the Social Security Act 1986, s 86(2), Sch 11.

SCHEDULES

Regulation 1(3)

SCHEDULE [1]

PART I
RULES

1 In these rules, unless the context otherwise requires—

    "patient" means the person in respect of whom a statement is given in accordance with these rules;

    "doctor" means a registered medical practitioner not being the patient;

    "2 weeks" means any period of 14 consecutive days.

2 The doctor's statement shall be in the form set out in Part II of this Schedule.

3 Where the patient is on the list of a doctor providing general medical services under the National Health Service Act 1977, or the National Health Service (Scotland) Act 1978, and is being attended by such a doctor, the doctor's statement shall be on a form provided by the Secretary of State for the purpose and shall be signed by that doctor.

4 In any other case, the doctor's statement shall be on a form provided by the Secretary of State for the purpose and shall be signed by the doctor attending the patient.

5 Every doctor's statement shall be completed in ink or other indelible substance and shall contain the following particulars:—

    (a)   the patient's name;

    (b)   the date of the examination on which the doctor's statement is based;

    (c)   the diagnosis of the patient's disorder in respect of which the doctor is advising the patient to refrain from work or, as the case may be, which has caused the patient's absence from work;

    (d)   the date on which the doctor's statement is given;

    (e)   the address of the doctor,

and shall bear, opposite the words "Doctor's signature", the signature of the doctor making the statement written after there have been entered the patient's name and the doctor's diagnosis.

6 Subject to rules 7 and 8 below, the diagnosis of the disorder in respect of which the doctor is advising the patient to refrain from work or, as the case may be, which has caused the patient's absence from work shall be specified as precisely as the doctor's knowledge of the patient's condition at the time of the examination permits.

7 The diagnosis may be specified less precisely where, in the doctor's opinion, a disclosure of the precise disorder would be prejudicial to the patient's well-being, or to the patient's position with his employer.

8 In the case of an initial examination by a doctor in respect of a disorder stated by the patient to have caused incapacity for work, where—

    (a) there are no clinical signs of that disorder, and

    (b) in the doctor's opinion, the patient need not refrain from work,

instead of specifying a diagnosis "unspecified" may be entered.

9 A doctor's statement must be given on a date not later than one day after the date of the examination on which it is based, and no further doctor's statement based on the same examination shall be furnished other than a doctor's statement by way of replacement of an original which has been lost or mislaid, in which case it shall be clearly marked "duplicate".

10 Where, in the doctor's opinion, the patient will become fit to resume work on a day not later than 2 weeks after the date of the examination on which the doctor's statement is based, the doctor's statement shall specify that day.

11 Subject to rules 12 and 13 below, the doctor's statement shall specify the minimum period during which, in the doctor's opinion, the patient should, by reason of his disorder, refrain from work.

12 The period specified shall begin on the date of the examination on which the doctor's statement is based and shall not exceed 6 months unless the patient has, on the advice of a doctor, refrained from work for at least 6 months immediately preceding that date.

13 Where—

    (a) the patient has, on the advice of a doctor, refrained from work for at least 6 months immediately preceding the date of the examination on which the doctor's statement is based, and

    (b) in the doctor's opinion, it will be necessary for the patient to refrain from work for the foreseeable future,

instead of specifying a period, the doctor may, having regard to the circumstances of the particular case, enter, after the word "until", the words 'further notice".

14 The Notes set out in Part III of this Schedule shall accompany the form of doctor's statement provided by the Secretary of State. **[1269]**

NOTE

Schedule heading: Schedule numbered Sch 1 by SI 1992/247, reg 6(1), (4).

PART II
FORM OF DOCTOR'S STATEMENT

DOCTOR'S STATEMENT

In confidence to

Mr/Mrs/Miss ....

I examined you today/yesterday and advised you that:

(a) you need not refrain from work   (b) you should refrain from work

                                        for.......................

                                        OR until ....

Diagnosis of your disorder causing absence from work ....

Doctor's remarks

Doctor's signature   Date of signing

[1270]

Part III
NOTES

The following notes shall accompany the form of doctor's statement provided by the Secretary of State:—

On the doctor's statement:—

(1) After the words "you should refrain from work for", the period entered must not exceed 6 months unless the patient has, on the advice of a doctor, already refrained from work for a continuous period of 6 months.

(2) After the words "you should refrain from work until"—

    (a)   if the patient is being given a date when he can return to work, the date entered should not be more than 2 weeks after the date of the examination;

    (b)   if the patient has already been incapable of work for at least 6 months and recovery of capacity for work in the foreseeable future is not expected, "further notice" may be entered.   **[1271]**

[SCHEDULE 1A

Regulation 2(1)

PART I
RULES

1 In these rules, unless the context otherwise requires—

    "patient" means the person in respect of whom a statement is given in accordance with these rules;

    "doctor" means a registered medical practitioner not being the patient;

    "special statement" means the form prescribed in Part II of this Schedule.

2 Where a doctor advises a patient to refrain from work on the basis of a written report which he has received from another doctor or where a doctor has not issued a statement since the claimant was examined and he wishes to issue a statement more than a day after the examination he shall use the special statement.

3 The special statement shall be completed in the manner described in paragraph 5 of Part I to Schedule 1.

4 Subject to rules 5 and 6 below, the diagnosis of the patient's disorder in respect of which the doctor is advising the patient to refrain from work or as the case may be, which has caused the patient's absence from work shall be specified as precisely as the doctor's knowledge of the patient's condition permits.

5 The diagnosis may be specified less precisely where in the doctor's opinion, a disclosure of the precise disorder would be prejudicial to the patient's well being, or to the patient's position with his employer.

6 In a case of a disorder stated by the patient to have caused incapacity for work, where—

    (a)   no clinical signs have been found of that disorder, and

    (b)   in the doctor's opinion, the patient need not refrain from work,

instead of specifying a diagnosis "unspecified" may be entered.

7 Part B of the special statement must only be given on a date not later than one month after the date of the written report on which the special statement is based and that part shall only be used where the patient is being advised to refrain from work for a specified period of not more than one month.]   **[1272]**

NOTE

Added by SI 1992/247, reg 6(1), (5), Sch 2.

PART II
FORM OF SPECIAL STATEMENT

[FOR SOCIAL SECURITY AND STATUTORY   Special Statement
SICK PAY PURPOSES ONLY   by the Doctor

In confidence to

Mr/Mrs/Miss/Ms...

(A) I examined you on the following dates

....

....

of...

....

and advised you that you should refrain from work

From........................ to ....

Diagnosis of your disorder causing absence from work...........

Doctor's remarks

Doctor's signature   Date of signing

(B) I have not examined you but, on the basis of a recent written report from—
Doctor........................(Name if known)

....

....

....

....(Address)

I have advised you that you should refrain from work for/until................................

The special circumstances in which this form may be used are described in the handbook "Medical Evidence for Social Security and Statutory Sick Pay purposes".]   **[1273]**

NOTE
Added by SI 1992/247, reg 6(1), (5), Sch 2.

REPORTING OF INJURIES, DISEASES AND DANGEROUS OCCURRENCES REGULATIONS 1985
(SI 1985/2023)

NOTES
Made: 17 December 1985.
Authority: Health and Safety at Work etc Act 1974, ss 15(1), (2), (3)(a), (4), (6)(a), (b), (9), Sch 3, paras 15(1), 16, 20.

ARRANGEMENT OF REGULATIONS

1 Citation and commencement

These Regulations may be cited as the Reporting of Injuries, Diseases and Dangerous Occurrences Regulations 1985 and shall come into operation on 1st April 1986.

[1274]

2 Interpretation

(1) In these Regulations, unless the context otherwise requires—

"approved" means approved for the time being for the purposes of these Regulations by the Health and Safety Executive;

"dangerous occurrence" means an occurrence which arises out of or in connection with work and is of a class specified in—

 (a) Part I of Schedule 1;

 (b) Part II of Schedule 1 and takes place at a mine;

 (c) Part III of Schedule 1 and takes place at a quarry;

 (d) Part IV of Schedule 1 and takes place on a railway;

"mine" or "quarry" means a mine or, as the case may be, a quarry within the meaning of section 180 of the Mines and Quarries Act 1954 and for the purposes of these Regulations includes a closed tip within the meaning of section 2(2)(b) of the Mines and Quarries (Tips) Act 1969 which is associated with that mine or that quarry;

"operator" means in relation to a vehicle to which paragraph 13 or 14 of Schedule 1, Part I applies—

 (a) a person who holds, or is required by section 60 of the Transport Act 1968 to hold, an operator's licence for the use of that vehicle for the carriage of goods on a road; or

 (b) where no such licence is required, the keeper of the vehicle;

"railway" means a railway having a gauge of 350 millimetres or more used for the purposes of public transport, whether passenger, goods, or other traffic and includes—

 (a) a tramway;

 (b) a railway laid on a beach or pier; and

 (c) a railway providing communication between the top and bottom of a cliff;

"responsible person" means—

 (a) in the case of—

  (i) a mine, the manager of that mine;

  (ii) a quarry, the owner of that quarry;

  (iii) a closed tip, the owner of the mine or quarry with which that tip is associated;

  (iv) a pipe-line within the meaning of section 65 of the Pipe-lines Act 1962, the owner of that pipe-line;

  (v) a vehicle to which paragraph 13 or 14 of Schedule 1, Part I applies, the operator of the vehicle;

 (b) where sub-paragraph (a) above does not apply, in the case of any event (other than a dangerous occurrence) reportable under Regulation 3, or any case of disease reportable under Regulation 5, involving—

  (i) an employee at work (including any person who is to be treated as an employee by virtue of any relevant statutory provision), his employer;

  (ii) a person (excluding one who is to be treated as an employee by virtue of any relevant statutory provision) undergoing training for employment, the person whose undertaking makes the immediate provision of that training;

(c) in any other case, the person for the time being having control of the premises in connection with the carrying on by him of any trade, business or other undertaking (whether for profit or not) at which, or in connection with the work at which, the accident or dangerous occurrence reportable under Regulation 3, or case of disease reportable under Regulation 5, happened;

"training" includes work experience received as part of a training programme; it does not include training on a course at a university, polytechnic, college, school or similar educational or technical institute where that body is the immediate provider of the training; but it does include training at a skillcentre, training centre or other training establishment run by the [Training Commission].

"work" means work as an employee, as a self-employed person or as a person undergoing training for employment (whether or not under any scheme administered by the [Training Commission]).

(2) In these Regulations, unless the context otherwise requires, any reference to—

(a) a numbered Regulation or Schedule is a reference to the Regulation or Schedule in these Regulations so numbered;

(b) a numbered paragraph is a reference to the paragraph so numbered in the Regulation or Schedule in which that reference appears; and

(c) an accident or a dangerous occurrence which arises out of or in connection with work shall include a reference to an accident, or as the case may be, a dangerous occurrence attributable to the manner of conducting an undertaking, the plant or substances used for the purposes of an undertaking and the condition of the premises so used or any part of them.

[1275]

NOTE
Para (1): words in square brackets substituted by virtue of the Employment Act 1988, s 24.

3 Notification and reporting of injuries and dangerous occurrences

(1) Subject to Regulation 10, where any person as a result of an accident arising out of or in connection with work, dies or suffers any of the injuries or conditions specified in paragraph (2) or where there is a dangerous occurrence, the responsible person shall—

(a) forthwith notify the enforcing authority thereof by the quickest practicable means; and

(b) within 7 days send a report thereof to the enforcing authority on a form approved for the purposes of this Regulation.

(2) The injuries and conditions referred to in paragraph (1) are—

(a) fracture of the skull, spine or pelvis;

(b) fracture of any bone—

(i) in the arm or wrist, but not a bone in the hand; or
(ii) in the leg or ankle, but not a bone in the foot;

(c) amputation of—

(i) a hand or foot; or
(ii) a finger, thumb or toe, or any part thereof if the joint or bone is completely severed;

(d) the loss of sight of an eye, a penetrating injury to an eye, or a chemical or hot metal burn to an eye;

(e) either injury (including burns) requiring immediate medical treatment, or loss of consciousness, resulting in either case from an electric shock from any electrical circuit or equipment, whether or not due to direct contact;

(f) loss of consciousness resulting from lack of oxygen;

(g) decompression sickness (unless suffered during an operation to which the Diving Operations at Work Regulations 1981 apply) requiring immediate medical treatment;

(h) either acute illness requiring medical treatment, or loss of consciousness, resulting in either case from the absorption of any substance by inhalation, ingestion or through the skin;

(i) acute illness requiring medical treatment where there is reason to believe that this resulted from exposure to a pathogen or infected material;

(j) any other injury which results in the person injured being admitted immediately into hospital for more than 24 hours.

(3) Subject to Regulation 10, where a person at work is incapacitated for work of a kind which he might reasonably be expected to do, either under his contract of employment, or, if there is no such contract, in the normal course of his work, for more than 3 consecutive days (excluding the day of the accident but including any days which would not have been working days) because of an injury (other than one specified in paragraph (2)) resulting from an accident at work the responsible person shall within 7 days of the accident send a report thereof to the enforcing authority on a form approved for the purposes of this Regulation. **[1276]**

4 Reporting of the death of an employee

Subject to Regulation 10, where an employee, as a result of an accident at work, has suffered an injury or condition reportable under Regulation 3 which is a cause of his death within one year of the date of that accident, the employer shall inform the enforcing authority in writing of the death as soon as it comes to his knowledge, whether or not the accident has been reported under Regulation 3. **[1277]**

5 Reporting of cases of disease

(1) Subject to paragraphs (2) and (3) and to Regulation 10, where a person at work suffers from one of the diseases specified in column 1 of Schedule 2 and his work involves one of the activities specified in the corresponding entry in column 2 of that Schedule, the responsible person shall forthwith send a report thereof to the enforcing authority on a form approved for the purposes of this Regulation.

(2) Paragraph (1) shall apply only if—

(a) in the case of an employee or a person undergoing training, the responsible person has received a written statement prepared by a registered medical practitioner diagnosing the disease as one of those specified in column 1 of Schedule 2; or

(b) in the case of a self-employed person, that person has been informed by a registered medical practitioner that he is suffering from a disease so specified.

(3) In the case of a self-employed person, it shall be a sufficient compliance with paragraph (1) if that person makes arrangements for the report to be sent to the enforcing authority by some other person. **[1278]**

6 Reporting of gas incidents

(1) Whenever a supplier of flammable gas through a fixed pipe distribution system or a filler, importer or supplier (other than by means of retail trade) of a refillable container containing liquefied petroleum gas receives notification of any death, or any injury or condition specified in Regulation 3(2) which has arisen out of or in connection with the gas supplied, filled or imported, as the case may be, by that person, he shall forthwith notify the Executive of the incident, and shall within 14 days send a report of it to the Executive on a form approved for the purposes of this Regulation.

(2) Whenever a supplier of flammable gas through a fixed pipe distribution system has in his possession sufficient information for it to be reasonable for him to decide that a gas fitting as defined by section 48(1) of the Gas Act 1972 or any flue or ventilation used in connection with that fitting, by reason of its design, construction, manner of installation, modification or servicing, is or has been likely to cause death, or any injury or condition specified in Regulation 3(2) by reason of—

    (a) accidental leakage of gas;

    (b) inadequate combustion of gas; or

    (c) inadequate removal of the products of combustion of gas,

he shall within 14 days send a report of it to the Executive on a form approved for the purposes of this Regulation, unless he has previously reported such information.

(3) Nothing which is notifiable or reportable elsewhere in these Regulations shall be reportable under this Regulation.

(4) In this Regulation "liquefied petroleum gas" means commercial butane (that is, a hydrocarbon mixture consisting predominantly of butane, butylene or any mixture thereof) or commercial propane (that is, a hydrocarbon mixture consisting predominantly of propane, propylene or any mixture thereof) or any mixture of commercial butane and commercial propane.   **[1279]**

7 Records

(1) The responsible person shall keep a record of—

    (a) any event which is required to be reported under Regulation 3, which shall contain the particulars specified in Part I of Schedule 3; and

    (b) any case of disease required to be reported under Regulation 5, which shall contain the particulars specified in Part II of that Schedule.

(2) Any person sending a form to the Executive under Regulation 6 shall keep a record of the information provided on that form.

(3) Any record of deaths or injuries at work which an employer is required to keep by virtue of any other enactment shall, if it covers the injuries recordable under these Regulations and includes the particulars specified in Schedule 3, be sufficient for the requirements of paragraph (1)(a).

(4) The records referred to in paragraph (1) shall be kept at the place where the work to which they relate is carried on or, if this is not reasonably practicable, at the usual place of business of the responsible person and an entry in either of such records shall be kept for at least 3 years from the date on which it was made.

(5) The responsible person shall send to the enforcing authority such extracts from the records required to be kept under paragraph (1) as the enforcing authority may from time to time require.   **[1280]**

8 Additional provisions relating to mines and quarries

The provisions of Schedule 4 (which contains additional provisions relating to mines and quarries) shall have effect.   **[1281]**

9 Requirement for further information

The Executive may, with the approval of the Commission, by notice in writing served on any person who has furnished a report under Regulation 3 or 5, require that person to give to the Executive in an approved form such of the information specified in Schedule 5 as may be specified in the notice within such time as may be specified in that notice.   **[1282]**

10 Restrictions to the application of Regulations 3, 4 and 5

(1) The requirements of Regulation 3 relating to any death, injury or condition shall not apply to a patient when undergoing treatment in a hospital or in the surgery of a doctor or a dentist.

(2) The requirements of Regulations 3 and 4 relating to the death, injury or condition of a person as a result of an accident, shall apply to an accident arising out of or in connection with the movement of a vehicle on a road (within the meaning of section 196(1) of the Road Traffic Act 1972) only if that person—

(a) was killed or suffered an injury or condition as a result of exposure to a substance being conveyed by the vehicle; or

(b) was either himself engaged in, or was killed or suffered an injury or condition as a result of the activities of another person who was at the time of the accident engaged in, work connected with the loading or unloading of any article or substance onto or off the vehicle; or

(c) was either himself engaged in, or was killed or suffered an injury or condition as a result of the activities of another person who was at the time of the accident engaged in, work on or alongside a road, being work concerned with the construction, demolition, alteration, repair or maintenance of—

(i) the road or the markings or equipment thereon;

(ii) the verges, fences, hedges or other boundaries of the road;

(iii) pipes or cables on, under, over or adjacent to the road; or

(iv) buildings or structures adjacent to or over the road.

(3) The requirements of Regulations 3, 4 and 5 relating to any death, injury or condition, or case of disease, shall not apply to a member of the armed forces of the Crown or visiting forces who was on duty at the relevant time.

(4) Regulations 3, 4 and 5 shall not apply to anything which is required to be notified under any of the enactments or instruments specified in Schedule 6.

(5) Regulation 3(1)(a) shall not apply to a self-employed person who is injured at premises of which he is the owner or occupier, but Regulation 3(1)(b) shall apply to such a self-employed person (other than in the case of death) and it shall be sufficient compliance with that sub-paragraph if that self-employed person makes arrangements for the report to be sent to the enforcing authority by some other person.   **[1283]**

11 Defence in proceedings for an offence contravening these Regulations

It shall be a defence in proceedings against any person for an offence under these Regulations for that person to prove that he was not aware of the event requiring him to notify or send a report to the enforcing authority and that he had taken all reasonable steps to have all such events brought to his notice.   **[1284]**

12 Extension outside Great Britain

These Regulations shall apply to any activity to which sections 1 to 59 and 80 to 82 of the Health and Safety at Work etc Act 1974 apply by virtue of articles 6 and 7 of the Health and Safety at Work etc Act 1974 (Application outside Great Britain) Order 1977 as they apply to any such activity in Great Britain.   **[1285]**

13 (*Contains repeals, revocations, modifications and savings.*)

SCHEDULES

SCHEDULE 1

Regulation 2(1)

DANGEROUS OCCURENCES

PART I
GENERAL

1 Lifting machinery etc

The collapse of, the overturning of, or the failure of any load bearing part of—

(a) any lift, hoist, crane, derrick or mobile powered access platform, but not any winch, teagle, pulley block, gin wheel, transporter or runway;
(b) any excavator; or
(c) any pile driving frame or rig having an overall height, when operating, of more than 7 metres.

2 Passenger carrying amusement device

The following incidents at a fun fair (whether or not a travelling fun fair) while the relevant device is in use or under test—

(a) the collapse of, or the failure of any load bearing part of, any amusement device provided as part of the fun fair which is designed to allow passengers to move or ride on it or inside it; or
(b) the failure of any safety arrangement connected with such a device, which is designed to restrain or support passengers.

3 Pressure vessels

Explosion, collapse or bursting of any closed vessel, including a boiler or boiler tube, in which the internal pressure was above or below atmospheric pressure, which might have been liable to cause the death of, or any of the injuries or conditions covered by Regulation 3(2) to, any person, or which resulted in the stoppage of the plant involved for more than 24 hours.

4 Electrical short circuit

Electrical short circuit or overload attended by fire or explosion which resulted in the stoppage of the plant involved for more than 24 hours and which, taking into account the circumstances of the occurrence, might have been liable to cause the death of, or any of the injuries or conditions covered by Regulation 3(2) to, any person.

5 Explosion or fire

An explosion or fire occurring in any plant or place which resulted in the stoppage of that plant or suspension of normal work in that place for more than 24 hours, where such explosion or fire was due to the ignition of process materials, their by-products (including waste) or finished products.

6 Escape of flammable substances

The sudden, uncontrolled release of one tonne or more of highly flammable liquid, within the meaning of Regulation 2(2) of the Highly Flammable Liquids and Liquefied Petroleum Gases Regulations 1972, flammable gas or flammable liquid above its boiling point from any system or plant or pipe-line.

7 Collapse of scaffolding

A collapse or partial collapse of any scaffold which is more than 5 metres high which results in a substantial part of the scaffold falling or over-turning; and where the scaffold is slung or suspended, a collapse or partial collapse of the suspension arrangements (including any outrigger) which causes a working platform or cradle to fall more than 5 metres.

8 Collapse of building or structure

Any unintended collapse or partial collapse of—

(a) any building or structure under construction, reconstruction, alteration or demolition, or of any false-work, involving a fall of more than 5 tonnes of material; or

(b) any floor or wall of any building being used as a place of work, not being a building under construction, reconstruction, alteration or demolition.

9 Escape of a substance or pathogen

The uncontrolled or accidental release or the escape of any substance or pathogen from any apparatus, equipment, pipework, pipe-line, process plant, storage vessel, tank, in-works conveyance tanker, land-fill site, or exploratory land drilling site, which having regard to the nature of the substance or pathogen and the extent and location of the release or escape, might have been liable to cause the death of, any of the injuries or conditions covered by Regulation 3(2) to, or other damage to the health of, any person.

10 Explosives

Any ignition or explosion or explosives, where the ignition or explosion was not intentional.

11 Freight containers

Failure of any freight container or failure of any load bearing part thereof while it is being raised, lowered or suspended and in this paragraph "freight container" means a container within the meaning of Regulation 2(1) of The Freight Containers (Safety Convention) Regulations 1984.

12 Pipe-lines

Either of the following incidents in relation to a pipe-line as defined by section 65 of the Pipe-lines Act 1962—

(a) the bursting, explosion or collapse of a pipe-line or any part thereof; or

(b) the unintentional ignition of anything in a pipe-line, or of anything which immediately before it was ignited was in a pipe-line.

13 Conveyance of dangerous substances by road

(1) Any incident—

(a) in which a road tanker or tank container used for [the carriage of] a dangerous substance . . .—

(i) overturns; or

(ii) suffers serious damage to the tank in which the dangerous substance is being [carried]; or

(b) in which there is, in relation to such a road tanker or tank container—

(i) an uncontrolled release or escape of the dangerous substance being [carried]; or

(ii) a fire which involves the dangerous substance being [carried];

(2) In this paragraph, "[carriage]", "road tanker", "tank container" and "dangerous substance" has in each case the meaning assigned to it by Regulation 2(1) of [the Road Traffic (Carriage of Dangerous Substances in Road Tankers and Tank Containers) Regulations 1992].

14 (1) Any incident involving a vehicle conveying a dangerous substance by road, other than a vehicle to which paragraph 13 applies, where there is—

(a) an uncontrolled release or escape from any package or container of the dangerous substance being conveyed; or

(b) a fire which involves the dangerous substance being conveyed.

(2) In this paragraph "dangerous substance" means a substance which is dangerous for conveyance as defined in Regulation 2(1) of the Classification, Packaging and Labelling of Dangerous Substances Regulations 1984.

15 Breathing apparatus

Any incident where breathing apparatus, while being used to enable the wearer to breathe independently of the surrounding environment, malfunctions in such a way as to be likely either to deprive the wearer of oxygen or, in the case of use in a contaminated atmosphere, to expose the wearer to the contaminant, to the extent in either case of posing a danger to his health, except that this paragraph shall not apply to such apparatus while it is being—

(a) used in a mine; or

(b) maintained or tested.

16 Overhead electric lines

Any incident in which plant or equipment either comes into contact with an uninsulated overhead electric line in which the voltage exceeds 200 volts, or causes an electrical discharge from such an electric line by coming into close proximity to it, unless in either case the incident was intentional.

17 Locomotives

Any case of an accidental collision between a locomotive or a train and any other vehicle at a factory or at dock premises which might have been liable to cause the death of, or any of the injuries or conditions covered by Regulation 3(2) to, any person. **[1286]**

NOTE

Para 13: words in square brackets substituted, and words omitted revoked, by the Road Traffic (Carriage of Dangerous Substances in Road Tankers and Tank Containers) Regulations 1992, SI 1992/743, reg 30(3), Sch 5, Pt II, para 1.

(Pts II–IV (Dangerous occurrences reportable in relation respectively to mines, quarries and railways) not printed.)
(Sch 2 (Reportable diseases) not printed.)

SCHEDULE 3

Regulation 7

RECORDS

PART I
PARTICULARS TO BE KEPT IN RECORDS OF ANY EVENT WHICH IS REPORTABLE UNDER REGULATION 3

1 Date and time of accident or dangerous occurrence.

2 The following particulars of the person affected:—
   (a) full name;
   (b) occupation;
   (c) nature of injury or condition.

3 Place where the accident or dangerous occurrence happened.

4 A brief description of the circumstances. **[1287]**

PART II
PARTICULARS TO BE KEPT IN RECORDS OF INSTANCES OF ANY OF THE DISEASES SPECIFIED IN SCHEDULE 2 AND REPORTABLE UNDER REGULATION 5

1 Date of diagnosis of the disease.

2 Occupation of the person affected.

3 Name or nature of the disease. **[1288]**

(Sch 4 not printed.)

SCHEDULE 5

Regulation 9

MATTERS WHICH THE EXECUTIVE WITH THE APPROVAL OF THE COMMISSION MAY REQUIRE TO BE NOTIFIED

1 Further details of the circumstances leading up to the reported incident.

2 Further details about the nature or design or both of any plant involved in the reported incident.

3 Safety systems and procedures for the control of the plant or substance involved in the reported incident.

4 Qualifications, experience and training of staff having use or control of any plant or substance or concerned with safety systems or procedures.

5 Design and operation documentation.

6 Arrangements for the protection of personnel from any plant or substance connected with the reported incident.

7 Details of any examination of, or tests carried out on, any plant or installation involved in the reported incident.

8 Any available information about levels of exposure of persons at the work place to airborne substances.   **[1289]**

(Sch 6 not printed.)

STATUTORY MATERNITY PAY (GENERAL) REGULATIONS 1986

(SI 1986/1960)

NOTES
Made: 17 November 1986.
Authority: Social Security Act 1986, ss 46(4), (7), (8), 47(1), (3), (6), (7), 48(3), (6), 50(1), (2), (4), (5), 51(1), (4), 54(1), 83(1), 84(1), Sch 4, paras 6, 8, 12(3) (see now Social Security Contributions and Benefits Act 1992, Pt XII).

ARRANGEMENT OF REGULATIONS

PART I
INTRODUCTION

PART I

INTRODUCTION

1 Citation, commencement and interpretation

(1) These regulations may be cited as the Statutory Maternity Pay (General) Regulations 1986 and shall come into operation in the case of regulations 1, 22 and 23 on 15th March 1987, and in the case of the remainder of the regulations on 6th April 1987.

(2) In these regulations, unless the context otherwise requires—

"the 1975 Act" means the Social Security Act 1975;
"the 1978 Act" means the Employment Protection (Consolidation) Act 1978;
"the 1986 Act" means the Social Security Act 1986.
["the Contributions and Benefits Act" means the Social Security Contributions and Benefits Act 1992.]

(3) Unless the context otherwise requires, any references in these regulations to—

(a) a numbered regulation is a reference to the regulation bearing that number in these regulations and any reference in a regulation to a numbered paragraph is a reference to the paragraph of that regulation bearing that number;

(b) any provision made by or contained in an enactment or instrument shall be construed as a reference to that provision as amended or extended by any enactment or instrument and as including a reference to any provision which it re-enacts or replaces, or which may re-enact or replace it, with or without modifications.   **[1290]**

NOTE
    Para (2): definition "the Contributions and Benefits Act" added by the Social Security (Miscellaneous Provisions) Amendment (No 2) Regulations 1992, SI 1992/2595, reg 12.

PART II

ENTITLEMENT

2 The maternity pay period

(1) Subject to paragraph (3), where a woman gives notice to her employer that she intends to stop work and does in fact stop work because of her pregnancy in a week which is later than the 12th week before the expected week of confinement, then the first week in the maternity pay period shall be the week following the week in which she stopped work, or the 6th week before the expected week of confinement, whichever is the earlier.

(2) The maternity pay period shall end not later than the end of the 11th week immediately following the expected week of confinement and subject thereto shall be for a period of 18 consecutive weeks.

(3) Where—
  (a) a woman is confined before the 11th week before the expected week of confinement, or
  (b) is confined after the 12th week but before the 6th week before the expected week of confinement and the confinement occurs in a week which precedes that mentioned in a notice given to her employer as being the week she intends to give up work,

the first week in the maternity pay period shall be the week after the week in which she is confined.   **[1291]**

3 Contract of service ended for the purpose of avoiding liability for statutory maternity pay

(1) A former employer shall be liable to make payments of statutory maternity pay to any woman who was employed by him for a continuous period of at least 8 weeks and whose contract of service with him was brought to an end by the former employer solely or mainly for the purpose of avoiding liability for statutory maternity pay.

(2) In order to determine the amount payable by the former employer—
  (a) the woman shall be deemed for the purposes of Part V of the 1986 Act to have been employed by him from the date her employment with him ended until the end of the week immediately preceding the 14th week before the expected week of confinement on the same terms and conditions of employment as those subsisting immediately before her employment ended, and
  (b) her normal weekly earnings for the period of 8 weeks immediately preceding the 14th week before the expected week of confinement shall for those purposes be calculated by reference to her normal weekly earnings for the period of 8 weeks ending with the last day in respect of which she was paid under her former contract of service.   **[1292]**

NOTE
"Part V of the 1986 Act": see now the Social Security Contributions and Benefits Act 1992, Pt XII.

4 Modification of entitlement provisions

(1) In relation to a woman who—
  (a) has been in employed earner's employment with an employer for a continuous period of at least 8 weeks, and

(b) is dismissed by that employer for a reason mentioned in paragraph (a) or (b) of section 60(1) of the 1978 Act, but

(c) is not offered a new contract of service which complies with section 60(3) of that Act, or is offered such a contract but declines to accept it,

section 46(2)(a) and (b) of the 1986 Act shall have effect as if for the conditions there set out there were substituted the conditions that—

(i) she would but for her dismissal have been in employment with the employer who dismissed her for a period of at least 26 weeks ending with the week immediately preceding the 14th week before the expected week of confinement, and

(ii) her normal weekly earnings from that employment for the period of 8 weeks ending with the last day in respect of which she was paid in accordance with the contract of service with the employer are not less than the lower earnings limit in force under section 4(1)(a) of the 1975 Act in the last of the 8 weeks.

(2) In relation to a woman in employed earner's employment who was confined before the 14th week before the expected week of confinement section 46(2)(a) and (b) of the 1986 Act shall have effect as if for the conditions there set out, there was substituted the conditions that—

(a) she would but for her confinement have been in employed earner's employment with an employer for a continuous period of at least 26 weeks ending with the week immediately preceding the 14th week before the expected week of confinement, and

(b) her normal weekly earnings for the period of 8 weeks ending with the week immediately preceding the week of her confinement are not less than the lower earnings limit in force under section 4(1)(a) of the 1975 Act immediately before the commencement of the week of her confinement.

[(3) In relation to a woman to whom either paragraph (1) or paragraph (2) applies, section 48 of the 1986 Act shall be modified so that—

(a) subsection (2) has effect as if the reference to the period of 8 weeks immediately preceding the 14th week before the expected week of confinement was a reference—

(i) in a case to which paragraph (1) applies, to the period of 8 weeks ending with the last day in respect of which she was paid in accordance with her contract of service with her employer, or

(ii) in a case to which paragraph (2) relates, to the period of 8 weeks immediately preceding the week in which her confinement occurred;

(b) subsection (4) has effect as if the words "or would but for her dismissal or confinement have been" were inserted after the words "expected week of confinement has been"; and

(c) subsection (5) has effect as if there were added at the end of the subsection the words—

"and for the purpose of this subsection—

(a) a contract of service which ended before the end of the week immediately preceding the 14th week before the expected week of confinement shall be deemed to have continued until the end of that week; and

(b) in any week which falls—

(i) after the week preceding the week in which her employment ended or confinement occurred, but

(ii) before the 14th week before the expected week of confinement,

the woman shall be deemed to have been employed under her contract of service for the same number of hours weekly as that which her contract involved in the week preceding the week in which her employment ended or her confinement occurred.]   **[1293]**

5 Treatment of more than one contract of service as one

Where 2 or more contracts of service exist concurrently between one employer and one employee, they shall be treated as one for the purposes of Part V of the 1986 Act, except where, by virtue of regulation 11 of the Social Security (Contributions) Regulations 1979 the earnings from those contracts of service are not aggregated for the purposes of earnings-related contributions.   **[1294]**

6 Lower rate of statutory maternity pay

The lower rate of statutory maternity pay is a weekly rate of [£47.95].   **[1295]**

7 Liability of Secretary of State to pay statutory maternity pay

(1) Where—

    (a) an adjudicating authority has determined that an employer is liable to make payments of statutory maternity pay to a woman, and

    (b) the time for appealing against that determination has expired, and

    (c) no appeal against the determination has been lodged or leave to appeal against the determination is required and has been refused,

then for any week in respect of which the employer was liable to make payments of statutory maternity pay but did not do so, and for any subsequent weeks in the maternity pay period the liability to make those payments shall, notwithstanding section 46(3) of the 1986 Act, be that of the Secretary of State and not the employer.

(2) In paragraph (1) adjudicating authority means, as the case may be, the Chief or any other adjudication officer, a Social Security Appeal Tribunal or the Chief or any other Social Security Commissioner.

(3) Liability to make payments of statutory maternity pay shall, notwithstanding section 46(3) of the 1986 Act, be a liability of the Secretary of State and not the employer as from the week in which the employer first becomes insolvent until the end of the maternity pay period.

(4) For the purposes of paragraph (3) an employer shall be taken to be insolvent if, and only if—

    (a) in England and Wales—

        (i) he has been adjudged bankrupt or has made a composition or arrangement with his creditors;

        (ii) he has died and his estate falls to be administered in accordance with an order under section 421 of the Insolvency Act 1986; or

(iii) where an employer is a company, a winding-up order or an administration order is made or a resolution for voluntary winding-up is passed with respect to it, or a receiver or manager of its undertaking is duly appointed, or possession is taken by or on behalf of the holders of any debentures secured by a floating charge, of any property of the company comprised in or subject to the charge or a voluntary arrangement proposed for the purposes of Part I of the Insolvency Act 1986 is approved under that Part;

(b) in Scotland—

(i) an award of sequestration is made on his estate or he executes a trust deed for his creditors or enters into a composition contract;

(ii) he has died and a judicial factor appointed under section 11A of the Judicial Factors (Scotland) Act 1889 is required by that section to divide his insolvent estate among his creditors; or

(iii) where the employer is a company, a winding-up order or an administration order is made or a resolution for voluntary winding-up is passed with respect to it or a receiver of its undertaking is duly appointed or a voluntary arrangement proposed for the purposes of Part I of the Insolvency Act 1986 is approved under that Part.

[1296]

NOTE

"Section 46(3) of the 1986 Act": see now the Social Security Contributions and Benefits Act 1992, s 164(3).

8 Work after confinement

(1) Where in the week immediately preceding the 14th week before the expected week of confinement a woman had 2 or more employers but one or more of them were not liable to make payments to her of statutory maternity pay ("non-liable employer"), section 47(6) of the 1986 Act shall not apply in respect of any week after the week of confinement but within the maternity pay period in which she works only for a non-liable employer.

(2) Where after her confinement a woman—

(a) works for an employer who is not liable to pay her statutory maternity pay and is not a non-liable employer, but

(b) before the end of her maternity pay period ceases to work for that employer,

the person who before she commenced work was liable to make payments of statutory maternity pay to her shall, notwithstanding section 46 of the 1986 Act, not be liable to make such payments to her for any weeks in the maternity pay period after she ceases work. [1297]

NOTE

"Section 47(6) of the 1986 Act": see now the Social Security Contributions and Benefits Act 1992, s 165(6); s 46 of the 1986 Act is now s 164 of the 1992 Act.

9 No liability to pay statutory maternity pay

Notwithstanding the provisions of section 46(1) of the 1986 Act, no liability to make payments of statutory maternity pay to a woman shall arise in respect of a week within the maternity pay period for any part of which she is detained in legal custody or sentenced to a term of imprisonment (except where the sentence is suspended), or of any subsequent week within that period. [1298]

NOTE

"Section 46(1) of the 1986 Act": see now the Social Security Contributions and Benefits Act 1992, s 164(1).

---

10 Death of woman

An employer shall not be liable to make payments of statutory maternity pay in respect of a woman for any week within the maternity pay period which falls after the week in which she dies. **[1299]**

PART III

CONTINUOUS EMPLOYMENT AND NORMAL WORKING HOURS

11 Continuous employment

(1) Subject to the following provisions of this regulation, where in any week a woman is, for the whole or part of the week,—

   (a) incapable of work in consequence of sickness or injury, or

   (b) absent from work on account of a temporary cessation of work, or

   (c) absent from work in circumstances such that, by arrangement or custom, she is regarded as continuing in the employment of her employer for all or any purpose, or

   (d) absent from work wholly or partly because of pregnancy or confinement,

and returns to work for her employer after the incapacity for or absence from work, that week shall be treated for the purposes of Part V of the 1986 Act as part of a continuous period of employment with that employer, notwithstanding that no contract of service exists with that employer in respect of that week.

(2) Incapacity for work which lasts for more than 26 consecutive weeks shall not count for the purposes of paragraph (1)(a).

(3) Paragraph (1)(d) shall only apply to a woman who—

   (a) has a contract of service with the same employer both before and after the confinement but not during any period of absence from work due to her confinement and the period between those contracts does not exceed 26 weeks, or

   (b) returns to work in accordance with section 45(1) of the 1978 Act or in pursuance of an offer made in circumstances described in section 56A(2) of that Act after a period of absence from work wholly or partly occasioned by pregnancy or confinement.

   [(3A) Where a woman who is pregnant—

   (a) is an employee in an employed earner's employment in which the custom is for the employer—

     (i) to offer work for a fixed period of not more than 26 consecutive weeks;

     (ii) to offer work for such period on 2 or more occasions in a year for periods which do not overlap; and

     (iii) to offer the work available to those persons who had worked for him during the last or a recent such period, but

   (b) is absent from work—

     (i) wholly or partly because of the pregnancy or her confinement, or

     (ii) because of incapacity arising from some specific disease or bodily or mental disablement, then in her case paragraph (1) shall apply as if the words "and returns to work for an employer after the incapacity for or absence from work" were omitted and paragraph (4) shall not apply.]

(4) Where a woman is employed under a contract of service for part only of the week immediately preceding the 14th week before the expected week of confinement, the whole of that week shall count in computing any period of continuous employment for the purposes of Part V of the 1986 Act.   **[1300]**

NOTES
Commencement: 6 April 1990 (para (3A)): 6 April 1987 (remainder).
Para (3A): inserted by SI 1990/622, reg 2.

12 Continuous employment and unfair dismissal

(1) This regulation applies to a woman in relation to whose dismissal an action is commenced which consists—

    (a) of the presentation by her of a complaint under section 67(1) of the 1978 Act; or

    (b) of her making a claim in accordance with a dismissals procedure agreement designated by an order under section 65 of that Act; or

    (c) of any action taken by a conciliation officer under section 134(3) of that Act.

(2) If in consequence of an action of the kind specified in paragraph (1) a woman is reinstated or re-engaged by her employer or by a successor or associated employer of that employer the continuity of her employment shall be preserved for the purposes of Part V of the 1986 Act and any week which falls within the interval beginning with the effective date of termination and ending with the date of reinstatement or re-engagement, as the case may be, shall count in the computation of her period of continuous employment.

(3) In this regulation—

"successor" and "dismissals procedure agreement" have the same meanings as in section 30(3) and (4) of the Trade Union and Labour Relations Act 1974, and

"associated employer" shall be construed in accordance with section 153(4) of the 1978 Act.   **[1301]**

13 Continuous employment and stoppages of work

(1) Where for any week or part of a week a woman does no work because there is, within the meaning of section 19 of the 1975 Act a stoppage of work due to a trade dispute at her place of employment the continuity of her employment shall, subject to paragraph (2), be treated as continuing throughout the stoppage but, subject to paragraph (3), no such week shall count in the computation of her period of employment.

(2) Subject to paragraph (3), where during the stoppage of work a woman is dismissed from her employment, the continuity of her employment shall not be treated in accordance with paragraph (1) as continuing beyond the commencement of the day she stopped work.

(3) The provisions of paragraph (1) to the extent that they provide that a week in which a stoppage of work occurred shall not count in the computation of a period of

employment, and paragraph (2) shall not apply to a woman who proves that at no time did she have a direct interest in the trade dispute in question.   **[1302]**

NOTE
"Section 19 of the 1975 Act": see now the Social Security Contributions and Benefits Act 1992, s 27.

14 Change of employer

A woman's employment shall, notwithstanding the change of employer, be treated as continuous employment with the second employer where—

  (a) the employer's trade or business or an undertaking (whether or not it is an undertaking established by or under an Act of Parliament) is transferred from one person to another;

  (b) by or under an Act of Parliament, whether public or local and whenever passed, a contract of employment between any body corporate and the woman is modified and some other body corporate is substituted as her employer;

  (c) on the death of her employer, the woman is taken into the employment of the personal representatives or trustees of the deceased;

  (d) the woman is employed by partners, personal representatives or trustees and there is a change in the partners, or, as the case may be, personal representatives or trustees;

  (e) the woman is taken into the employment of an employer who is, at the time she entered his employment, an associated employer of her previous employer, and for this purpose "associated employer" shall be construed in accordance with section 153(4) of the 1978 Act;

  (f) on the termination of her employment with an employer she is taken into the employment of another employer and [those employers are the governors of a school maintained by a local education authority and that authority].   **[1303]**

NOTE
Para (f): words in square brackets substituted by the Statutory Maternity Pay (General) Amendment Regulations 1990, SI 1990/622, reg 3.

15 Reinstatement after service with the armed forces etc

If a woman who is entitled to apply to her former employer under the Reserve Forces (Safeguard of Employment) Act 1985 enters the employment of that employer not later than the 6 month period mentioned in section 1(4)(b) of that Act, her previous period of employment with that employer (or if there was more than one such period, the last of those periods) and the period of employment beginning in the said period of 6 months shall be treated as continuous.   **[1304]**

16 Normal working weeks

(1) For the purposes of section 48(5) of the 1986 Act, a woman's contract of service shall be treated as not normally involving or having involved employment for less than 16 hours weekly where she is normally employed for 16 hours or more weekly.

(2) Where a woman's relations with her employer were governed for a continuous period of at least 2 years by a contract of service which normally involved employment for not less than 16 hours weekly and this period was followed by a further period, ending with the week immediately preceding the 14th week before the expected week of confinement, in which her relations with that employer were

governed by a contract of service which normally involved employment for less than 16 hours, but not less than 8 hours weekly, then her contract of service shall be treated for the purpose of section 48(5) of the 1986 Act as not normally involving or having involved employment for less than 16 hours weekly.

(3) Where a woman's relations with her employer are or were governed for a continuous period of at least 2 years by a contract of service which involved

    (a) for not more than 26 weeks in that period, employment for 8 hours or more but less than 16 hours weekly, and

    (b) for the whole of the remainder of that period employment for not less than 16 hours weekly,

the contract of service shall be treated for the purposes of section 48(5) of the 1986 Act as not normally involving or having involved employment for less than 16 hours weekly.   **[1305]**

NOTE

"Section 48(5) of the 1986 Act": see now the Social Security Contributions and Benefits Act 1992, s 166(5).

16A   Meaning of "week"

[Where a woman has been in employed earner's employment with the same employer in each of 26 consecutive weeks (but no more than 26 weeks) ending with the week immediately preceding the 14th week before the expected week of confinement then for the purpose of determining whether that employment amounts to a continuous period of at least 26 weeks, the first of those 26 weeks shall be a period commencing on the first day of her employment with the employer and ending at midnight on the first Saturday thereafter or on that day where her first day is a Saturday.]   **[1306]**

NOTES

Commencement: 6 April 1990.
Inserted by SI 1990/622, reg 4.

PART IV
GENERAL PROVISIONS

17 Meaning of "employee"

(1) In a case where, and in so far as, a woman over the age of 16 is treated as an employed earner by virtue of the Social Security (Categorisation of Earners) Regulations 1978 she shall be treated as an employee for the purposes of Part V of the 1986 Act and in a case where, and in so far as, such a woman is treated otherwise than as an employed earner by virtue of those regulations, she shall not be treated as an employee for the purposes of Part V.

(2) Any woman who is in employed earner's employment within the meaning of the 1975 Act under a contract of apprenticeship shall be treated as an employee for the purposes of Part V.

(3) A woman who is in employed earner's employment within the meaning of the 1975 Act but whose employer—

    (a) does not fulfil the conditions prescribed in regulation 119(1)(b) of the Social Security (Contributions) Regulations 1979 as to residence or presence in Great Britain, or

    (b) is a woman who, by reason of any international treaty to which the United

Kingdom is a party or of any international convention binding the United Kingdom—

(i) is exempt from the provisions of the 1975 Act, or

(ii) is a woman against whom the provisions of that Act are not enforceable,

shall not be treated as an employee for the purposes of Part V of the 1986 Act.

[1307]

18 Treatment of two or more employers as one

(1) In a case where the earnings paid to a woman in respect of 2 or more employments are aggregated and treated as a single payment of earnings under regulation 12(1) of the Social Security (Contributions) Regulations 1979, the employers of the woman in respect of those employments shall be treated as one for all purposes of Part V of the 1986 Act.

(2) Where 2 or more employers are treated as one under the provisions of paragraph (1), liability for statutory maternity pay payable by them to a woman shall be apportioned between them in such proportions as they may agree or, in default of agreement, in the proportions which the woman's earnings from each employment bear to the amount of the aggregated earnings.   **[1308]**

19 Payments to be treated as contractual remuneration

For the purposes of paragraph 12(1) and (2) of Schedule 4 to the 1986 Act, the payments which are to be treated as contractual remuneration are sums payable under the contract of service—

(a) by way of remuneration;

(b) for incapacity for work due to sickness or injury, and

(c) by reason of pregnancy or confinement.   **[1309]**

NOTE
  "1986 Act, Sch 4, para 12": see now the Social Security Contributions and Benefits Act 1992, Sch 13, para 3.

20 Meaning of "earnings"

(1) ...

[(2) For the purposes of section 171(4) of the Contributions and Benefits Act, the expression "earnings" refers to gross earnings and includes any remuneration or profit derived from a woman's employment except any payment or amount which is excluded from the computation of a person's earnings under regulation 19 or 19B of the Social Security (Contributions) Regulations 1979.]

(3) ...

(4) For the purposes of section 50(3) of the 1986 Act the expression "earnings" includes also—

(a) any sum payable in respect of arrears of pay in pursuance of an order for reinstatement or re-engagement under the 1978 Act;

(b) any sum payable by way of pay in pursuance of an order under the 1978 Act for the continuation of a contract of employment;

(c) any sum payable by way of remuneration in pursuance of a protective award under the Employment Protection Act 1975;

(d) any sum payable by way of statutory sick pay, including sums payable in accordance with regulations made under section 1(5) of the Social Security and Housing Benefits Act 1982.

(5), (6) ... **[1310]**

NOTES

Commencement: 16 November 1992 (para (2)); 6 April 1987 (remainder).

Paras (1), (3), (5), (6): revoked by the Social Security (Miscellaneous Provisions) Amendment (No 2) Regulations 1992, SI 1992/2595, reg 13(1), (2), (4).

Para (2): substituted by SI 1992/2595, reg 13(1), (3).

"Section 50(3) of the 1986 Act": see now the Social Security Contributions and Benefits Act 1992, s 171(4).

21 Normal weekly earnings

(1) For the purposes of Part V of the 1986 Act, a woman's normal weekly earnings shall be calculated in accordance with the following provisions of this regulation.

(2) In this regulation—

"the appropriate date" means the first day of the 14th week before the expected week of confinement, or the first day in the week in which the woman is confined, whichever is the earlier, or in the case of a woman in respect of whom section 46(2) of the 1986 Act is modified in accordance with regulation 4(1), the first day of the week immediately following the last week in which she was employed under a contract of service by the employer who dismissed her;

"normal pay day" means a day on which the terms of a woman's contract of service require her to be paid, or the practice in her employment is for her to be paid, if any payment is due to her; and

"day of payment" means a day on which the woman was paid.

(3) Subject to paragraph (4), the relevant period for the purposes of section 50(3) of the 1986 Act is the period between—

(a) the last normal pay day to fall before the appropriate date; and

(b) the last normal pay day to fall at least 8 weeks earlier than the normal pay day mentioned in sub-paragraph (a),

including the normal pay day mentioned in sub-paragraph (a) but excluding that first mentioned in sub-paragraph (b).

(4) In a case where a woman has no identifiable normal pay day, paragraph (3) shall have effect as if the words "day of payment" were substituted for the words "normal pay day" in each place where they occur.

(5) In a case where a woman has normal pay days at intervals of or approximating to one or more calendar months (including intervals of or approximating to a year) her normal weekly earnings shall be calculated by dividing her earnings in the relevant period by the number of calendar months in that period (or, if it is not a whole number, the nearest whole number), multiplying the result by 12 and dividing by 52.

(6) In a case to which paragraph (5) does not apply and the relevant period is not an exact number of weeks, the woman's normal weekly earnings shall be calculated by dividing her earnings in the relevant period by the number of days in the relevant period and multiplying the result by 7. **[1311]**

NOTE

"Section 46(2) of the 1986 Act": see now the Social Security Contributions and Benefits Act 1992, s 164(2); s 50(3) of the 1986 Act is now s 171(4) of the 1992 Act.

[21A Effect of statutory maternity pay on invalidity benefit

[(1) For the purpose of determining a woman's entitlement to invalidity pension under section 15 of the 1975 Act or under section 15 of the Social Security Pensions Act 1975, a day which falls within the maternity pay period shall, notwithstanding paragraph 11 of Schedule 4 to the 1986 Act, be treated as a day of incapacity for work for the purpose of determining whether it forms part of a period of interruption of employment where—

    (a) on that day she was incapable of work by reason of some specific disease or bodily or mental disablement, work for this purpose being work which the woman can reasonably be expected to do; and

    (b) that day is not treated under section 17(2) of the 1975 Act as a day which is not a day of incapacity for work, and

    (c) the day immediately preceding the first day in the maternity pay period falls within either a period of interruption of employment or a period of entitlement to statutory sick pay for the purposes of Part I of the Social Security and Housing Benefits Act 1982; and

    (d) the woman either satisfied the contribution conditions specified for sickness benefit on the first day of incapacity for work to fall within that period of interruption of employment or would have satisfied those conditions had a claim for sickness benefit been made on the first or any subsequent day of incapacity for work falling within that period of entitlement.

    (1A) Any day which, by virtue of paragraph (1), forms part of a period of interruption of employment shall be further treated, for the purposes of determining entitlement to invalidity pension under section 15 of the 1975 Act, as being a day on which the woman has been entitled to sickness benefit.

    (1B) For the purposes of this regulation, "period of interruption of employment" has the same meaning as it has in the 1975 Act by virtue of section 17(1)(d) of that Act.

    (1C) The reference to a maternity pay period in paragraph (1) is to a maternity pay period which commenced on or after 6th May 1990.]

    (2) Where by virtue of paragraph (1) a woman is entitled to invalidity pension for any week (including part of a week), the total amount of invalidity pension (including any increase for a dependant) and invalidity allowance (invalidity benefit) payable to her for that week shall be reduced by an amount equivalent to any statutory maternity pay to which she is entitled in accordance with Part V of the 1986 Act for the same week, and only the balance, if any, of the invalidity benefit shall be payable to her].   **[1312]**

NOTES

Commencement: 6 May 1990 (paras (1), (1A)–(1C)); 6 April 1988 (remainder).
Inserted by SI 1988/532, reg 3.
Paras (1), (1A)-(1C): substituted for para (1) as originally enacted by SI 1990/622, reg 6.
"Section 15 of the 1975 Act": see now the Social Security Contributions and Benefits Act 1992, s 33.
"Section 15 of the Social Security Pensions Act 1975": see now the Social Security Contributions and Benefits Act 1992, s 40.
"1986 Act, Sch 4, para 11": see now the Social Security Contributions and Benefits Act 1992, Sch 13, para 1.
"Section 17 of the 1975 Act": see now the Social Security Contributions and Benefits Act 1992, s 57.
"Part I of the Social Security and Housing Benefits Act 1982": see now the Social Security Contributions and Benefits Act 1992, Pt XI.

PART V

ADMINISTRATION

22 Evidence of expected week of confinement or of confinement

(1) A woman shall in accordance with the following provisions of this regulation, provide the person who is liable to pay her statutory maternity pay with evidence as to—

    (a) the week in which the expected date of confinement occurs, and

    (b) where her entitlement to statutory maternity pay depends upon the fact of her confinement, the week in which she was confined.

(2) For the purpose of paragraph (1)(b) a certificate of birth shall be sufficient evidence that the woman was confined in the week in which the birth occurred.

(3) The evidence shall be submitted to the person who will be liable to make payments of statutory maternity pay not later than the end of the third week of the maternity pay period so however that where the woman has good cause the evidence may be submitted later than that date but not later than the end of the 13th week of the maternity pay period.

(4) For the purposes of paragraph (3) evidence contained in an envelope which is properly addressed and sent by prepaid post shall be deemed to have been submitted on the day on which it was posted.   **[1313]**

23 Notice of absence from work

(1) Where a woman is confined before the beginning of the 14th week before the expected week of confinement, she shall be entitled to payments of statutory maternity pay only if—

    (a) she gives notice to the person who will be liable to pay it that her absence from work with him is wholly because of her confinement, and

    (b) that notice is given within 21 days of the date she was confined or if in the particular circumstances that is not practicable, as soon as is reasonably practicable thereafter; and

    (c) where the person so requests, the notice is in writing.

(2) Where a woman is confined before the date stated in a notice provided in accordance with section 46(4) of the 1986 Act as being the date her absence from work is due to begin, she shall be entitled to payments of statutory maternity pay only if—

    (a) she gives a further notice to the person who will be liable to pay it specifying the date she was confined and the date her absence from work wholly or partly because of pregnancy or confinement began, and

    (b) that further notice is given within 21 days of the date she was confined or if in the particular circumstances that is not practicable, as soon as is reasonably practicable thereafter; and

    (c) where the person so requests, the notice is in writing.

(3) For the purposes of this regulation, a notice contained in an envelope which is properly addressed and sent by prepaid post shall be deemed to be given on the date on which it is posted.

(4) Subject to paragraph (5), section 46(4) of the 1986 Act shall not apply to a woman who either—

    (a) leaves, for a reason wholly unconnected with her pregnancy, her employment with the person who will be liable to pay her statutory maternity pay, after the beginning of the 15th week before the expected week of confinement; or

(b) is dismissed, but not unfairly dismissed under section 60 of the 1978 Act, from her employment by the person who will be liable to pay statutory maternity pay and has not at the time of her dismissal given him notice that she is going to be absent from work with him because of her pregnancy or confinement.

(5) A woman who is exempted from section 46(4) of the 1986 Act by paragraph (4) but who is confined before the 11th week before the expected week of confinement shall be entitled to payments of statutory maternity pay only if she gives the person who will be liable to pay it notice specifying the date she was confined.   **[1314]**

NOTE
"Section 46(4) of the 1986 Act": see now the Social Security Contributions and Benefits Act 1992, s 164(4).

24 Notification of employment after confinement

A woman who after the date of confinement but within the maternity pay period commences work in employed earner's employment with a person who is not liable to make payments of statutory maternity pay to her and is not a non-liable employer for the purposes of regulation 8(1), shall within 7 days of the day she commenced work inform any person who is so liable of the date she commenced work.   **[1315]**

5 Provision of information in connection with determination of questions

Any woman claiming to be entitled to statutory maternity pay, or any other person who is a party to proceedings arising under the 1986 Act relating to statutory maternity pay, shall, if she receives notification from the Secretary of State that any information is required from her for the determination of any question arising in connection therewith, furnish that information to the Secretary of State within 10 days of receiving that notification.   **[1316]**

[25A Provision of information relating to claims for certain other benefits

(1) Where an employer who has been given notice in accordance with Section 46(4) of the 1986 Act or regulation 23 by a woman who is or has been an employee—

(a) decides that he has no liability to make payments of statutory maternity pay to her, or

(b) has made one or more payments of statutory maternity pay to her but decides, before the end of the maternity pay period and for a reason specified in paragraph (3), that he has no liability to make further payments to her,

then, in connection with the making of a claim by the woman for a maternity allowance or incapacity benefit, he shall furnish her with the information specified in the following provisions of this regulation.

(2) Where the employer decides he has no liability to make payments of statutory maternity pay to the woman, he shall furnish her with details of the decision and the reasons for it.

(3) Where the employer decides he has no liability to make further payments of statutory maternity pay to the woman because either she has within the maternity pay

period been detained in legal custody or sentenced to a term of imprisonment which was not suspended, or for part of a week within the maternity pay period she was not present in a member State, he shall furnish her with—

(a) details of his decision and the reasons for it; and

(b) details of the last week in respect of which a liability to pay statutory maternity pay arose and the total number of weeks within the maternity pay period in which such a liability arose.

(4) The employer shall—

(a) return to the woman any maternity certificate provided by her in support of the notice referred to in paragraph (1); and

(b) comply with any requirements imposed by the preceding provisions of this regulation—

(i) in a case to which paragraph (2) applies, within 7 days of the decision being made, or, if earlier, within 21 days of the day the woman gave notice of her intended absence or of her confinement if that had occurred; or

(ii) in a case to which paragraph (3) refers, within 7 days of being notified of the woman's detention or sentence or, as the case may be, absence from a member State.

(5) In this regulation, "incapacity benefit" means sickness benefit, invalidity pension or a severe disablement allowance.]   **[1317]**

NOTES
Commencement: 6 April 1990
Inserted by SI 1990/622, reg 7.
"Section 46(4) of the 1986 Act": see now the Social Security Contributions and Benefits Act 1992, s 164(4).

26 Records to be maintained by employers

(1) Every employer shall maintain for 3 years after the end of the tax year in which the maternity pay period ends a record in relation to any woman who is or was an employee of his of—

(a) the date of the first day of absence from work wholly or partly because of pregnancy or confinement as notified by her and, if different, the date of the first day when such absence commenced;

(b) the weeks in that tax year in which statutory maternity pay was paid and the amount paid in each week; and

(c) any week in that tax year which was within her maternity pay period but for which no payment of statutory maternity pay was made to her and the reasons no payment was made.

(2) Except where he was not liable to make a payment of statutory maternity pay and subject to paragraphs (3) and (4), every employer shall retain for 3 years after the end of the tax year in which the maternity pay period ends any medical certificate or other evidence relating to the expected week of confinement, or as the case may be, the confinement which was provided to him by a woman who is or was an employee of his.

(3) Where an employer returns a medical certificate to an employee of his for the purpose of enabling her to make a claim for benefit under the 1975 Act, it shall be sufficient for the purposes of paragraph (2) if he retains a copy of that certificate.

(4) An employer shall not retain any certificate of birth provided to him as evidence of confinement by a woman who is or was an employee of his, but shall retain a record of the date of birth.   **[1318]**

PART VI
PAYMENT

27 Payment of statutory maternity pay

Payment of statutory maternity pay may be made in a like manner to payments of remuneration but shall not include payments in kind or by way of the provision of board or lodgings or of services or other facilities. **[1319]**

28 Rounding to avoid fractional amounts

Where any payment of statutory maternity pay is made for any week at the higher rate specified in section 48(2) of the 1986 Act and the amount due for the week includes a fraction of a penny, the payment shall be rounded to the next whole number of pence. **[1320]**

NOTE
"Section 48(2) of the 1986 Act": see now the Social Security Contributions and Benefits Act 1992, s 166(2).

29 Time when statutory maternity pay is to be paid

(1) In this regulation, "pay day" means a day on which it has been agreed, or it is the normal practice between an employer or former employer and a woman who is or was an employee of his, that payments by way of remuneration are to be made, or, where there is no such agreement or normal practice, the last day of a calendar month.

(2) In any case where—
(a) a decision has been made by an adjudication officer, appeal tribunal or Commissioner in proceedings under Part III of the 1975 Act as a result of which a woman is entitled to an amount of statutory maternity pay; and
(b) the time for bringing an appeal against the decision has expired and either—
(i) no such appeal has been brought; or
(ii) such an appeal has been brought and has been finally disposed of,
that amount of statutory maternity pay shall be paid within the time specified in paragraph (3).

(3) Subject to paragraphs (4) and (5), the employer or former employer shall pay the amount not later than the first pay day after—
(a) where an appeal has been brought, the day on which the employer or former employer receives notification that it has been finally disposed of;
(b) where leave to appeal has been refused and there remains no further opportunity to apply for leave, the day on which the employer or former employer receives notification of the refusal; and
(c) in any other case, the day on which the time for bringing an appeal expires.

(4) Subject to paragraph (5), where it is impracticable, in view of the employer's or former employer's methods of accounting for and paying remuneration, for the requirement of payment referred to in paragraph (3) to be met by the pay day referred to in that paragraph, it shall be met not later than the next following pay day.

(5) Where the employer or former employer would not have remunerated the woman for her work in the week in question as early as the pay day specified in paragraph (3) or (if it applies) paragraph (4), the requirement of payment shall be met

on the first day on which the woman would have been remunerated for her work in that week. **[1321]**

30 Payments by the Secretary of State

Where the Secretary of State becomes liable in accordance with regulation 7 to make payments of statutory maternity pay to a woman, the first payment shall be made as soon as reasonably practicable after he becomes so liable, and payments thereafter shall be made at weekly intervals, by means of an instrument of payment or by such other means as appears to the Secretary of State to be appropriate in the circumstances of any particular case. **[1322]**

31 Persons unable to act

(1) Where in the case of any woman—

(a) statutory maternity pay is payable to her or she is alleged to be entitled to it;

(b) she is unable for the time being to act; and

(c) either—

(i) no receiver has been appointed by the Court of Protection with power to receive statutory maternity pay on her behalf, or

(ii) in Scotland, her estate is not being administered by any tutor, curator or other guardian acting or appointed in terms of law,

the Secretary of State may, upon written application to him by a person who, if a natural person, is over the age of 18, appoint that person to exercise, on behalf of the woman any right to which she may be entitled under Part V of the 1986 Act and to deal on her behalf with any sums payable to her.

(2) Where the Secretary of State has made an appointment under paragraph (1)—

(a) he may at any time in his absolute discretion revoke it;

(b) the person appointed may resign his office after having given one month's notice in writing to the Secretary of State of his intention to do so; and

(c) the appointment shall terminate when the Secretary of State is notified that a receiver or other person to whom paragraph (1)(c) applies has been appointed.

(3) Anything required by Part V of the 1986 Act to be done by or to any woman who is unable to act may be done by or to the person appointed under this regulation to act on her behalf, and the receipt of the person so appointed shall be a good discharge to the woman's employer or former employer for any sum paid. **[1323]**

PART VII

OFFENCES

32 Penalties

Any person who without reasonable excuse contravenes, or fails to comply with any provision of regulations [25] [25A], 26 or 29, shall be guilty of an offence under the 1986 Act and shall be liable on summary conviction to a penalty not exceeding—

(a) for any one offence, level 3 on the standard scale, or

(b) except in relation to regulation 29, for an offence of continuing any such contravention or failure after conviction, £40 for each day on which it is continued. **[1324]**

NOTE
 Figure in first pair of square brackets inserted by the Social Security (Miscellaneous Provisions) Amendment Regulations 1992, SI 1992/247, reg 8; figure in second pair of square brackets substituted by the Social Security (Miscellaneous Provisions) Amendment Regulations 1991, SI 1991/2284, reg 25.

WAGES COUNCILS (PRESERVATION OF ACCRUED RIGHTS UNDER WAGES ORDERS) ORDER 1986

(SI 1986/2282)

NOTES
 Made: 18 December 1986.
 Authority: Wages Act 1986, Sch 6, para 6.
 The enabling provision of the Wages Act 1986 is repealed (without any transitional or saving provisions) as from 30 August 1993 by the Trade Union Reform and Employment Rights Act 1993, but as at 1 September 1993 this Order had not been revoked.

1 Citation and commencement

This Order may be cited as the Wages Councils (Preservation of Accrued Rights under Wages Orders) Order 1986 and shall come into operation on 28th January 1987.

[1325]

2 Preservation of accrued rights

Where a worker has accrued any right to annual holidays or to any annual holiday remuneration under any provision of an order under section 14 of the Wages Councils Act 1979 ("the 1979 Act") before that order ceases to have effect in relation to him under section 24(2) or (3) of the 1986 Act, that provision shall, notwithstanding that cessation in the effect of the order, continue in force in relation to that worker for the purpose of preserving the effect of any such right. **[1326]**

3 Transitional provisions

Notwithstanding the repeal of the 1979 Act by the 1986 Act, the 1979 Act, and anything having effect under that Act in relation to a provision continued in force in accordance with paragraph 2 of this Order, shall continue to have effect in relation to that provision as so continued in force as if that repeal had not come into force.

[1327]

4 Where the 1979 Act continues to have effect in relation to a provision of an order made under that Act in accordance with paragraph 3 of this Order, it shall have effect as if references to an officer acting for the purposes of Parts III and IV of that Act were references to an officer acting for the purposes of Part II of the 1986 Act.

[1328]

5 Retrospective effect

Paragraphs 2, 3 and 4 of this Order shall apply whether an order under section 14 of the 1979 Act ceases to have effect in relation to a worker before, on or after the date on which this Order comes into operation. **[1329]**

STATUTORY MATERNITY PAY (COMPENSATION OF EMPLOYERS) REGULATIONS 1987

(SI 1987/91)

NOTES

Made: 27 January 1987.

Authority: Social Security Act 1986, ss 49(1), 84(1), Sch 4, paras 1, 5 (see now Social Security Contributions and Benefits Act 1992, Pt XII).

ARRANGEMENT OF REGULATIONS

1 Citation, commencement and interpretation

(1) These regulations may be cited as the Statutory Maternity Pay (Compensation of Employers) Regulations 1987 and shall come into force on 6th April 1987.

(2) In these regulations—

"contributions payments" means any payments which an employer is required, by or under any enactment, to make in discharge of any liability in respect of primary or secondary Class 1 contributions;
"regulation 2", "regulation 3", "regulation 4" and "regulation 5" mean, respectively, regulations 2, 3, 4 and 5 of these regulations;

. . .

and other expressions have the same meaning as in the Social Security Act 1986.

(3) For the purposes of regulations 4 and 5 "the Secretary of State" shall include a reference to the Commissioners of Inland Revenue acting on his behalf. **[1330]**

NOTE

Para (2): definition "statutory sick pay" revoked by the Statutory Maternity Pay (Compensation of Employers) Amendment Regulations 1991, SI 1991/641, reg 2(a).

2 Right of employers to prescribed amount

An employer who has made a payment of statutory maternity pay shall be entitled to an amount, determined in accordance with the provisions of regulation 3, which he shall be entitled to deduct or, as the case may be, receive in accordance with the provisions of regulation 4 or 5. **[1331]**

3 Determination of the amount an employer shall be entitled to under regulation 2

In respect of a payment of statutory maternity pay made in the tax year commencing [6th April 1991], [or in any subsequent tax year,] an employer shall be entitled under regulation 2 to an amount equal to [4.5 per cent] of the payment, that percentage being the total amount of secondary Class 1 contributions estimated by the Secretary of State as to be paid in respect of statutory maternity pay . . . by all employers in that year, expressed as a percentage of the total amount of statutory maternity pay . . . estimated by him to be paid by all employers in that year.   **[1332]**

4 Deductions from contributions payments

An employer who has made a payment of statutory maternity pay may recover—

    (i)   the amount so paid, and
    (ii) the amount determined in accordance with regulation 3,

by making one or more deductions from his contributions payments except where and insofar as—

    (a) the contributions payments relate to earnings paid before the beginning of the income tax month in which the payment of statutory maternity pay was made;

    (b) the contributions payments are made by him later than 6 years after the end of the tax year in which the payment of statutory maternity pay was made;

    (c) the amount of the payment of statutory maternity pay or the amount determined in accordance with regulation 3 have been paid to him under regulation 5 by the Secretary of State; or

    (d) the employer has made a request in writing under regulation 5 that the amount of the payment of statutory maternity pay or the amount determined in accordance with regulation 3 be paid to him and he has not received notification by the Secretary of State that the request is refused.

[1333]

5 Payments to employers by the Secretary of State

(1)   If the total amount which an employer is or would otherwise be entitled to deduct under regulation 4 exceeds the total amount which the employer is liable to pay by way of primary and secondary Class 1 contributions in respect of the earnings paid in an income tax month, and the Secretary of State is satisfied that that is so, then provided that the employer has in writing requested him to do so, the Secretary of State shall pay the employer such amount as the employer was unable to deduct.

(2) If an employer is not liable to pay any primary or secondary Class 1 contributions but would otherwise be entitled to deduct any amount under regulation 4, and the Secretary of State is satisfied that that is so, then provided the employer has in writing requested him to so do, the Secretary of State shall pay the employer that amount.   **[1334]**

6 Date when certain contributions are to be treated as paid

Where an employer has made a deduction from a contributions payment under regulation 4, the date on which it is to be treated as having been paid for the purposes of paragraph 5 of Schedule 4 to the Social Security Act 1986 (amount deducted to be treated as paid and received towards discharging liability in respect of Class 1 contributions) is—

(a) in a case where the deduction did not extinguish the contributions payment, the date on which the remainder of the contributions payment or, as the case may be, the first date on which any part of the remainder of the contributions payment, was paid; and

(b) in a case where the deduction extinguished the contributions payment, the fourteenth day after the end of the income tax month during which there were paid the earnings in respect of which the contributions payment was payable.   **[1335]**

NOTE

"Para 5 of Sch 4 to the Social Security Act 1986": see now the Social Security and Contributions and Benefits Act 1992, s 167(4).

STATUTORY MATERNITY PAY (MEDICAL EVIDENCE) REGULATIONS 1987

(SI 1987/235)

NOTES

Made: 19 February 1987.

Authority: Social Security Act 1986, ss 49, 84(1), Sch 4, para 6 (see now the Social Security Contributions and Benefits Act 1992).

1 Citation, commencement and interpretation

(1) These regulations may be cited as the Statutory Maternity Pay (Medical Evidence) Regulations 1987 and shall come into force on 15th March 1987.

(2) In these regulations, unless the context otherwise requires—

"the Act" means the Social Security Act 1986;

"registered midwife" means a midwife who is registered as a midwife with the United Kingdom Central Council for Nursing, Midwifery and Health Visiting under the Nurses, Midwives and Health Visitors' Act 1979;

"doctor" means a registered medical practitioner;

"signature" means, in relation to any statement or certificate given in accordance with these regulations, the name by which the person giving that statement or certificate, as the case may be, is usually known (any name other than the surname being either in full or otherwise indicated) written by that person in his own handwriting; and "signed" shall be construed accordingly.   **[1336]**

2 Evidence of pregnancy and confinement

The evidence as to pregnancy and the expected date of confinement which a woman is required to provide to a person who is liable to pay her statutory maternity pay shall be furnished in the form of a maternity certificate given by a doctor or by a registered midwife, not earlier than the beginning of the 14th week before the expected week of confinement, in accordance with the rules set out in Part I of the Schedule to these regulations—

(a) in the appropriate form as set out in Part II of that Schedule, or

(b) in a form substantially to the like effect with such variations as the circumstances may require.   **[1337]**

SCHEDULE

Regulation 2

PART I
RULES

1 In these rules any reference to a woman is a reference to the woman in respect of whom a maternity certificate is given in accordance with these rules.

2 A maternity certificate shall be given by a doctor or registered midwife attending the woman and shall not be given by the woman herself.

3 The maternity certificate shall be on a form provided by the Secretary of State for the purpose and the wording shall be that set out in the appropriate part of the form specified in Part II of this Schedule.

4 Every maternity certificate shall be completed in ink or other indelible substance and shall contain the following particulars—

    (a) the woman's name;
    (b) the week in which the woman is expected to be confined or, if the maternity certificate is given after confinement, the date of that confinement and the date the confinement was expected to take place . . .;
    (c) the date of the examination on which the maternity certificate is based;
    (d) the date on which the maternity certificate is signed; and
    (e) the address of the doctor or where the maternity certificate is signed by a [registered midwife the personal identification number given to her by the United Kingdom Central Council for Nursing, Midwifery and Health Visiting ("UKCC") on her registration in Part 10 of the register maintained under section 10 of the Nurses, Midwives and Health Visitors Act 1979 and the expiry date of that registration],

and shall bear opposite the word "Signature", the signature of the person giving the maternity certificate written after there has been entered on the maternity certificate the woman's name and the expected date or, as the case may be, the date of the confinement.

5 After a maternity certificate has been given, no further maternity certificate based on the same examination shall be furnished other than a maternity certificate by way of replacement of an original which has been lost or mislaid, in which case it shall be clearly marked "duplicate". **[1338]**

NOTE
    Para 4: words omitted from para (b) revoked, and words in square brackets in para (e) substituted, by the Social Security (Miscellaneous Provisions) Amendment Regulations 1991, SI 1991/2284, reg 23.

[PART II
FORM OF CERTIFICATE

MATERNITY CERTIFICATE

Please fill in this form in ink
Name of patient ....

Fill in this part if you are giving the certificate before the confinement.	*Fill in this part if you are giving the certificate after the confinement.*
Do not fill this in more than 14 weeks before the week the baby is expected.	
I certify that I examined you on the date given below. In my opinion you can expect to have your baby in the week that includes............/........../...........	I certify that I attended you in connection with the birth which took place on....../......./......when you were delivered of a child [ ] children.
Week means a period of 7 days starting on a Sunday and ending on a Saturday.	In my opinion your baby was expected in the week that includes....../........./......

Date of examination...../......./.....
Date of signing......./......./......
Signature...................

Registered midwives

Please give your UKCC Personal
Identification Number and the expiry date of
your registration with the UKCC.

Doctors
Please stamp your name and address here if
the form has not been stamped by the Family
Health Service Authority in whose medical
list you are included.]

[1339]

NOTES
Commencement: 1 November 1991.
Substituted by SI 1991/2284, reg 24.

CONTROL OF SUBSTANCES HAZARDOUS TO HEALTH REGULATIONS 1988

(SI 1988/1657)

NOTES
Made: 26 September 1988.
Authority: Health and Safety at Work etc Act 1974, ss 15(1), (2), (3)(a), (4), (5)(b), (6)(b), (9), 82(3)(a),
Sch 3, paras 1(1), (2), 2, 6(1), 8, 9, 11, 13(1), (3), 14, 15(1), 16.

ARRANGEMENT OF SECTIONS

1 Citation and commencement

These Regulations may be cited as the Control of Substances Hazardous to Health
Regulations 1988 and shall come into force on 1st October 1989. **[1340]**

NOTE
Commencement: 1 October 1989.

2 Interpretation

(1) In these Regulations, unless the context otherwise requires—

"the 1974 Act" means the Health and Safety at Work etc. Act 1974;

"approved" means approved for the time being in writing by the Health and Safety Commission or the Health and Safety Executive as the case may be;

"approved list" means the list published by the Health and Safety Commission entitled "Information Approved for the Classification, Packaging and Labelling of Dangerous Substances (2nd edition)" as revised or re-issued from time to time;

["carcinogen" means—

(a) any substance or preparation which if classified in accordance with the classification provided for by regulation 5 of the Classification, Packaging and Labelling of Dangerous Substances Regulations 1984 (SI 1984/1244, amended by SI 1986/1922, SI 1988/766, SI 1989/2208 and SI 1990/1255) would be required to be labelled with the risk phrase R45 (may cause cancer) or R49 (may cause cancer by inhalation), whether or not the substance or preparation is required to be classified in accordance with those Regulations; or

(b) any substance or preparation listed in Schedule 10 and any substance or preparation arising from a process specified in that Schedule which is a substance hazardous to health;]

"fumigation" means an operation in which a substance is released into the atmosphere so as to form a gas to control or kill pests or other undesirable organisms and "fumigate" and "fumigant" shall be construed accordingly;

"maximum exposure limit" for a substance hazardous to health means the maximum exposure limit for that substance set out in Schedule 1 in relation to the reference period specified therein when calculated by a method approved by the Health and Safety Commission;

"micro-organism" includes any microscopic biological entity which is capable of replication;

"occupational exposure standard" for a substance hazardous to health means the standard approved by the Health and Safety Commission for that substance in relation to the specified reference period when calculated by a method approved by the Health and Safety Commission;

"substance" means any natural or artificial substance whether in solid or liquid form or in the form of a gas or vapour (including micro-organisms);

"substance hazardous to health" means any substance (including any preparation) which is—

(a) a substance which is listed in Part 1A of the approved list as dangerous for supply within the meaning of the Classification, Packaging and Labelling Regulations 1984 and for which the general indication of nature of risk is specified as very toxic, toxic, harmful, corrosive or irritant;

(b) a substance for which a maximum exposure limit is specified in Schedule 1 or for which the Health and Safety Commission has approved an occupational exposure standard;

(c) a micro-organism which creates a hazard to the health of any person;

(d) dust of any kind, when present at a substantial concentration in air;

(e) a substance, not being a substance mentioned in sub-paragraphs (a) to (d) above, which creates a hazard to the health of any person which is comparable with the hazards created by substances mentioned in those sub-paragraphs.

(2) In these Regulations, any reference to an employee being exposed to a substance hazardous to health is a reference to the exposure of that employee to a substance hazardous to health arising out of or in connection with work which is under the control of his employer.

(3) In these Regulations, unless the context otherwise requires—

    (a) a reference to a numbered regulation or Schedule is a reference to the regulation or Schedule in these Regulations so numbered; and

    (b) a reference to a numbered paragraph is a reference to the paragraph so numbered in the regulation or Schedule in which that reference appears.

NOTES   **[1341]**

Commencement: 1 October 1989.

Para (1): definition "carcinogen" added by the Control of Substances Hazardous to Health (Amendment) Regulations 1992, SI 1992/2382, reg 2(1), Sch 1, para 1.

3 Duties under these regulations

(1) Where any duty is placed by these Regulations on an employer in respect of his employees, he shall, so far as is reasonably practicable, be under a like duty in respect of any other person, whether at work or not, who may be affected by the work carried on by the employer except that the duties of the employer—

    (a) under regulation 11 (health surveillance) shall not extend to persons who are not his employees; and

    (b) under regulations 10 and 12(1) and (2) (which relate respectively to monitoring and information, training etc.) shall not extend to persons who are not his employees, unless those persons are on the premises where the work is being carried on.

(2) These Regulations shall apply to a self-employed person as they apply to an employer and an employee and as if that self-employed person were both an employer and employee, except that regulations 10 and 11 shall not apply to a self-employed person.

(3) The duties imposed by these Regulations shall not extend to the master or crew of a sea-going ship or to the employer of such persons in relation to the normal shipboard activities of a ship's crew under the direction of the master.   **[1342]**

NOTE

Commencement: 1 October 1989.

4 Prohibitions relating to certain substances

(1) Those substances described in column 1 of Schedule 2 are prohibited to the extent set out in the corresponding entry in column 2 of that Schedule.

(2) The importation into the United Kingdom of the following substances and articles is prohibited, namely—

    (a) 2-naphthylamine, benzidine, 4-aminodiphenyl, 4-nitrodiphenyl, their salts and any substance containing any of those compounds in a total concentration [equal to or greater than 0.1 per cent. by mass];

    (b) matches made with white phosphorous,

and any contravention of this paragraph shall be punishable under the Customs and Excise Management Act 1979 and not as a contravention of a health and safety regulation.

(3) A person shall not supply during the course of or for use at work any substance or article [specified in paragraph (2)].

[(4) A person shall not supply during the course of or for use at work, benzene or any substance containing benzene unless its intended use is not prohibited by item 11 of Schedule 2.]   **[1343]**

NOTES
Commencement: 1 January 1992 (para (4)); 1 October 1989 (remainder).
By virtue of the Health and Safety (Miscellaneous Modifications) Regulations 1993, SI 1993/745, reg 3(1) (in force on 14 April 1993), para (2) ceased to have effect insofar as it relates to the importation of the substances and articles specified therein into the United Kingdom from any EC member State.
Para (2): words in square brackets substituted by SI 1992/2382, reg 2(1), Sch 1, para 2.
Para (3): words in square brackets substituted by SI 1993/745, reg 3(2).
Para (4): added by the Control of Substances Hazardous to Health (Amendment) Regulations 1991, SI 1991/2431, reg 2(1).

5 Application of regulations 6 to 12

(1) Regulations 6 to 12 shall have effect with a view to protecting persons against risks to their health, whether immediate or delayed, arising from exposure to substances hazardous to health except—

  (a) where and to the extent that the following Regulations apply, namely—

    (i) the Control of Lead at Work Regulations 1980,
    (ii) the Control of Asbestos at Work Regulations 1987;

  (b) where the substance is hazardous to health solely by virtue of its radioactive, explosive or flammable properties, or solely because it is at a high or low temperature or a high pressure;

  (c) where the risk to health is a risk to the health of a person to whom the substance is administered in the course of his medical treatment;

  (d) below ground in any mine within the meaning of section 180 of the Mines and Quarries Act 1954.

(2) In paragraph 1(c) "medical treatment" means medical or dental examination or treatment which is conducted under the direction of a registered medical or dental practitioner and includes any such examination, treatment or administration of any substance conducted for the purpose of research.

(3) Nothing in these Regulations shall prejudice any requirement imposed by or under any enactment relating to public health or the protection of the environment.
    [1344]

NOTE
Commencement: 1 October 1989.

6 Assessment of health risks created by work involving substances hazardous to health

(1) Subject to regulation 17(1) (which relates to transitional provisions), an employer shall not carry on any work which is liable to expose any employees to any substance hazardous to health unless he has made a suitable and sufficient assessment of the risks created by that work to the health of those employees and of the steps that need to be taken to meet the requirements of these Regulations.

(2) The assessment required by paragraph (1) shall be reviewed [regularly, and] forthwith if—

  (a) there is reason to suspect that the assessment is no longer valid; or

  (b) there has been a significant change in the work to which the assessment relates, and, where as a result of the review, changes in the assessment are required, those changes shall be made.

[1345]

NOTES

Commencement: 1 October 1989.

Para (2): words in square brackets added by SI 1992/2382, reg 2(1), Sch 1, para 3.

7 Prevention or control of exposure to substances hazardous to health

(1) Every employer shall ensure that the exposure of his employees to substances hazardous to health is either prevented or, where this is not reasonably practicable, adequately controlled.

(2) So far as is reasonably practicable, the prevention or adequate control of exposure of employees to a substance hazardous to health [except to a carcinogen] shall be secured by measures other than the provision of personal protective equipment.

[(2A) Without prejudice to the generality of paragraph (1), where the assessment made under regulation 6 shows that it is not reasonably practicable to prevent exposure to a carcinogen by using an alternative substance or process, adequate control of exposure to the carcinogen shall be achieved by the application of all the following measures, namely—

(a) the total enclosure of the process and handling systems unless this is not reasonably practicable;

(b) plant, processes and systems of work which minimise the generation of, or suppress and contain, spills, leaks, dust, fumes and vapours of carcinogens;

(c) limitation of the quantities of a carcinogen at the place of work;

(d) keeping the number of persons who might be exposed to a carcinogen to a minimum;

(e) prohibiting eating, drinking and smoking in areas that may be contaminated by carcinogens;

(f) the provision of hygiene measures including adequate washing facilities and regular cleaning of walls and surfaces;

(g) the designation of those areas and installations which may be contaminated by carcinogens, and the use of suitable and sufficient warning signs; and

(h) the safe storage, handling and disposal of carcinogens and use of closed and clearly labelled containers.]

(3) Where the measures taken in accordance with [paragraph (2) or (2A), as the case may be,] do not prevent, or provide adequate control of, exposure to substances hazardous to the health of employees, then, in addition to taking those measures, the employer shall provide those employees with such suitable personal protective equipment as will adequately control their exposure to substances hazardous to health.

[(3A) Any personal protective equipment provided by an employer in pursuance of this regulation shall comply with any enactment (whether in an Act or instrument) which implements in Great Britain any provision on design or manufacture with respect to health or safety in any relevant Community directive listed in Schedule 1 to the Personal Protective Equipment at Work Regulations 1992 which is applicable to that item of personal protective equipment.]

(4) Where there is exposure to a substance for which a maximum exposure limit is specified in Schedule 1, the control of exposure shall, so far as the inhalation of that substance is concerned, only be treated as being adequate if the level of exposure

is reduced so far as is reasonably practicable and in any case below the maximum exposure limit.

(5) Without prejudice to the generality of paragraph (1), where there is exposure to a substance for which an occupational exposure standard has been approved, the control of exposure shall, so far as the inhalation of that substance is concerned, be treated as being adequate if—

(a) that occupational exposure standard is not exceeded; or

(b) where that occupational exposure standard is exceeded, the employer identifies the reasons for the standard being exceeded and takes appropriate action to remedy the situation as soon as is reasonably practicable.

(6) Subject to regulation 17(2) (which relates to transitional provisions), where respiratory protective equipment is provided in pursuance of this regulation, then it shall—

(a) be suitable for the purpose; and

(b) [complies with paragraph (3A) or, where no requirement is imposed by virtue of that paragraph,] be of a type approved or shall conform to a standard approved, in either case, by the Health and Safety Executive.

[(6A) In the event of the failure of a control measure which might result in the escape of carcinogens into the workplace, the employer shall ensure that—

(a) only those persons who are responsible for the carrying out of repairs and other necessary work are permitted in the affected area and they are provided with appropriate respiratory protective equipment and protective clothing; and

(b) employees and other persons who may be affected are informed of the failure forthwith.]

(7) In this regulation, "adequate" means adequate having regard only to the nature of the substance and the nature and degree of exposure to substances hazardous to health and "adequately" shall be construed accordingly.   **[1346]**

NOTES

Commencement: 1 January 1993 (paras (2A), (3A), (6A)); 1 October 1989 (remainder).

Para (2): words in square brackets inserted by SI 1992/2382, reg 2(1), Sch 1, para 4.

Paras (2A), (6A): inserted by SI 1992/2382, reg 2(1), Sch 1, para 4.

Para (3): words in square brackets substituted by SI 1992/2382, reg 2(1), Sch 1, para 4.

Para (3A): inserted by the Personal Protective Equipment at Work Regulations 1992, SI 1992/2966, reg 14(1), Sch 2, para 19.

Para (6): words in square brackets in sub-para (b) inserted by SI 1992/2966, reg 14(1), Sch 2, para 20.

8 Use of control measures etc

(1) Every employer who provides any control measure, personal protective equipment or other thing or facility pursuant to these regulations shall take all reasonable steps to ensure that it is properly used or applied as the case may be.

(2) Every employee shall make full and proper use of any control measure, personal protective equipment or other thing or facility provided pursuant to these regulations [and shall take all reasonable steps to ensure it is returned after use to any accommodation provided for it] and, if he discovers any defect therein, he shall report it forthwith to his employer.   **[1347]**

NOTES

Commencement: 1 October 1989.

Para (2): words in square brackets inserted by SI 1992/2966, reg 14(1), Sch 2, para 21.

9 Maintenance, examination and test of control measures etc

(1) Every employer who provides any control measure to meet the requirements of regulation 7 shall ensure that it is maintained in an efficient state, in efficient working order and in good repair.

(2) Subject to regulation 17(3) (which relates to transitional provisions), where engineering controls are provided to meet the requirements of regulation 7, the employer shall ensure that thorough examinations and tests of those engineering controls are carried out—

    (a) in the case of local exhaust ventilation plant, at least once every 14 months, or for local exhaust ventilation plant used in conjunction with a process specified in column 1 of Schedule 3, at the interval specified in the corresponding entry in column 2 of that Schedule;

    (b) in any other case, at suitable intervals.

(3) Where respiratory protective equipment (other than disposable respiratory protective equipment) is provided to meet the requirements of regulation 7, the employer shall ensure that at suitable intervals thorough examinations and, where appropriate, tests of that equipment are carried out.

(4) Every employer shall keep a suitable record of the examinations and tests carried out in pursuance of paragraphs (2) and (3) and of any repairs carried out as a result of those examinations and tests, and that record or a suitable summary thereof shall be kept available for at least 5 years from the date on which it was made.

[1348]

NOTE
Commencement: 1 October 1989.

10 Monitoring exposure at the workplace

(1) In any case in which—

    (a) it is requisite for ensuring the maintenance of adequate control of the exposure of employees to substances hazardous to health; or

    (b) it is otherwise requisite for protecting the health of employees,

the employer shall ensure that the exposure of employees to substances hazardous to health is monitored in accordance with a suitable procedure.

(2) Where a substance or process is specified in column 1 of Schedule 4, monitoring shall be carried out at the frequency specified in the corresponding entry in column 2 of that Schedule.

(3) The employer shall keep a suitable record of any monitoring carried out for the purpose of this regulation and that record or a suitable summary thereof shall be kept available—

    (a) where the record is representative of the personal exposures of identifiable employees, for at least [40 years];

    (b) in any other case, for at least 5 years.

[1349]

NOTES
Commencement: 1 October 1989.
Para (3): words in square brackets substituted by SI 1992/2382, reg 2(1), Sch 1, para 5.

11 Health surveillance

(1) Where it is appropriate for the protection of the health of his employees who are, or are liable to be, exposed to a substance hazardous to health, the employer shall ensure that such employees are under suitable health surveillance.

(2) Health surveillance shall be treated as being appropriate where—

(a) the employee is exposed to one of the substances and is engaged in a process specified in Schedule 5, unless that exposure is not significant; or

(b) the exposure of the employee to a substance hazardous to health is such that an identifiable disease or adverse health effect may be related to the exposure, there is a reasonable likelihood that the disease or effect may occur under the particular conditions of his work and there are valid techniques for detecting indications of the disease or the effect.

(3) The employer shall ensure that a health record, containing particulars approved by the Health and Safety Executive, in respect of each of his employees to whom paragraph (1) relates is made and maintained and that that record or a copy thereof is kept in a suitable form for at least [40 years] from the date of the last entry made in it.

(4) Where an employer who holds records in accordance with paragraph (3) ceases to trade, he shall forthwith notify the Health and Safety Executive thereof in writing and offer those records to the Executive.

(5) Subject to regulation 17(4) (which relates to transitional provisions), if an employee is exposed to a substance specified in Schedule 5 and is engaged in a process specified therein, the health surveillance required under paragraph (1) shall include medical surveillance under the supervision of an employment medical adviser or appointed doctor at intervals of not more than 12 months or at such shorter intervals as the employment medical adviser or appointed doctor may require.

(6) Where an employee is subject to medical surveillance in accordance with paragraph (5) and an employment medical adviser or appointed doctor has certified in the health record of that employee that in his professional opinion that employee should not be engaged in work which exposes him to that substance or that he should only be so engaged under conditions specified in the record, the employer shall not permit the employee to be engaged in such work except in accordance with the conditions, if any, specified in the health record, unless that entry has been cancelled by an employment medical adviser or appointed doctor.

(7) Where an employee is subject to medical surveillance in accordance with paragraph (5) and an employment medical adviser or appointed doctor has certified by an entry in his health record that medical surveillance should be continued after his exposure to that substance has ceased, the employer shall ensure that the medical surveillance of that employee is continued in accordance with that entry while he is employed by the employer, unless that entry has been cancelled by an employment medical adviser or appointed doctor.

(8) On reasonable notice being given, the employer shall allow any of his employees access to the health record which relates to him.

(9) An employee to whom this regulation applies shall, when required by his employer and at the cost of the employer, present himself during his working hours for such health surveillance procedures as may be required for the purposes of paragraph (1) and, in the case of an employee who is subject to medical surveillance in accordance with paragraph (5), shall furnish the employment medical adviser or

appointed doctor with such information concerning his health as the employment medical adviser or appointed doctor may reasonably require.

(10) Where, for the purpose of carrying out his functions under these regulations, an employment medical adviser or appointed doctor requires to inspect any workplace or any record kept for the purposes of these Regulations, the employer shall permit him to do so.

(11) Where an employee or an employer is aggrieved by a decision recorded in the health record by an employment medical adviser or appointed doctor to suspend an employee from work which exposes him to a substance hazardous to health (or to impose conditions on such work), he may, by an application in writing to the Executive within 28 days of the date on which he was notified of the decision, apply for that decision to be reviewed in accordance with a procedure approved for the purposes of this paragraph by the Health and Safety Commission, and the result of that review shall be notified to the employee and employer and entered in the health record in accordance with the approved procedure.

(12) In this regulation—

"appointed doctor" means a fully registered medical practitioner who is appointed for the time being in writing by the Health and Safety Executive for the purposes of this regulation;
"employment medical adviser" means an employment medical adviser appointed under section 56 of the 1974 Act;
"health surveillance" includes biological monitoring.   **[1350]**

NOTES
Commencement: 1 October 1989.
Para (3): words in square brackets substituted by SI 1992/2382, reg 2(1), Sch 1, para 5.

12 Information, instruction and training for persons who may be exposed to substances hazardous to health

(1) An employer who undertakes work which may expose any of his employees to substances hazardous to health shall provide that employee with such information, instruction and training as is suitable and sufficient for him to know—

(a) the risks to health created by such exposure; and
(b) the precautions which should be taken.

(2) Without prejudice to the generality of paragraph (1), the information provided under that paragraph shall include—

(a) information on the results of any monitoring of exposure at the workplace in accordance with regulation 10 and, in particular, in the case of any substance hazardous to health specified in Schedule 1, the employee or his representatives shall be informed forthwith, if the results of such monitoring show that the maximum exposure limit has been exceeded; and
(b) information on the collective results of any health surveillance undertaken in accordance with regulation 11 in a form calculated to prevent it from being identified as relating to any particular person.

(3) Every employer shall ensure that any person (whether or not his employee) who carries out any work in connection with the employer's duties under these regulations has the necessary information, instruction and training.   **[1351]**

NOTE
Commencement: 1 October 1989.

13 Provisions relating to certain fumigations

(1) This regulation shall apply to fumigations in which the fumigant used or intended to be used is hydrogen cyanide, ethylene oxide, phosphine or methyl bromide, except that this regulation shall not apply to fumigations using the fumigant specified in column 1 of Schedule 6 when the nature of the fumigation is that specified in the corresponding entry in column 2 of that Schedule.

(2) An employer shall not undertake any fumigation to which this regulation applies unless he has—

 (a) notified the persons specified in Part I of Schedule 7 of his intention to undertake the fumigation; and

 (b) provided to those persons the information specified in Part II of that Schedule,

at least 24 hours in advance, or such shorter time in advance, as the persons required to be notified may agree.

(3) An employer who undertakes a fumigation to which this regulation applies shall ensure that, before the fumigant is released, suitable warning notices have been affixed at all points of reasonable access to the premises or to those parts of the premises in which the fumigation is to be carried out and that after the fumigation has been completed, and the premises are safe to enter, those warning notices are removed. **[1352]**

NOTE
Commencement: 1 October 1989.

14 Exemption certificates

(1) Subject to paragraph (2) and to any of the provisions imposed by the European Communities in respect of the protection of workers from the risks related to exposure to chemical, physical and biological agents at work, the Executive may, by a certificate in writing, exempt any person or class of persons or any substance or class of substances from all or any of the requirements or prohibitions imposed by these Regulations and any such exemption may be granted subject to conditions and to a limit of time and may be revoked by a certificate in writing at any time.

(2) The Executive shall not grant any such exemption unless having regard to the circumstances of the case and, in particular, to—

 (a) the conditions, if any, which it proposes to attach to the exemption; and

 (b) any other requirements imposed by or under any enactments which apply to the case,

it is satisfied that the health and safety of persons who are likely to be affected by the exemption will not be prejudiced in consequence of it. **[1353]**

NOTE
Commencement: 1 October 1989.

15 Extension outside Great Britain

These Regulations shall apply to any work outside Great Britain to which sections 1 to 59 and 80 to 82 of the 1974 Act apply by virtue of Article 7 of the Health and Safety at Work etc. Act 1974 (Application outside Great Britain) Order 1977 as they apply to work in Great Britain. **[1354]**

NOTE
Commencement: 1 October 1989.

16 Defence in proceedings for contravention of these Regulations

In any proceedings for an offence consisting of a contravention of these Regulations it shall be a defence for any person to prove that he took all reasonable precautions and exercised all due diligence to avoid the commission of that offence.   **[1355]**

NOTE
Commencement: 1 October 1989.

17 Transitional provisions

(1) Where work which is liable to expose employees to substances hazardous to health was commenced before 1st October 1989 or within 3 months after that date, it shall be a sufficient compliance with regulation 6(1) if the assessment required by that regulation is made before 1st January 1990.

(2) Until 1st January 1990, respiratory protective equipment required to be approved in accordance with regulation 7(6) need not be so approved, but until that date any such equipment which was required to be approved under any regulation revoked by these Regulations shall be approved in accordance with those Regulations or in accordance with the said regulation 7(6).

(3) Where, in respect of the engineering controls to which regulation 9(2) applies, immediately before 1st October 1989 local exhaust ventilation plant was required to be thoroughly examined and tested under any of the relevant statutory provisions then in force, the first thorough examination and test under regulation 9(2) shall not be required until the date on which it would have next been required under the former provision had that provision not been revoked.

(4) Where, in respect of an employee to whom regulation 11(1) applies, immediately before 1st October 1989 the employee was subject to health surveillance under any of the relevant statutory provisions then in force, he shall not be required to be medically examined for the first time under regulation 11(5) until the date on which he would have next been required to be so examined under the former provision had that provision not been revoked.   **[1356]**

NOTE
Commencement: 1 October 1989.

18 Modifications relating to the Ministry of Defence etc

(1) In this regulation, any reference to—

(a) "visiting forces" is a reference to visiting forces within the meaning of any provision of Part I of the Visiting Forces Act 1952; and

(b) "headquarters or organisation" is a reference to a headquarters or organisation designated for the purposes of the International Headquarters and Defence Organisations Act 1964.

(2) The Secretary of State for Defence may, in the interests of national security, by a certificate in writing exempt—

(a) Her Majesty's Forces;

(b) visiting forces;

(c) any member of a visiting force working in or attached to any headquarters or organisation; or

(d) any person engaged in work involving substances hazardous to health, if that person is under the direct supervision of a representative of the Secretary of State for Defence, from all or any of the requirements or prohibitions imposed by these regulations and any such exemption may be granted subject to conditions and to a limit of time and may be revoked at any time by a certificate in writing, except that, where any such exemption is granted, suitable arrangements shall be made for the assessment of the health risks created by the work involving substances hazardous to health and for adequately controlling the exposure to those substances of persons to whom the exemption relates.

(3) Regulation 11(11) shall not apply in relation to—

    (a) Her Majesty's Forces;

    (b) visiting forces; or

    (c) any member of a visiting force working in or attached to any headquarters or organisation.   **[1357]**

19 (*Contains repeals, revocations and savings.*)

SCHEDULES
(*Schs 1, 2 omitted.*)

SCHEDULE 3

Regulation 9(2)(a)

FREQUENCY OF THOROUGH EXAMINATION AND TEST OF LOCAL EXHAUST VENTILATION PLANT USED IN CERTAIN PROCESSES

Column 1 *Process*	Column 2 *Minimum Frequency*
Processes in which blasting is carried out in or incidental to the cleaning of metal castings, in connection with their manufacture.	Every month.
Processes, other than wet processes, in which metal articles (other than of gold, platinum or iridium) are ground, abraded or polished using mechanical powder, in any room for more than 12 hours in any week.	Every 6 months.
Processes giving off dust or fume in which non-ferrous metal castings are produced.	Every 6 months.
Jute cloth manufacture.	Every month.

[1358]

NOTE

    Commencement: 1 October 1989.

SCHEDULE 4

SPECIFIC SUBSTANCES AND PROCESSES FOR WHICH MONITORING IS REQUIRED

Regulation 10(2)

Column 1 *Substance or Process*	Column 2 *Minimum Frequency*
Vinyl chloride monomer.	Continuous or in accordance with a procedure approved by the Health and Safety Commission.

Vapour or spray given off from vessels at which an electrolytic chromium process is carried on, except trivalent chromium.	Every 14 days

[1359]

NOTE
        Commencement: 1 October 1989.

SCHEDULE 5

Regulation 11(2)(a) and (5)

MEDICAL SURVEILLANCE

Column 1 *Substances for which medical surveillance is appropriate*	Column 2 *Processes*
Vinyl chloride monomer (VCM).	In manufacture, production, reclamation, storage, discharge, transport, use or polymerisation.
Nitro or amino derivatives of phenol and of benzene or its homologues.	In the manufacture of nitro or amino derivatives of phenol and of benzene or its homologues and the making of explosives with the use of any of these substances.
Potassium or sodium chromate or dichromate.	In manufacture.
1-Naphthylamine and its salts Orthotolidine and its salts. Dianisidine and its salts.	In manufacture, formation or use of these substances.
Dichlorbenzidine and its salts.	In manufacture.
Auramine, Magenta.	
Carbon disulphide. Disulphur dichloride. Benzene, including benzol. Carbon tetrachloride. Trichlorethylene.	Processes in which these substances are used, or given off as vapour, in the manufacture of indiarubber or of articles or goods made wholly or partially of indiarubber.
Pitch.	In manufacture of blocks of fuel consisting of coal, coal dust, coke or slurry with pitch as a binding substance.

[1360]

NOTE
        Commencement: 1 October 1989.

(Schs 6, 7 (Fumigations excepted from reg 13 and Notification requirements for fumigations) Schs 8, 9 (Repeals and revocations) omitted)).

[SCHEDULE 10

OTHER SUBSTANCES AND PROCESSES TO WHICH THE DEFINITION OF "CARCINOGEN" RELATES

Regulation 2(1)

Aflatoxins
Arsenic and inorganic arsenic compounds
Beryllium and beryllium compounds
Bichromate manufacture involving the roasting of chromite ore
Electrolytic chromium processes, excluding passivation, which involve hexavalent chromium compounds

Mustard gas (B,B'Dichlorodiethyl sulphide)
Calcining, sintering or smelting of nickel copper matte or acid leaching or electrorefining of
  roasted matte
Ortho-toluidine
Coal soots, coal tar, pitch and coal tar fumes
The following mineral oils—

(i) unrefined and mildly refined vacuum distillates;
(ii) catalytically cracked petroleum oils with final boiling points above 320°C;
(iii) used engine oils;

Auramine manufacture
Leather dust in boot and shoe manufacture, arising during preparation and finishing
Hard wood dusts
Isopropyl alcohol manufacture (strong acid process)
Rubber manufacturing and processing giving rise to rubber process dust and rubber
  fume
Magenta manufacture
4–Nitrobiphenyl]   **[1361]**

NOTES
Commencement: 1 January 1993.
This Schedule was added by SI 1992/2382, reg 2(3), Sch 3.

HEALTH AND SAFETY INFORMATION FOR EMPLOYEES REGULATIONS 1989

(SI 1989/682)

Made: 18 April 1989.
Authority: Health and Safety at Work etc Act 1974, s 15(1), (2), (3)(a), (4)(a), (5)(b), (6)(b), Sch 3,
para 15(1).

ARRANGEMENT OF SECTIONS

1 Citation and commencement

These Regulations may be cited as the Health and Safety Information for Employees
Regulations 1989 and shall come into force on 18th October 1989.   **[1362]**

NOTE
Commencement: 18 October 1989.

2 Interpretation and application

(1) In these Regulations, unless the context otherwise requires—

"the 1974" Act means the Health and Safety at Work etc Act 1974;
"the approved poster" and "the approved leaflet" have the meanings assigned
  by regulation 3;
"employment medical advisory service" means the employment medical
  advisory service referred to in section 55 of the 1974 Act;
"ship" has the meaning assigned to it by section 742 of the Merchant Shipping
  Act 1894.

(2) Any reference in these Regulations to the enforcing authority for premises is a reference to the enforcing authority which has responsibility for the enforcement of section 2 of the 1974 Act in relation to the main activity carried on in those premises.

(3) Any reference in these Regulations to—

(a) a numbered regulation is a reference to the regulation so numbered in these Regulations;

(b) a numbered paragraph is a reference to the paragraph so numbered in the regulation in which the reference appears.

(4) These Regulations shall have effect for the purpose of providing information to employees relating to health, safety and welfare but they shall not apply in relation to the master and crew of a sea going ship.   **[1363]**

NOTE
Commencement: 18 October 1989.

3 Meaning of and revisions to the approved poster and leaflet

(1) In these Regulations "the approved poster" or "the approved leaflet" means, respectively, a poster or leaflet in the form approved and published for the purposes of these Regulations by the Health and Safety Executive, as revised from time to time in accordance with paragraph (2).

(2) The Health and Safety Executive may approve a revision (in whole or in part) to the form of poster or leaflet; and where it does so it shall publish the revised form of poster or leaflet and issue a notice in writing specifying the date the revision was approved.

(3) Such a revision shall not take effect until nine months after the date of its approval, but during that time the employer may use the approved poster or the approved leaflet incorporating that revision for the purposes of regulation 4(1).

                                                                              [1364]

NOTE
Commencement: 18 October 1989.

4 Provision of poster or leaflet

(1) An employer shall, in relation to each of his employees—

(a) ensure that the approved poster is kept displayed in a readable condition—

(i) at a place which is reasonably accessible to the employee while he is at work, and

(ii) in such a position in that place as to be easily seen and read by that employee; or

(b) give to the employee the approved leaflet.

(2) An employer shall be treated as having complied with paragraph (1)(b) from the date these Regulations come into force or the date the employee commences employment with him (if later) if he gives to the employee the approved leaflet as soon as is reasonably practicable after that date.

(3) Where the form of poster or leaflet is revised pursuant to regulation 3(2), then on or before the date the revision takes effect—

(a) an employer relying on compliance with paragraph (1)(a) shall ensure that the approved poster displayed is the one as revised;

(b) an employer relying on compliance with paragraph (1)(b) shall either give to the employees concerned fresh approved leaflets (as so revised) or bring the revision to their notice in writing.   **[1365]**

NOTE
Commencement: 18 October 1989.

5 Provision of further information

(1) An employer relying on compliance with regulation 4(1)(a) shall, subject to paragraph (2), ensure that the following information is clearly and indelibly written on the poster in the appropriate space—

(a) the name of the enforcing authority for the premises where the poster is displayed and the address of the office of that authority for the area in which those premises are situated; and

(b) the address of the office of the employment medical advisory service for the area in which those premises are situated.

(2) Where there is a change in any of the matters referred to in paragraph (1) it shall be sufficient compliance with that paragraph for the corresponding amendment to the poster to be made within six months from the date thereof.

(3) An employer who gives to his employee a leaflet pursuant to regulation 4(1)(b) shall give with the leaflet a written notice containing—

(a) the name of the enforcing authority for the premises where the employee works, and the address of the office of that authority for the area in which those premises are situated; and

(b) the address of the office of the employment medical advisory service for the area in which those premises are situated.

(4) Where the employee works in more than one location he shall, for the purposes of paragraph (3), be treated as working at the premises from which his work is administered, and if his work is administered from two or more premises, the employer may choose any one of them for the purpose of complying with that paragraph.

(5) Where an employer relies on compliance with regulation 4(1)(b) and there is a change in any of the matters referred to in paragraph (3) the employer shall within six months of the date thereof give to the employee a written notice specifying the change.   **[1366]**

NOTE
Commencement: 18 October 1989.

6 Exemption certificates

(1) Subject to paragraph (2) the Health and Safety Executive may, by a certificate in writing, exempt any person or class of persons from all or any of the requirements imposed by these Regulations and any such exemption may be granted subject to conditions and to a limit of time and may be revoked in writing at any time.

(2) The Executive shall not grant any such exemption unless, having regard to the circumstances of the case, and in particular to—

(a) the conditions if any, which it proposes to attach to the exemption; and

(b) any other requirements imposed by or under any enactment which apply to the case;

it is satisfied that the health, safety and welfare of persons who are likely to be affected by the exemption will not be prejudiced in consequence of it.   **[1367]**

NOTE
Commencement: 18 October 1989.

7 Defence

In any proceedings for an offence for a contravention of these Regulations it shall be a defence for the accused to prove that he took all reasonable precautions and exercised all due diligence to avoid the commission of that offence.   **[1368]**

NOTE
Commencement: 18 October 1989.

8 (*Contains repeals, revocations and modifications.*)
(*Schedule omitted.*)

SEX DISCRIMINATION ACT 1975 (EXEMPTION OF SPECIAL TREATMENT FOR LONE PARENTS) ORDER 1989

(SI 1989/2140)

NOTES
Made: 17 November 1989.
Authority: Employment Act 1989, ss 8, 28.

1 Citation and commencement

This Order may be cited as The Sex Discrimination Act 1975 (Exemption of Special Treatment for Lone Parents) Order 1989 and shall come into force on 19th December 1989.   **[1369]**

NOTE
Commencement: 19 December 1989.

2 Interpretation

In this Order—

> "child of that lone parent" means a person who for the purposes of any regulations made in pursuance of section 20(1)(a) of the Social Security Act 1986 is—
> (a) a child or young person for whom that lone parent is responsible, and
> (b) a member of the same household as that lone parent; and
> "Employment Training" means the arrangements known by that name made under section 2 of the Employment and Training Act 1973.   **[1370]**

NOTES
Commencement: 19 December 1989.
"Section 20(1)(a) of the Social Security Act 1986": see now the Social Security Contributions and Benefits Act 1992, s 123(1).

3 Exemption of Special Treatment

With respect to Employment Training, section 8 of the Employment Act 1989 shall apply to any special treatment afforded—

> (a) by the making of any payment, in connection with the participation of a lone parent in Employment Training, to a person having the care of a child of that lone parent, or

(b)   by the fixing of any special condition for the participation of lone parents
in Employment Training.   **[1371]**

NOTE
Commencement: 19 December 1989.

INDUSTRIAL TRIBUNALS (INTEREST) ORDER 1990
(SI 1990/479)

NOTES
Made: 6 March 1990.
Authority: Employment Protection (Consolidation) Act 1978, Sch 9, paras 1, 6A.

ARRANGEMENT OF ARTICLES

1   Citation, commencement and transitional provisions

(1) This Order may be cited as the Industrial Tribunals (Interest) Order 1990 and
shall come into force on 1st April 1990.

(2) Where a relevant decision day or a day to be treated as if it were a relevant
decision day would, but for this paragraph of this Article, fall on a day before 1st
April 1990, the relevant decision day or day to be treated as if it were that day shall
be 1st April 1990.   **[1372]**

NOTE
Commencement: 1 April 1990.

2   Interpretation

(1) In this Order, except in so far as the context otherwise requires—

"appellate court" means the Employment Appeal Tribunal, the High Court, the
Court of Appeal, the Court of Session or the House of Lords as the case
may be;

"the calculation day" in relation to a relevant decision means the day
immediately following the expiry of the period of 42 days beginning with
the relevant decision day;

"interest" means simple interest which accrues from day to day;

"relevant decision" in relation to a tribunal means any award or other
determination of the tribunal by virtue of which one party to proceedings
before the tribunal is required to pay a sum of money, excluding a sum
representing costs or expenses, to another party to those proceedings;

"Rules of Procedure" means rules having effect in relation to proceedings before a tribunal by virtue of any regulations or order made pursuant to an enactment;

"the stipulated rate of interest" has the meaning assigned to it in Article 4 below;

"tribunal" means in England and Wales an industrial tribunal (England and Wales) established in pursuance of the Industrial Tribunals (England and Wales) Regulations 1965 and in Scotland an industrial tribunal (Scotland) established in pursuance of the Industrial Tribunals (Scotland) Regulations 1965.

(2) For the purposes of this Order a sum of money is required to be paid by one party to proceedings to another such party if, and only if, an amount of money required to be so paid is:—

(a) specified in an award or other determination of a tribunal or, as the case may be, in an order or decision of an appellate court; or

(b) otherwise ascertainable solely by reference to the terms of such an award or determination or, as the case may be, solely by reference to the terms of such an order or decision,

but where a tribunal or, as the case may be, appellate court has made a declaration as to entitlement under a contract nothing in this Order shall be taken to provide for interest to be payable on any payment under that contract in respect of which no obligation to make the payment has arisen under that contract before the declaration was made.

(3) In this Order, except in so far as the context otherwise requires, "decision day" means the day signified by the date recording the sending of the document which is sent to the parties recording an award or other determination of a tribunal and "relevant decision day", subject to Article 5, 6 and 7 below, means the day so signified in relation to a relevant decision.

(4) In this Order "party" includes the Secretary of State where he has elected to appear as if he were a party in accordance with a Rule of Procedure entitling him so to elect.   **[1373]**

NOTE
Commencement: 1 April 1990.

3 Computation of interest

(1) Subject to paragraphs (2) and (3) of this Article and to Article 11 below, where the whole or any part of a sum of money payable by virtue of a relevant decision of a tribunal remains unpaid on the calculation day the sum of money remaining unpaid on the calculation day shall carry interest at the stipulated rate of interest from the calculation day (including that day).

(2) Where, after the calculation day, a party pays to another party some but not all of such a sum of money remaining unpaid on the calculation day, then beginning with the day on which the payment is made interest shall continue to accrue only on that part of the sum of money which then remains unpaid.

(3) For the purposes of the computation of interest under this Order, there shall be disregarded—

(a) any part of a sum of money which pursuant to the Employment Protection (Recoupment of Unemployment Benefit and Supplementary Benefit) Regulations 1977 has been claimed by the Secretary of State in a recoupment notice; and

(b) any part of a sum of money which the party required to pay the sum of money is required, by virtue of any provision contained in or having effect under any enactment, to deduct and pay over to a public authority in respect of income tax or contributions under Part I of the Social Security Act 1975.

[1374]

NOTE
Commencement: 1 April 1990.

4 Rate of interest

The stipulated rate of interest shall be the rate of interest specified in section 17 of the Judgments Act 1838 on the relevant decision day. **[1375]**

NOTES
Commencement: 1 April 1990.
The specified rate was 15% until 31 March 1993. As from 1 April 1993, the rate is 8%.

5 Reviews

Where a tribunal reviews its decision pursuant to the Rules of Procedure and the effect of the review, or of any re-hearing which takes place as a result of the review, is that a sum of money payable by one party to another party is confirmed or varied the relevant decision day shall be the decision day of the decision which is the subject of the review. **[1376]**

NOTE
Commencement: 1 April 1990.

6 Decisions on remission to a tribunal

Where an appellate court remits a matter to a tribunal for re-assessment of the sum of money which would have been payable by virtue of a previous relevant decision or by virtue of an order of another appellate court, the relevant decision day shall be the decision day of that previous relevant decision or the day on which the other appellate court promulgated its order, as the case may be. **[1377]**

NOTE
Commencement: 1 April 1990.

7 Appeals from relevant decisions

Where, on an appeal from a relevant decision, or on a further appeal arising from a relevant decision an appellate court makes an order which confirms or varies the sum of money which would have been payable by virtue of that relevant decision if there had been no appeal, the relevant decision day shall be the decision day of that relevant decision. **[1378]**

NOTE
Commencement: 1 April 1990.

8 Other appeals

(1) This Article applies in relation to any order made by an appellate court on an appeal from a determination of any issue by a tribunal which is not a relevant decision, or on any further appeal arising from such a determination, where the effect of the order is that for the first time in relation to that issue one party to the proceedings is

required to pay a sum of money, other than a sum representing costs or expenses, to another party to the proceedings.

(2) Where this Article applies in relation to an order, Articles 3 and 4 above shall apply to the sum of money payable by virtue of the order as if it was a sum of money payable by virtue of a relevant decision and as if the day on which the appellate court promulgated the order was the relevant decision day. **[1379]**

NOTE
Commencement: 1 April 1990.

9 Where, on an appeal from an order in relation to which Article 8 applies or on a further appeal arising from such an order, an appellate court makes an order which confirms or varies the sum of money which would have been payable by virtue of the order in relation to which Article 8 applies if there had been no appeal, the day to be treated as the relevant decision day shall be the day on which the order in relation to which Article 8 applies was promulgated. **[1380]**

NOTE
Commencement: 1 April 1990.

10 Reviews by the Employment Appeal Tribunal

Where the Employment Appeal Tribunal reviews an order to which Article 8 above applies, the day to be treated as the relevant decision day shall be the day on which the order reviewed was promulgated. **[1381]**

NOTE
Commencement: 1 April 1990.

11 Variations of the sum of money on appeal etc

Where a sum of money payable by virtue of a relevant decision is varied under one of the procedures referred to in Articles 5, 6 and 7 above, or a sum of money treated as being so payable by virtue of Article 8 above is varied under one of the procedures referred to in Articles 6, 9 and 10 above, the reference in paragraph (1) of Article 3 above, to a sum of money payable by virtue of a relevant decision shall be treated as if it were a reference to that sum as so varied. **[1382]**

NOTE
Commencement: 1 April 1990.

12 Notices

(1) Where a decision of a tribunal is a relevant decision and a copy of a document recording that decision is sent to all parties entitled to receive that decision, it shall be the duty of the Secretary of the Central Office of the Industrial Tribunals (England and Wales) or the Secretary of the Central Office of the Industrial Tribunals (Scotland), as the case may be, to cause a notice containing the matters detailed in paragraph (2) below to accompany that document.

(2) The notice referred to in paragraph (1) above shall specify the decision day, the stipulated rate of interest and the calculation day in respect of the decision concerned.

(3) The failure to discharge the duty under paragraph (1) above correctly or at all shall have no effect on the liability of one party to pay to another party any sum of money which is payable by virtue of this Order.   **[1383]**

NOTE
Commencement: 1 April 1990.

STATUTORY SICK PAY (SMALL EMPLOYERS' RELIEF) REGULATIONS 1991

(SI 1991/428)

NOTES
Made: 4 March 1991.
Authority: Social Security and Housing Benefits Act 1982, ss 9(1B), (1D), 26(1), (5), 47; Statutory Sick Pay Act 1991, s 2(4) (see now the Social Security Contributions and Benefits Act 1992, ss 158(2), (3), 163(1), (6), 175(1)).

1 Citation, commencement and interpretation

(1) These Regulations may be cited as the Statutory Sick Pay (Small Employers' Relief) Regulations 1991 and shall come into force on 6th April 1991.

(2) In these Regulations—

"the Act" means the Social Security and Housing Benefits Act 1982;
"the day in question" means a day in respect of which an employer is liable to make a payment of statutory sick pay to an employee of his;
"the qualifying tax year" means the tax year preceding the tax year in which falls the day in question;
"the specified day" means, in relation to a particular employee, the first day of incapacity for work in a period of incapacity for work on which the entitlement threshold is exceeded;
"income tax month" means the period beginning on the 6th day of any calendar month and ending on the 5th day of the following calendar month.

[1384]

NOTE
Commencement: 6 April 1991.

2 Employer's Contributions Payments

(1) Subject to the following provisions of this regulation, an employer is a small employer where the amount of his contributions payments for the qualifying tax year did not exceed [£16,000].

(2) For the purposes of this regulation, the amount of an employer's contributions payments shall be determined without regard to any deductions that may be made from them under section 9 of the Act or under any other enactment or any instrument.

(3) Where in the qualifying tax year an employer has contributions payments in one or more but less than 12 of the income tax months, the amount of his contributions payments for that tax year shall be estimated by adding together all of those payments, dividing the total amount by the number of those months in which he has those payments and multiplying the resulting figure by 12.

(4) Where in the qualifying tax year an employer has no contributions payments, but does have such payments in one or more income tax months which fall both—

(a) in the tax year in which the specified day falls, and
(b) before the specified day or, where there is more than one such day in that tax year, before the first of those days,

then the amount of his contributions payments for the qualifying tax year shall be estimated in accordance with paragraph (3) above but as if the amount of the contributions payments falling in those months had fallen instead in the corresponding tax months in the qualifying tax year.

(5) Paragraph (6) below applies where an employer has made two or more elections under regulation 2A of the Income Tax (Employments) Regulations 1973 to be treated as a different employer in respect of each of the groups of employees specified in the election.

(6) The different employers covered by each of the elections of the employer first mentioned in paragraph (5) above shall be treated for the purposes of section 9(1B) to (1E) of the Act as one employer.   **[1385]**

NOTES
Commencement: 6 April 1991.
Para (1): sum in square brackets substituted by SI 1992/797, reg 2(a).
"Sections 9(1B) to (1E) of the Act": see now the Social Security Contributions and Benefits Act 1992, ss 158(2), (3), 159.

3 Number of weeks

The prescribed number of weeks for the purposes of section 9(1B)(b) of the Act is 6.
                                                                              [1386]
NOTES
Commencement: 6 April 1991.
"Section 9(1B)(b) of the Act": see now the Social Security Contributions and Benefits Act 1992, s 158(2).

[4 Change in the appropriate rate where there are different weekly rates in the same period of incapacity for work

(1) In any case where the employee's entitlement to statutory sick pay is calculated by reference to two different weekly rates in the same period of incapacity for work, the entitlement threshold is to be calculated as set out in section 9(1B)(b) of the Act, but—

(a) as if R represents the appropriate weekly rate set out in section 7 of the Act at the time the calculation falls to be made; and
(b) from the amount which results from the calculation W x R there is deducted a sum, calculated in accordance with paragraph (2) of this regulation.

(2) The sum referred to in paragraph (1)(b) of this regulation is a sum equal to the difference between the appropriate weekly rate at the time the calculation falls to be made and the appropriate weekly rate which applied at the beginning of the period of incapacity for work multiplied by—

$$\frac{A}{Y}$$

where—

A is the number of days of incapacity for work for which the employer was liable to pay statutory sick pay at the lower of the two rates applying during the period of incapacity for work; and
Y is the number of qualifying days in the employee's week.

(3) In any case where the employee's entitlement to statutory sick pay is calculated by reference to three different weekly rates in the same period of incapacity for work, the entitlement threshold shall be calculated in accordance with paragraph (1) but as though the sum referred to in paragraph (1)(b) were the aggregate of—

   (a) a sum calculated in accordance with paragraph (2); and

   (b) a sum equal to the difference between the appropriate weekly rate at the time the calculation falls to be made and the appropriate weekly rate which applied second during the period of incapacity for work multiplied by—

$$\frac{B}{Y}$$

where—

      B is the number of days of incapacity for work for which the employer was liable to pay statutory sick pay at the second of the three rates applying during the period of incapacity for work; and

      Y is the number of qualifying days in the employee's week.

(4) In any case where the employee's entitlement to statutory sick pay is calculated by reference to four different weekly rates in the same period of incapacity for work, the entitlement threshold shall be calculated in accordance with paragraph (1) but as though the sum referred to in paragraph (1)(b) were the aggregate of—

   (a) a sum calculated in accordance with paragraph (2); and

   (b) a sum calculated in accordance with paragraph (3); and

   (c) a sum equal to the difference between the appropriate weekly rate at the time the calculation falls to be made and the appropriate weekly rate which applied third during the period of incapacity for work multiplied by—

$$\frac{C}{Y}$$

where—

      C is the number of days of incapacity for work for which the employer was liable to pay statutory sick pay at the third of the four rates applying during the period of incapacity for work; and

      Y is the number of qualifying days in the employee's week.]   **[1387]**

NOTES

Commencement: 6 April 1992.
Added by SI 1992/797, reg 2(b).
"Section 9(1B)(b) of the Act": see now the Social Security Contributions and Benefits Act 1992, s 158(2).

SEX DISCRIMINATION ACT 1975 (EXEMPTION OF SPECIAL TREATMENT FOR LONE PARENTS) ORDER 1991

(SI 1991/2813)

NOTES

Made: 12 December 1991.
Authority: Employment Act 1989, ss 8, 28.

1 Citation and commencement

This Order may be cited as the Sex Discrimination Act 1975 (Exemption of Special Treatment for Lone Parents) Order 1991 and shall come into force on 14th January 1992.   **[1388]**

NOTE

Commencement: 14 January 1992.

2 Interpretation

In this Order—

"the Council" means the National Council for One Parent Families;

"the Return to Work Programme" means arrangements known by that name made under section 2 of the Employment and Training Act 1973 for the provision by or on behalf of the Council of training and other assistance to persons wishing to obtain employment.   **[1389]**

NOTE

Commencement: 14 January 1992.

3 Exemption of special treatment

With respect to the Return to Work Programme, section 8 of the Employment Act 1989 shall apply to any special treatment afforded to or in respect of lone parents—

(a) by the fixing of any special condition for participation in the Programme, or

(b) by the making of any payment in respect of the care of a child of a lone parent while that lone parent is participating in the Programme.   **[1390]**

NOTE

Commencement: 14 January 1992.

MANAGEMENT OF HEALTH AND SAFETY AT WORK REGULATIONS 1992

(SI 1992/2051)

NOTES

Made: 26 August 1992.

Authority: Health and Safety at Work etc Act 1974, ss 15(1), (2), (5), (9), 47(2), 52(2), (3), Sch 3, paras 6(1), 7, 8(1), 14, 15(1), 16.

The Regulations implement EC Directive 89/391 (below, paras **[2185]–[2205]**). See also the Approved Code of Practice (not printed in this work) issued by the Health and Safety Commission in conjunction with these Regulations.

ARRANGEMENT OF REGULATIONS

1 Citation, commencement and interpretation

(1) These Regulations may be cited as the Management of Health and Safety at Work Regulations 1992 and shall come into force on 1st January 1993.

(2) In these Regulations—

"the assessment" means, in the case of an employer, the assessment made by him in accordance with regulation 3(1) and changed by him where necessary in accordance with regulation 3(3); and, in the case of a self-employed person, the assessment made by him in accordance with regulation 3(2) and changed by him where necessary in accordance with regulation 3(3);

"employment business" means a business (whether or not carried on with a view to profit and whether or not carried on in conjunction with any other business) which supplies persons (other than seafarers) who are employed in it to work for and under the control of other persons in any capacity;

"fixed-term contract of employment" means a contract of employment for a specific term which is fixed in advance or which can be ascertained in advance by reference to some relevant circumstance; and

"the preventive and protective measures" means the measures which have been identified by the employer or by the self-employed person in consequence of the assessment as the measures he needs to take to comply with the requirements and prohibitions imposed upon him by or under the relevant statutory provisions.

(3) Any reference in these Regulations to—

(a) a numbered regulation is a reference to the regulation in these Regulations so numbered; or

(b) a numbered paragraph is a reference to the paragraph so numbered in the regulation in which the reference appears.   **[1391]**

NOTE
Commencement: 1 January 1993.

2 Disapplication of these Regulations

These Regulations shall not apply to or in relation to the master or crew of a seagoing ship or to the employer of such persons in respect of the normal ship-board activities of a ship's crew under the direction of the master.   **[1392]**

NOTE
Commencement: 1 January 1993.

3 Risk assessment

(1) Every employer shall make a suitable and sufficient assessment of—

(a) the risks to the health and safety of his employees to which they are exposed whilst they are at work; and

(b) the risks to the health and safety of persons not in his employment arising out of or in connection with the conduct by him of his undertaking,

for the purpose of identifying the measures he needs to take to comply with the requirements and prohibitions imposed upon him by or under the relevant statutory provisions.

(2) Every self-employed person shall make a suitable and sufficient assessment of—

(a) the risks to his own health and safety to which he is exposed whilst he is at work; and

(b) the risks to the health and safety of persons not in his employment arising out of or in connection with the conduct by him of his undertaking,

for the purpose of identifying the measures he needs to take to comply with the requirements and prohibitions imposed upon him by or under the relevant statutory provisions.

(3) Any assessment such as is referred to in paragraph (1) or (2) shall be reviewed by the employer or self-employed person who made it if—

(a) there is reason to suspect that it is no longer valid; or

(b) there has been a significant change in the matters to which it relates;

and where as a result of any such review changes to an assessment are required, the employer or self-employed person concerned shall make them.

(4) Where the employer employs five or more employees, he shall record—

(a) the significant findings of the assessment; and

(b) any group of his employees identified by it as being especially at risk.

NOTE **[1393]**
Commencement: 1 January 1993.

4 Health and safety arrangements

(1) Every employer shall make and give effect to such arrangements as are appropriate, having regard to the nature of his activities and the size of his undertaking, for the effective planning, organisation, control, monitoring and review of the preventive and protective measures.

(2) Where the employer employs five or more employees, he shall record the arrangements referred to in paragraph (1). **[1394]**

NOTE
Commencement: 1 January 1993.

5 Health surveillance

Every employer shall ensure that his employees are provided with such health surveillance as is appropriate having regard to the risks to their health and safety which are identified by the assessment. **[1395]**

NOTE
Commencement: 1 January 1993.

6 Health and safety assistance

(1) Every employer shall, subject to paragraphs (6) and (7), appoint one or more competent persons to assist him in undertaking the measures he needs to take to comply with the requirements and prohibitions imposed upon him by or under the relevant statutory provisions.

(2) Where an employer appoints persons in accordance with paragraph (1), he shall make arrangements for ensuring adequate co-operation between them.

(3) The employer shall ensure that the number of persons appointed under paragraph (1), the time available for them to fulfil their functions and the means at

their disposal are adequate having regard to the size of his undertaking, the risks to which his employees are exposed and the distribution of those risks throughout the undertaking.

(4) The employer shall ensure that—

    (a) any person appointed by him in accordance with paragraph (1) who is not in his employment—

        (i) is informed of the factors known by him to affect, or suspected by him of affecting, the health and safety of any other person who may be affected by the conduct of his undertaking, and

        (ii) has access to the information referred to in regulation 8; and

    (b) any person appointed by him in accordance with paragraph (1) is given such information about any person working in his undertaking who is—

        (i) employed by him under a fixed-term contract of employment, or

        (ii) employed in an employment business,

as is necessary to enable that person properly to carry out the function specified in that paragraph.

(5) A person shall be regarded as competent for the purposes of paragraph (1) where he has sufficient training and experience or knowledge and other qualities to enable him properly to assist in undertaking the measures referred to in that paragraph.

(6) Paragraph (1) shall not apply to a self-employed employer who is not in partnership with any other person where he has sufficient training and experience or knowledge and other qualities properly to undertake the measures referred to in that paragraph himself.

(7) Paragraph (1) shall not apply to individuals who are employers and who are together carrying on business in partnership where at least one of the individuals concerned has sufficient training and experience or knowledge and other qualities—

    (a) properly to undertake the measures he needs to take to comply with the requirements and prohibitions imposed upon him by or under the relevant statutory provisions; and

    (b) properly to assist his fellow partners in undertaking the measures they need to take to comply with the requirements and prohibitions imposed upon them by or under the relevant statutory provisions.   **[1396]**

NOTE
Commencement: 1 January 1993.

7 Procedures for serious and imminent danger and for danger areas

(1) Every employer shall—

    (a) establish and where necessary give effect to appropriate procedures to be followed in the event of serious and imminent danger to persons at work in his undertaking;

    (b) nominate a sufficient number of competent persons to implement those procedures insofar as they relate to the evacuation from premises of persons at work in his undertaking; and

    (c) ensure that none of his employees has access to any area occupied by him to which it is necessary to restrict access on grounds of health and safety unless the employee concerned has received adequate health and safety instruction.

(2) Without prejudice to the generality of paragraph (1)(a), the procedures referred to in that sub-paragraph shall—

    (a)   so far as is practicable, require any persons at work who are exposed to serious and imminent danger to be informed of the nature of the hazard and of the steps taken or to be taken to protect them from it;

    (b)   enable the persons concerned (if necessary by taking appropriate steps in the absence of guidance or instruction and in the light of their knowledge and the technical means at their disposal) to stop work and immediately proceed to a place of safety in the event of their being exposed to serious, imminent and unavoidable danger; and

    (c)   save in exceptional cases for reasons duly substantiated (which cases and reasons shall be specified in those procedures), require the persons concerned to be prevented from resuming work in any situation where there is still a serious and imminent danger.

(3) A person shall be regarded as competent for the purposes of paragraph (1)(b) where he has sufficient training and experience or knowledge and other qualities to enable him properly to implement the evacuation procedures referred to in that sub-paragraph.   **[1397]**

NOTE
Commencement: 1 January 1993.

8 Information for employees

Every employer shall provide his employees with comprehensible and relevant information on—

    (a)   the risks to their health and safety identified by the assessment;

    (b)   the preventive and protective measures;

    (c)   the procedures referred to in regulation 7(1)(a);

    (d)   the identity of those persons nominated by him in accordance with regulation 7(1)(b); and

    (e)   the risks notified to him in accordance with regulation 9(1)(c).   **[1398]**

NOTE
Commencement: 1 January 1993.

9 Co-operation and co-ordination

(1) Where two or more employers share a workplace (whether on a temporary or a permanent basis) each such employer shall—

    (a)   co-operate with the other employers concerned so far as is necessary to enable them to comply with the requirements and prohibitions imposed upon them by or under the relevant statutory provisions;

    (b)   (taking into account the nature of his activities) take all reasonable steps to co-ordinate the measures he takes to comply with the requirements and prohibitions imposed upon him by or under the relevant statutory provisions with the measures the other employers concerned are taking to comply with the requirements and prohibitions imposed upon them by or under the relevant statutory provisions; and

    (c)   take all reasonable steps to inform the other employers concerned of the risks to their employees' health and safety arising out of or in connection with the conduct by him of his undertaking.

(2) Paragraph (1) shall apply to employers sharing a workplace with self-employed persons and to self-employed persons sharing a workplace with other self-

employed persons as it applies to employers sharing a workplace with other employers; and the references in that paragraph to employers and the reference in the said paragraph to their employees shall be construed accordingly.   **[1399]**

NOTE
Commencement: 1 January 1993.

10 Persons working in host employers' or self-employed persons' undertakings

(1) Every employer and every self-employed person shall ensure that the employer of any employees from an outside undertaking who are working in his undertaking is provided with comprehensible information on—

(a) the risks to those employees' health and safety arising out of or in connection with the conduct by that first-mentioned employer or by that self-employed person of his undertaking; and

(b) the measures taken by that first-mentioned employer or by that self-employed person in compliance with the requirements and prohibitions imposed upon him by or under the relevant statutory provisions insofar as the said requirements and prohibitions relate to those employees.

(2) Paragraph (1) shall apply to a self-employed person who is working in the undertaking of an employer or a self-employed person as it applies to employees from an outside undertaking who are working therein; and the reference in that paragraph to the employer of any employees from an outside undertaking who are working in the undertaking of an employer or a self-employed person and the references in the said paragraph to employees from an outside undertaking who are working in the undertaking of an employer or a self-employed person shall be construed accordingly.

(3) Every employer shall ensure that any person working in his undertaking who is not his employee and every self-employed person (not being an employer) shall ensure that any person working in his undertaking is provided with appropriate instructions and comprehensible information regarding any risks to that person's health and safety which arise out of the conduct by that employer or self-employed person of his undertaking.

(4) Every employer shall—

(a) ensure that the employer of any employees from an outside undertaking who are working in his undertaking is provided with sufficient information to enable that second-mentioned employer to identify any person nominated by that first-mentioned employer in accordance with regulation 7(1)(b) to implement evacuation procedures as far as those employees are concerned; and

(b) take all reasonable steps to ensure that any employees from an outside undertaking who are working in his undertaking receive sufficient information to enable them to identify any person nominated by him in accordance with regulation 7(1)(b) to implement evacuation procedures as far as they are concerned.

(5) Paragraph (4) shall apply to a self-employed person who is working in an employer's undertaking as it applies to employees from an outside undertaking who are working therein; and the reference in that paragraph to the employer of any employees from an outside undertaking who are working in an employer's undertaking and the references in the said paragraph to employees from an outside undertaking who are working in an employer's undertaking shall be construed accordingly.   **[1400]**

NOTE

Commencement: 1 January 1993.

11 Capabilities and training

(1) Every employer shall, in entrusting tasks to his employees, take into account their capabilities as regards health and safety.

(2) Every employer shall ensure that his employees are provided with adequate health and safety training—

    (a) on their being recruited into the employer's undertaking; and

    (b) on their being exposed to new or increased risks because of—

        (i) their being transferred or given a change of responsibilities within the employer's undertaking,

        (ii) the introduction of new work equipment into or a change respecting work equipment already in use within the employer's undertaking,

        (iii) the introduction of new technology into the employer's undertaking, or

        (iv) the introduction of a new system of work into or a change respecting a system of work already in use within the employer's undertaking.

(3) The training referred to in paragraph (2) shall—

    (a) be repeated periodically where appropriate;

    (b) be adapted to take account of any new or changed risks to the health and safety of the employees concerned; and

    (c) take place during working hours.   **[1401]**

NOTE

Commencement: 1 January 1993.

12 Employees' duties

(1) Every employee shall use any machinery, equipment, dangerous substance, transport equipment, means of production or safety device provided to him by his employer in accordance both with any training in the use of the equipment concerned which has been received by him and the instructions respecting that use which have been provided to him by the said employer in compliance with the requirements and prohibitions imposed upon that employer by or under the relevant statutory provisions.

(2) Every employee shall inform his employer or any other employee of that employer with specific responsibility for the health and safety of his fellow employees—

    (a) of any work situation which a person with the first-mentioned employee's training and instruction would reasonably consider represented a serious and immediate danger to health and safety; and

    (b) of any matter which a person with the first-mentioned employee's training and instruction would reasonably consider represented a shortcoming in the employer's protection arrangements for health and safety,

insofar as that situation or matter either affects the health and safety of that first-mentioned employee or arises out of or in connection with his own activities at work, and has not previously been reported to his employer or to any other employee of that employer in accordance with this paragraph.   **[1402]**

NOTE

Commencement: 1 January 1993.

13 Temporary workers

(1) Every employer shall provide any person whom he has employed under a fixed-term contract of employment with comprehensible information on—

    (a) any special occupational qualifications or skills required to be held by that employee if he is to carry out his work safely; and

    (b) any health surveillance required to be provided to that employee by or under any of the relevant statutory provisions,

and shall provide the said information before the employee concerned commences his duties.

(2) Every employer and every self-employed person shall provide any person employed in an employment business who is to carry out work in his undertaking with comprehensible information on—

    (a) any special occupational qualifications or skills required to be held by that employee if he is to carry out his work safely; and

    (b) any health surveillance required to be provided to that employee by or under any of the relevant statutory provisions.

(3) Every employer and every self-employed person shall ensure that every person carrying on an employment business whose employees are to carry out work in his undertaking is provided with comprehensible information on—

    (a) any special occupational qualifications or skills required to be held by those employees if they are to carry out their work safely; and

    (b) the specific features of the jobs to be filled by those employees (insofar as those features are likely to affect their health and safety);

and the person carrying on the employment business concerned shall ensure that the information so provided is given to the said employees.   **[1403]**

NOTE
Commencement: 1 January 1993.

14 Exemption certificates

(1) The Secretary of State for Defence may, in the interests of national security, by a certificate in writing exempt—

    (a) any of the home forces, any visiting force or any headquarters from those requirements of these Regulations which impose obligations on employers; or

    (b) any member of the home forces, any member of a visiting force or any member of a headquarters from the requirements imposed by regulation 12;

and any exemption such as is specified in sub-paragraph (a) or (b) of this paragraph may be granted subject to conditions and to a limit of time and may be revoked by the said Secretary of State by a further certificate in writing at any time.

(2) In this regulation—

    (a) "the home forces" has the same meaning as in section 12(1) of the Visiting Forces Act 1952;

    (b) "headquarters" has the same meaning as in article 3(2) of the Visiting Forces and international Headquarters (Application of Law) Order 1965;

(c) "member of a headquarters" has the same meaning as in paragraph 1(1) of the Schedule to the international Headquarters and Defence Organisations Act 1964; and

(d) "visiting force" has the same meaning as it does for the purposes of any provision of Part 1 of the Visiting Forces Act 1952.   **[1404]**

NOTE
Commencement: 1 January 1993.

15 Exclusion of civil liability

Breach of a duty imposed by these Regulations shall not confer a right of action in any civil proceedings.   **[1405]**

NOTE
Commencement: 1 January 1993; see reg 1(1).

16 Extension outside Great Britain

(1) These Regulations shall, subject to regulation 2, apply to and in relation to the premises and activities outside Great Britain to which sections 1 to 59 and 80 to 82 of the Health and Safety at Work etc Act 1974 apply by virtue of the Health and Safety at Work etc Act 1974 (Application Outside Great Britain) Order 1989 as they apply within Great Britain.

(2) For the purposes of Part I of the 1974 Act, the meaning of "at work" shall be extended so that an employee or a self-employed person shall be treated as being at work throughout the time that he is present at the premises to and in relation to which these Regulations apply by virtue of paragraph (1); and, in that connection, these Regulations shall have effect subject to the extension effected by this paragraph.

[1406]

NOTE
Commencement: 1 January 1993.

17 Modification of instrument

The Safety Representatives and Safety Committees Regulations 1977 shall be modified to the extent specified in the Schedule to these Regulations.   **[1407]**

NOTE
Commencement: 1 January 1993.

(*Schedule amends SI 1977/500.*)

HEALTH AND SAFETY (DISPLAY SCREEN EQUIPMENT) REGULATIONS 1992

(SI 1992/2792)

NOTES
Made: 5 November 1992.
Authority: Health and Safety at Work etc Act 1974, ss 15(1), (2), (5)(b), (9), 82(3)(a), Sch 3, paras 1(1)(a), (c), (2), 7, 8(1), 9, 14.
These Regulations implement EC Directive 90/270 (see paras **[2218]**–**[2231]** post). See also the Guidance notes on these Regulations issued by the Health and Safety Executive.

ARRANGEMENT OF REGULATIONS

1 Citation, commencement, interpretation and application

(1) These Regulations may be cited as the Health and Safety (Display Screen Equipment) Regulations 1992 and shall come into force on 1st January 1993.

(2) In these Regulations—

(a) "display screen equipment" means any alphanumeric or graphic display screen, regardless of the display process involved;

(b) "operator" means a self-employed person who habitually uses display screen equipment as a significant part of his normal work;

(c) "use" means use for or in connection with work;

(d) "user" means an employee who habitually uses display screen equipment as a significant part of his normal work; and

(e) "workstation" means an assembly comprising—

(i) display screen equipment (whether provided with software determining the interface between the equipment and its operator or user, a keyboard or any other input device),

(ii) any optional accessories to the display screen equipment,

(iii) any disk drive, telephone, modem, printer, document holder, work chair, work desk, work surface or other item peripheral to the display screen equipment, and

(iv) the immediate work environment around the display screen equipment.

(3) Any reference in these Regulations to—

(a) a numbered regulation is a reference to the regulation in these Regulations so numbered; or

(b) a numbered paragraph is a reference to the paragraph so numbered in the regulation in which the reference appears.

(4) Nothing in these Regulations shall apply to or in relation to—

(a) drivers' cabs or control cabs for vehicles or machinery;

(b) display screen equipment on board a means of transport;

(c) display screen equipment mainly intended for public operation;

(d) portable systems not in prolonged use;

(e) calculators, cash registers or any equipment having a small data or measurement display required for direct use of the equipment; or

(f) window typewriters.   **[1408]**

NOTE

Commencement: 1 January 1993.

2 Analysis of workstations

(1) Every employer shall perform a suitable and sufficient analysis of those work-stations which—

    (a) (regardless of who has provided them) are used for the purposes of his undertaking by users; or

    (b) have been provided by him and are used for the purposes of his undertaking by operators,

for the purpose of assessing the health and safety risks to which those persons are exposed in consequence of that use.

(2) Any assessment made by an employer in pursuance of paragraph (1) shall be reviewed by him if—

    (a) there is reason to suspect that it is no longer valid; or

    (b) there has been a significant change in the matters to which it relates;

and where as a result of any such review changes to an assessment are required, the employer concerned shall make them.

(3) The employer shall reduce the risks identified in consequence of an assessment to the lowest extent reasonably practicable.

(4) The reference in paragraph (3) to "an assessment" is a reference to an assessment made by the employer concerned in pursuance of paragraph (1) and changed by him where necessary in pursuance of paragraph (2).   **[1409]**

NOTE

Commencement: 1 January 1993.

3 Requirements for workstations

(1) Every employer shall ensure that any workstation first put into service on or after 1st January 1993 which—

    (a) (regardless of who has provided it) may be used for the purposes of his undertaking by users; or

    (b) has been provided by him and may be used for the purposes of his undertaking by operators,

meets the requirements laid down in the Schedule to these Regulations to the extent specified in paragraph 1 thereof.

(2) Every employer shall ensure that any workstation first put into service on or before 31st December 1992 which—

    (a) (regardless of who provided it) may be used for the purposes of his undertaking by users; or

    (b) was provided by him and may be used for the purposes of his undertaking by operators,

meets the requirements laid down in the Schedule to these Regulations to the extent specified in paragraph 1 thereof not later than 31st December 1996.   **[1410]**

NOTE

Commencement: 1 January 1993.

4 Daily work routine of users

Every employer shall so plan the activities of users at work in his undertaking that their daily work on display screen equipment is periodically interrupted by such breaks or changes of activity as reduce their workload at that equipment.   **[1411]**

NOTE
Commencement: 1 January 1993.

5 Eyes and eyesight

(1) Where a person—

- (a) is already a user on the date of coming into force of these Regulations; or
- (b) is an employee who does not habitually use display screen equipment as a significant part of his normal work but is to become a user in the undertaking in which he is already employed,

his employer shall ensure that he is provided at his request with an appropriate eye and eyesight test, any such test to be carried out by a competent person.

(2) Any eye and eyesight test provided in accordance with paragraph (1) shall—

- (a) in any case to which sub-paragraph (a) of that paragraph applies, be carried out as soon as practicable after being requested by the user concerned; and
- (b) in any case to which sub-paragraph (b) of that paragraph applies, be carried out before the employee concerned becomes a user.

(3) At regular intervals after an employee has been provided with an eye and eyesight test in accordance with paragraphs (1) and (2), his employer shall, subject to paragraph (6), ensure that he is provided with a further eye and eyesight test of an appropriate nature, any such test to be carried out by a competent person.

(4) Where a user experiences visual difficulties which may reasonably be considered to be caused by work on display screen equipment, his employer shall ensure that he is provided at his request with an appropriate eye and eyesight test, any such test to be carried out by a competent person as soon as practicable after being requested as aforesaid.

(5) Every employer shall ensure that each user employed by him is provided with special corrective appliances appropriate for the work being done by the user concerned where—

- (a) normal corrective appliances cannot be used; and
- (b) the result of any eye and eyesight test which the user has been given in accordance with this regulation shows such provision to be necessary.

(6) Nothing in paragraph (3) shall require an employer to provide any employee with an eye and eyesight test against that employee's will.   **[1412]**

NOTE
Commencement: 1 January 1993.

6 Provision of training

(1) Where a person—

- (a) is already a user on the date of coming into force of these Regulations; or
- (b) is an employee who does not habitually use display screen equipment as a significant part of his normal work but is to become a user in the undertaking in which he is already employed,

his employer shall ensure that he is provided with adequate health and safety training in the use of any workstation upon which he may be required to work.

(2) Every employer shall ensure that each user at work in his undertaking is provided with adequate health and safety training whenever the organisation of any workstation in that undertaking upon which he may be required to work is substantially modified.

[1413]

NOTE

Commencement: 1 January 1993.

7 Provision of information

(1) Every employer shall ensure that operators and users at work in his undertaking are provided with adequate information about—

    (a) all aspects of health and safety relating to their workstations; and

    (b) such measures taken by him in compliance with his duties under regulations 2 and 3 as relate to them and their work.

(2) Every employer shall ensure that users at work in his undertaking are provided with adequate information about such measures taken by him in compliance with his duties under regulations 4 and 6(2) as relate to them and their work.

(3) Every employer shall ensure that users employed by him are provided with adequate information about such measures taken by him in compliance with his duties under regulations 5 and 6(1) as relate to them and their work.

[1414]

NOTE

Commencement: 1 January 1993.

8 Exemption certificates

(1) The Secretary of State for Defence may, in the interests of national security, exempt any of the home forces, any visiting force or any headquarters from any of the requirements imposed by these Regulations.

(2) Any exemption such as is specified in paragraph (1) may be granted subject to conditions and to a limit of time and may be revoked by the Secretary of State for Defence by a further certificate in writing at any time.

(3) In this regulation—

    (a) "the home forces" has the same meaning as in section 12(1) of the Visiting Forces Act 1952;

    (b) "headquarters" has the same meaning as in article 3(2) of the Visiting Forces and International Headquarters (Application of Law) Order 1965; and

    (c) "visiting force" has the same meaning as it does for the purposes of any provision of Part I of the Visiting Forces Act 1952.

[1415]

NOTE

Commencement: 1 January 1993.

9 Extension outside Great Britain

These Regulations shall, subject to regulation 1(4), apply to and in relation to the premises and activities outside Great Britain to which sections 1 to 59 and 80 to 82 of the Health and Safety at Work etc Act 1974 apply by virtue of the Health and

Safety at Work etc Act 1974 (Application Outside Great Britain) Order 1989 as they apply within Great Britain.   **[1416]**

NOTE
Commencement: 1 January 1993.

THE SCHEDULE

Regulation 3
(WHICH SETS OUT THE MINIMUM REQUIREMENTS FOR WORKSTATIONS WHICH ARE CONTAINED IN THE ANNEX TO COUNCIL DIRECTIVE 90/270/EEC ON THE MINIMUM SAFETY AND HEALTH REQUIREMENTS FOR WORK WITH DISPLAY SCREEN EQUIPMENT)

1 Extent to which employers must ensure that workstations meet the requirements laid down in this schedules

An employer shall ensure that a workstation meets the requirements laid down in this Schedule to the extent that—

(a) those requirements relate to a component which is present in the workstation concerned;

(b) those requirements have effect with a view to securing the health, safety and welfare of persons at work; and

(c) the inherent characteristics of a given task make compliance with those requirements appropriate as respects the workstation concerned.

2 Equipment

(a) *General comment*

The use as such of the equipment must not be a source of risk for operators or users.

(b) *Display screen*

The characters on the screen shall be well-defined and clearly formed, of adequate size and with adequate spacing between the characters and lines.

The image on the screen should be stable, with no flickering or other forms of instability.

The brightness and the contrast between the characters and the background shall be easily adjustable by the operator or user, and also be easily adjustable to ambient conditions.

The screen must swivel and tilt easily and freely to suit the needs of the operator or user.

It shall be possible to use a separate base for the screen or an adjustable table.

The screen shall be free of reflective glare and reflections liable to cause discomfort to the operator or user.

(c) *Keyboard*

The keyboard shall be tiltable and separate from the screen so as to allow the operator or user to find a comfortable working position avoiding fatigue in the arms or hands.

The space in front of the keyboard shall be sufficient to provide support for the hands and arms of the operator or user.

The keyboard shall have a matt surface to avoid reflective glare.

The arrangement of the keyboard and the characteristics of the keys shall be such as to facilitate the use of the keyboard.

The symbols on the keys shall be adequately contrasted and legible from the design working position.

(d) *Work desk or work surface*

The work desk or work surface shall have a sufficiently large, low-reflectance surface and allow a flexible arrangement of the screen, keyboard, documents and related equipment.

The document holder shall be stable and adjustable and shall be positioned so as to minimise the need for uncomfortable head and eye movements.

There shall be adequate space for operators or users to find a comfortable position.

(e) *Work chair*

The work chair shall be stable and allow the operator or user easy freedom of movement and a comfortable position.

The seat shall be adjustable in height.

The seat back shall be adjustable in both height and tilt.

A footrest shall be made available to any operator or user who wishes one.

3 Environment

(a) *Space requirements*

The workstation shall be dimensioned and designed so as to provide sufficient space for the operator or user to change position and vary movements.

(b) *Lighting*

Any room lighting or task lighting provided shall ensure satisfactory lighting conditions and an appropriate contrast between the screen and the background environment, taking into account the type of work and the vision requirements of the operator or user.

Possible disturbing glare and reflections on the screen or other equipment shall be prevented by co-ordinating workplace and workstation layout with the positioning and technical characteristics of the artificial light sources.

(c) *Reflections and glare*

Workstations shall be so designed that sources of light, such as windows and other openings, transparent or translucid walls, and brightly coloured fixtures or walls cause no direct glare and no distracting reflections on the screen.

Windows shall be fitted with a suitable system of adjustable covering to attenuate the daylight that falls on the workstation.

(d) *Noise*

Noise emitted by equipment belonging to any workstation shall be taken into account when a workstation is being equipped, with a view in particular to ensuring that attention is not distracted and speech is not disturbed.

(e) *Heat*

Equipment belonging to any workstation shall not produce excess heat which could cause discomfort to operators or users.

(f) *Radiation*

All radiation with the exception of the visible part of the electromagnetic spectrum shall be reduced to negligible levels from the point of view of the protection of operators' or users' health and safety.

(g) *Humidity*

An adequate level of humidity shall be established and maintained.

4 Interface between computer and operator/user

In designing, selecting, commissioning and modifying software, and in designing tasks using display screen equipment, the employer shall take into account the following principles:

(a) software must be suitable for the task;

(b) software must be easy to use and, where appropriate, adaptable to the level of knowledge or experience of the operator or user; no quantitative or qualitative checking facility may be used without the knowledge of the operators or users;

(c) systems must provide feedback to operators or users on the performance of those systems;

(d) systems must display information in a format and at a pace which are adapted to operators or users;

(e) the principles of software ergonomics must be applied, in particular to human data processing.   **[1417]**

NOTE
Commencement: 1 January 1993.
Council Directive 90/270/EEC: OJ No L156, 21.6.90, p 14.

MANUAL HANDLING OPERATIONS REGULATIONS 1992
(SI 1992/2793)

NOTES
Made: 5 November 1992.
Authority: Health and Safety at Work etc Act 1974 (referred to in these Regulations as "the 1974 Act"), ss 15(1), (2), (3)(a), (5)(a), (9), 80(1), (2)(a), (4), Sch 3, paras 1(1)(a), (c), 8.
These Regulations implement EC Directive 90/269 (see paras **[2206]**–**[2217]** post). See also Guidance notes on these Regulations issued by the Health and Safety Executive.

ARRANGEMENT OF REGULATIONS

1 Citation and commencement

These Regulations may be cited as the Manual Handling Operations Regulations 1992 and shall come into force on 1st January 1993.   **[1418]**

NOTE
Commencement: 1 January 1993.

2 Interpretation

(1) In these Regulations, unless the context otherwise requires—

"injury" does not include injury caused by any toxic or corrosive substance which—

(a) has leaked or spilled from a load;
(b) is present on the surface of a load but has not leaked or spilled from it; or
(c) is a constituent part of a load;

and "injured" shall be construed accordingly;

"load" includes any person and any animal;

"manual handling operations" means any transporting or supporting of a load (including the lifting, putting down, pushing, pulling, carrying or moving thereof) by hand or by bodily force.

(2) Any duty imposed by these Regulations on an employer in respect of his employees shall also be imposed on a self-employed person in respect of himself.
[1419]

NOTE
Commencement: 1 January 1993.

3 Disapplication of Regulations

These Regulations shall not apply to or in relation to the master or crew of a sea-going ship or to the employer of such persons in respect of the normal ship-board activities of a ship's crew under the direction of the master.   **[1420]**

NOTE
Commencement: 1 January 1993.

4 Duties of employers

(1) Each employer shall—

    (a) so far as is reasonably practicable, avoid the need for his employees to undertake any manual handling operations at work which involve a risk of their being injured; or

    (b) where it is not reasonably practicable to avoid the need for his employees to undertake any manual handling operations at work which involve a risk of their being injured—

        (i) make a suitable and sufficient assessment of all such manual handling operations to be undertaken by them, having regard to the factors which are specified in column 1 of Schedule 1 to these Regulations and considering the questions which are specified in the corresponding entry in column 2 of that Schedule,

        (ii) take appropriate steps to reduce the risk of injury to those employees arising out of their undertaking any such manual handling operations to the lowest level reasonably practicable, and

        (iii) take appropriate steps to provide any of those employees who are undertaking any such manual handling operations with general indications and, where it is reasonably practicable to do so, precise information on—

            (aa) the weight of each load, and

            (bb) the heaviest side of any load whose centre of gravity is not positioned centrally.

(2) Any assessment such as is referred to in paragraph (1)(b)(i) of this regulation shall be reviewed by the employer who made it if—

    (a) there is reason to suspect that it is no longer valid; or

    (b) there has been a significant change in the manual handling operations to which it relates;

and where as a result of any such review changes to an assessment are required, the relevant employer shall make them. **[1421]**

NOTE
Commencement: 1 January 1993.

5 Duty of employees

Each employee while at work shall make full and proper use of any system of work provided for his use by his employer in compliance with regulation 4(1)(b)(ii) of these Regulations. **[1422]**

NOTE
Commencement: 1 January 1993.

6 Exemption certificates

(1) The Secretary of State for Defence may, in the interests of national security, by a certificate in writing exempt—

(a) any of the home forces, any visiting force or any headquarters from any requirement imposed by regulation 4 of these Regulations; or

(b) any member of the home forces, any member of a visiting force or any member of a headquarters from the requirement imposed by regulation 5 of these Regulations;

and any exemption such as is specified in sub-paragraph (a) or (b) of this paragraph may be granted subject to conditions and to a limit of time and may be revoked by the said Secretary of State by a further certificate in writing at any time.

(2) In this regulation—

(a) "the home forces" has the same meaning as in section 12(1) of the Visiting Forces Act 1952;

(b) "headquarters" has the same meaning as in article 3(2) of the Visiting Forces and International Headquarters (Application of Law) Order 1965;

(c) "member of a headquarters" has the same meaning as in paragraph 1(1) of the Schedule to the International Headquarters and Defence Organisations Act 1964; and

(d) "visiting force" has the same meaning as it does for the purposes of any provision of Part I of the Visiting Forces Act 1952. **[1423]**

NOTE
Commencement: 1 January 1993.

7 Extension outside Great Britain

These Regulations shall, subject to regulation 3 hereof, apply to and in relation to the premises and activities outside Great Britain to which sections 1 to 59 and 80 to 82 of the Health and Safety at Work etc Act 1974 apply by virtue of the Health and Safety at Work etc Act 1974 (Application Outside Great Britain) Order 1989 as they apply within Great Britain. **[1424]**

NOTE
Commencement: 1 January 1993.

8 Repeals and revocations

(1) The enactments mentioned in column 1 of Part I of Schedule 2 to these Regulations are repealed to the extent specified in the corresponding entry in column 3 of that part.

(2) The Regulations mentioned in column 1 of Part II of Schedule 2 to these Regulations are revoked to the extent specified in the corresponding entry in column 3 of that part.   **[1425]**

NOTE
  Commencement: 1 January 1993.

SCHEDULES

SCHEDULE 1

Regulation 4(1)(b)(i)

FACTORS TO WHICH THE EMPLOYER MUST HAVE REGARD AND QUESTIONS HE MUST CONSIDER WHEN MAKING AN ASSESSMENT OF MANUAL HANDLING OPERATIONS

Column 1 *Factors*	Column 2 *Questions*

1 The tasks	**Do they involve:**
	 —holding or manipulating loads at distance from trunk?
	 —unsatisfactory bodily movement or posture, especially:
	   —twisting the trunk?
	   —stooping?
	   —reaching upwards?
	 —excessive movement of loads, especially:
	   —excessive lifting or lowering distances?
	   —excessive carrying distances?
	 —excessive pushing or pulling of loads?
	 —risk of sudden movement of loads?
	 —frequent or prolonged physical effort?
	 —insufficient rest or recovery periods?
	 —a rate of work imposed by a process?

2 The loads	**Are they:** —heavy? —bulky or unwieldy? —difficult to grasp? —unstable, or with contents likely to shift? —sharp, hot or otherwise potentially damaging?
3 The working environment	**Are there:** —space constraints preventing good posture? —uneven, slippery or unstable floors? —variations in level of floors or work surfaces? —extremes of temperature or humidity? —conditions causing ventilation problems or gusts of wind? —poor lighting conditions?

Column 1 *Factors*	Column 2 *Questions*
4 Individual capability	**Does the job:** —require unusual strength, height, etc? —create a hazard to those who might reasonably be considered to be pregnant or to have a health problem? —require special information or training for its safe performance?
5 Other factors	**Is movement or posture hindered by personal protective equipment or by clothing?**

[1426]

NOTE
  Commencement: 1 January 1993.

(Sch 2 (repeals and revocations) omitted.)

FUNDS FOR TRADE UNION BALLOTS REGULATIONS (REVOCATION) REGULATIONS 1993

(SI 1993/233)

NOTES
  Made: 8 February 1993.
  Authority: Trade Union and Labour Relations (Consolidation) Act 1992, s 115.
  The Funds for Trade Union Ballots Regulations 1984, as amended, are printed at paras **[1188]–[1210]** ante.

ARRANGEMENT OF REGULATIONS

1 Citation and commencement

These Regulations may be cited as the Funds for Trade Union Ballots Regulations (Revocation) Regulations 1993 and shall come into force on 1st April 1993. **[1427]**

NOTE
  Commencement: 1 April 1993.

2 Interpretation

In these Regulations "the 1984 Regulations" means the Funds for Trade Union Ballots Regulations 1984, and expressions used in these Regulations and in the 1984 Regulations have the same meanings in these Regulations as in the 1984 Regulations. **[1428]**

NOTE
  Commencement: 1 April 1993.

3 Revocation

(1) The 1984 Regulations and the Regulations mentioned in paragraph (2) shall be revoked on 1st April 1996.

(2) Those Regulations are—

The Funds for Trade Union Ballots (Amendment) Regulations 1988
The Funds for Trade Union Ballots (Amendment No. 2) Regulations 1988
The Funds for Trade Union Ballots (Amendment) Regulations 1990. **[1429]**

NOTE
Commencement: 1 April 1996.

4 Progressive reduction in refunds payable during period before revocation

(1) The total amount of the payments made to a trade union by the Certification Officer under regulations 14 to 18 of the 1984 Regulations in respect of the expenditure incurred on a ballot shall be reduced—

   (a) by a quarter, if the date of the ballot falls after 31st March 1993 but before 1st April 1994;

   (b) by a half, if the date of the ballot falls after 31st March 1994 but before 1st April 1995; and

   (c) by three-quarters, if the date of the ballot falls after 31st March 1995.

(2) Paragraph (1) shall apply in relation to payments made in respect of arrangements to hold a ballot which is not proceeded with as if, for the words "the date of the ballot", there were substituted the words "the date which would have been the date of the ballot, had the ballot been held,". **[1430]**

NOTE
Commencement: 1 April 1993.

5 No payments if statutory requirement not satisfied

Nothing in the 1984 Regulations shall be construed as requiring or permitting the Certification Officer to make payments towards the expenditure incurred in respect of a ballot, or in respect of arrangements to hold a ballot which is not proceeded with, if the Certification Officer considers that any statutory requirement applying in relation to the conduct of the ballot has not been complied with. **[1431]**

NOTE
Commencement: 1 April 1993.

UNFAIR DISMISSAL (INCREASE OF COMPENSATION LIMIT) ORDER 1993

(SI 1993/1348)

NOTES
Made: 25 May 1993.
Authority: Employment Protection (Consolidation) Act 1978, ss 75(2), 154(3), (4).

1 Citation, commencement and revocation

(1) This Order may be cited as the Unfair Dismissal (Increase of Compensation Limit) Order 1993 and shall come into force on 1st June 1993.

(2) Subject to article 3(2), the Unfair Dismissal (Increase of Compensation Limit) Order 1991 ("the 1991 Order") is revoked.   **[1432]**

NOTE
Commencement: 1 June 1993.

2 Increase of limits

Subject to article 3, the limit of compensation specified in section 75(1) of the 1978 Act is increased to £11,000.   **[1433]**

NOTE
Commencement: 1 June 1993.

3 Transitional provisions

(1) The increase specified in article 2 shall have effect where the appropriate date falls on or after the date this Order comes into force.

(2) Notwithstanding the revocation of the 1991 Order, the limits set by or, as the case may be, preserved by articles 2 and 3 of that Order shall continue to have effect as provided by that Order where the appropriate date falls before the date this Order comes into force.

(3) In this article, "the appropriate date" means—

    (a) in the case of a complaint presented under section 67 of the 1978 Act (complaint of unfair dismissal), the effective date of termination;

    (b) in the case of a complaint presented under section 174 of the Trade Union and Labour Relations (Consolidation) Act 1992 ("the 1992 Act") (complaint of unreasonable exclusion or expulsion from a trade union), the date of the refusal of the application for, or of the expulsion from, membership, as the case may be;

    (c) in the case of a complaint presented under section 66 of the 1992 Act (complaint of unjustifiable discipline by a trade union), the date of determination which the individual claims constituted an infringement of his right;

    (d) in the case of a complaint presented under section 63 of the Sex Discrimination Act 1975 or under section 54 of the Race Relations Act 1976, the date on which the act complained of was done;

    (e) in the case of a complaint presented under section 137(2) (refusal of employment on the grounds related to union membership) or section 138(2) (refusal of service of employment agency on grounds related to union membership) of the 1992 Act, the date of the conduct, (as determined by section 139 of the 1992 Act) to which the complaint relates;

and "effective date of determination" has the same meaning as in section 55(4) of the 1978 Act except in a case in which section 55(5) or (6) of that Act would have effect so as to treat a later date as the effective date of termination, in which case that later date shall be the effective date for the purposes of this article.   **[1434]**

NOTE
Commencement: 1 June 1993.

TRADE UNION REFORM AND EMPLOYMENT RIGHTS ACT 1993 (COMMENCEMENT NO 1 AND TRANSITIONAL PROVISIONS) ORDER 1993

(SI 1993/1908)

NOTES

Made: 27 July 1993.

Authority: Trade Union Reform and Employment Rights Act 1993, s 52, Sch 9, para 1.

ARRANGEMENT OF ARTICLES

1 Citation and interpretation

(1) This Order may be cited as the Trade Union Reform and Employment Rights Act 1993 (Commencement No 1 and Transitional Provisions) Order 1993.

(2) In this Order—

(i) "the 1978 Act" means the Employment Protection (Consolidation) Act 1978;

(ii) "the 1992 Act" means the Trade Union and Labour Relations (Consolidation) Act 1992, and

(iii) "the 1993 Act" means the Trade Union Reform and Employment Rights Act 1993.   **[1435]**

2 Commencement

(1) The provisions of the 1993 Act which are specified in Schedule 1 to this Order shall come into force on 30 August 1993.

(2) The provisions of the 1993 Act which are specified in Schedule 2 to this Order shall come into force on 30 November 1993.

(3) The provisions of the 1993 Act which are specified in Schedule 3 to this Order shall come into force on 1 January 1994.

(4) The remaining provisions of Part 1 of the 1993 Act (section 7(2) and (3)) and section 51 and Schedule 10 (repeals), so far as that section and that Schedule relate to sections 115 and 116 of the 1992 Act shall come into force on 1 April 1996.

                                                                    [1436]

3 Transitional Provisions

(1) The amendments of the 1992 Act made by section 1 (election scrutineer to check register) and section 2 (counting of election votes etc by independent person) of the 1993 Act shall apply to any election ballot held on or after 30 August 1993, other than a ballot in relation to which the scrutineer begins to carry out his functions in relation to the ballot before that date.

(2) The amendments of the 1992 Act made by section 3 of and Schedule 1 to the 1993 Act (political fund ballots) shall have effect only in relation to ballots in which votes may only be cast on or after 30 August 1993 and shall not have effect in relation to a ballot in any case in which—

   (a) the approval of the Certification Officer for the union's political ballot rules was sought after 1 January 1993;

   (b) the Certification Officer approved the political ballot rules before 1 July 1993, and

   (c) the voting in the ballot is completed on or before 31 December 1993.

(3) The amendments of the 1992 Act made by sections 4 (ballots for union amalgamations and transfers of engagements) and 5 (ballots for union amalgamations and transfers of engagements: notice not to include influential material) of the 1993 Act shall have effect only in relation to ballots in which votes may only be cast on or after 30 August 1993 and shall not have effect in relation to a ballot in any case in which—

   (a) the Certification Officer approved the instrument of amalgamation or transfer of engagements before 1 July 1993, and

   (b) the voting in the ballot is completed on or before 31 December 1993.

(4) The amendments of the 1992 Act made by section 6 of the 1993 Act (confidentiality of trade unions register of members' names and addresses) shall have effect in relation to—

   (a) any Chapter IV election held on or after 30 August 1993, other than an election in relation to which the scrutineer begins to carry out his functions before that date,

   (b) any Chapter VI ballot in which votes may only be cast on or after 30 August 1993, except a ballot in any case in which—

      (i) the approval of the Certification Officer for the union's political ballot rules was sought after 1 January 1993;

      (ii) the Certification Officer approved the political ballot rules before 1 July 1993, and

      (iii) the voting in the ballot is completed on or before 31 December 1993.

   (c) any Chapter VII ballot in which votes may only be cast on or after 30 August 1993, except a ballot in any case in which—

      (i) the Certification Officer approved the instrument of amalgamation or transfer of engagements before 1 July 1993, and

      (ii) the voting in the ballot is completed on or before 31 December 1993.

(5) The amendments of the 1992 Act made by section 13 of the 1993 Act (action short of dismissal: non-infringing actions) shall have effect only in relation to action taken on or after 30 August 1993.

(6) Where a subscription deduction is treated, by virtue of paragraph 2 of Schedule 9 to the 1993 Act, as an authorised deduction for the purposes of the section substituted for section 68 of the 1992 Act by section 15 of the 1993 Act (right not to suffer deduction of unauthorised or excessive subscriptions) the amount of that deduction shall be treated, for the purposes of the substituted section, as not exceeding the permitted amount.

(7) The amendments of the 1992 Act made by section 17 of the 1993 Act (requirement of postal ballot) shall have effect only in relation to ballots in which votes may only be cast on or after 30 August 1993.

(8) The amendments of the 1992 Act made by section 18(2) of the 1993 Act (notice of ballot and sample voting papers for employers) shall have effect only in relation to ballots of which the opening day falls on or after 6 September 1993.

(9) The amendments of the 1992 Act made by sections 19 (ballot result for employers) and 20 (scrutiny of ballot) of the 1993 Act shall have effect only in relation to ballots in which votes may only be cast on or after 30 August 1993.

(10)(a) The amendments of the 1992 Act made by section 21 of the 1993 Act (notice of industrial action for employers) shall have effect in relation to an act by a trade union to induce a person to take part, or continue to take part in industrial action if (in the case of continuous action) the intended date for any of the affected employees to begin to take part in the action, or (in the case of discontinuous action) the first of the dates for any of the affected employees to take part in the action, falls after 6 September 1993.

(b) Where those amendments apply to such an act of inducement to take part, or continue to take part, in industrial action but the amendments made to the 1992 Act by section 19 of the 1993 Act (ballot result for employers) are not in force in relation to the ballot in respect of that industrial action, the appropriate period (as defined in section 234A(4) of the 1992 Act) shall be regarded as beginning—

(i) if the union satisfies the requirement of section 231 (ballot result for members) of the 1992 Act in relation to the ballot on or after 30 August 1993, with the day on which it satisfies that requirement; or

(ii) if the union satisfies that requirement before 30 August 1993, on 30 August 1993.

(11) The amendments of the 1978 Act made by sections 24(2) and (3) (to the extent that they are brought into force by this Order), 28, 29 and 30 of and paragraphs 2 to 10 of Schedule 5 to the 1993 Act shall apply to any dismissal where the effective date of termination (as defined in the 1978 Act) in relation to that dismissal falls on or after 30 August 1993. The amendments of the 1978 Act made by paragraph 1 of Schedule 5 to the 1993 Act shall apply to any detriment to which the employee was subjected on or after 30 August 1993.

(12) The amendments set out in section 34 (redundancy consultation procedures) of the 1993 Act shall not have effect in relation to any dismissal which takes effect within 90 days after section 34 comes into force. **[1437]**

SCHEDULE 1

Article 2(1)

PROVISIONS COMING INTO FORCE ON 30 AUGUST 1993

Provision	Subject Matter of Provision
Part I of the 1993 Act, except sections 7, 8, 9 and 14	Trade Unions etc
Section 24(2) and (3), except for the purpose of giving effect to section 60(a) to (f) of the 1978 Act	Dismissal rights
Section 28	Rights to claim unfair dismissal and not to suffer detriment in health and safety cases

Provision	Subject Matter of Provision
Section 29	Dismissal on ground of assertion of statutory rights
Section 30	Compensation for unfair dismissal when reinstatement or re-engagement ordered
Section 33	Amendments of transfer of undertakings regulations
Section 34	Redundancy consultation procedures
Section 35	Repeal of Part II of the Wages Act 1986
Section 36(3), for the purpose of inserting section 128(5) of the 1978 Act	Regulations to provide for industrial tribunal chairman to act alone
Section 38	Extension of power to confer on industrial tribunals jurisdiction in respect of contracts of employment etc
Section 39	Agreements not to take proceedings before industrial tribunal
Section 40	Restriction of publicity in cases involving sexual misconduct: industrial tribunals
Section 41	Restriction of publicity in cases involving sexual misconduct: Employment Appeal Tribunal
Section 43	Functions of ACAS
Section 44	Fees for exercise of functions by ACAS
Section 47	Employment and training functions of Scottish Enterprise and Highlands and Islands Enterprise
Section 48	Interpretation
Section 49(1), so far as it relates to the amendments effected by Schedule 7 specified below	Miscellaneous amendments
Section 49(2), so far as it relates to the amendments effected by Schedule 8 specified below	Consequential amendments
Section 50, so far as it relates to the transitional provisions and savings effected by Schedule 9 specified below	Transitional provisions and savings
Section 51, so far as it relates to the repeals and revocations specified in relation to Schedule 10 in the table below	Repeals and revocations
Schedule 1	Political fund ballots
Schedule 5	Employment protection in health and safety cases
Schedule 6	Compromise contracts
In Schedule 7, paragraphs 1, 2, 13, 14 to 27	Miscellaneous amendments
In Schedule 8, paragraphs 2, 6, 7, 11, 14, 20(a), 21, 24, 26(a)(i), 29, 32(b), 36 to 41, 43(b), 46, 47, 49, 52 to 61, 62(b), 63, 64(b) and (c), 65, 66(b), 67 to 75, 78 to 84 and 86 to 89. In addition paragraphs 16 (so far as it relates to section 60A(1) of the 1978 Act) and 76 and 77 (so far as they relate to section 57A of the 1978 Act).	Consequential amendments
In Schedule 9, paragraphs 1, 2, 4 and 5	Transitional provisions and savings
In Schedule 10 the repeals and revocations specified in the table below	Repeals and revocations

TABLE

Chapter or number	Short Title	Extent of Repeal or Revocation
9 & 10 Eliz 2 c.34	Factories Act 1961	Section 117(5)(b).
1965 c.19 (N.I.)	Contracts of Employment and Redundancy Payments Act (Northern Ireland) 1965	Sections 23 and 23A In section 29(1), the words "(except section 23)".
		Section 32(4).
		Section 54(2).
		In Schedule 5, paragraph 2.
1968 c.73	Transport Act 1968	Section 94(10)
1975 c.24	House of Commons Disqualification Act 1975	In Part III of Schedule 1, the first entry beginning "Member of a Wages Council".
1975 c.25	Northern Ireland Assembly Disqualification Act 1975	In Part III of Schedule 1, the first entry beginning "Member of a Wages Council".
S.I. 1976/1043 (N.I. 16).	Industrial Relations (Northern Ireland) Order 1976.	In Schedule 5, in Part II, paragraphs 19, 20 and 23(3).
1978 c.44	Employment Protection (Consolidation) Act 1978	In section 18, in subsection (1), the words "council or", subsection (2)(a), in subsection (3)(a), the words "(a) or", and in subsection (5), the words"council or".
		In section 53(4), the words "against his employer".
		In section 55(5) and (6), ", 64A".
		Section 64A.
		Section 93(4).
		Sections 94 and 95.
		In section 100(1), the words "(except section 94)".
		In section 123(4) the words ", maternity pay under Part III of this Act".
		In section 149(1)(c), "64A(1),".
		In Schedule 12, paragraph 13.
		In Schedule 13, in paragraph 11(1), ", 64A(1)"
1980 c.42	Employment Act 1980	Section 8(1). In Schedule 1, paragraphs 10, 21(a) and 32.
S.I. 1981/1794	Transfer of Undertakings (Protection of Employment) Regulations 1981	In Regulation 2(1), in the definition of "undertaking", the words from "but does not" to the end.
		Regulation 11(7).

Chapter or number	Short Title	Extent of Repeal or Revocation
1986 c.48	Wages Act 1986	Section 9(3)
		Part II.
		Section 31(a) and (b).
		In section 33, in subsection (2) the entries relating to sections 24 and 25(1) to (3), in subsection (4) the words from "Part II (excluding" to "relating to Part ll;" and in subsection (7) the words from "paragraphs 5" to "thereto,".
		Schedules 2 and 3.
		In Schedule 4, paragraphs 5 to 7.
		In Schedule 6, paragraphs 1 to 8.
1988 c.1	Income and Corporation Taxes Act 1988	In Section 175(4), the words "Part II of the Wages Act 1986,".
1990 c.35	Enterprise and New Towns (Scotland) Act 1990	In section 2(3), the word "and" at the end of paragraph (b).
1992 c.24	Offshore Safety (Protection Against Victimisation) Act 1992	The whole Act.
1992 c.52	Trade Union and Labour Relations (Consolidation) Act 1992	Section 24(4).
		In section 34(5), the second sentence.
		In section 43(1), the word "and" at the end of paragraph (b).
		In section 52(1), the word "and" at the end of paragraph (c).
		In section 65(2), the word "or" at the end of paragraph (d).
		In section 65(7), the word "and" following the definition of "contract of employment".
		In section 74(3), the word "and" at the end of the entry relating to section 77
		In section 78(1), the word "and" at the end of paragraph (c).
		In section 118(4), the word "and" at the end of paragraph (c).
		In section 135(3), the word "and" at the end of paragraph (c).
		In section 154, the words "and 64A".
		In section 188(4), the word "and" at the end of paragraph (d).

Chapter or number	Short Title	Extent of Repeal or Revocation
		Section 190(3).
		In section 209, the words from "and in particular" to the end.
		In section 246, the definition of "place of work".
		In section 249(2), the first sentence.
		Section 256(4).
		Section 273(4)(c).
		Section 283.
		In section 299, the entries relating to "the Commissioner" and "redundancy".
		In Schedule 2, paragraphs 15 and and 34(3).

[1439]

SCHEDULE 2

Article 2(2)

PROVISIONS COMING INTO FORCE ON 30 NOVEMBER 1993

Provision	Subject Matter of Provision
Section 14	Right not to be excluded from or expelled from union
Section 49(2), so far as it relates to the amendments effected by Schedule 8 specified below	Consequential amendments
Section 51, so far as it relates to the repeals effected by Schedule 10 specified below	Repeals
Schedule 8, paragraphs 48, 50 and 51	Consequential amendments
Schedule 10, the repeals specified in the table below	Repeals

[1440]

TABLE

Chapter	Short Title	Extent of Repeal
c.52	Trade Union Reform and Labour Relations (Consolidation) Act 1992	Section 67(9). In section 288(1)(b), the word "unreasonable".
		In section 290(e) the word "unreasonable" and the words "where employment subject to union membership agreement".
		In section 291, subsection (1) and, in subsection (2), the words "any other provision of".

[1441]

SCHEDULE 3

Article 2(3)

PROVISIONS COMING INTO FORCE ON 1 JANUARY 1994

Provision	Subject Matter of Provision
Section 8	Annual return to contain additional information
Section 9	Statement to members following annual return
Section 49(2), so far as it relates to the amendments effected by Schedule 8 specified below	Consequential amendments
Section 51, so far as it relates to the repeals effected by Schedule 10 specified below	Repeals
Schedule 8, paragraphs 42, 43(a), 44, 45, 62(a), 64(a) and 66(a)	Consequential amendments
In Schedule 10, the repeal in section 32(3) of the 1992 Act of the word "and" at the end of paragraph (b)	Repeals

[1442]

TRADE UNION BALLOTS AND ELECTIONS (INDEPENDENT SCRUTINEER QUALIFICATIONS) ORDER 1993

(SI 1993/1909)

NOTES
Made: 27 July 1993.
Authority: Trade Union and Labour Relations (Consolidation) Act 1992, ss 49(2), 75(2), 100A(2), 226B(2).

ARRANGEMENT OF ARTICLES

1 Citation, commencement and interpretation

(1) This Order may be cited as the Trade Union Ballots and Elections (Independent Scrutineer Qualifications) Order 1993 and shall come into force on 30 August 1993.

(2) In this Order, unless the context otherwise requires—

"an individual potentially qualified to be a scrutineer" means an individual who satisfies the requirement specified in either paragraph (a) of article 3 or paragraph (a) of article 4;

"the 1992 Act" means the Trade Union and Labour Relations (Consolidation) Act 1992;

"the relevant provisions" means the provisions of sections 49(2)(a), 75(2)(a), 100A(2)(a) and 226B(2)(a) of the 1992 Act.   **[1443]**

NOTE
Commencement: 30 August 1993.

2 Qualifications

An individual satisfies the condition specified for the purposes of the relevant provisions in relation to a ballot or election, (as the case may be), if he satisfies the condition specified in article 3 or 4.

[1444]

NOTE
Commencement: 30 August 1993.

3 An individual satisfies this condition if—

(a) he has in force a practising certificate issued by the Law Society of England and Wales or the Law Society of Scotland; and
(b) he is not disqualified from satisfying this condition by virtue of article 5.

[1445]

NOTE
Commencement: 30 August 1993.

4 An individual satisfies this condition if—

(a) he is qualified to be an auditor of a trade union by virtue of section 34(1) of the 1992 Act; and
(b) he is not disqualified from satisfying this condition by virtue of article 5.

[1446]

NOTE
Commencement: 30 August 1993.

5 (1) An individual potentially qualified to be a scrutineer does not satisfy the condition specified in article 3 or 4 if he or any existing partner of his has—

(a) during the preceding 12 months, been a member, an officer or an employee of the trade union proposing to hold the ballot or election; or
(b) in acting at any time as a scrutineer for any trade union, knowingly permitted any member, officer or employee of the trade union to assist him in carrying out any of the functions referred to in sections 49(3), 75(3), 100A(3) and 226B(1) of the 1992 Act.

(2) References in this article to an officer shall be construed as not including an auditor.

[1447]

NOTE
Commencement: 30 August 1993.

6 A partnership satisfies the condition specified for the purposes of the relevant provisions in relation to a ballot or election, (as the case may be), if—

(a) every member of the partnership is an individual potentially qualified to be a scrutineer; and
(b) no member of the partnership is disqualified from being a scrutineer by virtue of article 5.

[1448]

NOTE
Commencement: 30 August 1993.

7 Persons specified by name

The following persons are specified for the purposes of the relevant provisions—

     Electoral Reform Ballot Services Limited;
     The Industrial Society; and
     Unity Security Balloting Services Limited.   **[1449]**

NOTE
     Commencement: 30 August 1993.

8 The Trade Union Ballots and Elections (Independent Scrutineer Qualifications) Order 1988 is hereby revoked.   **[1450]**

NOTE
     Commencement: 30 August 1993.

EMPLOYMENT PROTECTION (CONTINUITY OF EMPLOYMENT) REGULATIONS 1993
(SI 1993/2165)

NOTES
     Made: 3 September 1993.
     Authority: Employment Protection (Consolidation) Act 1978, Sch 13, para 20.

1 Citation, commencement and revocation

(1) These Regulations may be cited as the Employment Protection (Continuity of Employment) Regulations 1993 and shall come into force on 4th October 1993.

     (2) As from that date the Labour Relations (Continuity of Employment) Regulations 1976 shall be revoked.   **[1451]**

NOTE
     Commencement: 4 October 1993.

2 Interpretation

In these Regulations, "the 1978 Act" means the Employment Protection (Consolidation) Act 1978.   **[1452]**

NOTE
     Commencement: 4 October 1993.

3 Application

(1) These Regulations apply to any action taken in relation to the dismissal of an employee which consists of—

     (a) the presentation by him of a relevant complaint of dismissal, or
     (b) his making a claim in accordance with a dismissal procedures agreement designated by an order under section 65 of the 1978 Act, or
     (c) any action taken by a conciliation officer under his relevant conciliation powers, or
     (d) the making of a relevant compromise contract.

     (2) In this regulation—

     "relevant complaint of dismissal" means a complaint under section 67 of the 1978 Act, a complaint under section 63 of the Sex Discrimination Act 1975 ("the 1975 Act") arising out of a dismissal or a complaint under section 54 of the Race Relations Act) 1976 ("the 1976 Act") arising out of a dismissal;

"relevant compromise contract" means—

    (a) any agreement authorised by section 140(2)(fb) of the 1978 Act to refrain from instituting or continuing any proceedings specified in section 134(1) of that Act before an industrial tribunal,

    (b) any contract authorised by section 77(4)(aa) of the 1975 Act settling a complaint arising out of a dismissal, or

    (c) any contract authorised by section 72(4)(aa) of the 1976 Act settling a complaint arising out of a dismissal;

"relevant conciliation powers" means section 134(3) of the 1978 Act, section 64(2) of the 1975 Act or section 55(2) of the 1976 Act. **[1453]**

NOTE

Commencement: 4 October 1993.

4 Continuity of employment where employee re-engaged

(1) The provisions of this regulation shall have effect to preserve the continuity of a person's period of employment for the purposes of Schedule 13 to the 1978 Act and for the purposes of that Schedule as applied by subsection (5) of section 281 and subsection (2) of section 282 of the Trade Union and Labour Relations (Consolidation) Act 1992 to those sections.

(2) If in consequence of any action to which these Regulations apply a dismissed employee is reinstated or re-engaged by his employer or by a successor or associated employer of the employer the continuity of that employee's period of employment shall be preserved and, accordingly, the period beginning with the date on which the dismissal to which the action relates takes effect and ending with the date of reinstatement or re-engagement, as the case may be, shall count in the computation of the employee's period of continuous employment. **[1454]**

NOTE

Commencement: 4 October 1993.

5 Exclusion of operation of paragraph 12 of Schedule 13 to the 1978 Act where redundancy or equivalent payment repaid

(1) Where—

    (a) in consequence of any action to which these Regulations apply a dismissed employee is reinstated or re-engaged by his employer or by a successor or associated employer of the employer, and

    (b) the terms upon which he is so reinstated or re-engaged include provision for him to repay the amount of a redundancy payment or an equivalent payment paid in respect of the relevant dismissal,

paragraph 12 of Schedule 13 to the 1978 Act (which requires the continuity of the period of employment to be treated as broken in redundancy cases where a redundancy payment or an equivalent payment is paid and he is subsequently re-engaged) shall not apply if that provision is complied with.

(2) For the purposes of this regulation the cases in which a redundancy payment shall be treated as having been paid are cases mentioned in sub-paragraphs (3)(a) and (3)(b) of paragraph 12 of Schedule 13 to the 1978 Act. **[1455]–[2000]**

NOTE

Commencement: 4 October 1993.

PART 3
EUROPEAN COMMUNITY
MATERIALS

EUROPEAN COMMUNITY MATERIALS

SECTION A: CONSTITUTIONAL MATERIALS

TREATY ESTABLISHING THE EUROPEAN COMMUNITY (TREATY OF ROME)

[25 March 1957]

GENERAL NOTE

Only those Articles of particular relevance to Employment Law are printed here. These include those relating to the free movement of persons and the right of establishment; the legislative powers of the Community and the powers of the Court of Justice. Articles 100A, 118A and 118B were added, and Articles 100 and 235 amended, by the Single European Act 1986. Further amendments are made, prospectively, by the (Maastricht) Treaty on European Union of 7 February 1992.

The Community was originally the European Economic Community but was redesignated the European Community by the Single European Act.

References throughout the Treaty to the European Parliament were substituted for references to the former European Assembly by the Single European Act.

Article 119 prospectively amended by a Protocol to the Treaty of European Union. The Protocol on Social Policy and Agreement on Social Policy (the "Social Chapter Protocol" and "Social Chapter") adopted at Maastricht are printed below, paras **[2064]–[2075]**. For the coming into force of the Treaty and Protocols see the note to the Treaty, below.

PART 1: PRINCIPLES

* * * * *

Article 5

Member States shall take all appropriate measures, whether general or particular, to ensure fulfilment of the obligations arising out of this Treaty or resulting from action taken by the institutions of the Community. They shall facilitate the achievement of the Community's tasks.

They shall abstain from any measure which could jeopardise the attainment of the objectives of this Treaty.　　　　　　　　　　　　　　　　　　　**[2001]**

* * * * *

PART 2: FOUNDATIONS OF THE COMMUNITY
[PART 3: COMMUNITY POLICIES]

NOTE

Title prospectively substituted by the Treaty on European Union.

TITLE III—FREE MOVEMENT OF PERSONS, SERVICES AND CAPITAL
CHAPTER 1—WORKERS

Article 48

1 Freedom of movement for workers shall be secured within the Community by the end of the transitional period at the latest.

2 Such freedom of movement shall entail the abolition of any discrimination based on nationality between workers of the Member States as regards employment, remuneration and other conditions of work and employment.

3 It shall entail the right, subject to limitations justified on grounds of public policy, public security or public health:

    (a) to accept offers of employment actually made;
    (b) to move freely within the territory of Member States for this purpose;
    (c) to stay in a Member State for the purpose of employment in accordance with the provisions governing the employment of nationals of that State laid down by law, regulation or administrative action;
    (d) to remain in the territory of a Member State after having been employed in that State, subject to conditions which shall be embodied in implementing regulations to be drawn up by the Commission.

4 The provisions of this Article shall not apply to employment in the public service. **[2002]**

Article 49

As soon as this Treaty enters into force, the Council shall, acting on a proposal from the Commission and after consulting the Economic and Social Committee, issue directives or make regulations setting out the measures required to bring about, by progressive stages, freedom of movement for workers, as defined in Article 48, in particular:

[As soon as this Treaty enters into force, the Council shall, acting in accordance with the procedure referred to in Article 189b and after consulting the Economic and Social Committee, issue directives or make regulations setting out the measures required to bring about, by progressive stages, freedom of movement for workers, as defined in Article 48, in particular:]

    (a) by ensuring close co-operation between national employment services;
    (b) by systematically and progressively abolishing those administrative procedures and practices and those qualifying periods in respect of eligibility for available employment, whether resulting from national legislation or from agreements previously concluded between Member States, the maintenance of which would form an obstacle to liberalisation of the movement of workers;
    (c) by systematically and progressively abolishing all such qualifying periods and other restrictions provided for either under national legislation or under agreements previously concluded between Member States as imposed on workers of other Member States conditions regarding the free choice of employment other than those imposed on workers of the State concerned;
    (d) by setting up appropriate machinery to bring offers of employment into touch with applications for employment and to facilitate the achievement of a balance between supply and demand in the employment market in such a way as to avoid serious threats to the standard of living and level of employment in the various regions and industries. **[2003]**

NOTE

  Words in italics prospectively replaced by words in square brackets by Title II D (10) of the Treaty on European Union.

Article 50

Member States shall, within the framework of a joint programme, encourage the exchange of young workers. **[2004]**

Article 51

The Council shall, acting unanimously on a proposal from the Commission, adopt such measures in the field of social security as are necessary to provide freedom of movement for workers; to this end, it shall make arrangements to secure for migrant workers and their dependants:

    (a) aggregation, for the purpose of acquiring and retaining the right to benefit and of calculating the amount of benefit, of all periods taken into account under the laws of the several countries;

    (b) payment of benefits to persons resident in the territories of Member States.
                                                                          [2005]

* * * * *

CHAPTER 3—SERVICES

Article 59

Within the framework of the provisions set out below, restrictions on freedom to provide services within the Community shall be progressively abolished during the transitional period in respect of nationals of Member States who are established in a State of the Community other than that of the person for whom the services are intended.

The Council may, acting unanimously on a proposal from the Commission, extend the provisions of this Chapter to nationals of a third country who provide services and who are established within the Community.   **[2006]**

Article 60

Services shall be considered to be "services" within the meaning of this Treaty where they are normally provided for remuneration, in so far as they are not governed by the provisions relating to freedom of movement for goods, capital and persons.

"Services" shall in particular include:

    (a) activities of an industrial character,
    (b) activities of a commercial character;
    (c) activities of craftsmen;
    (d) activities of the professions.

Without prejudice to the provisions of the Chapter relating to the right of establishment, the person providing a service may, in order to do so, temporarily pursue his activity in the State where the service is provided, under the same conditions as are imposed by that State on its own nationals.   **[2007]**

* * * * *

PART 3: POLICY OF THE COMMUNITY

TITLE I—COMMON RULES

[TITLE V—COMMON RULES ON COMPETITION, TAXATION AND APPROXIMATION OF LAWS]

CHAPTER 3—APPROXIMATION OF LAWS

Article 100

The Council shall, acting unanimously on a proposal from the Commission, issue directives for the approximation of such provisions laid down by law, regulation or administrative action in Member States as directly affect the establishment or functioning of the common market. The European Parliament and the Economic and Social Committee shall be consulted in the case of directives whose implementation would, in one or more Member States, involve the amendment of legislation.

[The Council shall, acting unanimously on a proposal from the Commission and after consulting the European Parliament and the Economic and Social Committee, issue directives for the approximation of such laws, regulations or administrative provisions of the Member States as directly affect the establishment or functioning of the common market.] **[2008]**

NOTE

Words in italics prospectively replaced by words in square brackets by the Treaty on European Union, Title II D (21).

[Article 100a

1 By way of derogation from Article 100 and save where otherwise provided in this Treaty, the following provisions shall apply for the achievement of the objectives set out in Article 8a. The Council shall, acting by a qualified majority on a proposal from the Commission in co-operation with the European Parliament and after consulting the Economic and Social Committee, adopt the measures for the approximation of the provisions laid down by law, regulation or administrative action in Member States which have as their object the establishment and functioning of the internal market.

[1 By way of derogation from Article 100 and save where otherwise provided in this Treaty, the following provisions shall apply for the achievement of the objectives set out in Article 7a. The Council shall, acting in accordance with the procedure referred to in Article 189b and after consulting the Economic and Social Committee, adopt the measures for the approximation of the provisions laid down by law, regulation or administrative action in Member States which have as their object the establishment and functioning of the internal market.]

2 Paragraph 1 shall not apply to fiscal provisions, to those relating to the free movement of persons nor to those relating to the rights and interests of employed persons.

3 The Commission, in its proposals envisaged in paragraph 1 concerning health, safety, environmental protection and consumer protection, will take as a base a high level of protection.

4 If, after the adoption of a harmonisation measure by the Council acting by a qualified majority, a Member State deems it necessary to apply national provisions on grounds of major needs referred to in Article 36, or relating to protection of the environment or the working environment, it shall notify the Commission of these provisions.

The Commission shall confirm the provisions involved after having verified that they are not a means of arbitrary discrimination or a disguised restriction on trade between Member States.

By way of derogation from the procedure laid down in Articles 169 and 170, the Commission or any Member State may bring the matter directly before the Court of Justice if it considers that another Member State is making improper use of the powers provided for in this Article.

5 The harmonisation measures referred to above shall, in appropriate cases, include a safeguard clause authorising the Member States to take, for one or more of the non-economic reasons referred to in Article 36, provisional measures subject to a Community control procedure.] **[2009]**

NOTES

This Art added by the Single European Act, February 1986, Art 3 (1).

Para 1: words in italics prospectively replaced by words in square brackets by the Treaty on European Union, Title II D (22).

* * * * *

TITLE III—SOCIAL POLICY

[TITLE VIII—SOCIAL POLICY, EDUCATION, VOCATIONAL TRAINING AND YOUTH]

CHAPTER 1—SOCIAL PROVISIONS

NOTE
Title prospectively substituted by the Treaty on European Union, Title II D (32).

Article 117

Member States agree upon the need to promote improved working conditions and an improved standard of living for workers, so as to make possible their harmonisation while the improvement is being maintained.

They believe that such a development will ensue not only from the functioning of the common market, which will favour the harmonisation of social systems, but also from the procedures provided for in this Treaty and from the approximation of provisions laid down by law, regulation or administrative action.   [2010]

Article 118

Without prejudice to the other provisions of this Treaty and in conformity with its general objectives, the Commission shall have the task of promoting close cooperation between Member States in the social field, particlarly in matters relating to:

—employment;
—labour law and working conditions;
—basic and advanced vocational training;
—social security;
—prevention of occupational accidents and diseases;
—occupational hygiene;
—the right of association, and the collective bargaining between employers and workers.

To this end, the Commission shall act in close contact with Member States by making studies, delivering opinions and arranging consultations both on problems arising at national level and on those of concern to international organisations.

Before delivering the opinions provided for in this Article, the Commission shall consult the Economic and Social Committee.   [2011]

[Article 118a

1 Member States shall pay particular attention to encouraging improvements, especially in the working environment, as regards the health and safety of workers, and shall set as their objective the harmonisation of conditions in this area, while maintaining the improvements made.

2 In order to help achieve the objective laid down in the first paragraph, the Council, acting by a qualified majority on a proposal from the Commission, in co-operation with the European Parliament and after consulting the Economic and Social Committee, shall adopt, by means of directives, minimum requirements for gradual implementation, having regard to the conditions and technical rules obtaining in each of the Member States.

[2 In order to help achieve the objective laid down in the first paragraph, the Council, acting in accordance with the procedure referred to in Article 189c and after consulting the Economic and Social Committee, shall adopt by means of directives, minimum requirements for gradual implementation, having regard to the conditions and technical rules obtaining in each of the Member States.]

Such directives shall avoid imposing administrative, financial and legal constraints in a way which would hold back the creation and development of small and medium-sized undertakings.

3 The provisions adopted pursuant to this Article shall not prevent any Member State from maintaining or introducing more stringent measures for the protection of working conditions compatible with this Treaty.] **[2012]**

NOTES

This Art added by the Single European Act, February 1986, Art 21.

Para 2: words in italics prospectively replaced by words in square brackets by the Treaty on European Union, Title II D (33).

[Article 118b

The Commission shall endeavour to develop the dialogue between management and labour at European level which could, if the two sides consider it desirable, lead to relations based on agreement.] **[2013]**

NOTE

This Art added by the Single European Act, February 1986, Art 22.

Article 119

Each Member State shall during the first stage ensure and subsequently maintain the application of the principle that men and women should receive equal pay for equal work.

For the purpose of this Article, "pay" means the ordinary basic or minimum wage or salary and any other consideration, whether in cash or in kind, which the worker receives, directly or indirectly, in respect of his employment from his employer.

Equal pay without discrimination based on sex means:

(a) that pay for the same work at piece rates shall be calculated on the basis of the same unit of measurement;

(b) that pay for work at time rates shall be the same for the same job. **[2014]**

NOTE

Protocol 2 to the Treaty on European Union, which will come into force concurrently with the Treaty, provides:

"2 PROTOCOL CONCERNING ARTICLE 119 OF THE TREATY ESTABLISHING THE EUROPEAN COMMUNITY

THE HIGH CONTRACTING PARTIES,

HAVE AGREED UPON the following provision, which shall be annexed to the Treaty establishing the European Community:

For the purposes of Article 119 of this Treaty, benefits under occupational social security schemes shall not be considered as remuneration if and so far as they are attributable to periods of employment prior to 17 May 1990, except in the case of workers or those claiming under them who have before that date initiated legal proceedings or introduced an equivalent claim under the applicable national law."

Article 120

Member States shall endeavour to maintain the existing equivalence between paid holiday schemes. **[2015]**

Article 121

The Council may, acting unanimously and after consulting the Economic and Social Committee, assign to the Commission tasks in connection with the implementation of common measures, particularly as regards social security for the migrant workers referred to in Articles 48 to 51.   **[2016]**

* * * * *

PART 5: INSTITUTIONS OF THE COMMUNITY

TITLE I—PROVISIONS GOVERNING THE INSTITUTIONS

CHAPTER 1—THE INSTITUTIONS

Section 4 —The Court of Justice

Article 164

The Court of Justice shall ensure that in the interpretation and application of this Treaty the law is observed.   **[2017]**

Article 165

[The Court of Justice shall consist of 13 Judges.]

The Court of Justice shall sit in plenary session. It may, however, form chambers, each consisting of three or five Judges, either to undertake certain preparatory inquiries or to adjudicate on particular categories of case in accordance with rules laid down for these purposes.

[Whenever the Court of Justice hears cases brought before it by a Member State or by one of the institutions of the Community or, to the extent that the Chambers of the Court do not have the requisite jurisdiction under the Rules of Procedure, has to give preliminary rulings on questions submitted to it pursuant to Article 177, it shall sit in plenary session.]

[The Court of Justice shall sit in plenary session when a Member State or a Community institution that is a party to the proceedings so requests.]

Should the Court of Justice so request, the Council may, acting unanimously, increase the number of Judges and make the necessary adjustments to the second and third paragraphs of this Article and to the second paragraph of Article 167.   **[2018]**

NOTES

First paragraph, and words in italics in third paragraph, substituted by the Act of Accession (Spain and Portugal) (OJ No L302, 15 November 1985, p 23), Art 17. Words in italics prospectively substituted by words in square brackets immediately following by the Treaty on European Union, Title II E (49).

Article 166

[The Court of Justice shall be assisted by six Advocates-General.]

It shall be the duty of the Advocate-General, acting with complete impartiality and independence, to make, in open court, reasoned submissions on cases brought before the Court of Justice, in order to assist the Court in the performance of the task assigned to it in Article 164.

Should the Court of Justice so request, the Council may, acting unanimously, increase the number of Advocates-General and make the necessary adjustments to the third paragraph of Article 167.   **[2019]**

NOTES

First paragraph amended by the Act of Accession (Spain and Portugal) (OJ No L302, 15 November 1985, p 23), Art 18.

Article 167

The Judges and Advocates-General shall be chosen from persons whose independence is beyond doubt and who possess the qualifications required for appointment to the highest judicial offices in their respective countries or who are jurisconsults of recognised competence; they shall be appointed by common accord of the Governments of the Member States for a term of six years.

[Every three years there shall be a partial replacement of the Judges. Seven and six Judges shall be replaced alternately.]

[Every three years there shall be a partial replacement of the Advocates-General. Three Advocates-General shall be replaced on each occasion.]

Retiring Judges and Advocates-General shall be eligible for reappointment.

The Judges shall elect the President of the Court of Justice from among their number of a term of three years. He may be re-elected.　　　　　　　**[2020]**

NOTES

First and second paragraphs amended by the Act of Accession (Spain and Portugal) (OJ No L302, 15 November 1985, p 23), Art 19.

* * * * *

Article 169

If the Commission considers that a Member State has failed to fulfil an obligation under this Treaty, it shall deliver a reasoned opinion on the matter after giving the State concerned the opportunity to submit its observations.

If the State concerned does not comply with the opinion within the period laid down by the Commission, the latter may bring the matter before the Court of Justice.
　　　　　　　[2021]

Article 170

A Member State which considers that another Member State has failed to fulfil an obligation under this Treaty may bring the matter before the Court of Justice.

Before a Member State brings an action against another Member State for an alleged infringement of an obligation under this Treaty, it shall bring the matter before the Commission.

The Commission shall deliver a reasoned opinion after each of the States concerned has been given the opportunity to submit its own case and its observations on the other party's case both orally and in writing.

If the Commission has not delivered an opinion within three months of the date on which the matter was brought before it, the absence of such opinion shall not prevent the matter from being brought before the Court of Justice.　　　　**[2022]**

Article 171

[1] If the Court of Justice finds that a Member State has failed to fulfil an obligation under this Treaty, the State shall be required to take the necessary measures to comply with the judgment of the Court of Justice.

[2 If the Commission considers that the Member State concerned has not taken such measures it shall, after giving that State the opportunity to submit its observations, issue a reasoned opinion specifying the points on which the Member State concerned has not complied with the judgment of the Court of Justice.

If the Member State concerned fails to take the necessary measures to comply with the Court's judgment within the time-limit laid down by the Commission, the latter may bring the case before the Court of Justice. In so doing it shall specify the amount of the lump sum or penalty payment to be paid by the Member State concerned which it considers appropriate in the circumstances.

If the Court of Justice finds that the Member State concerned has not complied with its judgment it may impose a lump sum or penalty payment on it.

This procedure shall be without prejudice to Article 170.]   **[2023]**

NOTE
    Original Article numbered as para 1, and para 2 prospectively added by the Treaty on Euopean Union, Title II E (51).

Article 172

Regulations made by the Council pursuant to the provisions of this Treaty may give the Court of Justice unlimited jurisdiction in regard to the penalties provided for in such regulations.

[Regulations adopted jointly by the European Parliament and the Council, and by the Council, pursuant to the provisions of this Treaty, may give the Court of Justice unlimited jurisdiction with regard to the penalties provided for in such regulations.]   **[2024]**

NOTE
    This Art prospectively substituted by words in square brackets by the Treaty on European Union, Title II E (52).

Article 173

The Court of Justice shall review the legality of acts of the Council and the Commission other than recommendations or opinions. It shall for this purpose have jurisdiction in actions brought by a Member State, the Council or the Commission on grounds of lack of competence, infringement of an essential procedural requirement, infringement of this Treaty or of any rule relating to its application, or misuse of powers.

Any natural or legal person may, under the same conditions, institute proceedings against a decision addressed to that person or against a decision which, although in the form of a regulation or a decision addressed to another person, is of direct and individual concern to the former.

The proceedings provided for in this Article shall be instituted within two months of the publication of the measure, or of its notification to the plaintiff, or, in the absence thereof, of the day on which it came to the knowledge of the latter, as the case may be.

[The Court of Justice shall review the legalility of acts adopted jointly by the European Parliament and the Council, of acts of the Council, of the Commission and of the ECB, other than recommendations and opinions, and of acts of the European Parliament intended to produce legal effects vis-à-vis third parties.

It shall for this purpose have jurisdiction in actions brought by a Member State, the Council or the Commission on grounds of lack of competence, infringement of an essential procedural requirement, infringement of this Treaty or of any rule relating to its application, or misuse of powers.

The Court shall have jurisdiction under the same conditions in actions brought by the European Parliament and by the ECB for the purpose of protecting their prerogatives.

Any natural or legal person may, under the same conditions, institute proceedings against a decision addressed to that person or against a decision which, although in the form of a regulation or a decision addressed to another person, is of direct and individual concern to the former.

The proceedings provided for in this Article shall be instituted within two months of the publication of the measure, or of its notification to the plaintiff, or, in the absence thereof, of the day on which it came to the knowledge of the latter, as the case may be.]   **[2025]**

NOTE

This Art prospectively replaced by words in square brackets by the Treaty on European Union, Title II E (53).

Article 174

If the action is well founded, the Court of Justice shall declare that act concerned to be void.

In the case of a regulation, however, the Court of Justice shall, if it considers this necessary, state which of the effects of the regulation which it has declared void shall be considered as definitive.   **[2026]**

* * * * *

Article 177

The Court of Justice shall have jurisdiction to give preliminary rulings concerning:

  (a) the interpretation of this Treaty;
  (b) the validity and interpretation of acts of the institutions of the Community [and of the ECB];
  (c) the interpretation of the statutes of bodies established by an act of the Council, where those statutes so provide.

Where such a question is raised before a court or tribunal of a Member State, that court or tribunal may, if it considers that a decision on the question is necessary to enable it to give judgment, request the Court of Justice to give a ruling thereon.

Where any such question is raised in a case pending before a court or tribunal of a Member State, against whose decisions there is no judicial remedy under national law, that court or tribunal shall bring the matter before the Court of Justice.   **[2027]**

NOTE

Words in square brackets in para (b) prospectively added by the Treaty on European Union, Title II E (56).

* * * * *

CHAPTER 2—PROVISIONS COMMON TO SEVERAL INSTITUTIONS

Article 189

In order to carry out their task *the Council and the Commission shall, in accordance with the provisions of this Treaty,* [and in accordance with the provisions of this Treaty, the European Parliament acting jointly with the Council, the Council and the Commission shall] make regulations, issue directives, take decisions, make recommendations or deliver opinions.

A regulation shall have general application. It shall be binding in its entirety and directly applicable in all Member States.

A directive shall be binding, as to the result to be achieved, upon each Member State to which it is addressed, but shall leave to the national authorities the choice of form and methods.

A decision shall be binding in its entirety upon those to whom it is addressed.

Recommendations and opinions shall have no binding force.   **[2028]**

NOTE
Words in italics prospectively replaced by words in square brackets by the Treaty on European Union, Title II E (60).

[Article 189a

1 Where, in pursuance of this Treaty, the Council acts on a proposal from the Commission, unanimity shall be required for an act constituting an amendment to that proposal, subject to Article 189b(4) and (5).

2 As long as the Council has not acted, the Commission may alter its proposal at any time during the procedures leading to the adoption of a Community act.]
                                                                              [2029]

NOTE
This Art prospectively inserted by the Treaty on European Union, Title II E (61).

[Article 189b

1 Where reference is made in this Treaty to this Article for the adoption of an act, the following procedure shall apply.

2 The Commission shall submit a proposal to the European Parliament and the Council.

The Council, acting by a qualified majority after obtaining the opinion of the European Parliament, shall adopt a common position. The common position shall be communicated to the European Parliament. The Council shall inform the European Parliament fully of the reasons which led it to adopt its common position. The Commission shall inform the European Parliament fully of its position.

If, within three months of such communication, the European Parliament:

(a) approves the common position, the Council shall definitively adopt the act in question in accordance with that common position;

(b) has not taken a decision, the Council shall adopt the act in question in accordance with its common position;

(c) indicates, by an absolute majority of its component members, that it intends to reject the common position, it shall immediately inform the Council. The Council may convene a meeting of the Conciliation Committee referred to in paragraph 4 to explain further its position. The European Parliament shall thereafter either confirm, by an absolute majority of its component members, its rejection of the common position, in which event the proposed act shall be deemed not to have been adopted, or propose amendments in accordance with subparagraph (d) of this paragraph;

(d) proposes amendments to the common position by an absolute majority of its component members, the amended text shall be forwarded to the Council and to the Commission, which shall deliver an opinion on those amendments.

3 If, within three months of the matter being referred to it, the Council, acting by a qualified majority, approves all the amendments of the European Parliament, it shall amend its common position accordingly and adopt the act in question; however, the Council shall act unanimously on the amendments on which the Commission has delivered a negative opinion. If the Council does not approve the act in question, the President of the Council, in agreement with the President of the European Parliament, shall forthwith convene a meeting of the Conciliation Committee.

4 The Conciliation Committee, which shall be composed of the members of the Council or their representatives and an equal number of representatives of the European Parliament, shall have the task of reaching agreement on a joint text, by a qualified majority of the members of the Council or their representatives and by a majority of the representatives of the European Parliament. The Commission shall take part in the Conciliation Committee's proceedings and shall take all the necessary initiatives with a view to reconciling the positions of the European Parliament and the Council.

5 If, within six weeks of its being convened, the Conciliation Committee approves a joint text, the European Parliament, acting by an absolute majority of the votes cast, and the Council, acting by a qualified majority, shall have a period of six weeks from that approval in which to adopt the act in question in accordance with the joint text. If one of the two institutions fails to adopt the proposed act, it shall be deemed not to have been adopted.

6 Where the Conciliation Committee does not approve a joint text, the proposed act shall not be deemed not to have been adopted unless the Council, acting by a qualified majority within six weeks of expiry of the period granted to the Conciliation Committee, confirms the common position to which it agreed before the conciliation procedure was initiated, possibly with amendments proposed by the European Parliament. In this case, the act in question shall be finally adopted unless the European Parliament, within six weeks of the date of confirmation by the Council, rejects the text by an absolute majority of its component members, in which case the proposed act shall be deemed not to have been adopted.

7 The periods of three months and six weeks referred to in this Article may be extended by a maximum of one month and two weeks respectively by common accord of the European Parliament and the Council. The period of three months referred to in paragraph 2 shall be automatically extended by two months where paragraph 2(c) applies.

8 The scope of the procedure under this Article may be widened, in accordance with the procedure provided for in Article N(2) of the Treaty on European Union, on the basis of a report to be submitted to the Council by the Commission by 1996 at the latest.] **[2030]**

NOTE

This Art prospectively inserted by the Treaty on European Union, Title II E (61).

[Article 189c

Where reference is made in this Treaty to this Article for the adoption of an act, the following procedure shall apply:

   (a) The Council, acting by a qualified majority on a proposal from the Commission and after obtaining the opinion of the European Parliament, shall adopt a common position.
   (b) The Council's common position shall be communicated to the European Parliament. The Council and the Commission shall inform the European Parliament fully of the reasons which led the Council to adopt its common position and also of the Commission's position.

If, within three months of such communication, the European Parliament approves this common position or has not taken a decision within that period, the Council shall definitively adopt the act in question in accordance with the common position.

(c) The European Parliament may, within the period of three months referred to in point (b), by an absolute majority of its component members, propose amendments to the Council's common position. The European Parliament may also, by the same majority, reject the Council's common position. The result of the proceedings shall be transmitted to the Council and the Commission.

If the European Parliament has rejected the Council's common position, unanimity shall be required for the Council to act on a second reading.

(d) The Commission shall, within a period of one month, re-examine the proposal on the basis of which the Council adopted its common position, by taking into account the amendments proposed by the European Parliament.

The Commission shall forward to the Council, at the same time as its re-examined proposal, the amendments of the European Parliament which it has not accepted, and shall express its opinion on them. The Council may adopt these amendments unanimously.

(e) The Council, acting by a qualified majority, shall adopt the proposal as re-examined by the Commission.

Unanimity shall be required for the Council to amend the proposal as re-examined by the Commission.

(f) In the cases referred to in points (c), (d) and (e), the Council shall be required to act within a period of three months. If no decision is taken within this period, the Commission proposal shall be deemed not to have been adopted.

(g) The periods referred to in points (b) and (f) may be extended by a maximum of one month by common accord between the Council and the European Parliament.]   **[2031]**

NOTE

This Art prospectively inserted by the Treaty on European Union, Title II E (61).

* * * * *

PART 6: GENERAL AND FINAL PROVISIONS

Article 235

If action by the Community should prove necessary to attain, in the course of the operation of the common market, one of the objectives of the Community and this Treaty has not provided the necessary powers, the Council shall, acting unanimously on a proposal from the Commission and after consulting the [European Parliament], take the appropriate measures.   **[2032]**

NOTE

Words in square brackets substituted by the Single European Act, February 1986.

* * * * *

COMMUNITY CHARTER OF THE FUNDAMENTAL SOCIAL RIGHTS OF WORKERS

[10 December 1989]

NOTE

This "Social Charter" was adopted by the Heads of Government of all member states of the Community except the United Kingdom. There is no express legal position for such a charter in the Treaty and it does not have any direct legal status except as instructions to the Commission to prepare a programme of measures to implement its objectives. It is included for its general interest and because of the importance of the Community instruments it may generate and has generated.

THE HEADS OF STATE AND GOVERNMENT OF THE
MEMBER STATES OF THE EUROPEAN COMMUNITY
MEETING AT STRASBOURG
ON 10 DECEMBER 1989

Whereas, under the terms of Article 117 of the EEC Treaty, the Member States have agreed on the need to promote improved living and working conditions for workers so as to make possible their harmonization while the improvement is being maintained;

Whereas following on from the conclusions of the European Councils of Hanover and Rhodes the European Council of Madrid considered that, in the context of the establishment of the single European market, the same importance must be attached to the social aspects as to the economic aspects and whereas, therefore, they must be developed in a balanced manner;

Having regard to the Resolutions of the European Parliament of 15 March 1989 and 14 September 1989 and to the Opinion of the Economic and Social Committee of 22 February 1989;

Whereas the completion of the internal market is the most effective means of creating employment and ensuring maximum well-being in the Community; whereas employment development and creation must be given first priority in the completion of the internal market; whereas it is for the Community to take up the challenges of the future with regard to economic competitiveness, taking into account, in particular, regional imbalances;

Whereas the social consensus contributes to the strengthening of the competitiveness of undertakings and of the economy as a whole and to the creation of employment; whereas in this respect it is an essential condition for ensuring sustained economic development;

Whereas the completion of the internal market must favour the approximation of improvements in living and working conditions, as well as economic and social cohesion within the European Community, while avoiding distortions of competition;

Whereas the completion of the internal market must offer improvements in the social field for workers of the European Community, especially in terms of freedom of movement, living and working conditions, health and safety at work, social protection, education and training;

Whereas, in order to ensure equal treatment, it is important to combat every form of discrimination, including discrimination on grounds of sex, colour, race, opinion and beliefs, and whereas, in a spirit of solidarity, it is important to combat social exclusion;

Whereas it is for Member States to guarantee that workers from non-member countries and members of their families who are legally resident in a Member State of the European Community are able to enjoy, as regards their living and working conditions, treatment comparable to that enjoyed by workers who are nationals of the Member State concerned;

Whereas inspiration should be drawn from the Conventions of the International Labour Organisation and from the European Social Charter of the Council of Europe;

Whereas the Treaty, as amended by the Single European Act, contains provisions laying down the powers of the Community relating, *inter alia,* to the freedom of movement of workers (Articles 7, 48-51), to the right of establishment (Articles 52-58), to the social field under the conditions laid down in Articles 117-122—in particular as regards the improvement of health and safety in the working environment (Article 118a), the development of the dialogue between management and labour at European level (Article 118b), equal pay for men and women for equal work (Article 119)—to the general principles for implementing a common vocational training policy (Article 128), to economic and social cohesion (Article 130a to 130e) and, more generally, to the approximation of legislation (Articles 100, 100a and 235); whereas the implementation of the Charter must not entail an extension of the Community's powers as defined by the Treaties;

Whereas the aim of the present Charter is on the one hand to consolidate the progress made in the social field, through action by the Member States, the two sides of industry and the Community;

Whereas its aim is on the other hand to declare solemnly that the implementation of the Single European Act must take full account of the social dimension of the Community and that it is necessary in this context to ensure at appropriate levels the development of the social rights of workers of the European Community, especially employed workers and self-employed persons;

Whereas, in accordance with the conclusions of the Madrid European Council, the respective roles of Community rules, national legislation and collective agreements must be clearly established;

Whereas, by virtue of the principle of subsidiarity, responsibility for the initiatives to be taken with regard to the implementation of these social rights lies with the Member States or their constituent parts and, within the limits of its powers, with the European Community; whereas such implementation may take the form of laws, collective agreements or existing practices at the various appropriate levels and whereas it requires in many spheres the active involvement of the two sides of industry;

Whereas the solemn proclamation of fundamental social rights at European Community level may not, when implemented, provide grounds for any retrogression compared with the situation currently existing in each Member State.

HAVE ADOPTED THE FOLLOWING DECLARATION CONSTITUTING THE "COMMUNITY CHARTER OF THE FUNDAMENTAL SOCIAL RIGHTS OF WORKERS":   **[2033]**

TITLE I—FUNDAMENTAL SOCIAL RIGHTS OF WORKERS

FREEDOM OF MOVEMENT

1 Every worker of the European Community shall have the right to freedom of movement throughout the territory of the Community, subject to restrictions justified on grounds of public order, public safety or public health.   **[2034]**

2 The right to freedom of movement shall enable any worker to engage in any occupation or profession in the Community in accordance with the principles of equal treatment as regards access to employment, working conditions and social protection in the host country.   **[2035]**

3 The right of freedom of movement shall also imply:

—harmonisation of conditions of residence in all Member States, particularly those concerning qualifications;
—elimination of obstacles arising from the non-recognition of diplomas or equivalent occupational qualifications;
—improvement of the living and working conditions of frontier workers.   **[2036]**

EMPLOYMENT AND REMUNERATION

4 Every individual shall be free to choose and engage in an occupation according to the regulations governing each occupation.   **[2037]**

5 All employment shall be fairly remunerated.

To this effect, in accordance with arrangements applying in each country:

—workers shall be assured of an equitable wage, i.e. a wage sufficient to enable them to have a decent standard of living;
—workers subject to terms of employment other than an open-ended full time contract shall receive an equitable reference wage;
—wages may be withheld, seized or transferred only in accordance with the provisions of national law; such provisions should entail measures enabling

the worker concerned to continue to enjoy the necessary means of subsistence for himself and his family.   **[2038]**

6 Every individual must be able to have access to public placement services free of charge.   **[2039]**

IMPROVEMENT OF LIVING AND WORKING CONDITIONS

7 The completion of the internal market must lead to an improvement in the living and working conditions of workers in the European Community. This process must result from an approximation of these conditions while the improvement is being maintained, as regards in particular the duration and organisation of working time and forms of employment other than open-ended contracts, such as fixed-term contracts, part-time working, temporary work and seasonal work.

The improvement must cover, where necessary, the development of certain aspects of employment regulations such as procedures for collective redundancies and those regarding bankruptcies.   **[2040]**

8 Every worker of the European Community shall have a right to a weekly rest period and to annual paid leave, the duration of which must be harmonised in accordance with national practices while the improvement is being maintained.

[2041]

9 The conditions of employment of every worker of the European Community shall be stipulated in laws, in a collective agreement or in a contract of employment, according to arrangements applying in each country.   **[2042]**

SOCIAL PROTECTION

According to the arrangements applying in each country:

10 Every worker of the European Community shall have a right to adequate social protection and shall, whatever his status and whatever the size of the undertaking in which he is employed, enjoy an adequate level of social security benefits.

Persons who have been unable either to enter or re-enter the labour market and have no means of subsistence must be able to receive sufficient resources and social assistance in keeping with their particular situation.   **[2043]**

FREEDOM OF ASSOCIATION AND COLLECTIVE BARGAINING

11 Employers and workers of the European Community shall have the right of association in order to constitute professional organisations or trade unions of their choice for the defence of their economic and social interests.

Every employer and every worker shall have the freedom to join or not to join such organisations without any personal or occupational damage being thereby suffered by him.   **[2044]**

12 Employers or employers' organisations, on the one hand, and workers' organisations, on the other, shall have the right to negotiate and conclude collective agreements under the conditions laid down by national legislation and practice.

The dialogue between the two sides of industry at European level which must be developed, may, if the parties deem it desirable, result in contractual relations, in particular at inter-occupational and sectoral level.   **[2045]**

13 The right to resort to collective action in the event of a conflict of interests shall include the right to strike, subject to the obligations arising under national regulations and collective agreements.

In order to facilitate the settlement of industrial disputes the establishment and utilisation at the appropriate levels of conciliation, mediation and arbitration procedures should be encouraged in accordance with national practice.   **[2046]**

14 The internal legal order of the Member States shall determine under which conditions and to what extent the rights provided for in Articles 11 to 13 apply to the armed forces, the police and the civil service.   **[2047]**

VOCATIONAL TRAINING

15 Every worker of the European Community must be able to have access to vocational training and to receive such training throughout his working life. In the conditions governing access to such training there may be no discrimination on grounds of nationality.

The competent public authorities, undertakings or the two sides of industry each within their own sphere of competence, should set up continuing and permanent training systems enabling every person to undergo retraining more especially through leave for training purposes, to improve his skills or to acquire new skills, particularly in the light of technical developments.   **[2048]**

EQUAL TREATMENT FOR MEN AND WOMEN

16 Equal treatment for men and women must be assured. Equal opportunities for men and women must be developed.

To this end, action should be intensified wherever necessary to ensure the implementation of the principle of equality between men and women as regards in particular access to employment, remuneration, working conditions, social protection, education, vocational training and career development.

Measures should also be developed enabling men and women to reconcile their occupational and family obligations.   **[2049]**

INFORMATION, CONSULTATION AND PARTICIPATION FOR WORKERS

17 Information, consultation and participation for workers must be developed along appropriate lines, taking account of the practice in force in the various Member States.

This shall apply especially in companies or groups of companies having establishments or companies in several Member States of the European Community.   **[2050]**

18 Such information, consultation and participation must be implemented in due time, particularly in the following cases:

—when technological changes which, from the point of view of working conditions and work organisation, have major implications for the work force are introduced into undertakings;
—in connection with restructuring operations in undertakings or in cases of mergers having an impact on the employment of workers;
—in cases of collective redundancy procedures;
—when transfrontier workers in particular are affected by employment policies pursued by the undertaking where they are employed.   **[2051]**

HEALTH PROTECTION AND SAFETY AT THE WORKPLACE

19 Every worker must enjoy satisfactory health and safety conditions in his working environment. Appropriate measures must be taken in order to achieve further harmonisation of conditions in this area while maintaining the improvements made.

These measures shall take account, in particular, of the need for the training, information, consultation and balanced participation of workers as regards the risks incurred and the steps taken to eliminate or reduce them.

The provisions regarding implementation of the internal market shall help to ensure such protection.   [2052]

PROTECTION OF CHILDREN AND ADOLESCENTS

20 Without prejudice to such rules as may be more favourable to young people, in particular those ensuring their preparation for work through vocational training, and subject to derogations limited to certain light work, the minimum employment age must not be lower than the minimum school-leaving age and, in any case, not lower than 15 years.   [2053]

21 Young people who are in gainful employment must receive equitable remuneration in accordance with national practice.   [2054]

22 Appropriate measures must be taken to adjust labour regulations applicable to young workers so that their specific needs regarding development, vocational training and access to employment are met.

The duration of work must, in particular, be limited—without it being possible to circumvent this limitation through recourse to overtime—and night work prohibited in the case of workers of under eighteen years of age, save in the case of certain jobs laid down in national legislation or regulations.   [2055]

23 Following the end of compulsory education, young people must be entitled to receive initial vocational training of a sufficient duration to enable them to adapt to the requirements of their future working life; for young workers, such training should take place during working hours.   [2056]

ELDERLY PERSONS

According to the arrangements applying in each country:

24 Every worker of the European Community must, at the time of retirement, be able to enjoy resources affording him or her a decent standard of living.   [2057]

25 Every person who has reached retirement age but who is not entitled to a pension or who does not have other means of subsistence, must be entitled to sufficient resources and to medical and social assistance specifically suited to his needs.   [2058]

DISABLED PERSONS

26 All disabled persons, whatever the origin and nature of their disablement, must be entitled to additional concrete measures aimed at improving their social and professional integration.

These measures must concern, in particular, according to the capacities of the beneficiaries, vocational training, ergonomics, accessibility, mobility, means of transport and housing.   [2059]

TITLE II—IMPLEMENTATION OF THE CHARTER

27 It is more particularly the responsibility of the Member States, in accordance with the national practices, notably through legislative measures or collective agreements, to guarantee the fundamental social rights in this Charter and to implement the social measures indispensable to the smooth operation of the internal market as part of a strategy of economic and social cohesion.   **[2060]**

28 The European Council invites the Commission to submit as soon as possible initiatives which fall within its powers, as provided for in the Treaties, with a view to the adoption of legal instruments for the effective implementation, as and when the internal market is completed, of those rights which come within the Community's area of competence.   **[2061]**

29 The Commission shall establish each year, during the last three months, a report on the application of the Charter by the Member States and by the European Community.   **[2062]**

30 The report of the Commission shall be forwarded to the European Council, the European Parliament and the Economic and Social Committee.   **[2063]**

TREATY ON EUROPEAN UNION
(TREATY OF MAASTRICHT)
[7 February 1992]

GENERAL NOTE
The parts of the Treaty on European Union relevant to this work are amendments to the Treaty of Rome, which is printed above incorporating the relevant amendments; Protocol 2, on Article 119 of the Treaty of Rome, which is printed in a note to that Article, above, para **[2014]**; and Protocol 14, which is printed below.
The Treaty was to come into force on 1 January 1993 if all member states had ratified it in good time, but this was not achieved. It will now come into force one month after the month in which the final ratification is deposited. At the time of going to press, litigation in the German Constitutional Court was delaying the German ratification process possibly until November 1993.

14 PROTOCOL ON SOCIAL POLICY

THE HIGH CONTRACTING PARTIES,

NOTING that eleven Member States, that is to say the Kingdom of Belgium, the Kingdom of Denmark, the Federal Republic of Germany, the Hellenic Republic, the Kingdom of Spain, the French Republic, Ireland, the Italian Republic, the Grand Duchy of Luxembourg, the Kingdom of the Netherlands and the Portuguese Republic, wish to continue along the path laid down in the 1989 Social Charter; that they have adopted among themselves an Agreement to this end; that this Agreement is annexed to this Protocol; that this Protocol and the said Agreement are without prejudice to the provisions of this Treaty, particularly those relating to social policy which constitute an integral part of the "acquis communautaire":   **[2064]**

1 Agree to authorise those eleven Member States to have recourse to the institutions, procedures and mechanisms of the Treaty for the purposes of taking among themselves and applying as far as they are concerned the acts and decisions required for giving effect to the abovementioned Agreement.

2 The United Kingdom of Great Britain and Northern Ireland shall not take part in the deliberations and the adoption by the Council of Commission proposals made on the basis of this Protocol and the abovementioned Agreement.

By way of derogation from Article 148(2) of the Treaty, acts of the Council which are made pursuant to this Protocol and which must be adopted by a qualified majority shall be deemed to be so adopted if they have received at least forty-four votes in favour. The unanimity of the members of the Council, with the exception of the United Kingdom of Great Britain and Northern Ireland, shall be necessary for acts of the Council which must be adopted unanimously and for those amending the Commission proposal.

Acts adopted by the Council and any financial consequences other than administrative costs entailed for the institutions shall not be applicable to the United Kingdom of Great Britain and Northern Ireland.

3 This Protocol shall be annexed to the Treaty establishing the European Community. **[2065]**

AGREEMENT ON SOCIAL POLICY CONCLUDED BETWEEN THE MEMBER STATES OF THE EUROPEAN COMMUNITY WITH THE EXCEPTION OF THE UNITED KINGDOM OF GREAT BRITAIN AND NORTHERN IRELAND

The undersigned eleven HIGH CONTRACTING PARTIES, that is to say the Kingdom of Belgium, the Kingdom of Denmark, the Federal Republic of Germany, the Hellenic Republic, the Kingdom of Spain, the French Republic, Ireland, the Italian Republic, the Grand Duchy of Luxembourg, the Kingdom of the Netherlands and the Portuguese Republic (hereinafter referred to as "the Member States"),

WISHING to implement the 1989 Social Charter on the basis of the "acquis communautaire",

CONSIDERING the Protocol on social policy,

HAVE AGREED as follows: **[2066]**

Article 1

The Community and the Member States shall have as their objectives the promotion of employment, improved living and working conditions, proper social protection, dialogue between management and labour, the development of human resources with a view to lasting high employment and the combatting of exclusion. To this end the Community and the Member States shall implement measures which take account of the diverse forms of national practices, in particular in the field of contractual relations, and the need to maintain the competitiveness of the Community economy. **[2067]**

Article 2

1 With a view to achieving the objectives of Article 1, the Community shall support and complement the activities of the Member States in the following fields:

—improvement in particular of the working environment to protect workers' health and safety;

—working conditions;

—the information and consultation of workers;

—equality between men and women with regard to labour market opportunities and treatment at work;

—the integration of persons excluded from the labour market, without prejudice to Article 127 of the Treaty establishing the European Community (hereinafter referred to as "the Treaty").

2 To this end, the Council may adopt, by means of directives, minimum requirements for gradual implementation, having regard to the conditions and technical rules obtaining in each of the Member States. Such directives shall avoid imposing administrative, financial and legal constraints in a way which would hold back the creation and development of small and medium-sized undertakings.

The Council shall act in accordance with the procedure referred to in Article 189c of the Treaty after consulting the Economic and Social Committee.

3 However, the Council shall act unanimously on a proposal from the Commission, after consulting the European Parliament and the Economic and Social Committee, in the following areas:

—social security and social protection of workers;
—protection of workers where their employment contract is terminated;
—representation and collective defence of the interests of workers and employers, including co-determination, subject to paragraph 6;
—conditions of employment for third-country nationals legally residing in Community territory;
—financial contributions for promotion of employment and job-creation, without prejudice to the provisions relating to the Social Fund.

4 A Member State may entrust management and labour, at their joint request, with the implementation of directives adopted pursuant to paragraphs 2 and 3.

In this case, it shall ensure that, no later than the date on which a directive must be transposed in accordance with Article 189, management and labour have introduced the necessary measures by agreement, the Member State concerned being required to take any necessary measure enabling it at any time to be in a position to guarantee the results imposed by that directive.

5 The provisions adopted pursuant to this Article shall not prevent any Member State from maintaining or introducing more stringent protective measures compatible with the Treaty.

6 The provisions of this Article shall not apply to pay, the right of association, the right to strike or the right to impose lock-outs. **[2068]**

Article 3

1 The Commission shall have the task of promoting the consultation of management and labour at Community level and shall take any relevant measure to facilitate their dialogue by ensuring balanced support for the parties.

2 To this end, before submitting proposals in the social policy field, the Commission shall consult management and labour on the possible direction of Community action.

3 If, after such consultation, the Commission considers Community action advisable, it shall consult management and labour on the content of the envisaged proposal. Management and labour shall forward to the Commission an opinion or, where appropriate, a recommendation.

4 On the occasion of such consultation, management and labour may inform the Commission of their wish to initiate the process provided for in Article 4. The duration of the procedure shall not exceed nine months, unless the management and labour concerned and the Commission decide jointly to extend it. **[2069]**

Article 4

1 Should management and labour so desire, the dialogue between them at Community level may lead to contractual relations, including agreements.

2 Agreements concluded at Community level shall be implemented either in accordance with the procedures and practices specific to management and labour and the Member States or, in matters covered by Article 2, at the joint request of the signatory parties, by a Council decision on a proposal from the Commission.

The Council shall act by qualified majority, except where the agreement in question contains one or more provisions relating to one of the areas referred to in Article 2(3), in which case it shall act unanimously. **[2070]**

Article 5

With a view to achieving the objectives of Article 1 and without prejudice to the other provisions of the Treaty, the Commission shall encourage co-operation between the Member States and facilitate the co-ordination of their action in all social policy fields under this Agreement. **[2071]**

Article 6

1 Each Member State shall ensure that the principle of equal pay for male and female workers for equal work is applied.

2 For the purpose of this Article, "pay" means the ordinary basic or minimum wage or salary and any other consideration, whether in cash or in kind, which the worker receives directly or indirectly, in respect of his employment, from his employer.

Equal pay without discrimination based on sex means:

(a) that pay for the same work at piece rates shall be calculated on the basis of the same unit of measurement;

(b) that pay for work at time rates shall be the same for the same job.

3 This Article shall not prevent any Member State from maintaining or adopting measures providing for specific advantages in order to make it easier for women to pursue a vocational activity or to prevent or compensate for disadvantages in their professional careers. **[2072]**

Article 7

The Commission shall draw up a report each year on progress in achieving the objectives of Article 1, including the demographic situation in the Community. It shall forward the report to the European Parliament, the Council and the Economic and Social Committee.

The European Parliament may invite the Commission to draw up reports on particular problems concerning the social situation. **[2073]**

DECLARATIONS

1 Declaration on Article 2(2)

The eleven High Contracting Parties note that in the discussions on Article 2(2) of the Agreement it was agreed that the Community does not intend, in laying down minimum requirements for the protection of the safety and health of employees, to discriminate in a manner unjustified by the circumstances against employees in small and medium-sized undertakings. **[2074]**

2 Declaration on Article 4(2)

The eleven High Contracting Parties declare that the first of the arrangements for application of the agreements between management and labour at Community level — referred to in Article 4(2) — will consist in developing, by collective bargaining according to the rules of each Member State, the content of the agreements, and that consequently this arrangement implies no obligation on the Member States to apply the agreements directly or to work out rules for their transposition, nor any obligation to amend national legislation in force to facilitate their implementation. **[2075]**

SECTION B: REGULATIONS, DIRECTIVES AND RECOMMENDATIONS

REGULATION No 1612/68 OF THE COUNCIL
of 15 October 1968
on freedom of movement for workers within the Community

THE COUNCIL OF THE EUROPEAN COMMUNITIES.

Having regard to the Treaty establishing the European Economic Community, and in particular Article 49 thereof;

Having regard to the proposal from the Commission;

Having regard to the Opinion of the European Parliament;

Having regard to the Opinion of the Economic and Social Committee;

Whereas freedom of movement for workers should be secured within the Community by the end of the transitional period at the latest; whereas the attainment of this objective entails the abolition of any discrimination based on nationality between workers of the Member States as regards employment, remuneration and other conditions of work and employment, as well as the right of such workers to move freely within the Community in order to pursue activities as employed persons subject to any limitations justified on grounds of public policy, public security or public health;

Whereas by reason in particular of the early establishment of the customs union and in order to ensure the simultaneous completion of the principal foundations of the Community, provisions should be adopted to enable the objectives laid down in Articles 48 and 49 of the Treaty in the field of freedom of movement to be achieved and to perfect measures adopted successively under Regulation No 15 on the first steps for attainment of freedom of movement and under Council Regulation No 38/64/EEC of 25 March 1964 on freedom of movement for workers within the Community;

Whereas freedom of movement constitutes a fundamental right of workers and their families; whereas mobility of labour within the Community must be one of the means by which the worker is guaranteed the possibility of improving his living and working conditions and promoting his social advancement, while helping to satisfy the requirements of the economies of the Member States; whereas the right of all workers in the Member States to pursue the activity of their choice within the Community should be affirmed;

Whereas such right must be enjoyed without discrimination by permanent, seasonal and frontier workers and by those who pursue their activities for the purpose of providing services;

Whereas the right of freedom of movement, in order that it may be exercised, by objective standards, in freedom and dignity, requires that equality of treatment shall be ensured in fact and in law in respect of all matters relating to the actual pursuit of activities as employed persons and to eligibility for housing, and also that obstacles to the mobility of workers shall be eliminated, in particular as regards the worker's right to be joined by his family and the conditions for the integration of that family into the host country;

Whereas the principle of non-discrimination between Community workers entails that all nationals of Member States have the same priority as regards employment as is enjoyed by national workers;

*****

HAS ADOPTED THIS REGULATION: **[2076]**

NOTE

Parts of the Preamble relating to those parts of the Regulation not reproduced here are omitted.

PART 1: EMPLOYMENT AND WORKERS' FAMILIES

TITLE I—ELIGIBILITY FOR EMPLOYMENT

Article 1

1 Any national of a Member State, shall, irrespective of his place of residence, have the right to take up an activity as an employed person, and to pursue such activity,

within the territory of another Member State in accordance with the provisions laid down by law, regulation or administrative action governing the employment of nationals of that State.

2 He shall, in particular, have the right to take up available employment in the territory of another Member State with the same priority as nationals of that State. **[2077]**

Article 2

Any national of a Member State and any employer pursuing an activity in the territory of a Member State may exchange their applications for and offers of employment, and may conclude and perform contracts of employment in accordance with the provisions in force laid down by law, regulation or administrative action, without any discrimination resulting therefrom. **[2078]**

Article 3

1 Under this Regulation, provisions laid down by law, regulation or administrative action or administrative practices of a Member State shall not apply:

—where they limit application for and offers of employment, or the right of foreign nationals to take up and pursue employment or subject these to conditions not applicable in respect of their own nationals; or

—where, though applicable irrespective of nationality, their exclusive or principal aim or effect is to keep nationals of other Member States away from the employment offered.

This provision shall not apply to conditions relating to linguistic knowledge required by reason of the nature of the post to be filled.

2 There shall be included in particular among the provisions or practices of a Member State referred to in the first subparagraph of paragraph 1 those which:

(a) prescribe a special recruitment procedure for foreign nationals;
(b) limit or restrict the advertising of vacancies in the press or through any other medium or subject it to conditions other than those applicable in respect of employers pursuing their activities in the territory of that Member State;
(c) subject eligibility for employment to conditions of registration with employment offices or impede recruitment of individual workers, where persons who do not reside in the territory of that State are concerned. **[2079]**

Article 4

1 Provisions laid down by law, regulation or administrative action of the Member States which restrict by number or percentage the employment of foreign nationals in any undertaking, branch of activity or region, or at a national level, shall not apply to nationals of the other Member States.

2 When in a Member State the granting of any benefit to undertakings is subject to a minimum percentage of national workers being employed, nationals of the other Member States shall be counted as national workers, subject to the provisions of the Council Directive of 15 October 1963. **[2080]**

Article 5

A national of a Member State who seeks employment in the territory of another Member State shall receive the same assistance there as that afforded by the employment offices in that State to their own nationals seeking employment. **[2081]**

Article 6

1 The engagement and recruitment of a national of one Member State for a post in another Member State shall not depend on medical, vocational or other criteria which are discriminatory on grounds of nationality by comparison with those applied to nationals of the other Member State who wish to pursue the same activity.

2 Nevertheless, a national who holds an offer in his name from an employer in a Member State other than that of which he is a national may have to undergo a vocational test, if the employer expressly requests this when making his offer of employment. [2082]

TITLE II—EMPLOYMENT AND EQUALITY OF TREATMENT

Article 7

1 A worker who is a national of a Member State may not, in the territory of another Member State, be treated differently from national workers by reason of his nationality in respect of any conditions of employment and work, in particular as regards remuneration, dismissal, and should he become unemployed, reinstatement or re-employment;

2 He shall enjoy the same social and tax advantages as national workers.

3 He shall also, by virtue of the same right and under the same conditions as national workers, have access to training in vocational schools and retraining centres.

4 Any clause of a collective or individual agreement or of any other collective regulation concerning eligibility for employment, employment, remuneration and other conditions of work or dismissal shall be null and void in so far as it lays down or authorises discriminatory conditions in respect of workers who are nationals of the other Member States. [2083]

Article 8

A worker who is a national of a Member State and who is employed in the territory of another Member State shall enjoy equality of treatment as regards membership of trade unions and the exercise of rights attaching thereto, including the right to vote; he may be excluded from taking part in the management of bodies governed by public law and from holding an office governed by public law. Furthermore, he shall have the right of eligibility for workers' representative bodies in the undertaking. The provisions of this Article shall not affect laws or regulations in certain Member States which grant more extensive rights to workers coming from the other Member States.

2 ... [2084]

Article 9

1 A worker who is a national of a Member State and who is employed in the territory of another Member State shall enjoy all the rights and benefits accorded to national workers in matters of housing, including ownership of the housing he needs.

2 Such worker may, with the same right as nationals, put his name down on the housing lists in the region in which he is employed, where such lists exist; he shall enjoy the resultant benefits and priorities.

If his family has remained in the country whence he came, they shall be considered for this purpose as residing in the said region, where national workers benefit from a similar presumption. [2085]

TITLE III—WORKERS' FAMILIES

Article 10

1 The following shall, irrespective of their nationality, have the right to install themselves with a worker who is a national of one Member State and who is employed in the territory of another Member State:

  (a) his spouse and their descendants who are under the age of 21 years or are dependants;

  (b) dependent relatives in the ascending line of the worker and his spouse.

2 Member States shall facilitate the admission of any member of the family not coming within the provisions of paragraph 1 if dependent on the worker referred to above or living under his roof in the country whence he comes.

3 For the purposes of paragraphs 1 and 2, the worker must have available for his family housing considered as normal for national workers in the region where he is employed; this provision, however must not give rise to discrimination between national workers and workers from the other Member States. **[2086]**

Article 11

Where a national of a Member State is pursuing an activity as an employed or self-employed person in the territory of another Member State, his spouse and those of the children who are under the age of 21 years or dependent on him shall have the right to take up any activity as an employed person throughout the territory of that same State, even if they are not nationals of any Member State. **[2087]**

* * * * *

NOTE

The remainder of this Regulation, which relates to the obligations of Member States, is omitted.

DIRECTIVE No 75/117 OF THE COUNCIL
of 10 February 1975

on the approximation of the laws of the Member States relating to the application of the principle of equal pay for men and women

THE COUNCIL OF THE EUROPEAN COMMUNITIES.

Having regard to the Treaty establishing the European Economic Community, and in particular Article 100 thereof:

Having regard to the proposal from the Commission;

Having regard to the Opinion of the European Parliament;

Having regard to the Opinion of the Economic and Social Committee;

Whereas implementation of the principle that men and women should receive equal pay contained in Article 119 of the Treaty is an integral part of the establishment and functioning of the common market;

Whereas it is primarily the responsibility of the Member States to ensure the application of this principle by means of appropriate laws, regulations and administrative provisions;

Whereas the Council resolution of January 21, 1974 concerning a social action programme, aimed at making it possible to harmonise living and working conditions while the improvement is being maintained and at achieving a balanced social and economic development of the Community, recognised that priority should be given to action taken on behalf of women as regards access to employment and vocational training and advancement, and as regards working conditions, including pay;

Whereas it is desirable to reinforce the basic laws by standards aimed at facilitating the practical application of the principle of equality in such a way that all employees in the Community can be protected in these matters;

Whereas differences continue to exist in the various Member States despite the efforts made to apply the resolution of the conference of the Member States of December 30, 1961 on equal pay for men and women and whereas, therefore, the national provisions should be approximated as regards application of the principle of equal pay.

HAS ADOPTED THIS DIRECTIVE [2088]

Article 1

The principle of equal pay for men and women outlined in Article 119 of the Treaty, hereinafter called "principle of equal pay", means, for the same work or for work to which equal value is attributed, the elimination of all discrimination on grounds of sex with regard to all aspects and conditions of remuneration.

In particular, where a job classification system is used for determining pay, it must be based on the same criteria for both men and women and so drawn up as to exclude any discrimination on grounds of sex. [2089]

Article 2

Member States shall introduce into their national legal systems such measures as are necessary to enable all employees who consider themselves wronged by failure to apply the principle of equal pay to pursue their claims by judicial process after possible recourse to other competent authorities. [2090]

Article 3

Member States shall abolish all discrimination between men and women arising from laws, regulations or administrative provisions which is contrary to the principle of equal pay. [2091]

Article 4

Member States shall take the necessary measures to ensure that provisions appearing in collective agreements, wage scales, wage agreements or individual contracts of employment which are contrary to the principle of equal pay shall be, or may be declared, null and void or may be amended. [2092]

Article 5

Member States shall take the necessary measures to protect employees against dismissal by the employer as a reaction to a complaint within the undertaking or to any legal proceedings aimed at enforcing compliance with the principle of equal pay. [2093]

Article 6

Member States shall, in accordance with their national circumstances and legal systems, take the measures necessary to ensure that the principle of equal pay is applied. They shall see that effective means are available to take care that this principle is observed. [2094]

Article 7

Member States shall take care that the provisions adopted pursuant to this Directive together with the relevant provisions already in force, are brought to the attention of employees by all appropriate means, for example at their place of employment. [2095]

Article 8

1 Member States shall put into force the laws, regulations and administrative provisions necessary in order to comply with this Directive within one year of its notification and shall immediately inform the Commission thereof.

2 Member States shall communicate to the Commission the texts of the laws, regulations and administrative provisions which they adopt in the field covered by this Directive. **[2096]**

Article 9

Within two years of the expiry of the one-year period referred to in Article 8, Member States shall forward all necessary information to the Commission to enable it to draw up a report on the application of this Directive for submission to the Council. **[2097]**

Article 10

This Directive is addressed to the Member States. **[2098]**

DIRECTIVE No 75/129 OF THE COUNCIL
of 17 February 1975

on the approximation of the laws of the Member States relating to collective redundancies

THE COUNCIL OF THE EUROPEAN COMMUNITIES,

Having regard to the Treaty establishing the European Economic Community, and in particular Article 100 thereof;

Having regard to the proposal from the Commission;

Having regard to the Opinion of the European Parliament;

Having regard to the Opinion of the Economic and Social Committee;

Whereas it is important that greater protection should be afforded to workers in the event of collective redundancies while taking into account the need for balanced economic and social development within the Community;

Whereas, despite increasing convergence, differences still remain between the provisions in force in the Member States of the Community concerning the practical arrangements and procedures for such redundancies and the measures designed to alleviate the consequences of redundancy for workers;

Whereas these differences can have a direct effect on the functioning of the common market;

Whereas the Council resolution of January 21, 1974 concerning a social action programme makes provision for a Directive on the approximation of Member States' legislation on collective redundancies;

Whereas this approximation must therefore be promoted while the improvement is being maintained within the meaning of Article 117 of the Treaty.

HAS ADOPTED THIS DIRECTIVE: **[2099]**

SECTION I—DEFINITIONS AND SCOPE

Article 1

1 For the purposes of this Directive:

    (a) "collective redundancies" means dismissals effected by an employer for one or more reasons not related to the individual workers concerned where, according to the choice of the Member States, the number of redundancies is:

—either, over a period of 30 days:

(1) at least 10 in establishments normally employing more than 20 and less than 100 workers;
(2) at least 10 per cent of the number of workers in establishments normally employing at least 100 but less than 300 workers;
(3) at least 30 in establishments normally employing 300 workers or more;

—or, over a period of 90 days, at least 20, whatever the number of workers normally employed in the establishments in question;

(b) "workers' representatives" means the workers' representatives provided for by the laws or practices of the Member States.

[For the purpose of calculating the number of redundancies provided for in the first subparagraph of point (a), terminations of an employment contract which occur on the employer's initiative for one or more reasons not related to the individual workers concerned shall be assimilated to redundancies, provided that there are at least five redundancies.]

2 This Directive shall not apply to:

(a) collective redundancies effected under contracts of employment concluded for limited periods of time or for specific tasks except where such redundancies take place prior to the date of expiry or the completion of such contracts;
(b) workers employed by public administrative bodies or by establishments governed by public law (or, in Member States where this concept is unknown, by equivalent bodies);
(c) the crews of sea-going vessels;
(d) *workers affected by the termination of an establishment's activities where that is the result of a judicial decision.*   **[2100]**

NOTE
Words in square brackets added, and words in italics revoked, by Council Directive 92/56/EEC, Art 1(1). The deadline for implementing Directive 92/56 is 24 June 1994.

Section II—*Consultation Procedure* [Information and Consultation]

Article 2

1 Where an employer is contemplating collective redundancies, he shall begin consultations with the workers' representatives with a view to reaching an agreement.

2 These consultations shall, at least, cover ways and means of avoiding collective redundancies or reducing the number of workers affected, and mitigating the consequences.

3 To enable the workers' representatives to make constructive proposals the employer shall supply them with all relevant information and shall in any event give in writing the reasons for the redundancies, the number of workers to be made redundant, the number of workers normally employed and the period over which the redundancies are to be effected.

The employer shall forward to the competent public authority a copy of all the written communications referred to in the preceding subparagraph.

[1 Where an employer is contemplating collective redundancies, he shall begin consultations with the workers' representatives in good time with a view to reaching an agreement.

2 These consultations shall, at least, cover ways and means of avoiding collective redundancies or reducing the number of workers affected, and of mitigating the consequences by recourse to accompanying social measures aimed, inter alia, at aid for redeploying or retraining workers made redundant.

Member States may provide that the workers' representatives may call upon the services of experts in accordance with national legislation and/or practice.

3 To enable workers' representatives to make constructive proposals, the employer shall in good time during the course of the consultations:

    (a) supply them with all relevant information and
    (b) in any event notify them in writing of:
        (i) the reasons for the projected redundancies;
        (ii) the number and categories of workers to be made redundant;
        (iii) the number and categories of workers normally employed;
        (iv) the period over which the projected redundancies are to be effected;
        (v) the criteria proposed for the selection of the workers to be made redundant in so far as national legislation and/or practice confers the power therefor upon the employer;
        (vi) the method for calculating any redundancy payments other than those arising out of national legislation and/or practice.

The employer shall forward to the competent public authority a copy of, at least, the elements of the written communication which are provided for in the first subparagraph, point (b), subpoints (i) to (v).

4 The obligations laid down in paragraphs 1, 2 and 3 shall apply irrespective of whether the decision regarding collective redundancies is being taken by the employer or by an undertaking controlling the employer.

In considering alleged breaches of the information, consultation and notification requirements laid down by this Directive, account shall not be taken of any defence on the part of the employer on the ground that the necessary information has not been provided to the employer by the undertaking which took the decision leading to collective redundancies.]   **[2101]**

NOTE
    Words in italics replaced by words in square brackets by Council Directive 92/56/EEC, Art 1(2). The deadline for implementing Directive 92/56 is 24 June 1994.

SECTION III—PROCEDURE FOR COLLECTIVE REDUNDANCIES

Article 3

1 Employers shall notify the competent public authority in writing of any projected redundancies.

[However, Member States may provide that in the case of planned collective redundancies arising from termination of the establishment's activities as a result of a judicial decision, the employer shall be obliged to notify the competent public authority in writing only if the latter so requests.]

This notification shall contain all relevant information concerning the projected collective redundancies and the consultations with workers' representatives provided for in Article 2, and particularly the reasons for the redundancies, the number of workers to be made redundant, the number of workers normally employed and the period over which the redundancies are to be effected.

2 Employers shall forward to the workers' representatives a copy of the notification provided for in paragraph 1.

The workers' representatives may send any comments they may have to the competent public authority.　　　　　　　　　　　　　**[2102]**

NOTE

　　Words in square brackets added by Council Directive 92/56/EEC, Art 1(3). The deadline for implementing Directive 92/56 is 24 June 1994.

Article 4

1 Projected collective redundancies notified to the competent public authority shall take effect not earlier than 30 days after the notification referred to in Article 3(1) without prejudice to any provisions governing individual rights with regard to notice of dismissal.

Member States may grant the competent public authority the power to reduce the period provided for in the preceding subparagraph.

2 The period provided for in paragraph 1 shall be used by the competent public authority to seek solutions in the problems raised by the projected collective redundancies.

3 Where the initial period provided for in paragraph 1 is shorter than 60 days, Member States may grant the competent public authority the power to extend the initial period to 60 days following notification where the problems raised by the projected collective redundancies are not likely to be solved within the initial period.

Member States may grant the competent public authority wider powers of extension.

The employer must be informed of the extension and the grounds for it before expiry of the initial period provided for in paragraph 1.

[**4** Member States need not apply this Article to collective redundancies arising from the termination of the establishment's activities where this is the result of a judicial decision.]　　　　　　　　　　　　　**[2103]**

NOTE

　　Para 4: added by Council Directive 92/56/EEC, Art 1(4). The deadline for implementing Directive 92/56 is 24 June 1994.

Section IV—Final Provisions

Article 5

This Directive shall not affect the right of Member States to apply or to introduce laws, regulations or administrative provisions which are more favourable to workers [or to promote or allow the application of collective agreements more favourable to workers.]　　　　　　　　　　　　　**[2104]**

NOTE

　　Words in square brackets added by Council Directive 92/56/EEC, Art 1(5). The deadline for implementing Directive 92/56 is 24 June 1994.

[Article 5a

Member States shall ensure that judicial and/or administrative procedures for the enforcement of obligations under this Directive are available to the workers' representatives and/or workers.]　　　　　　　　　**[2105]**

NOTE

This Art added by Council Directive 92/56/EEC, Art 1(6). The deadline for implementing Directive 92/56 is 24 June 1994.

Article 6

1 Member States shall bring into force the laws, regulations and administrative provisions needed in order to comply with this Directive within two years following its notification and shall forthwith inform the Commission thereof.

2 Member States shall communicate to the Commission the texts of the laws, regulations and administrative provisions which they adopt in the field covered by this Directive.   [2106]

Article 7

Within two years following expiry of the two year period laid down in Article 6, Member States shall forward all relevant information to the Commission to enable it to draw up a report for submission to the Council on the application of this Directive.

[2107]

Article 8

This Directive is addressed to the Member States.   [2108]

NOTES

For the domestic implementation of this Directive see the Trade Union and Labour Relations (Consolidation) Act 1992, ss 188-198, paras **[856]–[866]**.

DIRECTIVE No 76/207 OF THE COUNCIL
of 9 February 1976

on the implementation of the principle of equal treatment for men and women as regards access to employment, vocational training and promotion, and working conditions

THE COUNCIL OF THE EUROPEAN COMMUNITIES.

Having regard to the Treaty establishing the European Economic Community, and in particular Article 235 thereof;

Having regard to the proposal from the Commission;

Having regard to the opinion of the European Parliament;

Having regard to the opinion of the Economic and Social Committee;

Whereas the Council, in its resolution of 21 January 1974 concerning a social action programme included among the priorities action for the purpose of achieving equality between men and women as regards access to employment and vocational training and promotion and as regards working conditions, including pay;

Whereas, with regard to pay, the Council adopted on 10 February 1975 Directive 75/117/EEC on the approximation of the laws of the Member States relating to the application of the principle of equal pay for men and women;

Whereas Community action to achieve the principle of equal treatment for men and women in respect of access to employment and vocational training and promotion and in respect of other working conditions also appears to be necessary; whereas, equal treatment for male and female workers constitutes one of the objectives of the Community, in so far as the harmonization of living and working conditions while maintaining their improvement are *inter alia* to be furthered; whereas the Treaty does not confer the necessary specific powers for this purpose;

Whereas the definition and progressive implementation of the principle of equal treatment in matters of social security should be ensured by means of subsequent instruments

HAS ADOPTED THIS DIRECTIVE: [2109]

Article 1

1 The purpose of this Directive is to put into effect in the Member States the principle of equal treatment for men and women as regards access to employment, including promotion, and to vocational training and as regards working conditions and, on the conditions referred to in paragraph 2, social security. This principle is hereinafter referred to as "the principle of equal treatment".

2 With a view to ensuring the progressive implementation of the principle of equal treatment in matters of social security, the Council, acting on a proposal from the Commission, will adopt provisions defining its substance, its scope and the arrangements for its application.   **[2110]**

Article 2

1 For the purposes of the following provisions, the principle of equal treatment shall mean that there shall be no discrimination whatsoever on grounds of sex either directly or indirectly by reference in particular to marital or family status.

2 This Directive shall be without prejudice to the right of Member States to exclude from its field of application those occupational activities and, where appropriate, the training leading thereto, for which, by reason of their nature of the context in which they are carried out, the sex of the worker constitutes a determining factor.

3 This Directive shall be without prejudice to provisions concerning the protection of women, particularly as regards pregnancy and maternity.

4 This Directive shall be without prejudice to measures to promote equal opportunity for men and women, in particular by removing existing inequalities which affect women's opportunities in the areas referred to in Article 1(1).   **[2111]**

Article 3

1 Application of the principle of equal treatment means that there shall be no discrimination whatsoever on grounds of sex in the conditions, including selection criteria, for access to all jobs or posts, whatever the sector or branch of activity, and to all levels of the occupational hierarchy.

2 To this end, Member States shall take the measures necessary to ensure that:

  (a) any laws, regulations and administrative provisions contrary to the principle of equal treatment shall be abolished;

  (b) any provisions contrary to the principle of equal treatment which are included in collective agreements, individual contracts of employment, internal rules of undertakings, or in rules governing the independent occupations and professions shall be, or may be declared, null and void or may be amended:

  (c) those laws, regulations and administrative provisions contrary to the principle of equal treatment when the concern for protection which originally inspired them is no longer well founded shall be revised; and that where similar provisions are included in collective agreements labour and management shall be requested to undertake the desired revision.   **[2112]**

Article 4

Application of the principle of equal treatment with regard to access to all types and to all levels, of vocational guidance, vocational training, advanced vocational training and retraining, means that Member States shall take all necessary measures to ensure that:

  (a) any laws, regulations and administrative provisions contrary to the principle of equal treatment shall be abolished;

(b) any provisions contrary to the principle of equal treatment which are included in collective agreements, individual contracts of employment, internal rules of undertakings or in rules governing the independent occupations and professions shall be, or may be declared, null and void or may be amended;

(c) without prejudice to the freedom granted in certain Member States to certain private training establishments, vocational guidance, vocational training, advanced vocational training and retraining shall be accessible on the basis of the same criteria and at the same levels without any discrimination on grounds of sex. **[2113]**

Article 5

1 Application of the principle of equal treatment with regard to working conditions, including the conditions governing dismissal, means that men and women shall be guaranteed the same conditions without discrimination on grounds of sex.

2 To this end, Member States shall take the measures necessary to ensure that:

(a) any laws, regulations and administrative provisions contrary to the principle of equal treatment shall be abolished;

(b) any provisions contrary to the principle of equal treatment which are included in collective agreements, individual contracts of employment, internal rules of undertakings or in rules governing the independents occupations and professions shall be, or may be declared, null and void or may be amended;

(c) those laws, regulations and administrative provisions contrary to the principle of equal treatment when the concern for protection which originally inspired them is no longer well founded shall be revised; and that where similar provisions are included in collective agreements labour and management shall be requested to undertake the desired revision.

[2114]

Article 6

Member States shall introduce into their national legal systems such measures as are necessary to enable all persons who consider themselves wronged by failure to apply to them the principle of equal treatment within the meaning of Articles 3, 4 and 5 to pursue their claims by judicial process after possible recourse to other competent authorities. **[2115]**

Article 7

Member States shall take the necessary measures to protect employees against dismissal by the employer as a reaction to a complaint within the undertaking or to any legal proceedings aimed at enforcing compliance with the principle of equal treatment. **[2116]**

Article 8

Member States shall take care that the provisions adopted pursuant to this Directive, together with the relevant provisions already in force, are brought to the attention of employees by all appropriate means, for example at their place of employment.**[2117]**

Article 9

1 Member States shall put into force the laws, regulations and administrative provisions necessary in order to comply with this Directive within 30 months of its notification and shall immediately inform the Commission thereof.

However, as regards the first part of Article 3(2)(c) and the first part of Article 5(2)(c), Member States shall carry out a first examination and if necessary a first revision of the laws, regulations and administrative provisions referred to therein within four years of notification of this Directive.

2 Member States shall periodically assess the occupational activities referred to in Article 2(2) in order to decide, in the light of social developments, whether there is justification for maintaining the exclusions concerned. They shall notify the Commission of the results of this assessment.

3 Member States shall also communicate to the Commission the texts of laws, regulations and administrative provisions which they adopt in the field covered by this Directive.   **[2118]**

Article 10
Within two years following expiry of the 30-month period laid down in the first subparagraph of Article 9(1), Member States shall forward all necessary information to the Commission to enable it to draw up a report on the application of this Directive for submission to the Council.   **[2119]**

Article 11
This Directive is addressed to the Member States.   **[2120]**

DIRECTIVE No 77/187 OF THE COUNCIL
of 14 February 1977
on the approximation of the laws of the Member States relating to the safeguarding of employees' rights in the event of transfers of undertakings, businesses or parts of businesses

THE COUNCIL OF THE EUROPEAN COMMUNITIES,

Having regard to the Treaty establishing the European Economic Community, and in particular Article 100 thereof;

Having regard to the proposal from the Commission;

Having regard to the opinion of the European Parliament;

Having regard to the opinion of the Economic and Social Committee;

Whereas economic trends are bringing in their wake at both national and Community level, changes in the structure of undertakings, through transfers of undertakings, businesses or parts of businesses to other employers as a result of legal transfers or mergers;

Whereas it is necessary to provide for the protection of employees in the event of a change of employer, in particular, to ensure that their rights are safeguarded;

Whereas differences still remain in the Member States as regards the extent of the protection of employees in this respect and these differences should be reduced;

Whereas these differences can have a direct effect on the functioning of the common market;

Whereas it is therefore necessary to promote the approximation of laws in this field while maintaining the improvement described in Article 117 of the Treaty.

HAS ADOPTED THIS DIRECTIVE: **[2121]**

SECTION I—SCOPE AND DEFINITIONS

Article 1
1 This Directive shall apply to the transfer of an undertaking, business or part of a business to another employer as a result of a legal transfer or merger.

2 This Directive shall apply where and in so far as the undertaking, business or part of the business to be transferred is situated within the territorial scope of the Treaty.

3 This Directive shall not apply to sea-going vessels. **[2122]**

Article 2

For the purposes of this Directive:

    (a) "transferor" means any natural or legal person who, by reason of a transfer within the meaning of Article 1(1), ceases to be the employer in respect of the undertaking, business or part of the business;

    (b) "transferee" means any natural or legal person who, by reason of a transfer within the meaning of Article 1(1), becomes the employer in respect of the undertaking, business or part of the business;

    (c) "representatives of the employees" means the representatives of the employees provided for by the laws or practice of the Member States, with the exception of members of administrative, governing or supervisory bodies of companies who represent employees on such bodies in certain Member States. **[2123]**

SECTION II—SAFEGUARDS OF EMPLOYEES' RIGHTS

Article 3

1 The transferor's rights and obligations arising from a contract of employment or from an employment relationship existing on the date of a transfer within the meaning of Article 1(1) shall, by reason of such transfer, be transferred to the transferee.

Member States may provide that, after the date of transfer within the meaning of Article 1(1) and in addition to the transferee, the transferor shall continue to be liable in respect of obligations which arose from a contract of employment or an employment relationship.

2 Following the transfer within the meaning of Article 1(1), the transferee shall continue to observe the terms and conditions agreed in any collective agreement on the same terms applicable to the transferor under that agreement, until the date of termination or expiry of the collective agreement or the entry into force or application of another collective agreement.

Member States may limit the period for observing such terms and conditions, with the proviso that it shall not be less than one year.

3 Paragraphs 1 and 2 shall not cover employees' rights to old-age, invalidity or survivors' benefits under supplementary company or inter company pension schemes outside the statutory social security schemes in Member States.

Member States shall adopt the measures necessary to protect the interests of employees and of persons no longer employed in the transferor's business at the time of the transfer within the meaning of Article 1(1) in respect of rights conferring on them immediate or prospective entitlement to old-age benefits, including survivors' benefits, under supplementary schemes referred to in the first subparagraph. **[2124]**

Article 4

1 The transfer of an undertaking, business or part of a business shall not in itself constitute grounds for dismissal by the transferor or the transferee. This provision shall not stand in the way of dismissals that may take place for economic, technical or organizational reasons entailing changes in the work force.

Member States may provide that the first subparagraph shall not apply to certain specific categories of employees who are not covered by the laws or practice of the Member States in respect of protection against dismissal.

2 If the contract of employment or the employment relationship is terminated because the transfer within the meaning of Article 1(1) involves a substantial change in working conditions to the detriment of the employee, the employer shall be regarded as having been responsible for termination of the contract of employment or of the employment relationship.   **[2125]**

Article 5

1 If the business preserves its autonomy, the status and function, as laid down by the laws, regulations or administrative provisions of the Member States, of the representatives or of the representation of the employees affected by the transfer within the meaning of Article 1(1) shall be preserved.

The first subparagraph shall not apply if, under the laws, regulations, administrative provisions or practice of the Member States, the conditions necessary for the reappointment of the representatives of the employees or for the reconstruction of the representation of the employees are fulfilled.

2 If the term of office of the representatives of the employees affected by a transfer within the meaning of Article 1(1) expires as a result of the transfer, the representatives shall continue to enjoy the protection provided by the laws, regulations, administrative provisions or practice of the Member States.   **[2126]**

SECTION III—INFORMATION AND CONSULTATION

Article 6

1 The transferor and the transferee shall be required to inform the representatives of their respective employees affected by a transfer within the meaning of Article 1(1) of the following:

    —the reasons for the transfer,
    —the legal, economic and social implications of the transfer for the employees,
    —measures envisaged in relation to the employees.

The transferor must give such information to the representatives of his employees in good time before the transfer is carried out.

The transferee must give such information to the representatives of his employees in good time, and in any event before his employees are directly affected by the transfer as regards their conditions of work and employment.

2 If the transferor or the transferee envisages measures in relation to his employees, he shall consult his representatives of the employees in good time on such measures with a view to seeking agreement.

3 Member States whose laws, regulations or administrative provisions provide that representatives of the employees may have recourse to an arbitration board to obtain a decision on the measures to be taken in relation to employees may limit the obligations laid down in paragraphs 1 and 2 to cases where the transfer carried out gives rise to a change in the business likely to entail serious disadvantages for a considerable number of the employees.

The information and consultations shall cover at least the measures envisaged in relation to the employees.

The information must be provided and consultations take place in good time before the change in the business as referred to in the first subparagraph is effected.

4 Member States may limit the obligations laid down in paragraphs 1, 2 and 3 to undertakings or businesses which, in respect of the number of employees, fulfil the conditions for the election or designation of a collegiate body representing the employees.

5 Member States may provide that where there are no representatives of the employees in an undertaking or business, the employees concerned must be informed in advance when a transfer within the meaning of Article 1(1) is about to take place.

[2127]

SECTION IV—FINAL PROVISIONS

Article 7

This Directive shall not affect the right of Member States to apply or introduce laws, regulations or administrative provisions which are more favourable to employees.

[2128]

Article 8

1 Member States shall bring into force the laws, regulations and administrative provisions needed to comply with this Directive within two years of its notification and shall forthwith inform the Commission thereof.

2 Member States shall communicate to the Commission the texts of the laws, regulations and administrative provisions which they adopt in the field covered by this Directive. **[2129]**

Article 9

Within two years following expiry of the two-year period laid down in Article 8, Member States shall forward all relevant information to the Commission in order to enable it to draw up a report on the application of this Directive for submission to the Council. **[2130]**

Article 10

This Directive is addressed to the Member States. **[2131]**

NOTES

For the domestic implementation of this Directive, see the Transfer of Undertakings (Protection of Employment) Regulations 1981, SI 1981/1794, paras **[1137]–[1149]**.

DIRECTIVE No 79/7 OF THE COUNCIL
of 19 December 1978

on the progressive implementation of the principle of equal treatment for men and women in matters of social security

THE COUNCIL OF THE EUROPEAN COMMUNITIES,

Having regard to the Treaty establishing the European Economic Community, and in particular Article 235 thereof;

Having regard to the proposal from the Commission;

Having regard to the opinion of the European Parliament;

Having regard to the opinion of the Economic and Social Committee;

Whereas Article 1(2) of Council Directive 76/207/EEC of 9 February 1976 on the implementation of the principle of equal treatment for men and women as regards access to employment, vocational training and promotion, and working conditions provides that, with a view to ensuring the progressive implementation of the principle of equal treatment in matters of social security, the Council, acting on a proposal from the Commission, will adopt provisions defining its substance, its scope and the arrangements for its application; whereas the Treaty does not confer the specific powers required for this purpose;

Whereas the principle of equal treatment in matters of social security should be implemented in the first place in the statutory schemes which provide protection against the risks of sickness, invalidity, old age, accidents at work, occupational diseases and unemployment, and in social assistance in so far as it is intended to supplement or replace the abovementioned schemes;

Whereas the implementation of the principle of equal treatment in matters of social security does not prejudice the provisions relating to the protection of women on the ground of maternity; whereas, in this respect, Member States may adopt specific provisions for women to remove existing instances of unequal treatment,

HAS ADOPTED THIS DIRECTIVE: [2132]

Article 1

The purpose of this Directive is the progressive implementation, in the field of social security and other elements of social protection provided for in Article 3, of the principle of equal treatment for men and women in matters of social security, hereinafter referred to as 'the principle of equal treatment'. [2133]

Article 2

This Directive shall apply to the working population—including self-employed persons, workers and self-employed persons whose activity is interrupted by illness, accident or involuntary unemployment and persons seeking employment—and to retired or invalided workers and self-employed persons. [2134]

Article 3

1 This Directive shall apply to:

    (a) statutory schemes which provide protection against the following risks:
        —sickness,
        —invalidity,
        —old age,
        —accidents at work and occupational diseases,
        —unemployment;
    (b) social assistance, in so far as it is intended to supplement or replace the schemes referred to in (a).

2 This Directive shall not apply to the provisions concerning survivors' benefits nor to those concerning family benefits, except in the case of family benefits granted by way of increases of benefits due in respect of the risks referred to in paragraph 1(a).

3 With a view to ensuring implementation of the principle of equal treatment in occupational schemes, the Council, acting on a proposal from the Commission, will adopt provisions defining its substance, its scope and the arrangements for its application. [2135]

Article 4

1 The principle of equal treatment means that there shall be no discrimination whatsoever on ground of sex either directly, or indirectly by reference in particular to marital or family status, in particular as concerns:

—the scope of the schemes and the conditions of access thereto,
—the obligation to contribute and the calculation of contributions,
—the calculation of benefits including increases due in respect of a spouse and for dependants and the conditions governing the duration and retention of entitlement to benefits.

2 The principle of equal treatment shall be without prejudice to the provisions relating to the protection of women on the grounds of maternity. **[2136]**

Article 5

Member States shall take the measures necessary to ensure that any laws, regulations and administrative provisions contrary to the principle of equal treatment are abolished. **[2137]**

Article 6

Member States shall introduce into their national legal systems such measures as are necessary to enable all persons who consider themselves wronged by failure to apply the principle of equal treatment to pursue their claims by judicial process, possibly after recourse to other competent authorities. **[2138]**

Article 7

1 This Directive shall be without prejudice to the right of Member States to exclude from its scope:

(a) the determination of pensionable age for the purposes of granting old-age and retirement pensions and the possible consequences thereof for other benefits;

(b) advantages in respect of old-age pension schemes granted to persons who have brought up children; the acquisition of benefit entitlements following periods of interruption of employment due to the bringing up of children;

(c) the granting of old-age or invalidity benefit entitlements by virtue of the derived entitlements of a wife;

(d) the granting of increases of long-term invalidity, old-age, accidents at work and occupational disease benefits for a dependent wife;

(e) the consequences of the exercise, before the adoption of this Directive, of a right of option not to acquire rights to incur obligations under a statutory scheme.

2 Member States shall periodically examine matters excluded under paragraph 1 in order to ascertain, in the light of social developments in the matter concerned, whether there is justification for maintaining the exclusions concerned. **[2139]**

Article 8

1 Member States shall bring into force the laws, regulations and administrative provisions necessary to comply with this Directive within six years of its notification. They shall immediately inform the Commission thereof.

2 Member States shall communicate to the Commission the text of laws, regulations and administrative provisions which they adopt in the field covered by this Directive, including measures adopted pursuant to Article 7(2).

They shall inform the Commission of their reasons for maintaining any existing provisions on the matters referred to in Article 7(1) and of the possibilities for reviewing them at a later date. **[2140]**

Article 9

Within seven years of notification of this Directive, Member States shall forward all information necessary to the Commission to enable it to draw up a report on the application of this Directive for submission to the Council and to propose such further measures as may be required for the implementation of the principle of equal treatment.   **[2141]**

Article 10

This Directive is addressed to the Member States.   **[2142]**

DIRECTIVE No 80/987 OF THE COUNCIL
of 20 October 1980

on the approximation of the laws of the Member States relating to the protection of employees in the event of the insolvency of their employer

THE COUNCIL OF THE EUROPEAN COMMUNITIES,

Having regard to the Treaty establishing the European Economic Community, and in particular Article 100 thereof,

Having regard to the proposal from the Commission,

Having regard to the opinion of the European Parliament,

Having regard to the opinion of the Economic and Social Committee,

Whereas it is necessary to provide for the protection of employees in the event of the insolvency of their employer, in particular in order to guarantee payment of their outstanding claims, while taking account of the need for balanced economic and social development in the Community;

Whereas differences still remain between the Member States as regards the extent of the protection of employees in this respect; whereas efforts would be directed towards reducing these differences, which can have a direct effect on the functioning of the common market;

Whereas the approximation of laws in this field should, therefore, be promoted while the improvement within the meaning of Article 117 of the Treaty is maintained;

Whereas as a result of the geographical situation and the present job structures in that area, the labour market in Greenland is fundamentally different from that of the other areas of the Community;

Whereas to the extent that the Hellenic Republic is to become a member of the European Economic Community on 1 January 1981 in accordance with the Act concerning the Conditions of Accession of the Hellenic Republic and the Adjustments to the Treaties, it is appropriate to stipulate in the Annex to the Directive under the heading "Greece", those categories of employees whose claims may be excluded in accordance with Article 1(2) of the Directive,

HAS ADOPTED THIS DIRECTIVE: **[2143]**

SECTION I—SCOPE AND DEFINITIONS

Article 1

1 This Directive shall apply to employees' claims arising from contracts of employment or employment relationships and existing against employers who are in a state of insolvency within the meaning of Article 2(1).

2 Member States may, by way of exception, exclude claims by certain categories of employee from the scope of this Directive, by virtue of the special nature of the employee's contract of employment or employment relationship or of the existence of other forms of guarantee offering the employee protection equivalent to that resulting from this Directive.

The categories of employee referred to in the first subparagraph are listed in the Annex.

3 This Directive shall not apply to Greenland. This exception shall be re-examined in the event of any development in the job structures in that region.

[2144]

Article 2

1 For the purposes of this Directive, an employer shall be deemed to be in a state of insolvency:

(a) where a request has been made for the opening of proceedings involving the employer's assets, as provided for under the laws, regulations and administrative provisions of the Member State concerned, to satisfy collectively the claims of creditors and which make it possible to take into consideration the claims referred to in Article 1(1), and

(b) where the authority which is competent pursuant to the said laws, regulations and administrative provisions has:

—either decided to open the proceedings,

—or established that the employer's undertaking or business has been definitively closed down and that the available assets are insufficient to warrant the opening of the proceedings.

2 This Directive is without prejudice to national law as regards the definition of the terms "employee", "employer", "pay", "right conferring immediate entitlement" and "right conferring prospective entitlement". **[2145]**

SECTION II—PROVISIONS CONCERNING GUARANTEE INSTITUTIONS

Article 3

1 Member States shall take the measures necessary to ensure that guarantee institutions guarantee, subject to Article 4, payment of employees' outstanding claims resulting from contracts of employment or employment relationships and relating to pay for the period prior to a given date.

2 At the choice of the Member States, the date referred to in paragraph 1 shall be:

—either that of the onset of the employer's insolvency;

—or that of the notice of dismissal issued to the employee concerned on account of the employer's insolvency;

—or that of the onset of the employer's insolvency or that on which the contract of employment or the employment relationship with the employee concerned was discontinued on account of the employer's insolvency. **[2146]**

Article 4

1 Member States shall have the option to limit the liability of guarantee institutions, referred to in Article 3.

2 When Member States exercise the option referred to in paragraph 1, they shall:

—in the case referred to in Article 3(2), first indent, ensure the payment of outstanding claims relating to pay for the last three months of the contract of employment or employment relationship occurring within a period of six months preceding the date of the onset of the employer's insolvency;

—in the case referred to in Article 3(2), second indent, ensure the payment of outstanding claims relating to pay for the last three months of the contract of employment or employment relationship preceding the date of the notice of dismissal issued to the employee on account of the employer's insolvency;

—in the case referred to in Article 3(2), third indent, ensure the payment of outstanding claims relating to pay for the last 18 months of the contract of employment or employment relationship preceding the date of the onset of the employer's insolvency or the date on which the contract of employment or the employment relationship with the employee was discontinued on account of the employer's insolvency. In this case, Member States may limit the liability to make payment to pay corresponding to a period of eight weeks or to several shorter periods totalling eight weeks.

3 However, in order to avoid the payment of sums going beyond the social objective of this Directive, Member States may set a ceiling to the liability for employees' outstanding claims.

When Member States exercise this option, they shall inform the Commission of the methods used to set the ceiling.   **[2147]**

Article 5
Member States shall lay down detailed rules for the organization, financing and operation of the guarantee institutions, complying with the following principles in particular:

  (a) the assets of the institutions shall be independent of the employers' operating capital and be inaccessible to proceedings for insolvency;

  (b) employers shall contribute to financing, unless it is fully covered by the public authorities;

  (c) the institutions' liabilities shall not depend on whether or not obligations to contribute to financing have been fulfilled.   **[2148]**

SECTION III—PROVISIONS CONCERNING SOCIAL SECURITY

Article 6
Member States may stipulate that Articles 3, 4 and 5 shall not apply to contributions due under national statutory social security schemes or under supplementary company or inter-company pension schemes outside the national statutory social security schemes.   **[2149]**

Article 7
Member States shall take the measures necessary to ensure that non-payment of compulsory contributions due from the employer, before the onset of his insolvency, to their insurance institutions under national statutory social security schemes does not adversely affect employees' benefit entitlement in respect of these insurance institutions inasmuch as the employees' contributions were deducted at source from the remuneration paid.   **[2150]**

Article 8
Member States shall ensure that the necessary measures are taken to protect the interests of employees and of persons having already left the employer's undertaking or business at the date of the onset of the employer's insolvency in respect of rights

conferring on them immediate or prospective entitlement to old-age benefits, including survivors' benefits, under supplementary company or inter-company pension schemes outside the national statutory social security schemes.   **[2151]**

SECTION IV—GENERAL AND FINAL PROVISIONS

Article 9

This Directive shall not affect the option of Member States to apply or introduce laws, regulations or administrative provisions which are more favourable to employees.

[2152]

Article 10

This Directive shall not affect the option of Member States:

(a) to take the measures necessary to avoid abuses;
(b) to refuse or reduce the liability referred to in Article 3 or the guarantee obligation referred to in Article 7 if it appears that fulfilment of the obligation is unjustifiable because of the existence of special links between the employee and the employer and of common interests resulting in collusion between them.   **[2153]**

Article 11

1 Member States shall bring into force the laws, regulations and administrative provisions necessary to comply with this Directive within 36 months of its notification. They shall forthwith inform the Commission thereof.

2 Member States shall communicate to the Commission the texts of the laws, regulations and administrative provisions which they adopt in the field governed by this Directive.

[2154]

Article 12

Within 18 months of the expiry of the period of 36 months laid down in Article 11(1), Member States shall forward all relevant information to the Commission in order to enable it to draw up a report on the application of this Directive for submission to the Council.

[2155]

Article 13

This Directive is addressed to the Member States.   **[2156]**

ANNEX

Categories of employee whose claims may be excluded from the scope of this Directive, in accordance with Article 1(2)

I Employees having a contract of employment, or an employment relationship, of a special nature

A GREECE

The master and the members of a crew of a fishing vessel, if and to the extent that they are remunerated by a share in the profits or gross earnings of the vessel.

B   IRELAND

    1   Out-workers (ie persons doing piece-work in their own homes), unless they have a written contract of employment.

    2   Close relatives of the employer, without a written contract of employment, whose work has to do with a private dwelling or farm in, or on, which the employer and the close relatives reside.

    3   Persons who normally work for less than 18 hours a week for one or more employers and who do not derive their basic means of subsistence from the pay for this work.

    4   Persons engaged in share fishing on a seasonal, casual or part-time basis.

    5   The spouse of the employer.

C   NETHERLANDS

Domestic servants employed by a natural person and working less than three days a week for the natural person in question.

D   UNITED KINGDOM

    1   The master and the members of the crew of a fishing vessel who are remunerated by a share in the profits or gross earnings of the vessel.

    2   The spouse of the employer.

II Employees covered by other forms of guarantee

A   GREECE

The crews of sea-going vessels.

B   IRELAND

    1   Permanent and pensionable employees of local or other public authorities or statutory transport undertakings.

    2   Pensionable teachers employed in the following: national schools, secondary schools, comprehensive schools, teachers' training colleges.

    3   Permanent and pensionable employees of one of the voluntary hospitals funded by the Exchequer.

C   ITALY

    1   Employees covered by benefits laid down by law guaranteeing that their wages will continue to be paid in the event that the undertaking is hit by an economic crisis.

    2   The crews of sea-going vessels.

D   UNITED KINGDOM

    1   Registered dock workers other than those wholly or mainly engaged in work which is not dock work.

    2   The crews of sea-going vessels.   **[2157]**

DIRECTIVE No 86/378 OF THE COUNCIL
of 24 July 1986

on the implementation of the principle of equal treatment for men and women in occupational social security schemes

THE COUNCIL OF THE EUROPEAN COMMUNITIES,

Having regard to the Treaty establishing the European Economic Community, and in particular Articles 100 and 235 thereof,

Having regard to the proposal from the Commission,

Having regard to the opinion of the European Parliament,

Having regard to the opinion of the Economic and Social Committee,

Whereas the Treaty provides that each Member State shall ensure the application of the principle that men and women should receive equal pay for equal work; whereas "pay" should be taken to mean the ordinary basic or minimum wage or salary and any other consideration, whether in cash or in kind, which the worker receives, directly or indirectly, from his employer in respect of his employment;

Whereas, although the principle of equal pay does indeed apply directly in cases where discrimination can be determined solely on the basis of the criteria of equal treatment and equal pay, there are also situations in which implementation of this principle implies the adoption of additional measures which more clearly define its scope;

Whereas Article 1(2) of Council Directive 76/207/EEC of 9 February 1976 on the implementation of the principle of equal treatment for men and women as regards access to employment, vocational training and promotion, and working conditions provides that, with a view to ensuring the progressive implementation of the principle of equal treatment in matters of social security, the Council, acting on a proposal from the Commission, will adopt provisions defining its substance, its scope and the arrangements for its application; whereas the Council adopted to this end Directive 79/7/EEC of 19 December 1978 on the progressive implementation of the principle of equal treatment for men and women in matters of social security;

Whereas Article 3(3) of Directive 79/7/EEC provides that, with a view to ensuring implementation of the principle of equal treatment in occupational schemes, the Council, acting on a proposal from the Commission, will adopt provisions defining its substance, its scope and the arrangements for its application;

Whereas the principle of equal treatment should be implemented in occupational social security schemes which provide protection against the risks specified in Article 3(1) of Directive 79/7/EEC as well as those which provide employees with any other consideration in cash or in kind within the meaning of the Treaty;

Whereas implementation of the principle of equal treatment does not prejudice the provisions relating to the protection of women by reason of maternity,

HAS ADOPTED THIS DIRECTIVE: [2158]

Article 1

The object of this Directive is to implement, in occupational social security schemes, the principle of equal treatment for men and women, hereinafter referred to as "the principle of equal treatment".   [2159]

Article 2

1 "Occupational social security schemes" means schemes not governed by Directive 79/7/EEC whose purpose is to provide workers, whether employees or self-employed, in an undertaking or group of undertakings, area of economic activity or occupational sector or group of such sectors with benefits intended to supplement the benefits provided by statutory social security schemes or to replace them, whether membership of such schemes is compulsory or optional.

2 This Directive does not apply to:

(a) individual contracts,

(b) schemes having only one member,

(c) in the case of salaried workers, insurance schemes offered to participants individually to guarantee them:

—either additional benefits, or
—a choice of date on which the normal benefits will start, or a choice between several benefits.   **[2160]**

Article 3

This Directive shall apply to members of the working population including self-employed persons, persons whose activity is interrupted by illness, maternity, accident or involuntary unemployment and persons seeking employment, and to retired and disabled workers.   **[2161]**

Article 4

This Directive shall apply to:
(a) occupational schemes which provide protection against the following risks:
—sickness,
—invalidity,
—old age, including early retirement,
—industrial accidents and occupational diseases,
—unemployment;
(b) occupational schemes which provide for other social benefits, in cash or in kind, and in particular survivors' benefits and family allowances, if such benefits are accorded to employed persons and thus constitute a consideration paid by the employer to the worker by reason of the latter's employment.   **[2162]**

Article 5

1 Under the conditions laid down in the following provisions, the principle of equal treatment implies that there shall be no discrimination on the basis of sex, either directly or indirectly, by reference in particular to marital or family status, especially as regards:

—the scope of the schemes and the conditions of access to them;
—the obligation to contribute and the calculation of contributions;
—the calculation of benefits, including supplementary benefits due in respect of a spouse or dependants, and the conditions governing the duration and retention of entitlement to benefits.

2 The principle of equal treatment shall not prejudice the provisions relating to the protection of women by reason of maternity.   **[2163]**

Article 6

1 Provisions contrary to the principle of equal treatment shall include those based on sex, either directly or indirectly, in particular by reference to marital or family status for:
(a) determining the persons who may participate in an occupational scheme;
(b) fixing the compulsory or optional nature of participation in an occupational scheme;
(c) laying down different rules as regards the age of entry into the scheme or the minimum period of employment or membership of the scheme required to obtain the benefits thereof;
(d) laying down different rules, except as provided for in subparagraphs (h)

and (i), for the reimbursement of contributions where a worker leaves a scheme without having fulfilled the conditions guaranteeing him a deferred right to obtain long-term benefits;

(e) setting different conditions for the granting of benefits or restricting such benefits to workers of one or other of the sexes;

(f) fixing different retirement ages;

(g) suspending the retention or acquisition of rights during periods of maternity leave or leave for family reasons which are granted by law or agreement and are paid by the employer;

(h) setting different levels of benefit, except insofar as may be necessary to take account of actuarial calculation factors which differ according to sex in the case of benefits designated as contribution-defined;

(i) setting different levels of worker contribution; setting different levels of employer contribution in the case of benefits designated as contribution-defined, except with a view to making the amount of those benefits more nearly equal;

(j) laying down different standards or standards applicable only to workers of a specified sex, except as provided for in subparagraphs (h) and (i), as regards the guarantee or retention of entitlement to deferred benefits when a worker leaves a scheme.

2 Where the granting of benefits within the scope of this Directive is left to the discretion of the scheme's management bodies, the latter must take account of the principle of equal treatment.

[2164]

Article 7

Member States shall take all necessary steps to ensure that:

(a) provisions contrary to the principle of equal treatment in legally compulsory collective agreements, staff rules of undertakings or any other arrangements relating to occupational schemes are null and void, or may be declared null and void or amended;

(b) schemes containing such provisions may not be approved or extended by administrative measures.

[2165]

Article 8

1 Member States shall take all necessary steps to ensure that the provisions of occupational schemes contrary to the principle of equal treatment are revised by 1 January 1993.

2 This Directive shall not preclude rights and obligations relating to a period of membership of an occupational scheme prior to revision of that scheme from remaining subject to the provisions of the scheme in force during that period.

[2166]

Article 9

Member States may defer compulsory application of the principle of equal treatment with regard to:

(a) determination of pensionable age for the purposes of granting old-age or retirement pensions, and the possible implications for other benefits:
—either until the date on which such equality is achieved in statutory schemes,
—or, at the latest, until such equality is required by a directive.

(b) survivors' pensions until a directive requires the principle of equal treatment in statutory social security schemes in that regard;
(c) the application of the first subparagraph of Article 6(1)(i) to take account of the different actuarial calculation factors, at the latest until the expiry of a thirteen-year period as from the notification of this Directive. **[2167]**

Article 10

Member States shall introduce into their national legal systems such measures as are necessary to enable all persons who consider themselves injured by failure to apply the principle of equal treatment to pursue their claims before the courts, possibly after bringing the matters before other competent authorities. **[2168]**

Article 11

Member States shall take all the necessary steps to protect worker against dismissal where this constitutes a response on the part of the employer to a complaint made at undertaking level or to the institution of legal proceedings aimed at enforcing compliance with the principle of equal treatment. **[2169]**

Article 12

1 Member States shall bring into force such laws, regulations and administrative provisions as are necessary in order to comply with this Directive at the latest three years after notification thereof. They shall immediately inform the Commission thereof.

2 Member States shall communicate to the Commission at the latest five years after notification of this Directive all information necessary to enable the Commission to draw up a report on the application of this Directive for submission to the Council. **[2170]**

Article 13

This Directive is addressed to the Member States. **[2171]**

NOTES
For the prospective domestic implementation of this Directive see the Social Security Act 1989, s 23 and Sch 5, paras **[566]**, **[567]**. Although the deadline for implementation of the Directive was 1 January 1993, at the time of going to press the relevant parts of the 1989 Act have not been brought into effect.

COUNCIL RECOMMENDATION No 86/379

of 24 July 1986

on the employment of disabled people in the Community

THE COUNCIL OF THE EUROPEAN COMMUNITIES,
Having regard to the Treaty establishing the European Economic Community, and in particular Article 235 thereof;
Having regard to the draft recommendation submitted by the Commission;
Having regard to the opinion of the European Parliament;
Having regard to the opinion of the Economic and Social Committee;
Whereas the Council Resolution of 21 January 1974 concerning a social action programme provides for, *inter alia,* the implementation of a programme for the vocational and social integration of handicapped persons;
Whereas the Council Resolution of 27 June 1974 established the initial Community action programme for the vocational rehabilitation of handicapped persons;

Whereas the Resolution of the Council and of the Representatives of the Governments of the Member States, meeting within the Council, of 21 December 1981 on the social integration of handicapped people invites Member States to ensure that handicapped people do not shoulder an unfair burden of the effects, in particular from the point of view of employment, of economic difficulties and to promote measures to prepare handicapped people for an active life, but does not provide for a concerted or concentrated Community effort in this regard;

Whereas, for the purpose of this Recommendation, 'disabled people' includes all people with serious disabilities which result from physical, mental or psychological impairments;

Whereas disabled people have the same right as all other workers to equal opportunity in training and employment;

Whereas, in a period of economic crisis, action at European and Community levels should be not only continued but also intensified in order to promote the achievement of equal opportunity by means of positive and coherent policies;

Whereas these policies should take account of the aspirations of disabled people for a fully active and independent life;

Whereas the European Parliament, in its resolution of 11 March 1981, stressed the need to promote at Community level the economic, social and vocational integration of disabled people;

Whereas the provisions of fair opportunities for disabled people in the field of employment and vocational training appears necessary for the achievement of one of the objectives of the Community; whereas the Treaty has not provided for the powers of action required for the adoption of this Recommendation, other than those of Article 235, **[2172]**

I HEREBY RECOMMENDS MEMBER STATES:

1 To take all appropriate measures to promote fair opportunities for disabled people in the field of employment and vocational training, including initial training and employment as well as rehabilitation and resettlement.

The principle of fair opportunity for disabled people should be applied in respect of:

> (a) access to employment and vocational training, whether normal or special, including guidance, placement and follow-up services;
> (b) retention in that employment or vocational training and protection from unfair dismissal;
> (c) opportunities for promotion and in-service training.

2 To this end, to continue and, if necessary, intensify and re-examine their policies to help disabled people, where appropriate after consulting disabled people's organizations and both sides of industry; such policies should take account of measures and specific activities implemented in the other Member States which have proved effective and worthwhile.

These policies should provide in particular for:

> (a) *Elimination of negative discrimination by:*
> > (i) reviewing laws, regulations and administrative provisions to ensure that they are not contrary to the principle of fair opportunity for disabled people;
> > (ii) taking appropriate measures to avoid as far as possible dismissals linked to a disability;
> > (iii) limiting exceptions to the principle of equal treatment in access to training or employment to the cases justified on the ground of a specific incompatibility between a particular activity forming part of a job or course of training and a particular disability; if necessary, it should be possible to have this incompatibility confirmed by a medical certificate; any such exception should be reviewed periodically in order to establish whether it continues to be justified;

(iv) seeking to ensure that any tests required for access to vocational training courses and any tests required during or at the end of such courses are designed in such a way that candidates with disabilities are not thereby disadvantaged;

(v) seeking to ensure that disabled people can go before the competent bodies to establish their rights and can receive the necessary assistance to do so in accordance with national law and practice.

(b) *Positive action for disabled people, including:*

(i) bearing in mind differences in sectors and enterprises, the fixing by Member States, where appropriate and after consultation of disabled people's organizations and both sides of industry, of realistic percentage targets for the employment of disabled people in public or private enterprises having a minimum number of employees; such a minimum might be set at between 15 and 50. Measures should also be adopted for making these targets public and achieving them;

(ii) the making available, in each Member State, of a guide or code of good practice for the employment of disabled people, incorporating positive measures already adopted in the Member State concerned and corresponding in spirit with the provisions of this Recommendation; the Annex comprises a guideline framework for such a guide or code, setting out examples of positive action;

the guide or code of good practice should be circulated as widely as possible and refer to the public and private sectors;

it should describe clearly the contribution which the recipients of the guide or code can and should make in putting into practice the national policy on disabled people; it should include information and advice on the support that is available from public services;

(iii) provision whereby the Member States encourage the public and private enterprises to take all appropriate measures for the employment of disabled people which correspond in spirit with the guide or code of good practice; Member States should establish the means for making these policies, and the annual progress made in their implementation, known to the public, according to existing procedures for disseminating information in the social field;

(iv) provision whereby the employer and the rehabilitation services cooperate in the resettlement, with the same enterprise as far as possible, of any employee who becomes disabled.

3 To report to the Commission on the measures they have taken to implement this Recommendation with a view to enabling the Commission to present the report referred to in II.3.   **[2173]**

II INVITES THE COMMISSION:

1 To co-ordinate the exchange of information and experience on the rehabilitation and employment of disabled people between national authorities; agencies designated for the purpose by the Member States will also be involved in this exchange.

2 To maintain appropriate aid from the European Social Fund to assist disabled people of whatever age.

3 To report to the Council on the application of this Recommendation within two years of its adoption.   **[2173A]**

ANNEX

Guideline framework for positive action to promote the employment and vocational training of disabled people

Set out below are a number of possible measures, proposed by the Commission, which Member States should consider in implementing this Recommendation and in particular in drawing up a guide or code of good practice. **[2174]**

SECTION I

ASPECTS CONCERNING THE WORKING LIFE OF DISABLED PEOPLE

1 Job creation

(a) *Concerted projects*

Ensuring that disabled people are given a full and fair opportunity to benefit from projects such as regional development programmes, local employment initiatives and action to promote the setting-up of cooperatives or of small or medium-sized enterprises.

(b) *New technology*

Stimulating new employment opportunities by means of national initiatives both in the new technology sector itself and in the use of new technologies as aids to make employment possible in other fields.

In this connection, promoting projects to enable disabled people to take on tele-work.

Studying the specific risks to employment resulting from new technological developments and taking appropriate action.

Adapting work stations to the needs of disabled people.

(c) *Other activities*

Promoting and supporting projects which train and prepare disabled people to create their own business or which identify new employment opportunities in the media or in services on behalf of other disabled people.

Identifying other sectors (such as tertiary services, including tourism and catering, agriculture or horticulture and forestry) which have good prospects and are suitable for people with various disabilities.

Implementing schemes for creating new jobs for disabled people in these fields.

Drawing up special national policies for the re-employment of mentally handicapped workers who lose their jobs because of changes in the character of the employment market.

Creating more opportunities for part-time employment for disabled workers. **[2175]**

2 Sheltered employment

(a) *General*

Reviewing the situation in each Member State in regard to sheltered employment and sheltered occupation and drawing up plans for the future of this sector.

(b) *Quantitative side*

Arranging that plans should assess future demand and the need to develop or reduce such provision.

(c) *Qualitative side*
Seeing that the review takes into consideration the following points:
—improving the quality of less successful workshops or centres so that they approximate to the best;
—introducing new forms of activity (for example, in the computer sector) which are both more interesting and likely to be more successful commercially;
—increasing the amount of training available in workshops;
—developing the transitional role of workshops, ie their function as assessment and personal development centres coming between basic education or a period of unemployment and entry to the open labour market;
—reducing segregation by developing sheltered posts or groups within normal enterprises, or mixed cooperatives.   **[2176]**

3 Transition, vocational rehabilitation and vocational training

Enabling disabled trainees to enrol in integrated training courses in normal establishments wherever possible and desirable.

Giving a high priority to improving the availability and quality of vocational preparation and training for disabled people, with particular regard to the following aims:
—giving equal consideration to the needs of workers who incur disability through accident or disease and to the needs of young people whose disability is congenital or was incurred in childhood or adolescence;
—adapting the content of the training courses available to match more realistically the needs of the labour market;
—strengthening direct links between training establishments and local representatives of both sides of industry;
—improving training methods, in particular by developing the use of new technologies as training aids and by introducing modular training and, where appropriate, distant learning facilities;
—encouraging experimentation in course structure and design so as to facilitate the coordination of theoretical and practical training;
—improving all aspects of access to training courses;
—encouraging disabled trainees to take, as far as possible, a more active part in planning their own training programmes;
—guaranteeing continuity of vocational training and preparation for employment by promoting inter-professional cooperation and creating multidisciplinary teams.   **[2177]**

4 Guidance, assessment and placement

(a) *Guidance*
Providing at regional level, as part of the general guidance services, educational and vocational guidance services with a clear responsibility to meet the needs of disabled people.
Providing, in the case of general, rather than specialized, guidance services, for staff to be trained to understand and deal with the special needs of people with disabilities.

(b) *Assessment*
Identifying effective assessment methods and introducing those methods as far as possible.
Giving priority to the principles that:

—the disabled person himself (and, where appropriate, his family) should participate actively in assessment;

—every client should be encouraged to opt for the best level of training and highest vocational goal of which he is capable.

(c) *Placement services*

Setting up at regional level, as part of the general placement services, placement services to help suitably trained disabled people to find a job.

Ensuring that these services also follow and support the disabled person in the job, at least for an initial period.

Implementing training programmes for disabled people's placement officers.   **[2178]**

5 Employers and workers' organizations

(a) *Incentives to employers*

Encouraging employers to make greater use of funds from public sources. Where appropriate, making such funds available, in accordance with national policies and situations, to cover, or contribute towards covering, the special costs to an employer of taking on a disabled worker.

The eligible expenditure should include adaptations to machinery or equipment, provision of access facilities and additional staff costs.

The grants should apply both when a worker is re-employed after incurring a disability and for new recruitments.

In the case of new recruitments, envisaging a contribution from public funds to the worker's salary over a given period of induction training.

(b) *Workers' organizations*

Encouraging trade unions to give any necessary support to disabled workers and to ensure that their interests are properly catered for in representative structures.   **[2179]**

6 Social security

Ensuring that disabled workers who lose their jobs or who cannot find employment after vocational rehabilitation do not find themselves thereafter, purely because of their disability, financially worse off than other workers in similar circumstances.

Ensuring that benefit systems do not act as disincentives to part-time employment, to trial periods of employment or to the gradual take-up of a job or return to it, whenever any of these patterns is desirable from the disabled worker's and employer's point of view.   **[2180]**

SECTION II

GENERAL ASPECTS

1 The supporting environment

Ensuring that disabled people live in an environment which makes it possible for them to benefit from further education and training and to make their full contribution to the economy.

Effectively implementing existing legislation and where necessary introducing new legislation to promote:

—suitable housing (wherever possible integrated in the open community),

—adequate transport to places of training and work,

—access to and within the workplace, especially in the office sector.

Ensuring that measures aimed at guaranteeing fair opportunities for the disabled are not regarded as discriminatory against the able-bodied.

Recognizing the need for flexibility in the conditions of employment of persons looking after a disabled person. [2181]

2 Information and advice

(a) *Assistance for disabled people*

Developing, for the benefit of disabled people, their families and the professionals (whether case-workers or administrators) concerned, a system of information and advice covering technical aids and other questions of importance to disabled people.

Extending the system, which could consist of specialized centres or of services developed in existing centres with wider functions, below the national level to regional and local levels over time as resources permit.

(b) *Information campaign*

Undertaking coordinated action to inform and advise politicians, both sides of industry and the general public of the capacities and the needs of disabled people. In particular, making audio-visual material on disability problems widely available through appropriate channels such as interest groups and training schemes run by both sides of industry. [2182]

3 Social research

Encouraging and coordinating social research—for which national data bases should be established—both in order to analyse needs and possibilities and to evaluate the effectiveness of measures undertaken. [2183]

4 Consultation, coordination and participation

Continuing and developing systems of national, regional and local authorities' consultation, coordination and participation, including in this exercise the public services and agencies, the voluntary organizations, independent professionals, the two sides of industry and the media as well as disabled people and their families.

Giving particular priority to the active involvement of disabled people, whether in a representative or personal capacity, in the taking and implementation of decisions concerning them. [2184]

DIRECTIVE No 89/391 OF THE COUNCIL
of 12 June 1989
on the introduction of measures to encourage improvements in the safety and health of workers at work

THE COUNCIL OF THE EUROPEAN COMMUNITIES,

Having regard to the Treaty establishing the European Economic Community, and in particular Article 118a thereof,

Having regard to the proposal from the Commission, drawn up after consultation with the Advisory Committee on Safety, Hygiene and Health Protection at Work,

In cooperation with the European Parliament,

Having regard to the opinion of the Economic and Social Committtee,

Whereas Article 118a of the Treaty provides that the Council shall adopt, by means of Directives, minimum requirements for encouraging improvements, especially in the working environment, to guarantee a better level of protection of the safety and health of workers;

Whereas this Directive does not justify any reduction in levels of protection already achieved in individual Member States, the Member State being committed, under the Treaty, to encouraging improvements in conditions in this area and to harmonising conditions while maintaining the improvements made;

Whereas it is known that workers can be exposed to the effects of dangerous environmental factors at the work place during the course of their working life;

Wheareas, pursuant to Article 118a of the Treaty, such Directives must avoid imposing administrative, financial and legal constraints which would hold back the creation and development of small and medium-sized undertakings;

Whereas the communication from the Commission on its programme concerning safety, hygiene and health at work provides for the adoption of Directives designed to guarantee the safety and health of workers;

Whereas the Council, in its resolution of 21 December 1987 on safety, hygiene and health at work, took note of the Commission's intention to submit to the Council in the near future a Directive on the organisation of the safety and health of workers at the work place;

Whereas in February 1988 the European Parliament adopted four resolutions following the debate on the internal market and worker protection; whereas these resolutions specifically invited the Commission to draw up a framework Directive to serve as a basis for more specific Directives covering all the risks connected with safety and health at the work place;

Whereas Member States have a responsibility to encourage improvements in the safety and health of workers on their territory; whereas taking measures to protect the health and safety of workers at work also helps, in certain cases, to preserve the health and possibly the safety of persons residing with them;

Whereas Member States' legislative systems covering safety and health at the work place differ widely and need to be improved; whereas national provisions on the subject, which often include technical specifications and/or self-regulatory standards, may result in different levels of safety and health protection and allow competition at the expense of safety and health;

Whereas the incidence of accidents at work and occupational diseases is still too high; whereas preventive measures must be introduced or improved without delay in order to safeguard the safety and health of workers and ensure a higher degree of protection;

Whereas, in order to ensure an improved degree of protection, workers and/or their representatives must be informed of the risks to their safety and health and of the measures required to reduce or eliminate these risks; whereas they must also be in a position to contribute, by means of balanced participation in accordance with national laws and/or practices, to seeing that the necessary protective measures are taken;

Whereas information, dialogue and balanced participation on safety and health at work must be developed between employers and workers and/or their representatives by means of appropriate procedures and instruments, in accordance with national laws and/or practices;

Whereas the improvement of workers' safety, hygiene and health at work is an objective which should not be subordinated to purely economic considerations;

Whereas employers shall be obliged to keep themselves informed of the latest advances in technology and scientific findings concerning work-place design, account being taken of the inherent dangers in their undertaking, and to inform accordingly the workers' representatives exercising participation rights under this Directive, so as to be able to guarantee a better level of protection of workers' health and safety;

Whereas the provisions of this Directive apply, without prejudice to more stringent present or future Community provisions, to all risks, and in particular to those arising from the use at work of chemical, physical and biological agents covered by Directive 80/1107/EEC, as last amended by Directive 88/642/EEC;

Whereas, pursuant to Decision 74/325/EEC, the Advisory Committee on Safety, Hygiene and Health Protection at Work is consulted by the Commission on the drafting of proposals in this field;

Whereas a Committee composed of members nominated by the Member States needs to be set up to assist the Commission in making the technical adaptations to the individual Directives provided for in this Directive.

HAS ADOPTED THIS DIRECTIVE:

SECTION I—GENERAL PROVISIONS

Article 1

Object

1 The object of this Directive is to introduce measures to encourage improvements in the safety and health of workers at work.

2 To that end it contains general principles concerning the prevention of occupational risks, the protection of safety and health, the elimination of risk and accident factors, the informing, consultation, balanced participation in accordance with national laws and/or practices and training of workers and their representatives, as well as general guidelines for the implementation of the said principles.

3 This Directive shall be without prejudice to existing or future national and Community provisions which are more favourable to protection of the safety and health of workers at work. **[2186]**

Article 2

Scope

1 This Directive shall apply to all sectors of activity, both public and private (industrial, agricultural, commercial, administrative, service, educational, cultural, leisure, etc).

2 This Directive shall not be applicable where characteristics peculiar to certain specific service activities, such as the armed forces or the police, or to certain specific activities in the civil protection services inevitably conflict with it.

In that event, the safety and health of workers must be ensured as far as possible in the light of the objectives of this Directive. **[2187]**

Article 3

Definitions

For the purposes of this Directive, the following terms shall have the following meanings:

    (a) worker: any person employed by an employer, including trainees and apprentices but excluding domestic servants;

    (b) employer: any natural or legal person who has an employment relationship with the worker and has responsibility for the undertaking and/or establishment;

    (c) workers' representative with specific responsibility for the safety and health of workers: any person elected, chosen or designated in accordance with national laws and/or practices to represent workers where problems arise relating to the safety and health protection of workers at work;

    (d) prevention: all the steps or measures taken or planned at all stages of work in the undertaking to prevent or reduce occupational risks. **[2188]**

Article 4

1 Member States shall take the necessary steps to ensure that employers, workers and workers' representatives are subject to the legal provisions necessary for the implementation of this Directive.

2 In particular, Member States shall ensure adequate controls and supervision. **[2189]**

SECTION II—EMPLOYERS' OBLIGATIONS

Article 5

General provision

1 The employer shall have a duty to ensure the safety and health of workers in every aspect related to the work.

2 Where, pursuant to Article 7(3), an employer enlists competent external services or persons, this shall not discharge him from his responsibilities in this area.

3 The workers' obligations in the field of safety and health at work shall not affect the principle of the responsibility of the employer.

4 This Directive shall not restrict the option of Member States to provide for the exclusion or the limitation of employers' responsibility where occurances are due to unusual and unforeseeable circumstances, beyond the employers' control, or to exceptional events, the consequences of which could not have been avoided despite the exercise of all due care.

Member States need not exercise the option referred to in the first sub-paragraph.

[2190]

Article 6

General obligations on employers

1 Within the context of his responsibilities, the employer shall take the measures necessary for the safety and health protection of workers, including prevention of occupational risks and provision of information and training, as well as provision of the necessary organisation and means.

The employer shall be alert to the need to adjust these measures to take account of changing circumstances and aim to improve existing situations.

2 The employer shall implement the measures referred to in the first subparagraph of paragraph 1 on the basis of the following general principles of prevention:

   (a) avoiding risks;
   (b) evaluating the risks which cannot be avoided;
   (c) combating the risk at source;
   (d) adapting the work to the individual, especially as regards the design of work places, the choice of work equipment and the choice of working and production methods, with a view, in particular, to alleviating monotonous work and work at a predetermined work-rate and to reducing their effect on health;
   (e) adapting to technical progress;
   (f) replacing the dangerous by the non-dangerous or the less dangerous;
   (g) developing a coherent overall prevention policy which covers technology, organisation of work, working conditions, social relationships and the influence of factors related to the working environment;
   (h) giving collective protective measures priority over individual protective measures;
   (i) giving appropriate instructions to the workers.

3 Without prejudice to the other provisions of this Directive, the employers shall, taking into account the nature of the activities of the enterprise and/or establishment:

   (a) evaluate the risks to the safety and health of workers, *inter alia* in the choice of work equipment, the chemical substances or preparations used, and the fitting-out of work places.

Subsequent to this evaluation and as necessary, the preventive measures and the working and production methods implemented by the employer must:

—assure an improvement in the level of protection afforded to workers with regard to safety and health,

—be integrated into all the activities of the undertaking and/or establishment and at all hierarchical levels;

(b) where he entrusts tasks to a worker, take into consideration the worker's capabilities as regards health and safety;

(c) ensure that the planning and introduction of new technologies are the subject of consultation with the workers and/or their representatives, as regards the consequences of the choice of equipment, the working conditions and the working environment for the safety and health of workers;

(d) take appropriate steps to ensure that only workers who have received adequate instructions may have access to areas where there is serious and specific danger.

4 Without prejudice to the other provisions of this Directive, where several undertakings share a work place, the employers shall co-operate in implementing the safety, health and occupational hygiene provisions and, taking into account the nature of the activities, shall coordinate their actions in matters of the protection and prevention of occupational risks, and shall inform one another and their respective workers and/or workers' representatives of these risks.

5 Measures related to safety, hygiene and health at work may in no circumstances involve the workers in financial cost.   **[2191]**

Article 7

Protective and preventive services

1 Without prejudice to the obligations referred to in Articles 5 and 6, the employer shall designate one or more workers to carry out activities related to the protection and prevention of occupational risks for the undertaking and/or establishment.

2 Designated workers may not be placed at any disadvantage because of their activities related to the protection and prevention of occupational risks.

Designated workers shall be allowed adequate time to enable them to fulfil their obligations arising from this Directive.

3 If such protective and preventive measures cannot be organised for lack of competent personnel in the undertaking and/or establishment, the employer shall enlist competent external services or persons.

4 Where the employer enlists such services or persons, he shall inform them of the factors known to affect, or suspected of affecting, the safety and health of the workers and they must have access to the information referred to in Article 10(2).

5 In all cases:

—the workers designated must have the necessary capabilities and the necessary means,

—the external services or persons consulted must have the necessary aptitudes and the necessary personal and professional means, and

—the workers designated and the external services or persons consulted must be sufficient in number

to deal with the organisation of protective and preventive measures, taking into account the size of the undertaking and/or establishment and/or the hazards to which the workers are exposed and their distribution throughout the entire undertaking and/or establishment.

6 The protection from, and prevention of, the health and safety risks which form the subject of this Article shall be the responsibility of one or more workers, of one service or of separate services whether from inside or outside the undertaking and/or establishment.

The worker(s) and/or agency(ies) must work together whenever necessary.

7 Member States may define, in the light of the nature of the activities and size of the undertakings, the categories or undertakings in which the employer, provided he is competent, may himself take responsibility for the measures referred to in paragraph 1.

8 Member States shall define the necessary capabilities and aptitudes referred to in paragraph 5.

They may determine the sufficient number referred to in paragraph 5.   **[2192]**

Article 8

First aid, fire-fighting and evacuation of workers, serious and imminent danger
1 The employer shall:

—take the necessary measures for first aid, fire-fighting and evacuation of workers, adapted to the nature of the activities and the size of the undertaking and/or establishment and taking into account other persons present;
—arrange any necessary contacts with external services, particularly as regards first aid, emergency medical care, rescue work and fire-fighting.

2 Pursuant to paragraph 1, the employer shall, *inter alia,* for first aid, fire-fighting and the evacuation of workers, designate the workers required to implement such measures.

The number of such workers, their training and the equipment available to them shall be adequate, taking account of the size and/or specific hazards of the undertaking and/or establishment.

3 The employer shall:

(a) as soon as possible, inform all workers who are, or may be, exposed to serious and imminent danger of the risk involved and of the steps taken or to be taken as regards protection;
(b) take action and give instructions to enable workers in the event of serious, imminent and unavoidable danger to stop work and/or immediately to leave the work place and proceed to a place of safety;
(c) save in exceptional cases for reasons duly substantiated, refrain from asking workers to resume work in a working situation where there is still a serious and imminent danger.

4 Workers who, in the event of serious, imminent and unavoidable danger, leave their workstation and/or a dangerous area may not be placed at any disadvantage because of their action and must be protected against any harmful and unjustified consequences, in accordance with national laws and/or practices.

5 The employer shall ensure that all workers are able, in the event of serious and imminent danger to their own safety and/or that of other persons, and where the immediate superior responsible cannot be contacted, to take the appropriate steps in the light of their knowledge and the technical means at their disposal, to avoid the consequences of such danger.

Their actions shall not place them at any disadvantage, unless they acted carelessly or there was negligence on their part.   **[2193]**

Article 9

Various obligations on employers

1 The employer shall:

   (a) be in possession of an assessment of the risks to safety and health at work, in including those facing groups of workers exposed to particular risks;

   (b) decide on the protective measures to be taken and, if necessary, the protective equipment to be used;

   (c) keep a list of occupational accidents resulting in a worker being unfit for work for more than three working days;

   (d) draw up, for the responsible authorities and in accordance with national laws and/or practices, reports on occupational accidents suffered by his workers.

2 Member States shall define, in the light of the nature of the activities and size of the undertaking, the obligations to be met by the different categories of undertakings in respect of the drawing-up of the documents provided for in paragraph 1 (a) and (b) and when preparing the documents provided for in paragraph 1 (c) and (d). [2194]

Article 10

Worker information

1 The employer shall take appropriate measures so that workers and/or their representatives in the undertaking and/or establishment receive in accordance with national laws and/or practices which may take account, *inter alia*, of the size of the undertaking and/or establishment, all the necessary information concerning:

   (a) the safety and health risks and protective and preventive measures and activities in respect of both the undertaking and/or establishment in general and each type of workstation and/or job;

   (b) the measures taken pursuant to Article 8(2).

2 The employer shall take appropriate measures so that employers of workers from any outside undertakings and/or establishments engaged in work in his undertaking and/or establishment receive, in accordance with national laws and/or practices, adequate information concerning the points referred to in paragraph 1 (a) and (b) which is to be provided to the workers in question.

3 The employer shall take appropriate measures so that workers with specific functions in protecting the safety and health of workers, or workers' representatives with specific responsibility for the safety and health of workers shall have access, to carry out their functions and in accordance with national laws and/or practices, to:

   (a) the risk assessment and protective measures referred to in Article 9(1)(a) and (b);

   (b) the list and reports referred to in Article 9(1)(c) and (d);

   (c) the information yielded by protective and preventive measures, inspection agencies and bodies responsible for safety and health. [2195]

Article 11

Consultation and participation of workers

1 Employers shall consult workers and/or their representatives and allow them to take part in discussions on all questions relating to safety and health at work.

This presupposes:

—the consultation of workers,

—the right of workers and/or their representatives to make proposals,
—balanced participation in accordance with national laws and/or practices.

2 Workers or workers' representatives with specific responsibility for the safety and health of workers shall take part in a balanced way, in accordance with national laws and/or practices, or shall be consulted in advance and in good time by the employer with regard to:

(a) any measure which may substantially affect safety and health;
(b) the designation of workers referred to in Articles 7(1) and 8(2) and the activities referred to in Article 7(1);
(c) the information referred to in Articles 9(1) and 10;
(d) the enlistment, where appropriate, of the competent services or persons outside the undertaking and/or establishment, as referred to in Article 7(3);
(e) the planning and organisation of the training referred to in Article 12.

3 Workers' representatives with specific responsibility for the safety and health of workers shall have the right to ask the employer to take appropriate measures and to submit proposals to him to that end to mitigate hazards for workers and/or to remove sources of danger.

4 The workers referred to in paragraph 2 and the workers' representatives referred to in paragraphs 2 and 3 may not be placed at a disadvantage because of their respective activities referred to in paragraphs 2 and 3.

5 Employers must allow workers' representatives with specific responsibility for the safety and health of workers adequate time off work, without loss of pay, and provide them with the necessary means to enable such representatives to exercise their rights and functions deriving from this Directive.

6 Workers and/or their representatives are entitled to appeal, in accordance with national law and/or practice, to the authority responsible for safety and health protection at work if they consider that the measures taken and the means employed by the employer are inadequate for the purposes of ensuring safety and health at work.

Workers' representatives must be given the opportunity to submit their observations during inspection visits by the competent authority. **[2196]**

Article 12

Training of workers

1 The employer shall ensure that each worker receives adequate safety and health training, in particular in the form of information and instructions specific to his workstation or job:

—on recruitment,
—in the event of a transfer or a change of job,
—in the event of the introduction of new work equipment or a change in equipment,
—in the event of the introduction of any new technology.

The training shall be:

—adapted to take account of new or changed risks, and
—repeated periodically if necessary.

2 The employer shall ensure that workers from outside undertakings and/or establishments engaged in work in his undertaking and/or establishment have in fact received appropriate instructions regarding health and safety risks during their activities in his undertaking and/or establishment.

3 Workers' representatives with a specific role in protecting the safety and health of workers shall be entitled to appropriate training.

4 The training referred to in paragraphs 1 and 3 may not be at the workers' expense or at that of the workers' representatives.

The training referred to in paragraph 1 must take place during working hours.

The training referred to in paragraph 3 must take place during working hours or in accordance with national practice either within or outside the undertaking and/or the establishment.   **[2197]**

SECTION III—WORKERS' OBLIGATIONS

Article 13

1 It shall be the responsibility of each worker to take care as far as possible of his own safety and health and that of other persons affected by his acts or commissions at work in accordance with his training and the instructions given by his employer.

2 To this end, workers must in particular, in accordance with their training and the instructions given by their employer:

  (a) make correct use of machinery, apparatus, tools, dangerous substances, transport equipment and other means of production;

  (b) make correct use of the personal protective equipment supplied to them and, after use, return it to its proper place;

  (c) refrain from disconnecting, changing or removing arbitrarily safety devices fitted, eg to machinery, apparatus, tools, plant and buildings, and use such safety devices correctly;

  (d) immediately inform the employer and/or the workers with specific responsibility for the safety and health of workers of any work situation they have reasonable grounds for considering represents a serious and immediate danger to safety and health and of any shortcomings in the protection arrangements;

  (e) co-operate, in accordance with national practice, with the employer and/or workers with specific responsibility for the safety and health of workers, for as long as may be necessary to enable any tasks or requirements imposed by the competent authority to protect the safety and health of workers at work to be carried out;

  (f) co-operate, in accordance with national practice, with the employer and/or workers with specific responsibility for the safety and health of workers, for as long as may be necessary to enable the employer to ensure that the working environment and working conditions are safe and pose no risk to safety and health within their field of activity.   **[2198]**

SECTION IV—MISCELLANEOUS PROVISIONS

Article 14

Health surveillance

1 To ensure that workers receive health surveillance appropriate to the health and safety risks they incur at work, measures shall be introduced in accordance with national law and/or practices.

2 The measures referred to in paragraph 1 shall be such that each worker, if he so wishes, may receive health surveillance at regular intervals.

3 Health surveillance may be provided as part of a national health system.
[2199]

Article 15

Risk groups

Particularly sensitive risk groups must be protected against the dangers which specifically affect them.   [2200]

Article 16

Individual Directives—Amendments—General scope of this Directive

1 The Council, acting on a proposal from the Commission based on Article 118a of the Treaty, shall adopt individual Directives, *inter alia,* in the areas listed in the Annex.

2 This Directive and, without prejudice to the procedure referred to in Article 17 concerning technical adjustments, the individual Directives may be amended in accordance with the procedure provided for in Article 118a of the Treaty.

3 The provisions of this Directive shall apply in full to all the areas covered by the individual Directives, without prejudice to more stringent and/or specific provisions contained in these individual Directives.   [2201]

Article 17

Committee

1 For the purely technical adjustments to the individual Directives provided for in article 16(1) to take account of:

—the adoption of Directives in the field of technical harmonisation and standardisation, and/or

—technical progress, changes in international regulations or specifications, and new findings,

the Commission shall be assisted by a committee composed of the representatives of the Member States and chaired by the representative of the Commission.

2 The representative of the Commission shall submit to the committee a draft of the measures to be taken.

The committee shall deliver its opinion on the draft within a time limit which the chairman may lay down according to the urgency of the matter.

The opinion shall be delivered by the majority laid down in Article 148(2) of the Treaty in the case of decisions which the Council is required to adopt on a proposal from the Commission.

The votes of the representatives of the Member States within the committee shall be weighted in the manner set out in that Article. The chairman shall not vote.

3 The Commission shall adopt the measures envisaged if they are in accordance with the opinion of the committee.

If the measures envisaged are not in accordance with the opinion of the committee, or if no opinion is delivered, the Commission shall, without delay, submit to the Council a proposal relating to the measures to be taken. The Council shall act by a qualified majority.

If, on the expiry of three months from the date of the referral to the Council, the Council has not acted, the proposed measures shall be adopted by the Commission.   [2202]

Article 18

Final provisions

1 Member States shall bring into force the laws, regulations and administrative provisions necessary to comply with this Directive by 31 December 1992.

They shall forthwith inform the Commission thereof.

2 Member States shall communicate to the Commission the texts of the provisions of rational law which they have already adopted or adopt in the field covered by this Directive.

3 Member States shall report to the Commission every five years on the practical implementation of the provisions of this Directive, indicating the points of view of employers and workers.

The Commission shall inform the European Parliament, the Council, the Economic and Social Committee and the Advisory Committee on Safety, Hygiene and Health Protection at Work.

4 The Commission shall submit periodically to the European Parliament, the Council and the Economic and Social Committee a report on the implementation of this Directive, taking into account paragraphs 1 to 3. [2203]

Article 19

This Directive is addressed to the Member States. [2204]

ANNEX

List of areas referred to in Article 16(1)

—Work places
—Work equipment
—Personal protective equipment
—Work with visual display units
—Handling of heavy loads involving risk of back injury
—Temporary or mobile work sites
—Fisheries and agriculture [2205]

NOTE
For the domestic implementation of this Directive see the Management of Health and Safety at Work Regulations 1992, SI 1992/2051, paras **[1391]–[1407]**.

DIRECTIVE No 90/269 OF THE COUNCIL

of 29 May 1990

on the minimum health and safety requirements for the manual handling of loads where there is a risk particularly of back injury to workers (fourth individual Directive within the meaning of Article 16 (1) of Directive 89/391/EEC)

THE COUNCIL OF THE EUROPEAN COMMUNITIES,

Having regard to the Treaty establishing the European Economic Community, and in particular Article 118a thereof

Having regard to the Commission proposal submitted after consultation with the Advisory Committee on Safety, Hygiene and Health Protection at Work,

In cooperation with the European Parliament,

Having regard to the opinion of the Economic and Social Committee,

Whereas Article 118a of the Treaty provides that the Council shall adopt, by means of

Directives, minimum requirements for encouraging improvements, especially in the working environment, to guarantee a better level of protection of the health and safety of workers;

Whereas, pursuant to that Article, such Directives must avoid imposing administrative, financial and legal constraints in a way which would hold back the creation and development of small and medium-sized undertakings;

Whereas the Commission communication on its programme concerning safety, hygiene and health at work, provides for the adoption of Directives designed to guarantee the health and safety of workers at the workplace;

Whereas the Council, in its resolution of 21 December 1987 on safety, hygiene and health at work, took note of the Commission's intention of submitting to the Council in the near future a Directive on protection against the risks resulting from the manual handling of heavy loads;

Whereas compliance with the minimum requirements designed to guarantee a better standard of health and safety at the workplace is essential to ensure the health and safety of workers;

Whereas this Directive is an individual Directive within the meaning of Article 16 (1) of Council Directive 89/391/EEC of 12 June 1989 on the introduction of measures to encourage improvements in the health and safety of workers at work; whereas therefore the provisions of the said Directive are fully applicable to the field of the manual handling of loads where there is a risk particularly of back injury to workers, without prejudice to more stringent and/or specific provisions set out in this Directive;

Whereas this Directive constitutes a practical step towards the achievement of the social dimension of the internal market;

Whereas, pursuant to Decision 74/325/EEC, the Advisory Committee on Safety, Hygiene and Health Protection at Work shall be consulted by the Commission with a view to drawing up proposals in this field.

HAS ADOPTED THIS DIRECTIVE: **[2206]**

Section I
General Provisions

Article 1

Subject

1 This Directive, which is the fourth individual Directive within the meaning of Article 16 (1) of Directive 89/391/EEC, lays down minimum health and safety requirements for the manual handling of loads where there is a risk particularly of back injury to workers.

2 The provisions of Directive 89/391/EEC shall be fully applicable to the whole sphere referred to in paragraph 1, without prejudice to more restrictive and/or specific provisions contained in this Directive. **[2207]**

Article 2

Definition

For the purposes of this Directive, 'manual handling of loads' means any transporting or supporting of a load, by one or more workers, including lifting, putting down, pushing, pulling, carrying or moving of a load, which, by reason of its characteristics or of unfavourable ergonomic conditions, involves a risk particularly of back injury to workers. **[2208]**

Section II
Employers' Obligations

Article 3

General provision

1 The employer shall take appropriate organizational measures, or shall use the appropriate means, in particular mechanical equipment, in order to avoid the need for the manual handling of loads by workers.

2 Where the need for the manual handling of loads by workers cannot be avoided, the employer shall take the appropriate organizational measures, use the appropriate means or provide workers with such means in order to reduce the risk involved in the manual handling of such loads, having regard to Annex I.   **[2209]**

Article 4
Organization of workstations
Wherever the need for manual handling of loads by workers cannot be avoided, the employer shall organize workstations in such a way as to make such handling as safe and healthy as possible and;
  (a) assess, in advance if possible, the health and safety conditions of the type of work involved, and in particular examine the characteristics of loads, taking account of Annex I;
  (b) take care to avoid or reduce the risk particularly of back injury to workers, by taking appropriate measures, considering in particular the characteristics of the working environment and the requirements of the activity, taking account of Annex I.   **[2210]**

Article 5
Reference to Annex II
For the implementation of Article 6 (3) (b) and Articles 14 and 15 of Directive 89/391/EEC, account should be taken of Annex II.   **[2211]**

Article 6
Information for, and training of, workers
1 Without prejudice to Article 10 of Directive 89/391/EEC, workers and/or their representatives shall be informed of all measures to be implemented, pursuant to this Directive, with regard to the protection of safety and of health.
   Employers must ensure that workers and/or their representatives receive general indications and, where possible, precise information on:
   —the weight of a load,
   — the centre of gravity of the heaviest side when a package is eccentrically loaded.
2 Without prejudice to Article 12 of Directive 83/391/EEC, employers must ensure that workers receive in addition proper training and information on how to handle loads correctly and the risks they might be open to particularly if these tasks are not performed correctly, having regard to Annexes I and II.   **[2211A]**

Article 7
Consultation of workers and workers' participation
Consultation and participation of workers and/or of their representatives shall take place in accordance with Article 11 of Directive 89/391/EEC on matters covered by this Directive, including the Annexes thereto.   **[2212]**

SECTION III

MISCELLANEOUS PROVISIONS

Article 8
Adjustment of the Annexes
Alterations of a strictly technical nature to Annexes I and II resulting from technical progress and changes in international regulations and specifications or knowledge in

the field of the manual handling of loads shall be adopted in accordance with the procedure for in Article 17 of Directive 89/391/EEC.   [2213]

Article 9

Final provisions

1 Member States shall bring into force the laws, regulations and administrative provisions needed to comply with this Directive not later than 31 December 1992.

They shall forthwith inform the Commission thereof.

2 Member States shall communicate to the Commission the text of the provisions of national law which they adopt, or have adopted, in the field covered by this Directive.

3 Member States shall report to the Commission every four years on the practical implementation of the provisions of this Directive, indicating the points of view of employers and workers.

The Commission shall inform the European Parliament, the Council, the Economic and Social Committee and the Advisory Committee on Safety, Hygiene and Health Protection at Work thereof.

4 The Commission shall report periodically to the European Parliament, the Council and the Economic and Social Committee on the implementation of the Directive in the light of paragraphs 1, 2 and 3.   [2214]

Article 10

This Directive is addressed to the Member States.   [2215]

ANNEX I [*]

REFERENCE FACTORS

(Article 3(2), Article 4(a) and (b) and Article 6 (2))

1 Characteristics of the load

The manual handling of a load may present a risk particularly of back injury if it is:

—too heavy or too large,

—unwieldy or difficult to grasp,

—unstable or has contents likely to shift,

—positioned in a manner requiring it to be held or manipulated at a distance from the trunk, or with a bending or twisting of the trunk,

—likely, because of its contours and/or consistency, to result in injury to workers, particularly in the event of a collision.

2 Physical effort required

A physical effort may present a risk particularly of back injury if it is:

—too strenuous,

—only achieved by a twisting movement of the trunk,

—likely to result in a sudden movement of the load,

—made with the body in an unstable posture.

3 Characteristics of the working environment

The characteristics of the work environment may increase a risk particularly of back injury if:

—there is not enough room, in particular vertically, to carry out the activity,

—the floor is uneven, thus presenting tripping hazards, or is slippery in relation to the workers' footwear,

—the place of work or the working environment prevents the handling of loads at a safe height or with good posture by the worker,
—there are variations in the level of the floor or the working surface, requiring the load to be manipulated on different levels,
—the floor or foot rest is unstable,
—the temperature, humidity or ventilation is unsuitable.

4 Requirements of the activity

The activity may present a risk particularly of back injury if it entails one or more of the following requirements:

—over-frequent or over-prolonged physical effort involving in particular the spine,
—an insufficient bodily rest or recovery period,
—excessive lifting, lowering or carrying distances,
—a rate of work imposed by a process which cannot be altered by the worker.

[2216]

[*] With a view to multi-factor analysis, reference may be made simultaneously to the various factors listed in Annexes I and II.

ANNEX II [*]

INDIVIDUAL RISK FACTORS

(Articles 5 and 6 (2))

The worker may be at risk if he/she:

—is physically unsuited to carry out the task in question,
—is wearing unsuitable clothing, footwear or other personal effects,
—does not have adequate or appropriate knowledge or training.   **[2217]**

[*] With a view to multi-factor analysis, reference may be made simultaneously to the various factors listed in Annexes I and II.

NOTE
For the domestic implementation of this Directive see the Manual Handling Operations Regulations 1992, SI 1992/2793, paras **[1418]–[1426]**.

DIRECTIVE No 90/270 OF THE COUNCIL

of 29 May 1990

on the minimum safety and health requirements for work with display screen equipment (fifth individual Directive within the meaning of Article 16(1) of Directive 89/391/EEC)

THE COUNCIL OF THE EUROPEAN COMMUNITIES,
Having regard to the Treaty establishing the European Economic Community, and in particular Article 118a thereof,
Having regard to the Commission proposal drawn up after consultation with the Advisory Committee on Safety, Hygiene and Health Protection at Work,
In cooperation with the European Parliament,
Having regard to the opinion of the Economic and Social Committee.
Whereas Article 118a of the Treaty provides that the Council shall adopt, by means of Directives, minimum requirements designed to encourage improvements, especially in the working environment, to ensure a better level of protection of workers' safety and health;
Whereas, under the terms of that Article, those Directives shall avoid imposing administrative, financial and legal constraints, in a way which would hold back the creation and development of small and medium-sized undertakings;

Whereas the communication from the Commission on its programme concerning safety, hygiene and health at work provides for the adoption of measures in respect of new technologies; whereas the Council has taken note thereof in its resolution of 21 December 1987 on safety, hygiene and health at work;

Whereas compliance with the minimum requirements for ensuring a better level of safety at workstations with display screens is essential for ensuring the safety and health of workers;

Whereas this Directive is an individual Directive within the meaning of Article 16 (1) of Council Directive 89/391/EEC of 12 June 1989 on the introduction of measures to encourage improvements in the safety and health of workers at work; whereas the provisions of the latter are therefore fully applicable to the use by workers of display screen equipment, without prejudice to more stringent and/or specific provisions contained in the present Directive;

Whereas employers are obliged to keep themselves informed of the latest advances in technology and scientific findings concerning workstation design so that they can make any changes necessary so as to be able to guarantee a better level of protection of workers' safety and health;

Whereas the ergonomic aspects are of particular importance for a workstation with display screen equipment;

Whereas this Directive is a practical contribution towards creating the social dimension of the internal market;

Whereas, pursuant to Decision 74/325/EEC, the Advisory Committee on Safety, Hygiene and Health Protection at work shall be consulted by the Commission on the drawing-up of proposals in this field,

HAS ADOPTED THIS DIRECTIVE: [2218]

SECTION I

GENERAL PROVISIONS

Article 1

Subject

1 This Directive, which is the fifth individual Directive within the meaning of Article 16 (1) of Directive 89/391/EEC, lays down minimum safety and health requirements for work with display screen equipment as defined in Article 2.

2 The provisions of Directive 89/391/EEC are fully applicable to the whole field referred to in paragraph 1, without prejudice to more stringent and/or specific provisions contained in the present Directive.

3 This Directive shall not apply to:

(a) drivers' cabs or control cabs for vehicles or machinery;
(b) computer systems on board a means of transport;
(c) computer systems mainly intended for public use;
(d) 'portable' systems not in prolonged use at a workstation;
(e) calculators, cash registers and any equipment having a small data or measurements display required for direct use of the equipment;
(f) typewriters of traditional design, of the type known as 'typewriter with window.'   [2219]

Article 2

Definitions

For the purpose of this Directive, the following terms shall have the following meanings:

(a) *display screen equipment:* an alphanumeric or graphic display screen, regardless of the display process employed;
(b) *workstation:* an assembly comprising display screen equipment, which may be provided with a keyboard or input device and/or software determining the operator/machine interface, optional accessories, peripherals including the diskette drive, telephone, modem, printer,

document holder, work chair and work desk or work surface, and the immediate work environment;

(c) *worker:* any worker as defined in Article 3 (a) of Directive 89/391/EEC who habitually uses display screen equipment as a significant part of his normal work. **[2220]**

SECTION II

EMPLOYERS' OBLIGATIONS

Article 3

Analysis of workstations

1 Employers shall be obliged to perform an analysis of workstations in order to evaluate the safety and health conditions to which they give rise for their workers, particularly as regards possible risks to eyesight, physical problems and problems of mental stress.

2 Employers shall take appropriate measures to remedy the risks found, on the basis of the evaluation referred to in paragraph 1, taking account of the additional and/or combined effects of the risks so found. **[2221]**

Article 4

Workstations put into service for the first time

Employers must take the appropriate steps to ensure that workstations first put into service after 31 December 1992 meet the minimum requirements laid down in the Annex. **[2222]**

Article 5

Workstations already put into service

Employers must take the appropriate steps to ensure that workstations already put into service on or before 31 December 1992 are adapted to comply with the minimum requirements laid down in the Annex not later than four years after that date. **[2223]**

Article 6

Information for, and training of, workers

1 Without prejudice to Article 10 of Directive 89/391/EEC, workers shall receive information on all aspects of safety and health relating to their workstation, in particular information on such measures applicable to workstations as are implemented under Articles 3, 7 and 9.

In all cases, workers or their representatives shall be informed of any health and safety measure taken in compliance with this Directive.

2 Without prejudice to Article 12 of Directive 89/391/EEC, every worker shall also receive training in use of the workstation before commencing this type of work and whenever the organization of the workstation is substantially modified. **[2224]**

Article 7

Daily work routine

The employer must plan the worker's activities in such a way that daily work on a display screen is periodically interrupted by breaks or changes of activity reducing the workload at the display screen. **[2225]**

Article 8

Worker consultation and participation

Consultation and participation of workers and/or their representatives shall take place in accordance with Article 11 of Directive 89/391/EEC on the matters covered by this Directive, including its Annex. **[2226]**

Article 9

Protection of workers' eyes and eyesight

1 Workers shall be entitled to an appropriate eye and eyesight test carried out by a person with the necessary capabilities:

—before commencing display screen work,

—at regular intervals thereafter, and

—if they experience visual difficulties which may be due to display screen work.

2 Workers shall be entitled to an opthalmological examination if the results of the test referred to in paragraph 1 show that this is necessary.

3 If the results of the test referred to in paragraph 1 or of the examination referred to in paragraph 2 show that it is necessary and if normal corrective appliances cannot be used, workers must be provided with special corrective appliances appropriate for the work concerned.

4 Measures taken pursuant to this Article may in no circumstances involve workers in additional financial cost.

5 Protection of workers' eyes and eyesight may be provided as part of a national health system. **[2227]**

SECTION III

MISCELLANEOUS PROVISIONS

Article 10

Adaptions to the Annex

The strictly technical adaptions to the Annex to take account of technical progress, developments in international regulations and specifications and knowledge in the field of display screen equipment shall be adopted in accordance with the procedure laid down in Article 17 of Directive 89/391/EEC. **[2228]**

Article 11

Final provisions

1 Member States shall bring into force the laws, regulations and administrative provisions necessary to comply with this Directive by 31 December 1992.

They shall forthwith inform the Commission thereof.

2 Member States shall communicate to the Commission the texts of the provisions of national law which they adopt, or have already adopted, in the field covered by this Directive.

3 Member States shall report to the Commission every four years on the practical implementation of the provisions of this Directive, indicating the points of view of employers and workers.

The Commission shall inform the European Parliament, the Council, the Economic and Social Committee and the Advisory Committee on Safety, Hygiene and Health Protection at Work.

4 The Commission shall submit a report on the implementation of this Directive at regular intervals to the European Parliament, the Council and the Economic and Social Committee, taking into account paragraphs 1, 2 and 3.   [2229]

Article 12

This Directive is addressed to the Member States.   [2230]

ANNEX

MINIMUM REQUIREMENTS

(Articles 4 and 5)

Preliminary remark

The obligations laid down in this Annex shall apply in order to achieve the objectives of this Directive and to the extent that, firstly, the components concerned are present at the workstation, and secondly, the inherent requirements or characteristics of the task do not preclude it.

1 EQUIPMENT

(a) **General comment**
The use as such of the equipment must not be a source of risk for workers.

(b) **Display screen**
The characters on the screen shall be well-defined and clearly formed, of adequate size and with adequate spacing between the characters and lines.
The image on the screen should be stable, with no flickering or other forms of instability.
The brightness and/or the contrast between the characters and the background shall be easily adjustable by the operator, and also be easily adjustable to ambient conditions.
The screen must swivel and tilt easily and freely to suit the needs of the operator.
It shall be possible to use a separate base for the screen or an adjustable table.
The screen shall be free of reflective glare and reflections liable to cause discomfort to the user.

(c) **Keyboard**
The keyboard shall be tiltable and separate from the screen so as to allow the worker to find a comfortable working position avoiding fatigue in the arms or hands.
The space in front of the keyboard shall be sufficient to provide support for the hands and arms of the operator.
The keyboard shall have a matt surface to avoid reflective glare.
The arrangement of the keyboard and the characteristics of the keys shall be such as to facilitate the use of the keyboard.
The symbols on the keys shall be adequately contrasted and legible from the design working position.

(d) **Work desk or work surface**
The work desk or work surface shall have a sufficiently large, low-reflectance surface and allow a flexible arrangement of the screen, keyboard, documents and related equipment.
The document holder shall be stable and adjustable and shall be positioned so as to minimize the need for uncomfortable head and eye movements.

There shall be adequate space for workers to find a comfortable position.

(e) **Work chair**
The work chair shall be stable and allow the operator easy freedom of movement and a comfortable position.
The seat shall be adjustable in height.
The seat back shall be adjustable in both height and tilt.
A footrest shall be made available to any one who wishes for one.

2 ENVIRONMENT

(a) **Space requirements**
The workstation shall be dimensioned and designed so as to provide sufficient space for the user to change position and vary movements.

(b) **Lighting**
Room lighting and/or spot lighting (work lamps) shall ensure satisfactory lighting conditions and an appropriate contrast between the screen and the background environment, taking into account the type of work and the user's vision requirements.
Possible disturbing glare and reflections on the screen or other equipment shall be prevented by coordinating workplace and workstation layout with the positioning and technical characteristics of the artificial light sources.

(c) **Reflections and glare**
Workstations shall be so designed that sources of light such as windows and other openings, transparent or translucid walls, and brightly coloured fixtures or walls cause no direct glare and [no distracting] reflections on the screen.
Windows shall be fitted with a suitable system of adjustable covering to attenuate the daylight that falls on the workstation.

(d) **Noise**
Noise emitted by equipment belonging to workstation(s) shall be taken into account when a workstation is being equipped, in particular so as not to distract attention or disturb speech.

(e) **Heat**
Equipment belonging to workstation(s) shall not produce excess heat which could cause discomfort to workers.

(f) **Radiation**
All radiation with the exception of the visible part of the electromagnetic spectrum shall be reduced to negligible levels from the point of view of the protection of workers' safety and health.

(g) **Humidity**
An adequate level of humidity shall be established and maintained.

3 OPERATOR/COMPUTER INTERFACE

In designing, selecting, commissioning and modifying software, and in designing tasks using display screen equipment, the employer shall take into account the following principles:
  (a) software must be suitable for the task;
  (b) software must be easy to use and, where appropriate, adaptable to the operator's level of knowledge or experience; no quantitative or qualitative checking facility may be used without the knowledge of the workers;
  (c) systems must provide feedback to workers on their performance;
  (d) systems must display information in a format and at a pace which are adapted to operators;
  (e) the principles of software ergonomics must be applied, in particular to human data processing. **[2231]**

NOTES
Words in square brackets are a correction of the original text as published in OJ(L) 156 of 21 June 1990; see OJ(L) 171/30.
For the domestic implementation of this Directive see the Health and Safety (Display Screen Equipment) Regulations 1992, SI 1992/2792, paras **[1408]**–**[1417]**.

DIRECTIVE No 91/533 OF THE COUNCIL

of 14 October 1991

on an employer's obligation to inform employees of the conditions applicable to the contract or employment relationship

THE COUNCIL OF THE EUROPEAN COMMUNITIES,

Having regard to the Treaty establishing the European Economic Community, and in particular Article 100 thereof,

Having regard to the proposal from the Commission,

Having regard to the opinion of the European Parliament,

Having regard to the opinion of the Economic and Social Committee.

Whereas the development, in the Member States, of new forms of work has led to an increase in the number of types of employment relationship;

Whereas, faced with this development, certain Member States have considered it necessary to subject employment relationships to formal requirements; whereas these provisions are designed to provide employees with improved protection against possible infringements of their rights and to create greater transparency on the labour market;

Whereas the relevant legislation of the Member States differs considerably on such fundamental points as the requirement to inform employees in writing of the main terms of the contract or employment relationship;

Whereas differences in the legislation of Member States may have a direct effect on the operation of the common market;

Whereas Article 117 of the Treaty provides for the Member States to agree upon the need to promote improved working conditions and an improved standard of living for workers, so as to make possible their harmonisation while the improvement is being maintained;

Whereas point 9 of the Community Charter of Fundamental Social Rights for Workers, adopted at the Strasbourg European Council on 9 December 1989 by the Heads of State and Government of 11 Member States, states:

'The conditions of employment of every worker of the European Community shall be stipulated in laws, a collective agreement or a contract of employment, according to arrangements applying in each country.';

Whereas it is necessary to establish at Community level the general requirement that every employee must be provided with a document containing information on the essential elements of his contract or employment relationship;

Whereas, in view of the need to maintain a certain degree of flexibility in employment relationships, Member States should be able to exclude certain limited cases of employment relationship from this Directive's scope of application;

Whereas the obligation to provide information may be met by means of a written contract, a letter of appointment or one or more other documents or, if they are lacking, a written statement signed by the employer;

Whereas, in the case of expatriation of the employee, the latter must, in addition to the main terms of this contract or employment relationship, be supplied with relevant information connected with his secondment;

Whereas, in order to protect the interests of employees with regard to obtaining a document, any change in the main terms of the contract or employment relationship must be communicated to them in writing;

Whereas it is necessary for Member States to guarantee that employees can claim the rights conferred on them by this Directive;

Whereas Member States are to adopt the laws, regulations and legislative provisions necessary to comply with this Directive or are to ensure that both sides of industry set up the necessary provisions by agreement, with Member States being obliged to take the necessary steps enabling them at all times to guarantee the results imposed by this Directive,

HAS ADOPTED THIS DIRECTIVE: **[2232]**

Article 1

Scope

1 This Directive shall apply to every paid employee having a contract or employment relationship defined by the law in force in a Member State and/or governed by the law in force in a Member State.

2 Member States may provide that this Directive shall not apply to employees having a contract or employment relationship:

(a) – with a total duration not exceeding one month, and/or
 – with a working week not exceeding eight hours; or
(b) of a casual and/or specific nature provided, in these cases, that its non-application is justified by objective considerations. **[2233]**

Article 2

Obligation to provide information

1 An employer shall be obliged to notify an employee to whom this Directive applies, hereinafter referred to as 'the employee', of the essential aspects of the contract or employment relationship.

2 The information referred to in paragraph 1 shall cover at least the following:

(a) the identities of the parties;
(b) the place of work; where there is no fixed or main place of work, the principle that the employee is employed at various places and the registered place of business or, where appropriate, the domicile of the employer;
(c) (i) the title, grade, nature or category of the work for which the employee is employed; or
(ii) a brief specification or description of the work;
(d) the date of commencement of the contract or employment relationship;
(e) in the case of a temporary contract or employment relationship, the expected duration thereof;
(f) the amount of paid leave to which the employee is entitled or, where this cannot be indicated when the information is given, the procedures for allocating and determining such leave;
(g) the length of the periods of notice to be observed by the employer and the employee should their contract or employment relationship be terminated or, where this cannot be indicated when the information is given, the method for determining such periods of notice;
(h) the initial basic amount, the other component elements and the frequency of payment of the remuneration to which the employee is entitled;
(i) the length of the employee's normal working day or week;
(j) where appropriate;
(i) the collective agreements governing the employee's conditions of work;
or
(ii) in the case of collective agreements concluded outside the business by special joint bodies or institutions, the name of the competent body or joint institution within which the agreements were concluded.

3 The information referred to in paragraph 2(f), (g), (h) and (i) may, where appropriate, be given in the form of a reference to the laws, regulations and administrative or statutory provisions or collective agreements governing those particular points. **[2234]**

Article 3

Means of information

1 The information referred to in Article 2(2) may be given to the employee, not later than two months after the commencement of employment, in the form of:

(a) a written contract of employment; and/or

(b) a letter of engagement; and/or

(c) one or more other written documents, where one of these documents contains at least all the information referred to in Article 2(2)(a), (b), (c), (d), (h) and (i).

2 Where none of the documents referred to in paragraph 1 is handed over to the employee within the prescribed period, the employer shall be obliged to give the employee, not later than two months after the commencement of employment, a written declaration signed by the employer and containing at least the information referred to in Article 2(2).

Where the document(s) referred to in paragraph 1 contain only part of the information required, the written declaration provided for in the first subparagraph of this paragraph shall cover the remaining information.

3 Where the contract or employment relationship comes to an end before expiry of a period of two months as from the date of the start of work, the information provided for in Article 2 and in this Article must be made available to the employee by the end of this period at the latest. **[2235]**

Article 4

Expatriate employees

1 Where an employee is required to work in a country or countries other than the Member State whose law and/or practice governs the contract or employment relationship, the document(s) referred to in Article 3 must be in his/her possession before his/her departure and must include at least the following additional information:

(a) the duration of the employment abroad;

(b) the currency to be used for the payment of remuneration;

(c) where appropriate, the benefits in cash or kind attendant on the employment abroad;

(d) where appropriate, the conditions governing the employee's repatriation.

2 The information referred to in paragraph 1(b) and (c) may, where appropriate, be given in the form of a reference to the laws, regulations and administrative or statutory provisions or collective agreements governing those particular points.

3 Paragraphs 1 and 2 shall not apply if the duration of the employment outside the country whose law and/or practice governs the contract or employment relationship is one month or less. **[2236]**

Article 5

Modification of aspects of the contract or employment relationship

1 Any change in the details referred to in Articles 2(2) and 4(1) must be the subject of a written document to be given by the employer to the employee at the earliest opportunity and not later than one month after the date of entry into effect of the change in question.

2 The written document referred to in paragraph 1 shall not be compulsory in the event of a change in the laws, regulations and administrative or statutory provisions or collective agreements cited in the documents referred to in Article 3, supplemented, where appropriate, pursuant to Article 4(1).

[2236A]

Article 6

Form and proof of the existence of a contract or employment relationship and procedural rules

This Directive shall be without prejudice to national law and practice concerning:
—the form of the contract or employment relationship,
—proof as regards the existence and content of a contract or employment relationship,
—the relevant procedural rules.

[2236B]

Article 7

More favourable provisions

This Directive shall not affect Member States' prerogative to apply or to introduce laws, regulations or administrative provisions which are more favourable to employees or to encourage or permit the application of agreements which are more favourable to employees.

[2237]

Article 8

Defence of rights

1 Member States shall introduce into their national legal systems such measures as are necessary to enable all employees who consider themselves wronged by failure to comply with the obligations arising from this Directive to pursue their claims by judicial process after possible recourse to other competent authorities.

2 Member States may provide that access to the means of redress referred to in paragraph 1 are subject to the notification of the employer by the employee and the failure by the employer to reply within 15 days of notification.

However, the formality of prior notification may in no case be required in the cases referred to in Article 4, neither for workers with a temporary contract or employment relationship, nor for employees not covered by a collective agreement or by collective agreements relating to the employment relationship.   **[2238]**

Article 9

Final provisions

1 Member States shall adopt the laws, regulations and administrative provisions necessary to comply with this Directive no later than 30 June 1993 or shall ensure by that date that the employers' and workers' representatives introduce the required provisions by way of agreement, the Member States being obliged to take the necessary steps enabling them at all times to guarantee the results imposed by this Directive.

They shall forthwith inform the Commission thereof.

2 Member States shall take the necessary measures to ensure that, in the case of employment relationships in existence upon entry into force of the provisions that they adopt, the employer gives the employee, on request, within two months of receiving that request; any of the documents referred to in Article 3, supplemented, where appropriate, pursuant to Article 4(1).

3 When Member States adopt the measures referred to in paragraph 1, such measures shall contain a reference to this Directive or shall be accompanied by such reference on the occasion of their official publication. The methods of making such a reference shall be laid down by the Member States.

4 Member States shall forthwith inform the Commission of the measures they take to implement this Directive.   **[2239]**

Article 10
This Directive is addressed to the Member States.   **[2240]**

NOTE
For the domestic implementation of this Directive see the Employment Protection (Consolidation) Act 1978, ss 1-6 and 11, as respectively substituted and amended by the Trade Union Reform and Employment Rights Act 1993, s 26, Sch 4.

COMMISSION RECOMMENDATION
of 27 November 1991
on the protection of the dignity of women and men at work
(OJ(L) 49/92)

THE COMMISSION OF THE EUROPEAN COMMUNITIES
    Having regard to the Treaty establishing the European Economic Community and the second indent of Article 155 thereof;
    Whereas unwanted conduct of a sexual nature, or other conduct based on sex affecting the dignity of women and men at work, including the conduct of superiors and colleagues, is unacceptable and may, in certain circumstances, be contrary to the principle of equal treatment within the meaning of Articles 3, 4 and 5 of Council Directive 76/207/EEC of 9 February 1976 on the implementation of the principle of equal treatment for men and women as regards access to employment, vocational training and promotion and working conditions, a view supported by case law in some Member States;
    Whereas, in accordance with the Council Recommendation of 13 December 1984 on the promotion of positive action for women, many Member States have carried out a variety of positive action measures and actions having a bearing, inter alia, on respect for the dignity of women at the workplace;
    Whereas the European Parliament, in its resolution of 11 June 1986 on violence against women, has called upon national governments, equal opportunities committees and trade unions to carry out concerted information campaigns to create a proper awareness of the individual rights of all members of the labour force;
    Whereas the Advisory Committee on Equal Opportunities for Women and Men, in its opinion of 20 June 1988, has unanimously recommended that there should be a Recommendation and code of conduct on sexual harassment in the workplace covering harassment of both sexes;
    Whereas the Commission in its Action Programme relating to the implementation of the Community Charter of Basic Social Rights for workers undertook to examine the protection of workers and their dignity at work, having regard to the reports and recommendations prepared on various aspect of implementation of Community law;
    Whereas the Council, in its Resolution of 29 May 1990 on the protection of the dignity of women and men at work , affirms that conduct based on sex affecting the dignity of women and men at work, including conduct of superiors and colleagues, constitutes an intolerable violation of the dignity of workers or trainees, and calls on the Member States and the institutions and organs of the European Communities to develop positive measures designed to create a climate at work in which women and men respect one another's human integrity;
    Whereas the Commission, in its Third Action Programme on Equal Opportunities for Women and Men, 1991-1995 and pursuant to paragraph 3.2 of the said Council Resolution of 29 May 1990, resolved to draw up a code of conduct on the protection of the dignity of women and men at work, based on experience and best practice in the Member States, to provide

guidance on initiating and pursuing positive measures designed to create a climate at work in which women and men respect one another's human integrity;

Whereas the European Parliament, on 22 October 1991, adopted a Resolution on the protection of the dignity of women and men at work;

Whereas the Economic and Social Committee, on 30 October 1991, adopted an Opinion on the protection of the dignity of women and men at work;

RECOMMENDS AS FOLLOWS   [2241]

Article 1

It is recommended that the Member State take action to promote awareness that conduct of a sexual nature, or other conduct based on sex affecting the dignity of women and men at work, including conduct of superiors and colleagues, is unacceptable if:

(a) such conduct is unwanted, unreasonable and offensive to the recipient;

(b) a person's rejection of or submission to such conduct on the part of employers or workers (including superiors or colleagues) is used explicitly or implicitly as a basis for a decision which affects that person's access to vocational training, access to employment, continued employment, promotion, salary or other employment decisions; and/or

(c) such conduct creates an intimidating, hostile or humiliating work environment for the recipient;

and that such conduct may, in certain circumstances, be contrary to the principle of equal treatment within the meaning of Articles 3, 4 and 5 of Directive 76/207/EEC.

[2242]

Article 2

It is recommended that Member States should take action, in the public sector, to implement the Commission's Code of Practice on the protection of the dignity of women and men at work, annexed hereto. The action of the Member States, in thus initiating and pursuing positive measures designed to create a climate at work in which women and men respect one another's human integrity, should serve as an example to the private sector.   [2243]

Article 3

It is recommended that Member States encourage employers and employee representatives to develop measures to implement the Commission's Code of Practice on the protection of the dignity of women and men at work.   [2244]

Article 4

The Member States shall inform the Commission within three years of the date of this Recommendation of the measures taken to give effect to it, in order to allow the Commission to draw up a report on all such measures. The Commission shall, within this period, ensure the widest possible circulation of the Code of Practice. The report should examine the degree of awareness of the Code, its perceived effectiveness, its degree of application and the extent of its use in collective bargaining between the social partners.   [2245]

Article 5

This Recommendation is addressed to the Member States.   [2246]

PROTECTING THE DIGNITY OF WOMEN
AND MEN AT WORK
A code of practice on measures to combat sexual harassment

1 Introduction

This Code of Practice is issued in accordance with the Resolution of the Council of Ministers on the protection of the dignity of women and men at work, and to accompany the Commission's Recommendations on this issue.

Its purpose is to give practical guidance to employers, trade unions, and employees on the protection of the dignity of women and men at work. The Code is intended to be applicable in both the public and the private sector and employers are encouraged to follow the recommendations contained in the Code in a way which is appropriate to the size and structure of their organisation. It may be particularly relevant for small and medium-sized enterprises to adapt some of the practical steps to their specific needs.

The aim is to ensure that sexual harassment does not occur and, if it does occur, to ensure that adequate procedures are readily available to deal with the problem and prevent its recurrence. The Code thus seeks to encourage the development and implementation of policies and practices which establish working environments free of sexual harassment and in which women and men respect one another's human integrity.

The expert report carried out on behalf of the Commission found that sexual harassment is a serious problem for many working women in the European Community and research in Member States has proven beyond doubt that sexual harassment at work is not an isolated phenomenon. On the contrary, it is clear that for millions of women in the European Community, sexual harassment is an unpleasant and unavoidable part of their working lives. Men too may suffer sexual harassment and should, of course, have the same rights as women to the protection of their dignity.

Some specific groups are particularly vulnerable to sexual harassment. Research in several Member States, which documents the link between the risk of sexual harassment and the recipient's perceived vulnerability, suggests that divorced and separated women, young women and new entrants to the labour market and those with irregular or precarious employment contracts, women in non-traditional jobs, women with disabilities, lesbians and women from racial minorities are disproportionately at risk. Gay men and young men are also vulnerable to harassment. It is undeniable that harassment on grounds of sexual orientation undermines the dignity at work of those affected and it is impossible to regard such harassment as appropriate workplace behaviour.

Sexual harassment pollutes the working environment and can have a devastating effect upon the health, confidence, morale and performance of those affected by it. The anxiety and stress produced by sexual harassment commonly leads to those subjected to it taking time off work due to sickness, being less efficient at work, or leaving their job to seek work elsewhere. Employees often suffer the adverse consequences of the harassment itself and short- and long-term damage to their employment prospects if they are forced to change jobs. Sexual harassment may also have a damaging impact on employees not themselves the object of unwanted behaviour but who are witness to it or have a knowledge of the unwanted behaviour.

There are also adverse consequences arising from sexual harassment for employers. It has a direct impact on the profitability of the enterprise where staff take sick leave or resign their posts because of sexual harassment, and on the economic efficiency of the enterprise where employees' productivity is reduced by having to work in a climate in which individuals' integrity is not respected.

In general terms, sexual harassment is an obstacle to the proper integration of women into the labour market and the Commission is committed to encouraging the development of comprehensive measures to improve such integration. **[2247]**

2 Definition

Sexual harassment means "unwanted conduct of a sexual nature, or other conduct based on sex affecting the dignity of women and men at work". This can include unwelcome physical, verbal or non-verbal conduct.

Thus, a range of behaviour may be considered to constitute sexual harassment. It is unacceptable if such conduct is unwanted, unreasonable and offensive to the recipient; a person's rejection of or submission to such conduct on the part of employers or workers (including superiors or colleagues) is used explicitly or implicitly as a basis for a decision which affects that person's access to vocational training or to employment, continued employment, promotion, salary or any other employment decisions; and/or such conduct creates an intimidating, hostile or humiliating working environment for the recipient.

The essential characteristic of sexual harassment is that it is unwanted by the recipient, that it is for each individual to determine what behaviour is acceptable to them and what they regard as offensive. Sexual attention becomes sexual harassment if it is persisted in once it has been made clear that it is regarded by the recipient as offensive, although one incident of harassment may constitute sexual harassment if sufficiently serious. It is the unwanted nature of the conduct which distinguishes sexual harassment from friendly behaviour, which is welcome and mutual. **[2248]**

3 The law and employers' responsibilities

Conduct of a sexual nature or other conduct based on sex affecting the dignity of women and men at work may be contrary to the principle of equal treatment within the meaning of Articles 3, 4 and 5 of Council Directive 76/207/EEC of 9 February 1976 on the implementation of the principle of equal treatment for men and women as regards access to employment, vocational training and promotion and working conditions. This principle means that there shall be no discrimination whatsoever on grounds of sex either directly or indirectly by reference in particular to marital or family status.

In certain circumstances, and depending upon national law, sexual harassment may also be a criminal offence or may contravene other obligations imposed by the law, such as health and safety duties, or a duty, contractual or otherwise, to be a good employer. Since sexual harassment is a form of employee misconduct, employers have a responsibility to deal with it as they do with any other form of employee misconduct as well as to refrain from harassing employees themselves. Since sexual harassment is a risk to health and safety, employers have a responsibility to take steps to minimise the risk as they do with other hazards. Since sexual harassment often entails an abuse of power, employers may have a responsibility for the misuse of the authority they delegate.

This Code, however, focuses on sexual harassment as a problem of sex discrimination. Sexual harassment is sex discrimination because the gender of the recipient is the determining factor in who is harassed. Conduct of a sexual nature or other conduct based on sex affecting the dignity of women and men at work in some Member States already has been found to contravene national equal treatment laws and employers have a responsibility to seek to ensure that the work environment is free from such conduct.

As sexual harassment is often a function of women's status in the employment hierarchy, policies to deal with sexual harassment are likely to be most effective where they are linked to a broader policy to promote equal opportunities and to improve the position of women. Advice on steps which can be taken generally to implement an equal opportunities policy is set out in the Commission's Guide to Positive Action.

Similarly, a procedure to deal with complaints of sexual harassment should be regarded as only one component of a strategy to deal with the problem. The prime objective should be to change behaviour and attitudes, to seek to ensure the prevention of sexual harassment. **[2249]**

4 Collective bargaining

The majority of the recommendations contained in this Code are for action by employers, since employers have clear responsibilities to ensure the protection of the dignity of women and men at work.

Trade unions also have responsibilities to their members and they can and should play an important role in the prevention of sexual harassment in the workplace. It is recommended that the question of including appropriate clauses in agreements is examined in the context of the collective bargaining process, with the aim of achieving a work environment free from unwanted conduct of a sexual nature or other conduct based on sex affecting the dignity of women and men at work and free from victimisation of a complainant or of a person wishing to give, or giving, evidence in the event of a complaint. **[2249A]**

5 Recommendations to employers

The policies and procedures recommended below should be adopted, where appropriate, after consultation or negotiation with trade unions or employee representatives. Experience suggests that strategies to create and maintain a working environment in which the dignity of employees is respected are most likely to be effective where they are jointly agreed.

It should be emphasised that a distinguishing characteristic of sexual harassment is that employees subjected to it often will be reluctant to complain. An absence of complaints about sexual harassment in a particular organisation, therefore, does not necessarily mean an absence of sexual harassment. It may mean that the recipients of sexual harassment think that there is no point in complaining because nothing will be done about it, or because it will be trivialised or the complainant subjected to ridicule, or because they fear reprisals. Implementing the preventative and procedural recommendations outlined below should facilitate the creation of a climate at work in which such concerns have no place. **[2250]**

A Prevention

(i) Policy statements

As a first step in showing senior management's concern and their commitment to dealing with the problem of sexual harassment, employers should issue a policy statement which expressly states that all employees have a right to be treated with dignity, that sexual harassment at work will not be permitted or condoned and that employees have a right to complain about it should it occur.

It is recommended that the policy statement makes clear what is considered inappropriate behaviour at work, and explain that such behaviour, in certain circumstances, may be unlawful. It is advisable for the statement to set out a positive duty on managers and supervisors to implement the policy and to take corrective action to ensure compliance with it. It should also place a positive duty on all employees to comply with the policy and to ensure that their colleagues are treated with respect and dignity.

In addition, it is recommended that the statement explains the procedure which should be followed by employees subjected to sexual harassment at work in order to obtain assistance and to whom they should complain; that it contain an undertaking that allegations of sexual harassment will be dealt with seriously, expeditiously and . confidentially; and that employees will be protected against victimisation or retaliation for bringing a complaint of sexual harassment.

It should also specify that appropriate disciplinary measures will be taken against employees found guilty of sexual harassment.

(ii) Communicating the policy

Once the policy has been developed, it is important to ensure that it is communicated effectively to all employees, so that they are aware that they have a right to complain and to whom they should complain; that their complaint will be dealt with promptly and fairly; and so that employees are made aware of the likely consequences of engaging in sexual harassment. Such communication will highlight management's commitment to eliminating sexual harassment, thus enhancing a climate in which it will not occur.

(iii) Responsibility

All employees have a responsibility to help ensure a working environment in which the dignity of employees is respected and managers (including supervisors) have a particular duty to ensure that sexual harassment does not occur in work areas for which they are responsible. It is recommended that managers should explain the organisation's policy to their staff and take steps to positively promote the policy. Managers should also be responsive and supportive to any member of staff who complains about sexual harassment; provide full and clear advice on the procedure to be adopted; maintain confidentiality in any cases of sexual harassment; and ensure that there is no further problem of sexual harassment or any victimisation after a complaint has been resolved.

(iv) Training

An important means of ensuring that sexual harassment does not occur and that, if it does occur, the problem is resolved efficiently is through the provision of training for managers and supervisors. Such training should aim to identify the factors which contribute to a working environment free of sexual harassment and to familiarise participants with their responsibilities under the employer's policy and any problems they are likely to encounter.

In addition, those playing an official role in any formal complaints procedure in respect of sexual harassment should receive specialist training, such as that outlined above.

It is also good practice to include information as to the organisation's policy on sexual harassment and procedures for dealing with it as part of appropriate induction and training programmes. **[2251]**

B Procedures

The development of clear and precise procedures to deal with sexual harassment once it has occurred is of great importance. The procedures should ensure the resolution of problems in an efficient and effective manner. Practical guidance for employees on how to deal with sexual harassment when it occurs and with its aftermath will make it more likely that it will be dealt with at an early stage. Such guidance should of course draw attention to an employee's legal rights and to any time limits within which they must be exercised.

(i) Resolving problems informally

Most recipients of harassment simply want the harassment to stop. Both informal and formal methods of resolving problems should be available.

Employees should be advised that, if possible, they should attempt to resolve the problem informally in the first instance. In some cases, it may be possible and sufficient for the employee to explain clearly to the person engaging in the unwanted conduct that the behaviour in question is not welcome, that it offends them or makes them uncomfortable, and that it interferes with their work.

In circumstances where it is too difficult or embarrassing for an individual to do this on their own behalf, an alternative approach would be to seek support from, or for an initial approach to be made by, a sympathetic friend or confidential counsellor.

If the conduct continues or if it is not appropriate to resolve the problem informally, it should be raised through the formal complaints procedure.

(ii) Advice and assistance

It is recommended that employers should designate someone to provide advice and assistance to employees subjected to sexual harassment, where possible, with responsibilities to assist in the resolution of any problems, whether through informal or formal means. It may be helpful if the officer is designated with the agreement of the trade unions or employees, as this is likely to enhance their acceptability. Such officers could be selected from personnel departments or equal opportunities departments for example. In some organisations they are designated as "confidential counsellors" or "sympathetic friends". Often such a role may be played by someone from the employee's trade union or by women's support groups.

Whatever the location of this responsibility in the organisation, it is recommended that the designated officer receives appropriate training in the best means of resolving problems and in the detail of the organisation's policy and procedures, so that they can perform their role effectively. It is also important that they are given adequate resources to carry out their function, and protection against victimisation for assisting any recipient of sexual harassment.

(iii) Complaints procedure

It is recommended that, where the complainant regards attempts at informal resolution as inappropriate, where informal attempts at resolution have been refused, or where the outcome has been unsatisfactory, a formal procedure for resolving the complaint should be provided. The procedure should give employees confidence that the organisation will take allegations of sexual harassment seriously.

By its nature sexual harassment may make the normal channels of complaint difficult to use because of embarassment, fears of not being taken seriously, fears of damage to reputation, fears of reprisal or the prospect of damaging the working environment. Therefore, a formal procedure should specify to whom the employee should bring a complaint, and it should also provide an alternative if in the particular circumstances the normal grievance procedure may not be suitable, for example because the alleged harasser is the employee's line manager. It is also advisable to make provision for employees to bring a complaint in the first instance to someone of their own sex, should they so choose.

It is good practice for employers to monitor and review complaints of sexual harassment and how they have been resolved, in order to ensure that their procedures are working effectively.

(iv) Investigations

It is important to ensure that internal investigations of any complaints are handled with sensitivity and with due respect for the rights of both the complainant and the alleged harasser. The investigation should be seen to be independent and objective. Those carrying out the investigation should not be connected with the allegation in any way, and every effort should be made to resolve complaints speedily—grievances should be handled promptly and the procedure should set a time limit within which complaints will be processed, with due regard for any time limits set by national legislation for initiating a complaint through the legal system.

It is recommended as good practice that both the complainant and the alleged harasser have the right to be accompanied and/or represented, perhaps by a representative of their trade union or a friend or colleague; that the alleged harasser be given full details of the nature of the complaint and the opportunity to respond; and that strict confidentiality be maintained throughout any investigation into an allegation. Where it is necessary to interview witnesses, the importance of confidentiality should be emphasised.

It must be recognised that recounting the experience of sexual harassment is difficult and can damage the employee's dignity. Therefore, a complainant should not be required to repeatedly recount the events complained of where this is unnecessary.

The investigation should focus on the facts of the complaint and it is advisable for the employer to keep a complete record of all meetings and investigations.

(v) Disciplinary offence

It is recommended that violations of the organisation's policy protecting the dignity of employees at work should be treated as a disciplinary offence; and the disciplinary rules should make clear what is regarded as inappropriate behaviour at work. It is also good practice to ensure that the range of penalties to which offenders will be liable for violating the rule is clearly stated and also to make it clear that it will be considered a disciplinary offence to victimise or retaliate against an employee for bringing a complaint of sexual harassment in good faith.

Where a complaint is upheld and it is determined that it is necessary to relocate or transfer one party, consideration should be given, wherever practicable, to allowing the complainant to choose whether he or she wishes to remain in their post or be transferred to another location. No element of penalty should be seen to attach to a complainant whose complaint is upheld and in addition, where a complaint is upheld, the employer should monitor the situation to ensure that the harassment has stopped.

Even where a complaint is not upheld, for example because the evidence is regarded as inconclusive, consideration should be given to transferring or rescheduling the work of one of the employees concerned rather than requiring them to continue to work together against the wishes of either party.   **[2252]**

6 Recommendations to trade unions

Sexual harassment is a trade union issue as well as an issue for employers. It is recommended as good practice that trade unions should formulate and issue clear policy statements on sexual harassment and take steps to raise awareness of the problem of sexual harassment in the workplace, in order to help create a climate in which it is neither condoned nor ignored. For example, trade unions could aim to give all officers and representatives training on equality issues, including dealing with sexual harassment and include such information in union-sponsored or approved training courses, as well as information on the union's policy. Trade unions should consider declaring that sexual harassment is inappropriate behaviour and educating members and officials about its consequences is recommended as good practice.

Trade unions should also raise the issue of sexual harassment with employers and encourage the adoption of adequate policies and procedures to protect the dignity of women and men at work in the organisation. It is advisable for trade unions to inform members of their right not to be sexually harassed at work and provide members with clear guidance as to what to do if they are sexually harassed, including guidance on any relevant legal rights.

Where complaints arise, it is important for trade unions to treat them seriously and sympathetically and ensure that the complainant has the opportunity of representation if a complaint is to be pursued. It is important to create an environment in which members feel able to raise such complaints knowing they will receive a sympathetic and supportive response from local union representatives. Trade unions could consider designating specially-trained officials to advise and counsel members with complaints of sexual harassment and act on their behalf if required. This will provide a focal point for support. It is also a good idea to ensure that there are sufficient female representatives to support women subjected to sexual harassment.

It is recommended too, where the trade union is representing both the complainant and the alleged harasser for the purpose of the complaints procedure, that it be made clear that the union is not condoning offensive behaviour by providing representation. In any event, the same official should not represent both parties.

It is good practice to advise members that keeping a record of incidents by the harassed worker will assist in bringing any formal or informal action to a more effective conclusion; and that the union wishes to be informed of any incident of sexual harassment and that such information will be kept confidential. It is also good practice for the union to monitor and review the union's record in responding to complaints and in representing alleged harassers and the harassed, in order to ensure its responses are effective.   **[2253]**

7 Employees' responsibilities

Employees have a clear role to play in helping to create a climate at work in which sexual harassment is unacceptable. They can contribute to preventing sexual harassment through an awareness and sensitivity towards the issue and by ensuring that standards of conduct for themselves and for colleagues do not cause offence.

Employees can do much to discourage sexual harassment by making it clear that they find such behaviour unacceptable and by supporting colleagues who suffer such treatment and are considering making a complaint.

Employees who are themselves recipients of harassment should, where practicable, tell the harasser that the behaviour is unwanted and unacceptable. Once the offender understands clearly that the behaviour is unwelcome, this may be enough to put an end to it. If the behaviour is persisted in, employees should inform management and/or their employee representative through the appropriate channels and request assistance in stopping the harassment, whether through informal or formal means.   **[2254]**

DIRECTIVE No 92/56 OF THE COUNCIL

of 24 June 1992

amending Directive 75/129 on the approximation of the laws of the Member States relating to collective redundancies

THE COUNCIL OF THE EUROPEAN COMMUNITIES

Having regard to the Treaty establishing the European Economic Community, and in particular Article 100 thereof,

Having regard to the proposal from the Commission,

Having regard to the opinion of the European Parliament,

Having regard to the opinion of the Economic and Social Committee

Whereas the Community Charter of the Fundamental Social Rights of Workers, adopted at the Regulation Council meeting held in Strasbourg on 9 December 1989 by the Heads of State or Government of 11 Member States, states *inter alia* in point 7, first paragraph, first sentence, and second paragraph; in point 17, first paragraph; and in point 18, third indent:

"**7** The completion of the internal market must lead to an improvement in the living and working conditions of workers in the European Community (. . .).

The improvement must cover, where necessary, the development of certain aspects of employment regulations such as procedures for collective redundancies and those regarding bankruptcies.

17 Information, consultation and participation for workers must be developed along appropriate lines, taking account of the practices in force in the various Member States.

(. . .)

18 Such information, consultation and participation must be implemented in due time, particularly in the following cases:

(— . . .)

(— . . .)

—in cases of collective redundancy procedures;

(— . . .);"

Whereas, in order to calculate the number of redundancies provided for in the definition of collective redundancies within the meaning of Council Directive 75/129/EEC of 17 February 1975 on the approximation of the laws of the Member States relating to collective redundancies other forms of termination of employment contracts on the initiative of the employer should be equated to redundancies, provided that there are at least five redundancies;

Whereas it should be stipulated that Directive 75/129/EEC applies in principle also to collective redundancies resulting where the establishment's activities are terminated as a result of a judicial decision;

Whereas the Member States should be given the option of stipulating that workers' representatives may call on experts on grounds of the technical complexity of the matters which are likely to be the subject of the informing and consulting;

Whereas the provisions of Directive 75/129/EEC should be clarified and supplemented as regards the employer's obligations regarding the informing and consulting of workers' representatives;

Whereas it is necessary to ensure that employers' obligations as regards information, consultation and notification apply independently of the fact that the decision on collective redundancies emanates from the employer or from an undertaking which controls that employer;

Whereas Member States should ensure that workers' representatives and/or workers have at their disposal administrative and/or judicial procedures in order to ensure that the obligations laid down in Directive 75/129/EEC are fulfilled,

HAS ADOPTED THIS DIRECTIVE   [2255]

Article 1

* * * * *   [2256]

NOTE

This Article amends Directive 75/129, paras **[2099]–[2108]**

Article 2

1 Member States shall bring into force the laws, regulations and administrative provisions necessary to adoption or shall ensure, at the latest two years after adoption, that the employers' and workers' representatives introduce the required provisions by way of agreement, the Member States being obliged to take the necessary steps enabling them at all times to guarantee the results imposed by this Directive.

They shall immediately inform the Commission thereof.

2 When Member States adopt the provisions referred to in paragraph 1, such provisions shall contain a reference to this Directive or shall be accompanied by such reference at the time of their official publication. The procedure for such reference shall be adopted by Member States.

3 Member States shall forward to the Commission the text of any fundamental provisions of national law already adopted or being adopted in the area governed by this Directive.   **[2257]**

Article 3

This Directive is addressed to the Member States.   **[2258]**

COUNCIL RECOMMENDATION
of 27 July 1992
concerning the promotion of participation by employed persons in profits and enterprise results (including equity participation)
(OJ/(L) 245/92)

THE COUNCIL OF THE EUROPEAN COMMUNITIES,

Having regard to the Treaty establishing the European Economic Community, and in particular Article 235 thereof,

Having regard to the proposal for a Recommendation from the Commission,

Having regard to the Opinion of the European Parliament,

Having regard to the Opinion of the Economic and Social Committee,

Whereas in its communication concerning the Action Programme relating to the implementation of the Community Charter of the Fundamental Social Rights of Workers the Commission announced its intention to submit a Community instrument on equity sharing and financial participation by employed persons;

Whereas a report on the promotion of participation by employed persons in profits and enterprise results in the Member States has been prepared; whereas this report has established that there is a great variety in the types of scheme encountered in the Community, including cash payments, share-based and deferred profit-sharing schemes and various types of particular share-ownership schemes for employed persons;

Whereas encouragement of financial participation in enterprises by employed persons, without discrimination on grounds of sex or nationality, may be seen as a means of achieving a wider distribution of the wealth generated by enterprises which the employed persons have helped to produce; whereas, furthermore, the promotion of enterprise schemes for the financial participation of employed persons in enterprises encourages in particular greater involvement of employed persons in the progress of their companies;

Whereas, while the body of empirical research into the effects of such schemes in practice does not yet provide overwhelming evidence of strong overall advantages, there are sufficient indications that such schemes produce a number of positive effects, particularly on the motivation and productivity of employed persons and on the competitiveness of enterprises;

Whereas it is appropriate to promote a wider spread of financial participation schemes within the Community, without seeking active harmonisation or a reduction in the existing wide range of available schemes;

Whereas account should be taken of the important role and the extensive responsibilities of management and labour in this area; whereas the interest and active involvement of management and labour in this Community initiative are a precondition for its ultimate success;

Whereas the present action appears necessary to attain, in the course of the operation of the common market, one of the objectives of the Community. **[2259]**

I HEREBY INVITES THE MEMBER STATES:

1 to acknowledge the potential benefits of a wider use, individually or collectively, of a broad variety of schemes to increase the participation of employed persons in profits and enterprise results by means of profit-sharing, employee share-ownership or a combination of both;

2 to take account of the role and the responsibility of management and labour in this context, in accordance with national law and/or practice. **[2260]**

II HEREBY RECOMMENDS THE MEMBER STATES TO:

1 ensure that legal structures are adequate to allow the introduction of the financial participation schemes referred to in this Recommendation;

2 consider the possibility of according incentives such as fiscal or other financial advantages to encourage the introduction of certain schemes;

3 encourage the use of such schemes by facilitating the supply of adequate information to all relevant parties;

4 take account of experience gained in other Member States when deciding on which participation schemes to promote;

5 ensure that in the context of the laws, regulations and practice possibly existing in the Member States the parties concerned have a wide range of options or arrangements available, the implementation of which would, when suitable, be the subject of consultations between employers and employed persons or their representatives;

6 ensure that this choice can be made at a level which, taking account of national collective bargaining legislation and/or practices, is as close as possible to the employed person and the enterprise;

7 contemplate and/or encourage consideration of the points set out in the Annex when new financial participation schemes are being prepared or when existing schemes are being reviewed;

8 examine, after a period of three years following the adoption of this Recommendation, the data available at a national level on the development of financial participation by employed persons and to communicate the results to the Commission;

9 enhance management and labour's awareness of the above matters. **[2261]**

III NOTES THAT THE COMMISSION INTENDS:

to submit a report to the European Parliament, the Council and the Economic and Social Committee on the application of this Recommendation within four years of its adoption, on the basis of the information supplied to it by the Member States.
[2262]

ANNEX

Points referred to in section II, point 7

1 Regularity: the application of participation schemes on a regular basis and the granting of "bonuses" at least once a year.

2 Predetermined formula: the definition, in a clear way and before the beginning of each reference period, of the formula for calculating the amounts allocated to employed persons.

3 Maintaining wage negotiations: the existence of financial participation schemes should not stand in the way of normal negotiations dealing with wages and conditions of employment or of setting wages and working conditions through such negotiations.

The question of the agreement on new provisions in the field of the financial participation of employed persons may be taken up in the normal negotiations dealing with wage-setting and working conditions, without replacing them.

4 Voluntary participation: the opportunity for both enterprises and employed persons to express a choice, within the framework of any laws, regulations or agreements which may exist in the Member States, on the adoption of a participation scheme or on the financial participation scheme or arrangements in which they wish to participate.

5 Calculation of amounts allocated to employed persons: the amount of bonuses should not generally be fixed in advance, but determined on the basis of a predetermined formula reflecting the enterprise's performance during a certain period (expressed in terms of profits or any other indicator) the performance measure(s) chosen to measure the performances being clearly specified.

6 Amounts: the formula for calculating bonuses should be such that it will produce the expected incentive, although it should not exceed a specific ceiling (in relative or absolute terms) in order to avoid wide fluctuations in income.

7 Risks: employees should be made aware of the risks inherent in financial participation schemes; apart from the risks of income fluctuation inherent in participation schemes, employed persons may be exposed to additional risk if their participation takes the form of investments that are relatively undiversified; in this context, the possibility of providing for mechanisms to protect against the risk of depreciation in the value of assets merits consideration.

8 Beneficiaries: beneficiaries are primarily employed persons, ie wage-earners covered by employment contracts; as far as possible, access to participation schemes should be open to all persons employed by the enterprise.

More generally, workers in similar objective situations should have equal rights with regard to access to participation schemes.

9 Enterprise type: participation schemes may be instituted by both privately-owned firms and public enterprises, as long as suitable indicators of enterprise results or profits are, or can be, made available.

10 Size of enterprises:
    (a) small and medium-sized enterprises should have adequate opportunities to be able to implement financial participation schemes; in particular, it is important to ensure that administrative constraints are few in number and that, if needed at all, minimum financial requirements are not too high;
    (b) in larger enterprises, especially multinational companies, it may be useful to link all or part of employee benefits to the performance of a separate profit unit rather than to overall enterprise results;

    (c) the size of enterprises may also affect the choice of the most appropriate scheme.

11 Complexity: complex participation schemes should be avoided.

12 Information and training: to ensure the success of any type of participation scheme, substantial efforts will be required to provide relevant information and, if need be, training for all employed persons concerned.   **[2263]**

DIRECTIVE No 92/85 OF THE COUNCIL
of 19 October 1992
on the introduction of measures to encourage improvements in the safety and health of pregnant workers and workers who have recently given birth or are breastfeeding (tenth individual Directive within the meaning of Article 16(1) of Directive 89/391)

THE COUNCIL OF THE EUROPEAN COMMUNITIES,

    Having regard to the Treaty establishing the European Economic Community, and in particular Article 118a thereof,

    Having regard to the proposal from the Commission, drawn up after consultation with the Advisory Committee on Safety, Hygiene and Health Protection at work,

    In cooperation with the European Parliament,

    Having regard to the opinion of the Economic and Social Committee,

    Whereas Article 118a of the Treaty provides that the Council shall adopt, by means of directives, minimum requirements for encouraging improvements, especially in the working environment, to protect the safety and health of workers;

    Whereas this Directive does not justify any reduction in levels of protection already achieved in individual Member States, the Member States being committed, under the Treaty, to encouraging improvements in conditions in this area and to harmonizing conditions while maintaining the improvements made;

    Whereas, under the terms of Article 118a of the Treaty, the said directives are to avoid imposing administrative, financial and legal constraints in a way which would hold back the creation and development of small and medium-sized undertakings;

    Whereas, pursuant to Decision 74/325/EEC, as last amended by the 1985 Act of Accession, the Advisory Committee on Safety, Hygiene and Health Protection at Work is consulted by the Commission on the drafting of proposals in this field;

    Whereas the Community Charter of the fundamental social rights of workers, adopted at the Strasbourg European Council on 9 December 1989 by the Heads of State or Government of 11 Member States, lays down, in paragraph 19 in particular, that:

    'Every worker must enjoy satisfactory health and safety conditions in his working environment. Appropriate measures must be taken in order to achieve further harmonization of conditions in this area while maintaining the improvements made';

    Whereas the Commission, in its action programme for the implementation of the Community Charter of the fundamental social rights of workers, has included among its aims the adoption by the Council of a Directive on the protection of pregnant women at work;

    Whereas Article 15 of Council Directive 89/391/EEC of 12 June 1989 on the introduction of measures to encourage improvements in the safety and health of workers at work provides that particularly sensitive risk groups must be protected against the dangers which specifically affect them;

    Whereas pregnant workers, workers who have been recently given birth or who are breastfeeding must be considered a specific risk group in many respects, and measures must be taken with regard to their safety and health;

    Whereas the protection of the safety and health of pregnant workers, workers who have recently given birth or workers who are breastfeeding should not treat women on the labour market unfavourably nor work to the detriment of directives concerning equal treatment for men and women;

    Whereas some types of activities may pose a specific risk, for pregnant workers, workers who have recently given birth or workers who are breastfeeding, of exposure to dangerous agents, processes or working conditions; whereas such risks must therefore be assessed and the result of such assessment communicated to female workers and/or their representatives;

Whereas, further, should the result of this assessment reveal the existence of a risk to the safety or health of the female worker, provision must be made for such worker to be protected;

Whereas pregnant workers and workers who are breastfeeding must not engage in activities which have been assessed as revealing a risk of exposure, jeopardising safety and health, to certain particularly dangerous agents or working conditions;

Whereas provision should be made for pregnant workers, workers who have recently given birth or workers who are breastfeeding not to be required to work at night where such provision is necessary from the point of view of their safety and health;

Whereas the vulnerability of pregnant workers, workers who have recently given birth or who are breastfeeding makes it necessary for them to be granted the right to maternity leave of at least 14 continuous weeks, allocated before and/or after confinement, and renders necessary the compulsory nature of maternity leave of at least two weeks, allocated before and/or after confinement;

Whereas the risk of dismissal for reasons associated with their condition may have harmful effects on the physical and mental state of pregnant workers, workers who have recently given birth or who are breastfeeding; whereas provision should be made for such dismissal to be prohibited;

Whereas measures for the organization of work concerning the protection of the health of pregnant workers, workers who have recently given birth or workers who are breastfeeding would serve no purpose unless accompanied by the maintenance of rights linked to the employment contract, including maintenance of payment and/or entitlement to an adequate allowance;

Whereas, moreover, provision concerning maternity leave would also serve no purpose unless accompanied by the maintenance of rights linked to the employment contract and/or entitlement to an adequate allowance;

Whereas the concept of an adequate allowance in the case of maternity leave must be regarded as a technical point of reference with a view to fixing the minimum level of protection and should in no circumstances be interpreted as suggesting an analogy between pregnancy and illness.

HAS ADOPTED THIS DIRECTIVE   **[2264]**

SECTION I
PURPOSE AND DEFINITIONS

Article 1

Purpose

1 The purpose of this Directive, which is the tenth individual Directive within the meaning of Article 16 (1) of Directive 89/391/EEC, is to implement measures to encourage improvements in the safety and health at work of pregnant workers and workers who have recently given birth or who are breastfeeding.

2 The provisions of Directive 89/391/EEC, except for Article 2 (2) thereof, shall apply in full to the whole area covered by paragraph 1, without prejudice to any more stringent and/or specific provisions contained in this Directive.

3 This Directive may not have the effect of reducing the level of protection afforded to pregnant workers, workers who have recently given birth or who are breastfeeding as compared with the situation which exists in each Member State on the date on which this Directive is adopted.   **[2265]**

Article 2

Definitions

For the purposes of this Directive:

    (a) *pregnant worker* shall mean a pregnant worker who informs her employer of her condition, in accordance with national legislation and/or national practice;

(b) *worker who has recently given birth* shall mean a worker who has recently given birth within the meaning of national legislation and/or national practice and who informs her employer of her condition, in accordance with that legislation and/or practice;

(c) *worker who is breastfeeding* shall mean a worker who is breastfeeding within the meaning of national legislation and/or national practice and who informs her employer of her condition, in accordance with that legislation and/or practice.   **[2266]**

SECTION II

GENERAL PROVISIONS

Article 3

Guidelines

1 In consultation with the Member States and assisted by the Advisory Committee on Safety, Hygiene and Health Protection at Work, the Commission shall draw up guildelines on the assessment of the chemical, physical and biological agents and industrial process considered hazardous for the safety or health of workers within the meaning of Article 2.

The guidelines referred to in the first subparagraph shall also cover movements and postures, mental and physical fatigue and other types of physical and mental stress connected with the work done by workers within the meaning of Article 2.

2 The purpose of the guidelines referred to in paragraph 1 is to serve as a basis for the assessment referred to in Article 4 (1).

To this end, Member States shall bring these guidelines to the attention of all employers and all female workers and/or their representatives in the respective Member State.   **[2267]**

Article 4

Assessment and information

1 For all activities liable to involve a specific risk of exposure to the agents, processes or working conditions of which a non-exhaustive list is given in Annex 1, the employer shall assess the nature, degree and duration of exposure, in the undertaking and/or establishment concerned, or workers within the meaning of Article 2, either directly or by way of the protective and preventative services referred to in Article 7 of Directive 89/391/EEC, in order to:

—assess any risks to the safety or health and any possible effect on the pregnancies or breastfeeding of workers within the meaning of Article 2,

—decide what measures should be taken.

2 Without prejudice to Article 10 of Directive 89/391/EEC, workers within the meaning of Article 2 and workers likely to be in one of the situations referred to in Article 2 in the undertaking and/or establishment concerned and/or their representatives shall be informed of the results of the assessment referred to in paragraph 1 and of all measures to be taken concerning health and safety at work.   **[2268]**

Article 5

Action further to the results of the assessment

1 Without prejudice to Article 6 of Directive 89/391/EEC, if the results of the assessment referred to in Article 4(1) reveal a risk to the safety or health or an effect on the pregnancy or breastfeeding of a worker within the meaning of Article 2, the employer shall take the necessary measures to ensure that, by temporarily adjusting the working conditions and/or the working hours of the worker concerned, the exposure of that worker to such risks is avoided.

2 If the adjustment of her working conditions and/or working hours is not technically and/or objectively feasible, or cannot reasonably be required on duly substantiated grounds, the employer shall take the necessary measures to move the worker concerned to another job.

3 If moving her to another job is not technically and/or objectively feasible or cannot reasonably be required on duly substantiated grounds, the worker concerned shall be granted leave in accordance with national legislation and/or national practice for the whole of the period necessary to protect her safety or health.

4 The provisions of this Article shall apply *mutatis mutandis* to the case where a worker pursuing an activity which is forbidden pursuant to Article 6 becomes pregnant or starts breastfeeding and informs her employer thereof.   **[2269]**

Article 6
Cases in which exposure is prohibited

In addition to the general provisions concerning the protection of workers, in particular those relating to the limit values for occupational exposure:

1 pregnant workers within the meaning of Article 2(a) may under no circumstances be obliged to perform duties for which the assessment has revealed a risk of exposure, which would jeopardize safety or health, to the agents and working conditions listed in Annex II, Section A;

2 workers who are breastfeeding, within the meaning of Article 2 (c), may under no circumstances be obliged to perform duties for which the assessment has revealed a risk of exposure, which would jeopardize safety or health, to the agents and working conditions listed in Annex II, Section B.   **[2270]**

Article 7
Night work

1 Member States shall take the necessary measures to ensure that workers referred to in Article 2 are not obliged to perform night work during their pregnancy and for a period following childbirth which shall be determined by the national authority competent for safety and health, subject to submission, in accordance with the procedures laid down by the Member States, of a medical certificate stating that this is necessary for the safety or health of the worker concerned.

2 The measures referred to in paragraph 1 must entail the possibility, in accordance with national legislation and/or national practice, of:

    (a) transfer to daytime work; or

    (b) leave from work or extension of maternity leave where such a transfer is not technically and/or objectively feasible or cannot reasonably be required on duly substantiated grounds.   **[2271]**

Article 8
Maternity leave

1 Member States shall take the necessary measures to ensure that workers within the meaning of Article 2 are entitled to a continuous period of maternity leave of at least 14 weeks allocated before and/or after confinement in accordance with national legislation and/or practice.

2 The maternity leave stipulated in paragraph 1 must include compulsory maternity leave of at least two weeks allocated before and/or after confinement in accordance with national legislation and/or practice. **[2272]**

Article 9

Time off for ante-natal examinations

Member States shall take the necessary measures to ensure that pregnant workers within the meaning of Article 2 (a) are entitled to, in accordance with national legislation and/or practice, time off, without loss of pay, in order to attend ante-natal examinations, if such examinations have to take place during working hours. **[2273]**

Article 10

Prohibition of dismissal

In order to guarantee workers, within the meaning of Article 2, the exercise of their health and safety protection rights as recognized under this Article, it shall be provided that:

1 Member States shall take the necessary measures to prohibit the dismissal of workers, within the meaning of Article 2, during the period from the beginning of their pregnancy to the end of the maternity leave referred to in Article 8 (1) save in exceptional cases not connected with their condition which are permitted under national legislation and/or practice and, where applicable, provided that the competent authority has given its consent;

2 if a worker, within the meaning of Article 2, is dismissed during the period referred to in point 1, the employer must cite duly substantiated grounds for her dismissal in writing;

3 Member States shall take the necessary measures to protect workers, within the meaning of Article 2, from consequences of dismissal which is unlawful by virtue of point 1. **[2274]**

Article 11

Employment rights

In order to guarantee workers within the meaning of Article 2 the exercise of their health and safety protection rights as recognized in this Article, it shall be provided that:

1 in the cases referred to in Articles 5, 6 and 7, the employment rights relating to the employment contract, including the maintenance of a payment to, and/or entitlement to an adequate allowance for, workers within the meaning of Article 2, must be ensured in accordance with national legislation and/or national practice;

2 in the case referred to in Article 8, the following must be ensured:

    (a) the rights connected with the employment contract of workers within the meaning of Article 2, other than those referred to in point (b) below;
    (b) maintenance of a payment to, and/or entitlement to an adequate allowance for, workers within the meaning of Article 2;

3 the allowance referred to in point 2 (b) shall be deemed adequate if it guarantees income at least equivalent to that which the worker concerned would receive in the event of a break in her activities on grounds connected with her state of health, subject to any ceiling laid down under national legislation;

4 Member States may make entitlement to pay or the allowance referred to in points 1 and 2 (b) conditional upon the worker concerned fulfilling the conditions of eligibility for such benefits laid down under national legislation.

These conditions may under no circumstances provide for periods of previous employment in excess of 12 months immediately prior to the presumed date of confinement.   **[2275]**

NOTE
See further the Statement set out in the Notes at the end of this Directive.

Article 12

Defence of rights

Member States shall introduce into their national legal systems such measures as are necessary to enable all workers who should themselves wronged by failure to comply with the obligations arising from this Directive to pursue their claims by judicial process (and/or, in accordance with national laws and/or practices) by recourse to other competent authorities.   **[2276]**

NOTE
This Art is printed as in the *Official Journal*: presumably the word "consider" ought to have been inserted after the word "should": Ed.

Article 13

Amendments to the Annexes

1 Strictly technical adjustments to Annex I as a result of technical progress, changes in international regulations or specifications and new findings in the area covered by this Directive shall be adopted in accordance with the procedure laid down in Article 17 of Directive 89/391/EEC.

2 Annex II may be amended only in accordance with the procedure laid down in Article 118a of the Treaty.   **[2277]**

Article 14

Final provisions

1 Member States shall bring into force the laws, regulations and administrative provisions necessary to comply with this Directive not later than two years after the adoption thereof or ensure, at the latest two years after the adoption of this Directive, that the two sides of industry introduce the requisite provisions by means of collective agreements, with Member States being required to make all the necessary provisions to enable them at all times to guarantee the results laid down by this Directive. They shall forthwith inform the Commission thereof.

2 When Member States adopt the measure referred to in paragraph 1, they shall contain a reference of this Directive or shall be accompanied by such reference on the occasion of their official publication. The methods of making such a reference shall be laid down by the Member States.

3 Member States shall communicate to the Commission the texts of the essential provisions of national law which they have already adopted or adopt in the field governed by this Directive.

4 Member States shall report to the Commission every five years on the practical implementation of the provisions of this Directive, indicating the points of view of the two sides of industry.

However, Member States shall report for the first time to the Commission on the practical implementation of the provisions of this Directive, indicating the points of view of the two sides of industry, four years after its adoption.

The Commission shall inform the European Parliament, the Council, the Economic and Social Committee and the Advisory Committee on Safety, Hygiene and Health Protection at Work.

5 The Commission shall periodically submit to the European Parliament, the Council and the Economic and Social Committee a report on the implementation of this Directive, taking into account paragraphs 1, 2 and 3.

6 The Council will re-examine this Directive, on the basis of an assessment carried out on the basis of the reports referred to in the second subparagraph of paragraph 4 and, should the need arise, of a proposal, to be submitted by the Commission at the latest five years after adoption of the Directive. **[2278]**

Article 15

The Directive is addressed to the Member States. **[2279]**

ANNEX I

NON-EXHAUSTIVE LIST OF AGENTS, PROCESSES AND WORKING CONDITIONS
(referred to in Article 4 (1))

A AGENTS

1 Physical agents where these are regarded as agents causing foetal lesions and/or likely to disrupt placental attachment, and in particular:

    (a)   shocks, vibration or movement;
    (b)   handling of loads entailing risks, particularly of a dorsolumbar nature;
    (c)   noise;
    (d)   ionising radiation;
    (e)   non-ionising radiation;
    (f)   extremes of cold or heat;
    (g)   movements and postures, travelling — either inside or outside the establishment — mental and physical fatigue and other physical burdens connected with the activity of the worker within the meaning of Article 2 of the Directive.

2 Biological agents

Biological agents of risk groups 2, 3 and 3 [*] within the meaning of Article 2 (d) numbers 2, 3 and 4 of Directive 90/679/EEC, in so far as it is known that these agents or the therapeutic measures necessitated by such agents endanger the health of pregnant women and the unborn child and in so far as they do not yet appear in Annex II.

---

* text printed as in the *Official Journal*.

3 Chemical agents

The following chemical agents in so far as it is known that they endanger the health of pregnant women and the unborn child and in so far as they do not yet appear in Annex II:

    (a)   substances labelled R 40, R 45, R 46, and R 47 under Directive 67/548/EEC in so far as they do not yet appear in Annex II;
    (b)   chemical agents in Annex I to Directive 90/394/EEC;
    (c)   mercury and mercury derivatives;
    (d)   antimitotic drugs;
    (e)   carbon monoxide;
    (f)   chemical agents of known and dangerous percutaneous absorption.

B PROCESSES

Industrial processes listed in Annex I to Directive 90/394/EEC.

C WORKING CONDITIONS

Underground mining work. **[2280]**

ANNEX II

NON-EXHAUSTIVE LIST OF AGENTS AND WORKING CONDITIONS
(referred to in Article 6)

A PREGNANT WORKERS WITHIN THE MEANING OF ARTICLE 2 (A)

1 Agents

    (a) Physical agents

        Work in hyperbaric atmosphere, eg pressurized enclosures and underwater diving.

    (b) Biological agents

        The following biological agents:

        —toxoplasma,
        —rubella virus,

        unless the pregnant workers are proved to be adequately protected against such agents by immunization.

    (c) Chemical agents

        Lead and lead derivatives in so far as these agents are capable of being absorbed by the human organism.

2 Working conditions

Underground mining work.

B WORKERS WHO ARE BREASTFEEDING WITHIN THE MEANING OF ARTICLE 2 (C)

1 Agents

    (a) Chemical agents

        Lead and lead derivatives in so far as these agents are capable of being absorbed by the human organism.

2 Working conditions

Underground mining work.   **[2281]–[2999]**

NOTES

    For the prospective domestic implementation of parts of this Directive see the Trade Union Reform and Employment Rights Act 1993, ss 23-25 and Schs 2 and 3, substituting and amending relevant provisions of the Employment Protection (Consolidation) Act 1978. As to the scope and interpretation inter alia of Article 11(3) of the Directive, the Council and Commission issued the following formal statement at the 1608th meeting of the Council on 19 October 1992 (OJ(L) 348/92, p 8):

    THE COUNCIL AND THE COMMISSION stated that:

    "In determining the level of the allowances referred to in Article 11(2) (b) and (3), reference shall be made, for purely technical reasons, to the allowance which a worker would receive in the event of a break in her activities on grounds connected with her state of health. Such a reference is not intended in any way to imply that pregnancy and childbirth be equated with sickness. The national social security legislation of all Member States provides for an allowance to be paid during an absence from work due to sickness. The link with such allowance in the chosen formulation is simply intended to serve as a concrete, fixed reference amount in all Member States for the determination of the minimum amount of maternity allowance payable. In so far as allowances are paid in individual Member States which exceed those provided for in the Directive, such allowances are, of course, retained. This is clear from Article 1 (3) of the Directive.".

PART 4
STATUTORY CODES OF PRACTICE

STATUTORY CODES OF PRACTICE

THE INDUSTRIAL RELATIONS CODE OF PRACTICE 1972 (NOTE)

NOTE

This Code, which was the first and most broad of the Statutory Codes in the employment field, was in part superseded by later ACAS Codes. It was revoked in its entirety by the Employment Codes of Practice (Revocation) Order 1991, SI 1991/1264, with effect from 1 June 1991.

For ease of reference, the paragraphs of this former Code which have had most influence on decisions of Tribunals are reproduced in this note. The full Code can be found in earlier editions of this work.

"**46** If redundancy becomes necessary, management in consultation, as appropriate, with employees or their representatives, should:

    (i)   give as much warning as practicable to the employees concerned and to the Department of Employment;

    (ii)   consider introducing schemes for voluntary redundancy, retirement, transfer to other establishments within the undertaking, and a phased rundown of employment;

    (iii) establish which employees are to be made redundant and the order of discharge;

    (iv) offer help to employees in finding other work in co-operation, where appropriate, with the Department of Employment, and allow them reasonable time off for the purpose;

    (v)   decide how and when to make the facts public, ensuring that no announcement is made before the employees and their representatives and trade unions have been informed.

65 Consultation means jointly examining and discussing problems of concern to both management and employees. It involves seeking mutually acceptable solutions through a genuine exchange of views and information."   **[3000]**

A.C.A.S. CODE OF PRACTICE 1

DISCIPLINARY PRACTICE AND PROCEDURES IN EMPLOYMENT (1977)

NOTES

Authority: Employment Protection Act 1975, s 6. (Now the Trade Union and Labour Relations (Consolidation) Act 1992, ss 199, 200. For the legal statutes of the Code see ibid, s 207.)

This Code supersedes paragraphs 130 to 133 (inclusive) of the Industrial Relations Code of Practice. It was brought into force on 20 June 1977 by the Employment Protection Code of Practice (Disciplinary Practice and Procedures) Order 1977, SI 1977/867. A draft code which would have replaced this Code was prepared by ACAS in 1987 and submitted to the Secretary of State for Employment. but was not approved. The draft code was developed into a Handbook published by ACAS in 1988, "Discipline at Work", which although it has no formal legal status is of considerable influence in tribunal proceedings to which it is relevant. Copies may be obtained from ACAS.

Introduction

1 This document gives practical guidance on how to draw up disciplinary rules and procedures and how to operate them effectively. Its aim is to help employers and trade unions as well as individual employees—both men and women—wherever they are employed regardless of the size of the organisation in which they work. In the smaller establishments it may not be practicable to adopt all the detailed provisions, but most of the features listed in paragraph 10 could be adopted and incorporated into a simple procedure.   **[3001]**

Why have disciplinary rules and procedures?

2 Disciplinary rules and procedures are necessary for promoting fairness and order in the treatment of individuals and in the conduct of industrial relations. They also assist an organisation to operate effectively. Rules set standards of conduct at work; procedure helps to ensure that the standards are adhered to and also provides a fair method of dealing with alleged failures to observe them.   **[3002]**

3 It is important that employees know what standards of conduct are expected of them and the Contracts of Employment Act 1972 (as amended by the Employment Protection Act 1975) requires employers to provide written information for their employees about certain aspects of their disciplinary rules and procedures.[1] **[3003]**

4 The importance of disciplinary rules and procedures has also been recognised by the law relating to dismissals, since the grounds for dismissal and the way in which the dismissal has been handled can be challenged before an industrial tribunal.[2] Where either of these is found by a tribunal to have been unfair the employer may be ordered to reinstate or re-engage the employees concerned and may be liable to pay compensation to them. **[3004]**

Formulating policy

5 Management is responsible for maintaining discipline within the organisation and for ensuring that there are adequate disciplinary rules and procedures. The initiative for establishing these will normally lie with management. However, if they are to be fully effective the rules and procedures need to be accepted as reasonable both by those who are to be covered by them and by those who operate them. Management should therefore aim to secure the involvement of employees and all levels of management when formulating new or revising existing rules and procedures. In the light of particular circumstances in different companies and industries trade union officials[3] may or may not wish to participate in the formulation of the rules but they should participate fully with management in agreeing the procedural arrangements which will apply to their members and in seeing that these arrangements are used consistently and fairly. **[3005]**

Rules

6 It is unlikely that any set of disciplinary rules can cover all circumstances that may arise: moreover the rules required will vary according to particular circumstances such as the type of work, working conditions and size of establishment. When drawing up rules the aim should be to specify clearly and concisely those necessary for the efficient and safe performance of work and for the maintenance of satisfactory relations within the workforce and between employees and management. Rules should not be so general as to be meaningless. **[3006]**

7 Rules should be readily available and management should make every effort to ensure that employees know and understand them. This may be best achieved by

---

[1] Contracts of Employment Act 1972, s 4 (2) as amended by the Employment Protection Act, Sch 16, Pt II requires employers to provide employees with a written statement of the main terms and conditions of their employment. Such statements must also specify any disciplinary rules applicable to them and indicate the person to whom they should apply if they are dissatisfied with any disciplinary decision. The statement should explain any further steps which exist in any procedure for dealing with disciplinary decisions or grievances. The employer may satisfy these requirements by referring the employees to a reasonably accessible document which provides the necessary information. [See now the Employment Protection (Consolidation) Act 1978, ss 1–6, as substituted from 30 November 1993 by the Trade Union Reform and Employment Rights Act 1993, s 26, Sch 4: Ed.]
[2] The Trade Union and Labour Relations Act 1974, Sch I, para 21 (4), as amended by the Employment Protection Act 1975, Sch 16, Pt III specifies that a complaint of unfair dismissal has to be presented to an Industrial Tribunal before the end of the 3-month period beginning with the effective date of termination. [See now the Employment Protection (Consolidation) Act 1978, s 67: Ed.]
[3] Throughout this Code, trade union official has the meaning assigned to it by s 30 (1) of the Trade Union and Labour Relations Act 1974 and means, broadly, officers of the union, its branches and sections, and anyone else, including fellow employees, appointed or elected under the union's rules to represent members. [See now the Trade Union and Labour Relations (Consolidation) Act 1992, s 119: Ed.]

giving every employee a copy of the rules and by explaining them orally. In the case of new employees this should form part of an induction programme. **[3007]**

8 Employees should be made aware of the likely consequences of breaking rules and in particular they should be given a clear indication of the type of conduct which may warrant summary dismissal. **[3008]**

Essential features of disciplinary procedures

9 Disciplinary procedures should not be viewed primarily as a means of imposing sanctions. They should also be designed to emphasise and encourage improvements in individual conduct. **[3009]**

10 Disciplinary procedures should:
- (a) Be in writing.
- (b) Specify to whom they apply.
- (c) Provide for matters to be dealt with quickly.
- (d) Indicate the disciplinary actions which may be taken.
- (e) Specify the levels of management which have the authority to take the various forms of disciplinary action, ensuring that immediate superiors do not normally have the power to dismiss without reference to senior management.
- (f) Provide for individuals to be informed of the complaints against them and to be given an opportunity to state their case before decisions are reached.
- (g) Give individuals the right to be accompanied by a trade union representative or by a fellow employee of their choice.
- (h) Ensure that, except for gross misconduct, no employees are dismissed for a first breach of discipline.
- (i) Ensure that disciplinary action is not taken until the case has been carefully investigated.
- (j) Ensure that individuals are given an explanation for any penalty imposed.
- (k) Provide a right of appeal and specify the procedure to be followed.

[3010]

The procedure in operation

11 When a disciplinary matter arises, the supervisor or manager should first establish the facts promptly before recollections fade, taking into account the statements of any available witnesses. In serious cases consideration should be given to a brief period of suspension while the case is investigated and this suspension should be with pay. Before a decision is made or penalty imposed the individual should be interviewed and given the opportunity to state his or her case and should be advised of any rights under the procedure, including the right to be accompanied. **[3011]**

12 Often supervisors will give informal oral warnings for the purpose of improving conduct when employees commit minor infringements of the established standards of conduct. However, where the facts of a case appear to call for disciplinary action, other than summary dismissal, the following procedure should normally be observed:
- (a) In the case of minor offences the individual should be given a formal oral warning or if the issue is more serious, there should be a written warning setting out the nature of the offence and the likely consequences of further offences. In either case the individual should be advised that the warning constitutes the first formal stage of the procedure.
- (b) Further misconduct might warrant a final written warning which should

contain a statement that any recurrence would lead to suspension or dismissal or some other penalty, as the case may be.

(c) The final step might be disciplinary transfer, or disciplinary suspension without pay (but only if these are allowed for by an express or implied condition of the contract of employment), or dismissal, according to the nature of the misconduct. Special consideration should be given before imposing disciplinary suspension without pay and it should not normally be for a prolonged period. **[3012]**

13 Except in the event of an oral warning, details of any disciplinary action should be given in writing to the employee and if desired, to his or her representative. At the same time the employee should be told of any right of appeal, how to make it and to whom. **[3013]**

14 When determining the disciplinary action to be taken the supervisor or manager should bear in mind the need to satisfy the test of reasonableness in all the circumstances. So far as possible, account should be taken of the employee's record and any other relevant factors. **[3014]**

15 Special consideration should be given to the way in which disciplinary procedures are to operate in exceptional case. For example:

(a) *Employees to whom the full procedure is not immediately available.* Special provisions may have to be made for the handling of disciplinary matters among nightshift workers, workers in isolated locations or depots or others who may pose particular problems for example because no one is present with the necessary authority to take disciplinary action or no trade union representative is immediately available.

(b) *Trade union officials.* Disciplinary action against a trade union official can lead to a serious dispute if it is seen as an attack on the union's functions. Although normal disciplinary standards should apply to their conduct as employees, no disciplinary action beyond an oral warning should be taken until the circumstances of the case have been discussed with a senior trade union representative or full-time official.

(c) *Criminal offences outside employment.* These should not be treated as automatic reasons for dismissal regardless of whether the offence has any relevance to the duties of the individual as an employee. The main considerations should be whether the offence is one that makes the individual unsuitable for his or her type of work or unacceptable to other employees. Employees should not be dismissed solely because a charge against them is pending or because they are absent through having been remanded in custody. **[3015]**

Appeals

16 Grievance procedures are sometimes used for dealing with disciplinary appeals through it is normally more appropriate to keep the two kinds of procedure separate since the disciplinary issues are in general best resolved within the organisation and need to be dealt with more speedily than others. The external stages of a grievance procedure may however, be the appropriate machinery for dealing with appeals against disciplinary action where a final decision within the organisation is contested or where the matter becomes a collective issue between management and a trade union. **[3016]**

17 Independent arbitration is sometimes an appropriate means of resolving disciplinary issues. Where the parties concerned agree, it may constitute the final stage of procedure.   **[3017]**

Records

18 Records should be kept, detailing the nature of any breach of disciplinary rules, the action taken and the reasons for it, whether an appeal was lodged, its outcome and any subsequent developments. These records should be carefully safeguarded and kept confidential.   **[3018]**

19 Except in agreed special circumstances breaches of disciplinary rules should be disregarded after a specific period of satisfactory conduct.   **[3019]**

Further action

20 Rules and procedures should be reviewed periodically in the light of any developments in employment legislation or industrial relation practice and, if necessary, revised in order to ensure their continuing relevance and effectiveness. Any amendments and additional rules imposing new obligations should be introduced only after reasonable notice has been given to all employees and where appropriate, their representatives have been informed.   **[3020]**

A.C.A.S. CODE OF PRACTICE 2

DISCLOSURE OF INFORMATION TO TRADE UNIONS FOR COLLECTIVE BARGAINING PURPOSES (1977)

NOTES
    Authority: Employment Protection Act 1975, s 6. (Now the Trade Union and Labour Relations (Consolidation) Act 1992, ss 199, 200. For the legal status of the Code see ibid, s 207).
    This Code supersedes paragraphs 96 to 98 (inclusive) of the former Industrial Relations Code of Practice. It was brought into force on 22 August 1977 by the Employment Protection Code of Practice (Disclosure of Information) Order 1977, SI 1977/937.]

Introduction

1 Under the Employment Protection Act 1975 the Advisory, Conciliation and Arbitration Service (ACAS) may issue Codes of Practice containing such practical guidance as the Service thinks fit for the purpose of promoting the improvement of industrial relations. In particular, the Service has a duty to provide practical guidance on the application of sections 17 and 18 of the Act in relation to the disclosure of information by employers to trade unions for the purpose of collective bargaining.   **[3021]**

2 The Act and the Code apply to employers operating in both the public and private sectors of industry. They do not apply to collective bargaining between employers' associations and trade unions, although the parties concerned may wish to follow the guidelines contained in the Code.   **[3022]**

3 The information which employers may have a duty to disclose under section 17 is information which it would be in accordance with good industrial relations practice to disclose. In determining what would be in accordance with good industrial relations practice regard is to be had to any relevant provisions of the Code. However, the Code imposes no legal obligations on an employer to disclose any specific item of information. Failure to observe the Code does not by itself render anyone liable to proceedings, but the Act requires any relevant provisions to be taken into account in proceedings before the Central Arbitration Committee.[1]   **[3023]**

Provisions of the Act

4 The Act places a general duty on an employer to disclose at all stages of collective bargaining information requested by representatives of independent trade unions. The unions must be either recognised by the employer for collective bargaining purposes, or fall within the scope of an ACAS recommendation for recognition. The representative of the union is an official or other person authorised by the union to carry on such collective bargaining.   **[3024]**

5 The information requested has to be in the employer's possession, or in the possession of any associated employer, and must relate to the employer's undertaking. The information to be disclosed is that without which a trade union representative would be impeded to a material extent in bargaining and which it would be in accordance with good industrial relations practice to disclose for the purpose of collective bargaining. In determining what is in accordance with good industrial relations practice, any relevant provisions of this Code are to be taken into account.
                              [3025]

6 No employer is required to disclose any information which: would be against the interests of national security; would contravene a prohibition imposed by or under an enactment; was given to an employer in confidence, or was obtained by the employer in consequence of the confidence reposed in him by another person; relates to an individual unless he has consented to its disclosure; would cause substantial injury to the undertaking (or national interest in respect of Crown employment) for reasons other than its effect on collective bargaining; or was obtained for the purpose of any legal proceedings.   **[3026]**

7 In providing information the employer is not required to produce original documents for inspection or copying. Nor is he required to compile or assemble information which would entail work or expenditure out of reasonable proportion to the value of the information in the conduct of collective bargaining. The union representative can request that the information be given in writing by the employer or be confirmed in writing. Similarly, an employer can ask the trade union representative to make the request for information in writing or confirm it in writing.
                              [3027]

8 If the trade union considers that an employer has failed to disclose to its representatives information which he was required to disclose by section 17 of the Act, it may make a complaint to the Central Arbitration Committee.[2] The Committee may ask the Advisory, Conciliation and Arbitration Service to conciliate. If conciliation does not lead to a settlement of the complaint the Service shall inform the Committee accordingly who shall proceed to hear and determine the complaint. If the complaint is upheld by the Committee it is required to specify the information that should have been disclosed and a period of time within which the employer ought to disclose the information. If the employer does not disclose the information within

---

[1] 'Employment Protection Act 1975, s 18, See paragraphs 6 and 7 of this Code. [Section 18 has now been re-enacted as s 182 of the Trade Union and Labour Relations (Consolidation) Act 1992: Ed.]
[2] Further information can be obtained from the Secretary of the Committee at 1 The Abbey Garden, London SW1P 3SE. [Now at 39 Grosvenor Place, London SW1X 7BD: Ed]

the specified time the union may present a further complaint to the Committee and may also present a claim for improved terms and conditions. If the further complaint is upheld by the Committee an award, which would have effect as part of the contract of employment, may be made against the employer on the terms and conditions specified in the claim, or other terms and conditions which the Committee considers appropriate.   **[3028]**

Providing information

9 The absence of relevant information about an employer's undertaking may to a material extent impede trade unions in collective bargaining; particularly if the information would influence the formulation, presentation or pursuance of a claim, or the conclusion of an agreement. The provision of relevant information in such circumstances would be in accordance with good industrial relations practice. **[3029]**

10 To determine what information will be relevant negotiators should take account of the subject-matter of the negotiations and the issues raised during them; the level at which negotiations take place (department, plant, division, or company level); the size of the company; and the type of business the company is engaged in.
[3030]

11 Collective bargaining within an undertaking can range from negotiations on specific matters arising daily at the work place affecting particular sections of the workforce, to extensive periodic negotiations on terms and conditions of employment affecting the whole workforce in multiplant companies. The relevant information and the depth, detail and form in which it could be presented to negotiators will vary accordingly. Consequently, it is not possible to compile a list of items that should be disclosed in all circumstances. Some examples of information relating to the undertaking which could be relevant in certain collective bargaining situations and given below:

    (i) *Pay and benefits:* principles and structure of payment systems; job evaluation systems and grading criteria; earnings and hours analysed according to work-group, grade, plant, sex, out-workers and home-workers, department or division, giving, where appropriate, distributions and make-up of pay showing any additions to basic rate of salary; total pay bill; details of fringe benefits and non-wage labour costs.

    (ii) *Conditions of service:* policies on recruitment, redeployment, redundancy, training, equal opportunity, and promotion; appraisal systems; health, welfare and safety matters.

    (iii) *Manpower:* numbers employed analysed according to grade, department, location, age and sex; labour turnover; absenteeism; overtime and short-time; manning standards; planned changes in work methods, materials, equipment or organisation; available manpower plans; investment plans.

    (iv) *Performance:* productivity and efficiency data; savings from increased productivity and output; return on capital invested; sales and state of order book.

    (v) *Financial:* cost structures; gross and net profits; sources of earnings; assets; liabilities; allocation of profits; details of government financial assistance; transfer prices; loans to parent or subsidiary companies and interest charged.   **[3031]**

12 These examples are not intended to represent a check list of information that should be provided for all negotiations. Nor are they meant to be an exhaustive list of types of information as other items may be relevant in particular negotiations.
[3032]

Restrictions on the duty to disclose

13 Trade unions and employers should be aware of the restrictions on the general duty to disclose information for collective bargaining.[3]   **[3033]**

14 Some examples of information which if disclosed in particular circumstances might cause substantial injury are: cost information on individual products; detailed analysis of proposed investment, marketing or pricing policies; and price quotas or the make-up of tender prices. Information which has to be made available publicly, for example under the Companies Acts, would not fall into this category.   **[3034]**

15 Substantial injury may occur if, for example, certain customers would be lost to competitors, or suppliers would refuse to supply necessary materials, or the ability to raise funds to finance the company would be seriously impaired as a result of disclosing certain information. The burden of establishing a claim that disclosure of certain information would cause substantial injury lies with the employer.   **[3035]**

Trade union responsibilities

16 Trade unions should identify and request the information they require for collective bargaining in advance of negotiations whenever practicable. Misunderstandings can be avoided, costs reduced, and time saved, if requests state as precisely as possible all the information required, and the reasons why the information is considered relevant. Requests should conform to an agreed procedure. A reasonable period of time should be allowed for employers to consider a request and to reply.   **[3036]**

17 Trade unions should keep employers informed of the names of the representative authorised to carry on collective bargaining on their behalf.   **[3037]**

18 Where two or more trade unions are recognised by an employer for collective bargaining purposes they should co-ordinate their requests for information whenever possible.   **[3038]**

19 Trade unions should review existing training programmes or establish new ones to ensure negotiators are equipped to understand and use information effectively.   **[3039]**

Employers' responsibilities[4]

20 Employers should aim to be as open and helpful as possible in meeting trade union requests for information. Where a request is refused, the reasons for the refusal should be explained as far as possible to the trade union representatives concerned and be capable of being substantiated should the matter be taken to the Central Arbitration Committee.   **[3040]**

21 Information agreed as relevant to collective bargaining should be made available as soon as possible once a request for the information has been made by an authorised trade union representative. Employers should present information in a form and style which recipients can reasonably be expected to understand.   **[3041]**

---

[3] Employment Protection Act 1975, s 18. See paragraphs 6 and 7 of this Code. [Section 18 has now been re-enacted as s 182 of the Trade Union and Labour Relations (Consolidation) Act 1992: Ed.]
[4] The Stock Exchange has drawn attention to the need for employers to consider any obligations which they may have under their Listing Agreement.

Joint arrangements for disclosure of information

22 Employers and trade unions should endeavour to arrive at a joint understanding on how the provisions on the disclosure of information can be implemented most effectively. They should consider what information is likely to be required, what is available, and what could reasonably be made available. Consideration should also be given to the form in which the information will be presented, when it should be presented and to whom. In particular, the parties should endeavour to reach an understanding on what information could most appropriately be provided on a regular basis.   **[3042]**

23 Procedures for resolving possible disputes concerning any issues associated with the disclosure of information should be agreed. Where possible such procedures should normally be related to any existing arrangements within the undertaking or industry and the complaint, conciliation and arbitration procedure described in the Act.[5]   **[3043]**

HEALTH AND SAFETY COMMISSION
CODE OF PRACTICE: SAFETY
REPRESENTATIVES AND SAFETY
COMMITTEES (1978)

NOTES
    This Code of Practice was issued under s 16 of the Health and Safety at Work etc Act 1974, and came into force on 1 October 1978. It has the legal effect indicated in that section. For the Safety Representatives and Safety Committees Regulations 1977, see above, paras **[1057]–[1069]**.

1 The Safety Representatives and Safety Committees Regulations 1977 concern safety representatives appointed in accordance with Section 2(4) of the Act and cover:

    (a)   prescribed cases in which recognised trade unions may appoint safety representatives from amongst the employees;

    (b)   prescribed functions of safety representatives.

Section 2(6) of the Act requires an employer to consult with safety representatives with a view to the making and maintenance of arrangements which will enable him and his employees to cooperate effectively in promoting and developing measures to ensure the health and safety at work of the employees, and in checking the effectiveness of such measures. Under section 2(4) safety representatives are required to represent the employees in those consultations.   **[3044]**

2 This Code of Practice has been approved by the Health and Safety Commission with the consent of the Secretary of State. It relates to the requirements placed on safety representatives by section 2(4) of the Act and on employers by the Regulations and takes effect on the date the Regulations come into operation.   **[3045]**

3 The employer, the recognised trade unions concerned and safety representatives should make full and proper use of the existing agreed industrial relations machinery to reach the degree of agreement necessary to achieve the purpose of the Regulations and in order to resolve any differences.   **[3046]**

Interpretation

4   (a)   In this Code, "the 1974 Act" means the Health and Safety at Work etc. Act 1974 and "the Regulations" mean the Safety Representatives and

---

[5] Employment Protection Act 1975, ss 19 to 21. See paragraph 8 in this Code. [Sections 19 to 21 have now been re-enacted as ss 183 to 185 of the Trade Union and Labour Relations (Consolidation) Act 1992: Ed.]

Safety Committees Regulations 1977;
(b) words and expressions which are defined in the Act or in the Regulations have the same meaning in this Code unless the context requires otherwise.
[3047]

Functions of safety representatives

5 In order to fulfil their functions under section 2(4) of the Act safety representatives should:

(a) take all reasonably practical steps to keep themselves informed of:
  (i) the legal requirements relating to the health and safety of persons at work, particularly the group or groups of persons they directly represent,
  (ii) the particular hazards of the workplace and the measures deemed necessary to eliminate or minimise the risk deriving from these hazards, and
  (iii) the health and safety policy of their employer and the organisation and arrangements for fulfilling that policy;
(b) encourage cooperation between their employer and his employees in promoting and developing essential measures to ensure the health and safety of employees and in checking the effectiveness of these measures;
(c) bring to the employer's notice normally in writing any unsafe or unhealthy conditions or working practices or unsatisfactory arrangements for welfare at work which come to their attention whether on an inspection or day to day observation. The report does not imply that all other conditions and working practices are safe and healthy or that the welfare arrangements are satisfactory in all other respects.

Making a written report does not preclude the bringing of such matters to the attention of the employer or his representative by a direct oral approach in the first instance, particularly in situations where speedy remedial action is necessary. It will also be appropriate for minor matters to be the subject of direct oral discussion without the need for a formal written approach. **[3048]**

Information to be provided by employers

6 The Regulations require employers to make information within their knowledge available to safety representatives necessary to enable them to fulfil their functions. Such information should include:

(a) information about the plans and performance of their undertaking and any changes proposed insofar as they affect the health and safety at work of their employees;
(b) information of a technical nature about hazards to health and safety and precautions deemed necessary to eliminate or minimise them, in respect of machinery, plant, equipment, processes, systems of work and substances in use at work, including any relevant information provided by consultants or designers or by the manufacturer, importer or supplier of any article or substance used, or proposed to be used, at work by their employees;
(c) information which the employer keeps relating to the occurrence of any accident, dangerous occurrence or notifiable industrial disease and any statistical records relating to such accidents, dangerous occurrences or cases of notifiable industrial disease;
(d) any other information specifically related to matters affecting the health

and safety at work of his employees, including the results of any measurements taken by the employer or persons acting on his behalf in the course of checking the effectiveness of his health and safety arrangements;

(e) information on articles or substances which an employer issues to home-workers.　　　　　　　　　　　　　　　　　　　　　　　　　　　　　　[3049]

HEALTH AND SAFETY COMMISSION CODE OF PRACTICE: TIME OFF FOR THE TRAINING OF SAFETY REPRESENTATIVES (1978)

NOTES

This Code of Practice is issued under s 16 of the Health and Safety at Work etc Act 1974, and came into force on 1 October 1978. It has the legal effect indicated in that section. For the Safety Representatives and Safety Committees Regulations 1977, see above, paras **[1057]–[1069]**.

Preface

This document sets out a Code of Practice, which has been approved by the Health and Safety Commission, relating to the time off with pay which a safety representative is to be permitted to take during his working hours for the purpose of undergoing training approved by the TUC or by independent unions. It should be read in conjunction with the Safety Representatives and Safety Committees Regulations 1977, with particular reference to Regulation 4, which sets out the functions of a safety representative and the time off for training necessary to perform these functions.

The Advisory, Conciliation and Arbitration Service has also prepared a Code of Practice on Time Off for trade union duties and activities generally under Section 57 of the Employment Protection Act. However, this Code, approved by the Health and Safety Commission, is concerned with time off for training of safety representatives appointed under the Regulations.

Issues which may arise are covered by paragraph 3 of the Code of Practice on Safety Representatives approved by the Health and Safety Commission. The Schedule to the Regulations deals with the computation of pay for the time off allowed. Regulation 11 contains provisions as to reference of complaints to industrial tribunals about time off and the payment to be made.

To complement training approved by the TUC or by independent unions for safety representatives, an employer should make such arrangements as are necessary to provide training in the technical hazards of the workplace and relevant precautions on safe methods of work, and on his organisation and arrangements for health and safety.　　　　　　　　　　　　　　　　　　　　　　　　　　　　　　　[3050]

Code of Practice

1 The function of safety representatives appointed by recognised trade unions as set out in Section 2(4) of the Health and Safety at Work etc Act 1974 is to represent employees in consultations with employers about health and safety matters. Regulations 4(1) of the Safety Representatives and Safety Committees Regulations (SI 1977/500) prescribes other functions of safety representatives appointed under those Regulations.　　　　　　　　　　　　　　　　　　　　　　　　　[3051]

2 Under Regulations 4(2)(b) of those Regulations the employer has a duty to permit those safety representatives such time off with pay during the employee's working hours as shall be necessary for the purpose of "undergoing such training in aspects of those functions as may be reasonable in all the circumstances".   **[3052]**

3 As soon as possible after their appointment safety representatives should be permitted time off with pay to attend basic training facilities approved by the TUC or by the independent union or unions which appointed the safety representatives. Further training, similarly approved, should be undertaken where the safety representative has special responsibilities or where such training is necessary to meet changes in circumstances or relevant legislation.   **[3053]**

4 With regard to the length of training required, this cannot be rigidly prescribed, but basic training should take into account the function of safety representatives placed on them by the Regulations. In particular, basic training should provide an understanding of the role of safety representatives, of safety committees, and of trade union policies and practices in relation to:

(a) the legal requirements relating to the health and safety of persons at work, particularly the group or class of persons they directly represent;
(b) the nature and extent of workplace hazards, and the measures necessary to eliminate or minimise them;
(c) the health and safety policy of employers, and organisation and arrangements for fulfilling those policies.

Additionally, safety representatives will need to acquire new skills in order to carry out their functions, including safety inspections, and in using basic sources of legal and official information and information provided by or through the employer on health and safety matters.   **[3054]**

5 Trade unions are responsible for appointing safety representatives and when the trade union wishes a safety representative to receive training relevant to his functions it should inform management of the course it has approved and supply a copy of the syllabus, indicating its contents, if the employer asks for it. It should normally give at least a few weeks' notice of the safety representatives it has nominated for attendance. The number of safety representatives attending training courses at any one time should be that which is reasonable in the circumstances, bearing in mind such factors as the availability of relevant courses and the operational requirements of the employer. Unions and management should endeavour to reach agreement on the appropriate numbers and arrangements and refer any problems which may arise to the relevant agreed procedures.   **[3055]**

COMMISSION FOR RACIAL EQUALITY: CODE OF PRACTICE FOR THE ELIMINATION OF RACIAL DISCRIMINATION AND THE PROMOTION OF EQUALITY OF OPPORTUNITY IN EMPLOYMENT (1983)

NOTES
    This Code of Practice was made by the Commission for Racial Equality under s 47 of the Race Relations Act 1976. and came into effect on 1 April 1984 (see the Race Relations Code of Practice Order 1983, SI 1983/1081). For the legal effect of the Code see s 47 of the 1976 Act, above, para **[209]**.

1.1 This Code aims to give practical guidance which will help employers, trade unions, employment agencies and employees to understand not only the provisions of the Race Relations Act and their implications, but also how best they can implement policies to eliminate racial discrimination and to enhance equality of opportunity.

1.2 The Code does not impose any legal obligations itself, nor is it an authoritative statement of the law—that can only be provided by the courts and tribunals. If, however, its recommendations are not observed this may result in breaches of the law where the act or omission falls within any of the specific prohibitions of the Act. Moreover its provisions are admissible in evidence in any proceedings under the Race Relations Act before an Industrial Tribunal and if any provision appears to the Tribunal to be relevant to a question arising in the proceedings it must be taken into account in determining that question. If employers take the steps that are set out in the Code to prevent their employees from doing acts of unlawful discrimination they may avoid liability for such acts in any legal proceedings brought against them. *References to the appropriate Sections of the Race Relations Act 1976 are therefore given in the margin to the Code.**

1.3 Employees of all racial groups have a right to equal opportunity. Employees ought to provide it. To do so is likely to involve some expenditure at least in staff time and effort. But if a coherent and effective programme of equal opportunity is developed it will help industry to make full use of the abilities of its entire workforce. It is therefore particularly important for all those concerned—employers, trade unions and employees alike—to co-operate with goodwill in adopting and giving effect to measures for securing such equality. We welcome the commitment already made by the CBI and TUC to the principle of equal opportunity. The TUC has recommended a model equal opportunity clause for inclusion in collective agreements and the CBI has published a statement favouring the application by companies of constructive equal opportunity policies.

1.4 A concerted policy to eliminate both race and sex discrimination often provides the best approach. Guidance on equal opportunity between men and women is the responsibility of the Equal Opportunities Commission. **[3056]**

2 The application of the Code

2.1 The Race Relations Act applies to all employers. The Code itself is not restricted to what is required by law, but contains recommendations as well. Some of its detailed provisions may need to be adapted to suit particular circumstances. Any adaptations that are made, however, should be fully consistent with the Code's general intentions.

2.2 Small firms

In many small firms employers have close contact with their staff and there will therefore be less need for formality in assessing whether equal opportunity is being achieved, for example, in such matters as arrangements for monitoring. Moreover it may not be reasonable to expect small firms to have the resources and administrative systems to carry out the Code's detailed recommendations. In complying with the Race Relations Act, small firms should, however, ensure that their practices are consistent with the Code's general intentions. **[3057]**

* [Printed here in brackets at the end of the relevant section: Ed.]

3 Unlawful discrimination

3.1 The Race Relations Act 1976 makes it unlawful to discriminate against a person, directly or indirectly, in the field of employment (s 4).

Direct discrimination consists of treating a person, on racial grounds,[1] less favourably than others are or would be treated in the same or similar circumstances.

Segregating a person from others on racial grounds constitutes less favourable treatment (s 1 (1)(a)).

3.2 Indirect discrimination consists of applying in any circumstances covered by the Act a requirement or condition which, although applied equally to persons of all racial groups, is such that a considerably smaller proportion of a particular racial group can comply with it and it cannot be shown to be justifiable on other than racial grounds. Possible examples are:

—a rule about clothing or uniforms which disproportionately disadvantages a racial group and cannot be justified;
—an employer who requires higher language standards than are needed for safe and effective performance of the job.

3.3 The definition of indirect discrimination is complex, and it will not be spelt out in full in every relevant Section of the Code. Reference will be only to the terms "indirect discrimination" or "discriminate indirectly".

3.4 Discrimination by victimisation is also unlawful under the Act. For example, a person is victimised if he or she is given less favourable treatment than others in the same circumstances because it is suspected or known that he or she has brought proceedings under the Act, or given evidence or information relating to such proceedings, or alleged that discrimination has occurred.

Many of the Code's provisions show the close link between equal opportunity and good employment practice. For example, selection criteria which are relevant to job requirements and carefully observed selection procedures not only help to ensure that individuals are appointed according to their suitability for the job and without regard to racial group; they are also part of good employment practice. In the absence of consistent selection procedures and criteria, decisions are often too subjective and racial discrimination can easily occur.   **[3058]**

5 Positive action

Opportunities for employees to develop their potential through encouragement, training and careful assessment are also part of good employment practice. Many employees from the racial minorities have potential which, perhaps because of previous discrimination and other causes of disadvantage, they have not been able to realise, and which is not reflected in their qualifications and experience. Where members of particular racial groups have been under-represented over the previous twelve months in particular work, employers and specified training bodies are allowed under the Act to encourage them to take advantage of opportunities for doing that work and to provide training to enable them to attain the skills needed for it. In the case of employers, such training can be provided for persons currently in their employment (as defined by the Act) and in certain circumstances for others too, for example if they have been designated as training bodies. This Code encourages

---

[1] Racial grounds are the grounds of race, colour, nationality—including citizenship—or ethnic or national origins, and groups defined by reference to these grounds are referred to as racial groups.

employers to make use of these provisions, which are covered in detail in paragraphs 1.44 and 1.45 (ss 37 & 38). **[3059]**

6 Guidance papers

The guidance papers referred to in the footnotes contain additional guidance on specific issues but do not form part of the statutory Code. **[3060]**

PART 1

THE RESPONSIBILITIES OF EMPLOYERS

1.1 Responsibility for providing equal opportunity for all job applicants and employees rests primarily with employers. To this end it is recommended that they should adopt, implement and monitor an equal opportunity policy to ensure that there is no unlawful discrimination and that equal opportunity is genuinely available.

 1.2 This policy should be clearly communicated to all employees—eg through notice boards, circulars, contracts of employment or written notifications to individual employees.

 1.3 An equal opportunity policy aims to ensure:
- (a) *that no job applicant or employee receives less favourable treatment than another on racial grounds;*
- (b) *that no applicant or employee is placed at a disadvantage by requirements or conditions which have a disproportionately adverse effect on his or her racial group and which cannot be shown to be justifiable on other than racial grounds;*
- (c) *that, where appropriate and where permissible under the Race Relations Act, employees of under-represented racial groups are given training and encouragement to achieve equal opportunity within the organisation.*

 1.4 In order to ensure that an equal opportunity policy is fully effective, the following action by employers is recommended:
- (a) allocating overall responsibility for the policy to a member of senior management;
- (b) discussing and, where appropriate, agreeing with trade union or employee representatives the policy's contents and implementation;
- (c) ensuring that the policy is known to all employees and if possible, to all job applicants;
- (d) providing training and guidance for supervisory staff and other relevant decision makers (such as personnel and line managers, foremen, gatekeepers and receptionists) to ensure that they understand their position in law and under company policy;
- (e) examining and regularly reviewing existing procedures and criteria and changing them where they find that they are actually or potentially unlawfully discriminatory;
- (f) making an initial analysis of the workforce and regularly monitoring the application of the policy with the aid of analyses of the ethnic origins of the workforce and of job applicants in accordance with the guidance in paragraphs 1.34–1.35.

Recruitment, promotion, transfer, training and dismissal

Sources of recruitment

Advertisements

1.5 *When advertising job vacancies it is unlawful for employers:*
to publish an advertisement which indicates, or could reasonably be understood as indicating, an intention to discriminate against applicants from a particular racial group. (For exceptions see the Race Relations Act (s 29).)

1.6 It is therefore recommended that:

(a) employers should not confine advertisements unjustifiably to those areas or publications which would exclude or disproportionately reduce the numbers of applicants of a particular racial group;

(b) employers should avoid prescribing requirements such as length of residence or experience in the UK and where a particular qualification is required it should be made clear that a fully comparable qualification obtained overseas is as acceptable as a UK qualification.

1.7 In order to demonstrate their commitment to equality of opportunity it is recommended that where employers send literature to applicants, this should include a statement that they are equal opportunity employers.

Employment agencies

1.8 *When recruiting through employment agencies, job centres, careers offices and schools, it is unlawful for employers:*

(a) *to give instructions to discriminate, for example by indicating that certain groups will or will not be preferred. (For exceptions see the Race Relations Act);*

(b) *to bring pressure on them to discriminate against members of a particular racial group. (For exceptions, as above.)*

1.9 In order to avoid indirect discrimination it is recommended that employers should not confine recruitment unjustifiably to those agencies, job centres, careers offices and schools which, because of their particular source of applicants, provide only or mainly applicants of a particular racial group.

Other sources

1.10 *It is unlawful to use recruitment methods which exclude or disproportionately reduce the numbers of applicants of a particular racial group and which cannot be shown to be justifiable.* It is therefore recommended that employers should not recruit through the following methods:

(a) recruitment, solely or in the first instance, through the recommendations of existing employees where the workforce concerned is wholly or predominantly white or black and the labour market is multiracial;

(b) procedures by which applicants are mainly or wholly supplied through trade unions where this means that only members of a particular racial group, or a disproportionately high number of them, come forward.

Sources for promotion and training

1.11 *It is unlawful for employers to restrict access to opportunities for promotion or training in a way which is discriminatory* (ss 4, 28). It is therefore recommended that:

— job and training vacancies and the application procedure should be made known to all eligible employees, and not in such a way as to exclude or disproportionately reduce the numbers of applicants from a particular racial group.

Selection for recruitment, promotion, transfer, training and dismissal

1.12 *It is unlawful to discriminate[2], not only in recruitment, promotion, transfer and training, but also in the arrangements made for recruitment and in the ways of affording access to opportunities for promotion, transfer or training.*

Selection criteria and tests

1.13 In order to avoid direct or indirect discrimination it is recommended that selection criteria and tests are examined to ensure that they are related to job requirements and are not unlawfully discriminatory (s 4, 28). (See Introduction, para 3.2). For example:

   (a) a standard of English higher than that needed for the safe and effective performance of the job or clearly demonstrable career pattern should not be required, or a higher level of educational qualification than is needed;

   (b) in particular, employers should not disqualify applicants because they are unable to complete an application form unassisted unless personal completion of the form is a valid test of the standard of English required for safe and effective performance of the job;

   (c) overseas degrees, diplomas and other qualifications which are comparable with UK qualifications should be accepted as equivalents, and not simply be assumed to be of an inferior quality;

   (d) selection tests which contain irrelevant questions or exercises on matters which may be unfamiliar to racial minority applicants should not be used (for example, general knowledge questions on matters more likely to be familiar to indigenous applicants);

   (e) selection tests should he checked to ensure that they are related to the job's requirements, ie an individual's test markings should measure ability to do or train for the job in question.

Treatment of applicants, shortlisting, interviewing and selection

1.14 In order to avoid direct or indirect discrimination it is recommended that:

   (a) gate, reception and personnel staff should be instructed not to treat casual or formal applicants from particular racial groups less favourably than others. These instructions should be confirmed in writing;

   (b) in addition, staff responsible for shortlisting, interviewing and selecting candidates should be:

      — clearly informed of selection criteria and of the need for their consistent application;

---

[2] It should be noted that discrimination in selection to achieve "racial balance" is not allowed. The clause in the 1968 Race Relations Act which allowed such discrimination for the purpose of securing or preserving a reasonable balance of persons of different racial groups in the establishment is not included in the 1976 Race Relations Act.

—given guidance or training on the effects which generalised assumptions and prejudices about race can have on selection decisions;

—made aware of the possible misunderstandings that can occur in interviews between persons of different cultural background;

(c) wherever possible, shortlisting and interviewing should not be done by one person alone but should at least be checked at a more senior level.

Genuine occupational qualification

1.15 *Selection on racial grounds is allowed in certain jobs where being of a particular racial group is a genuine occupational qualification for that job* (s 5(2)(d)). An example is where the holder of a particular job provides persons of a racial group with personal services promoting their welfare, and those services can most effectively be provided by a person of that group.

Transfers and training

1.16 In order to avoid direct or indirect discrimination (s 4(2)(b)) it is recommended that:

(a) staff responsible for selecting employees for transfer to other jobs should be instructed to apply selection criteria without unlawful discrimination;

(b) industry or company agreements and arrangements of custom and practice on job transfers should be examined and amended if they are found to contain requirements or conditions which appear to be indirectly discriminatory. For example, if employees of a particular racial group are concentrated in particular sections, the transfer arrangements should be examined to see if they are unjustifiably and unlawfully restrictive and amended if necessary;

(c) staff responsible for selecting employees for training, whether induction, promotion or skill training should be instructed not to discriminate on racial grounds;

(d) selection criteria for training opportunities should be examined to ensure that they are not indirectly discriminatory.

Dismissal (including redundancy) and other detriment

1.17 *It is unlawful to discriminate on racial grounds in dismissal, or other detriment to an employee.* (s 4(2)(c)).

It is therefore recommended that:

(a) staff responsible for selecting employees for dismissal, including redundancy, should be instructed not to discriminate on racial grounds;

(b) selection criteria for redundancies should be examined to ensure that they are not indirectly discriminatory.

Performance appraisals

1.18 *It is unlawful to discriminate on racial grounds in appraisals of employee performance.* (s 4(2))

1.19 It is recommended that:

(a) staff responsible for performance appraisals should be instructed not to discriminate on racial grounds;

(b) assessment criteria should be examined to ensure that they are not unlawfully discriminatory.

Terms of employment, benefits, facilities and services

1.20 *It is unlawful to discriminate on racial grounds in affording terms of employment and providing benefits, facilities and services for employees.* (s 4(2)) It is therefore recommended that:

(a) all staff concerned with these aspects of employment should be instructed accordingly;

(b) the criteria governing eligibility should be examined to ensure that they are not unlawfully discriminatory.

1.21 In addition, employees may request extended leave from time to time in order to visit relations in their countries of origin or who have emigrated to other countries. Many employers have policies which allow annual leave entitlement to be accumulated, or extra unpaid leave to be taken to meet these circumstances. Employers should take care to apply such policies consistently and without unlawful discrimination.

Grievance, disputes and disciplinary procedures

1.22 *It is unlawful to discriminate in the operation of grievance, disputes and disciplinary procedures,* (ss 2, 4(2)) for example by victimising an individual through disciplinary measures because he or she has complained about racial discrimination, or given evidence about such a complaint. Employers should not ignore or treat lightly grievances from members of particular racial groups on the assumption that they are over-sensitive about discrimination.

1.23 It is recommended that:

in applying disciplinary procedures consideration should be given to the possible effect on an employee's behaviour of the following:

—racial abuse or other racial provocation;

—communication and comprehension difficulties;

—differences in cultural background or behaviour.

Cultural and religious needs

1.24 Where employees have particular cultural and religious needs which conflict with existing work requirements, it is recommended that employers should consider whether it is reasonably practicable to vary or adapt these requirements to enable such needs to be met. For example, it is recommended that they should not refuse employment to a turbanned Sikh because he could not comply with unjustifiable uniform requirements.

Other examples of such needs are:

(a) observance of prayer times and religious holidays;[3]

(b) wearing of dress such as sarees and the trousers worn by Asian women.

1.25 *Although the Act does not specifically cover religious discrimination, work requirements would generally be unlawful if they have a disproportionately adverse*

---

[3] The CRE has issued a guidance paper entitled—"Religious Observance by Muslim Employees".

effect on particular racial groups and cannot be shown to be justifiable.[4]
(ss 4(2), 28)

Communications and language training for employees

1.26 Although there is no legal requirement to provide language training, difficulties in communication can endanger equal opportunity in the workforce. In addition, good communications can improve efficiency, promotion prospects and safety and health and create a better understanding between employers, employees and unions. Where the workforce includes current employees whose English is limited it is recommended that steps are taken to ensure that communications are as effective as possible.

1.27 These should include, where reasonably practicable:

(a) provision of interpretation and translation facilities, for example, in the communications of grievance and other procedures, and of terms of employment;

(b) training in English language and in communication skills;[5]

(c) training for managers and supervisors in the background and culture of racial minority groups;

(d) the use of alternative or additional methods of communication, where employees find it difficult to understand health and safety requirements, for example:
  —safety signs; translations of safety notices;
  —instructions through interpreters;
  —instruction combined with industrial language training.

Instructions and pressure to discriminate

1.28 *It is unlawful to instruct or put pressure on others to discriminate on racial grounds.* (ss 30, 31)

(a) An example of an unlawful instruction is:
  —an instruction from a personnel or line manager to junior staff to restrict the numbers of employees from a particular racial groups in any particular work;

(b) An example of pressure to discriminate is:
  —an attempt by a shop steward or group of workers to induce an employer not to recruit members of particular racial groups, for example by threatening industrial action.

1.29 *It is also unlawful to discriminate in response to such instructions or pressure.*

1.30 The following recommendations are made to avoid unlawful instructions and pressure to discriminate:

(a) guidance should be given to all employees, and particularly those in positions of authority or influence on the relevant provisions of the law;

---

[4] Genuinely necessary safety requirements may not constitute unlawful discrimination.
[5] Industrial language training is provided by a network of Local Education Authority units throughout the country. Full details of the courses and the comprehensive services offered by these units are available from the National Centre for Industrial Language Training, The Havelock Centre, Havelock Road, Southall, Middx.

(b) decision-makers should be instructed not to give way to pressure to discriminate;

(c) giving instructions or bringing pressure to discriminate should be treated as a disciplinary offence.

Victimisation

1.31 *It is unlawful to victimise individuals who have made allegations or complaints of racial discrimination or provided information about such discrimination, for example by disciplining them or dismissing them.* (s 2) (See Introduction, para 3.4.)

1.32 It is recommended that:

—guidance on this aspect of the law should be given to all employees and particularly to those in positions of influence or authority.

Monitoring equal opportunity[6]

1.33 It is recommended that employers should regularly monitor the effects of selection decisions and personnel practices and procedures in order to assess whether equal opportunity is being achieved.

1.34 The information needed for effective monitoring may be obtained in a number of ways. It will best be provided by records showing the ethnic origins of existing employees and job applicants. It is recognised that the need for detailed information and the methods of collecting it will vary according to the circumstances of individual establishments. For example, in small firms or in firms in areas with little or no racial minority settlement it will often be adequate to assess the distribution of employees from personal knowledge and visual identification .

1.35 It is open to employers to adopt the method of monitoring which is best suited to their needs and circumstances, but whichever method is adopted, they should be able to show that it is effective. In order to achieve the full commitment of all concerned the chosen method should be discussed and agreed, where appropriate, with trade union or employee representatives.

1.36 Employers should ensure that information on individuals' ethnic origins is collected for the purpose of monitoring equal opportunity alone and is protected from misuse.

1.37 The following is the comprehensive method recommended by the CRE[7].

Analyses should be carried out of:

(a) the ethnic composition of the workforce of each plant, department, section, shift and job category, and changes in distribution over periods of time;

(b) selection decisions for recruitment, promotion, transfer and training, according to the racial group of candidates, and reasons for these decisions.

1.38 Except in cases where there are large numbers of applicants and the burden on resources would be excessive, reasons for selection and rejection should be recorded at each stage of the selection process, e.g. initial shortlisting and final decisions. Simple categories of reasons for rejection should be adequate for the early sifting stages.

---

[6] See the CRE's guidance paper on "Monitoring an Equal Opportunity Policy".
[7] This is outlined in detail in "Monitoring an Equal Opportunity Policy".

1.39 Selection criteria and personnel procedures should be reviewed to ensure that they do not include requirements or conditions which constitute or may lead to unlawful indirect discrimination.

1.40 This information should be carefully and regularly analysed and, in order to identify areas which may need particular attention, a number of key questions should be asked.

1.41 Is there evidence that individuals from any particular racial group:

(a) do not apply for employment or promotion, or that fewer apply than might be expected?

(b) are not recruited or promoted at all, or are appointed in a significantly lower proportion than their rate of application?

(c) are under-represented in training or in jobs carrying higher pay, status or authority?

(d) are concentrated in certain shifts, sections or departments?

1.42 If the answer to any of these questions is yes, the reasons for this should be investigated. If direct or indirect discrimination is found action must be taken to end it immediately. (ss 4, 28)

1.43 It is recommended that deliberate acts of unlawful discrimination by employees are treated as disciplinary offences.

Positive action[8]

1.44 *Although they are not legally required, positive measures are allowed by the law to encourage employees and potential employees and provide training for employees who are members of particular racial groups which have been under-represented[9] in particular work.* (s 38) (See Introduction, para 5.) Discrimination at the point of selection for work, however, is not permissible in these circumstances.

1.45 Such measures are important for the development of equal opportunity. It is therefore recommended that, where there is under-representation of particular racial groups in particular work, the following measures should be taken wherever appropriate and reasonably practicable:

(a) job advertisements designed to reach members of these groups and to encourage their applications: for example, through the use of the ethnic minority press, as well as other newspapers;

(b) use of the employment agencies and careers offices in areas where these groups are concentrated;

(c) recruitment and training schemes for school leavers designed to reach members of these groups;

(d) encouragement to employees from these groups to apply for promotion or transfer opportunities;

---

[8] The CRE has issued a guidance paper on Positive Action, entitled—"Equal Opportunity in Employment— Why Positive Action?"

[9] A racial group is under-represented if, at any time during the previous twelve months, either there was no one of that group doing the work in question, or there were disproportionately few in comparison with the group's proportion in the workforce at that establishment, or in the population from which the employer normally recruits for work at that establishment.

  (e)   training for promotion or skill training for employees of these groups who lack particular expertise but show potential: supervisory training may include language training.   **[3061]**

PART 2

THE RESPONSIBILITIES OF INDIVIDUAL EMPLOYEES

2.1 While the primary responsibility for providing equal opportunity rests with the employer, individual employees at all levels and of all racial groups have responsibilities too. Good race relations depend on them as much as on management, and so their attitudes and activities are very important.

2.2 *The following actions by individual employees would he unlawful* .

  (a) *discrimination in the course of their employment against fellow employees or job applicants on racial grounds* (ss 4, 33), for example, in selection decisions for recruitment, promotion, transfer and training;

  (b) *inducing, or attempting to induce other employees, unions or management to practice unlawful discrimination* (s 31). For example, they should not refuse to accept other employees from particular racial groups or refuse to work with a supervisor of a particular racial group;

  (c) *victimising individuals who have made allegations or complaints of racial discrimination or provided information about such discrimination* (s 2). (See Introduction, para 3.4.)

2.3 To assist in preventing racial discrimination and promoting equal opportunity it is recommended that individual employees should:

  (a) co-operate in measures introduced by management designed to ensure equal opportunity and non-discrimination;

  (b) where such measures have not been introduced, press for their introduction (through their trade union where appropriate);

  (c) draw the attention of management and, where appropriate, their trade unions to suspected discriminatory acts or practices;

  (d) refrain from harassment or intimidation of other employees on racial grounds, for example, by attempting to discourage them from continuing employment. Such action may be unlawful if it is taken by employees against those subject to their authority.

2.4 In addition to the responsibilities set out above individual employees from the racial minorities should recognise that in many occupations advancement is dependent on an appropriate standard of English. Similarly an understanding of the industrial relations procedures which apply is often essential for good working relationships.

2.5 They should therefore:

  (a) where appropriate, seek means to improve their standards of English;

  (b) co-operate in industrial language training schemes introduced by employers and/or unions;

  (c) co-operate in training or other schemes designed to inform them of industrial relations procedures, company agreements, work rules, etc;

  (d) where appropriate, participate in discussions with employers and unions, to find solutions to conflicts between cultural or religious needs and production needs.   **[3062]**

PART 3

THE RESPONSIBILITIES OF TRADE UNIONS

3.1 Trade unions, in common with a number of other organisations, have a dual role as employers and providers of services specifically covered by the Race Relations Act.

3.2 In their role as employer, unions have the responsibilities set out in Part 1 of the Code. They also have a responsibility to ensure that their representatives and members do not discriminate against any particular racial group in the admission or treatment of members, or as colleagues, supervisors, or subordinates.

3.3 In addition, trade union officials at national and local level and shopfloor representatives at plant level have an important part to play on behalf of their members in preventing unlawful discrimination and in promoting equal opportunity and good race relations. Trade unions should encourage and press for equal opportunity policies so that measures to prevent discrimination at the workforce can be introduced with the clear commitment of both management and unions.

Admission of members

3.4 *It is unlawful for trade unions to discriminate on racial grounds:*
  (a) *by refusing membership;*
  (b) *by offering less favourable terms of membership.* (s 11(2))

Treatment of members

3.5 *It is unlawful for trade unions to discriminate on racial grounds against existing members:*
  (a) *by varying their terms of membership. depriving them of membership or subjecting them to any other detriment* (s 11(3));
  (b) *by treating them less favourably in the benefits, facilities or services provided.* These may include:
    training facilities; ·
    welfare and insurance schemes;
    entertainment and social events;
    processing of grievances;
    negotiations;
    assistance in disciplinary or dismissal procedures.

3.6 In addition, it is recommended that unions ensure that in cases where members of particular racial groups believe that they are suffering racial discrimination, whether by the employer or the union itself, serious attention is paid to the reasons for this belief and that any discrimination which may be occurring is stopped.

Disciplining union members who discriminate

3.7 It is recommended that deliberate acts of unlawful discrimination by union members are treated as disciplinary offences.

Positive action

3.8 *Although they are not legally required, positive measures are allowed by the law to encourage and provide training for members of particular racial groups which have been under-represented*[10] *in trade union membership or in trade union posts* (s 38(3), (4), (5)). (Discrimination at the point of selection, however, is not permissible in these circumstances.)

3.9 It is recommended that, wherever appropriate and reasonably practicable, trade unions should:

(a) encourage individuals from these groups to join the union. Where appropriate, recruitment material should be translated into other languages;

(b) encourage individuals from these groups to apply for union posts and provide training to help fit them for such posts.

Training and information

3.10 Training and information play a major part in the avoidance of discrimination and the promotion of equal opportunity. It is recommended that trade unions should:

(a) provide training and information for officers, shop stewards and representatives on their responsibilities for equal opportunity. This training and information should cover:

the Race Relations Act and the nature and causes of discrimination;

the backgrounds of racial minority groups and communication needs;

the effects of prejudice;

equal opportunity policies; avoiding discrimination when representing members.

(b) ensure that members and representatives, whatever their racial group, are informed of their role in the union, and of industrial relations and union procedures and structures. This may be done, for example:

through translation of material;

through encouragement to participate in industrial relations courses and industrial language training.

Pressure to discriminate

3.11 *It is unlawful for trade union members or representatives to induce or to attempt to induce those responsible for employment decisions to discriminate* (s 31):

(a) *in the recruitment, promotion, transfer, training or dismissal of employees;*

(b) *in terms of employment, benefits, facilities or services.*

3.12 For example, they should not:

(a) restrict the numbers of a particular racial group in a section, grade or department

(b) resist changes designed to remove indirect discrimination, such as those in craft apprentice schemes, or in agreements concerning seniority rights or mobility between departments.

---

[10] A racial group is under-represented in trade union membership, if at any time during the previous twelve months no persons of that group were in membership, or disproportionately few in comparison with the proportion of persons of that group among those eligible for membership (s 38(5)). Under-representation in trade union posts applies under the same twelve month criteria where there were no persons of a particular racial group in those posts or disproportionately few in comparison with the proportion of that group in the organisation (s 38(4)).

Victimisation

3.13 *It is unlawful to victimise individuals who have made allegations or complaints of racial discrimination or provided information about such discrimination* (s 2). (See Introduction, para 3.4.)

Avoidance of discrimination

3.14 *Where unions are involved in selection decisions for recruitment, promotion, training or transfer, for example through recommendation or veto, it is unlawful for them to discriminate on racial grounds* (ss 31, 33).

3.15 It is recommended that they should instruct their members accordingly and examine their procedures and joint agreements to ensure that they do not contain indirectly discriminatory requirements or conditions, such as:
unjustifiable restriction on transfers between departments or irrelevant and unjustifiable selection criteria which have a disproportionately adverse effect on particular racial groups.

Union involvement in equal opportunity policies

3.16 It is recommended that:
(a) unions should co-operate in the introduction and implementation of full equal opportunity policies, as defined in paras 1.3 & 1.4;
(b) unions should negotiate the adoption of such policies where they have not been introduced or the extension of existing policies where these are too narrow;
(c) unions should co-operate with measures to monitor the progress of equal opportunity policies, or encourage management to introduce them where they do not already exist. Where appropriate (See paras 1.33-1.35) this may be done through analysis of the distribution of employees and job applicants according to ethnic origin;
(d) where monitoring shows that discrimination has occurred or is occurring, unions should co-operate in measures to eliminate it;
(e) although positive action[11] is not legally required, unions should encourage management to take such action where there is under-representation of particular racial groups in particular jobs, and where management itself introduces positive action representatives should support it;
(f) similarly, where there are communication difficulties, management should be asked to take whatever action is appropriate to overcome them.[3063]

PART 4

THE RESPONSIBILITIES OF EMPLOYMENT AGENCIES

4.1 Employment agencies, in their role as employers, have the responsibilities outlined in Part 1 of the Code. In addition, they have responsibilities as suppliers of job applicants to other employers.

4.2 *It is unlawful for employment agencies: (For exceptions see Race Relations Act)*

(a) *to discriminate on racial grounds in providing services to clients* (s 14(1));
(b) *to publish job advertisements indicating, or which might be understood to*

---

[11] See 1.44—Positive Action recommendations.

*indicate that applications from any particular group will not be considered
or will be treated more favourably or less favourably than others* (s 29);

(c) *to act on directly discriminatory instructions from employers to the effect
that applicants from a particular racial group will be rejected or preferred
or that their numbers should be restricted* (s 14(1));

(d) *to act on indirectly discriminatory instructions from employers i.e. that
requirements or conditions should be applied that would have a
disproportionately adverse effect on applicants of a particular racial
group and which cannot be shown to be justifiable* (ss 14(1), 16(1)(b)).

4.3 It is recommended that agencies should also avoid indicating such conditions
or requirements in job advertisements unless they can be shown to be justifiable.
Examples in each case may be those relating to educational qualifications or
residence.

4.4 It is recommended that staff should be given guidance on their duty not to
discriminate and on the effect which generalised assumptions and prejudices can have
on their treatment of members of particular racial group.

4.5 In particular staff should be instructed:

(a) not to ask employers for racial preferences;

(b) not to draw attention to racial origin when recommending applicants unless
the employer is trying to attract applicants of a particular racial group under
the exceptions in the Race Relations Act;

(c) to report a client's refusal to interview an applicant for reasons that are
directly or indirectly discriminatory to a supervisor, who should inform
the client that discrimination is unlawful. If the client maintains this refusal
the agency should inform the applicant of his or her right to complain to
an industrial tribunal and to apply to the CRE for assistance. An internal
procedure for recording such cases should be operated;

(d) to inform their supervisor if they believe that an applicant, though
interviewed, has been rejected on racial grounds. If the supervisor is
satisfied that there are grounds for this belief, he or she should arrange for
the applicant to be informed of the right to complain to an industrial
tribunal and to apply to the CRE for assistance. An internal procedure for
recording such cases should be operated

(e) to treat job applicants without discrimination. For example, they should
not send applicants from particular racial groups to only those employers
who are believed to be willing to accept them, or restrict the range of job
opportunities for such applicants because of assumptions about their
abilities based on race or colour.

4.6 It is recommended that employment agencies should discontinue their
services to employers who give unlawful discriminatory instructions and who refuse
to withdraw them.

4.7 It is recommended that employment agencies should monitor the
effectiveness of the measures they take for ensuring that no unlawful discrimination
occurs. For example, where reasonably practicable they should make periodic checks
to ensure that applicants from particular racial groups are being referred for suitable
jobs for which they are qualified at a similar rate to that for other comparable
applicants. **[3064]**

EQUAL OPPORTUNITIES COMMISSION: CODE OF PRACTICE FOR THE ELIMINATION OF DISCRIMINATION ON THE GROUNDS OF SEX AND MARRIAGE AND THE PROMOTION OF EQUALITY OF OPPORTUNITY IN EMPLOYMENT (1985)

GENERAL NOTE

This Code of Practice was issued by the Equal Opportunities Commission under s 56A of the Sex Discrimination Act 1975 and was brought into effect on 30 April 1985 by the Sex Discrimination Code of Practice Order 1985, SI 1985/387. The Legal Annex. which summarises the relevant provisions of the 1975 Act, is omitted. For the legal effect of the Code see s 56A of the 1975 Act, above, para **[141]**.

INTRODUCTION

1 The EOC issues this Code of Practice for the following purposes:

(a) for the elimination of discrimination in employment

(b) to give guidance as to what steps it is reasonably practicable for employers to take to ensure that their employees do not in the course of their employment act unlawfully contrary to the Sex Discrimination Act (SDA)

(c) for the promotion of equality of opportunity between men and women in employment.

The SDA prohibits discrimination against men, as well as against women. It also requires that married people should not be treated less favourably than single people of the same sex.

It should be noted that the provisions of the SDA—and therefore of this Code— apply to the UK-based subsidiaries of foreign companies.   **[3065]**

2 The Code gives guidance to employers, trade unions and employment agencies on measures which can be taken to achieve equality. The chances of success of any organisation will clearly be improved if it seeks to develop the abilities of all employees, and the Code shows the close link which exists between equal opportunity and good employment practice. In some cases, an initial cost may be involved, but this should be more than compensated for by better relationships and better use of human resources.   **[3066]**

Small businesses

3 The Code has to deal in general terms and it will be necessary for employers to adapt it in a way appropriate to the size and structure of their organisations. Small businesses, for example, will require much simpler procedures than organisations with complex structures and it may not always be reasonable for them to carry out all the Code's detailed recommendations. In adapting the Code's recommendations, small firms should, however, ensure that their practices comply with the Sex Discrimination Act.   **[3067]**

Employers' responsibility

4 *The primary responsibility at law rests with each employer to ensure that there is no unlawful discrimination.* It is important, however, that measures to eliminate discrimination or promote equality of opportunity should be understood and supported by all employees. Employers are therefore recommended to involve their employees in equal opportunity policies. **[3068]**

Individual employees' responsibility

5 While the main responsibility for eliminating discrimination and providing equal opportunity is that of the employer, individual employees at all levels have responsibilities too. They must not discriminate or knowingly aid their employer to do so. **[3069]**

Trade union responsibility

6 The full commitment of trade unions is essential for the elimination of discrimination and for the successful operation of an equal opportunities policy. Much can be achieved by collective bargaining and throughout the Code it is assumed that all the normal procedures will be followed. **[3070]**

7 It is recommended that unions should co-operate in the introduction and implementation of equal opportunities policies where employers have decided to introduce them, and should urge that such policies be adopted where they have not yet been introduced. **[3071]**

8 Trade Unions have a responsibility to ensure that their representatives and members do not unlawfully discriminate on grounds of sex or marriage in the admission or treatment of members. The guidance in this Code also applies to trade unions in their role as employers. **[3072]**

Employment agencies

9 Employment agencies have a responsibility as suppliers of job applicants to avoid unlawful discrimination on the grounds of sex or marriage in providing services to clients. The guidance in this Code also applies to employment agencies in their role as employers. **[3073]**

Definitions

10 For ease of reference, the main employment provisions of the Sex Discrimination Act, including definitions of direct and indirect sex and marriage discrimination, are provided in a Legal Annex to this Code. **[3074]**

PART 1

THE ROLE OF GOOD EMPLOYMENT PRACTICES IN
ELIMINATING SEX AND MARRIAGE DISCRIMINATION

11 This section of the Code describes those good employment practices which will help to eliminate unlawful discrimination. It recommends the establishment and use of consistent criteria for selection, training, promotion, redundancy and dismissal which are made known to all employees. Without this consistency, decisions can be subjective and leave the way open for unlawful discrimination to occur. **[3075]**

Recruitment

12 It is unlawful: UNLESS THE JOB IS COVERED BY AN EXCEPTION: * TO
DISCRIMINATE DIRECTLY OR INDIRECTLY ON THE GROUNDS OF SEX
OR MARRIAGE

—IN THE ARRANGEMENTS MADE FOR DECIDING WHO SHOULD BE
OFFERED A JOB
—IN ANY TERMS OF EMPLOYMENT
—BY REFUSING OR OMITTING TO OFFER A PERSON EMPLOYMENT

[Section 6(1)(a); 6(1)(b); 6(1)(c)]   **[3076]**

13 It is therefore recommended that:

(a) each individual should be assessed according to his or her personal
capability to carry out a given job. It should not be assumed that men only
or women only will be able to perform certain kinds of work;

(b) any qualifications or requirements applied to a job which effectively
inhibit applications from one sex or from married people should be retained
only if they are justifiable in terms of the job to be done;
[Section 6 (1) (a) together with section 1 (1) (b) or 3 (1) (b)]

(c) any age limits should be retained only if they are necessary for the job. An
unjustifiable age limit could constitute unlawful indirect discrimination,
for example, against women who have taken time out of employment for
child-rearing;

(d) where trade unions uphold such qualifications or requirements as union
policy, they should amend that policy in the light of any potentially
unlawful effect.   **[3077]**

Genuine occupational qualifications (GOQs)

14 It is unlawful: EXCEPT FOR CERTAIN JOBS WHEN A PERSON'S SEX IS
A GENUINE OCCUPATIONAL QUALIFICATION (GOQ) FOR THAT JOB to
select candidates on the ground of sex.

[Section 7(2); 7(3) and 7(4)]   **[3078]**

15 There are very few instances in which a job will qualify for a GOQ on the
ground of sex. However, exceptions may arise for example, where considerations of
privacy and decency or authenticity are involved. The SDA expressly states that the
need of the job for strength and stamina does not justify restricting it to men. When
a GOQ exists for a job, it applies also to promotion, transfer or training for that job,but
cannot be used to justify a dismissal.   **[3079]**

16 In some instances, the GOQ will apply to some of the duties only. A GOQ
will not be valid, however, where members of the appropriate sex are already
employed in sufficient numbers to meet the employer's likely requirements without
undue inconvenience. For example, in a job where sales assistants may be required
to undertake changing room duties, it might not be lawful to claim a GOQ in respect
of *all* the assistants on the grounds that any of them might be required to undertake
changing room duties from time to time.   **[3080]**

17 It is therefore recommended that:

— A job for which a GOQ was used in the past should be re-examined if the
post falls vacant to see whether the GOQ still applies. Circumstances may
well have changed, rendering the GOQ inapplicable.   **[3081]**

---

* There are a number of exceptions to the requirements of the SDA, that employers must not discriminate
against their employees or against potential employees.

Sources of recruitment

18 It is unlawful: UNLESS THE JOB IS COVERED BY AN EXCEPTION:

— TO DISCRIMINATE ON GROUNDS OF SEX OR MARRIAGE IN THE ARRANGEMENTS MADE FOR DETERMINING WHO SHOULD BE OFFERED EMPLOYMENT WHETHER RECRUITING BY ADVERT-ISEMENTS, THROUGH EMPLOYMENT AGENCIES, JOB-CENTRES, OR CAREER OFFICES.

— TO IMPLY THAT APPLICATIONS FROM ONE SEX OR FROM MARRIED PEOPLE WILL NOT BE CONSIDERED.

[Section 6(1) (a)]

— TO INSTRUCT OR PUT PRESSURE ON OTHERS TO OMIT TO REFER FOR EMPLOYMENT PEOPLE OF ONE SEX OR MARRIED PEOPLE UNLESS THE JOB IS COVERED BY AN EXCEPTION .

[Sections 39 and 40]

It is also unlawful WHEN ADVERTISING JOB VACANCIES,

— TO PUBLISH OR CAUSE TO BE PUBLISHED AN ADVERTISE-MENT WHICH INDICATES OR MIGHT REASONABLY BE UNDERSTOOD AS INDICATING AN INTENTION TO DIS-CRIMINATE UNLAWFULLY ON GROUNDS OF SEX OR MARRIAGE.

[Section 38]   **[3082]**

19 It is therefore recommended that:

Advertising

(a) job advertising should be carried out in such a way as to encourage applications from suitable candidates of both sexes. This can be achieved both by wording of the advertisements and, for example, by placing advertisements in publications likely to reach both sexes. All advertising material and accompanying literature relating to employment or training issues should be reviewed to ensure that it avoids presenting men and women in stereotyped roles. Such stereotyping tends to perpetuate sex segregation in jobs and can also lead people of the opposite sex to believe that they would be unsuccessful in applying for particular jobs;

(b) where vacancies are filled by promotion or transfer, they should be published to all eligible employees in such a way that they do not restrict applications from either sex;

(c) recruitment solely or primarily by word of mouth may unnecessarily restrict the choice of applicants available. The method should be avoided in a workforce predominantly of one sex, if in practice it prevents members of the opposite sex from applying;

(d) where applicants are supplied through trade unions and members of one sex only come forward, this should be discussed with the unions and an alternative approach adopted.   **[3083]**

Careers service schools

20 When notifying vacancies to the Careers Service, employers should specify that these are open to both boys and girls. This is especially important when a job has traditionally been done exclusively or mainly by one sex. If dealing with single sex schools, they should ensure, where possible, that both boys' and girls' schools are approached; it is also a good idea to remind mixed schools that jobs are open to boys and girls.   **[3084]**

Selection methods

Tests

21 (a) If selection tests are used, they should be specifically related to job and/
or career requirements and should measure an individual's actual or
inherent ability to do or train for the work or career.

(b) Tests should be reviewed regularly to ensure that they remain relevant and
free from any unjustifiable bias, either in content or in scoring mechanism.

[3085]

Application and Interviewing

22 It is unlawful: UNLESS THE JOB IS COVERED BY AN EXCEPTION:

TO DISCRIMINATE ON GROUNDS OF SEX OR MARRIAGE BY REFUSING
OR DELIBERATELY OMITTING TO OFFER EMPLOYMENT.

[Section 6(1)(c)]   **[3086]**

23 It is therefore recommended that:

(a) employers should ensure that personnel staff, line managers and all other
employees who may come into contact with job applicants, should be
trained in the provisions of the SDA, including the fact that it is unlawful
to instruct or put pressure on others to discriminate;

(b) applications from men and women should be processed in exactly the same
way. For example, there should not be separate lists of male and female or
married and single applicants. All those handling applications and
conducting interviews should be trained in the avoidance of unlawful
discrimination and records of interviews kept, where practicable, showing
why applicants were or were not appointed;

(c) questions should relate to the requirements of the job. Where it is necessary
to assess whether personal circumstances will affect performance of the
job (for example, where it involves unsocial hours or extensive travel) this
should be discussed objectively without detailed questions based on
assumptions about marital status, children and domestic obligations.
Questions about marriage plans or family intentions should not be asked,
as they could be construed as showing bias against women. Information
necessary for personnel records can be collected after a job offer has been
made.   **[3087]**

Promotion, transfer and training

24 It is unlawful: UNLESS THE JOB IS COVERED BY AN EXCEPTION, FOR
EMPLOYERS TO DISCRIMINATE DIRECTLY OR INDIRECTLY ON THE
GROUNDS OF SEX OR MARRIAGE IN THE WAY THEY AFFORD ACCESS
TO OPPORTUNITIES FOR PROMOTION, TRANSFER OR TRAINING.

[Section 6(2)(a)]   **[3088]**

25 It is therefore recommended that:

(a) where an appraisal system is in operation, the assessment criteria should
be examined to ensure that they are not unlawfully discriminatory and the
scheme monitored to assess how it is working in practice;

(b) when a group of workers predominantly of one sex is excluded from an
appraisal scheme, access to promotion, transfer and training and to other
benefits should be reviewed, to ensure that there is no unlawful indirect
discrimination;

   (c) promotion and career development patterns are reviewed to ensure that the traditional qualifications are justifiable requirements for the job to be done. In some circumstances, for example, promotion on the basis of length of service could amount to unlawful indirect discrimination, as it may unjustifiably affect more women than men;

   (d) when general ability and personal qualities are the main requirements for promotion to a post, care should be taken to consider favourably candidates of both sexes with differing career patterns and general experience;

   (e) rules which restrict or preclude transfer between certain jobs should be questioned and changed if they are found to be unlawfully discriminatory. Employees of one sex may be concentrated in sections from which transfers are traditionally restricted without real justification;

   (f) policies and practices regarding selection for training, day release and personal development should be examined for unlawful direct and indirect discrimination. Where there is found to be an imbalance in training as between sexes, the cause should be identified to ensure that it is not discriminatory;

   (g) age limits for access to training and promotion should be questioned.

[3089]

Health and safety legislation

26 Equal treatment of men and women may be limited by statutory provisions which require men and women to be treated differently. For example, the Factories Act 1961 places restrictions on the hours of work of female manual employees, although the Health and Safety Executive can exempt employers from these restrictions, subject to certain conditions. The Mines and Quarries Act 1954 imposes limitations on women's work and there are restrictions where there is special concern for the unborn child (e.g. lead and ionising radiation). However the broad duties placed on employers by the Health and Safety at Work, etc, Act 1974 makes no distinctions between men and women. Section 2(1) requires employers to ensure, so far as is reasonably practicable, the health and safety and welfare at work of *all* employees.

SPECIFIC HEALTH AND SAFETY REQUIREMENTS UNDER EARLIER LEGISLATION ARE UNAFFECTED BY THE ACT.

It is therefore recommended that

   — company policy should be reviewed and serious consideration given to any significant differences in treatment between men and women, and there should be well-founded reasons if such differences are maintained or introduced.   **[3090]**

Terms of employment, benefits, facilities and services

27 It is unlawful: UNLESS THE JOB IS COVERED BY AN EXCEPTION: TO DISCRIMINATE ON THE GROUNDS OF SEX OR MARRIAGE, DIRECTLY OR INDIRECTLY, IN THE TERMS ON WHICH EMPLOYMENT IS OFFERED OR IN AFFORDING ACCESS TO ANY BENEFITS*, FACILITIES OR SERVICES.

[*Sections 6(1) (b); 6(2) (a); 29*]   **[3091]**

---

* Certain provisions relating to death and retirement are exempt from the Act. [This is now subject to the amendments made by the Sex Discrimination Act 1986, s 2: Ed.]

28 It is therefore recommended that:

(a) all terms of employment, benefits, facilities and services are reviewed to ensure that there is no unlawful discrimination on grounds of sex or marriage. For example, part-time work, domestic leave, company cars and benefits for dependants should be available to both male and female employees in the same or not materially different circumstances.

[3092]

29 In an establishment where part-timers are solely or mainly women, unlawful indirect discrimination may arise if, as a group, they are treated less favourably than other employees without justification.

It is therefore recommended that:

(b) where part-time workers do not enjoy pro-rata pay or benefits with full-time workers, the arrangements should be reviewed to ensure that they are justified without regard to sex. **[3093]**

Grievances, disciplinary procedures and victimisation

30 It is unlawful: TO VICTIMISE AN INDIVIDUAL FOR A COMPLAINT MADE IN GOOD FAITH ABOUT SEX OR MARRIAGE DISCRIMINATION OR FOR GIVING EVIDENCE ABOUT SUCH A COMPLAINT.

[Section 4(1); 4(2); and 4(3)] **[3094]**

31 It is therefore recommended that:

(a) particular care is taken to ensure that an employee who has in good faith taken action under the Sex Discrimination Act or the Equal Pay Act does not receive less favourable treatment than other employees, for example by being disciplined or dismissed;

(b) employees should be advised to use the internal procedures, where appropriate, but this is without prejudice to the individual's right to apply to an industrial tribunal within the statutory time limit, i.e. before the end of the period of three months beginning when the act complained of was done. (There is no time limit if the victimisation is continuing);

(c) particular care is taken to deal effectively with all complaints of discrimination, victimisation or harassment. It should not be assumed that they are made by those who are over-sensitive. **[3095]**

Dismissals, redundancies and other unfavourable treatment of employees

32 It is unlawful: TO DISCRIMINATE DIRECTLY OR INDIRECTLY ON GROUNDS OF SEX OR MARRIAGE IN DISMISSALS OR BY TREATING AN EMPLOYEE UNFAVOURABLY IN ANY OTHER WAY.

[Section 6(2)(b)]

It is therefore recommended that:

(a) care is taken that members of one sex are not disciplined or dismissed for performance or behaviour which would be overlooked or condoned in the other sex;

(b) redundancy procedures affecting a group of employees predominantly of one sex should be reviewed, so as to remove any effects which could be disproportionate and unjustifiable;

(c)   conditions of access to voluntary redundancy benefit* should be made available on equal terms to male and female employees in the same or not materially different circumstances;

(d)   where there is down-grading or short-time working (for example, owing to a change in the nature or volume of an employer's business) the arrangements should not unlawfully discriminate on the ground of sex;

(e)   all reasonably practical steps should be taken to ensure that a standard of conduct or behaviour is observed which prevents members of either sex from being intimidated, harassed or otherwise subjected to unfavourable treatment on the ground of their sex.   **[3096]**

PART 2

THE ROLE OF GOOD EMPLOYMENT PRACTICES IN PROMOTING EQUALITY OF OPPORTUNITY

33 This section of the Code describes those employment practices which help to promote equality of opportunity. It gives information about the formulation and implementation of equal opportunities policies. While such policies are not required by law, their value has been recognised by a number of employers who have voluntarily adopted them. Others may wish to follow this example.   **[3097]**

Formulating and equal opportunities policy

34 An equal opportunities policy will ensure the effective use of human resources in the best interests of both the organisation and its employees. It is a commitment by an employer to the development and use of employment procedures and practices which do not discriminate on grounds of sex or marriage and which provide genuine equality of opportunity for all employees. The detail of the policy will vary according to size of the organisation.   **[3098]**

Implementing the policy

35 An equal opportunities policy must be seen to have the active support of management at the highest level. To ensure that the policy is fully effective, the following procedure is recommended:

(a)   the policy should be clearly stated and, where appropriate, included in a collective agreement;

(b)   overall responsibility for implementing the policy should rest with senior management;

(c)   the policy should be made known to all employees and, where reasonably practicable, to all job applicants.   **[3099]**

36 Trade unions have a very important part to play in implementing genuine equality of opportunity and they will obviously be involved in the review of established procedures to ensure that these are consistent with the law.   **[3100]**

Monitoring

37 It is recommended that the policy is monitored regularly to ensure that it is working in practice. Consideration could be given to setting up a joint Management/Trade Union Review Committee.   **[3101]**

---

* Certain provisions relating to death and retirement are exempt from the Act. [See note to para 27 of the Code: Ed.]

38 In a small firm with a simple structure it may be quite adequate to assess the distribution and payment of employees from personal knowledge. **[3102]**

39 In a large and complex organisation a more formal analysis will be necessary, for example, by sex, grade and payment in each unit. This may need to be introduced by stages as resources permit. Any formal analysis should be regularly updated and available to Management and Trade Unions to enable any necessary action to be taken. **[3103]**

40 Sensible monitoring will show, for example, whether members of one sex :

    (a) do not apply for employment or promotion, or that fewer apply than might be expected;

    (b) are not recruited, promoted or selected for training and development or are appointed/selected in a significantly lower proportion than their rate of application;

    (c) are concentrated in certain jobs, sections or departments. **[3104]**

Positive action

Recruitment, training and promotion

41 Selection for recruitment or promotion must be on merit, irrespective of sex. However, the Sex Discrimination Act does allow certain steps to redress the effects of previous unequal opportunities. Where there have been few or no members of one sex in particular work in their employment for the previous 12 months, the Act allows employers to give special encouragement to, and provide specific training for, the minority sex. Such measures are usually described as Positive Action.

[Section 48] **[3105]**

42 Employers may wish to consider positive measures such as:

    (a) training their own employees (male or female) for work which is traditionally the preserve of the other sex, for example, training women for skilled manual or technical work;

    (b) positive encouragement to women to apply for management posts— special courses may be needed;

    (c) advertisements which encourage application from the minority sex but make it clear that selection will be on merit without reference to sex;

    (d) notifying job agencies, as part of a Positive Action Programme that they wish to encourage members of one sex to apply for vacancies, where few or no members of that sex are doing the work in question. In these circumstances, job agencies should tell both men and women about the posts and, in addition, let the under-represented sex know that applications from them are particularly welcome. Withholding information from one sex in an attempt to encourage applications from the opposite sex would be unlawful. **[3106]**

Other working arrangements

43 There are other forms of action which could assist both employer and employee by helping to provide continuity of employment to working parents, many of whom will have valuable experience or skills.

Employers may wish to consider with their employees whether:

    (a) certain jobs can be carried out on a part-time or flexi-time basis;

    (b) personal leave arrangements are adequate and available to both sexes. It should not be assumed that men may not need to undertake domestic responsibilities on occasion, especially at the time of childbirth;

(c) child-care facilities are available locally or whether it would be feasible to establish nursery facilities on the premises or combine with other employers to provide them

(d) residential training could be facilitated for employees with young children. For example, where this type of training is necessary, by informing staff who are selected well in advance to enable them to make childcare and other personal arrangements; employers with their own residential training centres could also consider whether childcare facilities might be provided;

(e) the statutory maternity leave provisions could be enhanced, for example, by reducing the qualifying service period, extending the leave period, or giving access to part-time arrangements on return.

These arrangements, and others, are helpful to both sexes but are of particular benefit to women in helping them to remain in gainful employment during the years of child-rearing.   **[3107]**

A.C.A.S CODE OF PRACTICE: TIME OFF FOR TRADE UNION DUTIES AND ACTIVITIES (1991)

NOTE

Authority: Employment Protection Act 1975, s 6 (now the Trade Union and Labour Relations (Consolidation) Act 1992, ss 199, 200).

The original ACAS Code on this subject was issued in 1977 and came into force on 1 April 1978 (SI 1977/2076). It was revised, following amendments to the substantive law made by the Employment Act 1989, s 14, and in the light of comments received in a consultation exercise. The current Code came into force on 13 May 1991 (see SI 1991/968). For the legal status of the Code see the Trade Union and Labour Relations (Consolidation) Act 1992, s 207 (TULR(C) A 1992). The Annex, which reproduces the relevant statutory provisions, is omitted.

Introduction

1 Under s 6 of the Employment Protection Act 1975 the Advisory, Conciliation and Arbitration Service (ACAS) has a duty to provide practical guidance on the time off to be permitted by an employer:

(a) to a trade union official in accordance with section 27 of the Employment Protection (Consolidation) Act 1978 [now TULR(C) A 1992, s 168]; and

(b) to a trade union member in accordance with section 28 of the Employment Protection (Consolidation) Act 1978 [now TULR(C) A 1992, s 170].

This Code, which replaces the Code of Practice issued by the Service in 1978, is intended to provide such guidance.   **[3108]**

The background

2 The Employment Protection Act 1975 gave trade union officials a statutory right to reasonable paid time off form employment to carry out trade union duties and to undertake trade union training. Union officials and members were also given a statutory right to reasonable unpaid time off when taking part in trade union activities. These rights were subsequently re-enacted as sections 27 and 28 of the Employment Protection (Consolidation) Act 1978 [now TULR(C) A 1992, ss 168–170].   **[3109]**

3 Section 14 of the Employment Act 1989, which came into force on 26th February 1990, amends the statutory provisions. In particular, it introduces restrictions on the range of issues for which paid time off for trade union duties can be claimed to those covered by recognition agreements between employers and trade unions. Additionally union duties must relate to the official's own employer and not, for example, to any associated employer. **[3110]**

General purpose of the Code

4 The general purposes of the statutory provisions and this Code of Practice is to aid and improve the effectiveness of relationships between employers and trade unions. Employers and unions have joint responsibility to ensure that agreed arrangements seek to specify how reasonable time off for union duties and activities and for training can work to their mutual advantage. **[3111]**

Structure of the Code

5 Section 1 of this Code provides guidance on time off for trade union duties. Section 2 deals with time off for training of trade union officials. Section 3 considers time off for trade union activities. In each case the amount and frequency of time off, and the purposes for which and any conditions subject to which time off may be taken, are to be those that are reasonable in all the circumstances. Section 4 describes the responsibilities which employers and trade unions share in considering reasonable time off. Section 5 notes the advantages of reaching formal agreements with time off. Section 6 deals with industrial action and section 7 with methods of appeal. **[3112]**

6 The annex of this Code reproduces the relevant statutory provisions on time off. To help differentiate between these and practical guidance, the summary of statutory provisions relating to time off which appears in the main text of the Code is in bold type. Practical guidance is in ordinary type. While every effort has been made to ensure that the summary of the statutory provisions included in this Code is accurate, only the courts can interpret the law authoritatively. **[3113]**

Status of the Code

7 The provisions of this Code are admissible in evidence and may be taken into account in determining any question arising during industrial proceedings relating to time off for trade union duties and activities. However, failure to observe any provision of the Code does not of itself render a person liable to any proceedings.

[3114]

Section 1. Time off for trade union duties

ENTITLEMENT

8 Employees who are officials of an independent trade union recognised by their employer are to be permitted reasonable time off during working hours to carry out certain trade union duties. **[3115]**

9 An official is an employee who has been elected or appointed in accordance with the rules of the union to be a representative of all or some of the union's members in the particular company or workplace. **[3116]**

10 Officials are entitled to time off where the duties are concerned with:

- negotiations with the employer about matters which fall within section

29(1) of the Trade Union and Labour Relations Act 1974 (TULRA) [now TULR(C) A 1992, s 244] and for which the union is recognised for the purposes of collective bargaining by the employer; or
- any other functions on behalf of employees of the employer which are related to matters falling within s 29(1) TULRA and which the employer has agreed the union may perform.

Matters falling within s 29(1) TULRA are listed in the sub-headings of paragraph 12 below.   **[3117]**

11 An independent trade union is recognised by an employer when it is recognised to any extent for the purposes of collective bargaining. Where a trade union is not so recognised by an employer, employees have no statutory right to time off to undertake any duties.   **[3118]**

Examples of trade union duties

12 Subject to the recognition or other agreement, trade union officials should be allowed to take reasonable time off for duties concerned with negotiations or, where their employer has agreed, for duties concerned with other functions related to or connected with:

(a) terms and conditions of employment, or the physical conditions in which workers are required to work. Examples could include:
- pay
- hours of work
- holidays and holiday pay
- sick pay arrangements
- pensions
- vocational training
- equal opportunities
- notice periods
- the working environment
- utilisation of machinery and other equipment;

(b) engagement or non-engagement, or termination or suspension of employment or the duties of employment, of one or more workers. Examples could include:
- recruitment and selection policies
- human resource planning
- redundancy and dismissal arrangements;

(c) allocation of work or the duties of employment as between workers or groups of workers. Examples could include:
- job grading
- job evaluation
- job descriptions
- flexible working practices;

(d) matters of discipline. Examples could include:
- disciplinary procedures
- arrangements for representing trade union members at internal interviews
- arrangements for appearing on behalf of trade union members, or as witnesses, before agreed outside bodies or industrial tribunals;

(e) trade union membership or non-membership. Examples could include:
- representational arrangements
- any union involvement in the induction of new workers;

(f) facilities for officials of trade unions. Examples could include any agreed arrangements for the provisions of:
   ● accommodation
   ● equipment
   ● names of new workers to the union;
(g) machinery for negotiation or consultation and other procedures. Examples could include arrangements for:
   ● collective bargaining
   ● grievance procedures
   ● joint consultation
   ● communicating with members
   ● communicating with other union officials also concerned with collective bargaining with the employer. **[3119]**

13 The duties of an official of a recognised trade union must be connected with or related to negotiations or the performance of functions both in time and subject matter. Reasonable time off may be sought, for example to:
   ● prepare for negotiations
   ● inform members of progress
   ● explain outcomes to members
   ● prepare for meetings with the employer about matters for which the trade union has only representational rights. **[3120]**

PAYMENT FOR TIME OFF FOR TRADE UNION DUTIES

14 An employer who permits officials time off for trade union duties must pay them for the time off taken. The employer must pay either the amount that the officials would have earned had they worked during the time off taken or, where earnings vary with the work done, an amount calculated by reference to the average hourly earnings for the work they are employed to do. There is no statutory requirement to pay for time of where the duty is carried out at a time when the official would not otherwise have been at work. **[3121]**

Section 2. Training of officials in aspects of industrial relations

ENTITLEMENT

15 Employees who are officials of an independent trade union recognised by their employer are to be permitted reasonable time off during working hours to undergo training relevant to the carrying out of their trade union duties.[1] These duties must be concerned with:

   ● negotiations with the employer about matters which fall within s 29(1) TULRA and for which the union is recognised to any extent for the purposes of collective bargaining by the employer; or
   ● any other functions on behalf of employees of the employer which are related to matters falling within s 29(1) TULRA and [now TULR(C)A 1992, s 244] and which the employer has agreed the union may perform.

Matters falling within s 29(1) TULRA are set out in paragraph 12 above. **[3122]**

---

[1] Section 1 of this Code gives a more complete summary of the statutory entitlement of officials to time off to undertake trade union duties.

What is relevant industrial relations training ?

16 Training should be in aspects of industrial relations relevant to the duties of an official. There is no one recommended syllabus for training as an official's duties will vary according to:

- collective bargaining arrangements at the place of work, particularly the scope of the recognition or other agreement
- the structure of the union
- the role of the official.   **[3123]**

17 The training must also be approved by the Trades Union Congress or by the independent trade union of which the employee is an official.   **[3124]**

18 Trade union officials are more likely to carry out their duties effectively if they possess skills and knowledge relevant to their duties. In particular, employers should be prepared to consider releasing trade union officials for initial training in basic representational skills as soon as possible after their election or appointment, bearing in mind that suitable courses may be infrequent. Reasonable time off could also be considered, for example:

- for further training particularly where the official has special responsibilities
- where there are proposals to change the structure and topics of negotiations about matters for which the union is recognised; or where significant changes in the organisation of work are being contemplated
- where legislative change may affect the conduct of industrial relations at the place of work and may require the reconsideration of existing agreements.   **[3125]**

PAYMENT FOR TIME OFF FOR TRAINING

19 An employer who permits time off for officials to attend training relevant to their duties at the workplace must pay them for the time off taken. The employer must pay either the amount that the officials would have earned had they worked during the time off taken or, where earnings vary with the work done, an amount calculated by reference to the average hourly earnings for the work that they are employed to do. There is no statutory requirement to pay for time off where training is undertaken at a time when the official would not otherwise have been at work.   **[3126]**

Section 3. Time off for trade union activities

ENTITLEMENT

20 To operate effectively and democratically, trade unions need the active participation of members. It can be very much in employers' interests that such participation is assured. An employee who is a member of an independent trade union recognised by the employer in respect of that description of employee is to be permitted reasonable time off during working hours to take part in any trade union activity.   **[3127]**

What are examples of trade union activities?

21 The activities of a trade union member can be, for example:

- attending workplace meetings to discuss and vote on the outcome of negotiations with the employer

- meeting full-time officials to discuss issues relevant to the workplace
- voting in properly conducted ballots on industrial action
- voting in union elections.   **[3128]**

22 Where the member is acting as a representative of a recognised union activities can be, for example, taking part in:

- branch, area or regional meetings of the union where the business of the union is under discussion
- meetings of official policy making bodies such as the executive committee or annual conference
- meetings with full-time officials to discuss issues relevant to the workplace.   **[3129]**

23 There is no right to time off for trade union activities which themselves consist of industrial action.   **[3130]**

PAYMENT FOR TIME OFF FOR TRADE UNION ACTIVITIES

24 There is no requirement that union members or representatives be paid for time off taken on trade union activities. Nevertheless employers may want to consider payment in certain circumstances, for example to ensure that workplace meeting, are fully representative.   **[3131]**

Section 4. The responsibilities of employers and trade unions

GENERAL CONSIDERATIONS

25 The amount and frequency of time off should be reasonable in all the circumstances. Although the statutory provisions apply to all employers without exception as to size and type of business or service, trade unions should be aware of the wide variety of difficulties and operational requirements to be taken into account when seeking or agreeing arrangements for time off, for example:

- the size of the organisation and the number of workers
- the production process
- the need to maintain a service to the public
- the need for safety and security at all times.   **[3132]**

26 Employers in turn should have in mind the difficulties for trade union officials and members in ensuring representation and communications with, for example:

- shift workers
- part-time workers
- those employed at dispersed locations
- workers with particular domestic commitments.   **[3133]**

27 For time off arrangements to work satisfactorily trade unions should:

- ensure that officials are aware of their role, responsibilities and functions
- inform management, in writing, as soon as possible of appointments or resignations of officials
- ensure that officials receive any appropriate written credentials promptly.   **[3134]**

28 Employers should consider making available to officials the facilities necessary for them to perform their duties efficiently and communicate effectively with their members, fellow lay officials and full-time officers. Where resources permit the facilities could include:

- accommodation for meetings
- access to a telephone and other office equipment
- the use of notice boards
- where the volume of the official's work justifies it, the use of dedicated office space.   **[3135]**

REQUESTING TIME OFF

29 Trade union officials and members requesting time off to pursue their industrial relations duties or activities should provide management with as much notice as possible and give details of:

- the purpose of such time off
- the intended location
- the timing and duration of time off required.   **[3136]**

30 In addition, officials who request paid time off to undergo relevant training should:

- give at least a few weeks' notice to management of nominations for training courses
- if asked to do so, provide a copy of the syllabus or prospectus indicating the contents of the training course.   **[3137]**

31 When deciding whether request for paid time off should be granted, consideration would need to be given as to their reasonableness, for example to ensure adequate cover for safety or to safeguard the production process or the provision of service. Similarly managers and unions should seek to agree a mutually convenient time which minimises the effect on production or services. Where workplace meetings are requested consideration should be given to holding them, for example:

- towards the end of a shift or the working week
- before or after a meal break.   **[3138]**

32 Employers need to consider each application for the time off on its merits; they might also need to consider the reasonableness of the request in relation to agreed time off already taken or in prospect.   **[3139]**

Section 5. Agreements on time off

33 To take account of the wide variety of circumstances and problems which can arise, there can be positive advantages for employers and trade unions in establishing agreements on time off in ways which reflect their own situations. A formal agreement can help to:

- provide clear guidelines against which applications for time off can be determined
- avoid misunderstanding
- facilitate better planning
- ensure fair and reasonable treatment.   **[3140]**

34 Agreements could specify:

- the amount of time off permitted
- the occasions on which time off can be taken
- in what circumstances time off will be paid

- to whom time off will be paid
- the procedure for requesting time off. **[3141]**

35 In addition, it would be sensible for agreements to make clear:

- arrangements for the appropriate payment to be made when time off relates in part to union duties and in part to union activities
- whether payment (to which there would be no statutory entitlement) might be made to shift and part-time employees undertaking trade union duties outside their normal working hours. **[3142]**

36 Agreements for time off and other facilities for union representation should be consistent with wider agreements which deal with such matters as constituencies, number of representatives and the election of officials. **[3143]**

37 In smaller organisations, it might be thought more appropriate for employers and unions to reach understandings about how requests for time off are to be made; and more broadly to agree flexible arrangements which can accommodate their particular circumstances. **[3144]**

38 The absence of a formal agreement on time off, however, does not in itself deny an individual any statutory entitlement. Nor does any agreement supersede statutory entitlement to time off. **[3145]**

Section 6. Industrial action

39 Employers and unions have a responsibility to use agreed procedures to settle problems and avoid industrial action. Time off may therefore be permitted for this purpose particularly where there is a dispute. **There is no right to time off for trade union activities which themselves consist of industrial action.** However, where an official is not taking part in industrial action but represents members involved, normal arrangements for time off with pay for the official should apply. **[3146]**

Section 7. Making a complaint

40 Every effort should be made to resolve any dispute or grievance in relation to time off work for union duties or activities. There is advantage in agreeing ways in which such disputes can be settled and any appropriate procedures to resolve disputes should be followed. Where the grievance remains unresolved, trade union officials or members have a right to complain to an industrial tribunal that their employer has failed to allow reasonable time off or, in the case of an official, has failed to pay for all or part of the time off taken. Such complaints may be resolved by conciliation by ACAS and if this is successful, no tribunal hearing will be necessary. ACAS assistance may also be sought without the need for a formal complaint to a tribunal. **[3147]**

* * * * *

NOTE

The Annex, which reproduces the relevant statutory provisions (now re-enacted in the Trade Union and Labour Relations (Consolidation) Act 1992) is omitted.

CODE OF PRACTICE: TRADE UNION BALLOTS ON INDUSTRIAL ACTION (1991)

NOTE

Authority: Employment Act 1980, s 3 (as amended by the Employment Act 1988, s 18); Employment Act 1990, s 12. (See now the Trade Union and Labour Relations (Consolidation) Act 1992, ss 201, 202.)

This Code was made by the Secretary of State for Employment, and came into force on 20 May 1991 (SI 1991/989). It replaces the previous Code issued in 1990, which had in part been superseded by changes in the relevant legislation enacted by the Employment Act 1990. For the legal status of the Code see the Trade Union and Labour Relations (Consolidation) Act 1992, s 207 (TULR(C)A 1992).

Preamble

The legal framework within which the Code will operate is explained in the *Annex* and in the main text of the Code. While every effort has been made to ensure that explanations included in the Code are accurate, only the courts can give authoritative interpretations of the law.

The Code's provisions apply equally to men and to women, but for simplicity the masculine pronoun is used throughout. Wherever it appears in the Code the word "court" is used to mean the High Court in England and Wales and the Court of Session in Scotland, but without prejudice to the Code's relevance to any proceedings before any other court.

Passages in this Code which are printed [in italics] are re-statements of provisions in primary legislation.   **[3148]**

SECTION A: INTRODUCTION

1 The purpose of this Code is to provide practical guidance to promote the improvement of industrial relations and desirable practices in relation to the conduct by trade unions of ballots about industrial action.   **[3149]**

2 The Code should assist unions and their members who are directly involved in such ballots, and employers, and their customers and suppliers, who may be affected by industrial action organised by a union.   **[3150]**

3 A union is only legally responsible for organising industrial action if it "authorises or endorses" the action. Authorisation would take place before the industrial action starts, and endorsement after it has previously started as unofficial action.[1]   **[3151]**

Scope

4 The Code is concerned with ballots on industrial action which may protect a union from an application to the court by:—

   (a)   a member (under section 1 of the Employment Act 1988 [now TULR(C)A 1992, s 62); or

   (b)   an employer, or customer or supplier of an employer, who may be damaged by a union's inducement of members to break or interfere with the performance of contracts of employment or for services (relying on section 10 of the Trade Union Act 1984 [now TULR(C)A 1992, s 226]).   **[3152]**

5 Failure to hold a ballot which satisfies the requirements of section 11 of the Trade Union Act 1984 (as it has effect following amendments made by the

---

[1] A note on trade union liability is set out in the **Annex** to the Code.

Employment Act 1988 and changes made to the law on industrial action balloting in the Employment Act 1990) [now consolidated as TULR(C)A 1992, ss 227–232] will deprive the union of protection against legal action by an employer, customer or supplier, or by a member.   **[3153]**

6 The Code does not apply to union election ballots or ballots on union political funds. Separate statutory requirements have to be met in respect of such ballots.
     [3154]

Legal Status

7 *The Code itself imposes no legal obligations and failure to observe it does not by itself render anyone liable to proceedings. But section 3(8) of the Employment Act 1980 [now TULR(C)A 1992, s 207(3)] provides that any provisions of the Code are to be admissible in evidence and are to be taken into account in proceedings before any court where it considers them relevant.*   **[3155]**

SECTION B: WHETHER AN INDUSTRIAL ACTION BALLOT WOULD BE APPROPRIATE

Observing procedure agreements

8 An industrial action ballot should not take place until:—

  (a) any agreed procedures, either formal or informal, which might lead to the resolution of a dispute without the need for industrial action have been completed; or

  (b) where no such procedures are available or have been exhausted, consideration has been given to resolving the dispute by other means, including where practicable seeking assistance from the Advisory, Conciliation and Arbitration Service (ACAS).   **[3156]**

Other relevant considerations

9 A union should hold a ballot on industrial action only if:—

  (a) it is contemplating authorising or endorsing industrial action; and

  (b) it would be lawful for the union to organise the industrial action concerned if the statutory requirements in respect of the ballot were satisfied.[1]   **[3157]**

10 A union may wish to obtain its members' views about something other than their willingness to take part in, or continue with, industrial action—for example its negotiating position or an offer made by an employer. Such a ballot should be combined with an industrial action ballot only when the union is contemplating the authorisation or endorsement of industrial action.   **[3158]**

Informing the employer (or employers)

11 So far as practicable, a union should inform every employer whose workers may be given entitlement to vote of its intention to hold the ballot.   **[3159]**

---

[1] It is unlawful, for example, for a trade union to organise secondary action, unlawful picketing or action to further a dispute which does not come within the definition of a "trade dispute" set out in s 29 of the Trade Union and Labour Relations Act 1974 (as amended by the Employment Act 1982) [now TULR(C)A 1992, s 244].

Balloting by more than one union

12 Wherever more than one union decided that it wishes to ballot members working for the same employer in connection with the same dispute or potential dispute, the arrangements for the different ballots should be co-ordinated so that, as far as practicable, they are held at the same time and the results are announced simultaneously.   **[3160]**

SECTION C: PREPARING FOR AN INDUSTRIAL ACTION BALLOT

Establishing entitlement to vote (the "balloting constituency")

13 *The law requires that entitlement to vote in the ballot must be given to all the union's members who it is reasonable at the time of the ballot for the union to believe will be induced (whether that inducement will be successful or not) to take part in or continue with the industrial action, and to no other member.*[1]   **[3161]**

14 The relevant individual, individuals or body in the union who would authorise or endorse the industrial action, with which the ballot is concerned should have responsibility for establishing the proper "balloting constituency" for the ballot in accordance with the statutory requirements described in paragraph 13 above. **[3162]**

Reviewing the "balloting constituency"

15 *The law requires that, in some circumstances, one or more separate place of work ballots must be held. The law requires that certain conditions must be satisfied wherever a union proposes to conduct an industrial action ballot in such a way that votes by its members in the "balloting constituency" who have different places of work*[2] *are to be aggregated. They will be satisfied if, at the time of the ballot, it is reasonable for the union to believe (and it does believe) that those whose votes are to be aggregated form a group consisting of:—*

    (a) *all of its members;*
    (b) *all of its members employed by one or more employers; or*
    (c) *members who each share a "common distinguishing factor". For these purposes a "factor" is one which relates to the member's terms and conditions of employment or occupational description but which is not consequent upon the member's place of work alone. It is "common" if it is shared with one or more of the other members in the group whose votes are to be aggregated. It is "distinguishing" if it is not shared with any member employed by the same employer who is not entitled to vote.*

                                                        [3163]

16 *Where the "balloting constituency" covers members of a union with different places of work then, to the extent that the requirements described in paragraph 15 are not satisfied, a separate place of work ballot (or ballots) will be necessary. It will*

---

[1] The union may choose whether or not to give a vote to any "overseas member", ie any member (other than a merchant seaman or offshore worker) who is outside Great Britain for the whole of the voting period. However, members who are in Northern Ireland throughout the voting period for an industrial action ballot and who will be called upon to take part in, or continue with, the industrial action must be given entitlement to vote in the ballot if: (i) their place of work is in Great Britain and the ballot is of members at their place of work; or (ii) the industrial action to which the ballot relates will involve members in Great Britain as well as Northern Ireland. Members required to be given entitlement to vote by either of these requirements do not count as "overseas members" for the purposes of the law on industrial action balloting.

[2] In this context "place of work" means the premises occupied by an employer at which a member works or with which he has the closest connection.

be unlawful for the union to organise industrial action at any such place of work where a majority of those voting have not voted "yes" in response to the relevant required question (or questions) (see paragraph 27 below).   **[3164]**

17 Aggregation of votes by those properly given entitlement to vote in a ballot across different places of work would satisfy the statutory requirements if (and to the extent that) such aggregation covered, **for example:**—

(a) all of the union's members employed in a particular occupation by the same employer or a number of employers; **or**

(b) all of a union's members who share a particular term or condition of employment because their terms and conditions are determined by the same established collective bargaining arrangements.[3]   **[3165]**

*The process of review

18 The union should review against the statutory requirements described in paragraphs 15 and 16 above any part of the "balloting constituency" for which it proposes to aggregate votes across different places of work. The relevant individual, individuals or body in the union who would authorise or endorse the industrial action should decide if votes are going to be aggregated in this way.   **[3166]**

The balloting method

19 *The law requires that a ballot must be conducted by:*

(a) *postal voting;*

(b) *members casting votes at their workplace or a place more convenient to them; or*

(c) *a mix of these methods as permitted by the law.*

The law allows a union to give any or all of those entitled to vote the opportunity of voting either by post or at their workplace or a place more convenient to them as they choose.   **[3167]**

20 A union is free to decide which of these methods, or what mix of methods, will be used for the ballot. It should, however, consider the guidance set out below and apply its recommendations:—

(a) "fully-postal" balloting should be the preferred choice wherever the ballot is about the authorisation of industrial action by a union or wherever the "balloting constituency" (see paragraph 13 above) covers all the members of the union, unless this is impracticable in the time available (for example because it is necessary to obtain members' views sooner than its use would allow);

(b) "semi-postal" balloting—where voting papers are made available at the workplace or some other more convenient location, but are returned by voters by post to a central point for counting—should normally be the choice in circumstances where a "fully-postal" ballot is not considered practicable;

(c) "workplace balloting"—where votes are cast at the workplace or at some other more convenient location might be a suitable method where, for example:—

only a few union members are entitled to vote and/or the locations where balloting would actually take place are few; or speed of obtaining the voters' response is of the essence.   **[3168]**

---

[3] Other such "common distinguishing factors" could apply in particular circumstances. Votes can be aggregated across groups with different common factors provided that they are "distinguishing factors" for each group as described in paragraph 15 above.

21 Where the union decided to use "workplace" balloting in accordance with the Code, the employer (or employers) of the union's members given entitlement to vote should consider whether the provision of such facilities as would assist the proper conduct of the ballot, in accordance with good industrial relations practices and the requirements of the law, should be made available to the union.[4] **[3169]**

Arrangements for independent scrutiny

22 Whatever method of balloting is used, the union should ensure that adequate arrangements are made for independent scrutiny to oversee the ballot and for an independent scrutineer to report on its conduct. Any such report should be in writing, and be made available to the union's members on demand after the ballot has taken place. **[3170]**

23 Any person or body eligible to act as an independent scrutineer for statutory union election and political fund ballots would be suitable to act as an independent scrutineer for an industrial action ballot. Where it is not practicable to make such arrangements, the union should consider other arrangements, such as having the ballot scrutinised by one or more individuals who are neither directly affected by the dispute or potential dispute to which the ballot relates, nor, union officials who regularly represent any of those entitled to vote in the ballot. **[3171]**

Preparing voting papers

24 *The law requires that whatever the voting method adopted, votes must be recorded only by the individual voter marking a voting paper.* **[3172]**

25 *The law requires that the voting papers must:*

(a) *make clear whether voters are being asked if they are prepared to take part in an industrial action which consists of a strike, or of action short of a strike; and*

(b) *specify the person or description of persons who the union intends to have authority to call for industrial action to which the ballot relates, in the event of a vote in favour of industrial action.*[5] **[3173]**

26 *A ballot will not give a union protection against legal proceedings brought by an employer, customer or supplier, or by a member, if action is called by a person not specified on the voting paper (or by a person of a description not so specified) before it is first called by a specified person, unless, where it is possible to do so, the call by the unspecified person is effectively repudiated.*[6] **[3174]**

---

[4] Section 2 of the Employment Act 1980 puts an obligation on employers to comply as far as reasonable practicable with a request to use their premises for the purpose of giving their employees a convenient opportunity of voting in a secret ballot on industrial action. This statutory obligation applies to employers who have more than 20 employees, where an independent trade union which is recognised to some extent for collective bargaining purposes proposes that a qualifying ballot should be held and the application for use of premises is made by an authorised representative of the trade union. It does not require the employer to do anything more than permit premises to be used; there is no obligation, for example, to allow employees time off work to vote in a workplace (or any other) ballot. Employers may, however, consider that it will accord with good industrial relations practice to make facilities available. [Section 2 is now TULR(C)A 1992, s 116; it is repealed (prospectively) by the Trade Union Reform and Employment Rights Act 1993, s 51, Sch 10: Ed.]

[5] For this purpose, the person or description of persons so specified need not be authorised under the union's rules to call on members to take industrial action, but must be among these for whose acts the union is responsible in law. The **Annex** to the Code describes when a union is to be held responsible for a relevant act.

[6] The **Annex** to the Code contains a short explanation of "repudiation".

*Presentation of question (or questions) on voting papers

27 *While the question (or questions) may be framed in different ways, the law requires that the voter must be asked whether he is willing to take part in or continue with the industrial action the union may authorise or endorse. If the union's inducement of a voter might be to take strike or non-strike action, separate questions in respect of each type of action must appear on the voting paper.* **[3175]**

28 The relevant required question (or questions) should be simply expressed and appear on the voting paper separately from any other question that might also appear. Voters should not be misled or confused by the framing of the required question (or questions). They should not be led to believe, for example, that they are being asked to agree to an opinion about the union's view of the merits of the dispute or potential dispute. Nor should a voter be asked if he is prepared to "support" industrial action as part of the question which asks him if he is prepared to take part in or continue with it. **[3176]**

*Presentation of information on voting papers

29 The union should ensure that neither the required question (or questions), nor anything else which appears on the voting paper, is presented in a way which might encourage a voter to answer one way rather than another as a result of that presentation. **[3177]**

*Statement which must appear on every voting paper

30 *The law requires that the following words must appear on every voting paper:—*
    "If you take part in a strike or other industrial action, you may be in breach of your contract of employment".
    This statement must not be qualified or commented upon by anything else on the voting paper. **[3178]**

*Examples of voting papers

31 The union should include on the voting papers information to protect the security of the balloting process. Examples of voting papers containing such information are set out in *Figure 1* and *Figure 2* of the Code. The first example is of a voting paper for a postal ballot on taking part in industrial action short of a strike. The second is of a voting paper for a workplace ballot on taking part in a strike and/or non-strike industrial action. In both cases factual information as indicated would appear in the square brackets. **[3179]**

Printing and distribution of the voting papers

32 Arrangements for the production and distribution of the voting papers should be such as to ensure that no mistakes are made which might invalidate the ballot through a failure to satisfy the statutory requirements. The union should seek the advice of any independent scrutineer appointed in connection with the ballot about appropriate arrangements for the printing and distribution of voting papers and be guided by and such advice offered. **[3180]**

FIGURE 1: EXAMPLE OF VOTING PAPER FOR POSTAL BALLOT ON TAKING NON-STRIKE ACTION

[VOTING PAPER NUMBER]

[NAME OF THE TRADE UNION]

If you take part in a strike or other industrial action, you may be in breach of your contract of employment.

ARE YOU PREPARED TO TAKE PART IN INDUSTRIAL ACTION SHORT OF A STRIKE?

YES ☐   NO ☐

If the result of this ballot is in favour of taking industrial action, the following will have the authority to call for industrial action: **[DETAILS OF RELEVANT PERSON, PERSONS, AND/OR DESCRIPTION OF PERSONS]**.

If your vote is to count, this voting paper must be returned to **[FULL ADDRESS OF LOCATION TO WHICH THE VOTING PAPER IS TO BE RETURNED]** by **[FULL DATE AND TIME AS APPROPRIATE]**. Please use the enclosed pre-paid envelope provided for this purpose.

The law requires your union to ensure that in this ballot: (i) your vote will be secret; (ii) you are allowed to vote without interference from, or constraint imposed by, the union or any of its members, officials or employees; (iii) you are able to vote at no direct cost to yourself; and (iv) your vote is accurately and fairly counted in determining the result of the ballot.

[3180.1]

FIGURE 2: EXAMPLE OF VOTING PAPER FOR WORKPLACE BALLOT ON TAKING STRIKE AND/OR NON-STRIKE ACTION

[VOTING PAPER NUMBER]

[NAME OF THE TRADE UNION]

If you take part in a strike or other industrial action, you may be in breach of your contract of employment.

ARE YOU PREPARED TO TAKE PART IN INDUSTRIAL ACTION CONSISTING OF A STRIKE?

YES ☐   NO ☐

ARE YOU PREPARED TO TAKE PART IN INDUSTRIAL ACTION SHORT OF A STRIKE?

YES ☐   NO ☐

If the result of this ballot is in favour of taking industrial action, the following will have the authority to call for industrial action: **[DETAILS OF RELEVANT PERSON, PERSONS, AND/OR DESCRIPTION OF PERSONS]**.

Votes may be cast in this ballot at **[DETAILS OF LOCATION]** from **[APPROPRIATE DATE AND TIME]** to **[APPROPRIATE DATE AND TIME]**.

The law requires your union to ensure that in this ballot: (i) your vote will be secret; (ii) you are allowed to vote without interference from, or constraint imposed by, the union or any of its members, officials or employees; (iii) you are able to vote at no direct cost to yourself; and (iv) your vote is accurately and fairly counted in determining the result of the ballot.

[3180.2]

33 If there is no independent scrutineer (see paragraphs 22 and 23 above), or if a union decides that it cannot follow the advice offered by such a scrutineer, it should in any case consider:—

    (a) numbering all voting papers in a continuous sequence that can, if necessary, be checked later against the roll of those voting. This should be done in a manner consistent with the requirement to allow voters to cast their votes in secret (see paragraph 36(d) in Section D of the Code);

    (b) printing the voting papers on a security background to prevent duplication;

    (c) whether the arrangements proposed for printing (or otherwise preparing) the voting papers, and for their distribution to those entitled to vote in the ballot, offer all concerned sufficient assurance of security.   **[3181]**

Communication with members

34 A union should give relevant information to its members entitled to vote in the ballot, including:—

    (a) the background to the ballot and the issues to which the dispute relates;

    (b) how the voting papers will be distributed and returned;

    (c) the nature and timing of the industrial action which the union may be prepared to authorise or endorse on the ballot result;

    (d) any consideration in respect of turnout or size of the majority vote in the ballot that will be relevant to the decision on whether to authorise or endorse industrial action after the ballot;

    (e) the potential consequences for workers of taking industrial action.

A union is free to communicate with its members in a lawful manner and by lawful means. In connection with a ballot, it should consider doing so by special notices or meetings.   **[3182]**

35 A union should take steps to ensure that any information it supplies to members in connection with the ballot is accurate and does not mislead voters in the process of forming their opinions about which way to vote. The union should consider:—

    (a) preparing a standard statement for inclusion with information issued in connection with the ballot about the possible effects on individual workers of taking industrial action (such as employees' loss of their right to take a case of unfair dismissal to an industrial tribunal if they are dismissed while taking industrial action); and

    (b) making arrangements which will enable it to review any information which its members, officials or employees propose to issue in connection with a ballot or ballot voting papers to ensure its factual accuracy.   **[3183]**

SECTION D: HOLDING AN INDUSTRIAL ACTION BALLOT

36 *The law requires that in an industrial action ballot:-*

    (a) the method of voting must be by the marking of a voting paper by the person voting. No other method of voting will satisfy the statutory requirements; for example a "show of hands" is not sufficient even if it appears to show overwhelming support for taking industrial action;

    (b) every person properly entitled to vote must be allowed to do so without interference from, or constraint imposed by, the union or any of its members, officials or employees;

    (c) as far as reasonable practicable, every person properly entitled to vote must be:—

> (i)   allowed to do so without incurring any direct cost to himself;
>
> (ii) given a voting paper and a convenient opportunity to vote; and
>
> (d)   as far as reasonable practicable the ballot must be conducted in such a way as to ensure that those voting do so in secret.   **[3184]**

Avoiding interference with, or constraint on, those entitled to vote

37 The union should ensure that all of its members, officials and employees who might—even inadvertently—interfere with or constrain those entitled to vote in an industrial action ballot are aware of the potential consequences (ie that the ballot will fail to satisfy the statutory requirements) if their behaviour is regarded as having either of these effects.   **[3185]**

Enabling those properly entitled to vote to do so at no direct cost to themselves

38 The union should make arrangements so that:—

   (a) where "fully-" or "semi-postal" balloting methods are used, those properly entitled to vote are supplied with pre-paid reply envelopes with the voting paper so that they do not have to incur any postal costs themselves in order to vote;

   (b) where the "workplace" balloting method is used, the time allowed for voters to collect their voting papers and to cast votes is outside the normal working hours of those properly entitled to vote if that is necessary to ensure that they do not risk losing pay as a consequence of participating in the ballot.   **[3186]**

Ensuring that all those entitled to vote receive a voting paper and have a convenient opportunity to vote

39 Whatever method of balloting is adopted, the union should make arrangements so that:—

   (a) each of its members properly entitled to vote (see paragraph 13 in Section C of the Code) is on the relevant voters' list, and is supplied with a voting paper[1]; and

   (b) advice is given to those entitled to vote, well in advance, of where, when and how the balloting will take place.   **[3187]**

*Period to be allowed for "postal" and "semi-postal" balloting

40 For "fully-" and "semi-postal" balloting the period between distribution of voting papers and the date by which completed voting papers should be returned should allow at least:—

   (a) 7 days if voting papers are distributed and returned by first class post;

   (b) 14 days if second class post is used for either the distribution or return of voting papers.   **[3188]**

---

[1] If "semi-postal" balloting is used, special arrangements may be needed for members who are on holiday, sickness or maternity leave during the time when the balloting will be taking place so that they can receive voting papers.

*Checks on number of voting papers for return by post

41 The union should establish an appropriate checking system so that:—

    (a) no-one properly entitled to vote (see paragraph 13 in Section C of the Code) is accidentally disenfranchised; and

    (b) no uncompleted voting paper comes into the hands of anyone not properly entitled to vote who might use it to cast a vote to which he is not entitled.

Advice on these matters should be sought from any independent scrutineer appointed in connection with the ballot (see paragraphs 22 and 23 in Section C of the Code).

[3189]

*Arrangements for "workplace" balloting

42 For "workplace" balloting:-

    (a) postal voting papers should be provided to anyone properly entitled to vote who is known to be unable either to collect his voting paper at the time or location where they are issued or to cast his vote at the location where "workplace" balloting is to take place; any such special distribution of any voting paper should be recorded so as to avoid duplicating its issue and to allow sufficient time for its return when completed;

    (b) arrangements for independent scrutiny (see paragraphs 22 and 23 of Section C of the Code) should be made for every location where votes are cast;

    (c) the actual issue of voting papers to voters should not be entrusted to one member of the union alone (unless that person is acting as an independent scrutineer of the ballot), nor to anyone who is directly affected by the dispute or potential dispute to which the ballot relates or who is a union official who regularly represents any of those entitled to vote in the ballot;

    (d) everyone properly entitled to vote (see paragraph 13 in Section C of the Code) should be advised where and when balloting will take place, and what identification will be required in order to establish entitlement to vote at the location where his vote may be cast;

    (e) the time allowed for balloting should take into account the working hours of all those properly entitled to vote and allow them adequate time to cast their votes if they wish to do so.   **[3190]**

Ensuring secrecy of voting

43 In all ballots, conducted by whatever method, any list of those entitled to vote should be complied, and the voting papers themselves handled, so as to preserve the anonymity of the voter so far as this is consistent with the proper conduct of the ballot.

[3191]

*"Fully-" and "semi-postal" ballots

44 The union should take sufficient steps to ensure that a voter's anonymity is preserved when a voting paper is returned by post. This means, for example, that:—

    (a) envelopes in which voting papers are to be posted should have no distinguishing marks from which the identity of the voter could be established;

    (b) the procedures for counting voting papers returned by post (see paragraphs 48 and 40 in Section E of the Code) should not prejudice the statutory requirement for secret voting.   **[3192]**

*"Workplace" ballots

45 The union should make the following arrangements:—

  (a) voting should take place in a room or area where there is privacy for the voter to mark his voting paper and cast his vote;

  (b) no-one should be allowed in that room or area at the time when voting is taking place except those issuing voting papers, any independent scrutineer appointed in connection with the ballot, and those properly entitled to vote; once the voter has cast his vote he should leave the room or area;

  (c) a single, secure and locked receptacle ("ballot box") should be provided in the room or area used for voting at the time when voting is taking place, with its key held by someone not directly involved with the result of the ballot, such as an independent scrutineer overseeing the balloting process; completed voting papers should be placed in that receptacle by the voter personally;

  (d) if the completed voting papers are to be taken out of a "ballot box" and then posted (or otherwise sent) all together to a central location for counting, then each voter should be given a sealable envelope in which to put his completed voting paper, the envelope should be placed into a locked "ballot box" as described above, and at the end of the voting period all such envelopes should be transferred unopened to the central location.   **[3193]**

SECTION E: FOLLOWING AN INDUSTRIAL ACTION BALLOT

46 *The law requires that the union must:*—

  (a) *ensure that the votes given in an industrial action ballot are fairly and accurately counted; any inaccuracy in such counting may only be disregarded if it is both accidental and on a scale which could not affect the result of the ballot; and*

  (b) *observe its obligations in connection with the notification of details for the result of an industrial action ballot to all those properly entitled to vote in that ballot.*   **[3194]**

47 Even if the result of a properly-conducted ballot shows that a majority of those voting are willing to take part in (or continue with) industrial action, there is no statutory obligation on the union to authorise or endorse industrial action.   **[3195]**

Counting votes accurately and fairly

48 The union should consider and apply the following procedures:—

  (a) destruction of all unused or unissued voting papers as soon as possible after the time allowed for voting has passed and the necessary information for checking the number of voting papers issued and used has been prepared;

  (b) rejection of completed voting papers received after the official close of voting or the time set for receipt of such papers;

  (c) settlement well in advance of the actual ballot of the organisational arrangements for conducting the counting of votes cast, and making available equipment or facilities needed in the conduct of the count to those concerned;

  (d) proper briefing of all those involved in the counting process, particularly those doing the actual counting of completed voting papers, as to their responsibilities, including the statutory requirements described in paragraph 46 above;

(e) delaying the counting of votes at any one location until all the voting papers to be counted at that location have been received;

(f) storage of all voting papers received by post at the counting location in a locked and secure room as soon as they arrive, and keeping them under such secure conditions until removed for counting;

(g) making an individual—someone who is neither directly affected by the dispute or potential dispute to which the ballot relates, nor is a union official who regularly represents any of those entitled to vote in the ballot—responsible for adjudicating on any voting paper which those doing the actual counting propose to reject as "spoiled", and ensuring that those doing the actually counting refer any such voting paper about which they are in doubt to the adjudicator;

(h) if voting papers arrive at the counting location in envelopes, regular removal of such envelopes from the counting area once they have been opened and voting papers removed for counting;

(i) locking and securing the counting room during the period during which votes are to be counted whenever counting staff are not actually at work;

(j) ensuring that counting staff are not disturbed or distracted by any person with a particular interest in the result of the ballot during the process of the count;

(k) storage of voting papers, once counted, under secure conditions (ie so that they cannot be tampered with in any way and are available for checking if necessary) for at least 6 months after the ballot;

(l) where ballot boxes (or equivalent receptacles) are to be transferred from a voting location to any other place before votes are counted, this should be done in such a way as to avoid the possibility of interference. **[3196]**

Independent scrutiny

49 The union should consider the appointment of one or more independent scrutineers (see paragraphs 22 and 23 in Section C of the Code) and seek advice from them about suitable arrangements to meet the requirements for accurate and fair counting of votes. The union should also consider putting the counting exercise as a whole into the hands of an independent scrutineer. **[3197]**

Announcing details of the result of a ballot

50 *The law requires that a union must, as soon as reasonable practicable after holding an industrial action ballot, take steps to inform all those properly entitled to vote[1] of the number of:—*

(a) *votes cast in the ballot;*

(b) *individuals answering "Yes" to the required question (or questions);*

(c) *individuals answering "No" to the required question (or questions); and*

(d) *spoiled ballot papers.*

---

[1] If overseas members of a trade union have been given entitlement to vote in an industrial action ballot the detailed information about its result need not be sent to them, but the information supplied to non-overseas members in accordance with the statutory requirements must distinguish between votes cast, individuals voting, and spoiled ballot papers to show which details relate to overseas, and which to non-overseas, members. (For this purpose, members in Northern Ireland required to be given entitlement to vote do not count as "overseas members"—see the footnote to paragraph 13 in Section C of the Code.)

Where separate place of work ballots are required (see paragraphs 15 and 16 in Section C of the Code) these details must be notified separately for each such place of work to those entitled to vote at that place.   **[3198]**

51 To help ensure that its result can be notified as required, the union should consider, for example:—

  (a) designating a "Returning Officer" for the centralised count of votes cast in the ballot (or separate "Returning Offices" for counts conducted at different locations) to whom the results will be notified in the form required prior to their announcement;

  (b) organising the counting of votes in such a way that the information required to satisfy the relevant statutory requirements can be easily obtained after the counting process is completed;

  (c) utilising its own journals, local communications news-sheets, company or union branch noticeboards to publicise the details of the ballot result.
    [3199]

52 The union should not proceed to authorise or endorse industrial action without first taking steps to satisfy the statutory requirements for notifying details of the result of a ballot.   **[3200]**

*Responding to requests for details of the ballot

53 The union should respond positively (and in writing when so requested) to a request from any employer whose workers participated in the industrial action ballot, and/or any employers' association representing such employers, for such details of the ballot result as the law requires a union to provide to those entitled to vote in the ballot.   **[3201]**

Deciding on action a union may take after a ballot indicated a majority prepared to take part in (or continue with) industrial action

54 The union should consider all options other than authorising or endorsing industrial action as a means of resolving the dispute or potential dispute which led to the ballot being held.   **[3202]**

*Relevant considerations

55 In considering what action might be taken the individual, individuals or body who would authorise or endorse the industrial action on behalf of the union should take into account, for example:—

  (a) the serious consequences (such as risk of dismissal from employment) which may follow for union members if they embark on industrial action on the union's instruction or advice;

  (b) any changes in circumstances, such as developments in negotiations or in the offer made by the employer, since the time when the ballot was taken;

  (c) the willingness of the employer (or employers) concerned to enter into further negotiations or discussions;

  (d) the possibilities of using the services of the Advisory, Conciliation and Arbitration Service (ACAS);

  (e) the size of that majority and the number of those voting in the ballot relative to those given entitlement to vote;

(f) *that four weeks is allowed from the date of the ballot (ie the last day on which votes may be cast in the ballot) during which the industrial action may be induced.*[1] **[3203]**

If the union decides to authorise or endorse industrial action

56 If the union decides to authorise or endorse industrial action by its members, it should inform:—

(a) all its members concerned of its decision to authorise or endorse industrial action, and its reasons for doing so, before inducing them to take or continue that action; and

(b) any employer whose workers' industrial action has been authorised or endorsed of the union's decision to do so, allowing sufficient time before any consequent inducement by the union takes place for the employer to make any necessary arrangements to ensure that there is no risk to the health and safety of other workers, or the general public, as a result of the consequences of "official" industrial action. **[3204]**

Seeking union members' views after a union has authorised or endorsed industrial action

57 There is not statutory obligation on a union to ballot, or otherwise consult, its members before it decides to withdraw authorisation or endorsement of industrial action. However, if a union decides to seek its members' views about continuing with industrial action it has authorised or endorse, the same standards should be applied to the process of seeking their views as are set out in this Code. **[3205]**

ANNEX: TRADE UNION LIABILITY

1 *Section 15 of the Employment Act 1982 (as amended by the Employment Act 1990, s 6) [now TULR(C)A 1992, s 21] lays down when a union is to be held responsible for the act of inducing or threatening a breach or interference with a contract when there is no immunity. The union will be held liable for any such act which is done, authorised or endorsed by:—*

— *its Executive Committee, General Secretary or President;*
— *any person having power under the union's rules to do, authorise or endorse acts of the kind in question; or*
— *any other committee or other official*[2] *of the union (whether employed by it or not).*

---

[1] The law provides that, in certain circumstances, a union may be allowed to make its first call for industrial action more than four weeks after the date of the ballot. The circumstances occur where an injunction granted by a court or an undertaking given by the union to the court prohibits the union from calling for industrial action during some part, or the whole, of the four weeks following the date of the ballot, and the injunction subsequently lapses or is set aside or the union is released from its undertaking. In such circumstances, a union may apply forthwith to the court for an order which, if granted, would provide that the period during which the prohibition had effect would not count towards the four week limit. An order granting the extension will not be made if, on the basis of any submissions which may be made, it appears to the court that: (i) the result of the ballot no longer represents the views of the union members concerned; or (ii) an event has occurred, or is likely to occur, as a result of which those members would vote against industrial action if another ballot were to be held. In any case, under no circumstances will a union have immunity, or protection from legal proceedings brought by a union member, if it first calls for industrial action more than 12 weeks after the date of the ballot.

[2] An "official of the union" is any person who is an officer of the union or of a branch or section of the union or any person who is elected or appointed in accordance with the union's own rules to be a representative of its members, including any person so elected or appointed who is an employee of the same employer as the members, or one or more of the members, he is elected to represent—eg a shop steward.

A union will be held responsible for such an act by such a body or person regardless of any provisions to the contrary in its own rules, or anything in any other contract or rule of law. **[3206]**

2 *For these purposes:—*

    (a) a "committee of the union" is any group of persons constituted in accordance with the rules of the union; and

    (b) a relevant act will be held to have been done (or authorised or endorsed) by an official if it was done (or authorised or endorsed) by a group of persons, or any member of a group, to which an official belonged at the relevant time if the group's purposes included organising or co-ordinating industrial action. **[3207]**

3 *A union will not, however, be responsible in law for such an act of any committee or official (except an act of its Executive Committee, General Secretary or President or of an official or committee having power under the union's rules) if its Executive Committee, General Secretary or President repudiates the act as soon as reasonable practicable after it has come to the attention of any of them, and the union takes the steps which the law requires to make that repudiation effective. But, the union will not be considered to have "effectively repudiated" an act if the Executive Committee, General Secretary or President subsequently behave in a manner which is inconsistent with the repudiation.* **[3208]**

4 The fact that a union is responsible for organising industrial action to which immunity does not apply does not prevent legal action also being taken against the individual organisers of that action. **[3209]**

"Immunity"

5 A trade union which organises (ie authorises or endorses) industrial action without satisfying the requirements of section 10 of the Trade Union Act 1984 (as amended by the Employment Act of 1988 and 1990) [now TULR(C)A 1992, s 226] will have no "immunity". Without "immunity" the trade union will be at risk of legal action by any employer (and/or a customer or supplier of such an employer) who suffers (or may suffer) damage as a consequence of the trade union's unlawful inducement to his workers to break or interfere with the performance of contracts. Such legal action might result in a court order requiring the trade union not to proceed with, and/or desist from, the unlawful inducement of its members to take part or continue with the action and/or to pay damages for the effects of its unlawful inducement. **[3210]**

Section 1 of the Employment Act 1988

6 If any of the requirements of section 1 of the Employment Act 1988 (as amended by the Employment Act 1990) [now TULR(C)A 1992, s 62] are not satisfied a member of the trade union who is, or is likely to be, induced by the union to take industrial action may apply to the court. Such legal action might result in a court order requiring the trade union to take steps to ensure that there is no, or no further, unlawful inducement to members to take part or continue to take part in the action, and that no member does anything after the order is made as a result of unlawful inducement prior to the making of the order. The Commissioner for the Rights of Trade Union Members may assist a member of the trade union in connection with such proceedings. **[3211]**

Section 11 of the Trade Union Act 1984

7 Failure to satisfy any one of the requirements of section 11 of the Trade Union Act 1984 (as it has effect following amendments made by the Employment Act 1988 and changes made to the law on industrial action balloting in the Employment Act 1990) [now consolidated as ss 227–232 of TULR(C)A 1992] will deprive the trade union of protection against legal action by an employer, customer or supplier, or by a member of the union.   **[3212]**

Contempt and other proceedings

8 If a court order issued following legal proceedings as described in paragraph 5 and paragraph 6 above is not obeyed, anyone who sought it can go back to court and ask that those concerned be declared in contempt of court. The Commissioner for the Rights of Trade Union Members may assist a member of the trade union in connection with such contempt proceedings. A union found in contempt of court may face heavy fines, or other penalties which the court may consider appropriate.   **[3123]**

9 In addition, any member of the union may have grounds for legal action against the union's trustees if they have caused or permitted the unlawful application of union funds or property, and the Commissioner for the Rights of Trade Union Members may assist a member of the trade union in connection with such proceedings.   **[3214]**

CODE OF PRACTICE: PICKETING (1992)

NOTES

Authority: Employment Act 1980, s 3 (as amended by the Employment Act 1988, s 18). (See now the Trade Union and Labour Relations (Consolidation) Act 1992, ss 201, 202.)

This Code was made by the Secretary of State for Employment, and came into force on 1 May 1992 (see SI 1992/476) Following resolutions of the House of Commons on 19 February 1992 and of the House of Lords on 21 February 1992.

This Code replaces the previous Code on the subject issued in 1980.

For the legal status of the Code see the Trade Union and Labour Relations (Consolidation) Act 1992, s 207 (TULR(C)A 1992).

Preamble

The legal framework within which the Code will operate is explained in its text. While every effort has been made to ensure that explanations included in the Code are accurate, only the courts can give authoritative interpretations of the law.

The Code's provisions apply equally to men and to women, but for simplicity the masculine pronoun is used throughout. Wherever it appears in the Code, the word "court" is used to mean the High Court in England and Wales and the Court of Session in Scotland, but without prejudice to the Code's relevance to any proceedings before any other court.

Passages in this Code which are printed [in italics] outline or re-state provisions in primary legislation.

On the day on which this Code of Practice comes into operation in pursuance of an order under section 3(5) of the Employment Act 1980, the Code of Practice "Picketing" which came into effect on 17 December 1980 ceases to have effect subject to any transitional provisions or savings made by the order.   **[3215]**

Section A. Introduction

1 The purpose of this Code is to provide practical guidance on picketing in trade disputes for those:

- contemplating, organising or taking part in a picket or activities associated with picketing, such as assemblies of demonstrations; and/or
- employers, workers or members of the general public who may be affected by a picket or any associated activities.   **[3216]**

2 There is no legal "right to picket" as such, but attendance for the purpose of peaceful picketing has long been recognised to be a lawful activity. However, the law imposes certain limits on how, where and for what purpose such picketing can be undertaken. These limits help ensure proper protection for those who may be affected by picketing—including those who wish to cross a picket line and go to work. **[3217]**

3 It is a **civil** wrong, actionable in the civil courts, to persuade someone to break his contract of employment, or to secure the breaking of a commercial contract. But the law exempts from this liability those acting in contemplation or futherance of a trade dispute, including—in certain circumstances—pickets themselves.   **[3218]**

4 This exemption is provided by means of special "statutory immunities" to prevent liability arising to such **civil law** proceedings. These immunites—which are explained in more detail in Section B of this Code—have the effect that trade unions and individuals can, in certain circumstances, organise or conduct a picket without fear of being successfully sued in the courts. However, this protection applies only to acts of inducing breach, or interference with the performance, of contracts, or threatening to do either of these things.   **[3219]**

5 These "statutory immunities" afford no protection for a picket, anyone involved in activities associated with picketing, or anyone organising a picket who commits some other kind of civil wrong—such as trespass or nuisance.[1] Nor do they protect anyone—whether a picket, an employee who decides to take industrial action or to break his contract of employment because he is persuaded to do so by a picket, or anyone else—from the consequences which may follow if they choose to take industrial action or break their contracts of employment. These could include, for example, loss of wages, or other disciplinary action or dismissal from employment.   **[3220]**

6 The **criminal** law applies to pickets just as it applies to everyone else. No picket, person involved in activities associated with picketing or person organising a picket, has any exemption from the provisions of the criminal law as this applies, for example, to prevent obstruction, preserve public order, or regulate assemblies or demonstrations.   **[3221]**

7 This Code outlines aspects of the law on picketing—although it is, of course, for the courts and industrial tribunals to interpret and apply the law in particular cases. Sections B and C, respectively, outline provisions of the civil and criminal law and, where relevant, give guidance on good practice. Section D describes the role of the police in enforcing the law. Sections E, F and G also give guidance on good practice in relation to the conduct of particular aspects of picketing and of certain activities associated with picketing.   **[3222]**

8 *The Code itself imposes no legal obligations and failure to observe it does not by itself render anyone liable to proceedings. But statute law provides that any provisions of the Code are to be admissible in evidence and taken into account in*

---

[1] See the further explanation in paragraph 27 in Section B of the Code.

proceedings before any court, industrial tribunal or the Central Arbitration Committee where they consider them relevant.   **[3223]**

Section B. Picketing and the Civil Law

9 *The law sets out the basic rules which must be observed if picketing is to be carried out, or organised, lawfully. To keep to these rules, attendance for the purpose of picketing may only:*

(i)   *be taken in contemplation or furtherance of a trade dispute;*

(ii) *be carried out by a person attending at or near his own place of work; a trade union official, in addition to attending at or near his own place of work, may also attend at or near the place of work of a member of his trade union whom he is accompanying on the picket line and whom he represents.*

Furthermore, the only purpose involved must be peacefully to obtain or communicate information, or peacefully to persuade a person to work or not to work.   **[3224]**

10 Picketing commonly involves persuading workers to break, or interfere with the performance of, their contracts of employment by not going into work. Picketing can also disrupt the business of the employer who is being picketed by interfering with the performance of a commercial contract which the employer has with a customer or supplier. If pickets follow the rules outlined in paragraph 9, however, they may have the protection against civil proceedings afforded by the "statutory immunities". These rules, and immunities, are explained more fully in paragraphs 11 to 30 below.   **[3225]**

In contemplation or furtherance of a trade dispute

11 *Picketing is lawful only if it is carried out in contemplation or furtherance of a "trade dispute". A "trade dispute" is defined in law so as to cover the matters which normally occasion disputes between employers and workers—such as terms and conditions of employment, the allocation of work, matters of discipline, trade union recognition.*   **[3226]**

"Secondary" action

12 *The "statutory immunities" do not apply to protect a threat of, or call for or other inducement of "secondary" industrial action. The law defines "secondary" action— which is sometimes referred to as "sympathy" or "solidarity" action—as that by workers whose employer is not a party to the trade dispute to which the action relates.*
                                                                              [3227]

13 However, a worker employed by a party to a trade dispute, picketing at his own place of work may try to persuade another worker, not employed by that employer, to break, or interfere with the performance of, the second worker's contract of employment, and/or to interfere with the performance of a commercial contract. This could happen, for example, if a picket persuaded a lorry driver employed by another employer not to cross the picket line and deliver goods to be supplied, under a commercial contract, to the employer in dispute. Such an act by a picket would be an unlawful inducement to take secondary action unless provision was made to the contrary.   **[3228]**

14 *Accordingly, the law contains provisions which make it lawful for a peaceful picket, at the picket's own place of work, to seek to persuade workers other than those* *employed by the picket's own employer not to work, or not to work normally. To have such protection, the peaceful picketing must be done:*

(a) by a worker employed by the employer who is party to the dispute;[2] or

(b) by a trade union official whose attendance is lawful (see paragraphs 22-23 below).   **[3229]**

15 Where an entrance or exit is used jointly by the workers of more than one employer, the workers who are not involved in the dispute to which a picket relates should not be interfered with by picketing activities. Particular care should be taken to ensure that picketing does not involve calls for a breach, or interference with the performance, of contracts by employees of other employer(s) who are not involved in the dispute. Observing this principle will help avoid consequences which might otherwise be damaging and disruptive to good industrial relations.   **[3230]**

Attendance at or near a picket's own place of work

16 *It is lawful for a person to induce breach, or interference with the performance, of a contract in the course of attendance for the purpose of picketing only if he pickets at or near his own place of work.*   **[3231]**

17 The expression "at or near his own place of work" is not further defined in statute law. The provisions means that, except for those covered by paragraphs 22 and 23 below, lawful picketing must be limited to attendance at, or near, an entrance to or exit from the factory, site or office at which the picket works. Picketing should be confined to a location, or locations, as near as practicable to the place of work.
[3232]

18 The law does not enable a picket to attend lawfully at an entrance to, or exit from, *any* place of work other than his own. This applies even, for example, if those working at the other place of work are employed by the same employer, or are covered by the same collective bargaining arrangements as the picket.   **[3233]**

19 *The law identifies two specific groups in respect of which particular arrangements apply. These groups are:*

● *those (eg mobile workers) who work at more than one place; and*

● *those for whom it is impracticable to picket at their own place of work because of its location.*

The law provides that it is lawful for such workers to picket those premises of their employer from which they work, or those from which their work is administered. In the case of lorry drivers, for example, this will usually mean, in practice, the premises of their employer from which their vehicles operate.   **[3234]**

20 Special provisions also apply to people who are not in work, and who have lost their jobs for reasons connected with the dispute which has occasioned the picketing. This might arise, for example, where the dismissal of a group of employees has led directly to the organisation of a picket, or where an employer has dismissed employees because they refuse to work normally, and some or all of those dismissed then wish to set up a picket. *In such cases the law provides that it is lawful for a worker to picket at his former place of work. This special arrangement ceases to apply, however, to any worker who subsequently takes a job at another place of work.*
[3235]

---

[2] However, the peaceful picketing may be done by a worker who is not in employment but was last employed by the employer in dispute in certain circumstances—see paragraph 20.

21 The law does not protect anyone who pickets without permission on or inside any part of premises which are private property. The law will not, therefore, protect pickets who trespass, or those who organise such trespass, from being sued in the civil courts. **[3236]**

Trade union officials

22 For the reasons described in Section F of this Code, it may be helpful to the orderly organisation and conduct of picketing for a trade union official[3] to be present on a picket line where his members are picketing. *The law provides that it is lawful for trade union official to picket at any place of work provided that:*

(i) *he is accompanying members of his trade union who are picketing lawfully at or near their own place of work; and*

(ii) *he personally represents those members.* **[3237]**

23 If these conditions are satisfied, then a trade union official has the same legal protection as other pickets who picket lawfully at or near their own place of work. *However, the law provides that an official—whether a lay official or an employee of the union—is regarded for this purpose as representing only those members of his union whom he has been specifically* appointed or elected to represent. An official cannot, therefore, claim that he represents a group of members simply because they belong to his trade union. He must represent and be responsible for them in the normal course of his trade union duties. For example, it is lawful for an official—such as a shop steward—who represents members at a particular place of work to be present on a picket line where those members are picketing lawfully; for a branch official to be present only where members of his branch are lawfully picketing; for a national official who represents a particular trade group or section within the union, to be present wherever members of that trade group or section are lawfully picketing; for a regional official to be present only where members of his region are lawfully picketing; and for a national official such as a general secretary or president who represents the whole union to be present wherever any members of his union are picketing lawfully. **[3238]**

Lawful purposes of picketing

24 In no circumstances does a picket have power, under the law, to require other people to stop, or to compel them to listen or to do what he asks them to do. A person who decides to cross a picket line must be allowed to do so. *In addition, the law provides a remedy for any union member who is disciplined by his union because he has crossed a picket line.*[4] **[3239]**

25 The *only* purposes of picketing declared lawful in statute are:

● *peacefully obtaining and communicating information: and*

● *peacefully persuading a person to work or not to work.* **[3240]**

26 The law allows pickets to seek to explain their case to those entering or leaving the picketed premises, and/or to ask them not to enter or leave the premises where the dispute is taking place. This may be done by speaking to people, or it may involve

---

[3] The law defines an "official of the union" as a person who is an officer of the union (or of a branch or section of the union), or who, not being such an officer, is a person elected or appointed in accordance with the rules of the union to be a representative of its members (or some of them), including any person so elected or appointed who is an employee of the same employer as the members, or one or more of the members, whom he is elected to represent. This could include, for example, a shop steward.

[4] A member disciplined for crossing a picket line is "unjustifiably disciplined"; the remedy for unjustifiable discipline is by complaint to an industrial tribunal. (See also paragraphs 60-61 in Section F of this Code.)

the distribution of leaflets or the carrying of banners or placards putting the pickets' case. **In all cases, however, any such activity must by carried out** *peacefully*.

[3241]

27 The law protects peaceful communication and persuasion. It does not give pickets, anyone organising or participating in any activity associated with picketing, or anyone organising a picket, protection against civil proceedings being brought against them for any conduct occurring during the picketing, or associated activity, which amounts to a separate civil wrong such as:

- unlawful threat or assault;
- harassment (ie threatening or unreasonable behaviour causing fear or apprehension to those in the vicinity);
- obstruction of a path, road, entrance or exit to premises;
- interference (eg because of noise or crowds) in the rights of those in neighbouring properties (ie "private nuisance");
- trespassing on private property.   **[3242]**

28 Both individual pickets, and anyone—including a union—organising a picket or associated activity, should be careful not to commit such civil wrongs. It is possible, for example, that material on placards carried by pickets—or, for that matter, by those involved in activities associated with picketing—could be defamatory or amount to a threat or harassment. Pickets will also have no legal protection if they do or say things, or make offensive gestures at people, which amount to unlawful threat or harassment. Section C of this Code explains that such actions may also give rise to prosecution under the criminal law.   **[3243]**

29 Similarly, if the noise or other disturbance caused to residents of an area by pickets, or by those associated with picketing activity, amounts to a civil wrong, those involved or responsible are not protected by the law from proceedings being brought against them   **[3244]**

30 Similar principles apply in respect of any breach of the criminal law by pickets, or their organiser. As explained in Section C of this Code, a picket, or anyone involved in an associated activity, who threatens or intimidates someone, or obstructs an entrance to a workplace, or causes a breach of the peace, commits a criminal offence. Where pickets commit a criminal offence, then in many circumstances they will not be acting peacefully; consequently, any immunity under the civil law will be lost.

[3245]

Seeking redress

31 An employer, a worker, or anyone else who is party to a contract which is, or may be, broken or interfered with by unlawful picketing has a civil law remedy. He may apply to the court for an order[5] preventing, or stopping the unlawful picketing, or its organisation. Such a person may also claim damages from those responsible where the activities of the unlawful picket have caused him loss. An order can be sought against the person—which could include a particular trade union or unions—on whose instructions or advice the unlawful picketing is taking place, or will take place.

[3246]

32 In making an order, the court has authority to require a trade union which has acted unlawfully to take such steps as are considered necessary to ensure that there is no further call for, or other organisation of, unlawful picketing. An order may be granted by the court on an interim basis, pending a full hearing of the case. **[3247]**

---

[5] An injunction in England and Wales; an interdict in Scotland.

33 If a court order is made, it can apply not only to the person or union named in the order, but to anyone else acting on his behalf or on his instructions. Thus an organiser of unlawful picketing cannot avoid liability, for example, merely by changing the people on the unlawful picket line from time to time. **[3248]**

34 Similarly, anyone who is wronged in any other way by a picket can seek an order from the court to get the unlawful act stopped or prevented, and/or for damages. Thus, for example, if picketing, or associated activities, give rise to unlawful disturbance to residents in the vicinity, one or more of the residents so affected can apply to the court for such an order and/or for damages. Such proceedings might be taken against individual pickets, or the person—including a union where applicable—responsible for the unlawful act. **[3249]**

35 If a court is not obeyed, or is ignored, those who sought it can go back to court and ask to have those concerned declared in contempt of court. Anyone who is found to be in contempt of court may face heavy fines, or other penalties, which the court may consider appropriate. For example, a union may be deprived of its assets through sequestration, where the union's funds are placed in the control of a person appointed by the court who may, in particular, pay any fines or legal costs arising from the court proceedings. Similarly, if a person knows that such an order had been made against someone, or some union, and yet aids and abets that person to disobey or ignore the order, he may also be found to be acting in contempt of court and liable to be punished by the court. **[3250]**

Determining whether a union is responsible

36 Pickets will usually attend at a place of work for the purpose of persuading others not to work, or not to work normally, and may thereby be inducing them to breach, or interfere with the performance of, contracts. The law lays down rules which determine whether a union will be held liable for any such acts of inducement which are unlawful. **[3251]**

37 *The law provides that a union will be held responsible for such an unlawful act if it is done, authorised or endorsed by:*

(a) *the union's principal executive committee, president, or general secretary;*
(b) *any person given power under the union's own rules to do, authorise or endorse acts of the kind in question; or*
(c) *any other committee of the union, or any official of the union[6]—including those who are employed by the union, and those, like shop stewards, who are not.[7]*

A union will be held responsible for such an act by such a body or person regardless of any provisions to the contrary in its own rules, or anything in any other contract or rule of law. **[3252]**

---

[6] See footnote on paragraph 22 for the relevant definition of "official". In this case, however, an act will also be taken to have been done by an "official of the union" if it was done (or authorised or endorsed) by a group of persons, or any member of a group, to which such an official belonged at the relevant time if the group's purposes included organising or co-ordinating industrial action.

[7] However, if an act which is done (or authorised or endorsed) by a union committee or official is "effectively repudiated" by the union's principal executive committee, president or general secretary, the union will not be held responsible in law. In order to avoid liability in this way, the act concerned must be repudiated by any of these as soon as reasonably practicable after it has come to their knowledge. In addition, the union must, without delay:

    (a) give written notice of the repudiation to the committee or official in question; and
    (b) do its best to give individual written notice of the fact and date of the repudiation to: (i) every member of the union who it has reason to believe is taking part—or might otherwise take part—in industrial action as a result of the act; and (ii) the employer of every such member.

38 Pickets may, of course, commit civil wrongs other than inducing breach, or interference with the performance, of contracts. The question of whether a union will be held responsible for those wrongs will be determined according to common law principles of liability, rather than by reference to the rules described in paragraph 37 above. **[3253]**

The need for a ballot

39 If what is done in the course of picketing amounts to a call for industrial action, and is an act for which the union is responsible in law, the union can only have the protection of statutory immunity if it has first held a properly-conducted secret ballot. **[3254]**

40 *The law requires that entitlement to vote in such a ballot must be given to all the union members who it is reasonable at the time of the ballot for the union to believe will be called upon to take part in, or continue with, the industrial action, and to no other member. The ballot must produce a majority of those voting which is in favour of taking, or continuing with, industrial action.* These, and other requirements of the law in respect of such ballots, are restated in the statutory Code of Practice "Trade Union Ballots on Industrial Action (1st Revision)". **[3255]**

Section C. Picketing and the Criminal Law

41 If a picket commits a criminal offence he is just as liable to be prosecuted as any other member of the public who breaks the law. The immunity provided under the civil law does not protect him in any way. **[3256]**

42 The criminal law protects the rights of every person to go about his lawful daily business free from interference by others. No one is under any obligation to stop when a picket asks him to do so, or, if he does stop, to comply with a request, for example, not to go into work. Everyone has the right, if he wishes to do so, to cross a picket line in order to go into his place of work or to deliver or collect goods. A picket may exercise peaceful persuasion, but if he goes beyond that and tries by means other than peaceful persuasion to deter another person from exercising those rights he may commit a criminal offence. **[3257]**

43 *Among other matters, it is a criminal offence for pickets (as for others):*

- *to use threatening, abusive or insulting words or behaviour, or disorderly behaviour within the sight or hearing of any person—whether a worker seeking to cross a picket line, an employer, an ordinary member of the public, or the police—likely to be caused harassment, alarm or distress by such conduct;*
- *to use threatening, abusive or insulting words or behaviour towards any person with intent to cause fear of violence or to provoke violence;*
- *to use or threaten unlawful violence;*
- to obstruct the highway or the entrance to premises or to seek physically to bar the passage of vehicles or persons by lying down in the road, linking arms across or circling in the road, or jostling or physically restraining those entering or leaving the premises;
- *to be in possession of an offensive weapon;*
- *intentionally or recklessly to damage property;*
- *to engage in violent, disorderly or unruly behaviour or to take any action which is likely to lead to a breach of the peace;*
- *to obstruct a police officer in the execution of his duty.* **[3258]**

44 A picket has no right under the law to require a vehicle to stop or to be stopped. The law allows him only to ask a driver to stop by words or signals. A picket may not physically obstruct a vehicle if the driver decides to drive on or, indeed, in any other circumstances. A driver must—as on all other occasions—exercise due care and attention when approaching or driving past a picket line, and may not drive in such a manner as to give rise to a reasonable foreseeable risk of injury.   **[3259]**

Section D. Role of the Police

45 It is not the function of the police to take a view of the merits of a particular trade dispute. They have a general duty to uphold the law and keep the peace, whether on the picket line or elsewhere. The law gives the police discretion to take whatever measures may reasonable be considered necessary to ensure that picketing remains peaceful and orderly.   **[3260]**

46 The police have no responsibility for enforcing the civil law. An employer cannot require the police to help in identifying the pickets against whom he wishes to seek an order from the civil court. Nor is it the job of the police to enforce the terms of an order. Enforcement of an order on the application of a plaintiff is a matter for the court and its officer. The police may, however, decide to assist the officers of the court if they think there may be a breach of the peace.   **[3261]**

47 As regards the **criminal law** the police have considerable discretionary powers to limit the numbers of pickets at any one place where they have reasonable cause to fear disorder.[8] The law does not impose a specific limit on the number of people who may picket at any one place; nor does this Code affect in any way the discretion of the police to limit the number of people on a particular picket line. It is for the police to decide, taking into account all the circumstances, whether the number of pickets at any particular place provides reasonable grounds for the belief that a breach of the peace is likely to occur. If a picket does not leave the picket line when asked to do so by the police, he is liable to be arrested for obstruction either of the highway or of a police officer in the execution of his duty if the obstruction is such as to cause, or be likely to cause, a breach of the peace.   **[3262]**

Section E. Limiting Numbers of Pickets

48 Violence and disorder on the picket line is more likely to occur if there are excessive numbers of pickets. Wherever large numbers of people with strong feelings are involved there is danger that the situation will get out of control, and that those concerned will run the risk of committing an offence, with consequent arrest and prosecution, or of committing a civil wrong which exposes them, or anyone organising them, to civil proceedings.   **[3263]**

49 This is particularly so wherever people seek by sheer weight of numbers to stop others going into work or delivering or collecting goods. In such cases, what is intended is not peaceful persuasion, but obstruction or harrassment—if not intimidation. Such a situation is often described as "mass picketing". In fact, it is not picketing in its lawful sense of an attempt at peaceful persuasion, and may will result in a breach of the peace or other criminal offences.   **[3264]**

50 Moreoever, anyone seeking to demonstrate support for those in dispute should keep well away from any picket line so as not to create a risk of a breach of the peace or other criminal offence being committed on that picket line. Just as with a picket

---

[8] In *Piddington v Bates* (1960) the High Court upheld the decision of a police constable in the circumstances of that case to limit the number of pickets to two.

itself, the numbers involved is any such demonstration should not be excessive, and the demonstration should be conducted lawfully. *Section 14 of the Public Order Act 1986 provides the police with the power to impose conditions (for example, as to numbers, location and duration) on public assemblies of 20 or more people where the assembly is likely to result in serious public disorder; or serious damage to property; or serious disruption to the life of the community; or if its purpose is to coerce.*   **[3265]**

51 Large numbers on a picket line are also likely to give rise to fear and resentment amongst those seeking to cross that picket line, even where no criminal offence is committed. They exacerbate disputes and sour relations not only between management and employees but between the pickets and their fellow employees. Accordingly pickets and their organisers should ensure that in general the number of pickets does not exceed six at any entrance to, or exit from, a workplace; frequently a smaller number will be appropriate.

Section F. Organisation of Picketing

52 Sections B and C of this Code outline aspects of the civil law and the criminal law, as they may apply to pickets, and to anyone, including a trade union, who organises a picket. While it is possible that a picket may be entirely "spontaneous", it is much more likely that it will be organised by an identifiable individual or group.   **[3266]**

53 Paragraphs 36-38 in Section B of this Code describe how to identify whether a trade union is, in fact, responsible in terms of civil law liability, for certain acts. As explained in these paragraphs, the law means, for example, that if such an act takes place in the course of picketing, and if a trade union official has done, authorised or endorsed the act, then the official's union will be responsible in law unless the act is "effectively repudiated" by the union's national leadership.   **[3269]**

Functions of the picket organiser

54 Wherever picketing is "official" (ie organised by a trade union), an experienced person, preferably a trade union official who represents those picketing, should always be in charge of the picket line. He should have a letter of authority from his union which he can show to the police officers or to people who want to cross the picket line. Even when he is not on the picket line himself he should be available to give the pickets advice if a problem arises.   **[3268]**

55 A picket should not be designated as an "official" picket unless it is actually organised by a trade union. Nor should pickets claim the authority and support of a union unless the union is prepared to accept the consequent responsibility. In particular, union authority and support should not be claimed by the pickets if the union has, in fact, repudiated calls to take industrial action made, or being made, in the course of the picketing.   **[3269]**

56 Whether a picket is "official" or "unofficial", an organiser of pickets should maintain close contact with the police. Advance consultation with the police is always in the best interests of all concerned. In particular the organiser and the pickets should seek directions from the police on the number of people who should be present on the picket line at any one time and on where they should stand in order to avoid obstructing the highway.   **[3270]**

57 The other main functions of the picket organiser should include ensuring that:

- the pickets understand the law and are aware of the provisions of this Code, and that the picketing is conducted peacefully and lawfully;
- badges or armbands, which authorised pickets should wear so that they are clearly identified, are distributed to such pickets and are worn while they are picketing;
- workers from other places of work do not join the picket line, and that any offers of support on the picket line from outsiders are refused;
- the number of pickets at any entrance to, or exit from, a place of work is not so great as to give rise to fear and resentment amongst those seeking to cross that picket line (see paragraph 51 in Section E of this Code);
- close contact with his own union office (if any), and with the officers of other unions if they are involved in the picketing, is established and maintained;
- such special arrangements as may be necessary for essential supplies, services or operations (see paragraphs 62-64 in Section G of this Code) are understood and observed by the pickets.   **[3271]**

Consultations with other trade unions

58 Where several unions are involved in a dispute, they should consult each other about the organisation of any picketing. It is important that they should agree how the picketing is to be carried out, how many pickets there should be from each union, and who should have overall responsibility for organising them.   **[3272]**

Right to cross picket lines

59 Everyone has the right to decide for himself whether he will cross a picket line. Disciplinary action should not be taken or threatened by a union against a member on the grounds that he has crossed a picket line.   **[3273]**

60 *If a union disciplines any member for crossing a picket line, the member will have been "unjustifiably disciplined". In such a case, the individual can make a complaint to an industrial tribunal. If the tribunal finds the complaint well-founded, it will make a declaration to that effect.*   **[3274]**

61 *If the union has not lifted the penalty imposed on the member, or if it has not taken all necessary steps to reverse anything done in giving effect to the penalty, an application for compensation should be made to the Employment Appeal Tribunal (EAT). In any other case, the individual can apply to an industrial tribunal for compensation. The EAT or tribunal will award whatever compensation it considers just and equitable in all the circumstances, subject to a specified maximum amount. Where the application is made to the EAT, there will normally be a specified minimum award.*   **[3275]**

Section G. Essential Supplies, Services and Operations

62 Pickets, and anyone organising a picket should take very great care to ensure that their activities do not cause distress, hardship or inconvenience to members of the public who are not involved in the dispute. Particular care should be taken to ensure that the movement of essential goods and supplies, the carrying out of essential maintenance of plant and equipment, and the provision of services essential to the life of the community are not impeded, still less prevented.   **[3276]**

63 The following list of essential supplies and services is provided as an illustration of the kind of activity which requires special protection to comply with the recommendations in paragraph 62 above. However, **the list is not intended to be comprehensive**. The supplies and services which may need to be protected in accordance with these recommendations could cover different activities in different circumstances. Subject to this *caveat*, "essential supplies, services and operations" include:

- the production, packaging, marketing and/or distribution of medical and pharmaceutical products;
- the provision of supplies and services essential to health and welfare institutions, eg hospitals, old people's homes;
- the provision of heating fuel for schools, residential institutions, medical institutions and private residential accommodation;
- the production and provision of other supplies for which there is a crucial need during a crisis in the interests of public health and safety (eg chlorine, lime and other agents for water purification; industrial and medical gases; sand and salt for road gritting purposes);
- activities necessary to the maintenance of plant and machinery;
- the proper care of livestock;
- necessary safety procedures (including such procedures as are necessary to maintain plant and machinery);
- the production, packaging, marketing and/or distribution of food and animal feeding stuffs;
- the operation of essential services, such as police, fire, ambulance, medical and nursing services, air safety, coastguard and air sea rescue services, and services provided by voluntary bodies (eg Red Cross and St John's ambulances, meals on wheels, hospital car service), and mortuaries, burial and cremation services.	**[3277]**

64 Arrangements to ensure these safeguards for essential supplies, services and operations should be agreed in advance between the pickets, or anyone organising the picket, and the employer, or employers, concerned.	**[3278]–[4000]**

PART 5
MISCELLANEOUS MATERIALS

MISCELLANEOUS MATERIALS

(a) International Law Materials

INTERNATIONAL LABOUR ORGANISATION CONVENTION (No 87) ON FREEDOM OF ASSOCIATION AND PROTECTION OF THE RIGHT TO ORGANISE (1948)

[Adopted, 9 July 1948; in force 4 July 1950.]

GENERAL NOTE

The preamble, and Articles 12, 13 and 17-21, which deal with ancillary and procedural matters, are omitted.

PART I

FREEDOM OF ASSOCIATION

Article 1

Each Member of the International Labour Organisation for which this Convention is in force undertakes to give effect to the following provisions. **[4001]**

Article 2

Workers and employers, without distinction whatsoever, shall have the right to establish and, subject only to the rules of the organisation concerned, to join organisations of their own choosing without previous authorisation. **[4002]**

Article 3

1 Workers' and employers' organisations shall have the right to draw up their constitutions and rules, to elect their representatives in full freedom, to organise their administration and activities and to formulate their programmes.

2 The public authorities shall refrain from any interference which would restrict this right or impede the lawful exercise thereof. **[4003]**

Article 4

Workers' and employers' organisations shall not be liable to be dissolved or suspended by administrative authority. **[4004]**

Article 5

Workers' and employers' organisations shall have the right to establish and join federations and confederations and any such organisation, federation or confederation shall have the right to affiliate with international organisations of workers and employers. **[4005]**

Article 6

The provisions of Articles 2, 3 and 4 hereof apply to federations and confederations of workers' and employers' organisations. **[4006]**

Article 7

The acquisition of legal personality by workers' and employers' organisations, federations and confederations shall not be made subject to conditions of such a character as to restrict the application of the provisions of Articles 2, 3 and 4 hereof. **[4007]**

Article 8

1 In exercising the rights provided for in this Convention workers and employers and their respective organisations, like other persons or organised collectivities, shall respect the law of the land.

2 The law of the land shall not be such as to impair, nor shall it be so applied as to impair, the guarantees provided for in this Convention. **[4008]**

Article 9

1 The extent to which the guarantees provided for in this Convention shall apply to the armed forces and the police shall be determined by national laws or regulations.

2 In accordance with the principle set forth in paragraph 8 of Article 19 of the Constitution of the International Labour Organisation the ratification of this Convention by any Member shall not be deemed to affect any existing law, award, custom or agreement in virtue of which members of the armed forces or the police enjoy any right guaranteed by this Convention. **[4009]**

Article 10

In this Convention the term 'organisation' means any organisation of workers or of employers for furthering and defending the interests of workers or of employers. **[4010]**

PART II

PROTECTION OF THE RIGHT TO ORGANISE

Article 11

Each Member of the International Labour Organisation for which this Convention is in force undertakes to take all necessary and appropriate measures to ensure that workers and employers may exercise freely the right to organise. **[4011]**

* * * * *

PART IV

FINAL PROVISIONS

Article 14

The formal ratifications of this Convention shall be communicated to the Director-General of the International Labour Office for registration. **[4012]**

Article 15

1 This Convention shall be binding only upon those Members of the International Labour Organisation whose ratifications have been registered with the Director-General.

2 It shall come into force twelve months after the date on which the ratifications of two Members have been registered with the Director-General.

3 Thereafter, this Convention shall come into force for any Member twelve months after the date on which its ratification has been registered. **[4013]**

Article 16

1 A Member which has ratified this Convention may denounce it after the expiration of ten years from the date on which the Convention first comes into force, by an act communicated to the Director-General of the International Labour Office for registration. Such denunciation shall not take effect until one year after the date on which it is registered.

2 Each Member which has ratified this Convention and which does not, within the year following the expiration of the period of ten years mentioned in the preceding paragraph, exercise the right of denunciation provided for in this article, will be bound for another period of ten years and, thereafter, may denounce this Convention at the expiration of each period of ten years under the terms provided for in this article. **[4014]**

*   *   *   *   *

INTERNATIONAL LABOUR ORGANISATION CONVENTION (No 98) ON THE RIGHT TO ORGANISE AND COLLECTIVE BARGAINING (1949)

[Adopted, I July 1949; in force 18 July 1951.]

GENERAL NOTE
The Preamble, and Articles 9, 10 and 12–16, which deal with ancillary and procedural matters, are omitted.

Article 1

1 Workers shall enjoy adequate protection against acts of anti-union discrimination in respect of their employment.

2 Such protection shall apply more particularly in respect of acts calculated to:

(a) Make the employment of a worker subject to the condition that he shall not join a union or shall relinquish trade union membership

(b) Cause the dismissal of or otherwise prejudice a worker by reason of union membership or because of participation in union activities outside working hours or, with the consent of the employer, within working hours. **[4015]**

Article 2

1 Workers' and employers' organisations shall enjoy adequate protection against any acts of interference by each other or each others' agents or members in their establishment functioning or administration.

2 In particular, acts which are designed to promote the establishment of workers' organisations under the domination of employers or employers' organisations, or to support workers' organisations by financial or other means, with the object of placing such organisations under the control of employers or employers' organisations, shall be deemed to constitute acts of interference within the meaning of this article.

[4016]

Article 3

Machinery appropriate to national conditions shall be established, where necessary, for the purpose of ensuring respect for the right to organise as defined in the preceding articles. **[4017]**

Article 4

Measures appropriate to national conditions shall be taken where necessary, to encourage and promote the full development and utilisation of machinery for voluntary negotiation between employers or employers' organisations and workers' organisations, with a view to the regulation of terms and conditions of employment by means of collective agreements. **[4018]**

Article 5

1 The extent to which the guarantees provided for in this Convention shall apply to the armed forces and the police shall be determined by national laws or regulations.

2 In accordance with the principle set forth in paragraph 8 of Article 19 of the Constitution of the International Labour Organisation the ratification of this Convention by any Member shall not be deemed to affect any existing law, award, custom or agreement in virtue of which members of the armed forces or the police enjoy any right guaranteed by this Convention. **[4019]**

Article 6

This Convention does not deal with the position of public servants engaged in the administration of the State, nor shall it be construed as prejudicing their rights or status in any way. **[4020]**

Article 7

The formal ratifications of this Convention shall be communicated to the Director General of the International Labour Office for registration.   **[4021]**

Article 8

1 This Convention shall be binding only upon those Members of the International Labour Organisation whose ratifications have been registered with the Director-General.

2 It shall come into force twelve months after the date on which the ratifications of two Members have been registered with the Director-General.

3 Thereafter, this Convention shall come into force for any Member twelve months after the date on which its ratification has been registered.   **[4022]**

* * * * *

Article 11

1 A Member which has ratified this Convention may denounce it after the expiration of ten years from the date on which the Convention first comes into force, by an act communicated to the Director-General of the International Labour Office for registration. Such denunciation shall not take effect until one year after the date on which it is registered.

2 Each Member which has ratified this Convention and which does not, within the year following the expiration of the period of ten years mentioned in the preceding paragraph, exercise the right of denunciation provided for in this article, will be bound for another period of ten years and, thereafter, may denounce this Convention at the expiration of each period of ten years under the terms provided for in this Article.   **[4023]**

* * * * *

THE EUROPEAN CONVENTION FOR THE PROTECTION OF HUMAN RIGHTS AND FUNDAMENTAL FREEDOMS (1950)

[Signed 4 November 1950; in force 3 September 1953.]

NOTE
Only those articles of the Convention of particular relevance to employment law are reproduced here.

Article 1

The High Contracting Parties shall secure to everyone within their jurisdiction the rights and freedoms defined in Section 1 of this Convention.   **[4024]**

SECTION 1

* * * * *

Article 9

1 Everyone has the right to freedom of thought, conscience and religion; this right includes freedom to change his religion or belief, and freedom, either alone or in community with others and in public or private, to manifest his religion or belief, in worship, teaching, practice and observance.

2 Freedom to manifest one's religion or beliefs shall be subject only to such limitations as are prescribed by law and are necessary in a democratic society in the interests of public safety, for the protection of public order, health or morals, or for the protection of the rights and freedoms of others. **[4025]**

* * * * *

Article 11

1 Everyone has the right to freedom of peaceful assembly and to freedom of association with others, including the right to form and to join trade unions for the protection of his interests.

2 No restrictions shall be placed on the exercise of these rights other than such as are prescribed by law and are necessary in a democratic society in the interests of national security or public safety, for the prevention of disorder or crime, for the protection of health or morals or for the protection of the rights and freedoms of others. This article shall not prevent the imposition of lawful restrictions on the exercise of these rights by members of the armed forces, of the police or of the administration of the State. **[4026]**

* * * * *

Article 13

Everyone whose rights and freedoms as set forth in this Convention are violated shall have an effective remedy before a national authority notwithstanding that the violation has been committed by persons acting in an official capacity. **[4027]**

Article 14

The enjoyment of the rights and freedoms set forth in this Convention shall be secured without discrimination on any ground such as sex, race, colour, language, religion, political or other opinion, national or social origin, association with a national minority, property, birth or other status. **[4028]**

* * * * *

THE EUROPEAN SOCIAL CHARTER (1961)
[Signed, 18th October 1961; in force 26th February 1965]

GENERAL NOTE
Those Parts of the Charter most relevant to Employment Law are reproduced here.

PART I

The Contracting Parties accept as the aim of their policy, to be pursued by all appropriate means, both national and international in character, the attainment of conditions in which the following rights and principles may be effectively realised:

(1) Everyone shall have the opportunity to earn his living in an occupation freely entered upon.

(2) All workers have the right to just conditions of work.

(3) All workers have the right to safe and healthy working conditions.

(4) All workers have the right to a fair remuneration sufficient for a decent standard of living for themselves and their families.

(5) All workers and employers have the right to freedom of association in national or international organisations for the protection of their economic and social interests.

(6) All workers and employers have the right to bargain collectively.

(7) Children and young persons have the right to a special protection against the physical and moral hazards to which they are exposed.

(8) Employed women, in case of maternity, and other employed women as appropriate, have the right to a special protection in their work.

(9) Everyone has the right to appropriate facilities for vocational guidance with a view to helping him choose an occupation suited to his personal aptitude and interests.

(10) Everyone has the right to appropriate facilities for vocational training.

(11) Everyone has the right to benefit from any measures enabling him to enjoy the highest possible standard of health attainable.

(12) All workers and their dependents have the right to social security.

(13) Anyone without adequate resources has the right to social and medical assistance.

(14) Everyone has the right to benefit from social welfare services.

(15) Disabled persons have the right to vocational training, rehabilitation and resettlement, whatever the origin and nature of their disability.

(16) The family as a fundamental unit of society has the right to appropriate social, legal and economic protection to ensure its full development.

(17) Mothers and children, irrespective of marital status and family relations, have the right to appropriate social and economic protection.

(18) The nationals of any one of the Contracting Parties have the right to engage in any gainful occupation in the territory of any one of the others on a footing of equality with the nationals of the latter, subject to restrictions based on cogent economic or social reasons.

(19) Migrant workers who are nationals of a Contracting Party and their families have the right to protection and assistance in the territory of any other Contracting Party.   **[4029]**

PART II

The Contracting Parties undertake, as provided for in Part III, to consider themselves bound by the obligations laid down in the following articles and paragraphs.

The Right to Work

Article 1

With a view to ensuring the effective exercise of the right to work, the Contracting Parties undertake.

(1) to accept as one of their primary aims and responsibilities the achievement and maintenance of as high and stable a level of employment as possible, with a view to the attainment of full employment;

(2) to protect effectively the right of the worker to earn his living in an occupation freely entered upon;

(3) to establish or maintain free employment services for all workers;

(4) to provide or promote appropriate vocational guidance, training and rehabilitation. **[4030]**

The Right to Just Conditions of Work

Article 2

With a view to ensuring the effective exercise of the right to just conditions of work, the Contracting Parties undertake:

(1) to provide for reasonable daily and weekly working hours, the working week to be progressively reduced to the extent that the increase of productivity and other relevant factors permit;

(2) to provide for public holidays with pay;

(3) to provide for a minimum of two weeks annual holiday with pay;

(4) to provide for additional paid holidays or reduced working hours for workers engaged in dangerous or unhealthy occupations as prescribed;

(5) to ensure a weekly rest period which shall, as far as possible, coincide with the day recognised by tradition or custom in the country or region concerned as a day of rest. **[4031]**

The Right to Sale and Healthy Working Conditions

Article 3

With a view to ensuring the effective exercise of the right to safe and healthy working conditions, the Contracting Parties undertake:

(1) to issue safety and health regulations;

(2) to provide for the enforcement of such regulations by measures of supervision;

(3) to consult, as appropriate, employers' and workers' organisations on measures intended to improve industrial safety and health. **[4032]**

The Right to a Fair Remuneration

Article 4

With a view to ensuring the effective exercise of the right to a fair remuneration, the Contracting Parties undertake;

(1) to recognise the right of workers to a remuneration such as will give them and their families a decent standard of living;

(2) to recognise the right of workers to an increased rate of remuneration for overtime work subject to exceptions in particular cases;

(3) to recognise the right of men and women workers to equal pay for work of equal value;

(4) to recognise the right of all workers to a reasonable period of notice for termination of employment;

(5) to permit deductions from wages only under conditions and to the extent prescribed by national laws or regulations or fixed by collective agreements or arbitration awards.

The exercise of these rights shall be achieved by freely concluded collective agreements, by statutory wage-fixing machinery, or by other means appropriate to national conditions. [4033]

The Right to Organise

Article 5

With a view to ensuring or promoting the freedom of workers and employers to form local, national or international organisations for the protection of their economic and social interests and to join those organisations, the Contracting Parties undertake that national law shall not be such as to impair, nor shall it be so applied as to impair, this freedom. The extent to which the guarantees provided for in this article shall apply to the police shall be determined by national laws or regulations. The principle governing the application to the members of the armed forces of these guarantees and the extent to which they shall apply to persons in this category shall equally be determined by national laws or regulations. [4034]

The Right to Bargain Collectively

Article 6

With a view to ensuring the effective exercise of the right to bargain collectively, the Contracting Parties undertake:

(1) to promote joint consultation between workers and employers;
(2) to promote, where necessary and appropriate, machinery for voluntary negotiations between employers or employers' organisations and workers' organisations, with a view to the regulation of terms and conditions of employment by means of collective agreements;
(3) to promote the establishment and use of appropriate machinery for conciliation and voluntary arbitration for the settlement of labour disputes;

and recognise:

(4) the right to workers and employers to collective action in cases of conflicts of interest, including the right to strike, subject to obligations that might arise out of collective agreements previously entered into. [4035]

The Right of Children and Young Persons to Protection

Article 7

With a view to ensuring the effective exercise of the right of children and young persons to protection, the Contracting Parties undertake:

(1) to provide that the minimum age of admission to employment shall be 15 years, subject to exceptions for children employed in prescribed light work without harm to their health, morals or education;
(2) to provide that a higher minimum age of admission to employment shall be fixed with respect to prescribed occupations regarded as dangerous or unhealthy;
(3) to provide that persons who are still subject to compulsory education shall not be employed in such work as would deprive them of the full benefit of their education;
(4) to provide that the working hours of persons under 16 years of age shall be limited in accordance with the needs of their development, and particularly with their need for vocational training;

(5) to recognise the right of young workers and apprentices to a fair wage or other appropriate allowances;

(6) to provide that the time spent by young persons in vocational training during the normal working hours with the consent of the employer shall be treated as forming part of the working day;

(7) to provide that employed persons of under 18 years of age shall be entitled to not less than three weeks' annual holiday with pay;

(8) to provide that persons under 18 years of age shall not be employed in night work with the exception of certain occupations provided for by national laws or regulations;

(9) to provide that persons under 18 years of age employed in occupations prescribed by national laws or regulations shall be subject to regular medical control;

(10) to ensure special protection against physical and moral dangers to which children and young persons are exposed, and particularly against those resulting directly or indirectly from their work. **[4036]**

The Right of Employed Women to Protection

Article 8

With a view to ensuring the effective exercise of the right of employed women to protection, the Contracting Parties undertake:

(1) to provide either by paid leave, by adequate social security benefits or by benefits from public funds for women to take leave before and after childbirth up to a total of at least 12 weeks;

(2) to consider it as unlawful for an employer to give a woman notice of dismissal during her absence on maternity leave or to give her notice of dismissal at such a time that the notice would expire during such absence

(3) to provide that mothers who are nursing their infants shall be entitled to sufficient time off for this purpose;

(4) (a) to regulate the employment of women workers on night work in industrial employment;

    (b) to prohibit the employment of women workers in underground mining, and appropriate, on all other work which is unsuitable for them by reason of its dangerous, unhealthy, or arduous nature.

[4037]

* * * * *

(b) Employment Appeal Tribunal Practice Directions

EMPLOYMENT APPEAL TRIBUNAL PRACTICE DIRECTION: APPEAL PROCEDURE (17 February 1981)

1. The Employment Appeal Tribunal Rules 1980 (SI 1980 No 2035) (hereinafter called "The Rules") came into operation on 1 February 1981. **[4038]**

2. By virtue of paragraph 7(2) of Schedule 11 to the Employment Protection (Consolidation) Act 1978, the Appeal Tribunal has power, subject to the Rules, to regulate its own procedure. **[4039]**

3. Where the Rules do not otherwise provide, the following procedure will be followed in all appeals to the Appeal Tribunal. **[4040]**

4. Appeals out of time

(a) By virtue of rule 3(1) of the rules every appeal under section 136 of the Employment Protection (Consolidation) Act 1978 or section 4 of the Employment Act 1980 to the Employment Appeal Tribunal shall be instituted by serving on the tribunal, within 42 days of the date on which the document recording the decision or order appealed from was sent to the appellant, a notice of appeal as prescribed in the Rules.

(b) Every notice of appeal not delivered within 42 days of the date on which the document recording the decision or order appealed from was sent to the appellant must be accompanied by an application for an extension of time, setting out the reasons for the delay.

(c) Applications for an extension of time for appealing cannot be considered until a notice of appeal has been presented.

(d) Unless otherwise ordered, the application for extension of time will be considered and determined as though it were an interlocutory application.

(e) In determining whether to extend the time for appealing, particular attention will be paid to the guidance contained in *Marshall v Harland & Wolff Ltd* [1972] ICR 97, and to whether any excuse for the delay has been shown.

(f) It is not necessarily a good excuse for delay in appealing that legal aid has been applied for, or that support is being sought, (eg from the Equal Opportunities Commission, or from a trade union). In such cases the intending appellant should at the earliest possible moment, and at the latest within the time limit for appealing, inform the registrar, and the other party, of his intentions, and seek the latter's agreement to an extension of time for appealing.

(g) Time for appealing runs from the date on which the document recording the decision or order of the industrial tribunal was sent to the appellant, notwithstanding that the assessment of compensation has been adjourned, or an application has been made for a review.

(h) In any case of doubt or difficulty, notice of appeal should be presented in time, and an application made to the registrar for directions.   **[4041]**

5. Institution of appeal

(a) Subject to Rule 3(2) of the Rules, if it appears to the registrar that a Notice of Appeal or application gives insufficient particulars or lacks clarity either as to the question of law or the grounds of an appeal, the registrar may postpone his direction under that Rule pending amplification or clarification of the Notice of Appeal, as regards the question of law or grounds of appeal, by the intended appellant.

(b) An appellant will not ordinarily be allowed to contend that "the decision was contrary to the evidence," or that "there was no evidence to support the decision," or to advance similar contentions, unless full and sufficient particulars identifying the particular matters relied upon have been supplied to the Appeal Tribunal.

(c) It will not be open to the parties to reserve a right to amend, alter or add to any pleading. Any such right is not inherent and may only be exercised if permitted by order for which an interlocutory application should be made as soon as the need for alteration is known.   **[4042]**

6. Special procedure

(a) Where an appeal has not been rejected pursuant to Rule 3(2) but nevertheless the Appeal Tribunal considers that it is doubtful whether the grounds of appeal disclose an arguable point of law, the president or a judge may direct that the matter be set down before a Division of the Appeal Tribunal for hearing of a preliminary point to enable the appellant to show cause why the appeal should not be dismissed on the ground that it does not disclose a fairly arguable point of law.

(b) The respondent will be given notice of the hearing but since it will be limited to the preliminary point he will not be required to attend the hearing or permitted to take part in it.

(c) If the appellant succeeds in showing cause, the hearing will be adjourned and the appeal will be set down for hearing before a different Division of the Appeal Tribunal in the usual way.

(d) If the appellant does not show cause, the appeal will be dismissed.

(e) The decision as to whether this procedure will be adopted in any particular case will be in the discretion of the president or a judge. **[4043]**

7. Interlocutory applications

(a) On receipt of an interlocutory application the registrar will submit a copy of the application to the other side, and will indicate that if it is not intended to oppose the application it may be unnecessary for the parties to be heard and that the appropriate order may be made in their absence. Where the application is opposed the registrar will also in appropriate cases give the parties an opportunity of agreeing to the application being decided on the basis of written submissions.

(b) Save where the president or a judge directs otherwise, every interlocutory application to strike out pleadings or to debar a party from taking any further part in the proceedings pursuant to Rules 16 or 21 will be heard on the day appointed for the hearing of the appeal, but immediately preceding the hearing thereof. **[4044]**

8. Meeting for directions

On every appeal from the decision of the certification officer, and, if necessary on any other appeal, so soon as the answer is delivered, or if a cross-appeal, the reply, the registrar will appoint a day when the parties shall meet on an appointment for directions and the appeal tribunal will give such directions, including a date for hearing, as it deems necessary. **[4045]**

9. Right to inspect the register and certain documents and to take copies

Where, pursuant to the direction dated 31 March 1976, a document filed at the Employment Appeal Tribunal has been inspected and a photographic copy of the document is bespoken, a copying fee of 25p for each page will be charged. **[4046]**

10. Listing of appeals

A. England and Wales
(a) When the respondent's answer has been received and a copy served on the

appellant, the case will be put in the list of cases for hearing. At the beginning of each calendar month a list will be prepared of cases to be heard on specified dates in the next following calendar month. That list will also include a number of cases which are liable to be taken in each specified week of the relevant month. The parties or their representatives will be notified as soon as the list is prepared. When cases in the list with specified dates are settled or withdrawn, cases warned for the relevant week will be substituted and the parties notified as soon as possible.

(b) A party finding that the date which has been given causes serious difficulties may apply to the listing officer before the 15th of the month in which the case first appears in the list. No change will be made unless the listing officer agrees, but every reasonable effort will be made to accommodate parties in difficulties. Changes after the 15th of the month in which the list appears will not be made other than on application to the President of the Employment Appeal Tribunal; arrangements for the making of such an application should be made through the listing officer.

(c) Other cases may be put in the list by the listing officer with the consent of the parties at shorter notice, eg where other cases have been settled or withdrawn or where it appears that they will take less time than originally estimated. Parties who wish their cases to be taken as soon as possible and at short notice should notify the listing officer.

(d) Each week an up-to-date list for the following week will be prepared including any changes which have been made (in particular specifying cases which by then have been given fixed dates).

(e) The monthly list and the weekly list will appear in the Daily Cause List and will also be displayed in Room 6 at the Royal Courts of Justice and at No 4, St James's Square, London, SW1. It is important that parties or their advisors should inspect the weekly list as well as the monthly list.

(f) If cases are settled or to be withdrawn notice should be given at once to the listing officer so that other cases may be given fixed dates.

B. Scotland
When the respondent's answer has been received and a copy served on the appellant both parties will be notified in writing that the appeal will be ready for hearing in approximately six weeks. The proposed date of hearing will be notified to the parties three or four weeks ahead. Any party who wishes to apply for a different date must do so within seven days of receipt of such notification. Thereafter a formal notice of the date fixed for the hearing will be issued not less than 14 days in advance. This will be a peremptory diet. It will not be discharged except by the judge on cause shown. **[4047]**

11. Admissibility of documents

(a) Where, pursuant to Rules 9 or 13 an application is made by a party to an appeal to put in at the hearing of the appeal any document which was not before the industrial tribunal, including a note of evidence given before the industrial tribunal (other than the chairman's note), the application shall be submitted in writing with copies of the document(s) sought to be made admissible at the hearing.

(b) The registrar will forthwith communicate the nature of the application and of the document(s) sought to be made admissible to the other party and where appropriate, to the chairman of the industrial tribunal, for comment.

(c) A copy of the comment will be forwarded to the party making the application, by the registrar who will either dispose of it in accordance with the Rules or refer it to the appeal tribunal for a ruling at the hearing. In the case of comments received from the chairman of the industrial tribunal a copy will be sent to both parties.

[4048]

12. Complaints of bias, etc.

(a) The appeal tribunal will not normally consider complaints of bias or of the conduct of an industrial tribunal unless full and sufficient particulars are set out in the grounds of appeal.

(b) In any such case the registrar may inquire of the party making the complaint whether it is the intention to proceed with the complaint in which case the registrar will give appropriate directions for the hearing.

(c) Such directions may include the filing of affidavits dealing with the matters upon the basis of which the complaint is made or for the giving of further particulars of the complaint on which the party will seek to rely.

(d) On compliance with any such direction the registrar will communicate the complaint together with the matters relied on in support of the complaint to the chairman of the industrial tribunal so that he may have an opportunity of commenting upon it.

(e) No such complaint will be permitted to be developed upon the hearing of the appeal, unless the appropriate procedure has been followed.

(f) A copy of any affidavit or direction for particulars to be delivered thereunder will be communicated to the other side.   **[4049]**

13. Exhibits and documents for use at the hearing

(a) The appeal tribunal will prepare copies of all documents for use of the judges and members at the hearing in addition to those which the registrar is required to serve on the parties under the Rules. It is the responsibility of parties or their advisers to ensure that all documents submitted for consideration at the hearing are capable of being reproduced legibly by photographic process.

(b) In Scotland a copy of the Chairman's Notes will not be supplied to the parties except on application to the Appeal Tribunal on cause shown In England and Wales copies will only be sent to the parties if in the view of the Appeal Tribunal all or part of such notes are necessary for the purpose of the appeal or on application to the tribunal on cause shown. Chairman's Notes are supplied for the use of the Appeal Tribunal and not for the parties to embark on a "fishing" expedition to establish further grounds of appeal.

(c) It is the duty of parties and their solicitors to ensure that only those documents which are relevant to the point of law raised in the appeal, and which are likely to be referred to, are included in the documents before the tribunal.

(d) It will be the responsibility of the parties or their advisers to ensure that all exhibits and documents used before the industrial tribunal, and which are considered to be relevant to the appeal, are sent to the appeal tribunal immediately on request. This will enable the appeal tribunal to number and prepare sufficient copies, together with an index, for the judges and members at least a week before the day appointed for the hearing.

(e) A copy of the index will be sent to the parties or their representatives prior to the hearing so that they may prepare their bundles in the same order.   **[4050]**

EMPLOYMENT APPEAL TRIBUNAL
PRACTICE DIRECTION: PRELIMINARY
HEARING (15 July 1985)

1. Many of the appeals brought before the Employment Appeal Tribunal involve a complaint that the industrial tribunal reached an unreasonable conclusion upon the facts. It has been decided that the arrangements for the hearing of such appeals could be improved by introducing an opportunity for the appeal tribunal to determine, at a preliminary stage, first, whether the appeal raises a sufficiently arguable case to give the appeal tribunal jurisdiction to entertain it at all; and secondly (if it does), what directions are required for the subsequent listing and hearing of the appeal in the light of the indications obtained at such preliminary hearing as to the salient issues involved and the probable length of the argument. Accordingly, for an experimental period beginning on 1 October 1985, the following listing arrangements will be applied to all appeals which appear to the registrar to depend solely or principally upon a plea that the industrial tribunal took an erroneous view of the evidence or reached an unreasonable conclusion upon the facts.   **[4051]**

2. Such appeals will be listed for a preliminary hearing to be attended by both parties, at which the appeal tribunal will receive submissions from each side as to whether or not the grounds of appeal disclose a fairly arguable case. If satisfied that such a case is established, the appeal tribunal will give the appropriate directions to enable the appeal to proceed to a full hearing at the soonest possible subsequent date. If not so satisfied, the appeal tribunal will dismiss the appeal, stating the view summarily that it has no jurisdiction to entertain it. Preliminary hearings will be listed on the assumption that the total hearing time will not exceed one hour.   **[4052]**

3. Any appeal listed for preliminary hearing under this direction may be vacated and a fresh date obtained for its substantive hearing if the parties make an agreed application in writing to that effect, to be received not later than 15 days before the date fixed for the preliminary hearing. Any such agreed application should include an agreed estimate by the parties of the probable length of the hearing (including in such estimate an allowance of one hour for deliberation by the tribunal and delivery of the judgment).   **[4053]**

4. This direction does not apply to appeal hearings in Scotland. These arrangements suspend the current "Special Procedure".   **[4054]**

(c) Miscellaneous materials

TRADES UNION CONGRESS: PRINCIPLES
GOVERNING RELATIONS
BETWEEN UNIONS
(THE "BRIDLINGTON PRINCIPLES". Adopted 1939)

NOTES

These are the well-known "Bridlington Principles" approved at the Bridlington Congress of the TUC in 1939 and subsequently amended, most recently in 1979. They have no statutory force but govern important aspects of relationships between trades unions which are affiliated to the TUC. (See now however Trade Union Reform and Employment Rights Act 1993, s 14.)

Preface

The following Principles constitute a code of conduct accepted as morally binding by affiliated organisations. They are not intended by such organisations or by the Trade Union Congress to be a legally enforceable contract. The Principles include the main text and the Notes and both are to be read together as having equal status and validity. **[4055]**

Principle 1

Each union shall consider developing joint working agreements with unions with whom they are in frequent contact, and in particular developing (a) procedures for resolving particular issues and (b) specific arrangements concerning spheres of influence, transfers of members and benefit rights, recognition of cards, and demarcation of work. Unions should also ensure that members and officials are made fully aware of the terms of existing agreements, and of the importance of following the agreed procedures for the avoidance and settlement of disputes.

NOTES ON PRINCIPLE 1

(a) *Procedures for resolving particular issues* are usually between two unions, cover all the members, and are capable of dealing with any issue that arises between the two unions. They normally provide for an unresolved issue to be processed through the district, regional and national levels of the procedure. They may also provide for arbitration by a third party (for example, by the TUC) if the final stage of the procedure has been exhausted without agreement being reached. Such agreements may also incorporate joint standing committees to review relations between the unions and to promote closer working arrangements.

(b) *Specific arrangements* concerning:

    (i)   spheres of influence (trade union organisation and representation);
    (ii) transfers of members and benefit rights;
    (iii) recognition of cards;
    (iv) demarcation of work

are usually between two unions but may be on a wider basis (for example, between a number of unions on the trade union side of a joint negotiating body), particularly when they relate to spheres of influence concerning trade union organisation. They generally apply to members in a particular establishment or industry though in the case of agreements concerning the conditions for the transfer of members (and benefit rights), they will normally apply to all the members of the signatory unions.

(c) *Advice and assistance:* The General Council will assist unions in drawing up such agreements and procedures and, if requested, will be pleased to arrange meetings between unions.

(d) *Mergers:* Mergers between affiliated unions in frequent contact with one another are in general a desirable means of strengthening trade union organisation and the General Council will therefore be glad to provide advice and assistance to unions considering mergers.

Affiliated unions should consult other affiliates with an interest when they are considering a merger with a non-affiliated organisation. In the event of disagreement it is open to any affiliated union involved to refer the matter to the TUC for advice and conciliation but not adjudication by a Disputes Committee unless by agreement between all the affiliated unions concerned.

Affiliated unions will of course appreciate that it is a matter of good trade union practice not to intervene in any way in a ballot being conducted by other unions about a merger.

(e) *Sole Negotiating Rights and Union Membership Agreements:* When making sole negotiating rights or union membership agreements or arrangements affiliated unions should have regard to the interest of other unions which may be affected and should consider their position in the drafting of such agreements. Where unions cannot resolve these matters between themselves they may be referred to the TUC for advice and conciliation and if necessary to a Disputes Committee for adjudication. **[4056]**

Principle 2

No one who is or has recently been a member of any affiliated union should be accepted into membership in another without enquiry of his present or former union. The present or former union shall be under an obligation to reply within 21 days of the enquiry, stating:

(a) whether the applicant has tendered his resignation;
(b) whether he is clear on the books;
(c) whether he is under discipline or penalty;
(d) whether there are any other reasons why the applicant should not be accepted.

If the present or former union objects to the transfer, and the enquiring union considers the objection to be unreasonable, the enquiring union shall not accept the applicant into membership but shall maintain the status quo with regard to membership. If the problem cannot be mutually resolved it should be referred to the TUC for adjudication.

A union should not accept an applicant into membership if no reply has been received 21 days after the enquiry, but in such circumstances a union may write again to the present or former union, sending a copy of the letter to the head office of the union if the correspondence is with a branch, stating that if no reply is received within a further 14 days they intend to accept the applicant into membership. Where the union to which application is being made is dealing directly with the head office of the present or former union, a copy of this communication may be sent to the TUC.

NOTES ON PRINCIPLE 2

(a) Where unions are in frequent contact, they should advise one another of the appropriate level at which membership enquiries should be made.

(b) No member should be allowed to escape his financial obligations by leaving one union while in arrears and by joining another.

(c) The reference to "recently" in the first sentence of Principle 2 shall normally be understood to apply to applicants who have contributed to an affiliated union during the preceding 52 weeks. Unions should however appreciate that this is intended merely as a guide and much difficulty will be avoided if enquiries are made in all cases where previous trade union membership is known. **[4057]**

Principle 3

Each union shall use an enquiry form as proposed by the General Council in the case of all enquiries under Principle 2 above, and forward reasoned replies on any such form as they may receive from an enquiring union. **[4058]**

Principle 4

A union shall not accept a member of another union where that union objects to the transfer (see Principle 2 above), or where enquiry shows that the member is:

(a) under discipline;
(b) engaged in a trade dispute;
(c) in arrears with contributions.

NOTES ON PRINCIPLE 4

(a) It should be a general understanding that both national and local officials of trade unions should refrain from speaking or acting adversely to the interests of any other union during any period in which the members of the latter union are participating in a trade dispute. Much trouble could be avoided if unions about to participate in a trade dispute would take care to inform other unions whose members would be likely to be affected thereby.

(b) With regard to the question of arrears in (c) above, a number of affiliated unions have a rule or rules excluding members who have been in arrears for a specified period of time. However, although a union with such a rule regards an individual in such arrears as being no longer a member entitled to participate in the work of the union, it does not necessarily mean that the union regards the individual as being automatically free to join another organisation. Any union which considers that another union has unreasonably objected to a transfer on the grounds of arrears (or for any other reason) should not therefore accept an individual into membership, but should refer the matter to the TUC for adjudication.   **[4059]**

Principle 5

No union shall commence organising activities at any establishment or undertaking in respect of any grade or grades of workers in which another union has the majority of workers employed and negotiates wages and conditions, unless by arrangement with that union.

NOTE ON PRINCIPLE 5

Where a union has membership but does not have a majority in respect of any grade or grades of workers and/or does not negotiate terms and conditions of employment for such grade or grades, another union wishing to organise should engage in consultation as soon as it is aware (or has drawn to its attention by the existing union) that another union has membership in the grade or grades concerned before it commences organising activities. If there is no agreement, and the matter is referred by either union to the TUC and a Disputes Committee adjudicates, the Disputes Committee will have regard to the following factors:

(i) the efforts which the union opposing the entry of another union or unions has itself made in trying to secure or retain a majority membership, the period over which any such efforts have been made, the extent and causes of any difficulties encountered by that union, and the likely prospect of that union securing or regaining a majority membership and/or negotiating rights;
(ii) any existing collective bargaining or other representation arrangements in the establishment, company or industry.   **[4060]**

Principle 6

Each union shall include in its membership form questions on the lines of the TUC model form in regard to past or present membership of another union.

The essential questions on the model form are as follows:

Are you, or have you been a member of any other trade union or unions? (*See Note below*) Give the name of the union or unions, together with the name of the branch or branches of that union or those unions of which you are or were formerly a member. (*See Note below*)

If you are a member of any other trade union and are not in benefit, please state the amount of your arrears.

Each union should also include in its membership form a note pointing out that *dual membership* is valid only if the two unions concerned have jointly agreed to it.

NOTE ON PRINCIPLE 6

Failure by a union to include the necessary questions and note on its application form will make it impossible for a union to pursue the course of enquiry laid down, and will be regarded by a Disputes Committee as an important factor in determining any complaint brought against such a union.   **[4061]**

Principle 7

In cases of inter-union disputes (whether relating to trade union membership, trade union recognition, demarcation of work, or any other difficulty) no official strike should take place before the TUC has been able to examine the issue.

If a dispute (short of a strike) emerges between two or more unions there is an obligation on the unions concerned to notify the TUC forthwith of the circumstances so that it can be dealt with by a TUC Disputes Committee.   **[4062]**

Principle 8

If an inter-union dispute has led to an unauthorised stoppage of work there is an obligation on the union or unions concerned to take immediate and energetic steps to get their members to resume normal working; the union or unions concerned are also required to notify the TUC as soon as possible of the dispute and of the steps they have taken, or are taking, to secure a resumption of work.   **[4063]**

APPENDIX: REGULATIONS GOVERNING PROCEDURE IN REGARD TO DISPUTES BETWEEN AFFILIATED ORGANISATIONS

A. In the event of a dispute arising between affiliated unions, there should be a normal maximum period of *eight weeks* in which the unions concerned should have made efforts to resolve the issues between them including a meeting at national level.

B. On receiving a complaint the General Secretary or any person to whom he delegates authority shall ascertain whether the complainant union has taken the matter up with the head office of the respondent union, and no dispute between unions shall be heard by a Disputes Committee (see Regulation E below) until the General Secretary or any person to whom he delegates authority is assured that the unions have made an effort to settle the dispute between themselves, including holding a meeting between national officials, although in exceptional circumstances this requirement may be waived.

In the case of alleged poaching, the effort at settlement should include an examination of the specific cases.

C. If there is machinery within the industry for the settlement of disputes, no dispute between unions shall be heard by a Disputes Committee unless the General Secretary or any person to whom he delegates authority is assured that such machinery has been tried and has failed to settle the dispute, although in exceptional circumstances this requirement may be waived.

D. Where it appears to the General Secretary or any person to whom he delegates authority that agreement might be reached by conciliation at an informal conference under the chairmanship of a member of the General Council or the General Secretary or any person appointed by the General Secretary, efforts shall be made to persuade the disputants to follow this method. If the unions concerned agree to attend an informal conference, they will be expected to agree within *14 days* on a date for the conference which is convenient to the TUC and the unions.

E. Where he considers it appropriate, the General Secretary may refer a dispute between affiliated organisations to a Disputes Committee. A Disputes Committee shall consist of not less than three persons appointed by or under the authority of the General Secretary, being members of a panel comprising all members of the General Council and experienced union officials nominated by affiliated organisations. A member of the General Council shall act as Chairman of a Disputes Committee. Where the General Secretary or the General Council decides that an investigation on the spot will be useful, the Disputes Committee shall, so far as is practicable, include members of the panel who live in a region adjacent to the locality of the dispute. No person shall be appointed as a member of a Disputes Committee who is himself, or who is a member of a union which is, immediately involved in the dispute.

F. There shall be a Secretary to the Disputes Committees of the Congress ("the Secretary"), appointed by the General Secretary. The Secretary may delegate any of his duties or functions under these Regulations to such persons as he sees fit, provided always that the Secretary shall remain responsible thereof to the General Secretary.

G. The Secretary shall require the complainant union to furnish (if they have not already done so) explicit particulars of the complaint.

(1) In a case of alleged poaching of members the following particulars shall be provided, so far as applicable to the case:

    (a) the names of the persons concerned, their places of work, and their grade or occupation;
    (b) the date of joining the complainant union
    (c) the date up to which contributions have been paid;
    (d) arrears, if any; and
    (e) letters of resignation or applications for transfer, if any.

In ordinary circumstances there shall be no hearing by a Disputes Committee until these particulars or at least (a), (b), (c) and (d) are in the hands of the Secretary.

(2) In cases concerning recognition, demarcation, or wages and conditions of employment the complainant union shall provide the following particulars, so far as they are relevant to the case:

    (f) its agreement(s) with the employer or federation of employers concerned;
    (g) the extent of membership among the grade of workers concerned; (h) its agreement(s) with the union(s) with whom it is in dispute; and
    (i) a description of the work in dispute.

H. Subject to Regulations A, B, C, D, and G above, the complaint with full particulars shall be conveyed by the TUC to the respondent union with a request for their comments. The respondent union shall send a considered reply to the TUC within *21 days*.

(1) In a complaint of poaching, the respondent union shall be asked definitely whether the workers concerned are members of their union and if so, shall be required to provide the following particulars:

    (a) original application forms
    (b) the date of acceptance into the union (if not included above); and
    (c) applications for transfers, if any.

(2) In cases concerning recognition, demarcation of work, or wages and conditions of employment the respondent union shall provide the following particulars, so far as they are relevant to the case:

    (d) its agreement(s) with the employer or federation of employers concerned;
    (e) the extent of its membership among the grade of workers concerned;
    (f) its agreement(s) with the union(s) with whom it is in dispute; and
    (g) a description of the work in dispute.

I. The reply of the respondent union shall be sent by the TUC to the complainant union which shall within *21 days* inform the TUC whether it wishes to pursue the complaint.

J. Where a union wishes to pursue the complaint the TUC will inform the respondent union, and both unions will be expected to agree within *14 days* on a date for a Disputes Committee hearing which is convenient to the TUC and the unions.

K. The General Secretary shall be empowered in the case of unnecessary or wilful delay on the part of either union at any stage in the procedure to fix a date for a Disputes Committee hearing.

L. In addition to the information provided under the preceding Regulations, unions shall endeavour (wherever possible) to submit a written statement of their case to the Secretary at least seven days before the date of the hearing.

M. At the hearing of the complaint before the Disputes Committee no new complaint may be raised without the consent of the Disputes Committee. In the event of such a consent being granted the disputants shall be given a fair opportunity to prepare and present their cases on the new matter.

N. At the hearing, corroborative evidence may be produced. Originals or copies of all documents read or quoted by the disputants shall be handed to the Secretary and copies of such documents supplied to the other disputants and to the Disputes Committee.

O. A Disputes Committee shall investigate the causes and circumstances of the dispute and shall give to the disputants a full opportunity to submit factual information and to present their views to the Disputes Committee. With the agreement of the disputants the Disputes Committee may discuss with such local union representatives and management representatives as it considers appropriate. The Disputes Committee shall otherwise conduct its proceedings in such manner as it sees fit.

P. The basic approach of the Disputes Committee shall be to seek to obtain an agreed settlement, whether of a permanent or an interim character, which is acceptable to all the disputants; and the Disputes Committee may at any time make such recommendations as it sees fit. But whenever the Disputes Committee considers it to be necessary, it shall make an award. In deciding the dispute the Disputes Committee shall have general regard to the interests of the trade union Movement and to the declared principles or declared policy of Congress but shall in particular be guided by the *Principles Governing Relations Between Unions* [above], as amended by the General Council and adopted by the Congress from time to time.

Q. The General Secretary shall send copies of the award of the Disputes Committee to all the disputants and to the General Council. **[4064]**

A SUGGESTED METHOD FOR ASSESSING LOSS OF PENSION RIGHTS UNDER AN OCCUPATIONAL SCHEME FOLLOWING A FINDING OF UNFAIR DISMISSAL BY AN INDUSTRIAL TRIBUNAL

(Government Actuary's Department) (**Note**) **[4065]**

GENERAL NOTE

This article was printed in full in previous editions but is now seriously out of date as a result of changes in interest and inflation patterns and in pensions legislation. It is therefore omitted. The article has been largely superseded by a new publication prepared by a committee of Industrial Tribunal Chairmen: "Industrial Tribunals: Compensation for Loss of Pension Rights" (HMSO, 2nd edn, 1991, £4.50; ISBN 0 11 361324 5). This publication is not reproduced for reasons of space. It has no official status, but is a helpful analysis of the problems and is influential in tribunal proceedings concerning the loss of pension rights.

(d) Useful addresses

1. ADVISORY, CONCILIATION AND ARBITRATION SERVICE

Northern Region
Westgate House, Westgate Road, Newcastle upon Tyne NE1 1TJ
Tel: 091 261 2191 Fax: 091 232 5452

Cumbria	Tyne and Wear	Cleveland
Northumberland	Durham	

Yorkshire and Humberside Region
Commerce House, St Alban's Place, Leeds LS2 8HH
Tel: Leeds (0532) 431371 Fax: (0532) 446678

North Yorkshire	South Yorkshire	Humberside
West Yorkshire		

London Region
Clifton House, 83–117 Euston Road, London NW1 2RB
Tel: 071 388 5100 Fax: 071 388 9722

South East Region
Westminster House, Fleet Road, Fleet, Hants, GU13 8PD
Tel: Fleet (0251) 811868 Fax: (0252) 617006

Cambridgeshire	Herefordshire	Hampshire
Norfolk	Essex	(except
Suffolk	Berkshire	Ringwood)
Oxfordshire	Surrey	Isle of Wight
Buckinghamshire	Kent	East Sussex
Bedfordshire		West Sussex

South West Region
Regent House, 27a Regent Street, Clifton, Bristol BS8 4HR
Tel: Bristol (0272) 744066 Fax: (0272) 744078

Gloucestershire	Cornwall	Dorset
Avon	Devon	Ringwood
Wiltshire	Somerset	

Midlands Region
Leonard House, 319/323 Bradford Street, Birmingham, B5 6ET
Tel: 021 622 5050 Fax: 021 631 2331

Northamptonshire	West Midlands	Warwickshire
Shropshire	Hereford and	
Staffordshire	Worcester	

Nottingham Office: Anderson House, Clinton Avenue, Nottingham NG5 1AW

Tel: Nottingham (0602) 693355 Fax: (0622) 693085

| Derbyshire (except High Peak District) | Nottinghamshire Leicestershire | Lincolnshire |

North West Region Boulton House, 17–21 Chorlton Street, Manchester M1 3HY

Tel: 061 228 3222 Fax: 061 228 7975

| Lancashire Cheshire | High Peak District of Derbyshire | Greater Manchester |

Merseyside Office: Cressington House, 249 St Mary's Road, Garston, Liverpool L19 0NF
Tel: 051 427 8881 Fax: 051 427 2715

Scotland Franborough House, 123–157 Bothwell Street, Glasgow G2 7JR
Tel: 041 204 2677 Fax: 041 221 4697

Wales Phase 1, Ty Glas Road, Llanishen, Cardiff CF4 5PH
Tel: Cardiff (0222) 762636 Fax: (0222) 751334

Head Office 27 Wilton Street, London SW1X 7AZ
(including WRU) Tel: 071 210 3000 Fax: 071 210 3708

2. CENTRAL ARBITRATION COMMITTEE
   39 Grosvenor Place, London, SW1X 7BD
   Tel: 071 210 3738

3. CERTIFICATION OFFICE FOR TRADE UNIONS AND EMPLOYERS' ASSOCIATIONS
   27 Wilton Street, London SW1X 7AZ
   Tel: 071 210 3734

4. COMMISSION FOR RACIAL EQUALITY
   Elliott House, 10–12 Allington Street, London SW1E 5EH
   Tel: 071 828 7022

5. THE COMMISSIONER FOR THE RIGHTS OF TRADE UNION MEMBERS
   First Floor, Bank Chambers, 2A Rylands Street, Warrington, Cheshire, WA1 1EN (0925) 415771

6. EMPLOYMENT APPEAL TRIBUNAL
   Central Office
   58 Victoria Embankment, London EC4Y 0DS
   Tel: 071 273 1041 Fax: 071 273 1045

   Divisional Office
   11 Melville Crescent, Edinburgh
   Tel: 031 225 3963 Fax: 031 220 6694

7. EQUAL OPPORTUNITIES COMMISSION
   Overseas House, Quay Street, Manchester M3 3HN
   Tel: 061 833 9244

8. INDUSTRIAL TRIBUNALS

(1) England and Wales

(a) Central Office

Central Office of the Industrial Tribunals
Southgate Street, Bury St Edmunds, Suffolk IP33 2AQ
Tel: 0284 762300 Fax: 0284 766334

(b) Regional and other offices

Birmingham ROIT
Phoenix House, 1/3 Newhall Street, Birmingham B3 3NH
Tel: 021 236 6051 Fax: 021 236 6029

Bristol ROIT
1st Floor, The Crescent Centre, Temple Beck, Bristol BS1 6EZ
Tel: 0272 298261 Fax: 0272 253452

Exeter OIT
Renslade House, Bonhay Road, Exeter EX4 4BX
Tel: 0392 79665

Bury St Edmunds ROIT
Southgate Street, Bury St Edmunds, Suffolk IP33 2AQ
Tel: 0284 762171

Bedford OIT
8/10 Howard Street, Bedford MK40 3HS
Tel: 0234 51306

Cardiff ROIT
1–6 St Andrews Place, Cardiff CF1 3BE
Tel: 0222 372693 Fax: 0222 225906

Shrewsbury OIT
Prospect House, Belle Vue Road, Shrewsbury SY3 7AR
Tel: 0743 58341

Leeds ROIT
11 Albion Street, Leeds LS1 5ES
Tel: 0532 459741 Fax: 0532 428843

Sheffield OIT
14 East Parade, Sheffield S1 2ET
Tel: 0742 760348

London North ROIT
19/29 Woburn Place, London WC1H 0LU
Tel: 071 273 3000/071 273 8602 Fax: 071 278 5068

London South ROIT
Montague Court, 101 London Road, Croydon CR0 2RF
Tel: 081 667 9131 Fax: 081 649 9470

Ashford OIT
Tufton House, Tufton Street, Ashford, Kent TN23 1RJ
Tel: 0233 621346

Manchester ROIT
14–22 The Parsonage, Manchester M3 2JA
Tel: 061 833 0581 Fax: 061 832 0249

Liverpool OIT
1 Union Court, Cook Street, Liverpool L2 4UJ
Tel: 051 236 9397

Newcastle ROIT
3rd Floor, Plummer House, Market Street East, Newcastle upon Tyne NE1 6NF
Tel: 091 232 8865 Fax: 091 222 1680

Nottingham ROIT
7th Floor, Birbeck House, Trinity Square, Nottingham NG1 4AX
Tel: 0602 475701 Fax: 0602 507612

Leicester OIT
31–33 Millstone Lane, Leicester LE1 5JS
Tel: 0533 530119

Southampton ROIT
3rd Floor, Dukes Keep, Marsh Lane, Southampton SO1 1EX
Tel: 0703 639555 Fax: 0703 635506

Brighton OIT
St James House, New England Street, Brighton BN1 4GQ
Tel: 0273 571488

Reading OIT
30–31 Friar Street, Reading RG1 1DY
Tel: 0734 594917/9

(2) Scotland

(a) *Central office*

Central Office of the Industrial Tribunals
St Andrews House, 141 West Nile Street, Glasgow G1 2RU
Tel: 041 331 1601 Fax: 041 332 3316

(b) *Other offices*

Aberdeen OIT
252 Union Street, Aberdeen AB1 1TN
Tel: 0224 643307

Dundee OIT
13 Albert Square, Dundee DD1 1DD
Tel: 0382 21578

Edinburgh OIT
124–125 Princes Street, Edinburgh EH2 4AD
Tel: 031 226 5584

[4066]

INDEX